ROTHMANS RUGBY UNION YEARBOOK 1994-95

Editor: Stephen Jones
Statistician: John Griffiths

ROTHMANS

HEADLINE

First published in 1994
by HEADLINE BOOK PUBLISHING

Cover photographs. Action from the 1994 Five Nations Championship.
Front: Scott Quinnell on his way to a try for Wales against France at Cardiff Arms Park.
Wales won 24-15 and went on to take the Championship, *Back:* England scrum-half
Dewi Morris clears the ball in the 18-14 victory over France at Parc des Princes.

All photographs by Colorsport

10 9 8 7 6 5 4 3 2 1

ISBN 0-7472-7850-4

Photoset by Cylinder Typesetting Limited, London

Printed and bound in Great Britain by
The Bath Press, Avon

HEADLINE BOOK PUBLISHING
A division of Hodder Headline PLC
338 Euston Road
London NW1 3BH

CONTENTS

EDITORIAL PREFACE

Warm thanks are due, once again, to all contributors to this, the 23rd edition of the *Rothmans Rugby Union Yearbook;* to all the readers who wrote in with suggestions for improvements and to everyone in rugby, especially officials, who help with its compilation.

Thanks are also due to Chris Rhys, for his work in compiling the ever-growing section on international tours; and to Caroline North, house editor, for her invaluable work in the production of the Yearbook.

The main statistical sections of the Yearbook are, as usual, complete up until 1 May 1994. However, in order to provide the most up-to-date coverage possible, we have included the touring parties, Test appearances and results of the summer tours made by the five home countries in this edition for quick reference. As always, full statistical details of those tours will be included next year. The next edition will also carry full coverage of the 1995 World Cup.

Stephen Jones *Editor*
John Griffiths *Statistician*

SENSE OF EXPECTATION TEMPERED BY GLOBAL INCONSISTENCIES

REVIEW OF THE 1993-94 SEASON
The Editor

There is a discernible rise in the momentum and the sense of expectation in rugby as the 1995 World Cup approaches. Every team with aspirations is working furiously already, while the Rugby World Cup body battles through its minefields of organisation. The fact that England's tour of South Africa in May and June 1994 went off without extraneous problems suggests that the alternative venues nominated will not be needed and the probability of a spectacular competition looms.

Not all the omens are good, however. The 1995 World Cup will give even more impetus to the rampant commercialism in the game, and will also, yet again, increase substantially the pressure on the competing players. Those demands reached breaking point years ago and yet they are still increasing.

So it is extremely disappointing to note that rugby administration has been so slow to develop a coherent response, applying across the board, to either the problem of amateurism or to those commitments. Almost every country has its own agenda, almost every country applies only those by-laws which suit. The inconsistency of treatment of players is potentially disastrous and causes no end of bad feeling among the players themselves. Surely, since the game now generates so much enjoyment, fascination and finance on the backs of the players, it would be appropriate to look after their interests far better. To give them a code of conduct and a code of commerce to be followed by every international squad throughout the world would be a start.

It is also high time that the game confronted the problem of discipline. In one sense, there is no problem in that the level of dirty play throughout the game has receded considerably over the years. However, lurid incidents in the top games are highlighted unmercifully in the media; and quite properly, too. The response from unions and team managements is inadequate. Too many team hierarchies allow their own men to escape with neither suspension nor condemnation. There was the escape of Tim Rodber, dismissed in the appalling Eastern Province-England match – Rodber was brutally provoked, but then unleashed a barrage of lefts and rights. He should have been suspended, if only because his absolution sent out precisely the wrong signals – just as, for example, the escape of Jamie Joseph sent out the wrong signals.

Joseph, the All Black flanker who went out of his way to stamp on the ankle of Kyran Bracken of England in the Test in the autumn of 1993, at first evaded admonishment. He did not play in a subsequent tour match against the Barbarians, although the New Zealand management refused to confirm that they had taken internal action and suspended him. It was the kind of head-in-the-sand approach which characterised the reaction to most incidents of rough play during the season. There is no shame, no sign of weakness, in condemning any player (your own, or an opponent) perceived in dirty play. If players are allowed to get away with it, if disputes are allowed to fester and if light sentences or no sentence at all form the judicial precedent, then the game is in trouble. The stakes are now far too high for rugby's dereliction of its disciplinary duty to continue. The worst-case scenario is for the World Cup to go up in flames before a watching world. Rugby's image would take 20 years to recover from that.

The game is still doing its best to recover from the attention of the laws committee of the International Rugby Board. Remember the high rhetoric which accompanied their imposition (on a game which did not need or want it) of the experimental law relating to ruck and maul? People wittered away about the ball being in play for longer, about the prospect of more action and more tries. Even after the experiment had been in existence for a year, there were still those unwilling to accept the evidence of their own eyes – as well as the evidence of the disappearing try – that the experiment had been an unmitigated disaster which produced nothing whatsoever that was good for the game.

So what happened when the experiment came up for review at the IRB meeting in March 1994? The IRB revealed the weakness of their position by abandoning that part of the experiment dealing with the ruck (and giving a tortuous, nonsensical explanation to mask their retreat) but retained it for the maul, thereby continuing to rob the game of its dynamic. It was half improvement, half shameless cop-out. The result was that the game improved but only to a tiny degree, that refereeing interpretations became even more difficult, and that we are stuck with the mish-mash for the World Cup.

It is also high time that the laws committee stopped bleating that they are only taking into account the views of the game in general. Nothing of the sort. The IRB, on the subject of the laws or in any other area, can only be said to be reflecting the views of rugby at large if they take into account a wider range of those views, if they introduce formal consultation with leading players, referees and coaches at IRB level. At the moment, they receive only patchy reaction, transmitted through bureaucratic channels by each individual union. Not good enough, not good enough at all.

The balance of the game on the field was difficult to determine as the summer tours of 1994 drew to a close. England achieved a marvellous victory over New Zealand at a boiling Twickenham in the autumn; they played brilliantly and with complete authority in beating South Africa in Pretoria. Yet they also subsided tamely to Ireland at Twickenham and could easily have lost to Scotland at Murrayfield. The evidence

New England manager Jack Rowell marks the end of his brilliantly successful tenure at Bath as he raises the Pilkington Cup to acknowledge the appreciation of the Twickenham crowd.

seems clear – at their best, England have a team of dedication and forward power. But compared with, say, Australia at their best, they have a disturbing lack of an all-round game, of a killing, attacking machine. England and a vision of total rugby do not sit down together at the same table. Perhaps the influence of Jack Rowell, the new team manager, will help the vision to develop.

And if the season as a whole found England in unpredictable form, then there was something all too predictable about Scotland and Ireland. It is a measure of the awful Irish season that they could record a victory at Twickenham and yet still finish in the red, hammered throughout Australia on their tour. Scotland, who were humiliated at home by the touring New Zealanders in the autumn, suffering their record defeat, have still not found themselves. They really should stop thrashing around at half-back and instal and remotivate Craig Chalmers and Gary Armstrong. They should also stop proclaiming their readiness to expand their game and actually do something about it – outstanding moves by Scottish back divisions in the last decade are as rare as world-class bursts of spin bowling by Americans.

New Zealand's problem is the lack of plan B. When a team of sufficient forward power and motivation lines up against the All Blacks, they find them far more vulnerable than they used to be. If the typical and unchanging Kiwi game is stopped then they are as beatable as any team – even though the pride, the energy and the dedication of the All Blacks is as strong as ever. Australia would still, probably, be favourites for the World Cup, shading the South Africans. But their chances took a dive in May when both their brilliant centres, Tim Horan and Jason Little, were badly injured in the same match, the Super-10 final in Durban against Natal. Little was out jogging within months, on the road to recovery. Sadly, Horan's appallingly complicated knee injury calls into question whether he can regain his superb best form in time for the World Cup. Yet if the pair can regain their stride, then the strength of Australia's squad is still most impressive.

Wales, at least, made a genuine advance. Robert Norster, Alan Davies and Gareth Jenkins, their hierarchy, were far too wise and realistic to be carried away when Wales won their first three Five Nations matches, against Scotland, France and Ireland – the French match was a passionate affair which woke Cardiff Arms Park from its slumbers – and when they arrived at Twickenham with the Grand Slam beckoning. They were second-best at Twickenham, won the title on points difference and marched off for their summer tour, still with weaknesses (notably in the line-out) but with morale and confidence growing apace. For that, the team management and Ieuan Evans, the captain, deserve vast credit. Evans, for his dignity and inspiration as captain and for his superb form on the right wing, is now to be compared with Welsh greats of any era. So is Phil Davies, the key forward of the European season who was, tragically, below fitness at

The joyful Canadian team revel in their 26-24 victory over Wales in November. From this low point Wales went on to take the Five Nations Championship.

Twickenham. Scott Quinnell, the young player of the year, could easily join them in time.

The season brought a welcome world title for England. The English women avenged their defeat at the hands of the USA in the previous World Cup final with an outstanding victory in the finals of the 1994 competition. This time, the US forwards had no answer to the scrum-maging power of the England pack in a final watched by a splendidly large crowd. After the final, the England captain, Karen Almond, announced her retirement from the captaincy. She has been the kingpin of the national team for so long, not only with her astute play at fly-half, but also through the good sense and zeal with which she has fought the corner for the women's game over the years.

But if the tournament was a triumph for England, then it was also a triumph for the Scottish organisers, landed with the job at short notice, and for the women's game itself. Interest in women's rugby is still growing at a remarkable rate around the world, and indeed, also creates a problem: the workload on administrators has become ridiculously high and it is small wonder that the British game is attempting to establish formal links with the men's game to tap into some of the resources and expertise.

Elsewhere, the game threw up extraordinary sights – the heroic scale of the Super-10 events; the glorious end to the long tenure of Jack Rowell as Bath coach as Bath re-established themselves yet again with a convincing double, a tribute to their endless motivation and skills. And, not least, the incredible boom in the game at all levels, especially in mini-rugby. The game at all the myriad mini levels is expanding so quickly throughout the British Isles that rugby can hardly cope. It is a credit to the coaches and parents.

Cardiff, at last, won a trophy, beating Llanelli in the Welsh Cup final. Swansea, expertly coached by Mike Ruddock, won the League title and Treorchy, desperately trying to put rugby in the Rhondda back on the map, proudly ascend to Division 1 for 1994-95. Yet again, the game faced the new season with only the pressure of expectation to daunt.

ROTHMANS FIVE PLAYERS OF THE YEAR

The basis for selection for the Rothmans Five Players of the Year was the European season 1993-94. No sooner had the British Lions returned from their tour of New Zealand than several of them were facing the same opponents for either England or Scotland. Australia pitched camp in France, Japan and Canada flitted into Wales and the Five Nations formbook was ripped to shreds. The choice of our panel of contributors reflects those packed nine months.

The five players are **Philippe Sella,** the French centre who just goes on and on, this year beating Serge Blanco's world record tally of 93 caps and reaching the magical century on tour in New Zealand this summer; **Phil Davies,** the Llanelli forward, a stalwart for club and country, who was at the heart of the Welsh revival; **Ben Clarke,** the England back-row forward, a colossal presence in New Zealand who enhanced his reputation here when moving to openside; **Tim Horan,** the centre, tough, talented and the backbone of the Australian side; and **Nigel Redman,** the lock whom England found, once again, they could not do without.

NB: No player can be nominated more than once. Career details given are correct up to 30 April 1994.

Previous nominations
1989-90: **Will Carling, Patrice Lagisquet, Steve McDowell, David Sole, Paul Ackford**
1990-91: **Dean Richards, Gary Armstrong, Wade Dooley, Serge Blanco, Rory Underwood**
1991-92: **Peter Winterbottom, Jonathan Webb, David Campese, Simon Poidevin, Marc Cecillon**
1992-93: **Gavin Hastings, Laurent Cabannes, Phil Kearns, Jean-Baptiste Lafond, Waisale Serevi**

PHILIPPE SELLA

French rugby is characterised by chaos. At its worst, this trait sees captains sacked, coaches dismissed, presidents toppled, committees squabbling and psychopaths heading for an early bath. At its best the same impulse breeds the most breathtaking rugby played in the world: the rulebook is forgotten, cautious voices gagged and full rein given to wild, romantic instinct.

So much for the background. In a perverse way it's perhaps fittingly ironic that the one player who has straddled several eras of France's turbulent past should be a model of stability, composure and consistency. While all around have lost their heads in one way or another Philippe Sella has retained his. He eclipsed Serge Blanco's world record total of 93 caps in the Second Test against Australia in November. By

Philippe Sella.

the season's end – another full one at that – Sella had 98 caps to his name. The century was a certainty for Sella, 32, will play on until his body finally gives up. Not too many bets have been taken on when this might be. Sella's lungs and joints have probably been screaming for surrender for years but he has taken no notice: his physical durability is remarkable. He won his first 45 caps on the trot and has completed 71 out of a possible 73 internationals. 'Philippe is like a bullet,' said Franck Mesnel, his longstanding partner in the French centre. 'When he falls he doesn't just hit the ground, he ricochets off it.'

Sella may have lost some of the searing pace of old, and with it the confidence to pin back his ears and steam through the slenderest of gaps. With age has come wisdom. He is a superb player and a rock in defence. 'He has the strength of a bull but the touch of a piano-player,' says Jacques Fouroux, his old international coach.

Fame and achievement have had no impact on this most revered of French players. 'He is a star of the shadows,' as his club coach, Charly Nieucel, puts it. Sella has played for Agen throughout his career after moving there from the small village club Clairac. He won his first cap against Romania in 1982 although, as he was concussed in the game, he has little memory of it. Our own memories of his glorious career will never fade.

Philippe Sella *Born Bourran, France, 14 February 1962; centre; plays for Agen; 98 caps for France since first cap against Romania in 1982.*

PHIL DAVIES

In season 1993-94 others may have taken the headlines – Nigel Walker for his pace, Scott Quinnell for his precocious talent – but only one man truly epitomised the new-found soul of Welsh rugby. Phil Davies has suffered for his country and now his countrymen have repaid the debt by responding to his indomitable presence. Only in the final Five Nations game, against England, did they falter. Significantly, Davies was nursing an injury.

But consider his collective performances in the three other games. Davies was recalled to the colours against Scotland. Suddenly the Welsh pack began to breathe fire. Pumping the bellows in where the heat was at its fiercest was Davies. The scrum which had creaked against Canada was now set in concrete; the line-out which had twitched and disintegrated found a focus; the all-round loose driving and mauling developed an energy and purpose which had seemed beyond them. 'Phil was immense,' said team manager Robert Norster, who knows a thing or two himself about producing displays of that magnitude.

Davies himself is a man of few words. He now admits that he wishes he'd been even more sparing with his comments back in 1990 when he told the then manager, Ron Waldron, what he could do with his Welsh jersey. 'It was a difficult time for me,' said Davies. 'But after that I never lost sight of my ambition to play for Wales again.'

Injuries have also hampered his career. Even so, by the end of the Five Nations season he was within sight of Graham Price's record for a Welsh forward of 41 caps. Davies has slotted into several positions – No 8, blindside and second row. His nomadic existence is confined to the pitch: he has played all his club rugby for Llanelli. He is set to see out his days with his head buried between the front row's legs. 'I wouldn't get in the back row any longer,' he says. 'But at least I've proved them all wrong about being too small for the second row.'

At 6 feet 5 inches, a comparative dwarf by modern standards, Davies has shown that the undervalued skills of timing and co-ordinated support still have a significant part to play in the line-out. Davies played for Wales in the 1987 and 1991 World Cups and was bitterly disappointed to miss out on Lions selection in 1989. Now those dark days are behind both Davies and his country.

Phil Davies *Born Seven Sisters, Wales, 19 October 1963; lock or back row; plays for Llanelli; 39 caps since first cap against England in 1985.*

Phil Davies.

BEN CLARKE

John Kirwan still bears the marks. So, too, do a host of others who have met Ben Clarke. There are those, like Kirwan, who were lined up for a mighty hit many yards away but simply had no chance. The target was sighted, the radar locked in, the ground devoured and the enemy felled. There are others who have met Clarke in more favourable circumstances, grinning and obliging, still the modest, hugely likeable man. Neither type will forget the encounter in a hurry.

Ben Clarke.

Clarke, the fledgling international, grew into a man and athlete of real stature before our very eyes in the 1992-93 season. We may not be taking too many liberties in tracing that moment of flowering to the – or, rather, *the* – tackle on Kirwan in the Second All Blacks-British Lions Test. By the time Kirwan had managed to haul himself off the ground, wondering who had clobbered him and how, the match had swung the Lions' way and Clarke's name was being etched into the history books.

Not many Brits have moved Kiwis to compliment and none come harder to impress than Colin Meads. 'You can take the rest home,' growled Pinetree, 'but leave that Clarke here.'

There might be the odd – very odd – sceptic claiming that Clark, 26, did not make as big an impression in his second full international season as in his first. They could not be more wrong. If anything his achievements were even more astonishing, for he played out of position. How would Brian Moore have fared at tight-head prop? Clarke, by preference a No 8, was asked to replace the irreplaceable Peter Winterbottom at openside. His heart probably sank when the news was broken but he did not complain. New Zealand were the only ones doing the complaining, being on the receiving end once again in November of Clarke's ferocious commitment and quite remarkable athleticism. He flitted back and forth between the two positions during the Championship.

He has honed his game brilliantly since he surged through the ranks, moving from junior club Bishop's Stortford, where his father is club chairman, to Saracens and from there to Bath. Battling for a place there ahead of a fearsome retinue of back-row men put the spice on Clarke's competitive nature. The club say they weren't that impressed when he first arrived. Few would venture a similar opinion these days. Just ask John Kirwan.

Ben Clarke *Born Bishop's Stortford, England, 15 April 1968; back-row forward; plays for Bath; 9 caps since first cap against South Africa in 1992.*

TIM HORAN

In a small, private room in the autumn of 1989, Australian lock Peter FitzSimons performed one of the great services to the game of rugby football. No, nothing to do with drawing up a great tactical battle-plan – he is a second row, remember. What FitzSimons and a couple of his mates did was to pin Tim Horan to the floor and make him swear an oath of allegiance to the 15-a-side code. Their concern about Horan's commitment extended for just a couple of years, until after the World Cup. Thankfully, Horan, perhaps for fear of another grilling from Peter 'Thumbscrews' FitzSimons, has remained true to his oath.

For that the rugby world is grateful, because Horan's star has never dimmed. We hope he will make a complete recovery from the appalling

Tim Horan.

knee injury suffered in the Super-10 final in May 1994. He was only a teenager on the night that his team-mates took such decisive action. He had, though, just scored two tries in a 32-15 victory over France. Five years later the scenario was much the same. On a fitful tour of North America and France, Horan, almost alone, stood out from the middling level of performance of those around him. In the First Test against France in Bordeaux he moved body and soul in trying to inspire his colleagues to the victory they threatened but never delivered. Horan, winning his 32nd cap that afternoon, ran some dazzling angles in attack and was as unyielding as ever in defence.

Given such sustained levels of achievement it's no surprise that the most commonly heard sound in the Australian camp in recent years has been the rustle of Rugby League chequebooks. Many times they have come to lure the Queenslander; many times they have been resisted. Horan, who had now established himself as consistently the finest centre in the world, would be an ideal capture for League. His work rate is immense, his dynamic thrust almost irresistible and, as France found out, his tackling without fault. New Zealand almost battered him to death with the ferocity of their attacks in the second half of that magnificent 1991 World Cup semi-final, but Horan, standing alongside his great boyhood mate and partner, Jason Little, gave not an inch. It has been like that ever since Horan, still only 24, first came to prominence with the Australian Schools side, followed by the Under-21s. From there he rapidly swung into the view of FitzSimons and his buddies. They took care of the rest.

Tim Horan *Born Queensland, Australia, 15 May 1970: centre; plays for Southern Districts, 33 caps since first cap against New Zealand in 1989.*

NIGEL REDMAN

He's been hauled into the knacker's yard, he's been beaten with iron bars in training, he's been dropped after being cited as Man of the Match, and yet still he comes back for more. Nigel Redman is not a man who lies down and dies.

His return to prominence this season, ten years after winning his first cap against Australia as 20-year-old, has been truly heartening. His success will please those who value integrity, durability and dwarves. With the passing of the new laws, we thought that the modern game would henceforth be peopled by those on eye level with giraffes. Redman, in a heroic performance against New Zealand, showed that theory to be nonsense. He may be only 6 feet 4 inches tall but he more than compensated for what nature had denied him with a dextrous display, debunking forever another myth: namely, that front-five forwards are lumpy old grunters and nothing more.

Physically robust as he is, Redman's game is based on great technical subtlety and intelligence. Allied to that comes a huge degree of athletic ability which sees him time and again breathing life into movements which seem to be dying on their feet. Of course Redman is also a grafter, a mean, no-nonsense operator who bonds together his own side's loose mauls and then somehow wriggles an interfering arm into the opposition's.

It may seem strange to pay tribute to one who was effectively dropped for the opening two Championship matches against Scotland and Ireland. After scaling the mountain against the All Blacks, for which he was singled out by New Zealand coach Laurie Mains, Redman was omitted when Bayfield returned from injury. This was the eighth time in his career that he'd suffered such a fate. And yet the selectors got it wrong. England had no core, no one who would stand firm and hold the team together. Recall number nine came for the match in Paris – Redman's 15th cap – and suddenly the England pack were a different outfit.

Redman, 30, was born in Cardiff and was one of the Ninian Park faithful as a boy. He took to rugby only in his mid-teens, when the family moved to Weston. From there it was England Colts and then Bath. His first cap arrived after just 17 games for the club. Ten years and numerous club trophies later, nothing much has changed. No matter what the tape-measure might say, Nigel Redman is a huge man.

Nigel Redman *Born Cardiff, 16 August 1964; second row; plays for Bath; 16 caps since first cap against Australia in 1984.*

Nigel Redman.

TOURS 1993

BRITISH ISLES TO NEW ZEALAND 1993

A case of so near yet so far – that was the verdict on the 1993 Lions in New Zealand. The record of seven wins from 13 games made the class of '93 statistically the least successful Lions to visit the country. Yet, but for one refereeing decision, the tour would have turned into a resounding triumph.

The Lions were leading 18-17 in the First Test when referee Brian Kinsey saw an offence as a ruck formed after a tackle one minute from time. The ball was emerging on the Lions' side but, to the dismay of the visitors, who expected a decision in their favour, the referee awarded the penalty to the All Blacks. According to Mr Kinsey, Dean Richards had prevented the tackled player from moving away from the ball. Grant Fox duly kicked the goal that, as it turned out, cost the Lions the series.

The Lions party was one of the most popular bunches of players to tour New Zealand. Captain Gavin Hastings was a fine ambassador and an inspiring leader who commanded the respect of his colleagues and the New Zealand public. Others to impress were Ben Clarke, Scott Gibbs, Nick Popplewell and Dewi Morris. Clarke emerged as the tour's outstanding player, pushing himself into the world-class rankings with his polished performances in all three back-row positions.

On the field the team showed immense character to overhaul a 0-20 deficit against the Maoris at Wellington, and there was another spirited display when the Lions returned to New Zealand's capital to win the Second Test. But at times the tourists were badly let down by their tight forwards. The surrender against Waikato and defeats at Hawke's Bay and Auckland exposed the folly of selecting Scottish forwards who had had mediocre Five Nations matches. And although Jason Leonard eventually crossed the front row to fill in admirably as an emergency tight-head, there was no doubt that the omission of Jeff Probyn was a costly mistake.

Finally, the tourists had an interesting retort to those iconoclasts who warn that Lions tours are becoming an anachronism. To a man, the Lions agreed that such tours should continue.

THE TOURING PARTY

Manager G Cooke **Coach** I R McGeechan **Assistant Coach** R Best
Captain A G Hastings

FULL-BACKS

A G Hastings (Watsonians & Scotland)
A Clement (Swansea & Wales)

THREEQUARTERS

R Underwood (Leicester & England)

T Underwood (Leicester & England)
I Hunter (Northampton & England)
I C Evans (Llanelli & Wales)
W D C Carling (Harlequins & England)
J C Guscott (Bath & England)
I S Gibbs (Swansea & Wales)

S Hastings (Watsonians & Scotland)
*R M Wallace (Garryowen & Ireland)
*V J G Cunningham (St Mary's Coll & Ireland)

HALF-BACKS

S Barnes (Bath & England)
C R Andrew (Wasps & England)
R N Jones (Swansea & Wales)
C D Morris (Orrell & England)
*A D Nicol (Dundee HSFP & Scotland)

FORWARDS

J Leonard (Harlequins & England)
N J Popplewell (Greystones & Ireland)
A P Burnell (London Scottish & Scotland)
P H Wright (Boroughmuir & Scotland)

B C Moore (Harlequins & England)
K S Milne (Heriot's FP & Scotland)
W A Dooley (Preston Grasshoppers & England)
M C Bayfield (Northampton & England)
D F Cronin (London Scottish & Scotland)
A I Reed (Bath & Scotland)
M J Galwey (Shannon & Ireland)
M C Teague (Moseley & England)
P J Winterbottom (Harlequins & England)
R E Webster (Swansea & Wales)
D Richards (Leicester & England)
B B Clarke (Bath & England)
*M O Johnson (Leicester & England)

Replacement during tour

TOUR RECORD

All matches Played 13 Won 7 Lost 6 Points for 314 Against 285
International matches Played 3 Won 1 Lost 2 Points for 51 Against 57

SCORING DETAILS

All matches
For: 33T 19C 33PG 4DG 314 Pts
Against: 31T 17C 30PG 2DG 285 Pts

International matches
For: 2T 1C 12PG 1DG 51 Pts
Against: 5T 4C   8PG   –   57 Pts

MATCH DETAILS

1993	OPPONENTS	VENUE	RESULT
22 May	North Auckland	Whangarei	W 30-17
26 May	North Harbour	Auckland	W 29-13
29 May	NZ Maoris	Wellington	W 24-20
2 June	Canterbury	Christchurch	W 28-10
5 June	Otago	Dunedin	L 24-37
8 June	Southland	Invercargill	W 34-16
12 June	NEW ZEALAND	Christchurch	L 18-20
16 June	Taranaki	New Plymouth	W 49-25
19 June	Auckland	Auckland	L 18-23
22 June	Hawke's Bay	Napier	L 17-29
26 June	NEW ZEALAND	Wellington	W 20-7
29 June	Waikato	Hamilton	L 10-38
3 July	NEW ZEALAND	Auckland	L 13-30

Appearances: 9 – G Hastings*, Guscott**; 8 – Clarke*, Milne**, Teague**, Barnes**, Morris*, Leonard*; 7 – Andrew, Evans, R Underwood, Gibbs, Winterbottom, Bayfield, Popplewell, Moore, Clement*, Webster*, Galwey*, Carling*, Burnell*; 6 – T Underwood, Reed, Richards, Cronin, Jones, Wright; 5 – Wallace; 4 – Johnson; 3 – Cunningham, S Hastings*, Dooley; 1 – Nicol*, Hunter   * includes appearances as a replacement
Scorers: 101 – G Hastings (1T 12C 24PG); 33 – Barnes (6C 7PG); 24 – Andrew (2T 1C 2PG 2DG); 20 – Evans (4T); 15 – Underwood (3T); 13 – Clement (2T 1DG); 10 – Guscott, Webster, T Underwood, Cunningham, Gibbs, 2 pen tries (all 2T); 8 – Carling (1T 1DG); 5 – Teague, Galwey, Reed, Richards, Cronin, Jones, Wallace, S Hastings (all 1T)

MATCH 1 22 May, Okara Park, Whangarei

North Auckland 17 (1G 2T)   British Lions 30 (2G 2PG 2T)
North Auckland: W B Johnston; T Going, C M Going, M B Seymour, D Manako; A Monaghan, R L J le Bas; L Davies, D Te Puni, C K Barrell, I D Jones (*capt*), E Jones,

G L Taylor, K Tuipolotu, A D Going *Replacements* R C Hilton-Jones for Tuipolotu (58 mins); L Sigley for Te Puni (77 mins)
Scorers *Tries:* Te Puni, Seymour, T Going   *Conversion:* Johnston
British Lions: Clement; Hunter, Guscott, S Hastings, R Underwood; Barnes *(capt)*, Jones; Leonard, Moore, Wright, Cronin, Reed, Galwey, Clarke, Webster
Replacements G Hastings for Hunter (38 mins); Burnell for Wright (temp)
Scorers *Tries:* Guscott, S Hastings, Clement, Underwood   *Conversions:* Barnes, G Hastings   *Penalty Goals:* Barnes, G Hastings
Referee L L McLachlan (Otago)

MATCH 2   26 May, Mount Smart Stadium, Auckland

North Harbour 13 (1G 2PG)   **British Lions 29** (3G 1PG 1T)
North Harbour: I R Calder; E J Rush, F E Bunce, W K Little, R M Kapa; J Carter, A D Strachan; R O Williams, G W Dowd, K G Boroevich, B P Larsen, D W Mayhew, A Perelini, R S Turner *(capt)*, L J Barry *Replacement* D George for Larsen (78 mins)
Scorers *Try:* Perelini   *Conversion:* Carter   *Penalty Goals:* Carter (2)
British Lions: G Hastings *(capt)*; Evans, Gibbs, Carling, T Underwood; Andrew, Morris; Popplewell, Milne, Burnell, Bayfield, Dooley, Teague, Richards, Winterbottom
Replacement Webster for Richards (55 mins)
Scorers *Tries:* Underwood, Andrew, Evans, Webster   *Conversions:* Hastings (3)
Penalty Goal: Hastings
Referee A G Riley (Waikato)

MATCH 3   29 May, Athletic Park, Wellington

NZ Maoris 20 (2G 2PG)   **British Lions 24** (3G 1PG)
NZ Maoris: S C Doyle; E J Rush, G N Konia, R D Ellison, A Prince; S Hirini, S T Forster; G M Hurunui, N J Hewitt, K G Boroevich, M S B Cooksley, J N Coe, J W Joseph, A R B Pene *(capt)*, Z V Brooke
Scorers *Tries:* Prince, Hirini   *Conversions:* Hirini (2)   *Penalty Goals:* Hirini (2)
British Lions: G Hastings *(capt)*; Evans, Carling, S Hastings, R Underwood; Barnes, Morris; Popplewell, Moore, Wright, Cronin, Dooley, Teague, Clarke, Winterbottom
Replacements Leonard for Popplewell (51 mins); Guscott for Carling (74 mins)
Scorers *Tries:* Evans, Underwood, G Hastings   *Conversions:* G Hastings (3)
Penalty Goal: G Hastings
Referee G Lempriere (Manawatu)

MATCH 4   2 June, Lancaster Park, Christchurch

Canterbury 10 (1G 1PG)   **British Lions 28** (1G 1PG 1DG 3T)
Canterbury: A Lawry; P Bale, S Philpott, K D Hansen, S J Cleave; G P Coffey, G T M Bachop; G A Halford, M G Hammett, S J Loe, C L England, M R McAtamney, T J Blackadder, R H Penney *(capt)*, G R Smith *Replacements* W K Maunsell for Hansen (4 mins); T Kele for Halford (62 mins)
Scorers *Try:* Smith   *Conversion:* Coffey   *Penalty Goal:* Coffey
British Lions: Clement; Wallace, Guscott, Gibbs, T Underwood; Andrew, Jones; Leonard, Milne, Burnell, Reed, Bayfield, Galwey, Richards *(capt)*, Clarke
Replacement Barnes for Andrew (76 mins)
Scorers *Tries:* Guscott, Galwey, Underwood, Andrew   *Conversion:* Andrew
Penalty Goal: Andrew   *Dropped Goal:* Andrew
Referee J A E Taylor (Counties)

MATCH 5   5 June, Carisbrook, Dunedin

Otago 37 (3G 1PG 1DG 2T)   **British Lions 24** (1G 4PG 1T)

Otago: J K R Timu; A R H Bell, M C G Ellis, J A Leslie, P J Cooke; S J Bachop, S T Forster; N Moore, D E Latta (*capt*), M A Mika, A M Rich, G Macpherson, J W Joseph, A R B Pene, J A Kronfeld
Scorers *Tries:* Cooke (2), Leslie, Latta, Timu   *Conversions:* Bell (3)
Penalty Goal: Bell   *Dropped Goal:* Bachop
British Lions: G Hastings (*capt*); Evans, Guscott, Carling, R Underwood; Barnes, Morris; Popplewell, Milne, Burnell, Bayfield, Dooley, Teague, Richards, Winterbottom
Replacements S Hastings for Carling (10 mins); Clement for S Hastings (47 mins); Galwey for Bayfield (78 mins)
Scorers *Tries:* Richards, Evans   *Conversion:* G Hastings   *Penalty Goals:* G Hastings (4)
Referee C J Hawke (South Canterbury)

MATCH 6   8 June, Homestead Rugby Stadium, Invercargill

Southland 16 (2PG 2T)   **British Lions 34** (2G 4PG 1DG 1T)
Southland: S Forrest; P J Johnston, A G James, G J Beardsley, J A Cormack; S D Culhane, B D Murrell; R J Palmer, D Heaps, C C Corbett, M B Tinnock, W A Miller, B J Morton, R T Smith, P W Henderson (*capt*) *Replacements* S P Hayes for Heaps (70 mins); R Bekhuis for Tinnock (74 mins)
Scorers *Tries:* Cormack, Johnston   *Penalty Goals:* Culhane (2)
British Lions: G Hastings (*capt*); Wallace, Gibbs, Clement, T Underwood; Andrew, Jones; Leonard, Moore, Wright, Cronin, Reed, Teague, Galwey, Webster
Replacements Barnes for Andrew (67 mins); Guscott for Gibbs (69 mins); Morris for Barnes (79 mins)
Scorers *Tries:* penalty try, Reed, Clement   *Conversions:* Hastings (2)
Penalty Goals: Hastings (4)   *Dropped Goal:* Clement
Referee M L Fitzgibbon (Canterbury)

MATCH 7   12 June, Lancaster Park, Christchurch   1st Test
NEW ZEALAND 20 (5PG 1T)   BRITISH ISLES 18 (6PG)

Grant Fox won the praise of the New Zealanders but broke the Lions' hearts with his pinpoint accurate kicks. His first-minute garryowen led to Frank Bunce's controversial try when Ieuan Evans, who made an awkward catch as the ball descended, was adjudged to have lost possession as he was bundled over the line by the All Blacks. Fox also landed five penalties, including one in the last minute after Dean Richards fell foul of the referee for a tackle offence which was hotly disputed.

Gavin Hastings showed for most of the match that anything Fox could do he could better. The Lions captain belted over penalties in the tenth, 17th, 35th, 48th, 53rd and 71st minutes to give his side the lead until the game entered its dying moments. His contribution equalled the record for most points by a Lion in a Test and took him past Phil Bennett's record haul of most points in Lions Tests.

NEW ZEALAND: J K R Timu (Otago); E Clarke (Auckland), F E Bunce (North Harbour), W K Little (North Harbour), V L Tuigamala (Auckland); G J Fox (Auckland), A D Strachan (North Harbour); C W Dowd (Auckland), S B T Fitzpatrick (Auckland) (*capt*), O M Brown (Auckland), I D Jones (North Auckland), R M Brooke (Auckland), J W Joseph (Otago), Z V Brooke (Auckland), M N Jones (Auckland)
Replacement M J A Cooper (Waikato) for Little (79 mins)
Scorers *Try:* Bunce   *Penalty Goals:* Fox (5)
BRITISH ISLES: G Hastings (*capt*); Evans, Guscott, Carling, R Underwood; Andrew,

Andy Reed of the Lions tackles All Black Va'aiga Tuigamala in the dramatic First Test in Christchurch.

Morris; Popplewell, Milne, Burnell, Reed, Bayfield, Clarke, Richards, Winterbottom
Scorer *Penalty Goals:* Hastings (6)
Referee B Kinsey (Australia)

MATCH 8   16 June, Rugby Park, New Plymouth

Taranaki 25 (2G 2PG 1T)   **British Lions 49** (4G 2PG 3T)
Taranaki: K J Crowley; D J Murfitt, K F Mahon, T Martin, K W Eynon; J B Cameron,
W R Dombroski; M R Allen *(capt)*, S R McDonald, G L Slater, D B O'Sullivan, J Roche,
A W Slater, N Hill, F Mahoni
Scorers *Tries:* O'Sullivan, A Slater, McDonald   *Conversions:* Crowley (2)
Penalty Goals: Crowley (2)
British Lions: Clement; Wallace, Cunningham, Gibbs, T Underwood; Barnes *(capt)*,
Jones; Wright, Moore, Leonard, Cronin, Johnson, Teague, Galwey, Webster
Replacements Clarke for Galwey (33 mins); Nicol for Jones (77 mins); Milne for Teague
(77 mins)
Scorers *Tries:* Cronin, Teague, Cunningham (2), Jones, Wallace, Gibbs
Conversions: Barnes (4)   *Penalty Goals:* Barnes (2)
Referee S Walsh (Wellington)

MATCH 9   19 June, Eden Park, Auckland

Auckland 23 (6PG 1T)   **British Lions 18** (1G 2PG 1T)
Auckland: S P Howarth; J J Kirwan, L Stensness, W R R Sotutu, E Clarke; G J Fox,
J A Hewett; C W Dowd, S B T Fitzpatrick, O M Brown, B T Jackson, R Fromont,
R M Brooke, Z V Brooke *(capt)*, M N Jones *Replacement* C Adams for Howarth (10 mins)
Scorers *Try:* Kirwan   *Penalty Goals:* Fox (6)
British Lions: G Hastings *(capt)*; Evans, Guscott, Gibbs, R Underwood; Andrew,
Morris; Popplewell, Moore, Burnell, Johnson, Bayfield, Webster, Clarke, Winterbottom
Replacements Carling for Hastings (40 mins); Milne for Moore (temp)
Scorers *Tries:* penalty try, Evans   *Conversion:* Hastings   *Penalty Goals:* Hastings,
Andrew
Referee D J Bishop (Southland)

MATCH 10   22 June, McLean Park, Napier

Hawke's Bay 29 (1G 3PG 1DG 2T)   **British Lions 17** (3PG 1DG 1T)
Hawke's Bay: J B Cunningham; A Hamilton, G N Konia, M R Paewai, F P Davis;
S Kerr, N M Weber; T G Taylor, N J Hewitt *(capt)*, O H Crawford, J Fowler,
W Davison, D J Watts, S Tremain, G J Falcon
Scorers *Tries:* Hewitt, Weber, Tremain   *Conversion:* Kerr
Penalty Goals: Cunningham (2), Kerr   *Dropped Goal:* Kerr
British Lions: Clement; Wallace, Cunningham, Carling, T Underwood; Barnes *(capt)*,
Jones; Wright, Milne, Leonard, Cronin, Reed, Teague, Galwey, Webster
Scorers *Try:* Webster   *Penalty Goals:* Barnes (3)   *Dropped Goal:* Carling
Referee P D O'Brien (North Otago)

MATCH 11   26 June, Athletic Park, Wellington   2nd Test

NEW ZEALAND 7 (1G)   BRITISH ISLES 20 (4PG 1DG 1T)

There were 11 England internationals, an all-time record for a Lions
Test side, in the team which levelled the series. The Lions registered
only their sixth Test victory on New Zealand soil and recorded their
highest score and biggest winning margin for Tests against the All Blacks.
     Gavin Hastings had been struggling with a hamstring injury before
the Test. The worries about his fitness became rife when he spilled a

steepling kick from Grant Fox and permitted Eroni Clarke to score a try after 12 minutes. Thereafter, however, the Lions pack took total control of the match while Jason Leonard, in the unaccustomed role of tighthead prop, proved as solid as the proverbial rock in the scrums. Rory Underwood provided the moment of excitement of the second half, sprinting along the touchline for a corner try that took the Lions 17-7 clear on the hour.

NEW ZEALAND: J K R Timu (Otago); J J Kirwan (Auckland), F E Bunce (North Harbour), E Clarke (Auckland), V L Tuigamala (Auckland); G J Fox (Auckland), J P Preston (Wellington); C W Dowd (Auckland), S B T Fitzpatrick (Auckland) (*capt*), O M Brown (Auckland), R M Brooke (Auckland), M S B Cooksley (Counties), J W Joseph (Otago), Z V Brooke (Auckland), M N Jones (Auckland) *Replacement* I D Jones (North Auckland) for Cooksley (40 mins)
Scorers *Try:* Clarke   *Conversion:* Fox
BRITISH ISLES: G Hastings (*capt*); Evans, Guscott, Gibbs, R Underwood; Andrew, Morris; Popplewell, Moore, Leonard, Johnson, Bayfield, Clarke, Richards, Winterbottom *Replacement* Teague for Winterbottom (temp)
Scorers *Try:* Underwood   *Penalty Goals:* Hastings (4)   *Dropped Goal:* Andrew
Referee P Robin (France)

MATCH 12   29 June, Rugby Park, Hamilton

Waikato 38 (2G 3PG 3T)   **British Lions 10** (1G 1PG)
Waikato: M J A Cooper; D M Wilson, A Collins, D R Ellison, W S Warlow; I D Foster, S J Crabb; C M Stevenson, W D Gatland, D W Stevenson, S B Gordon, B L Anderson, R M Jerram, J E P Mitchell (*capt*), D I Monkley *Replacement* M G Russell for Anderson (71 mins)
Scorers *Tries:* Wilson, Monkley (2), Collins, Gatland   *Conversions:* Cooper (2) *Penalty Goals:* Cooper (3)
British Lions: Clement; Wallace, Cunningham, Carling (*capt*), T Underwood; Barnes, Jones; Wright, Milne, Burnell, Cronin, Reed, Teague, Galwey, Webster
Scorers *Try:* Carling   *Conversion:* Barnes   *Penalty Goal:* Barnes
Referee T R Marshall (Canterbury)

MATCH 13   3 July, Eden Park, Auckland   3rd Test
NEW ZEALAND 30 (3G 3PG)   BRITISH ISLES 13 (1G 2PG)

The Lions were on top for 27 minutes, building up a 10-0 lead. The thousand or so loyal supporters who had followed the tour and the millions who maintained midnight vigils before televisions back in Britain hoped that the platform for a famous series victory had been established. It had not. For the first time in the rubber the All Blacks' back row won the battle for the equivalent of soccer's midfield, and instead it was New Zealand who reached half-time nursing a slender 14-10 lead, thanks to tries by Frank Bunce and Sean Fitzpatrick converted by the metronomic Grant Fox.

The Lions launched a mighty offensive to mark the start of the second half. The All Blacks, bursting with pride, displayed the kind of spirit which had characterised their approach to the 1987 World Cup win. For the Lions the uphill task became an impossible one when further

Scott Gibbs beats John Timu to score a try for the Lions in the third and deciding Test in Auckland. The All Blacks won 30–13 to deny the Lions an historic series victory.

goals from Fox and a blindside try scored by Jon Preston crowned New Zealand's best display of the series.

NEW ZEALAND: J K R Timu (Otago); J J Kirwan (Auckland), F E Bunce (North Harbour), L Stensness (Auckland), V L Tuigamala (Auckland); G J Fox (Auckland), J P Preston (Wellington); C W Dowd (Auckland), S B T Fitzpatrick (Auckland) (*capt*), O M Brown (Auckland), R M Brooke (Auckland), I D Jones (North Auckland), J W Joseph (Otago), A R B Pene (Otago), M N Jones (Auckland) *Replacements* M S B Cooksley (Counties) for I Jones (20 mins); Z V Brooke (Auckland) for M Jones (73 mins)
Scorers *Tries:* Bunce, Fitzpatrick, Preston   *Conversions:* Fox (3)   *Penalty Goals:* Fox (3)
BRITISH ISLES: G Hastings (*capt*); Evans, Guscott, Gibbs, R Underwood; Andrew, Morris; Popplewell, Moore, Leonard, Johnson, Bayfield, Clarke, Richards, Winterbottom
Scorers *Try:* Gibbs   *Conversion:* Hastings   *Penalty Goals:* Hastings (2)
Referee P Robin (France)

ENGLAND TO CANADA 1993

With 16 of their senior players on tour with the Lions in New Zealand, England sent what was effectively the A team on a short five-match tour of Canada in May and June. No caps were awarded for the two-Test series against the team which had reached the quarter-finals of the 1991 World Cup.

The visit should have given England's selectors an early opportunity to assess the form of the likely contenders for places in the 1995 World Cup squad. But in truth, players who were tired after a long domestic season showed little relish for more representative rugby. Hard grounds and the heavy tackling which is a feature of the Canadian game took their toll on the visitors, who had to summon four replacements for injured players.

Kyran Bracken was the only tourist who really enhanced a claim for a full international place. In the chase for Dewi Morris's scrum-half shirt he leapfrogged Matt Dawson, whose tour was barely ten minutes old before a hamstring injury put him out of action. Bracken's distribution and vision in the second international definitely gave the tourists the necessary edge to tie the series.

The tour also revealed the line-out promise of Bristol's Andy Blackmore, while his partner Martin Johnson showed that he was fit to be a Lion: as the squad prepared to fly home at the end of the tour Johnson boarded an aeroplane for New Zealand, to replace Wade Dooley in the Lions Test pack.

THE TOURING PARTY
Manager P A Rossborough   **Coach** M A C Slemen   **Assistant Coach** K Richardson
Captain C J Olver

FULL-BACKS

D Pears (Harlequins)
A J Buzza (Wasps)

THREEQUARTERS

S T Hackney (Leicester)

N D Beal (Northampton)
C Oti (Wasps)
A A Adebayo (Bath)
J Fletcher (Tynedale)
P R de Glanville (Bath)
D P Hopley (Wasps)

G C Childs (Wasps)
***S Potter** (Leicester)

HALF-BACKS

A P Challinor (Harlequins)
P J Grayson (Waterloo)
***S M Douglas** (Newcastle Gosforth)
M J S Dawson (Northampton)
K P P Bracken (Bristol)

FORWARDS

G C Rowntree (Leicester)
M P Hynes (Orrell)
D J Garforth (Leicester)
V E Ubogu (Bath)

C J Olver (Northampton)
K A Dunn (Wasps)
M O Johnson (Leicester)
A G Blackmore (Bristol)
A C W Snow (Harlequins)
N C Redman (Bath)
J P Hall (Bath)
***M I Rennell** (Bedford)
T A K Rodber (Northampton)
M J Greenwood (Wasps)
D Ryan (Wasps)
S O Ojomoh (Bath)
N A Back (Leicester)
***R S R Langhorn** (Harlequins)
* Replacement during tour

TOUR RECORD
All matches Played 5 Won 4 Lost 1 Points for 123 Against 57
International matches Played 2 Won 1 Lost 1 Points for 31 Against 29
(England did not award caps because 16 players were on the British Lions tour)

SCORING DETAILS

All matches

For:	13T	5C	15PG	1DG	123 Pts
Against:	4T	2C	10PG	1DG	57 Pts

International matches

For:	2T	–	7PG	–	31 Pts
Against:	1T	–	7PG	1DG	29 Pts

MATCH DETAILS

1993	OPPONENTS	VENUE	RESULT
22 May	British Columbia	Victoria	W 26-10
26 May	BC President's XV	Vancouver	W 26-11
29 May	CANADA	Vancouver	L 12-15
2 June	Ontario	Toronto	W 40-7
5 June	CANADA	Ottawa	W 19-14

Appearances: 4 – Hopley*, Beal**, Adebayo*; 3 – Pears, Oti, Challinor, Rowntree, Olver, Ubogu, Blackmore, Johnson, Hall, Ojomoh, Back, Potter, Bracken*, Fletcher*; 2 – Buzza, Hackney, Grayson, Douglas, Hynes, Dunn, Garforth, Redman, Snow, Greenwood, Langhorn, Rennell; 1 – de Glanville, Dawson, Childs *includes appearances as a replacement
Scorers: 26 – Grayson (4C 6PG); 23 – Pears (1C 7PG); 19 – Challinor (2T 2PG 1DG); 10 – Adebayo, Potter (both 2T); 5 – Hopley, Bracken, Hackney, Rennell, Greenwood, Beal, Douglas (all 1T)

MATCH 1 22 May, Victoria

British Columbia 10 (1G 1PG) **England XV 26** (1G 2PG 1DG 2T)
British Columbia: S Stewart; S Gray, M Williams, M Doyle, B Ebl; J Graf, C Tynan (*capt*); J Hayes, M Cardinal, D Jackart, J Knauer, I Cooper, I Gordon, C McKenzie, G MacKinnon *Replacements* G Rees for Ebl (55 mins); B Breen for Gordon (75 mins)
Scorers *Try:* McKenzie *Conversion:* Rees *Penalty Goal:* Tynan
England XV: Pears; Beal, de Glanville, Hopley, Oti; Challinor, Dawson; Rowntree, Olver (*capt*), Ubogu, Blackmore, Johnson, Hall, Ojomoh, Back *Replacements* Bracken for Dawson (10 mins); Adebayo for de Glanville (35 mins)
Scorers *Tries:* Hopley, Bracken, Adebayo *Conversion:* Pears *Penalty Goals:* Pears (2)
Dropped Goal: Challinor
Referee K Morrison (Victoria)

MATCH 2 26 May, Thunderbird Stadium, Vancouver

BC President's XV 11 (2PG 1T) **England XV 26** (1G 3PG 2T)
BC President's XV: B Jordan; S MacKinnon, T Toews, R Toews, R Wheeldon; R Ross,

29

I McKay (*capt*); K Wirachowski, J Benko, P Szabo, I Cooper, A Wilson, A Phillips, M Schmid, R Robson *Replacements* I Kennedy for Phillips (30 mins); T Murdy for Cooper (47 mins)
Scorers *Try:* MacKinnon *Penalty Goals:* Ross (2)
England XV: Buzza; Hackney, Fletcher, Childs, Adebayo; Grayson, Douglas; Hynes, Dunn, Garforth, Redman (*capt*), Snow, Greenwood, Langhorn, Rennell
Replacement Hopley for Adebayo (75 mins)
Scorers *Tries:* Hackney, Rennell, Adebayo *Conversion:* Grayson
Penalty Goals: Grayson (3)
Referee C Marsden (Vancouver)

MATCH 3   29 May, Swangard Stadium, Vancouver

CANADA 15 (4PG 1DG)   ENGLAND 12 (4PG)

Canada, who had beaten a Scotland XV two years earlier, added the scalp of another representative side from the Home Unions. England's pack won plenty of possession, Andy Blackmore's aerial superiority at the line-out was unchallenged and the front row remained rock-solid against Canada's experienced front five. It was their backs who let England down. They were ponderous in attack and the Canadian back row had a field day, mowing them down with thunderous tackles.

The Canadians used John Graf, a former scrum-half, as partner to Chris Tynan, and their star kicker, Gareth Rees, was accommodated at centre. There, his burly presence played a part in Canada's aggressive defence, though it was his last-minute penalty that won the match. A touch-judge intervened to accuse Neil Back of foul play when the score was 12-12. Rees, never one to lack a big-match temperament, nervelessly placed the goal.

CANADA: S Stewart (UBC Old Boys); J Loveday (Calgary Irish), S Gray (Vancouver Kats), G Rees (Oak Bay Castaways), D Lougheed (Toronto Welsh); J Graf (UBC Old Boys), C Tynan (Vancouver Meralomas); E Evans (IBM Tokyo), K Svoboda (Ajax Wanderers) (*capt*), D Jackart (UBC Old Boys), A Charron (Ottawa Irish), J Knauer (Vancouver Meralomas), B Breen (Vancouver Meralomas), C McKenzie (UBC Old Boys), G Ennis (Suntory Tokyo)
Scorers *Penalty Goals:* Rees (4) *Dropped Goal:* Graf
ENGLAND: Pears; Buzza, Potter, Hopley, Oti; Challinor, Bracken; Rowntree, Olver (*capt*), Ubogu, Johnson, Blackmore, Hall, Ojomoh, Back *Replacement* Beal for Buzza (3 mins)
Scorers *Penalty Goals:* Pears (4)
Referee A R MacNeill (Australia)

MATCH 4   2 June, Toronto

Ontario 7 (1G)   **England XV 40** (3G 3PG 2T)
Ontario: G Pettigrew; C Smith, S Bryan, J O'Meara, W Lyttleton; S Pettigrew, C Wilson; M Jacques, S Hendry, J Ashley, T Gibson, I Middleton (*capt*), J Tomlinson, P Ross, J Hutchinson
Scorers *Try:* Smith *Conversion:* G Pettigrew
England XV: Beal; Hackney, Potter, Fletcher, Adebayo; Grayson, Douglas; Hynes, Dunn, Garforth, Redman (*capt*), Snow, Greenwood, Langhorn, Rennell
Scorers *Tries:* Potter (2), Greenwood, Beal, Douglas *Conversions:* Grayson (3)
Penalty Goals: Grayson (3)
Referee I Hyde-Lay (British Columbia)

MATCH 5   5 June, Twin Elm Rugby Park, Ottawa

CANADA 14 (3PG 1T)   ENGLAND 19 (3PG 2T)

Sixteen points from Paul Challinor on an overcast day in Ottawa helped England square the mini-series. The tourists used their strong men – Steve Ojomoh, Victor Ubogu and Jon Hall – as battering rams to tie Canada's back row into the rucks and mauls. The tactic was effective and, as a result, the pressure on the England backs, who had been tackled into submission in the First Test, was reduced.

England's pack went well throughout the afternoon and at their heels Kyran Bracken played with considerable maturity. The scrum-half's quick presence of mind created the decisive score which took his side 19-11 clear 11 minutes into the second half. Hall put in a big tackle near Canada's line, England's forwards won possession and Bracken made the opening for Challinor to score his second try of the match.

CANADA: S Stewart (UBC Old Boys); J Loveday (Ottawa Irish), S Gray (Vancouver Kats), G Rees (Oak Bay Castaways), D Lougheed (Toronto Welsh); J Graf (UBC Old Boys), C Tynan (Vancouver Meralomas); E Evans (IBM Tokyo), K Svoboda (Ajax Wanderers), D Jackart (UBC Old Boys), J Knauer (Vancouver Meralomas), N Hadley (UBC Old Boys) (*capt*), A Charron (Ottawa Irish), G Ennis (Suntory Tokyo), G MacKinnon (Ex-Britannia Lions) *Replacement* J Hutchinson (York Yeomen) for MacKinnon (77 mins)
Scorers *Try:* MacKinnon   *Penalty Goals:* Rees (3)
ENGLAND: Pears; Adebayo, Potter, Hopley, Oti; Challinor, Bracken; Rowntree, Olver (*capt*), Ubogu, Johnson, Blackmore, Hall, Ojomoh, Back *Replacements* Beal for Pears (27 mins); Fletcher for Challinor (58 mins)
Scorers *Tries:* Challinor (2)   *Penalty Goals:* Challinor (2), Pears
Referee A R MacNeill (Australia)

WALES TO ZIMBABWE AND NAMIBIA 1993

'What this tour will have done is lay a foundation for next season,' said manager Robert Norster, summing up Wales' successful unbeaten tour of Southern Africa. True, heat and altitude problems induced a sluggish performance by the Welsh forwards in their opening match of the trip against Zimbabwe. But a ten-try romp a couple of days later against the Zimbabwe B side quickly set a lively tone which was sustained for the rest of the tour. The backs revelled behind a dominant pack and took every opportunity to show their fine finishing skills.

Neil Jenkins revealed his versatility on tour, appearing as centre, full-back and fly-half respectively in the three internationals. Not even Jenkins, though, could catch the exciting Zimbabwean wing, Victor Olonga, who brought the house down in the Harare Test when he loped 80 metres for a sensational try in the closing moments of the second international.

Although the Tests were comfortably won in the end, Wales did have a struggle early on in the Windhoek Test against Namibia. They fell behind in the second minute of the game and trailed 14-17 at half-time before Jenkins rescued Wales with his boot. He kicked 13 points in the match and thus brought to 100 his points tally in cap internationals.

Robin McBryde, the Swansea hooker, received his marching orders in the match against Namibia B, which was watched by a mere 600 spectators. Mr Theunissen, the referee, dismissed him for allegedly punching an opponent. The consensus was that the referee might have been visually challenged.

Wales gave emphatic notice of their growing potential with a convincing win against the South African Barbarians in the final match of the tour. The victory was achieved with style. Forwards and backs joined in an impressive display to create eight tries. Jenkins, with seven more accurate kicks, brought his tour points haul to 89 points, a new record for a Welsh team on tour.

THE TOURING PARTY

Manager R L Norster   **Coach** A Davies   **Assistant Coach** G Jenkins
Captain G O Llewellyn

FULL-BACKS

M A Rayer (Cardiff)
I W Jones (Llanelli)

THREEQUARTERS

W T Proctor (Llanelli)
R A Bidgood (Newport)
S D Hill (Cardiff)
H Woodland (Neath)
N Boobyer (Llanelli)

HALF-BACKS

N R Jenkins (Pontypridd)
A Davies (Cardiff)
R H StJ B Moon (Llanelli)
R Howley (Bridgend)

FORWARDS

M Griffiths (Cardiff)
I Buckett (Swansea)
H Williams-Jones (SW Police)
J D Davies (Neath)
A E H Lamerton (Llanelli)
R McBryde (Swansea)
G O Llewellyn (Neath)
A H Copsey (Llanelli)
P T Davies (Llanelli)
P Arnold (Swansea)
A Williams (Maesteg)
E W Lewis (Llanelli)
R L Jones (Llanelli)
M A Perego (Llanelli)
S Davies (Swansea)

TOUR RECORD

All matches   Played 6   Won 6   Points for 282   Against 90
International matches   Played 3   Won 3   Points for 115   Against 50

SCORING DETAILS

All matches

For:	40T	26C	9PG	1DG	282 Pts
Against:	9T	6C	11PG	–	90 Pts

International matches

For:	15T	8C	7PG	1DG	115 Pts
Against:	4T	3C	8PG	–	50 Pts

MATCH DETAILS

1993	OPPONENTS	VENUE	RESULT
22 May	ZIMBABWE	Bulawayo	W 35-14
25 May	Zimbabwe B	Harare	W 64-13
29 May	ZIMBABWE	Harare	W 42-13
2 June	Namibia B	Windhoek	W 47-10
5 June	NAMIBIA	Windhoek	W 38-23
9 June	South African Barbarians	Windhoek	W 56-17

Appearances: 6 – S Davies*, Hill*, Jenkins; 5 – Boobyer, Proctor, Rayer; 4 – A Davies*, P Davies*, Griffiths, Lamerton, Lewis, Llewellyn, Moon, Perego; 3 – Arnold, Bidgood, J Davies, L Jones, Williams*, Williams-Jones; 2 – Buckett, Copsey, Howley, I Jones, McBryde, Woodland *includes appearances as a replacement
Scorers: 89 – Jenkins (2T 26C 9PG); 25 – Proctor (5T); 20 – I Jones (4T); 15 – Boobyer, Hill, Rayer (all 3T); 10 – J Davies, P Davies, S Davies, Howley, Lewis, Llewellyn, Moon (all 2T); 8 – A Davies (1T 1DG); 5 – Arnold, Bidgood, Buckett, McBryde, Perego

MATCH 1   22 May, Bulawayo   1st Test

ZIMBABWE 14 (3PG 1T) **WALES 35** (3G 2PG 1DG 1T)
ZIMBABWE: I Noble (Old Miltonians); D Nash (Mat Busters), M Letcher (Old Hararians), D Walters (Old Miltonians) *(capt)*, V Olonga (Old Miltonians); C Brown (Harare Sports Club), S Day (Old Miltonians); G Snyder (Harare Sports Club), B Beattie (Old Miltonians), A Garvey (Old Miltonians), R Demblon (Old Hararians), T Tabvuma (Old Miltonians), S Landman (Harare Sports Club), B Dawson (Old Miltonians), E Fargnoli (Old Miltonians)
Scorers *Try:* Olonga *Penalty Goals:* Walters (3)
WALES: Rayer; Hill, Bidgood, Jenkins, Proctor; A Davies, Moon; Griffiths, Lamerton, Williams-Jones, P Davies, Llewellyn *(capt)*, Perego, L Jones, Lewis
Scorers *Tries:* P Davies, Hill, Moon, Proctor *Conversions:* Jenkins (3)
Penalty Goals: Jenkins (2) *Dropped Goal:* A Davies
Referee I Rogers (South Africa)

MATCH 2   25 May, Harare

Zimbabwe B 13 (1PG 2T) **Wales XV 64** (7G 3T)
Zimbabwe B: T Tambo; A Jani, D Maidza, G Whittal, D Nash; W Veltman, E MacMillan; D Johnstone, P Albasini *(capt)*, T Erlank, B Chivandire, M Fick, G Cheromo, M Malaniphy, D Kirkman
Scorers *Tries:* Chivandire, Kirkman *Penalty Goal:* Veltman
Wales XV: I Jones; Hill, Boobyer, Woodland, Rayer; Jenkins, Howley; Buckett, McBryde, J Davies, Arnold, Copsey, A Williams, S Davies *(capt)*, Perego
Scorers *Tries:* Jones (2), Rayer (2), Howley, Buckett, Boobyer, Hill, Arnold, Jenkins
Conversions: Jenkins (7)
Referee K Shadwick (Zimbabwe)

MATCH 3   29 May, Harare   2nd Test

ZIMBABWE 13 (1G 2PG) **WALES 42** (3G 2PG 3T)
ZIMBABWE: I Noble (Old Miltonians); W Schultz (Karoi), M Letcher (Old Hararians), D Walters (Old Miltonians) *(capt)*, V Olonga (Old Miltonians); C Brown (Harare Sports Club), G Snyder (Harare Sports Club), B Beattie (Old Miltonians), E MacMillan (Old Hararians); G Snyder (Harare Sports Club), B Beattie (Old Miltonians), A Garvey (Old Miltonians), R Demblon (Old Hararians), T Tabvuma (Old Miltonians), S Landman (Harare Sports Club), B Dawson (Old Miltonians), D Kirkman (Old Miltonians)
Replacements E Chimbima (Old Hararians) for Schultz (33 mins); B Chivandire (Old Hararians) for Landman (53 mins)
Scorers *Try:* Olonga *Conversion:* Noble *Penalty Goals:* Noble (2)
WALES: Jenkins; Hill, Boobyer, Bidgood, Proctor; A Davies, Moon; Griffiths, Lamerton, J Davies, Arnold, Llewellyn *(capt)*, S Davies, L Jones, Lewis
Scorers *Tries:* Llewellyn (2), Bidgood, J Davies, S Davies, Jenkins
Conversions: Jenkins (3) *Penalty Goals:* Jenkins (2)
Referee I Anderson (South Africa)

MATCH 4   2 June, Windhoek

Namibia B 10 (1G 1PG) **Wales XV 47** (6G 1T)
Namibia B: D Gous; R Gous, N Du Plessis, E Isaacs, S von Skalkvake; N Horn,

H Husselman; R Esterhuizen, A von Tonder, W Otto, A Hwisamen, J Jordan, P du Plooy (*capt*), G Rich, F Francis
Scorers *Try:* R Gous   *Conversion:* Horn   *Penalty Goal:* Horn
Wales XV: Rayer; Hill, Boobyer, Woodland, Proctor; Jenkins, Howley; Buckett, McBryde, Williams-Jones, Arnold, Copsey, S Davies (*capt*), A Williams, Perego
Replacements A Davies for Hill (44 mins); P Davies for Williams (53 mins)
Scorers *Tries:* Proctor (2), Boobyer (2), McBryde, Howley, Rayer
Conversions: Jenkins (6)
Referee P Theunissen (Namibia)

MATCH 5   5 June Windhoek   Test Match

NAMIBIA 23 (2G 3PG)   **WALES 38** (2G 3PG 3T)
NAMIBIA: J Coetzee (Police); G Mans (Wanderers) (*capt*), H Snyman (Wanderers), M Marais (Police), E Meyer (United); M Booysen (United), B Buitendag (Transnamib); C Derks (Transnamib), S Smith (United), A van Wyk (United), D Kotze (Transnamib), B Malgas (Transnamib), J Barnard (Wanderers), H Brink (Transnamib), K Goosen (Oranjemund)
Scorers *Tries:* Coetzee, Kotze   *Conversions:* Coetzee (2)   *Penalty Goals:* Coetzee (3)
WALES: Rayer; Hill, Bidgood, Boobyer, Proctor; Jenkins, Moon; Griffiths, Lamerton, Williams-Jones, P Davies, Llewellyn (*capt*), S Davies, L Jones, Lewis
Scorers *Tries:* Lewis (2), Hill, Proctor, Moon   *Conversions:* Jenkins (2)
Penalty Goals: Jenkins (3)
Referee K W McCartney (Scotland)

MATCH 6   9 June, Windhoek

South African Barbarians 17 (2G 1PG)   **Wales XV 56** (5G 2PG 3T)
South African Barbarians: C Dirks (Transvaal); G Mans (Namibia), H L Müller (Orange Free State), H Snyman (Namibia), A Alexander (Border); J Stransky (Natal), J P Roux (Transvaal); G R Kebble (Natal), J Allan (Natal) (*capt*), M H Hurter (Western Transvaal), R J Kruger (Orange Free State), J J Strydom (Transvaal), R J Opperman (Orange Free State), G Teichmann (Natal), J Barnard (Namibia)
Replacements C Derks (Namibia) for Kebble (40 mins); J Coetzee (Namibia) for Mans (76 mins)
Scorers *Tries:* Barnard, Stransky   *Conversions:* Stransky (2)   *Penalty Goal:* Stransky
Wales XV: Rayer; I Jones, Boobyer, Jenkins, Proctor; A Davies, Moon; Griffiths, Lamerton, J Davies, S Davies, P Davies, Llewellyn (*capt*), Lewis, Perego
Replacements Hill for Proctor (39 mins); Williams for Perego (66 mins)
Scorers *Tries:* Jones (2), Proctor, Perego, P Davies, J Davies, S Davies, A Davies
Conversions: Jenkins (5)   *Penalty Goals:* Jenkins (2)
Referee F Burger (South Africa)

FRANCE TO SOUTH AFRICA 1993

France used their first tour of the Republic since 1980 to develop fresh talent. Didier Camberabero, Franck Mesnel and Jean-Baptiste Lafond, three of the senior players who had helped the side to become the 1993 European champions, were discarded as the French selectors attempted to build a squad for the 1995 Rugby World Cup.

The discovery of the tour was undoubtedly Olivier Merle, the 20-stone former shot-putter. He showed considerable potential alongside Olivier Roumat in the Test pack, although his lack of experience in the loose was occasionally more of a hindrance than a help to the French cause. There was also a welcome return to the side by Alain Penaud, whose commitment to free-running rugby excited the South African spectators.

France faced a demanding itinerary in the five-match run-up to the Tests. Besides a draw with Free State, they lost to the South African B team and to Northern Transvaal, and their preparations were disrupted early in the tour by the loss of their captain, Jeff Tordo. He suffered appalling facial injuries when he was raked by Gary Pagel in the Western Province match. Tordo required 50 stitches and plastic surgery. Pagel was initially suspended for the rest of the season, but had his ban halved on appeal.

Tordo's biggest contribution since becoming captain had been to instil the side with pride and higher standards of discipline. Olivier Roumat, his successor, continued the good work.

THE TOURING PARTY

Manager G Laporte   **Coach** P Berbizier   **Assistant Coach** C Mombet
Captain J-F Tordo, replaced by O Roumat

FULL-BACKS

J-L Sadourny (Colomiers)
O Campan (Agen)

THREEQUARTERS

P Hontas (Biarritz)
P Saint-André (Montferrand)
P Bernat-Salles (Pau)
D Berty (Toulouse)
P Sella (Agen)
T Lacroix (Dax)
H Couffignal (Colomiers)
P Bondouy (Narbonne)

HALF-BACKS

A Penaud (Brive)
P Montlaur (Agen)
A Hueber (Toulon)
J Cazalbou (Toulouse)

FORWARDS

L Armary (Lourdes)

L Seigne (Agen)
S Graou (Auch)
E Menieu (SBUC Bordeaux)
J-F Tordo (Nice)
J-M Gonzalez (Bayonne)
O Roumat (Dax)
A Benazzi (Agen)
O Merle (Grenoble)
Y Lemeur (Racing Club de France)
P Benetton (Agen)
L Cabannes (Racing Club de France)
L Loppy (Toulon)
J-M Lhermet (Montferrand)
M Cecillon (Bourgoin)
X Blond (Racing Club de France)
*L Verge (Bègles-Bordeaux)
*C Deslandes (Racing Club de France)

*Replacements during tour

TOUR RECORD

All matches   Played 8   Won 4   Drawn 2   Lost 2   Points for 169   Against 159
International matches   Played 2   Won 1   Drawn 1   Points for 38   Against 37

SCORING DETAILS

All matches						International matches					
For:	14T	9C	22PG	5DG	169 Pts	For:	1T	–	7PG	4DG	38 Pts
Against:	12T	6C	29PG	–	159 Pts	Against:	2T	–	9PG	–	37 Pts

MATCH DETAILS

1993	OPPONENTS	VENUE	RESULT
9 June	Eastern Province	Port Elizabeth	W 18-8
12 June	Western Province	Cape Town	W 12-6
15 June	South Africa B	East London	L 22-35
19 June	Orange Free State	Bloemfontein	D 22-22
22 June	Northern Transvaal	Pretoria	L 19-38
26 June	SOUTH AFRICA	Durban	D 20-20
29 June	Development XV	Welkom	W 38-13
3 July	SOUTH AFRICA	Johannesburg	W 18-17

Appearances: 7 – Gonzalez**; 6 – Roumat, Graou*; 5 – Benetton*, Cecillon*, Lhermet*, Merle, Campan**, Lacroix; 4 – Armary, Blond, Cabannes, Loppy, Menieu, Bernat-Salles, Berty, Bondouy, Cazalbou, Couffignal, Hontas, Hueber, Montlaur, Penaud, Sadourny, Saint-André, Sella; 3 – Lemeur, Verge; 2 – Benazzi*, Seigne; 1 – Deslandes, Tordo   * includes appearances as a replacement
Scorers: 51 – Montlaur (13PG 6C); 36 – Lacroix (3C 9PG 1DG); 20 – Berty (4T); 19 – Penaud (2T 3DG); 10 – Bondouy (2T); 8 – Hueber (1T 1DG); 5 – Loppy, Hontas, Saint-André, Merle Sella (all 1T)

MATCH 1   9 June, Boet Erasmus Stadium, Port Elizabeth

Eastern Province 8 (1PG 1T)   France XV 18 (1G 1PG 1DG 1T)
Eastern Province: A Fourie; E Truter, M Knoetze, H Fuls, T Markow; G Miller, G Wright (*capt*); F Erasmus, H Brown, W Meyer, N Meyer, A Geldenhuys, M Wood, M Mostert, E van der Bergh
Scorer *Try:* Miller   *Penalty Goal:* Miller
France XV: Sadourny; Hontas, Lacroix, Couffignal, Bernat-Salles; Penaud, Cazalbou; Menieu, Gonzalez, Seigne, Lemeur, Roumat (*capt*), Lhermet, Blond, Cabannes
Scorers *Tries:* Penaud (2)   *Conversion:* Lacroix   *Penalty Goal:* Lacroix
Dropped Goal: Penaud
Referee I Anderson (Transvaal)

MATCH 2   12 June, Newlands, Cape Town

Western Province 6 (2PG)   France XV 12 (4PG)
Western Province: G Lawless; C Williams, T Linee, C Scholtz, S Berridge; L Sherrell, A Kirsten; G Pagel, A Patterson, K Andrews, L Blom, N Wegner, A Aitken, C Strauss (*capt*), S Burger *Replacement* Trytsman for Blom (12 mins)
Scorer *Penalty Goals:* Sherrell (2)
France XV: Campan; Berty, Bondouy, Lacroix, Saint-André; Montlaur, Hueber; Armary, Tordo (*capt*), Graou, Merle, Roumat, Loppy, Cecillon, Lhermet
Replacement Gonzalez for Tordo (15 mins)
Scorer *Penalty Goals:* Montlaur (4)
Referee S Neethling (Boland)

MATCH 3   15 June, Basil Kenyon Stadium, East London

South Africa B 35 (3G 3PG 1T)   France XV 22 (2G 1PG 1T)
South Africa B: H Reece-Edwards; C Williams, H Fuls, F A Meiring, D Oosthuysen; H Honiball, J van der Westhuizen; G R Kebble, J Allan, L Müller, J J Strydom, N Wegner, R J Kruger, A Richter (*capt*), I Macdonald *Replacement* A Cloete for Macdonald (78 mins)
Scorers *Tries:* Macdonald, van der Westhuizen (2), Williams
Conversions: Reece-Edwards (3)   *Penalty Goals:* Reece-Edwards (3)
France XV: Penaud; Bernat-Salles, Sella, Bondouy, Saint-André; Montlaur, Hueber; Menieu, Gonzalez, Seigne, Roumat (*capt*), Benazzi, Benetton, Blond, Cabannes
Replacement Cecillon for Benazzi (35 mins)
Scorers *Tries:* Hueber, Bondouy, Sella   *Conversions:* Montlaur (2)
Penalty Goal: Montlaur
Referee F Burger (Western Province)

MATCH 4   19 June, Free State Stadium, Bloemfontein

Orange Free State 22 (1G 5PG)   France XV 22 (2G 1PG 1T)
Orange Free State: H Truter; I Beneke, A Pawson, H Müller, C Badenhorst; J de Beer,
H Martens; J J Styger, A Bester, D Theron, D van Zyl, A Cloete, R J Kruger,
P G Human (capt), J Beukes Replacement A Fourie for Bester (78 mins)
Scorers Try: de Beer   Conversion: de Beer   Penalty Goals: de Beer (4), Truter
France XV: Sadourny; Hontas, Couffignal, Sella (capt), Berty; Lacroix, Cazalbou;
Armary, Verge, Graou, Lemeur, Merle, Loppy, Cecillon, Lhermet
Scorers Tries: Berty (2), Merle   Conversions: Lacroix (2)   Penalty Goal: Lacroix
Referee A L Adams (Northern Transvaal)

MATCH 5   22 June, Loftus Versveld, Pretoria

Northern Transvaal 38 (2G 8PG)   FRANCE XV 19 (1G 4PG)
Northern Transvaal: J J van der Walt; D Oosthuysen, J Claassens, F A Meiring,
F P Naude; C Maree, C Breytenbach; J Barnard, C Rossouw, R van Niekerk, P Schutte,
J Gouws, G Combrinck, A Richter (capt), K Otto
Scorers Tries: Breytenbach, van der Walt   Conversions: Maree (2)
Penalty Goals: Maree (8)
FRANCE XV: Campan; Berty, Bondouy, Couffignal, Hontas; Montlaur, Cazalbou;
Graou, Verge, Menieu, Roumat (capt), Merle, Loppy, Blond, Benetton
Replacements Benazzi for Roumat (41 mins); Gonzalez for Benazzi (75 mins);
Lhermet for Benetton (40 mins)
Scorers Try: Bondouy   Conversion: Montlaur   Penalty Goals: Montlaur (4)
Referee I Rogers (Natal)

MATCH 6   26 June, King's Park, Durban   1st Test

SOUTH AFRICA 20 (5PG 1T)   FRANCE 20 (3PG 2DG 1T)

South Africa entered the Test as favourites after lacklustre French
performances in their three preceding tour matches. But France, who
dominated the line-outs and had the better of the loose play, were never
behind in a game that they should easily have won.

Yet for all the confidence France displayed, they were never able to
establish a winning lead. Both sides relied heavily on their kickers to
accumulate points and the only tries scored came in the second quarter
of the match.

France were 9-6 ahead when Alain Penaud made a lovely blindside
break which opened the path for Philippe Saint-André to score. Uli
Schmidt crossed for South Africa's try after a ruck near the French line
to make the score 11-14 at the break. The kickers landed five penalties
in the second half to tie the scores.

SOUTH AFRICA: J T J van Rensburg (Transvaal); J T Small (Natal), H T Fuls
(Eastern Province), P G Müller (Natal), J Olivier (Northern Transvaal); H P le Roux
(Transvaal), R J du Preez (Natal); W G Hills (Northern Transvaal), U L Schmidt
(Transvaal), K S Andrews (Western Province), J J Wiese (Transvaal), R G Visagie
(Natal), J F Pienaar (Transvaal) (capt), C P Strauss (Western Province), I Macdonald
(Transvaal)
Scorers Try: Schmidt   Penalty Goals: van Rensburg (5)
France: Sadourny; Bernat-Salles, Lacroix, Sella, Saint-André; Penaud, Hueber;
Armary, Gonzalez, Graou, Merle, Roumat (capt), Benetton, Cecillon, Cabannes
Replacement Campan for Bernat-Salles (50 mins)

Scorers *Try:* Saint André   *Penalty Goals:* Lacroix (3)   *Dropped Goals:* Hueber, Penaud
Referee S R Hilditch (Ireland)

MATCH 7   29 June, Welkom Stadium, Welkom

Development XV 13 (1PG 2T)   **France XV 38** (3G 4PG 1T)
Development XV: I Oktober; A Alexander, P Treu, T Zweni, F Amsterdam;
R Hendricks, A Coetzee; K Bezuidenhout, P Stubbs, M Hurter, S Goedhals, M Potgieter,
B Peterson, R Britton, C Lutz
Scorers *Tries:* Hendricks, Coetzee   *Penalty Goal:* Hendricks
France XV: Campan; Hontas, Bondouy, Couffignal, Berty; Montlaur, Cazalbou;
Menieu, Gonzalez, Verge, Lemeur, Deslandes, Loppy, Blond, Lhermet
Replacements Graou for Gonzalez (44 mins); Benetton for Blond (60 mins)
Scorers *Tries:* Hontas, Loppy, Berty (2)   *Conversions:* Montlaur (3)
Penalty Goals: Montlaur (4)
Referee P Lombaard (Northern Orange Free State)

MATCH 8   3 July, Ellis Park, Johannesburg   2nd Test
SOUTH AFRICA 17 (4PG 1T)   FRANCE 18 (4PG 2DG)

The Springboks began the deciding Test of the series with a sparkling exhibition of attacking rugby matching the bright spectacle of South Africa's first floodlit rugby international. James Small ran in for a splendid try in the seventh minute and soon afterwards Theo van Rensburg stretched the lead to eight points with the first of his four successful kicks at goal.

South Africa then surrendered the advantage by conceding a succession of penalties for impetuosity. France could not break the Springbok defence to score a try, but Thierry Lacroix was in deadly kicking form. His second penalty put France ahead 9-8 at the interval and in the second half he shared the honours with van Rensburg to bring France their fourth Test win on South African soil.

Olivier Roumat, for his aerial superiority at line-outs and the strong influence he exerted on his team, was unanimously declared the player of the series.

SOUTH AFRICA: J T J van Rensburg (Transvaal); J T Small (Natal), P G Müller (Natal),
H T Fuls (Eastern Province), J Olivier (Northern Transvaal); H P le Roux (Transvaal),
R J du Preez (Natal); W G Hills (Northern Transvaal), U L Schmidt (Transvaal),
K S Andrews (Western Province), J J Strydom (Transvaal), N Wegner
(Western Province), J F Pienaar (Transvaal) *(capt)*, C P Strauss (Western Province),
D Lotter (Transvaal) *Replacement* J J Styger (Orange Free State) for Hills (8 mins)
Scorers *Try:* Small   *Penalty Goals:* van Rensburg (4)
FRANCE: Sadourny; Bernat-Salles, Lacroix, Sella, Saint-André; Penaud, Hueber;
Armary, Gonzalez, Graou, Merle, Roumat *(capt)*, Benetton, Cecillon, Cabannes
Replacement Campan for Sadourny (50 mins)
Scorers *Penalty Goals:* Lacroix (4)   *Dropped Goals:* Penaud, Lacroix
Referee E F Morrison (England)

WESTERN SAMOA TO NEW ZEALAND 1993

Western Samoa's first Test tour to New Zealand left both nations wanting more regular playing contact in the near future. Peter Fatialofa's tourists, who were warmly welcomed at all eight of the tour match venues, impressed everyone with their skilful handling and bone-juddering tackling and showed that none of the qualities they had paraded during the 1991 Rugby World Cup had deteriorated.

The Samoans collected the staggering total of 200 points without reply in their two opening matches, running up a world record win for a major tour when they swept Marlborough aside by 128 points in Blenheim. Their only defeat before the Test was against the New Zealand shadow XV, which included several All Blacks.

The Test was the culmination of the visit and attracted a crowd of 40,000 to Auckland's Eden Park. A hard, physical contest was punctuated by penalty awards and stoppages for injuries. Altogether, four full bench reserves won caps as temporary replacements while players received attention to cuts. Mark Allen, the Taranaki prop, came on twice and Matthew Cooper won a cap standing in for Va'aiga Tuigamala as Grant Fox shuffled about preparing to kick one of his record seven penalty goals for New Zealand.

The biggest cheer of the Test was reserved for the Samoans' try early in the second half. Sila Vaifale made a scorching 40-metre break from deep inside his own half. He was eventually overhauled but managed to set up second-phase ball. Darren Kellett raced away and sent Anetelea Aiolupo over for a try. That move, executed at top speed, was typical of the passages of play that led to many of the 67 tour tries scored by the Samoans.

THE TOURING PARTY

Manager T Simi   **Coach** P Schuster   **Assistant Coach** S Patu
Technical Adviser B G Williams   **Captain** P Fatialofa

FULL-BACKS

A Aiolupo (Moataa)
T Meleisea (Marist St Joseph)

THREEQUARTERS

A Ieremia (SCOPA & Wellington)
L Koko (Moataa & Wellington)
B Lima (Marist St Joseph & Auckland)
T Vaega (Moataa & Auckland)
M Vaeono (Police)
D Kellett (Vailele & Auckland)
L Langkilde (King Country)
*T Samania (Moataa & King Country)

HALF-BACKS

F Saena (Moataa & Auckland)

K Sio (SCOPA)
J Tonu'u (Apia & Auckland)
M Vaea (North Harbour)
*T Nu'uali'ita (Auckland)

FORWARDS

T Leiasamaiavao (Wellington)
S To'omalatai (Vaiala & Otago)
P Lilomaiava (Marist St Joseph)
A Leu'u (Vailele & Counties)
P Fatialofa (Apia & Auckland)
V Ala'alatoa (Apia & Manly, NSW)
P Solaese (Vaiala)
M Keenan (London Irish)
P Leavasa (Apia & Hawke's Bay)
M Birtwistle (Auckland)
L Falaniko (Marist St Joseph)

S Vaifale (Hawke's Bay)
S Tatupu (Auckland)
H Schuster (Apia)
A Perelini (Moataa & North Harbour)

D Kaleopa (Moataa)
M Iupeli (Vaimoso)
* Replacement during tour

TOUR RECORD

All matches   Played 9   Won 7   Lost 2   Points for 455   Against 131
International matches   Played 1   Lost 1   Points for 13   Against 35

SCORING DETAILS

All matches
For: 67T   45C   10PG   455 Pts
Against: 13T   9C   16PG   131 Pts

International matches
For: 1T   1C   2PG   13 Pts
Against: 2T   2C   7PG   35 Pts

MATCH DETAILS

1993	OPPONENTS	VENUE	RESULT
4 July	Buller-West Coast	Westport	W 72-0
7 July	Marlborough	Blenheim	W 128-0
11 July	NZ Universities	Wellington	W 48-10
14 July	Wanganui	Wanganui	W 30-0
18 July	New Zealand XV	Rotorua	L 13-37
21 July	Counties	Pukekohe	W 41-22
24 July	King Country	Te Kuiti	W 57-21
27 July	Poverty Bay	Gisborne	W 53-6
31 July	NEW ZEALAND	Auckland	L 13-35

Appearances: 7 – Vaega*, Fatialofa*, Falaniko*, Kellett*, Iupeli**, Ieremia**; 6 – Lima, Keenan, Koko, Tatupu*; 5 – Vaifale, Perelini, Leiasamaiavao, Leu'u, Tonu'u, Sio*, Vaeono*, Kaleopa*; 4 – Aiolupo, Saena, To'omalatai, Leavasa, Langkilde*, Lilomaiava*, Birtwistle*; 3 – Samania, Ala'alatao, Meleisea; 2 – Vaea, Schuster, Nu'uali'ita, Solaese*
* includes appearances as a replacement
Scorers: 95 – Kellett (5T 26C 6PG); 41 – Samania (2T 11C 3PG); 40 – Koko (8T); 34 – Saena (3T 8C 1PG); 30 – Tonu'u, Lima (both 6T); 25 – Vaega, Iupeli, Vaeono, Lima (all 5T); 20 – Ieremia (4T); 15 – Aiolupo, Tatupu (both 3T); 10 – Meleisea, Leiasamaiavao (both 2T); 5 – Vaifale, Perelini, Keenan, To'omalatai, Fatialofa, Lilomaiava, Sio, Vaea (all 1T)

MATCH 1   4 July, Victoria Square, Westport

Buller-West Coast 0   Western Samoa XV 72 (6G 6T)
Buller-West Coast: M Fitzgerald; G O'Dea, R Cook, K Roache, D Masterson; M Foster, C Alexander; W Iafeta, P Beveridge, J Brazil, G Elley, M Burrow, R Best, T Stuart, G O'Conor
Western Samoa XV: Aiolupo; Lima, Vaega, Meleisea, Sio; Saena, Vaea; Fatialofa (*capt*), To'omalatai, Ala'alatao, Keenan, Falaniko, Vaifale, Iupeli, Perelini
Scorers *Tries:* Iupeli (2), Lima (2), Fatialofa, To'omalatai, Keenan, Perelini, Vaea, Meleisea, Aiolupo (2)   *Conversions:* Saena (6)
Referee D J Bishop (Southland)

MATCH 2   7 July, Lansdowne Park, Blenheim

Marlborough 0   Western Samoa XV 128 (14G 6T)
Marlborough: B Clarke; R Burrows, E Manu, K Boyd, T Sloan; C Forsyth, W Young; A Holdaway, B Foster, P Macdonald, F Marfell (*capt*), J Foliaki, M Davidson, M Kerr, H Gledhill *Replacement* C Wood for Forsyth
Western Samoa XV: Saena; Koko, Langkilde, Ieremia (*capt*), Vaeono; Kellett, Tonu'u; Lilomaiava, Leiasamaiavao, Leu'u, Leavasa, Keenan, Tatupu, Schuster, Perelini
Replacements Vaega for Ieremia; Solaese for Leu'u
Scorers *Tries:* Koko (4), Kellett (3), Saena (3), Vaeono (3), Ieremia (3), Tonu'u (2), Tatupu, Leiasamaiavao   *Conversions:* Kellett (12), Saena (2)
Referee P O'Brien (Southland)

MATCH 3   11 July, Athletic Park, Wellington

NZ Universities 10 (1G 1PG)   **Western Samoa XV 48** (5G 1PG 2T)
NZ Universities: M C G Ellis; P J Alston, J A Leslie, S R Cottrell, D M Wilson;
J J Holland, J A Hewett (*capt*); N Moore, R P Nesdale, M A Mika, J Cullen,
P O'Shannessey, J A Kronfeld, J W Campbell, B P Timmins *Replacement* S D Surridge
for Timmins
Scorers *Try:* Ellis   *Conversion:* Holland   *Penalty Goal:* Holland
Western Samoa XV: Saena; Lima, Vaega, Ieremia, Koko; Kellett, Tonu'u; Leu'u,
To'omalatai, Fatialofa (*capt*), Falaniko, Keenan, Perelini, Tatupu, Vaifale
Replacement Iupeli for Tatupu
Scorers *Tries:* Tonu'u (3), Vaega (2), Koko, Iupeli   *Conversions:* Kellett (5)
Penalty Goal: Kellett
Referee G K Wahlstrom (Auckland)

MATCH 4   14 July, Spriggens Park, Wanganui

Wanganui 0   Western Samoa XV 30 (2G 2PG 2T)
Wanganui: J Hamlin; S Selby, C Osborne, T Combs, J Hainsworth; G Lennox (*capt*),
P Mitchell; T Cundy, A Bull, A Smith, G Stantiall, H Gordon, N Bell, G Carey,
D Thompson *Replacement* M Paranihi for Hainsworth
Western Samoa XV: Saena; Vaeono, Meleisea, Sio, Langkilde; Kellett, Vaea;
Leiasamaiavao, Lilomaiava, Solaese, Falaniko, Birtwistle, Leavasa, Kaleopa (*capt*),
Iupeli *Replacements* Ieremia for Sio; Fatialofa for Solaese
Scorers *Tries:* Iupeli, Lilomaiava, Vaeono, Meleisea   *Conversions:* Kellett (2)
Penalty Goals: Kellett, Saena
Referee R T A Ross (North Harbour)

MATCH 5   18 July, Rotorua International Stadium, Rotorua

New Zealand XV 37 (3G 2PG 2T)   **Western Samoa XV 13** (1PG 2T)
New Zealand XV: S P Howarth (Auckland); A R Prince (Nelson Bays), E Clarke
(Auckland); W K Little (North Harbour), E J Rush (North Harbour); S J Bachop
(Otago), G T M Bachop (Canterbury); K G Boroevich (North Harbour) (*capt*),
N J Hewitt (Hawke's Bay), G H Purvis (Waikato), B P Larsen (North Harbour),
S B Gordon (Waikato), R M Jerram (Waikato), R S Turner (North Harbour),
D I Monkley (Waikato)
Scorers *Tries:* Boroevich, S J Bachop, Rush, Clarke, Turner   *Conversions:* Howarth (3)
Penalty Goals: Howarth (2)
Western Samoa XV: Aiolupo; Lima, Vaega, Ieremia, Koko; Kellett, Tonu'u;
Fatialofa (*capt*), To'omalatai, Leu'u, Leavasa, Falaniko, Perelini, Tatupu, Vaifale
Replacements Vaeono for Koko; Kaleopa for Tatupu
Scorers *Tries:* Vaega, Vaifale   *Penalty Goal:* Kellett
Referee T R Marshall (Canterbury)

MATCH 6   21 July, Pukekohe Stadium

Counties 22 (2G 1PG 1T)   **Western Samoa XV 41** (4G 1PG 2T)
Counties: D R Sheppard; L Erenavula, C A Hassan, S Palelei, L Foai; D Love, M Scott;
H M R Maxwell, A T Roose, T Barchard, J N Coe, M S B Cooksley, J Paramore,
E F Brain (*capt*), O W John
Scorers *Tries:* Foai (2), Coe   *Conversions:* Love (2)   *Penalty Goal:* Love
Western Samoa XV: Aiolupo; Vaeono, Vaega, Sio, Lima; Samania, Nu'uali'ita;
Fatialofa (*capt*), Leiasamaiavao, Ala'alatoa, Birtwistle, Keenan, Vaifale, Kaleopa, Iupeli
Replacements Ieremia for Sio; Langkilde for Samania
Scorers *Tries:* Lima (2), Vaega (2), Samania, Iupeli   *Conversions:* Samania (4)
Penalty Goal: Samania
Referee M W Thompson (Auckland)

MATCH 7   24 July, Te Kuiti

King Country 21 (1G 3PG 1T)   **Western Samoa XV 57** (7G 1PG 1T)
King Country: F H J Walker; M Seavill, J G R Rika, R A M Watts, M Coll; H C Coffin,
C N Wills; T Stuart, P L Mitchell (*capt*), P H Coffin, L Warren, D Coleman, W Henare,
W G Paalvast, D Anglesey
Scorers *Tries:* Seavill, Mitchell   *Conversion:* H C Coffin   *Penalty Goals:* H C Coffin (3)
Western Samoa XV: Samania; Koko, Vaega, Ieremia, Lima; Kellett, Tonu'u; Leu'u,
Leiasamaiavao, Fatialofa (*capt*), Falaniko, Keenan, Tatupu, Kaleopa, Iupeli
Replacement Birtwistle for Falaniko
Scorers *Tries:* Lima (2), Kellett (2), Tonu'u, Ieremia, Koko, Leiasamaiavao
Conversions: Kellett (4), Samania (3)   *Penalty Goal:* Kellett
Referee J F Norton (King Country)

MATCH 8   27 July, U-Bix Rugby Park, Gisborne

Poverty Bay 6 (2PG)   **Western Samoa XV 53** (6G 2PG 1T)
Poverty Bay: S R Brown; G Lexmond, M Turei, S D Fitzsimons, R Lexmond;
D Sutton, A Willock; M Nepia, B Te Kani, Q Carmichael, M Atkinson, G L F Williams,
C Brownlie, M Dudley (*capt*), J J J Martin *Replacements* W Maxwell for Sutton; D Ria for
Carmichael
Scorer *Penalty Goals:* Sutton (2)
Western Samoa XV: Langkilde; Meleisea, Vaeono, Sio, Koko; Samania, Nu'uali'ita;
Lilomaiava, To'omalatai, Ala'alatoa, Leavasa, Falaniko, Iupeli, Schuster, Kaleopa
(*capt*) *Replacements* Kellett for Samania; Tatupu for Schuster; Birtwistle for Leavasa
Scorers *Tries:* Koko (2), Tatupu (2), Sio, Samania, Vaeono   *Conversions:* Samania (4),
Kellett (2)   *Penalty Goals:* Samania (2)
Referee B Smallridge (Auckland)

MATCH 9   31 July, Eden Park, Auckland   Test Match

NEW ZEALAND 35 (2G 7PG)   **WESTERN SAMOA 13** (1G 2PG)
NEW ZEALAND: J K R Timu (Otago); J J Kirwan (Auckland), F E Bunce
(North Harbour), L Stensness (Auckland), V L Tuigamala (Auckland); G J Fox
(Auckland), J P Preston (Wellington); G H Purvis (Waikato), S B T Fitzpatrick
(Auckland) (*capt*), C W Dowd (Auckland), I D Jones (North Auckland), R M Brooke
(Auckland), J W Joseph (Otago), A R B Pene (Otago), M N Jones (Auckland)
Replacements Z V Brooke (Auckland) for Joseph; W K Little (North Harbour) for
Stensness; M R Allen (Taranaki) for Purvis and Dowd (temp); M J A Cooper for
Tuigamala (temp)
Scorers *Tries:* Stensness, Z Brooke   *Conversions:* Fox (2)   *Penalty Goals:* Fox (7)
WESTERN SAMOA: Aiolupo; Lima, Vaega, Ieremia, Koko; Kellett, Tonu'u; Leu'u,
Leiasamaiavao, Fatialofa (*capt*), Birtwistle, Keenan, Vaifale, Tatupu, Perelini
Replacements Sio for Vaega; Falaniko for Birtwistle, Iupeli for Vaifale
(temp); Lilomaiava for Fatialofa (temp)
Scorers *Try:* Aiolupo   *Conversion:* Kellett   *Penalty Goals:* Kellett (2)
Referee J M Fleming (Scotland)

SOUTH AFRICA TO AUSTRALIA 1993

Eyebrows were raised when the Springbok selectors named several
veterans for the tour who had been dropped from the international team
after the draw with France in Durban. Critics argued that three Tests
against Australia would be the ideal opportunity for South Africa to
blood the players who would represent their country in the 1995 Rugby
World Cup.

Controversies over selection gave way to false confidence as the tourists opened their visit with a series of meaningless runaway wins against weak Australian state sides. The 90-3 defeat of South Australia was a new record for a South African touring side, overtaking the 83-0 thrashing inflicted on Nelson Bays in New Zealand in 1981. There followed the 19-12 First Test win in Sydney, which was more meaningful from the South African point of view. It hinted that the Springboks were back on a course to break Australia and New Zealand's world rugby duopoly.

The Sydney win, however, proved a false dawn. Australia pulled their act together to come from behind to win the Test series and, by the end of the tour, the Springboks were looking distinctly ragged. Their inability to impose any design on line-out tactics – a failing which has haunted them since their return from rugby isolation – let them down again in the last two internationals.

Besides the technical flaws, bad habits spawned by the internecine rivalry of the domestic Currie Cup competition crept into the tourists' tactics. Professional fouls, ranging from deliberate collapsing at mauls to illegal protective blocking in open play, did not escape referee Ed Morrison's beady eyes in the Tests and showed that the South Africans still had much to learn before claiming a coveted place among rugby's top tier.

On the credit side, there was the discovery of Joel Stransky as a possible fly-half successor to Naas Botha. In sharp contrast to the former captain, Stransky looked an exciting prospect with a lively commitment to the running, handling game which South Africa's stodgy forward-orientated approach badly needs.

THE TOURING PARTY

Manager J P Engelbrecht   **Coach** I McIntosh   **Assistant Coach** Z M J Pienaar
Captain J F Pienaar   **Vice-captain** C P Strauss

FULL-BACKS

J T J van Rensburg (Transvaal)
H Reece-Edwards (Natal)

THREEQUARTERS

J Olivier (Northern Transvaal)
C Williams (Western Province)
P G Müller (Natal)
H W Honiball (Natal)
H T Fuls (Eastern Province)
T Linee (Western Province)
J T Small (Natal)
D E Oosthuysen (Northern Transvaal)

HALF-BACKS

H P le Roux (Transvaal)
J Stransky (Natal)
R J du Preez (Natal)

J van der Westhuizen (Northern Transvaal)
*A J Joubert (Natal)

FORWARDS

W G Hills (Northern Transvaal)
J J Styger (Orange Free State)
U L Schmidt (Transvaal)
J Allan (Natal)
K S Andrews (Western Province)
S B Swart (Transvaal)
J J Strydom (Transvaal)
J J Wiese (Transvaal)
N Wegner (Western Province)
R G Visagie (Natal)
J F Pienaar (Transvaal)
R J Kruger (Orange Free State)
D Lotter (Transvaal)

I Macdonald (Transvaal)
C P Strauss (Western Province)
A Richter (Northern Transvaal)

*S Atherton (Natal)
*P H Rodgers (Transvaal)
Replacement during tour

TOUR RECORD
All matches Played 12 Won 9 Lost 3 Points for 527 Against 147
International matches Played 3 Won 1 Lost 2 Points for 51 Against 59

SCORING DETAILS
All matches

For: 75T 49C 18PG – 527 Pts
Against: 15T 9C 18PG – 147 Pts

International matches

For: 7T 5C 2PG – 51 Pts
Against: 4T 3C 11PG – 59 Pts

MATCH DETAILS

1993	OPPONENTS	VENUE	RESULT
14 July	Western Australia	Perth	W 71-8
17 July	S Australian Invitation XV	Adelaide	W 90-3
21 July	Victoria	Melbourne	W 78-3
24 July	New South Wales	Sydney	L 28-29
27 July	NSW Country	Orange	W 41-7
31 July	AUSTRALIA	Sydney	W 19-12
4 Aug	Australian Capital Territory	Canberra	W 57-10
8 Aug	Queensland	Brisbane	W 17-3
11 Aug	Queensland Country	Mackay	W 63-5
14 Aug	AUSTRALIA	Brisbane	L 20-28
18 Aug	Sydney	Sydney	W 31-20
21 Aug	AUSTRALIA	Sydney	L 12-19

Appearances: 9 – Honiball**; 8 – Swart, Andrews**; 7 – Williams*, Styger**, Richter*, Macdonald*, Allan*; 6 – Reece-Edwards, Small, Fuls, Strauss, van der Westhuizen, Wiese, Wegner, Pienaar, Oosthuysen, Müller, Olivier, le Roux, du Preez, Schmidt, Strydom, Lotter, Stransky, Kruger; 5 – Linee; 4 – Visagie; 3 – Hills, van Rensburg, Joubert; 2 – Rodgers, Atherton *includes appearances as a replacement
Scorers: 73 – Reece-Edwards (3T 17C 8PG); 58 – Stransky (1T 22C 3PG); 55 – van der Westhuizen (11T); 40 – Kruger, du Preez (both 8T); 35 – Williams (7T); 30 – Joubert (2T 4C 4PG); 25 – Small (5T); 22 – van Rensburg (1T 4C 3PG); 20 – Allan, Macdonald, Richter (all 4T); 15 – Oosthuysen, Olivier (both 3T); 14 – le Roux (2T 2C); 10 – Müller (2T); 5 – Wiese, Pienaar, Schmidt, Visagie, Lotter, Strauss, Linee (all 1T)

MATCH 1 14 July, WACA Cricket Oval, Perth

Western Australia 8 (1PG 1T) South African XV 71 (8G 3T)
Western Australia: R Smith; P Morton, D Hamilton, S Bunce, E Saaga; T Fearn, M Ryburn; S Porter, A Box, M Hudson, G Thompson, T Thomas, G Thomas, H Nguruve, P Roberts (capt)
Scorers *Try:* Hamilton *Penalty Goal:* Fearn
South Africa XV: Reece-Edwards; Small, Honiball, Fuls, Williams; Stransky, van der Westhuizen; Styger, Allan, Swart, Wiese, Wegner, Pienaar (capt), Richter, Macdonald
Scorers *Tries:* van der Westhuizen (4), Small (2), Macdonald (2), Williams, Wiese, Richter *Conversions:* Stransky (8)
Referee W Erickson

MATCH 2 17 July, Thebarton Oval, Adelaide

South Australian Invitation XV 3 (1PG) South Africa XV 90 (10G 4T)
South Australian Invitation XV: A Lawson; S Fonua, S Elliott, R Tuhou, R Sadler; D Emtage, M Catchpole; M Florey, N Edwards, W Matthews, J Hyland, N Porter, B Pillinger, P Jackson, D Rees (capt) *Replacements* T Grigg for Fonua (60 mins); O Porter for Florey (78 mins)

Scorer *Penalty Goal:* Emtage
South Africa XV: Reece-Edwards; Oosthuysen, Honiball, Müller, Olivier; le Roux,
du Preez; Andrews, Schmidt, Hills, Visagie, Strydom, Lotter, Strauss *(capt)*, Kruger
Replacement Williams for le Roux (75 mins)
Scorers *Tries:* du Preez (4), Kruger (2), Reece-Edwards, Visagie, Lotter, Strauss,
Olivier, Müller, Oosthuysen, le Roux   *Conversions:* Reece-Edwards (10)
Referee S Young

MATCH 3   21 July, Olympic Park, Melbourne

Victoria 3 (1PG)   **South Africa XV 78** (9G 3T)
Victoria: P Gascoigne; T Hogan, J Goodman, R Sanders, C McGregor; P Henara, J Dix;
N Raikuna, C Smith, M L'Hullier, S Hughes, C Clyne, D Williams *(capt)*, N Potae,
C Freighter
Scorer *Penalty Goal:* Goodman
South Africa XV: van Rensburg; Williams, Honiball, Linee, Oosthuysen; Stransky,
du Preez; Styger, Allan, Andrews, Visagie, Wiese, Kruger, Richter *(capt)*, Macdonald
Scorers *Tries:* du Preez (4), Williams (3), Richter (2), Kruger (2), Allan
Conversions: Stransky (9)
Referee J Allan

MATCH 4   24 July, Waratah Rugby Stadium, Sydney

New South Wales 29 (3G 1PG 1T)   **South Africa XV 28** (2G 3PG 1T)
New South Wales: T P Kelaher; D I Campese, R C Tombs, M Burke, A Murdoch;
S Bowen, N C Farr-Jones; E J A McKenzie, P N Kearns *(capt)*, A J Daly, W W Waugh,
T P Kava, M Brial, B T Gavin, A Dempsey *Replacement* S Payne for Farr-Jones (57 mins)
Scorers *Tries:* Murdoch (2), Tombs, Kelaher   *Conversions:* Kelaher (3)
Penalty Goal: Kelaher
South Africa XV: van Rensburg; Small, Müller, Fuls, Olivier; le Roux,
van der Westhuizen; Swart, Schmidt, Hills, Wegner, Strydom, Pienaar *(capt)*, Strauss,
Lotter *Replacement* Honiball for Müller (75 mins)
Scorers *Tries:* van der Westhuizen, le Roux, van Rensburg
Conversions: van Rensburg (2)   *Penalty Goals:* van Rensburg (3)
Referee B Leask

MATCH 5   27 July, Wade Park, Orange

NSW Country 7 (1G)   **South Africa XV 41** (2G 4PG 3T)
NSW Country: D Munday; M Crawford, P O'Brien, C Coffey, D Earp; J Trevaskis,
S Merrick; M Prior, J Ives, K Whiteman, N Cobcroft, J Nowland, A McCalman *(capt)*,
J Fenwicke, J Langford *Replacements* W DeJong, C Derwin, P Townsend
Scorers *Try:* O'Brien   *Conversion:* Trevaskis
South Africa XV: Reece-Edwards; Oosthuysen, Honiball, Linee, Williams; le Roux,
van der Westhuizen; Andrews, Allan, Styger, Wiese, Visagie, Macdonald, Richter
(capt), Kruger
Scorers *Tries:* Reece-Edwards (2), Oosthuysen, van der Westhuizen, Kruger
Conversions: Reece-Edwards (2)   *Penalty Goals:* Reece-Edwards (4)
Referee K O'Halloran

MATCH 6   31 July, Sydney Football Stadium   1st Test

AUSTRALIA 12 (4PG)   SOUTH AFRICA 19 (2G 1T)

Sheer determination to win carried South Africa to a decisive floodlit
victory by three tries to nil. Trailing 9-0 to three penalties kicked by
Marty Roebuck in the first half-hour, the Springboks stunned the

capacity crowd of 41,190 with two scores before the break. First, Pieter Müller took advantage of a gaffe by David Campese, and on the stroke of half-time James Small stepped through some feeble tackling for a corner try. Theo van Rensburg's goal-kicks converted South Africa into a 14-9 lead.

Marty Roebuck pulled the Wallabies back to 14-12 with another penalty 15 minutes after the interval, but the aggressive defence of the South Africans was so well organised that the Australians never looked like scoring a try. Six minutes from time, Heinrich Fuls slotted a kick into the path of James Small, who gathered the ball to score his second try.

AUSTRALIA: M C Roebuck (Eastwood & NSW); D I Campese (Randwick & NSW), J S Little (Souths & Queensland), T J Horan (Souths & Queensland), D Smith (Souths & Queensland); S Bowen (Souths & NSW), N C Farr-Jones (Sydney U & NSW); A J Daly (Randwick & NSW), P N Kearns (Randwick & NSW) (*capt*), E J A McKenzie (Randwick & NSW), B T Gavin (Easts & NSW), R J McCall (Brothers & Queensland), W W Waugh (Randwick & NSW), G Morgan (Souths & Queensland), D J Wilson (Easts & Queensland)
Scorer *Penalty Goals:* Roebuck (4)
SOUTH AFRICA: van Rensburg; Small, Müller, Fuls, Olivier; Stransky, du Preez; Hills, Schmidt, Swart, Wegner, Strydom, Pienaar (*capt*), Strauss, Lotter
Replacements Andrews for Hills (5 mins); Allan for Schmidt (79 mins)
Scorers *Tries:* Small (2), Müller   *Conversions:* van Rensburg (2)
Referee L L McLachlan (New Zealand)

MATCH 7   4 August, Bruce Stadium, Canberra

Australian Capital Territory 10 (1G 1PG)   **South Africa XV 57** (5G 4PG 2T)
Australian Capital Territory: A Apps; V Crowe, P Cornish, J Swan, D Grimmond; R Hayes, G Gregan; A Hayes, J Taylor (*capt*), C Hutchinson, A Harley, M McGuiness, J Ross, G Emmery, P Docherty *Replacements* G Didier, D McLachlan
Scorers *Try:* R Hayes   *Conversion:* Cornish   *Penalty Goal:* Cornish
South Africa XV: Reece-Edwards; Williams, Honiball, Linee, Oosthuysen; le Roux, van der Westhuizen; Styger, Allan, Swart, Wiese, Visagie, Kruger, Richter, Macdonald
Scorers *Tries:* van der Westhuizen (2), Williams (2), Allan, Kruger, Richter
Conversions: Reece-Edwards (5)   *Penalty Goals:* Reece-Edwards (4)
Referee A Cole

MATCH 8   8 August, Ballymore Oval, Brisbane

Queensland 3 (1PG)   **South Africa XV 17** (2G 1PG)
Queensland: M Pini; D Smith, J S Little, T J Horan, P V Carozza; P Howard, P J Slattery (*capt*); M Ryan, D V Nucifora, D J Crowley, R J McCall, G Morgan, D J Wilson, S J S Scott-Young, I Tabua *Replacements* B Fielke for Carozza (45 mins); A Moors for Tabua (57 mins); A Herbert for Pini (78 mins)
Scorer *Penalty Goal:* Pini
South Africa XV: Reece-Edwards; Small, Müller, Fuls, Olivier; Stransky, du Preez; Andrews, Schmidt, Swart, Wegner, Strydom, Pienaar (*capt*), Strauss, Lotter
Replacements Styger for Swart (31 mins); Richter for Pienaar (75 mins)
Scorers *Tries:* Schmidt, Olivier   *Conversions:* Stransky (2)   *Penalty Goal:* Stransky
Referee P Marshall

MATCH 9   11 August, Quarry Hill Rugby Park, Mackay

Queensland Country 5 (1T)   **South Africa XV 63** (4G 7T)
Queensland Country: R Leeson; B Lea, M Hood, R Constable, B Fielke; M Catchpole

(*capt*), A Gold; G Brown, M Holt, R Blackley, R Korst, S Thorn, G Hislop, M Cockbain, M Murray
Scorer *Try:* Constable
South Africa XV: Joubert; Oosthuysen, Honiball, Linee, Williams; le Roux, van der Westhuizen; Rodgers, Allan, Swart, Atherton, Wiese, Kruger, Richter (*capt*), Macdonald *Replacement* Andrews for Swart (40 mins)
Scorers *Tries:* Joubert (2), van der Westhuizen (2), Kruger (2), Allan (2), Williams, Oosthuysen, Macdonald *Conversions:* Joubert (2), le Roux (2)
Referee B Fienberg

MATCH 10   14 August, Ballymore, Brisbane   2nd Test

AUSTRALIA 28 (2G 3PG 1T)   SOUTH AFRICA 20 (2G 2PG)

Australia squared the rubber with a spirited performance which restored the morale of the world champions after their lacklustre effort in Sydney a fortnight earlier. They ran up their highest score for a Test against South Africa and relaxed their strong grip on the game only in the last ten minutes after James Small had become the first Springbok to be sent off in an international. Small received his marching orders for dissent when the Aussies were already home and dry, 28-13 ahead.

The tourists could find no answer to the driving play of the Australian pack. Ilie Tabua, on his Test debut, showed that his tackles and skills in the loose were every bit as effective as those of Willie Ofahengaue, the injured flanker whose place he filled. Behind the scrum, Jason Little and Tim Horan were as imaginative as ever in attack and scored the Australian tries.

AUSTRALIA: M C Roebuck (Eastwood & NSW); D I Campese (Randwick & NSW), J S Little (Souths & Queensland), T J Horan (Souths & Queensland), D Smith (Souths & Queensland); S Bowen (Souths & NSW), N C Farr-Jones (Sydney U & NSW); A J Daly (Randwick & NSW), P N Kearns (Randwick & NSW) (*capt*), E J A McKenzie (Randwick & NSW), R J McCall (Brothers & Queensland), G Morgan (Souths & Queensland), I Tabua (Brothers & Queensland), B T Gavin (Easts & NSW), D J Wilson (Easts & Queensland) *Replacement* A G Herbert (GPS & Queensland) for Little (79 mins)
Scorers *Tries:* Little (2), Horan *Conversions:* Roebuck (2) *Penalty Goals:* Roebuck (3)
SOUTH AFRICA: Reece-Edwards; Small, Müller, Fuls, Olivier; Stransky, du Preez; Andrews, Schmidt, Swart, Wegner, Strydom, Pienaar (*capt*), Strauss, Lotter
Scorers *Tries:* Stransky, Olivier *Conversions:* Stransky (2) *Penalty Goals:* Stransky (2)
Referee E F Morrison (England)

MATCH 11   18 August, Penrith Stadium, Sydney

Sydney 20 (1G 1PG 2T)   **South Africa XV 31** (2G 4PG 1T)
Sydney: M Burke; D K Junee, A Murdoch, R C Tombs (*capt*), P Jorgensen; T Wallace, A Eckert; M N Hartill, M Bell, A Blades, W W Waugh, J Hearn, S Talbot, M Guberina, A Dempsey *Replacement* R Muik
Scorers *Tries:* Murdoch, Wallace, Eckert *Conversion:* Wallace *Penalty Goal:* Burke
South Africa XV: Joubert; Oosthuysen, Honiball, Linee, Williams; le Roux, van der Westhuizen; Styger, Allan, Rodgers, Wiese, Atherton, Lotter, Richter (*capt*), Kruger *Replacement* Macdonald
Scorers *Tries:* Linee, van der Westhuizen, Macdonald *Conversions:* Joubert (2) *Penalty Goals:* Joubert (4)
Referee M Keogh

MATCH 12   21 August, Sydney Football Stadium   3rd Test

AUSTRALIA 19 (1G 4PG)   **SOUTH AFRICA 12** (1G 1T)

Nick Farr-Jones, who had emerged from retirement earlier in the season when Peter Slattery was injured, bowed out of Test rugby with a display of technical brilliance which was an inspiration to the Wallabies. At times he played like an extra flanker to supplement his pack's work in the tight and loose; he was careful to protect his half-back partner, Scott Bowen, in the rare moments of Springbok pressure and his tactical vision was as clear as ever.

Penalties by Marty Roebuck in the fourth, 14th, 54th and 59th minutes to a try by James Small gave Australia a 12-5 lead as the Test entered its final quarter. Then a typical show of magic by David Campese, popping up in midfield to float a cut-out pass to Tim Horan, led to a try which Roebuck converted. Although François Pienaar scored another South African try near no-side, it came too late to prevent Australia clinching the series.

AUSTRALIA: M C Roebuck (Eastwood & NSW); D I Campese (Randwick & NSW), J S Little (Souths & Queensland), T J Horan (Souths & Queensland), D Smith (Souths & Queensland); S Bowen (Souths & NSW), N C Farr-Jones (Sydney U & NSW); A J Daly (Randwick & NSW), P N Kearns (Randwick & NSW) (*capt*), E J A McKenzie (Randwick & NSW), R J McCall (Brothers & Queensland), G Morgan (Souths & Queensland), I Tabua (Brothers & Queensland), B T Gavin (Easts & NSW), D J Wilson (Easts & Queensland) *Replacement* M Burke (Eastwood & NSW) for Smith (38 mins)
Scorers *Try:* Horan   *Conversion:* Roebuck   *Penalty Goals:* Roebuck (4)
SOUTH AFRICA: Joubert; Small, Müller, Fuls, Olivier; Stransky, du Preez; Andrews, Schmidt, Swart, Wegner, Strydom, Pienaar (*capt*), Strauss, Macdonald *Replacements* Styger for Swart (45 mins); Honiball for Müller (48 mins)
Scorers *Tries:* Small, Pienaar   *Conversion:* Stransky
Referee E F Morrison (England)

NEW ZEALAND TO BRITAIN 1993

The All Blacks, a mixture of emerging talent and old hands – but minus Grant Fox and Michael Jones – romped through a series of easy wins against inferior scratch sides in the lead-up to the Tests. Three of the wins were particularly impressive. London Division were sent packing 39-12 in the tour opener, though the visitors did not really move into top gear until reaching Scotland. There, the South were overwhelmed at Gala by the staggering margin of 84-5 – the biggest-ever New Zealand victory in Britain or Ireland – and the Scots were still cowering ten days later when the All Blacks powered to a 51-15 win in the Murrayfield international. Nevertheless, the most important match for New Zealand was the disastrous defeat against England at Twickenham.

Capacity crowds attended everywhere the All Blacks played. The tourists, true to type, relied on the direct forward approach tactically, yet possessed backs who showed fine handling skills. The threequarters were good finishers but, arguably, were given fewer opportunities to excel than they deserved.

Young Jeff Wilson was the tour's golden boy. Selected ahead of seasoned wing John Kirwan, Wilson showed that his unexpected promotion was thoroughly justified. He possessed pace, had an uncanny sense of anticipation, and proved a useful goal-kicker. Moreover, his modesty and cheerfulness marked him out as one of the most likeable of players to emerge from a nation that traditionally breeds unsmiling giants for its rugby teams.

On occasions the New Zealanders' scant regard for bodies on the floor, especially at rucks, led to criticism of their methods. Phil de Glanville received 15 stitches to an eye wound after being raked early in the match at Redruth, and Kyran Bracken was stamped on by Jamie Joseph in England's win at Twickenham. The management's subsequent failure to make public the disciplinary action taken against Joseph for his cynical foul incensed the New Zealand Rugby executive, who sacked Neil Gray, the manager, soon after the tour party returned home.

THE TOURING PARTY

Manager N Gray **Coach** L W Mains **Assistant Coach** E W Kirton
Captain S B T Fitzpatrick **Medical Officer** Dr J Mayhew

FULL-BACKS

S P Howarth (Auckland)
J K R Timu (Otago)

THREEQUARTERS

M J A Cooper (Waikato)
V L Tuigamala (Auckland)
J W Wilson (Otago)
E J Rush (North Harbour)
E Clarke (Auckland)
F E Bunce (North Harbour)
L Stensness (Auckland)
M J Berry (Wellington)

HALF-BACKS

M C G Ellis (Otago)
S J Bachop (Otago)
J P Preston (Wellington)
S Forster (Otago)

FORWARDS

M R Allen (Taranaki)

C W Dowd (Auckland)
G H Purvis (Waikato)
O M Brown (Auckland)
S B T Fitzpatrick (Auckland)
N J Hewitt (Hawke's Bay)
S B Gordon (Waikato)
R M Brooke (Auckland)
I D Jones (North Auckland)
R T Fromont (Auckland)
J W Joseph (Otago)
Z V Brooke (Auckland)
L J P Barry (North Harbour)
P W Henderson (Southland)
J E P Mitchell (Waikato)
A R B Pene (Otago)
*B P Larsen (North Harbour)
*M R Brewer (Otago)

Replacement during tour

TOUR RECORD

All matches Played 13 Won 12 Lost 1 Points for 386 Against 156
International matches Played 2 Won 1 Lost 1 Points for 60 Against 30

SCORING DETAILS

All matches

For:	42T	31C	36PG	2DG	386 Pts
Against:	5T	1C	39PG	4DG	156 Pts

International matches

For:	7T	5C	5PG	–	60 Pts
Against:	–	–	9PG	1DG	30 Pts

MATCH DETAILS

1993	OPPONENTS	VENUE	RESULT
23 Oct	London-SE Division	Twickenham	W 39-12
26 Oct	Midland Division	Leicester	W 12-6
30 Oct	South-West Division	Redruth	W 19-15
2 Nov	Northern Division	Liverpool	W 27-21
7 Nov	England A	Gateshead	W 26-12
10 Nov	South of Scotland	Galashiels	W 84-5
13 Nov	Scotland A	Hawick	W 20-9
16 Nov	Scottish Development XV	Edinburgh	W 31-12
20 Nov	SCOTLAND	Murrayfield	W 51-15
23 Nov	England Emerging Players	Gloucester	W 30-19
27 Nov	ENGLAND	Twickenham	L 9-15
30 Nov	Combined Services	Devonport	W 13-3
4 Dec	Barbarians	Cardiff	W 25-12

Appearances: 9 – Z Brooke**, Wilson; 8 – Larsen*, Ellis*, Clarke*, Jones, Gordon; 7 – Allen*, Fitzpatrick, Tuigamala, Bunce, Timu, Forster, Dowd, Pene, Brown; 6 – Howarth, Cooper*, Hewitt, Bachop, Rush, Mitchell, Preston, Fromont, Purvis, Stensness, Joseph; 5 – Berry, Barry, Henderson; 1 – Brewer* * includes appearance as a replacement
Scorers: 81 – Howarth (3T 15C 12PG); 76 – Cooper (11C 18PG); 58 – Wilson (6T 5C 6PG); 33 – Ellis (6T 1DG); 25 – Z Brooke (5T); 20 – Hewitt (4T); 18 – Bachop (3T 1DG); 15 – Rush (3T); 10 – Mitchell (2T); 5 – Clarke, Jones, Tuigamala, Timu, Bunce, Preston, Dowd, Berry, Barry, Joseph

MATCH 1   23 October, Twickenham

London-SE Division 12 (1G 1T)   **New Zealand XV 39** (4G 2PG 1T)
London-SE Division: G H Davies (Wasps); T Underwood (Leicester), W D C Carling (Harlequins), D P Hopley (Wasps), C Oti (Wasps); C R Andrew (Wasps) *(capt)*, S M Bates (Wasps); J Leonard (Harlequins), B C Moore (Harlequins), J A Probyn (Wasps), A C W Snow (Harlequins), D Ryan (Wasps), M J Greenwood (Wasps), C M A Sheasby (Harlequins), R H J Jenkins (London Irish)
Scorers *Tries:* Jenkins, Oti   *Conversion:* Andrew
New Zealand XV: Cooper; Wilson, Bunce, Berry, Tuigamala; Bachop, Forster; Dowd, Fitzpatrick *(capt)*, Brown, Jones, Gordon, Joseph, Pene, Henderson *Replacement* Z Brooke for Henderson (temp – twice)
Scorers *Tries:* Bachop (2), Wilson (2), Berry   *Conversions:* Cooper (4)
Penalty Goals: Cooper (2)
Referee P Thomas (France)

MATCH 2   26 October, Welford Road, Leicester

Midland Division 6 (2PG)   **New Zealand XV 12** (4PG)
Midland Division: J Steele (Northampton); S T Hackney (Leicester), S Potter (Leicester), I Bates (Leicester), H Thorneycroft (Northampton); A P Challinor (Harlequins), M J S Dawson (Northampton); G C Rowntree (Leicester), C J Olver (Northampton), G S Pearce (Northampton), M O Johnson (Leicester), S J Lloyd (Moseley), J M Wells (Leicester), D Richards (Leicester) *(capt)*, N A Back (Leicester)
Scorer *Penalty Goals:* Steele (2)
New Zealand XV: Howarth; Timu, Clarke, Stensness, Rush; Ellis, Preston; Allen, Hewitt, Purvis, Jones, Fromont, Z Brooke *(capt)*, Mitchell, Barry *Replacement* Cooper for Stensness (50 mins)
Scorers *Penalty Goals:* Howarth (2), Cooper (2)
Referee B W Stirling (Ireland)

MATCH 3   30 October, Recreation Ground, Redruth

South-West Division 15 (4PG 1DG)   **New Zealand XV 19** (1G 4PG)
South-West Division: J E B Callard (Bath); P Hull (Bristol), P R de Glanville (Bath),

N D Beal (Northampton), A E Lumsden (Bath); M J Catt (Bath), K P P Bracken (Bristol); C J Clark (Oxford U & Bath), R G R Dawe (Bath), V E Ubogu (Bath), N C Redman (Bath), A G Blackmore (Bristol), J P Hall (Bath) (*capt*), B B Clarke (Bath), R A Robinson (Bath) *Replacements* P Holford (Gloucester) for de Glanville (15 mins); S O Ojomoh for Robinson (65 mins); D Sims (Gloucester) for Blackmore (79 mins) **Scorers** *Penalty Goals:* Callard (4)   *Dropped Goal:* Hull
New Zealand XV: Timu; Wilson, Bunce, Cooper, Tuigamala; Bachop, Preston; Dowd, Fitzpatrick (*capt*), Brown, Jones, Gordon, Henderson, Pene, Joseph
Replacement Z Brooke for Joseph (78 mins)
Scorers *Try:* Joseph   *Conversion:* Cooper   *Penalty Goals:* Cooper (4)
Referee C Thomas (Wales)

MATCH 4   2 November, Anfield Stadium, Liverpool

Northern Division 21 (7PG)   New Zealand XV 27 (2G 1PG 2T)
Northern Division: I Hunter (Northampton); J Mallinder (Sale), M R Fielden (Northampton), K G Simms (Liverpool St Helens) (*capt*), R Underwood (Leicester & RAF); P J Grayson (Northampton), D Scully (Wakefield); M P Hynes (Orrell), G J French (Orrell), S McMain (Sheffield), J Dixon (West Hartlepool), D Baldwin (Sale), T A K Rodber (Northampton), A Macfarlane (Sale), N Ashurst (Orrell) *Replacement* C Cusani (Orrell) for Baldwin (40 mins)
Scorer *Penalty Goals:* Grayson (7)
New Zealand XV: Howarth; Wilson, Clarke, Berry, Rush; Ellis, Forster; Allen, Hewitt, Purvis, Larsen, Fromont, Z Brooke (*capt*), Mitchell, Barry
Scorers *Tries:* Ellis (2), Hewitt, Rush   *Conversions:* Wilson (2)
Penalty Goal: Wilson
Referee J M Fleming (Scotland)

MATCH 5   7 November, International Stadium, Gateshead

England A 12 (4PG)   New Zealand XV 26 (2G 3PG 1DG)
England A: J E B Callard (Bath); I Hunter (Northampton), D P Hopley (Wasps), M J Catt (Bath), P Hull (Bristol); S Barnes (Bath), K P P Bracken (Bristol); G C Rowntree (Leicester), R G R Dawe (Bath), A R Mullins (Harlequins), N C Redman (Bath), D Sims (Gloucester), J P Hall (Bath) (*capt*), T A K Rodber (Northampton), N A Back (Leicester) *Replacement* S O Ojomoh (Bath) for Redman (temp)
Scorer *Penalty Goals:* Callard (4)
New Zealand XV: Timu; Wilson, Bunce, Cooper, Tuigamala; Ellis, Forster; Dowd, Fitzpatrick (*capt*), Brown, Jones, Gordon, Larsen, Pene, Z Brooke
Scorers *Tries:* Wilson, Timu   *Conversions:* Cooper (2)   *Penalty Goals:* Cooper (3)
Dropped Goal: Ellis
Referee R J Megson (Scotland)

MATCH 6   10 November, Netherdale, Galashiels

South of Scotland 5 (1T)   New Zealand XV 84 (9G 2PG 3T)
South of Scotland: M Dods (Gala); A G Stanger (Hawick), S A Nichol (Selkirk), A G Shiel (Melrose), G Parker (Melrose); C M Chalmers (Melrose), B W Redpath (Melrose); G R Isaac (Gala), J A Hay (Hawick), H Hunter (Gala), R Brown (Melrose) (*capt*), G W Weir (Melrose), D J Turnbull (Hawick), B Renwick (Hawick), J Amos (Gala) *Replacement* S McColm (Selkirk) for Hunter (6 mins)
Scorer *Try:* Parker
New Zealand XV: Howarth; Clarke, Berry, Stensness, Rush; Bachop, Preston; Allen, Hewitt, Purvis, Gordon, Fromont, Larsen, Mitchell, Z Brooke (*capt*) *Replacement* Ellis for Berry (26 mins)
Scorers *Tries:* Z Brooke (4), Hewitt (2), Howarth (2), Ellis, Bachop, Preston, Mitchell
Conversions: Howarth (9)   *Penalty Goals:* Howarth (2)
Referee D Matthews (England)

MATCH 7   13 November, Mansfield Park, Hawick

Scotland A 9 (1PG 2DG)   **New Zealand XV 20** (5PG 1T)
Scotland A: M Dods (Gala); K M Logan (Stirling County), I C Jardine (Stirling County),
S Nichol (Selkirk), G Parker (Melrose); D S Wyllie (Stewart's-Melville FP) (*capt*),
B W Redpath (Melrose); A G J Watt (Glasgow High/Kelvinside), K D McKenzie
(Stirling County), D Herrington (Dundee HSFP), D S Munro
(Glasgow High/Kelvinside), A E D Macdonald (Heriot's FP), D J McIvor
(Edinburgh Acads), C D Hogg (Melrose), R I Wainwright (Edinburgh Acads)
Scorers *Penalty Goal:* Dods   *Dropped Goals:* Wyllie (2)
New Zealand XV: Timu; Wilson, Bunce, Cooper, Tuigamala; Ellis, Forster; Dowd,
Fitzpatrick (*capt*), Brown, Jones, Gordon, Joseph, Pene, Henderson
Replacements Allen for Dowd (14 mins); Larsen for Gordon (37 mins)
Scorers *Try:* Ellis   *Penalty Goals:* Cooper (5)
Referee A J Spreadbury (England)

MATCH 8   16 November, Myreside, Edinburgh

Scottish Development XV 12 (4PG)   **New Zealand XV 31** (2G 4PG 1T)
Scottish Development XV: C Glasgow (Heriot's FP); D A Stark (Boroughmuir),
F Harrold (London Scottish), R MacNaughton (Northampton), C Dalglish (Gala);
K A Bray (Harlequins), D Patterson (Edinburgh Acads); J Manson (Dundee HSFP),
J A Hay (Hawick) (*capt*), D Herrington (Dundee HSFP), S Campbell (Dundee HSFP),
N G B Edwards (Northampton), P Walton (Northampton), F Wallace
(Glasgow High/Kelvinside), I R Smith (Gloucester) *Replacement* S McIntosh
(West of Scotland) for Stark (57 mins)
Scorer *Penalty Goals:* Bray (4)
New Zealand XV: Howarth; Wilson, Clarke, Stensness, Rush; Bachop, Preston; Allen,
Hewitt, Purvis, Fromont, Larsen, Joseph, Mitchell (*capt*), Barry
Scorers *Tries:* Rush, Barry, Mitchell   *Conversions:* Howarth (2)
Penalty Goals: Howarth (4)
Referee G Black (Ireland)

MATCH 9   20 November, Murrayfield   Test Match

SCOTLAND 15 (5PG)   NEW ZEALAND 51 (5G 2PG 2T)

Although the appalling weaknesses of Scotland must be taken into
account, New Zealand made rugby football look simple. Their drives
and incessant support, all carried out at speed and with the matter-of-
fact ease of a training session, put Scotland to the sword. It was a near-
perfect technical display which had coaches up and down the land
delighting at the efficiency of the All Blacks.

The tourists went ahead in the third minute, led 22-9 at the interval,
and were still committed to all-out attack at the final whistle. The total
was their highest for a cap match in Europe, and Scotland conceded 50
points for the first time in their 122-year Test history. In addition, Jeff
Wilson became the youngest player since 1882 to score a hat-trick of
tries on his debut in a major international.

SCOTLAND: A G Hastings (Watsonians) (*capt*); A G Stanger (Hawick), I C Jardine
(Stirling County), A G Shiel (Melrose), S Hastings (Watsonians); C M Chalmers
(Melrose), A D Nicol (Dundee HSFP); A G J Watt (Glasgow High/Kelvinside),
K S Milne (Heriot's FP), A P Burnell (London Scottish), D F Cronin (London Scottish),
A E D Macdonald (Heriot's FP), D J McIvor (Edinburgh Acads), G W Weir (Melrose),

R I Wainwright (Edinburgh Acads) *Replacements* D S Wyllie (Stewart's-Melville FP) for Chalmers (59 mins); C D Hogg (Melrose) for Cronin (62 mins); B W Redpath (Melrose) for Nicol (temp); K M Logan (Stirling County) for G Hastings (temp) **Scorers** *Penalty Goals:* G Hastings (4), Chalmers
NEW ZEALAND: Timu; Wilson, Bunce, Cooper, Tuigamala; Ellis, Forster; Dowd, Fitzpatrick (*capt*), Brown, Jones, Gordon, Joseph, Pene, Z Brooke *Replacement* Clarke for Cooper (78 mins)
Scorers *Tries:* Wilson (3), Ellis (2), Brooke, Bunce *Conversions:* Cooper (4), Wilson *Penalty Goals:* Cooper (2)
Referee F Burger (South Africa)

MATCH 10 23 November, Kingsholm, Gloucester

England Emerging Players 19 (3PG 2T) **New Zealand XV 30** (3G 2PG 1DG)
England Emerging Players: A P Challinor (Harlequins); P Holford (Gloucester), N D Beal (Northampton), D P Hopley (Wasps), P Hull (Bristol); M J Catt (Bath), M J S Dawson (Northampton); C J Clark (Oxford U & Bath), K A Dunn (Wasps), J Mallett (Bath), D Sims (Gloucester), R West (Gloucester), C M A Sheasby (Harlequins), D Ryan (Wasps) (*capt*), S O Ojomoh (Bath)
Scorers *Tries:* Sims, Challinor *Penalty Goals:* Challinor (3)
New Zealand XV: Howarth; Clarke, Berry, Stensness, Rush; Bachop, Preston; Allen, Hewitt, Purvis, Larsen, Fromont, Barry, Mitchell (*capt*), Henderson
Scorers *Tries:* Rush, Clarke, Howarth *Conversions:* Howarth (3)
Penalty Goals: Howarth (2) *Dropped Goal:* Bachop
Referee D Mene (France)

MATCH 11 27 November, Twickenham Test Match
ENGLAND 15 (4PG 1DG) NEW ZEALAND 9 (3PG)

England's back row of Tim Rodber, Dean Richards and Ben Clarke were immense, drawing down a white curtain on every front to prevent an All Black repeat of the Murrayfield massacre. They took on the New Zealanders at their own game – and won. Tight marking, helped a little by the referee's blind eye to offside at set pieces, and sheer courage were the main ingredients of England's winning recipe.

Jon Callard kicked his important penalties for England in the 16th, 28th, 49th and 70th minutes and Rob Andrew dropped a goal on the hour. In contrast Jeff Wilson, having been cast as the hero of Murrayfield, was now seen as villain: he missed five kickable goals, leaving the tourists to grieve for Grant Fox or even the injured Matt Cooper.

No tries were scored, but that was irrelevant to a partisan crowd and the jubilant England team and management. Victory gave Will Carling a full set of wins against the seven other senior nations of the International Board.

ENGLAND: J E B Callard (Bath); T Underwood (Leicester), W D C Carling (Harlequins) (*capt*), P R de Glanville (Bath), R Underwood (Leicester & RAF); C R Andrew (Wasps), K P P Bracken (Bristol); J Leonard (Harlequins), B C Moore (Harlequins), V E Ubogu (Bath), M O Johnson (Leicester), N C Redman (Bath), T A K Rodber (Northampton), D Richards (Leicester), B B Clarke (Bath)
Scorers *Penalty Goals:* Callard (4) *Dropped Goal:* Andrew
NEW ZEALAND: Timu; Wilson, Bunce, Clarke, Tuigamala; Ellis, Forster; Dowd, Fitzpatrick (*capt*), Brown, Jones, Gordon, Joseph, Pene, Z Brooke

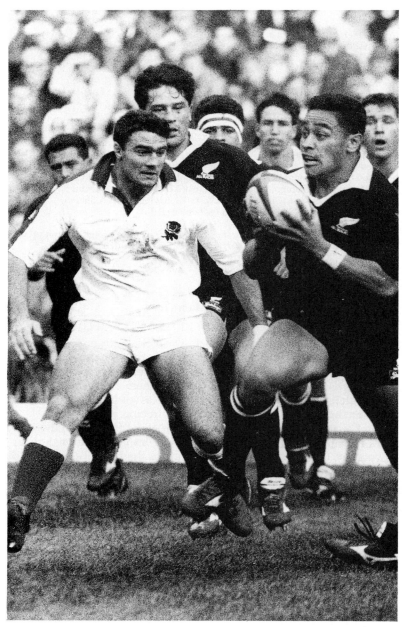

Ben Clarke of England moves in to tackle Eroni Clarke in England's thrilling defeat of New Zealand at Twickenham in November.

Scorer *Penalty Goals:* Wilson (3)
Referee F Burger (South Africa)

MATCH 12   30 November, Devonport Services Ground, Devonport

Combined Services 3 (1PG)   **New Zealand XV 13** (1G 2PG)
Combined Services: Cpl P Hull (RAF); Cpl S Bartliff (Army), SAC G Sharpe (RAF), ABS D Sibson (Royal Navy), Flt Lt R Underwood (RAF); Flt Lt A Johnson (RAF), Sgt S Worrall (RAF) *(capt)*; Cpl T Billett (RAF), Capt J Brammer (Army), Sgt J Fowers (Army), Cpl R Armstrong (Royal Navy), Sgt B Richardson (RAF), Flt Lt C Moore (RAF), L Cpl M Watson (Army), Capt R Wainwright (Army)
Replacement L/Sgt S Berryman (Army) for Watson (35 mins)
Scorer *Penalty Goal:* Worrall
New Zealand XV: Howarth; Clarke, Berry, Stensness, Rush; Bachop, Preston; Allen, Hewitt, Purvis, Larsen, Fromont, Barry, Mitchell *(capt)*, Henderson
Scorers *Try:* Hewitt   *Conversion:* Howarth   *Penalty Goals:* Howarth (2)
Referee D Davies (Wales)

MATCH 13   4 December, Cardiff Arms Park

Barbarians 12 (4PG)   **New Zealand XV 25** (2G 2PG 1T)
Barbarians: A Clement (Swansea & Wales); A G Stanger (Hawick & Scotland), S Hastings (Watsonians & Scotland) *(capt)*, I S Gibbs (Swansea & Wales), N Walker (Cardiff & Wales); E P Elwood (Lansdowne & Ireland), G Armstrong (Jedforest & Scotland); N J Popplewell (Greystones & Ireland), T J Kingston (Dolphin & Ireland), E J A McKenzie (Paris University Club, NSW & Australia), P S Johns (Dungannon & Ireland), O Roumat (Dax & France), R I Wainwright (Edinburgh Acads & Scotland), L S Quinnell (Llanelli & Wales), N A Back (Leicester)
Replacements R Howley (Cardiff) for Armstrong (62 mins); C Scholtz (Stellenbosch University & Western Province) for Gibbs (79 mins)
Scorer *Penalty Goals:* Elwood (4)
New Zealand XV: Timu; Wilson, Bunce, Stensness, Tuigamala; Ellis, Forster; Dowd, Fitzpatrick *(capt)*, Brown, Jones, Gordon, Larsen, Pene, Z Brooke
Replacement Brewer for Larsen (73 mins)
Scorers *Tries:* Dowd, Tuigamala, Jones   *Conversions:* Wilson (2)
Penalty Goals: Wilson (2)
Referee P Robin (France)

SOUTH AFRICA TO ARGENTINA 1993

South Africa's selectors disposed of the old faithfuls and adopted a bold youth policy for the six-match tour. After only two wins in ten Tests, Prof Daan Swiegers and his selection panel axed several established players and introduced seven new Springboks as part of a World Cup strategy for 1995.

The tourists had an early setback, losing by a point to a Buenos Aires XV in the second match of the visit, but thereafter difficulties were relatively few. One problem not resolved by the Springboks, however, was their tendency to concede points after establishing commanding leads.

In the First Test, for example, South Africa were 29-10 ahead at the break but gave away 16 points without adding to their own total in the second half. Moreover, Santiago Meson, who contributed 21 of the Pumas' points, could have levelled the scores: his last-minute, wind-assisted penalty attempt landed metres short to let the Springboks escape with a narrow win.

There were no scares a week later when the tourists wrapped up the mini-series with a 52-23 victory before a crowd of 35,000. Gavin Johnson, who had been sent out as a replacement from Britain, where he was touring with the South African Barbarians, scored 22 points on his Test debut to equal the Springbok record for most individual points in an international.

THE TOURING PARTY

Manager J Engelbrecht **Coach** I McIntosh **Assistant Coach** Z M J Pienaar
Captain J F Pienaar

FULL-BACKS

A J Joubert (Natal)
C Dirks (Transvaal)
*G Johnson (Transvaal)

THREEQUARTERS

J Olivier (Northern Transvaal)
J T Small (Natal)
C Williams (Western Province)
P G Müller (Natal)
H P le Roux (Transvaal)
H T Fuls (Eastern Province)

HALF-BACKS

J Stransky (Natal)
H W Honiball (Natal)
J H van der Westhuizen (Northern Transvaal)
H J Martens (Orange Free State)

FORWARDS

K S Andrews (Western Province)
S B Swart (Transvaal)
W J Bartmann (Natal)
G R Kebble (Natal)
A-H le Roux (Orange Free State)
J Allan (Natal)
N Drotske (Orange Free State)
J J Strydom (Transvaal)
N Wegner (Western Province)
S Atherton (Natal)
J F Pienaar (Transvaal)
R J Kruger (Northern Transvaal)
M Andrews (Natal)
C P Strauss (Western Province)
G Teichmann (Natal)

Replacement during tour

TOUR RECORD

All matches   Played 6   Won 5   Lost 1   Points for 243   Against 152
International matches   Played 2   Won 2   Points for 81   Against 49

SCORING DETAILS

All matches
For: 32T 19C 15PG –   243 Pts
Against: 11T 11C 24PG 1DG   152 Pts

International matches
For: 11T 7C 4PG –   81 Pts
Against: 4T 4C 6PG 1DG 49 Pts

MATCH DETAILS

1993	OPPONENTS	VENUE	RESULT
27 Oct	Provincial XV	Cordoba	W 55-37
30 Oct	Buenos Aires XV	Buenos Aires	L 27-28
3 Nov	Tucumán	Tucumán	W 40-12
6 Nov	ARGENTINA	Buenos Aires	W 29-26
9 Nov	Provincial XV	Rosario	W 40-26
13 Nov	ARGENTINA	Buenos Aires	W 52-23

Scorers: 35 – Honiball (7C 7PG); 31 – Stransky (8C 5PG); 27 – Johnson (2T 4C 3PG); 25 – Strauss (5T); 20 – Olivier, Small (both 4T); 15 – Williams (3T); 10 – Dirks, Kruger, H P le Roux, Joubert, van der Westhuizen (all 2T); 5 – Müller, Martens, Wegner, Fuls (all 1T)

MATCH 1   27 October, Cordoba

Provincial XV 37 (4G 3PG)   **South African XV 55** (3G 3PG 5T)
Provincial XV *Tries:* Dragotto (2), Sagrera, Irozoqui   *Conversions:* Luna (4)
Penalty Goals: Luna (3)
South Africa XV *Tries:* Strauss (3), Dirks, Kruger, H P le Roux, Williams, Olivier
Conversions: Honiball (3)   *Penalty Goals:* Honiball (3)

MATCH 2   30 October, Buenos Aires

Buenos Aires XV 28 (1G 7PG)   **South Africa XV 27** (2G 1PG 2T)
Buenos Aires XV *Try:* Villalonga   *Conversion:* Arbizu   *Penalty Goals:* Arbizu (7)
South Africa XV *Tries:* Olivier (2), Müller, Joubert   *Conversions:* Stransky (2)
Penalty Goal: Stransky

MATCH 3   3 November, Tucumán

Tucumán 12 (4PG)   **South Africa XV 40** (4G 4PG)
Tucumán *Penalty Goals:* Meson (4)
South Africa XV *Tries:* Dirks, Martens, Williams, Olivier   *Conversions:* Honiball (4)
Penalty Goals: Honiball (4)

MATCH 4   6 November, Ferrocaril Oeste Stadium, Buenos Aires   1st Test

ARGENTINA 26 (2G 4PG)   **SOUTH AFRICA 29** (3G 1PG 1T)
ARGENTINA: S Meson (Tucumán RC); M Teran (Tucumán RC), S Salvat (Alumni),
D Cuesta Silva (San Isidro Club), G Jorge (Pucara); L Arbizu (Belgrano) *(capt)*,
G Camardon (Alumni); M Corral (San Isidro Club), R le Fort (Tucumán RC), P Noreiga
(Hindu), P Sporleder (Curupayti), G Llanes (La Plata), R N Perez (Duendas Rosario),
G Ugartemendia (Los Matreros), P Fernandez-Bravo (Tucumán RC)
Replacement S Peretti (Buenos Aires Cricket & Rugby Club) for le Fort (65 mins)
Scorers *Tries:* Cuesta Silva, Meson   *Conversions:* Meson (2)   *Penalty Goals:* Meson (4)
SOUTH AFRICA: Joubert; Small, Fuls, Müller, Olivier; Stransky,
van der Westhuizen; Swart, Allan, Kebble, Strydom, Atherton, Pienaar *(capt)*,
Strauss, Kruger *Replacement* K S Andrews for Swart (46 mins)
Scorers *Tries:* Small (2), van der Westhuizen, Joubert   *Conversions:* Stransky (3)
Penalty Goal: Stransky
Referee W D Bevan (Wales)

MATCH 5   9 November, Rosario

Provincial XV 26 (2G 4PG)   **South Africa XV 40** (3G 3PG 2T)
Provincial XV *Tries:* Oviedo, del Castillo   *Conversions:* Crexell (2)
Penalty Goals: Crexell (4)
South Africa XV *Tries:* Johnson, Kruger, Wegner, Fuls, H P le Roux
Conversions: Stransky (3)   *Penalty Goals:* Stransky (3)

MATCH 6   13 November, Ferrocaril Oeste Stadium, Buenos Aires   2nd Test

ARGENTINA 23 (2G 2PG 1DG)   **SOUTH AFRICA 52** (4G 3PG 3T)
ARGENTINA: S Meson (Tucumán RC); M Teran (Tucumán RC), S Salvat (Alumni),
D Cuesta Silva (San Isidro Club), G Jorge (Pucara); L Arbizu (Belgrano) *(capt)*,
G Camardon (Alumni); M Corral (San Isidro Club), R le Fort (Tucumán RC), P Noreiga
(Hindu), P Sporleder (Curupayti), G Llanes (La Plata), M Bertranou
(Los Todos, Mendoza), G Ugartemendia (Los Matreros), P Fernandez-Bravo
(Tucumán RC) *Replacements* R Bullrich (Newman) for Camardon (50 mins); L Criscuolo
(Alumni) for Salvat (60 mins)
Scorers *Tries:* Camardon, Jorge   *Conversions:* Meson (2)   *Penalty Goals:* Meson (2)
Dropped Goal: Arbizu

SOUTH AFRICA: Johnson; Small Müller, Fuls, Williams; Honiball,
van der Westhuizen; Kebble, Drotske, K S Andrews, Strydom, Atherton, Pienaar *(capt)*,
Strauss, Kruger *Replacement* Allan for Pienaar (40 mins)
Scorers *Tries:* Strauss (2), Small (2), van der Westhuizen, Williams, Johnson
Conversions: Johnson (4) *Penalty Goals:* Johnson (3)
Referee W D Bevan (Wales)

AUSTRALIA TO NORTH AMERICA AND FRANCE 1993

Australia's trip was, incredibly, the last tour they have scheduled
before the 1995 World Cup (all six of their Test engagements for 1994
were due to be at home). As in 1989, when Tim Horan, Jason Little, Phil
Kearns, Tony Daly and Rod McCall came through to establish reputations as world-class players during the previous Australian visit to
France, the tour was viewed primarily as a World Cup planning exercise.

Bob Dwyer's teams for the provincial matches featured blends of the
uncapped and senior members of the squad. Most notable among the
newcomers was scrum-half Mark Catchpole, whose father, Ken, was
the leading player in that position in the 1960s. When it came to the
Tests, though, Dwyer took no chances and fell back on his tried and
tested regulars.

The Wallabies looked uncomfortable, despite beating the US Eagles
in a non-cap international in stifling conditions in Riverside. Before the
party departed for France, there was a win against a depleted Canadian
side in the full Test in Calgary.

At times the Aussies struggled in France. Tight discipline, sound
defence and Thierry Lacroix's second-half penalty brought France a
16-13 triumph in the Bordeaux Test; then the tourists crashed to a midweek defeat against Provence-Littoral in Toulon. Yet in the Second
Test, played under floodlights in Paris, the world champions gave a
stunning team performance, brilliantly orchestrated by Michael
Lynagh, their captain. The 24-3 victory was their biggest winning
margin in a Test against France and it was also the heaviest defeat
inflicted on France by an international team at Parc des Princes since
the ground was redeveloped in the early 1970s.

THE TOURING PARTY

Manager J Breen **Coach** R Dwyer **Assistant Coaches** R Templeton, J Howard
Captain M P Lynagh

FULL-BACKS

M C Roebuck (New South Wales)
M Burke (New South Wales)

THREEQUARTERS

D I Campese (New South Wales)
D Smith (Queensland)
B P J Lea (Queensland)

A Murdoch (New South Wales)
J S Little (Queensland)
T J Horan (Queensland)
P W Howard (Queensland)
R Constable (Queensland)

HALF-BACKS

M P Lynagh (Queensland)

S **Bowen** (New South Wales)
P J **Slattery** (Queensland)
M **Catchpole** (Queensland)
★T M **Wallace** (New South Wales)

FORWARDS

A J **Daly** (New South Wales)
D J **Crowley** (Queensland)
E J A **McKenzie** (New South Wales)
M N **Hartill** (New South Wales)
P N **Kearns** (New South Wales)
D V **Nucifora** (Queensland)
G J **Morgan** (Queensland)

R J **McCall** (Queensland)
W W **Waugh** (New South Wales)
T P **Kava** (New South Wales)
A **Dempsey** (New South Wales)
M C **Brial** (New South Wales)
F **Finau** (New South Wales)
D J **Wilson** (Queensland)
I **Tabua** (Queensland)
B T **Gavin** (New South Wales)
M **Bell** (New South Wales)
A **Skeggs** (Queensland)
★B **Robinson** (Queensland)

Replacement during tour

TOUR RECORD
All matches Played 11 Won 9 Lost 2 Points for 313 Against 182
International matches Played 3 Won 2 Lost 1 Points for 80 Against 35

SCORING DETAILS

All matches

For: 32T 18C 39PG –   313 Pts
Against: 13T   9C 31PG 2DG 182 Pts

International matches

For: 9T 4C 9PG –   80 Pts
Against: 3T 1C 4PG 2DG 35 Pts

MATCH DETAILS

1993	OPPONENTS	VENUE	RESULT
2 Oct	USA Eagles	Riverside	W 26-22
6 Oct	Canada B	Calgary	W 40-3
9 Oct	CANADA	Calgary	W 43-16
16 Oct	Aquitaine XV	Dax	W 30-15
20 Oct	South-West XV	Agen	W 20-19
23 Oct	Languedoc-Roussillon XV	Narbonne	W 35-18
26 Oct	South-East XV	Grenoble	W 24-23
30 Oct	FRANCE	Bordeaux	L 13-16
2 Nov	Provence-Littoral XV	Toulon	L 15-21
6 Nov	FRANCE	Paris	W 24-3
11 Nov	French Barbarians	Clermont-Ferrand	W 43-26

Appearances: 8 – Little*, Roebuck*, Morgan*; 7 – Lynagh, McKenzie, McCall, Wilson, Campese, Horan, Gavin, Smith*, Slattery*, Daly*; 6 – Nucifora*, Murdoch*, Brial*, Howard**, Crowley**; 5 – Burke, Lea, Tabua, Finau, Kearns, Catchpole, Hartill*; 4 – Waugh, Kava; 3 – Bowen, Dempsey; 2 – Constable, Bell*; 1 – Robinson, Wallace, Skeggs
* includes appearances as a replacement
Scorers: 106 – Roebuck (2T 9C 26PG); 57 – Lynagh (9C 13PG); 25 – Lea (5T); 20 – Campese, Murdoch (both 4T); 15 – Morgan (3T); 10 – Smith, Horan, Gavin (all 2T); 5 – Burke, Little, Howard, Daly, Tabua, Wilson, Bowen, Catchpole (all 1T)

MATCH 1 2 October, Riverside

USA Eagles 22 (1G 5PG) **Australia XV 26** (3G 1T)
USA Eagles: M Sika (BYU, Hawaii); G Hein (Old Blues), E Schram (Manly, NSW), M Scharrenberg (Chicago Sting), R Schurfeld (Belmont Shore); C O'Brien (Old Blues), A Bachelet (California RFC); C Lippert (OMBAC), T Billups (Old Blues), D James (Old Blues), K Swords (Beacon Hill) *(capt)*, R Randell (United RFC), C Campbell (Life College), R Tardits (Mystic River), J Wilkerson (Belmont Shore) *Replacement* S Hiatt (Old Blues) for Schram (65 mins)
Scorers *Try:* Schurfeld *Conversion:* O'Brien *Penalty Goals:* O'Brien (5)
Australia XV: Burke; Lea, Little, Howard, Smith; Lynagh *(capt)*, Slattery; Daly, Nucifora, McKenzie, McCall, Waugh, Tabua, Finau, Wilson

Scorers *Tries:* Tabua, Lea, Wilson, Howard   *Conversions:* Lynagh (3)
Referee G Gadjovich (Canada)

MATCH 2   6 October, Kingsland Rugby Park, Calgary

Canada B 3 (1PG)   **Australia XV 40** (2G 2PG 4T)
Canada B: S MacKinnon (British Columbia); C Smith (Ontario), R Toews
(British Columbia), D Clarke (Newfoundland), R Wheeldon (British Columbia);
J Penaluna (British Columbia), S Armstrong (Quebec); K Wirachowski (British Columbia),
M Cardinal (British Columbia), R Bice (British Columbia), J Knauer (British Columbia)
(*capt*), I Middleton (Ontario), J Tomlinson (Ontario), I Cooper (British Columbia),
I Phillips (British Columbia) *Replacement* S Gray (British Columbia) for Clarke
(32 mins)
Scorer *Penalty Goal:* MacKinnon
Australia XV: Roebuck; Lea, Burke, Horan, Murdoch; Bowen, Catchpole; Skeggs, Bell,
Hartill, Kava, Morgan, Dempsey, Gavin (*capt*), Brial *Replacements* Howard for Horan
(46 mins); Smith for Lea (60 mins); Crowley for Hartill (70 mins)
Scorers *Tries:* Murdoch (2), Morgan, Smith, Lea, Roebuck   *Conversions:* Roebuck (2)
Penalty Goals: Roebuck (2)
Referee P Higgens (Ontario)

MATCH 3   9 October, Kingsland Rugby Park, Calgary   Test

CANADA 16 (2PG 2T)   **AUSTRALIA 43** (2G 3PG 4T)
CANADA: S Stewart (UBC Old Boys, Vancouver, BC); J Loveday (Calgary Irish,
Alberta), M Williams (Vancouver Meralomas, BC) (*capt*), I Stuart (Vancouver Rowing
Club, BC), S Gray (Vancouver Kats, BC); J Graf (UBC Old Boys, BC), I MacKay
(Vancouver Kats, BC); P Szabo (Pocomo, BC), I Kennedy (Vancouver Meralomas, BC),
D Jackart (UBC Old Boys, BC), C Whittaker (James Bay, Victoria, BC), A Charron
(Ottawa Irish, Ontario), J Hutchinson (York Yeomen, Toronto, Ontario), C McKenzie
(UBC Old Boys, BC), I Gordon (James Bay, Victoria, BC) *Replacement* M Cardinal
(James Bay, Victoria, BC) for Kennedy (58 mins)
Scorers *Tries:* Kennedy, Jackart   *Penalty Goals:* Graf (2)
AUSTRALIA: Roebuck; Campese, Horan, Little, Smith; Lynagh (*capt*), Slattery; Daly,
Kearns, McKenzie, Morgan, McCall, Wilson, Gavin, Tabua *Replacements* Crowley for
Daly (62 mins); Kearns for Nucifora (68 mins)
Scorers *Tries:* Campese (3), Smith, Horan, Daly   *Conversions:* Lynagh (2)
Penalty Goals: Lynagh (3)
Referee W D Bevan (Wales)

MATCH 4   16 October, Parc Municipal, Dax

Aquitaine XV 15 (5PG)   **Australia XV 30** (3G 3PG)
Aquitaine XV: R Dourthe (Dax); W Téchoueyres (SBUC Bordeaux), P Lopez (Pau),
C Coeurveille (Biarritz), P Hontas (Biarritz); S Prosper (Mont de Marsan),
G Accoceberry (Bègles-Bordeaux) (*capt*); S Simon (Bègles-Bordeaux), A Fabre
(Tyrosse), L Verge (Bègles-Bordeaux), P Beraud (Dax), F Sentenac (SBUC Bordeaux),
O Magne (Dax), C Dongieu (Bayonne), A Agueb (SBUC Bordeaux)
Replacement E Vergniol (Dax) for Coeurville (26 mins)
Scorer *Penalty Goals:* Prosper (5)
Australia XV: Roebuck; Campese, Little, Howard, Murdoch; Bowen, Slattery;
Crowley, Kearns (*capt*), Hartill, Waugh, Morgan, Tabua, Finau, Dempsey
Scorers *Tries:* Murdoch, Little, Bowen   *Conversions:* Roebuck (3)
Penalty Goals: Roebuck (3)
Referee A J Spreadbury (England)

MATCH 5   20 October, Stade Armandie, Agen

South-West XV 19 (1G 4PG)   **Australia XV 20** (5PG 1T)
South-West XV: S Viars (Brive); S Ougier (Toulouse), L Salinas (Lourdes),
H Couffignal (Colomiers), G Bouic (Agen); P Montlaur (Agen), F Galthié (Colomiers)
(capt); L Toussaint (Castres), C Urios (Castres), L Seigne (Merignac), C Porcu (Auch),
F Grec (Lourdes), J Diaz (Castres), N Hallinger (Colomiers), A Benazzi (Agen)
Replacement T Bourdet (Castres) for Grec (52 mins)
Scorers *Try:* Bourdet   *Conversion:* Montlaur   *Penalty Goals:* Montlaur (4)
Australia XV: Burke; Smith, Constable, Horan, Lea; Lynagh (capt), Catchpole;
Crowley, Nucifora, McKenzie, McCall, Kava, Brial, Gavin, Wilson *Replacements* Howard
for Constable (18 mins); Daly for Crowley (55 mins)
Scorers *Try:* Horan   *Penalty Goals:* Lynagh (5)
Referee M Darroque (Armagnac-Bigorre)

MATCH 6   23 October, Parc des Sports et de l'Amitié, Narbonne

Languedoc-Roussillon XV 18 (1G 2PG 1T)   **Australia XV 35** (3G 3PG 1T)
Languedoc-Roussillon: T Clavieres (Narbonne); P Fabre (Montpellier), A Hyardet
(Béziers), P Bondouy (Narbonne), J-V Bertrand (Narbonne); J-M Lescure (Narbonne),
A Macabiau (Perpignan) (capt); J Puginier (Perpignan), P Laurent (Perpignan),
P Gallart (Béziers), J-F Gourragne (Béziers), F Dejean (Narbonne), M Lievremont
(Perpignan), S Dispagne (Narbonne), G Majoral (Perpignan) *Replacement* P Amalric
(Perpignan) for Clavieres (74 mins); A Foury for Dejean (temp)
Scorers *Tries:* Laurent, Lievremont   *Conversion:* Lescure   *Penalty Goals:* Lescure (2)
Australia XV: Burke; Campese, Little, Horan, Murdoch; Lynagh (capt), Slattery;
Daly, Kearns, McKenzie, McCall,. Morgan, Tabua, Gavin, Wilson *Replacements* Roebuck
for Burke (54 mins); Hartill for McKenzie (77 mins)
Scorers *Tries:* Morgan (2), Burke, Murdoch   *Conversions:* Lynagh (3)
Penalty Goals: Lynagh (3)
Referee J Dumé (Côte d'Argent)

MATCH 7   26 October, Stade Lesdiguieres, Grenoble

South-East XV 23 (2G 3PG)   **Australia XV 24** (1G 4PG 1T)
South-East XV: J-B Lafond (Stade Français); A Gomez (Paris University Club),
F Mesnel (Racing Club de France), F Velo (Grenoble), P Berot (LOU Lyon);
D Aucagne (Paris University Club), P Ladouce (Montferrand); L Benezech
(Racing Club de France), C Ducluzeau (Montferrand), F Heyer (LOU Lyon), Y Brouzet
(Grenoble), Y Lemeur (Racing Club de France), B Simond (Rumilly), X Blond
(Racing Club de France), J-M Lhermet (Montferrand) *Replacement* E Joliveau (Dijon)
for Simond (6 mins)
Scorers *Tries:* Gomez, Lafond   *Conversions:* Aucagne (2)   *Penalty Goals:* Aucagne (3)
Australia XV: Roebuck; Lea, Murdoch, Howard, Smith; Bowen, Catchpole; Crowley,
Nucifora, Hartill, Kava (capt), Waugh, Dempsey, Brial, Finau *Replacements* Little for
Howard (22 mins); Howard for Bowen (22 mins); Morgan for Dempsey (41 mins); Bell
for Nucifora (56 mins)
Scorers *Tries:* Lea (2)   *Conversion:* Roebuck   *Penalty Goals:* Roebuck (4)
Referee K W McCartney (Scotland)

MATCH 8   30 October, Parc Lescure, Bordeaux   **1st Test**

FRANCE 16 (1G 1PG 2DG)   **AUSTRALIA 13** (1G 2PG)
FRANCE: J-L Sadourny (Colomiers); P Bernat-Salles (Pau), P Sella (Agen), T Lacroix
(Dax), P Saint-André (Montferrand); A Penaud (Brive), A Hueber (Toulon); L Armary
(Lourdes), J-M Gonzalez (Bayonne), L Seigne (Merignac), O Merle (Grenoble),
O Roumat (Dax) (capt), P Benetton (Agen), M Cecillon (Bourgoin), A Benazzi (Agen)
Scorers *Try:* Hueber   *Conversion:* Lacroix   *Penalty Goal:* Lacroix

Dropped Goals: Penaud, Sadourny
AUSTRALIA: Burke; Campese, Little Horan, Murdoch; Lynagh (*capt*), Slattery; Daly, Kearns, McKenzie, McCall, Morgan, Tabua, Gavin, Wilson *Replacement* Brial for Tabua (40 mins)
Scorers *Try:* Gavin   *Conversion:* Lynagh   *Penalty Goals:* Lynagh (2)
Referee D J Bishop (New Zealand)

MATCH 9   2 November, Stade Mayol, Toulon

Provence-Littoral XV 21 (1G 3PG 1T)   **Australia XV 15** (5PG)
Provence-Littoral XV: E N'Tamack (Toulouse); P Escalle (Castres), M Marfaing (Narbonne), Y Delaigue (Toulon), D Jaubert (Toulon); G Merceron (Toulon), J Cazalbou (Toulouse); M Perie (Toulon), E Dasalmartini (Toulon), C Califano (Toulouse), T Devergie (Grenoble), B Motteroz (Toulon), C Moni (Nice), T Louvet (Toulon) (*capt*), F Pelous (Graulhet) *Replacement* B Lapiatte (Toulon) for Perie (42 mins)
Scorers *Tries:* Escalle, Marfaing   *Conversion:* Merceron   *Penalty Goals:* Merceron (3)
Australia XV: Roebuck; Campese, Constable, Howard, Smith; Wallace, Catchpole; Hartill, Nucifora, Crowley, Kava (*capt*), Waugh, Finau, Robinson, Brial
Replacement Murdoch for Constable (49 mins); Slattery for Catchpole (temp)
Scorers *Penalty Goals:* Roebuck (5)
Referee J-R Barrabes (Languedoc)

MATCH 10   6 November, Parc des Princes, Paris   2nd Test

FRANCE 3 (1PG)   **AUSTRALIA 24** (1G 4PG 1T)
FRANCE: J-L Sadourny (Colomiers); P Bernat-Salles (Pau), P Sella (Agen), T Lacroix (Dax), P Saint-André (Montferrand); A Penaud (Brive), A Hueber (Toulon); L Armary (Lourdes), J-M Gonzalez (Bayonne), L Seigne (Merignac), O Merle (Grenoble), O Roumat (Dax) (*capt*), P Benetton (Agen), M Cecillon (Bourgoin), A Benazzi (Agen)
Replacement S Graou (Auch) for Seigne (79 mins)
Scorer *Penalty Goal:* Lacroix
AUSTRALIA: Roebuck; Campese, Little, Horan, Smith; Lynagh (*capt*), Slattery; Daly, Kearns, McKenzie, McCall, Morgan, Brial, Gavin, Wilson
Scorers *Tries:* Roebuck, Gavin   *Conversion:* Roebuck   *Penalty Goals:* Roebuck (4)
Referee D J Bishop (New Zealand)

MATCH 11   11 November, Stade Marcel Michelen, Clermont-Ferrand

French Barbarians 26 (2G 4PG)   **Australia XV 43** (2G 8PG 1T)
French Barbarians: E N'Tamack (Toulouse); P Saint-André (Montferrand & France), F Mesnel (Racing Club de France & France), D Codorniou (Narbonne & France), P Lagisquet (Biarritz & France); D Charvet (Racing Club de France & France), N C Farr-Jones (Sydney U & Australia); G Lascubé (Biarritz & France), M Dal Maso (Agen), P Gallart (Béziers & France), A Benazzi (Agen & France), G W Whetton (Castres & New Zealand), R Pool-Jones (Biarritz), H Chaffardon (Grenoble), E Champ (Toulon & France) (*capt*) *Replacement* F Galthié (Colomiers & France) for Farr-Jones (65 mins); J-M Lhermet (Montferrand & France) for Champ (temp)
Scorers *Tries:* Saint-André, Dal Maso   *Conversions:* Charvet (2)
Penalty Goals: Charvet (4)
Australia XV: Roebuck; Campese, Little, Horan, Lea; Lynagh (*capt*), Catchpole; Daly, Nucifora, McKenzie, McCall, Morgan, Finau, Gavin, Wilson
Scorers *Tries:* Lea, Catchpole, Campese   *Conversions:* Roebuck (2)
Penalty Goals: Roebuck (8)
Referee S R Hilditch (Ireland)

JAPAN TO WALES 1993

Too much earth and wind but not enough fire was the story of the third Japanese short tour of Wales. Ankle-deep mud and gales wrecked constructive play at several of the tour venues and not even the likes of Ian Williams, the former Australian wing, Tupo Fa'amasino, late of Western Samoa, and Bruce Ferguson, the ex-Fijian lock, could inject spirit into a side which showed that Japanese rugby had gone into sharp decline.

Previous Japanese teams had demonstrated that they were rugby's living embodiment of the adage that necessity is the mother of invention. Vertically compromised on the field, they had used plenty of ploys to ensure a share of possession. Their inspired tricks had bamboozled opponents and fascinated crowds. The 1993 tourists, in contrast, lacked initiative and were unable to attract a sponsor for the visit.

True, there were good wins at Narberth, Pontypridd and, despite the sending-off of their prospective Buddhist monk Hirofumi Ouchi, at Dunvant. But any Japanese pretensions to breaking into the higher echelons of rugby's world order evaporated in the game against Wales at Cardiff, where they were taken apart. Wales posted their highest-ever score and biggest winning margin for a cap match, and Ieuan Evans' try in the 45th second was the quickest scored by a Welshman in a major international.

THE TOURING PARTY

Manager Z Shirai   **Coach** O Koyabu
Assistant Coaches M Sakai, M Fujiwara   **Captain** M Kunda

FULL-BACKS	FORWARDS
T Maeda (NTT Kansai)	O Ota (NEC)
T Matsuda (Toshiba)	K Kimura (Toyota Motor)
THREEQUARTERS	K Takahashi (Toyota Motor)
Y Yoshida (Isetan)	M Nakamura (Mitsubishi)
T Fujihara (Doshisha U)	M Kunda (Toshiba)
I Williams (Kobe Steel)	E Hirotsu (Kobe Steel)
M Fujikake (World)	Y Sakuraba (Nippon Steel)
T Fa'amasino (ex-Wellington)	H Kaneshiro (Toyota Motor)
F Kutsuki (Toyota Motor)	B Ferguson (Hino Motor)
HALF-BACKS	H Kajihara (Toshiba)
S Aoki (Ricoh)	S Kaleta (Ricoh)
K Matsuo (World)	S Nakashima (NEC)
Y Nagatomo (Suntory)	S Latu (Sanyo)
R Onitsuka (Doshisha U)	S Ono (Toshiba Fuchu)
	H Ouchi (Ryukoku U)

TOUR RECORD

All matches   Played 6   Won 3   Lost 3   Points for 111   Against 197
International matches   Played 1   Lost 1   Points for 5   Against 55

SCORING DETAILS

All matches					International matches				
For:	16T 11C 3PG	–	111 Pts		For:	1T	–	–	5 Pts

Against: 28T 15C 8PG 1DG 197 Pts   Against: 9T 5C –   55 Pts

MATCH DETAILS

1993	OPPONENTS	VENUE	RESULT
29 Sept	Wales A	Llanelli	L 5-61
2 Oct	Dunvant	Dunvant	W 24-23
6 Oct	East Wales	Abertillery	L 12-38
9 Oct	West Wales	Narberth	W 26-10
12 Oct	Heineken Select XV	Pontypridd	W 39-10
16 Oct	WALES	Cardiff	L 5-55

Appearances: 6 – Fujikake; 5 – Yoshida, Sakuraba, Kaleta, Ferguson; 4 – Matsuda, Fa'amasino, Nagatomo, Ota, Kunda, Latu, Aoki*, Maeda, Ouchi; 3 – Nakamura, Kaneshiro, Onitsuka*, Fujihara, Takahashi, Williams; 2 – Matsuo, Nakashima, Kimura, Hirotsu, Ono, Kutsuki * includes appearance as a replacement
Scorers: 18 – Nagatomo (6C 2PG), Maeda (1T 5C 1PG); 15 – Fujihara (3T); 10 – Williams, Fujikake, Ouchi (all 3T); 5 – Matsuda, Fa'amasino, Kunda, Nakamura, Kaneshiro, Latu (all 1T)

MATCH 1   29 September, Stradey Park, Llanelli

Wales A 61 (4G 1PG 6T) **Japan XV 5** (1T)
Wales A: M Back (Pontypridd); S Hill (Cardiff), R A Bidgood (Newport), N R Jenkins (Pontypridd), N Walker (Cardiff); A Davies (Cardiff) *(capt)*, R Howley (Cardiff); R L Evans (Llanelli), G R Jenkins (Swansea), H Williams-Jones (Llanelli), A H Copsey (Llanelli), P Arnold (Swansea), H Taylor (Cardiff), L S Quinnell (Llanelli), L Jones (Llanelli) *Replacement* G Wilkins (Bridgend) for Bidgood (65 mins)
Scorers *Tries:* Arnold (2), Jenkins (2), Davies (2), Walker, Quinnell, Back, Wilkins *Conversions:* Jenkins (2), Davies (2) *Penalty Goal:* Jenkins
Japan XV: Matsuda; Williams, Fujikake, Fa'amasino, Yoshida; Matsuo, Nagatomo; Ota, Kunda *(capt)*, Nakamura, Sakuraba, Kaneshiro, Kaleta, Nakashima, Latu
Replacements Onitsuka for Nagatomo (46 mins); Aoki for Fujikake (63 mins)
Scorer *Try:* Kaneshiro
Referee D Matthews (Lancashire RU)

MATCH 2   2 October, Broadacre, Dunvant

Dunvant 23 (2G 3PG) **Japan XV 24** (3G 1PG)
Dunvant: D Evans; C Young, N Bolton, W Lloyd, P Farnworth; M Thomas, N Lloyd; M Waygood, D Morris, R Llewellyn, D Niblo, D Crane *(capt)*, C Davies, P Morris, C Butler *Replacement* P Hopkins for Farnworth (65 mins)
Scorers *Tries:* P Morris, N Lloyd *Conversions:* Thomas (2) *Penalty Goals:* Thomas (3)
Japan XV: Maeda; Fujihara, Fujikake, Fa'amasino, Yoshida; Aoki *(capt)*, Onitsuka; Kimura, Hirotsu, Nakamura, Sakuraba, Ferguson, Kaleta, Ouchi, Ono
Scorers *Tries:* Fujikake, Ouchi, Fujihara *Conversions:* Maeda (3)
Penalty Goal: Maeda
Referee J Bacigalupo (Scotland)

MATCH 3   6 October, Abertillery Park, Abertillery

East Wales 38 (3G 4PG 1T) **Japan XV 12** (1G 1T)
East Wales: L Evans (Treorchy); D Manley (Pontypridd), J Hewitt (Cardiff), S Lewis (Pontypridd), A Harries (Newbridge); D Rees (Newport), A Booth (Cardiff); N Bezani (Pontypridd), J Humphreys (Cardiff), P Sedgemore (Cardiff), A Rees (Cardiff), D Jones (Cardiff), H Stone (Cardiff), O Williams (Cardiff) *(capt)*, M Budd (Cardiff)
Replacements A Moore (Cardiff) for Booth (49 mins); P Thomas (Pontypridd) for Stone (47 mins)
Scorers *Tries:* Harries (3), Humphreys *Conversions:* Evans (3) *Penalty Goals:* Evans (4)
Japan XV: Maeda; Fujihara, Fujikake, Fa'amasino, Yoshida; Matsuo, Onitsuka; Ota, Kunda *(capt)*, Takahashi, Kaneshiro, Ferguson, Kaleta, Latu, Nakashima
Scorers *Tries:* Fa'amasino, Fujihara *Conversion:* Maeda
Referee B Campsall (Yorkshire RU)

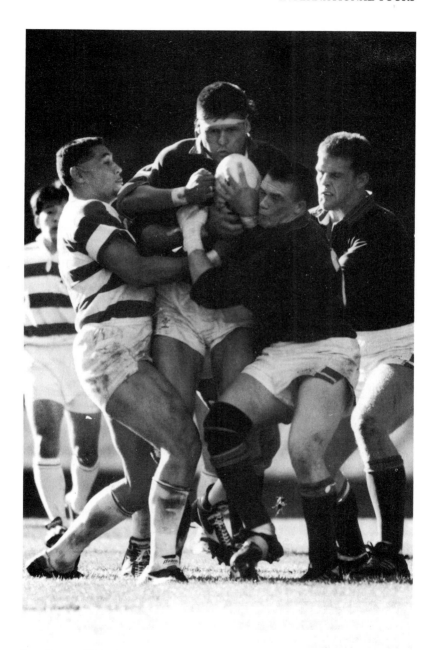

Tony Copsey of Wales has possession in the Test against the touring Japanese at Cardiff. Wales beat the visitors 55-5, recording their biggest-ever win and margin in a cap match.

MATCH 4   9 October, Lewis Lloyd Ground, Narberth

West Wales 10 (2T)   **Japan XV 26** (3G 1T)
West Wales: D Weatherley (Swansea); S Barclay (Swansea), J Jardine (Aberavon), I Lewis (Swansea), G Willis (Bridgend); M Lewis (Bridgend), Rhodri Jones (Neath); I Buckett (Swansea), A Thomas (Neath), R Shaw (Swansea), G O Llewellyn (Neath) (*capt*), P Jones (Llanelli), I Davies (Swansea), A Williams (Maesteg), A Varney (Neath) *Replacements* H Harries (Cardiff) for Rhodri Jones (46 mins); Iwan Jones (Swansea) for Davies (46 mins)
Scorers *Tries:* Barclay, Rhodri Jones
Japan XV: Matsuda; Maeda, Fujikake, Fa'amasino, Yoshida; Aoki, Nagatomo; Ota, Kunda (*capt*), Takahashi, Sakuraba, Ferguson, Kaleta, Latu, Ouchi
Scorers *Tries:* Kunda, Maeda, Ouchi, Latu   *Conversions:* Nagatomo (2), Maeda
Referee R McDowall (Ireland)

MATCH 5   12 October, Pontypridd

Heineken Select XV 10 (1G 1DG)   **Japan XV 39** (4G 2PG 1T)
Heineken Select XV: R Boobyer (Tondu); D Howells (Bonymaen), M Tatchell (Tondu), T Manseivata (Pyle), R Rees (Tumble); M Dacey (Bonymaen), R Lewis (Blackwood); M King (Kidwelly), L Phillips (Abercynon), J Pugh (Builth Wells) (*capt*), P Clapham (Kenfig Hill), P Nolan (Bonymaen), A Myers (Bonymaen), N Edwards (Abercynon), D Edwards (Kenfig Hill) *Replacements* M Clement (Bonymaen) for Lewis (74 mins); P Owen (Kenfig Hill) for Clapham (60 mins); C West (Pontypridd United) for N Edwards (40 mins)
Scorers *Try:* Nolan   *Conversion:* Tatchell   *Dropped Goal:* Dacey
Japan XV: Matsuda; Williams, Fujikake, Kutsuki, Fujihara; Maeda, Nagatomo; Kimura, Hirotsu, Nakamura, Sakuraba, Kaneshiro, Ouchi, Ono, Ferguson
Scorers *Tries:* Fujihara, Fujikake, Matsuda, Nakamura, Williams
Conversions: Nagatomo (4)   *Penalty Goals:* Nagatomo (2)
Referee S Lander (Liverpool)

MATCH 6   16 October, Cardiff Arms Park   **Test Match**

WALES 55 (5G 4T)   **JAPAN 5** (1T)
WALES: A Clement (Swansea); I C Evans (Llanelli) (*capt*), I S Gibbs (Swansea), N R Jenkins (Pontypridd), N Walker (Cardiff); A Davies (Cardiff), R H St J B Moon (Llanelli); M Griffiths (Cardiff), A E H Lamerton (Llanelli), J D Davies (Neath), A H Copsey (Llanelli), G O Llewellyn (Neath), S Davies (Swansea), E W Lewis (Llanelli), L Jones (Llanelli) *Replacements* M A Rayer (Cardiff) for Walker (27 mins); R A Bidgood (Newport) for Evans (73 mins)
Scorers *Tries:* Evans (2), Gibbs (2), Jenkins, Moon, Lewis, Rayer, Clement
Conversions: Jenkins (5)
JAPAN: Matsuda; Williams, Fujikake, Kutsuki, Yoshida; Aoki, Nagatomo; Ota, Kunda (*capt*), Takahashi, Sakuraba, Ferguson, Kaleta, Latu, Ouchi
Scorer *Try:* Williams
Referee E F Morrison (England)

SCOTLAND TO FIJI, TONGA AND WESTERN SAMOA 1993

Scotland's tour to the South Pacific ended in defeat as Western Samoa avenged their Murrayfield loss in the 1991 World Cup quarter-finals. The Samoans won the rematch in Apia by 28-11, but overall the Scots' tour was an undoubted success.

Not only did they win all six of their matches before the Apia defeat but they found strength in depth. Scotland toured without most of their recognised first-choice players from the previous season's International Championship. Seven Scots were away with the Lions in New Zealand and more than a dozen others were unavailable, which persuaded the Scottish Rugby Union not to recognise the three Tests as cap internationals, and in certain positions the selectors had to draw deep from the limited reservoir for third and fourth choices.

Andy Nicol, Dundee High School FP's international scrum-half, marked himself down as a possible future national captain through the manner of his leadership on and off the field, though his own game dipped a little, and his fellow cap, Gregor Townsend, recovered from a poor start to his tour. The 20-year-old Gala fly-half was left out against Fiji, the tour selectors preferring Ally Donaldson, Currie's Edinburgh and Scotland A fly-half, but Townsend responded to the challenge by playing himself into the Test team through a tidy performance in the 21-5 win over the Tongan President's XV in Nuku'alofa. His accurate kicking was particularly influential in that result.

Doddie Weir, the Melrose No 8, relished his role as the only player remaining from Scotland's first-choice Championship XV the previous season, but his club and international colleague, Carl Hogg, had a frustrating tour. Not only had he to play second fiddle to Weir but his nose was so severely broken by a brutal stiff-arm tackle during the midweek match in Apia that he had to be flown to Auckland for an operation.

Two Glasgow High/Kelvinside forwards, Shade Munro and Murray Wallace, came home with reputations substantially enhanced, as did at least five more of the 19 uncapped players among the 30 original tourists. Munro, who might have had a dozen caps or more by 1993 but for a severe leg fracture in 1990, was the most consistent of the four locks in the squad, though it was only for the Samoan Test that he broke through to depose Chris Gray as front jumper, whereas Wallace, who had played only one district game for Glasgow before he went on tour, emerged as one who could go all the way in his preferred role as open-side flanker. When he switched from the blind side for the last quarter of the midweek match against the Fijian Juniors he scored two tries, and he established himself as a serious challenger to Ian Smith, though the Gloucester cap held on for all three Tests.

Gary Isaac, Gala's loose head, and Steve Ferguson, from Second Division Peebles, responded to the demands in establishing themselves as the Test props. Richie Dixon, the Scottish forwards' coach, awarded the Border pair high praise, especially after the 23-9 win over Tonga, for the way they had locked in to ensure scrummage command.

Ian Jardine, the Stirling County centre who had been on the verge for half a dozen years, emerged as the midfield rock in the Test matches, especially in stemming the Samoan tide that threatened to engulf the Scots in the final match, and Rob MacNaughton, the Northampton centre who, like Wallace, was chosen for the tour after only one district game, showed much promise, though he did not make Test selection. Another of the Melrose contingent, Bryan Redpath, was a worthy deputy for Nicol at scrum-half. The Borderer was a doughty competitor blessed with a swift service.

Scotland won all three matches in Fiji and the two in Tonga, and they continued their winning ways against the Western Samoa President's XV. By then the success of the tour was assured. For all that it had turned into more of a development tour, the players mainly responded well to the coaches, David Johnston and Dixon, and victory in the final match would have been the icing on the cake. Western Samoa, however, proved too strong, even though the Scottish forwards maintained their scrummage power for a pushover try for Nicol.

THE TOURING PARTY

Captain A D Nicol   **Manager** A M Hosie
Coach D I Johnston   **Assistant Coach** J R Dixon

FULL-BACKS

K M Logan (Stirling County)
A C Redpath (Melrose)

THREEQUARTERS

I C Glasgow (Heriot's FP)
N J Grecian (London Scottish)
I C Jardine (Stirling County)
J A Kerr (Haddington)
R C MacNaughton (Northampton)
K R Milligan (Stewart's-Melville FP)
M Moncrieff (Gala)
S A Nichol (Selkirk)
D S Wyllie (Stewart's-Melville FP)

HALF-BACKS

A Donaldson (Currie)
A D Nicol (Dundee HSFP)
B W Redpath ((Melrose)
G P J Townsend (Gala)

FORWARDS

K Armstrong (Jedforest)
*I Corcoran (Gala)
S W Ferguson (Peebles)
C A Gray (Nottingham)
J A Hay (Hawick)
C D Hogg (Melrose)
G R Isaac (Gala)
P M Jones (Gloucester)
A E D Macdonald (Heriot's FP)
D J McIvor (Edinburgh Acads)
D S Munro (Glasgow High/Kelvinside)
M W Scott (Edinburgh Acads)
R Scott (London Scottish)
I R Smith (Gloucester)
M I Wallace (Glasgow High/Kelvinside)
G W Weir (Melrose)
G D Wilson (Boroughmuir)
* Replacement during tour

TOUR RECORD

All matches   Played 7   Won 6   Lost 1   Points for 174   Against 66
International matches   Played 3   Won 2   Lost 1   Points for 55   Against 43

SCORING DETAILS

All matches

For:	22T	8C	16PG	–	174 Pts
Against:	8T	4C	6PG	–	66 Pts

International matches

For:	6T	2C	7PG	–	55 Pts
Against:	5T	3C	4PG	–	43 Pts

MATCH DETAILS

1993	OPPONENTS	VENUE	RESULT
22 May	Fiji B	Nadi	W 14-7
26 May	Fiji Juniors	Suva	W 51-3

29 May	FIJI	Suva	W 21-10
2 June	Tonga President's XV	Nuku'alofa	W 21-5
5 June	TONGA	Nuku'alofa	W 23-5
9 June	W Samoa President's XV	Apia	W 33-8
12 June	WESTERN SAMOA	Apia	L 11-28

Appearances: 6 – Weir**; 5 – Hay*, Logan*, McIvor, A D Nicol*, R Scott; 4 – Donaldson*, Ferguson, Grecian, Gray, Hogg*, Isaac, Jardine, Moncrieff, S A Nichol, Smith, Townsend, Wilson*, Wyllie*; 3 – Jones, Kerr, Macdonald*, MacNaughton, Munro, A C Redpath, B W Redpath, Wallace; 2 – Armstrong, Corcoran*, Milligan, M W Scott; 1 – Glasgow
* includes appearances as a replacement
Scorers: 30 – Townsend (1T 2C 7PG); 25 – Donaldson (2C 7PG); 20 – A D Nicol (4T); 16 – Grecian (1T 4C 1PG); 15 – Hogg (3T); 10 – Kerr, Logan, Wallace, Weir (all 2T); 5 – Gray, Hay (both 1T); 3 – Wyllie (1DG), 3 penalty tries

MATCH 1   22 May, A D Patel Stadium, Nadi

Fiji B 7 (1G)   **Scotland 14** (3PG 1T)
Fiji B *Try:* I Kunaqio   *Conversion:* I Saukuru
Scotland: Logan; Moncrieff, Jardine, MacNaughton, Kerr; Donaldson, B W Redpath; Isaac, Hay, Wilson, Gray, R Scott, McIvor, Weir, Smith (*capt*)
Scorers *Try:* Kerr   *Penalty Goals:* Donaldson (3)
Referee B M Kinsey (Australia)

MATCH 2   26 May, National Stadium, Suva

Fiji Juniors 3 (1PG)   **Scotland 51** (4G 1PG 4T)
Fiji Juniors: *Penalty Goal:* A Dreu
Scotland: A C Redpath; Grecian, S A Nichol, Wylie, Milligan; Townsend, A D Nicol (*capt*); Jones, M W Scott, Ferguson, Macdonald, Munro, Armstrong, Hogg, Wallace
Scorers *Tries:* Grecian, Hogg (3), A D Nicol (2), Wallace (2)   *Conversions:* Grecian (4)
Penalty Goal: Grecian
Referee W Erickson (Australia)

MATCH 3   29 May, National Stadium, Suva

FIJI 10 (1G 1PG)   **SCOTLAND 21** (1G 3PG 1T)
FIJI: T Vonolagi; W Komaitai, V Raulini, E Nauga, T Lovo; E Rokowailoa, W Serevi; M Taga (*capt*), A Rabitu, I Naituku, P Naruma, A Nadolo, I Tawake, E Tuvunivona, S Vololagi
Scorers *Try:* Rokowailoa   *Conversion:* Serevi   *Penalty Goal:* Serevi
SCOTLAND: Logan; Grecian, Jardine, S A Nichol, Moncrieff; Donaldson, A D Nicol (*capt*); Isaac, Hay, Ferguson, Gray, R Scott, McIvor, Weir, Smith
Scorers *Tries:* Hay, Logan   *Conversion:* Donaldson   *Penalty Goals:* Donaldson (3)
Referee B M Kinsey (Australia)

MATCH 4   2 June, Teufaiva Stadium, Nuku'alofa

Tongan President's XV 5 (1T)   **Scotland 21** (1G 3PG 1T)
Tongan President's XV *Try:* E Tulikaki
Scotland: A C Redpath; Milligan, MacNaughton, Wyllie (*capt*), Kerr; Townsend, B W Redpath; Jones, M W Scott, Wilson, Munro, R Scott, Armstrong, Hogg, Wallace
Replacements Logan for Milligan; Donaldson for MacNaughton; Hay for M W Scott; Weir (temp)
Scorers *Tries:* Townsend, pen try   *Conversion:* Townsend   *Penalty Goals:* Townsend (3)
Referee T R Marshall (New Zealand)

MATCH 5   5 June, Teufaiva Stadium, Nuku'alofa

TONGA 5 (1T)   **SCOTLAND 23** (1G 2PG 2T)
TONGA: I Tapueluelu; A Uasi, T Tu'ineau, M Lavaka, T Va'enuku; E Vunipola,

69

A Tulikaki; V Moa, F Masila, E Talakai, T Loto'ahea, I Fatani, I Fenukitau, M Manukia (*capt*), F Fakaongo *Replacement* L Fotu for Tapueluelu; T Levaki for Moa; M Vunipola for Tulikaka
Scorer *Try:* Lavaka
SCOTLAND: A C Redpath; Moncrieff, S A Nichol, Jardine, Logan; Townsend, A D Nicol (*capt*); Isaac, Hay, Ferguson, Gray, R Scott, McIvor, Weir, Smith
Replacements Hogg for Scott; Wyllie (temp); Wilson (temp)
Scorers *Tries:* Logan Weir, pen try   *Conversion:* Townsend
Penalty Goals: Townsend (2)
Referee L L McLachlan (New Zealand)

MATCH 6   9 June, Apia

Western Samoa President's XV 8 (1PG 1T)   **Scotland 33** (1G 1PG 1DG 4T)
Western Samoa President's XV *Try:* P Paulo   *Penalty Goal:* A Leaupepe
Scotland: Grecian; Glasgow, MacNaughton, Wyllie, Kerr; Donaldson, B W Redpath; Jones, Corcoran, Wilson, Gray (*capt*), Macdonald, McIvor, Hogg, Wallace
Replacements A D Nicol for Redpath; Weir for Hogg
Scorers *Tries:* Gray, Kerr, A D Nicol, Weir, pen try   *Conversion:* Donaldson
Penalty Goal: Donaldson   *Dropped Goal:* Wyllie
Referee T R Marshall (New Zealand)

MATCH 7   12 June, Apia

WESTERN SAMOA 28 (2G 3PG 1T)   **SCOTLAND 11** (2PG 1T)
WESTERN SAMOA: A Aiolupo; L Koko, T Vaega, A Ieremia, B Lima; D Kellett, J Tonu'u; P Fatialofa (*capt*), T Leasamaivao, A Leu'u, P Leavasa, L Falaniko, S Vaifale, D Kaleopa, M Iupeli *Replacements* S To'omalatai for Leu'u; J Schuster for Vaifale
Scorers *Tries:* D Kaleopa, Lima, Vaega   *Conversions:* Kellett (2)
Penalty Goals: Kellett (3)
SCOTLAND: Grecian; Moncrieff, S A Nichol, Jardine, Logan; Townsend, A D Nicol (*capt*); Isaac, Hay, Ferguson, Munro, R Scott, McIvor, Weir, Smith *Replacements* Corcoran for Hay; Macdonald for Scott
Scorers *Try:* A D Nicol   *Penalty Goals:* Townsend (2)
Referee L L McLachlan (New Zealand)

OTHER TOURS

Tonga to Australia 1993
Played 4   Won 2   Lost 2   Points for 51   Against 89
Beat New South Wales Country 11-5, lost to Australian Capital Territory 8-29, LOST TO AUSTRALIA 14-52, beat Queensland Country 18-3

4 July, Ballymore, Brisbane   Test Match

AUSTRALIA 52 (4G 3PG 3T)   **TONGA 14** (2G)
AUSTRALIA: M C Roebuck (NSW); D I Campese (NSW), J S Little (Queensland), T J Horan (Queensland), P V Carozza (Queensland); M P Lynagh (Queensland) (*capt*), P J Slattery (Queensland); A J Daly (NSW), P N Kearns (NSW), E J A McKenzie (NSW), R J McCall (Queensland), G Morgan (Queensland), T Coker (Queensland), B T Gavin (NSW), D J Wilson (Queensland) *Replacement* B Johnstone (Queensland) for Slattery (15 mins)
Scorers *Tries:* Campese (2), Little, Carozza, Gavin, Johnstone, Morgan
Conversions: Roebuck (3), Lynagh   *Penalty Goals:* Roebuck (3)
TONGA: T Vave; A Taufa, T Tu'Ineau, M Lavaka, T Va'enuku; E Vunipola, M Vunipola; S Latu, R Kapeli, F Masila, I Fatani, F Mafi, I Fenukitau, M Manukia,

(*capt*), F Mahoni *Replacements* F Manukia for Tu'Ineau (39 mins); T Kolo for E Vunipola (71 mins)
Scorers *Tries:* Fenukitau, pen try   *Conversions:* Vave (2)
Referee B Leask (Queensland)

Ireland Development Team to Zimbabwe, Namibia and South Africa 1993

Played 7   Won 6   Lost 1   Points for 219   Against 103
Beat Mashonaland 22-10, beat Zimbabwe A 20-6, beat Namibia B 38-21,
lost to Namibia A 19-33, beat South African Central Provinces 53-15, beat South African
Rural Provinces 23-18, beat South African Development XV 44-0

Auckland to England and Scotland 1993

Played 7   Won 6   Lost 1   Points for 236   Against 100
Beat Scottish Exiles 33-12, beat Edinburgh 27-21, lost to Scottish Districts XV 19-24,
beat Bedford 51-3, beat Bristol 44-7, beat West Hartlepool 34-8, beat Wasps 28-25

South African Barbarians to Britain 1993

Played 8   Won 8   Points for 293   Against 137
Beat Gloucester 15-11, beat Leicester 24-18, beat Newport 58-31, beat Northampton
51-23, beat Ulster 22-6, beat Bristol 45-13, beat Cornwall 44-12, beat Bath 34-23

STOP PRESS TOURS 1994

Test appearances are included in the touring parties. Full details of the following tours will be given in the next edition of the Yearbook.

ENGLAND TO SOUTH AFRICA 1994

THE TOURING PARTY
Manager J Rowell   **Assistant Manager** J Elliott   **Coaches** R Best & L Cusworth
Captain W D C Carling

FULL-BACKS
 P A Hull (Bristol & RAF) *SA* 1,2
 D Pears (Harlequins)
 *J E B Callard (Bath)

THREEQUARTERS
 A A Adebayo (Bath)
 T Underwood (Leicester) *SA* 1,2
 R Underwood (Leicester & RAF) *SA* 1,2
 D P Hopley (Wasps)
 W D C Carling (Harlequins) *SA* 1,2
 M J Catt (Bath)
 P R de Glanville (Bath) *SA* 1,2
 S Potter (Leicester)

HALF-BACKS
 C R Andrew (Wasps) *SA* 1,2
 S Barnes (Bath)
 C D Morris (Orrell) *SA* 1,2
 S M Bates (Wasps)

FORWARDS
 J Leonard (Harlequins) *SA* 1,2
 G C Rowntree (Leicester)
 V E Ubogu (Bath) *SA* 1,2
 J Mallett (Bath)
 R G R Dawe (Bath)
 B C Moore (Harlequins) *SA* 1,2
 M C Bayfield (Northampton) *SA* 1,2
 N C Redman (Bath) *SA* 1,2
 M O Johnson (Leicester)
 M D Poole (Leicester)
 *S Shaw (Bristol)
 T A K Rodber (Northampton & Army) *SA* 1,2
 S O Ojomoh (Bath) *SA* 1(R),2
 L B N Dallaglio (Wasps)
 B B Clarke (Bath) *SA* 1,2
 D Richards (Leicester) *SA* 1
 D Ryan (Wasps)
 Replacement during tour

MATCH DETAILS

1994	OPPONENTS	VENUE	RESULT
18 May	Orange Free State	Bloemfontein	L 11-22
21 May	Natal	Durban	L 6-21
25 May	Western Transvaal	Potchefstroom	W 26-24
28 May	Transvaal	Johannesburg	L 21-24
31 May	South Africa A	Kimberley	L 16-19
4 June	SOUTH AFRICA	Pretoria	W 32-15
7 June	Eastern Province	Port Elizabeth	W 31-13
11 June	SOUTH AFRICA	Cape Town	L 9-27

Tour record: Played 8   Won 3   Lost 5   Points for 152   Against 165
International matches: Played 2   Won 1   Lost 1   Points for 41   Against 42

IRELAND TO AUSTRALIA 1994

THE TOURING PARTY
Manager F Sowman   **Assistant Manager** L G Butler   **Coach** G Murphy
Captain M T Bradley

FULL-BACKS
 C M P O'Shea (Lansdowne) *A* 1,2
 J E Staples (L Irish)

THREEQUARTERS
 S P Geoghegan (L Irish) *A* 1,2
 J Bell (Ballymena & Loughboro U) *A* 1,2

Ben Clarke scores for England in the marvellous First Test victory, by 32-15, against South Africa in Pretoria. Captain Carling registers his approval.

N Woods (Blackrock Coll) *A* 1,2
P P A Danaher (Garryowen) *A* 1,2
M J Field (Malone) *A* 1(R)
M P Ridge (Blackrock Coll)
B Walsh (Cork Const)

HALF-BACKS
E P Elwood (Lansdowne) *A* 1,2
A N McGowan (Blackrock Coll)
M T Bradley (Cork Const) *A* 1,2
A C P Rolland (Blackrock Coll)
*N Hogan (Terenure Coll)

FORWARDS
P J Soden (Cork Const)
P M Clohessy (Young Munster) *A* 1,2
J J Fitzgerald (Young Munster) *A* 1,2

G F Halpin (London Irish)
T J Kingston (Dolphin)
K G M Wood (Garryowen) *A* 1,2
G M Fulcher (Cork Const) *A* 2
M J Galwey (Shannon) *A* 1
N P J Francis (Old Belvedere) *A* 1,2
J Davidson (Dungannon)
P J Hogan (Garryowen)
W D McBride (Malone) *A* 1(R)
D Corkery (Cork Const) *A* 1,2
B F Robinson (Ballymena) *A* 1,2
V C P Costello (St Mary's Coll)
P S Johns (Dungannon) *A* 1,2
R K Wilson (Instonians)
*B Cronin (Garryowen)
*S Byrne (Blackrock Coll)
Replacement during tour

MATCH DETAILS

1994	OPPONENTS	VENUE	RESULT
18 May	Western Australia	Perth	W 64-8
22 May	New South Wales	Sydney	L 18-55
25 May	Australian Capital Territory	Canberra	L 9-22
29 May	Queensland	Brisbane	L 26-29
1 June	Australian XV	Mount Isa	L 9-57
5 June	AUSTRALIA	Brisbane	L 13-33
8 June	New South Wales Country	Lismore	W 20-18
11 June	AUSTRALIA	Brisbane	L 18-32

Tour record: Played 8   Won 2   Lost 6   Points for 177   Against 254
International matches: Played 2   Lost 2   Points for 31   Against 65

WALES TO CANADA AND THE SOUTH SEAS 1994

THE TOURING PARTY
Manager R L Norster   **Coach** A B C Davies   **Captain** I C Evans

FULL-BACKS
M A Rayer (Llanelli) *C, Fj, WS*
A Clement (Swansea) *C*(R), *Tg, WS*

THREEQUARTERS
I C Evans (Llanelli) *C, Fj, Tg, WS*
G Wilkins (Bridgend) *Tg*
D Manley (Pontypridd)
W T Proctor (Llanelli) *C, Fj, WS*
M R Hall (Cardiff) *C, Tg*
N G Davies (Llanelli) *C, Fj, Tg*(R), *WS*
N Boobyer (Llanelli) *Fj, Tg*

HALF-BACKS
A Davies (Cardiff) *Fj*
N R Jenkins (Pontypridd) *C, Tg, WS*
R H StJ B Moon (Llanelli) *C, Fj, WS*
P John (Pontypridd) *Tg*

FORWARDS
R L Evans (Llanelli) *C, Fj, WS*
I Buckett (Swansea) *Tg*
J D Davies (Neath) *C, WS*
H Williams-Jones (Llanelli) *Fj, Tg, WS*(R)
R C McBryde (Swansea) *Fj*
G R Jenkins (Swansea) *C, Tg, WS*
P Arnold (Swansea) *Fj*
P T Davies (Llanelli) *C, Fj*(R), *WS*
G O Llewellyn (Neath) *C, Tg, WS*
A H Copsey (Llanelli) *Fj, Tg, WS*(R)
H T Taylor (Cardiff) *C, Fj, Tg, WS*(R)
E W Lewis (Llanelli) *Fj, WS*
R G Collins (Pontypridd) *C, Fj, Tg, WS*
L S Quinnell (Llanelli) *C, WS*
S M Williams (Neath) *Tg*

MATCH DETAILS

1994	OPPONENTS	VENUE	RESULT
8 June	Canadian Select XV	Hamilton	W 28-19
11 June	CANADA	Toronto	W 33-15
18 June	FIJI	Suva	W 23-8
22 June	TONGA	Nuku'alofa	W 18-9
25 June	WESTERN SAMOA	Apia	L 9-34

Tour record: Played 5   Won 4   Lost 1   Points for 111   Against 85
International matches: Played 4   Won 3   Lost 1   Points for 83   Against 66

SCOTLAND TO ARGENTINA 1994

THE TOURING PARTY

Manager F McLeod   **Coaches** D W Morgan & R Dixon   **Captain** A I Reed

FULL-BACKS
M Dods (Gala) *Arg* 1,2
R J S Shepherd (Edinburgh Acads)

THREEQUARTERS
K M Logan (Stirling Co) *Arg* 1,2
C A Joiner (Melrose) *Arg* 1,2
C S Dalgleish (Gala)
I C Jardine (Stirling Co) *Arg* 1,2
S A Nichol (Selkirk) *Arg* 2(R)
A G Shiel (Melrose) *Arg* 1,2

HALF-BACKS
G P J Townsend (Gala) *Arg* 1,2
D W Hodge (Watsonians)
B W Redpath (Melrose) *Arg* 1,2
D Patterson (Edinburgh Acads)

FORWARDS
A V Sharp (Bristol) *Arg* 1,2
A P Burnell (L Scottish) *Arg* 1,2
S W Ferguson (Peebles)
A G J Watt (Glasgow H/K) *Arg* 2(R)
K D McKenzie (Stirling Co) *Arg* 1,2
S J Brotherstone (Melrose)
A I Reed (Bath) *Arg* 1,2
D S Munro (Glasgow H/K) *Arg* 1,2
J F Richardson (Edinburgh Acads)
S J Campbell (Dundee HSFP)
P Walton (Northampton) *Arg* 1,2
I R Smith (Gloucester) *Arg* 1,2
D J McIvor (Edinburgh Acads)
F S Wallace (Glasgow H/K)
S J Reid (Boroughmuir)
C D Hogg (Melrose) *Arg* 1,2

MATCH DETAILS

1994	OPPONENTS	VENUE	RESULT
25 May	Buenos Aires XV	Buenes Aires	D 24-24
28 May	Cuyo XV	Mendoza	L 11-25
31 May	Cordoba XV	Cordoba	W 40-15
4 June	ARGENTINA	Buenos Aires	L 15-16
7 June	Rosario	Rosario	L 16-27
11 June	ARGENTINA	Buenos Aires	L 17-19

Tour record: Played 6   Won 1   Drawn 1   Lost 4   Points for 123   Against 126
International matches: Played 2   Lost 2   Points for 32   Against 35

FRANCE TO CANADA AND NEW ZEALAND 1994

THE TOURING PARTY

Manager G Laporte **Coach** P Berbizier **Captain** P Saint-André

FULL-BACKS
J-L Sadourny (Colomiers) C, NZ 1,2
S Viars (Brive) C(R), NZ 1(t)

THREEQUARTERS
P Saint-André (Montferrand) C, NZ 1,2
E N'Tamack (Toulouse) C, NZ 1,2
W Téchoueyres (SBUC)
L Leflamand (Lyon)
P Sella (Agen) C, NZ 1,2
Y Delaigue (Toulon) NZ 2(R)
F Mesnel (RCF)
T Lacroix (Dax) C, NZ 1,2
*P Carbonneau (Toulouse)

HALF-BACKS
B Bellot (Graulhet)
C Deylaud (Toulouse) C, NZ 1,2
A Macabiau (Perpignan) C
G Accoceberry (Bègles) NZ 1,2

*F Galthié (Colomiers)

FORWARDS
L Seigne (Merignac) C
L Benezech (RCF) C, NZ 1,2
L Armary (Lourdes) NZ 1(t), 2(t)
C Califano (Toulouse) NZ 1,2
J-M Gonzalez (Bayonne) C, NZ 1,2
J-F Tordo (Nice)
O Merle (Grenoble) C, NZ 1,2
O Roumat (Dax) C, NZ 1,2
O Brouzet (Grenoble) NZ, 2(R)
A Benazzi (Agen) C, NZ 1,2
X Blond (RCF) NZ 2(R)
L Cabannes (RCF) C, NZ 1,2
P Benetton (Agen) C, NZ 1,2
L Loppy (Toulon)
S Dispagne (Narbonne)
M Cecillon (Bourgoin) NZ 1(R)

* *Replacement during tour*

MATCH DETAILS

1994	OPPONENTS	VENUE	RESULT
1 June	Canada A	Toronto	W 34-31
4 June	CANADA	Ottawa	L 16-18
8 June	Northland	Whangarei	W 28-23
11 June	N Harbour	Auckland	L 23-27
15 June	Wairarapa Bush	Masterton	W 53-9
18 June	New Zealand XV	Wanganui	W 33-25
22 June	Nelson Bays	Nelson	W 46-18
26 June	NEW ZEALAND	Christchurch	W 22-8
29 June	Hawke's Bay	Napier	L 25-30
3 July	NEW ZEALAND	Auckland	W 23-20

Tour record: Played 10 Won 7 Lost 3 Points for 303 Against 209
International matches: Played 3 Won 2 Lost 1 Points for 61 Against 46

WALES WIN THE TITLE BUT GO OUT WITH A WHIMPER

THE INTERNATIONAL CHAMPIONSHIP 1994
Mick Cleary *The Observer*

We all peered into our crystal balls and all we could see was 'le crunch' in Paris. There could be no other rational outcome. England and France were such strong favourites for the Championship that the other three seemed to be there just to provide the backdrop for the most important element of the Five Nations – having a great time.

If there was drama in the tournament, it did not walk hand in hand with quality. The excitement came purely from the shredding of expectations: from seeing, on one hand, humbled Wales rise from the ashes of defeat by Canada to come within 80 minutes of a Grand Slam; on the other the heart-stopping finale to the Scotland-England game. And what about the boys in green once again refusing to be intimidated by the English rose? That match too saw a one-point margin of victory.

And so we had our adrenaline fix as favourites crumbled and matches swung wildly one way and another. For the purists, though, there was nothing but despair. Once again a paltry total of 20 tries was recorded, the same as in the preceding season and far below the average for the past decade. The common denominator over these two years? The new laws. The result was that we entered the final weekend with an absurd scenario in prospect: that France, if they lost to Scotland, could finish bottom of the table yet with the highest number of tries scored while England, if they knocked over six penalty goals or more against Wales, could have taken the title without having crossed the try-line.

Those long-suffering supporters in Wales will care little for such aesthetic agonising. All they cared about was the scoreboard. Yet the truly uplifting thing about the Welsh revival was that it was achieved in style – both on and off the pitch. Even if the small-minded ones couldn't get their act together in the committee rooms, the Welsh playing hierarchy made up for the inadequacies and were a credit to the sport. Alan Davies and Bob Norster conducted themselves with great dignity throughout. Skipper Ieuan Evans must also take a bow. Out where it counts Wales unearthed some men of steel in the their front row: the born-again Phil Davies and the new kid on the block (and a chip off the old one), Scott Quinnell. Wales did not reach their ultimate destination but they travelled much further than anyone dared imagine.

England, if they had risked investing in imagination, would have landed the big prize. They were the best-equipped team in every department except one – self-belief. Only in years to come might they realise what escaped them here. It was Geoff Cooke's last Championship. He had had a massive influence on English rugby and only the bitter and twisted on the English committee were not able to recognise that.

The Irish had an Irish sort of season – delirious one moment, crushingly disappointing the next. Victory at Twickenham for the first time in 12 years was offset by only one point gained at home. Their Celtic cousins, Scotland, were grateful for such small mercies. After their All Black trauma they were relieved just to get the one point, although they rued the one that got away against England. It took their selectors too long to settle on the right front five and Armstrong's return showed just how much they rely on the Jedforest genius.

France threatened to cut loose but never really did. They might have scored a hatful of tries against Ireland in the opening game, but were too casual, a failing which pursued them throughout the Championship.

In the end points difference, in use for only the second year, settled the issue. In theory it seemed like a good idea. In practice it proved a nonsense. Wales, having been comprehensively beaten by England, went up the steps at Twickenham to collect the trophy.

FINAL TABLE

	P	W	D	L	F	A	Pts
Wales	4	3	0	1	78	51	6
England	4	3	0	1	60	49	6
France	4	2	0	2	84	69	4
Ireland	4	1	1	2	49	70	3
Scotland	4	0	1	3	38	70	1

Johnson, Richards and Clarke gather in support of Dewi Morris in the Championship decider at Twickenham. The game was England's but the title went to Wales.

15 January, Cardiff Arms Park
WALES 29 (1G 4PG 2T)   **SCOTLAND 6** (2PG)

The clouds may have hung low over Cardiff but there was nothing but sunshine in the hearts of Welsh supporters. The gloom which had infused their hearts since that wretched defeat against Canada was dispelled here by a performance of spirit, tenacity and no little skill.

Nine changes had been made in the wake of the Canadian defeat, three of them positional. Eight Llanelli players were selected, five of them in the forwards. It was here that the game was won. On a filthy, rain-sodden day, two players, Phil Davies and Scott Quinnell, stood head and shoulders above the rest. As others scrambled and slithered to grasp control, this pair were order personified.

The forward exchanges had threatened to degenerate in an early bust-up after which Welsh hooker Garin Jenkins was lucky to stay on the field. Scotland were unfortunate to lose the foraging Morrison with a broken leg after 18 minutes although the arrival of Weir did enhance their line-out.

Behind the scrum, Wales were slick and composed. Davies and Hall combined well in the Welsh centre, while Moon and Jenkins were robustly effective at half-back. In contrast Chalmers looked below form, the Scottish line only beginning to function when Townsend moved infield after Chalmers' departure through injury in the 52nd minute.

Wales led 12-3 at half-time, with four penalty goals by Jenkins to one by Hastings. The first try, a quarter of an hour into the second half, was a gem. Moon drove the blind side, the ball was switched back and Clement came in as the extra man to send Rayer, who had come on as an early replacement for Walker, slithering in at the corner. Wales' final flurry, with two tries in two minutes, gave a truer reflection of the gulf between the teams. Clement was again involved before Moon and Jenkins sent Rayer in for his second try. Then, in overtime, Nigel Davies chipped a ball perfectly into the path of Ieuan Evans, who nudged it past Hastings into the in-goal, where he fell triumphantly upon it.

WALES: A Clement (Swansea); I C Evans (Llanelli) (*capt*), M R Hall (Cardiff), N G Davies (Llanelli), N Walker (Cardiff); N R Jenkins (Pontypridd), R H St J B Moon (Llanelli); R L Evans (Llanelli), G R Jenkins (Swansea), J D Davies (Neath), P T Davies (Llanelli), G O Llewellyn (Neath), E W Lewis (Llanelli), L S Quinnell (Llanelli), M A Perego (Llanelli) *Replacement* M A Rayer (Cardiff) for Walker
Scorers *Tries:* Rayer (2), I Evans   *Conversion:* N Jenkins   *Penalty Goals:* N Jenkins (4)
SCOTLAND: A G Hastings (Watsonians) (*capt*); A G Stanger (Hawick), G P J Townsend (Gala), I C Jardine (Stirling County), K M Logan (Stirling County); C M Chalmers (Melrose), A D Nicol (Dundee HSFP); P H Wright (Boroughmuir), K S Milne (Heriot's FP), A P Burnell (London Scottish), N G B Edwards (Northampton), D S Munro (Glasgow High/Kelvinside), D J Turnbull (Hawick), R I Wainwright (Edinburgh Acads), I R Morrison (London Scottish) *Replacements* G W Weir (Melrose) for Morrison; D S Wyllie (Stewart's-Melville FP) for Chalmers
Scorer *Penalty Goals:* A G Hastings (2)
Referee P Robin (France)

15 January, Parc des Princes
FRANCE 35 (3G 3PG 1T)   **IRELAND 15** (5PG)

Paris has been spiritual home to many a lost soul down the years. On this basis its population probably includes a good few Irish rugby players. Once again they travelled in hope of ending a long, losing sequence; once again they returned with nothing to declare. Twenty-two years have passed since they won in the French capital.

There were commendable traits in the Irish play: the sustained vigour of Francis in the line-out, the electricity of Geoghegan on the wing and the executioner's swing of Elwood's right boot. The Lansdowne fly-half slotted five penalty goals and kept his side in contention at many crucial junctures, just when it looked as if they would be swamped. Indeed, France only really stretched clear with two tries in the last few minutes. In fact they might have had another at the very death, but Benetton hung on to the ball too long. Such profligacy was the theme of the day, for unyielding as the Irish were in the tackle, the French might well have scored eight tries. So often the last critical pass was not given or the decisive option taken. Would that Ireland had so many chances, for it is now 14 years since they last scored a try at the Parc des Princes.

They embarked upon a damage-limitation operation, the ball rarely travelling beyond Elwood's outside boot. In contrast France took every opportunity to play with a flourish. Berbizier had worked hard to inject some steel and self-discipline into his men: here they unearthed some traditional flair. Sadourny ran free from full-back, linking well with the speedy Bernat-Salles. The opening try, though, was prosaic, Benetton snaffling a loose Irish line-out tap to plunge over just before half-time. Elwood was nibbling away to keep Ireland in touch 16-12 at the interval.

The traffic in the second half was all one way. Lacroix forced his way over the corner early on. For all the pressure the scores did not come until the dying moments, when first Saint-André cruised round Wallace to be followed by the giant Merle crashing through on the whistle after a collective 50-metre drive.

FRANCE: J-L Sadourny (Colomiers); P Bernat-Salles (Pau), P Sella (Agen), T Lacroix (Dax), P Saint-André (Montferrand); A Penaud (Brive), F Galthié (Colomiers); L Armary (Lourdes), J-M Gonzalez (Bayonne), P Gallart (Béziers), O Merle (Grenoble), O Roumat (Dax) (*capt*), P Benetton (Agen), M Cecillon (Bourgoin), A Benazzi (Agen)
Scorers *Tries:* Benetton, Saint-André, Lacroix, Merle   *Conversions:* Lacroix (3)
Penalty Goals: Lacroix (3)
IRELAND: C P O'Shea (Lansdowne); R M Wallace (Garryowen), V J G Cunningham (St Mary's Coll), P P A Danaher (Garryowen), S P Geoghegan (London Irish); E P Elwood (Lansdowne), M T Bradley (Cork Const) (*capt*); N J Popplewell (Greystones), T J Kingston (Dolphin), P M Clohessy (Young Munster), P S Johns (Dungannon), N P J Francis (Old Belvedere), M J Galwey (Shannon), B F Robinson (Ballymena), K D O'Connell (Sunday's Well) *Replacements* R Saunders (London Irish) for Bradley (temp); G F Halpin (London Irish) for Clohessy
Scorer *Penalty Goals:* Elwood (5)
Referee J M Fleming (Scotland)

5 February, Murrayfield
SCOTLAND 14 (2PG 1DG 1T)   ENGLAND 15 (5PG)

An entire nation sank to its knees as surely as if Jon Callard's last-second kick had landed in their collective crotch rather than between the Murrayfield posts. Elation had turned to abject despair in the time it took for the 40-metre penalty goal to sail from its centre-field position through the uprights. That score swiftly and cruelly cancelled out Townsend's towering dropped goal which moments earlier had seemed to settle the game in Scotland's favour.

No wonder Gavin Hastings was in tears afterwards, a condition which drew small-minded rebuke from some commentators. If he hadn't been watery-eyed then the whole country would have wanted to know why not. This was the second time in six months that his dreams of glory had been shattered by a last fling of the dice. If anything the pain was worse than that experienced in Christchurch with the Lions. Then the sides had been even on paper. Here Scotland had not been given a prayer.

They almost pulled it off against much-vaunted opponents supposedly just limbering up for a putative Grand Slam showdown with the French four weeks later. It was hard to pinpoint a precise reason why one side rose above themselves and the other lurched into disarray. Walton and Sharp did beef up the Scottish pack but there was little clear pattern from anyone on the day, for the game which ended in spectacular and memorable drama contained neither spectacle nor abiding memory for much of its 80 minutes. True, there was Wainwright's well-taken try on the half-hour to admire as well as the exhilarating approach work of England in the opening quarter of an hour. But these uplifting moments were swamped by long passages in which errors dominated. Of course, any match which features Gary Armstrong is sure to raise the spirits. Only a clawing tackle by Hall prevented him scoring in the first half. Gavin Hastings had a poor day with the boot, landing only two from seven attempts. Callard showed no such frailty. Such was the slender difference between the teams: tears for one, cheers for the other.

SCOTLAND: A G Hastings (Watsonians) (*capt*); A G Stanger (Hawick), S Hastings (Watsonians), D S Wyllie (Stewart's-Melville FP), K M Logan (Stirling County); G P J Townsend (Gala), G Armstrong (Jedforest); A V Sharp (Bristol), K S Milne (Heriot's FP), A P Burnell (London Scottish), D S Munro (Glasgow High/Kelvinside), A I Reed (Bath), P Walton (Northampton), G W Weir (Melrose), R I Wainwright (Edinburgh Acads) *Replacements* I C Jardine (Stirling County) for S Hastings; B W Redpath (Melrose) for Armstrong (temp); I R Smith (Gloucester) for Wainwright
Scorers *Try:* Wainwright   *Penalty Goals:* A G Hastings (2)   *Dropped Goal:* Townsend
ENGLAND: J E B Callard (Bath); T Underwood (Leicester), W D C Carling (Harlequins) (*capt*), P R de Glanville (Bath), R Underwood (Leicester & RAF); C R Andrew (Wasps), J Leonard (Harlequins), K P P Bracken (Bristol); J Leonard (Harlequins), B C Moore (Harlequins), V E Ubogu (Bath), M C Bayfield (Northampton), M O Johnson (Leicester), J P Hall (Bath), B B Clarke (Bath), N A Back (Leicester)
Scorer *Penalty Goals:* Callard (5)
Referee L L McLachlan (New Zealand)

5 February, Lansdowne Road
IRELAND 15 (5PG)   WALES 17 (4PG 1T)

For once the assassin fired a blank. For 12 months Eric Elwood had been called up to do a job. Nearly every time he had hit the target. Here, seven minutes from the final whistle, it was no more than 15 metres away. He swung back that deadly boot of his . . . and missed.

If Wales were granted a stay of execution, they just about deserved it. They finished the match in much stronger, more purposeful fashion than their opponents, and in scoring the game's only try after 25 minutes provided one of the afternoon's few crisp attacking movements.

If there was little for the neutral to savour, there was once again plenty for the partisan Welsh to cheer, not least the warhorse qualities of Phil Davies in the pack and the muscular hustling of their back row. Any sweat expended up front was invariably put to good use behind, through either the probing punts of Jenkins or the subtle midfield passing of Hall and Davies. It was the latter's delicious long, floated pass to his partner in the centre which created the space for Jenkins' try.

Unfortunately Davies was not to finish the match, the Llanelli centre retiring with a muscle strain. He was joined in the treatment room by Tony Clement with a similar complaint and the unfortunate Proctor, who sustained a broken jaw when trying to tackle Johns. More disturbing was the late shoulder injury to Ieuan Evans which was eventually to keep him from the French game.

Ireland's pains were all metaphorical. They suffered from a paucity of ambition, a condition brought about perhaps by a lack of faith in their own abilities. Geoghegan was so desperate for any action that at one point he hurled himself into a ruck and started pulling out any red shirt he could get his hands on. He summed up Ireland's approach: forced to act the bouncer when he should have been the star turn. So often they have wriggled into contention and even dominance through the trusted boot of their fly-half, but here Elwood proved he was only human.

IRELAND: C P O'Shea (Lansdowne); R M Wallace (Garryowen), M C McCall (Bangor), P P A Danaher (Garryowen), S P Geoghegan (London Irish); E P Elwood (Lansdowne), M T Bradley (Cork Const) (*capt*); N J Popplewell (Greystones), T J Kingston (Dolphin), P M Clohessy (Young Munster), M J Galwey (Shannon), N P J Francis (Old Belvedere), B F Robinson (Ballymena), P S Johns (Dungannon), W D McBride (Malone)
Scorer *Penalty Goals:* Elwood (5)
WALES: A Clement (Swansea); I C Evans (Llanelli) (*capt*), M R Hall (Cardiff), N G Davies (Llanelli), W T Proctor (Llanelli); N R Jenkins (Pontypridd), R H St J B Moon (Llanelli); R L Evans (Llanelli), G R Jenkins (Swansea), J D Davies (Neath), P T Davies (Llanelli), G O Llewellyn (Neath), E W Lewis (Llanelli), L S Quinnell (Llanelli), M A Perego (Llanelli) *Replacements* S D Hill (Cardiff) for Proctor; M Rayer (Cardiff) for Clement; R N Jones (Swansea) for N Davies
Scorer *Try:* N Jenkins   *Penalty Goals:* N Jenkins (4)
Referee A J Spreadbury (England)

19 February, Twickenham
ENGLAND 12 (4PG)   IRELAND 13 (1G 2PG)

Defeat was unexpected: so too was the manner of it. This was no great Celtic uprising, rather a triumph of adventure over inhibition, of poise over dishevelment and, above all else, of self-belief over self-doubt. Even though the scores were so close and even though England might claim that the award of the decisive penalty was harsh, there could be few real grumbles. Ireland were worthy winners. England lost at home for the first time in six years in the Championship and for the fourth match in succession they failed to score a try.

The worrying signs of hesitancy which had been detected in England's play at Murrayfield surfaced again here. With the great enforcer Dean Richards still injured on the sidelines, the pack struggled to gain any control. The towering Bayfield was a giant only on the tape measure. His lack of match fitness and sharpness following a long lay-off really told.

England, through Johnson, Rodber and the impressive debutant Ojomoh, did win plenty of ball. What they did with it, though, once again brought furrows to the brows of their supporters. They stuck rigidly to route one for attack, Andrew walloping the ball great distances downfield. This tactic is painful to watch at the best of times; here the anguish was compounded by the fact that it was badly executed. When Callard was actually called into the line, he too could do no more than chip the ball lamely ahead.

All the zip and sparkle came from Ireland, at no time more so than when they scored their try just before half-time. Ireland won an England restart 22 and nudged the ball forward before releasing the backs. A couple of snappy dummy runs in the centre created the space for Geoghegan on the wide outside. He was not going to waste his first pass of the year and cruised easily outside Tony Underwood and through Callard's tackle. Geoghegan was also involved in the crucial last penalty. He thumped the ball out of his own 22 before flattening Andrew on the England 22 with a follow-up tackle. The referee favoured Ireland. On the day they deserved his generosity.

ENGLAND: J E B Callard (Bath); T Underwood (Leicester), W D C Carling (Harlequins) (*capt*), P R de Glanville (Bath), R Underwood (Leicester & RAF); C R Andrew (Wasps), K P P Bracken (Bristol); J Leonard (Harlequins), B C Moore (Harlequins), V E Ubogu (Bath), M O Johnson (Leicester), M C Bayfield (Northampton), T A K Rodber (Northampton & Army), S O Ojomoh (Bath), N A Back (Leicester)
Scorer *Penalty Goals:* Callard (4)
IRELAND: C P O'Shea (Lansdowne); R M Wallace (Garryowen), M J Field (Malone), P P A Danaher (Garryowen), S P Geoghegan (London Irish); E P Elwood (Lansdowne), M T Bradley (Cork Const) (*capt*); N J Popplewell (Greystones), T J Kingston (Dolphin), P M Clohessy (Young Munster), M J Galwey (Shannon), N P J Francis (Old Belvedere), B F Robinson (Ballymena), P S Johns (Dungannon), W D McBride (Malone)
Replacement K D O'Connell (Sunday's Well) for Robinson (temp)
Scorers *Try:* Geoghegan   *Conversion:* Elwood   *Penalty Goals:* Elwood (2)
Referee P Thomas (France)

19 February, Cardiff Arms Park
WALES 24 (1G 4PG 1T)   FRANCE 15 (1G 1PG 1T)

The torments of the November nightmare gave way to a bright, joyous dawn. Who would dared have speculate at that dark hour that Welsh supporters would soon be dreaming of a possible Grand Slam?

The Welsh have never been too good at contemplating reality, preferring either to sink into a trough of despair or to soar to fanciful heights. After this display they deserved their moment of ecstasy. They had not beaten France for 12 years and encouraging as their shows in the Championship had been to date, no one expected such a victory here. Their first back-to-back wins since 1988 had only just been secured and with the loss of their talismanic captain, Ieuan Evans, to injury, there was caution, if not apprehension in the air.

The fears were groundless. For Wales were mighty and none more so than No 8 Scott Quinnell, whose father played a bit of rugby in his day. Those days have haunted Wales for many years. Now was the hour for young Wales to stand up. Quinnell typified the surging pride and raw power of the new generation.

If there was one area of the game in which you would have expected an assured measure of parity, if not dominance, from the French it was the back row. Quinnell ripped those cosy assessments to shreds. He was yards quicker than anyone in a blue shirt and with the ball in his hands he was unstoppable. His try in the 14th minute is already etched in Arms Park folklore. He latched on to a loose line-out ball near halfway, handed off, dummied and blasted through tackles before planting the ball over the line. Magnificent.

The Welsh forwards so pressurised their opponents that Jenkins was able to nudge them into a comfortable 17-3 half-time lead. When the tide turned it made for a fascinating contest and a few cardiac arrests in the Principality. Tries by Roumat and Sella closed the scores to just two points. But the day was destined to be tinged in a glorious red. Walker, the Olympic hurdler, scored a suitably exuberant try, picking up the ball 40 metres from the line. After just one stride it was obvious that no one would catch him. The celebrations began before he had even touched down. As well they might.

WALES: M A Rayer (Cardiff); S D Hill (Cardiff), M R Hall (Cardiff), A Clement (Swansea), N Walker (Cardiff); N R Jenkins (Pontypridd), R H St J B Moon (Llanelli); R L Evans (Llanelli), G R Jenkins (Swansea), J D Davies (Neath), P T Davies (Llanelli), G O Llewellyn (Neath) (*capt*), E W Lewis (Llanelli), L S Quinnell (Llanelli), M A Perego (Llanelli)
Scorers *Tries:* Quinnell, Walker   *Conversion:* N Jenkins   *Penalty Goals:* N Jenkins (4)
FRANCE: J-L Sadourny (Colomiers); E N'Tamack (Toulouse), P Sella (Agen), T Lacroix (Dax), P Saint-André (Montferrand); A Penaud (Brive), F Galthié (Colomiers); L Armary (Lourdes), J-M Gonzalez (Bayonne), P Gallart (Béziers), O Merle (Grenoble), O Roumat (Dax) (*capt*), P Benetton (Agen), M Cecillon (Bourgoin), A Benazzi (Agen)
Scorers *Tries:* Roumat, Sella   *Conversion:* Lacroix   *Penalty Goal:* Lacroix
Referee L L McLachlan (New Zealand)

Above: Scrum-half Rupert Moon gets the ball away for Wales, the eventual champions, in their 17-15 win against Ireland at Lansdowne Road.
Below: Abdel Benazzi of France scores the only try of the match against England in Paris. England won 18-14 through the deadly boot of Rob Andrew.

5 March, Parc des Princes
FRANCE 14 (3PG 1T)   ENGLAND 18 (5PG 1DG)

Once again the England team failed to score a try and once again not one of them gave a damn. This time they were on safer ground in claiming that the end justified the means. Victory in Paris had proved beyond the other countries for a number of years; for England it has become almost a formality. This was their fourth in a row at the Parc and their seventh in succession against France.

They have had the evil eye on their opponents by virtue of one simple factor – being themselves. That is, pragmatic, unflappable, controlled and courageous. Some might say boring, but that would be unfairly judgemental. In this arena the clash of styles – Anglo-Saxon sang-froid trying to contain and counter Gallic passion and flair – has always been utterly compelling. And so it was again. For all that France threw at England, and in the opening quarter of an hour, they might well have scored a couple of tries, there was always that sense that England just would not wilt.

England had made five changes after the Irish defeat. Geoff Cooke announced one more in the week leading up to the game – that of manager. The players could have given him no better leaving present. All the changes in selection fulfilled Cooke's faith in them. Furthermore, Rob Andrew, an icon of the Cooke era, hit a groove of perfection. His kicking from hand, and from ground, was superb. All five place-kicks as well as the dropped goal soared through the posts. Pears was a rock at full-back, Redman injected the necessary snarl into the pack, Morris was a bulldog at the base of the scrum and Hunter had the characteristic clatter of two from the back. Ojomoh too impressed.

France were profligate near the line. Even Benazzi might have been denied his try 15 minutes into the second half: as he charged down the blind side his foot went into touch but was not spotted. Justice of a minor sort was done when the ball fell over as Lacroix attempted the conversion. The French half-backs were wretchedly indecisive and their captain, Roumat, anonymous on his home patch. Lacroix, as against Wales, was fallible with kicking. His head drooped long before the end: Andrew's, and indeed England's, was held high.

FRANCE: J-L Sadourny (Colomiers); W Téchoueyres (SBUC Bordeaux), P Sella (Agen), T Lacroix (Dax), P Saint-André (Montferrand); A Penaud (Brive), F Galthié (Colomiers); L Benezech (Racing Club de France), J-M Gonzalez (Bayonne), P Gallart (Béziers), O Merle (Grenoble), O Roumat (Dax) (*capt*), A Benazzi (Agen), P Benetton (Agen), L Cabannes (Racing Club de France)
Scorers *Try:* Benazzi   *Penalty Goals:* Lacroix (3)
ENGLAND: D Pears (Harlequins); I G Hunter (Northampton), W D C Carling (Harlequins) (*capt*), P R de Glanville (Bath), R Underwood (Leicester & RAF); C R Andrew (Wasps), C D Morris (Orrell); J Leonard (Harlequins), B C Moore (Harlequins), V E Ubogu (Bath), M O Johnson (Leicester), N C Redman (Bath), T A K Rodber (Northampton & Army), S O Ojomoh (Bath), B B Clarke (Bath)
Scorer *Penalty Goals:* Andrew (5)   *Dropped Goal:* Andrew
Referee S R Hilditch (Ireland)

5 March, Lansdowne Road
IRELAND 6 (2PG)   SCOTLAND 6 (2PG)

The elements couldn't make up their mind in the Fair City. Nor could the players. As the weather switched without warning from bright, warm sunshine one minute to driving, sleet-tinged rain the next, the teams themselves seemed to crash along, unsure of what style of game they ought to be playing.

To be fair, Scotland in the first half did set down their markers and stick fairly closely to them. Into the teeth of the gale they showed commendable resolve and control in mauling their way downfield. Then, as soon as they had the wind in their favour, they went to pieces, losing composure and direction. Only one man stood out from this mass of frenetic nothingness: Gary Armstrong.

Put him before an audience of a sympathetic few and he will quake to the tips of his toes. Stick him in front of a pack of demented Irishmen trying to rip his eyeballs from their sockets and he will just smile his watery smile and get stuck in. Here he showed he had the brain to match his ample brawn. He unfalteringly chose the right option at the right moment. When the situation called for him to bang around the edges, sucking in the defence, he did it. But when the play cried out for a subtle nudge of the ball downfield he had the vision, as well as the skills, to carry it out. He even played on with the hand injury which was eventually to rule him out of the final match of the Championship. Such was Armstrong's total involvement that he also managed to head-butt his own captain, who had to leave the field for four stitches.

All Armstrong's efforts came to naught. Scotland just did not have the pace behind the scrum to take penetrating advantage of the discomfort he had caused in the Irish defence. Great man that he is, and unshakable as he might be in defence, Gavin Hastings just does not have the legs of old. He did at least convert the only two penalty opportunities presented to him at the start of the second half. Elwood, for once, was not as reliable: three chances went begging in the first half before he ceded the duties to O'Shea. He too missed.

IRELAND: C P O'Shea (Lansdowne); R M Wallace (Garryowen), M J Field (Malone), P P A Danaher (Garryowen), S P Geoghegan (London Irish); E P Elwood (Lansdowne), M T Bradley (Cork Const) (*capt*); N J Popplewell (Greystones), T J Kingston (Dolphin), P M Clohessy (Young Munster), M J Galwey (Shannon), N P J Francis (Old Belvedere), B F Robinson (Ballymena), P S Johns (Dungannon), W D McBride (Malone)
Scorer *Penalty Goals:* Elwood (2)
SCOTLAND: A G Hastings (Watsonians) (*capt*); A G Stanger (Hawick), S Hastings (Watsonians), D S Wyllie (Stewart's-Melville FP), K M Logan (Stirling County); G P J Townsend (Gala), G Armstrong (Jedforest); A V Sharp (Bristol), K S Milne (Heriot's FP), A P Burnell (London Scottish), D S Munro (Glasgow High/Kelvinside), A I Reed (Bath), P Walton (Northampton), G W Weir (Melrose), I R Smith (Gloucester)
Replacement M Dods (Gala) for G Hastings (temp)
Scorer *Penalty Goals:* G Hastings (2)
Referee E F Morrison (England)

19 March, Twickenham
ENGLAND 15 (1G 1PG 1T)   **WALES 8** (1PG 1T)
It was the 100th encounter between these old enemies, the Queen was in attendance, the Grand Slam and Triple Crown were up for grabs and England finally slipped the leash and left their inhibitions behind. It ought to have been a mighty occasion. And yet it wasn't.

True, England really did put together some magnificent passages of play, but the overriding sense at the end of the day was one of anti-climax. For all their early promise England just fizzled out. When Rory Underwood hit the perfect angle to take a scoring pass from de Glanville after ten minutes it looked as if the 16-point deficit England needed to make up to claim the Championship on points difference was there for the taking. And so it was. But the mind is a funny thing. No matter how the legs may be pumping, and the hands whizzing the ball around, if the old brain is not used to really letting rip, then it has a habit of closing in on itself. England were too accustomed to playing it tight to have the deep self-belief to really go for broke when it mattered.

They had the perfect platform on which to work. The return from injury of the colossal Dean Richards, restored for his first game of the tournament, made a huge difference. The young Welsh cub Scott Quinnell suddenly found out what old beasts live out there in the jungle. He was not alone in being overawed. The whole Welsh team seemed daunted by what lay before them. It was Englishmen who made all the running: Rodber crunching round the fringes and jumping well in the line-out; Redman grafting tirelessly and Morris bouncing about furiously to take the honours in the clash of the two combative scrum-halves. Behind the scrum the Underwoods looked far more potent than they had done all year and de Glanville finally came of age with a mature performance in the centre.

Rodber effectively put the match beyond the reach of Wales at the start of the second half when he moved up to snatch a Welsh throw at the line-out and plunged over. Wales did rally and deserved their late try from Walker. The Cardiff winger showed in this game that he is not just a pair of pretty legs. His tackling was exemplary. The laurels on the day went to England, the trophy to Wales.

ENGLAND: I Hunter (Northampton); T Underwood (Leicester), W D C Carling (Harlequins) (*capt*), P R de Glanville (Bath), R Underwood (Leicester & RAF); C R Andrew (Wasps), C D Morris (Orrell); J Leonard (Harlequins), B C Moore (Harlequins), V E Ubogu (Bath), M O Johnson (Leicester), N C Redman (Bath), T A K Rodber (Northampton & Army), D Richards (Leicester), B B Clarke (Bath) *Replacement* M J Catt (Bath) for Andrew
Scorers *Tries:* R Underwood, Rodber   *Conversion:* Andrew   *Penalty Goal:* Andrew
WALES: M A Rayer (Cardiff); I C Evans (Llanelli) (*capt*), M R Hall (Cardiff), N G Davies (Llanelli), N Walker (Cardiff); N R Jenkins (Pontypridd), R H St J B Moon (Llanelli), R L Evans (Llanelli), G R Jenkins (Swansea), J D Davies (Neath), P T Davies (Llanelli), G O Llewellyn (Neath), E W Lewis (Llanelli), L S Quinnell (Llanelli), M A Perego (Llanelli) *Replacement* A H Copsey (Llanelli) for Lewis
Scorers *Try:* Walker   *Penalty Goal:* N Jenkins

19 March, Murrayfield
SCOTLAND 12 (4PG)   FRANCE 20 (2G 2PG)

France were probably grateful that the Scots had decided to knock the old Murrayfield to the ground and erect a magnificent new stadium. Whatever it was about the old place, the French did not like it. They had not won there since 1978. Here, among new concrete, cantilevered surroundings they seemed quite at home. They did not even play particularly well in consigning Scotland to defeat and the wooden spoon.

The French had reverted to type coming into the match. Calm and consistent in method and selection throughout the season, they went back to those days of panic and made wholesale changes after their defeat by England. The half-backs were axed and so too was the captain, Roumat. Yanne Delaigue, son of a former international, won his first cap in the centre and for one glorious moment in the first half it looked as if France had discovered their old selves and were going to run riot. Delaigue made a delicious break in midfield, floating clear of the markers, and, when he was eventually tracked down, kicked delicately ahead for Sadourny to score in the corner.

But as happened so often in the season, expectations went unfulfilled. No one player had the class to wrench the game his way; no unit was able to completely subdue its opposition. Even the Hastings brothers, each celebrating their 50th cap, were muted. The Scottish back row, with Walton to the fore, did well to set up some impressive drives, gaining the position and exerting the pressure from which Hastings was able to slot over three penalty goals when France were forced into infringement. Scotland closed to within a point but Lacroix edged France back to a four-point advantage by half-time.

The early signs of the second half were that Scotland were beginning to pick up some momentum, invariably through the quick taps and charges of Milne. But 15 minutes into the half Townsend looped on his centres and threw a pass to the wing. Unfortunately, the wing was wearing a French jersey and Saint-André set off on a gleeful 50-metre run to the line. Scotland finished their season on a mistake. Somehow it seemed fitting.

SCOTLAND: A G Hastings (Watsonians) (*capt*); A G Stanger (Hawick), S Hastings (Watsonians), D S Wyllie (Stewart's-Melville FP), K M Logan (Stirling County); G P J Townsend (Gala), B W Redpath (Melrose); A V Sharp (Bristol), K S Milne (Heriot's FP), A P Burnell (London Scottish), D S Munro (Glasgow High/Kelvinside), A I Reed (Bath), P Walton (Northampton), G W Weir (Melrose), I R Smith (Gloucester)
Scorer *Penalty Goals:* G Hastings (4)
FRANCE: J-L Sadourny (Colomiers); W Téchoueyres (SBUC Bordeaux), P Sella (Agen), Y Delaigue (Toulon), P Saint-André (Montferrand) (*capt*); T Lacroix (Dax), A Macabiau (Perpignan); L Benezech (Racing Club de France), J-M Gonzalez (Bayonne), L Seigne (Merignac), O Brouzet (Grenoble), P Benetton (Agen), A Benazzi (Agen), L Cabannes (Racing Club de France) *Replacement* P Montlaur (Agen) for Lacroix
Scorers *Tries:* Sadourny, Saint-André   *Conversions:* Lacroix, Montlaur
Penalty Goals: Lacroix (2)
Referee W D Bevan (Wales)

RESULTS OF INTERNATIONAL MATCHES (up to 31 March 1994)

Cap matches only.
Years for Five Nations' matches are for the second half of the season: eg 1972 means season 1971-72. Years for matches against touring teams from the Southern Hemisphere refer to the actual year of the match.
Points-scoring was first introduced in 1886, when an International Board was formed by Scotland, Ireland and Wales. Points values varied between countries until 1890, when England agreed to join the Board, and uniform values were adopted.
WC indicates a fixture played during the Rugby World Cup.

Northern Hemisphere seasons	Try	Conversion	Penalty goal	Dropped goal	Goal from mark
1890-91	1	2	2	3	3
1891-92 to 1892-93	2	3	3	4	4
1893-94 to 1904-05	3	2	3	4	4
1905-06 to 1947-48	3	2	3	4	3
1948-49 to 1970-71	3	2	3	3	3
1971-72 to 1991-92	4	2	3	3	3*
1992-93 onwards	5	2	3	3	–

★The goal from mark ceased to exist when free kick clause was introduced, 1977-78.

ENGLAND v SCOTLAND
Played 111   England won 55, Scotland won 39, Drawn 17

1871 Raeburn Place (Edinburgh) **Scotland** 1G 1T to 1T
1872 The Oval (London) **England** 1G 1DG 2T to 1DG
1873 Glasgow **Drawn** no score
1874 The Oval **England** 1DG to 1T
1875 Raeburn Place **Drawn** no score
1876 The Oval **England** 1G 1T to 0
1877 Raeburn Place **Scotland** 1 DG to 0
1878 The Oval **Drawn** no score
1879 Raeburn Place **Drawn** Scotland 1DG England 1G
1880 Manchester **England** 2G 3T to 1G
1881 Raeburn Place **Drawn** Scotland 1G 1T England 1DG 1T
1882 Manchester **Scotland** 2T to 0
1883 Raeburn Place **England** 2T to 1T
1884 Blackheath (London) **England** 1G to 1T
1885 No Match
1886 Raeburn Place **Drawn** no score
1887 Manchester **Drawn** 1T each
1888 No Match
1889 No Match
1890 Raeburn Place **England** 1G 1T to 0
1891 Richmond (London) **Scotland** 9-3
1892 Raeburn Place **England** 5-0
1893 Leeds **Scotland** 8-0
1894 Raeburn Place **Scotland** 6-0
1895 Richmond **Scotland** 6-3
1896 Glasgow **Scotland** 11-0

1897 Manchester **England** 12-3
1898 Powderhall (Edinburgh) **Drawn** 3-3
1899 Blackheath **Scotland** 5-0
1900 Inverleith (Edinburgh) **Drawn** 0-0
1901 Blackheath **Scotland** 18-3
1902 Inverleith **England** 6-3
1903 Richmond **Scotland** 10-6
1904 Inverleith **Scotland** 6-3
1905 Richmond **Scotland** 8-0
1906 Inverleith **England** 9-3
1907 Blackheath **Scotland** 8-3
1908 Inverleith **Scotland** 16-10
1909 Richmond **Scotland** 18-8
1910 Inverleith **England** 14-5
1911 Twickenham **England** 13-8
1912 Inverleith **Scotland** 8-3
1913 Twickenham **England** 3-0
1914 Inverleith **England** 16-15
1920 Twickenham **England** 13-4
1921 Inverleith **England** 18-0
1922 Twickenham **England** 11-5
1923 Inverleith **England** 8-6
1924 Twickenham **England** 19-0
1925 Murrayfield **Scotland** 14-11
1926 Twickenham **Scotland** 17-9
1927 Murrayfield **Scotland** 21-13
1928 Twickenham **England** 6-0
1929 Murrayfield **Scotland** 12-6
1930 Twickenham **Drawn** 0-0
1931 Murrayfield **Scotland** 28-19
1932 Twickenham **England** 16-3

1933 Murrayfield **Scotland** 3-0
1934 Twickenham **England** 6-3
1935 Murrayfield **Scotland** 10-7
1936 Twickenham **England** 9-8
1937 Murrayfield **England** 6-3
1938 Twickenham **Scotland** 21-16
1939 Murrayfield **England** 9-6
1947 Twickenham **England** 24-5
1948 Murrayfield **Scotland** 6-3
1949 Twickenham **England** 19-3
1950 Murrayfield **Scotland** 13-11
1951 Twickenham **England** 5-3
1952 Murrayfield **England** 19-3
1953 Twickenham **England** 26-8
1954 Murrayfield **England** 13-3
1955 Twickenham **England** 9-6
1956 Murrayfield **England** 11-6
1957 Twickenham **England** 16-3
1958 Murrayfield **Drawn** 3-3
1959 Twickenham **Drawn** 3-3
1960 Murrayfield **England** 21-12
1961 Twickenham **England** 6-0
1962 Murrayfield **Drawn** 3-3
1963 Twickenham **England** 10-8
1964 Murrayfield **Scotland** 15-6
1965 Twickenham **Drawn** 3-3
1966 Murrayfield **Scotland** 6-3
1967 Twickenham **England** 27-14
1968 Murrayfield **England** 8-6

1969 Twickenham **England** 8-3
1970 Murrayfield **Scotland** 14-5
1971 Twickenham **Scotland** 16-15
1971 Murrayfield **Scotland** 26-6
Special Centenary match – non-championship
1972 Murrayfield **Scotland** 23-9
1973 Twickenham **England** 20-13
1974 Murrayfield **Scotland** 16-14
1975 Twickenham **England** 7-6
1976 Murrayfield **Scotland** 22-12
1977 Twickenham **England** 26-6
1978 Murrayfield **England** 15-0
1979 Twickenham **Drawn** 7-7
1980 Murrayfield **England** 30-18
1981 Twickenham **England** 23-17
1982 Murrayfield **Drawn** 9-9
1983 Twickenham **Scotland** 22-12
1984 Murrayfield **Scotland** 18-6
1985 Twickenham **England** 10-7
1986 Murrayfield **Scotland** 33-6
1987 Twickenham **England** 21-12
1988 Murrayfield **England** 9-6
1989 Twickenham **Drawn** 12-12
1990 Murrayfield **Scotland** 13-7
1991 Twickenham **England** 21-12
1991 Murrayfield *WC* **England** 9-6
1992 Murrayfield **England** 25-7
1993 Twickenham **England** 26-12
1994 Murrayfield **England** 15-14

ENGLAND v IRELAND
Played 107 England won 61, Ireland won 38, Drawn 8

1875 The Oval (London) **England** 1G
    1DG 1T to 0
1876 Dublin **England** 1G 1T to 0
1877 The Oval **England** 2G 2T to 0
1878 Dublin **England** 2G 1T to 0
1879 The Oval **England** 2G 1DG 2T to 0
1880 Dublin **England** 1G 1T to 1T
1881 Manchester **England** 2G 2T to 0
1882 Dublin **Drawn** 2T each
1883 Manchester **England** 1G 3T to 1T
1884 Dublin **England** 1G to 0
1885 Manchester **England** 2T to 1T
1886 Dublin **England** 1T to 0
1887 Dublin **Ireland** 2G to 0
1888 No Match
1889 No Match
1890 Blackheath (London) **England** 3T
    to 0
1891 Dublin **England** 9-0
1892 Manchester **England** 7-0
1893 Dublin **England** 4-0
1894 Blackheath **Ireland** 7-5
1895 Dublin **England** 6-3
1896 Leeds **Ireland** 10-4
1897 Dublin **Ireland** 13-9
1898 Richmond (London) **Ireland** 9-6

1899 Dublin **Ireland** 6-0
1900 Richmond **England** 15-4
1901 Dublin **Ireland** 10-6
1902 Leicester **England** 6-3
1903 Dublin **Ireland** 6-0
1904 Blackheath **England** 19-0
1905 Cork **Ireland** 17-3
1906 Leicester **Ireland** 16-6
1907 Dublin **Ireland** 17-9
1908 Richmond **England** 13-3
1909 Dublin **England** 11-5
1910 Twickenham **Drawn** 0-0
1911 Dublin **Ireland** 3-0
1912 Twickenham **England** 15-0
1913 Dublin **England** 15-4
1914 Twickenham **England** 17-12
1920 Dublin **England** 14-11
1921 Twickenham **England** 15-0
1922 Dublin **England** 12-3
1923 Leicester **England** 23-5
1924 Belfast **England** 14-3
1925 Twickenham **Drawn** 6-6
1926 Dublin **Ireland** 19-15
1927 Twickenham **England** 8-6
1928 Dublin **England** 7-6
1929 Twickenham **Ireland** 6-5

Ireland's Simon Geoghegan beats Tony Underwood of England to the ball in the 1994 encounter between the two countries, in which Ireland recorded a 13-12 win.

1930 Dublin **Ireland** 4-3
1931 Twickenham **Ireland** 6-5
1932 Dublin **England** 11-8
1933 Twickenham **England** 17-6
1934 Dublin **England** 13-3
1935 Twickenham **England** 14-3
1936 Dublin **Ireland** 6-3
1937 Twickenham **England** 9-8
1938 Dublin **England** 36-14
1939 Twickenham **Ireland** 5-0
1947 Dublin **Ireland** 22-0
1948 Twickenham **Ireland** 11-10
1949 Dublin **Ireland** 14-5
1950 Twickenham **England** 3-0
1951 Dublin **Ireland** 3-0
1952 Twickenham **England** 3-0
1953 Dublin **Drawn** 9-9
1954 Twickenham **England** 14-3
1955 Dublin **Drawn** 6-6
1956 Twickenham **England** 20-0
1957 Dublin **England** 6-0
1958 Twickenham **England** 6-0
1959 Dublin **England** 3-0
1960 Twickenham **England** 8-5
1961 Dublin **Ireland** 11-8
1962 Twickenham **England** 16-0
1963 Dublin **Drawn** 0-0
1964 Twickenham **Ireland** 18-5
1965 Dublin **Ireland** 5-0
1966 Twickenham **Drawn** 6-6

1967 Dublin **England** 8-3
1968 Twickenham **Drawn** 9-9
1969 Dublin **Ireland** 17-15
1970 Twickenham **England** 9-3
1971 Dublin **England** 9-6
1972 Twickenham **Ireland** 16-12
1973 Dublin **Ireland** 18-9
1974 Twickenham **Ireland** 26-21
1975 Dublin **Ireland** 12-9
1976 Twickenham **Ireland** 13-12
1977 Dublin **England** 4-0
1978 Twickenham **England** 15-9
1979 Dublin **Ireland** 12-7
1980 Twickenham **England** 24-9
1981 Dublin **England** 10-6
1982 Twickenham **Ireland** 16-15
1983 Dublin **Ireland** 25-15
1984 Twickenham **England** 12-9
1985 Dublin **Ireland** 13-10
1986 Twickenham **England** 25-20
1987 Dublin **Ireland** 17-0
1988 Twickenham **England** 35-3
1988 Dublin **England** 21-10
    Non-championship match
1989 Dublin **England** 16-3
1990 Twickenham **England** 23-0
1991 Dublin **England** 16-7
1992 Twickenham **England** 38-9
1993 Dublin **Ireland** 17-3
1994 Twickenham **Ireland** 13-12

ENGLAND v WALES
Played 100   England won 40, Wales won 48, Drawn 12

1881 Blackheath (London) **England** 7G
    1DG 6T to 0
1882 No Match
1883 Swansea **England** 2G 4T to 0
1884 Leeds **England** 1G 2T to 1G
1885 Swansea **England** 1G 4T to 1G 1T
1886 Blackheath **England** 1GM 2T to 1G
1887 Llanelli **Drawn** no score
1888 No Match
1889 No Match
1890 Dewsbury **Wales** 1T to 0
1891 Newport **England** 7-3
1892 Blackheath **England** 17-0
1893 Cardiff **Wales** 12-11
1894 Birkenhead **England** 24-3
1895 Swansea **England** 14-6
1896 Blackheath **England** 25-0
1897 Newport **Wales** 11-0
1898 Blackheath **England** 14-7
1899 Swansea **Wales** 26-3
1900 Gloucester **Wales** 13-3
1901 Cardiff **Wales** 13-0
1902 Blackheath **Wales** 9-8
1903 Swansea **Wales** 21-5

1904 Leicester **Drawn** 14-14
1905 Cardiff **Wales** 25-0
1906 Richmond (London) **Wales** 16-3
1907 Swansea **Wales** 22-0
1908 Bristol **Wales** 28-18
1909 Cardiff **Wales** 8-0
1910 Twickenham **England** 11-6
1911 Swansea **Wales** 15-11
1912 Twickenham **England** 8-0
1913 Cardiff **England** 12-0
1914 Twickenham **England** 10-9
1920 Swansea **Wales** 19-5
1921 Twickenham **England** 18-3
1922 Cardiff **Wales** 28-6
1923 Twickenham **England** 7-3
1924 Swansea **England** 17-9
1925 Twickenham **England** 12-6
1926 Cardiff **Drawn** 3-3
1927 Twickenham **England** 11-9
1928 Swansea **England** 10-8
1929 Twickenham **England** 8-3
1930 Cardiff **England** 11-3
1931 Twickenham **Drawn** 11-11
1932 Swansea **Wales** 12-5

93

1933 Twickenham **Wales** 7-3
1934 Cardiff **England** 9-0
1935 Twickenham **Drawn** 3-3
1936 Swansea **Drawn** 0-0
1937 Twickenham **England** 4-3
1938 Cardiff **Wales** 14-8
1939 Twickenham **England** 3-0
1947 Cardiff **England** 9-6
1948 Twickenham **Drawn** 3-3
1949 Cardiff **Wales** 9-3
1950 Twickenham **Wales** 11-5
1951 Swansea **Wales** 23-5
1952 Twickenham **Wales** 8-6
1953 Cardiff **England** 8-3
1954 Twickenham **England** 9-6
1955 Cardiff **Wales** 3-0
1956 Twickenham **Wales** 8-3
1957 Cardiff **England** 3-0
1958 Twickenham **Drawn** 3-3
1959 Cardiff **Wales** 5-0
1960 Twickenham **England** 14-6
1961 Cardiff **Wales** 6-3
1962 Twickenham **Drawn** 0-0
1963 Cardiff **England** 13-6
1964 Twickenham **Drawn** 6-6
1965 Cardiff **Wales** 14-3
1966 Twickenham **Wales** 11-6
1967 Cardiff **Wales** 34-21

1968 Twickenham **Drawn** 11-11
1969 Cardiff **Wales** 30-9
1970 Twickenham **Wales** 17-13
1971 Cardiff **Wales** 22-6
1972 Twickenham **Wales** 12-3
1973 Cardiff **Wales** 25-9
1974 Twickenham **England** 16-12
1975 Cardiff **Wales** 20-4
1976 Twickenham **Wales** 21-9
1977 Cardiff **Wales** 14-9
1978 Twickenham **Wales** 9-6
1979 Cardiff **Wales** 27-3
1980 Twickenham **England** 9-8
1981 Cardiff **Wales** 21-19
1982 Twickenham **England** 17-7
1983 Cardiff **Drawn** 13-13
1984 Twickenham **Wales** 24-15
1985 Cardiff **Wales** 24-15
1986 Twickenham **England** 21-18
1987 Cardiff **Wales** 19-12
1987 Brisbane *WC* **Wales** 16-3
1988 Twickenham **Wales** 11-3
1989 Cardiff **Wales** 12-9
1990 Twickenham **England** 34-6
1991 Cardiff **England** 25-6
1992 Twickenham **England** 24-0
1993 Cardiff **Wales** 10-9
1994 Twickenham **England** 15-8

ENGLAND v FRANCE

Played 70 England won 39, France won 24, Drawn 7

1906 Paris **England** 35-8
1907 Richmond (London) **England** 41-13
1908 Paris **England** 19-0
1909 Leicester **England** 22-0
1910 Paris **England** 11-3
1911 Twickenham **England** 37-0
1912 Paris **England** 18-8
1913 Twickenham **England** 20-0
1914 Paris **England** 39-13
1920 Twickenham **England** 8-3
1921 Paris **England** 10-6
1922 Twickenham **Drawn** 11-11
1923 Paris **England** 12-3
1924 Twickenham **England** 19-7
1925 Paris **England** 13-11
1926 Twickenham **England** 11-0
1927 Paris **France** 3-0
1928 Twickenham **England** 18-8
1929 Paris **England** 16-6
1930 Twickenham **England** 11-5
1931 Paris **France** 14-13
1947 Twickenham **England** 6-3
1948 Paris **France** 15-0
1949 Twickenham **England** 8-3
1950 Paris **France** 6-3
1951 Twickenham **France** 11-3
1952 Paris **England** 6-3
1953 Twickenham **England** 11-0
1954 Paris **France** 11-3
1955 Twickenham **France** 16-9

1956 Paris **France** 14-9
1957 Twickenham **England** 9-5
1958 Paris **England** 14-0
1959 Twickenham **Drawn** 3-3
1960 Paris **Drawn** 3-3
1961 Twickenham **Drawn** 5-5
1962 Paris **France** 13-0
1963 Twickenham **England** 6-5
1964 Paris **England** 6-3
1965 Twickenham **England** 9-6
1966 Paris **France** 13-0
1967 Twickenham **France** 16-12
1968 Paris **France** 14-9
1969 Twickenham **England** 22-8
1970 Paris **France** 35-13
1971 Twickenham **Drawn** 14-14
1972 Paris **France** 37-12
1973 Twickenham **England** 14-6
1974 Paris **Drawn** 12-12
1975 Twickenham **France** 27-20
1976 Paris **France** 30-9
1977 Twickenham **France** 4-3
1978 Paris **France** 15-6
1979 Twickenham **England** 7-6
1980 Paris **England** 17-13
1981 Twickenham **France** 16-12
1982 Paris **England** 27-15
1983 Twickenham **France** 19-15
1984 Paris **France** 32-18
1985 Twickenham **Drawn** 9-9

1986 Paris **France** 29-10
1987 Twickenham **France** 19-15
1988 Paris **France** 10-9
1989 Twickenham **England** 11-0
1990 Paris **England** 26-7

1991 Twickenham **England** 21-19
1991 Paris *WC* **England** 19-10
1992 Paris **England** 31-13
1993 Twickenham **England** 16-15
1994 Paris **England** 18-14

ENGLAND v NEW ZEALAND
Played 17   England won 4, New Zealand won 13, Drawn 0

1905 Crystal Palace (London) **New Zealand** 15-0
1925 Twickenham **New Zealand** 17-11
1936 Twickenham **England** 13-0
1954 Twickenham **New Zealand** 5-0
1963 *1* Auckland **New Zealand** 21-11
    2 Christchurch **New Zealand** 9- 6
    New Zealand won series 2-0
1964 Twickenham **New Zealand** 14-0
1967 Twickenham **New Zealand** 23-11
1973 Twickenham **New Zealand** 9-0

1973 Auckland **England** 16-10
1978 Twickenham **New Zealand** 16-6
1979 Twickenham **New Zealand** 10-9
1983 Twickenham **England** 15-9
1985 *1* Christchurch **New Zealand** 18-13
    2 Wellington **New Zealand** 42-15
    New Zealand won series 2-0
1991 Twickenham *WC* **New Zealand** 18-12
1993 Twickenham **England** 15-9

ENGLAND v SOUTH AFRICA
Played 10   England won 3, South Africa won 6, Drawn 1

1906 Crystal Palace (London) **Drawn** 3-3
1913 Twickenham **South Africa** 9-3
1932 Twickenham **South Africa** 7-0
1952 Twickenham **South Africa** 8-3
1961 Twickenham **South Africa** 5-0
1969 Twickenham **England** 11-8

1972 Johannesburg **England** 18-9
1984 *1* Port Elizabeth **South Africa** 33-15
    2 Johannesburg **South Africa** 35-9
    South Africa won series 2-0
1992 Twickenham **England** 33-16

ENGLAND v AUSTRALIA
Played 18   England won 6, Australia won 12, Drawn 0

1909 Blackheath (London) **Australia** 9-3
1928 Twickenham **England** 18-11
1948 Twickenham **Australia** 11-0
1958 Twickenham **England** 9-6
1963 Sydney **Australia** 18-9
1967 Twickenham **Australia** 23-11
1973 Twickenham **England** 20-3
1975 *1* Sydney **Australia** 16-9
    2 Brisbane **Australia** 30-21
    Australia won series 2-0

1976 Twickenham **England** 23-6
1982 Twickenham **England** 15-11
1984 Twickenham **Australia** 19-3
1987 Sydney *WC* **Australia** 19-6
1988 *1* Brisbane **Australia** 22-16
    2 Sydney **Australia** 28-8
    Australia won series 2-0
1988 Twickenham **England** 28-19
1991 Sydney **Australia** 40-15
1991 Twickenham *WC* **Australia** 12-6

ENGLAND v NEW ZEALAND NATIVES
Played 1   England won 1

1889 Blackheath **England** 1G 4T to 0

ENGLAND v RFU PRESIDENT'S XV
Played 1   President's XV won 1

1971 Twickenham **President's XV** 28-11

ENGLAND v ARGENTINA
Played 5   England won 3, Argentina won 1, Drawn 1

1981 *1* Buenos Aires **Drawn** 19-19
    2 Buenos Aires **England** 12-6
    England won series 1-0 with 1 draw

1990 *1* Buenos Aires **England** 25-12
    2 Buenos Aires **Argentina** 15-13
    Series drawn 1-1
1990 Twickenham **England** 51-0

ENGLAND v ROMANIA
Played 2   England won 2

1985 Twickenham **England** 22-15	1989 Bucharest **England** 58-3

ENGLAND v JAPAN
Played 1   England won 1

1987 Sydney *WC* **England** 60-7

ENGLAND v UNITED STATES
Played 2   England won 2

1987 Sydney *WC* **England** 34-6	1991 Twickenham *WC* **England** 37-9

ENGLAND v FIJI
Played 3   England won 3

1988 Suva **England** 25-12	1991 Suva **England** 28-12
1989 Twickenham **England** 58-23	

ENGLAND v ITALY
Played 1   England won 1

1991 Twickenham *WC* **England** 36-6

ENGLAND v CANADA
Played 1   England won 1

1992 Wembley **England** 26-13

SCOTLAND v IRELAND
Played 106   Scotland won 55, Ireland won 45, Drawn 5, Abandoned 1

1877 Belfast **Scotland** 4G 2DG 2T to 0	1898 Belfast **Scotland** 8-0
1878 No Match	1899 Inverleith (Edinburgh) **Ireland** 9-3
1879 Belfast **Scotland** 1G 1DG 1T to 0	1900 Dublin **Drawn** 0-0
1880 Glasgow **Scotland** 1G 2DG 2T to 0	1901 Inverleith **Scotland** 9-5
1881 Belfast **Ireland** 1DG to 1T	1902 Belfast **Ireland** 5-0
1882 Glasgow **Scotland** 2T to 0	1903 Inverleith **Scotland** 3-0
1883 Belfast **Scotland** 1G 1T to 0	1904 Dublin **Scotland** 19-3
1884 Raeburn Place (Edinburgh) **Scotland** 2G 2T to 1T	1905 Inverleith **Ireland** 11-5
	1906 Dublin **Scotland** 13-6
1885 Belfast **Abandoned** Ireland 0 Scotland 1T	1907 Inverleith **Scotland** 15-3
	1908 Dublin **Ireland** 16-11
1885 Raeburn Place **Scotland** 1G 2T to 0	1909 Inverleith **Scotland** 9-3
1886 Raeburn Place **Scotland** 3G 1DG 2T to 0	1910 Belfast **Scotland** 14-0
	1911 Inverleith **Ireland** 16-10
1887 Belfast **Scotland** 1G 1GM 2T to 0	1912 Dublin **Ireland** 10-8
1888 Raeburn Place **Scotland** 1G to 0	1913 Inverleith **Scotland** 29-14
1889 Belfast **Scotland** 1DG to 0	1914 Dublin **Ireland** 6-0
1890 Raeburn Place **Scotland** 1DG 1T to 0	1920 Inverleith **Scotland** 19-0
1891 Belfast **Scotland** 14-0	1921 Dublin **Ireland** 9-8
1892 Raeburn Place **Scotland** 2-0	1922 Inverleith **Scotland** 6-3
1893 Belfast **Drawn** 0-0	1923 Dublin **Scotland** 13-3
1894 Dublin **Ireland** 5-0	1924 Inverleith **Scotland** 13-8
1895 Raeburn Place **Scotland** 6-0	1925 Dublin **Scotland** 14-8
1896 Dublin **Drawn** 0-0	1926 Murrayfield **Ireland** 3-0
1897 Powderhall (Edinburgh) **Scotland** 8-3	1927 Dublin **Ireland** 6-0
	1928 Murrayfield **Ireland** 13-5

1929 Dublin **Scotland** 16-7
1930 Murrayfield **Ireland** 14-11
1931 Dublin **Ireland** 8-5
1932 Murrayfield **Ireland** 20-8
1933 Dublin **Scotland** 8-6
1934 Murrayfield **Scotland** 16-9
1935 Dublin **Ireland** 12-5
1936 Murrayfield **Ireland** 10-4
1937 Dublin **Ireland** 11-4
1938 Murrayfield **Scotland** 23-14
1939 Dublin **Ireland** 12-3
1947 Murrayfield **Ireland** 3-0
1948 Dublin **Ireland** 6-0
1949 Murrayfield **Ireland** 13-3
1950 Dublin **Ireland** 21-0
1951 Murrayfield **Ireland** 6-5
1952 Dublin **Ireland** 12-8
1953 Murrayfield **Ireland** 26-8
1954 Belfast **Ireland** 6-0
1955 Murrayfield **Scotland** 12-3
1956 Dublin **Ireland** 14-10
1957 Murrayfield **Ireland** 5-3
1958 Dublin **Ireland** 12-6
1959 Murrayfield **Ireland** 8-3
1960 Dublin **Scotland** 6-5
1961 Murrayfield **Scotland** 16-8
1962 Dublin **Scotland** 20-6
1963 Murrayfield **Scotland** 3-0
1964 Dublin **Scotland** 6-3
1965 Murrayfield **Ireland** 16-6

1966 Dublin **Scotland** 11-3
1967 Murrayfield **Ireland** 5-3
1968 Dublin **Ireland** 14-6
1969 Murrayfield **Ireland** 16-0
1970 Dublin **Ireland** 16-11
1971 Murrayfield **Ireland** 17-5
1972 No Match
1973 Murrayfield **Scotland** 19-14
1974 Dublin **Ireland** 9-6
1975 Murrayfield **Scotland** 20-13
1976 Dublin **Scotland** 15-6
1977 Murrayfield **Scotland** 21-18
1978 Dublin **Ireland** 12-9
1979 Murrayfield **Drawn** 11-11
1980 Dublin **Ireland** 22-15
1981 Murrayfield **Scotland** 10-9
1982 Dublin **Ireland** 21-12
1983 Murrayfield **Ireland** 15-13
1984 Dublin **Scotland** 32-9
1985 Murrayfield **Ireland** 18-15
1986 Dublin **Scotland** 10-9
1987 Murrayfield **Scotland** 16-12
1988 Dublin **Ireland** 22-18
1989 Murrayfield **Scotland** 37-21
1990 Dublin **Scotland** 13-10
1991 Murrayfield **Scotland** 28-25
1991 Murrayfield *WC* **Scotland** 24-15
1992 Dublin **Scotland** 18-10
1993 Murrayfield **Scotland** 15-3
1994 Dublin **Drawn** 6-6

SCOTLAND v WALES

Played 98   Scotland won 42, Wales won 54, Drawn 2

1883 Raeburn Place (Edinburgh)
       Scotland (3G to 1G
1884 Newport **Scotland** 1DG 1T to 0
1885 Glasgow **Drawn** no score
1886 Cardiff **Scotland** 2G 8T to 0
1887 Raeburn Place **Scotland** 4G 8T to 0
1888 Newport **Wales** 1T to 0
1889 Raeburn Place **Scotland** 2T to 0
1890 Cardiff **Scotland** 1G 2T to 1T
1891 Raeburn Place **Scotland** 15-0
1892 Swansea **Scotland** 7-2
1893 Raeburn Place **Wales** 9-0
1894 Newport **Wales** 7-0
1895 Raeburn Place **Scotland** 5-4
1896 Cardiff **Wales** 6-0
1897 No Match
1898 No Match
1899 Inverleith (Edinburgh) **Scotland**
       21-10
1900 Swansea **Wales** 12-3
1901 Inverleith **Scotland** 18-8
1902 Cardiff **Wales** 14-5
1903 Inverleith **Scotland** 6-0
1904 Swansea **Wales** 21-3
1905 Inverleith **Wales** 6-3
1906 Cardiff **Wales** 9-3
1907 Inverleith **Scotland** 6-3

1908 Swansea **Wales** 6-5
1909 Inverleith **Wales** 5-3
1910 Cardiff **Wales** 14-0
1911 Inverleith **Wales** 32-10
1912 Swansea **Wales** 21-6
1913 Inverleith **Wales** 8-0
1914 Cardiff **Wales** 24-5
1920 Inverleith **Scotland** 9-5
1921 Swansea **Scotland** 14-8
1922 Inverleith **Drawn** 9-9
1923 Cardiff **Scotland** 11-8
1924 Inverleith **Scotland** 35-10
1925 Swansea **Scotland** 24-14
1926 Murrayfield **Scotland** 8-5
1927 Cardiff **Scotland** 5-0
1928 Murrayfield **Wales** 13-0
1929 Swansea **Wales** 14-7
1930 Murrayfield **Scotland** 12-9
1931 Cardiff **Wales** 13-8
1932 Murrayfield **Wales** 6-0
1933 Swansea **Scotland** 11-3
1934 Murrayfield **Wales** 13-6
1935 Cardiff **Wales** 10-6
1936 Murrayfield **Wales** 13-3
1937 Swansea **Scotland** 13-6
1938 Murrayfield **Scotland** 8-6
1939 Cardiff **Wales** 11-3

1947 Murrayfield **Wales** 22-8
1948 Cardiff **Wales** 14-0
1949 Murrayfield **Scotland** 6-5
1950 Swansea **Wales** 12-0
1951 Murrayfield **Scotland** 19-0
1952 Cardiff **Wales** 11-0
1953 Murrayfield **Wales** 12-0
1954 Swansea **Wales** 15-3
1955 Murrayfield **Scotland** 14-8
1956 Cardiff **Wales** 9-3
1957 Murrayfield **Scotland** 9-6
1958 Cardiff **Wales** 8-3
1959 Murrayfield **Scotland** 6-5
1960 Cardiff **Wales** 8-0
1961 Murrayfield **Scotland** 3-0
1962 Cardiff **Scotland** 8-3
1963 Murrayfield **Wales** 6-0
1964 Cardiff **Wales** 11-3
1965 Murrayfield **Wales** 14-12
1966 Cardiff **Wales** 8-3
1967 Murrayfield **Scotland** 11-5
1968 Cardiff **Wales** 5-0
1969 Murrayfield **Wales** 17-3
1970 Cardiff **Wales** 18-9

1971 Murrayfield **Wales** 19-18
1972 Cardiff **Wales** 35-12
1973 Murrayfield **Scotland** 10-9
1974 Cardiff **Wales** 6-0
1975 Murrayfield **Scotland** 12-10
1976 Cardiff **Wales** 28-6
1977 Murrayfield **Wales** 18-9
1978 Cardiff **Wales** 22-14
1979 Murrayfield **Wales** 19-13
1980 Cardiff **Wales** 17-6
1981 Murrayfield **Scotland** 15-6
1982 Cardiff **Scotland** 34-18
1983 Murrayfield **Wales** 19-15
1984 Cardiff **Scotland** 15-9
1985 Murrayfield **Wales** 25-21
1986 Cardiff **Wales** 22-15
1987 Murrayfield **Scotland** 21-15
1988 Cardiff **Wales** 25-20
1989 Murrayfield **Scotland** 23-7
1990 Cardiff **Scotland** 13-9
1991 Murrayfield **Scotland** 32-12
1992 Cardiff **Wales** 15-12
1993 Murrayfield **Scotland** 20-0
1994 Cardiff **Wales** 29-6

SCOTLAND v FRANCE

Played 65   Scotland won 30, France won 32, Drawn 3

1910 Inverleith (Edinburgh)
    Scotland 27-0
1911 Paris **France** 16-15
1912 Inverleith **Scotland** 31-3
1913 Paris **Scotland** 21-3
1914 No Match
1920 Paris **Scotland** 5-0
1921 Inverleith **France** 3-0
1922 Paris **Drawn** 3-3
1923 Inverleith **Scotland** 16-3
1924 Paris **France** 12-10
1925 Inverleith **Scotland** 25-4
1926 Paris **Scotland** 20-6
1927 Murrayfield **Scotland** 23-6
1928 Paris **Scotland** 15-6
1929 Murrayfield **Scotland** 6-3
1930 Paris **France** 7-3
1931 Murrayfield **Scotland** 6-4
1947 Paris **France** 8-3
1948 Murrayfield **Scotland** 9-8
1949 Paris **Scotland** 8-0
1950 Murrayfield **Scotland** 8-5
1951 Paris **France** 14-12
1952 Murrayfield **France** 13-11
1953 Paris **France** 11-5
1954 Murrayfield **France** 3-0
1955 Paris **France** 15-0
1956 Murrayfield **Scotland** 12-0
1957 Paris **Scotland** 6-0
1958 Murrayfield **Scotland** 11-9
1959 Paris **France** 9-0
1960 Murrayfield **France** 13-11
1961 Paris **France** 11-0
1962 Murrayfield **France** 11-3

1963 Paris **Scotland** 11-6
1964 Murrayfield **Scotland** 10-0
1965 Paris **France** 16-8
1966 Murrayfield **Drawn** 3-3
1967 Paris **Scotland** 9-8
1968 Murrayfield **France** 8-6
1969 Paris **Scotland** 6-3
1970 Murrayfield **France** 11-9
1971 Paris **France** 13-8
1972 Murrayfield **Scotland** 20-9
1973 Paris **France** 16-13
1974 Murrayfield **Scotland** 19-6
1975 Paris **France** 10-9
1976 Murrayfield **France** 13-6
1977 Paris **France** 23-3
1978 Murrayfield **France** 19-16
1979 Paris **France** 21-17
1980 Murrayfield **Scotland** 22-14
1981 Paris **France** 16-9
1982 Murrayfield **Scotland** 16-7
1983 Paris **France** 19-15
1984 Murrayfield **Scotland** 21-12
1985 Paris **France** 11-3
1986 Murrayfield **Scotland** 18-17
1987 Paris **France** 28-22
1987 Christchurch *WC* **Drawn** 20-20
1988 Murrayfield **Scotland** 23-12
1989 Paris **France** 19-3
1990 Murrayfield **Scotland** 21-0
1991 Paris **France** 15-9
1992 Murrayfield **Scotland** 10-6
1993 Paris **France** 11-3
1994 Murrayfield **France** 20-12

SCOTLAND v NEW ZEALAND
Played 17   Scotland won 0, New Zealand won 15, Drawn 2

1905 Inverleith (Edinburgh)	1981 *1* Dunedin **New Zealand** 11-4
New Zealand 12-7	*2* Auckland **New Zealand** 40-15
1935 Murrayfield **New Zealand** 18-8	*New Zealand won series 2-0*
1954 Murrayfield **New Zealand** 3-0	1983 Murrayfield **Drawn** 25-25
1964 Murrayfield **Drawn** 0-0	1987 Christchurch *WC* **New Zealand** 30-3
1967 Murrayfield **New Zealand** 14-3	1990 *1* Dunedin **New Zealand** 31-16
1972 Murrayfield **New Zealand** 14-9	*2* Auckland **New Zealand** 21-18
1975 Auckland **New Zealand** 24-0	*New Zealand won series 2-0*
1978 Murrayfield **New Zealand** 18-9	1991 Cardiff *WC* **New Zealand** 13-6
1979 Murrayfield **New Zealand** 20-6	1993 Murrayfield **New Zealand** 51-15

SCOTLAND v SOUTH AFRICA
Played 8   Scotland won 3, South Africa won 5, Drawn 0

1906 Glasgow **Scotland** 6-0	1960 Port Elizabeth **South Africa** 18-10
1912 Inverleith **South Africa** 16-0	1961 Murrayfield **South Africa** 12-5
1932 Murrayfield **South Africa** 6-3	1965 Murrayfield **Scotland** 8-5
1951 Murrayfield **South Africa** 44-0	1969 Murrayfield **Scotland** 6-3

SCOTLAND v AUSTRALIA
Played 14   Scotland won 7, Australia won 7, Drawn 0

1927 Murrayfield **Scotland** 10-8	1982 *1* Brisbane **Scotland** 12-7
1947 Murrayfield **Australia** 16-7	*2* Sydney **Australia** 33-9
1958 Murrayfield **Scotland** 12-8	*Series drawn 1-1*
1966 Murrayfield **Scotland** 11-5	1984 Murrayfield **Australia** 37-12
1968 Murrayfield **Scotland** 9-3	1988 Murrayfield **Australia** 32-13
1970 Sydney **Australia** 23-3	1992 *1* Sydney **Australia** 27-12
1975 Murrayfield **Scotland** 10-3	*2* Brisbane **Australia** 37-13
1981 Murrayfield **Scotland** 24-15	*Australia won series 2-0*

SCOTLAND v SRU PRESIDENT'S XV
Played 1   Scotland won 1

1973 Murrayfield **Scotland** 27-16

SCOTLAND v ROMANIA
Played 6   Scotland won 4, Romania won 2

1981 Murrayfield **Scotland** 12-6	1987 Dunedin *WC* **Scotland** 55-28
1984 Bucharest **Romania** 28-22	1989 Murrayfield **Scotland** 32-0
1986 Bucharest **Scotland** 33-18	1991 Bucharest **Romania** 18-12

SCOTLAND v ZIMBABWE
Played 2   Scotland won 2

1987 Wellington *WC* **Scotland** 60-21	1991 Murrayfield *WC* **Scotland** 51-12

SCOTLAND v FIJI
Played 1   Scotland won 1

1989 Murrayfield **Scotland** 38-17

SCOTLAND v ARGENTINA
Played 1   Scotland won 1

1990 Murrayfield **Scotland** 49-3

SCOTLAND v JAPAN
Played 1   Scotland won 1

1991 Murrayfield *WC* **Scotland** 47-9

SCOTLAND v WESTERN SAMOA
Played 1   Scotland won 1

1991 Murrayfield *WC* **Scotland** 28-6

IRELAND v WALES
Played 97   Ireland won 33, Wales won 58, Drawn 6

1882 Dublin **Wales** 2G 2T to 0	1935 Belfast **Ireland** 9-3
1883 No Match	1936 Cardiff **Wales** 3-0
1884 Cardiff **Wales** 1DG 2T to 0	1937 Belfast **Ireland** 5-3
1885 No Match	1938 Swansea **Wales** 11-5
1886 No Match	1939 Belfast **Wales** 7-0
1887 Birkenhead **Wales** 1DG 1T to 3T	1947 Swansea **Wales** 6-0
1888 Dublin **Ireland** 1G 1DG 1T to 0	1948 Belfast **Ireland** 6-3
1889 Swansea **Ireland** 2T to 0	1949 Swansea **Ireland** 5-0
1890 Dublin **Drawn** 1G each	1950 Belfast **Wales** 6-3
1891 Llanelli **Wales** 6-4	1951 Cardiff **Drawn** 3-3
1892 Dublin **Ireland** 9-0	1952 Dublin **Wales** 14-3
1893 Llanelli **Wales** 2-0	1953 Swansea **Wales** 5-3
1894 Belfast **Ireland** 3-0	1954 Dublin **Wales** 12-9
1895 Cardiff **Wales** 5-3	1955 Cardiff **Wales** 21-3
1896 Dublin **Ireland** 8-4	1956 Dublin **Ireland** 11-3
1897 No Match	1957 Cardiff **Wales** 6-5
1898 Limerick **Wales** 11-3	1958 Dublin **Wales** 9-6
1899 Cardiff **Ireland** 3-0	1959 Cardiff **Wales** 8-6
1900 Belfast **Wales** 3-0	1960 Dublin **Wales** 10-9
1901 Swansea **Wales** 10-9	1961 Cardiff **Wales** 9-0
1902 Dublin **Wales** 15-0	1962 Dublin **Drawn** 3-3
1903 Cardiff **Wales** 18-0	1963 Cardiff **Ireland** 14-6
1904 Belfast **Ireland** 14-12	1964 Dublin **Wales** 15-6
1905 Swansea **Wales** 10-3	1965 Cardiff **Wales** 14-8
1906 Belfast **Ireland** 11-6	1966 Dublin **Ireland** 9-6
1907 Cardiff **Wales** 29-0	1967 Cardiff **Ireland** 3-0
1908 Belfast **Wales** 11-5	1968 Dublin **Ireland** 9-6
1909 Swansea **Wales** 18-5	1969 Cardiff **Wales** 24-11
1910 Dublin **Wales** 19-3	1970 Dublin **Ireland** 14-0
1911 Cardiff **Wales** 16-0	1971 Cardiff **Wales** 23-9
1912 Belfast **Ireland** 12-5	1972 No Match
1913 Swansea **Wales** 16-13	1973 Cardiff **Wales** 16-12
1914 Belfast **Wales** 11-3	1974 Dublin **Drawn** 9-9
1920 Cardiff **Wales** 28-4	1975 Cardiff **Wales** 32-4
1921 Belfast **Wales** 6-0	1976 Dublin **Wales** 34-9
1922 Swansea **Wales** 11-5	1977 Cardiff **Wales** 25-9
1923 Dublin **Ireland** 5-4	1978 Dublin **Wales** 20-16
1924 Cardiff **Ireland** 13-10	1979 Cardiff **Wales** 24-21
1925 Belfast **Ireland** 19-3	1980 Dublin **Ireland** 21-7
1926 Swansea **Wales** 11-8	1981 Cardiff **Wales** 9-8
1927 Dublin **Ireland** 19-9	1982 Dublin **Ireland** 20-12
1928 Cardiff **Ireland** 13-10	1983 Cardiff **Wales** 23-9
1929 Belfast **Drawn** 5-5	1984 Dublin **Wales** 18-9
1930 Swansea **Wales** 12-7	1985 Cardiff **Ireland** 21-9
1931 Belfast **Wales** 15-3	1986 Dublin **Wales** 19-12
1932 Cardiff **Ireland** 12-10	1987 Cardiff **Ireland** 15-11
1933 Belfast **Ireland** 10-5	1987 Wellington *WC* **Wales** 13-6
1934 Swansea **Wales** 13-0	1988 Dublin **Wales** 12-9

1989 Cardiff **Ireland** 19-13
1990 Dublin **Ireland** 14-8
1991 Cardiff **Drawn** 21-21

1992 Dublin **Wales** 16-15
1993 Cardiff **Ireland** 19-14
1994 Dublin **Wales** 17-15

IRELAND v FRANCE
Played 67   Ireland won 25, France won 37, Drawn 5

1909 Dublin **Ireland** 19-8	1963 Dublin **France** 24-5
1910 Paris **Ireland** 19-8	1964 Paris **France** 27-6
1911 Cork **Ireland** 25-5	1965 Dublin **Drawn** 3-3
1912 Paris **Ireland** 11-6	1966 Paris **France** 11-6
1913 Cork **Ireland** 24-0	1967 Dublin **France** 11-6
1914 Paris **Ireland** 8-6	1968 Paris **France** 16-6
1920 Dublin **France** 15-7	1969 Dublin **Ireland** 17-9
1921 Paris **France** 20-10	1970 Paris **France** 8-0
1922 Dublin **Ireland** 8-3	1971 Dublin **Drawn** 9-9
1923 Paris **France** 14-8	1972 Paris **Ireland** 14-9
1924 Dublin **Ireland** 6-0	1972 Dublin **Ireland** 24-14
1925 Paris **Ireland** 9-3	*Non-championship match*
1926 Belfast **Ireland** 11-0	1973 Dublin **Ireland** 6-4
1927 Paris **Ireland** 8-3	1974 Paris **France** 9-6
1928 Belfast **Ireland** 12-8	1975 Dublin **Ireland** 25-6
1929 Paris **Ireland** 6-0	1976 Paris **France** 26-3
1930 Belfast **France** 5-0	1977 Dublin **France** 15-6
1931 Paris **France** 3-0	1978 Paris **France** 10-9
1947 Dublin **France** 12-8	1979 Dublin **Drawn** 9-9
1948 Paris **Ireland** 13-6	1980 Paris **France** 19-18
1949 Dublin **France** 16-9	1981 Dublin **France** 19-13
1950 Paris **Drawn** 3-3	1982 Paris **France** 22-9
1951 Dublin **Ireland** 9-8	1983 Dublin **Ireland** 22-16
1952 Paris **Ireland** 11-8	1984 Paris **France** 25-12
1953 Belfast **Ireland** 16-3	1985 Dublin **Drawn** 15-15
1954 Paris **France** 8-0	1986 Paris **France** 29-9
1955 Dublin **France** 5-3	1987 Dublin **France** 19-13
1956 Paris **France** 14-8	1988 Paris **France** 25-6
1957 Dublin **Ireland** 11-6	1989 Dublin **France** 26-21
1958 Paris **France** 11-6	1990 Paris **France** 31-12
1959 Dublin **Ireland** 9-5	1991 Dublin **France** 21-13
1960 Paris **France** 23-6	1992 Paris **France** 44-12
1961 Dublin **France** 15-3	1993 Dublin **France** 21-6
1962 Paris **France** 11-0	1994 Paris **France** 35-15

IRELAND v NEW ZEALAND
Played 12   Ireland won 0, New Zealand won 11, Drawn 1

1905 Dublin **New Zealand** 15-0	1976 Wellington **New Zealand** 11-3
1924 Dublin **New Zealand** 6-0	1978 Dublin **New Zealand** 10-6
1935 Dublin **New Zealand** 17-9	1989 Dublin **New Zealand** 23-6
1954 Dublin **New Zealand** 14-3	1992 *1* Dunedin **New Zealand** 24-21
1963 Dublin **New Zealand** 6-5	*2* Wellington **New Zealand** 59-6
1973 Dublin **Drawn** 10-10	*New Zealand won series 2-0*
1974 Dublin **New Zealand** 15-6	

IRELAND v SOUTH AFRICA
Played 10   Ireland won 1, South Africa won 8, Drawn 1

1906 Belfast **South Africa** 15-12	1965 Dublin **Ireland** 9-6
1912 Dublin **South Africa** 38-0	1970 Dublin **Drawn** 8-8
1931 Dublin **South Africa** 8-3	1981 *1* Cape Town **South Africa** 23-15
1951 Dublin **South Africa** 17-5	*2* Durban **South Africa** 12-10
1960 Dublin **South Africa** 8-3	*South Africa won series 2-0*
1961 Cape Town **South Africa** 24-8	

IRELAND v AUSTRALIA

Played 14   Ireland won 6, Australia won 8, Drawn 0

1927 Dublin **Australia** 5-3	2 Sydney **Ireland** 9-3
1947 Dublin **Australia** 16-3	*Ireland won series 2-0*
1958 Dublin **Ireland** 9-6	1981 Dublin **Australia** 16-12
1967 Dublin **Ireland** 15-8	1984 Dublin **Australia** 16-9
1967 Sydney **Ireland** 11-5	1987 Sydney *WC* **Australia** 33-15
1968 Dublin **Ireland** 10-3	1991 Dublin *WC* **Australia** 19-18
1976 Dublin **Australia** 20-10	1992 Dublin **Australia** 42-17
1979 *1* Brisbane **Ireland** 27-12	

IRELAND v NEW ZEALAND NATIVES

Played 1   New Zealand Natives won 1

1888 Dublin **New Zealand Natives**
    4G 1T to 1G 1T

IRELAND v IRU PRESIDENT'S XV

Played 1   Drawn 1

1974 Dublin **Drawn** 18-18

IRELAND v ROMANIA

Played 2   Ireland won 2

1986 Dublin **Ireland** 60-0	1993 Dublin **Ireland** 25-3

IRELAND v CANADA

Played 1   Ireland won 1

1987 Dunedin *WC* **Ireland** 46-19

IRELAND v TONGA

Played 1   Ireland won 1

1987 Brisbane *WC* **Ireland** 32-9

IRELAND v WESTERN SAMOA

Played 1   Ireland won 1

1988 Dublin **Ireland** 49-22

IRELAND v ITALY

Played 1   Ireland won 1

1988 Dublin **Ireland** 31-15

IRELAND v ARGENTINA

Played 1   Ireland won 1

1990 Dublin **Ireland** 20-18

IRELAND v NAMIBIA

Played 2   Namibia won 2

1991 *1* Windhoek **Namibia** 15-6	2 Windhoek **Namibia** 26-15
	Namibia won series 2-0

IRELAND v ZIMBABWE

Played 1   Ireland won 1

1991 Dublin *WC* **Ireland** 55-11

IRELAND v JAPAN

Played 1   Ireland won 1

1991 Dublin *WC* **Ireland** 32-16

WALES v FRANCE

Played 68   Wales won 37, France won 28, Drawn 3

1908 Cardiff **Wales** 36-4	1963 Paris **France** 5-3
1909 Paris **Wales** 47-5	1964 Cardiff **Drawn** 11-11
1910 Swansea **Wales** 49-14	1965 Paris **France** 22-13
1911 Paris **Wales** 15-0	1966 Cardiff **Wales** 9-8
1912 Newport **Wales** 14-8	1967 Paris **France** 20-14
1913 Paris **Wales** 11-8	1968 Cardiff **France** 14-9
1914 Swansea **Wales** 31-0	1969 Paris **Drawn** 8-8
1920 Paris **Wales** 6-5	1970 Cardiff **Wales** 11-6
1921 Cardiff **Wales** 12-4	1971 Paris **Wales** 9-5
1922 Paris **Wales** 11-3	1972 Cardiff **Wales** 20-6
1923 Swansea **Wales** 16-8	1973 Paris **France** 12-3
1924 Paris **Wales** 10-6	1974 Cardiff **Drawn** 16-16
1925 Cardiff **Wales** 11-5	1975 Paris **Wales** 25-10
1926 Paris **Wales** 7-5	1976 Cardiff **Wales** 19-13
1927 Swansea **Wales** 25-7	1977 Paris **France** 16-9
1928 Paris **France** 8-3	1978 Cardiff **Wales** 16-7
1929 Cardiff **Wales** 8-3	1979 Paris **France** 14-13
1930 Paris **Wales** 11-0	1980 Cardiff **Wales** 18-9
1931 Swansea **Wales** 35-3	1981 Paris **France** 19-15
1947 Paris **Wales** 3-0	1982 Cardiff **Wales** 22-12
1948 Swansea **France** 11-3	1983 Paris **France** 16-9
1949 Paris **France** 5-3	1984 Cardiff **France** 21-16
1950 Cardiff **Wales** 21-0	1985 Paris **France** 14-3
1951 Paris **France** 8-3	1986 Cardiff **France** 23-15
1952 Swansea **Wales** 9-5	1987 Paris **France** 16-9
1953 Paris **Wales** 6-3	1988 Cardiff **France** 10-9
1954 Cardiff **Wales** 19-13	1989 Paris **France** 31-12
1955 Paris **Wales** 16-11	1990 Cardiff **France** 29-19
1956 Cardiff **Wales** 5-3	1991 Paris **France** 36-3
1957 Paris **Wales** 19-13	1991 Cardiff **France** 22-9
1958 Cardiff **France** 16-6	*Non-championship match*
1959 Paris **France** 11-3	1992 Cardiff **France** 12-9
1960 Cardiff **France** 16-8	1993 Paris **France** 26-10
1961 Paris **France** 8-6	1994 Cardiff **Wales** 24-15
1962 Cardiff **Wales** 3-0	

WALES v NEW ZEALAND

Played 15   Wales won 3, New Zealand won 12, Drawn 0

1905 Cardiff **Wales** 3-0	1972 Cardiff **New Zealand** 19-16
1924 Swansea **New Zealand** 19-0	1978 Cardiff **New Zealand** 13-12
1935 Cardiff **Wales** 13-12	1980 Cardiff **New Zealand** 23-3
1953 Cardiff **Wales** 13-8	1987 Brisbane *WC* **New Zealand** 49-6
1963 Cardiff **New Zealand** 6-0	1988 *1* Christchurch **New Zealand** 52-3
1967 Cardiff **New Zealand** 13-6	*2* Auckland **New Zealand** 54-9
1969 *1* Christchurch **New Zealand** 19-0	*New Zealand won series 2-0*
2 Auckland **New Zealand** 33-12	1989 Cardiff **New Zealand** 34-9
New Zealand won series 2-0	

WALES v SOUTH AFRICA

Played 7   Wales won 0, South Africa won 6, Drawn 1

1906 Swansea **South Africa** 11-0	1960 Cardiff **South Africa** 3-0
1912 Cardiff **South Africa** 3-0	1964 Durban **South Africa** 24-3
1931 Swansea **South Africa** 8-3	1970 Cardiff **Drawn** 6-6
1951 Cardiff **South Africa** 6-3	

WALES v AUSTRALIA
Played 16   Wales won 8, Australia won 8, Drawn 0

1908 Cardiff **Wales** 9-6	2 Sydney **Australia** 19-17
1927 Cardiff **Australia** 18-8	*Australia won series 2-0*
1947 Cardiff **Wales** 6-0	1981 Cardiff **Wales** 18-13
1958 Cardiff **Wales** 9-3	1984 Cardiff **Australia** 28-9
1966 Cardiff **Australia** 14-11	1987 Rotorua *WC* **Wales** 22-21
1969 Sydney **Wales** 19-16	1991 Brisbane **Australia** 63-6
1973 Cardiff **Wales** 24-0	1991 Cardiff *WC* **Australia** 38-3
1975 Cardiff **Wales** 28-3	1992 Cardiff **Australia** 23-6
1978 *1* Brisbane **Australia** 18-8	

WALES v NEW ZEALAND NATIVES
Played 1   Wales won 1

1888 Swansea **Wales** 1G 2T to 0

WALES v NEW ZEALAND ARMY
Played 1   New Zealand Army won 1

1919 Swansea **New Zealand Army** 6-3

WALES v ROMANIA
Played 2   Romania won 2

1983 Bucharest **Romania** 24-6	1988 Cardiff **Romania** 15-9

WALES v FIJI
Played 2   Wales won 2

1985 Cardiff **Wales** 40-3	1986 Suva **Wales** 22-15

WALES v TONGA
Played 2   Wales won 2

1986 Nuku'Alofa **Wales** 15-7	1987 Palmerston North *WC* **Wales** 29-16

WALES v WESTERN SAMOA
Played 3   Wales won 2, Western Samoa won 1

1986 Apia **Wales** 32-14	1991 Cardiff *WC* **Western Samoa** 16-13
1988 Cardiff **Wales** 28-6	

WALES v CANADA
Played 2   Wales won 1, Canada won 1

1987 Invercargill *WC* **Wales** 40-9	1993 Cardiff **Canada** 26-24

WALES v UNITED STATES
Played 1   Wales won 1

1987 Cardiff **Wales** 46-0

WALES v NAMIBIA
Played 3   Wales won 3

1990 *1* Windhoek **Wales** 18-9	1993 Windhoek **Wales** 38-23
2 Windhoek **Wales** 34-30	
Wales won series 2-0	

WALES v BARBARIANS
Played 1   Barbarians won 1

1990 Cardiff **Barbarians** 31-24

WALES v ARGENTINA
Played 1   Wales won 1

1991 Cardiff *WC* **Wales** 16-7

WALES v ZIMBABWE
Played 2   Wales won 2

1993 *1* Bulawayo **Wales** 35-14   2 Harare **Wales** 42-13
Wales won series 2-0

WALES v JAPAN
Played 1   Wales won 1

1993 Cardiff **Wales** 55-5

FRANCE v NEW ZEALAND
Played 28   France won 5, New Zealand won 23, Drawn 0

1906 Paris **New Zealand** 38-8
1925 Toulouse **New Zealand** 30-6
1954 Paris **France** 3-0
1961 *1* Auckland **New Zealand** 13-6
    2 Wellington **New Zealand** 5-3
    3 Christchurch **New Zealand** 32- 3
    New Zealand won series 3-0
1964 Paris **New Zealand** 12-3
1967 Paris **New Zealand** 21-15
1968 *1* Christchurch **New Zealand** 12-9
    2 Wellington **New Zealand** 9-3
    3 Auckland **New Zealand** 19-12
    New Zealand won series 3-0
1973 Paris **France** 13-6
1977 *1* Toulouse **France** 18-13
    2 Paris **New Zealand** 15-3
    Series drawn 1-1
1979 *1* Christchurch **New Zealand** 23-9
    2 Auckland **France** 24-19
    Series drawn 1-1

1981 *1* Toulouse **New Zealand** 13-9
    2 Paris **New Zealand** 18-6
    New Zealand won series 2-0
1984 *1* Christchurch **New Zealand** 10-9
    2 Auckland **New Zealand** 31-18
    New Zealand won series 2-0
1986 Christchurch **New Zealand** 18-9
1986 *1* Toulouse **New Zealand** 19-7
    2 Nantes **France** 16-3
    Series drawn 1-1
1987 Auckland *WC* **New Zealand** 29-9
1989 *1* Christchurch **New Zealand** 25-17
    2 Auckland **New Zealand** 34-20
    New Zealand won series 2-0
1990 *1* Nantes **New Zealand** 24-3
    2 Paris **New Zealand** 30-12
    New Zealand won series 2-0

FRANCE v SOUTH AFRICA
Played 23   France won 5, South Africa won 13, Drawn 5

1913 Bordeaux **South Africa** 38-5
1952 Paris **South Africa** 25-3
1958 *1* Cape Town **Drawn** 3-3
    2 Johannesburg **France** 9-5
    France won series 1-0, with 1 draw
1961 Paris **Drawn** 0-0
1964 Springs (SA) **France** 8-6
1967 *1* Durban **South Africa** 26-3
    2 Bloemfontein **South Africa** 16-3
    3 Johannesburg **France** 19-14
    4 Cape Town **Drawn** 6-6
    South Africa won series 2-1, with 1 draw
1968 *1* Bordeaux **South Africa** 12-9

    2 Paris **South Africa** 16-11
    South Africa won series 2-0
1971 *1* Bloemfontein **South Africa** 22-9
    2 Durban **Drawn** 8-8
    South Africa won series 1-0, with 1 draw
1974 *1* Toulouse **South Africa** 13-4
    2 Paris **South Africa** 10-8
    South Africa won series 2-0
1975 *1* Bloemfontein **South Africa** 38-25
    2 Pretoria **South Africa** 33-18
    South Africa won series 2-0
1980 Pretoria **South Africa** 37-15

1992 *1* Lyons **South Africa** 20-15
2 Paris **France** 29-16
Series drawn 1-1

1993 *1* Durban **Drawn** 20-20
2 Johannesburg **France** 18-17
France won series 1-0 with 1 draw

FRANCE v AUSTRALIA
Played 25   France won 13, Australia won 10, Drawn 2

1928 Paris **Australia** 11-8
1948 Paris **France** 13-6
1958 Paris **France** 19-0
1961 Sydney **France** 15-8
1967 Paris **France** 20-14
1968 Sydney **Australia** 11-10
1971 *1* Toulouse **Australia** 13-11
2 Paris **France** 18-9
Series drawn 1-1
1972 *1* Sydney **Drawn** 14-14
2 Brisbane **France** 16-15
France won series 1-0, with 1 draw
1976 *1* Bordeaux **France** 18-15
2 Paris **France** 34-6
France won series 2-0
1981 *1* Brisbane **Australia** 17-15

2 Sydney **Australia** 24-14
Australia won series 2-0
1983 *1* Clermont-Ferrand **Drawn** 15-15
2 Paris **France** 15-6
France won series 1-0, with 1 draw
1986 Sydney **Australia** 27-14
1987 Sydney *WC* **France** 30-24
1989 *1* Strasbourg **Australia** 32-15
2 Lille **France** 25-19
Series drawn 1-1
1990 *1* Sydney **Australia** 21-9
2 Brisbane **Australia** 48-31
3 Sydney **France** 28-19
Australia won series 2-1
1993 *1* Bordeaux **France** 16-13
2 Paris **Australia** 24-3
Series drawn 1-1

FRANCE v UNITED STATES
Played 5   France won 4, United States won 1

1920 Paris **France** 14-5
1924 Paris **United States** 17-3
1976 Chicago **France** 33-14

1991 *1* Denver **France** 41-9
2 Colorado Springs **France** 10-3★
★Abandoned after 43 mins
France won series 2-0

FRANCE v ROMANIA
Played 40 France won 30, Romania won 8, Drawn 2

1924 Paris **France** 59-3
1938 Bucharest **France** 11-8
1957 Bucharest **France** 18-15
1957 Bordeaux **France** 39-0
1960 Bucharest **Romania** 11-5
1961 Bayonne **Drawn** 5-5
1962 Bucharest **Romania** 3-0
1963 Toulouse **Drawn** 6-6
1964 Bucharest **France** 9-6
1965 Lyons **France** 8-3
1966 Bucharest **France** 9-3
1967 Nantes **France** 11-3
1968 Bucharest **Romania** 15-14
1969 Tarbes **France** 14-9
1970 Bucharest **France** 14-3
1971 Béziers **France** 31-12
1972 Constanza **France** 15-6
1973 Valence **France** 7-6
1974 Bucharest **Romania** 15-10
1975 Bordeaux **France** 36-12

1976 Bucharest **Romania** 15-12
1977 Clermont-Ferrand **France** 9-6
1978 Bucharest **France** 9-6
1979 Montauban **France** 30-12
1980 Bucharest **Romania** 15-0
1981 Narbonne **France** 17-9
1982 Bucharest **Romania** 13-9
1983 Toulouse **France** 26-15
1984 Bucharest **France** 18-3
1986 Lille **France** 25-13
1986 Bucharest **France** 20-3
1987 Wellington *WC* **France** 55-12
1987 Agen **France** 49-3
1988 Bucharest **France** 16-12
1990 Auch **Romania** 12-6
1991 Bucharest **France** 33-21
1991 Béziers *WC* **France** 30-3
1992 Le Havre **France** 25-6
1993 Bucharest **France** 37-20
1993 Brive **France** 51-0

FRANCE v NEW ZEALAND MAORIS
Played 1   New Zealand Maoris won 1

1926 Paris **New Zealand Maoris** 12-3

FRANCE v GERMANY
Played 15   France won 13, Germany won 2

1927 Paris **France** 30-5	1934 Hanover **France** 13-9
1927 Frankfurt **Germany** 17-16	1935 Paris **France** 18-3
1928 Hanover **France** 14-3	1936 *1* Berlin **France** 19-14
1929 Paris **France** 24-0	2 Hanover **France** 6-3
1930 Berlin **France** 31-0	*France won series 2-0*
1931 Paris **France** 34-0	1937 Paris **France** 27-6
1932 Frankfurt **France** 20-4	1938 Frankfurt **Germany** 3-0
1933 Paris **France** 38-17	1938 Bucharest **France** 8-5

FRANCE v ITALY
Played 17   France won 17

1937 Paris **France** 43-5	1960 Treviso **France** 26-0
1952 Milan **France** 17-8	1961 Chambéry **France** 17-0
1953 Lyons **France** 22-8	1962 Brescia **France** 6-3
1954 Rome **France** 39-12	1963 Grenoble **France** 14-12
1955 Grenoble **France** 24-0	1964 Parma **France** 12-3
1956 Padua **France** 16-3	1965 Pau **France** 21-0
1957 Agen **France** 38-6	1966 Naples **France** 21-0
1958 Naples **France** 11-3	1967 Toulon **France** 60-13
1959 Nantes **France** 22-0	

FRANCE v BRITISH XVs
Played 5   France won 2, British XVs won 3

1940 Paris **British XV** 36-3	1946 Paris **France** 10-0
1945 Paris **France** 21-9	1989 Paris **British XV** 29-27
1945 Richmond **British XV** 27-6	

FRANCE v NEW ZEALAND ARMY
Played 1   New Zealand Army won 1

1946 Paris **New Zealand Army** 14-9

FRANCE v ARGENTINA
Played 26   France won 21, Argentina won 4, Drawn 1

1949 *1* Buenos Aires **France** 5-0	2 Paris **France** 13-6
2 Buenos Aires **France** 12-3	*France won series 2-0*
France won series 2-0	1985 *1* Buenos Aires **Argentina** 24-16
1954 *1* Buenos Aires **France** 22-8	2 Buenos Aires **France** 23-15
2 Buenos Aires **France** 30-3	*Series drawn 1-1*
France won series 2-0	1986 *1* Buenos Aires **Argentina** 15-13
1960 *1* Buenos Aires **France** 37-3	2 Buenos Aires **France** 22-9
2 Buenos Aires **France** 12-3	*Series drawn 1-1*
3 Buenos Aires **France** 29-6	1988 *1* Buenos Aires **France** 18-15
France won series 3-0	2 Buenos Aires **Argentina** 18-6
1974 *1* Buenos Aires **France** 20-15	*Series drawn 1-1*
2 Buenos Aires **France** 31-27	1988 *1* Nantes **France** 29-9
France won series 2-0	2 Lille **France** 28-18
1975 *1* Lyons **France** 29-6	*France won series 2-0*
2 Paris **France** 36-21	1992 *1* Buenos Aires **France** 27-12
France won series 2-0	2 Buenos Aires **France** 33-9
1977 *1* Buenos Aires **France** 26-3	*France won series 2-0*
2 Buenos Aires **Drawn** 18-18	1992 Nantes **Argentina** 24-20
France won series 1-0, with 1 draw	
1982 *1* Toulouse **France** 25-12	

FRANCE v CZECHOSLOVAKIA
Played 2   France won 2

1956 Toulouse **France** 28-3   1968 Prague **France** 19-6

FRANCE v FIJI
Played 3   France won 3

1964 Paris **France** 21-3   1991 Grenoble *WC* **France** 33-9
1987 Auckland *WC* **France** 31-16

FRANCE v JAPAN
Played 1   France won 1

1973 Bordeaux **France** 30-18

FRANCE v ZIMBABWE
Played 1   France won 1

1987 Auckland *WC* **France** 70-12

FRANCE v CANADA
Played 1   France won 1

1991 Agen *WC* **France** 19-13

NEW ZEALAND v SOUTH AFRICA
Played 38   New Zealand won 16, South Africa won 20, Drawn 2

1921 *1* Dunedin **New Zealand** 13-5
    2 Auckland **South Africa** 9-5
    3 Wellington **Drawn** 0-0
    Series drawn 1-1, with 1 draw
1928 *1* Durban **South Africa** 17-0
    2 Johannesburg **New Zealand** 7-6
    3 Port Elizabeth **South Africa** 11-6
    4 Cape Town **New Zealand** 13-5
    Series drawn 2-2
1937 *1* Wellington **New Zealand** 13-7
    2 Christchurch **South Africa** 13-6
    3 Auckland **South Africa** 17-6
    South Africa won series 2-1
1949 *1* Cape Town **South Africa** 15-11
    2 Johannesburg **South Africa** 12-6
    3 Durban **South Africa** 9-3
    4 Port Elizabeth **South Africa** 11-8
    South Africa won series 4-0
1956 *1* Dunedin **New Zealand** 10-6
    2 Wellington **South Africa** 8-3
    3 Christchurch **New Zealand** 17-10
    4 Auckland **New Zealand** 11-5
    New Zealand won series 3-1
1960 *1* Johannesburg **South Africa** 13-0

2 Cape Town **New Zealand** 11-3
3 Bloemfontein **Drawn** 11-11
4 Port Elizabeth **Drawn** 8-3
South Africa won series 2-1, with 1 draw
1965 *1* Wellington **New Zealand** 6-3
    2 Dunedin **New Zealand** 13-0
    3 Christchurch **South Africa** 19-16
    4 Auckland **New Zealand** 20-3
    New Zealand won series 3-1
1970 *1* Pretoria **South Africa** 17-6
    2 Cape Town **New Zealand** 9-8
    3 Port Elizabeth **South Africa** 14-3
    4 Johannesburg **South Africa** 20-17
    South Africa won series 3-1
1976 *1* Durban **South Africa** 16-7
    2 Bloemfontein **New Zealand** 15-9
    3 Cape Town **South Africa** 15-10
    4 Johannesburg **South Africa** 15-14
    South Africa won series 3-1
1981 *1* Christchurch **New Zealand** 14-9
    2 Wellington **South Africa** 24-12
    3 Auckland **New Zealand** 25-22
    New Zealand won series 2-1
1992 Johannesburg **New Zealand** 27-24

NEW ZEALAND v AUSTRALIA
Played 97   New Zealand won 66, Australia won 26, Drawn 5

1903 Sydney **New Zealand** 22-3   1907 *1* Sydney **New Zealand** 26-6
1905 Dunedin **New Zealand** 14-3   *2* Brisbane **New Zealand** 14-5

3 Sydney **Drawn** 5-5
New Zealand won series 2-0, with 1 draw
1910 *1* Sydney **New Zealand** 6-0
2 Sydney **Australia** 11-0
3 Sydney **New Zealand** 28-13
New Zealand won series 2-1
1913 *1* Wellington **New Zealand** 30-5
2 Dunedin **New Zealand** 25-13
3 Christchurch **Australia** 16-5
New Zealand won series 2-1
1914 *1* Sydney **New Zealand** 5-0
2 Brisbane **New Zealand** 17-0
3 Sydney **New Zealand** 22-7
New Zealand won series 3-0
1929 *1* Sydney **Australia** 9-8
2 Brisbane **Australia** 17-9
3 Sydney **Australia** 15-13
Australia won series 3-0
1931 Auckland **New Zealand** 20-13
1932 *1* Sydney **Australia** 22-17
2 Brisbane **New Zealand** 21-3
3 Sydney **New Zealand** 21-13
New Zealand won series 2-1
1934 *1* Sydney **Australia** 25-11
2 Sydney **Drawn** 3-3
Australia won series 1-0, with 1 draw
1936 *1* Wellington **New Zealand** 11-6
2 Dunedin **New Zealand** 38-13
New Zealand won series 2-0
1938 *1* Sydney **New Zealand** 24-9
2 Brisbane **New Zealand** 20-14
3 Sydney **New Zealand** 14-6
New Zealand won series 3-0
1946 *1* Dunedin **New Zealand** 31-8
2 Auckland **New Zealand** 14-10
New Zealand won series 2-0
1947 *1* Brisbane **New Zealand** 13-5
2 Sydney **New Zealand** 27-14
New Zealand won series 2-0
1949 *1* Wellington **Australia** 11-6
2 Auckland **Australia** 16-9
Australia won series 2-0
1951 *1* Sydney **New Zealand** 8-0
2 Sydney **New Zealand** 17-11
3 Brisbane **New Zealand** 16-6
New Zealand won series 3-0
1952 *1* Christchurch **Australia** 14-9
2 Wellington **New Zealand** 15-8
Series drawn 1-1
1955 *1* Wellington **New Zealand** 16-8
2 Dunedin **New Zealand** 8-0
3 Auckland **Australia** 8-3
New Zealand won series 2-1
1957 *1* Sydney **New Zealand** 25-11
2 Brisbane **New Zealand** 22-9
New Zealand won series 2-0
1958 *1* Wellington **New Zealand** 25-3
2 Christchurch **Australia** 6-3
3 Auckland **New Zealand** 17-8
New Zealand won series 2-1
1962 *1* Brisbane **New Zealand** 20-6
2 Sydney **New Zealand** 14-5
New Zealand won series 2-0

1962 *1* Wellington **Drawn** 9-9
2 Dunedin **New Zealand** 3-0
3 Auckland **New Zealand** 16-8
New Zealand won series 2-0, with 1 draw
1964 *1* Dunedin **New Zealand** 14-9
2 Christchurch **New Zealand** 18- 3
3 Wellington **Australia** 20-5
New Zealand won series 2-1
1967 Wellington **New Zealand** 29-9
1968 *1* Sydney **New Zealand** 27-11
2 Brisbane **New Zealand** 19-18
New Zealand won series 2-0
1972 *1* Wellington **New Zealand** 29-6
2 Christchurch **New Zealand** 30-17
3 Auckland **New Zealand** 38-3
New Zealand won series 3-0
1974 *1* Sydney **New Zealand** 11-6
2 Brisbane **Drawn** 16-16
3 Sydney **New Zealand** 16-6
New Zealand won series 2-0, with 1 draw
1978 *1* Wellington **New Zealand** 13-12
2 Christchurch **New Zealand** 22-6
3 Auckland **Australia** 30-16
New Zealand won series 2-1
1979 Sydney **Australia** 12-6
1980 *1* Sydney **Australia** 13-9
2 Brisbane **New Zealand** 12-9
3 Sydney **Australia** 26-10
Australia won series 2-1
1982 *1* Christchurch **New Zealand** 23-16
2 Wellington **Australia** 19-16
3 Auckland **New Zealand** 33-18
New Zealand won series 2-1
1983 Sydney **New Zealand** 18-8
1984 *1* Sydney **Australia** 16-9
2 Brisbane **New Zealand** 19-15
3 Sydney **New Zealand** 25-24
New Zealand won series 2-1
1985 Auckland **New Zealand** 10-9
1986 *1* Wellington **Australia** 13-12
2 Dunedin **New Zealand** 13-12
3 Auckland **Australia** 22-9
Australia won series 2-1
1987 Sydney **New Zealand** 30-16
1988 *1* Sydney **New Zealand** 32-7
2 Brisbane **Drawn** 19-19
3 Sydney **New Zealand** 30-9
New Zealand won series 2-0, with 1 draw
1989 Auckland **New Zealand** 24-12
1990 *1* Christchurch **New Zealand** 21-6
2 Auckland **New Zealand** 27-17
3 Wellington **Australia** 21-9
New Zealand won series 2-1
1991 *1* Sydney **Australia** 21-12
2 Auckland **New Zealand** 6-3
1991 Dublin *WC* **Australia** 16-6
1992 *1* Sydney **Australia** 16-15
2 Brisbane **Australia** 19-17
3 Sydney **New Zealand** 26-23
Australia won series 2-1
1993 Dunedin **New Zealand** 25-10

109

NEW ZEALAND v UNITED STATES
Played 2   New Zealand won 2

1913 Berkeley **New Zealand** 51-3	1991 **New Zealand** 46-6

NEW ZEALAND v ROMANIA
Played 1   New Zealand won 1

1981 Bucharest **New Zealand** 14-6

NEW ZEALAND v ARGENTINA
Played 7   New Zealand won 6, Drawn 1

1985 *1* Buenos Aires **New Zealand** 33-20	2 Wellington **New Zealand** 49-12
2 Buenos Aires **Drawn** 21-21	*New Zealand won series 2-0*
New Zealand won series 1-0, with 1 draw	1991 *1* Buenos Aires **New Zealand** 28-14
1987 Wellington *WC* **New Zealand** 46-15	2 Buenos Aires **New Zealand** 36-6
	New Zealand won series 2-0
1989 *1* Dunedin **New Zealand** 60-9	

NEW ZEALAND v ITALY
Played 2   New Zealand won 2

1987 Auckland *WC* **New Zealand** 70-6	1991 Leicester *WC* **New Zealand** 31-21

NEW ZEALAND v FIJI
Played 1   New Zealand won 1

1987 Christchurch *WC* **New Zealand** 74-13

NEW ZEALAND v CANADA
Played 1   New Zealand won 1

1991 Lille *WC* **New Zealand** 29-13

NEW ZEALAND v WORLD XVs
Played 3   New Zealand won 2, World XV won 1

1992 *1* Christchurch **World XV** 28-14	*3* Auckland **New Zealand** 26-15
2 Wellington **New Zealand** 54-26	*New Zealand won series 2-1*

NEW ZEALAND v WESTERN SAMOA
Played 1   New Zealand won 1

1993 Auckland **New Zealand** 35-13

SOUTH AFRICA v AUSTRALIA
Played 32   South Africa won 22, Australia won 10, Drawn 0

1933 *1* Cape Town **South Africa** 17-3	1956 *1* Sydney **South Africa** 9-0
2 Durban **Australia** 21-6	2 Brisbane **South Africa** 9-0
3 Johannesburg **South Africa** 12-3	*South Africa won series 2-0*
4 Port Elizabeth **South Africa** 11-0	1961 *1* Johannesburg **South Africa** 28-3
5 Bloemfontein **Australia** 15-4	2 Port Elizabeth **South Africa** 23-11
South Africa won series 3-2	*South Africa won series 2-0*
1937 *1* Sydney **South Africa** 9-5	1963 *1* Pretoria **South Africa** 14-3
2 Sydney **South Africa** 26-17	2 Cape Town **Australia** 9-5
South Africa won series 2-0	3 Johannesburg **Australia** 11-9
1953 *1* Johannesburg **South Africa** 25-3	4 Port Elizabeth **South Africa** 22-6
2 Cape Town **Australia** 18-14	*Series drawn 2-2*
3 Durban **South Africa** 18-8	1965 *1* Sydney **Australia** 18-11
4 Port Elizabeth **South Africa** 22-9	2 Brisbane **Australia** 12-8
South Africa won series 3-1	*Australia won series 2-0*

1969 *1* Johannesburg **South Africa** 30-11
 2 Durban **South Africa** 16-9
 3 Cape Town **South Africa** 11-3
 4 Bloemfontein **South Africa** 19-8
 South Africa won series 4-0
1971 *1* Sydney **South Africa** 19-11
 2 Brisbane **South Africa** 14-6

3 Sydney **South Africa** 18-6
South Africa won series 3-0
1992 Cape Town **Australia** 26-3
1993 *1* Sydney **South Africa** 19-12
 2 Brisbane **Australia** 28-20
 3 Sydney **Australia** 19-12
Australia won series 2-1

SOUTH AFRICA v WORLD XVs
Played 3 South Africa won 3

1977 Pretoria **South Africa** 45-24
1989 *1* Cape Town **South Africa** 20-19

2 Johannesburg **South Africa** 22-16
South Africa won series 2-0

SOUTH AFRICA v SOUTH AMERICA
Played 8 South Africa won 7, South America won 1

1980 *1* Johannesburg **South Africa** 24-9
 2 Durban **South Africa** 18-9
 South Africa won series 2-0
1980 *1* Montevideo **South Africa** 22-13
 2 Santiago **South Africa** 30-16
 South Africa won series 2-0

1982 *1* Pretoria **South Africa** 50-18
 2 Bloemfontein **South America** 21-12
 Series drawn 1-1
1984 *1* Pretoria **South Africa** 32-15
 2 Cape Town **South Africa** 22-13
 South Africa won series 2-0

SOUTH AFRICA v UNITED STATES
Played 1 South Africa won 1

1981 Glenville **South Africa** 38-7

SOUTH AFRICA v NEW ZEALAND CAVALIERS
Played 4 South Africa won 3, New Zealand Cavaliers won 1

1986 *1* Cape Town **South Africa** 21-15
 2 Durban **New Zealand Cavaliers**
 19-18

3 Pretoria **South Africa** 33-18
4 Johannesburg **South Africa** 24-10
South Africa won series 3-1

SOUTH AFRICA v ARGENTINA
Played 2 South Africa won 2

1993 *1* Buenos Aires **South Africa** 29-26

2 Buenos Aires **South Africa** 52-23
South Africa won series 2-0

AUSTRALIA v UNITED STATES
Played 5 Australia won 5

1912 Berkeley **Australia** 12-8
1976 Los Angeles **Australia** 24-12
1983 Sydney **Australia** 49-3

1987 Brisbane *WC* **Australia** 47-12
1990 Brisbane **Australia** 67-9

AUSTRALIA v NEW ZEALAND MAORIS
Played 10 Australia won 4, New Zealand Maoris won 4, Drawn 2

1928 Wellington **New Zealand Maoris**
 9-8
1931 Palmerston North **Australia** 14-3
1936 Palmerston North **Australia** 31-6
1946 Hamilton **New Zealand Maoris** 20-0
1949 *1* Sydney **New Zealand Maoris**
 12-3
 2 Brisbane **Drawn** 8-8

3 Sydney **Australia** 18-3
Series drawn 1-1, with 1 draw
1958 *1* Brisbane **Australia** 15-14
 2 Sydney **Drawn** 3-3
 3 Melbourne **New Zealand Maoris**
 13-6
Series drawn 1-1, with 1 draw

AUSTRALIA v FIJI
Played 15   Australia won 12, Fiji won 2, Drawn 1

1952 *1* Sydney **Australia** 15-9
    2 Sydney **Fiji** 17-15
    Series drawn 1-1
1954 *1* Brisbane **Australia** 22-19
    2 Sydney **Fiji** 18-16
    Series drawn 1-1
1961 *1* Brisbane **Australia** 24-6
    2 Sydney **Australia** 20-14
    3 Melbourne **Drawn** 3-3
    Australia won series 2-0, with 1 draw

1972 Suva **Australia** 21-19
1976 *1* Sydney **Australia** 22-6
    2 Brisbane **Australia** 21-9
    3 Sydney **Australia** 27-17
    Australia won series 3-0
1980 Suva **Australia** 22-9
1984 Suva **Australia** 16-3
1985 *1* Brisbane **Australia** 52-28
    2 Sydney **Australia** 31-9
    Australia won series 2-0

AUSTRALIA v TONGA
Played 3   Australia won 2, Tonga won 1

1973 *1* Sydney **Australia** 30-12
    2 Brisbane **Tonga** 16-11
    Series drawn 1-1

1993 Brisbane **Australia** 52-14

AUSTRALIA v JAPAN
Played 3   Australia won 3

1975 *1* Sydney **Australia** 37-7
    2 Brisbane **Australia** 50-25
    Australia won series 2-0

1987 Sydney *WC* **Australia** 42-23

AUSTRALIA v ARGENTINA
Played 9   Australia won 5, Argentina won 3, Drawn 1

1979 *1* Buenos Aires **Argentina** 24-13
    2 Buenos Aires **Australia** 17-12
    Series drawn 1-1
1983 *1* Brisbane **Argentina** 18-3
    2 Sydney **Australia** 29-13
    Series drawn 1-1
1986 *1* Brisbane **Australia** 39-19

    2 Sydney **Australia** 26-0
    Australia won series 2-0
1987 *1* Buenos Aires **Drawn** 19-19
    2 Buenos Aires **Argentina** 27-19
    Argentina won series 1-0, with 1 draw
1991 Llanelli *WC* **Australia** 32-19

AUSTRALIA v WESTERN SAMOA
Played 1   Australia won 1

1991 Pontypool *WC* **Australia** 9-3

AUSTRALIA v ITALY
Played 3   Australia won 3

1983 Rovigo **Australia** 29-7
1986 Brisbane **Australia** 39-18

1988 Rome **Australia** 55-6

AUSTRALIA v CANADA
Played 3   Australia won 3

1985 *1* Sydney **Australia** 59-3
    2 Brisbane **Australia** 43-15
    Australia won series 2-0

1993 Calgary **Australia** 43-16

AUSTRALIA v KOREA
Played 1   Australia won 1

1987 Brisbane **Australia** 65-18

WORLD CUP WINNERS
New Zealand once: 1987
Australia once: 1991

GRAND SLAM WINNERS
England 10 times: 1913, 1914, 1921, 1923, 1924, 1928, 1957, 1980, 1991, 1992.
Wales 8 times: 1908, 1909, 1911, 1950, 1952, 1971, 1976, 1978.
France 4 times: 1968, 1977, 1981, 1987. Scotland 3 times: 1925, 1984, 1990.
Ireland once: 1948.

TRIPLE CROWN WINNERS
Wales 17 times: 1893, 1900, 1902, 1905, 1908, 1909, 1911, 1950, 1952, 1965, 1969, 1971, 1976, 1977, 1978, 1979, 1988. England 17 times: 1883, 1884, 1892, 1913, 1914, 1921, 1923, 1924, 1928, 1934, 1937, 1954, 1957, 1960, 1980, 1991, 1992. Scotland 10 times: 1891, 1895, 1901, 1903, 1907, 1925, 1933, 1938, 1984, 1990. Ireland 6 times: 1894, 1899, 1948, 1949, 1982, 1985.

INTERNATIONAL CHAMPIONSHIP WINNERS

Year	Winner	Year	Winner	Year	Winner	Year	Winner
1883	England	1911	Wales	1939	{ England / Wales / Ireland	1969	Wales
1884	England	1912	{ England / Ireland			1970	{ France / Wales
1885*	—			1947	{ Wales / England	1971	Wales
1886	{ England / Scotland	1913	England			1972*	—
		1914	England	1948	Ireland	1973	Quintuple tie
1887	Scotland			1949	Ireland		
1888*	—	1920	{ England / Scotland / Wales	1950	Wales	1974	Ireland
1889*	—			1951	England	1975	Wales
1890	{ England / Scotland	1921	England	1952	Wales	1976	Wales
1891	Scotland	1922	Wales	1953	England	1977	France
1892	England	1923	England	1954	{ England / France / Wales	1978	Wales
1893	Wales	1924	England			1979	Wales
1894	Ireland	1925	Scotland	1955	{ France / Wales	1980	England
1895	Scotland	1926	{ Scotland / Ireland			1981	France
1896	Ireland	1927	{ Scotland / Ireland	1956	Wales	1982	Ireland
1897*	—			1957	England	1983	{ France / Ireland
1898*	—	1928	England	1958	England		
1899	Ireland	1929	Scotland	1959	France	1984	Scotland
1900	Wales	1930	England	1960	{ France / England	1985	Ireland
1901	Scotland	1931	Wales	1961	France	1986	{ France / Scotland
1902	Wales	1932	{ England / Wales / Ireland	1962	France		
1903	Scotland			1963	England	1987	France
1904	Scotland	1933	Scotland	1964	{ Scotland / Wales	1988	{ Wales / France
1905	Wales	1934	England				
1906	{ Ireland / Wales	1935	Ireland	1965	Wales	1989	France
1907	Scotland	1936	Wales	1966	Wales	1990	Scotland
1908	Wales	1937	England	1967	France	1991	England
1909	Wales	1938	Scotland	1968	France	1992	England
1910	England					1993	France
						1994**	Wales

*Matches not completed, for various reasons
**Indicates winners of the Five Nations Trophy (introduced 1993) on points difference.

Wales have won the title outright most times, 22; England have won it 20 times, Scotland 13, Ireland 10, and France 10.

A INTERNATIONALS 1993-94

18 December 1993, Rovigo
Italy 18 (6PG)   Scotland A 15 (5PG)

Italy: P Vaccari; R Crotti, M Bonomi, G Filizzola, M Ravazzola; D Dominguez, U Castellato (*capt*); Massimo Cuttitta, C Orlandi, F Properzi-Curti, G Croci, M Giacheri, A Sagorlon, D Beretta, C Checchainato
Scorer *Penalty Goals:* Dominguez (6)
Scotland A: M Dods (Gala); K R Milligan (Stewart's-Melville FP), S A Nichol (Selkirk), I C Jardine (Stirling County), K M Logan (Stirling County); D S Wyllie (Stewart's-Melville FP), B W Redpath (Melrose); A V Sharp (Bristol), K D McKenzie (Stirling County) (*capt*), P H Wright (Boroughmuir), P Walton (Northampton), D S Munro (Glasgow High/Kelvinside), A Macdonald (Heriot's FP), D McIntosh (Pontypridd), C D Hogg (Melrose)
Scorer *Penalty Goals:* Dods (5)
Referee D Roelands (Belgium)

28 December 1993, Millbrae
Scotland A 24 (3G 1PG)   Ireland A 9 (3PG)

Scotland A: K M Logan (Stirling County); K R Milligan (Stewart's-Melville FP), S A Nichol (Selkirk), I C Jardine (Stirling County), D A Stark (Boroughmuir); G P J Townsend (Gala), A D Nicol (Dundee HSFP); A V Sharp (Bristol), K D McKenzie (Stirling County) (*capt*), P H Wright (Boroughmuir), D S Munro (Glasgow High/Kelvinside), G W Weir (Melrose), P Walton (Northampton), I R Morrison (London Scottish), R I Wainwright (Edinburgh Acads)
Scorers *Tries:* Morrison, Wainwright, Munro   *Conversions:* Townsend (3)
Penalty Goal: Townsend
Ireland A: C Clarke (Terenure Coll); S P Geoghegan (London Irish), D Dooley (London Irish), M C McCall (Bangor), N Woods (Blackrock Coll); A McGowan (Blackrock Coll), N Hogan (Terenure Coll) (*capt*); H Hurley (Old Wesley), K Wood (Garryowen), P M Clohessy (Young Munster), D Tweed (Ballymena), B J Rigney (Greystones), E Halvey (Shannon), P J Lawlor (Bective Rangers), L Toland (Old Crescent)
Scorer *Penalty Goals:* McGowan (3)
Referee D R Davies (Wales)

4 February 1994, Donnybrook
Ireland A 10 (1G 1PG)   Wales A 20 (1G 1PG 2T)

Ireland A: P Murray (Shannon); T Howe (Dungannon), B Walsh (Cork Const), M Field (Malone), N Woods (Blackrock Coll); P Burke (London Irish), N Hogan (Terenure Coll); P Soden (Cork Const), J McDonald (Malone) (*capt*), P Millar (Ballymena), J Etheridge (Blackrock Coll), D Tweed (Ballymena), E Halvey (Shannon), K McKee (Instonians), R Wilson (Instonians)
Scorers *Try:* Woods   *Conversion:* Burke   *Penalty Goal:* Burke
Wales A: I Jones (Llanelli); D Manley (Pontypridd), S Lewis (Pontypridd), M Wintle (Llanelli), G Wilkins (Bridgend); A Williams (Swansea), P John (Pontypridd) (*capt*); I Buckett (Swansea), B Williams (Neath), L Mustoe (Cardiff), P Arnold (Swansea), D Jones (Cardiff), A Gibbs (Newbridge), L Jones (Llanelli), H Taylor (Cardiff)
Scorers *Tries:* Manley, A Williams, John   *Conversion:* A Williams
Penalty Goals: A Williams
Referee B Campsall (England)

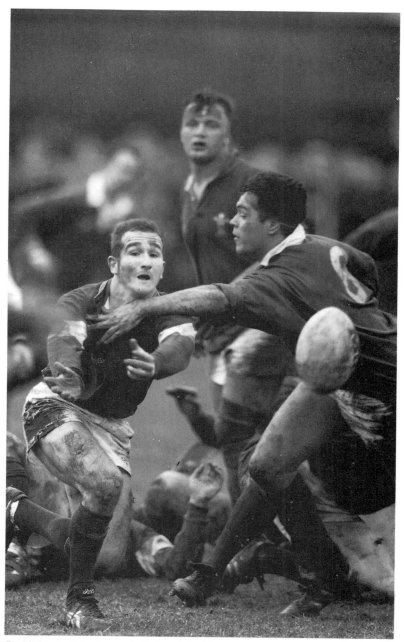

Paul John, the Wales A scrum-half, clears the ball despite the efforts of Roger Wilson of Ireland A.

5 February 1994, Piacenza
Italy A 9 (3PG)   England A 15 (1G 1PG 1T)

Italy A: S Pertile; R Crotti, N Aldrovanti, G Filizzola, M Gerosa; S Brolis, I Francescato (*capt*); M Dalsie, M Trevosiol, F Properzi, D Scaglia, D Sesenna, M Capuzzoni, G Cicino, D Arancio
Scorer *Penalty Goals:* Filizzola (3)
England A: P Hull (Bristol & RAF); A Adebayo (Bath), D P Hopley (Wasps), S Potter (Leicester), N D Beal (Northampton); A P Challinor (Harlequins), M J S Dawson (Northampton); C J Clark (Oxford U & Bath), K Dunn (Wasps), A R Mullins (Harlequins), N C Redman (Bath), A G Blackmore (Bristol), C Sheasby (Harlequins), D Ryan (Wasps) (*capt*), R H J Jenkins (London Irish) *Replacement* D Sims (Gloucester) for Blackmore (55 mins)
Scorers *Tries:* Adebayo, Sheasby   *Conversion:* Challinor   *Penalty Goal:* Challinor
Referee I Rogers (South Africa)

18 February 1994, Richmond
England A 29 (1G 3PG 1DG 2T)   Ireland A 14 (2PG 1DG 1T)

England A: P Hull (Bristol & RAF); A Adebayo (Bath), D P Hopley (Wasps), S Potter (Leicester), N D Beal (Northampton); A P Challinor (Harlequins), M J S Dawson (Northampton); C J Clark (Oxford U & Bath), K Dunn (Wasps), J Mallett (Bath), A Blackmore (Bristol), N C Redman (Bath), A Diprose (Saracens), D Ryan (Wasps) (*capt*), R H J Jenkins (London Irish)
Scorers *Tries:* Diprose, Ryan, Dawson   *Conversion:* Challinor
Penalty Goals: Challinor (3)   *Dropped Goal:* Challinor
Ireland A: J E Staples (London Irish); T Howe (Dungannon), B Walsh (Cork Const), M C McCall (Bangor), N Woods (Blackrock Coll); D Humphreys (Queen's U, Belfast), A C Rolland (Blackrock Coll); P Soden (Cork Const), J McDonald (Malone) (*capt*), P Millar (Ballymena), J Etheridge (Blackrock Coll), D Tweed (Ballymena), P Hogan (Garryowen), R Wilson (Instonians), K McKee (Instonians) *Replacement* V Costello (St Mary's Coll, Dublin) for Tweed (74 mins)
Scorers *Try:* McKee   *Penalty Goals:* Humphreys (2)   *Dropped Goal:* Humphreys
Referee D Gillet (France) *Replaced by* D Sainsbury (London) (15 mins)

20 February 1994, Rennes
France A 9 (3PG)   Scotland A 12 (3PG 1DG)

France A: L Labit (Castres); L Leflamand (Lyon), C Coeurveille (Biarritz), F Velo (Grenoble), P Fabre (Toulouse); C Deylaud (Toulouse), G Accoceberry (Bègles) (*capt*); L Benezech (Racing Club de France), L Landreau (Grenoble), L Seigne (Merignac), F Pelous (Graulhet), T Bourdet (Perpignan), G Pages (Castres), C Moni (Nice), O Brouzet (Grenoble)
Scorer *Penalty Goals:* Labit (3)
Scotland A: M Dods (Gala); K R Milligan (Stewart's-Melville FP), R Shepherd (Edinburgh Acads), I C Jardine (Stirling County), D A Stark (Boroughmuir); C M Chalmers (Melrose), B W Redpath (Melrose); P H Wright (Boroughmuir), K D McKenzie (Stirling County) (*capt*), D Herrington (Dundee HSFP), N G B Edwards (Northampton), S Campbell (Dundee HSFP), D McIvor (Edinburgh Acads), S Reid (Boroughmuir), C Hogg (Melrose)
Scorers *Penalty Goals:* Dods (3)   *Dropped Goal:* Chalmers
Referee S Piercy (England)

5 March 1994, Stade Jean Bouin, Paris
France A 20 (3PG 2DG 1T)   England A 8 (1PG 1T)

France A: L Labit (Castres); L Leflamand (Lyon), F Velo (Grenoble), Y Delaigue (Toulon), S Viars (Brive); G Merceron (Toulon), A Macabiau (Perpignan) (*capt*); E Menieu (Clermont-Ferrand), M de Rougemont (Toulon), S Graou (Auch), F Pelous (Graulhet), O Brouzet (Grenoble), M Lievremont (Perpignan), C Moni (Nice), X Blond (Racing Club de France)
Scorers *Try:* Velo   *Penalty Goals:* Labit (3)   *Dropped Goals:* Merceron, Macabiau
England A: J E B Callard (Bath); T Underwood (Leicester), D P Hopley (Wasps), S Potter (Leicester), N D Beal (Northampton); A P Challinor (Harlequins), S M Bates (Wasps) (*capt*); G Holmes (Wasps), K Dunn (Wasps), J Mallett (Bath), M C Bayfield (Northampton), A G Blackmore (Bristol), M J Greenwood (Wasps), A Diprose (Saracens), N A Back (Leicester) *Replacements* L Dallaglio (Wasps) for Bayfield (56 mins); P Hull (Bristol & RAF) for Potter (60 mins); D Garforth (Leicester) for Holmes (65 mins)
Scorers *Try:* Back   *Penalty Goal:* Callard
Referee D Leslie (Scotland)

18 March 1994, Cardiff
Wales A 21 (3G)   France A 8 (1PG 1T)

Wales A: I Jones (Llanelli); D Manley (Pontypridd), N Boobyer (Llanelli), S Lewis (Pontypridd), G Wilkins (Bridgend); M McCarthy (Neath), P John (Pontypridd) (*capt*); I Buckett (Swansea), B Williams (Neath), L Mustoe (Cardiff), P Arnold (Swansea), D Jones (Cardiff), H Taylor (Cardiff), S Williams (Neath), L Jones (Llanelli) *Replacements* L Evans (Treorchy) for I Jones (6 mins); G Jones (Llanelli) for L Jones (79 mins)
Scorers *Tries:* Wilkins, L Jones, Evans   *Conversions:* Evans (3)
France A: L Labit (Castres); S Viars (Brive), H Couffignol (Colomiers), F Velo (Grenoble), L Leflamand (Lyon); V Etcheto (Bègles), G Accoceberry (Bègles) (*capt*); E Menieu (Clermont-Ferrand), C Urios (Castres), S Graou (Auch), H Moirin (Toulouse), T Devergie (Grenoble), L Loppy (Toulon), C Moni (Nice), S Despagne (Montauban) *Replacement* M de Rougemont (Toulon) for Moni (50 mins)
Scorers *Try:* Leflamand   *Penalty Goal:* Labit
Referee C Muir (Scotland)

OTHER INTERNATIONAL MATCHES 1993-94

19 June, Twin Elm Park, Winnipeg
CANADA 20 (1G 1PG 2T)   USA 9 (3PG)

CANADA: D S Stewart (UBC Old Boys, Vancouver); J Loveday (Calgary Irish), S Gray (Vancouver Kats), G L Rees (Oak Bay Castaways, Victoria), D Lougheed (Toronto Welsh); J Graf (UBC Old Boys, Vancouver), C J C Tynan (Meralomas, Vancouver); K Wirachowski (Velox Vahallians, BC), K Svoboda (Ajax Wanderers, Ontario) (capt), D Jackart (UBC Old Boys, Vancouver), J Knauer (Meralomas, Vancouver), A J Charron (Ottawa Irish), I Gordon (James Bay, Victoria Island), C McKenzie (UBC Old Boys, Vancouver), B Breen (Meralomas, Vancouver) *Replacements* P Szabo (Pocomo) for Jackart; C Whittaker (James Bay, Victoria) for Gordon
Scorers *Tries:* Jackart (2), Loveday   *Conversion:* Rees   *Penalty Goal:* Rees
USA: M Sika (BYU-Hawaii); G Hein (Old Blues), W Chai (Old Blues), B Geraghty (Life), C Schlereth (St Louis Bombers); C O'Brien (Old Blues), A Bachelet (California RC); T Petersen (Old Blues), T Billups (Old Blues), D James (Old Blues), K Swords (Beacon Hill) (capt), A Ridnell (Old Puget Sound), D Gonzales (OMBAC), D Steinbauer (Sacramento), C Campbell (Old Puget Sound) *Replacement* J Schraml (Milwaukee) for Billups
Scorer *Penalty Goals:* O'Brien (3)
Referee N Saito (Japan)

17 July, Carisbrook, Dunedin   BLEDISLOE CUP
NEW ZEALAND 25 (5PG 2T)   AUSTRALIA 10 (1G 1PG)

NEW ZEALAND: J K R Timu (Otago); J J Kirwan (Auckland), F E Bunce (North Harbour), L Stensness (Auckland), V L Tuigamala (Auckland); G J Fox (Auckland), J P Preston (Wellington); C E Dowd (Auckland), S B T Fitzpatrick (Auckland) (capt), O M Brown (Auckland), M S B Cooksley (Counties), R M Brooke (Auckland), J W Joseph (Otago), A R B Pene (Otago), M N Jones (Auckland)
Scorers *Tries:* Fitzpatrick, Bunce   *Penalty Goals:* Fox (5)
AUSTRALIA: T P Kelaher (NSW); D I Campese (NSW), J S Little (Queensland), T J Horan (Queensland), P V Carozza (Queensland); P Howard (Queensland), N C Farr-Jones (NSW); A J Daly (NSW), P N Kearns (NSW) (capt), E J A McKenzie (NSW), R J McCall (Queensland), G Morgan (Queensland), T Coker (Queensland), B T Gavin (NSW), D J Wilson (Queensland) *Replacement* A G Herbert (Queensland) for Carozza (57 mins)
Scorers *Try:* Horan   *Conversion:* Kelaher   *Penalty Goal:* Kelaher
Referee W D Bevan (Wales)

17 October, Brive
FRANCE 51 (6G 3PG)   ROMANIA 0

FRANCE: J-L Sadourny (Colomiers); P Bernat-Salles (Pau), P Sella (Agen), T Lacroix (Dax), D Berty (Toulouse); A Penaud (Brive), A Hueber (Toulon); L Armary (Lourdes), J-M Gonzalez (Bayonne), S Graou (Auch), O Merle (Grenoble), O Roumat (Dax) (capt), P Benetton (Agen), M Cecillon (Bourgoin), L Loppy (Toulon) *Replacements* L Seigne (Merignac) for Armary (56 mins); O Campan (Agen) for Sella (56 mins)
Scorers *Tries:* Bernat-Salles (3), Sella, Merle, Loppy   *Conversions:* Lacroix (6)
Penalty Goals: Lacroix (3)

ROMANIA: G Solomie (Dinamo Bucharest); A Mitocaru (U Timisoara), M Nedelcu (Steaua Bucharest), N Fulina (Farul Constanta), M Dumitru (Metro-Rapid Bucharest); F Ion (Dinamo Bucharest), M Foca (Farul Constanta); G Leonte (Vienne, France), G Ion (Dinamo Bucharest), G Vlad (Grivita Rosie), H Dumitras (Pau, France) *(capt)*, C Cojocariu (Bayonne, France), I Seceleanu (Sibiu), T Brinza (Cluj), G Dinu (ASPTT, Paris) *Replacements* A Girbu (Farul Constanta) for Seceleanu (48 mins); N Marin (Farul Constanta) for Dinu (60 mins)
Referee J M Fleming (Scotland)

10 November, Cardiff Arms Park
WALES 24 (8PG) CANADA 26 (2G 4PG)

WALES: A Clement (Swansea); I C Evans (Llanelli) *(capt)*, I S Gibbs (Swansea), N R Jenkins (Pontypridd), W T Proctor (Llanelli); A Davies (Cardiff), R H St J B Moon (Llanelli); M Griffiths (Cardiff), G R Jenkins (Swansea), J D Davies (Neath), A H Copsey (Llanelli), G O Llewellyn (Neath), L S Quinnell (Llanelli), E W Lewis (Llanelli), R L Jones (Llanelli)
Scorer *Penalty Goals:* Jenkins (8)
CANADA: M Williams (Meralomas, Vancouver); R Toews (Meralomas, Vancouver), S Gray (Vancouver Kats), I Stuart (Vancouver Rowing Club), D S Stewart (UBC Old Boys, Vancouver); G L Rees (Oxford U), C J C Tynan (Cambridge U); P Szabo (Pocomo), I Kennedy (Meralomas, Vancouver), D Jackart (UBC Old Boys, Vancouver), J Knauer (Meralomas, Vancouver), A J Charron (Ottawa Irish), I Gordon (James Bay, Victoria Island), C McKenzie (UBC Old Boys, Vancouver), J Hutchinson (York Yeomen, Toronto) *Replacement* I Mackay (Vancouver Kats) for Tynan (43 mins)
Scorers *Tries:* Stuart, Charron *Conversions:* Rees (2) *Penalty Goals:* Rees (4)
Referee O E Doyle (Ireland)

13 November, Lansdowne Road, Dublin
IRELAND 25 (1G 6PG) ROMANIA 3 (1PG)

IRELAND: C M O'Shea (Lansdowne); R M Wallace (Garryowen), V J G Cunningham (St Mary's Coll), P P A Danaher (Garryowen), S P Geoghegan (London Irish); E P Elwood (Lansdowne), M T Bradley (Cork Const) *(capt)*; N J Popplewell (Greystones), T J Kingston (Dolphin), G F Halpin (London Irish), P S Johns (Dungannon), N P J Francis (Old Belvedere), M J Galwey (Shannon), B T Robinson (Ballymena), W D McBride (Malone) *Replacement* P D McCarthy (Cork Const) for Popplewell (77 mins)
Scorers *Try:* Geoghegan *Conversion:* Elwood *Penalty Goals:* Elwood (6)
ROMANIA: V Brici (Farul Constanta); C Sasu (Farul Constanta), G Solomie (Dinamo Bucharest), N Fulina (Farul Constanta), L Colceriu (Steaua Bucharest); S Rosu (Sibiu), D Neaga (Dinamo Bucharest); G Leonte (Vienne, France), C Gheorghe (Grivita Rosie), G Vlad (Grivita Rosie), T Oroian (Steaua Bucharest), A Girbu (Farul Constanta), H Dumitras (Pau, France) *(capt)*, A Guranescu (Dinamo Bucharest), T Brinza (Cluj) *Replacements* C Cojocariu (Bayonne, France) for Girbu (43 mins); N Marin (Farul Constanta) for Cojocariu (temp replacement)
Scorer *Penalty Goal:* Rosu
Referee R Yeman (Wales)

NATIONAL TRIAL MATCHES 1994

IRELAND
1 January 1994, Lansdowne Road

Whites 25 (2G 2PG 1T)   **Blues 14** (3PG 1T)

Whites: C M P O'Shea (Lansdowne); R M Wallace (Garryowen), P P A Danaher (Garryowen), V J G Cunningham (St Mary's Coll), S P Geoghegan (London Irish); E P Elwood (Lansdowne), M T Bradley (Cork Const) (*capt*); N J Popplewell (Greystones), T J Kingston (Dolphin), P M Clohessy (Young Munster), P S Johns (Dungannon), D Tweed (Ballymena), C Pim (Old Wesley), N P Mannion (Lansdowne), B F Robinson (Ballymena) *Replacement* A C Rolland (Blackrock Coll) for Bradley (79 mins)
Scorers *Tries:* Geoghegan, Cunningham, Kingston   *Conversions:* Elwood (2)
Penalty Goals: Elwood (2)
Blues: J E Staples (London Irish); T Howe (Dungannon), B Walsh (Cork Const), M C McCall (Bangor) (*capt*), N Woods (Blackrock Coll); A McGowan (Blackrock Coll), A Matchett (Ballymena); P Soden (Cork Const), K Wood (Garryowen), G Halpin (London Irish), J Etheridge (Blackrock Coll), B J Rigney (Greystones), E Halvey (Shannon), S McKinty (Bangor), K O'Connell (Sunday's Well) *Replacements* S Jameson (St Mary's Coll) for Rigney (40 mins); K Potts (St Mary's Coll) for Halvey (66 mins)
Scorers *Try:* Woods   *Penalty Goals:* McGowan (3)
Referee B Stirling (Ulster)

SCOTLAND
3 January 1994, Murrayfield

Blues 24 (1G 4PG 1T)   **Reds 14** (3PG 1T)

Blues: A G Hastings (Watsonians) (*capt*); A G Stanger (Hawick), S Hastings (Watsonians), I C Jardine (Stirling County), K M Logan (Stirling County); G P J Townsend (Gala), A D Nicol (Dundee HSFP); A V Sharp (Bristol), K S Milne (Heriot's FP), P H Wright (Boroughmuir), D S Munro (Glasgow High/Kelvinside), G W Weir (Melrose), D J Turnbull (Hawick), R I Wainwright (Edinburgh Acads), I R Morrison (London Scottish) *Replacement* Watt (Reds) for Sharp (40 mins)
Scorers *Tries:* Townsend, S Hastings   *Conversion:* A G Hastings
Penalty Goals: A G Hastings (4)
Reds: M Dods (Gala); K R Milligan (Stewart's-Melville FP), S A Nichol (Selkirk), D S Wyllie (Stewart's-Melville FP), D A Stark (Boroughmuir); C M Chalmers (Melrose), B W Redpath (Melrose); A G J Watt (Glasgow High/Kelvinside), K D McKenzie (Stirling County) (*capt*), D W Herrington (Dundee HSFP), N G B Edwards (Northampton), A E D Macdonald (Heriot's FP), P Walton (Northampton), C D Hogg (Melrose), I R Smith (Gloucester) *Replacements* Sharp (Blues) for Watt (40 mins); R J S Shepherd (Edinburgh Acads) for Nichol (48 mins)
Scorers *Try:* Walton   *Penalty Goals:* Dods (2), Chalmers
Referee K W McCartney (Hawick)

WORLD CUP QUALIFIERS

The final stages of the 1995 Rugby World Cup will be contested by 16 nations in South Africa. Australia (the holders), England (runners-up), New Zealand (third), Scotland (fourth) and France, Ireland, Canada and Western Samoa (beaten quarter-finalists) qualify for the 1995 tournament on the strength of their performances in the last World Cup. South Africa qualify as host nation, leaving a further seven places to be settled before the end of 1994.

Results and qualifiers to June 1994

AMERICAS ZONE

North

| 12 Mar 1994 | Bermuda | 3 | United States | 60 | (Devonshire) |

United States forward to play-off

South

26 Sept 1993	Chile	24	Paraguay	25	(Santiago)
2 Oct 1993	Paraguay	3	Uruguay	67	(Ascunción)
9 Oct 1993	Uruguay	14	Chile	6	(Montevideo)
11 Oct 1993	Argentina	70	Chile	7	(Buenos Aires)
16 Oct 1993	Argentina	51	Paraguay	3	(Buenos Aires)
23 Oct 1993	Uruguay	10	Argentina	19	(Montevideo)

Argentina forward to play-off

Play-off

| 28 May 1994 | United States | 22 | Argentina | 28 | (Long Beach) |
| 20 June 1994 | Argentina | 16 | United States | 11 | (Buenos Aires) |

ARGENTINA QUALIFY FOR FINALS

AFRICAN ZONE

North

26 Oct 1993	Tunisia	16	Ivory Coast	19	(Tunis)
28 Oct 1993	Tunisia	5	Morocco	6	(Tunis)
30 Oct 1993	Morocco	3	Ivory Coast	15	(Tunis)

Morocco and Ivory Coast forward to play-off

South

3 July 1993	Kenya	7	Zimbabwe	42	(Nairobi)
3 July 1993	Namibia	64	Gulf States	20	(Nairobi)
7 July 1993	Kenya	9	Namibia	60	(Nairobi)
7 July 1993	Zimbabwe	50	Gulf States	21	(Nairobi)

10 July 1993	Kenya	24	Gulf States	23	(Nairobi)
10 July 1993	Namibia	41	Zimbabwe	16	(Nairobi)

Namibia and Zimbabwe forward to play-off

Play-off

14 June 1994	Morocco	17	Ivory Coast	9	(Casablanca)
14 June 1994	Namibia	25	Zimbabwe	20	(Casablanca)
16 June 1994	Morocco	9	Zimbabwe	21	(Casablanca)
16 June 1994	Ivory Coast	13	Namibia	12	(Casablanca)
18 June 1994	Morocco	16	Namibia	16	(Casablanca)
18 June 1994	Ivory Coast	17	Zimbabwe	10	(Casablanca)

IVORY COAST QUALIFY FOR FINALS

EUROPEAN ZONE

East

1 May 1993	Germany	31	Lithuania	5	(Berlin)
8 May 1993	Latvia	5	Germany	27	(Riga)
29 May 1993	Lithuania	6	Latvia	7	(Siauliai)

Germany forward to Eastern play-off

24 May 1993	Russia	15	Georgia	9	(Gdansk)
27 May 1993	Poland	23	Georgia	6	(Gdansk)
29 May 1993	Poland	5	Russia	41	(Gdansk)

Russia forward to Eastern play-off

Play-off

2 May 1994	Romania	60	Germany	6	(Bucharest)
4 May 1994	Russia	69	Germany	5	(Bucharest)
7 May 1994	Romania	30	Russia	0	(Bucharest)

FINAL TABLE

	P	W	L	F	A	Pts
Romania	2	2	0	90	6	4
Russia	2	1	1	69	35	2
Germany	2	0	2	11	129	0

ROMANIA QUALIFY FOR FINALS

Romanian Appearances
Full-back: V Brici [*G*, *Ru*]
Threequarters: L Colceriu [*G*, *Ru*]; R Cioca [*G*, *Ru*]; N Fulina [*G*, *Ru*]; G Solomie [*G*]; N Racean [*G*(R), *Ru*]; V Flutur [*G*(R)]
Half-backs: N Nichitean [*G*, *Ru*]; D Neaga [*G*, *Ru*]
Forwards: G Vlad [*G*, *Ru*]; G Leonte [*G*, *Ru*]; V Ionescu [*G*(R)]; C Gheorghe [*G*]; G Ion [*Ru*]; S Ciorescu [*G*, *Ru*]; C Cojocariu [*G*(R), *Ru*]; T Oroian [*G*, *Ru*]; C Draguceanu [(*G*, *Ru*]; A Guranescu [*G*, *Ru*]; T Brinza (*capt*) [*G*]
D Neaga was captain against Russia

Central

30 May 1993	Hungary	8	Israel	67	(Budapest)

Israel forward to pre-qualifying round

31 Oct 1993	Israel	10	Sweden	26	(Den Haag)

31 Oct 1993	Holland	42	Czech Reps	6	(Den Haag)
3 Nov 1993	Holland	56	Israel	0	(Apeldoorn)
3 Nov 1993	Sweden	7	Czech Reps	34	(Apeldoorn)
6 Nov 1993	Holland	31	Sweden	6	(Amsterdam)
6 Nov 1993	Israel	0	Czech Reps	28	(Amsterdam)

Holland and Czech Reps forward to play-off

Play-off

14 May 1994	Holland	33	Czech Reps	9	(Brescia)
18 May 1994	Italy	104	Czech Reps	8	(Viadana)
21 May 1994	Italy	63	Holland	9	(Calvisano)

FINAL TABLE

	P	W	L	F	A	Pts
Italy	2	2	0	167	17	4
Holland	2	1	1	42	72	2
Czech Reps	2	0	2	17	137	0

ITALY QUALIFY FOR FINALS

Italian Appearances

Full-back: P Vaccari [*Cz, H*]

Threequarters: M Gerosa [*Cz*]; N Aldrovandi [*Cz, H*]; E G Filizzola [*Cz*]; M Ravazzolo [*Cz, H*]; M Bonomi [*H*]; Marcello Cuttitta [*H*]

Half-backs: L Troiani [Cz];, D Dominguez [*H*]; A Troncon [*Cz, H*(R)]; I Francescato [*H*]

Forwards: A Castellani [*Cz*]; C Orlandi [*Cz, H*]; G Grespan [*Cz*]; F Properzi-Curti [*H*]; A Sagorlon [*Cz*(R)]; P Pedroni [*Cz, H*]; R Favaro [*Cz*(R)]; M Giovanelli [*Cz, H*]; O Arancio [*Cz, H*]; M Giacheri [*Cz, H*]; C De Rossi [*H*(R)]; C Checchinato [*Cz*]; Massimo Cuttitta [*Cz*(R), *H*]; J M Gardner [*H*]

West

Oct 1992	Andorra	3	Denmark	0	(Andorra)
Oct 1992	Denmark	8	Switzerland	3	(Andorra)
Oct 1992	Andorra	0	Switzerland	14	(Andorra)

Switzerland forward to pre-qualifying round

11 May 1993	Spain	40	Switzerland	0	(Lisbon)
11 May 1193	Portugal	8	Belgium	3	(Lisbon)
13 May 1993	Belgium	3	Spain	67	(Lisbon)
13 May 1993	Portugal	32	Switzerland	0	(Lisbon)
16 May 1993	Portugal	15	Spain	37	(Lisbon)
16 May 1993	Belgium	42	Switzerland	3	(Lisbon)

Spain and Portugal forward to play-off

Play-off

17 May 1994	Portugal	11	Wales	102	(Lisbon)
21 May 1994	Spain	0	Wales	54	(Madrid)
29 May 1994	Spain	35	Portugal	19	(Madrid)

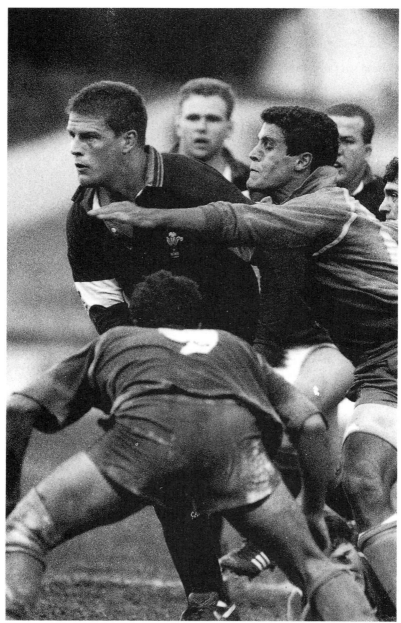

Gareth Llewellyn of Wales in action as the Welsh beat Spain by 54-0 in Madrid in the play-off round of the European Zone (West), from which Wales qualified for the World Cup in 1995.

FINAL TABLE

	P	W	L	F	A	Pts
Wales	2	2	0	156	11	4
Spain	2	1	1	35	73	2
Portugal	2	0	0	30	137	0

WALES QUALIFY FOR FINALS

Welsh Appearances:
Full-backs: M A Rayer [Pt]; A Clement [Sp]
Threequarters: I C Evans (capt) [Pt, Sp]; M R Hall [Pt, Sp]; N G Davies [Pt, Sp];
N Walker [Pt, Sp]
Half-backs: N R Jenkins [Pt, Sp]; R N Jones [Pt]; R H StJ B Moon [Sp]
Forwards: R L Evans [Pt, Sp]; G R Jenkins [Pt, Sp]; J D Davies [Pt, Sp];
A H Copsey [Pt, Sp(R)]; G O Llewellyn [Pt, Sp]; P Arnold [Sp]; E W Lewis [Pt, Sp];
L S Quinnell [Pt, Sp]; H T Taylor [Pt]; M A Perego [Sp]

*Romania, Italy and Wales meet in a further play-off in September-October 1994 to determine
which pools they will join for the Rugby World Cup finals.*

PACIFIC ZONE

| 12 June 1993 | Fiji | 11 | Tonga | 24 | (Suva) |
| 17 July 1993 | Tonga | 10 | Fiji | 15 | (Nuku'alofa) |

TONGA QUALIFY FOR FINALS

ASIAN ZONE

*The tournament to decide the Asian qualifier for the World Cup finals is scheduled for October
1994 in Malaysia.*

AN HISTORIC WIN FOR ITALY AS NUMBERS SWELL

THE FIRA CHAMPIONSHIP 1993-94
Chris Rhys

There were two significant events in the 1993-94 FIRA Championship. The first concerned the excellent news that no fewer than 28 countries took part in the Championship – easily a record and hugely encouraging news for the growth of the game in general. As a result, although the Championship was run on its usual lines, the plan is now to rank all countries in a classification from 1 to 28 in order to introduce a more geographical plan for 1994-95, and thence to groups on merit in 1995-96. These modifications have become necessary due to the rise in numbers of participants from the old Iron Curtain bloc.

The other major feat was that Italy, for the first time ever, beat France in an international. They had been trying since 1936, and had managed only a couple of draws until the historic day, 11 November 1993, when France were beaten 16-9 at Treviso. Italy conquered a French team including nine full internationals by a 54th-minute penalty try and 11 points from the boot of Diego Dominguez to three penalties from Olivier Campan. In the 58 years and 45 previous encounters between the countries, France had 43 wins, the draws occurring in 1968 and 1983.

Earlier France had beaten Romania 51-0 with a full international complement who were about to take on the touring Australians. They scored six tries – from Philippe Bernat-Salles (3), Philippe Sella, Olivier Merle and Leon Loppy – all converted by Thierry Lacroix, who also added three penalties. However, the roulette continued later in the season when Romania beat Italy 26-12, a try from Gheorge Leonte and 21 points from Neculai Nichitean proving too much for the visitors.

Russia fell away a little, though France found them by no means easy to beat in their narrow 11-9 win in Moscow. Spain, who beat Morocco 48-17 to qualify for a place in the top group, lost all their four games but showed spirit in losing causes in both the senior group and the World Cup qualifiers.

Group A Pool 1
RESULTS

1993	Venue	Result			
17 Oct	Brive	France	51	Romania	0
6 Nov	Moscow	Russia	19	Italy	30
11 Nov	Treviso	Italy	16	France	9
1994					
20 Mar	Sarlat	France	49	Spain	3
10 Apr	Madrid	Spain	9	Russia	16
24 Apr	Zaragoza	Spain	3	Romania	11
7 May	Bucharest	Romania	30	Russia	0

7 May	Parma	Italy	62	Spain	15
14 May	Bucharest	Romania	26	Italy	12
28 May	Moscow	Russia	9	France	11

Group A Pool 2
RESULTS

1993	Venue	Result			
2 Oct	Tunis	Tunisia	15	Germany	6
21 Nov	Chicciu (Romania)	Germany	32	Belgium	16
1994					
29 Jan	Brussels	Belgium	18	Morocco	14
26 Mar	Hanover	Germany	35	Morocco	18
9 Apr	Vise	Belgium	10	Portugal	8
17 Apr	Lisbon	Portugal	18	Germany	20
30 Apr	Casablanca	Morocco	20	Portugal	15
4 May	Casablanca	Morocco	25	Tunisia	10
7 May	Lisbon	Portugal	16	Tunisia	18
14 May	Tunis	Tunisia	16	Belgium	16

A1 FINAL TABLE

	P	W	D	L	F	A	Pts
France	4	3	0	1	120	28	10
Italy	4	3	0	1	120	69	10
Romania	4	3	0	1	67	66	10
Russia	4	1	0	3	44	80	6
Spain	4	0	0	4	30	138	4

A2 FINAL TABLE

	P	W	D	L	F	A	Pts
Germany	4	3	0	1	93	68	10
Tunisia	4	2	1	1	60	63	9
Belgium	4	2	1	1	60	70	9
Morocco	4	2	0	2	77	78	8
Portugal	4	0	0	4	57	68	4

Group B Pool 1
RESULTS

1993	Venue	Result			
11 Sept	Nassjo	Sweden	25	Andorra	6
17 Oct	Viskov	Czech Rep	19	Poland	18
31 Oct	*Den Haag	Holland	42	Czech Rep	6
3 Nov	*Apeldoorn (Holland)	Czech Rep	34	Sweden	6
6 Nov	*Amsterdam	Holland	31	Sweden	6
6 Nov	Sochaczcew	Poland	30	Andorra	10
1994					
26 Mar	Andorra	Andorra	10	Holland	49
16 Apr	Karlskrona	Sweden	18	Poland	25
23 Apr	Prague	Czech Rep	56	Andorra	0
30 Apr	Lublin	Poland	13	Holland	10
7 May	Vanersborg	Sweden	6	Holland	44
7 May	Andorra	Andorra	w/o	Sweden	

Also World Cup qualifiers

Group B Pool 2
RESULTS

1993	Venue	Result			
16 Oct	Miskolc	Hungary	3	Ukraine	41
23 Oct	Vienna	Austria	11	Slovenia	14
13 Nov	Szekesfehervar	Hungary	w/o	Austria	
1994					
16 Apr	Sisak	Croatia	41	Austria	12
23 Apr	Zagreb	Croatia	77	Slovenia	10

1 May	Sisak	Croatia	13	Ukraine	23
7 May	Ljubliana	Slovenia	26	Ukraine	41
14 May	Ljubliana	Slovenia	28	Hungary	17
15 May	Vienna	Austria	0	Ukraine	72
28 May	Budapest	Hungary	5	Croatia	31

B1 FINAL TABLE

	P	W	D	L	F	A	Pts
Holland	5	4	0	1	176	41	13
Poland	4	3	0	1	86	57	10
Czech Rep	4	2	0	2	115	67	8
Sweden	6	1	0	5	62	140	8
Andorra	5	1	0	4	26	160	7

B2 FINAL TABLE

	P	W	D	L	F	A	Pts
Ukraine	4	4	0	0	177	42	12
Croatia	4	3	0	1	162	50	10
Slovenia	4	2	0	2	78	146	8
Hungary	4	1	0	3	25	100	7
Austria	4	0	0	4	23	127	4

Group C Pool 1
RESULTS

1993	Venue	Result			
31 Oct	Cessange	Luxembourg	10	Georgia	10
6 Nov	Riga	Latvia	10	Switzerland	0
1994					
30 Apr	Luxembourg	Luxembourg	10	Latvia	25
15 May	Tiblisi	Georgia	w/o	Latvia	
15 May	Luxembourg	Luxembourg	8	Switzerland	17

Group C Pool 2
RESULTS

1993	Venue	Result			
10 Oct	Sjaulai	Lithuania	6	Moldavia	22
6 Nov	Gabrovo	Bulgaria	9	Lithuania	9
27 Nov	Gabrovo	Bulgaria	11	Denmark	7
1994					
23 Apr	Kishinev	Moldavia	42	Bulgaria	3
7 May	Copenhagen	Denmark	69	Lithuania	6
29 May	Copenhagen	Denmark	w/o	Moldavia	

C1 FINAL TABLE

	P	W	D	L	F	A	Pts
Latvia	3	2	0	1	35	10	7
Georgia	2	1	1	0	10	10	6
Switzerland	2	1	0	1	17	18	4
Luxembourg	3	0	1	2	28	52	4

C2 FINAL TABLE

	P	W	D	L	F	A	Pts
Moldavia	3	2	0	1	64	9	7
Denmark	3	2	0	1	76	17	7
Bulgaria	3	1	1	1	23	58	6
Lithuania	3	0	1	2	21	100	4

OTHER INTERNATIONAL TOURNAMENTS 1993-94

CURRIE CUP FINAL

Natal 15 (5PG) **Transvaal 21** (1G 3PG 1T)
Natal: A Joubert; C van der Westhuizen, R Muir, P Müller, J Small; J Stransky, K Putt; G Kebble, J Allan, L Müller, S Atherton, M Andrews, W Bartmann (*capt*), A Blakeway, G Teichmann
Scorer *Penalty Goals:* Stransky (5)
Transvaal: G Johnson; P Hendriks, B Fourie, J Mulder, C Dirks; H le Roux, J Roux; B Swart, U Schmidt, H Rodgers, K Wiese, H Strydom, I Macdonald, R Strauli, F Pienaar (*capt*) *Replacement* D Lotter for Pienaar (46 mins)
Scorers *Tries:* Johnson, Schmidt *Conversion:* Johnson *Penalty Goals:* Johnson (3)
Referee F Burger (SARFU)

THE SUPER-10 SERIES 1994

The Super-10 tournament is a marvel of the ambition and energy of the rugby authorities in the Southern Hemisphere. The top provincial teams in South Africa, New Zealand and Australia join with the champions of the Pacific – in 1994, Western Samoa. The demands on players participating are obviously immense; so is the commercial and marketing activity which surrounds the whole event. The future is not assured because of the commitments which will be demanded of the players in 1995, World Cup year. Yet the cross-pollination provided by the event, the exposure of the players to different playing cultures, seems sure to increase the lead which the Southern Hemisphere has over the Northern.

The 1994 tournament was suitably exciting. It was soured by the refusal of New South Wales to travel to Durban for the key match against Natal. There was a state of emergency in Natal at the time and NSW obviously had to be concerned about the safety of their players. But when the other teams had made uneventful visits to the province, and when the England tour had also proceeded there with no hint of trouble, the NSW decision looked alarmist and precipitate. They tried to have the Natal game switched to a neutral venue but ultimately had to concede the match and the points.

The Pool matches brought some outstanding rugby. In Pool B, Western Samoa, conceding home advantage to Auckland, won a memorable victory over the mighty Aucklanders. Natal won away at Waikato and in Auckland against the Samoans, and thoroughly deserved their passage to the final. In Pool A, Transvaal hammered Otago at home but their form on the road was disappointing. They lost heavily to Queensland and to North Harbour, the surprise packet for the whole event. Waikato were a disappointment, given their excellent form of the previous season, and Eastern Province, new to the series, found it all too much for them. Queensland lost heavily to Otago in

New Zealand but recovered well, finding a hard-nosed team improving all the way.

The final, with Natal enjoying home field advantage, was no classic, and obviously, the Queensland joy was tempered drastically by the loss of both Jason Little and Tim Horan during the match. Little made a good recovery from a nasty ligament injury but Horan had to have the ligaments of his knee completely rebuilt after dislocating his kneecap. His future remains in doubt. Queensland did well to pull themselves together. They had scored tries through Barry Lea and Sam Scott-Young in the early stages, were still 12-0 ahead at half-time and were in full control. Yet a try by Cabous van der Westhuizen, the Natal left wing, just after the hour hurried Natal back to 10-12 and the noise level at the remarkable Kings Park Stadium grew. Yet Queensland's experienced forwards rallied, and Michael Lynagh kicked two penalties and a dropped goal in the closing stages to secure the trophy.

RESULTS

Points are awarded as follows: win – 4 points; draw – 2 points; defeat by a margin of 7 points or less – 1 point; defeat by a margin of more than 7 points – 0 points

Pool A: Transvaal 35, Eastern Province 15; Transvaal 44, Otago 19; Eastern Province 10, Queensland 41; Otago 24, Queensland 18; Eastern Province 21, North Harbour 31; Queensland 21, Transvaal 10; North Harbour 23, Otago 19; Otago 57, Eastern Province 24; North Harbour 19, Transvaal 6; Queensland 13, North Harbour 10

Pool B: Waikato 16, New South Wales 43; Auckland 27, Waikato 10; New South Wales 25, Western Samoa 23; Western Samoa 32, Waikato 16; Natal-New South Wales not played; Auckland 13, Western Samoa 15; Waikato 24, Natal 30; Waikato 24, Natal 30; Western Samoa 26, Natal 48; New South Wales 22, Auckland 19; Natal 14, Auckland 12

	P	W	D	L	F	A	Pts
Queensland*	4	3	0	1	85	61	13
North Harbour	4	3	0	1	95	56	13
Otago	4	2	0	3	119	109	9
Transvaal	4	2	0	2	95	74	8
Eastern Province	4	0	0	4	70	164	0

If two teams are tied on points, the group winner is determined on result of the pool match played between them, so Queensland qualified for final.

	P	W	D	L	F	A	Pts
Natal*	3	3	0	0	92	62	16
New South Wales*	3	3	0	1	90	58	12
Western Samoa	4	2	0	2	96	102	9
Auckland	4	1	0	3	71	62	7
Waikato	4	0	0	4	66	132	1

Natal were awarded 4 points after New South Wales refused to travel to Durban.

FINAL   14 May 1994, Kings Park, Durban

Natal 10 (1G 1PG)   **Queensland 21** (1G 2PG 1DG 1T)
Natal: A Joubert; C van der Westhuizen, J Thomson, P Müller, J Small; H Honiball, R du Preez; G Kebble, J Allan, A Garvey, J Slade, S Atherton, W Bartmann (*capt*), G Teichmann, A Blakeway *Replacement* A Marinos for Müller
Scorers *Try:* van der Westhuizen   *Conversion:* Joubert   *Penalty Goal:* Joubert
Queensland: M Pini; D Smith, T Horan, J Little, B Lea; M Lynagh, P Slattery (*capt*); C Lillicrap, M Foley, A Skeggs, R McCall, G Morgan, D Wilson, S Scott-Young, I Tabua *Replacements* J Eales for Tabua; A Herbert for Horan; P Carozza for Little
Scorers *Tries:* Lea, Scott-Young   *Conversion:* Lynagh   *Penalty Goals:* Lynagh (2)
Dropped Goal: Lynagh
Referee G Wahlstrom (New Zealand)

FRENCH CLUB CHAMPIONSHIP FINAL

28 June, Parc des Princes
Toulouse 22 (1G 3PG 2DG)   **Montferrand 16** (1G 3PG)

As ever, this was a marvellous occasion, quite the most atmospheric rugby match of the European season. There was hardly a neutral, it seemed, wedged into the Parc des Princes among the vociferous, painted, partisan support from Toulouse and Montferrand.

But there was also the match to do justice to the occasion. It was fast-moving, relentlessly hard fought and entertaining and that remarkable institution, Toulouse, surged to victory. Toulouse, who had fought their way past Narbonne and Dax in the quarter- and semi-finals respectively, launched a long and sustained attack immediately on the opening whistle. The pace hardly dropped afterwards.

Montferrand, who had beaten Toulon and the highly fancied Grenoble in the last two rounds before the final, missed a glorious early chance of a try through sheer over-eagerness. They did lead 9-0 in the first half with three penalties from Pradier at scrum-half, but Toulouse, surging back to the attack, were back at 9-6 by half-time with a penalty and dropped goal from Deylaud, the fly-half.

Toulouse's pack were dominant in the second half. Deylaud kicked an equalising penalty, although there was an aberration on the road to glory soon afterwards, Juillet of Montferrand scoring near the posts after a breakaway attack. The conversion made it 16-9. Toulouse came back with a try by Cazalbou and a conversion and another dropped goal from Deylaud. Among some dramatic attacking and counter-attacking in the later stages, Deylaud kicked another penalty to seal the match.

Toulouse: J Dupuy; E N'Tamack, P Carbonneau, O Carbonneau, D Berty; C Deylaud, J Cazalbou; C Califano, P Solua, C Portolan, H Miorin, F Belot, J-L Cester, A Cigagna (*capt*), R Sonnes *Replacements* D Lacroix for P Carbonneau; C Guiter for Soula
Scorers *Try:* Cazalbou   *Conversion:* Deylaud   *Penalty Goals:* Deylaud (3)
Dropped Goals: Deylaud (2)
Montferrand: G Darlet; P Saint-André, F Ribeyrolles, R Saint-André, F Bertrank; E Nicol, M Pradier; E Menieu, P Marocco, C Duchene, E Lecomte, J-P Versailles, A Costes, C Juillet, J-M Lhermet (*capt*)
Scorers *Try:* Juillet   *Conversion:* Pradier   *Penalty Goals:* Pradier (3)
Referee M Desclaux (FFR)

SEVENS TOURNAMENTS 1993-94
Michael Austin

THE 1994 CATHAY PACIFIC-HONG KONG BANK SEVENS

An inspirational performance by Eric Rush, the New Zealand captain, guided his side to a 32-20 victory in the Hong Kong Sevens and forced Australia once again to become reluctant runners-up. In the process the All Blacks revealed some richly talented young players. Rush scored two of New Zealand's five tries as Australia were cruelly reminded of their defeat by England in the World Cup Sevens final at Murrayfield a year earlier. New Zealand's fourth Hong Kong title, but their first since 1989, was achieved in a rousing final characterised by their familiar mixture of speed, precise handling and unwavering commitment. Not for the first time in the tournament, a star was born.

Jonah Lomu, aged 18, from Tonga, who had yet to play senior rugby, was rated by Rush, a globe-trotting veteran and shrewd judge, as 'a bigger, faster but younger Va'aiga Tuigamala'. Lomu's rise continued in remarkable fashion. He won his first cap for New Zealand in the home series against France in 1994. In Hong Kong, His stunning strength and pace, allied to the running of Luke Erenavula and the subtlety of Joe Tauiwi, brushed Australia aside in the climax to the competition at the new £75 million stadium in front of a crowd of 40,000.

David Campese, for once, was on the receiving end as Lomu forcefully handed him off during a dazzling run for the final try. Campese, aged 31, who has been playing in Hong Kong for a decade, said that it was his last tournament but that he planned to continue at 15-a-side level until the World Cup in South Africa in May 1995. 'You have to go when your body can no longer do what your mind wants it to do,' he remarked. Ultimately, Campese became a limping passenger, suffering a recurrence of a hamstring injury sustained in a group match against Japan. Always a man to air an opinion, he said he could not understand why England continue to snub Hong Kong. The organisers too were dismayed that of the major countries only England chose not to support the event.

Of the other Home Unions, Scotland, the sevens inventors, were disappointing, even in the Plate competition, in which they lost to Japan. In the main tournament, they had lost to Hong Kong and beaten Argentina. Eric Elwood, Ireland's play-maker, suffered a back injury in their opening match and the team failed to reproduce the impressive form of Murrayfield and Hong Kong the previous year. England did have a limited representation in five of the World Sevens-winning squad, who played for the Hong Kong RFU President's team which reached the quarter-finals, beating Singapore and Ireland before losing honourably to the holders, Western Samoa. First-half tries from Derek

The inspirational captain, Eric Rush, pictured after New Zealand's 32-20 victory against Australia in the Hong Kong Sevens final.

Stark and Chris Sheasby guided the President's side into a 14-12 half-time lead before they succumbed by 21-12.

Australia, who beat the Samoans 20-17 with an extra-time penalty goal from Campese in an exhausting semi-final, scored first, fell behind and then rallied brilliantly against New Zealand as they sought their first title since 1988. Jim Williams ran in a try and, late in the match, David Wilson, George Gregan and Williams also scored. They shook New Zealand to the extent that Glen Osborne chose to kick a short-range penalty for the winners. It was a dual-purpose kick, designed to both produce points and consume vital seconds.

New Zealand reached the final by dealing impressively with Fiji, a win which avenged the three consecutive final defeats by Waisale Serevi's team between 1990 and 1992.

Portugal, coached by Andy Cushing, the former London Scottish sevens expert, showed their potential by beating Thailand and Romania to reach the Bowl final, where they lost to Hong Kong. Korea were popular winners of the Plate, defeating the American Eagles, who had previously eliminated Ireland. It was a typical tournament of sun, fun, tries and the occasional spree – notably New Zealand's 64-point win over Malaysia, South Africa's by 63 over Thailand and Western Samoa's 61-point romp against Sri Lanka.

Pool A: Western Samoa 61, Sri Lanka 0; American Eagles 24, Sri Lanka 14; Western Samoa 33, American Eagles 10 **Pool B:** Ireland 40, Singapore 0; President's VII 45, Singapore 0; President's VII 22, Ireland 7 **Pool C:** Hong Kong 15, Scotland 5; Argentina 26, Hong Kong 5; Scotland 24, Argentina 14 **Pool D:** Australia 29, Taiwan 0; Japan 17, Taiwan 12; Australia 54, Japan 0 **Pool E:** New Zealand 64, Malaysia 0; Tonga 45, Malaysia 7; New Zealand 38, Tonga 5 **Pool F:** France 26, Papua New Guinea 5; Papua New Guinea 26, Romania 5; France 40, Romania 5 **Pool G:** South Africa 63, Thailand 0; Canada 35, Thailand 0; South Africa 20, Thailand 7 **Pool H:** Fiji 56, Portugal 7; South Korea 26, Portugal 10; Fiji 33, South Korea 0

BOWL: Final: Hong Kong 26, Portugal 12
PLATE: Final: Korea 26, American Eagles 21
CUP: Quarter-finals: Western Samoa 21, President's VII 12; Australia 43, Argentina 0; New Zealand 21, France 12; Fiji 14, South Africa 12 **Semi-finals:** Australia 20, Western Samoa 17 (*sudden death, 17-17 at full-time*); New Zealand 28, Fiji 14
Final: New Zealand 32, Australia 20

Teams in the final
New Zealand: L Erenavula, G Osborne, J Tauiwi, P Woods; D Seymour, E Rush (*capt*), J Lomu
Scorers *Tries:* Rush (2), Lomu, Erenavula, Osborne   *Conversions:* Osborne (2)
Penalty Goal: Osborne
Australia: J Little, T Horan, D Campese (*capt*), G Gregan; I Tabua, D Wilson, J Williams *Replacement* J Fenwicke for Tabua
Scorers *Tries:* Williams (2), Wilson, Gregan
Referee D Mene (France)

THE MIDDLESEX SEVENS 1994
(Sponsored by Save & Prosper)

Bath, the team to beat from the start in the Middlesex Sevens, duly completed a unique treble, adding the Sevens title, for the first time, to a League and Cup double. It was a remarkable performance, even by their standards. They beat Orrell 19-12 through a try by Jonathan Callard, soon to be enlisted as a replacement on England's tour of South Africa. Callard, scoring three tries and ten conversions, shared with team-mate Audley Lumsden (seven tries) the distinction of being the tournament's top scorer with 35 points. Paul Johnson levelled the final against Bath at 12-12 with a try before Callard ended his own season and that of his club on the highest possible note.

On the way to the final, Bath kept Loughborough University and Saracens scoreless, having conceded points only in the second half of their opening game, against London Scottish. They had led 21-0 at half-time and won 28-26, coasting along with more in reserve than the score indicated. Orrell's familiar heavy industry of the 15-a-side game and their willingness to move the ball was enhanced by the pace of England Under-21 team-mates Jim Naylor and Austin Healey, a newcomer from Waterloo. After eliminating well-fancied Bristol, they squeezed past Fiji Spartans and Rosslyn Park by identical 10-7 scores in deteriorating weather before a crowd of 48,000.

Qualifiers from the six preliminary competitions included Rosslyn Park, who eliminated Northampton, beaten finalists the previous season, by 26-12, and Harlequins, champions 13 times in the tournament. Loughborough University distinguished themselves by beating Zimbabwe, another entry on the honours board at Ashby Road, while Saracens knocked out Wasps, the holders, who proceeded to win the Plate competition.

RESULTS
Sixth round: Northampton 12, Rosslyn Park 26; Harlequins 19, Richmond 12; Orrell 17, Bristol 12 *(aet)*; Blackheath 7, Fiji Spartans 21; Zimbabwe 12, Loughborough University 21; Bath 28, London Scottish 26; Gloucester 12, London Irish 17; Saracens 17, Wasps 5
Seventh round: Rosslyn Park 21, Harlequins 10; Orrell 10, Fiji Spartans 7; Loughborough University 0, Bath 24; London Irish 5, Saracens 26
Semi-finals: Rosslyn Park 7, Orrell 10; Bath 19, Saracens 0
Final: Bath 19, Orrell 12
Plate Final: Wasps 22, Northampton 12

Teams in the final
Bath: A Lumsden, E Rayner, J Callard *(capt)*, I Sanders; E Peters, G Adams, M Haag
Scorers *Tries:* Rayner, Lumsden, Callard   *Conversions:* Callard (2)
Orrell: J Naylor, I Wynn, P Johnson *(capt)*, A Healey; M Farr, J Clayton, H Parr
Scorers *Tries:* Naylor, Johnson   *Conversion:* Johnson
Referee K Ricketts

WINNERS

1926 **Harlequins**	1949 **Heriot's FP**	1972 **London Welsh**
1927 **Harlequins**	1950 **Rosslyn Park**	1973 **London Welsh**
1928 **Harlequins**	1951 **Richmond II**	1974 **Richmond**
1929 **Harlequins**	1952 **Wasps**	1975 **Richmond**
1930 **London Welsh**	1953 **Richmond**	1976 **Loughborough Colls**
1931 **London Welsh**	1954 **Rosslyn Park**	1977 **Richmond**
1932 **Blackheath**	1955 **Richmond**	1978 **Harlequins**
1933 **Harlequins**	1956 **London Welsh**	1979 **Richmond**
1934 **Barbarians**	1957 **St Luke's College**	1980 **Richmond**
1935 **Harlequins**	1958 **Blackheath**	1981 **Rosslyn Park**
1936 **Sale**	1959 **Loughborough Colls**	1982 **Stewart's-Melville FP**
1937 **London Scottish**	1960 **London Scottish**	1983 **Richmond**
1938 **Metropolitan Police**	1961 **London Scottish**	1984 **London Welsh**
1939 **Cardiff**	1962 **London Scottish**	1985 **Wasps**
1940 **St Mary's Hospital**	1963 **London Scottish**	1986 **Harlequins**
1941 **Cambridge U**	1964 **Loughborough Colls**	1987 **Harlequins**
1942 **St Mary's Hospital**	1965 **London Scottish**	1988 **Harlequins**
1943 **St Mary's Hospital**	1966 **Loughborough Colls**	1989 **Harlequins**
1944 **St Mary's Hospital**	1967 **Harlequins**	1990 **Harlequins**
1945 **Notts**	1968 **London Welsh**	1991 **London Scottish**
1946 **St Mary's Hospital**	1969 **St Luke's College**	1992 **Western Samoa**
1947 **Rosslyn Park**	1970 **Loughborough Colls**	1993 **Wasps**
1948 **Wasps**	1971 **London Welsh**	1994 **Bath**

Harlequins have won the title 13 times, Richmond 9 (including one by their second VII), London Welsh 8, London Scottish 7, St Mary's Hospital and Loughborough Colleges 5 each, Rosslyn Park and Wasps 4 each, Blackheath and St Luke's College (now Exeter University) twice, Barbarians, Sale, Met Police, Cardiff, Cambridge University, Notts (now Nottingham), Heriot's FP, Stewart's-Melville FP, Western Samoa and Bath once each

WORTHINGTON WELSH SEVENS 1993-94
(for the Snelling Trophy)

28 August 1993, Cardiff RFC Ground, Cardiff Arms Park

Preliminary round: Cross Keys 26, Abertillery 10; Pontypool 7, Pontypridd 21
First round: Cross Keys 5, Pontypridd 33; Aberavon 14, Neath 35; Swansea 31, Newbridge 7; Penarth 24, Tredegar 12; Ebbw Vale 14, Llanelli 33; South Wales Police 24, Newport 10; Bridgend 52, Glamorgan Wanderers 0; Cardiff 33, Maesteg 7
Second round: Pontypridd 26, Neath 7; Swansea 33, Penarth 14; Llanelli 5, South Wales Police 26; Bridgend 28, Cardiff 19
Final: South Wales Police 24, Pontypridd 14

Teams in the final
South Wales Police: C Hillman *(capt)*, R Collins, J Apsee; S Evans, P Phillips, J Price, C Higgs
Pontypridd: M Rowley, M Spiller, S Lewis; N Jenkins, P John *(capt)*, G Jones, D Manley *Replacement* P Thomas for Lewis
Referee R G Davies (Dunvant)
Man of the Tournament: R Collins (South Wales Police) **Leading scorer:** N Jenkins (Pontypridd) 62 points

ENGLAND UNDER COOKE LEAVES BEHIND RUGBY'S BACKWATERS

THE 1993-94 SEASON IN ENGLAND
David Hands *The Times*

When history comes to cast a critical eye on England's achievements between 1988 and 1994, they may come to be described as the Cooke years rather than the Carling years. Will Carling was the captain and public face of the England team which won two Grand Slams and reached a World Cup final; Geoff Cooke the team manager and organiser whose clear vision and strength of character helped make the playing achievements possible and whose resignation was the best-kept secret of the 1993-94 season in England.

His announcement, at the end of February, concluded a six-and-a-half-year period in which English rugby emerged from the backwaters to become a major international force. Cooke created a vibrant team which served as a model for youngsters and a prop to the expanding organisation of the Rugby Football Union at Twickenham. Though the rumourmongers claimed that Cooke jumped before he was pushed, and cited a furore within the RFU committee, which retained Cooke only on a narrow majority at the start of the season, Cooke himself said he was 'tired of living inside a goldfish bowl'.

His legacy is a framework via which international aspirants can be identified far earlier than before; greatly enhanced fitness levels; an emphasis on continuity and loyalty which, even when overplayed, was better than what preceded it, and a direct honesty, sometimes amounting to bluntness, about the requirements to compete at the highest level.

His successor, at least until the World Cup is over, is Jack Rowell, who coached Gosforth to Cup success in 1976 but whose name and reputation rests firmly on the magnificent machine he created at Bath, which has dominated domestic rugby for a decade. His calibre, as coach and motivator, has been proved at all but the highest level, but as important as anything are the standards he had laid down consistently over the years of Bath's success and which will now be applied to England.

Yet the 1993-94 season was neither fish nor fowl. A reshaped team flattered to deceive by beating New Zealand before the hurly-burly of the Five Nations Championship. That the All Blacks contributed towards their own downfall by playing a non-kicking fly-half and were without their injured goal-kicker mattered little to England, who were forced themselves to introduce Kyran Bracken, the Bristol scrum-half, to international rugby only 48 hours before the match. His response was so good that it carried him, somewhat precipitately, into the games against Scotland and Ireland where England salvaged a one-point win in the first and nothing from the second.

That England could have played so effectively against New Zealand and, subsequently, France and Wales and in so disorganised a manner against the weakest teams in the Championship was frustrating for the players and the management. There were mitigating factors: the comparative inexperience of many of the team after the loss from the previous season of such players as Jonathan Webb, Peter Winterbottom, Wade Dooley, Jeff Probyn, Jeremy Guscott and Mike Teague; injuries at various stages of the season to Dean Richards, Tim Rodber and Ben Clarke. It is easy, too, to forget the wearying demands of non-stop rugby: summer tours, the introduction of a home-and-away league system, the mediocre quality of much of the club rugby on offer and the continued stifling effect of the ruck-maul law.

All of these led to an intense scrutiny of the structure of the game played in England, both official and unofficial. The RFU president, Ian Beer, established a commission led by Bill Bishop to look into the governing body itself and recommend change. At the same time the RFU's competitions committee was looking closely at the playing structure of the game. One of the new team management's primary aims will be to reduce the load on international squad players during the domestic season leading up to the 1995 World Cup.

In the circumstances it was surprising that a handful of clubs could genuinely sit down and debate the formation of an Anglo-Welsh League, but the report produced by Bob Taylor for the Senior Clubs Association knocked that idea on the head. In the meantime two clubs dominated the season: Bath and Leicester. The Tigers did themselves no favours by losing very early in the season to Northampton and Harlequins, but they became the first team to stop Bath's charge towards a fourth consecutive League title at Welford Road. To win the title, however, they also had to beat Bath at the Recreation Ground, and that proved a game too far. Bath were left to offer their own tribute, his fifth League title in seven years, to Rowell, their departing coach, whose position now passes to Brian Ashton, who was once himself an assistant England coach and is certain to sustain the quality of rugby with which Bath have now become synonymous.

One of their secrets is their ability to regenerate players: no club or country would have wished to be without the injured Guscott all season but Bath survived better than England. They survived, too, the retirement of Gareth Chilcott, the prop who became part of local legend, and the temporary absence of Philip de Glanville, whose savage raking and subsequent eye injury during the game at Redruth between the South-West and the All Blacks led to a somewhat ineffectual 'summit' on violence between RFU and New Zealand representatives. At the season's end Richard Hill, England's most-capped scrum-half, also retired and for company he had John Olver, the Northampton hooker and occupant of many an England replacement bench, and Fred Howard, one of the best referees to be produced by England in the last generation.

The England team which beat Wales at Twickenham. L-R, back row: R J Megson (touch-judge), K W McCartney (touch-judge), J M Fleming (referee), V E Ubogu, K P P Bracken (replacement), M J Catt (replacement), B B Clarke, T A K Rodber, M O Johnson, D Richards, N C Redman, S O Ojomoh (replacement), J Leonard, G C Rowntree (replacement), G D Cooke (manager), R Best (coach); front row: C D Morris, T Underwood, B C Moore, R Underwood, W D C Carling (capt), I Hunter, P R de Glanville, J E B Callard (replacement), R G R Dawe (replacement), C R Andrew.

ENGLISH INTERNATIONAL PLAYERS
(up to 31 March 1994)

ABBREVIATIONS

A – Australia; *Arg* – Argentina; *C* – Canada; *F* – France; *Fj* – Fiji; *I* – Ireland; *It* – Italy; *J* – Japan; *M* – Maoris; *NZ* – New Zealand; *R* – Romania; *S* – Scotland; *SA* – South Africa; *US* – United States; *W* – Wales; (C) – Centenary match v Scotland at Murrayfield, 1971 (non-championship); *P* – England v President's Overseas XV at Twickenham in RFU's Centenary season, 1970-71; (R) – Replacement; (t) – temporary replacement. Entries in square brackets [ ] indicate appearances in the World Cup.

Note: Years given for Five Nations' matches are for second half of season; eg 1972 means season 1971-72. Years for all other matches refer to the actual year of the match. When a series has taken place, figures have been used to denote the particular matches in which players have featured. Thus 1984 *SA* 2 indicates that a player appeared in the second Test of the series.

Aarvold, C D (Cambridge U, W Hartlepool, Headingley, Blackheath) 1928 *A, W, I, F, S,* 1929 *W, I, F,* 1931 *W, S, F,* 1932 *SA, W, I, S,* 1933 *W*
Ackford, P J (Harlequins) 1988 *A,* 1989 *S, I, F, W, R, Fj,* 1990 *I, F, W, S, Arg* 3, 1991 *W, S, I, F, A,* [*NZ, It, F, S, A*]
Adams, A A (London Hospital) 1910 *F*
Adams, F R (Richmond) 1875 *I, S,* 1876 *S,* 1877 *I,* 1878 *S,* 1879 *S, I*
Adey, G J (Leicester) 1976 *I, F*
Adkins, S J (Coventry) 1950 *I, F, S,* 1953 *W, I, F, S*
Agar, A E (Harlequins) 1952 *SA, W, S, I, F,* 1953 *W, I*
Alcock, A (Guy's Hospital) 1906 *SA*
Alderson, F H R (Hartlepool R) 1891 *W, I, S,* 1892 *W, S,* 1893 *W*
Alexander, H (Richmond) 1900 *I, S,* 1901 *W, I, S,* 1902 *W, I*
Alexander, W (Northern) 1927 *F*
Allison, D F (Coventry) 1956 *W, I, S, F,* 1957 *W,* 1958 *W, S*
Allport, A (Blackheath) 1892 *W,* 1893 *I,* 1894 *W, I, S*
Anderson, S (Rockcliff) 1899 *I*
Anderson, W F (Orrell) 1973 *NZ* 1
Anderton, C (Manchester FW) 1889 *M*
Andrew, C R (Cambridge U, Nottingham, Wasps, Toulouse) 1985 *R, F, S, I, W,* 1986 *W, S, I, F,* 1987 *I, F, W,* [*J* (R), *US*], 1988 *S, I* 1,2, *A* 1,2, *Fj, A,* 1989 *S, I, F, W, R, Fj,* 1990 *I, F, W, S, Arg* 3, 1991 *W, S, I, F, Fj, A,* [*NZ, It, US, F, S, A*], 1992 *S, I, F, W, C, SA,* 1993 *F, W, NZ,* 1994 *S, I, F, W*
Archer, H (Bridgwater A) 1909 *W, F, I*
Armstrong, R (Northern) 1925 *W*
Arthur, T G (Wasps) 1966 *W, I*
Ashby, R C (Wasps) 1966 *I, F,* 1967 *A*
Ashcroft, A (Waterloo) 1956 *W, I, S, F,* 1957 *W, I, F, S,* 1958 *W, A, I, F, S,* 1959 *I, F, S*
Ashcroft, A H (Birkenhead Park) 1909 *A*
Ashford, W (Richmond) 1897 *W, I,* 1898 *S, W*
Ashworth, A (Oldham) 1892 *I*
Askew, J G (Cambridge U) 1930 *W, I, F*
Aslett, A R (Richmond) 1926 *W, I, F, S,* 1929 *S, F*
Assinder, E W (O Edwardians) 1909 *A, W*
Aston, R L (Blackheath) 1890 *S, I*
Auty, J R (Headingley) 1935 *S*

Back, N A (Leicester) 1994 *S, I*
Bailey, M D (Cambridge U, Wasps) 1984 *SA* 1,2, 1987 [*US*], 1989 *Fj,* 1990 *I, F, S* (R)
Bainbridge, S (Gosforth, Fylde) 1982 *F, W,* 1983 *F, W, S, I, NZ,* 1984 *S, I, F, W,* 1985 *NZ* 1,2, 1987 *F, W, S,* [*J, US*]
Baker, D G S (OMTs) 1955 *W, I, F, S*
Baker, E M (Moseley) 1895 *W, I, S,* 1896 *W, I, S,* 1897 *W*
Baker, H C (Clifton) 1887 *W*
Bance, J F (Bedford) 1954 *S*
Barley, B (Wakefield) 1984 *I, F, W, A,* 1988 *A* 1,2, *Fj*
Barnes, S (Bristol, Bath) 1984 *A,* 1985 *R* (R), *NZ* 1,2, 1986 *S* (R), *F* (R), 1987 *I* (R), 1988 *Fj,* 1993 *S, I*
Barr, R J (Leicester) 1932 *SA, W, I*
Barrett, E I M (Lennox) 1903 *S*
Barrington, T J M (Bristol) 1931 *W, I*
Barrington-Ward, L E (Edinburgh U) 1910 *W, I, F, S*

Barron, J H (Bingley) 1896 *S,* 1897 *W, I*
Bartlett, J T (Waterloo) 1951 *W*
Bartlett, R M (Harlequins) 1957 *W, I, F, S,* 1958 *I, F, S*
Barton, J (Coventry) 1967 *I, F, W,* 1972 *F*
Batchelor, T B (Oxford U) 1907 *F*
Bates, S M (Wasps) 1989 *R*
Bateson, A H (Otley) 1930 *W, I, F, S*
Bateson, H D (Liverpool) 1879 *I*
Batson, T (Blackheath) 1872 *S,* 1874 *S,* 1875 *I*
Batten, J M (Cambridge U) 1874 *S*
Baume, J L (Northern) 1950 *S*
Baxter, J (Birkenhead Park) 1900 *W, I, S*
Bayfield, M C (Northampton) 1991 *Fj, A,* 1992 *S, I, F, W, C, SA,* 1993 *F, W, S, I,* 1994 *S, I*
Bazley, R C (Waterloo) 1952 *I, F,* 1953 *W, I, F, S,* 1955 *W, I, F, S*
Beaumont, W B (Fylde) 1975 *I, A* 1(R),2, 1976 *A, W, S, I, F,* 1977 *S, I, F, W,* 1978 *F, W, S, I, NZ,* 1979 *S, I, F, W, NZ,* 1980 *I, F, W, S,* 1981 *W, S, I, F, Arg* 1,2, 1982 *A, S*
Bedford, H (Morley) 1889 *M,* 1890 *S, I*
Bedford, L L (Headingley) 1931 *W, I*
Beer, I D S (Harlequins) 1955 *F, S*
Beese, M C (Liverpool) 1972 *W, I, F*
Bell, F J (Northern) 1900 *W*
Bell, H (New Brighton) 1884 *I*
Bell, J L (Darlington) 1878 *I*
Bell, P J (Blackheath) 1968 *W, I, F, S*
Bell, R W (Northern) 1900 *W, I, S*
Bendon, G J (Wasps) 1959 *W, I, F, S*
Bennett, N O (St Mary's Hospital, Waterloo) 1947 *W, S, F,* 1948 *A, W, I, S*
Bennett, W N (Bedford, London Welsh) 1975 *S, A* 1, 1976 *S* (R), 1979 *S, I, F, W*
Bennetts, B B (Penzance) 1909 *A, W*
Bentley, J (Sale) 1988 *I* 2, *A* 1
Bentley, J E (Gipsies) 1871 *S,* 1872 *S*
Berridge, M J (Northampton) 1949 *W, I*
Berry, H (Gloucester) 1910 *W, I, F, S*
Berry, J (Tyldesley) 1891 *W, I, S*
Berry, J T W (Leicester) 1939 *W, I, S*
Beswick, E (Swinton) 1882 *I, S*
Biggs, J M (UCH) 1878 *S,* 1879 *I*
Birkett, J G G (Harlequins) 1906 *S, F, SA,* 1907 *F, W, S,* 1908 *F, W, I, S,* 1910 *W, I, S,* 1911 *W, F, I, S,* 1912 *W, I, S, F*
Birkett, L (Clapham R) 1875 *S,* 1877 *I, S*
Birkett, R H (Clapham R) 1871 *S,* 1875 *S,* 1876 *S,* 1877 *I*
Bishop, C C (Blackheath) 1927 *F*
Black, B H (Blackheath) 1930 *W, I, F, S,* 1931 *W, I, S, F,* 1932 *S,* 1933 *W*
Blacklock, J H (Aspatria) 1898 *I,* 1899 *I*
Blakeway, P J (Gloucester) 1980 *I, F, W, S,* 1981 *W, S, I, F,* 1982 *I, F, W,* 1984 *I, F, W, SA* 1, 1985 *R, F, S, I*
Blakiston, A F (Northampton) 1920 *S,* 1921 *W, I, S, F,* 1922 *W,* 1923 *S, F,* 1924 *W, I, F, S,* 1925 *NZ, W, I, S, F*
Blatherwick, T (Manchester) 1878 *I*
Body, J A (Gipsies) 1872 *S,* 1873 *S*
Bolton, C A (United Services) 1909 *F*
Bolton, R (Harlequins) 1933 *W,* 1936 *S,* 1937 *S,* 1938 *W, I*
Bolton, W N (Blackheath) 1882 *I, S,* 1883 *W, I, S,* 1884

W, I, S, 1885 *I*, 1887 *I, S*
Bonaventura, M S (Blackheath) 1931 *W*
Bond, A M (Sale) 1978 *NZ*, 1979 *S, I, NZ*, 1980 *I*, 1982 *I*
Bonham-Carter, E (Oxford U) 1891 *S*
Bonsor, F (Bradford) 1886 *W, I, S*, 1887 *W, S*, 1889 *M*
Boobbyer, B (Rosslyn Park) 1950 *W, I, F, S*, 1951 *W, F*, 1952 *S, I, F*
Booth, L A (Headingley) 1933 *W, I, S*, 1934 *S*, 1935 *W, I, S*
Botting, I J (Oxford U) 1950 *W, I*
Boughton, H J (Gloucester) 1935 *W, I, S*
Boyle, C W (Oxford U) 1873 *S*
Boyle, S B (Gloucester) 1983 *W, S, I*
Boylen, F (Hartlepool R) 1908 *F, W, I, S*
Bracken, K P P (Bristol) 1993 *NZ*, 1994 *S, I*
Bradby, M S (United Services) 1922 *I, F*
Bradley, R (W Hartlepool) 1903 *W*
Bradshaw, H (Bramley) 1892 *S*, 1893 *W, I, S*, 1894 *W, I, S*
Brain, S E (Coventry) 1984 *SA* 2, *A* (R), 1985 *R, F, S, I, W, NZ* 1,2, 1986 *W, S, I, F*
Braithwaite, J (Leicester) 1905 *NZ*
Braithwaite-Exley, B (Headingley) 1949 *W*
Brettargh, A T (Liverpool OB) 1900 *W*, 1903 *I, S*, 1904 *W, I, S*, 1905 *I, S*
Brewer, J (Gipsies) 1876 *I*
Briggs, A (Bradford) 1892 *W, I, S*
Brinn, A (Gloucester) 1972 *W, I, S*
Broadley, T (Bingley) 1893 *W, S*, 1894 *W, I, S*, 1896 *S*
Bromet, W E (Richmond) 1891 *W, I*, 1892 *W, I, S*, 1893 *W, I, S*, 1895 *W, I, S*, 1896 *I*
Brook, P W P (Harlequins) 1930 *S*, 1931 *F*, 1936 *S*
Brooke, T J (Richmond) 1968 *F, S*
Brooks, F G (Bedford) 1906 *SA*
Brooks, M J (Oxford U) 1874 *S*
Brophy, T J (Liverpool) 1964 *I, F, S*, 1965 *W, I*, 1966 *W, I, F*
Brough, J W (Silloth) 1925 *NZ, W*
Brougham, H (Harlequins) 1912 *W, I, S, F*
Brown, A A (Exeter) 1938 *S*
Brown, L G (Oxford U, Blackheath) 1911 *W, F, I, S*, 1913 *SA, W, F, I, S*, 1914 *W, I, S, F*, 1921 *W, I, S, F*, 1922 *W*
Brown, T W (Bristol) 1928 *S*, 1929 *W, I, S, F*, 1932 *S*, 1933 *W, I, S*
Brunton, J (N Durham) 1914 *W, I, S*
Brutton, E B (Cambridge U) 1886 *S*
Bryden, C C (Clapham R) 1876 *I*, 1877 *S*
Bryden, H A (Clapham R) 1874 *S*
Buckingham, R A (Leicester) 1927 *F*
Bucknall, A L (Richmond) 1969 *SA*, 1970 *I, W, S, F*, 1971 *W, I, F, S* (2[1C])
Buckton, J R D (Saracens) 1988 *A* (R), 1990 *Arg* 1,2
Budd, A (Blackheath) 1878 *I*, 1879 *S, I*, 1881 *W, S*
Budworth, R T D (Blackheath) 1890 *W*, 1891 *W, S*
Bull, A G (Northampton) 1914 *W*
Bullough, E (Wigan) 1892 *W, I, S*
Bulpitt, M P (Blackheath) 1970 *S*
Bulteel, A J (Manchester) 1876 *I*
Bunting, W L (Moseley) 1897 *I, S*, 1898 *I, S, W*, 1899 *S*, 1900 *S*, 1901 *I, S*
Burland, D W (Bristol) 1931 *W, I, F*, 1932 *I, S*, 1933 *W, I, S*
Burns, B H (Blackheath) 1871 *S*
Burton, G W (Blackheath) 1879 *S, I*, 1880 *S*, 1881 *I, W, S*
Burton, H C (Richmond) 1926 *W*
Burton, M A (Gloucester) 1972 *W, I, F, S, SA*, 1974 *F, W*, 1975 *S, A* 1,2, 1976 *A, W, S, I, F*, 1978 *F, W*
Bush, J A (Clifton) 1872 *S*, 1873 *S*, 1875 *S*, 1876 *I, S*
Butcher, C J S (Harlequins) 1984 *SA* 1,2, *A*
Butcher, W V (Streatham) 1903 *S*, 1904 *W, I, S*, 1905 *W, I, S*
Butler, A G (Harlequins) 1937 *W, I*
Butler, P E (Gloucester) 1975 *A* 1, 1976 *F*
Butterfield, J (Northampton) 1953 *F, S*, 1954 *W, NZ, I, S, F*, 1955 *W, I, F, S*, 1956 *W, I, S, F*, 1957 *W, I, F, S*, 1958 *W, A, I, F, S*, 1959 *W, I, F, S*
Byrne, F A (Moseley) 1897 *W*
Byrne, J F (Moseley) 1894 *W, I, S*, 1895 *I, S*, 1896 *I*, 1897 *W, I, S*, 1898 *I, S, W*, 1899 *I*

Cain, J J (Waterloo) 1950 *W*
Callard, J E B (Bath) 1993 *NZ*, 1994 *S, I*

Campbell, D A (Cambridge U) 1937 *W, I*
Candler, P L (St Bart's Hospital) 1935 *W*, 1936 *NZ, W, I, S*, 1937 *W, I, S*, 1938 *W, S*
Cannell, L B (Oxford U, St Mary's Hospital) 1948 *F*, 1949 *W, I, F, S*, 1950 *W, I, F, S*, 1952 *SA, W*, 1953 *W, I, F*, 1956 *I, S, F*, 1957 *W, I*
Caplan, D W N (Headingley) 1978 *S, I*
Cardus, R M (Roundhay) 1979 *F, W*
Carey, G M (Blackheath) 1895 *W, I, S*, 1896 *W, I*
Carleton, J (Orrell) 1979 *NZ*, 1980 *I, F, W, S*, 1981 *W, S, I, F, Arg* 1,2, 1982 *A, S, I, F, W*, 1983 *F, W, S, I, NZ*, 1984 *S, I, F, W, A*
Carling, W D C (Durham U, Harlequins) 1988 *F, W, S, I* 1,2, *A2, Fj, A*, 1989 *S, I, F, W, Fj*, 1990 *I, F, W, S, Arg* 1,2,3, 1991 *W, S, I, F, Fj, A*, [*NZ, It, US, F, S, A*], 1992 *S, I, F, W, C, SA*, 1993 *F, W, S, I, NZ*, 1994 *S, I, F, W*
Carpenter, A D (Gloucester) 1932 *SA*
Carr, R S L (Manchester) 1939 *W, I, S*
Cartwright, V H (Nottingham) 1903 *W, I, S*, 1904 *W, S*, 1905 *W, I, S, NZ*, 1906 *W, I, S, F, SA*
Catcheside, H C (Percy Park) 1924 *W, I, F, S*, 1926 *W, I*, 1927 *I, S*
Catt, M J (Bath) 1994 *W*(R)
Cattell, R H B (Blackheath) 1895 *W, I, S*, 1896 *W, I, S*, 1900 *W*
Cave, J W (Richmond) 1889 *M*
Cave, W T C (Blackheath) 1905 *W*
Challis, R (Bristol) 1957 *I, F, S*
Chambers, E L (Bedford) 1908 *F*, 1910 *W, I*
Chantrill, B S (Bristol) 1924 *W, I, F, S*
Chapman, C E (Cambridge U) 1884 *W*
Chapman, F E (Hartlepool) 1910 *W, I, F, S*, 1912 *W*, 1914 *W, I*
Cheesman, W I (OMTs) 1913 *SA, W, F, I*
Cheston, E C (Richmond) 1873 *S*, 1874 *S*, 1875 *I, S*, 1876 *S*
Chilcott, G J (Bath) 1984 *A*, 1986 *I, F*, 1987 *F* (R), *W*, [*J, US, W*(R)], 1988 *I* 2(R), *Fj*, 1989 *I* (R), *F, W, R*
Christopherson, P (Blackheath) 1891 *W, S*
Clark, C W H (Liverpool) 1876 *I*
Clarke, A J (Coventry) 1935 *W, I, S*, 1936 *NZ, W, I*
Clarke, B B (Bath) 1992 *SA*, 1993 *F, W, S, I, NZ*, 1994 *S, F, W*
Clarke, S J S (Cambridge U, Blackheath) 1963 *W, I, F, S, NZ* 1,2, *A*, 1964 *NZ, W, I*, 1965 *I, F, S*
Clayton, J H (Liverpool) 1871 *S*
Clements, J W (O Cranleighans) 1959 *I, F, S*
Cleveland, C R (Blackheath) 1887 *W, S*
Clibborn, W G (Richmond) 1886 *W, I, S*, 1887 *W, I, S*
Clough, F J (Cambridge U, Orrell) 1986 *I, F*, 1987 [*J*(R), *US*]
Coates, C H (Yorkshire W) 1880 *S*, 1881 *S*, 1882 *S*
Coates, V H M (Bath) 1913 *SA, W, F, I, S*
Cobby, W (Hull) 1900 *W*
Cockerham, A (Bradford Olicana) 1900 *W*
Colclough, M J (Angoulême, Wasps, Swansea) 1978 *S, I*, 1979 *NZ*, 1980 *F, W, S*, 1981 *W, S, I, F*, 1982 *A, S, I, F, W*, 1983 *F, NZ*, 1984 *S, I, F, W*, 1986 *W, S, I, F*
Coley, E (Northampton) 1929 *F*, 1932 *W*
Collins, P J (Camborne) 1952 *S, I, F*
Collins, W E (O Cheltonians) 1874 *S*, 1875 *I, S*, 1876 *I, S*
Considine, S G U (Bath) 1925 *F*
Conway, G S (Cambridge U, Rugby, Manchester) 1920 *F, I, S*, 1921 *F*, 1922 *W, I, F, S*, 1923 *W, I, S, F*, 1924 *W, I, F, S*, 1925 *NZ*, 1927 *W*
Cook, J G (Bedford) 1937 *S*
Cook, P W (Richmond) 1965 *I, F*
Cooke, D A (Harlequins) 1976 *W, S, I, F*
Cooke, D H (Harlequins) 1981 *W, S, I, F*, 1984 *I*, 1985 *R, F, S, I, W, NZ* 1,2
Cooke, P (Richmond) 1939 *W, I*
Coop, T (Leigh) 1892 *S*
Cooper, J G (Moseley) 1909 *A, W*
Cooper, M J (Moseley) 1973 *F, S, NZ* 2 (R), 1975 *F, W*, 1976 *A, W*, 1977 *S, I, F, W*
Coopper, S F (Blackheath) 1900 *W*, 1902 *W, I*, 1905 *W, I, S*, 1907 *W*
Corbett, L J (Bristol) 1921 *F*, 1923 *W, I*, 1924 *W, I, F*, 1925 *NZ, W, I, S, F*, 1927 *W, I, S, F*
Corless, B J (Coventry, Moseley) 1976 *A, I* (R), 1977 *S, I, F, W*, 1978 *F, W, S, I*
Cotton, F E (Loughborough Colls, Coventry, Sale)

1971 *S* (2[1C]), *P*, 1973 *W, I, F, S, NZ* 2, *A*, 1974 *S, I*,
1975 *I, F, W*, 1976 *A, W, S, I, F*, 1977 *S, I, F, W*, 1978
S, I, 1979 *NZ*, 1980 *I, F, W, S*, 1981 *W*
Coulman, M J (Moseley) 1967 *A, I, F, S, W*, 1968 *W,
I, F, S*
Coulson, T J (Coventry) 1927 *W*, 1928 *A, W*
Court, E D (Blackheath) 1885 *W*
Coverdale, H (Blackheath) 1910 *F*, 1912 *I, F*, 1920 *W*
Cove-Smith, R (OMTs)1921 *S, F*, 1922 *I, F, S*, 1923
W, I, S, F, 1924 *W, I, S, F*, 1925 *NZ, W, I, S, F*, 1927
W, I, S, F,1928 *A, W, I, F, S*, 1929 *W, I*
Cowling, R J (Leicester) 1977 *S, I, F, W*, 1978 *F, NZ*,
1979 *S, I*
Cowman, A R (Loughborough Colls, Coventry) 1971 *S*
(2[1C]), *P*, 1973 *W, I*
Cox, N S (Sunderland) 1901 *S*
Cranmer, P (Richmond, Moseley) 1934 *W, I, S*, 1935
W, I, S, 1936 *NZ, W, I, S*, 1937 *W, I, S*, 1938 *W, I, S*
Creed, R N (Coventry) 1971 *P*
Cridlan, A G (Blackheath) 1935 *W, I, S*
Crompton, C A (Blackheath) 1871 *S*
Crosse, C W (Oxford U) 1874 *S*, 1875 *I*
Cumberlege, B S (Blackheath) 1920 *W, I, S*, 1921 *W, I,
S, F*, 1922 *W*
Cumming, D C (Blackheath) 1925 *S, F*
Cunliffe, F L (RMA) 1874 *S*
Currey, F I (Marlborough N) 1872 *S*
Currie, J D (Oxford U, Harlequins, Bristol) 1956 *W, I,
S, F*, 1957 *W, I, F, S*, 1958 *W, A, I, F, S*, 1959 *W, I,
F, S*, 1960 *W, I, F, S*, 1961 *SA*, 1962 *W, I, F*
Cusani, D A (Orrell) 1987 *I*
Cusworth, L (Leicester) 1979 *NZ*, 1982 *F, W*, 1983 *F,
W, NZ*, 1984 *S, I, F, W*, 1988 *F, W*

D'Aguilar, F B G (Royal Engineers) 1872 *S*
Dalton, T J (Coventry) 1969 *S* (R)
Danby, T (Harlequins) 1949 *W*
Danielli, J (Richmond) 1899 *W*, 1900 *I, S*, 1902 *I, S*,
1904 *I, S*
Darby, A J L (Birkenhead Park) 1899 *I*
Davenport, A (Ravenscourt Park) 1871 *S*
Davey, J (Redruth) 1908 *S*, 1909 *W*
Davey, R F (Teignmouth) 1931 *W*
Davidson, Jas (Aspatria) 1897 *S*, 1898 *S, W*, 1899 *I, S*
Davidson, Jos (Aspatria) 1899 *W, S*
Davies, G H (Cambridge U, Coventry, Wasps) 1981 *S,
I, F, Arg* 1,2, 1982 *A, S, I*, 1983 *F, W, S*, 1984 *S, SA*
1,2, 1985 *R* (R), *NZ* 1,2, 1986 *W, S, I, F*
Davies, P H (Sale) 1927 *I*
Davies, V G (Harlequins) 1922 *W*, 1925 *NZ*
Davies, W J A (United Services, RN) 1913 *SA, W, F,
I, S*, 1914 *I, S, F*,1920 *F, I, S*, 1921 *W, I, S, F*, 1922 *I,
F, S*, 1923 *W, I, S, F*
Davies, W P C (Harlequins) 1953 *S*, 1954 *NZ, I*, 1955
W, I, F, S, 1956 *W*, 1957 *F, S*, 1958 *W*
Davis, A M (Harlequins) 1963 *W, I, S, NZ* 1,2, 1964
NZ, W, I, F, S, 1966 *W*, 1967 *A*, 1969 *SA*, 1970 *I, W, S*
Dawe, R G R (Bath) 1987 *I, F, W*, [US]
Dawson, E F (RIEC) 1878 *I*
Day, H L V (Leicester) 1920 *W*, 1922 *W, F*, 1926 *S*
Dean, G J (Harlequins) 1931 *I*
Dee, J M (Hartlepool R) 1962 *S*, 1963 *NZ* 1
Devitt, Sir T G (Blackheath) 1926 *I, F*, 1928 *A, W*
Dewhurst, J H (Richmond) 1887 *W, I, S*, 1890 *W*
De Glanville, P R (Bath) 1992 *SA*(R), 1993 *W*(R), *NZ*,
1994 *S, I, F, W*
De Winton, R F C (Marlborough N) 1893 *W*
Dibble, R (Bridgwater A) 1906 *S, F, SA*, 1908 *F, W, I,
S*, 1909 *A, W, F, I, S*, 1910 *S*, 1911 *W, F, S*, 1912 *W,
I, S*
Dicks, J (Northampton) 1934 *W, I, S*, 1935 *W, I, S*,
1936 *S*, 1937 *I*
Dillon, E W (Blackheath) 1904 *W, I, S*, 1905 *W*
Dingle, A J (Hartlepool R) 1913 *I*, 1914 *S, F*
Dixon, P J (Harlequins, Gosforth) 1971 *P*, 1972 *W, I,
F, S*, 1973 *I, F, S*, 1974 *S, I, F, W*, 1975 *I*, 1976 *F*, 1977
S, I, F, W, 1978 *F, S, I, NZ*
Dobbs, G E B (Devonport A) 1906 *W, I*
Doble, S A (Moseley) 1972 *SA*, 1973 *NZ* 1, *W*
Dobson, D D (Newton Abbot) 1902 *W, I, S*, 1903 *W,
I, S*
Dobson, T H (Bradford) 1895 *S*
Dodge, P W (Leicester) 1978 *W, S, I, NZ*, 1979 *S, I, F,
W*, 1980 *W, S*, 1981 *W, S, I, F, Arg* 1,2, 1982 *A, S, F*,

W, 1983 *F, W, S, I, NZ*, 1985 *R, F, S, I, W, NZ* 1,2
Donnelly, M P (Oxford U) 1947 *I*
Dooley, W A (Preston Grasshoppers, Fylde) 1985 *R,
F, S, I, W, NZ* 2 (R), 1986 *W, S, I, F*, 1987 *F, W*, [A,
US, W], 1988 *F, W, S, I* 1,2, *A* 1,2, *Fj, A*, 1989 *S, I, F,
W, R, Fj*, 1990 *I, F, W, S, Arg* 1,2,3, 1991 *W, S, I, F,
[NZ, US, F, S, A]*, 1992 *S, I, F, W, C, SA*, 1993 *W,
S, I*
Dovey, B A (Rosslyn Park) 1963 *W, I*
Down, P J (Bristol) 1909 *A*
Dowson, A O (Moseley) 1899 *S*
Drake-Lee, N J (Cambridge U, Leicester) 1963 *W, I,
F, S*, 1964 *NZ, W, I*, 1965 *W*
Duckett, H (Bradford) 1893 *I, S*
Duckham, D J (Coventry) 1969 *I, F, S, W, SA*, 1970 *I,
W, S, F*, 1971 *W, I, F, S* (2[1C]), *P*, 1972 *W, I, F, S*,
1973 *NZ* 1, *W, I, F, S, NZ* 2, *A*, 1974 *S, I, F, W*, 1975
I, F, W, 1976 *A, W, S*
Dudgeon, H W (Richmond) 1897 *S*, 1898 *I, S, W*, 1899
W, I, S
Dugdale, J M (Ravenscourt Park) 1871 *S*
Dun, A F (Wasps) 1984 *W*
Duncan, R F H (Guy's Hospital) 1922 *I, F, S*
Dunkley, P E (Harlequins) 1931 *I, S*, 1936 *NZ, W, I, S*
Duthie, J (W Hartlepool) 1903 *W*
Dyson, J W (Huddersfield) 1890 *S*, 1892 *S*, 1893 *I, S*

Ebdon, P J (Wellington) 1897 *W, I*
Eddison, J H (Headingley) 1912 *W, I, S, F*
Edgar, C S (Birkenhead Park) 1901 *S*
Edwards, R (Newport) 1921 *W, I, S, F*, 1922 *W, F*,
1923 *W*, 1924 *W, F, S*, 1925 *NZ*
Egerton, D W (Bath) 1988 *I* 2, *A* 1, *Fj* (R), *A*, 1989 *Fj*,
1990 *I, Arg* 2 (R)
Elliot, C H (Sunderland) 1886 *W*
Elliot, E W (Sunderland) 1901 *W, I, S*, 1904 *W*
Elliot, W (United Services, RN) 1932 *I, S*, 1933 *W, I,
S*, 1934 *W, I*
Elliott, A E (St Thomas's Hospital) 1894 *S*
Ellis, J (Wakefield) 1939 *S*
Ellis, S S (Queen's House) 1880 *I*
Emmott, C (Bradford) 1892 *W*
Enthoven, H J (Richmond) 1878 *I*
Estcourt, N S D (Blackheath) 1955 *S*
Evans, B J (Leicester) 1988 *A* 2, *Fj*
Evans, E (Sale) 1948 *A*, 1950 *W*, 1951 *I, F, S*, 1952 *SA,
W, S, I, F*, 1953 *I, F, S*, 1954 *W, NZ, I, F*, 1956 *W, I,
S, F*, 1957 *W, I, F, S*, 1958 *W, A, I, F, S*
Evans, G W (Coventry) 1972 *S*, 1973 *W* (R), *F, S, NZ*
2, 1974 *S, I, F, W*
Evans, N L (RNEC) 1932 *W, I, S*, 1933 *W, I*
Evanson, A M (Richmond) 1883 *W, I, S*, 1884 *S*
Evanson, W A D (Richmond) 1875 *S*, 1877 *S*, 1878 *S*,
1879 *S, I*
Evershed, F (Blackheath) 1889 *M*, 1890 *W, S, I*, 1892
W, I, S, 1893 *W, I, S*
Eyres, W C T (Richmond) 1927 *I*

Fagan, A R St L (Richmond) 1887 *I*
Fairbrother, K E (Coventry) 1969 *I, F, S, W, SA*, 1970
I, W, S, F, 1971 *W, I, F*
Faithfull, C K T (Harlequins) 1924 *I*, 1926 *F, S*
Fallas, H (Wakefield T) 1884 *I*
Fegan, J H C (Blackheath) 1895 *W, I, S*
Fernandes, C W L (Leeds) 1881 *I, W, S*
Fidler, J H (Gloucester) 1981 *Arg* 1,2, 1984 *SA* 1,2
Field, E (Middlesex W) 1893 *W, I*
Fielding, K J (Moseley, Loughborough Colls) 1969 *I,
F, S, SA*, 1970 *F, I*, 1972 *W, I, F, S*
Finch, R T (Cambridge U) 1880 *S*
Finlan, J F (Moseley) 1967 *I, F, S, W, NZ*, 1968 *W, I*,
1969 *W, S*, 1970 *F*, 1973 *NZ* 1
Finlinson, H W (Blackheath) 1895 *W, I, S*
Finney, S (RIE Coll) 1872 *S*, 1873 *S*
Firth, F (Halifax) 1894 *W, I, S*
Fletcher, N C (OMTs) 1901 *W, I, S*, 1903 *S*
Fletcher, T (Seaton) 1897 *W*
Fletcher, W R B (Marlborough N) 1873 *S*, 1875 *S*
Fookes, E F (Sowerby Bridge) 1896 *W, I, S*, 1897 *W, I,
S*, 1898 *I, W*, 1899 *I, S*
Ford, P J (Gloucester) 1964 *W, I, F, S*
Forrest, J W (United Services, RN) 1930 *W, I, F, S*,
1931 *W, I, S, F*, 1934 *I, S*

Forrest, R (Wellington) 1899 *W*, 1900 *S*, 1902 *I*, *S*, 1903 *I*, *S*
Foulds, R T (Waterloo) 1929 *W*, *I*
Fowler, F D (Manchester) 1878 *S*, 1879 *S*
Fowler, H (Oxford U) 1878 *S*, 1881 *W*, *S*
Fowler, R H (Leeds) 1877 *I*
Fox, F H (Wellington) 1890 *W*, *S*
Francis, T E S (Cambridge U) 1926 *W*, *I*, *F*, *S*
Frankcom, G P (Cambridge U, Bedford) 1965 *W*, *I*, *F*, *S*
Fraser, E C (Blackheath) 1875 *I*
Fraser, G (Richmond) 1902 *W*, *I*, *S*, 1903 *W*, *I*
Freakes, H D (Oxford U) 1938 *W*, 1939 *W*, *I*
Freeman, H (Marlborough N) 1872 *S*, 1873 *S*, 1874 *S*
French, R J (St Helens) 1961 *W*, *I*, *F*, *S*
Fry, H A (Liverpool) 1934 *W*, *I*, *S*
Fry, T W (Queen's House) 1880 *I*, *S*, 1881 *W*
Fuller, H G (Bath) 1882 *I*, *S*, 1883 *W*, *I*, *S*, 1884 *W*

Gadney, B C (Leicester, Headingley) 1932 *I*, *S*, 1933 *I*, *S*, 1934 *W*, *I*, *S*, 1935 *S*, 1936 *NZ*, *W*, *I*, *S*, 1937 *S*, 1938 *W*
Gamlin, H T (Blackheath) 1899 *W*, *S*, 1900 *W*, *I*, *S*, 1901 *S*, 1902 *W*, *I*, *S*, 1903 *W*, *I*, *S*, 1904 *W*, *I*, *S*
Gardner, E R (Devonport Services) 1921 *W*, *I*, *S*, 1922 *W*, *I*, *F*, 1923 *W*, *I*, *S*, *F*
Gardner, H P (Richmond) 1878 *I*
Garnett, H W T (Bradford) 1877 *S*
Gavins, M N (Leicester) 1961 *W*
Gay, D J (Bath) 1968 *W*, *I*, *F*, *S*
Gent, D R (Gloucester) 1905 *NZ*, 1906 *W*, *I*, 1910 *W*, *I*
Genth, J S M (Manchester) 1874 *S*, 1875 *S*
George, J T (Falmouth) 1947 *S*, *F*, 1949 *I*
Gerrard, R A (Bath) 1932 *SA*, *W*, *I*, *S*, 1933 *W*, *I*, *S*, 1934 *W*, *I*, *S*, 1936 *NZ*, *W*, *I*, *S*
Gibbs, G A (Bristol) 1947 *F*, 1948 *I*
Gibbs, J C (Harlequins) 1925 *NZ*, 1926 *F*, 1927 *W*, *I*, *S*, *F*
Gibbs, N (Harlequins) 1954 *S*, *F*
Giblin, L F (Blackheath) 1896 *W*, *I*, 1897 *S*
Gibson, A S (Manchester) 1871 *S*
Gibson, C O P (Northern) 1901 *W*
Gibson, G R (Northern) 1899 *W*, 1901 *S*
Gibson, T A (Northern) 1905 *W*, *S*
Gilbert, F G (Devonport Services) 1923 *W*, *I*
Gilbert, R (Devonport A) 1908 *W*, *I*, *S*
Giles, J L (Coventry) 1935 *W*, *I*, 1937 *W*, *I*, 1938 *I*, *S*
Gittings, W J (Coventry) 1967 *NZ*
Glover, P B (Bath) 1967 *A*, 1971 *F*, *P*
Godfray, R E (Richmond) 1905 *NZ*
Godwin, H O (Coventry) 1959 *F*, *S*, 1963 *S*, *NZ* 1,2, *A*, 1964 *NZ*, *I*, *F*, *S*, 1967 *NZ*
Gordon-Smith, G W (Blackheath) 1900 *W*, *I*, *S*
Gotley, A L H (Oxford U) 1910 *F*, *S*, 1911 *W*, *F*, *I*, *S*
Graham, D (Aspatria) 1901 *W*
Graham, H J (Wimbledon H) 1875 *I*, *S*, 1876 *I*, *S*
Graham, J D G (Wimbledon H) 1876 *I*
Gray, A (Otley) 1947 *W*, *I*, *S*
Green, J (Skipton) 1905 *I*, 1906 *S*, *F*, *SA*, 1907 *F*, *W*, *I*, *S*
Green, J F (West Kent) 1871 *S*
Greenwell, J H (Rockcliff) 1893 *W*, *I*
Greenwood, J E (Cambridge U, Leicester) 1912 *F*, 1913 *SA*, *W*, *F*, *I*, *S*, 1914 *W*, *S*, *F*, 1920 *W*, *F*, *I*, *S*
Greenwood, J R H (Waterloo) 1966 *I*, *F*, *S*, 1967 *A*, 1969 *I*
Greg, W (Manchester) 1876 *I*, *S*
Gregory, G G (Bristol) 1931 *I*, *S*, *F*, 1932 *SA*, *W*, *I*, *S*, 1933 *W*, *I*, *S*, 1934 *W*, *I*, *S*
Gregory, J A (Blackheath) 1949 *W*
Grylls, W M (Redruth) 1905 *I*
Guest, R H (Waterloo) 1939 *W*, *I*, *S*, 1947 *W*, *I*, *S*, *F*, 1948 *A*, *W*, *I*, *S*, 1949 *F*, *S*
Guillemard, A G (West Kent) 1871 *S*, 1872 *S*
Gummer, C H A (Plymouth A) 1929 *F*
Gunner, C R (Marlborough N) 1876 *I*
Gurdon, C (Richmond) 1880 *I*, *S*, 1881 *I*, *W*, *S*, 1882 *I*, *S*, 1883 *S*, 1884 *W*, *S*, 1885 *I*, 1886 *W*, *I*
Gurdon, E T (Richmond) 1878 *S*, 1879 *I*, 1880 *S*, 1881 *I*, *W*, *S*, 1882 *S*, 1883 *W*, *I*, *S*, 1884 *W*, *I*, *S*, 1885 *W*, *I*, 1886 *S*
Guscott, J C (Bath) 1989 *R*, *Fj*, 1990 *I*, *F*, *W*, *S*, *Arg* 3, 1991 *W*, *S*, *I*, *F*, *Fj*, *A*, [*NZ*, *It*, *F*, *S*, *A*], 1992 *S*, *I*, *F*, *W*, *C*, *SA*, 1993 *F*, *W*, *S*, *I*

Haigh, L (Manchester) 1910 *W*, *I*, *S*, 1911 *W*, *F*, *I*, *S*
Hale, P M (Moseley) 1969 *SA*, 1970 *I*, *W*
Hall, C (Gloucester) 1901 *I*, *S*
Hall, J (N Durham) 1894 *W*, *I*, *S*
Hall, J P (Bath) 1984 *S* (R), *I*, *F*, *SA* 1,2, *A*, 1985 *R*, *F*, *S*, *I*, *W*, *NZ* 1,2, 1986 *W*, *S*, 1987 *I*, *F*, *W*, *S*, 1990 *Arg* 3, 1994 *S*
Hall, N M (Richmond) 1947 *W*, *I*, *F*, *S*, 1949 *W*, *I*, 1952 *SA*, *W*, *S*, *I*, *F*, 1953 *W*, *I*, *F*, *S*, 1955 *W*, *I*
Halliday, S J (Bath, Harlequins) 1986 *W*, *S*, 1987 *S*, 1988 *S*, *I* 1,2, *A* 1, *A*, 1989 *S*, *I*, *F*, *W*, *R*, *Fj* (R), 1990 *W*, *S*, 1991 [*US*, *S*, *A*], 1992 *S*, *I*, *F*, *W*
Hamersley, A St G (Marlborough N) 1871 *S*, 1872 *S*, 1873 *S*, 1874 *S*
Hamilton-Hill, E A (Harlequins) 1936 *NZ*, *W*, *I*
Hamilton-Wickes, R H (Cambridge U) 1924 *I*, 1925 *NZ*, *W*, *I*, *S*, *F*, 1926 *W*, *I*, *S*, 1927 *W*
Hammett, E D G (Newport) 1920 *W*, *F*, *S*, 1921 *W*, *I*, *S*, *F*, 1922 *W*
Hammond, C E L (Harlequins) 1905 *S*, *NZ*, 1906 *W*, *I*, *S*, *F*, 1908 *W*, *I*
Hancock, A W (Northampton) 1965 *F*, *S*, 1966 *F*
Hancock, G E (Birkenhead Park) 1939 *W*, *I*, *S*
Hancock, J H (Newport) 1955 *W*, *I*
Hancock, P F (Blackheath) 1886 *W*, *I*, 1890 *W*
Hancock, P S (Richmond) 1904 *W*, *I*, *S*
Handford, F G (Manchester) 1909 *W*, *F*, *I*, *S*
Hands, R H M (Blackheath) 1910 *F*, *S*
Hanley, J (Plymouth A) 1927 *W*, *S*, *F*, 1928 *W*, *I*, *F*, *S*
Hannaford, R C (Bristol) 1971 *W*, *I*, *F*
Hanvey, R J (Aspatria) 1926 *W*, *I*, *F*, *S*
Harding, E H (Devonport Services) 1931 *I*
Harding, R M (Bristol) 1985 *R*, *F*, *S*, 1987 *S*, [*A*, *J*, *W*], 1988 *I* 1(R),2, *A* 1,2, *Fj*
Harding, V S J (Saracens) 1961 *F*, *S*, 1962 *W*, *I*, *F*, *S*
Hardwick, P F (Percy Park) 1902 *I*, *S*, 1903 *W*, *I*, *S*, 1904 *W*, *I*, *S*
Hardy, E M P (Blackheath) 1951 *I*, *F*, *S*
Hare, W H (Nottingham, Leicester) 1974 *W*, 1978 *F*, *NZ*, 1979 *NZ*, 1980 *I*, *F*, *W*, *S*, 1981 *W*, *S*, *Arg* 1,2, 1982 *F*, *W*, 1983 *F*, *W*, *S*, *I*, *NZ*, 1984 *S*, *I*, *F*, *W*, *SA* 1,2
Harper, C H (Exeter) 1899 *W*
Harriman, A T (Harlequins) 1988 *A*
Harris, S W (Blackheath) 1920 *I*, *S*
Harris, T W (Northampton) 1929 *S*, 1932 *I*
Harrison, A C (Hartlepool R) 1931 *I*, *S*
Harrison, A L (United Services, RN) 1914 *I*, *F*
Harrison, G (Hull) 1877 *I*, *S*, 1879 *S*, *I*, 1880 *S*, 1885 *W*, *I*
Harrison, H C (United Services, RN) 1909 *S*, 1914 *I*, *S*, *F*
Harrison, M E (Wakefield) 1985 *NZ* 1,2, 1986 *S*, *I*, *F*, 1987 *I*, *F*, *W*, *S*, [*A*, *J*, *US*, *W*], 1988 *F*, *W*
Hartley, B C (Blackheath) 1901 *S*, 1902 *S*
Haslett, L W (Birkenhead Park) 1926 *I*, *F*
Hastings, G W D (Gloucester) 1955 *W*, *I*, *F*, *S*, 1957 *W*, *I*, *F*, *S*, 1958 *W*, *A*, *I*, *F*, *S*
Havelock, H (Hartlepool R) 1908 *F*, *W*, *I*
Hawcridge, J J (Bradford) 1885 *W*, *I*
Hayward, L W (Cheltenham) 1910 *I*
Hazell, D St G (Leicester) 1955 *W*, *I*, *F*, *S*
Hearn, R D (Bedford) 1966 *F*, *S*, 1967 *I*, *F*, *S*, *W*
Heath, A H (Oxford U) 1876 *S*
Heaton, J (Waterloo) 1935 *W*, *I*, *S*, 1939 *W*, *I*, *S*, 1947 *I*, *S*, *F*
Henderson, A P (Edinburgh Wands) 1947 *W*, *I*, *S*, *F*, 1948 *I*, *S*, *F*, 1949 *W*, *I*
Henderson, R S F (Blackheath) 1883 *W*, *S*, 1884 *W*, *S*, 1885 *W*
Heppell, W G (Devonport A) 1903 *I*
Herbert, A J (Wasps) 1958 *F*, *S*, 1959 *W*, *I*, *F*, *S*
Hesford, R (Bristol) 1981 *S* (R), 1982 *A*, *S*, *F* (R), 1983 *F* (R), 1985 *R*, *F*, *I*, *S*
Heslop, N J (Orrell) 1990 *Arg* 1,2,3, 1991 *W*, *S*, *I*, *F*, [*US*, *F*], 1992 *W*(R)
Hetherington, J G G (Northampton) 1958 *A*, *I*, 1959 *W*, *I*, *F*, *S*
Hewitt, E N (Coventry) 1951 *W*, *I*, *F*
Hewitt, W W (Queen's House) 1881 *I*, *W*, *S*, 1882 *I*
Hickson, J L (Bradford) 1887 *W*, *S*, *I*, 1890 *W*, *S*, *I*
Higgins, R (Liverpool) 1954 *W*, *NZ*, *I*, *S*, 1955 *W*, *I*, *F*, *S*, 1957 *W*, *I*, *F*, *S*, 1959 *W*
Hignell, A J (Cambridge U, Bristol) 1975 *A* 2, 1976 *A*,

Labuschagne, N A (Harlequins, Guy's Hospital) 1953 *W*, 1955 *W, I, F, S*
Lagden, R O (Richmond) 1911 *S*
Laird, H C C (Harlequins) 1927 *W, I, S,* 1928 *A, W, I, F, S,* 1929 *W, I*
Lambert, D (Harlequins) 1907 *F,* 1908 *F, W, S,* 1911 *W, F, I*
Lampkowski, M S (Headingley) 1976 *A, W, S, I*
Lapage, W N (United Services, RN) 1908 *F, W, I, S*
Larter, P J (Northampton, RAF) 1967 *A, NZ,* 1968 *W, I, F, S,* 1969 *I, F, S, W, SA,* 1970 *I, W, F, S,* 1971 *W, I, F, S* (2[1C]), *P,* 1972 *SA,* 1973 *NZ* 1, *W*
Law, A F (Richmond) 1877 *S*
Law, D E (Birkenhead Park) 1927 *I*
Lawrence, Hon H A (Richmond) 1873 *S,* 1874 *S,* 1875 *I, S*
Lawrie, P W (Leicester) 1910 *S,* 1911 *S*
Lawson, R G (Workington) 1925 *I*
Lawson, T M (Workington) 1928 *A, W*
Leadbetter, M M (Broughton Park) 1970 *F*
Leadbetter, V H (Edinburgh Wands) 1954 *S, F*
Leake, W R M (Harlequins) 1891 *W, I, S*
Leather, G (Liverpool) 1907 *I*
Lee, F H (Marlborough N) 1876 *S,* 1877 *I*
Lee, H (Blackheath) 1907 *F*
Le Fleming, J (Blackheath) 1887 *W*
Leonard, J (Saracens, Harlequins) 1990 *Arg* 1,2,3, 1991 *W, S, I, F, Fj, A,* [*NZ, It, US, F, S, A*], 1992 *S, I, F, W, C, SA,* 1993 *F, W, S, I, NZ* 1994 *S, I, F, W*
Leslie-Jones, F A (Richmond) 1895 *W, I*
Lewis, A O (Bath) 1952 *SA, W, S, I, F,* 1953 *W, I, F, S,* 1954 *F*
Leyland, R (Waterloo) 1935 *W, I, S*
Linnett, M S (Moseley) 1989 *Fj*
Livesay, R O'H (Blackheath) 1898 *W,* 1899 *W*
Lloyd, R H (Harlequins) 1967 *NZ,* 1968 *W, I, F, S*
Locke, H M (Birkenhead Park) 1923 *S, F,* 1924 *W, F, S,* 1925 *W, I, S, F,* 1927 *W, I, S*
Lockwood, R E (Heckmondwike) 1887 *W, I, S,* 1889 *M,* 1891 *W, I, S,* 1892 *W, I, S,* 1893 *W, I,* 1894 *W, I*
Login, S H M (RN Coll) 1876 *I*
Lohden, F C (Blackheath) 1893 *W*
Longland, R J (Northampton) 1932 *S,* 1933 *W, S,* 1934 *W, I, S,* 1935 *W, I, S,* 1936 *NZ, W, I, S,* 1937 *W, I, S,* 1938 *W, I, S*
Lowe, C N (Cambridge U, Blackheath) 1913 *SA, W, F, I, S,* 1914 *W, I, S, F,* 1920 *W, F, I, S,* 1921 *W, I, S, F,* 1922 *W, I, F, S,* 1923 *W, I, S, F*
Lowrie, F (Wakefield T) 1889 *M,* 1890 *W*
Lowry, W M (Birkenhead Park) 1920 *F*
Lozowski, R A P (Wasps) 1984 *A*
Luddington, W G E (Devonport Services) 1923 *W, I, S, F,* 1924 *W, I, F, S,* 1925 *W, I, S, F,* 1926 *W*
Luscombe, F (Gipsies) 1872 *S,* 1873 *S,* 1875 *I, S,* 1876 *I, S*
Luscombe, J H (Gipsies) 1871 *S*
Luxmoore, A F C C (Richmond) 1900 *S,* 1901 *W*
Luya, H F (Waterloo, Headingley) 1948 *W, I, S, F,* 1949 *W*
Lyon, A (Liverpool) 1871 *S*
Lyon, G H d'O (United Services, RN) 1908 *S,* 1909 *A*

McCanlis, M A (Gloucester) 1931 *W, I*
McFadyean, C W (Moseley) 1966 *I, F, S,* 1967 *A, I, F, S, W, NZ,* 1968 *W, I*
MacIlwaine, A H (United Services, Hull & E Riding) 1912 *W, I, S, F,* 1920 *I*
Mackie, O G (Wakefield T, Cambridge U) 1897 *S,* 1898 *I*
Mackinlay, J E H (St George's Hospital) 1872 *S,* 1873 *S,* 1875 *I*
MacLaren, W (Manchester) 1871 *S*
MacLennan, R R F (OMTs) 1925 *I, S, F*
McLeod, N F (RIE Coll) 1879 *S, I*
Madge, R J P (Exeter) 1948 *A, W, I, S*
Malir, F W S (Otley) 1930 *W, I, S*
Mangles, R H (Richmond) 1897 *W, I*
Manley, D C (Exeter) 1963 *W, I, F, S*
Mann, W E (United Services, Army) 1911 *W, F, I*
Mantell, N D (Rosslyn Park) 1975 *A* 1
Markendale, E T (Manchester R) 1880 *I*
Marques, R W D (Cambridge U, Harlequins) 1956 *W, I, S, F,* 1957 *W, I, F, S,* 1958 *W, A, I, F, S,* 1959 *W, I, F, S,* 1960 *W, I, F, S,* 1961 *SA, W*

Marquis, J C (Birkenhead Park) 1900 *I, S*
Marriott, C J B (Blackheath) 1884 *W, I, S,* 1886 *W, I, S,* 1887 *I*
Marriott, E E (Manchester) 1876 *I*
Marriott, V R (Harlequins) 1963 *NZ* 1,2, *A,* 1964 *NZ*
Marsden, G H (Morley) 1900 *W, I, S*
Marsh, H (RIE Coll) 1873 *S*
Marsh, J (Swinton) 1892 *I*
Marshall, H (Blackheath) 1893 *W*
Marshall, M W (Blackheath) 1873 *S,* 1874 *S,* 1875 *I, S,* 1876 *I, S,* 1877 *I, S,* 1878 *S, I*
Marshall, R M (Oxford U) 1938 *I, S,* 1939 *W, I, S*
Martin, C R (Bath) 1985 *F, S, I, W*
Martin, N O (Harlequins) 1972 *F* (R)
Martindale, S A (Kendal) 1929 *F*
Massey, E J (Leicester) 1925 *W, I, S*
Mathias, J L (Bristol) 1905 *W, I, S, NZ*
Matters, J C (RNE Coll) 1899 *S*
Matthews, J R C (Harlequins) 1949 *F, S,* 1950 *I, F, S,* 1952 *SA, W, S, I, F*
Maud, P (Blackheath) 1893 *W, I*
Maxwell, A W (New Brighton, Headingley) 1975 *A* 1, 1976 *A, W, S, I,* 1978 *F*
Maxwell-Hyslop, J E (Oxford U) 1922 *I, F, S*
Maynard, A F (Cambridge U) 1914 *W, I, S*
Meikle, G W C (Waterloo) 1934 *W, I, S*
Meikle, S S C (Waterloo) 1929 *S*
Mellish, F W (Blackheath) 1920 *W, F, I, S,* 1921 *W, I*
Melville, N D (Wasps) 1984 *A,* 1985 *I, W, NZ* 1,2, 1986 *W, S, I, F,* 1988 *F, W, S, I* 1
Merriam, L P B (Blackheath) 1920 *W, F*
Michell, A T (Oxford U) 1875 *I, S,* 1876 *I*
Middleton, B B (Birkenhead Park) 1882 *I,* 1883 *I*
Middleton, J A (Richmond) 1922 *S*
Miles, J H (Leicester) 1903 *W*
Millett, H (Richmond) 1920 *F*
Mills, F W (Marlborough N) 1872 *S,* 1873 *S*
Mills, S G F (Gloucester) 1981 *Arg* 1,2, 1983 *W,* 1984 *SA* 1, *A*
Mills, W A (Devonport A) 1906 *W, I, S, F, SA,* 1907 *F, W, I, S,* 1908 *F, W*
Milman, D L K (Bedford) 1937 *W,* 1938 *W, I, S*
Milton, C H (Camborne S of M) 1906 *I*
Milton, J G (Camborne S of M) 1904 *W, I, S,* 1905 *S,* 1907 *I*
Milton, W H (Marlborough N) 1874 *S,* 1875 *I*
Mitchell, F (Blackheath) 1895 *W, I, S,* 1896 *W, I, S*
Mitchell, W G (Richmond) 1890 *W, S, I,* 1891 *W, I, S,* 1893 *S*
Mobbs, E R (Northampton) 1909 *A, W, F, I, S,* 1910 *I, F*
Moberly, W O (Ravenscourt Park) 1872 *S*
Moore, B C (Nottingham, Harlequins) 1987 *S,* [*A, J, W*], 1988 *F, W, S, I* 1,2, *A* 1,2, *Fj, A,* 1989 *S, I, F, W, R, Fj,* 1990 *I, F, W, S, Arg* 1,2, 1991 *W, S, I, F, Fj, A,* [*NZ, It, F, S, A*], 1992 *S, I, F, W, C, SA,* 1993 *F, W, S, I, NZ,* 1994 *S, I, F, W*
Moore, E J (Blackheath) 1883 *I, S*
Moore, N J N H (Bristol) 1904 *W, I, S*
Moore, P B C (Blackheath) 1951 *W*
Moore, W K T (Leicester) 1947 *W, I,* 1949 *F, S,* 1950 *I, F, S*
Mordell, R J (Rosslyn Park) 1978 *W*
Morfitt, S (W Hartlepool) 1894 *W, I, S,* 1896 *W, I, S*
Morgan, J R (Hawick) 1920 *W*
Morgan, W G D (Medicals, Newcastle) 1960 *W, I, F, S,* 1961 *SA, W, I, F, S*
Morley, A J (Bristol) 1972 *SA,* 1973 *NZ* 1, *W, I,* 1975 *S, A* 1,2
Morris, A D W (United Services, RN) 1909 *A, W, F*
Morris, C D (Liverpool St Helens, Orrell) 1988 *A,* 1989 *S, I, F, W,* 1992 *S, I, F, W, C, SA,* 1993 *F, W, S, I,* 1994 *F, W*
Morrison, P H (Cambridge U) 1890 *W, S, I,* 1891 *I*
Morse, S (Marlborough N) 1873 *S,* 1874 *S,* 1875 *S*
Mortimer, W (Marlborough N) 1899 *W*
Morton, H J S (Blackheath) 1909 *I, S,* 1910 *W, I*
Moss, F (Broughton) 1885 *W, I,* 1886 *W*
Mullins, A R (Harlequins) 1989 *Fj*
Mycock, J (Sale) 1947 *W, I, S, F,* 1948 *A*
Myers, E (Bradford) 1920 *I, S,* 1921 *W, I,* 1922 *W, I, F, S,* 1923 *W, I, S, F,* 1924 *W, F, I, S,* 1925 *S, F*
Myers, H (Keighley) 1898 *I*

145

Nanson, W M B (Carlisle) 1907 *F, W*
Nash, E H (Richmond) 1875 *I*
Neale, B A (Rosslyn Park) 1951 *I, F, S*
Neale, M E (Blackheath) 1912 *F*
Neame, S (O Cheltonians) 1879 *S, I, 1880 I, S*
Neary, A (Broughton Park) 1971 *W, I, F, S (2[1C]), P, 1972 W, I, F, S, SA, 1973 NZ 1, W, I, F, S, NZ 2, A, 1974 S, I, F, W, 1975 I, F, W, S, A 1, 1976 A, W, S, I, F, 1977 I, 1978 F (R), 1979 S, I, F, W, NZ, 1980 I, F, W, S*
Nelmes, B G (Cardiff) 1975 *A 1,2, 1978 W, S, I, NZ*
Newbold, C J (Blackheath) 1904 *W, I, S, 1905 W, I, S*
Newman, S C (Oxford U) 1947 *F, 1948 A, W*
Newton, A W (Blackheath) 1907 *S*
Newton, P A (Blackheath) 1882 *S*
Newton-Thompson, J O (Oxford U) 1947 *S, F*
Nichol, W (Brighouse R) 1892 *W, S*
Nicholas, P L (Exeter) 1902 *W*
Nicholson, B E (Harlequins) 1938 *W, I*
Nicholson, E S (Leicester) 1935 *W, I, S, 1936 NZ, W*
Nicholson, E T (Birkenhead Park) 1900 *W, I*
Nicholson, T (Rockcliff) 1893 *I*
Ninnes, B F (Coventry) 1971 *W*
Norman, D J (Leicester) 1932 *SA, W*
North, E H G (Blackheath) 1891 *W, I, S*
Northmore, S (Millom) 1897 *I*
Novak, M J (Harlequins) 1970 *W, S, F*
Novis, A L (Blackheath) 1929 *S, F, 1930 W, I, F, 1933 I, S*

Oakeley, F E (United Services, RN) 1913 *S, 1914 I, S, F*
Oakes, R F (Hartlepool R) 1897 *W, I, S, 1898 I, S, W, 1899 W, S*
Oakley, L F L (Bedford) 1951 *W*
Obolensky, A (Oxford U) 1936 *NZ, W, I, S*
Ojomoh, S O (Bath) 1994 *I, F*
Old, A G B (Middlesbrough, Leicester, Sheffield) 1972 *W, I, F, S, SA, 1973 NZ 2, A, 1974 S, I, F, W, 1975 I, A 2, 1976 S, I, 1978 F*
Oldham, W L (Coventry) 1908 *S, 1909 A*
Olver, C J (Northampton) 1990 *Arg 3, 1991 [US], 1992 C*
O'Neill, A (Teignmouth, Torquay A) 1901 *W, I, S*
Openshaw, W E (Manchester) 1879 *I*
Orwin, J (Gloucester, RAF, Bedford) 1985 *R, F, S, I, W, NZ 1,2, 1988 F, W, S, I 1,2, A 1,2*
Osborne, R R (Manchester) 1871 *S*
Osborne, S H (Oxford U) 1905 *S*
Oti, C (Cambridge U, Nottingham, Wasps) 1988 *S, I 1, 1989 S, I, F, W, R, 1990 Arg 1,2, 1991 Fj, A, [NZ, It,]*
Oughtred, B (Hartlepool R) 1901 *S, 1902 W, I, S, 1903 W, I*
Owen, J E (Coventry) 1963 *W, I, F, S, A, 1964 NZ, 1965 W, I, F, S, 1966 I, F, S, 1967 NZ*
Owen-Smith, H G O (St Mary's Hospital) 1934 *W, I, S, 1936 NZ, W, I, S, 1937 W, I, S*

Page, J J (Bedford, Northampton) 1971 *W, I, F, S, 1975 S*
Pallant, J N (Notts) 1967 *I, F, S*
Palmer, A C (London Hospital) 1909 *I, S*
Palmer, F H (Richmond) 1905 *W*
Palmer, G V (Richmond) 1928 *I, F, S*
Palmer, J A (Bath) 1984 *SA 1,2, 1986 I (R)*
Pargetter, T A (Coventry) 1962 *S, 1963 F, NZ 1*
Parker, G W (Gloucester) 1938 *I, S*
Parker, Hon S (Liverpool) 1874 *S, 1875 S*
Parsons, E I (RAF) 1939 *S*
Parsons, M J (Northampton) 1968 *W, I, F, S*
Patterson, W M (Sale) 1961 *SA, S*
Pattisson, R M (Blackheath) 1883 *I, S*
Paul, J E (RIE Coll) 1875 *S*
Payne, A T (Bristol) 1935 *I, S*
Payne, C M (Harlequins) 1964 *I, F, S, 1965 I, F, S, 1966 W, I, F, S*
Payne, J H (Broughton) 1882 *S, 1883 W, I, S, 1884 I, 1885 W, I*
Pearce, G S (Northampton) 1979 *S, I, F, W, 1981 Arg 1,2, 1982 A, S, 1983 F, W, S, I, NZ, 1984 S, SA 2, A, 1985 R, F, S, I, W, NZ 1,2, 1986 W, S, I, F, 1987 I, F, W, S, [A, US, W], 1988 Fj, 1991 [US]*
Pears, D (Harlequins) 1990 *Arg 1,2, 1992 F(R), 1994 F*

Pearson, A W (Blackheath) 1875 *I, S, 1876 I, S, 1877 S, 1878 S, I*
Peart, T G A H (Hartlepool R) 1964 *F, S*
Pease, F E (Hartlepool R) 1887 *I*
Penny, S H (Leicester) 1909 *A*
Penny, W J (United Hospitals) 1878 *I, 1879 S, I*
Percival, L J (Rugby) 1891 *I, 1892 I, 1893 S*
Periton, H G (Waterloo) 1925 *W, 1926 W, I, F, S, 1927 W, I, S, F, 1928 A, I, F, S, 1929 W, I, S, F, 1930 W, I, F, S*
Perrott, E S (O Cheltonians) 1875 *I*
Perry, D G (Bedford) 1963 *F, S, NZ 1,2, A 1964 NZ, W, I, 1965 W, I, F, S, 1966 W, I, F*
Perry, S V (Cambridge U, Waterloo) 1947 *W, I, 1948 A, W, I, S, F*
Peters, J (Plymouth) 1906 *S, F, 1907 I, S, 1908 W*
Phillips, C (Birkenhead Park) 1880 *S, 1881 I, S*
Phillips, M S (Fylde) 1958 *A, I, F, S, 1959 W, I, F, S, 1960 W, I, F, S, 1961 W, 1963 W, I, F, S, NZ 1,2, A, 1964 NZ, W, I, F, S*
Pickering, A S (Harrogate) 1907 *I*
Pickering, R D A (Bradford) 1967 *I, F, S, W, 1968 F, S*
Pickles, R C W (Bristol) 1922 *I, F*
Pierce, R (Liverpool) 1898 *I, 1903 S*
Pilkington, W N (Cambridge U) 1898 *S*
Pillman, C H (Blackheath) 1910 *W, I, F, S, 1911 W, F, I, S, 1912 W, F, 1913 SA, W, F, I, S, 1914 W, I, S*
Pillman, R L (Blackheath) 1914 *F*
Pinch, J (Lancaster) 1896 *W, I, 1897 S*
Pinching, W W (Guy's Hospital) 1872 *S*
Pitman, I J (Oxford U) 1922 *S*
Plummer, K C (Bristol) 1969 *W, 1976 S, I, F*
Poole, F O (Oxford U) 1895 *W, I, S*
Poole, R W (Hartlepool R) 1896 *S*
Pope, E B (Blackheath) 1931 *W, S, F*
Portus, G V (Blackheath) 1908 *F, I*
Poulton, R W (later Poulton Palmer) (Oxford U, Harlequins, Liverpool) 1909 *F, I, S, 1910 W, 1911 S, 1912 W, I, S, 1913 SA, W, F, I, S, 1914 W, I, S, F*
Powell, D L (Northampton) 1966 *W, I, 1969 I, F, S, W, 1971 W, I, F, S (2[1C])*
Pratten, W E (Blackheath) 1927 *S, F*
Preece, I (Coventry) 1948 *I, S, F, 1949 F, S, 1950 W, I, F, S, 1951 W, I, F*
Preece, P S (Coventry) 1972 *SA, 1973 NZ 1, W, I, F, S, NZ 2, 1975 I, F, W, A 2, 1976 W (R)*
Preedy, M (Gloucester) 1984 *SA 1*
Prentice, F D (Leicester) 1928 *I, F, S*
Prescott, R E (Harlequins) 1937 *W, I, 1938 I, 1939 W, I, S*
Preston, N J (Richmond) 1979 *NZ, 1980 I, F*
Price, H L (Harlequins) 1922 *I, S, 1923 W, I, F*
Price, J (Coventry) 1961 *I*
Price, P L A (RIE Coll) 1877 *I, S, 1878 S*
Price, T W (Cheltenham) 1948 *S, F, 1949 W, I, F, S*
Probyn, J A (Wasps, Askeans) 1988 *F, W, S, I 1,2, A 1,2, A, 1989 S, I, R (R), 1990 I, F, W, S, Arg 1,2,3, 1991 W, S, I, F, Fj, A, [NZ, It, F, S, A], 1992 S, I, F, W, 1993 F, W, S, I*
Prout, D H (Northampton) 1968 *W, I*
Pullin, J V (Bristol) 1966 *W, 1968 W, I, F, S, 1969 I, F, S, W, SA, 1970 I, W, S, F, 1971 W, I, F, S (2[1C]), P, 1972 W, I, F, S, SA, 1973 NZ 1, W, I, F, S, NZ 2, A, 1974 S, I, F, W, 1975 I, W (R), S, A 1,2, 1976 F*
Purdy, S J (Rugby) 1962 *S*
Pyke, J (St Helens Recreation) 1892 *W*
Pym, J A (Blackheath) 1912 *W, I, S, F*

Quinn, J P (New Brighton) 1954 *W, NZ, I, S, F*

Rafter, M (Bristol) 1977 *S, F, W, 1978 F, W, S, I, NZ, 1979 S, I, F, NZ, 1980 W (R), 1981 W, Arg 1,2*
Ralston, C W (Richmond) 1971 *S (C), P, 1972 W, I, F, S, SA, 1973 NZ 1, W, I, F, S, NZ 2, A, 1974 S, I, F, W, 1975 I, F, S*
Ramsden, H E (Bingley) 1898 *W, S*
Ranson, J M (Rosslyn Park) 1963 *NZ 1,2, A, 1964 W, I, F, S*
Raphael, J E (OMTs) 1902 *W, I, S, 1905 W, S, NZ, 1906 W, S, F*
Ravenscroft, J (Birkenhead Park) 1881 *I*
Rawlinson, W C W (Blackheath) 1876 *S*
Redfern, S (Leicester) 1984 *I (R)*
Redman, N C (Bath) 1984 *A, 1986 S (R), 1987 I, S, [A,*

J, *W*], 1988 *Fj*, 1990 *Arg* 1,2, 1991 *Fj*, [*It*, *US*], 1993 *NZ*, 1994 *F*, *W*
Redmond, G F (Cambridge U) 1970 *F*
Redwood, B W (Bristol) 1968 *W*, *I*
Rees, G W (Nottingham) 1984 *SA* 2 (R), *A*, 1986 *I*, *F*, 1987 *F*, *W*, *S*, [*A*, *J*, *US*, *W*], 1988 *S* (R), *I* 1,2, *A* 1,2, *Fj*, 1989 *W* (R), *R* (R), *Fj* (R), 1990 *Arg* 3 (R), 1991 *Fj*, [*US*]
Reeve, J S R (Harlequins) 1929 *F*, 1930 *W*, *I*, *F*, *S*, 1931 *W*, *I*, *S*
Regan, M (Liverpool) 1953 *W*, *I*, *F*, *S*, 1954 *W*, *NZ*, *I*, *S*, *F*, 1956 *I*, *S*, *F*
Rendall, P A G (Wasps, Askeans) 1984 *W*, *SA* 2, 1986 *W*, *S*, 1987 *I*, *F*, *S*, [*A*, *J*, *W*], 1988 *F*, *W*, *S*, *I* 1,2, *A* 1,2, *A*, 1989 *S*, *I*, *F*, *W*, *R*, 1990 *I*, *F*, *W*, *S*, 1991 [*It* (R)]
Rew, H (Blackheath) 1929 *S*, *F*, 1930 *F*, *S*, 1931 *W*, *S*, *F*, 1934 *W*, *I*, *S*
Reynolds, F J (O Cranleighans) 1937 *S*, 1938 *I*, *S*
Reynolds, S (Richmond) 1900 *W*, *I*, *S*, 1901 *I*
Rhodes, J (Castleford) 1896 *W*, *I*, *S*
Richards, D (Leicester) 1986 *I*, *F*, 1987 *S*, [*A*, *J*, *US*, *W*], 1988 *F*, *W*, *S*, *I* 1, *A* 1,2, *Fj*, *A*, 1989 *S*, *I*, *F*, *W*, *R*, 1990 *Arg* 3, 1991 *W*, *S*, *I*, *F*, *Fj*, *A*, [*NZ*, *It*, *US*], 1992 *S*(R), *F*, *W*, *C*, 1993 *NZ*, 1994 *W*
Richards, E E (Plymouth A) 1929 *S*, *F*
Richards, J (Bradford) 1891 *W*, *I*, *S*
Richards, S B (Richmond) 1965 *W*, *I*, *F*, *S*, 1967 *A*, *I*, *F*, *S*, *W*
Richardson, J V (Birkenhead Park) 1928 *A*, *W*, *I*, *F*, *S*
Richardson, W R (Manchester) 1881 *I*
Rickards, C H (Gipsies) 1873 *S*
Rimmer, G (Waterloo) 1949 *W*, *I*, 1950 *W*, 1951 *W*, *I*, *F*, 1952 *SA*, *W*, 1954 *W*, *NZ*, *I*, *S*
Rimmer, L I (Bath) 1961 *SA*, *W*, *I*, *F*, *S*
Ripley, A G (Rosslyn Park) 1972 *W*, *I*, *F*, *S*, *SA*, 1973 *NZ* 1, *W*, *I*, *F*, *S*, *NZ* 2, *A*, 1974 *S*, *I*, *F*, *W*, 1975 *I*, *F*, *S*, *A* 1,2, 1976 *A*, *W*, *S*
Risman, A B W (Loughborough Coll) 1959 *W*, *I*, *F*, *S*, 1961 *SA*, *W*, *I*, *F*
Ritson, J A S (Northern) 1910 *F*, *S*, 1912 *F*, 1913 *SA*, *W*, *F*, *I*, *S*
Rittson-Thomas, G C (Oxford U) 1951 *W*, *I*, *F*
Robbins, G L (Coventry) 1986 *W*, *S*
Robbins, P G D (Oxford U, Moseley, Coventry) 1956 *W*, *I*, *S*, *F*, 1957 *W*, *I*, *F*, *S*, 1958 *W*, *A*, *I*, *S*, 1960 *W*, *I*, *F*, *S*, 1961 *SA*, *W*, 1962 *S*
Roberts, A D (Northern) 1911 *W*, *F*, *I*, *S*, 1912 *I*, *S*, *F*, 1914 *I*
Roberts, E W (RNE Coll) 1901 *W*, *I*, 1905 *NZ*, 1906 *W*, *I*, 1907 *S*
Roberts, G D (Harlequins) 1907 *S*, 1908 *F*, *W*
Roberts, J (Sale) 1960 *W*, *I*, *F*, *S*, 1961 *SA*, *W*, *I*, *F*, *S*, 1962 *W*, *I*, *F*, *S*, 1963 *W*, *I*, *F*, *S*, 1964 *NZ*
Roberts, R S (Coventry) 1932 *I*
Roberts, S (Swinton) 1887 *W*, *I*
Roberts, V G (Penryn, Harlequins) 1947 *F*, 1949 *W*, *I*, *F*, *S*, 1950 *I*, *F*, *S*, 1951 *W*, *I*, *F*, *S*, 1956 *W*, *I*, *S*, *F*
Robertshaw, A R (Bradford) 1886 *W*, *I*, *S*, 1887 *W*, *S*
Robinson, A (Blackheath) 1889 *M*, 1890 *W*, *S*, *I*
Robinson, E T (Coventry) 1954 *S*, 1961 *I*, *F*, *S*
Robinson, G C (Percy Park) 1897 *I*, *S*, 1898 *I*, 1899 *W*, 1900 *I*, *S*, 1901 *I*, *S*
Robinson, J J (Headingley) 1893 *S*, 1902 *W*, *I*, *S*
Robinson, R A (Bath) 1988 *A* 2, *Fj*, *A*, 1989 *S*, *I*, *F*, *W*
Robson, A (Northern) 1924 *W*, *I*, *F*, *S*, 1926 *W*
Robson, M (Oxford U) 1930 *W*, *I*, *F*, *S*
Rodber, T A K (Army, Northampton) 1992 *S*, *I*, 1993 *NZ*, 1994 *I*, *F*, *W*
Rogers, D P (Bedford) 1961 *I*, *F*, *S*, 1962 *W*, *I*, *F*, 1963 *W*, *I*, *F*, *S*, *NZ* 1,2, *A*, 1964 *NZ*, *W*, *I*, *F*, *S*, 1965 *W*, *I*, *F*, *S*, 1966 *W*, *I*, *F*, *S*, 1967 *A*, *S*, *W*, *NZ*, 1969 *I*, *F*, *S*, *W*
Rogers, J H (Moseley) 1890 *W*, *S*, *I*, 1891 *S*
Rogers, W L Y (Blackheath) 1905 *W*, *I*
Rollitt, D M (Bristol) 1967 *I*, *F*, *S*, *W*, 1969 *I*, *F*, *S*, *W*, 1975 *S*, *A* 1,2
Roncoroni, A D S (West Herts, Richmond) 1933 *W*, *I*, *S*
Rose, W M H (Cambridge U, Coventry, Harlequins) 1981 *I*, *F*, 1982 *A*, *S*, *I*, 1987 *I*, *F*, *W*, *S*, [*A*]
Rossborough, P A (Coventry) 1971 *W*, 1973 *NZ* 2, *A*, 1974 *S*, *I*, 1975 *I*, *F*
Rosser, D W A (Wasps) 1965 *W*, *I*, *F*, *S*, 1966 *W*
Rotherham, Alan (Richmond) 1883 *W*, 1884 *W*, *S*,

1885 *W*, *I*, 1886 *W*, *I*, *S*, 1887 *W*, *I*, *S*
Rotherham, Arthur (Richmond) 1898 *S*, *W*, 1899 *W*, *I*, *S*
Roughley, D (Liverpool) 1973 *A*, 1974 *S*, *I*
Rowell, R E (Leicester) 1964 *W*, 1965 *W*
Rowley, A J (Coventry) 1932 *SA*
Rowley, H C (Manchester) 1879 *S*, *I*, 1880 *I*, *S*, 1881 *I*, *W*, *S*, 1882 *I*, *S*
Royds, P M R (Blackheath) 1898 *S*, *W*, 1899 *W*
Royle, A V (Broughton R) 1889 *M*
Rudd, E L (Liverpool) 1965 *W*, *I*, *S*, 1966 *W*, *I*, *S*
Russell, R F (Leicester) 1905 *NZ*
Rutherford, D (Percy Park, Gloucester) 1960 *W*, *I*, *F*, 1965 *W*, *I*, *F*, *S*, 1966 *W*, *I*, *F*, *S*, 1967 *NZ*
Ryalls, H J (N Brighton) 1885 *W*, *I*
Ryan, D (Wasps) 1990 *Arg* 1,2, 1992 *C*
Ryan, P H (Richmond) 1955 *W*, *I*

Sadler, E H (Army) 1933 *I*, *S*
Sagar, J W (Cambridge U) 1901 *W*, *I*
Salmon, J L B (Harlequins) 1985 *NZ* 1,2, 1986 *W*, *S*, 1987 *I*, *F*, *W*, *S*, [*A*, *J*, *US*, *W*]
Sample, C H (Cambridge U) 1884 *I*, 1885 *I*, 1886 *S*
Sanders, D L (Harlequins) 1954 *W*, *NZ*, *I*, *S*, *F*, 1956 *W*, *I*, *S*, *F*
Sanders, F W (Plymouth A) 1923 *I*, *S*, *F*
Sandford, J R P (Marlborough N) 1906 *I*
Sangwin, R D (Hull and E Riding) 1964 *NZ*, *W*
Sargent, G A F (Gloucester) 1981 *I* (R)
Savage, K F (Northampton) 1966 *W*, *I*, *F*, *S*, 1967 *A*, *I*, *F*, *S*, *W*, *NZ*, 1968 *W*, *F*, *S*
Sawyer, C M (Broughton) 1880 *S*, 1881 *I*
Saxby, L E (Gloucester) 1932 *SA*, *W*
Schofield, J W (Manchester) 1880 *I*
Scholfield, J A (Preston Grasshoppers) 1911 *W*
Schwarz, R O (Richmond) 1899 *S*, 1901 *W*, *I*
Scorfield, E S (Percy Park) 1910 *F*
Scott, C T (Blackheath) 1900 *W*, *I*, 1901 *I*, *W*
Scott, E K (St Mary's Hospital, Redruth) 1947 *W*, 1948 *A*, *W*, *I*, *S*
Scott, F S (Bristol) 1907 *W*
Scott, H (Manchester) 1955 *F*
Scott, J P (Rosslyn Park, Cardiff) 1978 *F*, *W*, *S*, *I*, *NZ*, 1979 *S* (R), *I*, *F*, *W*, *NZ*, 1980 *I*, *F*, *W*, *S*, 1981 *W*, *S*, *I*, *F*, *Arg* 1,2, 1982 *I*, *F*, *W*, 1983 *F*, *W*, *S*, *I*, *NZ*, 1984 *S*, *I*, *F*, *W*, *SA* 1,2
Scott, J S M (Oxford U) 1958 *F*
Scott, M T (Cambridge U) 1887 *I*, 1890 *S*, *I*
Scott, W M (Cambridge U) 1889 *M*
Seddon, R L (Broughton R) 1887 *W*, *I*, *S*
Sellar, K A (United Services, RN) 1927 *W*, *I*, *S*, 1928 *A*, *W*, *I*, *F*
Sever, H S (Sale) 1936 *NZ*, *W*, *I*, *S*, 1937 *W*, *I*, *S*, 1938 *W*, *I*, *S*
Shackleton, I R (Cambridge U) 1969 *SA*, 1970 *I*, *W*, *S*
Sharp, R A W (Oxford U, Wasps, Redruth) 1960 *W*, *I*, *F*, *S*, 1961 *I*, *F*, 1962 *W*, *I*, *F*, 1963 *W*, *I*, *F*, *S*, 1967 *A*
Shaw, C H (Moseley) 1906 *S*, *SA*, 1907 *F*, *W*, *I*, *S*
Shaw, F (Cleckheaton) 1898 *I*
Shaw, J F (RNE Coll) 1898 *S*, *W*
Sheppard, A (Bristol) 1981 *W* (R), 1985 *W*
Sherrard, C W (Blackheath) 1871 *S*, 1872 *S*
Sherriff, G A (Saracens) 1966 *S*, 1967 *A*, *NZ*
Shewring, H E (Bristol) 1905 *I*, *NZ*, 1906 *W*, *S*, *F*, *SA*, 1907 *F*, *W*, *I*, *S*
Shooter, J H (Morley) 1899 *I*, *S*, 1900 *I*, *S*
Shuttleworth, D W (Headingley) 1951 *S*, 1953 *S*
Sibree, H J H (Harlequins) 1908 *F*, 1909 *I*, *S*
Silk, N (Harlequins) 1965 *W*, *I*, *F*, *S*
Simms, K G (Cambridge U, Liverpool, Wasps) 1985 *R*, *F*, *S*, *I*, *W*, 1986 *I*, *F*, 1987 *I*, *F*, *W*, [*A*, *J*, *W*], 1988 *F*, *W*
Simpson, C P (Harlequins) 1965 *W*
Simpson, P D (Bath) 1983 *NZ*, 1984 *S*, 1987 *I*
Simpson, T (Rockcliff) 1902 *S*, 1903 *W*, *I*, *S*, 1904 *I*, *S*, 1905 *I*, *S*, 1906 *S*, 1909 *F*
Skinner, M G (Harlequins) 1988 *F*, *W*, *S*, *I* 1,2, 1989 *Fj*, 1990 *I*, *F*, *W*, *S*, *Arg* 1,2, 1991 *Fj* (R), [*US*, *F*, *S*, *A*], 1992 *S*, *I*, *F*, *W*
Sladen, G M (United Services, RN) 1929 *W*, *I*, *S*
Slemen, M A C (Liverpool) 1976 *I*, *F*, 1977 *S*, *I*, *F*, *W*, 1978 *F*, *W*, *S*, *I*, *NZ*, 1979 *S*, *I*, *F*, *W*, *NZ*, 1980 *I*, *F*, *W*, *S*, 1981 *W*, *S*, *I*, *F*, 1982 *A*, *S*, *I*, *F*, *W*, 1983 *NZ*, 1984 *S*

147

Underwood, A M (Exeter) 1962 *W, I, F, S*, 1964 *I*
Underwood, R (Leicester, RAF) 1984 *I, F, W, A*, 1985 *R, F, S, I, W*, 1986 *W, I, F*, 1987 *I, F, W, S, [A, J, W]*, 1988 *F, W, S, I* 1,2, *A* 1,2, *Fj, A*, 1989 *S, I, F, W, R, Fj*, 1990 *I, F, W, S, Arg* 3, 1991 *W, S, I, F, Fj, A, [NZ, It, US, F, S, A]*, 1992 *S, I, F, W, SA*, 1993 *F, W, S, I, NZ*, 1994 *S, I, F, W*
Underwood, T (Leicester) 1992 *C, SA*, 1993 *S, I, NZ*, 1994 *S, I, W*
Unwin, E J (Rosslyn Park, Army) 1937 *S*, 1938 *W, I, S*
Unwin, G T (Blackheath) 1898 *S*
Uren, R (Waterloo) 1948 *I, S, F*, 1950 *I*
Uttley, R M (Gosforth) 1973 *I, F, S, NZ* 2, *A*, 1974 *I, F, W*, 1975 *F, W, S, A* 1,2, 1977 *S, I, F, W*, 1978 *NZ*, 1979 *S*, 1980 *I, F, W, S*

Valentine, J (Swinton) 1890 *W*, 1896 *W, I, S*
Vanderspar, C H R (Richmond) 1873 *S*
Van Ryneveld, C B (Oxford U) 1949 *W, I, F, S*
Varley, H (Liversedge) 1892 *S*
Vassall, H (Blackheath) 1881 *W, S*, 1882 *I, S*, 1883 *W*
Vassall, H H (Blackheath) 1908 *I*
Vaughan, D B (Headingley) 1948 *A, W, I, S*, 1949 *I, F, S*, 1950 *W*
Vaughan-Jones, A (Army) 1932 *I, S*, 1933 *W*
Verelst, C L (Liverpool) 1876 *I*, 1878 *I*
Vernon, G F (Blackheath) 1878 *S, I*, 1880 *I, S*, 1881 *I*
Vickery, G (Aberavon) 1905 *I*
Vivyan, E J (Devonport A) 1901 *W*, 1904 *W, I, S*
Voyce, A T (Gloucester) 1920 *I, S*, 1921 *W, I, S, F*, 1922 *W, I, F, S*, 1923 *W, I, S, F*, 1924 *W, I, F, S*, 1925 *NZ, W, I, S, F*, 1926 *W, I, F, S*

Wackett, J A S (Rosslyn Park) 1959 *W, I*
Wade, C G (Richmond) 1883 *W, I, S*, 1884 *W, S*, 1885 *W*, 1886 *W, I*
Wade, M R (Cambridge U) 1962 *W, I, F*
Wakefield, W W (Harlequins) 1920 *W, F, I, S*, 1921 *W, I, S, F*, 1922 *W, I, F, S*, 1923 *W, I, S, F*, 1924 *W, I, F, S*, 1925 *NZ, W, I, S, F*, 1926 *W, I, F, S*, 1927 *S, F*
Walker, G A (Blackheath) 1939 *W, I*
Walker, H W (Coventry) 1947 *W, I, S, F*, 1948 *A, W, I, S, F*
Walker, R (Manchester) 1874 *S*, 1875 *I*, 1876 *S*, 1879 *S*, 1880 *S*
Wallens, J N S (Waterloo) 1927 *F*
Walton, E J (Castleford) 1901 *W, I*, 1902 *I, S*
Walton, W (Castleford) 1894 *S*
Ward, G (Leicester) 1913 *W, F, S*, 1914 *W, I, S*
Ward, H (Bradford) 1895 *W*
Ward, J I (Richmond) 1881 *I*, 1882 *I*
Ward, J W (Castleford) 1896 *W, I, S*
Wardlow, C S (Northampton) 1969 *SA* (R), 1971 *W, I, F, S* (2[1C])
Warfield, P J (Rosslyn Park, Durham U) 1973 *NZ* 1, *W, I*, 1975 *I, F, S*
Warr, A L (Oxford U) 1934 *W, I*
Watkins, J A (Gloucester) 1972 *SA*, 1973 *NZ* 1, *W, NZ* 2, *A*, 1975 *F, W*
Watkins, J K (United Services, RN) 1939 *W, I, S*
Watson, F B (United Services, RN) 1908 *S*, 1909 *S*
Watson, J H D (Blackheath) 1914 *W, S, F*
Watt, D E J (Bristol) 1967 *I, F, S, W*
Webb, C S H (Devonport Services, RN) 1932 *SA, W, I, S*, 1933 *W, I, S*, 1935 *S*, 1936 *NZ, W, I, S*
Webb, J M (Bristol, Bath) 1987 *[A(R), J, US, W]*, 1988 *F, W, S, I* 1,2, *A* 1,2, *A*, 1989 *S, I, F, W*, 1991 *Fj, A, [NZ, It, F, S, A]*, 1992 *S, I, F, W, C, SA*, 1993 *F, W, S, I*
Webb, J W G (Northampton) 1926 *F, S*, 1929 *S*
Webb, R E (Coventry) 1967 *S, W, NZ*, 1968 *I, F, S*, 1969 *I, F, S, W*, 1972 *I, F*
Webb, St L H (Bedford) 1959 *W, I, F, S*
Webster, J G (Moseley) 1972 *W, I, SA*, 1973 *NZ* 1, *W, NZ* 2, 1974 *S, W*, 1975 *I, F, W*
Wedge, T G (St Ives) 1907 *F*, 1909 *W*
Weighill, R H G (RAF, Harlequins) 1947 *S, F*, 1948 *S, F*
Wells, C M (Cambridge U, Harlequins) 1893 *S*, 1894 *W, S*, 1896 *S*, 1897 *W, S*
West, B R (Loughborough Colls, Northampton) 1968 *W, I, F, S*, 1969 *SA*, 1970 *I, W, S*
Weston, H T F (Northampton) 1901 *S*
Weston, L E (W of Scotland) 1972 *F, S*

Weston, M P (Richmond, Durham City) 1960 *W, I, F, S*, 1961 *SA, W, I, F, S*, 1962 *W, I, F*, 1963 *W, I, F, S*, *NZ* 1,2, *A*, 1964 *NZ, W, I, F, S*, 1965 *F, S*, 1966 *S*, 1968 *F, S*
Weston, W H (Northampton) 1933 *I, S*, 1934 *I, S*, 1935 *W, I, S*, 1936 *NZ, W, S*, 1937 *W, I, S*, 1938 *W, I, S*
Wheatley, A A (Coventry) 1937 *W, I, S*, 1938 *W, S*
Wheatley, H F (Coventry) 1936 *I*, 1937 *S*, 1938 *W, S*, 1939 *W, I, S*
Wheeler, P J (Leicester) 1975 *F, W*, 1976 *A, W, S, I*, 1977 *S, I, F, W*, 1978 *F, W, S, I, NZ*, 1979 *S, I, F, W*, *NZ*, 1980 *I, F, W, S*, 1981 *W, S, I, F*, 1982 *A, S, I, F, W*, 1983 *F, S, I, NZ*, 1984 *S, I, F, W*
White, C (Gosforth) 1983 *NZ*, 1984 *S, I, F*
White, D F (Northampton) 1947 *W, I, S*, 1948 *I, F, S*, 1951 *S*, 1952 *SA, W, S, I, F*, 1953 *W, I, S*
Whiteley, E C P (O Alleynians) 1931 *S, F*
Whiteley, W (Bramley) 1896 *W*
Whitley, H (Northern) 1929 *W*
Wightman, B J (Moseley, Coventry) 1959 *W*, 1963 *W, I, NZ* 2, *A*
Wigglesworth, H J (Thornes) 1884 *I*
Wilkins, D T (United Services, RN, Roundhay) 1951 *W, I, F, S*, 1952 *SA, W, S, I, F*, 1953 *W, I, F, S*
Wilkinson, E (Bradford) 1886 *W, I, S*, 1887 *W, S*
Wilkinson, H (Halifax) 1929 *W, I, S*, 1930 *F*
Wilkinson, H J (Halifax) 1889 *M*
Wilkinson, P (Law Club) 1872 *S*
Wilkinson, R M (Bedford) 1975 *A* 2, 1976 *A, W, S, I, F*
Willcocks, T J (Plymouth) 1902 *W*
Willcox, J G (Oxford U, Harlequins) 1961 *I, F, S*, 1962 *W, I, F, S*, 1963 *W, I, F, S*, 1964 *NZ, W, I, S*
William-Powlett, P B R W (United Services, RN) 1922 *S*
Williams, C G (Gloucester, RAF) 1976 *F*
Williams, C S (Manchester) 1910 *F*
Williams, J E (O Millhillians, Sale) 1954 *F*, 1955 *W, I, F, S*, 1956 *I, S, F*, 1965 *W*
Williams, J M (Penzance-Newlyn) 1951 *I, S*
Williams, P N (Orrell) 1987 *S, [A, J, W]*
Williams, S G (Devonport A) 1902 *W, I, S*, 1903 *I, S*, 1907 *I, S*
Williams, S H (Newport) 1911 *W, F, I, S*
Williamson, R H (Oxford U) 1908 *W, I, S*, 1909 *A, F*
Wilson, A J (Camborne S of M) 1909 *I*
Wilson, C E (Blackheath) 1898 *I*
Wilson, C P (Cambridge U, Marlborough N) 1881 *W*
Wilson, D S (Met Police, Harlequins) 1953 *F*, 1954 *W, NZ, I, S, F*, 1955 *F, S*
Wilson, G S (Tyldesley) 1929 *W, I*
Wilson, K J (Gloucester) 1963 *F*
Wilson, R P (Liverpool OB) 1891 *W, I, S*
Wilson, W C (Richmond) 1907 *I, S*
Winn, C E (Rosslyn Park) 1952 *SA, W, S, I, F*, 1954 *W, S, F*
Winterbottom, P J (Headingley, Harlequins) 1982 *A, S, I, F, W*, 1983 *F, W, S, I, NZ*, 1984 *S, F, W, SA* 1,2, 1986 *W, S, I, F*, 1987 *I, F, W, [A, J, US, W]*, 1988 *F, W, S*, 1989 *R, Fj*, 1990 *I, F, W, S, Arg* 1,2,3, 1991 *W, S, I, F, A, [NZ, It, F, S, A]*, 1992 *S, I, F, W, C, SA*, 1993 *F, W, S, I*
Wintle, T C (Northampton) 1966 *S*, 1969 *I, F, S, W*
Wodehouse, N A (United Services, RN) 1910 *F*, 1911 *W, F, I, S*, 1912 *W, I, S, F*, 1913 *SA, W, F, I, S*
Wood, A (Halifax) 1884 *I*
Wood, A E (Gloucester, Cheltenham) 1908 *F, W, I*
Wood, G W (Leicester) 1914 *W*
Wood, R (Liversedge) 1894 *I*
Wood, R D (Liverpool OB) 1901 *I*, 1903 *W, I*
Woodgate, E E (Paignton) 1952 *W*
Woodhead, E (Huddersfield) 1880 *I*
Woodruff, C G (Harlequins) 1951 *W, I, F, S*
Woods, S M J (Cambridge U, Wellington) 1890 *W, S, I*, 1891 *W, I, S*, 1892 *W, I, S*, 1893 *W, I, S*, 1895 *W, I, S*
Woods, T (Bridgwater) 1908 *S*
Woods, T (United Services, RN) 1920 *S*, 1921 *W, I, S, F*
Woodward, C R (Leicester) 1980 *I* (R), *F, W, S*, 1981 *W, S, I, F, Arg* 1,2, 1982 *A, S, I, F, W*, 1983 *I, NZ*, 1984 *S, I, F, W*
Woodward, J E (Wasps) 1952 *SA, W, S*, 1953 *W, I, F, S*, 1954 *W, NZ, I, S, F*, 1955 *W, I*, 1956 *S*
Wooldridge, C S (Oxford U, Blackheath) 1883 *W, I, S*, 1884 *W, I, S*, 1885 *I*

Wordsworth, A J (Cambridge U) 1975 *A* 1 (R)
Worton, J R B (Harlequins, Army) 1926 *W*, 1927 *W*
Wrench, D F B (Harlequins) 1964 *F, S*
Wright, C C G (Cambridge U, Blackheath) 1909 *I, S*
Wright, F T (Edinburgh Acady, Manchester) 1881 *S*
Wright, I D (Northampton) 1971 *W, I, F, S* (R)
Wright, J C (Met Police) 1934 *W*
Wright, J F (Bradford) 1890 *W*
Wright, T P (Blackheath) 1960 *W, I, F, S*, 1961 *SA, W, I, F, S*, 1962 *W, I, F, S*
Wright, W H G (Plymouth) 1920 *W, F*
Wyatt, D M (Bedford) 1976 *S* (R)

Yarranton, P G (RAF, Wasps) 1954 *W, NZ, I*, 1955 *F, S*

Yiend, W (Hartlepool R, Gloucester) 1889 *M*, 1892 *W, I, S*, 1893 *I, S*
Young, A T (Cambridge U, Blackheath, Army) 1924 *W, I, F, S*, 1925 *NZ, F*, 1926 *I, F, S*, 1927 *I, S, F*, 1928 *A, W, I, F, S*, 1929 *I*
Young, J R C (Oxford U, Harlequins) 1958 *I*, 1960 *W, I, F, S*, 1961 *SA, W, I, F*
Young, M (Gosforth) 1977 *S, I, F, W*, 1978 *F, W, S, I, NZ*, 1979 *S*
Young, P D (Dublin Wands) 1954 *W, NZ, I, S, F*, 1955 *W, I, F, S*
Youngs, N G (Leicester) 1983 *I, NZ*, 1984 *S, I, F, W*

ENGLISH INTERNATIONAL RECORDS

Both team and individual records are for official England international matches up to 31 March 1994.

TEAM RECORDS

Highest score
60 v Japan (60-7) 1987 Sydney
v individual countries
51 v Argentina (51-0) 1990 Twickenham
28 v Australia (28-19) 1988 Twickenham
26 v Canada (26-13) 1992 Wembley
58 v Fiji (58-23) 1989 Twickenham
41 v France (41-13) 1907 Richmond
38 v Ireland (38-9) 1992 Twickenham
36 v Italy (36-6) 1991 Twickenham
60 v Japan (60-7) 1987 Sydney
16 v N Zealand (16-10) 1973 Auckland
58 v Romania (58-3) 1989 Bucharest
30 v Scotland (30-18) 1980 Murrayfield
33 v S Africa (33-16) 1992 Twickenham
37 v US (37-9) 1991 Twickenham
34 v Wales (34-6) 1990 Twickenham

28 v US { (34-6) 1987 Sydney
         { (37-9) 1991 Twickenham
28 v Wales (34-6) 1990 Twickenham

Longest winning sequence
10 matches – 1882-86

Highest score by opposing team
42 N Zealand (15-42) 1985 Wellington
by individual countries
19 Argentina (19-19) 1981 Buenos Aires
40 Australia (15-40) 1991 Sydney
13 Canada (26-13) 1992 Wembley
23 Fiji (58-23) 1989 Twickenham
37 France (12-37) 1972 Colombes
26 Ireland (21-26) 1974 Twickenham
 6 Italy (36-6) 1991 Twickenham
 7 Japan (60-7) 1987 Sydney
42 N Zealand (15-42) 1985 Wellington
15 Romania (22-15) 1985 Twickenham
33 Scotland (6-33) 1986 Murrayfield
35 S Africa (9-35) 1984 Johannesburg
 9 United States (37-9) 1991 Twickenham
34 Wales (21-34) 1967 Cardiff

Biggest winning points margin
55 v Romania (58-3) 1989 Bucharest
v individual countries
51 v Argentina (51-0) 1990 Twickenham
17 v Australia { (20-3) 1973 Twickenham
               { (23-6) 1976 Twickenham
13 v Canada (26-13) 1992 Wembley
35 v Fiji (58-23) 1989 Twickenham
37 v France (37-0) 1911 Twickenham
32 v Ireland (35-3) 1988 Twickenham
30 v Italy (36-6) 1991 Twickenham
53 v Japan (60-7) 1987 Sydney
13 v N Zealand (13-0) 1936 Twickenham
55 v Romania (58-3) 1989 Bucharest
20 v Scotland (26-6) 1977 Twickenham
17 v S Africa (33-16) 1992 Twickenham

Biggest losing points margin
27 v N Zealand (15-42) 1985 Wellington
27 v Scotland (6-33) 1986 Murrayfield
v individual countries
 2 v Argentina (13-15) 1990 Buenos Aires
25 v Australia (15-40) 1991 Sydney
25 v France (12-37) 1972 Colombes

22 v Ireland (0-22) 1947 Dublin
27 v N Zealand (15-42) 1985 Wellington
27 v Scotland (6-33) 1986 Murrayfield
26 v S Africa (9-35) 1984 Johannesburg
25 v Wales (0-25) 1905 Cardiff

No defeats v Canada, Fiji, Italy, Japan, Romania or United States

Longest losing sequence
7 matches – 1904-06
and 1971-72

Most tries by England in an international
13 v Wales 1881 Blackheath

Most tries against England in an international
8 by Wales (6-28) 1922 Cardiff

Most points by England in International Championship in a season – 118
in season 1991-92

Most tries by England in International Championship in a season – 20
in season 1913-14

INDIVIDUAL RECORDS

Most capped player
R Underwood   65   1984-94
in individual positions
Full-back
J M Webb   33   1987-93
Wing
R Underwood   65   1984-94
Centre
W D C Carling   47   1988-94
Fly-half
C R Andrew   56(57)[1]   1985-94
Scrum-half
R J Hill   29   1984-91
Prop
J A Probyn   37   1988-93
Hooker
B C Moore   50   1987-94

Lock
W A Dooley   55   1985-93
Flanker
P J Winterbottom   58   1982-93
No 8
D Richards   36   1986-94

[1]*Andrew has played once as a full-back*

Longest international career
G S Pearce 14 seasons 1978-79 to 1991-92

Most consecutive internationals – 36
J V Pullin 1968-75

Most internationals as captain – 40
W D C Carling 1988-94

Most points in internationals – 296
J M Webb (33 matches) 1987-93

Most points in International Championship in a season – 67
J M Webb (4 matches) 1991-92

Most points in an international – 24
J M Webb v Italy 1991 Twickenham

Most tries in internationals – 37
R Underwood (65 matches) 1984-94

Most tries in International Championship in a season – 8
C N Lowe (4 matches) 1913-14

Most tries in an international – 5
D Lambert v France 1907 Richmond
R Underwood v Fiji 1989 Twickenham

Most conversions in internationals – 41
J M Webb (33 matches) 1987-93

Most conversions in International Championship in a season – 11
J M Webb (4 matches) 1991-92

Most conversions in an international – 8
S D Hodgkinson v Romania 1989 Bucharest

Most dropped goals in internationals – 16
C R Andrew (57 matches) 1985-94

Most dropped goals in an international – 2
R Hiller v Ireland 1970 Twickenham
A G B Old v France 1978 Paris
A G B Old v France 1980 Paris
C R Andrew v Romania 1985 Twickenham
C R Andrew v Fiji 1991 Suva

Most penalty goals in internationals – 67
W H Hare (25 matches) 1974-84

Most penalty goals in International Championship in a season – 18
S D Hodgkinson (4 matches) 1990-91

Most penalty goals in an international – 7
S D Hodgkinson v Wales 1991 Cardiff

Most points on major tour – 56
S D Hodgkinson (4 matches) Argentina 1990
W H Hare scored 79 points on the N American tour of 1982, but this was not a major tour

---

Most points in a tour match – 36
W N Bennett v Western Australia 1975 Perth

Most tries in a tour match – 4
A J Morley v Western Australia 1975 Perth
P S Preece v New South Wales 1975 Sydney

R E Webb scored 4 tries v Canada in 1967, and J Carleton scored 4 against Mid-West at Cleveland in 1982, but these were not on major tours

Rob Andrew, England's most-capped fly-half, also holds the record for most dropped goals in Tests (16) and shares the record for most dropped goals in an international (2).

REARRANGED SOUTH-WEST STRIDE ON STRONGLY TO RETAIN TITLE

CIS INSURANCE DIVISIONAL CHAMPIONSHIP 1993-94

The South and South-West, unrecognisable from the limp, disorientated team of a few years earlier, retained the Divisional Championship and matched the name of the competition's new sponsor with a players' co-operative of their own. CIS agreed a £750,000 deal with the Rugby Football Union covering the Divisional and County Championships over three years, and they impressed instantly as enthusiastic and active sponsors, eagerly seeking to promote the game alongside their own company.

The competition itself survived a familiar quota of criticism of its role in the broader spectrum of the game in England. However, it reached a fitting climax in a rescheduled match at Twickenham in January, when an eighth change of lead brought the South and South-West a 25-17 victory over London. Circumstances had been unpropitious, as the original November date clashed with the weekend of the England A match against the All Blacks. Both divisional sides would have been diluted, which was ironically the case anyway when the game was eventually rearranged – in an increasingly crowded calendar there was virtually only one alternative day for the fixture, the New Year bank holiday, when several players had, not unreasonably, taken family holidays.

Jonathan Callard was the solitary current England player to appear in the match, watched by a crowd of 7,000, but it was a far from wasted exercise. The competition's long-term objective has been, in the words of Geoff Cooke, then the England manager, to take players outside their 'cosy club atmosphere'. The absence of Rob Andrew from London's team, for example, served to allow the promising Guy Gregory a first major opportunity, which he took impressively, kicking four penalty goals along the way.

A tense Bank Holiday Monday match also produced the first dropped goals by the South and South-West in 31 Championship matches stretching back to 1977. Nick Beal landed the first and Paul Hull sealed the result with a second after Paul Holford scored a skilfully worked try following a blindside sortie involving Richard Hill, Beal and Derek Eves.

After being 'locked into a cycle of defeat', as former captain Andy Robinson had described it two years earlier, the South and South-West remained unbeaten in six matches under the leadership first of Stuart Barnes, then Jon Hall and Graham Dawe. Their massive improvement was demonstrated by the fact that their victory over London was only their ninth in 31 games overall since 1977. The South and South-West's intent had been apparent in their opening game when they brushed aside the Midlands 31-3, recording their biggest victory in the Championship's history.

With the benefit of a second successive home game, this time at Gloucester, they beat the North, Callard's full-back performance against Hunter pointing his way towards the England team for the All Blacks match five weeks later. Callard proceeded to become the competition's leading points-scorer for the season with 39, edging out Paul Grayson of the North by a single point. The Bath full-back was still 12 points short of the competition record in a season, set by John Liley of the Midlands and Leicester two years earlier.

Audley Lumsden and Adedayo Adebayo of the South and South-West scored two tries in the tournament, along with Jim Mallinder of the North who, like the Midlands, saw few of their players press international claims via the divisional route. While Kyran Bracken, Mike Catt, Nigel Redman, John Mallett, Hull, Dawe and Hall thrust their names forward from the South and South-West, London provided several candidates, notably Damian Hopley, Rory Jenkins, Steve Bates and Lawrence Dallaglio. Hopley's try, with three minutes remaining, had beaten the North at Newcastle Gosforth in a match featuring excellent performances from Paul Grayson and Michael Fielden, the North backs, before London beat the Midlands 23-14 at Leicester with a 13-point contribution from Rob Andrew.

Blighted by two successive defeats, the North reached an unexpected peak to their season when they overpowered the Midlands 31-9 at Northampton. Grayson, playing on his home club ground, confirmed the fine impression made against London in amassing 16 of the North's points. The back row also made possible such an emphatic victory. Charles Vyvyan, late of Richmond and now of Wharfedale, prospered alongside Neil Ashurst and Andy Macfarlane to resist the dominance of the Midlands front five forwards, among whom Martin Johnson had an outstanding match.

Despite holding the All Blacks to 12-6, the Midlands picked up the wooden spoon. They lacked Martin Bayfield, the Northampton lock, throughout the Championship and used 28 players, nine of them new-comers. They made 14 changes, all except one through injury or unavailability. Darren Garforth, the Leicester prop, and Stuart Potter, his club-mate, rose above the disappointments by going on to play for England A, but at the end of the Championship the Midlands were next to bottom of the cumulative results list since the introduction of the competition. After 31 matches each, the North led the way with 18 wins, together with four titles. London had 17 victories, the Midlands 13 and the South and South-West nine.

During the season, the RFU Senior Clubs Association pledged support to the divisional system, though not to the County Championship, and there was a growing lobby for the divisions to play more matches against teams from overseas, and for the introduction of fixtures against Scottish district sides and Irish provinces to broaden the experience of players, rather than a domestic competition. Bill Beaumont, the former

England captain who led the North to title wins in 1977 and 1980, added another view. He believed that the North should select a team exclusively comprising players from clubs based within the area.

The North selected five Northampton players – Ian Hunter, John Fletcher, Tim Rodber, Grayson and Fielden – together with Tony Underwood of Leicester during the season. Beaumont's view was that the beneficial experience of playing in major matches should filter through and help to improve northern clubs rather than working to the advantage of those in other divisions.

Final Table

	P	W	D	L	F	A	Pts
South & South-West	3	3	0	0	85	36	6
London	3	2	0	1	62	60	4
North	3	1	0	2	68	60	2
Midlands	3	0	0	3	26	85	0

The North have won the Divisional Championship 4 times, London 3 times, Midlands and South & South-West twice each.

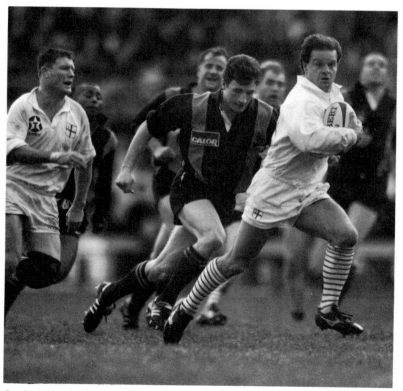

London's Huw Davies, with Buster White in support, breaks away from Mike Catt of the South and South-West in the Championship decider at Twickenham.

16 October, Newcastle Gosforth RFC

Northern Division 21 (1G 1PG 2DG 1T)   **London Division 22** (2G 1PG 1T)
Northern Division: I Hunter (Harlequins); J Mallinder (Sale), M R Fielden
(Northampton), K G Simms (Liverpool St Helens) (*capt*), J Sleightholme (Wakefield);
P Grayson (Northampton), D Scully (Wakefield); M P Hynes (Orrell), G J French
(Orrell), S McMain (Sheffield), D Baldwin (Sale), J Dixon (West Hartlepool),
T A K Rodber (Northampton & Army), A Macfarlane (Sale), N Ashurst (Orrell)
Scorers *Tries:* Mallinder, Fielden   *Conversion:* Grayson   *Penalty Goal:* Grayson
Dropped Goals: Grayson (2)
London Division: G H Davies (Wasps); T Underwood (Leicester), D P Hopley (Wasps),
W D C Carling (Harlequins), D O'Leary (Harlequins); C R Andrew (Wasps) (*capt*),
S M Bates (Wasps); J Leonard (Harlequins), B C Moore (Harlequins), J A Probyn
(Wasps), A C Snow (Harlequins), R Langhorn (Harlequins), M J Greenwood (Wasps),
D Ryan (Wasps), L Dallaglio (Wasps)
Scorers *Tries:* Underwood, Carling, Hopley   *Conversions:* Andrew (2)
Penalty Goal: Andrew
Referee E Murray (Scotland)

16 October, Bath RFC

South & South-West Division 31 (1G 3PG 3T)   **Midland Division 3** (1PG)
South & South-West Division: J E B Callard (Bath); A Adebayo (Bath), P R de Glanville
(Bath), N D Beal (Northampton), A E Lumsden (Bath); M J Catt (Bath), K P P Bracken
(Bristol); C J Clark (Oxford U & Bath), R G R Dawe (Bath), V E Ubogu (Bath),
N C Redman (Bath), A G Blackmore (Bristol), J P Hall (Bath) (*capt*), S O Ojomoh (Bath),
R A Robinson (Bath)
Scorers *Tries:* Lumsden (2), Beal, Adebayo   *Conversion:* Callard
Penalty Goals: Callard (3)
Midland Division: S D Hodgkinson (Moseley); S T Hackney (Leicester), S Potter
(Leicester), I Bates (Leicester), H Thorneycroft (Northampton); A P Challinor
(Harlequins), M J S Dawson (Northampton); G C Rowntree (Leicester), C J Olver
(Northampton), D J Garforth (Leicester), J Phillips (Northampton), S J Lloyd
(Moseley), C Barrow (Bristol), D Richards (Leicester) (*capt*), C Millhouse
(Northampton) *Replacements* A Kardooni (Leicester) for Dawson (33 mins); J C Harris
(Leicester) for Hodgkinson (58 mins)
Scorer *Penalty Goal:* Hodgkinson
Referee D Matthews (Liverpool)

23 October, Gloucester RFC

South & South-West Division 29 (1G 4PG 2T)   **Northern Division 16** (1G 2PG 1DG)
South & South-West Division: J E B Callard (Bath); P Holford (Gloucester),
P R de Glanville (Bath), N D Beal (Northampton), A Adebayo (Bath); P Hull
(Bristol & RAF), K P P Bracken (Bristol); C J Clark (Oxford U & Bath), K Dunn
(Wasps), D Hinkins (Bristol), D Sims (Gloucester), A G Blackmore (Bristol), J P Hall
(Bath) (*capt*), S O Ojomoh (Bath), D Eves (Bristol) *Replacement* G Adams (Bath) for
Ojomoh (temp)
Scorers *Tries:* Hull, Adebayo, Ojomoh   *Conversion:* Callard   *Penalty Goals:* Callard (4)
Northern Division: I Hunter (Northampton); J Mallinder (Sale), M R Fielden
(Northampton), K G Simms (Liverpool St Helens) (*capt*), J Sleightholme (Wakefield);
P Grayson (Northampton), D Scully (Wakefield); M P Hynes (Orrell), G J French
(Orrell), S McMain (Sheffield), D Baldwin (Sale), J Dixon (West Hartlepool),
C B Vyvyan (Wharfedale), A Macfarlane (Sale), N Ashurst (Orrell)
Replacement G Ainscough (Orrell) for Mallinder (70 mins)
Scorers *Try:* Mallinder   *Conversion:* Grayson   *Penalty Goals:* Grayson (2)
Dropped Goal: Grayson
Referee D McHugh (Ireland)

30 October, Leicester RFC

Midland Division 14 (2PG 1DG 1T)   **London Division 23** (2G 2PG 1DG)
Midland Division: J Steele (Northampton); E Saunders (Rugby), F E Packman (Northampton), I Bates (Leicester), H Thorneycroft (Northampton); J C Harris (Leicester), M J S Dawson (Northampton); G C Rowntree (Leicester), C J Olver (Northampton) (*capt*), D J Garforth (Leicester), M O Johnson (Leicester), S J Lloyd (Moseley), J M Wells (Leicester), C Barrow (Bristol), N A Back (Leicester)
Replacement S Purdy (Moseley) for Bates (39 mins)
Scorers *Try:* Saunders   *Penalty Goals:* Steele (2)   *Dropped Goal:* Packman
London Division: G H Davies (Wasps); D O'Leary (Harlequins), G Childs (Wasps), D P Hopley (Wasps), C Oti (Wasps); C R Andrew (Wasps) (*capt*), S M Bates (Wasps); J Leonard (Harlequins), B C Moore (Harlequins), A R Mullins (Harlequins), A C Snow (Harlequins), D Ryan (Wasps), M Greenwood (Wasps), C M A Sheasby (Harlequins), R H J Jenkins (London Irish)
Scorers *Tries:* Ryan, Sheasby   *Conversions:* Andrew (2)   *Penalty Goals:* Andrew (2)
Dropped Goal: Andrew
Referee A Spreadbury (Somerset)

6 November, Northampton RFC

Midland Division 9 (3PG)   **Northern Division 31** (2G 3PG 1DG 1T)
Midland Division: J Steele (Northampton); S T Hackney (Leicester), F E Packman (Northampton), S Purdy (Moseley), H Thorneycroft (Northampton); J C Harris (Leicester), A Kardooni (Leicester); G Baldwin (Northampton), R Cockerill (Leicester), M O Johnson (Leicester), S J Lloyd (Moseley), J M Wells (Leicester), D Richards (Leicester) (*capt*), C Millhouse (Northampton) *Replacement* I Skingsley (Bedford) for Lloyd (68 mins)
Scorer *Penalty Goals:* Steele (3)
Northern Division: M Jackson (Wakefield); R Underwood (Leicester & RAF), K G Simms (Liverpool St Helens) (*capt*), J Fletcher (Northampton), J Sleightholme (Wakefield); P Grayson (Northampton), D Scully (Wakefield); P Lancaster (West Hartlepool), S J Mitchell (West Hartlepool), S McMain (Sheffield), J Dixon (West Hartlepool), C Cusani (Orrell), C B Vyvyan (Wharfedale), A Macfarlane (Sale), N Ashurst (Orrell)
Scorers *Tries:* Ashurst, Sleightholme, Simms   *Conversions:* Grayson (2)
Penalty Goals: Grayson (3)   *Dropped Goal:* Grayson
Referee E Morrison (Bristol) *Replaced by* P Wakefield (London) (74 mins)

3 January, Twickenham

London Division 17 (4PG 1T)   **South & South-West Division 25** (1G 4PG 2DG)
London Division: A J Buzza (Wasps); D O'Leary (Harlequins), G H Davies (Wasps), F J Clough (Wasps), J Alexander (Harlequins); G Gregory (Nottingham), S M Bates (Wasps) (*capt*); G Holmes (Wasps), G Botterman (Saracens), J A Probyn (Wasps), A C Snow (Harlequins), A Diprose (Saracens), M J Greenwood (Wasps), C M A Sheasby (Harlequins), M White (Wasps)
Scorers *Try:* Alexander   *Penalty Goals:* Gregory (4)
South & South-West Division: J E B Callard (Bath); M Lloyd (Bath), M J Catt (Bath), N D Beal (Northampton), P Holford (Gloucester); P Hull (Bristol & RAF), R J Hill (Bath); C J Clark (Oxford U & Bath), R G R Dawe (Bath) (*capt*), D Hinkins (Bristol), A G Blackmore (Bristol), R West (Gloucester), S O Ojomoh (Bath), D Sims (Gloucester), D Eves (Bristol)
Scorers *Try:* Holford   *Conversion:* Callard   *Penalty Goals:* Callard (4)
Dropped Goals: Beal, Hull
Referee G Simmonds (Wales)

NOSTALGIC BATH RULE AGAIN

PILKINGTON CUP 1993-94
Michael Austin

7 May, Twickenham
Bath 21 (1G 3PG 1T)   Leicester 9 (3PG)

The showpiece that should have been never was. A world-record crowd of 68,000 for a club match saw a contest with so much passion, so much at stake, consigned to the realms of disappointment, despite the rarefied atmosphere. Bath won the title for the eighth time in 11 years, recording their third league and Cup double, and have still to lose a Twickenham final. Yet their decisive superiority in so many areas did not take them clear of a hugely under-achieving Leicester side until Catt ran in their second try with five minutes remaining.

Nostalgia ruled: this was Richard Hill's final game for Bath, and as their scrum-half and England's record cap-holder in his position with 29, he stood alone in having played in eight Cup-winning teams. Stuart Barnes, his half-back partner, was appearing in his eighth final, including two with Bristol, one of which ended in the 10-9 defeat by Bath exactly ten years earlier. Furthermore, for Jack Rowell, Bath's coach, it was the end of one era and the start of another as England's manager. Rowell, taciturn to those he does not know, outgoing towards those he trusts, held the trophy, smiled and waved goodbye. Bath had won 13 of the 18 titles on offer under his charge since 1984.

This was a final which will be remembered more for the cancelling out of the opposition, rather than for the production of positive play. Needle, ferocity and a touch of spite laced a contest in which Leicester patently lacked the cutting edge to create anything. Their resilience kept them roughly in contention until the second try, by Catt – following ground-earning thrusts by Hill and Clarke, de Glanville's ball-rescuing and Callard's weaving run – sealed the match. Garforth, the Leicester prop, had the ill luck to tap the ball on to Catt from Callard's pass with a despairing hand.

Callard, originally omitted from England's tour of South Africa before being enlisted as a replacement for the injured Pears, had been immaculate in kicking and defence. As for Leicester, their work rate was tremendous, their inspiration level bordering on zero. Even four attacking scrums produced an attritional approach, leaving the Underwood brothers lurking unused on the wings. Bath bottled up the midfield to the extent that Potter, a replacement tourist for Guscott, made no impression.

Far worse for Leicester, Harris, their fly-half, who scored three penalty goals before the interval and finished the season with 314 club points, missed three kicks from comfortable range in the second half. When

Mike Catt's attempt to reach the loose ball is thwarted by Leicester's John Wells in the 1994 Pilkington Cup final. Catt scored a try for Bath in their 21-9 win.

Leicester battled back in the final quarter, Harris booted wide the relatively easy kick which would have brought his side to within two points of Bath. Just as Harris had lost his admirable place-kicking rhythm in the weeks before the final, his team's form had also gone missing. They had the statistical consolation of having increased their Cup points aggregate to a record 1,608 with 766 against in 75 matches, compared with Bath's 1,222 (574 against) in 13 fewer games.

Swift extended his individual competition record to 22 tries when gathering a kick ahead by de Glanville and beating a defence on the turn – together with a slipping Rory Underwood – for the opening try after 48 minutes. It raised Swift's career aggregate to 368. Hall followed five previous captains for the club to have lifted the trophy: John Palmer, Roger Spurrell, Hill, Barnes and Andy Robinson.

Bath: J E B Callard; A H Swift, P R de Glanville, M J Catt, A A Adebayo; S Barnes, R J Hill; D Hilton, R G R Dawe, V E Ubogu, N C Redman, A I Reed, R A Robinson, B B Clarke, J P Hall (*capt*) *Replacement* S O Ojomoh for Robinson (49 mins)
Scorers *Tries:* Swift, Catt   *Conversion:* Callard   *Penalty Goals:* Callard (3)
Leicester: W A Kilford; T Underwood, S Potter, L S Boyle, R Underwood; J C Harris, A Kardooni; G C Rowntree, R Cockerill, D J Garforth, M O Johnson, M D Poole, J M Wells, D Richards (*capt*), N A Back
Scorer *Penalty Goals:* Harris (3)
Referee E F Morrison (Bristol Society)

Bath had survived somewhat shakily in a breathtaking and vibrant semi-final, televised live, against Harlequins in front of 8,000 spectators at the Stoop Memorial Ground. They won 26-25, through a try from Swift (his 50th for the club) and Callard's conversion from in front of the posts with three minutes remaining. The match was a classic, with multiple twists and turns. Bath led 19-0 after 24 minutes and threatened to run away with the game until Harlequins courageously scored the next 25 points. Bath's majestic moments included the first of Swift's two tries after four minutes when an attack went through nine separate phases, 31 pairs of hands and involved 13 Bath players.

Swift, aged 34, who had begun his senior career 18 years earlier with Fylde, said afterwards that he had never played in such a dramatic match. Other definitive figures were Barnes and Redman for Bath, who scored four tries to three, while Harlequins prospered on the work of Challinor, Thresher and Snow. Appropriately, Bath's route to Twickenham was via the London clubs, the exception being a fifth-round win over much-improved Bristol, who had inched back to 14-9 with three penalty goals from Tainton, the final scores of the match. Their other conquests were Wasps, who had the misfortune to be drawn at Bath as early as the fourth round, and Saracens, who enjoyed a good Cup run despite losing five players, O'Leary, Tarbuck, Peters, Cassell and Dooley, after their relegation the previous season.

Leicester, who had beaten Bath 9-6 in a League match the previous November, had a curious Cup run. While they won the semi-final at Orrell 31-18 and with considerable ease, they had struggled at Blackheath, where Back scored two tries, and in quelling Moseley at Welford Road. The interim tie yielded an overwhelming win over London Irish.

Orrell, yet to reach the final, suffered their fourth semi-final defeat since their first by London Scottish exactly 20 years earlier. With wind assistance, they led 15-9 at half-time against Leicester but were trailing 21-15 when Charles Cusani, their lock forward, was sent off for alleged stamping by Tony Spreadbury, an international referee. Whereas Harlequins had been drawn at home in each round and beat Basingstoke, West Hartlepool and Sale, Orrell achieved a more notable victory when they beat Gloucester at Kingsholm 10-3 in the quarter-finals. Langford converted the only try of the match, by Hamer, a wing, and kicked a penalty goal.

Northampton, beaten finalists three years earlier, had slipped into decline and suffered a fifth-round defeat at Gloucester, whose new director of rugby, Barrie Corless, had switched from Franklins Gardens the previous summer.

While clubs in lower leagues still found it realistic to bridge two divisions and eliminate a more fancied team, no top League side lost to one from the Second Division. Performances of special merit came from Wharfedale, the North Division 1 club which produced former England centre John Spencer. Wharfedale's Cup debut provided a 59-6 win at Scunthorpe, another at Walsall and a 20-point defeat of Sheffield at Abbeydale Park before they lost at Otley. Their pack included two outstanding players, Vyvyan, a Cambridge Blue, and Verity. Bradford & Bingley surprised Bedford, two leagues higher; Kettering, from Midlands East 1, won at Leeds, surmounting a gap of four divisions; York knocked out Kendal before breaking new ground and meeting Coventry. The previous season, Exeter had become the first club from the Third Division to qualify for the quarter-final since Wakefield four years earlier. This time they suffered the disappointment of falling at the first hurdle, to Clifton. Camp Hill, another centenary-celebrating club, suffered the same fate at Stourbridge.

With the advent of home and away matches in the top National Leagues, an additional round was introduced, enabling the number of participating clubs to be increased from 76 to 96. This gave all clubs in the new Division 5 North and South automatic entry into the first round. This expansion of the competition prompted the inclusion of ten new qualifiers, increasing the total participants to 228 in 23 seasons. In addition to Wharfedale, they were Alton, Broadstreet, Cambridge, Kendal, New Brighton, Scunthorpe, Stoke-on-Trent, Windsor and York. They were among the clubs benefiting from a revised sponsorship deal, worth £700,000 over three years. Pilkington's overall package of £1 million, covering Cup and Shield, allowed the RFU to achieve a long-held wish to stage both finals on the same day.

RESULTS

First Round
Alton 8, St Ives 23; Berry Hill 15, Henley 20; Bradford & Bingley 12, Tynedale 6; Brixham 17, Reading 14; Broadstreet 6, Birmingham Solihull 17; Camborne 22, Wimborne 14; Cheshunt 8, High Wycombe 14; Chiltern 8, Worthing 0; Durham City 14, Wolverhampton 8; Kettering 8, Widnes 3; Lichfield 9, Walsall 14; London Welsh 44, Windsor 0; Lydney 64, Maidstone 0; New Brighton 14, Wigton 8; North Walsham 22, Metropolitan Police 3; Nuneaton 9, Hereford 11; Old Mid-Whitgiftians 8, Bridgwater & Albion 12; Preston Grasshoppers 38, Stoke-on-Trent 0; Ruislip 5, Tabard 30; Scunthorpe 6, Wharfedale 59; Southend 11, Cambridge 20; Stockton 8, Syston 11; Stourbridge 15, Camp Hill 10; Stroud 12, Basingstoke 16; Westcombe Park 20, Ealing 16; Weston-super-Mare 10, Barking 39; Winnington Park 15, Rotherham 13; York 16, Kendal 15

Second Round
Amersham & Chiltern 5, London Welsh 23; Askeans 0, Basingstoke 6; Aspatria 17, Stourbridge 22; Bradford & Bingley 23, Bedford 15; Birmingham Solihull 7, Harrogate 3; Brixham 3, North Walsham 3 (*aet* – North Walsham qualified on 'away team' rule); Broughton Park 6, Morley 5; Camborne 20, Bridgwater & Albion 21; Coventry 33, York 19; Exeter 6, Clifton 9; Henley 65, St Ives 0; High Wycombe 9, Preston Grasshoppers 20; Leeds 6, Kettering 13; Lydney 11, Havant 16; New Brighton 17, Liverpool St Helens 12; Plymouth Albion 22, Barking 11; Redruth 6, Rosslyn Park 20; Richmond 21, Blackheath 23; Sheffield 9, Hereford 8; Syston 9, Fylde 15; Tabard 9, Sudbury 33; Walsall 17, Wharfedale 22; Westcombe Park 6, Cambridge 21; Winnington Park 37, Durham City 3

Third Round
Birmingham Solihull 13, Broughton Park 3; Blackheath 21, London Welsh 9; Bradford & Bingley 6, Fylde 13; Clifton

12, Bridgwater & Albion 24; Coventry 10, Preston Grasshoppers 5; Havant 24, Cambridge 13; Henley 17, North Walsham 3; Kettering 6, Stourbridge 13; New Brighton 3, Winnington Park 16; Rosslyn Park 38, Plymouth Albion 7; Sheffield 0, Wharfedale 20; Sudbury 6, Basingstoke 25

Fourth Round

Bath 24, Wasps 11; Blackheath 10, Leicester 16; Bristol 46, Henley 6; Harlequins 52, Basingstoke 3; Havant 13, London Irish 18; London Scottish 6, Fylde 8; Moseley 32, Winnington Park 6; Newcastle Gosforth 53, Bridgwater & Albion 10; Northampton 22, Waterloo 3; Nottingham 9, Gloucester 29; Orrell 55, Stourbridge 3; Otley 20, Wharfedale 5; Rosslyn Park 22, Coventry 15; Rugby 13, Sale 17; Saracens 26, Birmingham Solihull 3; Wakefield 17, West Hartlepool 18

Fifth Round

Bath 14, Bristol 9; Gloucester 11, Northampton 6; Harlequins 23, West Hartlepool 15; Leicester 43, London Irish 10; Moseley 15, Fylde 6; Newcastle Gosforth 7, Orrell 12; Otley 7, Sale 58; Rosslyn Park 12, Saracens 29

Quarter-finals

Gloucester 3, Orrell 10; Harlequins 26, Sale 13; Leicester 12, Moseley 6; Saracens 6, Bath 23

Semi-finals

Harlequins 25, Bath 26; Orrell 18, Leicester 31

Previous finals (all at Twickenham)

1972 Gloucester 17 Moseley 6
1973 Coventry 27 Bristol 15
1974 Coventry 26 London Scottish 6
1975 Bedford 28 Rosslyn Park 12
1976 Gosforth 23 Rosslyn Park 14
1977 Gosforth 27 Waterloo 11
1978 Gloucester 6 Leicester 3
1979 Leicester 15 Moseley 12
1980 Leicester 21 London Irish 9
1981 Leicester 22 Gosforth 15
1982 Gloucester 12 Moseley 12
      (title shared)
1983 Bristol 28 Leicester 22
1984 Bath 10 Bristol 9
1985 Bath 24 London Welsh 15
1986 Bath 25 Wasps 17
1987 Bath 19 Wasps 12
1988 Harlequins 28 Bristol 22
1989 Bath 10 Leicester 6
1990 Bath 48 Gloucester 6
1991 Harlequins 25, Northampton 13
      (aet)
1992 Harlequins 12, Bath 15 (aet)
1993 Leicester 23, Harlequins 16

COUNTY CUP WINNERS 1993-94

Berkshire	**Reading**
Buckinghamshire	**High Wycombe**
Cheshire	**Winnington Park**
Cornwall	**Launceston**
Cumbria	**Wigton**
Dorset/Wilts	**Sherborne**
Devon	**Exeter**
Durham	**Stockton**
Eastern Counties	**Sudbury**
East Midlands	**Stockwood Park**
Gloucestershire	**Gloucester Old Boys**
Hampshire	**Basingstoke**
Hertfordshire	**Tabard**
Kent	**Old Colfeians**
Lancashire	**Waterloo**
Leicestershire	**Loughboro' Students**
Middlesex	**Ealing**
North Midlands	**Camp Hill**
Northumberland	**Newcastle Gosforth**
Notts, Lincs & Derbys	**Scunthorpe**
Oxfordshire	**Henley**
Somerset	**Bridgwater & Albion**
Staffordshire	**Walsall**
Surrey	**Esher**
Sussex	**Horsham**
Warwickshire	**Barker's Butts**
Yorkshire	**Wakefield**

BATH CELEBRATE THE END OF THE ERA WITH LEAGUE BUSINESS AS USUAL

THE COURAGE LEAGUES 1993-94

Bath have won the title four times in succession and five times in all in the seven years in which the Courage Leagues have been in operation. They have lost only one League match per season in the last four seasons. Considering that we are now in the era when other clubs are trying to make a quantum leap, trying desperately to improve and expand in all areas and devoting huge resources along the way, then Bath's dominance is scarcely believable.

There were a few weeks in mid-season where they faltered just a little. The Recreation Ground became a mudheap in midwinter, and Bath's players did not train on a decent surface for two months. Their line-out became inefficient. They had already lost at Leicester, in a poor but hard-fought match at Welford Road, throwing the title race open and also raising the possibility that, in this last season under the coaching of Jack Rowell before he departed to take on the managership of England, Bath would finally lose some of their hegemony. Leicester waited impatiently.

But Bath found themselves in the run-in, beat Leicester convincingly in the mud at the Rec and stormed through to the title with a match to spare. Typically, they worked out their problems as they went along. For example, they found that Andy Reed, their Scottish international lock, finished the season so well that their line-out weakness became a strength.

At the other end of the table, Newcastle Gosforth and London Irish were relegated. Newcastle never quite came to terms with life in the top flight while London Irish are perhaps paying the price for their continued coaching upheavals. Over the years, they have sacked successful men. The truncated size of the top division is unfair on teams trying to establish themselves, especially on those which have been promoted and are trying to make the great leap forward to establish themselves among the élite of Division 1. The smaller the size of the division, the more self-perpetuating that élite will be. Moves to cut down numbers in the national divisions must be strongly resisted.

Happily for rugby in the north, West Hartlepool and Sale were promoted from Division 2. Happily, too, for those with a sense of rugby history, Coventry won Division 3 to reverse a long decline, and to do so in style.

PREVIOUS WINNERS OF THE COURAGE TROPHY
1987-88: **Leicester** (runners-up: Wasps); 1988-89: **Bath** (runners-up: Gloucester); 1989-90: **Wasps** (runners-up: Gloucester); 1990-91: **Bath** (runners-up: Wasps); 1991-92: **Bath** (runners-up: Orrell); 1992-93: **Bath** (runners-up: Wasps)

Captain Jon Hall shows off the Courage League Cup, won by Bath for the fourth successive season.

* points deducted for various reasons
† promotions/relegations made for disciplinary reasons

NATIONAL DIVISION

National 1

	P	W	D	L	F	A	Pts
Bath	18	17	0	1	431	181	34
Leicester	18	14	0	4	425	210	28
Wasps	18	10	1	7	362	340	21
Bristol	18	10	0	8	331	276	20
Northampton	18	9	0	9	305	342	18
Harlequins	18	8	0	10	333	287	16
Orrell	18	8	0	10	327	302	16
Gloucester	18	6	2	10	247	356	14
L Irish	18	4	0	14	217	391	8
Newcastle Gos	18	2	1	15	190	483	5

National 2

	P	W	D	L	F	A	Pts
Sale	18	13	2	3	438	160	28
W Hartlepool	18	13	2	3	389	271	28
Saracens	18	11	1	6	299	238	23
Wakefield	18	8	3	7	347	240	19
Moseley	18	9	1	8	266	220	19
Nottingham	18	8	1	9	254	326	17
Waterloo	18	6	2	10	231	346	14
L Scottish	18	6	0	12	232	325	12
Rugby	18	5	1	12	186	302	11
Otley	18	4	1	13	235	449	9

National 3

	P	W	D	L	F	A	Pts
Coventry	18	14	0	4	406	259	28
Fylde	18	13	0	5	339	219	26
Bedford	18	12	0	6	332	260	24
Blackheath	18	11	0	7	305	222	22
Rosslyn Pk	18	10	1	7	372	240	21
Exeter	18	9	1	8	308	271	19
Richmond	18	9	0	9	337	300	18
Morley	18	6	0	12	245	334	12
Havant	18	3	0	15	203	432	6
Redruth	18	2	0	16	178	488	4

National 4

	P	W	D	L	F	A	Pts
Clifton	18	16	2	0	477	205	34
Harrogate	18	14	2	2	479	219	30
Liverpool St H	18	11	1	6	396	275	23
Plymouth Alb	18	9	0	9	286	416	18
Aspatria	18	8	0	10	303	372	16
Leeds	18	7	0	11	243	318	14
Askeans	18	6	1	11	268	358	13
Broughton Pk	18	6	0	12	243	356	12
Sheffield	18	5	1	12	287	310	11
Sudbury	18	4	1	13	240	393	9

National 5 North

	P	W	D	L	F	A	Pts
Rotherham	12	10	1	1	335	142	21
Preston Grass	12	10	0	2	191	128	20
Walsall	12	7	0	5	166	148	14
Winnington Pk	12	6	1	5	227	132	13
Stourbridge	12	6	0	6	162	188	12
Stoke-on-Trent	12	5	1	6	153	167	11
Lichfield	12	5	0	7	118	138	10
Hereford	12	4	2	6	126	153	10
B'ham S'hull	12	5	0	7	128	162	10
Kendal	12	4	1	7	142	171	9
Nuneaton	12	4	1	7	122	200	9
Durham C	12	4	1	7	159	279	9
Bradford & B	12	4	0	8	189	210	8

National 5 South

	P	W	D	L	F	A	Pts
Reading	12	10	1	1	248	61	21
Lydney	12	7	2	3	181	111	16
Tabard	12	6	2	4	183	136	14
Camborne	12	6	2	4	197	180	14
Weston-s-Mare	12	7	0	5	163	180	14
L Welsh	12	5	3	4	216	140	13
Berry Hill	12	6	1	5	146	154	13
North Walsham	12	5	2	5	148	136	12
High Wycombe	12	5	1	6	120	173	11
Met Police	12	5	0	7	167	174	10
Basingstoke	12	5	0	7	191	210	10
Southend	12	3	0	9	203	208	6
Maidstone	12	1	0	11	86	386	2

LONDON DIVISION

London 1

	P	W	D	L	F	A	Pts
Barking	12	10	1	1	290	149	21
Ealing	12	9	0	3	271	141	18
Camberley	12	9	0	3	242	137	18
Sutton & Epsom	12	7	1	4	271	207	15
Harlow	12	6	0	6	223	217	12
Guildford & G	12	6	0	6	162	162	12
O Mid-Whitgift	12	6	0	6	143	163	12
Eton Manor	12	5	1	6	178	176	11
Streatham-Croy	12	5	1	6	166	183	11
O Colfeians	12	5	0	7	166	221	10
Thurrock	12	3	1	8	138	204	7
Dorking	12	3	0	9	171	220	6
O Alleynian	12	1	1	10	135	376	3

London 2 North

	P	W	D	L	F	A	Pts
Ruislip	12	9	2	1	196	95	20
O Verulamians	12	9	1	2	203	102	19
B'ps Stortford	12	9	1	2	175	131	17

Fran Clough of Wasps hands off Northampton's Nick Beal in the April League fixture at Sudbury. Wasps won the match 24-11.

	P	W	D	L	F	A	Pts
Cambridge	12	7	2	3	214	130	16
Cheshunt	12	8	1	3	190	96	15
Norwich	12	6	1	5	143	122	13
O Gaytonians	12	5	1	6	178	142	11
Chingford	12	4	2	6	178	120	10
Woodford	12	5	0	7	152	198	10
Finchley	12	4	1	7	107	146	9
Brentwood	12	3	1	8	103	223	7
Upper Clapton	12	1	1	10	51	226	3
O Edwardians	12	1	0	11	69	228	0

London 2 South

	P	W	D	L	F	A	Pts
Esher	12	10	2	0	387	95	22
Westcombe Pk	12	10	1	1	259	130	21
Thanet Wands	12	6	2	4	243	171	14
O Wimbledons	12	6	1	5	208	176	13
Horsham	12	6	1	5	205	196	13
Charlton Pk	12	6	1	5	172	208	13
Sidcup	12	6	0	6	208	174	12
O Blues	12	5	2	5	157	139	12
O Reigatian	12	4	2	6	124	162	10
O Juddian	12	5	0	7	230	292	10
Lewes	12	3	2	7	135	187	8
Worthing	12	4	0	8	107	163	6
KCS OB	12	0	0	12	94	436	0

London 3 North-East

	P	W	D	L	F	A	Pts
Romford & G Pk	12	12	0	0	310	63	24
Ipswich	12	9	1	2	212	81	19
Woodbridge	12	8	0	4	131	148	16
Braintree	12	7	0	5	140	112	14
Rochford	12	6	1	5	150	127	13
Colchester	12	6	0	6	131	101	12
Bury St Edmunds	12	6	0	6	165	146	12
Campion	12	5	1	6	161	236	11
Chelmsford	12	4	2	6	100	153	10
Basildon	12	4	1	7	170	206	9
Shelford	12	4	0	8	141	158	8
Westcliff	12	3	0	9	112	174	4
Saffron Walden	12	1	0	11	97	315	2

London 3 North-West

	P	W	D	L	F	A	Pts
Staines	12	11	0	1	291	96	22
Letchworth	12	10	0	2	267	102	18
Grasshoppers	12	9	0	3	211	133	18
O Merchant Ts	12	8	0	4	192	172	16
Hertford	12	7	0	5	154	171	14
Lensbury*	12	10	0	2	223	117	10
London NZ	12	5	0	7	158	180	10
Welwyn	12	5	0	7	162	236	10
O Elizabethans	12	4	0	8	172	193	8
O Albanians	12	4	0	8	155	230	8

	P	W	D	L	F	A	Pts
Kingsburians	12	3	0	9	113	178	6
Fullerians	12	2	0	10	83	200	4
O Meadonians	12	0	0	12	64	237	0

London 3 South-East

	P	W	D	L	F	A	Pts
Gravesend	12	12	0	0	315	57	24
Beckenham	12	9	0	3	165	73	18
Brockleians	12	8	0	4	213	94	16
Canterbury	12	8	0	4	206	103	16
Haywards Heath	12	7	0	5	145	139	14
O Beccehamian	12	6	0	6	151	116	12
Brighton	12	6	0	6	150	181	12
Chichester	12	5	1	6	120	161	11
E Grinstead	12	4	1	7	163	247	9
Erith	12	4	0	8	142	139	8
Gillingham Anc	12	4	0	8	105	231	8
Tunbridge W	12	3	0	9	111	264	6
Hove	12	1	0	11	91	272	2

London 3 South-West

	P	W	D	L	F	A	Pts
Portsmouth	12	9	2	1	224	104	20
O Guildfordians	12	8	1	3	223	117	17
Alton	12	8	1	3	230	139	17
Guy's Hosp	12	8	0	4	166	124	16
Purley	12	8	0	4	146	144	16
Warlingham	12	6	2	4	176	136	14
O Walcountians	12	5	4	3	180	148	14
O Emanuel	12	5	1	6	241	207	11
Eastleigh	12	4	0	8	99	210	8
Southampton	12	3	0	9	103	210	6
Cranleigh	12	2	0	10	110	244	4
Winchester	12	2	1	9	170	243	3
United Servs, Por	12	4	0	8	132	174	2

Eastern Counties 1

	P	W	D	L	F	A	Pts
Maldon	12	11	0	1	274	86	22
West Norfolk	12	10	0	2	240	99	20
Lowestoft & Yar	12	9	0	3	288	107	18
Wymondham	12	8	0	4	294	120	16
Canvey Island	12	9	0	3	191	150	16
Bancroft	12	6	1	5	157	148	13
Ely	12	5	1	6	141	231	11
Ravens	12	5	0	7	105	210	10
Upminster	12	4	1	7	98	159	9
Harwich & Dov	12	3	2	7	105	138	6
Newmarket	12	3	0	9	118	179	6
Cantabrigian	12	1	1	10	77	286	3
Wanstead	12	1	0	11	89	264	2

Eastern Counties 2

	P	W	D	L	F	A	Pts
Diss	12	11	0	1	292	56	22
Holt	12	10	0	2	253	92	20
E London	12	11	0	1	237	79	20
Thames Sports	12	6	2	4	172	117	14
Loughton	12	7	1	4	212	115	13
Clacton	12	6	1	5	140	160	13
Thetford	12	6	1	5	138	176	13
Lakenham Hewett	12	3	2	7	107	286	8
O Bealonians	12	3	0	9	139	194	6
O Palmerians	12	2	2	8	73	161	6
Met Pol Chigwell	12	2	2	8	109	236	6
Crusaders	12	4	0	8	130	206	4
Ipswich YMCA	12	1	1	10	113	237	3

Eastern Counties 3

	P	W	D	L	F	A	Pts
O Cooperians	11	11	0	0	237	69	22
Ilford Wands	11	9	0	2	219	87	18
Fakenham	11	7	0	4	148	101	14
S Wood Ferrers	11	6	1	4	148	82	13
Haverhill	11	6	0	5	198	84	12
Thurston	11	5	1	5	185	126	11
Stowmarket	11	5	1	5	125	89	11
Felixstowe	11	5	0	6	148	139	10
Beccles	11	4	1	6	192	161	9
Southwold	11	3	0	8	131	128	6
Redbridge	11	3	0	8	117	234	6
O Brentwoods	11	0	0	11	17	565	0
London Hosp*							−1

Eastern Counties 4

	P	W	D	L	F	A	Pts
Hadleigh	12	12	0	0	264	111	24
Broadland	12	8	1	3	144	133	17
Billericay	12	7	2	3	207	98	16
March	12	7	1	4	195	155	15
May & Baker	11	6	1	4	160	132	13
Witham	12	6	0	6	134	141	12
Brightlingsea	12	5	1	6	190	139	11
Ongar	11	5	0	6	106	147	10
Burnham-on-Cr	12	3	2	7	115	120	8
Wisbech	12	4	0	8	107	145	8
Dereham	12	4	0	8	141	187	8
Essex Police	12	4	0	8	132	215	8
Swaffham	12	2	0	10	105	277	4

Eastern Counties 5

	P	W	D	L	F	A	Pts
Mersea Island	11	9	2	0	248	43	20
Mayfield OB	10	9	1	0	205	47	17
Sawston	11	6	2	3	192	85	14
Stanford	10	6	1	3	281	118	13
Burwell	11	6	0	5	212	120	12
Essex U	10	5	1	4	308	179	11

Essex CC	10	5	1	4	232	166	11
Norwich Union	11	4	2	5	190	144	10
Dagenham	11	5	0	6	201	155	10
Leiston	11	2	0	9	120	290	4
Mistley	10	1	0	9	64	668	2
Watton	10	0	0	10	57	325	0

Hampshire 1

	P	W	D	L	F	A	Pts
Gosport	12	11	0	1	323	70	22
Jersey	12	11	0	1	348	101	20
Millbrook	12	10	0	2	343	96	20
Tottonians	12	8	0	4	166	106	14
Petersfield	12	7	0	5	222	173	14
Isle of Wight	12	7	0	5	173	149	14
Farnborough	12	5	0	7	159	178	10
Trojans	12	5	0	7	134	279	10
New Milton	12	4	0	8	126	274	8
Sandown & Sh'n	12	4	0	8	105	262	8
Fareham Hs	12	4	0	8	122	302	6
Andover	12	2	0	10	156	173	4
Romsey	12	0	0	12	84	298	0

Hampshire 2

	P	W	D	L	F	A	Pts
Esso	11	11	0	0	451	37	22
Guernsey	11	9	0	2	432	85	18
AC Delco	11	9	0	2	245	83	18
Fordingbridge	11	8	0	3	266	91	16
Ventnor	11	7	0	4	297	101	14
Overton	11	7	0	4	218	117	14
Waterlooville	11	5	0	6	83	291	10
Alresford	11	4	0	7	116	293	8
Fleet	11	3	0	8	108	290	6
Nomads	11	2	0	9	99	374	4
Ellingham	11	1	0	10	50	356	2
Basingstoke Ws	11	0	0	11	61	308	0

Hertfordshire 1

	P	W	D	L	F	A	Pts
St Albans	9	9	0	0	321	47	16
Datchworth	9	7	0	2	237	45	14
O Ashmoleans	9	7	0	2	166	73	14
Watford	9	6	0	3	112	89	12
Tring	9	6	0	3	271	89	10
O Stanfordians	9	4	0	5	85	154	8
Bacavians	9	3	0	6	74	158	6
Hatfield	9	2	0	7	24	274	4
Royston	9	1	0	8	59	179	0
QE II Hosp*	9	0	0	9	19	260	−2
Stevenage*							−3

Herts/Middlesex 1

	P	W	D	L	F	A	Pts
Barnet	12	10	0	2	210	119	20
O Millhillians	12	11	0	1	360	90	18
Hampstead	12	9	0	3	257	114	16

	P	W	D	L	F	A	Pts
Uxbridge	12	8	0	4	204	106	16
Haringey	12	8	0	4	214	179	16
St Mary's Hosp	12	7	0	5	237	233	14
Hendon	12	5	0	7	131	206	10
Harpenden	12	5	0	7	144	220	10
Hemel Hempst'd	12	4	0	8	147	180	8
Centaurs	12	4	0	8	128	162	8
Hitchin	12	3	0	9	118	235	6
Harrow	12	3	0	9	131	274	6
Antlers	12	1	0	11	98	261	2

Kent 1

	P	W	D	L	F	A	Pts
Park House	12	10	1	1	306	77	21
Sevenoaks	11	9	0	2	299	103	18
Dartfordians	12	8	1	3	286	182	17
Sheppey	12	7	1	4	215	150	15
Medway	11	7	0	4	199	144	14
Bromley	12	7	0	5	178	162	14
O Dunstonians	12	6	0	6	283	174	12
Met Pol Hayes	11	5	1	5	129	147	11
Betteshanger	12	5	0	7	144	259	10
Thames Poly	12	4	1	7	128	249	9
Snowdown CW	12	4	0	8	116	278	8
New Ash Green	12	1	1	10	82	212	3
Nat West Bank	11	0	0	11	91	319	0

Kent 2

	P	W	D	L	F	A	Pts
O Shooterhillians	12	10	0	2	234	63	20
O Elthamians	12	10	0	2	170	65	16
Dover	12	7	1	4	142	108	15
Folkestone	11	7	0	4	136	139	14
Deal	11	7	0	4	122	147	14
Vigo	12	6	1	5	113	109	13
Cranbrook	12	5	1	6	201	146	11
Midland Bank	12	5	0	7	187	165	10
Ashford	12	4	2	6	144	129	10
Sittingbourne	12	3	2	7	116	141	8
Bexley	12	4	0	8	110	211	8
Tonbridge	11	3	1	7	120	160	7
Lloyds Bank	11	1	0	10	54	266	2

Kent 3

	P	W	D	L	F	A	Pts
O Gravesendians	9	7	0	2	165	86	14
Whitstable	9	7	0	2	115	83	14
Darenth Valley	9	6	0	3	135	95	12
O Williamsonians	9	5	0	4	158	85	10
Linton	9	5	0	4	127	102	10
Lordswood	9	4	0	5	85	119	8
Citizens	9	4	0	5	67	102	8
Kent Police	9	3	0	6	119	96	6
STC Footscray	9	3	0	6	47	147	6
Orpington	9	1	0	8	72	175	2

Kent 4

	P	W	D	L	F	A	Pts
O Olavians	10	9	0	1	362	44	18
Greenwich	10	8	0	2	239	56	16
Edenbridge	10	6	0	4	148	77	12
Faversham	10	4	0	6	61	131	8
Westerham	10	2	0	8	23	291	4
Centurians	10	1	0	9	54	288	2

Middlesex 1

	P	W	D	L	F	A	Pts
Mill Hill	12	12	0	0	311	91	24
Roxeth Manor OB	12	9	0	3	143	93	18
O Hamptonians	12	8	0	4	291	139	16
Civil Service	12	8	0	4	217	102	16
Wembley	11	7	0	4	220	120	14
O Actonians	12	6	1	5	203	180	13
O Haberdashers	12	5	1	6	136	198	11
Twickenham	12	5	0	7	165	139	10
Sudbury Court	11	4	0	7	112	200	8
Hackney	12	3	1	8	126	219	7
O Islesworthians	12	3	1	8	93	211	7
O Abbotstonians★	12	3	2	7	133	243	4
H'smith & Fulham	12	1	0	11	75	290	2

Middlesex 2

	P	W	D	L	F	A	Pts
O Paulines	12	10	0	2	220	98	20
Belsize Pk	12	9	0	3	244	129	18
Pinner & Grams	12	9	0	3	209	113	18
Thamesians	12	9	1	2	290	150	15
Enfield Ignats	12	7	1	4	212	142	15
Barclays Bank	12	7	0	5	200	187	12
HAC	12	6	1	5	216	211	11
Feltham	12	4	2	6	126	161	10
O Grammarians	12	3	2	7	149	145	8
Hayes	12	4	0	8	145	199	8
L Cornish	12	3	1	8	118	184	7
Orleans FP	12	2	0	10	87	213	4
Osterley★	12	1	0	11	66	350	−2

Middlesex 3

	P	W	D	L	F	A	Pts
Bank of England	9	8	1	0	279	109	17
L Nigerians	9	8	0	1	282	80	16
L Exiles	8	6	0	2	227	94	12
St Nicholas OB	9	5	1	3	97	108	11
UCS OB	9	4	2	3	272	106	10
Northolt	9	3	1	5	144	138	7
O Tottonians	9	2	1	6	57	146	5
St Bart's Hosp	8	2	1	5	79	229	5
Royal Free Hosp	9	2	0	7	103	268	4
Quintin	9	0	1	8	53	315	1

Middlesex 4

	P	W	D	L	F	A	Pts
L French	8	8	0	0	265	67	16
Southgate	8	7	0	1	201	66	14
Meadhurst	7	4	0	3	154	73	8
Kodak	7	4	0	3	92	85	8
British Airways	6	3	0	3	106	113	6
St George's Hosp	6	2	0	4	75	115	4
Middlesex Hosp	6	1	0	5	27	189	2
Univ Coll	4	0	0	4	0	67	0
GWR	6	0	0	6	42	187	0

Surrey 1

	P	W	D	L	F	A	Pts
Wimbledon	12	10	0	2	258	60	20
Univ Vandals	12	10	0	2	218	66	20
O Whitgiftians	12	10	0	2	199	97	20
John Fisher OB	12	9	0	3	173	165	18
Shirley Wands	12	5	1	6	116	117	11
Kingston	12	5	0	7	143	149	10
Raynes Pk	12	4	2	6	85	114	10
Barnes	12	5	0	7	153	191	10
O Reedonians	12	5	0	7	122	222	10
Effingham	12	4	0	8	156	164	8
Chobham	12	4	0	8	130	160	8
O Rutlishians	12	4	0	8	146	189	8
Mitcham	12	1	1	10	67	272	3

Surrey 2

	P	W	D	L	F	A	Pts
O Cranleighans	12	12	0	0	247	95	22
Farnham	12	11	0	1	209	81	22
O Haileyburyians	12	8	0	4	237	192	16
Merton	12	7	1	4	165	99	15
Law Society	12	7	0	5	166	114	14
O Caterhamians	12	6	0	6	233	115	12
Bec OB	12	5	1	6	192	127	9
Cobham	12	4	1	7	129	135	9
Chipstead	12	5	2	5	218	107	8
O Tiffinians	12	4	0	8	163	131	8
Wandsworthians	12	4	0	8	115	274	8
Reigate & R'hill*	12	0	0	12	55	401	−2
Charing X/West H*							−10

Surrey 3

	P	W	D	L	F	A	Pts
Woking	12	11	1	0	291	79	23
L Fire Brigade	11	10	1	0	202	93	21
Battersea Irons	12	10	0	2	299	76	20
London Media	12	7	1	4	267	146	15
O Pelhamians	12	7	0	5	230	150	14
O Suttonians	11	5	0	6	143	137	10
Lightwater	12	4	2	6	169	168	10
O Bevonians	12	5	0	7	138	191	10
Haslemere	12	5	0	7	136	215	10
R Holloway Coll	11	3	0	8	154	206	6

Croydon	12	3	0	9	57	314	6
King's Coll Hosp	11	2	0	9	93	246	4
O Freemans	12	1	1	10	72	230	3

Surrey 4

	P	W	D	L	F	A	Pts
Egham	8	8	0	0	247	40	16
O Johnians	8	7	0	1	204	57	14
Surrey Pol	8	5	0	3	157	76	10
Surrey U	8	5	0	3	132	98	10
O Epsomians	8	5	0	3	156	124	10
Oxted	8	2	0	6	91	130	4
Racal-Decca	8	2	0	6	80	136	4
Economicals	8	1	0	7	73	137	2
Sun Alliance	8	1	0	7	28	370	2

Sussex 1

	P	W	D	L	F	A	Pts
H'field & Wald	11	10	1	0	373	41	21
Uckfield	11	10	0	1	216	74	20
Crawley	11	8	1	2	225	71	17
Bognor	11	8	0	3	204	142	16
Hastings & Bex	11	7	0	4	244	143	14
Seaford	11	5	0	6	122	174	10
Burgess Hill	11	4	0	7	143	236	8
Eastbourne	11	3	0	8	141	173	6
Crowborough	11	3	0	8	112	195	6
Ditchling	11	3	0	8	92	288	6
O Brightonians	11	2	0	9	87	199	4
BA Wingspan	11	2	0	9	71	294	4

Sussex 2

	P	W	D	L	F	A	Pts
Pulborough	7	7	0	0	166	42	14
Sunallon	7	6	0	1	173	51	12
St Francis	7	5	0	2	95	62	10
Hellingly	7	4	0	3	134	84	8
Sussex Police	7	2	0	5	75	125	4
Newick	7	2	0	5	82	144	4
Plumpton	7	2	0	5	53	129	4
Midhurst	7	0	0	7	44	185	0

SOUTH & SOUTH-WEST DIVISION

South-West 1

	P	W	D	L	F	A	Pts
Henley	12	12	0	0	328	125	24
Cheltenham	12	11	0	1	312	119	22
Newbury	12	8	1	3	173	165	17
St Ives	12	7	1	4	181	138	15
Barnstaple	12	7	0	5	161	142	14
Torquay	12	5	2	5	125	160	12
Salisbury	12	5	0	7	105	118	10
Stroud	12	4	2	6	165	237	10
Cinderford	12	4	1	7	140	167	9
Brixham	12	3	1	8	112	209	7
Maidenhead	12	3	0	9	139	177	6

	P	W	D	L	F	A	Pts
Sherborne	12	3	0	9	153	220	6
Gordon League	12	1	2	9	102	219	4

South-West 2

	P	W	D	L	F	A	Pts
Gloucester OB	12	12	0	0	343	83	24
Taunton	12	11	0	1	296	130	22
Matson	12	9	0	3	222	99	18
Bridgwater & Alb	12	9	0	3	251	135	18
Oxford	12	7	0	5	200	218	14
Clevedon	12	6	0	6	220	214	12
Aylesbury	12	6	0	6	194	210	12
Swanage & Ware	12	5	0	7	162	268	10
Combe Down	12	4	1	7	208	167	9
Banbury	12	2	2	8	129	223	6
Marlow	12	2	2	8	126	228	6
Penryn	12	2	1	9	131	254	5
Windsor	12	0	0	12	126	379	0

Southern Counties

	P	W	D	L	F	A	Pts
Bournemouth	12	12	0	0	293	64	24
Bracknell	12	10	0	2	294	90	20
Dorchester	12	9	0	3	267	111	18
Chippenham	12	7	1	4	182	149	15
Olney	12	7	0	5	230	169	14
Abbey	12	6	1	5	150	143	13
Wimborne	12	6	0	6	163	156	12
Bletchley	12	5	1	6	120	177	11
Bicester	12	3	2	7	185	199	8
Oxford Marath	12	3	2	7	164	195	8
Slough	12	3	1	8	75	228	7
Redingensians	12	2	0	10	68	276	4
Wootton Bass	12	1	0	11	125	359	2

Western Counties

	P	W	D	L	F	A	Pts
O Patesians	12	10	1	1	215	99	21
Tiverton	12	10	0	2	197	130	20
Launceston	12	8	0	4	204	110	16
Penzance-N'lyn	12	8	0	4	185	124	16
Devonport Servs	12	6	1	5	183	128	13
O Culverhaysians	12	6	0	6	178	207	12
Drybrook	12	5	0	7	140	181	10
Crediton	12	5	0	7	121	192	10
Spartans	12	4	1	7	132	160	9
Avonmouth OB	12	4	1	7	146	193	9
Bideford	12	3	1	8	128	163	7
Okehampton	12	3	1	8	80	132	7
Wiveliscombe	12	3	0	9	103	193	6

Cornwall & Devon

	P	W	D	L	F	A	Pts
Devon & C Pol	12	9	0	3	223	105	18
Exmouth	12	8	0	4	233	169	16

	P	W	D	L	F	A	Pts
Hayle	12	7	0	5	132	132	14
Paignton	12	6	1	5	177	134	13
Teignmouth	12	6	1	5	192	195	13
Truro	12	6	1	5	113	118	13
Sidmouth	12	6	1	5	167	178	13
Newquay Horns	12	6	0	6	180	161	12
Plymouth CS	12	5	2	5	109	153	12
S Molton	12	5	0	7	212	220	10
Veor	12	4	1	7	150	166	9
Ivybridge	12	4	1	7	131	176	9
Liskeard-Looe	12	2	0	10	85	197	4

Glos & Somerset

	P	W	D	L	F	A	Pts
Dings Crus	12	12	0	0	262	100	24
St Mary's OB	12	11	0	1	296	117	22
Keynsham	12	8	1	3	346	188	17
Hornets	12	7	0	5	258	120	14
Bristol H'quins	12	6	1	5	148	108	13
Whitehall	12	6	0	6	152	121	12
Thornbury	12	6	0	6	181	183	12
Oldfield OB	12	6	0	6	143	214	12
O Redcliffians	12	4	1	7	189	178	9
N Bristol	12	4	1	7	132	136	9
Cirencester	12	3	0	9	152	319	6
Frome	12	2	0	10	117	311	4
Coney Hill	12	1	0	11	67	348	2

Cornwall 1

	P	W	D	L	F	A	Pts
Saltash	10	9	1	0	319	48	19
Falmouth	10	6	1	3	247	104	13
Helston	10	6	1	3	207	72	13
St Austell	10	6	1	3	211	114	13
Bude	10	6	1	3	131	112	13
Wadebridge Cam	10	6	1	3	109	103	13
Bodmin	10	4	2	4	163	141	10
Illogan Park	10	4	0	6	91	156	8
Stithians	10	3	0	7	150	190	6
Redruth Albany	10	1	0	9	61	232	2
St Just*	10	0	0	10	41	458	−2

Bude w/o St Just

Cornwall 2

	P	W	D	L	F	A	Pts
St Agnes	10	10	0	0	217	73	20
Perranporth	10	8	0	2	110	62	16
St Day	10	5	0	5	132	112	10
Roseland	10	4	0	6	127	152	8
Camborne SoM	10	3	0	7	102	137	6
Lankelly Fowey	10	0	0	10	73	225	0

Devon 1

	P	W	D	L	F	A	Pts
Honiton	12	10	1	1	236	79	21
Newton Abbot	12	9	0	3	283	119	18

Tavistock	12	8	1	3	230	114	17
O Public Oaks	12	8	0	4	291	150	16
Topsham	12	8	0	4	222	89	16
O Plymothian	12	7	1	4	166	130	15
Kingsbridge	12	6	0	6	143	156	12
Exeter Saras	12	5	0	7	111	186	10
Ilfracombe	12	5	0	7	96	192	10
Withycombe	12	4	1	7	109	158	9
O Technicians	12	4	0	8	99	151	8
Dartmouth	12	1	0	11	92	251	2
Jesters	12	1	0	11	45	348	2

Devon 2

	P	W	D	L	F	A	Pts
Salcombe	11	10	0	1	327	79	20
Prince Rock	11	10	0	1	232	87	20
Torrington	11	9	0	2	246	111	18
Totnes	11	7	0	4	151	117	14
Cullompton	11	6	1	4	218	109	13
N Tawton	11	6	0	5	86	169	12
Plymouth Arg	11	4	0	7	135	173	8
Plymstock	11	4	0	7	114	185	8
St Columba	11	2	2	7	122	121	6
Tamar Saras	11	2	1	8	76	206	5
Devonport HSOB	11	2	0	9	72	212	4
Plymouth YMCA	11	2	0	9	96	306	4

Plympton and Victoria are to merge as one team and will rejoin the Leagues in 1994-95

Gloucester 1

	P	W	D	L	F	A	Pts
Stow-on-the-W	12	11	0	1	268	109	22
Cheltenham N	12	9	2	1	306	121	20
Bream	12	10	0	2	221	117	20
Longlevens	12	9	1	2	238	109	19
Cleve	12	7	1	4	322	114	15
Brockworth	12	7	0	5	200	194	14
Frampton Cott	12	5	1	6	163	263	11
O Richians	12	4	1	7	137	229	9
O Cryptians	12	2	2	8	119	243	6
Painswick	12	3	0	9	95	221	6
Widden OB	12	3	0	9	104	240	6
Saintbridge	12	3	0	9	115	266	6
Ashley Down OB	12	1	0	11	139	201	2

Gloucester 2

	P	W	D	L	F	A	Pts
Hucclecote OB	12	11	0	1	211	118	22
Barton Hill	12	10	1	1	279	69	21
O Bristolians	12	9	1	2	227	133	19
Cheltenham Saras	12	9	1	2	195	120	19
Chosen Hill FP	12	8	0	4	181	127	16
Cheltenham CS	12	5	1	6	146	118	11
Tetbury	12	4	3	5	195	193	11
Bristol Tele	12	5	0	7	137	190	10
Bristol Saras	12	4	1	7	122	142	9
Tredworth	12	3	1	8	178	197	7

Cotham Pk	12	3	1	8	109	213	7
Chipping Sod	12	1	0	11	105	221	2
Dursley	12	1	0	11	97	341	2

Gloucester 3

	P	W	D	L	F	A	Pts
Bishopston	12	10	1	1	259	53	21
Kingswood	12	10	1	1	231	111	21
Cainscross	12	10	0	2	279	125	20
Smiths (Ind)	12	9	0	3	212	125	18
Southmead	12	8	0	4	243	109	16
Westbury-on-S	12	7	0	5	182	109	14
Aretians	12	6	0	6	169	169	12
O Elizabethans	12	4	0	8	163	218	8
Gloucester CS	12	3	2	7	122	210	8
O Colstonians	12	3	1	8	127	157	7
Broad Plain	12	2	1	9	181	281	5
Bristol Aero Co	12	1	2	9	72	247	4
Gloucester AB	12	1	0	11	65	391	2

Gloucester 4

	P	W	D	L	F	A	Pts
Tewkesbury	12	12	0	0	272	62	24
Minchinhampton	12	9	1	2	259	105	19
Pilning	12	6	1	5	130	106	13
Glos Pol	12	6	0	6	126	137	12
Dowty	12	5	0	7	131	112	10
Newent	12	3	0	9	140	203	6
Wotton-u-Edge	12	0	1	11	29	362	1

Somerset 1

	P	W	D	L	F	A	Pts
Midsomer N	12	11	1	0	309	107	23
Yatton	12	9	1	2	192	111	19
Walcot OB	12	9	0	3	325	141	18
St B'dettes OB	12	9	0	3	219	129	18
Wellington	12	9	0	3	231	159	18
N Petherton	12	8	0	4	206	151	16
Minehead Barbs	12	5	0	7	125	199	10
Wells	12	4	0	8	134	153	8
Chard	12	4	0	8	107	213	8
O Sulians	12	4	0	8	131	253	8
Yeovil	12	2	0	10	143	209	4
Imperial	12	2	0	10	80	241	4
Stothert & Pitt	12	1	0	11	91	227	2

Somerset 2

	P	W	D	L	F	A	Pts
Tor	12	11	0	1	314	61	22
Gordano	12	11	0	1	244	88	22
Crewkerne	12	8	1	3	227	147	17
Blagdon	12	7	0	5	191	161	14
Westland	12	7	0	5	147	158	14
Winscombe	12	6	1	5	185	149	13
Chew Valley	12	6	0	6	167	148	12
Avon	12	5	0	7	105	186	10

Backwell	12	4	1	7	122	205	9
Bath O Eds	12	4	0	8	154	154	8
O Ashtonians	12	3	0	9	96	208	6
Avonvale	12	2	1	9	115	214	5
Bath Saras	12	2	0	10	107	295	4

Somerset 3

	P	W	D	L	F	A	Pts
St Brendan's OB	16	15	0	1	511	101	30
Cheddar Valley	16	14	0	2	493	110	28
Burnham-on-Sea	16	10	0	6	211	175	20
South-West Gas	16	7	1	8	200	253	15
Morganians	16	7	1	8	121	224	15
Castle Cary	16	7	0	9	172	297	14
Wincanton	16	5	0	11	261	347	10
Aller	16	3	0	13	149	385	6
Martock	16	3	0	13	136	362	2

Berks/Dorset/Wilts 1

	P	W	D	L	F	A	Pts
Devizes	12	12	0	0	327	46	24
Swindon	12	11	0	1	435	58	22
Swindon Coll	12	9	0	3	248	124	18
Melksham	12	7	0	5	274	151	14
Corsham	12	7	0	5	144	119	14
Supermarine	12	6	0	6	178	177	12
Weymouth	12	5	0	7	241	196	10
Marlborough	12	5	0	7	210	185	10
Lytchett M	12	5	0	7	201	219	10
Aldermaston	12	5	0	7	115	180	10
N Dorset	12	4	1	7	142	261	9
Bradford-on-A	12	1	1	10	98	208	3
Puddletown	12	0	0	12	34	723	0

Berks/Dorset/Wilts 2

	P	W	D	L	F	A	Pts
Blandford	12	12	0	0	342	91	24
Thatcham	12	10	1	1	219	83	21
Bournemouth U	12	9	0	3	253	156	18
Trowbridge	12	8	0	4	313	137	16
Calne	12	7	0	5	303	167	14
Oakmedians	12	6	1	5	172	191	13
Bridport	12	5	1	6	178	179	11
Poole	12	5	1	6	119	224	11
Westbury	12	4	0	8	152	180	8
Warminster	12	3	2	7	155	217	8
Tadley	12	3	1	8	173	146	7
Hungerford	12	2	1	9	122	222	5
Minety	12	0	0	12	32	540	0

Berks/Dorset/Wilts 3

	P	W	D	L	F	A	Pts
Berkshire S Hall	10	8	1	1	250	72	17
Pewsey Vale	10	6	1	3	137	104	13
Portcastrians	10	6	1	3	173	97	13
Colerne	10	5	0	5	129	103	10

Pioneers	10	3	1	6	116	115	7
Christchurch	10	0	0	10	50	364	0

Pewsey Vale promoted under Rule 11 (f)

Bucks & Oxon 1

	P	W	D	L	F	A	Pts
Amersham & C	12	12	0	0	493	63	24
Chinnor	12	10	0	2	293	122	20
Witney	12	8	0	4	193	110	16
Oxford OB	12	7	1	4	206	134	15
Milton Keynes	12	6	1	5	215	189	13
Grove	12	6	0	6	133	105	12
Drifters	12	5	2	5	132	141	12
Beaconsfield	12	6	0	6	180	193	12
Chesham	12	5	0	7	139	219	10
Pennanians	12	4	1	7	132	254	9
Abingdon	12	2	0	10	117	304	4
Littlemore*	12	3	1	8	128	282	3
Chipping Norton	12	1	0	11	56	301	2

Bucks & Oxon 2

	P	W	D	L	F	A	Pts
Phoenix	16	15	0	1	504	55	30
Buckingham	16	14	0	2	385	109	28
Gosford ABs	16	8	1	7	202	149	17
Wheatley	16	8	0	8	174	162	16
Harwell	16	8	0	8	169	267	16
Didcot	16	6	1	9	156	251	13
Cholsey	16	5	1	10	184	295	11
Thames Valley Pol	16	4	1	11	112	204	9
Winslow	16	2	0	14	59	453	4

NORTH DIVISION

North 1

	P	W	D	L	F	A	Pts
Wharfedale	12	12	0	0	327	77	24
Sandal	12	9	0	3	219	131	18
Hull Ionians	12	9	0	3	185	137	18
Manchester	12	8	0	4	208	159	16
Tynedale	12	7	0	5	255	168	14
Middlesbrough	12	7	0	5	161	141	14
Widnes	12	5	0	7	172	180	10
Huddersfield	12	5	0	7	164	148	8
Stockton	12	4	0	8	132	245	8
Wigton	12	3	1	8	184	271	7
Hartlepool R	12	3	0	9	135	248	6
Vale of Lune	12	3	0	9	90	265	6
Northern	12	2	1	9	166	228	5

North 2

	P	W	D	L	F	A	Pts
York	12	10	0	2	217	138	20
W Pk Bramhope	12	9	1	2	269	93	19
Bridlington	12	9	1	2	250	99	19
Macclesfield	12	9	1	2	250	104	19
Alnwick	12	7	2	3	200	93	16

O Crossleyans	12	7	0	5	170	153	14
West Pk St H	12	5	0	7	172	184	8
Birkenhead Pk	12	4	0	8	138	190	8
Northwich	12	4	0	8	131	214	8
Halifax	12	4	0	8	153	241	8
Lymm	12	3	1	8	142	233	7
Wigan	12	2	0	10	103	255	4
Carlisle	12	2	0	10	62	260	4

North-West 1

	P	W	D	L	F	A	Pts
New Brighton	12	10	1	1	310	87	21
Oldershaw	12	9	2	1	242	83	20
Chester	12	8	2	2	185	116	18
Sandbach	12	6	3	3	172	163	15
Sedgley Pk	12	5	2	5	201	134	12
Cockermouth	11	5	1	5	81	125	11
Stockport	11	5	0	6	140	153	10
Ashton-o-Mersey	11	5	0	6	128	143	10
Blackburn	12	5	0	7	127	169	10
Caldy	12	4	0	8	121	203	8
St Edwards OB	12	3	1	8	119	230	7
Merseyside Pol	11	3	0	8	106	191	6
Kirkby Lons*	12	2	0	10	108	243	2

North-West 2

	P	W	D	L	F	A	Pts
Wilmslow	12	11	0	1	312	95	22
Netherhall	12	9	0	3	250	90	18
O Aldwinians	12	9	0	3	186	131	18
Ruskin Pk	12	7	1	4	185	131	15
Rossendale	12	6	2	4	171	124	14
Egremont	12	6	0	6	173	165	12
Vagabonds	12	6	0	6	106	120	12
O Salians	12	4	1	7	85	116	9
Penrith	12	4	1	7	119	187	9
Ormskirk	12	6	0	6	192	250	8
Warrington	12	2	1	9	108	197	5
Rochdale	12	3	0	9	109	197	4
Wirral	12	2	0	10	104	297	4

Cumbria/Lancs North

	P	W	D	L	F	A	Pts
Fleetwood	12	9	1	2	327	94	19
Tyldesley	12	9	0	4	221	150	16
U Eden	12	8	0	4	190	137	16
Windermere	12	7	1	4	180	161	13
Calder Vale	12	6	1	5	167	155	13
Workington	12	6	0	6	175	189	12
St Benedict's	12	5	1	6	122	127	11
Vickers	12	6	0	6	163	172	10
Furness	12	4	1	7	120	154	9
Oldham	12	4	1	7	97	152	9
Moresby†	12	5	0	7	145	214	10
Metrovick	12	5	0	7	131	151	8
Smith Bros	12	2	0	10	97	279	4

Cumbria

	P	W	D	L	F	A	Pts
Keswick	8	7	0	1	245	62	14
Creighton	8	6	1	1	140	60	13
Carnforth	8	4	1	3	146	108	9
Millom	8	4	1	3	115	82	9
British Steel	8	3	1	4	128	107	7
Greengarth	8	2	2	4	110	140	6
Whitehaven	8	2	1	5	97	113	5
Ambleside	7	2	1	4	69	171	5
Silloth	7	1	0	6	23	230	2

Lancashire North 1

	P	W	D	L	F	A	Pts
De La S Salford	13	13	0	0	197	51	26
Bolton	13	11	0	2	327	122	22
Bury	13	9	0	4	182	109	18
Blackpool	12	8	1	3	123	90	17
Colne & Nelson	12	8	0	4	216	88	16
Thornton Cleve	13	7	0	6	232	122	14
Chorley	13	6	1	6	166	153	13
Burnage	12	5	1	6	81	145	11
Ashton-u-Lyne	12	5	1	6	90	155	11
Dukinfield	12	4	0	8	106	138	8
Eccles	13	3	0	10	97	185	6
O Bedians†	12	3	1	8	91	147	7
Broughton	12	1	1	10	88	232	3
Clitheroe	10	0	0	10	42	301	0

Lancashire North 2

	P	W	D	L	F	A	Pts
Heaton Moor	7	7	0	0	187	22	14
N Manchester	7	6	0	1	163	40	12
Littleborough	7	4	0	3	140	53	8
Shell Carr'ton	7	4	0	3	57	46	8
Marple	7	4	0	3	115	51	6
Lostock	7	2	0	5	52	141	4
Agecroft	7	1	0	6	42	145	2
British Aero*	7	0	0	7	25	283	−2

Cheshire/Lancs South

	P	W	D	L	F	A	Pts
Leigh	12	10	1	1	214	117	21
Aspull	11	9	0	2	265	90	18
Southport	12	8	1	3	201	124	17
Altrincham Kers	10	7	1	2	135	86	15
O Anselmians	11	6	2	3	161	159	14
Sefton	12	5	1	6	170	130	11
O Parkonians	12	5	1	6	122	139	11
Eagle	12	5	1	6	152	171	11
S Liverpool	11	5	0	6	159	129	10
Crewe & Nantwich	12	3	2	7	122	163	8
Liverpool Coll	12	4	0	8	83	149	8
St Mark's OB	12	2	2	8	146	234	6
Newton-le-W	11	0	0	11	47	286	0

Cheshire

	P	W	D	L	F	A	Pts
Pt Sunlight	9	9	0	0	213	22	18
Congleton	9	8	0	1	159	45	16
Prenton	9	6	0	3	168	90	12
Wallasey	8	6	0	2	127	61	12
Shell Stanlow	8	5	0	3	99	71	10
Bowdon	9	3	0	6	134	135	6
Holmes Chapel	9	2	0	7	85	164	4
Helsby	9	2	0	7	67	224	4
Hoylake*	9	2	0	7	93	163	2
Moore*	9	1	0	8	55	225	0

Lancashire South

	P	W	D	L	F	A	Pts
Didsbury Toc H†	8	6	0	2	183	70	12
Vulcan	8	7	0	1	175	71	14
Douglas (IoM)	7	5	1	1	119	71	11
Manchester YMCA	8	4	2	2	149	90	10
Birchfield	7	4	0	3	158	124	6
Mossley Hill	8	2	2	4	71	127	6
Hightown	8	2	1	5	75	123	3
Lucas	8	1	1	6	97	226	3
Halton	8	0	1	7	82	207	1

North-East 1

	P	W	D	L	F	A	Pts
Doncaster	12	11	0	1	232	70	22
Driffield	12	8	1	3	173	109	17
Pontefract	12	8	1	3	215	147	15
Blaydon	12	6	1	5	171	106	13
Thornensians	12	6	1	5	127	141	13
Keighley	12	6	1	5	121	170	13
Selby	12	6	0	6	124	175	12
O Brodleians	12	4	3	5	147	117	11
Roundhegians	12	6	1	5	140	152	11
Gateshead Fell	12	2	3	7	121	167	7
Morpeth	12	3	1	8	75	126	7
Redcar	12	3	0	9	98	210	6
Novocastrians	12	2	1	9	84	138	5

North-East 2

	P	W	D	L	F	A	Pts
Horden	12	10	1	1	262	123	21
Cleckheaton	12	10	0	2	310	133	20
Goole	12	8	1	3	189	109	17
Ashington	12	8	1	3	173	134	17
Blyth	12	6	1	5	173	129	13
Westoe	12	5	1	6	184	140	11
Whitby	12	5	1	6	110	177	11
Hull	12	6	0	6	170	147	10
Beverley	12	5	0	7	138	223	10
Ripon	12	4	0	8	94	194	8
Bramley	12	3	1	8	152	243	7
Rockcliff	12	3	0	9	127	184	6
Acklam	12	1	1	10	89	235	3

Durham & Northumberland 1

	P	W	D	L	F	A	Pts
Mowden Pk	12	12	0	0	256	76	24
Darlington†	12	6	0	6	195	162	12
W H'pool TDSOB	12	10	1	1	286	115	21
Ryton	12	7	1	4	224	166	15
Percy Pk	12	6	2	4	234	111	14
Sunderland	12	6	0	6	176	137	12
N Shields	12	5	1	6	193	161	11
Bishop Auckland	12	6	1	5	168	193	11
Guisborough	12	5	1	6	117	158	11
N Durham	12	5	0	7	156	203	10
Darlington RA	12	3	0	9	114	239	6
Seaham	12	2	1	9	134	305	5
Consett	12	1	0	11	104	331	2

Durham & Northumberland 2

	P	W	D	L	F	A	Pts
Ponteland	11	9	1	1	220	75	19
Wallsend	11	8	2	1	324	87	18
Winlaton Vulcans	11	7	2	2	154	69	16
Hartlepool	11	7	0	4	203	87	14
Wensleydale	11	7	0	4	184	84	14
Medicals	11	6	1	4	147	104	13
Chester-le-St	11	5	1	5	111	112	11
Seghill	11	4	0	7	146	277	8
H'pool BBOB	11	3	0	8	101	321	6
Houghton	11	3	0	8	148	218	4
Seaton Carew	11	1	2	8	59	207	4
N Aycliffe*	11	1	1	9	86	242	−1

Durham & Northumberland 3

	P	W	D	L	F	A	Pts
Billingham	9	8	0	1	266	59	16
Richmondshire	9	8	0	1	209	27	16
Barnard Castle	9	8	0	1	150	62	16
Sedgefield	9	5	0	4	166	117	10
Jarrovians	9	5	0	4	120	152	10
Wearside	9	3	1	5	102	116	7
Belmont	9	3	0	6	84	180	6
Prudhoe	9	3	0	6	94	194	6
H'pool Ath	9	0	2	7	36	148	2
Washington*	9	0	1	8	41	213	−1

Yorkshire 1

	P	W	D	L	F	A	Pts
N Ribblesdale	12	10	0	2	221	114	20
Wheatley Hills	12	8	2	2	206	98	18
B'ford Salem	12	8	0	4	145	150	16
Wath	12	7	1	4	192	143	15
O Otliensians	12	7	1	4	172	126	15
Ilkley	12	7	0	5	237	82	14
Leodiensians	12	7	0	5	210	165	14
Sheff Oaks	12	6	0	6	152	152	12
Hemsworth	12	6	0	6	137	185	12
Malton & Norton	12	5	0	7	140	203	10

	P	W	D	L	F	A	Pts
Pocklington	12	4	0	8	130	225	8
Yarnbury	12	1	0	11	94	197	2
York RI	12	0	0	12	93	289	0

Yorkshire 2

	P	W	D	L	F	A	Pts
Barnsley	12	11	0	1	245	91	22
Castleford	12	10	0	2	270	73	20
O Modernians	12	10	0	2	221	78	20
Northallerton	12	8	0	4	211	110	16
Halifax Vands	12	7	0	5	157	128	14
Sheffield Tigers	12	6	0	6	167	169	12
W Leeds	12	5	0	7	225	221	10
Scarborough	12	5	0	7	126	183	10
Hessle	12	4	0	8	117	141	8
Dinnington	12	4	0	8	165	220	8
Hud'field YMCA	12	3	0	9	106	175	6
Moortown	12	4	0	8	97	183	4
Leeds CSSA	12	1	0	11	79	414	2

Yorkshire 3

	P	W	D	L	F	A	Pts
Aireborough	12	12	0	0	291	54	24
Wibsey	12	10	1	1	362	124	21
Hullensians	12	9	0	3	189	106	18
Wetherby	12	8	1	3	184	130	17
Heath	12	7	1	4	136	134	15
Knottingley	12	7	0	5	152	107	14
O Rishworthians	12	5	1	6	175	126	11
Marist	12	4	1	7	140	179	9
Burley	12	3	1	8	114	213	7
Ossett	12	3	0	9	126	189	6
Leeds Corinths	12	4	0	8	86	177	6
Stanley Rodills	12	3	0	9	117	228	6
Leeds YMCA	12	0	0	12	56	361	0

Yorkshire 4

	P	W	D	L	F	A	Pts
Phoenix Pk	12	11	1	0	258	69	23
Skipton	12	11	1	0	150	63	23
Mosborough	12	8	0	4	227	102	16
Baildon	12	8	0	4	146	84	16
Hornsea	12	7	0	5	153	121	14
De La S Sheff	12	7	1	4	145	117	13
Withernsea	12	4	0	8	92	213	8
Knaresborough	12	4	1	7	121	136	7
Castle Coll	12	3	1	8	77	141	7
Yorks Main	12	4	0	8	105	169	6
Danum Phoenix	12	3	0	9	99	184	6
Rowntrees	12	3	0	9	91	195	6
BP Chemicals	12	2	1	9	67	137	5

Castle Coll have withdrawn from the League for 1994-95

Yorkshire 5

	P	W	D	L	F	A	Pts
Garforth	9	7	1	1	228	57	15
Stocksbridge	9	8	0	1	159	41	14
Adwick-le-St	9	7	0	2	178	82	14
Rawmarsh	9	6	1	2	163	78	11
New Earswick	9	4	0	5	143	112	8
Menwith Hill Qs	9	3	0	6	98	169	6
Harlow Nomads	9	4	0	5	82	141	4
Armthorpe M'ham	9	3	0	6	66	170	4
St James	9	2	0	7	47	122	2
Yorks CW	9	0	0	9	40	232	0

MIDLANDS DIVISION

Midlands 1

	P	W	D	L	F	A	Pts
Barkers Butts	12	10	0	2	180	86	20
Worcester	12	8	0	4	234	104	16
Burton	12	8	0	4	219	159	16
Syston	12	8	0	4	221	119	14
Leamington	12	7	0	5	189	150	14
Camp Hill	12	7	0	5	178	158	12
Bedworth	12	6	0	6	156	149	10
Mansfield	12	5	0	7	139	173	10
Derby	12	5	0	7	118	177	10
Westleigh	12	5	0	7	137	212	10
Wolverhampton	12	4	0	8	169	221	8
Towcestrians	12	3	0	9	123	218	6
Leighton Buzz	12	2	0	10	83	220	4

Midlands 2

	P	W	D	L	F	A	Pts
Whitchurch	12	10	1	1	178	85	21
Stafford	12	9	1	2	226	75	19
Stockwood Pk	12	8	0	4	188	145	16
Paviors	12	7	1	4	146	129	15
Bedford Ath	12	7	0	5	207	188	14
Matlock	12	5	1	6	164	124	11
Belgrave	12	5	1	6	138	112	11
Broad St	12	5	0	7	193	132	10
Keresley	12	5	0	7	148	192	10
Newark	12	5	0	7	163	222	10
Peterborough	12	4	0	8	143	187	8
Willenhall	12	4	0	8	128	255	8
Vipers	12	1	1	10	89	265	3

Midlands East 1

	P	W	D	L	F	A	Pts
Hinckley	12	10	0	2	223	97	20
Scunthorpe	12	9	0	3	172	109	18
Ampthill	12	8	1	3	198	142	17
Kettering	12	9	0	3	182	98	16
Stoneygate	12	7	0	5	121	117	14
Biggleswade	12	5	1	6	117	146	11
Chesterfield	12	5	1	6	110	140	11

	P	W	D	L	F	A	Pts
Stews & Lloyds	12	4	1	7	128	132	9
Northampton BB	12	4	0	8	111	162	8
Spalding	12	5	1	6	167	138	7
Amber Valley	12	3	1	8	112	164	7
Luton	12	2	1	9	121	184	5
Moderns*	12	3	1	8	119	252	3

Midlands West 1

	P	W	D	L	F	A	Pts
Sutton Coldfield	12	10	0	2	276	137	20
Bromsgrove	12	10	1	1	203	97	19
Newbold	12	8	0	4	172	105	16
Dudley	12	7	1	4	167	160	15
O Longtonians	12	7	0	5	178	133	14
O Halesonians	12	6	0	6	134	149	12
N'castle (Staffs)	12	5	1	6	113	176	11
Ludlow	12	4	2	6	123	137	10
King's Norton	12	5	0	7	102	121	10
O Leam'tonians	12	3	2	7	119	194	8
Aston O Edwards	12	3	1	8	178	212	5
Leek	12	3	1	8	174	212	5
Nuneaton O Eds	12	2	1	9	180	286	5

Midlands East 2

	P	W	D	L	F	A	Pts
Long Buckby	12	12	0	0	299	77	24
Wellingborough	12	10	0	2	288	120	20
Kibworth	12	8	1	3	176	134	17
Worksop	12	7	1	4	126	98	15
S Leicester	12	7	0	5	184	110	14
Lutterworth	12	6	0	6	132	108	12
Lincoln	12	6	0	6	159	146	12
Grimsby	12	5	1	6	138	164	11
W Bridgford	12	6	0	6	168	182	10
Mellish	12	5	0	7	117	187	10
Coalville	12	2	1	9	108	170	5
Kesteven	12	2	0	10	84	192	4
Dronfield	12	0	0	12	62	353	0

Midlands West 2

	P	W	D	L	F	A	Pts
O Laurentians	12	12	0	0	259	57	24
Newport	12	11	0	1	448	74	22
O Coventrians	12	9	0	3	244	192	18
Selly Oak	12	8	0	4	310	169	16
O Yardleians*	12	6	0	6	164	161	10
Dixonians	12	5	0	7	147	225	10
Woodrush	12	5	0	7	157	266	10
Kenilworth*	12	6	0	6	213	184	8
W Midlands Pol*	12	5	0	7	158	138	8
Tamworth*	12	5	0	7	168	231	8
Stratford-o-A	12	4	0	8	146	228	8
Shrewsbury	12	2	0	10	81	280	2
Coventry Welsh*	12	0	0	12	86	346	−2

East Midlands/Leics 1

	P	W	D	L	F	A	Pts
Huntingdon	12	9	1	2	261	110	19
Oadby Wygges	12	9	1	2	218	109	19
Market Bos'th*	12	11	0	1	308	87	18
St Neots	12	6	2	4	144	91	14
O Bosworthians	12	7	0	5	165	170	14
Northampton MO	12	6	1	5	153	134	13
Dunstablians	12	5	1	6	163	180	11
N'pton OS*	12	6	0	6	194	168	10
Aylestone St J	12	4	1	7	121	158	9
Loughborough	12	3	0	9	112	196	6
Daventry*	12	3	1	8	108	210	5
Melton Mowbray	12	2	1	9	103	224	5
Brackley*	12	2	1	9	64	277	3

East Midlands/Leics 2

	P	W	D	L	F	A	Pts
O Northamptons	12	11	0	1	338	64	22
Bedford Queens	12	10	1	1	244	66	21
Oakham	12	9	0	3	267	123	18
Wellingboro OG	12	8	2	2	189	119	18
Rushden & High	12	4	5	3	183	85	13
Bugbrooke	12	6	0	6	139	217	12
N'ton Casuals	12	4	3	5	133	131	11
Birstall	12	5	1	6	168	170	11
Aylestonians	12	4	3	5	157	164	11
Wigston	12	4	1	7	130	192	9
St Ives	12	2	2	8	117	219	6
O Ashbeians	12	2	0	10	95	204	4
New Parks OB	12	0	0	12	26	432	0

East Midlands/Leics 3

	P	W	D	L	F	A	Pts
Bedford Swifts	11	11	0	0	311	60	22
Colworth Hse	11	10	0	1	313	85	20
Corby	11	7	1	3	261	129	15
Oundle	11	7	1	3	159	104	15
Kempston	11	6	0	5	209	109	12
Deepings	11	6	0	5	170	153	12
Westwood	11	4	1	6	89	120	9
Anstey	11	4	1	6	136	178	9
O Newtonians	11	4	0	7	113	138	8
O Wellingburians	11	3	0	8	137	349	6
W Leicester	11	2	0	9	103	234	4
Burbage	11	0	0	11	36	378	0

East Midlands/Leics 4

	P	W	D	L	F	A	Pts
Vauxhall Motors	12	11	0	1	395	35	22
N'ton Heathens	12	9	0	3	224	131	18
Thorney	12	8	0	4	127	139	16
Braunstone T	12	7	0	5	209	123	14
Cosby	12	4	0	8	80	181	8
Clapham T'woods	12	3	0	9	111	323	6
Potton	12	0	0	12	64	278	0

North Midlands 1

	P	W	D	L	F	A	Pts
Luctonians	12	12	0	0	438	52	24
Telford	12	8	0	4	256	131	16
Five Ways O Eds	12	7	2	3	160	121	16
Veseyans	12	6	2	4	233	173	14
O Griffinians	12	6	2	4	210	167	14
Pershore	12	7	0	5	203	177	14
Kidderminster	12	7	0	5	186	165	14
O Centrals	12	5	1	6	170	179	11
Evesham	12	4	1	7	162	198	9
Bridgnorth	12	4	1	7	124	199	9
Droitwich	12	4	0	8	127	244	8
Warley	12	3	0	9	144	313	6
Redditch*	12	0	1	11	51	345	−1

North Midlands 2

	P	W	D	L	F	A	Pts
Edwardians	12	12	0	0	468	53	24
Malvern	12	11	0	1	426	104	20
Erdington	12	9	0	3	203	113	18
B'ham City Off	12	8	0	4	266	90	16
Ross-on-Wye	12	6	0	6	181	229	12
Tenbury	12	5	0	7	127	203	10
Bournville	12	4	1	7	104	226	9
Market Drayton	12	4	1	7	105	281	9
Kynoch	12	5	0	7	161	181	8
Bromyard	12	3	2	7	112	223	8
B'ham Welsh	12	3	0	9	131	235	6
O Salteians	12	3	0	9	88	248	6
O Moseleians	12	3	0	9	116	302	6

North Midlands 3

	P	W	D	L	F	A	Pts
Upton-on-S	10	10	0	0	210	73	20
Birmingham CS	10	8	0	2	212	61	16
Bishops Castle	10	7	1	2	139	73	15
Ledbury	10	6	1	3	170	77	13
Stourport	10	6	0	4	137	91	12
Birchfield	10	4	0	6	138	156	8
Yardley & Dist	10	4	0	6	98	144	8
Cleobury Mortimer	10	4	0	6	84	139	8
Witton	10	3	0	7	98	139	6
Oswestry	10	2	0	8	112	136	4
Thimblemill	10	0	0	10	39	348	0

Notts, Lincs & Derbys 1

	P	W	D	L	F	A	Pts
Ilkeston	12	12	0	0	250	92	24
Glossop	12	9	0	3	243	99	18
Stamford	12	6	2	4	162	109	14
Southwell	12	6	2	4	196	197	14
N'ham Casuals	12	7	1	4	228	172	13
Sleaford	12	6	1	5	115	134	13
Ashbourne	12	5	4	3	198	112	12
Bakewell Manns	12	6	0	6	178	169	12

East Leake	12	5	2	5	146	127	4
Long Eaton	12	5	0	7	185	155	2
M Rasen & Louth	12	3	0	9	138	262	2
Keyworth	12	2	0	10	112	274	2
Meden Vale	12	0	0	12	73	322	0

Notts, Lincs & Derbys 2

	P	W	D	L	F	A	Pts
Leesbrook	12	12	0	0	378	57	24
Melbourne	12	9	1	2	262	75	19
N'hamshire Cons	12	9	1	2	212	137	19
E Retford	12	9	0	3	243	110	18
Ashfield Swans	12	7	2	3	135	126	16
Rolls-Royce	12	5	1	6	196	154	11
Buxton	12	5	0	7	176	152	10
Boston	12	3	3	6	121	186	9
All Spartans	12	4	1	7	103	174	9
Bingham	12	3	1	8	60	212	5
Boots Ath	12	2	0	10	107	277	4
Nottinghamians	12	2	2	8	77	240	2
Stamford Coll	12	2	0	10	61	231	2

Notts, Lincs & Derbys 3

	P	W	D	L	F	A	Pts
N Kesteven	12	11	1	0	406	64	23
Barton & Dist	12	11	0	1	241	83	22
Derby Coll	12	7	0	5	178	142	14
Skegness	12	6	1	5	123	148	13
Belper	12	6	0	6	147	128	12
Cotgrave	12	6	0	6	158	153	12
Tupton	12	5	1	6	121	152	11
Gainsborough	12	4	2	6	127	123	10
Ollerton & B'coat	12	5	0	7	140	145	10
Horncastle	12	5	0	7	164	280	10
Bourne	12	4	0	8	189	220	8
Cleethorpes	12	4	0	8	87	261	8
Hope Valley	12	1	1	10	89	271	3

Notts, Lincs & Derbys 4

	P	W	D	L	F	A	Pts
Bolsover	10	8	1	1	142	79	17
Castle Don'ton	10	5	2	3	135	97	12
Yarborough Bs	10	5	2	3	121	75	12
Whitwell	10	6	0	4	154	110	12
Sutton B'ton Sc	10	3	1	6	116	119	7
Bilsthorpe	10	0	0	10	27	215	0

Staffs/Warwickshire 1

	P	W	D	L	F	A	Pts
Dunlop	12	12	0	0	273	75	24
Trinity Guild	12	11	0	1	343	92	22
Southam	12	9	0	3	196	79	18
Stoke OB	12	8	0	4	190	139	16
Manor Pk	12	6	0	6	126	113	12
GEC Coventry	12	6	0	6	146	144	12
O Wheatleyans	12	7	0	5	142	127	10

	P	W	D	L	F	A	Pts
GEC St Leonards	12	5	0	7	142	211	10
Trentham	12	3	1	8	93	144	7
Eccleshall	12	3	1	8	125	252	7
Uttoxeter	12	2	1	9	97	317	5
Coventry Saras	12	3	1	8	123	149	3
Handsworth	12	0	2	10	84	238	0

Staffs/Warwickshire 2

	P	W	D	L	F	A	Pts
Atherstone	12	11	0	1	320	36	22
Rugby St And	12	10	0	2	296	70	20
Silhillians	12	10	0	2	306	87	20
Pinley	12	8	1	3	209	139	17
Earlsdon	12	8	0	4	283	96	16
Berkswell & B	12	7	0	5	179	104	14
Spartans	12	7	1	4	206	125	13
Coventrians	12	4	1	7	71	172	9
Linley	12	2	3	7	117	166	7
Harbury	12	3	1	8	81	238	7
Cannock	12	2	1	9	128	219	5
Wednesbury	12	2	0	10	53	299	4
O Oaks	12	0	0	12	41	539	0

Staffs/Warwickshire 3

	P	W	D	L	F	A	Pts
Shipston-on-S	12	10	1	1	326	87	21

Warwicks Pol	12	9	0	3	183	66	18
Rubery Owen	12	8	0	4	238	111	16
Burntwood	12	8	0	4	190	114	14
Alcester	12	8	0	4	173	111	14
Wulfrun	12	6	0	6	172	187	12
Standard	12	4	3	5	137	162	11
Rugeley	12	4	1	7	165	198	9
Warwick	12	4	1	7	153	231	9
Wheaton Aston	12	5	0	7	190	248	8
Claverdon	12	4	1	7	161	175	7
O Warwickians	12	4	1	7	121	136	7
Michelin	12	0	0	12	37	420	0

Wulfrun join North Midlands 3 in 1994-95

Staffs/Warwickshire 4

	P	W	D	L	F	A	Pts
Bloxwich	8	7	1	0	184	36	15
Coventry Tech	8	5	1	2	104	69	11
Rugby Welsh	8	4	1	3	185	71	9
Stone	8	5	1	2	159	80	7
Ford	8	3	1	4	145	90	5
Shottery	8	4	1	3	88	101	5
Jaguar (Cov)	8	2	0	6	93	172	4
Cheadle	8	3	0	5	47	131	4
Fife Street	8	0	0	8	38	293	0

YORKSHIRE GO FORWARD WITH ENTERPRISE FROM THEIR BACKS

CIS INSURANCE COUNTY CHAMPIONSHIP 1993-94
Michael Austin

16 April, Twickenham
Durham 3 (1PG)   **Yorkshire 26** (2G 4PG)

Yorkshire's inventive back division left their signature on the County Championship, sponsored for the first time by the Co-operative Insurance Society. A crowd of 15,000, including 10,000 from schools and junior sections admitted free, saw Yorkshire lift the title for the 12th time.

Their performance was embellished by the skills of Michael Harrison, the former England captain, who had led Yorkshire to their previous success in 1987; by current captain Bryan Barley, Steve Burnhill and David Breakwell, a bold, running full-back. Breakwell initiated one of the finest tries at headquarters during the season with a dazzling break from deep within his own half. Charles Vyvyan committed four tacklers and handed on to Guy Easterby for Harrison to score on his final – albeit unscheduled – appearance for the county. Harrison, aged 38 and a member of Wakefield's second team as well as the newly appointed manager of England Emerging Players, had responded to a late call to play following the withdrawal of Jon Eagle through injury. After the match, Barley, too, announced his retirement at county level.

Durham had a far more severe pre-match setback when Jonathan Bland, their fly-half and captain of the 1989 Championship-winning team, failed a Friday-night fitness test. It was his two dropped goals in the final 12 minutes which had beaten favourites Cornwall in the semi-final before a crowd of 15,000 two months earlier. Bland's experience was sorely needed against a seasoned Yorkshire side which once again appreciated the place-kicking skills of Kevin Plant, aged 37. His injury-time touchline penalty goal against Gloucestershire at Otley had enabled Yorkshire to scramble into the final. This had denied the West Countrymen the opportunity to equal Lancashire's record of 16 title wins. Plant exposed Durham's indiscretions by landing four penalty goals, as well as converting the two tries – one by Barley, from a determined drive and support from Carroll, and the other by Harrison.

Outplayed but spirited, Durham struggled to curb the line-out authority of Christian Raducanu, the former Romanian lock forward, but trailed by 16-3 at half-time. They had lost to Yorkshire 30-8 in a League 1 North game earlier in the season and qualified for the semi-finals ahead of Lancashire and Northumberland – all three counties had two wins and one defeat – only on superior points difference.

After two successive all-northern finals, a new format for 1994-95 rules out a hat-trick. The London and South and South-West Divisions are to combine to produce two semi-finalists while the North and Midlands will each find their own champion to progress into the last four.

TEAMS IN THE FINAL

Durham: G D Spearman (Blaydon); O Evans (West Hartlepool), I Bell (Hartlepool Rovers), P J T Nickalls (Rosslyn Park), C A Mattison (Durham City); A Parker (West Hartlepool), S Kirkup (Durham City); R G Naisbitt (Stockton) (*capt*), I R Parnaby (Westoe), M Douthwaite (Stockton), G R Wanless (Durham City), C Aldus (Stockton), S Musgrove (Westoe), B Dixon (Stockton), D McKinnon (West Hartlepool)
Replacements K R McCallum (Durham City) for Evans (35 mins); J M A Brown (Novocastrians) for Spearman (75 mins)
Scorer *Penalty Goal:* Parker
Yorkshire: D Breakwell (Leeds); M E Harrison (Wakefield), B Barley (Sandal) (*capt*), S Burnhill (Cleckheaton), C Thornton (Leeds); K Plant (Rotherham), G Easterby (Harrogate); R Szabo (Wakefield), R Whyley (Harrogate), S McMain (Sheffield), I Carroll (Otley), C Raducanu (Bradford & Bingley), C West (Rotherham), C B Vyvyan (Wharfedale), N Hargreaves (Leeds)
Scorers *Tries:* Barley, Harrison *Conversions:* Plant (2) *Penalty Goals:* Plant (4)
Referee A Spreadbury (Somerset)

TEAMS IN THE SEMI-FINALS

15 January, Otley RFC
Yorkshire 13 (1G 2PG) **Gloucestershire 12** (3PG 1DG)

Yorkshire: T Stimpson (Durham U); J Eagle (Leeds), B Barley (Sandal) (*capt*), S Burnhill (Cleckheaton), C Thornton (Leeds); J Plant (Rotherham), A Crowley (Bradford & Bingley); P Wright (Middlesbrough), R Whyley (Harrogate), R Szabo (Wakefield), P Taylor (Harrogate), C Raducanu (Bradford & Bingley), C West (Rotherham), C B Vyvyan (Wharfedale), H Verity (Wharfedale)
Scorers *Try:* West *Conversion:* Plant *Penalty Goals:* Plant (2)
Gloucestershire: N Marment (Cheltenham); J Davies (Cheltenham), B Maslen (Gloucester), L Osborne (Berry Hill), D Cottrell (Bristol); M Hamlin (Moseley) (*capt*), G Shipton (Stroud); A Powles (Berry Hill), N Nelmes (Lydney), S Baldwin (Gloucester Old Boys), N Scrivens (Cirencester), J Brain (Cheltenham), I Patten (Bristol), D Mann (Matson), R Lewis (Lydney)
Scorer *Penalty Goals:* Hamlin (3) *Dropped Goal:* Hamlin
Referee N D Cousins (London)

5 February, Redruth RFC
Cornwall 9 (2PG 1DG) **Durham 14** (1PG 2DG 1T)

Cornwall: D Chapman (Camborne); D Weeks (Camborne), P S Gadsdon (Camborne), A W Mead (Redruth), I K Pollard (Camborne); J S Tucker (Launceston), R D Nancekivell (Launceston); A Ellery (Redruth), B P Andrew (Redruth), J W Pearce (St Ives), T F Adams (Camborne), A H Cook (Redruth) (*capt*), S D Berryman (Penzance/Newlyn), J Atkinson (St Ives), M Addinall (Penryn)
Scorer *Penalty Goals:* Chapman (2) *Dropped Goal:* Chapman
Durham: K R McCallum (Durham City); O Evans (West Hartlepool), I Bell (Hartlepool Rovers), P J T Nickalls (Rosslyn Park), C A Mattison (Durham City); J P Bland (Durham City), S Kirkup (Durham City); R G Naisbitt (Stockton) (*capt*), I R Parnaby (Westoe), M Douthwaite (Stockton), G R Wanless (Durham City), C Aldus (Stockton), S Musgrove (Westoe), B Dixon (Stockton), D McKinnon (West Hartlepool)
Replacement D Tweddle (Gateshead Fell) for Mattison (62 mins)

Scorers *Try:* McKinnon   *Penalty Goal:* Bland   *Dropped Goals:* Bland (2)
Referee S Lander (Liverpool)

DIVISIONAL ROUNDS

AREA NORTH

League 1

Durham 38, Northumberland 11;
Lancashire 3, Yorkshire 26; Durham 16,
Lancashire 22; Yorkshire 27,
Northumberland 3; Northumberland 30,
Lancashire 15; Yorkshire 30, Durham 8

	P	W	D	L	F	A	Pts
Yorkshire	3	3	0	0	83	14	6
Durham	3	1	0	2	62	63	2
Northumberland	3	1	0	2	44	80	2
Lancashire	3	1	0	2	40	72	2

League 2

Cheshire 15, Leicestershire 9;
Warwickshire 12, Cumbria 20;
Leicestershire 14, Cumbria 21;
Warwickshire 22, Cheshire 30; Cumbria
16, Cheshire 20; Leicestershire 28,
Warwickshire 17

	P	W	D	L	F	A	Pts
Cheshire	3	3	0	0	65	47	6
Cumbria	3	2	0	1	57	46	2
Leicestershire	3	1	0	2	51	53	2
Warwickshire	3	0	0	3	51	78	2

League 3

North Midlands 18, Staffordshire 25;
Notts, Lincs & Derbys 36, East Midlands
14; Notts, Lincs & Derbys 11, North
Midlands 31; Staffordshire 41, East
Midlands 29; East Midlands 5, North
Midlands 24; Staffordshire 18, Notts,
Lincs & Derbys 12

	P	W	D	L	F	A	Pts
Staffordshire	3	3	0	0	84	59	6
North Midlands	3	2	0	1	73	41	4
Notts, Lincs & Derbys	3	1	0	2	59	63	2
East Midlands	3	0	0	3	48	101	0

AREA SOUTH

League 1

Cornwall 19, Gloucestershire 17;
Hampshire 21, Middlesex 7; Cornwall
14, Hampshire 6; Middlesex 17,
Gloucestershire 26; Gloucestershire 35,
Hampshire 3; Middlesex 14, Cornwall 15

	P	W	D	L	F	A	Pts
Cornwall	3	3	0	0	48	37	6
Gloucestershire	3	2	0	1	78	39	4
Hampshire	3	1	0	2	30	56	2
Middlesex	3	0	0	3	38	62	0

League 2

Devon 15, Kent 14; Dorset & Wilts 16,
Surrey 29; Dorset & Wilts 20, Devon 10;
Kent 6, Surrey 13; Kent 32, Dorset &
Wilts 13; Surrey 6, Devon 6

	P	W	D	L	F	A	Pts
Surrey	3	2	1	0	48	28	5
Devon	3	1	1	1	31	40	3
Kent	3	1	0	2	52	41	2
Dorset & Wilts	3	1	0	2	49	71	2

League 3

Hertfordshire 24, Somerset 8; Sussex 17,
Buckinghamshire 7; Somerset 10,
Buckinghamshire 13; Sussex 20,
Hertfordshire 11; Somerset 19, Sussex 8;
Buckinghamshire 16, Hertfordshire 13

	P	W	D	L	F	A	Pts
Sussex	3	2	0	1	45	37	4
Buckinghamshire	3	2	0	1	36	40	4
Hertfordshire	3	1	0	2	48	44	2
Somerset	3	1	0	2	37	45	2

League 4

Berkshire 42, Eastern Counties 11;
Oxfordshire 36, Berkshire 12; Eastern
Counties 9, Oxfordshire 21

	P	W	D	L	F	A	Pts
Oxfordshire	2	2	0	0	57	21	4
Berkshire	2	1	0	1	54	47	2
Eastern Counties	2	0	0	2	20	63	0

ENGLISH COUNTY CHAMPIONS 1889-1993

FIRST SYSTEM

1889	**Yorkshire,** undefeated, declared champions by RU (scored 18G 17T to 1G 3T)	1890	**Yorkshire,** undefeated, declared champions (scored 10G 16T to 2G 4T)

SECOND SYSTEM

1891	**Lancashire** champions.	Group Winners — Yorkshire, Surrey, Gloucestershire.
1892	**Yorkshire** champions.	Group Winners — Lancashire, Kent, Midlands.
1893	**Yorkshire** champions.	Group Winners — Cumberland, Devon, Middlesex.
1894	**Yorkshire** champions.	Group Winners — Lancashire, Gloucestershire, Midlands.
1895	**Yorkshire** champions.	Group Winners — Cumberland, Devon, Midlands.

THIRD SYSTEM

	Champions	*Runners-up*	*Played at*
1896	**Yorkshire**	Surrey	Richmond
1897	**Kent**	Cumberland	Carlisle
1898	**Northumberland**	Midlands	Coventry
1899	**Devon**	Northumberland	Newcastle
1900	**Durham**	Devon	Exeter
1901	**Devon**	Durham	W Hartlepool
1902	**Durham**	Gloucestershire	Gloucester
1903	**Durham**	Kent	W Hartlepool
1904	**Kent**	Durham	Blackheath (2nd meeting)
1905	**Durham**	Middlesex	W Hartlepool
1906	**Devon**	Durham	Exeter
1907	**Devon** and **Durham** joint champions after drawn games at W Hartlepool and Exeter		
1908	**Cornwall**	Durham	Redruth
1909	**Durham**	Cornwall	W Hartlepool
1910	**Gloucestershire**	Yorkshire	Gloucester
1911	**Devon**	Yorkshire	Headingley
1912	**Devon**	Northumberland	Devonport
1913	**Gloucestershire**	Cumberland	Carlisle
1914	**Midlands**	Durham	Leicester
1920	**Gloucestershire**	Yorkshire	Bradford

FOURTH SYSTEM

	Champions	*Runners-up*	*Played at*
1921	**Gloucestershire** (31)	Leicester (4)	Gloucester
1922	**Gloucestershire** (19)	N Midlands (0)	Birmingham
1923	**Somerset** (8)	Leicester (6)	Bridgwater
1924	**Cumberland** (14)	Kent (3)	Carlisle
1925	**Leicestershire** (14)	Gloucestershire (6)	Bristol
1926	**Yorkshire** (15)	Hampshire (14)	Bradford
1927	**Kent** (22)	Leicestershire (12)	Blackheath
1928	**Yorkshire** (12)	Cornwall (8)	Bradford
1929	***Middlesex** (9)	Lancashire (8)	Blundellsands
1930	**Gloucestershire** (13)	Lancashire (7)	Blundellsands
1931	**Gloucestershire** (10)	Warwickshire (9)	Gloucester
1932	**Gloucestershire** (9)	Durham (3)	Blaydon
1933	**Hampshire** (18)	Lancashire (7)	Boscombe
1934	**E Midlands** (10)	Gloucester (0)	Northampton
1935	**Lancashire** (14)	Somerset (0)	Bath
1936	**Hampshire** (13)	Northumberland (6)	Gosforth
1937	**Gloucestershire** (5)	E Midlands (0)	Bristol
1938	**Lancashire** (24)	Surrey (12)	Blundellsands
1939	**Warwickshire** (8)	Somerset (3)	Weston
1947	†**Lancashire** (14)	Gloucestershire (3)	Gloucester
1948	**Lancashire** (5)	E Counties (0)	Cambridge

1949	**Lancashire (9)**	Gloucestershire (3)	Blundellsands
1950	**Cheshire (5)**	E Midlands (0)	Birkenhead Park
1951	**E Midlands (10)**	Middlesex (0)	Northampton
1952	**Middlesex (9)**	Lancashire (6)	Twickenham
1953	**Yorkshire (11)**	E Midlands (3)	Bradford
1954	**Middlesex (24)**	Lancashire (6)	Blundellsands
1955	**Lancashire (14)**	Middlesex (8)	Twickenham
1956	**Middlesex (13)**	Devon (9)	Twickenham
1957	**Devon (12)**	Yorkshire (3)	Plymouth
1958	**Warwickshire (16)**	Cornwall (8)	Coventry
1959	**Warwickshire (14)**	Gloucestershire (9)	Bristol
1960	**Warwickshire (9)**	Surrey (6)	Coventry
1961	o**Cheshire (5)**	Devon (3)	Birkenhead Park
1962	**Warwickshire (11)**	Hampshire (6)	Twickenham
1963	**Warwickshire (13)**	Yorkshire (10)	Coventry
1964	**Warwickshire (8)**	Lancashire (6)	Coventry
1965	**Warwickshire (15)**	Durham (9)	Hartlepool
1966	**Middlesex (6)**	Lancashire (0)	Blundellsands
1967	****Surrey** and **Durham**		
1968	**Middlesex (9)**	Warwickshire (6)	Twickenham
1969	**Lancashire (11)**	Cornwall (9)	Redruth
1970	**Staffordshire (11)**	Gloucestershire (9)	Burton-on-Trent
1971	**Surrey (14)**	Gloucestershire (3)	Gloucester
1972	**Gloucestershire (11)**	Warwickshire (6)	Coventry
1973	**Lancashire (17)**	Gloucestershire (12)	Bristol
1974	**Gloucestershire (22)**	Lancashire (12)	Blundellsands
1975	**Gloucestershire (13)**	E Counties (9)	Gloucester
1976	**Gloucester (24)**	Middlesex (9)	Richmond
1977	**Lancashire (17)**	Middlesex (6)	Blundellsands
1978	**N Midlands (10)**	Gloucestershire (7)	Moseley
1979	**Middlesex (19)**	Northumberland (6)	Twickenham
1980	**Lancashire (21)**	Gloucestershire (15)	Vale of Lune
1981	**Northumberland (15)**	Gloucestershire (6)	Gloucester
1982	**Lancashire (7)**	North Midlands (3)	Moseley

FIFTH SYSTEM

	Champions	*Runners-up*	*Played at*
1983	**Gloucestershire (19)**	Yorkshire (7)	Bristol
1984	**Gloucestershire (36)**	Somerset (18)	Twickenham
1985	**Middlesex (12)**	Notts, Lincs and Derbys (9)	Twickenham

SIXTH SYSTEM

	Champions	*Runners-up*	*Played at*
1986	**Warwickshire (16)**	Kent (6)	Twickenham
1987	**Yorkshire (22)**	Middlesex (11	Twickenham
1988	**Lancashire (23)**	Warwickshire (18)	Twickenham
1989	**Durham (13)**	Cornwall (9)	Twickenham
1990	**Lancashire (32)**	Middlesex (9)	Twickenham
1991	**Cornwall (29**	Yorkshire (20) (*aet*)	Twickenham
1992	**Lancashire (9)**	Cornwall (6)	Twickenham
1993	**Lancashire (9)**	Yorkshire (6)	Twickenham
1994	**Yorkshire (26)**	Durham (3)	Twickenham

*After a draw at Twickenham. †*After a draw, 8-8, at Blundellsands.* o*After a draw 0-0, at Plymouth.*
**Surrey and Durham drew 14 each at Twickenham and no score at Hartlepool and thus became joint champions. Lancashire have won the title 16 times, Gloucestershire 15, Yorkshire 12, Warwickshire 9, Middlesex 8, Durham 8 (twice jointly), Devon 7 (once jointly), Kent 3 times, Hampshire, East Midlands, Cheshire, Northumberland and Cornwall twice each, Surrey twice (once jointly), and Midlands (3rd System), Somerset, Cumberland, Leicestershire, Staffordshire and North Midlands once each.

A 'DOUBLE' FOR SPARKLING MALVERN

PILKINGTON SHIELD 1993-94
Michael Austin

7 May 1994, Twickenham
Malvern 8 (1PG 1T)   **Old Hamptonians 6** (2PG)

The Midlands produced their first winner of the RFU junior clubs knock-out competition when Malvern triumphed with a try and a penalty goal from David Grundy, a painter and decorator, playing on the right wing. Grundy had kicked the last-minute winning penalty goal from 40 metres which beat Hucclecote Old Boys, of Gloucester, by an identical score in the semi-final.

Malvern duly became the first winners of the Pilkington Shield – the tournament was under new sponsorship worth £300,000 over three years, succeeding the Provincial Insurance sponsorship. The format was similar, but playing the final as a curtain-raiser to the Pilkington Cup final was a welcome innovation. By the end, a crowd of 10,000 had assembled for the climax to a competition which began the previous September with 512 clubs and which demanded that those reaching Twickenham should pass just about unscathed through eight rigorous rounds.

Old Hamptonians, whose headquarters are only three miles from Twickenham, won all their matches, while the only blemish on Malvern's progress was a 9-9 quarter-final draw with Edwardians, the Birmingham club where Peter Jackson, the former Coventry and England wing, learned the game. Malvern qualified on the 'away team' rule. Hamptonians, fielding 12 old boys of Hampton School, had been assisted by Dick Best, the England coach, before the final while Barrie Corless, Gloucester's director of rugby, helped with Malvern's preparations. Malvern achieved a double with their promotion to North Midlands League 1, guided by fitness training from their centre, Rob James, a former Welsh decathlon champion.

The match featured two rallies which took the trophy to Malvern, whose smaller pack resisted being steamrollered by the Hamptonians heavyweights. Malvern fulfilled their pre-match promise to run the ball after Hamptonians established a three-point half-time lead through Gareth Prichard's penalty goal. Fittingly, the best move of the game, as sparkling as the spa water from their town, launched Grundy on a 22-metre run for the only try after 48 minutes. Prichard's second penalty goal four minutes later restored Hamptonians' lead before Grundy's 35-metre penalty kick from an awkward angle won the match with 22 minutes remaining. The other notable achievement belonged to Kidderminster Carolians, beaten in the semi-finals for the second successive season.

McBurney of Malvern wins a line-out in the Pilkington Shield final at Twickenham.

Malvern: S Fahey; D Grundy, G Richards, R James, A Johnstone; D Green, G Henderson; S Cooper, P Morewood, C Campion, A MacKelvie, A McBurney, S Dixon, A Ridley *(capt)* M Wolfe *Replacement* D Blinston for Wolfe (75 mins)
Scorer *Try:* Grundy   *Penalty Goal:* Grundy
Old Hamptonians: S Eggleton; A Maclenan, G Prichard, S Fox, A Mills-Leggett; N Bugler, E Turnill; A Glyn-Jones, S Zander *(capt)*, L Gallant, J Lumley-Kelly, R Bowden, J Clarke, N Cooke M Carmody
Scorer *Penalty Goals:* Prichard (2)
Referee A J Spreadbury (Somerset Society)

RESULTS

Third Round

London Division: Region 1 – Eastern Counties, Hertfordshire, Middlesex Old Hamptonians 57, London French 14; Belsize Park 27, Northolt 10; Feltham 5, Bank of England 53; Ilford Wanderers 46, Witham 5; St Albans 10, Barclays Bank 3 *(aet)*; St Nicholas Old Boys 12, Hayes 13; Ongar 9, May & Baker 3; London Hospital 20, Hadleigh 8; Loughton 64, Brightlingsea 3; Old Actonians 12, Datchworth 27
Region 2 – Hampshire, Surrey, Kent, Sussex Vigo 30, Folkestone 3; Old Caterhamians 18, Cranbrook 3; STC Footscray 22, London Fire Brigade 9; Chipstead 3, Old Pelhamians 6; Old Tiffinians 5, Trojans 10; Deal Wanderers 9, Esso 5; Old Suttonians 0, Woking 41; Battersea Ironsides 22, Old Brightonians 3; Overton 22, Ditchling 27; Linton 14, Bexley 7
Midland Division: Region 1 – North Midlands, Staffordshire, Warwickshire Bromyard 0, Atherstone 15; Spartans 0, Edwardians 0 *(Edwardians qualify on 'away team' rule)*; Birmingham City Officials 30, Yardley & District 6; Claverdon 0, Erdington 22; Cannock 6, Droitwich 10; Malvern 61, Bournville 3; Kidderminster Carolians 28, Burntwood 14
Region 2 – East Midlands, Leicestershire, Notts, Lincs, & Derbys Ledbury 17, Oundle 3; Vauxhall Motors 22, Barton & District 6; Melton Mowbray 45, Westwood 0; Oakham 60, North Kesteven 0; Wellingborough Old Grammarians 40, Ashfield Swans 0; Aylestone St James 43, Ollerton & Bevercoat 12; New Parks Old Boys 8, Anstey 30; Old Northamptonians 12, Bugbrooke 0

South-West Division: Region 1 – Berkshire, Buckinghamshire, Dorset & Wilts, Oxfordshire Beaconsfield 23, Thames Valley Police 9; Thatcham 19, Chesham 23; Blandford 25, Phoenix 23 *(aet)*; Trowbridge 49, Berkshire Shire Hall 8
Region 2 – Cornwall, Devon, Gloucestershire, Somerset Chipping Sodbury 5, Hucclecote Old Boys 14; Barton Hill Old Boys 44, Old Technicians 8; Chew Valley Old Boys 6, Bristol Telephones 18; Blagdon 24, St Agnes 35; Withcombe 0, Old Public Oaks 25; Dartmouth w/o, Ilfracombe w/d; North Petherton 23, Tredworth 20; Old Elizabethans 7, Bishopston 28; Prince Rock 13, Bodmin 16; Tetbury 24, Tor 20
North Division: Region 1 – Durham, Northumberland, Yorkshire Knottingley 13, Aireborough 20; Halifax Vandals 29, Richmondshire 3; Leeds Corinthians 20, Marist 14; Wibsey 33, Leeds CSSA 8; West Leeds 21, Burley 15; Hullensians 16, Wetherby 14; Wensleydale 28, Mosborough 3; North Shields 35, Phoenix Park 3
Region 2 – Cheshire, Cumbria, Lancashire Keswick 7, De La Salle (Salford) 3; Old Bedians 23, Gentlemen of Moore 7; Burnage 25, Dukinfield 0; Colne & Nelson 8, Sefton 6; Bolton 13, Wallasey 16; Old Anselmians 13, Bury 24; Old Parkonians 20, Congleton 10

Fourth Round

London Division: Old Pelhamians 11, Bank of England 12; Deal Wanderers 22, Ilford Wanderers 12; Linton 3, Woking 21; Old Caterhamians 13, Battersea Ironsides 3; London Hospital 19, Ongar 5; St Albans 24, Datchworth 12; Vigo 5, Loughton 19; Ditchling 7, Old Hamptonians 35; Hayes 12, Belsize Park 14; Trojans 24, STC Footscray 7

Midland Division: Melton Mowbray 23, Anstey 5; Atherstone 29, Droitwich 0; Wellingborough Old Grammarians 25, Erdington 7; Aylestone St James 3, Malvern 16; Kidderminster Carolians 17, Vauxhall Motors 6; Edwardians 11, Old Northamptonians 6; Ledbury 15, Oakham 16
South-West Division: Tetbury 6, Bishopston 12; Barton Hill Old Boys 20, North Petherton 0; Old Public Oaks 29, Bodmin 3; Bristol Telephones 0, St Agnes 10; Hucclecote Old Boys 29, Chesham 10; Dartmouth 20, Trowbridge 8; Blandford 3, Beaconsfield 21
North Division: Burnage 19, North Shields 10; Colne & Nelson 11, Wensleydale 8; Wallasey 0, Birmingham City Officers 10; Halifax Vandals 13, Old Parkonians 6; Wibsey 9, Bury 7; Leeds Corinthians 8, West Leeds 23; Old Bedians 3, Aireborough 22; Keswick 18, Hullensians 14

Fifth Round
South-West Division: Hucclecote Old Boys 11, Burnage 3; Dartmouth 6, Barton Hill Old Boys 13; St Agnes 16, Old Public Oaks 22; Beaconsfield 6, Bishopston 8
North Division: Aireborough 3, Keswick 6; Colne & Nelson 15, West Leeds 9; Halifax Vandals 14, Wibsey 21
Midland Division: Birmingham City Officials 8, Edwardians 25; Melton

Mowbray 10, Kidderminster Carolians 13; Oakham 5, Malvern 8; Wellingborough Old Grammarians 3, Atherstone 6
London Division: Loughton 17, Bank of England 8; Old Caterhamians 11, Belsize Park 9; Old Hamptonians 33, Deal Wanderers 13; St Albans 21, Trojans 0; Woking 3, London Hospital 0

Sixth Round
North & Midlands: Atherstone 3, Keswick 10; Edwardians 22, St Albans 0; Kidderminster Carolians 14, Colne & Nelson 0; Malvern 20, Wibsey 13
London & South-West: Barton Hill Old Boys 6, Hucclecote Old Boys 8; Bishopstone 11, Old Hamptonians 26; Loughton 6, Old Caterhamians 14; Old Public Oaks 10, Woking 3

Quarter-finals
North & Midlands: Edwardians 9, Malvern 9 (*Malvern qualify on 'away team' rule*); Keswick 17, Kidderminster Carolians 27
London & South-West: Hucclecote Old Boys 11, Old Public Oaks 6; Old Caterhamians 3, Old Hamptonians 15

Semi-finals
Malvern 8, Hucclecote Old Boys 6 (*at Coventry*); Old Hamptonians 10, Kidderminster Carolians 6 (*at Northampton*)

BARBARIANS PUSH ALL BLACKS TO THE LIMIT IN CARDIFF CLASSIC

THE BARBARIANS 1993-94
Geoff Windsor-Lewis

The highlight of the season was the match against the All Blacks at Cardiff, in which the Barbarians went down by 25 points to 12. After an impressive start, they conceded possession from which the All Blacks built up an imposing 17-point lead.

The home side rose to the occasion and gradually fought their way back by playing some impressive attacking rugby. Tony Clement encouraged his team-mates with some fine, uninhibited running and stylish attacking from full-back; Neil Back was the link for the whole side, and his ability to reach the breakdown and then take part in the succeeding move kept the Barbarians in the game when the All Blacks had a purple patch during the second half. Olivier Roumat had an outstanding all-round game, dominating the line-out and showing his speed in the open play.

Overall, the Barbarians could not quite match the team play of a touring side which had been together for 12 matches. Although Eric Elwood kept them in the game with four penalties from six attempts, they could not score the try that might have made all the difference. The New Zealand defence, and in particular John Timu, held out against all the efforts of a Barbarian side which came together late in the second half under Scott Hastings' positive leadership. Ian Jones rounded off the tour with the All Blacks' third try.

In September, the Barbarians returned to Exeter to celebrate that club's centenary at the County Ground. It was 85 years since the clubs had last met and the Barbarians produced some scintillating rugby with Michael Dods and Jon Sleightholme leading the way for a side which was determined to keep the pressure on until the end.

A strong team containing 12 internationals went down to a determined Newport side who made the most of frequent mistakes made in the Barbarian ranks. Perhaps the home side were given opportunities they did not expect, and the Barbarians could not raise their game in the second half although they were only two points behind.

Jez Harris, Leicester's long-serving fly-half, will long remember his contribution in a game in which Leicester convincingly beat the Barbarians in front of a packed house at Welford Road. Harris scored 26 points in a runaway victory, giving the home side the biggest win in history of the fixture, which began 84 years ago to the day. Against a home side rising to the occasion, Mike Rayer, Cardiff's full-back, impressed and played a part in both Barbarian tries, scored by Patrice Lagisquet and Jon Sleightholme. Stuart Potter and both Underwoods scored tries for Leicester, as did Graham Rowntree.

The Easter tour was notable for the inclusion of Kummer and De Vries, the first Dutchmen to play for the club. Over 100 Dutch rugby fans travelled to Cardiff to support the Dutch representation and were delighted when Kummer marked the occasion with a spectacular try-scoring dive under the posts. It was probably the first time that the Dutch national anthem had been heard at Cardiff Arms Park. The Barbarians possessed too much fire-power for Cardiff, Derek Stark scoring a hat-trick and Sleightholme scoring two tries on the other wing. Captain Craig Chalmers had opened the scoring with an early try and then kicked a penalty goal and five conversions in an impressive display by the Barbarians, their third successive victory over Cardiff.

The touring side, captained by Gavin Hastings, lost to Swansea on Easter Monday. A young Swansea team made the most of their opportunities and even though 11 tries were scored during the afternoon, the match never really caught alight and produced little rugby to remember.

The Barbarians, on the incentive of £300 for every try scored, have now pushed their total to £49,800, donated by their sponsors, Scottish Amicable, for the development of youth rugby.

In the close season, the club made a three-match tour of Zimbabwe, culminating in a match against the national side in Harare. In September, they were due to visit Bath to take part in the celebrations of 100 years of rugby football at the Recreation Ground, and then Paris to play the French Barbarians to celebrate the 50th anniversary of the Liberation of Paris by the Allied forces. The Barbarians will include representatives from Australia, New Zealand, Canada, America and South Africa. The match against the South African tourists, the last of their tour, was due to be held in Dublin for the first time.

RESULTS 1993-94

Played 7   Won 3   Lost 4   Drawn 0   Points for 243 (24G 5PG 12T)
Against 218 (19G 9PG 1DG 11T)

1993

28 Sept	**Beat Exeter** at County Ground, Exeter 59 (7G 2T) to 14 (2G)
5 Oct	**Lost to Newport** at Rodney Parade 19 (2G 1T) to 35 (3G 3PG 1T)
4 Dec	**Lost to New Zealand** at Cardiff Arms Park 12 (4PG) to 25 (2G 2PG 1T)
28 Dec	**Lost to Leicester** at Welford Road, Leicester 14 (2G) to 51 (6G 2PG 1DG)

1994

9 Mar	**Beat East Midlands** at Franklins Gardens, Northampton 55 (5G 4T) to 25 (1G 1PG 3T)

2 Apr	**Beat Cardiff** at Cardiff Arms Park 53 (5G 1PG 3T) to 27 (1G 4T)
4 Apr	**Lost to Swansea** at St Helen's, Swansea 31 (3G 2T) to 41 (4G 1PG 2T)

PLAYERS 1993-94

Abbreviations: *E* – Exeter; *N* – Newport; *NZ* – New Zealand; *L* – Leicester; *EM* – East Midlands; *SW1* – Cardiff; *SW2* – Swansea; (R) – Replacement; * – New Barbarian

Full-backs: *M Dods (Gala) [*E, N, EM*]; A Clement (Swansea & Wales) [*NZ*]; M A Rayer (Cardiff & Wales) [*L*]; I C Glasgow (Heriot's FP) [*SW1, SW2* (centre), *E* (fly-half)]; A G Hastings (Watsonians & Scotland) [*SW2*]

Threequarters: S P Geoghegan (London Irish & Ireland) [*E*]; S Hastings (Watsonians & Scotland) [*E, NZ*]; *S Potter (Leicester) [*E*]; J M Sleightholme (Wakefield) [*E, L, SW1*]; D A Stark (Boroughmuir & Scotland) [*N, EM, SW1, SW2*]; *P R de Glanville (Bath) [*N, L*]; M R Hall (Cardiff & Wales) [*N*]; H S Thorneycroft (Northampton) [*N*]; A G Stanger (Hawick & Scotland) [*NZ*]; I S Gibbs (Swansea & Wales) [*NZ*]; *N T Walker (Cardiff & Wales) [*NZ*]; H Woodland (Neath) [*L*]; *P Lagisquet (Bayonne & France) [*L*]; *M J Field (Malone & Ireland) [*EM, SW1, SW2*]; * M Ridge (Blackrock Coll & Ireland) [*EM*]; *N Woods (Blackrock Coll) [*EM*]; D S Wyllie (Stewart's-Melville FP & Scotland) [*SW1*]; *R Hennessy (London Irish) [*SW2*]; *C P Scholtz (Stellenbosch U) [*NZ*(R)]; *L Evans (Treorchy) [*SW2*(R)]

Half-backs: *D B Millard (London Scottish) [*E*]; A Davies (Cardiff & Wales) [*N*]; R H StJ B Moon (Llanelli & Wales) [*N*]; *E P Elwood (Lansdowne & Ireland) [*NZ*]; G Armstrong (Jedforest & Scotland) [*NZ*]; C M Chalmers (Melrose & Scotland) [*L, EM, SW1*]; R Howley (Cardiff) [*NZ*(R), *L*]; *A Rolland (Blackrock Coll & Ireland) [*EM*]; A D Nicol (Dundee HSFP & Scotland) [*SW1, SW2*]; R H Q B Moon (Rosslyn Park) [*EM*(R)]; *G P J Townsend (Gala & Scotland) [*SW2*]; *M de Maid (Pontypool) [*SW2*(R)]

Forwards: M S Linnett (Moseley & England) [*E, SW1, SW2*]; R G R Dawe (Bath & England) [*E*]; *P M Clohessy (Young Munster & Ireland) [*E, N*]; N Hadley (Wasps & Canada) [*E, N*]; S J Lloyd (Moseley) [*E*]; D J McIvor (Edinburgh Acads & Scotland) [*E, SW2*]; R A Robinson (Bath & England) [*E, L*]; E W Peters (Bath) [*E, N*(R)]; C J Hillman (South Wales Police) [*E*(R)]; *G Rowntree (Leicester) [*N, EM*]; *J N Murphy (Greystones & Ireland) [*N*]; N G B Edwards (Northampton & Scotland) [*N, SW1*]; K T Leahy (Wanderers & Ireland) [*N*]; R I Wainwright (Edinburgh Acads & Scotland) [*N, NZ*]; I R Smith (Gloucester & Scotland) [*N*]; N J Popplewell (Greystones & Ireland) [*NZ*]; T J Kingston (Dolphin & Ireland) [*NZ*]; *E J A McKenzie (Paris U, NSW & Australia) [*NZ, L*]; *P S Johns (Dungannon & Ireland) [*NZ, L*]; *O Roumat (Dax & France) [*NZ*]; *L S Quinnell (Llanelli & Wales) [*NZ*]; N A Back (Leicester & England) [*NZ*]; M Griffiths (Cardiff & Wales) [*L*]; N N Meek (Pontypridd & Wales) [*L, SW2*]; A E D MacDonald (Heriot's FP & Scotland) [*L, EM*]; C M A Sheasby (Harlequins) [*L*]; *S M Williams (Neath) [*L*]; *W J Mulcahy (Skerries) [*EM*]; A P Burnell (London Scottish & Scotland) [*EM, SW1*]; *M Poole (Leicester) [*EM*]; *J Hall (Bath & England) [*EM*]; *B F Robinson (Ballymena & Ireland) [*EM, SW1, SW2*(R)]; *D Eves (Bristol) [*EM*]; *Y Kummer (DIOK & Netherlands) [*SW1, SW2*(wing)]; D S Munro (Glasgow HSFP & Scotland) [*SW1, SW2*(R)]; *C Lion-Cachet (Oxford U & Western Province, SA) [*SW1*]; W D McBride (Malone & Ireland) [*SW1*]; *G de Vries (Hilversum) [*SW2*]; *H T Dumitras (Pau) [*SW2*]; *R West (Gloucester) [*SW2*]; *P F Crane (Newbridge) [*SW2*]; *M Greenwood (Wasps) [*SW2*]

OXFORD'S TERM-TIME FORM COMES THROUGH ON THE BIG DAY

THE VARSITY MATCH 1993 (*for the Bowring Bowl*)
Michael Austin

7 December, Twickenham
Oxford University 20 (3PG 2DG 1T)
Cambridge University 8 (1DG 1T)

Breaking the two-year-old mould of Cambridge victories, Oxford relished their 48th win in the series (Cambridge have three more) with a success which owed much to their back row in this 112th Varsity Match, contested in front of another packed crowd.

Lion-Cachet, the Johannesburg-born captain, Aitken, from Durban, and Martin, an English Students cap, made a massive contribution, alongside Fennell, the loose-head prop, who strode about Ubogu-style. Victory sustained the impression that Oxford, with ten wins from 15 previous matches, were better equipped than their opponents, who had managed seven successes from 16 games. Rees, the Canada fly-half of Welsh stock, scored 12 of Oxford's points with three penalty goals and a dropped goal, but it was the Dark Blues' collective ability to move into overdrive beyond Cambridge's capabilities that won them the match.

Roy, born in Cambridgeshire, and Bramley, a rougher-hewn Yorkshireman, played admirably for the Light Blues, winning the possession which gave them hope from the danger zone of 12-3 adrift soon after half-time. Rees, who has played for Wasps, Middlesex and British Columbia as well as Canada, opened the scoring for Oxford with an 18th-minute penalty goal. Cambridge, in considerable disarray, fell offside and Boyle, a Leicester and former Moseley centre, dropped a goal after du Toit had subtly switched direction in a series of attacking moves. Boyle's kick was a collector's item, veering between the posts from a lowering trajectory to take Oxford six points ahead.

The dropped goal habit was not lost on Kennedy, who responded with another before Rees continued the trend with a third for Oxford. Oxford 9, Cambridge 3 – three dropped goals and a penalty goal in all.

Then the try-scoring started, but typically in this time-honoured, tight match, it did not erupt. After Rees kicked a second penalty goal, Flood, the Cambridge centre, who played for England at schools, under-21 and students levels, made a classical break through the middle; Boyd, the University Club secretary and Kent Schools product, made considerable ground in support and scored a thrilling try. This was the distinctive high point of an otherwise low-key Cambridge performance. Their scent of a surprise victory at 12-8 down evaporated into a mere whiff and Rees kicked a third penalty goal after Bramley had been penalised amid a rare flurry of fisticuffs.

Kennedy, the Cambridge Scot playing at fly-half, had a kick charged down and du Toit took advantage of the friendly bounce to score an unchallenged try in the north-east corner. Oxford's win was complete, but Cambridge had the consolation of winning the other games, at Under-21 and second-team levels.

Oxford University: M T Joy (Marling GS, Stroud & Keble); R V Wintle (Cynffig CS, Bridgend & University), L S Boyle (Binswood Coll, Leamington Spa & Keble), E J Rayner (Dauntsey's & Oriel), T C S Watson (Radley & St Edmund Hall); G K Rees (St Michael's University School, Harrow & Keble), S F du Toit (Paul Roos Gymnasium, Cape Town & Christ Church); B Fennell (St Edward's, Oxford & Keble), D S Henderson (Glenalmond & Keble), C J Clark (Marlborough & Keble), J B B Daniell (Wanganui College, NZ, Eton & St Catherine's), D R Evans (Bro Myrddin CS, Carmarthen & St Anne's), C C Lion-Cachet (Pretoria HS, S Africa & Keble) *(capt)*, A D Aitken (Durban HS, S Africa & Keble), N F C Martin (King Edward's, Birmingham & Keble)
Scorers *Try:* du Toit   *Penalty Goals:* Rees (3)   *Dropped Goals:* Boyle, Rees
Cambridge University: A L Dalwood (St Albans School & St Edmund's); A R Arentsen (Cardiff HS & Corpus Christi), J P Flood (Stonyhurst & St Edmund's), A J Palfrey (St Cyres CS & Hughes Hall), A Boyd (St Olave's GS & Jesus); A J S Kennedy (Fettes & St John's), C J Tynan (Magee HS, Vancouver & Hughes Hall); T J Hughes (Harrow & Trinity), A J G Read (RGS, High Wycombe & Hughes Hall), P G Callow (Oakham & Fitzwilliam) *(capt)*, R A Bramley (Queen Elizabeth GS, Wakefield & St Edmund's), W S Roy (David Hughes School, Menai Bridge & Hughes Hall), P C M Irons (Wellington & Hughes Hall), A J Meadows (Sedbergh & St Edmund's), N D Richardson (King's, Worcester & St Edmund's) *Replacements* C W Thompson (Arnold & Magdalene) for Flood (59 mins); J F Duckworth (Bradford GS & St Edmund's) for Callow (temp)
Scorers *Try:* Boyd   *Dropped Goal:* Kennedy
Referee W D Bevan (Wales)

---

7 December, Stoop Memorial Ground

Oxford University Under-21s 10 (1G 1PG)   **Cambridge University Under-21s 12** (1G 1T)
Oxford University Under-21s: J J Sacree (St Edmund Hall); C J Smart (Trinity), T Gladstone (St Edmund Hall), J W Dargie (Brasenose), J S Tilley (Pembroke); M P Butler (St Edmund Hall), R C Brown (St Hugh's); G K T Hamp (Keble), T M Bennett-Britton (Oriel), D E Grant (Worcester), C P Smith (Keble), R J W Paul (Keble), M H Freer (Brasenose) *(capt)*, R S Yeabsley (Keble), A C J Bridgwood (Keble)
Scorers *Try:* Yeabsley   *Conversion:* Sacree   *Penalty Goal:* Sacree
Cambridge University Under-21s: T Walton (Downing); P T Maximan (Queens'), J Hurst (Homerton), A P Spencer (St John's), J E Butler (St John's); O W R Clayton (Magdalene), D M Maslen (Girton); D H G Fish (Trinity Hall), J G T Edwards (St Catharine's), E B R Simpson (Clare), J D Motts (Robinson) *(capt)*, A Nelstrop (Girton), R C Calvert (Pembroke), R D Earnshaw (St John's), M Holmes (Peterhouse)
Scorers *Tries:* Hurst, Walton   *Conversion:* Hurst
Referee S Lander (Liverpool)

---

2 December, Iffley Road, Oxford

Oxford University Greyhounds 20 (5PG 1T)   **Cambridge University LX Club 23** (6PG 1T)
Oxford University Greyhounds: G Allison (Templeton); J Bursell (New College), M Mermagen (Keble), E Dickinson (St Cross), J Brennand (St Anne's); C Jones (University), G Barber (Keble); R Tice (Wycliffe Hall) *(capt)*, G Cooper (Keble), A Bryce (Keble), R Yeabsley (Keble), P Coveney (Templeton), R Underhill (Green College), C Ritchie (Keble), A Bridgwood (Keble)
Scorers *Try:* Brennand   *Penalty Goals:* Mermagen (5)
Cambridge University LX Club: S Phillips (St Edmund's); W Thompson (Magadelene), P Bingham (St Edmund's), G Bird (Hughes Hall), T Walton (Downing); C Pring (Queens'), J Davies (Downing); J Duckworth (St Edmund's), T Keith-Roach (Jesus), J Tidball (Sidney Sussex), M Wright (Hughes Hall), T Dower (St John's), A McCracken (Downing) *(capt)*, E Rollitt (Magdalene), H Jones (Gonville & Caius)
Scorers *Try:* Jones   *Penalty Goals:* Thompson (6)
Referee P Dickens (East Midlands)

The annual match between Cambridge University LX Club and Oxford University Whippets was cancelled.

17 November, Iffley Road, Oxford
Oxford University 54 (3G 1PG 6T)   **Major Stanley's XV 8** (1PG 1T)

24 November, Grange Road, Cambridge
Cambridge University 31 (4G 1PG)   **M R Steele-Bodger's XV 43** (5G 1PG 1T)

A smiling Chad Lion-Cachet, Oxford's South African-born captain, with the Bowring Bowl after the Dark Blues' 20-8 win, their 48th in the series.

VARSITY MATCH RESULTS

112 Matches played   Oxford 48 wins   Cambridge 51 wins   13 Draws

*Match played at Oxford 1871-72; Cambridge 1872-73; The Oval 1873-74 to 1879-80; Blackheath 1880-81 to 1886-87; Queen's Club 1887-88 to 1920-21; then Twickenham.   *At this date no match could be won unless a goal was scored.*

Year	Winner	Score
1871-72	**Oxford**	1G 1T to 0
1872-73	**Cambridge**	1G 2T to 0
1873-74	Drawn	1T each
1874-75*	Drawn	Oxford 2T to 0
1875-76	**Oxford**	1T to 0
1876-77	**Cambridge**	1G 2T to 0
1877-78	**Oxford**	2T to 0
1878-79	Drawn	No score
1879-80	**Cambridge**	1G 1DG to 1DG
1880-81	Drawn	1T each
1881-82	**Oxford**	2G 1T to 1G
1882-83	**Oxford**	1T to 0
1883-84	**Oxford**	3G 4T to 1G
1884-85	**Oxford**	3G 1T to 1T
1885-86	**Cambridge**	2T to 0
1886-87	**Cambridge**	3T to 0
1887-88	**Cambridge**	1DG 2T to 0
1888-89	**Cambridge**	1G 2T to 0
1889-90	**Oxford**	1G 1T to 0
1890-91	Drawn	1G each
1891-92	**Cambridge**	2T to 0
1892-93	Drawn	No score
1893-94	**Oxford**	1T to 0
1894-95	Drawn	1G each
1895-96	**Cambridge**	1G to 0
1896-97	**Oxford**	1G 1DG to 1G 1T
1897-98	**Oxford**	2T to 0
1898-99	**Cambridge**	1G 2T to 0
1899-1900	**Cambridge**	2G 4T to 0
1900-01	**Oxford**	2G to 1G 1T
1901-02	**Oxford**	1G 1T to 0
1902-03	Drawn	1G 1T each
1903-04	**Oxford**	3G 1T to 2G 1T
1904-05	**Cambridge**	3G to 2G
1905-06	**Cambridge**	3G (15) to 2G 1T (13)
1906-07	**Oxford**	4T (12) to 1G 1T (8)
1907-08	**Oxford**	1G 4T (17) to 0
1908-09	Drawn	1G (5) each
1909-10	**Oxford**	4G 5T (35) to 1T (3)
1910-11	**Oxford**	4G 1T (23) to 3G 1T (18)
1911-12	**Oxford**	2G 3T (19) to 0
1912-13	**Cambridge**	2G (10) to 1T (3)
1913-14	**Cambridge**	1DG 3T (13) to 1T (3)
1914-18	*No matches*	
1919-20	**Cambridge**	1PG 1DG (7) to 1G (5)
1920-21	**Oxford**	1G 4T (17) to 1G 3T (14)
1921-22	**Oxford**	1G 2T (11) to 1G (5)
1922-23	**Cambridge**	3G 2T (21) to 1G 1T (8)
1923-24	**Oxford**	3G 2T (21) to 1G 1PG 2T (14)
1924-25	**Oxford**	1G 2T (11) to 2T (6)
1925-26	**Cambridge**	3G 6T (33) to 1T (3)
1926-27	**Cambridge**	3G 5T (30) to 1G (5)
1927-28	**Cambridge**	2G 2PG 2T (22) to 1G 3T (14)
1928-29	**Cambridge**	1G 3T (14) to 1PG 1DG 1T (10)
1929-30	**Oxford**	1G 1DG (9) to 0
1930-31	Drawn	Oxford 1PG (3) Cambridge 1T (3)
1931-32	**Oxford**	1DG 2T (10) to 1T (3)
1932-33	**Oxford**	1G 1T (8) to 1T (3)
1933-34	**Oxford**	1G (5) to 1T (3)
1934-35	**Cambridge**	2G 1PG 1DG 4T (29) to 1DG (4)
1935-36	Drawn	No score

Year	Winner	Score
1936-37	**Cambridge**	2T (6) to 1G (5)
1937-38	**Oxford**	1G 4T (17) to 1DG (4)
1938-39	**Cambridge**	1G 1PG (8) to 2PG (6)
1939-45	*War-time series*	
1945-46	**Cambridge**	1G 2T (11) to 1G 1PG (8)
1946-47	**Oxford**	1G 1DG 2T (15) to 1G (5)
1947-48	**Cambridge**	2PG (6) to 0
1948-49	**Oxford**	1G 1DG 2T (14) to 1G 1PG (8)
1949-50	**Oxford**	1T (3) to 0
1950-51	**Oxford**	1G 1PG (8) to 0
1951-52	**Oxford**	2G 1T (13) to 0
1952-53	**Cambridge**	1PG 1T (6) to 1G (5)
1953-54	Drawn	Oxford 1PG 1T (6) Cambridge 2PG (6)
1954-55	**Cambridge**	1PG (3) to 0
1955-56	**Oxford**	1PG 2T (9) to 1G (5)
1956-57	**Cambridge**	1G 1PG 1DG 1T (14) to 2PG 1T (9)
1957-58	**Oxford**	1T (3) to 0
1958-59	**Cambridge**	1G 1PG 3T (17) to 1PG 1T (6)
1959-60	**Oxford**	3PG (9) to 1PG (3)
1960-61	**Cambridge**	2G 1T (13) to 0
1961-62	**Cambridge**	1DG 2T (9) to 1DG (3)
1962-63	**Cambridge**	1G 1PG 1DG 1T (14) to 0
1963-64	**Cambridge**	2G 1PG 2T (19) to 1G 1PG 1DG (11)
1964-65	**Oxford**	2G 1PG 2T (19) to 1PG 1GM (6)
1965-66	Drawn	1G (5) each
1966-67	**Oxford**	1G 1T (8) to 1DG 1T (6)
1967-68	**Cambridge**	1T 1PG (6) to 0
1968-69	**Cambridge**	1T 1PG 1DG (9) to 2T (6)
1969-70	**Oxford**	3PG (9) to 2PG (6)
1970-71	**Oxford**	1G 1DG 2T (14) to 1PG (3)
1971-72	**Oxford**	3PG 3T (21) to 1PG (3)
1972-73	**Cambridge**	1G 1PG 1DG 1T (16) to 2PG (6)
1973-74	**Cambridge**	1PG 1DG 2T (14) to 1G 2PG (12)
1974-75	**Cambridge**	1G 2PG 1T (16) to 5PG (15)
1975-76	**Cambridge**	2G 5PG 1DG 1T (34) to 3PG 1DG (12)
1976-77	**Cambridge**	1G 3PG (15) to 0
1977-78	**Oxford**	4PG 1T (16) to 2PG 1T (10)
1978-79	**Cambridge**	2G 3PG 1T (25) to 1PG 1T (7)
1979-80	**Oxford**	2PG 1DG (9) to 1PG (3)
1980-81	**Cambridge**	3PG 1T (13) to 3PG (9)
1981-82	**Cambridge**	3PG (9) to 2PG (6)
1982-83	**Cambridge**	3PG 1DG 2T (20) to 1G 1PG 1T (13)
1983-84	**Cambridge**	4PG 2T (20) to 3PG (9)
1984-85	**Cambridge**	4G 2T (32) to 2PG (6)
1985-86	**Oxford**	1PG 1T (7) to 2PG (6)
1986-87	**Oxford**	3PG 2DG (15) to 1PG 1DG 1T (10)
1987-88	**Cambridge**	1DG 3T (15) to 2PG 1T (10)
1988-89	**Oxford**	2G 1DG 3T (27) to 1DG 1T (7)
1989-90	**Cambridge**	2G 2PG 1T (22) to 1G 1PG 1T (13)
1990-91	**Oxford**	2G 2PG 1DG (21) to 1G 2PG (12)
1991-92	**Cambridge**	2PG 1DG 2T (17) to 1DG 2T (11)
1992-93	**Cambridge**	1G 2PG 2DG (19) to 1PG 1DG 1T (11)
1993-94	**Oxford**	3PG 2DG 1T (20) to 1DG 1T (8)

THE WAR-TIME MATCHES

Year	Winner	Score		Winner	Score
1939-40	**Oxford**	1G 1DG 2T (15) to 1T (3) (at Cambridge)		**Cambridge**	2G 1T (13) to 0 (at Cambridge)
	Cambridge	1G 3T (14) to 2G 1T (13) (at Oxford)	1941-42	**Cambridge**	1PG 2T (9) to 1PG 1T (6) (at Cambridge)
1940-41	**Cambridge**	1G 2T (11) to 1G 1DG (9) (at Oxford)		**Cambridge**	1G 2PG 2T (17) to 1G 1T (8) (at Oxford)

1942-43	**Cambridge**	1G 1DG (9) to 0 (at Oxford)		**Oxford**	2T (6) to 1G (5)
	Cambridge	2G 2T (16) to			(at Oxford)
		1T (3) (at Cambridge)	1944-45	Drawn	1T (3) each (at Oxford)
1943-44	**Cambridge**	2G 1T (13) to		**Cambridge**	2G 2T (16) to
		1DG (4) (at Cambridge)			1DG (4) (at Cambridge)

OXFORD and CAMBRIDGE BLUES 1872-1993

(Each year indicates a separate appearance, and refers to the first half of the season. Thus 1879 refers to the match played in the 1879-80 season.) (R) indicates an appearance as a replacement; (t) denotes an appearance as a temporary replacement.

OXFORD

Abbott, J S	1954-55	Boobbyer, B	1949-50-51	Carey, W J	1894-95-96-97
Abell, G E B	1923-24-25-26	Booker, J L	1880	Carlyon, H B	1871
Adamson, J A	1928-29-31	Booth, J L	1956	Carroll, B M	1970-71
Adcock, J R L	1961	Bos, F H ten	1958-59-60	Carroll, P R	1968-69-70
Aitken, A D	1993	Boswell, J D	1885-86-87	Carter, C R	1885
Aitken, G G	1922-24	Botfield, A S G	1871	Cartwright, V H	1901-02-03-04
Aldridge, J E	1888	Botting, I J	1949-50	Cass, T	1961
Alexander, H	1897-98	Bourdillon, H	1873-74-75	Castens, H H	1886-87
Alexander, P C	1930	Bourns, C	1903	Cattell, R H B	1893
Allaway, R C P	1953-54-55	Bowers, J B	1932-34	Cave, H W	1881
Allen, C P	1881-82-83	Boyce, A W	1952-53	Cawkwell, G L	1946-47
Allen, T	1909	Boyd, A de H	1924	Chadwick, A J	1898-99
Allen, W C	1910	Boyd, E F	1912	Chambers, J C	1921
Allison, M G	1955	Boyle, D S	1967-68-69	Champain, F H B	1897-98-99
Almond, R G P	1937	Boyle, L S	1993	Champneys, F W	1874-75-76
Ashby, C J	1973	Brace, D O	1955-56	Charles, A E S	1932
Asher, A G G	1881-82-83-84	Bradby, G F	1882-85	Cheesman, W I	1910-11
Asquith, P R	1974	Bradford, C C	1887	Cheyne, H	1903-04
Atkinson, C C	1876	Branfoot, E P	1878-79	Chislett, J	1986-87
		Bray, C N	1979	Cholmondeley, F G	1871-73
Back, A	1878	Bray, K A	1989	Christopherson, P	1886-87-88
Badenoch, D F	1971	Bremridge, H	1876-77	Clark, C J	1993
Baden-Powell, F S	1873	Brett, J A	1935-36-37	Clark, R B	1978-79
Baggaley, J C	1953-54	Brett, P V	1978	Clarke, E J D	1973
Bain, D McL	1910-11-12-13	Brewer, R J	1965	Clarke, I A	1913
Bainbrigge, J H	1874-76-77	Brewer, T J	1951	Clauss, P R	1889-90-91
Baird, J S	1966-67	Bridge, D J W	1946-47-48	Clements, B S	1975
Baiss, R S H	1894-95	Brierley, H	1871	Cleveland, C R	1885-86
Baker, C D	1891-93	Britton, R B	1963-64	Cochran, P C	1889-91
Baker, D G S	1951-52	Bromet, W E	1889	Cohen, B A	1884
Baker, E M	1893-94-95-96	Brooks, A W	1980-81-82	Coker, J B H	1965
Baker, P	1980(R)	Brooks, M J	1873	Coker, T	1988-89
Baker, R T	1968	Brooks, W	1872	Cole, B W	1945
Balfour, E R	1893-94-95	Broster, L R	1912	Coleman, D J	1982-83
Bannerman, J MacD	1927-28	Broughton, R C	1965	Coles, D G G	1937-38
Barclay, S L	1990-91	Brown, L G	1910-11-12	Coles, P	1884-85-86
Barker, A C	1966-67	Brown, M E O	1988	Coles, S C	1954-56-57
Barnes, S	1981-82-83	Brunskill, R F	1873-74	Collingwood, J A	1961-62
Barr, D C A	1980	Bryan, T A	1975-76-77	Colville, A H	1892-93
Barry, C E	1897-98-99	Bryer, L W	1953	Conway-Rees, J	1891-92-93
Barry, D M	1968-69-70	Buchanan, F G	1909-10	Cook, D J	1988(R)-89
Barwick, W M	1880-81	Buckett, I M	1992	Cooke, J L	1968-69
Bass, R G	1961	Bucknall, A L	1965-66	Cooke, P	1936-37
Batchelor, T B	1906	Budge, K J	1977-78-79	Cooke, W R	1976
Bateson, H D	1874-75-77	Budworth, R T D	1887-88-89	Cookson, G H F	1891-92
Baxter, T J	1958-59	Bullard, G L	1950-51	Cooper, A H	1951
Beamish, S H	1971	Bullock, H	1910-11	Cooper, M McG	1934-35-36
Beare, A	1982	Bulpett, C W L	1871	Cooper, R A	1937
Bedford, T P	1965-66-67	Burnet, P J	1960	Cooper, R M	1946
Behn, A R	1968-69	Burrow, K C	1933	Cornish, W H	1876
Bell, D L	1970	Burse, R M	1974	Couper, T	1899-1900
Benson, E T	1928	Bush, A	1934	Court, E D	1882-83
Bentley, P J	1960	Bussell, J G	1903-04	Cousins, F C	1885-86
Berkeley, W V	1924-25-26	Butcher, W M	1954	Coutts, I D F	1913
Berry, C W	1883-84	Butler, F E R	1959-60	Coventry, R G T	1889-90-91
Bettington, R H B	1920-22	Button, E L	1936	Cowen, T J	1938
Bevan, J H	1946	Byers, R M	1926	Cowlishaw, F I	1890-91
Bibby, A J	1980-81			Cox, G V	1878
Binham, P A	1971	Caccia, H A	1926	Cozens-Hardy, B	1904-05-06
Birrell, H B	1953	Cadell, P R	1890	Crabbie, J E	1898-99-1900-01
Black, B H	1929	Cairns, A G	1899-1900-01	Craig, F J R	1963-64-65
Blair, A S	1884	Calcraft, W J	1986-87	Crane, C M	1985-86-87
Blencowe, L C	1907-08	Cameron, A J	1988	Cranmer, P	1933-34
Bloxham, C T	1934-35-36-37	Campbell, E	1919-20-21	Crawfurd, J W F A	1900
Blyth, P H	1885-86	Campbell, W	1987	Creese, N A H	1951
Bolton, W H	1873-74-75	Cannell, L B	1948-49-50	Cridlan, A G	1928-29-30
Bonham-Carter, C R	1990	Cardale, C F	1929-30	Croker, J R	1966-67
Bonham-Carter, E	1890-91	Carey, G M	1891-92-94	Crole, G B	1913-19

196

Name	Years
Jenkins, V G J	1930-31-32
Jesson, D	1957-58-59
Johnson, A M	1985-86-87
Johnson, P M	1968-70
Johnson, T F	1875
Johnstone, P G	1952-53-54
Jones, A M	1989
Jones, D K	1963
Jones, D R R	1972
Jones, G S A	1896
Jones, I C	1962-63-64
Jones, K W J	1931-32
Jones, L E	1991
Jones, R M	1991
Jones, R O P	1969-70-71
Jones, T O	1898
Jones, T W	1978-79
Jones, V W	1954
Joy, M T	1992-93
Joyce, A L	1984
Jupp, H B	1873
Kay, A R	1889-90-91
Kay, D C	1972-73
Kelly, H M	1932
Kendall-Carpenter, J MacG K	1948-49-50
Kennedy, A P	1985
Kennedy, N	1901
Kennedy, W D	1904
Kent, C P	1972-73-74-75
Kent, P C	1970
Kershaw, F	1898-99-1900-01
Key, K J	1885-86
Kindersley, R S	1882-83
King, B B H	1963
King, P E	1975
King, T W	1929
Kininmonth, P W	1947-48
Kirk, D E	1987-88
Kitson, J A	1895
Kittermaster, H J	1922-24
Kitto, R C M	1884-85-86-87
Knight, R L	1879
Knott, F H	1910-11-12-13
Koe, A P	1886
Kyrke, G V	1902-03
Kyrke-Smith, P St L	1973-74-75(R)
Lagden, R O	1909-10-11
Laidlaw, C R	1968-69
Lamb, R H	1962-63-64
Lamport, N K	1930-31-32
Landale, D F	1925-26
Lane, R O B	1887-88-89
Langley, P J	1949
Latham, H E	1907
Latter, A	1892
Law, A F	1875
Lawrence, W S	1954-56
Lawrie, A A	1903-05
Lawton, T	1921-22-23
Lee, F H	1874-75-76-77
Lee, J W	1973-74
Lee, R J	1972
Legge, D	1897
Lennox-Cook, J M	1945
Leslie, C F H	1880-81
Leslie, R E	1954
Leslie-Jones, F A	1894-95-96
Lewin, A J A	1962-63
Lewis, A K	1888
Lewis, D J	1950
Lewis, S M	1973
Light, B	1977
Lindsay, G C	1882-83-84-85
Lion-Cachet, C C	1992-93
Littlechild, E J F	1972
Littlewood, R B	1893
Lloyd, E A	1964-65-66
Lloyd, J E	1872-74
Lloyd, R	1908
Lombard, L T	1956-57-58
Longdon, J S	1889
Lorraine, H D B	1932-33-34
Loudoun-Shand, E G	1913-19
Love, R D	1972
Low, R C S	1933
Luce, F M	1899-1900
Luddington, R S	1980-81-82
Lumsden, A E	1992
Lusty, W	1927
Luyt, R E	1938
Lyle, A M P	1902-04-05
McBain, N S	1986-87
McCanlis, M A	1926-27
McClure, R N	1973
Macdonald, C P	1985-86
Macdonald, D A	1975-76
Macdonald, D S M	1974-75-76
Macdonald, G E	1922
Macdonald, N L	1926
Macdonald, N W	1984-85
MacEwen, G L	1895
McFarland, P R E	1967
MacGibbon, R R	1930-31
McGlashan, J R C	1945
McGrath, N F	1934-35-36
MacGregor, A	1871
Mackenzie, A O M	1880-81
Mackenzie, D W	1974
Mackenzie, F J C	1882-83
Mackintosh, C E W C	1925
MacLachlan, L P	1953
Maclachlan, N	1879-80
Macmillan, M	1876
McNeill, A	1884
MacNeill, H P	1982-83-84
McPartlin, J J	1960-61-62
Macpherson, G P S	1922-23-24
Macpherson, N M S	1928
McQuaid, A S J	1983
McShane, J M S	1933-35
Maddock, W P	1972
Mallalieu, J P W	1927
Mallett, N V H	1979
Malone, N G	1992
Marshall, H P	1921
Marshall, R M	1936-37-38
Martin, H	1907-08-09
Martin, N F C	1993
Marvin, T G R	1884-85
Mather, E G S	1933
Maxwell-Hyslop, J E	1920-21-22
Mayhew, P K	1937
Mead, B D	1972-73
Meadows, H J	1948
Merivale, G M	1874
Merriam, L P B	1913
Michell, A T	1871-72-73-74
Millerchip, C J	1981-82
Mills, D J	1983-84
Milton, N W	1905-06-07
Milward, A W	1991
Minns, P C	1930-31-32
Mitchell, M D	1977
Moberly, W O	1871-72-73
Moir, M J P	1977
Molohan, M J B	1928
Moloney, R J	1990
Monteath, J G	1912
Montgomery, J R	1958
Moorcroft, E K	1966
Moore, A P	1990
Moore, E J	1882-83
Moore, H B	1912-13
Moore, H R	1956
Moore, P B C	1945-46
Moresby-White, J M	1913-19
Morgan, A K	1963-64
Morgan, D J	1979
Morgan, F	1888
Morgan, R de R	1983
Morris, E G	1904
Morrison, W E A	1979-80
Mortimer, L	1892
Moubray, J J	1876-77-78
Muller, H	1938
Mullin, B J	1986-87
Mullins, R C	1894
Mulvey, R S	1968
Munro, P	1903-04-05
Murray, G C	1959
Nash, E H	1874-75
Nasser, B P	1992
Nelson, T A	1897-98
Nesbitt, J V	1904-05
Neser, V H	1919-20
Neville, T B	1971-72
Newman, A P	1973
Newman, S C	1946-47
Newton, H F	1895-96-97
Newton, P A	1879-80
Newton-Thompson, J O	1945-46
Nicholas, P L	1897-98-99
Nicholson, E S	1931-32-33-34
North, E G H	1888-89-90
Norwitz, E R	1988-89-90
Novis, A L	1927
Nunn, J A	1925-26
Obolensky, A	1935-37
O'Brien, T S	1983-84
O'Connor, A	1958
O'Mahony, B G	1992
O'Mahony, D P	1992
Odgers, W B	1901-02
Orpen, L J J	1898
Osborn, E C	1969
Osborne, S H	1900-01-02
Osler, S G	1931
Owen-Smith, H G O	1932-33
Page, H V	1884-85
Painter, P A	1967
Palmer, M S	1960
Parker, L	1905
Parker, T	1888
Parkin, W H	1890
Pask, R A	1991
Paterson, A M	1889-90
Paterson, L R	1886-87
Patterson, A R	1879-80-81
Patton, M B	1991-92
Payne, C M	1960
Peacock, M B	1880
Peacock, M F	1932-33
Peacock, N C	1987
Peake, H W	1871
Pearce, J K	1945
Pearson, S B	1983-84-85
Pearson, T S	1871
Peat, W H	1898
Peck, A Q	1981
Pennington, H H	1937-38
Percival, L J	1889-91
Percy, H R G	1936-38
Pether, S	1938
Phillips, C	1876-77-78-79
Phillips, E L	1933
Phillips, L R L	1984
Phillips, M S	1956-57-58-59
Phillips, P C	1938
Phillips, R H	1966-67-68
Pienaar, J H	1933-34-35
Pitman, I J	1921
Plant, W I	1958
Pleydell-Bouverie, Hon B	1923
Plumbridge, R A	1954-55-56
Podmore, G	1872
Pollard, D	1952
Poole, F O	1891-92-93-94
Poulton, R W	1909-10-11
Prescott, A E C	1928
Prescott, R E	1932
Preston, B W	1925
Price, H L	1920-21
Price, V R	1919-20-21
Pritchard, N S M	1985(R)

Prodger, J A	1955	Sharp, R G	1919	Thomson, F W	1912-13
		Shaw, C	1974-75	Thomson, J B	1983
Quinnen, P N	1974-75	Shearman, M	1878-79	Thomson, W J	1895-96
Quist-Arcton, E A K	1978-79	Sheffield, R W	1873-74	Thorburn, C W	1964
		Sheil, A G R	1958	Thorniley-Walker, M J	1967
Rahmatallah, F J	1976	Shillito, G V	1930	Thresher, P R	1991
Ramsay, A W	1952-53	Sidgwick, A	1872	Tongue, P K	1975
Ramsden, J E	1945	Siepmann, C A	1921	Torry, P J	1968-69
Raphael, J E	1901-02-03-04	Silk, N	1961-62-63	Travers, B H	1946-47
Rashleigh, W	1887-88	Sim, A C	1876	Tristram, H B	1882-83-84
Ravenscroft, J	1877-78	Simmie, M S	1965-66	Troup, D S	1928
Raymond, R L	1924	Simonet, P M	1984	Tudor, H A	1878-79-80-81
Rayner, E J	1993	Simpson, E P	1887	Turcan, H H	1928
Rayner-Wood, A C	1895-96	Simpson, H B	1920	Turner, A B	1884
Read, R F	1965	Skipper, D J	1952	Turner, F H	1908-09-10
Reed, D K	1984	Slater, N T	1960		
Reeler, I L	1955-56	Sloan, T	1908	Ubogu, V E	1987
Rees, G L	1993	Sloane, A D	1902	Unwin, G T	1894-95-96
Rees, H	1930	Small, H D	1949-50		
Rees, H J V	1913	Smith, A R	1894-95-96-97	Valentine, A C	1923-24-25
Rees, P S	1974-75-78	Smith, B A	1988-89	Van Der Merwe, W M	1989
Rees-Jones, G R	1933-34-35	Smith, I S	1923	Van Der Riet, E F	1920-21
Reid, C J	1896	Smith, J A	1892-93	Van Ryneveld, A J	1946-47-48
Reid, G A	1935-36	Smith, M J K	1954-55	Van Ryneveld, C B	1947-48-49
Reid, N	1912-13	Southee, E A	1913	Vassall, H	1879-80-81-82
Renwick, W N	1936-37	Speed, R R	1967-68-69	Vassall, H H	1906-07-08
Rice-Evans, W	1890	Spence, D O	1992	Vecqueray, A H	1877-78
Richards, C A L	1932	Spence, K M	1951-52	Vecqueray, G C	1873
Richards, S B	1962	Spencer, B L	1960	Vessey, S J R	1984-85-86-87-88
Richardson, J V	1925	Spragg, F F	1926	Vidal, R W S	1872
Richardson, W R	1881	Springman, P	1877-78	Vincent, A N	1848-49
Rigby, J P	1955-56	Squire, W H S	1882-83-84		
Rimmer, L I	1958	Stafford, P M W	1961-62	Wade, C G	1882-83-84
Risman, J M	1984-85-86	Stagg, P K	1961-62	Waide, S L	1932
Rittson-Thomas, G C	1949-50	Starmer-Smith, N C	1965-66	Wake, H B L	1922
Robbins, P G D	1954-55-56-57	Steel, J J	1953	Wakefield, W H	1891-92
Roberts, D G	1990	Steinthal, F E	1906	Wakelin, W S	1964
Roberts, G D	1907-08	Stevens, D T	1959	Waldock, F A	1919
Roberts, M G	1968	Stewart, A	1947-48	Waldock, H F	1919-20
Roberts, N T	1979-80-81	Stewart, W B	1892	Waldron, O C	1965-67
Roberts, S N J	1985-86	Steyn, S S L	1911-12	Walford, M M	1935-36-37
Roberts, W	1928-29-30-31	Stileman, W M C	1988-90	Walker, A	1880
Robertson, A M	1903	Still, E R	1871-73	Walker, J C	1955
Robertson, J W	1921	Stobie, A M	1945	Walker, J G	1879-80-81
Robertson, M A	1894-96	Stobie, W D K	1947	Walker, M	1950-51
Robinson, D A B	1952-53	Stone, T	1897	Wall, T W	1875-76-77
Robinson, R G	1976-77	Stoneman, B M	1962	Wallace, A C	1922-23-24-25
Robson, M	1929	Stoop, A D	1902-03-04	Walton, E J	1900-01
Rogers, W L Y	1898-1900	Strand-Jones, J	1899-1900-01	Ward, J M	1972
Rolfe, A J	1987	Stratton, J W	1897	Ware, M A	1961-62
Roos, G D	1936	Street, K P	1991-92	Warr, A L	1933-34
Rosier, J R H	1983	Strong, E L	1881-83	Waterman, J S	1974
Ross, W S	1980	Strong, W I N	1924-25	Wates, C S	1961
Rotherham, A	1882-83-84	Stuart-Watson, J L	1935	Watkins, L	1879
Roughead, W N	1924-25-26	Summerskill, W H J	1945	Watkinson, A F	1977-78
Rousseau, W P	1929	Surtees, E A	1885	Watson, P W	1954-55
Row, A W L	1921	Sutherland, I W	1938	Watson, T C S	1993
Rowley, J V D'A	1929	Sutherland, J G B	1885	Watt, K A	1976
Rucker, R W	1874-76	Sutton, M A	1945-46	Watts, I H	1937-38
Rudd, E L	1963-64	Swan, M W	1957	Watts, L D	1957-58
Russell, H	1872-73-74-75	Swanston, J F A	1897-98-99-1900	Webster, J G M	1980-81
Russell, J H	1929	Swanzy, A J	1901-02	Webster, J P	1982-83
Russell-Roberts, F D	1931	Swarbrick, D W	1946-47-48	Welsh, A R	1984
Rydon, R A	1985-86	Swayne, D H	1930-31	Wensley, S C	1988
		Sweatman, E A	1927	Wesche, V V G	1924
Sachs, D M	1962			Weston, B A G	1957
Sampson, D H	1945	Taberer, H M	1892	Weston, J W	1871
Sampson, H F	1910-11	Tahany, M P	1945	White, G L	1976-77
Sanctuary, C F S	1879-80	Tanner, T L	1931	White, N T	1905-06
Sandford, J R P	1902-03	Tapper, A D	1991	Whiteside, S D	1991
Saunders, C J	1951	Tarr, F N	1907-08-09	Whyte, A G D	1963
Sawtell, P R	1972	Tatham, W M	1881-82-83	Whyte, D J	1963
Sayer, J	1871	Taylor, E G	1926-27-28	Wilcock, R M	1962
Sayer, J B	1887	Taylor, G C	1990	Wilcock, S H	1957-58-59
Scholefield, B G	1920-21	Taylor, J A	1974	Wilkinson, J V S	1904
Scott, J S M	1957-58	Taylor, S C	1989	Wilkinson, W E	1891
Searle, J P	1981-82	Terry, H F	1900-01	Willcox, J G	1959-60-61-62
Seccombe, L S	1925	Theron, T P	1923	Williams, A D	1988-92
Selby, E	1891	Thomas, A C	1979	Williams, C D	1945
Sexton, C M	1976	Thomas, T R	1938	Williams, I M	1988
Seymour, T M	1971-73	Thomas, W E	1911-12	Williams, J R	1969
Shacksnovis, A	1922-23	Thomas, W L	1893-94	Williams, S R	1988(R)
Sharp, H S	1910-11	Thomson, B E	1951-52	Williamson, A C	1913
Sharp, R A W	1959-60-61	Thomson, C	1896	Williamson, R H	1906-07-08

Willis, D C	1975-76-77	Wilson, W G	1887	Woodrow, D K	1978-79-80
Willis, T G	1985-86-88	Wimperis, E J	1951	Wooldridge, C S	1882
Wilson, C T M	1948	Winn, C E	1950	Wordsworth, C R	1922-23-24
Wilson, D B	1874	Winn, R R	1953	Wordsworth, C W	1902
Wilson, G A	1946-48	Wintle, R V	1993	Wordsworth, J R	1885
Wilson, J	1967-68	Witney, N K J	1970-71	Wray, M O	1933-34
Wilson, J H G	1888-89-90	Wix, R S	1904-05-06-07	Wyatt, D M	1981
Wilson, N G C	1967	Wood, A E	1904	Wydell, H A	1951
Wilson, R W	1956	Wood, D E	1952-53	Wynter, E C C	1947
Wilson, S	1963-64	Wood, G F	1919		
Wilson, S E	1890	Woodhead, P G	1974	Young, J R C	1957-58

CAMBRIDGE

Aarvold, C D	1925-26-27-28	Bennett, G M	1897-98	Cake, J J	1988
Ackford, P J	1979	Bennett, N J	1981	Callow, P G	1992-93
Adams, G C A	1929	Benthall, E C	1912	Campbell, D A	1936
Adams, H F S	1884-85	Beringer, F R	1951-52	Campbell, H H	1946
Agnew, C M	1875-76	Beringer, G G	1975-76	Campbell, J A	1897-98-99
Agnew, G W	1871-72-73	Berman, J V	1966	Campbell, J D	1927
Agnew, W L	1876-77-78	Berry, S P	1971	Campbell, J W	1973-74
Albright, G S	1877	Bevan, G A J	1951	Campbell, R C C	1907
Alderson, F H R	1887-88	Bevan, J A	1877-80	Candler, P L	1934
Alexander, E P	1884-85-86	Bevan, W	1887	Cangley, B T G	1946
Alexander, J W	1905-06	Bickle, D J	1992	Carey, G V	1907-08
Allan, C J	1962	Biddell, C W	1980-81	Carpmael, W P	1885
Allan, J L F	1956	Biggar, M A	1971	Carris, H E	1929
Allchurch, T J	1980-81	Bird, D R J	1958-59	Carter, C P	1965
Allen, A D	1925-26-27	Birdwood, C R B	1932	Cave, J W	1887-88
Allen, D B	1975	Bishop, C C	1925	Cave, W T C	1902-03-04
Allen, J	1875-76	Black, M A	1897-98	Chadwick, W O	1936-37-38
Anderson, W T	1931-32	Blair, P C B	1910-11-12-13	Chalmers, P S	1979
Andrew, C R	1982-83-84	Blake, W H	1875	Chambers, E L	1904
Anthony, A J	1967	Boggon, R P	1956	Chapman, C E	1881-84
Archer, G M D	1950-51	Bole, E	1945-46-47	Chapman, E S	1879-80
Arentsen, A N	1993	Bonham-Carter, J	1873	Chapman, G M	1907-08-09
Arthur, T G	1962	Booth, A H	1989-90	Chapman, J M	1873
Ashcroft, A H	1908-09	Bordass, J H	1923-24	Chapple, M A	1991
Ashford, C L	1929	Borthwick, T J L	1985	Chilcott, E W	1883
Ashworth, J	1988-89	Boughton-Leigh, C E W	1878	Child, H H	1875-76
Askew, J G	1929-30-31	Boulding, P V	1975-76	Clarke, B D F	1978
Asquith, J P K	1953	Bowcott, H M	1927-28	Clarke, S J S	1962-63
Aston, R L	1889-90	Bowcott, J E	1933	Clayton, H R	1876-77-78
Atkinson, M L	1908-09	Bowen, R W	1968	Clayton, J R W	1971
Attfield, S J W	1982-84	Bowhill, J W	1888-89	Clements, J W	1953-54-55
		Bowman, J H	1933-34	Clifford, P H	1876-77-78
Back, F F	1871-72	Boyd, A	1993	Clough, F J	1984-85-86-87
Bailey, G H	1931	Boyd, C W	1909	Coates, C H	1877-78-79
Bailey, M D	1982-83-84-85	Boyd-Moss, R J	1980-81-82	Coates, V H M	1907
Bailey, R C	1982-83	Bramley, R A	1993	Cobby, W	1900
Balding, I A	1961	Brandram, R A	1896	Cock, T A	1899
Balfour, A	1896-97	Brash, J C	1959-60-61	Cocks, F W	1935
Bance, J F	1945	Brathwaite, G A	1934	Coghlan, G B	1926-27-28
Bannerman, C M	1990	Breakey, J N F	1974-75(R)-77	Cohen, A S	1922
Barker, R E	1966	Bree-Frink, F C	1888-89-90	Colbourne, G L	1883
Barlow, C S	1923-24-25-26	Briggs, P D	1962	Coley, M	1964
Barlow, R M M	1925	Bromet, E	1887-88	Collett, G F	1898
Barrow, C	1950	Brook, P W P	1928-29-30-31	Collier, R B	1960-61
Barter, A F	1954-55-56	Brookstein, R	1969	Collin, T	1871
Bartlett, R M	1951	Brooman, R J	1977-78	Collins, W O H	1931
Bateman-Champain, P J C	1937	Browell, H H	1877-78	Collis, W R F	1919-20
Bates, C S	1991	Brown, A C	1920-21	Collison, L H	1930
Batstone, G R D	1992	Brown, S L	1975-76	Combe, P H	1984-85
Batten, J M	1871-72-73-74	Browning, O C	1934	Considine, W C D	1919
Batty, P A	1919-20	Bruce Lockhart, J H	1910	Conway, G S	1919-20-21
Baxter, R	1871-72-73	Bruce Lockhart, L	1945-46	Cook, D D B	1920-21
Baxter, W H B	1912-13	Bruce Lockhart, R B	1937-38	Cook, S	1920-21
Bealey, R J	1874	Brutton, E B	1883-85-86	Cooke, S J	1981
Beard, P L	1987	Bryant, S S	1988	Cooper, H S	1881
Bearne, K R F	1957-58-59	Bryce, R D H	1965	Cooper, P T	1927-28
Beazley, T A G	1971	Bull, H A	1874-75	Cope, W	1891
Bedell-Sivright, D R	1899-1900-01-02	Bunting, W L	1894-95	Corry, T M	1966
Bedell-Sivright, J V	1900-01-02-03	Burns, S A	1992	Cosh, N J	1966
Beer, I D S	1952-53-54	Burt-Marshall, J	1905	Covell, G A B	1949
Bell, D S	1989	Burton, B C	1882-83	Cove-Smith, R	1919-20-21
Bell, R W	1897-98-99	Bush, J D	1983	Cox, F L	1879
Bell, S P	1894-95-96	Bussey, W M	1960-61-62	Craig, H J	1891
		Butler, E T	1976-77-78	Craigmile, H W C	1920
		Buzza, A J	1988-89	Crichton-Miller, D	1928

Williamson, P R	1984	Woodroffe, O P	1952	Yetts, R M	1879-80-81
Willis, H	1949-50-51	Woods, S M J	1888-89-90	Young, A B S	1919-20
Wilson, A H	1911-12-13	Wooller, W	1933-34-35	Young, A T	1922-23-24
Wilson, C P	1877-78-79-80	Wordley, S A	1988-89	Young, J S	1935
Wilton, C W	1936	Wordsworth, A J	1973-75	Young, J V	1906
Winthrop, W Y	1871	Wotherspoon, W	1888-89	Young, P D	1949
Wintle, T C	1960-61	Wrench, D F B	1960	Young, S K	1974
Withyman, T A	1985-86	Wright, C C G	1907-08	Young, W B	1935-36-37
Wood, G E	1974-75-76	Wrigley, P T	1877-78-79-80		
Wood, G E C	1919	Wyles, K T	1985-86		
Woodall, B J C	1951	Wynne, E H	1887		

VARSITY MATCH REFEREES

(From 1881, when referees first officiated at the match. Prior to this date, the match was controlled by a pair of umpires elected by the Universities.) Each year indicates a separate appearance, and refers to the first half of the season. Thus 1881 refers to the match played in the 1881-82 season.

Allan, M A	1933-34	Fleming, J M	1991	Morrison, E F	1992
Ashmore, H L	1891-92-93-95-96	Freethy, A E	1923-25-27-29-31-32	Murdoch, W C W	1952
Bean, A S	1948-49	Gadney, C H	1935-36-37-38-45-47	Norling, C	1977-78-81-88-89
Bevan, W D	1993	Gillespie, J I	1905	Pattinson, K A	1974
Bolton, W N	1882	Harnett, G H		Potter-Irwin, F C	1909-11-13-19
Boundy, L M	1958		1897-98-99-1900-01-02	Prideaux, L	1984
Burnett, D I H	1980-82	Hill, G R	1883-84-86-87-88-89-90	Quittenton, R C	1985-87
Burrell, R P	1963	Hosie, A M	1979	Sanson, N R	1976
Clark, K H	1973	Howard, F A	1986	Sturrock, J C	1921
Cooper, Dr P F	1951-53	Jeffares, R W	1930	Taylor, H H	1881
Crawford, S H	1920	John, K S	1956-67	Titcombe, M H	1969
Currey, F I	1885	Johnson, R F	1972	Trigg, J A F	1983
Dallas, J D	1910-12	Jones, T	1950	Vile, T H	1922-24-26-28
D'Arcy, D P	1968	Lamb, Air Cdre G C	1970	Walters, D G	
David, I	1954-55	Lambert, N H	1946		1957-60-61-62-64-65-66
Doyle, O E	1990	Lawrence, Capt H D	1894	Welsby, A	1975
Evans, G	1907	Lewis, R	1971	Williams, R C	1959
Findlay, J C	1904-08	Marsh, F W	1906	Williams, T	1903

A ROUGH DEAL FOR STUDENTS

RUGBY IN THE STUDENT SECTOR 1993-94
Harry Townsend

It is a sobering thought that, by the turn of the century, a third of all youngsters aged between 18 and 21 will be university students. They are the club players, referees and administrators of the future, and they need a better deal than they get at present. I'm sure that the government, when it 'universitised' almost 100 polytechnics and colleges, did not foresee the effect this would have on student sport.

Two years ago, students in England had six tiers of international representative rugby available: England Students, English Universities, English Colleges, British Polytechnics (BPSA) and even Combined Students and UAU. Roughly the same went for Wales, Scotland and Ireland. 'Universitisation' meant that within a year UAU rugby expanded from 41 to 135 participants and BPSA and British Colleges rugby went out of business.

Now, students can play for only England Students and English Universities, so international student rugby is available to only about 45 players each season. Although more divisional matches are planned, this is not the same as a national shirt. An expanded UAU also means extra pressure. Whereas two years ago a UAU final meant nine (or, in the north-west, 11) matches, a BPSA final eight and Colleges six, the UAU can now mean 13: one almost every week of term. Many students are linked to top clubs, some by bursaries, and so some are pressurised to withdraw from midweek UAU matches when a League fixture follows that weekend.

Another way to representative honours is through under-21 rugby. This season, five students also played for England Emerging Players, Darren O'Leary for England A and Kyran Bracken for England. All demand extra training and travel. The Divisional Under-21 Championship, the route to the England team, takes place on Sundays following the last three Five Nations rounds in which England are involved – weekends when club matches are low-key. Yet still clubs persuade ambitious youngsters (many of them students) to play on these Saturdays and then perform, heavy-legged, a day later to chase international ambitions.

While student, university and under-21 honours are attainable only by a tiny minority, that's where subsidies are principally allotted. Yet student rugby generally is for the average player, the club stalwart of the future, and that's where support is needed most.

Peter Drewett was appointed for two years as part-time technical administrator (higher education) and this has now been upgraded to a full-time post for a further two years. He works wonderfully hard, but it's not enough. RFU money, or external sponsorship, is needed to subsidise coaching and administration, provide grants, and fund realistic competition (a student league) for these players. The embryo Student League, their rugby education, foundered for this very lack of cash.

Representative matches: England Students 23, Ireland Students 17 (Bournemouth); England Students 22, Wales Students 29 (Oxford); France Students 36, England Students 17 (Dunkirk); Wales Students 18, France Students 6 (Cardiff); England Students Under-21s 37, Irish Exiles Under-21s 13; Combined Services Under-21s 16, England Students Under-21s 16 (Twickenham); Scottish Universities 3, English Universities 31 (Peffermill); English Universities 19, Welsh Universities 9 (Richmond); Welsh Universities 64, Scottish Universities 16 (Cardiff University); Irish Universities 39, Welsh Universities 0 (Old Belvedere); South of Scotland Under-21s 60, Scottish Universities 13 (Kelso); North & Midlands Under-21s 38, Scottish Universities 16 (Cupar); English Colleges 13, Irish Colleges 21 (Trojans).

COMMERCIAL UNION UAU CHAMPIONSHIP 1993-94

23 March, Twickenham
Northumbria University 13 (1G 2PG)
West London Institute 9 (3PG)

The 75th anniversary of the UAU broke new ground with the appearance at Twickenham not merely of two teams new to the final, but of two teams virtually new to the entire competition: Northumbria University in their debut year and West London Institute in their second.

West London had cruised almost effortlessly to the quarter-final, winning their five group matches 384-9 and play-off rounds against Cranfield (Shrivenham) 44-10, Westminster (walkover) and Hospitals Cup finalists Charing Cross/Westminster 41-9. Bath provided the first real test, West London scraping home 28-16 with extra-time tries by Andy Duggan and scrum-half Chris Mahon. Local rivals Roehampton Institute provided a highly motivated semi-final challenge, and although a late try by England A wing Darren O'Leary settled the issue 24-19, Roehampton showed that away victories over 1993 finalists Bristol and 1991 finalists Swansea had been no flukes.

Northumbria had lost a year earlier to Sheffield Hallam University 14-13 in the final of the BSSA Cup, and the previous year the same teams had met (as Newcastle Polytechnic and Sheffield Polytechnic) with the same result in the final of the former BPSA (British Polytechnics) Cup. Welsh Students prop Steve Bowen played in all three finals. Northumbria had made heavier weather of their group matches, crashing to Durham 29-5 with a depleted pack and beating Leeds Metropolitan by only 11-8. Then came a walkover against Chester and further play-off rounds against Liverpool (25-0) and Scottish qualifiers Edinburgh (11-9). Manchester were decisively beaten 40-5 in the quarter-final before sweet revenge was taken against Durham by 34-9.

Wet and windy Twickenham was the stage for these two new finalists, with the enthusiastic support of virtually the entire West

London campus matched by vocal coachloads from Northumbria. West London, despite the weather, spun the ball wide in their traditional free-running style in an attempt to stretch the heavyweight Northumbria pack and to get full-back O'Leary and wings Kemp and Francis on the end of scoring passes. Their early pressure paid off with a penalty goal by Saracens fly-half Andy Lee.

But tight marking and uncompromising tackling by the less adventurous Northumbria forced errors as wide-flung passes drifted and faltered. Scotland Under-21 full-back John Miller, one of eight Newcastle Gosforth players, snapped up an interception midway through the half to race 80 yards for a try which Joel Eley converted for Northumbria.

Dour defence by the north-east side, who were pinned on their line for much of the second half, countered the blockbusting runs of centre Glen Harrison and the bustling West London pack fired by England Students No 8 Richard Hill and scrum-half Mahon, but bungled penalties and hasty decisions gradually disrupted the pattern as frustration became evident. Commitment rather than artistry was the watchword, and the result hung in the balance until the final whistle. In the end Lee's two second-half penalties were matched by two from Eley to give Northumbria victory by 13-9.

Northumbria University: J Miller; D Bennett, M Tetlow, A Redpath, T Penn; J Eley, A Scott; R Fuller, D Hayes, S Bowen, J Fowler, S Owen, M Corry (*capt*), J Nicholson, J Ayton *Replacement* E Craig for Penn (78 mins)
Scorers *Try:* Miller   *Conversion:* Eley   *Penalty Goals:* Eley (2)
West London Institute: D O'Leary; M Kemp, S Burns, G Harrison, R Francis; C Mahon, A Lee; J Cooke, S Rodgers, O Pipe, D Ruffell, J Beddoe, C Clements, R Hill, A Dougan
Scorer *Penalty Goals:* Lee (3)
Referee E Sklar (UAR)

Loughborough have won the title 25 times, Durham 8, Liverpool and Swansea 7, Bristol 5, Cardiff and Manchester 4, Bangor and UWIST 2, Aberystwyth, Birmingham, Leeds, Newcastle and Northumbria once each.

Second XV final: Loughborough 18, West London Institute 9
Third XV final: Loughborough 30, Exeter 13

Although the 'universitisation' of the majority of Polytechnics and Colleges had taken place before last season began, only six of them (plus a number from Scotland) had taken part in the UAU Championship. Participants barely topped 50. But the writing was already on the wall for the likes of Loughborough and Durham, who had won all but three of the previous 20 titles, and although Loughborough won the Championship, five of the six English newcomers reached the quarter-finals. Most of the other eligible Institutes of Higher Education (IHEs) had taken part in the one and only year of the BSSA (effectively the British Polytechnics or BPSA) Cup.

This season the UAU coped manfully with 136 English and Welsh IHEs (of which 121 stayed the course) and nine Scottish, but the 'old guard' was effectively eased out as two teams virtually new to the competition reached Twickenham. Only Durham of the 'old guard' reached the semi-finals, beaten decisively 34-9 by Northumbria, while Roehampton Institute (also debutants) lost a hard-fought semi-final 'derby' to West London by 24-19. Loughborough, resisting the temptation of the 'one-off' selection of many top club players in residence, crashed 16-8 in the third-place play-off round to more new boys in Sheffield Hallam, who had won the previous two BSSA and BPSA finals against Northumbria. Swansea lost by a single point to Roehampton 18-17 in the quarter-finals and UAU rugby had been thrown wide open.

GROUP TABLES

The leading three from groups to which six, seven or eight participating teams are allocated (regardless of how many complete their programme), the leading two from groups allocated five teams and the leading one from groups allocated four teams qualify for the first play-off round. The top two from the Scottish Universities Championship go direct to the third play-off round.

'Tiers' indicate the number of teams an IHE can field in major sports each week, irrespective of playing strength, and do not affect the number of teams qualifying for the play-off rounds from any group.

GROUP 1: Midlands Tier 1 (North)

	P	W	D	L	F	A	Pts
Loughborough	5	5	0	0	195	26	10
Sheffield	5	3	1	1	110	33	7
Sheffield Hallam	5	2	1	2	81	26	5
Nottingham	5	2	0	3	111	79	4
Stafford (Stoke)	4	0	0	4	3	121	0
Nottingham Trent	4	0	0	4	10	225	0

GROUP 2: Midlands Tier 1 (South)

	P	W	D	L	F	A	Pts
Birmingham	5	5	0	0	134	35	10
Leicester	5	4	0	1	91	58	8
Oxford Brookes	5	2	0	3	78	67	4
Warwick	5	2	0	3	65	82	4
Coventry	5	2	0	3	80	119	4
De Montfort Leic	5	0	0	5	62	149	0

GROUP 3: Midlands Tier 2

	P	W	D	L	F	A	Pts
Cheltenham & Glos	6	6	0	0	243	31	12
Bedford	6	5	0	1	204	35	10
W'ton St Peters	6	4	0	2	150	117	8
Nene	6	3	0	3	85	78	6
Central England	6	1	0	5	99	110	2
Staffs (Stafford)	6	1	0	5	75	241	2
Aston	6	1	0	5	75	319	2

GROUP 4: Midlands Tier 3

	P	W	D	L	F	A	Pts
Harper Adams	3	3	0	0	120	24	6
Worcester	3	2	0	1	69	40	4
Derby	3	1	0	2	18	102	2
Newman	3	0	0	3	41	82	0

GROUP 5: South-West (West)

	P	W	D	L	F	A	Pts
Bristol	5	5	0	0	166	38	10
Exeter	5	4	0	1	220	48	8
St Mk & St John	5	2	0	3	76	96	4
Plymouth	5	2	0	3	51	108	4
W of England	5	2	0	3	51	179	4
Seale Hayne	5	0	0	5	46	141	0

GROUP 6: South-West (East)

	P	W	D	L	F	A	Pts
Bath	4	4	0	0	211	22	8
Portsmouth	4	3	0	1	77	65	6
Bournemouth	4	2	0	2	45	119	4
Southampton	4	1	0	3	75	89	2
Southampton Inst	4	0	0	4	24	137	0

GROUP 7: South (Central)

	P	W	D	L	F	A	Pts
W London Inst	5	5	0	0	384	9	10
RHBNC	5	4	0	1	93	97	8
Reading	5	3	0	2	102	85	6
Imperial	5	2	0	3	85	184	4
Brunel	5	1	0	4	47	153	2
Thames Valley	5	0	0	5	18	201	0

GROUP 8: South (South)

	P	W	D	L	F	A	Pts
W Sussex	6	5	0	1	163	16	10
Kent	6	5	0	1	112	45	10
Brighton	6	5	0	1	50	51	10
Surrey	6	3	0	3	41	83	6
Sussex	6	2	0	4	45	121	4
Canterbury	6	1	0	5	82	114	2
Greenwich	6	0	0	6	18	81	0

GROUP 9: South-East (North)

	P	W	D	L	F	A	Pts
N London	5	4	0	1	81	56	8
Hertford	5	4	0	1	81	66	8
UCL	5	3	0	2	73	66	6
Essex	5	2	0	3	82	80	4
Middlesex	5	1	0	4	77	92	2
E Anglia	5	0	0	5	42	76	0

GROUP 10: South-East (South)

	P	W	D	L	F	A	Pts
Roehampton	4	3	1	0	112	41	7
St Mary's Coll	4	3	0	1	73	45	6
Westminster	4	2	1	1	64	40	5
Kingston	4	1	0	3	47	62	2
Southampton	4	0	0	4	24	132	0

GROUP 11: London A

	P	W	D	L	F	A	Pts
King's College	4	4	0	0	126	26	8
Charing X/West	4	2	0	2	179	42	4
Q Mary Westfield	4	2	0	2	89	46	4
LSE	4	1	0	3	44	158	2
E London	4	1	0	3	47	213	2

GROUP 12: London B

	P	W	D	L	F	A	Pts
UMDS	1	1	0	0	8	0	2
Royal London	1	0	0	1	0	8	0

GROUP 13: London C

	P	W	D	L	F	A	Pts
St Mary's Hosp	3	3	0	0	62	3	6
Wye	3	2	0	1	95	56	4
St George's Hosp	3	1	0	0	25	41	2
UC Hosp	3	0	0	3	15	97	0

GROUP 14: London D

	P	W	D	L	F	A	Pts
Royal Ag	3	3	0	0	178	3	6
Cranfield Sh'ham	3	2	0	1	52	34	4
Cranfield (Beds)	3	1	0	2	30	74	2
De Montfort MK	3	0	0	3	7	156	0

GROUP 15: North-West Tier 1

	P	W	D	L	F	A	Pts
Liverpool	7	5	0	2	149	100	10
Manchester	7	4	1	2	125	56	9
Salford	7	3	2	3	106	91	8
Keele	7	4	0	3	95	89	8
Lancaster	7	3	0	4	50	68	6
Manchester Met	7	3	0	5	88	119	6
L'pool J Moores	7	2	1	4	104	159	5
UMIST	7	2	0	5	70	105	4

GROUP 16: North-East Tier 1

	P	W	D	L	F	A	Pts
Durham	6	6	0	0	265	34	12
Northumbria	6	5	0	1	160	51	10
Newcastle	6	3	0	3	153	89	6
Leeds Met	6	3	0	3	132	136	6
Leeds	6	3	0	3	123	169	6
Hull	6	1	0	5	78	172	2
Bradford	6	0	0	6	34	294	0

GROUP 17: North-West Tier 2

	P	W	D	L	F	A	Pts
Crewe & Als	5	4	0	1	223	41	8
Central Lancs	5	4	0	1	164	85	8
Chester	5	4	0	1	90	77	8
N Cheshire	5	2	0	3	40	33	4
St Martin's	4	0	0	4	27	162	0
Edge Hill	4	0	0	4	30	176	0

GROUP 18: North-East Tier 2

	P	W	D	L	F	A	Pts
Humberside	6	5	0	1	224	46	10
Ripon & York St J	6	5	0	1	74	37	10
Teesside	6	4	0	2	113	86	8
Bradford Ilkley	6	3	0	3	18	54	6
Huddersfield	6	2	0	4	51	88	4
New College	6	2	0	4	92	158	4
Sunderland	6	0	0	6	51	154	0

GROUP 19: Wales Tier 1

	P	W	D	L	F	A	Pts
Swansea	4	4	0	0	94	46	8
Cardiff Inst	4	3	0	1	136	57	6
Aberystwyth	4	1	0	3	70	100	2
UWCC	4	1	0	3	41	76	2
Glamorgan	4	1	0	3	60	122	2

GROUP 20: Wales Tier 2

	P	W	D	L	F	A	Pts
Gwent	5	4	0	1	138	21	8
Trinity	5	4	0	1	151	36	8
Lampeter	5	2	1	2	129	115	5
Swansea Inst	5	2	1	2	51	70	5
Bangor Normal	5	1	0	4	66	147	2
NE Wales	5	0	0	5	23	169	0

Scottish Universities Championship

Pool A

	P	W	D	L	F	A	Pts
St Andrews	4	3	0	1	40	32	6
Aberdeen	4	2	0	1	67	54	4
Napier	4	2	0	2	57	54	4
Stirling	4	2	0	2	35	47	4
Heriot Watt	4	1	0	3	42	54	2

Pool B

	P	W	D	L	F	A	Pts
Edinburgh	3	3	0	0	74	24	6
Dundee	3	2	0	1	45	23	4
Glasgow	3	1	0	2	40	56	2
Strathclyde	3	0	0	3	20	76	0

Scottish Universities Championship semi-finals: Edinburgh 38, Aberdeen 7;
St Andrews 19, Dundee 29
Scottish Universities Championship final: Dundee 13, Edinburgh 11 (*Dundee qualify for the Commercial Union Championship in first place, Edinburgh as runners-up*)

COMMERCIAL UNION UAU CHAMPIONSHIP
Knock-out Rounds
1st play-off round: Manchester w/o Teesside; Humberside 7, Leeds Metro 37;
Northumbria w/o Chester; Liverpool 43, Ripon and York St John 17; Central Lancs 13,
Salford 17; Durham w/o Keele; Crewe and Alsager 0, Newcastle 31; Cardiff Inst 50,
Oxford Brookes 10; Birmingham 12, UWCC 10; Worcester 0, Sheffield Hallam 35;
Loughborough 22, Wolverhampton St Peters 8; Sheffield w/o Bedford;
Swansea w/o Derby; Harper Adams 5, Leicester 10; Cheltenham and Gloucester w/o
Trinity; Gwent 29, RHBNC 0; Kent w/o London Hospital; St Mary's College 12,
Portsmouth 6; Roehampton 13, St Mark and St John 0; Bristol 26, Reading 0; UMDS 32,
Wye 3; Bath 28, UCL 14; West Sussex 22, Queen Mary Westfield 0; Exeter w/o
North London; St Mary's Hospital 12, Charing Cross/Westminster Hospital 14;
Royal Agricultural College 27, Hertfordshire 3; West London Institute 44,
Cranfield (Shrivenham) 10; King's College 12, Westminster 27
2nd play-off round: Manchester 13, Leeds Metropolitan 12; Northumbria 25,
Liverpool 0; Salford 3, Durham 48; Newcastle 15, Cardiff Inst 39; Birmingham 20,
Sheffield Hallam 28; Loughborough 41, Sheffield 6; Swansea 28, Leicester 8;
Cheltenham and Gloucester 18, Gwent 19; Kent 3, St Mary's College 12;
Roehampton 17, Bristol 11; UMDS 5, Bath 19; West Sussex 3, Exeter 15; Charing Cross/
Westminster Hospital 19, Royal Agricultural College 15; West London Institute w/o
Westminster
3rd play-off round: Manchester 37, Dundee 14; Edinburgh 9, Northumbria 11;
Durham 30, Cardiff Inst 22; Sheffield Hallam 16, Loughborough 8; Swansea 61,
Gwent 3; St Mary's College 9, Roehampton 14; Bath 21, Exeter 13;
Charing Cross/Westminster Hospital 9, West London Institute 41
Quarter-finals: Manchester 5, Northumbria 40; Durham 17, Sheffield Hallam 8;
Swansea 17, Roehampton 18; Bath 16, West London Institute 28
Semi-finals: Durham 9, Northumbria 34; Roehampton 19, West London Institute 24

COMMERCIAL UNION English Universities Inter-Divisional Tournament
23 January 1994, Loughborough University
Semi-finals: South-West 12, North 5; Midlands 20, South-East 5   **Final:** South-West
17, Midlands 10   **3rd and 4th Place:** North 37, South-East 10

COMMERCIAL UNION UAU Seven-a-side Tournament
13 March 1994, Newcastle Gosforth RFC
Semi-finals: Bristol 19, Swansea 5; Exeter 31, Nottingham 14   **Final:** Exeter 40,
Bristol 12   **3rd and 4th Place:** Swansea 24, Nottingham 7

SCOTTISH UNIVERSITIES Seven-a-side Tournament
4 May 1994, Glasgow University
Final: Dundee 26, St Andrews 7

YORKSHIRE UNIVERSITIES CUP
1st XV Semi-finals: Humberside 10, Sheffield Hallam 28; Teesside 5, Hull 54
1st XV Final (16 March 1994, Selby RFC): Sheffield Hallam 19, Hull 15
2nd XV Semi-finals: Humberside 5, Sheffield Hallam 45; Teesside 0, Sheffield 47
2nd XV Final (16 March 1994, Selby RFC): Sheffield Hallam 29, Sheffield 5

WORRALL'S HEROES RETAIN TITLE

THE SERVICES 1993-94
John Mace   *Daily Telegraph*

Inter-Services Tournament

For the first time the senior Inter-Services tournament had a single sponsor, Willis Corroon, who provided the Willis Corroon Bowl for the overall champions. The inaugural winners were the RAF, who thus retained their title, and the first recipient the RAF's skipper, Sgt Steve Worrall, who made his 24th Inter-Services appearance to top the tri-service list one ahead of Rory Underwood and two in front of the Army's Andy Hoon and the late Norman Bruce.

The Army defeated the Navy in a frenzied encounter marred by frequent stoppages for offences and attention to the walking wounded. The architects of the Army's victory were centre Steve Powley, who kicked six penalty goals, and their back row of Gareth James, Tim Rodber and Mike Watson. The Navy did well to weather the initial onslaught and were level at half-time but in the second half they committed too many offences and the soldiers had the better of the uncompromising exchanges.

The speed and skill of the RAF's backs plus a forthright first-half contribution from their forwards secured a hard-won victory over the Navy. They scored three early tries, one converted, to a dropped goal, but following the interval their pack faded as the Navy eight generated a fine head of steam. Despite this the airmen got a breakaway try before defending tenaciously to restrict the sailors to three penalty goals.

In the final game the RAF forwards, mindful that they had not lasted the pace against the Navy, kept going until the final whistle and dominated the more fancied Army pack for long periods. Paul Hull dropped a goal before the soldiers touched the ball and the RAF then added two converted tries and a penalty goal. The Army hit back with two tries but appeared to have lost touch when the RAF crossed again following the interval. But the RAF's concentration wavered and the Army closed the gap as ineffectual tackling let them in for two soft tries, one converted. A further penalty goal eased the RAF's anxiety but, as so often in the past, they were grateful for Steve Worrall's experience as he slowed the tempo and steered them to victory.

While the Combined Services' fighting performance against the All Blacks provided a fillip to the season and the Inter-Services matches were of a high standard, the effects of successive manpower cuts were felt as the Navy and RAF struggled to field Under-21 sides and the senior service were unable to raise a Colts team. There is general concern that the Navy and RAF might soon be unable to develop talent for their senior squads.

26 March, Twickenham
Royal Navy 6 (2PG)   **Army 18** (6PG)
for the Willis Corroon Trophy

Royal Navy: Sub Lt J R Coulton (RNAS Culdrose); Mne C White (HMS Warrior),
Sub Lt M Jarrett (RNEC Manadon), LWEM(R) D Oakley (HMS Raleigh),
Musn S Brown (HMS Warrior); LMEM G A Price (HMS Defiance), Cpl P Livingstone
(RM Stonehouse); PO(R) D Honey (HMS Battleaxe), POPT M R Clay
(HMS Temeraire), AEM S D Gay (HMS Centurion), LRO G Harrison
(HMS Atherstone), Mne D Cross (Comacchio Gp RM), Lt C B Palmer RM
(HMS Warrior), POPT S Jones (BRNC Dartmouth) (*capt*), Cpl R W Armstrong
(CTCRM Lympstone) *Replacement* Lt K Eyre RM (RM Stonehouse) for Coulton
Scorer *Penalty Goals:* Price (2)
Army: Cpl K Bowling (R Signals); Cpl S P Bartliff (R Signals), Capt A Glasgow (RE),
WO2 S Powley (REME), Capt J D Fenn (RLC); SSgt S Commander (RHA),
Bdr J Denwood (RHA); Sgt D Coghlan (RHA), Capt J Brammer (RE) (*capt*),
Sgt J Fowers (RHA), Lt D Dahinten (RHA), Lt A J K Newsham (RA), Capt G D James
(R Signals), Lt T A K Rodber (Green Howards), Cpt M Watson (REME)
Replacements Cpl D Hall (RMP) for Fowers (temp); Capt D Orr Ewing (Black Watch) for
Dahinten
Scorer *Penalty Goals:* Powley (6)
Referee G Davies (Liverpool Society)

13 April, Twickenham
Royal Navy 12 (3PG 1DG)   **Royal Air Force 22** (1G 3T)
for the Willis Corroon Hibernia Cup

Royal Navy: Lt K B Eyre RM (RM Stonehouse); Mne C White (HMS Warrior),
Sub Lt M Jarrett (RNEC Manadon), LWEM(R) D Oakley (HMS Raleigh),
Musn S Brown (HMS Warrior); LMEM G A Price (HMS Defiance), Cpl P Livingstone
(RM Stonehouse); PO(R) D Honey (HMS Battleaxe), POPT M R Clay
(HMS Temeraire), CPO W Lee (HMS Osprey), LRO G Harrison (HMS Atherstone),
Mne D Cross (Comacchio Gp RM), Lt C I M Dixon R M (RM Poole), POPT S Jones
(BRNC Dartmouth) (*capt*), Cpl R W Armstrong (CTCRM Lympstone)
Replacement Lt C B Palmer RM (HMS Warrior) for Jones (temp)
Scorer *Penalty Goals:* Price (3)   *Dropped Goal:* Price
Royal Air Force: Flt Lt R Underwood (Finningley); SAC S Crossland (Innsworth),
Cpl S Roke (Wittering), A/PO E Rayner (Oxford UAS), SAC G Sharp (Benson);
Cpl P Hull (Lyneham), Sgt S Worrall (Cottesmore) (*capt*); Cpl A Billett (St Athan),
Flt Lt R Miller (Wyton), JT B Williams (Brize Norton), Flt Lt R Burn (Lossiemouth),
Sgt B Richardson (CIO Ayr), Fg Off DS Williams (Locking), Cpl L Hibbert (Innsworth),
Cpl D Parsonage (Wittering)
Scorers *Tries:* Rayner (2), Roke, Underwood   *Conversion:* Worrall
Referee A Rowden (Berkshire Society)

20 April, Twickenham
Army 22 (1G 3T)   **Royal Air Force 28** (2G 2PG 1DG 1T)

Army: Cpl K Bowling (R Signals); Cpl S P Bartliffe (R Signals), Capt A Glasgow (RE),
WO2 S Powley (REME), Capt J D Fenn (RLC); SSgt S Commander (RHA),
Lt J H Merritt (R Signals); Cpl D Hall (RMP), Capt J Brammer (RE) (*capt*), Sgt J Fowers
(RHA), Lt D Dahinten (RHA), Lt A J K Newsham (RA), Capt G D James (R Signals),
Lt T A K Rodber (Green Howards), Cpl M Watson (REME) *Replacements* Sgt D Coghlan
(RHA) for Fowers; Cpl P R Curtis (R Signals) for James; Cfn P J Jinks (REME) for
Brammer
Scorers *Tries:* Rodber (2), Watson, Jinks   *Conversion:* Powley
Royal Air Force: Flt Lt R Underwood (Finningley); SAC S Crossland (Innsworth),
Cpl S Roke (Wittering), A/PO E Rayner (Oxford UAS), SAC G Sharp (Benson);

Cpl P Hull (Lyneham), Sgt S Worrall (Cottesmore) (*capt*); Cpl A Billett (St Athan), Flt Lt R Miller (Wyton), JT B Williams (Brize Norton), Flt Lt R Burn (Lossiemouth), Sgt B Richardson (CIO Ayr), Fg Off D Williams (Locking), Cpl L Hibbert (Innsworth), Cpl D Parsonage (Wittering) *Replacement* Cpl P Taylor (Northolt) for Richardson
Scorers *Tries:* Sharp (2), Rayner *Conversions:* Worrall (2) *Penalty Goals:* Worrall, Hull *Dropped Goal:* Hull
Referee G Hughes (Manchester Society)

Inter-Services Tournament Champions

The Army have won the Tournament outright 28 times, the Royal Navy 16 times and the Royal Air Force 14 times. The Army and the Royal Air Force have shared it on 2 occasions and there have been 9 triple ties.

1920	**RN**	1949	**Army and RAF**	1972	**Army**
1921	**RN**	1950	**Army**	1973	**RN**
1922	**RN**	1951	**RN**	1974	**RN**
1923	**RAF**	1952	**Army**	1975	Triple Tie
1924	Triple Tie	1953	**Army**	1976	**Army**
1925	**Army and RAF**	1954	Triple Tie	1977	**RN**
1926	**Army**	1955	**RAF**	1978	Triple Tie
1927	**RN**	1956	Triple Tie	1979	**RAF**
1928	**Army**	1957	**Army**	1980	**Army**
1929	**Army**	1958	**RAF**	1981	**RN**
1930	**Army**	1959	**RAF**	1982	**RAF**
1931	**RN**	1960	**Army**	1983	**Army**
1932	**Army**	1961	**RN**	1984	Triple Tie
1933	**Army**	1962	**RAF**	1985	**RAF**
1934	**Army**	1963	**Army**	1986	**RAF**
1935	Triple Tie	1964	**Army**	1987	**RN**
1936	**Army**	1965	**Army**	1988	**Army**
1937	**Army**	1966	**RN**	1989	**Army**
1938	**RN**	1967	**Army**	1990	**Army**
1939	**RN**	1968	**Army**	1991	**RAF**
1946	**Army**	1969	**Army**	1992	Triple Tie
1947	**RAF**	1970	**RN**	1993	**RAF**
1948	Triple Tie	1971	**RAF**	1994	**RAF**

Royal Navy v Army The Royal Navy have won 31, the Army 43, and 3 matches have been drawn (including matches before 1920) **Royal Navy v Royal Air Force** The Royal Navy have won 37, the Royal Air Force 28, and 4 matches have been drawn **Army v Royal Air Force** The Army have won 38, the Royal Air Force 23, and 8 matches have been drawn

Other Competitions

After their impressive showing against the All Blacks the Combined Services were hoping to regain the Securicor Trophy from the British Police but fielded a weak team and went down heavily to a side with four full and three A internationals. The Army won the Inter-Services Under-21 and Colts (Under-19) competitions but both competitions were affected by recruiting restrictions caused by the ongoing defence cuts. In the former the Royal Navy and Royal Air Force had to field several players who were still Colts while in the latter the Royal Navy were unable to raise a team at all.

Royal Marines Plymouth beat HMS Heron, the Naval Air Station from Yeovilton, to win the Royal Navy Cup for the first time, while

HMS Collingwood won the Navy Sevens tournament. The Royal Artillery headed Division 1 of the Army Inter-Corps Merit Table and the Royal Army Medical Corps won Division 2. Last season's losing finalists, the 7th Signals Regiment, ended the 7th Parachute Regiment Royal Horse Artillery's run of four consecutive victories in the final of the Army Major Units Cup competition. The 17th Battery Royal Artillery won the Minor Units Cup and the 2nd Signals Regiment captured the Army Sevens title.

In the RAF Inter-Command match Strike and Support fought a fitting 20-20 draw in the final meeting between the two formations. RAF Brize Norton won the Royal Air Force Inter-Station Cup and RAF Wittering took the Inter-Station Shield for units eliminated in the first round of the Cup competition. RAF Halton emerged as winners of the Binbrook Bomb in the RAF Sevens tournament.

Inter-Services Under-21 Tournament
Army 22, RAF 3; RN 10, RAF 20; RN 3, Army 36 **Winners:** Army

Inter-Services Colts (Under-19) Tournament
Army 17, RAF 5 **Winners:** Army

Combined Services Matches
Senior: Combined Services 19, Bristol 7; Combined Services 20, Bath 3; Combined Services 3, New Zealand 13; Combined Services 36, British Police 72 (*for the Securicor Trophy*)
Under-21: Combined Services 16, England Students 16 **Under-20:** Combined Services 12, Cardiff 48; Combined Services 9, Ogmore and District 52

Individual Service Competitions
ROYAL NAVY
Inter-Command Match: Royal Marines 38, Naval Air Command 3
Inter-Unit Cup: HMS Nelson 12, Royal Marines Plymouth 16
Inter-Unit Sevens: HMS Collingwood 14, HMS Nelson 0
ARMY
Inter Corps Merit Table: Division 1 winners: Royal Artillery **Division 2 winners:** Royal Army Medical Corps **Major Units Cup:** 7th Parachute Regiment Royal Horse Artillery 14, 7th Signal Regiment 20 **Minor Units Cup:** 17th Battery Royal Artillery 18, Infantry Training Battalion Strensall 15 **Inter-Unit Sevens:** 2 Signals Regiment 31, Royal Regiment of Wales 0
RAF
Inter-Command Match: Strike Command 20, Support Command 20
Inter-Station Cup: RAF Brize Norton 33, RAF Coningsby 10 **Inter-Station Shield:** RAF Wittering 11, RAF Aldergrove 8 **Inter-Station Sevens:** RAF Halton 15, RAF Lossiemouth 10

ENGLAND BOUNCE BACK TO A 'GRAND SLAM'

SCHOOLS RUGBY 1993-94
Michael Stevenson

England 18 Group provided the most positive and admirable reaction to last season's whitewash with their second 'Grand Slam' in three years, following improved form in their Australian summer tour. In the three matches prior to the Durham encounter with unbeaten Ireland, they defeated Wales (32-3), Scotland (22-12) and France 14-13), but there remained a general feeling that there was still some room for improvement.

Whether or not that was achieved, their 23-8 win against Ireland was a thoroughly workmanlike performance in horrendously difficult conditions. Andrew Blyth managed only two successful kicks out of 12 chances in the fiercely swirling wind and Richard Governey for Ireland one out of four. But a 3-1 try count was decisive. Eric Miller at No 8 and Denis Hickie on the wing were outstanding for the losers. The Hymers flanker Neil Spence scored England's first try; Blyth touched down and converted the second. Their third was by the Millfield fly-half Matthew Jones, after creative work by his scrum-half, Phil Harvey. Ireland's try was scored by Simon Doggett.

It is perhaps a sign of the times in rugby that the two England locks, Ben Kay and Chris Murphy, were 6 feet 7 inches and 6 feet 8 inches respectively, weighing in at 18 stone and 16 stone 12 pounds. (By way of contrast it is interesting to record that when Cowley High School went 55 matches unbeaten in the 1980s, they did not possess a single player over 6 feet.)

Prior to their defeat by England, Wales had prospered, beating Scottish Schools (35-8), Welsh Youth (30-13) and France (24-11), but it was clear evidence of Ireland's pedigree that they had overcome a deficit of 13 points shortly after half-time against Wales. Nick Walne had made the first try for Wales, scored by Andrew Thomas, and scored the second himself to open up what seemed to be a winning margin. Yet a couple of penalties by Richard Governey put Ireland within a single score and victory (by 14-13) came with a try by Stephen Bell and a third penalty by Governey.

The climax of England's campaign at 16 Group level was their Festival match against Wales at Twickenham, played alongside the two *Daily Mail* Cup finals. England had good wins at both first team and A team level against Portugal to encourage them, but the big match ended in an 11-11 draw after Wales had led 11-3 at the interval.

The semi-finals of the *Daily Mail* Under-18 Cup had seen *RGS Newcastle's* domination of *RGS Guildford* result in victory by 13-0, while *Mount St Mary's,* well beaten forward, had struggled to survive and win against Campion (13-8). This may have established Newcastle as favourites but Mount's class proved crucial as they won by 17-12 with a 2-0 try count. Their tries were scored by their speedy wing, James Bartle, and their excellent scrum-half, Charlie Harrison. All Newcastle's points – from a massive 50-yard dropped goal and three penalties – came from the boot of Philip Belgian. Some wonderfully dedicated tackling in the *Daily Mail* Under-15 final resulted in a 3-3 draw between *Bedford School* and *Wellington College, Berkshire.*

For the first time ever, *King's, Taunton* and *Loughborough GS* progressed beyond the quarter-finals of the Festival tournament at the Rosslyn Park Sevens to meet in the final, where King's triumphed 19-15 through a try in injury time by Andy Lister. It was appropriate that their coach should be Ray Codd, who captained Rosslyn Park from full-back in the early 1970s. In the Open category, *Millfield,* who enjoyed a wonderful season, beat *Ampleforth,* those notable sevens specialists, by 19-14, one of the Millfield try-scorers being Rhys Edwards, son of Gareth. The other tries were scored by Nick Buoy and, in extra time, Dinos Alexopoulos. Toby Mostyn scored both Ampleforth's tries. The Prep Schools' Sevens tournament at Rosslyn Park was won by *Cranmore.* Andrew Campbell and Cameron Norsworthy accounted for their 10-0 win and, remarkably, Campbell's try was his 81st of the season, an unbeaten one for Cranmore. *Dulwich* won the Junior title.

It is 23 years since two finalists have competed for the prestigious Ulster Bank Schools' Cup without either having previously won the competition. Both finalists this season, *Regent House* and *Wallace HS,* were viewed as underdogs in the semi-finals, but Regent saw off *Royal School, Dungannon* (21-12) and Wallace scraped home against Methodist College, Belfast (6-5). The final, in which Wallace enjoyed the edge forward, was not a classic as they were unable to turn pressure into points. An accurate diagonal kick by John Todd set up the game's only try, scored by Stephen Gardiner, and the other points came from penalties kicked by Gary Stewart for Regent and Stephen Doherty for Wallace, leaving Regent 8-3 winners.

Millfield had a fantastic season and are the unbeaten winners of the *Rugby World* Team of the Year Award with a record of P16, W16, F514, A118, including their five matches in the Ipswich 15-a-side tournament. Only once, against QEH Bristol (24-18), were they remotely extended and among their more gratifying victories they would surely include Sherborne (30-10), Llandovery (32-15), King's, Taunton at Ipswich (19-5) and Strade (36-7). They provided the England fly-half, Matthew Jones, and Philip Booth represented Wales Schools at prop.

It is only the second time in the history of the school that *Cranleigh* have won all their matches, the last occasion being 1955. Their 13 wins comprised 219 points scored to 79 conceded. Their coach, the former England fly-half Neil Bennett, was adamant that their success was not based on stars but on dedicated team-work. Predictably, therefore, they had few large winning margins, though they beat Brighton 37-3 and Epsom 24-9, their most noteworthy victory of all coming against Wellington, Berkshire (17-14).

Seaford College, too, had an outstanding record to report: W13, D1, F412, A97. As they had only 230 boys to choose from, this was a wonderful performance. The drawn game was against St George's, Weybridge (5-5) and among their most gratifying victories were those against Brighton (31-3), King Edward VI, Southampton (15-13), Chichester HS (8-6) and Christ's Hospital (21-10).

Both *Truro School* and *Kelly College* from the south-west prospered impressively. Truro drew with Kelly (8-8) and lost (12-15) away in the *Daily Mail* Cup to Colston's to set against 11 wins from 13 matches and a points record of 310 scored to 97 conceded. Truro contributed seven players to the Cornwall 18 Group and, remarkably, their right wing, Mark Cooper, scored a try in every match. Kelly College (W13, F393, A97) were rewarded with the selection of six players for the Devon 18 Group. Among their best wins were West Buckland (15-13), Exeter School (20-10), Plymouth College (17-3) and Wellington School, Somerset (39-13).

It is desperately hard, bearing in mind the horrendous problems of state schools with regard to finances and staffing, to compare the results of a team like *Hall Cross CS* from Doncaster with the consistently successful and long-established independent schools. Their record was W19, L3, F653 A128, and their coach, Mick Knight, regards their best performances as the defeats by Hymers (8-16) and 3-10 against QEGS, Wakefield, the best side they have met. Crossley Heath CS was the third side to beat them, by 9-24.

Rugby lost narrowly to Harrow but enjoyed their best season for years. On a strong circuit they managed 12 wins along with the one defeat, scoring 242 points to 112 against. They scored 31 tries and conceded only 16. Their final flourish to a wonderful term's rugby was a 10-28 away win against Radley and a 17-10 win against South Africa College HS from Cape Town.

Merchiston Castle enjoyed a great season north of the border (W12, L2, F376, A115) and benefited considerably from their pre-season tour to Australia. Their defeats were by Windsor Boys' HS (19-10) and RGS, Newcastle (10-0). *Loretto*'s record was similar (W11, D1, L2, F356, A153), but perhaps Merchiston could claim a moral victory over-all as they inflicted one of Loretto's two defeats. Top try-scorer for Loretto was Adam Lowles with 19 and their leading points-scorer was Richard Rait (101).

One of the more interesting of the numerous tours of the British Isles was made by Lindisfarne College from New Zealand. They won 8 out of 9 matches, losing only to *Blackrock College* in Dublin (9-11). The two other games in which the tourists were extended were also in Ireland –

against *Campbell College* (16-7) and *Dalriada School* (16-9). It was also pleasing to note the regular tour traffic between the UK and South Africa. Long may it continue.

The following players took part in the 18 Group international matches. Countries played against are shown in square brackets.
Abbreviations: *E* – England, *F* – France, *I* – Ireland, *S* – Scotland, *W* – Wales, (R) – Replacement

ENGLAND
Full-back: C Catling (Whitgift School) [*F, I, S, W*]
Threequarters: D Smyth (Hampton School) [*F, S, W*]; A Blyth (Rugby School) [*F, I, S, W*]; F Waters (Harrow School) [*F, I, S, W*]; M Wood (Sedburgh School) [*I, W*]; D Craig (Sherborne School) [*F, I*]; G Truelove (Durham School) [*S*]; B Stafford (Truro College) [*S*(R), *W*, (R)]
Half-backs: M Jones (Millfield School) [*F, I, S, W*]; P Harvey (Durham School) [*F, I, S, W*]
Forwards: S Beaufoy (Wyggeston QE College) [*F, I, S, W*]; P Greening (Gloucester College) [*F, I, S, W*]; B Kay (Merchant Taylors, Crosby) [*F, I, S, W*]; C Murphy (Hymers College) [*F, I, S, W*]; E Pearce (Clifton College) [*F, I, S, W*]; N Spence (Hymers College) [*F, I, S, W*]; R Winters (Haywards Heath College) [*F, I, W*]; G Wappett (Bradford GS) [*S*]
Greening was captain in all four matches

IRELAND
Full-back: J Lowe (Ballyclare HS) [*E, S, W*]
Threequarters: S Doggett (St Mary's) [*E, S, W*]; J Lacy (Clongowes Wood College) [*E, S, W*]; M Smyth (Terenure College) [*E, S, W*]; K McNamee (St Mary's) [*W*]; D Hickie (St Mary's) [*E, S*]
Half-backs: R Governey (Clongowes Wood College) [*E, S, W*]; S Bell (Friends School, Lisburn) [*E, S, W*]
Forwards: A McSweeney (CBC, Cork) [*E, S, W*]; R Sands (Royal School, Dungannon) [*E, S, W*]; R Sheehan (Garbally College) [*E, S, W*]; J Fitzgerald (PBC, Cork) [*E, S, W*]; D Lane (PBC, Cork) [*E, S, W*]; P Lynch (Clongowes Wood College) [*E, S, W*]; E Miller (Wesley College) [*E, S, W*]; D Shanley (St Michael's) [*W*(R)]; G Gannon (St Mary's) [*W*(R)]
Lynch was captain in all three matches

SCOTLAND
Full-back: K Baillie (Hutchesons' GS) [*E, F, I, W*]
Threequarters: D Bull (Stewart's-Melville) [*E, F, I, W*]; A Bulloch (Hutchesons' GS) [*E, F, I, W*]; A Taylor (George Heriot's) [*E, F, I, W*]; D Mallinson (George Watson's) [*F, W*]; D Ablett (Boroughmuir) [*E*]; J Wilson (Queen Victoria) [*I*]
Half-backs: G Dalgleish (Galashiels Academy) [*E, F, I, W*]; J Weston (Merchiston Castle) [*E, F, I, W*]
Forwards: P Fitzgerald (Dollar Academy) [*F, W*]; M Smith (Glasgow Academy) [*E, I*]; I Cornwall (Peebles HS) [*E*(R)]; M Bannerman (Hawick HS) [*E, F, I, W*]; D Bett (Dundee HS) [*E*(R)]; I McLaren (George Watson's) [*E*(R), *F, W*]; L Walker (Strathallan) [*E*]; R Watson (Perth Academy) [*I*]; L Walker (Strathallan) [*E*]; R Watson (Perth Academy) [*I*]; G Macfarlane (Kelvinside Academy) [*E, F, I, W*]; I Fullerton (Merchiston Castle) [*E, F, I, W*]; G Inglis (Hutchesons' GS) [*F, W*]; J Henderson (Strathallan) [*E, F, I, W*]; E Macdonald (Douglas Ewart HS) [*E, I*]; I Sinclair (Kelvinside Academy) [*E, F, I, W*]; I Hope (Dundee HS) [*E*(R)]
Weston was captain in all four matches

WALES

Full-back: G Watts (Llandovery College) [*E, F, I, S*]
Threequarters: M Garfield (Maesteg CS) [*E, F, I, S*]; N Walne (Caerleon CS)
[*E, F, I, S*]; J Funnell (Neath College) [*E, I*]; A Thomas (Gorseinon Tertiary College)
[*E, F, I, S*]; T Davies (Maesydderwen CS) [*F, S*]; L Davies (Neath Tertiary College)
[*I*(R)]
Half-backs: D Morris (Neath Tertiary College) [*E, F, I, S*]; D Hawkins
(Neath Tertiary College) [*E, F, S*]; G Downs (Ysgol Gyfun Rhydfelen) [*E*(R), *I*];
A Drought (Caerleon CS) [*E*(R)]
Forwards: P Booth (Millfield School) [*E, F, I, S*]; J Richards (Fishguard CS) [*E, F, I, S*];
G Alexander (Ysgol Gyfun Llanhari) [*E, F, I, S*]; S Gardiner
(Cross Keys Tertiary College) [*E, F, I, S*]; N Watkins (Neath Tertiary College)
[*E, F, I, S*]; N Thomas (Llandovery College) [*E, F, I, S*]; M Williams (Coed y Lan CS)
[*E, F, S*]; R Field (St David's College, Cardiff) [*E, F, I, S*]; J Ringer (St Cyres CS) [*I*];
G Gittings (Neath College) [*E*(R)]
Watts was captain in all four matches

MATCH DETAILS 1993-94 (18 Group)

20 December 1993, Myreside, Edinburgh

SCOTLAND 17 (4PG 1T) **FRANCE 21** (1G 3PG 1T)
SCOTLAND *Try:* Bull *Penalty Goals:* Mallinson (4)
FRANCE *Tries:* Crouzie, Gourdon *Conversion:* Reyes *Penalty Goals:* Reyes (3)
Referee J G Crothers

4 January 1994, Newport

WALES 35 (2G 2PG 3T) **SCOTLAND 8** (1PG 1T)
WALES *Tries:* A Thomas (2), Garfield, Gardiner, Williams *Conversions:* Morris (2)
Penalty Goals: Morris (2)
SCOTLAND *Try:* Bull *Penalty Goal:* Mallinson
Referee J Western (England)

18 February 1994, St Helen's, Swansea

WALES 24 (1G 3PG 1DG 1T) **FRANCE 11** (2PG 1T)
WALES *Tries:* Booth, Williams *Conversion:* Morris *Penalty Goals:* Morris (3)
Dropped Goal: Morris
FRANCE *Try:* Bisaro *Penalty Goals:* Reyes (2)
Referee A Watson (Ireland)

23 March 1994, Bournemouth

ENGLAND 32 (3G 2PG 1T) **WALES 3** (1PG)
ENGLAND *Tries:* Blyth (2), Wood, Kay *Conversions:* Blyth, Jones (2)
Penalty Goals: Jones (2)
WALES *Penalty Goal:* Morris
Referee D Haladjian (France)

30 March 1994, Poynder Park, Kelso

SCOTLAND 12 (1G 1T) **ENGLAND 22** (2G 1PG 1T)
SCOTLAND *Tries:* Bull, Ablett *Conversion:* Taylor
ENGLAND *Tries:* Jones, Kay, Catling *Conversions:* Blyth (2) *Penalty Goal:* Blyth
Referee H Lewis (Wales)

30 March 1994, Templeville Road, Dublin

IRELAND 14 (3PG 1T)   **WALES 13** (1PG 2T)
IRELAND *Try:* Bell   *Penalty Goals:* Governey (3)
WALES *Tries:* A Thomas, Walne   *Penalty Goal:* Morris
Referee R Clarke (Scotland)

2 April 1994, Cahors

FRANCE 13 (1G 2PG)   **ENGLAND 14** (3PG 1T)
FRANCE *Try:* Lajus   *Conversion:* Reyes   *Penalty Goals:* Reyes (2)
ENGLAND *Try:* Catling   *Penalty Goals:* Blyth (3)
Referee D L Roelands (Belgium)

4 April 1994, Thomond Park, Limerick

IRELAND 30 (6T)   **SCOTLAND 5** (1T)
IRELAND *Tries:* Hickie (4), Bell, Spence
SCOTLAND *Try:* Baillie
Referee C Thomas (Wales)

13 April 1994, Durham

ENGLAND 23 (1G 1PG 1DG 2T)   **IRELAND 8** (1PG 1T)
ENGLAND *Tries:* Blyth, Jones, Spence   *Conversion:* Blyth   *Penalty Goal:* Blyth
Dropped Goal: Jones
IRELAND *Try:* Doggett   *Penalty Goal:* Governey
Referee L D Crerar (Scotland)

ENGLAND EXCITE BUT STILL NEED A DASH OF FLEXIBILITY

COLTS AND YOUTH RUGBY 1993-94
Michael Stevenson

Ray Phillips celebrated his inaugural year as team manager of England Colts with some exciting and stimulating rugby which brought a considerable degree of success. The only setback in their four-match programme was a 15-10 defeat by Welsh Youth. He felt that both this match and the one against France, which resulted in an 11-11 draw, might well have been won had the plethora of possession provided by their powerful and efficient pack been used more wisely and constructively.

England possesses a superb system now, with all the age groups dovetailed, integrated and feeding each other. Sometimes, however, it seemed that tactical flexibility was lacking. If the ball-carrier has crashed two or three times and there is a hint of disarray in the opposition, then surely that is the time to let the ball flow in the backs. This did not happen as often as might have been hoped. Ray Phillips felt that 'The team did not play to their full potential . . . we lost to Wales despite dominating all the possession.' A similar picture emerged from the French game, as well as some poor decision-making and indifferent handling in the threequarters.

Scott Benton, the Yorkshire scrum-half, showed the sort of talent that might carry him eventually to a full England cap and, remarkably, Neil McCarthy of Somerset represented the Colts for the third season. But perhaps the most dramatic contribution came from Joseph Czerpak, who came on as a replacement and kicked a penalty to earn the draw against France with his first touch of the ball in international rugby.

Following a narrow 12-11 victory over Italy in Brescia, with tries by Benton and Reed, plus a conversion by Jowett, England met Wales with high hopes. Welsh Youth had also beaten Italy (24-14) but lost in France (28-8). Against England, scrum-half Kevin Mably profited from a charged-down kick to score the first Welsh try; the second, by Chris Stephens, came direct from a line-out. Scott Benton and Dean Jowett scored tries for England before a fine break by Arwel Thomas put Darren Davies in for the decider.

Ireland are improving fast at Colts (Under-18) level and won both their matches, against Wales (12-6) and Scotland (10-5).

The divisional preparations for the internationals saw the North defeat London and the South-East 18-9. In the semi-finals, London and the South-East had beaten the Midlands (22-12) while the North won against the South and South-West (13-0). It is a sign of the North's strength that they comfortably triumphed over a Northumberland Under-21 side prior to the semi-finals by 32-5, and with a formidable try count of 6-1.

Further preparation followed with the England trial at Castlecroft, squad weekends and games between England and the North and Midlands, London and the South-West and Loughborough Freshers. Yorkshire, providing the base for the North side, contributed five players to the 28-strong England squad and Gloucestershire three. Six players who had not taken part in the Divisional games were included in the squad: Archer (Newcastle Gosforth), Overend (Otley), Kinder and Ions (Durham University), Denny (Bristol University) and Binns (Birmingham University).

Yorkshire met Somerset in the semi-finals of the Colts' County Championship with a point to make as Somerset had beaten them in the previous year's final. It was a close-run thing, Yorkshire finally succeeding by 10-8 with a 2-1 try count. Their tries came from Nick Miller and Dean Jowett, while Somerset came agonising close to snatching the match through Richard Hale's penalty and a try by Alan Rochford.

Gloucestershire comfortably attended to Kent (20-6) in the other semi-final, and a close final was anticipated. It was sad that under 500 spectators attended the final at Twickenham, making it probable that future finals will be held at Castlecroft. The game was virtually decided in Yorkshire's favour by the interval; in a difficult swirling wind, Ian Shuttleworth contributed a try and two penalties, which, along with Nick Miller's try and two conversions by Dean Jowett, opened up a 20-3 half-time lead. Charles Heming had kicked a penalty for Gloucestershire.

In the second half, Stephen Hart added a third Yorkshire try and Shuttleworth kicked a second penalty in reply to Michael Crisp's dropped goal, taking the final score to 28-6 and snuffing out any chance of a Gloucestershire resurgence.

Among the clubs, few have done better than Thornensians, Moderns Under-17s and Old Crossleyans, but there is still that niggling suspicion that colts rugby is not given its proper due in all quarters. This, surely, is a shortsighted attitude. Pride of place, however, must go to Pontypridd, recently voted the Whitbread Youth Team of the Year. Their final record, P29 W26 D1 L2 F910 A218, makes wonderfully impressive reading.

Both the half-backs, Gareth Downes and Lee Jarvis, as well as Martyn Williams were rewarded with selection for Wales Schools 18 Group squad, and fly-half Jarvis established a new colts record. He played 24 matches and contributed 352 points, which included 19 tries to add to his accomplished goal-kicking. This comfortably beat the previous record of 308 set by the current senior fly-half, Neil Jenkins.

Pontypridd's young half-backs have played together since they were seven and the contribution of the Downes family is remarkable. Gareth's brother, Robert Downes, coaches the backs and three other Downes brothers, Carl, Jamie and Jeff, have all represented Pontypridd Colts. So far they have no plans to take over the world!

The following players took part in the Colts/Youth international matches. Countries played against are shown in square brackets.
Abbreviations: *E* – England, *F* – France, *I* – Ireland, *It* – Italy, *S* – Scotland, *Sp* – Spain, *W* – Wales, (R) – Replacement

ENGLAND
Full-backs: D Jowett (Old Brodleians) [*F, It, S, W*]; J Czerpak (Exeter U) [*F*(R)]
Threequarters: N Miller (Wakefield) [*F, It, S, W*]; M Denney (Bristol U) [*F, It, S, W*]; J Overend (Otley) [*F, It, S, W*]; S Reed (Leicester) [*F, It, S, W*]; C Kinder (Durham U) [*F*(R)]
Half-backs: A King (Rosslyn Park) [*F, It, S, W*]; S Benton (Morley) [*F, It, S, W*]; B Hyde (Cheltenham) [*F*(R)]
Forwards: A Collins (Bath) [*It, S, W*]; D Robbins (Swansea U) [*It, S, W*]; M Banner (Plymouth Albion) [*F*]; P Vickery (Redruth) [*F, S*(R)]; N McCarthy (Bath) [*F, It, S, W*]; G Archer (Newcastle Gosforth) [*F, It, S, W*]; R Kidman (Blackheath) [*It, S, W*]; B Wade (Morley) [*F, It, S, W*]; J Ions (Durham U) [*F, It, S, W*]; R Fidler (Gloucester) [*F, It, S, W*]; A Bennett (Blackheath) [*F, It*(R), *S*(R)]
Denney was captain in all four matches

IRELAND
Under-18s
Full-back: O Moran (Bohemians) [*S, W*]
Threequarters: G Corless (Tuam) [*S, W*]; T Lane (Clonmel) [*S, W*]; P Connella (Ennis) [*S, W*]; G Foley (Sligo) [*S, W*]; R Doyle (Old Christians) [*W*(R)]
Half-backs: A Finney (Portadown) [*S, W*]; T Tierney (Richmond) [*S, W*]
Forwards: R McArdle (Youghal) [*S, W*]; R McGarrigle (Limavady) [*S, W*]; L Johnston (Dromore) [*S, W*]; A Patterson (Ballymena) [*S*(R), *W* (R)]; P Humphrey (Richmond) [*S*(R)]; E Cullen (Wexford Wanderers) [*S, W*]; M Mullen (Monaghan) [*S, W*]; M Crowley (Highfield) [*S, W*]; G Sloan (Dromore) [*S, W*]; R Cogan (Highfield) [*S, W*]; G Williamson (Clogher Valley) [*W*(R)]
Cogan was captain in both matches

SCOTLAND
Under-19s
Full-back: C Richards (Jedforest) [*E, W*]
Threequarters: C MacRobert (Stirling County) [*E, W*]; C Murray (Hawick) [*E, W*]; D Cross (Corstorphine) [*E, W*]; H Gilmour (Heriot's FP) [*E, W*]; A Taylor (George Heriot's School) [*E*(R)]
Half-backs: M Duncan (Blaydon) [*E, W*]; D Paterson (Gala) [*E, W*]
Forwards: M McCluskie (Musselburgh) [*E, W*]; G Bulloch (Hutchesons'/Aloysians) [*E, W*]; B Stewart (Edinburgh Acads) [*E, W*]; S Begley (Blackheath) [*E, W*]; G Perrett (West of Scotland) [*E, W*]; T McVie (Edinburgh Acads) [*E, W*]; D McLeish (Hutchesons'/Aloysians) [*E, W*]; G Dall (Heriot's FP) [*E, W*]
Dall was captain in both matches

Under-18s
Full-back: S Tomlinson (Selkirk) [*I, Sp*]
Threequarters: G Caldwell (Ayr) [*I, Sp*]; A Wilson (Highland) [*I, Sp*]; R Kennedy (Stirling County) [*I, Sp*]; C Turnbull (Hawick PSA) [*I, Sp*]; A McLean (Boroughmuir) [*Sp*]
Half-backs: K Utterson (Kelso Harlequins) [*I, Sp*]; P Simpson (Kirkcaldy) [*I, Sp*]
Forwards: S Lithgow (St Andrews U) [*I, Sp*]; C Docherty (GHK) [*I, Sp*]; G Talac (Musselburgh) [*I, Sp*]; C Hunter (Livingston) [*I, Sp*]; S Murray (Preston Lodge FP) [*I, Sp*]; L Nixon (Tynedale) [*Sp*]; G Hayter (Moray) [*I*]; S Wands (Edinburgh Wands) [*I, Sp*]; W Spencer (Aberdeen U) [*I, Sp*]
Simpson was captain against Ireland, Docherty against Spain

WALES
Under-19s
Full-back: A Jones (Harlequins) [*E, F, It, S*]
Threequarters: R Jones (Neath Colts) [*E, F, It S*]; L Davies (Swansea) [*F*(R), *S*];
G Jones (Bridgend) [*E, F, It, S*]; D James (Cornelly) [*E, F, It, S*]; N Walsh (Maesteg)
[*F, It*]; C Wilkins (Cardiff) [*E*]
Half-backs: A Thomas (Trebannws) [*E, F, It, S*]; K Mably (Bridgend) [*E, S*]; S Powell
(Worcester) [*F, It*]
Forwards: L Manning (Bridgend) [*E, F, It, S*]; J Power (Rhigos) [*E, F, It, S*]; D Morris
(Neath) [*E, F, It, S*]; L Johnson (Neath Colts) [*F*(R)]; B Evans (Cardiff) [*S*(R)];
N Dawkins (Blaina) [*It*(R)]; S Ford (Cwmafan) [*E, F, It, S*]; C Stephens (Maesteg)
[*E, F, It, S*]; C Quinnell (Llanelli) [*E, F, It, S*]; D Davies (Cardiff) [*E, F*(R), *S*];
M Codd (Llanelli) [*E, S*]; G Thomas (Tondu) [*F, It*]; N Thomas (Maesteg) [*F, It*]
Richard Jones was captain in all four matches

Under-18s (v Ireland)
Full-back: C Quick (Coventry)
Threequarters: D Griffiths (Neath Colts); A Henderson (New Tredegar); W Jarvis
(Llanharan); G Aylward (Taibach) (R); J Pleece (RTB Ebbw Vale)
Half-backs: S Connor (Abertillery); L Thomas (Carmarthen Athletic)
Forwards: D Bowen (Swansea); J Kemble (Cardiff); B Grace (Kidwelly); L Banks
(Abertillery); J Sulway (Pontypool); A Fowler (Cardiff); M Buckingham (Llanelli);
G Green (Pontypool)
Kemble was captain

MATCH DETAILS 1993-94

27 February 1994, Newport

WELSH YOUTH 24 (3G 1PG)   **ITALIAN YOUTH 14** (3PG 1T)
WALES *Tries:* A Jones (2), Walsh   *Conversions:* A Thomas (3)
Penalty Goal: A Thomas
ITALY *Try:* Gnesini   *Penalty Goals:* Pilat (3)
Referee S Piercy (England)

12 March 1994, Le Puy

FRANCE JUNIORS 28 (1G 1PG 1DG 3T)   **WELSH YOUTH 8** (1PG 1T)
FRANCE *Tries:* Casteignede (2), Horta, Saunier   *Conversion:* Peclier
Penalty Goal: Peclier   *Dropped Goal:* Casteignede
WALES *Try:* Quinnell   *Penalty Goal:* A Thomas
Referee T Spreadbury (England)

12 March 1994, Brescia

ITALIAN YOUTH 11 (2PG 1T)   **ENGLAND COLTS 12** (1G 1T)
ITALY *Try:* Ambrosio   *Penalty Goals:* Pilat (2)
ENGLAND *Tries:* Benton, Reed   *Conversion:* Jowett
Referee L Crerar (Scotland)

27 March 1994, Cardiff Arms Park

WELSH YOUTH 15 (3T)   **ENGLAND COLTS 10** (2T)
WALES *Tries:* Mably, Stephens, D Davies
ENGLAND *Tries:* Jowett, Benton
Referee J Bacigalupo (Scotland)

2 April 1994, Beveridge Park, Kirkcaldy

SCOTLAND UNDER-18 11 (2PG 1T) **SPAIN UNDER-18 3**
SCOTLAND *Try:* Caldwell *Penalty Goals:* Utterson (2)
Referee A Lewis (Ireland)

3 April 1994, South Wales Police Ground, Bridgend

WELSH YOUTH UNDER-18 6 (2PG) **IRELAND YOUTH UNDER-18 12** (4PG)
WALES *Penalty Goals:* Jervis (2)
IRELAND *Penalty Goals:* Moran (4)
Referee J Wallis (England)

9 April 1994, Ravenhill, Belfast

SCOTLAND UNDER-18 5 (1T) **IRELAND UNDER-18 10** (1G 1PG)
SCOTLAND *Try:* Caldwell
IRELAND *Try:* Cogan *Conversion:* Moran *Penalty Goal:* Moran
Referee J Pearson (England)

9 April 1994, Blundellsands, Merseyside

ENGLAND COLTS 11 (2PG 1T) **SCOTLAND UNDER-19 6** (2PG)
ENGLAND *Try:* Reed *Penalty Goals:* Jowett (2)
SCOTLAND *Penalty Goals:* Richards (2)
Referee R Duhau (France)

16 April 1994, Bridgehaugh, Stirling

SCOTLAND UNDER-19 15 (3PG 2DG) **WELSH YOUTH 25** (2G 2PG 1T)
SCOTLAND *Penalty Goals:* Richards (3) *Dropped Goals:* Duncan (2)
WALES *Tries:* R Jones (2), James *Conversions:* A Thomas (2)
Penalty Goals: A Thomas (2)
Referee G Bordenave (France)

23 April 1994, Moseley

ENGLAND COLTS 11 (2PG 1T) **FRANCE JUNIORS 11** (2PG 1T)
ENGLAND *Try:* Benton *Penalty Goals:* King, Czerpak
FRANCE *Try:* Nadau *Penalty Goals:* Casteignede (2)
Referee A Lewis (Ireland)

A WOODEN SPOON SEASON FOR SCOTLAND AT MANY LEVELS

THE 1993-94 SEASON IN SCOTLAND
Bill McMurtrie *Glasgow Herald*

Scotland's international season was the worst since the Championship whitewash in 1985. Summing it up, Jock Steven, the Scottish Rugby Union president, said at the *Herald* awards dinner in May that even the soup spoon at his table place had been wooden. Only an uninspiring 6-6 draw with Ireland at Lansdowne Road broke a run of defeats which had started with the All Blacks' 51-15 victory at Murrayfield in November. New Zealand had opened their Scottish visit with an 84-5 win over the South of Scotland, the District champions for the third successive time. It was an ominous sign, and though Scotland A and the Scotland Development XV put up more heartening resistance the All Blacks' runaway win at Murrayfield was a severe body-blow to national pride.

A hefty 29-6 defeat followed in Cardiff in January, but Scotland almost pulled off a momentous result when Gregor Townsend struck a dropped goal for a 14-12 lead only minutes from the end of the Calcutta Cup match against England at Murrayfield. Yet there was time enough left for Jon Callard's saving penalty goal for the visitors. The draw in Dublin and the first French win at Murrayfield since 1978 rounded off a forgettable international season in which Scotland scored only one try, when Rob Wainwright galloped over from outside the English 22.

In such a season it was inevitable that Scotland should run through plenty of players, 31 in all, including seven new caps. Only Gavin Hastings, Tony Stanger, Kenny Milne and Paul Burnell played through every match while 11 others, including replacements, had only one appearance each. Nor were Scotland fortunate with injury. Craig Chalmers was replaced against both New Zealand and Wales, Andy Nicol also fell in Cardiff and Gary Armstrong came out of self-imposed exile from international rugby to play against England and Ireland before a hand injury struck him down. Equally cruel blows befell open-side wing forwards, an area, like scrum-half, where Scotland could ill afford losses: Iain Morrison, returning to international rugby after injury, broke a leg in the Cardiff international, and Wainwright's jaw was fractured in the next match after he had scored a try against England.

Scotland's A team enjoyed rare success, though only after defeats by New Zealand in Glasgow and Italy in Rovigo. Kevin McKenzie, Stirling County's hooker, took over the captaincy and led the back-up team to a 24-9 win over the Irish at Ayr and, better still, a 12-9 victory against France A in Rennes.

However, most of the younger international teams suffered a worse fate than even the senior XV. The Under-21s lost all four matches, as did the Schools, and the Under-19s were beaten in their two games.

The Scotland team which lost to Wales at Cardiff. L-R, back row: G W Weir (replacement), A V Sharp (replacement), D A Stark (replacement), P H Wright, I R Morrison, I C Jardine, N G B Edwards, R I Wainwright, D J Turnbull, K S Milne, A G Stanger, D S Wyllie (replacement), K D McKenzie (replacement); front row: C M Chalmers, G P J Townsend, A P Burnell, A G Hastings (capt), D S Munro, A D Nicol, K M Logan, B W Redpath (replacement).

Only the Under-18s broke the mould with an 11-3 victory over Spain at Kirkcaldy, but they could not consolidate their success, losing 5-10 to Ireland at Ravenhill.

South retained the McEwan's 70/- District title in a truncated championship played as knock-out instead of in the usual league format. The Borderers beat North and Midlands 37-13 at Riverside Park, Gala wing Chris Dalgleish scoring two tries on his District debut, and the South went on to a 28-14 win over Glasgow in the final at Melrose. But the champions then lost to the All Blacks as well as falling to Ulster (26-44 at Ravenhill) and 16-26 to Leinster (at Melrose) in the new series between the Scottish districts and the Irish provinces. Glasgow beat both Munster (22-17 at New Anniesland) and Connacht (47-25 in Galway), and Edinburgh, too, won their two matches – 13-8 against Leinster at Donnybrook, and 39-13 against Ulster at Hawkhill, Leith.

The South were also winners of the Under-21 and Under-18 District Championships, and the McEwan's 70/- National League title, too, stayed in the Borders: Melrose won it for the third successive season as well as taking the Bank of Scotland Border League for the fifth year in a row. Gala dominated the Border spring sevens, winning three of the five April prizes, including the prestigious Bell's Melrose tournament.

Boroughmuir regained the Alloa Cup in the unofficial national knock-out competition, beating Dundee High School FP by 42-18 in the final. Dundee, Alloa winners the previous year, had consolation as their second team beat Dunfermline 21-6 in the Tennents Midlands Cup final.

Glasgow broke the South's domination by winning the Bank of Scotland schools district title. The Schools Cup, too, stayed in the west, won by Marr College from Troon.

A FITTING FINALE FOR TELFER

McEWAN'S 70/- NATIONAL LEAGUE REVIEW

Melrose retained the McEwan's 70/- National League trophy for the fourth time in five years even though they lost at home in their opening match against Gala. The backlash was a 65-23 victory for the champions against Watsonians at the Greenyards the following week, and Melrose went on to win all of their remaining League games, tying up the title with a 74-10 victory over Currie at Malleny Park. It was the biggest score and winning margin Melrose had had in the 21 years of the competition, and it was, too, a fitting parting gift to Jim Telfer, who retired as the club's coach because of his appointment as the Scottish Rugby Union's director of rugby. Gary Parker, Melrose's effervescent wing, scored 190 of their 410 League points. He had 20 of the points against Watsonians, and surpassed that figure with 23 against Selkirk and 24 against Currie. His League tally included nine tries, a figure matched

Edinburgh Academicals' Rob Wainwright scored Scotland's only try of the Five Nations Championship, against England. He was later chosen to lead Scotland on their summer tour to Argentina, but injury ruled him out of the trip.

only by Gordon Waddell, the Gala wing. Derek Stark, Boroughmuir's international wing, had one try fewer.

No club could take advantage of the champions' defeat on the first day of the League season – even Gala could not maintain their early impetus. A 35-20 defeat by Heriot's at Goldenacre pulled Gala back, and even though the Netherdale club immediately responded with a 30-3 home win over another of the contenders, Edinburgh Academicals, they slipped too far off the champions' pace with further defeats, at home by Stirling County and away by Jedforest, who were revitalised by Gary Armstrong's decision to forsake outfield positions and return to his international role at scrum-half.

Gala, coached by Peter Dods, their former international full-back, finished second, though six points behind the champions. Edinburgh Academicals were third, and Heriot's were joint fourth along with Watsonians, who picked up once the Hastings brothers returned to the fold. Academicals had a golden chance to follow Gala's example two weeks after the champions' opening defeat. Melrose were 13 points down at Raeburn Place before they recovered to win 17-16, and Academicals' bid fell further away when they lost at Netherdale two weeks later.

Heriot's were handicapped from the first Saturday, losing 12-18 to Kelso at Poynder Park. Even so, they kept up with the pace by winning seven in a row, including that victory over Gala, but then slipped away by losing their last four matches.

Kelso, champions in 1988 and 1989, and Selkirk were relegated in a tight finish, the first time two Border clubs had gone down together. Selkirk's run of defeats was broken only by a 3-3 draw with Stewart's-Melville FP at Philiphaugh, but Kelso hung on until the last gasp. They grabbed a lifeline with a 15-10 win over Stew-Mel at Poynder Park before falling to another of the former champions, Boroughmuir, by 3-22 in what was effectively a relegation decider at Meggetland.

Glasgow High/Kelvinside, relegated the previous season with a plus points difference, bounced back up, winning the Second Division title with maximum points. Dundee High School FP made an immediate return to the top flight, losing only to GHK at Old Anniesland.

Nowhere was the contest for promotion tighter than in the Third Division, where five clubs took turns at leading the way. Gordonians were the first to come through, winning the division title, a sharp contrast to their relegation escapes in previous seasons, and Corstorphine edged out Kilmarnock in a head-to-head decider for the runners-up spot, as Hillhead/Jordanhill and Hutchesons'/Aloysians also failed to fulfil earlier promise.

Duns and Glenrothes won promotion from the Fifth Division only on points difference from Linlithgow. It was the third successive year Duns had taken a step up, and Annan, too, won promotion three seasons in a row. Annan, who, like GHK, won all of their season's League matches, took the Seventh Division championship to add to their victory in the Glasgow and District League's Second and First Divisions in the two previous seasons.

McEWAN'S 70/- NATIONAL LEAGUE 1993-94

Division 1	P	W	D	L	F	A	Pts
Melrose	13	12	0	1	410	192	24
Gala	12	9	0	3	274	214	18
Edinburgh Acs	13	8	1	4	265	183	17
Heriot's FP	12	7	0	5	230	224	14
Watsonians	13	7	0	6	276	337	14
Stirling County	12	6	1	5	227	163	13
Hawick	12	6	1	5	218	178	13
Jedforest	13	6	0	7	231	199	12
Currie	12	6	0	6	230	285	12
Stewart's-Mel	13	5	1	7	157	190	11
Boroughmuir	12	5	0	7	214	228	10
W of Scotland	13	4	1	8	235	279	9
Kelso	13	4	0	9	175	296	8
Selkirk	13	0	1	12	138	312	1

Previous champions: Hawick 10 times, 1973-74 to 1977-78, 1981-82, 1983-84 to 1986-87; Gala 3 times, 1979-80, 1980-81, 1982-83; Melrose 3 times, 1989-90, 1991-92, 1992-93; Kelso twice, 1987-88, 1988-89; Heriot's FP 1979-80; Boroughmuir 1990-91.

Division 2	P	W	D	L	F	A	Pts
Glasgow H/K	13	13	0	0	440	115	26
Dundee HSFP	12	11	0	1	395	80	22
Kirkcaldy	13	10	0	3	277	150	20
Edinburgh W	13	8	0	5	214	251	16
Musselburgh	13	7	0	6	204	185	14
Peebles	13	6	0	7	206	219	12
Glasgow Acs	13	5	1	7	237	276	11
Wigtownshire	13	5	0	8	172	241	10
Haddington	12	5	0	7	146	220	10
Grangemouth	13	4	1	8	201	293	9
Biggar	13	3	2	8	203	240	8
Preston Lodge	13	4	0	9	158	291	8
Clarkston	13	4	0	9	158	357	8
Ayr	13	3	0	10	168	261	6

Division 3	P	W	D	L	F	A	Pts
Gordonians	13	10	1	2	263	123	21
Corstorphine	13	10	0	3	237	161	20
Kilmarnock	13	9	1	3	277	129	19
Hillhead/J'hill	13	9	0	4	223	109	18
Hutchesons'/Al	13	8	0	5	216	159	16
Langholm	12	7	0	5	224	124	14
East Kilbride	13	7	0	6	190	192	14
Royal High	13	6	0	7	176	169	12
Stewartry	13	4	2	7	125	168	10

	P	W	D	L	F	A	Pts
Portobello FP	13	5	0	8	172	237	10
Dunfermline	12	4	1	7	153	228	9
Dumfries	13	4	1	8	148	240	9
Howe of Fife	13	3	0	10	161	309	6
Perthshire	13	1	0	12	86	303	2

Division 4	P	W	D	L	F	A	Pts
Trinity Acs	13	11	0	2	293	149	22
Edinburgh U	13	10	1	2	287	155	21
Dalziel HSFP	12	9	0	3	176	144	18
Livingston	12	8	0	4	215	157	16
Ardrossan Acs	12	7	1	4	145	148	15
Cambuslang	12	7	0	5	214	183	14
St Boswells	12	6	0	6	144	194	12
Morgan FP	12	5	0	7	179	173	10
Highland	13	5	0	8	191	239	10
Alloa	13	5	0	8	163	217	10
Aberdeen GSFP	13	4	0	9	251	249	8
North Berwick	13	4	0	9	158	267	8
Cartha QP	13	3	1	9	158	216	7
Leith Acs	13	2	1	10	122	205	5

Division 5	P	W	D	L	F	A	Pts
Duns	13	9	2	2	328	153	20
Glenrothes	13	10	0	3	288	168	20
Linlithgow	13	10	0	3	225	138	20
Falkirk	13	7	2	4	195	130	16
Berwick	13	8	0	5	184	138	16
Penicuik	13	7	0	6	241	209	14
Clydebank	13	5	1	7	134	176	11
Paisley	13	5	0	8	201	195	10
Irvine	13	5	0	8	158	198	10
Lismore	13	5	0	8	167	219	10
Madras FP	13	5	0	8	208	295	10
Hillfoots	13	5	0	8	160	275	10
Lenzie	13	4	0	9	204	296	8
Aberdeenshire	13	3	1	9	117	220	7

Division 6	P	W	D	L	F	A	Pts
Allan Glen's	13	12	0	1	372	96	24
Cumbernauld	13	12	0	1	270	106	24
Forrester FP	13	7	0	6	231	205	14
St Andrews U	13	7	0	6	197	328	14
Greenock W	13	6	1	6	322	250	13
Dunbar	13	6	1	6	230	184	13
Ross High	13	6	1	6	213	178	13
Murrayfield	13	6	0	7	301	225	12
Marr	13	6	0	7	215	191	12

Earlston	13	5	1	7	163	249	11
Waysiders/Dr	13	5	0	8	180	312	10
Harris FP	13	4	1	8	149	218	9
Moray	13	4	0	9	150	284	8
Lasswade	13	2	1	10	126	293	5

Division 7	P	W	D	L	F	A	Pts
Annan	12	12	0	0	501	78	24
Aberdeen U	12	8	0	4	312	170	16
Holy Cross	12	8	0	4	299	167	16
Garnock	12	8	0	4	184	121	16
Whitecraigs	12	6	1	5	158	177	13
Hyndland FP	12	6	1	5	149	220	13
Waid FP	12	6	0	6	236	195	12
Broughton FP	12	6	0	6	175	189	12
Panmure	12	4	2	6	194	228	10
Walkerburn	12	4	0	8	214	254	8
RAF Kinloss	12	4	0	8	160	245	8
Dalkeith	12	3	2	7	90	211	8
Montrose	12	0	0	12	99	516	0

Stirling University expelled from National League for failing to fulfil fixtures.

District League Champions (*promoted to Division 7*):
Glasgow: Cumnock

Edinburgh: Edinburgh Northern
North & Midlands: Lochaber

BANK OF SCOTLAND BORDER LEAGUE

	P	W	D	L	F	A	Pts
Melrose	11	10	0	1	355	119	20
Jedforest	12	7	1	4	289	139	15
Hawick	10	7	1	2	219	113	15
Gala	8	5	0	3	123	169	10
Kelso	12	4	0	8	209	265	8
Selkirk	10	2	0	8	124	200	4
Langholm	9	0	0	9	39	353	0

McEWAN'S DISTRICT CHAMPIONSHIP

	P	W	D	L	F	A	Pts
South	2	2	0	0	65	27	4
Glasgow	2	1	0	1	35	34	2
Edinburgh	2	1	0	1	34	46	2
North & Midlands	2	0	0	2	38	65	0

McEWAN'S 70/- DISTRICT CHAMPIONSHIP 1993-94

23 October, Hughenden
Glasgow 21 (6PG 1DG) **Edinburgh 6** (1PG 1DG)

Glasgow: K M Logan (Stirling County); A S M Turner (Stirling County), S McIntosh (West of Scotland), I C Jardine (Stirling County), R A G Porter (Edinburgh Acads); D N Barrett (West of Scotland), F H Stott (West of Scotland); A G J Watt (Glasgow High/Kelvinside), K D McKenzie (Stirling County), G B Robertson (Stirling County), J S Hamilton (Stirling County), D S Munro (Glasgow High/Kelvinside), F D Wallace (Glasgow High/Kelvinside), (capt), M I Wallace (Glasgow High/Kelvinside), J Brough (Stirling County) *Replacement* G T Mackay (Stirling County) for M I Wallace (65 mins)
Scorer *Penalty Goals:* Barrett (6)   *Dropped Goal:* Barrett
Edinburgh: I C Glasgow (Heriot's FP); K R Milligan (Stewart's-Melville FP), S Hastings (Watsonians) (capt), S R P Lineen (Boroughmuir), J A Kerr (Watsonians); D S Wyllie (Stewart's-Melville FP), D W Patterson (Edinburgh Acads); G D Wilson (Boroughmuir), A Robertson (Musselburgh), P H Wright (Boroughmuir), J F Richardson (Edinburgh Acads), A E D Macdonald (Heriot's FP), G J Drummond (Boroughmuir), D Mack (Currie), S J Reid (Boroughmuir)
Scorer *Penalty Goal:* Glasgow   *Dropped Goal:* Glasgow
Referee W W Calder (Selkirk)

23 October, Riverside Park, Jedburgh
South 37 (3G 2PG 2T) **North & Midlands 13** (1G 2PG)

South: M Dods (Gala); G A Parker (Melrose), S A Nichol (Selkirk), B A J Swan (Gala), C S Dalgleish (Gala); A G Shiel (Melrose), B W Redpath (Melrose); G R Isaac (Gala), J A Hay (Hawick), H A Hunter (Gala), R R Brown (Melrose) (capt), G W Weir (Melrose), D J Turnbull (Hawick), J P Amos (Gala), C D Hogg (Melrose)
Scorers *Tries:* Amos, Dalgleish (2), Dods, Shiel   *Conversions:* Parker (3)   *Penalty Goals:* Parker (2)
North & Midlands: S A D Burns (Edinburgh Acads) (capt); G Stirling (Stewart's-Melville FP), P R Rouse (Dundee HSFP), R J S Shepherd (Edinburgh Acads), J F Swanson (Edinburgh Acads); B R Easson (Boroughmuir), A Imrie (Stirling County); J J Manson (Dundee HSFP), M W Scott (Edinburgh Acads), D W Herrington (Dundee HSFP), B H Bell (Highland), S J Campbell (Dundee HSFP), D J McIvor (Dundee HSFP), D H Mitchell (Edinburgh Acads), R I Wainwright (Edinburgh Acads)   *Replacement* P W B Flockhart (Stewart's-Melville FP) for Rouse (66 mins)
Scorers *Try:* Scott   *Conversion:* Easson   *Penalty Goals:* Easson (2)
Referee R S Clark (Stewart's-Melville FP)

30 October, The Greenyards, Melrose (Championship Final)
South 28 (2G 2PG 1DG 1T)   **Glasgow 14** (3PG 1T)

South: M Dods (Gala); A G Stanger (Hawick), S A Nichol (Selkirk), A G Shiel (Melrose), G A Parker (Melrose); C M Chalmers (Melrose), B W Redpath (Melrose); G R Isaac (Gala), J A Hay (Hawick), H A Hunter (Gala), R R Brown (Melrose) (*capt*), G W Weir (Melrose), D J Turnbull (Hawick), J P Amos (Gala), C D Hogg (Melrose)
Replacement D W Hunter (Selkirk) for Dods (56 mins)
Scorers *Tries:* Chalmers, Nichol, Turnbull   *Conversions:* Parker (2)   *Penalty Goals:* Parker (2)
Dropped Goal Chalmers
Glasgow: K M Logan (Stirling County); A S M Turner (Stirling County), S McIntosh (West of Scotland), I C Jardine (Stirling County), R A G Porter (Edinburgh Acads); D N Barrett (West of Scotland), F H Stott (West of Scotland); A G J Watt (Glasgow High/Kelvinside), K D McKenzie (Stirling County), G B Robertson (Stirling County), J S Hamilton (Stirling County), D S Munro (Glasgow High/Kelvinside), F D Wallace (Glasgow High/Kelvinside), (*capt*), J D Busby (Glasgow High/Kelvinside), J Brough (Stirling County)
Scorer *Try:* Brough   *Penalty Goals:* Barrett (3)
Referee E F Morrison (England)

30 October, The Greenyards, Melrose (Third-place Play-off)
Edinburgh 28 (5PG 1DG 2T)   **North & Midlands 25** (4PG 1DG 2T)

Edinburgh: A G Hastings (Watsonians) (*capt*); D A Stark (Boroughmuir), S Hastings (Watsonians), S R P Lineen (Boroughmuir), J A Kerr (Watsonians); A Donaldson (Currie), D W Patterson (Edinburgh Acads); P H Wright (Boroughmuir), K S Milne (Heriot's FP), G D Wilson (Boroughmuir), A R Adamson (Edinburgh Acads), A E D Macdonald (Heriot's FP), S A Aitken (Watsonians), D Mack (Currie), S J Reid (Boroughmuir)
Replacement B Ward (Currie) for Mack (half-time)
Scorers *Tries:* A G Hastings, Lineen   *Penalty Goals:* Donaldson (4), A G Hastings   *Dropped Goal:* Donaldson
North & Midlands: S A D Burns (Edinburgh Acads) (*capt*); G Stirling (Stewart's-Melville FP), B Doney (Gordonians), R J S Shepherd (Edinburgh Acads), J F Swanson (Edinburgh Acads); B R Easson (Boroughmuir), A D Nicol (Dundee HSFP); J J Manson (Dundee HSFP), W Scott (Edinburgh Acads), D W Herrington (Dundee HSFP), J G Mathieson (Watsonians), S J Campbell (Dundee HSFP), D J McIvor (Edinburgh Acads), R I Wainwright (Edinburgh Acads), M Waite (Dundee HSFP)   *Replacement* G N Flockhart (Stirling County) (temp)
Scorers *Tries:* Burns, Wainwright   *Penalty Goals:* Easson (4)   *Dropped Goal:* Easson
Referee R J Megson (Edinburgh Wands)

SCOTTISH INTERNATIONAL PLAYERS
(up to 31 March 1994)

ABBREVIATIONS

A – Australia; *Arg* – Argentina; *E* – England; *F* – France; *Fj* – Fiji; *I* – Ireland; *J* – Japan; *NZ* – New Zealand; *R* – Romania; *SA* – South Africa; *W* – Wales; *WS* – Western Samoa; *Z* – Zimbabwe; (C) – Centenary match v England at Murrayfield, 1971 (non-championship); P – Scotland v President's Overseas XV at Murrayfield in SRU's Centenary season, 1972-73; (R) Replacement; (t) – temporary replacement. Entries in square brackets [ ] indicate appearances in the World Cup.

Note: Years given for Five Nations' matches are for second half of season; eg 1972 means season 1971-72. Years for all other matches refer to the actual year of the match. When a series has taken place, figures have been used to denote the particular matches in which players have featured. Thus 1981 *NZ* 1,2 indicates that a player appeared in the first and second Tests of the series. The abandoned game with Ireland at Belfast in 1885 is now included as a cap-match.

Abercrombie, C H (United Services) 1910 *I, E*, 1911 *F, W*, 1913 *F, W*
Abercrombie, J G (Edinburgh U) 1949 *F, W, I*, 1950 *F, W, I, E*
Agnew, W C C (Stewart's Coll FP) 1930 *W, I*
Ainslie, R (Edinburgh Inst FP) 1879 *I, E*, 1880 *I, E*, 1881 *E*, 1882 *I, E*
Ainslie, T (Edinburgh Inst FP) 1881 *E*, 1882 *I, E*, 1883 *W, I, E*, 1884 *W, I, E*, 1885 *W, I*,2
Aitchison, G R (Edinburgh Wands) 1883 *I*
Aitchison, T G (Gala) 1929 *W, I, E*
Aitken, A I (Edinburgh Inst FP) 1889 *I*
Aitken, G G (Oxford U) 1924 *W, I, E*, 1925 *F, W, I, E*, 1929 *F*
Aitken, J (Gala) 1977 *E, I, F*, 1981 *F, W, E, I, NZ*1,2, *R, A*, 1982 *E, I, F, W*, 1983 *F, W, E, NZ*,1984 *W, E, I, F, E*
Aitken, R (London Scottish) 1947 *W*
Allan, B (Glasgow Acads) 1881 *I*
Allan, J (Edinburgh Acads) 1990 *NZ*1, 1991 *W, I, R, [J, I, WS, E, NZ]*
Allan, J L (Melrose) 1952 *F, W, I*, 1953 *W*
Allan, J L F (Cambridge U) 1957 *I, E*
Allan, J W (Melrose) 1927 *F*, 1928 *I*, 1929 *F, W, I, E*, 1930 *F, E*, 1931 *F, W, I, E*, 1932 *SA, W, I*, 1934 *I, E*
Allan, R C (Hutchesons' GSFP) 1969 *I*
Allardice, W D (Aberdeen GSFP) 1947 *A*, 1948 *F, W, I*, 1949 *F, W, I, E*
Allen, H W (Glasgow Acads) 1873 *E*
Anderson, A H (Glasgow Acads) 1894 *I*
Anderson, D G (London Scottish) 1889 *I*, 1890 *W, I, E*, 1891 *W, E*, 1892 *W, E*
Anderson, E (Stewart's Coll FP) 1947 *I, E*
Anderson, J W (W of Scotland) 1872 *E*
Anderson, T (Merchiston) 1882 *I*
Angus, A W (Watsonians) 1909 *W*, 1910 *F, W, E*, 1911 *W, I*, 1912 *F, W, I, E, SA*, 1913 *F, W*, 1914 *E*, 1920 *F, W, I, E*
Anton, P A (St Andrew's U) 1873 *E*
Armstrong, G (Jedforest) 1988 *A*, 1989 *W, E, I, F, Fj, R*, 1990 *I, F, W, E, NZ* 1,2, *Arg*, 1991 *F, W, E, I, R, [J, I, WS, E, NZ]*, 1993 *I, F, W, E*, 1994 *E, I*
Arneil, R J (Edinburgh Acads, Leicester and Northampton) 1968 *I, E, A*,1969 *F, W, I, E, SA*, 1970 *F, W, I, E, A*, 1971 *F, W, I, E*(2[1C]), 1972 *F, W, E, NZ*
Arthur, A (Glasgow Acads) 1875 *E*, 1876 *E*
Arthur, J W (Glasgow Acads) 1871 *E*, 1872 *E*
Asher, A G G (Oxford U) 1882 *I*, 1884 *W, I, E*, 1885 *W*, 1886 *I, E*
Auld, W (W of Scotland) 1889 *W*, 1890 *W*
Auldjo, L J (Abertay) 1878 *E*

Bain, D McL (Oxford U) 1911 *E*, 1912 *F, W, E, SA*, 1913 *F, W, I, E*, 1914 *W, E*
Baird, G R T (Kelso) 1981 *A*, 1982 *E, I, F, W, A* 1,2, 1983 *I, F, W, E, NZ*, 1984 *W, E, I, F, A*, 1985 *I, W, E*, 1986 *F, W, E, I, R*, 1987 *E*, 1988 *I*
Balfour, A (Watsonians) 1896 *W, I, E*, 1897 *E*
Balfour, L M (Edinburgh Acads) 1872 *E*
Bannerman, E M (Edinburgh Acads) 1872 *E*, 1873 *E*
Bannerman, J M (Glasgow HSFP) 1921 *F, W, I, E*, 1922 *F, W, I, E*, 1923 *F, W, I, E*, 1924 *F, W, I, E*, 1925

F, W, I, E, 1926 *F, W, I, E*, 1927 *F, W, I, E, A*, 1928 *F, W, I, E*, 1929 *F, W, I, E*
Barnes, I A (Hawick) 1972 *W*, 1974 *F* (R), 1975 *E* (R), *NZ*, 1977 *I, F, W*
Barrie, R W (Hawick) 1936 *E*
Bearne, K R F (Cambridge U, London Scottish) 1960 *F, W*
Beattie, J A (Hawick) 1929 *F, W*, 1930 *W*, 1931 *F, W, I, E*, 1932 *SA, W, I, E*, 1933 *W, E, I*, 1934 *I, E*, 1935 *W, I, E, NZ*, 1936 *W, I, E*
Beattie, J R (Glasgow Acads) 1980 *I, F, W, E*, 1981 *F, W, E, I*, 1983 *F, W, E, NZ*, 1984 *E* (R), *R, A*, 1985 *I*, 1986 *F, W, E, I, R*, 1987 *I, F, W, E*
Bedell-Sivright, D R (Cambridge U, Edinburgh U) 1900 *W*, 1901 *W, I, E*, 1902 *W, I, E*, 1903 *W, I*, 1904 *W, I, E*, 1905 *NZ*, 1906 *W, I, E, SA*, 1907 *W, I, E*, 1908 *W, I*
Bedell-Sivright, J V (Cambridge U) 1902 *W*
Begbie, T A (Edinburgh Wands) 1881 *I, E*
Bell, D L (Watsonians) 1975 *I, F, W, E*
Bell, J A (Clydesdale) 1901 *W, I, E*, 1902 *W, I, E*
Bell, L H I (Edinburgh Acads) 1900 *E*, 1904 *W, I*
Berkeley, W V (Oxford U) 1926 *F*, 1929 *F, W, I*
Berry, C W (Fettesian-Lorettonians) 1884 *I, E*, 1885 *W, I* 1, 1887 *I, W, E*, 1888 *W, I*
Bertram, D M (Watsonians) 1922 *F, W, I, E*, 1923 *F, W, I, E*, 1924 *W, I, E*
Biggar, A G (London Scottish) 1969 *SA*, 1970 *F, I, E, A*, 1971 *F, W, I, E* (2[1C]), 1972 *F, W*
Biggar, M A (London Scottish) 1975 *I, F, W, E*, 1976 *W, E, I*, 1977 *I, F, W*, 1978 *F, W, E, NZ*, 1979 *W, E, I, F, NZ*, 1980 *I, F, W, E*
Birkett, G A (Harlequins, London Scottish) 1975 *NZ*
Bishop, J M (Glasgow Acads) 1893 *I*
Bisset, A A (RIE Coll) 1904 *W*
Black, A W (Edinburgh U) 1947 *F, W*, 1948 *E*, 1950 *W, I, E*
Black, W P (Glasgow HSFP) 1948 *F, W, I, E*, 1951 *E*
Blackadder, W F (W of Scotland) 1938 *E*
Blaikie, C F (Heriot's FP) 1963 *I, E*, 1966 *E*, 1968 *A*, 1969 *F, W, I, E*
Blair, P C B (Cambridge U) 1912 *SA*, 1913 *F, W, I, E*
Bolton, W H (W of Scotland) 1876 *E*
Borthwick, J B (Stewart's Coll FP) 1938 *W, I*
Bos, F H ten (Oxford U, London Scottish) 1959 *E*, 1960 *F, W, SA*, 1961 *F, SA, W, I, E*, 1962 *F, W, I, E*, 1963 *F, W, I, E*
Boswell, J D (W of Scotland) 1889 *W, I*, 1890 *W, I, E*, 1891 *W, I, E*, 1892 *W, I, E*, 1893 *I, E*, 1894 *I, E*
Bowie, T C (Watsonians) 1913 *I, E*, 1914 *I, E*
Boyd, G M (Glasgow HSFP) 1926 *E*
Boyd, J L (United Services) 1912 *E, SA*
Boyle, A C W (London Scottish) 1963 *F, W, I*
Boyle, A H W (St Thomas's Hospital, London Scottish) 1966 *A*, 1967 *F, NZ*, 1968 *F, W, I*
Brash, J C (Cambridge U) 1961 *E*
Breakey, R W (Gosforth) 1978 *E*
Brewis, N T (Edinburgh Inst FP) 1876 *E*, 1878 *E*, 1879 *I, E*, 1880 *I, E*
Brewster, A K (Stewart's-Melville FP) 1977 *E*, 1980 *I, F*, 1986 *E, I, R*
Brown, A H (Heriot's FP) 1928 *E*, 1929 *F, W*
Brown, A R (Gala) 1971 *E* (2[1C]), 1972 *F, W, E*

Brown, C H C (Dunfermline) 1929 *E*
Brown, D I (Cambridge U) 1933 *W, E, I*
Brown, G L (W of Scotland) 1969 *SA*, 1970 *F, W* (R), *I, E, A*, 1971 *F, W, I, E* (2[1C]), 1972 *F, W, E, NZ*, 1973 *E* (R), *P*, 1974 *W, E, I, F*, 1975 *I, F, W, E, A*, 1976 *F, W, E, I*
Brown, J A (Glasgow Acads) 1908 *W, I*
Brown, J B (Glasgow Acads) 1879 *I, E*, 1880 *I, E*, 1881 *I, E*, 1882 *I, E*, 1883 *W, I, E*, 1884 *W, I, E*, 1885 *I* 1,2, 1886 *W, I, E*
Brown, P C (W of Scotland, Gala) 1964 *F, NZ, W, I, E*, 1965 *I, E, SA*, 1966 *A*, 1969 *I, E*, 1970 *W, E*, 1971 *F, W, I, E* (2[1C]), 1972 *F, W, E, NZ*, 1973 *F, W, I, E, P*
Brown, T G (Heriot's FP) 1929 *W*
Brown, W D (Glasgow Acads) 1871 *E*, 1872 *E*, 1873 *E*, 1874 *E*, 1875 *E*
Brown, W S (Edinburgh Inst FP) 1880 *I, E*, 1882 *I, E*, 1883 *W, E*
Browning, A (Glasgow HSFP) 1920 *I*, 1922 *F, W, I*, 1923 *W, I, E*
Bruce, C R (Glasgow Acads) 1947 *F, W, I, E*, 1949 *F, W, I, E*
Bruce, N S (Blackheath, Army and London Scottish) 1958 *F, A, I, E*, 1959 *F, W, I, E*, 1960 *F, W, I, E, SA*, 1961 *F, SA, W, I, E*, 1962 *F, W, I, E*, 1963 *F, W, I, E*, 1964 *F, NZ, W, I, E*
Bruce, R M (Gordonians) 1947 *A*, 1948 *F, W, I*
Bruce-Lockhart, J H (London Scottish) 1913 *W*, 1920 *E*
Bruce-Lockhart, L (London Scottish) 1948 *E*, 1950 *F, W*, 1953 *I, E*
Bruce-Lockhart, R B (Cambridge U and London Scottish) 1937 *I*, 1939 *I, E*
Bryce, C C (Glasgow Acads) 1873 *E*, 1874 *E*
Bryce, R D H (W of Scotland) 1973 *I* (R)
Bryce, W E (Selkirk) 1922 *W, I, E*, 1923 *F, W, I, E*, 1924 *F, W, I, E*
Brydon, W R C (Heriot's FP) 1939 *W*
Buchanan, A (Royal HSFP) 1871 *E*
Buchanan, F G (Kelvinside Acads and Oxford U) 1910 *F*, 1911 *F, W*
Buchanan, J C R (Stewart's Coll FP) 1921 *W, I, E*, 1922 *W, I, E*, 1923 *F, W, I, E*, 1924 *F, W, I, E*, 1925 *F, I*
Buchanan-Smith, G A E (London Scottish, Heriot's FP) 1989 *Fj* (R), 1990 *Arg*
Bucher, A M (Edinburgh Acads) 1897 *E*
Budge, G M (Edinburgh Wands) 1950 *F, W, I, E*
Bullmore, H H (Edinburgh U) 1902 *I*
Burnell, A P (London Scottish) 1989 *E, I, F, Fj, R*, 1990 *I, F, W, E, Arg*, 1991 *F, W, E, I, R, [J, Z, I, WS, E, NZ]*, 1992 *E, I, F, W*, 1993 *I, F, W, E, NZ*, 1994 *W, E, I, F*
Burnet, P J (London Scottish and Edinburgh Acads) 1960 *SA*
Burnet, W (Hawick) 1912 *E*
Burnet, W A (W of Scotland) 1934 *W*, 1935 *W, I, E, NZ*, 1936 *W, I, E*
Burnett, J N (Heriot's FP) 1980 *I, F, W, E*
Burrell, G (Gala) 1950 *F, W, I*, 1951 *SA*

Cairns, A G (Watsonians) 1903 *W, I, E*, 1904 *W, I, E*, 1905 *W, I, E*, 1906 *W, I, E*
Calder, F (Stewart's-Melville FP) 1986 *F, W, E, I, R*, 1987 *I, F, W, E, [F, Z, R, NZ]*, 1988 *I, F, W, E*, 1989 *W, E, I, F, R*, 1990 *I, F, W, E, NZ* 1,2, 1991 *R, [J, WS, E, NZ]*
Calder, J H (Stewart's-Melville FP) 1981 *F, W, E, I, NZ* 1,2, *R, A*, 1982 *E, I, F, W, A* 1,2, 1983 *I, F, W, E, NZ*, 1984 *W, E, I, F, A*, 1985 *I, F, W*
Callander, G J (Kelso) 1984 *R*, 1988 *I, F, W, E, A*
Cameron, A (Glasgow HSFP) 1948 *W*, 1950 *I, E*, 1951 *F, W, I, E, SA*, 1953 *I, E*, 1955 *F, W, I, E*, 1956 *F, W, I*
Cameron, A D (Hillhead HSFP) 1951 *F*, 1954 *F, W*
Cameron, A W (Watsonians) 1887 *W*, 1893 *W*, 1894 *I*
Cameron, D (Glasgow HSFP) 1953 *I, E*, 1954 *F, NZ, I, E*
Cameron, N W (Glasgow U) 1952 *E*, 1953 *F, W*
Campbell, A J (Hawick) 1984 *I, F, R*, 1985 *I, F, W, E*, 1986 *F, W, E, I, R*, 1988 *F, W, A*
Campbell, G T (London Scottish) 1892 *W, I, E*, 1893 *I, E*, 1894 *W, I, E*, 1895 *W, I, E*, 1896 *W, I, E*, 1897 *I*, 1899 *I*, 1900 *E*
Campbell, H H (Cambridge U, London Scottish) 1947 *I, E*, 1948 *I, E*

Campbell, J A (W of Scotland) 1878 *E*, 1879 *I, E*, 1881 *I, E*
Campbell, J A (Cambridge U) 1900 *I*
Campbell, N M (London Scottish) 1956 *F, W*
Campbell-Lamerton, J R E (London Scottish) 1986 *F*, 1987 *[Z, R(R)]*
Campbell-Lamerton, M J (Halifax, Army, London Scottish) 1961 *F, SA, W, I*, 1962 *F, W, I, E*, 1963 *F, W, I, E*, 1964 *I, E*, 1965 *F, W, I, E, SA*, 1966 *F, W, I, E*
Carmichael, A B (W of Scotland) 1967 *I, NZ*, 1968 *F, W, I, E, A*, 1969 *F, W, I, E, SA*, 1970 *F, W, I, E, A*, 1971 *F, W, I, E* 2[1C]), 1972 *F, W, E, NZ*, 1973 *F, W, I, E, P*, 1974 *W, E, I, F*, 1975 *I, F, W, E, NZ, A*, 1976 *F, W, E, I*, 1977 *E, I*(R), *F, W*, 1978 *I*
Carmichael, J H (Watsonians) 1921 *F, W, I*
Carrick, J S (Glasgow Acads) 1876 *E*, 1877 *E*
Cassels, D Y (W of Scotland) 1880 *E*, 1881 *I*, 1882 *I, E*, 1883 *W, I, E*
Cathcart, C W (Edinburgh U) 1872 *E*, 1873 *E*, 1876 *E*
Cawkwell, G L (Oxford U) 1947 *E*
Chalmers, C M (Melrose) 1989 *W, E, I, F, Fj*, 1990 *I, F, W, E, NZ* 1,2, *Arg*, 1991 *F, W, E, I, R, [J, Z(R)], I, WS, E, NZ]*, 1992 *E, I, F, W, A* 1,2, 1993 *I, F, W, E, NZ*, 1994 *W*
Chalmers, T (Glasgow Acads) 1871 *E*, 1872 *E*, 1873 *E*, 1874 *E*, 1875 *E*, 1876 *E*
Chambers, H F T (Edinburgh U) 1888 *W, I*, 1889 *W, I*
Charters, R G (Hawick) 1955 *W, I, E*
Chisholm, D H (Melrose) 1964 *I, E*, 1965 *E, SA*, 1966 *F, I, E, A*, 1967 *F, W, NZ*, 1968 *F, W, I*
Chisholm, R W T (Melrose) 1955 *I, E*, 1956 *F, W, I, E*, 1958 *F, W, A, I*, 1960 *SA*
Church, W C (Glasgow Acads) 1906 *W*
Clark, R L (Edinburgh Wands, Royal Navy) 1972 *F, W, E, NZ*, 1973 *F, W, I, E, P*
Clauss, P R A (Oxford U) 1891 *W, I, E*, 1892 *W, E*, 1895 *I*
Clay, A T (Edinburgh Acads) 1886 *W, I, E*, 1887 *I, W, E*, 1888 *W*
Clunies-Ross, A (St Andrews U) 1871 *E*
Coltman, S (Hawick) 1948 *I*, 1949 *F, W, I, E*
Colville, A G (Merchistonians, Blackheath) 1871 *E*, 1872 *E*
Connell, G C (Trinity Acads and London Scottish) 1968 *E, A*, 1969 *F, E*, 1970 *F*
Cooper, M McG (Oxford U) 1936 *W, I*
Corcoran, I (Gala) 1992 *A* 1(R)
Cordial, I F (Edinburgh Wands) 1952 *F, W, I, E*
Cotter, J L (Hillhead HSFP) 1934 *I, E*
Cottington, G S (Kelso) 1934 *I, E*, 1935 *W, I*, 1936 *E W, I, E*, 1963 *F, W, I, E*
Coughtrie, S (Edinburgh Acads) 1959 *F, W, I, E*, 1962 *W, I, E*, 1963 *F, W, I, E*
Couper, J H (W of Scotland) 1896 *W, I*, 1899 *I*
Coutts, F H (Melrose, Army) 1947 *W, I, E*
Coutts, I D F (Old Alleynians) 1951 *F*, 1952 *E*
Cowan, R C (Selkirk) 1961 *F*, 1962 *F, W, I, E*
Cowie, W L K (Edinburgh Wands) 1953 *E*
Cownie, W B (Watsonians) 1893 *W, I, E*, 1894 *W, I, E*, 1895 *W, I, E*
Crabbie, G E (Edinburgh Acads) 1904 *W*
Crabbie, J E (Edinburgh Acads, Oxford U) 1900 *W*, 1902 *I*, 1903 *W, I*, 1904 *E*, 1905 *W*
Craig, J B (Heriot's FP) 1939 *W*
Cramb, R I (Harlequins) 1987 *[R(R)]*, 1988 *I, F, A*
Cranston, A G (Hawick) 1976 *W, E, I*, 1977 *E, I*, 1978 *F* (R), *W, E, NZ*, 1981 *NZ* 1,2
Crawford, J A (Army, London Scottish) 1934 *I*
Crawford, W H (United Services, RN) 1938 *W, I, E*, 1939 *W, E*
Crichton-Miller, D (Gloucester) 1931 *W, I, E*
Crole, G B (Oxford U) 1920 *F, W, I, E*
Cronin, D F (Bath, London Scottish) 1988 *I, F, W, E, A*, 1989 *W, E, I, F, Fj, R*, 1990 *I, F, W, E, NZ* 1,2, 1991 *W, E, I, R, [Z]*, 1992 *A* 2, 1993 *I, F, W, E, NZ*
Cross, M (Merchistonians) 1875 *E*, 1876 *E*, 1877 *I, E*, 1878 *E*, 1879 *I, E*, 1880 *I, E*
Cross, W (Merchistonians) 1871 *E*, 1872 *E*
Cumming, R S (Aberdeen U) 1921 *F, W*
Cunningham, G (Oxford U) 1908 *W, I*, 1909 *W, E*, 1910 *F, I, E*, 1911 *E*
Cunningham, R F (Gala) 1978 *NZ*, 1979 *W, E*
Currie, L R (Dunfermline) 1947 *A*, 1948 *F, W, I*, 1949 *F, W, I, E*
Cuthbertson, W (Kilmarnock, Harlequins) 1980 *I*,

1981 *W, E, I, NZ* 1,2, *R, A*, 1982 *E, I, F, W, A* 1,2, 1983 *I, F, W, NZ*, 1984 *W, E, A*

Dalgleish, A (Gala) 1890 *W, E*, 1891 *W, I*, 1892 *W*, 1893 *W*, 1894 *W, I*
Dalgleish, K J (Edinburgh Wands, Cambridge U) 1951 *I, E*, 1953 *F, W*
Dallas, J D (Watsonians) 1903 *E*
Davidson, J A (London Scottish, Edinburgh Wands) 1959 *E*, 1960 *I, E*
Davidson, J N G (Edinburgh U) 1952 *F, W, I, E*, 1953 *F, W*, 1954 *F*
Davidson, J P (RIE Coll) 1873 *E*, 1874 *E*
Davidson, R S (Royal HSFP) 1893 *E*
Davies, D S (Hawick) 1922 *F, W, I, E*, 1923 *F, W, I, E*, 1924 *F, E*, 1925 *W, I, E*, 1926 *F, W, I, E*, 1927 *F, W, I*
Dawson, J C (Glasgow Acads) 1947 *A*, 1948 *F, W*, 1949 *F, W, I*, 1950 *F, W, I, E*, 1951 *F, W, I, E, SA*, 1952 *F, W, I, E*, 1953 *E*
Deans, C T (Hawick) 1978 *F, W, E, NZ*, 1979 *W, E, I, F, NZ*, 1980 *I, F*, 1981 *F, W, E, I, NZ* 1,2, *R, A*, 1982 *I, F, W, A* 1,2, 1983 *I, F, W, E, NZ*, 1984 *E, I, F, A*, 1985 *I, F, W, E*, 1986 *F, W, E, I, R*, 1987 *I, F, W, E, [F, Z, R, NZ]*
Deans, D T (Hawick) 1968 *E*
Deas, D W (Heriot's FP) 1947 *F, W*
Dick, L G (Loughborough Colls, Jordanhill, Swansea) 1972 *W* (R), *E*, 1974 *W, E, I, F*, 1975 *I, F, W, E, NZ, A*, 1976 *F*, 1977 *E*
Dick, R C S (Cambridge U, Guy's Hospital) 1934 *W, I, E*, 1935 *W, I, E, NZ*, 1936 *W, I, E*, 1937 *W*, 1938 *W, I, E*
Dickson, G (Gala) 1978 *NZ*, 1979 *W, E, I, F, NZ*, 1980 *W*, 1981 *F*, 1982 *W* (R)
Dickson, M R (Edinburgh U) 1905 *I*
Dickson, W M (Blackheath, Oxford U) 1912 *F, W, E, SA*, 1913 *F, W, I*
Dobson, J (Glasgow Acads) 1911 *E*, 1912 *F, W, I, E, SA*
Dobson, J D (Glasgow Acads) 1910 *I*
Dobson, W G (Heriot's FP) 1922 *W, I, E*,
Docherty, J T (Glasgow HSFP) 1955 *F, W*, 1956 *E*, 1958 *F, W, A, I, E*
Dods, F P (Edinburgh Acads) 1901 *I*
Dods, J H (Edinburgh Acads) 1895 *W, I, E*, 1896 *W, I, E*, 1897 *I, E*
Dods, M (Gala) 1994 *I*(t)
Dods, P W (Gala) 1983 *I, F, W, E, NZ*, 1984 *W, E, I, F, R, A*, 1985 *I, F, W, E*, 1989 *W, E, I, F*, 1991 *I*(R), *R, [Z, NZ*(R)]
Donald, D G (Oxford U) 1914 *W, I*
Donald, R L H (Glasgow HSFP) 1921 *W, I, E*
Donaldson, W P (Oxford U, W of Scotland) 1893 *I*, 1894 *I*, 1895 *E*, 1896 *I, E*, 1899 *I*
Don-Wauchope, A R (Fettesian-Lorettonians) 1881 *E*, 1882 *E*, 1883 *W*, 1884 *W, I, E*, 1885 *W, I* 1,2, 1886 *W, I, E*, 1888 *I*
Don-Wauchope, P H (Fettesian-Lorettonians) 1885 *I* 1,2, 1886 *W*, 1887 *I, W, E*
Dorward, A F (Cambridge U, Gala) 1950 *F*, 1951 *SA*, 1952 *W, I, E*, 1953 *F, W, E*, 1955 *F, I*, 1956 *I, E*, 1957 *F, W, I, E*
Dorward, T F (Gala) 1938 *W, I, E*, 1939 *I, E*
Douglas, G (Jedforest) 1921 *W*
Douglas, J (Stewart's Coll FP) 1961 *F, SA, W, I, E*, 1962 *F, W, I, E*, 1963 *F, W, I*
Douty, P S (London Scottish) 1927 *A*, 1928 *F, W*
Drew, D (Glasgow Acads) 1871 *E*, 1876 *E*
Druitt, W A H (London Scottish) 1936 *W, I, E*
Drummond, A H (Kelvinside Acads) 1938 *W, I*
Drummond, C W (Melrose) 1947 *F, W, I, E*, 1948 *F, I, E*, 1950 *F, W, I, E*
Drybrough, A S (Edinburgh Wands, Merchistonians) 1902 *I*, 1903 *I*
Dryden, R H (Watsonians) 1937 *E*
Drysdale, D (Heriot's FP) 1923 *F, W, I, E*, 1924 *F, W, I, E*, 1925 *W, I, E*, 1926 *F, W, I, E*, 1927 *F, W, I, E, A*, 1928 *F, W, I, E*, 1929 *F*
Duff, P L (Glasgow Acads) 1936 *W, I*, 1938 *W, I, E*, 1939 *W*
Duffy, H (Jedforest) 1955 *F*
Duke, A (Royal HSFP) 1888 *W, I*, 1889 *W, I*, 1890 *W, I*

Duncan, A W (Edinburgh U) 1901 *W, I, E*, 1902 *W, I, E*
Duncan, D D (Oxford U) 1920 *F, W, I, E*
Duncan, M D F (W of Scotland) 1986 *F, W, E, R*, 1987 *I, F, W, E, [F, Z, R, NZ]*, 1988 *I, F, W, E, A*, 1989 *W*
Duncan, M M (Fettesian-Lorettonians) 1888 *W*
Dunlop, J W (W of Scotland) 1875 *E*
Dunlop, Q (W of Scotland) 1971 *E* (2[1C])
Dykes, A S (Glasgow Acads) 1932 *E*
Dykes, J C (Glasgow Acads) 1922 *F, E*, 1924 *I*, 1925 *F, W, I*, 1926 *F, W, I, E*, 1927 *F, W, I, E, A*, 1928 *F, I*, 1929 *F, W, I*
Dykes, J M (Clydesdale, Glasgow HSFP) 1898 *I, E*, 1899 *W, E*, 1900 *W, I*, 1901 *W, I, E*, 1902 *E*

Edwards, D B (Heriot's FP) 1960 *I, E, SA*
Edwards, N G B (Harlequins, Northampton) 1992 *E, I, F, W, A* 1, 1994 *W*
Elgie, M K (London Scottish) 1954 *NZ, I, E, W*, 1955 *F, W, I, E*
Elliot, C (Langholm) 1958 *E*, 1959 *F*, 1960 *F*, 1963 *E*, 1964 *F, NZ, W, I, E*, 1965 *F, W, I*
Elliot, M (Hawick) 1895 *W*, 1896 *E*, 1897 *I, E*, 1898 *I, E*
Elliot, T (Gala) 1905 *E*
Elliot, T (Gala) 1955 *W, I, E*, 1956 *F, W, I, E*, 1957 *F, W, I, E*, 1958 *W, A, I*
Elliot, T G (Langholm) 1968 *W, A*, 1969 *F, W*, 1970 *E*
Elliot, W I D (Edinburgh Acads) 1947 *F, W, E, A*, 1948 *F, W, I, E*, 1949 *F, W, I, E*, 1950 *F, W, I, E*, 1951 *F, W, I, E, SA*, 1952 *F, W, I, E*, 1954 *NZ, I, E, W*
Emslie, W D (Royal HSFP) 1930 *F*, 1932 *I*
Evans, H L (Edinburgh U) 1885 *I* 1,2
Ewart, E N (Glasgow Acads) 1879 *E*, 1880 *I, E*

Fahmy, Dr E C (Abertillery) 1920 *F, W, I, E*
Fasson, F H (London Scottish, Edinburgh Wands) 1900 *W*, 1901 *W, I*, 1902 *W, E*
Fell, A N (Edinburgh U) 1901 *W, I, E*, 1902 *W, E*, 1903 *W, E*
Ferguson, J H (Gala) 1928 *W*
Ferguson, W G (Royal HSFP) 1927 *A*, 1928 *F, W, I, E*
Fergusson, E A J (Oxford U) 1954 *F, NZ, I, E, W*
Finlay, A B (Edinburgh Acads) 1875 *E*
Finlay, J F (Edinburgh Acads) 1871 *E*, 1872 *E*, 1874 *E*, 1875 *E*
Finlay, N J (Edinburgh Acads) 1875 *E*, 1876 *E*, 1878 *E*, 1879 *I, E*, 1880 *I, E*, 1881 *I, E*
Finlay, R (Watsonians) 1948 *E*
Fisher, A T (Waterloo, Watsonians) 1947 *I, E*
Fisher, C D (Waterloo) 1975 *NZ, A*, 1976 *W, E, I*
Fisher, D (W of Scotland) 1893 *I*
Fisher, J P (Royal HSFP, London Scottish) 1963 *E*, 1964 *F, NZ, W, I, E*, 1965 *F, W, I, E, SA*, 1966 *F, W, I, E, A*, 1967 *F, W, I, E, NZ*, 1968 *F, W, I, E*
Fleming, C J N (Edinburgh Wands) 1896 *I, E*, 1897 *I*
Fleming, G R (Glasgow Acads) 1875 *E*, 1876 *E*
Fletcher, H N (Edinburgh U) 1904 *E*, 1905 *W*
Flett, A B (Edinburgh U) 1901 *W, I, E*, 1902 *W, I*
Forbes, J L (Watsonians) 1905 *W*, 1906 *I, E*
Ford, D St C (United Services, RN) 1930 *I, E*, 1931 *E*, 1932 *W, I*
Ford, J R (Gala) 1893 *I*
Forrest, J E (Glasgow Acads) 1932 *SA*, 1935 *E, NZ*
Forrest, J G S (Cambridge U) 1938 *W, I, E*
Forrest, W T (Hawick) 1903 *W, I, E*, 1904 *W, I, E*, 1905 *W, I*
Forsayth, H H (Oxford U) 1921 *F, W, I, E*, 1922 *W, I, E*
Forsyth, I W (Stewart's Coll FP) 1972 *NZ*, 1973 *F, W, I, E, P*
Forsyth, J (Edinburgh U) 1871 *E*
Foster, R A (Hawick) 1930 *W*, 1932 *SA, I, E*
Fox, J (Gala) 1952 *F, W, I, E*
Frame, J N M (Edinburgh U, Gala) 1967 *NZ*, 1968 *F, W, I, E*, 1969 *W, I, E, SA*, 1970 *F, W, I, E, A*, 1971 *F, W, I, E* (2[1C]), 1972 *F, W, E*, 1973 *P* (R)
France, C (Kelvinside Acads) 1903 *I*
Fraser, C F P (Glasgow U) 1888 *W*, 1889 *W*
Fraser, J W (Edinburgh Inst FP) 1881 *E*
Fraser, R (Cambridge U) 1911 *F, W, I, E*
French, J (Glasgow Acads) 1886 *W*, 1887 *I, W, E*
Frew, A (Edinburgh U) 1901 *W, I, E*
Frew, G M (Glasgow HSFP) 1906 *SA*, 1907 *W, I, E*,

1908 *W, I, E*, 1909 *W, I, E*, 1910 *F, W, I*, 1911 *I, E*
Friebe, J P (Glasgow HSFP) 1952 *E*
Fulton, A K (Edinburgh U, Dollar Acads) 1952 *F*, 1954 *F*
Fyfe, K C (Cambridge U, Sale, London Scottish) 1933 *W, E*, 1934 *E*, 1935 *W, I, E, NZ*, 1936 *W, E*, 1939 *I*

Gallie, G H (Edinburgh Acads) 1939 *W*
Gallie, R A (Glasgow Acads) 1920 *F, W, I, E*, 1921 *F, W, I, E*
Gammell, W B B (Edinburgh Wands) 1977 *I, F, W*, 1978 *W, E*
Geddes, I C (London Scottish) 1906 *SA*, 1907 *W, I, E*, 1908 *W, E*
Geddes, K I (London Scottish) 1947 *F, W, I, E*
Gedge, H T S (Oxford U, London Scottish, Edinburgh Wands) 1894 *W, I, E*, 1896 *E*, 1899 *W, E*
Gedge, P M S (Edinburgh Wands) 1933 *I*
Gemmill, R (Glasgow HSFP) 1950 *F, W, I, E*, 1951 *F, W, I*
Gibson, W R (Royal HSFP) 1891 *I, E*, 1892 *W, I, E*, 1893 *W, I, E*, 1894 *W, I, E*, 1895 *W, I, E*
Gilbert-Smith, D S (London Scottish) 1952 *E*
Gilchrist, J (Glasgow Acads) 1925 *F*
Gill, A D (Gala) 1973 *P*, 1974 *W, E, I, F*
Gillespie, J I (Edinburgh Acads) 1899 *E*, 1900 *W, E*, 1901 *W, I, E*, 1902 *W, I*, 1904 *I, E*
Gillies, A C (Watsonians) 1924 *W, I, E*, 1925 *F, W, E*, 1926 *F, W*, 1927 *F, W, I, E*
Gilray, C M (Oxford U, London Scottish) 1908 *E*, 1909 *W, E*, 1912 *I*
Glasgow, R J C (Dunfermline) 1962 *F, W, I, E*, 1963 *I, E*, 1964 *I, E*, 1965 *W, I*
Glen, W S (Edinburgh Wands) 1955 *W*
Gloag, L G (Cambridge U) 1949 *F, W, I, E*
Goodfellow, J (Langholm) 1928 *W, I, E*
Goodhue, F W J (London Scottish) 1890 *W, I, E*, 1891 *W, I, E*, 1892 *W, I, E*
Gordon, R (Edinburgh Wands) 1951 *W*, 1952 *F, W, I, E*, 1953 *W*
Gordon, R E (Royal Artillery) 1913 *F, W, I*
Gordon, R J (London Scottish) 1982 *A 1,2*
Gore, A C (London Scottish) 1882 *I*
Gossman, B M (W of Scotland) 1980 *W*, 1983 *F, W*
Gossman, J S (W of Scotland) 1980 *E* (R)
Gowans, J J (Cambridge U, London Scottish) 1893 *W*, 1894 *W, E*, 1895 *W, I, E*, 1896 *I, E*
Gowland, G C (London Scottish) 1908 *W*, 1909 *W, E*, 1910 *F, W, I, E*
Gracie, A L (Harlequins) 1921 *F, W, I, E*, 1922 *F, W, I, E*, 1923 *F, W, I, E*, 1924 *F*
Graham, I N (Edinburgh Acads) 1939 *I, E*
Graham, J (Kelso) 1926 *I, E*, 1927 *F, W, I, E, A*, 1928 *F, W, I, E*, 1930 *I, E*, 1932 *SA, W*
Graham, J H S (Edinburgh Acads) 1876 *E*, 1877 *I, E*, 1878 *I, E*, 1879 *I, E*, 1880 *I, E*, 1881 *I, E*
Grant, D (Hawick) 1965 *F, E, SA*, 1966 *F, W, I, E, A*, 1967 *F, W, I, E, NZ*, 1968 *F*
Grant, D M (East Midlands) 1911 *W, I*
Grant, M L (Harlequins) 1955 *F*, 1956 *F, W*, 1957 *F*
Grant, T O (Hawick) 1960 *I, E, SA*, 1964 *F, NZ, W*
Grant, W St C (Craigmount) 1873 *E*, 1874 *E*
Gray, C A (Nottingham) 1989 *W, E, I, F, Fj, R*, 1990 *I, F, W, E, NZ 1,2, Arg*, 1991 *F, W, E, I, [J, I, WS, E, NZ]*
Gray, D (W of Scotland) 1978 *E*, 1979 *I, F, NZ*, 1980 *I, F, W, E*, 1981 *W*
Gray, G L (Gala) 1935 *NZ*, 1937 *W, I, E*
Gray, T (Northampton, Heriot's FP) 1950 *F, E*, 1951 *F, E*
Greenlees, H D (Leicester) 1927 *A*, 1928 *F, W*, 1929 *I, E*, 1930 *E*
Greenlees, J R C (Cambridge U, Kelvinside Acads) 1900 *I*, 1902 *W, I, E*, 1903 *W, I, E*
Greenwood, J T (Dunfermline and Perthshire Acads) 1952 *F*, 1955 *F, W, I, E*, 1956 *F, W, I, E*, 1957 *F, W, E*, 1958 *F, W, A, I, E*, 1959 *F, W, I*
Greig, A (Glasgow HSFP) 1911 *I*
Greig, L L (Glasgow Acads, United Services) 1905 *NZ*, 1906 *SA*, 1907 *W*, 1908 *W, I*
Greig, R C (Glasgow Acads) 1893 *W*, 1897 *I*
Grieve, C F (Oxford U) 1935 *W*, 1936 *E*
Grieve, R M (Kelso) 1935 *W, I, E, NZ*, 1936 *W, I, E*
Gunn, A W (Royal HSFP) 1912 *F, W, I, SA*, 1913 *F*

Hamilton, A S (Headingley) 1914 *W*, 1920 *F*
Hamilton, H M (W of Scotland) 1874 *E*, 1875 *E*
Hannah, R S M (W of Scotland) 1971 *I*
Harrower, P R (London Scottish) 1885 *W*
Hart, J G M (London Scottish) 1951 *SA*
Hart, T M (Glasgow U) 1930 *W, I*
Hart, W (Melrose) 1960 *SA*
Harvey, L (Greenock Wands) 1899 *I*
Hastie, A J (Melrose) 1961 *W, I, E*, 1964 *I, E*, 1965 *E, SA*, 1966 *F, W, I, E, A*, 1967 *F, W, I, NZ*, 1968 *F, W*
Hastie, I R (Kelso) 1955 *F*, 1958 *F, E*, 1959 *F, W, I*
Hastie, J D H (Melrose) 1938 *W, I, E*
Hastings, A G (Cambridge U, Watsonians, London Scottish) 1986 *F, W, E, I, R*, 1987 *I, F, W, E, [F, Z, R, NZ]*, 1988 *I, F, W, E, A*, 1989 *Fj, R*, 1990 *I, F, W, E, NZ 1,2, Arg*, 1991 *F, W, E, I, [J, I, WS, E, NZ]*, 1992 *E, I, F, W, A 1*, 1993 *I, F, W, E, NZ*, 1994 *W, E, I, F*
Hastings, S (Watsonians) 1986 *F, W, E, I, R*, 1987 *I, F, W, [R]*, 1988 *I, F, W, A*, 1989 *W, E, I, F, Fj, R*, 1990 *I, F, W, E, NZ 1,2, Arg*, 1991 *F, W, E, I, [J, Z, I, WS, E, NZ]*, 1992 *E, I, F, W, A 1,2*, 1993 *I, F, W, E, NZ*, 1994 *E, I, F*
Hay, B H (Boroughmuir) 1975 *NZ, A*, 1976 *F*, 1978 *I, F, W, E, NZ*, 1979 *W, E, I, F, NZ*, 1980 *I, F, W, E*, 1981 *F, W, E, I, NZ 1,2*
Hay-Gordon, J R (Edinburgh Acads) 1875 *E*, 1877 *I, E*
Hegarty, C B (Hawick) 1978 *I, F, W, E*
Hegarty, J J (Hawick) 1951 *F*, 1953 *F, W, I, E*, 1955 *F*
Henderson, B C (Edinburgh Wands) 1963 *E*, 1964 *F, I, E*, 1965 *F, W, I, E*, 1966 *F, W, I, E*
Henderson, F W (London Scottish) 1900 *W, I*,
Henderson, I C (Edinburgh Acads) 1939 *I, E*, 1947 *F, W, E, A*, 1948 *I, E*
Henderson, J H (Oxford U, Richmond) 1953 *F, W, I, E*, 1954 *F, NZ, I, E, W*
Henderson, J M (Edinburgh Acads) 1933 *W, E, I*
Henderson, J Y M (Watsonians) 1911 *E*
Henderson, M M (Dunfermline) 1937 *W, I, E*
Henderson, N F (London Scottish) 1892 *I*
Henderson, R G (Newcastle Northern) 1924 *I, E*
Hendrie, K G P (Heriot's FP) 1924 *F, W, I*
Hendry, T L (Clydesdale) 1893 *W, I, E*, 1895 *I*
Henriksen, E H (Royal HSFP) 1953 *I*
Hepburn, D P (Woodford) 1947 *A*, 1948 *F, W, I, E*, 1949 *F, W, I, E*
Heron, G (Glasgow Acads) 1874 *E*, 1875 *E*
Hill, C C P (St Andrew's U) 1912 *F, I*
Hinshelwood, A J W (London Scottish) 1966 *F, W, I, E, A*, 1967 *F, W, I, E, NZ*, 1968 *F, W, I, E, A*, 1969 *F, W, I, SA*, 1970 *F, W*
Hodgson, C G (London Scottish) 1968 *I, E*
Hogg, C D (Melrose) 1992 *A 1,2*, 1993 *NZ*(R)
Hogg, C G (Boroughmuir) 1978 *F* (R), *W* (R)
Holms, W F (RIE Coll) 1886 *W, E*, 1887 *I, E*, 1889 *W, I*, 1890 *I, E*, 1939 *W, I, E*
Horsburgh, G B (London Scottish) 1937 *W, I, E*, 1938 *W, I, E*, 1939 *W, I, E*
Howie, D D (Kirkcaldy) 1912 *F, W, I, E, SA*, 1913 *F, W*
Howie, R A (Kirkcaldy) 1924 *F, W, I, E*, 1925 *W, I, E*
Hoyer-Millar, G C (Oxford U) 1953 *I*
Huggan, J L (London Scottish) 1914 *E*
Hume, J (Royal HSFP) 1912 *F*, 1920 *F*, 1921 *F, W, I, E*, 1922 *F*
Hume, J W G (Oxford U, Edinburgh Wands) 1928 *I*, 1930 *F*
Hunter, F (Edinburgh U) 1882 *I*
Hunter, I G (Selkirk) 1984 *I* (R), 1985 *F* (R), *W, E*
Hunter, J M (Cambridge U) 1947 *F*
Hunter, M D (Glasgow High) 1974 *F*
Hunter, W J (Hawick) 1964 *F, NZ, W*, 1967 *F, W, I, E*
Hutchison, W R (Glasgow HSFP) 1911 *E*
Hutton, A H M (Dunfermline) 1932 *I*
Hutton, J E (Harlequins) 1930 *E*, 1931 *F*

Inglis, H M (Edinburgh Acads) 1951 *F, W, I, E, SA*, 1952 *W, I*
Inglis, J M (Selkirk) 1952 *E*
Inglis, W M (Cambridge U, Royal Engineers) 1937 *W, I, E*, 1938 *W, I, E*
Innes, J R S (Aberdeen GSFP) 1939 *W, I, E*, 1947 *A*, 1948 *F, W, I, E*
Ireland, J C H (Glasgow HSFP) 1925 *W, I, E*, 1926 *F, W, I, E*, 1927 *F, W, I, E*
Irvine, A R (Heriot's FP) 1972 *NZ*, 1973 *F, W, I, E, P*,

MacEwan, N A (Gala, Highland) 1971 *F, W, I, E* (2[1C]), 1972 *F, W, E, NZ,* 1973 *F, W, I, E, P,* 1974 *W, E, I, F,* 1975 *W, E*
McEwan, W M C (Edinburgh Acads) 1894 *W, E,* 1895 *W, E,* 1896 *W, I, E,* 1897 *I, E,* 1898 *I, E,* 1889 *I, W, E,* 1900 *W, E*
MacEwen, R K G (Cambridge U, London Scottish) 1954 *F, NZ, I, W,* 1956 *F, W, I, E,* 1957 *F, W, I, E,* 1958 *W*
Macfarlan, D J (London Scottish) 1883 *W,* 1884 *W, I, E,* 1886 *W, I,* 1887 *I,* 1888 *I*
McFarlane, J L H (Edinburgh U) 1871 *E,* 1872 *E,* 1873 *E*
McGaughey, S K (Hawick) 1984 *R*
McGeechan, I R (Headingley) 1972 *NZ,* 1973 *F, W, I, E, P,* 1974 *W, E, I, F,* 1975 *I, F, W, E, NZ, A,* 1976 *F, W, E, I,* 1977 *E, I, F, W,* 1978 *I, F, W, NZ,* 1979 *W, E, I, F*
McGlashan, T P L (Royal HSFP) 1947 *F, I, E,* 1954 *F, NZ, I, E, W*
MacGregor, D G (Watsonians, Pontypridd) 1907 *W, I, E*
MacGregor, G (Cambridge U) 1890 *W, I, E,* 1891 *W, I, E,* 1893 *W, I, E,* 1894 *W, I, E,* 1896 *E*
MacGregor, I A A (Hillhead HSFP, Llanelli) 1955 *I, E,* 1956 *F, W, I, E,* 1957 *F, W, I*
MacGregor, J R (Edinburgh U) 1909 *I*
McGuinness, G M (W of Scotland) 1982 *A* 1,2, 1983 *I,* 1985 *I, F, W, E*
McHarg, A F (W of Scotland, London Scottish) 1968 *I, E, A,* 1969 *F, W, I, E,* 1971 *F, W, I, E* (2[1C]), 1972 *F, E, NZ,* 1973 *F, W, I, E, P,* 1974 *W, E, I, F,* 1975 *I, F, W, E, NZ, A,* 1976 *F, W, E, I,* 1977 *E, I, F, W,* 1978 *I, F, W, NZ,* 1979 *W, E*
McIndoe, F (Glasgow Acads) 1886 *W, I*
MacIntyre, I (Edinburgh Wands) 1890 *W, I, E,* 1891 *W, I, E*
McIvor, D J (Edinburgh Acads) 1992 *E, I, F, W,* 1993 *NZ*
Mackay, E B (Glasgow Acads) 1920 *W,* 1922 *E*
McKeating, E (Heriot's FP) 1957 *F, W,* 1961 *SA, W, I, E*
McKendrick, J G (W of Scotland) 1889 *I*
Mackenzie, A D G (Selkirk) 1984 *A*
Mackenzie, C J G (United Services) 1921 *E*
Mackenzie, D D (Edinburgh U) 1947 *W, I, E,* 1948 *F, W, I*
Mackenzie, D K A (Edinburgh Wands) 1939 *I, E*
Mackenzie, J M (Edinburgh U) 1905 *NZ,* 1909 *W, I, E,* 1910 *W, I, E,* 1911 *W, I*
Mackenzie, R C (Glasgow Acads) 1877 *I, E,* 1881 *I, E*
Mackie, G Y (Highland) 1975 *A,* 1976 *F, W,* 1978 *F*
MacKinnon, A (London Scottish) 1898 *I, E,* 1899 *I, W, E,* 1900 *E*
Mackintosh, C E W C (London Scottish) 1924 *F*
Mackintosh, H S (Glasgow U, W of Scotland) 1929 *F, W, I, E,* 1930 *F, W, I, E,* 1931 *F, W, I, E,* 1932 *SA, W, I, E*
MacLachlan, L P (Oxford U, London Scottish) 1954 *NZ, I, E, W*
Maclagan, W E (Edinburgh Acads) 1878 *E,* 1879 *I, E,* 1880 *I, E,* 1881 *I, E,* 1883 *I, E,* 1883 *W, I, E,* 1884 *W, I, E,* 1885 *W, I* 1,2, 1887 *I, W, E,* 1888 *W, I,* 1890 *W, I, E*
McLaren, A (Durham County) 1931 *F*
McLaren, E (London Scottish, Royal HSFP) 1923 *F, W, I, E,* 1924 *F*
McLauchlan, J (Jordanhill) 1969 *E, SA,* 1970 *F, W,* 1971 *F, W, I, E* (2[1C]), 1972 *F, W, E, NZ,* 1973 *F, W, I, E, P,* 1974 *W, E, I, F,* 1975 *I, F, W, E, NZ, A,* 1976 *F, W, E, I,* 1977 *W,* 1978 *I, F, W, E, NZ,* 1979 *W, E, I, F, NZ*
McLean, D I (Royal HSFP) 1947 *I, E*
Maclennan, W D (Watsonians) 1947 *F, I*
MacLeod, D A (Glasgow U) 1886 *I, E*
MacLeod, G (Edinburgh Acads) 1878 *E,* 1882 *I*
McLeod, H F (Hawick) 1954 *F, NZ, I, E, W,* 1955 *F, W, I, E,* 1956 *F, W, I, E,* 1957 *F, W, I, E,* 1958 *F, W, A, I, E,* 1959 *F, W, I, E,* 1960 *F, W, I, E, SA,* 1961 *F, SA, W, I, E,* 1962 *F, W, I, E*
MacLeod, K G (Cambridge U) 1905 *NZ,* 1906 *W, I, E, SA,* 1907 *W, I, E,* 1908 *I, E*
MacLeod, L M (Cambridge U) 1904 *W, I, E,* 1905 *W, I, NZ*

Macleod, W M (Fettesian-Lorettonians, Edinburgh Wands) 1886 *W, I*
McMillan, K H D (Sale) 1953 *F, W, I, E*
MacMillan, R G (London Scottish) 1887 *W, I, E,* 1890 *W, I, E,* 1891 *W, E,* 1892 *W, I, E,* 1893 *W, E,* 1894 *W, I, E,* 1895 *W, I, E,* 1897 *I, E*
MacMyn, D J (Cambridge U, London Scottish) 1925 *F, W, I, E,* 1926 *F, W, I, E,* 1927 *E, A,* 1928 *F*
McNeil, A S B (Watsonians) 1935 *I*
McPartlin, J J (Harlequins, Oxford U) 1960 *F, W,* 1962 *F, W, I, E*
Macphail, J A R (Edinburgh Acads) 1949 *E,* 1951 *SA*
Macpherson, D G (London Hospital) 1910 *I, E*
Macpherson, G P S (Oxford U, Edinburgh Acads) 1922 *F, W, I, E,* 1924 *W, E,* 1925 *F, W, E,* 1927 *F, W, I, E,* 1928 *F, W, E,* 1929 *I, E,* 1930 *F, W, I, E,* 1931 *W, E,* 1932 *SA, E*
Macpherson, N C (Newport, Mon) 1920 *W, I, E,* 1921 *F, E,* 1923 *I, E*
McQueen, S B (Waterloo) 1923 *F, W, I, E*
Macrae, D J (St Andrews U) 1937 *W, I, E,* 1938 *W, I, E,* 1939 *W, I, E*
Madsen, D F (Gosforth) 1974 *W, E, I, F,* 1975 *I, F, W, E,* 1976 *F,* 1977 *E, I, F, W,* 1978 *I*
Mair, N G R (Edinburgh U) 1951 *F, W, I, E*
Maitland, G (Edinburgh Inst FP) 1885 *W, I* 2
Maitland, R (Edinburgh Inst FP) 1881 *E,* 1882 *I, E,* 1884 *W,* 1885 *W*
Maitland, R P (Royal Artillery) 1872 *E*
Malcolm, A G (Glasgow U) 1888 *I*
Marsh, J (Edinburgh Inst FP) 1889 *W, I*
Marshall, A (Edinburgh Acads) 1875 *E*
Marshall, G R (Selkirk) 1988 *A* (R), 1989 *Fj,* 1990 *Arg,* 1991 *[Z]*
Marshall, J C (London Scottish) 1954 *F, NZ, I, E, W*
Marshall, K W (Edinburgh Acads) 1934 *W, I, E,* 1935 *W, I, E,* 1936 *W, E,* 1937 *E*
Marshall, T R (Edinburgh Acads) 1871 *E,* 1872 *E,* 1873 *E,* 1874 *E*
Marshall, W (Edinburgh Acads) 1872 *E*
Martin, H (Edinburgh Acads, Oxford U) 1908 *W, I, E,* 1909 *W, E*
Masters, W H (Edinburgh Inst FP) 1879 *I,* 1880 *I, E*
Maxwell, F T (Royal Engineers) 1872 *E*
Maxwell, G H H P (Edinburgh Acads, RAF, London Scottish) 1913 *I, E,* 1914 *W, I, E,* 1920 *W, E,* 1921 *F, W, I, E,* 1922 *F, E*
Maxwell, J M (Langholm) 1957 *I*
Mein, J (Edinburgh Acads) 1871 *E,* 1872 *E,* 1873 *E,* 1874 *E,* 1875 *E*
Melville, C L (Army) 1937 *W, I, E*
Menzies, H F (W of Scotland) 1893 *W, I,* 1894 *W, E*
Methuen, A (London Scottish) 1889 *W, I*
Michie, E J S (Aberdeen U, Aberdeen GSFP) 1954 *F, NZ, I, E,* 1955 *W, I, E,* 1956 *F, W, I, E,* 1957 *F, W, I, E*
Millar, J N (W of Scotland) 1892 *W, I, E,* 1893 *W,* 1895 *I, E*
Millar, R K (London Scottish) 1924 *I*
Millican, J G (Edinburgh U) 1973 *W, I, E*
Milne, C J B (Fettesian-Lorettonians, W of Scotland) 1886 *W, I, E*
Milne, D F (Heriot's FP) 1991 *[J(R)]*
Milne, I G (Heriot's FP, Harlequins) 1979 *I, F, NZ,* 1980 *I, F,* 1981 *NZ* 1,2, *R, A,* 1982 *E, I, F, W, A* 1,2, 1983 *I, F, W, E, NZ,* 1984 *W, E, I, F, A,* 1985 *F, W, E,* 1986 *F, W, E, I, R,* 1987 *I, F, W, E,* [*F, Z, NZ*], 1988 *A,* 1989 *W,* 1990 *I,* 1,2
Milne, K S (Heriot's FP) 1989 *W, E, I, F, Fj, R,* 1990 *I, F, W, E,* 1990 *NZ* 2, *Arg,* 1991 *F, W(R), E,* [*Z*], 1992 *E, I, F, W, A* 1, 1993 *I, F, W, E, NZ,* 1994 *W, E, I, F*
Milne, W M (Glasgow Acads) 1904 *I, E,* 1905 *W, I*
Milroy, E (Watsonians) 1910 *W,* 1911 *E,* 1912 *W, I, E, SA,* 1913 *F, W, I, E,* 1914 *I, E*
Mitchell, G W E (Edinburgh Wands) 1967 *NZ,* 1968 *F, W*
Mitchell, J G (W of Scotland) 1885 *W, I* 1,2
Moncreiff, F J (Edinburgh Acads) 1871 *E,* 1872 *E,* 1873 *E*
Monteith, H G (Cambridge U, London Scottish) 1905 *E,* 1906 *W, I, E, SA,* 1907 *W, I,* 1908 *E*
Monypenny, D B (London Scottish) 1899 *I, W, E*
Moodie, A R (St Andrew's U) 1909 *E,* 1910 *F,* 1911 *F*
Moore, A (Edinburgh Acads) 1990 *NZ* 2, *Arg,* 1991 *F,*

W, E

Morgan, D W (Stewart's-Melville FP) 1973 *W, I, E, P,* 1974 *I, F,* 1975 *I, F, W, E, NZ, A,* 1976 *F, W,* 1977 *I, F, W,* 1978 *I, F, W, E*

Morrison, I R (London Scottish) 1993 *I, F, W, E,* 1994 *W*

Morrison, M C (Royal HSFP) 1896 *W, I, E,* 1897 *I, E,* 1898 *I, E,* 1899 *I, W, E,* 1900 *W, E,* 1901 *W, I, E,* 1902 *W, I, E,* 1903 *W, I,* 1904 *W, I, E*

Morrison, R H (Edinburgh U) 1886 *W, I, E*

Morrison, W H (Edinburgh Acads) 1900 *W*

Morton, D S (W of Scotland) 1887 *I, W, E,* 1888 *W, I,* 1889 *W, I,* 1890 *I, E*

Mowat, J G (Glasgow Acads) 1883 *W, E*

Muir, D E (Heriot's FP) 1950 *F, W, I, E,* 1952 *W, I, E*

Munnoch, N M (Watsonians) 1952 *F, W, I*

Munro, D S (Glasgow High Kelvinside) 1994 *W, E, I, F*

Munro, P (Oxford, London Scottish) 1905 *W, I, E, NZ,* 1906 *W, I, E, SA,* 1907 *I, E,* 1911 *F, W, I*

Munro, R (St Andrews U) 1871 *E*

Munro, S (Ayr, W of Scotland) 1980 *I, F,* 1981 *F, W, E, I, NZ* 1,2, *R,* 1984 *W*

Munro, W H (Glasgow HSFP) 1947 *I, E*

Murdoch, W C W (Hillhead HSFP) 1935 *E, NZ,* 1936 *W, I,* 1939 *E,* 1948 *F, W, I, E*

Murray, G M (Glasgow Acads) 1921 *I,* 1926 *W*

Murray, H M (Glasgow U) 1936 *W, I*

Murray, K T (Hawick) 1985 *I, F, W*

Murray, R O (Cambridge U) 1935 *W, E*

Murray, W A K (London Scottish) 1920 *F, I,* 1921 *F*

Napier, H M (W of Scotland) 1877 *I, E,* 1878 *E,* 1879 *I, E*

Neill, J B (Edinburgh Acads) 1963 *E,* 1964 *F, NZ, W, I, E,* 1965 *F*

Neill, R M (Edinburgh Acads) 1901 *E,* 1902 *I*

Neilson, G T (W of Scotland) 1891 *W, I, E,* 1892 *W, E,* 1893 *W,* 1894 *W, I,* 1895 *W, I, E,* 1896 *W, I, E*

Neilson, J A (Glasgow Acads) 1878 *E,* 1879 *E*

Neilson, R T (W of Scotland) 1898 *I, E,* 1899 *I, W,* 1900 *I, E*

Neilson, T (W of Scotland) 1874 *E*

Neilson, W (Merchiston, Cambridge U, London Scottish) 1891 *W, E,* 1892 *W, I, E,* 1893 *I, E,* 1894 *E,* 1895 *W, I, E,* 1896 *I,* 1897 *I, E*

Neilson, W G (Merchistonians) 1894 *E*

Nelson, J B (Glasgow Acads) 1925 *F, W, I, E,* 1926 *F, W, I, E,* 1927 *F, W, I, E,* 1928 *I, E,* 1929 *F, W, I, E,* 1930 *F, W, I, E,* 1931 *F, W, I*

Nelson, T A (Oxford U) 1898 *E*

Nichol, J A (Royal HSFP) 1955 *W, I, E*

Nicol, A D (Dundee HSFP) 1992 *E, I, F, W, A* 1,2, 1993 *NZ,* 1994 *W*

Nimmo, C S (Watsonians) 1920 *E*

Ogilvy, C (Hawick) 1911 *I, E,* 1912 *I*

Oliver, G H (Hawick) 1987 [Z], 1990 *NZ* 2 (R), 1991 [Z]

Oliver, G K (Gala) 1970 *A*

Orr, C E (W of Scotland) 1887 *I, E, W,* 1888 *W, I,* 1889 *W, I,* 1890 *W, I, E,* 1891 *W, I, E,* 1892 *W, I, E*

Orr, H J (London Scottish) 1903 *W, I, E,* 1904 *W, I*

Orr, J E (W of Scotland) 1889 *I,* 1890 *W, I, E,* 1891 *W, I, E,* 1892 *W, I, E,* 1893 *I, E*

Orr, J H (Edinburgh City Police) 1947 *F, W*

Osler, F L (Edinburgh U) 1911 *F, W*

Park, J (Royal HSFP) 1934 *W*

Paterson, D S (Gala) 1969 *SA,* 1970 *I, E, A,* 1971 *F, W, I, E* (2[1C]), 1972 *W*

Paterson, G Q (Edinburgh Acads) 1876 *E*

Paterson, J R (Birkenhead Park) 1924 *F, W, I, E,* 1926 *F, W, I, E,* 1927 *F, W, I, E, A,* 1928 *F, W, I, E,* 1929 *F, W, I, E*

Patterson, D (Hawick) 1896 *W*

Pattullo, G L (Panmure) 1920 *F, W, I, E*

Paxton, I A M (Selkirk) 1981 *NZ* 1,2, *R, A,* 1982 *E, I, F, W, A* 1,2, 1983 *I, E, NZ,* 1984 *W, E, I, F,* 1985 *I* (R), *F, W, E,* 1986 *W, E, I, R,* 1987 *I, F, W, E,* [*F, Z, R, NZ*], 1988 *I, E, A*

Paxton, R E (Kelso) 1982 *I, A* 2 (R)

Pearson, J (Watsonians) 1909 *I, E,* 1910 *F, W, I, E,* 1911 *F,* 1912 *F, W, SA,* 1913 *I, E*

Pender, I M (London Scottish) 1914 *E*

Pender, N E K (Hawick) 1977 *I,* 1978 *F, W, E*

Penman, W M (RAF) 1939 *I*

Peterkin, W A (Edinburgh U) 1881 *E,* 1883 *I,* 1884 *W, I, E,* 1885 *W, I* 1,2

Petrie, A G (Royal HSFP) 1873 *E,* 1874 *E,* 1875 *E,* 1876 *E,* 1877 *I, E,* 1878 *E,* 1879 *I, E,* 1880 *I, E*

Philp, A (Edinburgh Inst FP) 1882 *E*

Pocock, E I (Edinburgh Wands) 1877 *I, E*

Pollock, J A (Gosforth) 1982 *W,* 1983 *E, NZ,* 1984 *E* (R), *I, F, R,* 1985 *F*

Polson, A H (Gala) 1930 *E*

Purdie, W (Jedforest) 1939 *W, I, E*

Purves, A B H L (London Scottish) 1906 *W, I, E, SA,* 1907 *W, I, E,* 1908 *W, I, E*

Purves, W D C L (London Scottish) 1912 *F, W, I, SA,* 1913 *I, E*

Rea, C W W (W of Scotland, Headingley) 1968 *A,* 1969 *F, W, I, SA,* 1970 *F, W, I, A,* 1971 *F, W, E* (2[1C])

Redpath, B W (Melrose) 1993 *NZ*(t), 1994 *E*(t), *F*

Reed, A I (Bath) 1993 *I, F, W, E,* 1994 *E, I, F*

Reid, C (Edinburgh Acads) 1881 *I, E,* 1882 *I, E,* 1883 *W, I, E,* 1884 *W, I, E,* 1885 *W, I* 1,2, 1886 *W, I, E,* 1887 *I, W, E,* 1888 *W, I*

Reid, J (Edinburgh Wands) 1874 *E,* 1875 *E,* 1876 *E,* 1877 *I, E*

Reid, J M (Edinburgh Acads) 1898 *I, E,* 1899 *I*

Reid, M F (Loretto) 1883 *I, E*

Reid-Kerr, J (Greenock Wand) 1909 *E*

Relph, W K L (Stewart's Coll FP) 1955 *F, W, I, E*

Renny-Tailyour, H W (Royal Engineers) 1872 *E*

Renwick, J M (Hawick) 1972 *F, W, E, NZ,* 1973 *F,* 1974 *W, E, I, F,* 1975 *I, F, W, E, NZ, A,* 1976 *F, W, E*(R), 1977 *I, F, W,* 1978 *I, F, W, E, NZ,* 1979 *W, E, I, F, NZ,* 1980 *I, F, W, E,* 1981 *F, W, E, I, NZ* 1,2, *R, A,* 1982 *E, I, F, W,* 1983 *I, F, W, E,* 1984 *R*

Renwick, W L (London Scottish) 1989 *R*

Renwick, W N (London Scottish, Edinburgh Wands) 1938 *E,* 1939 *W*

Ritchie, G (Merchistonians) 1871 *E*

Ritchie, G F (Dundee HSFP) 1932 *E*

Ritchie, J M (Watsonians) 1933 *W, E, I,* 1934 *W, I, E*

Ritchie, W T (Cambridge U) 1905 *I, E*

Robb, G H (Glasgow U) 1881 *I,* 1885 *W*

Roberts, G (Watsonians) 1938 *W, I, E,* 1939 *W, E*

Robertson, A H (W of Scotland) 1871 *E*

Robertson, A W (Edinburgh Acads) 1897 *E*

Robertson, D (Edinburgh Acads) 1875 *E*

Robertson, D D (Cambridge U) 1893 *W*

Robertson, I (London Scottish, Watsonians) 1968 *E,* 1969 *E, SA,* 1970 *F, W, I, E, A*

Robertson, I P M (Watsonians) 1910 *F*

Robertson, J (Clydesdale) 1908 *E*

Robertson, K W (Melrose) 1978 *NZ,* 1979 *W, E, I, F, NZ,* 1980 *W, E,* 1981 *F, W, E, I, R, A,* 1982 *E, I, F, A* 1,2, 1983 *I, F, W, E,* 1984 *E, I, F, R, A,* 1985 *I, F, W, E,* 1986 *I,* 1987 *F* (R), *W, E,* [*F, Z, NZ*], 1988 *E, A,* 1989 *E, I, F*

Robertson, L (London Scottish, United Services) 1908 *E,* 1911 *W,* 1912 *W, I, E, SA,* 1913 *W, I, E*

Robertson, M A (Gala) 1958 *F*

Robertson, R D (London Scottish) 1912 *F*

Robson, A (Hawick) 1954 *F,* 1955 *F, W, I, E,* 1956 *F, W, I, E,* 1957 *F, W, I, E,* 1958 *W, A, I, E,* 1959 *F, W, I, E,* 1960 *F*

Rodd, J A T (United Services, RN, London Scottish) 1958 *F, W, A, I, E,* 1960 *F, W,* 1962 *F,* 1964 *F, NZ, W,* 1965 *F, W, I*

Rogerson, J (Kelvinside Acads) 1894 *W*

Roland, E T (Edinburgh Acads) 1884 *I, E*

Rollo, D M D (Howe of Fife) 1959 *E,* 1960 *F, W, I, E, SA,* 1961 *F, SA, W, I, E,* 1962 *F, W, E,* 1963 *F, W, I, E,* 1964 *F, NZ, W, I, E,* 1965 *F, W, I, E, SA,* 1966 *F, W, I, E, A,* 1967 *F, W, E, NZ,* 1968 *F, W, I*

Rose, D M (Jedforest) 1951 *F, W, I, E, SA,* 1953 *F, W*

Ross, A (Kilmarnock) 1924 *F, W*

Ross, A (Royal HSFP) 1905 *W, I, E,* 1909 *W, I*

Ross, A R (Edinburgh U) 1911 *W,* 1914 *W, I, E*

Ross, E J (London Scottish) 1904 *W*

Ross, G T (Watsonians) 1954 *NZ, I, E, W*

Ross, I A (Hillhead HSFP) 1951 *F, W, I, E*

Ross, J (London Scottish) 1901 *W, I, E,* 1902 *W,* 1903 *E*

Ross, K I (Boroughmuir FP) 1961 *SA, W, I, E*, 1962 *F, W, I, E*, 1963 *F, W, E*
Ross, W A (Hillhead HSFP) 1937 *W, E*
Rottenburg, H (Cambridge U, London Scottish) 1899 *W, E*, 1900 *W, I, E*
Roughead, W N (Edinburgh Acads, London Scottish) 1927 *A*, 1928 *F, W, I, E*, 1930 *I, E*, 1931 *F, W, I, E*, 1932 *W*
Rowan, N A (Boroughmuir) 1980 *W, E*, 1981 *F, W, E, I*, 1984 *E*, 1985 *I*, 1987 [R], 1988 *I, F, W, E*
Rowand, R (Glasgow HSFP) 1930 *F, W*, 1932 *E*, 1933 *W, E, I*, 1934 *W*
Roy, A (Waterloo) 1938 *W, I, E*, 1939 *W, I, E*
Russell, W L (Glasgow Acads) 1905 *NZ*, 1906 *W, I, E*
Rutherford, J Y (Selkirk) 1979 *W, E, I, F, NZ*, 1980 *I, F, E*, 1981 *F, W, E, I, NZ* 1,2, *A*, 1982 *E, I, F, W, A* 1,2, 1983 *E, NZ*, 1984 *W, E, I, F, R*, 1985 *I, F, W, E*, 1986 *F, W, E, I, R*, 1987 *I, F, W, E*, [F]

Sampson, R W F (London Scottish) 1939 *W*, 1947 *W*
Sanderson, G A (Royal HSFP) 1907 *W, I, E*, 1908 *I*
Sanderson, J L P (Edinburgh Acads) 1873 *E*
Schulze, D G (London Scottish) 1905 *E*, 1907 *I, E*, 1908 *W, I, E*, 1909 *W, I, E*, 1910 *W, I, E*, 1911 *W*
Scobie, R M (Royal Military Coll) 1914 *W, I, E*
Scotland, K J F (Heriot's FP, Cambridge U, Leicester) 1957 *F, W, I, E*, 1958 *E*, 1959 *F, W, I, E*, 1960 *F, W, I, E*, 1961 *F, SA, W, I, E*, 1962 *F, W, I, E*, 1963 *F, W, I, E*, 1965 *F*
Scott, D M (Langholm, Watsonians) 1950 *I, E*, 1951 *W, I, E, SA*, 1952 *F, W, I*, 1953 *F*
Scott, J M B (Edinburgh Acads) 1907 *E*, 1908 *W, I, E*, 1909 *W, I, E*, 1910 *F, W, I, E*, 1911 *F, W, I*, 1912 *W, I, E, SA*, 1913 *W, I, E*
Scott, J S (St Andrews U) 1950 *E*
Scott, J W (Stewart's Coll FP) 1925 *F, W, I, E*, 1926 *F, W, I, E*, 1927 *F, W, I, E, A*, 1928 *F, W, E*, 1929 *E*, 1930 *F*
Scott, M (Dunfermline) 1992 *A 2*
Scott, R (Hawick) 1898 *I*, 1900 *I, E*
Scott, T (Langholm, Hawick) 1896 *W*, 1897 *I, E*, 1898 *I, E*, 1899 *I, W, E*, 1900 *W, I, E*
Scott, T M (Hawick) 1893 *E*, 1895 *W, I, E*, 1896 *W, E*, 1897 *I, E*, 1898 *I, E*, 1900 *W, I*
Scott, W P (W of Scotland) 1900 *I, E*, 1902 *I, E*, 1903 *W, I, E*, 1904 *W, I, E*, 1905 *W, I, E, NZ*, 1906 *W, I, E, SA*, 1907 *W, I, E*
Scoular, J G (Cambridge U) 1905 *NZ*, 1906 *W, I, E, SA*
Selby, J A R (Watsonians) 1920 *W, I*
Shackleton, J A P (London Scottish) 1959 *E*, 1963 *F, W*, 1964 *NZ, W*, 1965 *I, SA*
Sharp, A V (Bristol) 1994 *E, I, F*
Sharp, G (Stewart's FP, Army) 1960 *F*, 1964 *F, NZ, W*
Shaw, G D (Sale) 1935 *NZ*, 1936 *W*, 1937 *W, I, E*, 1939 *I*
Shaw, I (Glasgow HSFP) 1937 *I*
Shaw, J N (Edinburgh Acads) 1921 *W, I*
Shaw, R W (Glasgow HSFP) 1934 *W, I, E*, 1935 *W, I, E, NZ*, 1936 *W, I, E*, 1937 *W, I, E*, 1938 *W, I, E*, 1939 *W, I, E*
Shedden, D (W of Scotland) 1972 *NZ*, 1973 *F, W, I, E, P*, 1976 *W, E, I*, 1977 *I, F, W*, 1978 *I, F, W*
Shiel, A G (Melrose) 1991 [*I*(R), *WS*], 1993 *I, F, W, E, NZ*
Shillinglaw, R B (Gala, Army) 1960 *I, E, SA*, 1961 *F, SA*
Simmers, B M (Glasgow Acads) 1965 *F, W*, 1966 *A*, 1967 *F, W, I*, 1971 *F* (R)
Simmers, W M (Glasgow Acads) 1926 *W, I, E*, 1927 *F, W, I, E, A*, 1928 *F, W, I, E*, 1929 *F, W, I, E*, 1930 *F, W, I, E*, 1931 *F, W, I, E*, 1932 *SA, W, I, E*
Simpson, J W (Royal HSFP) 1893 *I, E*, 1894 *W, I, E*, 1895 *W, I, E*, 1896 *W, I, E*, 1897 *E*, 1899 *W, E*
Simpson, R S (Glasgow Acads) 1923 *I*
Simson, E D (Edinburgh U, London Scottish) 1902 *E*, 1903 *W, I, E*, 1904 *W, I, E*, 1905 *W, I, E, NZ*, 1906 *W, I, E*, 1907 *W, I, E*
Simson, J T (Watsonians) 1905 *NZ*, 1909 *W, I, E*, 1910 *F, W*, 1911 *I*
Simson, R F (London Scottish) 1911 *E*
Sloan, A T (Edinburgh Acads) 1914 *W*, 1920 *F, W, I, E*, 1921 *F, W, I, E*
Sloan, D A (Edinburgh Acads, London Scottish) 1950

F, W, E, 1951 *W, I, E*, 1953 *F*
Sloan, T (Glasgow Acads, Oxford U) 1905 *NZ*, 1906 *W, SA*, 1907 *W, E*, 1908 *W*, 1909 *I*
Smeaton, P W (Edinburgh Acads) 1881 *I*, 1883 *I, E*
Smith, A R (Oxford U) 1895 *W, I, E*, 1896 *W, I*, 1897 *I, E*, 1898 *I, E*, 1900 *I, E*
Smith, A R (Cambridge U, Gosforth, Ebbw Vale, Edinburgh Wands) 1955 *W, I, E*, 1956 *F, W, I, E*, 1957 *F, W, I, E*, 1958 *F, W, A, I*, 1959 *F, W, I, E*, 1960 *F, W, I, E, SA*, 1961 *F, SA, W, I, E*, 1962 *F, W, I, E*
Smith, D W C (London Scottish) 1949 *F, W, I, E*, 1950 *F, W, I*, 1953 *I*
Smith, E R (Edinburgh Acads) 1879 *I*
Smith, G K (Kelso) 1957 *I, E*, 1958 *F, W, A*, 1959 *F, W, I, E*, 1960 *F, W, I, E*, 1961 *F, SA, W, I, E*
Smith, H O (Watsonians) 1895 *W*, 1896 *W, I, E*, 1898 *I, E*, 1899 *W, I, E*, 1900 *E*, 1902 *E*
Smith, I R (Gloucester) 1992 *E, I, W, A* 1,2, 1994 *E*(R), *I, F*
Smith, I S (Oxford U, Edinburgh U) 1924 *W, I, E*, 1925 *F, W, I, E*, 1926 *F, W, I, E*, 1927 *F, I, E*, 1929 *F, W, I, E*, 1930 *F, W, I*, 1931 *F, W, I, E*, 1932 *SA, W, I, E*, 1933 *W, E, I*
Smith, I S G (London Scottish) 1969 *SA*, 1970 *F, W, I, E*, 1971 *F, W, I*
Smith, M A (London Scottish) 1970 *W, I, E, A*
Smith, R T (Kelso) 1929 *F, W, I, E*, 1930 *F, W, I*
Smith, S H (Glasgow Acads) 1877 *I*, 1878 *E*
Smith, T J (Gala) 1983 *E, NZ*, 1985 *I, F*
Sole, D M B (Bath, Edinburgh Acads) 1986 *F, W*, 1987 *I, F, W, E, [F, Z, R, NZ]*, 1988 *I, F, W, E, A*, 1989 *W, E, I, F, Fj, R*, 1990 *I, F, W, E, NZ* 1,2, *Arg*, 1991 *F, W, E, I, R, [J, I, WS, E, NZ]*, 1992 *E, I, F, W, A* 1,2
Somerville, D (Edinburgh Inst FP) 1879 *I*, 1882 *I*, 1883 *W, I, E*, 1884 *W*
Speirs, L M (Watsonians) 1906 *SA*, 1907 *W, I, E*, 1908 *W, I, E*, 1910 *F, W, E*
Spence, K M (Oxford U) 1953 *I*
Spencer, E (Clydedale) 1898 *I*
Stagg, P K (Sale) 1965 *F, W, E, SA*, 1966 *F, W, I, E, A*, 1967 *F, W, I, E, NZ*, 1968 *F, W, I, E, A*, 1969 *F, W, I* (R), *SA*, 1970 *F, W, I, E, A*
Stanger, A G (Hawick) 1989 *Fj, R*, 1990 *I, F, W, E, NZ* 1,2, *Arg*, 1991 *F, W, E, I, R, [J, Z, I, WS, E, NZ]*, 1992 *E, I, F, W, A* 1,2, 1993 *I, F, W, E, NZ*, 1994 *W, E, I, F*
Stark, D A (Boroughmuir) 1993 *I, F, W, E*
Steele, W C C (Langholm, Bedford, RAF, London Scottish) 1969 *E*, 1971 *F, W, I, E* (2[1C]), 1972 *F, W, E, NZ*, 1973 *F, W, I, E*, 1975 *I, F, W, E, NZ* (R), 1976 *W, E, I*, 1977 *E*
Stephen, A E (W of Scotland) 1885 *W*, 1886 *I*
Steven, P D (Heriot's FP) 1984 *A*, 1985 *F, W, E*
Steven, R (Edinburgh Wands) 1962 *I*
Stevenson, A K (Glasgow Acads) 1922 *F*, 1923 *F, W, E*
Stevenson, A M (Glasgow U) 1911 *F*
Stevenson, G D (Hawick) 1956 *E*, 1957 *F*, 1958 *F, W, A, I, E*, 1959 *W, I, E*, 1960 *W, I, E, SA*, 1961 *F, SA, W, I, E*, 1963 *F, W, I*, 1964 *E*, 1965 *F*
Stevenson, H J (Edinburgh Acads) 1888 *W, I*, 1889 *W, I*, 1890 *W, I, E*, 1891 *W, I, E*, 1892 *W, I, E*, 1893 *I, E*
Stevenson, L E (Edinburgh U) 1888 *W*
Stevenson, R C (London Scottish) 1897 *I, E*, 1898 *E*, 1899 *I, W, E*
Stevenson, R C (St Andrews U) 1910 *F, I, E*, 1911 *F, W, I*
Stevenson, W H (Glasgow Acads) 1925 *F*
Stewart, A K (Edinburgh U) 1874 *E*, 1876 *E*
Stewart, A M (Edinburgh Acads) 1914 *W*
Stewart, C A R (W of Scotland) 1880 *I, E*
Stewart, C E B (Kelso) 1960 *W*, 1961 *F*
Stewart, J (Glasgow HSFP) 1930 *F*
Stewart, J L (Edinburgh Acads) 1921 *I*
Stewart, M S (Stewart's Coll FP) 1932 *SA, W, I*, 1933 *W, E, I*, 1934 *W, I, E*
Stewart, W A (London Hospital) 1913 *F, W, I*, 1914 *W*
Steyn, S S L (Oxford U) 1911 *E*, 1912 *I*
Strachan, G M (Jordanhill) 1971 *E* (C) (R), 1973 *W, I, E, P*
Stronach, R S (Glasgow Acads) 1901 *W, E*, 1905 *W, I, E*
Stuart, C D (W of Scotland) 1909 *I*, 1910 *F, W, I, E*, 1911 *I, E*
Stuart, L M (Glasgow HSFP) 1923 *F, W, I, E*, 1924 *F,*

1928 E, 1930 I, E
Suddon, N (Hawick) 1965 W, I, E, SA, 1966 A, 1968 E, A, 1969 F, W, I, 1970 I, E, A
Sutherland, W R (Hawick) 1910 W, E, 1911 F, E, 1912 F, W, E, SA, 1913 F, W, I, E, 1914 W
Swan, J S (Army, London Scottish, Leicester) 1953 E, 1954 F, NZ, I, E, W, 1955 F, W, I, E, 1956 F, W, I, E, 1957 F, W, 1958 F
Swan, M W (Oxford U, London Scottish) 1958 F, W, A, I, E, 1959 F, W, I
Sweet, J B (Glasgow HSFP) 1913 E, 1914 I
Symington, A W (Cambridge U) 1914 W, E

Tait, A V (Kelso) 1987 [F(R), Z, R, NZ], 1988 I, F, W, E
Tait, J G (Edinburgh Acads) 1880 I, 1885 I 2
Tait, P W (Royal HSFP) 1935 E
Taylor, E G (Oxford U) 1927 W, A
Taylor, R C (Kelvinside-West) 1951 W, I, E, SA
Telfer, C M (Hawick) 1968 A, 1969 F, W, I, E, 1972 F, W, E, 1973 W, I, E, P, 1974 W, E, I, 1975 A, 1976 F
Telfer, J W (Melrose) 1964 F, NZ, W, I, E, 1965 F, W, I, 1966 F, W, I, E, 1967 W, I, E, 1968 E, A, 1969 F, W, I, E, SA, 1970 F, W, I
Tennent, J M (W of Scotland) 1909 W, I, E, 1910 F, W, E
Thom, D A (London Scottish) 1934 W, 1935 W, I, E, NZ
Thom, G (Kirkcaldy) 1920 F, W, I, E
Thom, J R (Watsonians) 1933 W, E, I
Thomson, A E (United Services) 1921 F, W, E
Thomson, A M (St Andrews U) 1949 I
Thomson, B E (Oxford U) 1953 F, W, I
Thomson, I H M (Heriot's FP, Army) 1951 W, I, 1952 F, W, I, 1953 I, E
Thomson, J S (Glasgow Acads) 1871 E
Thomson, R H (London Scottish) 1960 I, E, SA, 1961 F, SA, W, I, E, 1963 F, W, I, E, 1964 F, NZ, W
Thomson, W H (W of Scotland) 1906 SA
Thomson, W J (W of Scotland) 1899 W, E, 1900 W
Timms, A B (Edinburgh U, Edinburgh Wands) 1896 W, 1900 W, I, 1901 W, I, E, 1902 W, 1903 W, E, 1904 I, E, 1905 I, E
Tod, H B (Gala) 1911 F
Tod, J (Watsonians) 1884 W, I, E, 1885 W, I 1,2, 1886 W, I, E
Todd, J K (Glasgow Acads) 1874 E, 1875 E
Tolmie, J M (Glasgow HSFP) 1922 E
Tomes, A J (Hawick) 1976 E, I, 1977 E, 1978 I, F, W, E, NZ, 1979 W, E, I, F, NZ, 1980 F, W, E, 1981 F, W, E, I, NZ 1,2, R, A, 1982 E, I, F, W, A 1,2, 1983 I, F, W, 1984 W, E, I, F, R, A, 1985 W, E, 1987 I, F, E(R), [F, Z, R, NZ]
Torrie, T J (Edinburgh Acads) 1877 E
Townsend, G P J (Gala) 1993 E(R), 1994 W, E, I, F
Tukalo, I (Selkirk) 1985 I, 1987 I, F, W, E, [F, Z, R, NZ], 1988 F, W, E, A, 1989 W, E, I, F, Fj, 1990 I, F, W, E, NZ 1, 1991 I, R, [J, Z, I, WS, E, NZ], 1992 E, I, F, W, A 1,2
Turk, A S (Langholm) 1971 E (R)
Turnbull, D J (Hawick) 1987 [NZ], 1988 F, E, 1990 E (R), 1991 F, W, E, I, R, [Z], 1993 I, F, W, E, 1994 W
Turnbull, F O (Kelso) 1951 F, SA
Turnbull, G O (W of Scotland) 1896 I, E, 1897 I, E, 1904 W
Turnbull, P (Edinburgh Acads) 1901 W, I, E, 1902 W, I, E
Turner, F H (Oxford U, Liverpool) 1911 F, W, I, E, 1912 F, W, I, E, SA, 1913 F, W, I, E, 1914 I, E
Turner, J W C (Gala) 1966 W, A, 1967 F, W, I, E, NZ, 1968 F, W, I, E, A, 1969 F, 1970 E, A, 1971 F, W, I, E (2[1C])

Usher, C M (United Services, Edinburgh Wands) 1912 E, 1913 F, W, I, E, 1914 E, 1920 F, W, I, E, 1921 W, E, 1922 F, W, I, E

Valentine, A R (RNAS, Anthorn) 1953 F, W, I
Valentine, D D (Hawick) 1947 I, E
Veitch, J P (Royal HSFP) 1882 E, 1883 I, 1884 W, I, E, 1885 I 1,2, 1886 E
Villar, C (Edinburgh Wands) 1876 E, 1877 I, E

Waddell, G H (London Scottish, Cambridge U) 1957 E, 1958 F, W, A, I, E, 1959 F, W, I, E, 1960 I, E, SA, 1961 F, 1962 F, W, I, E
Waddell, H (Glasgow Acads) 1924 F, W, I, E, 1925 I, E, 1926 F, W, I, E, 1927 F, W, I, E, 1930 W
Wade, A L (London Scottish) 1908 E
Wainwright, R I (Edinburgh Acads) 1992 I(R), F, A 1,2, 1993 NZ, 1994 W, E
Walker, A (W of Scotland) 1881 I, 1882 E, 1883 W, I, E
Walker, A W (Cambridge U, Birkenhead Park) 1931 F, W, I, E, 1932 I
Walker, J G (W of Scotland) 1882 E, 1883 W
Walker, M (Oxford U) 1952 F
Wallace, A C (Oxford U) 1923 F, 1924 F, W, E, 1925 F, W, I, E, 1926 F
Wallace, W M (Cambridge U) 1913 E, 1914 W, I, E
Walls, W A (Glasgow Acads) 1882 E, 1883 W, I, E, 1884 W, I, E, 1886 W, I, E
Walter, M W (London Scottish) 1906 I, E, SA, 1907 W, I, 1908 W, I, 1910 I
Walton, P (Northampton) 1994 E, I, F
Warren, J R (Glasgow Acads) 1914 I
Warren, R C (Glasgow Acads) 1922 W, I, 1930 W, I, E
Waters, F H (Cambridge U, London Scottish) 1930 F, W, I, E, 1932 SA, W, I
Waters, J A (Selkirk) 1933 W, E, I, 1934 W, I, E, 1935 W, I, E, NZ, 1936 W, I, E, 1937 W, I, E
Waters, J B (Cambridge U) 1904 I, E
Watherston, J G (Edinburgh Wands) 1934 I, E
Watherston, W R A (London Scottish) 1963 F, W, I
Watson, D H (Glasgow Acads) 1876 E, 1877 I, E
Watson, W S (Boroughmuir) 1974 W, E, I, F, 1975 NZ, 1977 I, E, W, 1979 I, F
Watt, A G J (Glasgow High Kelvinside) 1991 [Z], 1993 I, NZ
Watt, A G M (Edinburgh Acads) 1947 F, W, I, A, 1948 F, W
Weatherstone, T G (Stewart's Coll FP) 1952 E, 1953 I, E, 1954 F, NZ, I, E, W, 1955 F, 1958 W, A, I, E, 1959 W, I, E
Weir, G W (Melrose) 1990 Arg, 1991 R, [J, Z, I, WS, E, NZ], 1992 E, I, F, W, A 1,2, 1993 I, F, W, E, NZ, 1994 W(R), E, I, F
Welsh, R (Watsonians) 1895 W, I, E, 1896 W
Welsh, R B (Hawick) 1967 I, E
Welsh, W B (Hawick) 1927 A, 1928 F, W, I, 1929 I, E, 1930 F, W, I, E, 1931 F, W, I, E, 1932 SA, W, I, E, 1933 W, E, I
Welsh, W H (Edinburgh U) 1900 I, E, 1901 W, I, E, 1902 W, I, E
Wemyss, A (Gala, Edinburgh Wands) 1914 W, I, 1920 F, E, 1922 F, W, I, E
West, L (Edinburgh U, West Hartlepool) 1903 W, I, E, 1905 I, E, 1906 W, I, E
Weston, V G (Kelvinside Acads) 1936 I, E
White, D B (Gala, London Scottish) 1982 F, W, A 1,2, 1987 W, E, [F, R, NZ], 1988 I, F, W, E, A, 1989 W, E, I, F, Fj, R, 1990 I, F, W, E, NZ 1,2, 1991 F, W, E, I, R, [J, Z, I, WS, E, NZ], 1992 E, I, F, W
White, D M (Kelvinside Acads) 1963 F, W, I, E
White, T B (Edinburgh Acads) 1888 W, I, 1889 W
Whittington, T P (Merchistonians) 1873 E
Whitworth, R J E (London Scottish) 1936 I
Whyte, D J (Edinburgh Wands) 1965 W, I, E, SA, 1966 F, W, I, E, A, 1967 F, W, I, E
Will, J G (Cambridge U) 1912 F, W, I, E, 1914 W, I, E
Wilson, A W (Dunfermline) 1931 F, I, E
Wilson, G A (Oxford U) 1949 F, W, E
Wilson, G R (Royal HSFP) 1886 E, 1890 W, I, E, 1891 I
Wilson, J H (Watsonians) 1953 I
Wilson, J S (St Andrews U) 1931 F, W, I, E, 1932 E
Wilson, J S (United Services, London Scottish) 1908 I, 1909 W
Wilson, R (London Scottish) 1976 E, I, 1977 E, I, F, 1978 I, F, 1981 R, 1983 I
Wilson, R L (Gala) 1951 F, W, I, E, SA, 1953 F, W, E
Wilson, R W (W of Scotland) 1873 E, 1874 E
Wilson, S (Oxford U, London Scottish) 1964 F, NZ, W, I, E, 1965 W, I, E, SA, 1966 F, W, I, A, 1967 F, W, I, E, NZ, 1968 F, W, I, E
Wood, A (Royal HSFP) 1873 E, 1874 E, 1875 E
Wood, G (Gala) 1931 W, I, 1932 W, I, E
Woodburn, J C (Kelvinside Acads) 1892 I
Woodrow, A N (Glasgow Acads) 1887 I, W, E

Wotherspoon, W (W of Scotland) 1891 *I*, 1892 *I*, 1893 *W*, *E*, 1894 *W*, *I*, *E*
Wright, F A (Edinburgh Acads) 1932 *E*
Wright, H B (Watsonians) 1894 *W*
Wright, K M (London Scottish) 1929 *F*, *W*, *I*, *E*
Wright, P H (Boroughmuir) 1992 *A* 1,2, 1993 *F*, *W*, *E*, 1994 *W*
Wright, R W J (Edinburgh Wands) 1973 *F*
Wright, S T H (Stewart's Coll FP) 1949 *E*
Wright, T (Hawick) 1947 *A*
Wyllie, D S (Stewart's-Melville FP) 1984 *A*, 1985 *W*

(R), *E*, 1987 *I*, *F*, [*F*, *Z*, *R*, *NZ*], 1989 *R*, 1991 *R*, [*J*(R), *Z*], 1993 *NZ*(R), 1994 *W*(R), *E*, *I*, *F*

Young, A H (Edinburgh Acads) 1874 *E*
Young, E T (Glasgow Acads) 1914 *E*
Young, R G (Watsonians) 1970 *W*
Young, T E B (Durham) 1911 *F*
Young, W B (Cambridge U, London Scottish) 1937 *W*, *I*, *E*, 1938 *W*, *I*, *E*, 1939 *W*, *I*, *E*, 1948 *E*

SCOTTISH INTERNATIONAL RECORDS

Both team and individual records are for official Scotland international matches, up to 31 March 1994.

TEAM RECORDS

Highest score
60 v Zimbabwe (60-21) 1987 Wellington

v individual countries
49 v Argentina (49-3) 1990 Murrayfield
24 v Australia (24-15) 1981 Murrayfield
33 v England (33-6) 1986 Murrayfield
38 v Fiji (38-17) 1989 Murrayfield
31 v France (31-3) 1912 Inverleith
37 v Ireland (37-21) 1989 Murrayfield
47 v Japan (47-9) 1991 Murrayfield
25 v N Zealand (25-25) 1983 Murrayfield
55 v Romania (55-28) 1987 Dunedin
10 v S Africa (10-18) 1960 Port Elizabeth
35 v Wales (35-10) 1924 Inverleith
28 v W Samoa (28-6) 1991 Murrayfield
60 v Zimbabwe (60-21) 1987 Wellington

Biggest winning points margin
46 v Argentina (49-3) 1990 Murrayfield

v individual countries
46 v Argentina (49-3) 1990 Murrayfield
 9 v Australia (24-15) 1981 Murrayfield
27 v England (33-6) 1986 Murrayfield
21 v Fiji (38-17) 1989 Murrayfield
28 v France (31-3) 1912 Inverleith
23 v Ireland (32-9) 1984 Dublin
38 v Japan (47-9) 1991 Murrayfield
No win v N Zealand
32 v Romania (32-0) 1989 Murrayfield
 6 v S Africa (6-0) 1906 Glasgow
25 v Wales (35-10) 1924 Inverleith
22 v W Samoa (28-6) 1991 Murrayfield
39 v Zimbabwe $\begin{cases} \text{(60-21) 1987 Wellington} \\ \text{(51-12) 1991 Murrayfield} \end{cases}$

Longest winning sequence
6 matches – 1925-26 and 1989-90

Highest score by opposing team
51 N Zealand (15-51) 1993 Murrayfield

by individual countries
 3 Argentina (49-3) 1990 Murrayfield
37 Australia $\begin{cases} \text{(12-37) 1984 Murrayfield} \\ \text{(13-37) 1992 Brisbane} \end{cases}$
30 England (18-30) 1980 Murrayfield
17 Fiji (38-17) 1989 Murrayfield
28 France (22-28) 1987 Parc de Princes
26 Ireland (8-26) 1953 Murrayfield
 9 Japan (47-9) 1991 Murrayfield
51 N Zealand (15-51) 1993 Murrayfield
28 Romania $\begin{cases} \text{(22-28) 1984 Bucharest} \\ \text{(55-28) 1987 Dunedin} \end{cases}$
44 S Africa (0-44) 1951 Murrayfield
35 Wales (12-35) 1972 Cardiff
 6 W Samoa (28-6) 1991 Murrayfield
21 Zimbabwe (60-21) 1987 Wellington

Biggest losing points margin
44 v S Africa (0-44) 1951 Murrayfield

v individual countries
25 v Australia (12-37) 1984 Murrayfield
20 v England (6-26) 1977 Twickenham
20 v France (3-23) 1977 Parc des Princes
21 v Ireland (0-21) 1950 Dublin
36 v N Zealand (15-51) 1993 Murrayfield
 6 v Romania $\begin{cases} \text{(22-28) 1984 Bucharest} \\ \text{(12-18) 1991 Bucharest} \end{cases}$
44 v S Africa (0-44) 1951 Murrayfield
23 v Wales $\begin{cases} \text{(12-35) 1972 Cardiff} \\ \text{(6-29) 1994 Cardiff} \end{cases}$
No defeat v Argentina, Fiji, Japan, Western Samoa or Zimbabwe

Longest losing sequence
17 matches – 1951-54

**Most tries by Scotland in an
international**
12 v Wales 1887 Raeburn Place
  (Edinburgh)

**Most tries against Scotland in an
international**
9 by S Africa (0-44) 1951 Murrayfield

**Most points by Scotland in
International Championship in a
season – 86**
in season 1983-84

**Most tries by Scotland in
International Championship in a
season – 17**
in season 1924-25

INDIVIDUAL RECORDS

Most capped player
J M Renwick 52 1972-84
C T Deans 52 1978-87
in individual positions
Full-back
A G Hastings 50[1] 1986-94
Wing
I Tukalo 37 1985-92
Centre
J M Renwick 51(52)[2] 1972-84
Fly-half
J Y Rutherford 42 1979-87
Scrum-half
R J Laidlaw 47 1980-88
Prop
A B Carmichael 50 1967-78
Hooker
C T Deans 52 1978-87
Lock
A J Tomes 48 1976-87

Scotland captain Gavin Hastings, 50 caps, is the holder of nine records for his country.

Flanker
J Jeffrey 40 1984-91
No 8
D B White 29(41)[3] 1982-92
[1]*A R Irvine, 51 caps, won 47 as a full-back and 4 as a wing*
[2]*Renwick played once, as a replacement, on the wing*
[3]*White won 5 caps as a flanker and 7 as a lock*

Longest international career
W C W Murdoch 14 seasons 1935-48

Most consecutive internationals – 49
A B Carmichael 1967-78

Most internationals as captain – 25
D M B Sole 1989-92

Most points in internationals – 466
A G Hastings (50 matches) 1986-94

Most points in International Championship in a season – 52
A G Hastings (4 matches) 1985-86

Most points in an international – 27
A G Hastings v Romania 1987
  Dunedin

Most tries in internationals – 24
I S Smith (32 matches) 1924-33

Most tries in International Championship in a season – 8
I S Smith (4 matches) 1924-25

Most tries in an international – 5
G C Lindsay v Wales 1887 Raeburn Place
(Edinburgh)

Most conversions in internationals – 60
A G Hastings (50 matches) 1986-94

Most conversions in International Championship in a season – 8
P W Dods (4 matches) 1983-84

Most conversions in an international – 8
A G Hastings v Zimbabwe 1987 Wellington
A G Hastings v Romania 1987 Dunedin

Most dropped goals in internationals – 12
J Y Rutherford (42 matches) 1972-82

Most dropped goals in an international – 2
R C MacKenzie v Ireland 1877 Belfast
N J Finlay v Ireland 1880 Glasgow
B M Simmers v Wales 1965 Murrayfield
D W Morgan v Ireland 1973 Murrayfield
B M Gossman v France 1983 Paris
J Y Rutherford v N Zealand 1983
  Murrayfield
J Y Rutherford v Wales 1985 Murrayfield
J Y Rutherford v Ireland 1987 Murrayfield

Most penalty goals in internationals – 102
A G Hastings (50 matches) 1986-94

Most penalty goals in International Championship in a season – 14
A G Hastings (4 matches) 1985-86

Most penalty goals in an international – 6
A G Hastings v France 1986 Murrayfield

Most points on major tour – 58
P W Dods (4 matches) N Zealand 1990
C D R Mair scored 100 points in the Far East in 1977, but this was not on a major tour

Most points in a tour match – 24
D W Morgan v Wellington 1975
  Wellington, NZ
A R Irvine v King Country 1981
  Taumarunui, NZ
A R Irvine v Wairarapa-Bush 1981
  Masterton, NZ
P W Dods scored 43 points v Alberta in 1985, but this was not on a major tour

Most tries in a tour match – 3
A R Smith v Eastern Transvaal 1960
  Springs, SA
K R F Bearne scored 5 tries v Ontario U in 1964, A J W Hinshelwood scored 5 v Quebec in 1964, and D E W Leckie scored 5 v Goshawks (Zimbabwe) in 1988, but these were not on a major tour

TWICKENHAM CONSOLATION FOR A REVIVAL WHICH SOMETIMES STALLED

THE 1993-94 SEASON IN IRELAND
Sean Diffley *Irish Independent*

Judging by the Irish norm, it wasn't a bad season. Two wins (remember Romania in November), two losses and a draw – and one of those defeats, by Wales, should have been a win but for the unconscionable width of the right-hand upright at the Lansdowne Road end of the ground. Eric Elwood, hitting everything with utter composure, managed to place that feasible match-winning kick wide of the yawning gap between the posts and, with William Tell accuracy, hit the upright instead.

But 14 days later came Twickenham and Ireland's cup of joy overflowed. It was only their tenth win at Twickenham since the first match between the two countries there in 1910. And it was, of course, the second win in succession over England, in itself a cause for vast celebration; but it was something more substantial this time. After all, this was an Irish squad struggling to escape the morass of recent seasons and an England squad which had valid reasons for claiming to be right up there with the world's leading sides. Only in Paris in the opening flurry in January were Ireland well beaten. But even in the Parc des Princes the Irish remained in touch until the last minutes, though that was due more to the d'Artagnan-style leadership of Olivier Roumat, who preferred elegance and graceful running to the more mundane job of kicking for points.

The basis of the Irish team last season was the solidity of the forwards, particularly the iron front row of Nick Popplewell, Terry Kingston and Peter Clohessy. It was only against Scotland, where Alan Sharp was a problem, that they looked a trifle uncomfortable. At Twickenham, Neil Francis left his eyrie for once to contribute his talent to the lineouts. And Paddy Johns at No 8 was another considerable force in the Championship. Fly-half Eric Elwood experienced a typical 'second season', being well policed by the opposition, who were more aware of what to expect. Yet he came through well, this deep-thinking player whose place-kicking and tactical kicking was first rate (though unlike John Cleese in *Fawlty Towers*, we won't mention the war or dwell on the miss against Wales).

Altogether then, 1993-94 marked a continuation of the Irish revival of the previous season and the earnest hope that the summer tour of Australia would add further to the experience of the squad and give an edge to the 1994-95 season and the forthcoming World Cup.

The domestic highlight was, of course, the new format of four divisions, instead of the two of the previous three seasons, in the Insurance Corporation All-Ireland League. And, as has been the case since the

The Ireland team which beat England at Twickenham. L-R, back row: P Robin (touch-judge), P Thomas (referee), E P Elwood, P M Clohessy, M J Field, R M Wallace, B F Robinson, P S Johns, N P J Francis, M J Galwey, S P Geoghegan, N J Popplewell, D Mene (touch-judge); front row: C M P O'Shea, P P A Danaher, M T Bradley (capt), M Cuddy (president), T J Kingston, W D McBride.

League was instituted four year ago, the title went to Munster, to the Limerick club Garryowen, to continue the complete Cork-Limerick dominance in Division 1 (the title was previously won by Cork Constitution, Garryowen and Young Munster). And once again the decisive game between the two front-runners was played, fortuitously, on the last Saturday of the competition, at Dooradoyle between Garryowen and Blackrock College. If Garryowen were deserving winnners, Blackrock, the Dublin side captained by Brendan Mullin, carved their own special niche. They had in successive seasons won their way to the League from Leinster, won Division 2 and promotion and then battled for Division 1 honours.

It was a long and rather over-burdened season with the extended ICL, the well-spread Irish Inter-Provincial Championship, the games against the Scottish regional sides and the end-of-season Provincial Cup competitions running well into May. The Irish-Scottish series will continue this season, although the matches themselves were hardly of a standard in their inaugural season to set the scene ablaze.

Ulster, Munster and Leinster shared the Inter-Provincial title, which means that Ulster have either won or shared it for the last ten seasons.

INSURANCE CORPORATION ALL-IRELAND LEAGUE 1993-94

Division 1	P	W	D	L	F	A	Pts
Garryowen	10	8	0	2	172	108	16
Cork Const	10	7	0	3	201	123	14
Blackrock Coll	10	7	0	3	137	99	14
Dungannon	10	5	0	5	181	130	10
Lansdowne	10	5	0	5	162	167	10
St Mary's Coll	10	5	0	5	157	163	10
Young Munster	10	5	0	5	102	149	10
Shannon	10	4	0	6	107	104	8
Old Wesley	10	4	0	6	114	138	8
Greystones	10	4	0	6	97	156	8
Wanderers	10	1	0	9	141	234	2

Division 2	P	W	D	L	F	A	Pts
Instonians	10	8	0	2	205	100	16
Sunday's Well	10	8	0	2	184	118	16
Ballymena	10	7	0	3	214	125	14
Old Belvedere	10	7	0	3	141	125	14
Bangor	10	5	0	5	122	189	10
Terenure Coll	10	4	1	5	149	112	9
Malone	10	4	1	5	125	141	9
Old Crescent	10	4	0	6	173	150	8
Dolphin	10	4	0	6	139	144	8
Galwegians	10	3	0	7	113	124	6
Ballina	10	0	0	10	72	309	0

Division 3	P	W	D	L	F	A	Pts
UC Dublin	12	11	0	1	246	81	22
Bective Rangers	12	10	0	2	306	109	20
City of Derry	12	10	0	2	231	130	20
DLS Palmerston*	11	7	1	3	150	143	15
NIFC	12	6	2	4	203	142	14
Clontarf	12	5	4	3	127	130	14
UC Cork*	11	5	0	6	137	163	10
Highfield	12	4	1	7	128	157	9
Corinthians	12	4	0	8	150	205	8
Athlone	12	3	2	7	88	156	8
Portadown	12	3	1	8	116	157	7
Collegians	12	2	1	9	103	223	5
Sligo	12	1	0	11	64	253	2

Division 3	P	W	D	L	F	A	Pts
Monkstown	10	9	0	1	262	69	18
Waterpark	10	8	0	2	248	82	16
Queen's U	10	8	0	2	240	92	16
Dublin U	10	7	0	3	248	114	14
Skerries	10	6	1	3	160	84	13
CIYMS	10	5	0	5	183	162	10
Ards	10	4	0	6	125	185	8
Bohemians	10	3	0	7	112	142	6
Westport	10	2	1	7	63	237	5
City of Armagh	10	2	0	8	96	305	4
UC Galway	10	0	0	10	44	309	0

*De La Salle Palmerston-UCC game was cancelled and no points awarded to either team.

WINNERS OF PROVINCIAL TOURNAMENTS

LEINSTER
Senior Cup: Terenure College **Schools Senior Cup:** St Mary's College **Schools Junior Cup:** Belvedere College

ULSTER
Senior Cup: Dungannon **Schools Senior Cup:** Regent House **Schools Medallion:** Dungannon Royal

MUNSTER
Senior Cup: Sunday's Well **Schools Senior Cup:** Crescent College **Schools Junior Cup:** Christian Brothers, Cork

CONNACHT
Senior Cup: Corinthians **Schools Senior Cup:** St Joseph's, Galway **Schools Junior Cup:** Garbally College

INTER-PROVINCIAL TOURNAMENT 1993

16 October, Ravenhill

Ulster 21 (1G 3PG 1T) **Exiles 3** (1PG)

Ulster: I Orr (City of Derry); I Gray (Queen's U), M McCall (Bangor), M Field (Malone), T Howe (Dungannon); D Humphreys (Queen's U), A Blair (Dungannon); D Millar (Dungannon), J McDonald (Malone), G Bell (Instonians), P Johns (Dungannon), D Tweed (Ballymena), S McKinty (Bangor), B Robinson (Ballymena), D McBride (Malone) *Replacement* S Smith (City of Derry) for Orr
Scorers *Tries:* Tweed, Millar *Conversion:* Humphreys *Penalty Goals:* Humphreys (3)
Exiles: *(London Irish unless stated):* J Staples; P Hopley (Wasps), K Orrell (Treorchy), D Dooley, S Geoghegan; P Burke, R Saunders; N Donovan, M Kernohan (Glasgow HS), G Halpin, M Keenan, J Etheridge (Blackrock Coll), J Cleary (Orrell), A Verling, D Kelly (Manchester) *Replacements* R Hennessy for Staples; M Dobson (Sale) for Kelly; K Rabbitt (Westpark) for Kernohan
Scorer *Penalty Goal:* Burke
Referee B Smith

16 October, Sportsground, Galway

Munster 15 (1G 1PG 1T) **Connacht 9** (3PG)

Munster: P Murray (Shannon); R Wallace (Garryowen), B Walsh (Cork Const), P Danaher (Garryowen), B Begley (Old Crescent); J Galvin (Shannon), M Bradley (Cork Const); J Fitzgerald (Young Munster), T Kingston (Dolphin), P Wallace (Blackrock Coll), M Galwey (Shannon), G Fulcher (Cork Const), P O'Hara (Cork Const), E Halvey (Shannon), B Cronin (Garryowen)
Scorers *Tries:* Wallace, Begley *Conversion:* Begley *Penalty Goal:* Begley
Connacht: A White (St Mary's Coll); C Leahy (Wanderers), S Tormey (Athlone/Ballinasloe), S Carty (Galwegians), G Curley (Athlone/Ballinasloe); M Cosgrave (Wanderers), B Comerford (Athlone/Ballinasloe); T Clancy (De La Salle Palmerston), W Mulcahy (Skerries), C Shanley (De La Salle Palmerston), T Coughlin (St Mary's Coll), S Jameson (St Mary's Coll), P Bradley (Wanderers), K Devlin (St Mary's Coll), N Mannion (Lansdowne)
Scorer *Penalty Goals:* White (3)
Referee O Doyle

23 October, London Irish RFC

Exiles 8 (1PG 1T) **Leinster 13** (1G 2PG)

Exiles *(London Irish unless stated):* R Hennessy; P Hopley (Wasps), S Burns, D Dooley, S Geoghegan; P Burke, R Saunders; N Donovan, M Kernohan (Glasgow HS), G Halpin, M Keenan, J Etheridge (Blackrock Coll), D Cleary (Orrell), A Verling, K Hickey (Coventry) *Replacements* J McFarland for Kernohan; N Malone (Leicester) for Hennessy
Scorers *Try:* Cleary *Penalty Goal:* Burke
Leinster: C O'Shea (Lansdowne); P Gavin (Old Belvedere), V Cunningham (St Mary's Coll), M Ridge (Blackrock Coll), D Wall (St Mary's Coll); A McGowan (St Mary's Coll), N Hogan (Terenure Coll); H Hurley (Old Wesley), J Murphy (Greystones), A McKeen (Lansdowne), B Rigney (Greystones), N Francis (Old Belvedere), A Doyle (Lansdowne), P Lawlor (Bective Rangers), K Potts (St Mary's Coll)
Scorers *Try:* Potts *Conversion:* McGowan *Penalty Goals:* McGowan, O'Shea
Referee A Watson

23 October, Sportsground, Galway

Connacht 10 (1G 1PG) **Ulster 39** (4G 2PG 1T)

Connacht: A White (St Mary's Coll); C Leahy (Wanderers), M Cosgrave (Wanderers), S Carty (Galwegians), G Curley (Athlone/Ballinasloe); E Elwood (Lansdowne), B Comerford (Athlone/Ballinasloe); T Clancy (De La Salle Palmerston), J O'Riordan (Wanderers), K Shanley (De La Salle Palmerston), T Coughlin (St Mary's Coll), S Jameson (St Mary's Coll), V Costello (St Mary's Coll), K Devlin (St Mary's Coll), N Mannion (Lansdowne) *Replacement* R Garvey (De La Salle Palmerston) for White

Scorers *Try:* Curley   *Conversion:* Elwood   *Penalty Goal:* Elwood
Ulster: C Wilkinson (Malone); I Gray (Queen's U), M McCall (Bangor), M Field (Malone), T Howe (Dungannon); D Humphreys (Queen's U), A Blair (Dungannon); D Millar (Dungannon), J McDonald (Malone), G Bell (Instonians), P Johns (Dungannon), D Tweed (Ballymena), S McKinty (Bangor), B Robinson (Ballymena), D McBride (Malone)
Scorers *Tries:* Blair, Wilkinson, Humphreys, McKinty, McBride   *Conversions:* McCall (4)   *Penalty Goals:* McCall (2)
Referee A Lewis

30 October, Musgrave Park, Cork

Munster 21 (1G 3PG 1T)   **Leinster 19** (1G 4PG)
Munster: P Murray (Shannon); R Wallace (Garryowen), P Danaher (Garryowen), B Walsh (Cork Const), K Murphy (Cork Const); G O'Sullivan (Garryowen), M Bradley (Cork Const); J Fitzgerald (Young Munster), T Kingston (Dolphin), P McCarthy (Cork Const), M Galwey (Shannon), G Fulcher (Cork Const), K O'Connell (Sunday's Well), B Cronin (Garryowen), E Halvey (Shannon) *Replacement* P Wallace (Blackrock Coll) for Fitzgerald
Scorers *Tries:* Danaher, Murphy   *Conversion:* O'Sullivan   *Penalty Goals:* O'Sullivan (3)
Leinster: C O'Shea (Lansdowne); N Woods (Blackrock Coll), V Cunningham (St Mary's Coll), M Ridge (Blackrock Coll), D Wall (St Mary's Coll); A McGowan (Blackrock Coll), N Hogan (Terenure Coll); H Hurley (Old Wesley), J Murphy (Greystones), A McKeen (Lansdowne), D Bursey (Old Wesley), N Francis (Old Belvedere), K Potts (St Mary's Coll), P Lawlor (Bective Rangers), R Love (Old Wesley)
Scorers *Try:* McGowan   *Conversion:* McGowan   *Penalty Goals:* McGowan (3), O'Shea
Referee S Hilditch

30 October, London Irish RFC

Exiles 42 (2G 4PG 2DG 2T)   **Connacht 12** (3PG 1DG)
Exiles (*London Irish unless stated*): R Hennessy; P Hopley (Wasps), S Burns, D Dooley, M Corcoran; N Malone (Leicester), R Saunders; N Donovan, M Kernohan (Glasgow HS), G Halpin, M Keenan, J Etheridge (Blackrock Coll), D Cleary (Orrell), D Erskine (Sale), K Hickey (Coventry) *Replacement* M Dawson (Racing Club de France) for Halpin
Scorers *Tries:* Cleary, Keenan, Hopley, Hickey   *Conversions:* Corcoran (2)   *Penalty Goals:* Corcoran (4)
Dropped Goals: Malone (2)
Connacht: A White (St Mary's Coll); C Leahy (Wanderers), M Cosgrave (Wanderers), S Carty (Galwegians), G Curley (Athlone/Ballinasloe); E Elwood (Lansdowne), B Comerford (Athlone/Ballinasloe); T Clancy (De La Salle Palmerston), W Mulcahy (Skerries), K Shanley (De La Salle Palmerston), T Coughlin (St Mary's Coll), S Jameson (St Mary's Coll), V Costello (St Mary's Coll), N Mannion (Lansdowne), K Devlin (Old Belvedere) *Replacements* R Rogers (Blackrock Coll) for Costello; J O'Riordan (Wanderers) for Mannion; D Kavanagh (Blackrock Coll) for Jameson; R Garvey (De La Salle Palmerston) for White
Scorers *Penalty Goals:* White (3)   *Dropped Goal:* Elwood
Referee D Lamont

27 November, Donnybrook, Dublin

Leinster 25 (2G 2PG 1T)   **Ulster 0**
Leinster: C O'Shea (Lansdowne); P Gavin (Old Belvedere), V Cunningham (St Mary's Coll), M Ridge (Blackrock Coll), N Woods (Blackrock Coll); A McGowan (Blackrock Coll), N Hogan (Terenure Coll); H Hurley (Old Wesley), S Byrne (Blackrock Coll), A McKeen (Lansdowne), B Rigney (Greystones), N Francis (Blackrock Coll), C Pim (Old Wesley), R Love (Old Wesley), P Lawlor (Bective Rangers)
Scorers *Tries:* O'Shea, Woods, Gavin   *Conversions:* O'Shea (2)   *Penalty Goals:* O'Shea (2)
Ulster: C Wilkinson (Malone); I Gray (Queen's U), M McCall (Bangor), M Field (Malone), T Howe (Dungannon); D Humphreys (Queen's U), A Blair (Dungannon); D Millar (Dungannon), J McDonald (Malone), G Bell (Instonians), P Johns (Dungannon), D Tweed (Ballymena), S McKinty (Bangor), B Robinson (Ballymena), D McBride (Malone) *Replacement* G Longwell (Queen's U) for Tweed
Referee S Lander (RFU)

27 November, Thomond Park, Limerick

Munster 34 (2G 5PG 1T)   **Exiles 19** (1G 4PG)
Munster: P Murray (Shannon); R Wallace (Garryowen), B Walsh (Cork Const), P Danaher (Garryowen), K Murphy (Cork Const); G O'Sullivan (Cork Const), M Bradley (Cork Const); P McCarthy (Cork Const), T Kingston (Dolphin), P Wallace (Blackrock Coll), M Galwey (Shannon), G Fulcher (Cork Const), E Halvey (Shannon), B Toland (Old Crescent), L Toland (Old Crescent) *Replacement* R Costello (Garryowen) for Fulcher
Scorers *Tries:* O'Sullivan, Halvey (2)   *Conversions:* O'Sullivan (2)   *Penalty Goals:* O'Sullivan (5)
Exiles (*London Irish unless stated*): J Staples; P Hopley (Wasps), R Hennessy, D Dooley, S Geoghegan; N Malone (Leicester), R Saunders; A Donovan, J McFarland, G Halpin, M Keenan, J Etheridge (Blackrock Coll), D Cleary (Orrell), A Verling, K Hickey (Coventry)
Scorer *Try:* Hopley   *Conversion:* Hopley   *Penalty Goals:* Hopley (4)
Referee G Crothers

18 December, Ravenhill

Ulster 24 (1G 1DG 1T)   **Munster 21** (7PG)
Ulster: C Wilkinson (Malone); R Carey (Dungannon), M McCall (Bangor), M Field (Malone), T Howe (Dungannon); D Humphreys (Queen's U), A Matchett (Ballymena); D Elliott (Bangor), J McDonald (Bangor), P Millar (Ballymena), D Tweed (Ballymena), P Johns (Dungannon), S McKinty (Bangor), R Robinson (Ballymena), D McBride (Malone) *Replacement* Jeremy Hastings (Dungannon) for McBride

Scorers *Tries:* Wilkinson, Howe *Conversion:* McCall *Penalty Goals:* McCall (3) *Dropped Goal:* Humphreys
Munster: P Murray (Shannon); R Wallace (Garryowen), P Danaher (Garryowen), B Walsh (Cork Const), K Murphy (Cork Const); G O'Sullivan (Cork Const), M Bradley (Cork Const); P Soden (Cork Const), T Kingston (Dolphin), P Wallace (Blackrock Coll), M Galwey (Shannon), G Fulcher (Cork Const), K O'Connell (Sunday's Well), L Dineen (Cork Const), E Halvey (Shannon)
Scorer *Penalty Goals:* O'Sullivan (7)
Referee G Black

18 December, Donnybrook, Dublin

Leinster 15 (5PG) **Connacht 11** (2PG 1T)
Leinster: C O'Shea (Lansdowne); P Gavin (Old Belvedere), V Cunningham (St Mary's Coll), M Ridge (Blackrock Coll), N Woods (Blackrock Coll); A McGowan (Blackrock Coll), N Hogan (Terenure Coll); H Hurley (Old Wesley), S Byrne (Blackrock Coll), A McKeen (Lansdowne), B Rigney (Greystones), N Francis (Old Belvedere), K Potts (St Mary's Coll), P Lawlor (Bective Rangers), R Love (Old Wesley) *Replacement* B Keane (St Mary's Coll) for McKeen
Scorer *Penalty Goals:* McGowan (5)
Connacht: A White (St Mary's Coll); N Furlong (Garryowen), M Cosgrave (Connacht), S Tormey (Old Belvedere), C Leahy (Wanderers); E Elwood (Lansdowne), D Reddan (Old Crescent); T Clancy (De La Salle Palmerston), W Mulcahy (Skerries), C Shanley (De La Salle Palmerston), T Coughlin (St Mary's Coll), S Jameson (St Mary's Coll), V Costello (St Mary's Coll), N Mannion (Lansdowne), K Devlin (St Mary's Coll)
Scorers *Try:* Leahy *Penalty Goals:* White (2)
Referee G Black

Final Table

	P	W	D	L	F	A	Pts
Leinster	4	3	0	1	72	40	6
Ulster	4	3	0	1	84	59	6
Munster	4	3	0	1	91	71	6
Exiles	4	1	0	3	72	80	2
Connacht	4	0	0	4	42	111	0

IRISH INTERNATIONAL PLAYERS
(up to 31 March 1994)

ABBREVIATIONS

A – Australia; *Arg* – Argentina; *C* – Canada; *E* – England; *F* – France; *It* – Italy; *J* – Japan; *M* – Maoris; *Nm* – Namibia; *NZ* – New Zealand; *R* – Romania; *S* – Scotland; *SA* – South Africa; *Tg* – Tonga; *W* – Wales; *WS* – Western Samoa; *Z* – Zimbabwe; *P* – Ireland v IRFU President's XV at Lansdowne Road in IRFU centenary season, 1974-75; (R) – Replacement; (t) – temporary replacement. Entries in square brackets [ ] indicate appearances in the World Cup. NIFC – North of Ireland Football Club; CIYMS – Church of Ireland Young Men's Society; KCH – King's College Hospital

Note: Years given for Five Nations' matches are for second half of season; eg 1972 means season 1971-72. Years for all other matches refer to the actual year of the match. When a series has taken place, figures have been used to denote the particular matches in which players have featured. Thus 1981 *SA* 2 indicates that a player appeared in the second Test of the series. The abandoned game with Scotland at Belfast in 1885 is now included as a cap match.

NB – The second of Ireland's two matches against France in 1972 was a non-championship match.

Abraham, M (Bective Rangers) 1912 *E, S, W, SA,* 1914 *W*
Adams, C (Old Wesley) 1908 *E,* 1909 *E, F,* 1910 *F,* 1911 *E, S, W, F,* 1912 *S, W, SA,* 1913 *W, F,* 1914 *F, E, S*
Agar, R D (Malone) 1947 *F, E, S, W,* 1948 *F,* 1949 *S, W,* 1950 *F, E, W*
Agnew, P J (CIYMS) 1974 *F* (R), 1976 *A*
Ahearne, T (Queen's Coll, Cork) 1899 *E*
Aherne, L F P (Dolphin, Lansdowne) 1988 *E* 2, *WS, It,* 1989 *F, W, E, S, NZ,* 1990 *E, S, F, W* (R), 1992 *E, S, F, A*
Alexander, R (NIFC, Police Union) 1936 *E, S, W,* 1937 *E, S, W,* 1938 *E, S, W,* 1939 *E, S, W*
Allen, C E (Derry, Liverpool) 1900 *E, S, W,* 1901 *E, S, W,* 1903 *S, W,* 1904 *E, S, W,* 1905 *E, S, W, NZ,* 1906 *E, S, W, SA,* 1907 *S, W*
Allen, G G (Derry, Liverpool) 1896 *E, S, W,* 1897 *E, S,* 1898 *E, S,* 1899 *E, W*
Allen, T C (NIFC) 1885 *E, S* 1
Allen, W S (Wanderers) 1875 *E*
Allison, J B (Edinburgh U) 1899 *E, S,* 1900 *E, S, W,* 1901 *E, S, W,* 1902 *E, S, W,* 1903 *S*
Anderson, F E (Queen's U, Belfast, NIFC) 1953 *F, E, S, W,* 1954 *NZ, F, E, S, W,* 1955 *F, E, S, W*
Anderson, H J (Old Wesley) 1903 *E, S,* 1906 *E, S*
Anderson, W A (Dungannon) 1984 *A,* 1985 *S, F, W, E,* 1986 *F, S, R,* 1987 *E, S, F, W, [W, C, Tg, A],* 1988 *F, W, E* 1,2, 1989 *F, W, E, NZ,* 1990 *E, S*
Andrews, G (NIFC) 1875 *E,* 1876 *E*
Andrews, H W (NIFC) 1888 *M,* 1889 *S, W*
Archer, A M (Dublin U, NIFC) 1879 *S*
Arigho, J E (Lansdowne) 1928 *F, E, W,* 1929 *F, E, S, W,* 1930 *F, E, S, W,* 1931 *F, E, S, W, SA*
Armstrong, W K (NIFC) 1960 *SA,* 1961 *E*
Arnott, D T (Lansdowne) 1876 *E*
Ash, W H (NIFC) 1875 *E,* 1876 *E,* 1877 *S*
Aston, H R (Dublin U) 1908 *E, W*
Atkins, A P (Bective Rangers) 1924 *F*
Atkinson, J M (NIFC) 1927 *F, A*
Atkinson, J R (Dublin U) 1882 *W, S*

Bagot, J C (Dublin U, Lansdowne) 1879 *S, E,* 1880 *E, S,* 1881 *S*
Bailey, A H (UC Dublin, Lansdowne) 1934 *W,* 1935 *E, S, W, NZ,* 1936 *E, S, W,* 1937 *E, S, W,* 1938 *E, S*
Bailey, N (Northampton) 1952 *E*
Bardon, M E (Bohemians) 1934 *E*
Barlow, M (Wanderers) 1875 *E*
Barnes, R J (Dublin U, Armagh) 1933 *W*
Barr, A (Methodist Coll, Belfast) 1898 *W,* 1899 *S,* 1901 *E, S*
Barry, N J (Garryowen) 1991 *Nm*2(R)
Beamish, C E St J (RAF, Leicester) 1933 *W, S,* 1934 *S, W,* 1935 *E, S, W, NZ,* 1936 *S, W,* 1938 *W*
Beamish, G R (RAF, Leicester) 1925 *E, S, W,* 1928 *F, E, S, W,* 1929 *F, E, S, W,* 1930 *F, S, W,* 1931 *F, E, S, W, SA,* 1932 *E, S, W,* 1933 *E, W, S*
Beatty, W J (NIFC, Richmond) 1910 *F,* 1912 *F, W*
Becker, V A (Lansdowne) 1974 *F, W*

Beckett, G G P (Dublin U) 1908 *E, S, W*
Bell, R J (NIFC) 1875 *E,* 1876 *E*
Bell, W E (Belfast Collegians) 1953 *F, E, S, W*
Bennett, F (Belfast Collegians) 1913 *S*
Bent, G C (Dublin U) 1882 *W, E*
Berkery, P J (Lansdowne) 1954 *W,* 1955 *W,* 1956 *S, W,* 1957 *F, E, S, W,* 1958 *A, E, S*
Bermingham, J J C (Blackrock Coll) 1921 *E, S, W, F*
Blackham, J C (Queen's Coll, Cork) 1909 *S, W, F,* 1910 *E, S, W*
Blake-Knox, S E F (NIFC) 1976 *E, S,* 1977 *F* (R)
Blayney, J J (Wanderers) 1950 *S*
Bond, A T W (Derry) 1894 *S, W*
Bornemann, W W (Wanderers) 1960 *E, S, W, SA*
Bowen, D St J (Cork Const) 1977 *W, E, S*
Boyd, C A (Dublin U) 1900 *S,* 1901 *S, W*
Boyle, C V (Dublin U) 1935 *NZ,* 1936 *E, S, W,* 1937 *E, S, W,* 1938 *W,* 1939 *W*
Brabazon, H M (Dublin U) 1884 *E,* 1885 *S* 1, 1886 *E*
Bradley, M J (Dolphin) 1920 *W, F,* 1922 *E, S, W, F,* 1923 *E, S, W, F,* 1925 *F, S, W,* 1926 *F, E, S, W,* 1927 *F, W*
Bradley, M T (Cork Constitution) 1984 *A,* 1985 *S, F, W, E,* 1986 *F, W, E, S, R,* 1987 *E, S, F, W, [W, C, Tg, A],* 1988 *S, F, W, E* 1, 1990 *W,* 1992 *NZ* 1,2, 1993 *S, F, W, E, R,* 1994 *F, W, E, S*
Bradshaw, G (Belfast Collegians) 1903 *W*
Bradshaw, R M (Wanderers) 1885 *E, S* 1,2
Brady, A M (UC Dublin, Malone) 1966 *S,* 1968 *E, S, W*
Brady, J A (Wanderers) 1976 *E, S*
Brady, J R (CIYMS) 1951 *S, W,* 1953 *F, E, S, W,* 1954 *W,* 1956 *W,* 1957 *F, E, S, W*
Bramwell, T (NIFC) 1928 *F*
Brand, T N (NIFC) 1924 *NZ*
Brennan, J I (CIYMS) 1957 *S, W*
Bresnihan, F P K (UC Dublin, Lansdowne, London Irish) 1966 *E, W,* 1967 *A* 1, *E, S, W, F,* 1968 *F, E, S, W, A,* 1969 *F, E, S, W,* 1970 *SA, F, E, S, W,* 1971 *F, E, S, W*
Brett, J T (Monkstown) 1914 *W*
Bristow, J R (NIFC) 1879 *E*
Brophy, N H (Blackrock Coll, UC Dublin, London Irish) 1957 *F, E,* 1959 *E, S, W, F,* 1960 *F, SA,* 1961 *S, W,* 1962 *E, S, W,* 1963 *E, W,* 1967 *E, S, W, F, A* 2
Brown, E L (Instonians) 1958 *F*
Brown, G S (Monkstown, United Services) 1912 *S, W, SA*
Brown, H (Windsor) 1877 *E*
Brown, T (Windsor) 1877 *E, S*
Brown, W H (Dublin U) 1899 *E*
Brown, W J (Malone) 1970 *SA, F, S, W*
Brown, W S (Dublin U) 1893 *S, W,* 1894 *E, S, W*
Browne, A W (Dublin U) 1951 *SA*
Browne, D (Blackrock Coll) 1920 *F*
Browne, H C (United Services and RN) 1929 *E, S, W*
Browne, W F (United Services and Army) 1925 *E, S, W,* 1926 *S, W,* 1927 *F, E, S, W, A,* 1928 *E, S*
Browning, D R (Wanderers) 1881 *E, S*
Bruce, S A M (NIFC) 1883 *E, S,* 1884 *E*
Brunker, A A (Lansdowne) 1895 *E, W*
Bryant, C H (Cardiff) 1920 *E, S*

252

Buchanan, A McM (Dublin U) 1926 *E, S, W,* 1927 *S, W, A*
Buchanan, J W B (Dublin U) 1882 *S,* 1884 *E, S*
Buckley, J H (Sunday's Well) 1973 *E, S*
Bulger, L Q (Lansdowne) 1896 *E, S, W,* 1897 *E, S,* 1898 *E, S, W*
Bulger, M J (Dublin U) 1888 *M*
Burges, J H (Rosslyn Park) 1950 *F, E*
Burgess, R B (Dublin U) 1912 *SA*
Burkitt, J C S (Queen's Coll, Cork) 1881 *E*
Burns, I J (Wanderers) 1980 *E* (R)
Butler, L G (Blackrock Coll) 1960 *W*
Butler, N (Bective Rangers) 1920 *E*
Byers, R M (NIFC) 1928 *S, W,* 1929 *E, S, W*
Byrne, E M J (Blackrock Coll) 1977 *S, F,* 1978 *F, W, E, NZ*
Byrne, N F (UC Dublin) 1962 *F*

Byrne, S J (UC Dublin, Lansdowne) 1953 *S, W,* 1955 *F*
Byron, W G (NIFC) 1896 *E, S, W,* 1897 *E, S,* 1898 *E, S, W,* 1899 *E, S, W*

Caddell, E D (Dublin U, Wanderers) 1904 *S,* 1905 *E, S, W, NZ,* 1906 *E, S, W, SA,* 1907 *E, S,* 1908 *S, W*
Cagney, S J (London Irish) 1925 *W,* 1926 *F, E, S, W,* 1927 *F,* 1928 *E, S, W,* 1929 *F, E, S, W*
Callan, C P (Lansdowne) 1947 *F, E, S, W,* 1948 *F, E, S, W,* 1949 *F, E*
Cameron, E D (Bective Rangers) 1891 *S, W*
Campbell, C E (Old Wesley) 1970 *SA*
Campbell, E F (Monkstown) 1899 *S, W,* 1900 *E, W*
Campbell, S B B (Derry) 1911 *E, S, W, F,* 1912 *F, E, S, W, SA,* 1913 *E, S, F*
Campbell, S O (Old Belvedere) 1976 *A,* 1979 *A* 1,2, 1980 *E, S, F, W,* 1981 *F, W, E, S, SA* 1, 1982 *W, E, S,*

Ireland captain Michael Bradley (34 caps) evades Kyran Bracken's tackle in Ireland's surprise 13-12 victory over England at Twickenham.

F, 1983 *S*, *F*, *W*, *E*, 1984 *F*, *W*
Canniffe, D M (Lansdowne) 1976 *W*, *E*
Cantrell, J L (UC Dublin, Blackrock Coll) 1976 *A*, *F*, *W*, *E*, *S*, 1981 *S*, *SA* 1,2, *A*
Carey, R W (Dungannon) 1992 *NZ* 1,2
Carpendale, M J (Monkstown) 1886 *S*, 1887 *W*, 1888 *W*, *S*
Carr, N J (Ards) 1985 *S*, *F*, *W*, *E*, 1986 *W*, *E*, *S*, *R*, 1987 *E*, *S*, *W*
Carroll, C (Bective Rangers) 1930 *F*
Carroll, R (Lansdowne) 1947 *F*, 1950 *S*, *W*
Casement, B N (Dublin U) 1875 *E*, 1876 *E*, 1879 *E*
Casement, F (Dublin U) 1906 *E*, *S*, *W*
Casey, J C (Young Munster) 1930 *S*, 1932 *E*
Casey, P J (UC Dublin, Lansdowne) 1963 *F*, *E*, *S*, *W*, *NZ*, 1964 *E*, *S*, *W*, *F*, 1965 *F*, *E*, *S*
Chambers, J (Dublin U) 1886 *E*, *S*, 1887 *E*, *S*, *W*
Chambers, R R (Instonians) 1951 *F*, *E*, *S*, *W*, 1952 *F*, *W*
Clancy, T P J (Lansdowne) 1988 *W*, *E* 1,2, *WS*, *It*, 1989 *F*, *W*, *E*, *S*
Clarke, C P (Terenure Coll) 1993 *F*, *W*, *E*
Clarke, D J (Dolphin) 1991 *W*, *Nm* 1,2, [*J*, *A*], 1992 *NZ* 2(R)
Clarke, J A B (Bective Rangers) 1922 *S*, *W*, *F*, 1923 *F*, 1924 *E*, *S*, *W*
Clegg, R J (Bangor) 1973 *F*, 1975 *E*, *S*, *F*, *W*
Clifford, J T (Young Munster) 1949 *F*, *E*, *S*, *W*, 1950 *F*, *E*, *S*, *W*, 1951 *F*, *E*, *SA*, 1952 *F*, *S*, *W*
Clinch, A D (Dublin U, Wanderers) 1892 *S*, 1893 *W*, 1895 *E*, *S*, *W*, 1896 *E*, *S*, *W*, 1897 *E*, *S*
Clinch, J D (Wanderers, Dublin U) 1923 *W*, 1924 *F*, *E*, *S*, *W*, *NZ*, 1925 *F*, *E*, *S*, 1926 *E*, *S*, *W*, 1927 *F*, 1928 *F*, *E*, *S*, *W*, 1929 *F*, *E*, *S*, *W*, 1930 *F*, *E*, *S*, *W*, 1931 *F*, *E*, *S*, *W*, *SA*
Clohessy, P M (Young Munster) 1993 *F*, *W*, *E*, 1994 *F*, *W*, *E*, *S*
Clune, J J (Blackrock Coll) 1912 *SA*, 1913 *W*, *F*, 1914 *F*, *E*, *W*
Coffey, J J (Lansdowne) 1900 *E*, 1901 *W*, 1902 *E*, *S*, *W*, 1903 *E*, *S*, *W*, 1905 *E*, *S*, *W*, *NZ*, 1906 *E*, *S*, *W*, *SA*, 1907 *E*, 1908 *W*, 1910 *F*
Cogan, W St J (Queen's Coll, Cork) 1907 *E*, *S*
Collier, S R (Queen's Coll, Belfast) 1883 *S*
Collins, P C (Lansdowne, London Irish) 1987 [*C*], 1990 *S* (R)
Collis, W R F (KCH, Harlequins) 1924 *F*, *W*, *NZ*, 1925 *F*, *E*, *S*, 1926 *F*
Collis, W S (Wanderers) 1884 *W*
Collopy, G (Bective Rangers) 1891 *S*, 1892 *S*
Collopy, R (Bective Rangers) 1923 *E*, *S*, *W*, *F*, 1924 *F*, *E*, *S*, *W*, *NZ*, 1925 *F*, *E*, *S*, *W*
Collopy, W P (Bective Rangers) 1914 *F*, *E*, *S*, *W*, 1921 *E*, *S*, *W*, *F*, 1922 *E*, *S*, *W*, *F*, 1923 *S*, *W*, *F*, 1924 *F*, *E*, *S*, *W*
Combe, A (NIFC) 1875 *E*
Condon, H C (London Irish) 1984 *S* (R)
Cook, H G (Lansdowne) 1884 *W*
Coote, P B (RAF, Leicester) 1933 *S*
Corcoran, J C (London Irish) 1947 *A*, 1948 *F*
Corken, T S (Belfast Collegians) 1937 *E*, *S*, *W*
Corley, H H (Dublin U, Wanderers) 1902 *E*, *S*, *W*, 1903 *E*, *S*, *W*, 1904 *E*, *S*
Cormac, H S T (Clontarf) 1921 *E*, *S*, *W*
Costello, P (Bective Rangers) 1960 *F*
Costello, R A (Garryowen) 1993 *S*
Cotton, J (Wanderers) 1889 *W*
Coulter, H H (Queen's U, Belfast) 1920 *E*, *S*, *W*
Courtney, A W (UC Dublin) 1920 *S*, *W*, *F*, 1921 *E*, *S*, *W*, *F*
Cox, H L (Dublin U) 1875 *E*, 1876 *E*, 1877 *E*, *S*
Craig, R G (Queen's U, Belfast) 1938 *S*, *W*
Crawford, E C (Dublin U) 1885 *E*, *S* 1
Crawford, W E (Lansdowne) 1920 *E*, *S*, *W*, *F*, 1921 *E*, *S*, *W*, *F*, 1922 *E*, *S*, 1923 *E*, *S*, *W*, *F*, 1924 *F*, *E*, *W*, *NZ*, 1925 *F*, *E*, *S*, *W*, 1926 *F*, *E*, *S*, *W*, 1927 *F*, *E*, *S*, *W*
Crean, T J (Wanderers) 1894 *E*, *S*, *W*, 1895 *E*, *S*, *W*, 1896 *E*, *S*, *W*
Crichton, R Y (Dublin U) 1920 *E*, *S*, *W*, *F*, 1921 *F*, 1922 *E*, 1923 *W*, *F*, 1924 *F*, *E*, *S*, *W*, *NZ*, 1925 *E*, *S*
Croker, E W D (Limerick) 1878 *E*
Cromey, G E (Queen's U, Belfast) 1937 *E*, *S*, *W*, 1938 *E*, *S*, *W*, 1939 *E*, *S*, *W*
Cronyn, A P (Dublin U, Lansdowne) 1875 *E*, 1876 *E*, 1880 *S*

Crossan, K D (Instonians) 1982 *S*, 1984 *F*, *W*, *E*, *S*, 1985 *S*, *F*, *W*, *E*, 1986 *E*, *S*, *R*, 1987 *E*, *S*, *F*, *W*, [*W*, *C*, *Tg*, *A*], 1988 *S*, *F*, *W*, *E* 1, *WS*, *It*, 1989 *W*, *S*, *NZ*, 1990 *E*, *S*, *F*, *W*, *Arg*, 1991 *E*, *S* , *Nm* 2, [*Z*, *J*, *S*], 1992 *W*
Crowe, J F (UC Dublin) 1974 *NZ*
Crowe, L (Old Belvedere) 1950 *E*, *S*, *W*
Crowe, M P (Lansdowne) 1929 *W*, 1930 *E*, *S*, *W*, 1931 *F*, *S*, *W*, *SA*, 1932 *S*, *W*, 1933 *W*, *S*, 1934 *E*
Crowe, P M (Blackrock Coll) 1935 *E*, 1938 *E*
Cullen, T J (UC Dublin) 1949 *F*
Cullen, W J (Monkstown and Manchester) 1920 *E*
Culliton, M G (Wanderers) 1959 *E*, *S*, *W*, *F*, 1960 *E*, *S*, *W*, *F*, *SA*, 1961 *E*, *S*, *W*, *F*, 1962 *S*, *F*, 1964 *E*, *S*, *W*, *F*
Cummins, W E A (Queen's Coll, Cork) 1879 *S*, 1881 *E*, 1882 *E*
Cunningham, D McC (NIFC) 1923 *E*, *S*, *W*, 1925 *F*, *E*, *W*
Cunningham, M J (UC Cork) 1955 *F*, *E*, *S*, *W*, 1956 *F*, *S*, *W*
Cunningham, V J G (St Mary's Coll) 1988 *E* 2, *It* 1990 *Arg* (R), 1991 *Nm* 1,2, [*Z*, *J*(R)], 1992 *NZ* 1,2, *A*, 1993 *S*, *F*, *W*, *E*, *R*, 1994 *F*
Cunningham, W A (Lansdowne) 1920 *W*, 1921 *E*, *S*, *W*, *F*, 1922 *E*, 1923 *S*, *W*
Cuppaidge, J L (Dublin U) 1879 *E*, 1880 *E*, *S*
Currell, J (NIFC) 1877 *S*
Curtis, A B (Oxford U) 1950 *F*, *E*, *S*
Curtis, D M (London Irish) 1991 *W*, *E*, *S*, *Nm* 1,2, [*Z*, *J*, *S*, *A*], 1992 *W*, *E*, *S*(R), *F*
Cuscaden, W A (Dublin U, Bray) 1876 *E*
Cussen, D J (Dublin U) 1921 *E*, *S*, *W*, *F*, 1922 *E*, 1923 *E*, *S*, *W*, *F*, 1926 *F*, *E*, *S*, *W*, 1927 *F*, *E*

Daly, J C (London Irish) 1947 *F*, *E*, *S*, *W*, 1948 *E*, *S*, *W*
Daly, M J (Harlequins) 1938 *E*
Danaher, P P A (Lansdowne, Garryowen) 1988 *S*, *F*, *W*, *WS*, *It*, 1989 *F*, *NZ* (R), 1990 *F*, 1992 *S*, *F*, *NZ* 1, *A*, 1993 *S*, *F*, *W*, *E*, *R*, 1994 *F*, *W*, *E*, *S*
Dargan, M J (Old Belvedere) 1952 *S*, *W*
Davidson, C T (NIFC) 1921 *F*
Davidson, I G (NIFC) 1899 *E*, 1900 *S*, *W*, 1901 *E*, *S*, *W*, 1902 *E*, *S*, *W*
Davidson, J C (Dungannon) 1969 *F*, *E*, *S*, *W*, 1973 *NZ*, 1976 *NZ*
Davies, F E (Lansdowne) 1892 *S*, *W*, 1893 *E*, *S*, *W*
Davis, J L (Monkstown) 1898 *E*, *S*
Davis, W J N (Edinburgh U, Bessbrook) 1890 *S*, *W*, *E*, 1891 *E*, *S*, *W*, 1892 *E*, *S*, 1895 *S*
Davison, W (Belfast Academy) 1887 *W*
Davy, E O'D (UC Dublin, Lansdowne) 1925 *W*, 1926 *F*, *E*, *S*, *W*, 1927 *F*, *E*, *S*, *W*, *A*, 1928 *F*, *E*, *S*, *W*, 1929 *F*, *E*, *S*, *W*, 1930 *F*, *E*, *S*, *W*, 1931 *F*, *E*, *S*, *W*, *SA*, 1932 *E*, *S*, *W*, 1933 *E*, *W*, *S*, 1934 *E*
Dawson, A R (Wanderers) 1958 *A*, *E*, *S*, *W*, *F*, 1959 *E*, *S*, *W*, *F*, 1960 *F*, *SA*, 1961 *E*, *S*, *W*, *F*, *SA*, 1962 *S*, *F*, *W*, 1963 *F*, *E*, *S*, *W*, *NZ*, 1964 *E*, *S*, *F*
Dean, P M (St Mary's Coll) 1981 *SA* 1,2, *A*, 1982 *W*, *E*, *S*, *F*, 1984 *A*, 1985 *S*, *F*, *W*, *E*, 1986 *F*, *W*, *R*, 1987 *E*, *S*, *F*, *W*, [*W*, *A*], 1988 *S*, *F*, *W*, *E* 1,2, *WS*, *It*, 1989 *F*, *W*, *E*, *S*
Deane, E C (Monkstown) 1909 *E*
Deering, M J (Bective Rangers) 1929 *W*
Deering, S J (Bective Rangers) 1935 *E*, *S*, *W*, *NZ*, 1936 *E*, *S*, *W*, 1937 *E*, *S*
Deering, S M (Garryowen, St Mary's Coll) 1974 *W*, 1976 *F*, *W*, *E*, *S*, 1977 *W*, *E*, 1978 *NZ*
de Lacy, H (Harlequins) 1948 *E*, *S*
Delaney, M G (Bective Rangers) 1895 *W*
Dennison, S P (Garryowen) 1973 *F*, 1975 *E*, *S*
Dick, C J (Ballymena) 1961 *W*, *F*, *SA*, 1962 *W*, 1963 *F*, *E*, *S*, *W*
Dick, J S (Queen's U, Belfast) 1962 *E*
Dick, J S (Queen's U, Cork) 1887 *E*, *S*, *W*
Dickson, J A N (Dublin U) 1920 *E*, *W*, *F*
Doherty, A E (Old Wesley) 1974 *P* (R)
Doherty, W D (Guy's Hospital) 1920 *E*, *S*, *W*, 1921 *E*, *S*, *W*, *F*
Donaldson, J A (Belfast Collegians) 1958 *A*, *E*, *S*, *W*
Donovan, T M (Queen's Coll, Cork) 1889 *S*
Dooley, J F (Galwegians) 1959 *E*, *S*, *W*
Doran, B R W (Lansdowne) 1900 *S*, *W*, 1901 *E*, *S*, *W*, 1902 *E*, *S*, *W*

Doran, E F (Lansdowne) 1890 *S, W*
Doran, G P (Lansdowne) 1899 *S, W,* 1900 *E, S,* 1902 *S, W,* 1903 *W,* 1904 *E*
Douglas, A C (Instonians) 1923 *F,* 1924 *E, S,* 1927 *A,* 1928 *S*
Downing, A J (Dublin U) 1882 *W*
Dowse, J C A (Monkstown) 1914 *F, S, W*
Doyle, J A P (Greystones) 1984 *E, S*
Doyle, J T (Bective Rangers) 1935 *W*
Doyle, M G (Blackrock Coll, UC Dublin, Cambridge U, Edinburgh Wands) 1965 *F, E, S, W, SA,* 1966 *F, E, S, W,* 1967 *A* 1, *E, S, W, F, A* 2, 1968 *F, E, S, W, A*
Doyle, T J (Wanderers) 1968 *E, S, W*
Duggan, A T A (Lansdowne) 1963 *NZ,* 1964 *F,* 1966 *W,* 1967 *A* 1, *S, W, A* 2, 1968 *F, E, S, W,* 1969 *F, E, S, W,* 1970 *SA, F, E, S, W,* 1971 *F, E, S, W,* 1972 *F* 2
Duggan, W (UC Cork) 1920 *S, W*
Duggan, W P (Blackrock Coll) 1975 *E, S, F, W,* 1976 *A, F, W, S, NZ,* 1977 *W, E, S, F,* 1978 *S, F, W, E, NZ,* 1979 *E, S, A* 1,2, 1980 *E,* 1981 *F, W, E, S, SA* 1,2, *A,* 1982 *W, E, S,* 1983 *S, F, W, E,* 1984 *F, W, E, S*
Duncan, W R (Malone) 1984 *W, E*
Dunlea, F J (Lansdowne) 1989 *W, E, S*
Dunlop, R (Dublin U) 1889 *W,* 1890 *S, W, E,* 1891 *E, S, W,* 1892 *E, S,* 1893 *W,* 1894 *W*
Dunn, P E F (Bective Rangers) 1923 *S*
Dunn, T B (NIFC) 1935 *NZ*
Dunne, M J (Lansdowne) 1929 *F, E, S,* 1930 *F, E, S, W,* 1932 *E, S, W,* 1933 *E, W, S,* 1934 *E, S, W*
Dwyer, P J (UC Dublin) 1962 *W,* 1963 *F, NZ,* 1964 *S, W*

Edwards, H G (Dublin U) 1877 *E,* 1878 *E*
Edwards, R W (Malone) 1904 *W*
Edwards, T (Lansdowne) 1888 *M,* 1890 *S, W, E,* 1892 *W,* 1893 *E*
Edwards, W V (Malone) 1912 *F, E*
Egan, J D (Bective Rangers) 1922 *S*
Egan, J T (Cork Constitution) 1931 *F, E, SA*
Egan, M S (Garryowen) 1893 *E,* 1895 *S*
Ekin, W (Queen's Coll, Belfast) 1888 *W, S*
Elliott, W R J (Bangor) 1979 *S*
Elwood, E P (Lansdowne) 1993 *W, E, R,* 1994 *F, W, E, S*
English, M A F (Lansdowne, Limerick Bohemians) 1958 *W, F,* 1959 *E, S, F,* 1960 *E, S,* 1961 *S, W, F,* 1962 *F, W,* 1963 *E, S, W, NZ*
Ennis, F N G (Wanderers) 1979 *A* 1 (R)
Ensor, A H (Wanderers) 1973 *W, F,* 1974 *F, W, E, S, P, NZ,* 1975 *E, S, F, W,* 1976 *A, F, W, E, NZ,* 1977 *E,* 1978 *S, F, W, E*
Entrican, J C (Queen's U, Belfast) 1931 *S*

Fagan, G L (Kingstown School) 1878 *E*
Fagan, W B C (Wanderers) 1956 *F, E, S*
Farrell, J L (Bective Rangers) 1926 *F, E, S, W,* 1927 *F, E, S, W, A,* 1928 *F, E, S, W,* 1929 *F, E, S, W,* 1930 *F, E, S, W,* 1931 *F, E, S, W, SA,* 1932 *E, S, W*
Feddis, N (Lansdowne) 1956 *E*
Feighery, C F P (Lansdowne) 1972 *F* 1, *E, F* 2
Feighery, T A O (St Mary's Coll) 1977 *W, E*
Ferris, H H (Queen's Coll, Belfast) 1901 *W*
Ferris, J H (Queen's Coll, Belfast) 1900 *E, S, W*
Field, M J (Malone) 1994 *E, S*
Finlay, J E (Queen's Coll, Belfast) 1913 *E, S, W,* 1920 *E, S, W*
Finlay, J C (NIFC) 1876 *E,* 1877 *E, S,* 1878 *E,* 1879 *S, E,* 1880 *S,* 1882 *S*
Finn, M C (UC Cork, Cork Constitution) 1979 *E,* 1982 *W, E, S, F,* 1983 *S, F, W, E,* 1984 *E, S, A,* 1986 *F*
Finn, R G A (UC Dublin) 1977 *F*
Fitzgerald, C (Glasgow U, Dungannon) 1902 *E,* 1903 *E, S*
Fitzgerald, C F (St Mary's Coll) 1979 *A* 1,2, 1980 *E, S, F, W,* 1982 *W, E, S, F,* 1983 *S, F, W, E,* 1984 *F, W, A,* 1985 *S, F, W, E,* 1986 *F, W, E, S*
Fitzgerald, D C (Lansdowne, De La Salle Palmerston) 1984 *E, S,* 1986 *W, E, S,* 1987 *E, S, F, W,* [*W, C, A*], 1988 *S, F, W, E* 1, 1989 *NZ* (R), 1990 *E, S, F, W, Arg,* 1991 *F, W, E, S, Nm* 1,2, [*Z, S, A*], 1992 *W, S*(R)
Fitzgerald, J (Wanderers) 1884 *W*
Fitzgerald, J J (Young Munster) 1988 *S, F,* 1990 *S, F, W,* 1991 *W, E, S,* [*J*]
Fitzgibbon, M J J (Shannon) 1992 *W, E, S, F, NZ* 1,2

Fitzpatrick, M P (Wanderers) 1978 *S,* 1980 *S, F, W,* 1981 *F, W, E, S, A,* 1985 *F* (R)
Fletcher, W W (Kingstown) 1882 *W, S,* 1883 *E*
Flood, R S (Dublin U) 1925 *W*
Flynn, M K (Wanderers) 1959 *F,* 1960 *F,* 1962 *E, S, F, W,* 1964 *E, S, W, F,* 1965 *F, E, S, W, SA,* 1966 *F, E, S,* 1972 *F* 1, *E, F* 2, 1973 *NZ*
Fogarty, T (Garryowen) 1891 *W*
Foley, B O (Shannon) 1976 *F, E,* 1977 *W, F* (R), 1980 *F, W,* 1981 *F, E, S, SA,* 1,2, *A*
Forbes, R E (Malone) 1907 *E*
Forrest, A J (Wanderers) 1880 *E, S,* 1881 *E, S,* 1882 *W, E,* 1883 *E,* 1885 *S* 2
Forrest, E G (Wanderers) 1888 *M,* 1889 *S, W,* 1890 *S, E,* 1891 *E,* 1893 *S,* 1894 *E, S, W,* 1895 *W,* 1897 *E, S*
Forrest, H (Wanderers) 1893 *S, W*
Fortune, J J (Clontarf) 1963 *NZ,* 1964 *E*
Foster, A R (Derry) 1910 *E, S, F,* 1911 *E, S, W, F,* 1912 *F, E, S, W,* 1914 *E, S, W,* 1921 *E, S, W*
Francis, N P J (Blackrock Coll, London Irish, Old Belvedere) 1987 [*Tg, A*], 1988 *WS, It,* 1989 *S,* 1990 *E, F, W,* 1991 *S, Nm* 1,2, [*Z, J, S, A*], 1992 *W, E, S,* 1993 *F, R,* 1994 *F, W, E, S*
Franks, J G (Dublin U) 1898 *E, S, W*
Frazer, E F (Bective Rangers) 1891 *S,* 1892 *S*
Freer, A E (Lansdowne) 1901 *E, S, W*
Fulton, J (NIFC) 1895 *S, W,* 1896 *E,* 1897 *E,* 1898 *W,* 1899 *E,* 1900 *W,* 1901 *E,* 1902 *E, S, W,* 1903 *E, S, W,* 1904 *E, S*
Furlong, J N (UC Galway) 1992 *NZ* 1,2

Gaffikin, W (Windsor) 1875 *E*
Gage, J H (Queen's U, Belfast) 1926 *S, W,* 1927 *S, W*
Galbraith, E (Dublin U) 1875 *E*
Galbraith, H T (Belfast Acad) 1890 *W*
Galbraith, R (Dublin U) 1875 *E,* 1876 *E,* 1877 *E*
Galwey, M J (Shannon) 1991 *F, W, Nm* 2(R), [*J*], 1992 *E, S, F, NZ* 1,2, *A,* 1993 *F, W, E, R,* 1994 *F, W, E, S*
Ganly, J B (Monkstown) 1927 *F, E, S, W, A,* 1928 *F, E, S, W,* 1929 *F, S,* 1930 *F*
Gardiner, F (NIFC) 1900 *E, S,* 1901 *E, W,* 1902 *E, S, W,* 1903 *E, W,* 1904 *E, S, W,* 1906 *E, S, W,* 1907 *S, W,* 1908 *S, W,* 1909 *E, S, F*
Gardiner, J B (NIFC) 1923 *E, S, W, F,* 1924 *F, E, S, W, NZ,* 1925 *F, E, S, W*
Gardiner, S (Belfast Albion) 1893 *E, S*
Gardiner, W (NIFC) 1892 *E, S,* 1893 *E, S, W,* 1894 *E, S, W,* 1895 *E, S, W,* 1896 *E, S, W,* 1897 *E, S,* 1898 *W, E, S, W*
Garry, M G (Bective Rangers) 1909 *E, S, W, F,* 1911 *E, S, W*
Gaston, J T (Dublin U) 1954 *NZ, F, E, S, W,* 1955 *W,* 1956 *F, E*
Gavin, T J (Moseley, London Irish) 1949 *F, E*
Geoghegan, S P (London Irish) 1991 *F, W, E, S, Nm* 1, [*Z, S, A*], 1992 *E, S, F, A,* 1993 *S, F, W, E, R,* 1994 *F, W, E, S*
Gibson, C M H (Cambridge U, NIFC) 1964 *E, S, W, F,* 1965 *F, E, S, W, SA,* 1966 *F, E, S, W,* 1967 *A* 1, *E, S, W, F, A* 2, 1968 *E, S, W, A,* 1969 *E, S, W,* 1970 *SA, F, E, S, W,* 1971 *F, E, S, W,* 1972 *F* 1, *E, F* 2, 1973 *NZ, E, S, W, F,* 1974 *F, W, E, S, P,* 1975 *E, S, F, W,* 1976 *A, F, W, E, S, NZ,* 1977 *W, E, S, F,* 1978 *F, W, E, NZ,* 1979 *S, A* 1,2
Gibson, M E (Lansdowne, London Irish) 1979 *F, W, E, S,* 1981 *W* (R), 1986 *R,* 1988 *S, F, W, E* 2
Gifford, H P (Wanderers) 1890 *S*
Gillespie, J C (Dublin U) 1922 *W, F*
Gilpin, F G (Queen's U, Belfast) 1962 *E, S, F*
Glass, D C (Belfast Collegians) 1958 *F,* 1960 *W,* 1961 *W, SA*
Glennon, B T (Lansdowne) 1993 *F*(R)
Glennon, J J (Skerries) 1980 *E, S,* 1987 *E, S, F,* [*W*(R)]
Godfrey, R P (UC Dublin) 1954 *S, W*
Goodall, K G (City of Derry, Newcastle U) 1967 *A* 1, *E, S, W, F, A* 2, 1968 *F, E, S, W, A,* 1969 *F, E, S,* 1970 *SA, F, E, S, W*
Gordon, A (Dublin U) 1884 *S*
Gordon, T G (NIFC) 1877 *E, S,* 1878 *E*
Gotto, R P C (NIFC) 1906 *SA*
Goulding, W J (Cork) 1879 *S*
Grace, T O (UC Dublin, St Mary's Coll) 1972 *F* 1, *E,* 1973 *NZ, E, S, W,* 1974 *E, S, P, NZ,* 1975 *E, S, F, W,* 1976 *A, F, W, E, S, NZ,* 1977 *W, E, S, F,* 1978 *S*
Graham, R I (Dublin U) 1911 *F*

Kennedy, H (Bradford) 1938 *S, W*
Kennedy, J M (Wanderers) 1882 *W*, 1884 *W*
Kennedy, K W (Queen's U, Belfast, London Irish) 1965 *F, E, S, W, SA*, 1966 *F, E, W*, 1967 *A* 1, *E, S, W, F, A* 2, 1968 *F, A*, 1969 *F, E, S, W*, 1970 *SA, F, E, S, W*, 1971 *F, E, S, W*, 1972 *F* 1, *E, F* 2, 1973 *NZ, E, S, W, F*, 1974 *F, W, E, S, P, NZ*, 1975 *F, W*
Kennedy, T J (St Mary's Coll) 1978 *NZ*, 1979 *F, W, E* (R), *A* 1,2, 1980 *E, S, F, W*, 1981 *SA* 1,2, *A*
Kenny, P (Wanderers) 1992 *NZ* 2(R)
Keogh, F S (Bective Rangers) 1964 *W, F*
Keon, J J (Limerick) 1879 *E*
Keyes, R P (Cork Constitution) 1986 *E*, 1991 [*Z, J, S, A*], 1992 *W, E, S*
Kidd, F W (Dublin U, Lansdowne) 1877 *E, S*, 1878 *E*
Kiely, M D (Lansdowne) 1962 *W*, 1963 *F, E, S, W*
Kiernan, M J (Dolphin, Lansdowne) 1982 *W*(R), *E, S, F*, 1983 *S, F, W, E*, 1984 *E, S, A*, 1985 *S, F, W, E*, 1986 *F, W, E, S, R*, 1987 *E, S, F, W*, [*W, C, A*], 1988 *S, F, W, E* 1,2, *WS*, 1989 *F, W, E, S*, 1990 *E, S, F, W, Arg*, 1991 *F*
Kiernan, T J (UC Cork, Cork Const) 1960 *E, S, W, F, SA*, 1961 *E, S, W, F, SA*, 1962 *E, W*, 1963 *F, S, W, NZ*, 1964 *E, S*, 1965 *F, E, S, W, SA*, 1966 *F, E, S, W*, 1967 *A* 1, *E, S, W, F, A* 2, 1968 *F, E, S, W, A*, 1969 *F, E, S, W*, 1970 *SA, F, E, S, W*, 1971 *F*, 1972 *F* 1, *E, F* 2, 1973 *NZ, E, S*
Killeen, G V (Garryowen) 1912 *E, S, W*, 1913 *E, S, W, F*, 1914 *E, S, W*
King, H (Dublin U) 1883 *E, S*
Kingston, T G (Dolphin) 1987 [*W, Tg, A*], 1988 *S, F, W, E* 1, 1990 *F, W*, 1991 [*J*], 1993 *F, W, E, R*, 1994 *F, W, E, S*
Knox, J H (Dublin U, Lansdowne) 1904 *W*, 1905 *E, S, W, NZ*, 1906 *E, S, W*, 1907 *W*, 1908 *S*
Kyle, J W (Queen's U, Belfast, NIFC) 1947 *F, E, S, W, A*, 1948 *F, E, S, W*, 1949 *F, E, S, W*, 1950 *F, E, S, W*, 1951 *F, E, S, W, SA*, 1952 *F, S, W, E*, 1953 *F, E, S, W*, 1954 *NZ, F*, 1955 *F, E, W*, 1956 *F, E, S, W*, 1957 *F, E, S, W*, 1958 *A, E, S*

Lambert, N H (Lansdowne) 1934 *S, W*
Lamont, R A (Instonians) 1965 *F, E, SA*, 1966 *F, E, S, W*, 1970 *SA, F, E, S, W*
Landers, M F (Cork Const) 1904 *W*, 1905 *E, S, W, NZ*
Lane, D (UC Cork) 1934 *S, W*, 1935 *E, S*
Lane, M F (UC Cork) 1947 *W*, 1949 *F, E, S, W*, 1950 *F, E, S, W*, 1951 *F, E, S, W, SA*, 1952 *F, S*, 1953 *F, E*
Lane, P (Old Crescent) 1964 *W*
Langan, D J (Clontarf) 1934 *W*
Langbroek, J A (Blackrock Coll) 1987 [*Tg*]
Lavery, P (London Irish) 1974 *W*, 1976 *W*
Lawler, P J (Clontarf) 1951 *S, SA*, 1952 *F, S, W, E*, 1953 *F*, 1954 *NZ, E, S*, 1956 *F, E*
Lawlor, P J (Bective Rangers) 1935 *E, S, W*, 1937 *E, S, W*
Lawlor, P J (Bective Rangers) 1990 *Arg*, 1992 *A*, 1993 *S*
Leahy, K T (Wanderers) 1992 *NZ* 1
Leahy, M W (UC Cork) 1964 *W*
Lee, S (NIFC) 1891 *E, S, W*, 1892 *E, S, W*, 1893 *E, S, W*, 1894 *E, S, W*, 1895 *E, W*, 1896 *E, S, W*, 1897 *E*, 1898 *E*
Le Fanu, V C (Cambridge U, Lansdowne) 1886 *E, S*, 1887 *E, W*, 1888 *S*, 1889 *W*, 1890 *E*, 1891 *E*, 1892 *E, S, W*
Lenihan, D G (UC Cork, Cork Const) 1981 *A*, 1982 *W, E, S, F*, 1983 *F, W, E*, 1984 *F, W, E, S, A*, 1985 *S, F, W, E*, 1986 *F, W, E, S, R*, 1987 *E, S, F, W*, [*W, C, Tg, A*], 1988 *S, F, W, E* 1,2, *WS, It*, 1989 *F, W, E, S, NZ*, 1990 *E, W, Arg*, 1991 *Nm* 2, [*Z, S, A*], 1992 *W*
L'Estrange, L P F (Dublin U) 1962 *E*
Levis, F H (Wanderers) 1884 *E*
Lightfoot, E J (Lansdowne) 1931 *F, E, S, W, SA*, 1932 *E, S, W*, 1933 *E, W, S*
Lindsay, H (Dublin U, Armagh) 1893 *E, S, W*, 1894 *E, S, W*, 1895 *E*, 1896 *E, S, W*, 1898 *E, S, W*
Little, T J (Bective Rangers) 1898 *W*, 1899 *E, S, W*, 1900 *S, W*, 1901 *E, S*
Lloyd, R A (Dublin U, Liverpool) 1910 *E, S*, 1911 *E, S, W, F*, 1912 *F, E, S, W, SA*, 1913 *E, S, W, F*, 1914 *F, E*, 1920 *E, S*
Lydon, C T J (Galwegians) 1956 *S*
Lyle, R K (Dublin U) 1910 *W, F*
Lyle, T R (Dublin U) 1885 *E, S* 1,2, 1886 *E*, 1887 *E, S*

Lynch, J F (St Mary's Coll) 1971 *F, E, S, W*, 1972 *F* 1, *E, F* 2, 1973 *NZ, E, S, W*, 1974 *F, W, E, S, P, NZ*
Lynch, L (Lansdowne) 1956 *S*
Lytle, J H (NIFC) 1894 *E, S, W*, 1895 *W*, 1896 *E, S, W*, 1897 *E, S*, 1898 *E, S*, 1899 *S*
Lytle, J N (NIFC) 1888 *M*, 1889 *W*, 1890 *E*, 1891 *E, S*, 1894 *E, S, W*
Lyttle, V J (Collegians, Bedford) 1938 *E*, 1939 *E, S*

McAleese, D R (Ballymena) 1992 *F*
McAllan, G H (Dungannon) 1896 *S, W*
Macaulay, J (Limerick) 1887 *E, S*
McBride, W D (Malone) 1988 *W, E* 1, *WS, It*, 1989 *S*, 1990 *F, W, Arg*, 1993 *S, F, W, E, R*, 1994 *W, E, S*
McBride, W J (Ballymena) 1962 *E, S, F, W*, 1963 *F, E, S, W, NZ*, 1964 *E, S, F*, 1965 *F, E, S, W, SA*, 1966 *F, E, S, W, NZ*, 1967 *A* 1, *E, S, W, F, A* 2, 1968 *F, E, S, W, A*, 1969 *F, E, S, W*, 1970 *SA, F, E, S, W*, 1971 *F, E, S, W*, 1972 *F* 1, *E, F* 2, 1973 *NZ, E, S, W, F*, 1974 *F, W, E, S, P, NZ*, 1975 *E, S, F, W*
McCall, B W (London Irish) 1985 *F* (R), 1986 *E, S*
McCall, M C (Bangor) 1992 *NZ* 1(R),2, 1994 *F*
McCallan, B (Ballymena) 1960 *E, S*
McCarten, R J (London Irish) 1961 *E, W, F*
McCarthy, E A (Kingstown) 1882 *W*
McCarthy, J S (Dolphin) 1948 *F, E, S, W*, 1949 *F, E, S, W*, 1950 *W*, 1951 *F, E, S, W, SA*, 1952 *F, S, W, E*, 1953 *F, E, S*, 1954 *NZ, F, E, S, W*, 1955 *F, E*
McCarthy, P D (Cork Const) 1992 *NZ* 1,2, *A*, 1993 *S, R*(R)
MacCarthy, St G (Dublin U) 1882 *W*
McCarthy, T (Cork) 1898 *W*
McClelland, T A (Queen's U, Belfast) 1921 *E, S, W, F*, 1922 *E, W, F*, 1923 *E, S, W, F*, 1924 *F, E, S, W, NZ*
McClenahan, R O (Instonians) 1923 *E, S, W*
McClinton, A N (NIFC) 1910 *W, F*
McCombe, W McM (Dublin U, Bangor) 1968 *F*, 1975 *E, S, F, W*
McConnell, A A (Collegians) 1947 *A*, 1948 *F, E, S, W*, 1949 *F, E*
McConnell, G (Derry, Edinburgh U) 1912 *F, E*, 1913 *W, F*
McConnell, J W (Lansdowne) 1913 *S*
McCormac, F M (Wanderers) 1909 *W*, 1910 *W, F*
McCormick, W J (Wanderers) 1930 *E*
McCoull, H C (Belfast Albion) 1895 *E, S, W*, 1899 *E*
McCourt, D (Queen's U, Belfast) 1947 *A*
McCoy, J J (Dungannon, Bangor, Ballymena) 1984 *W, A*, 1985 *S, F, W, E*, 1986 *F*, 1987 [*Tg*], 1988 *E* 2, *WS, It*, 1989 *F, W, E, S, NZ*
McCracken, H (NIFC) 1954 *W*
McDermott, S J (London Irish) 1955 *S, W*
Macdonald, J A (Methodist Coll, Belfast) 1875 *E*, 1876 *E*, 1877 *S*, 1878 *E*, 1879 *S*, 1880 *E*, 1881 *S*, 1882 *E, S*, 1883 *E, S*, 1884 *E, S*
McDonald, J P (Malone) 1987 [*C*], 1990 *E* (R), *S, Arg*
McDonnell, A C (Dublin U) 1889 *W*, 1890 *S, W*, 1891 *E*
McDowell, J C (Instonians) 1924 *F, NZ*
McFarland, B A T (Derry) 1920 *S, W, F*, 1922 *W*
McGann, B J (Lansdowne) 1969 *F, E, S, W*, 1970 *SA, F, E, S, W*, 1971 *F, E, S, W*, 1972 *F* 1, *E, F* 2, 1973 *NZ, E, S, W*, 1976 *F, W, E, S, NZ*
McGown, T M W (NIFC) 1899 *E, S*, 1901 *S*
McGrath, D G (UC Dublin, Cork Const) 1984 *S*, 1987 [*W, C, Tg, A*]
McGrath, N F (Oxford U, London Irish) 1934 *W*
McGrath, P J (UC Cork) 1965 *E, S, W, SA*, 1966 *F, E, S, W*, 1967 *A* 1, *A* 2
McGrath, R J M (Wanderers) 1977 *W, E, F* (R), 1981 *SA* 1,2, *A*, 1982 *W, E, S, F*, 1983 *S, F, W, E*, 1984 *F, W*
McGrath, T (Garryowen) 1956 *W*, 1958 *F*, 1960 *E, S, W, F*, 1961 *SA*
McGuire, E P (UC Galway) 1963 *E, S, W, NZ*, 1964 *E, S, W, F*
MacHale, S (Lansdowne) 1965 *F, E, S, W, SA*, 1966 *F, E, S, W*, 1967 *S, W, F*
McIldowie, G (Malone) 1906 *SA*, 1910 *E, S, W*
McIlrath, J A (Ballymena) 1976 *A, F, NZ*, 1977 *W, E*
McIlwaine, E H (NIFC) 1895 *S, W*
McIlwaine, E N (NIFC) 1875 *E*, 1876 *E*
McIlwaine, J E (NIFC) 1897 *E, S*, 1898 *E, S, W*, 1899 *E, W*
McIntosh, L M (Dublin U) 1884 *S*
MacIvor, C V (Dublin U) 1912 *F, E, S, W*, 1913 *E, S, F*

F, W, E, S, Nm 1,2, *[J, S, A]*, 1992 *W, E, S*
Murphy, C J (Lansdowne) 1939 *E, S, W,* 1947 *F, E*
Murphy, J G M W (London Irish) 1951 *SA,* 1952 *S, W, E,* 1954 *NZ,* 1958 *W*
Murphy, J J (Greystones) 1981 *SA* 1, 1982 *W* (R), 1984 *S*
Murphy, J N (Greystones) 1992 *A*
Murphy, K J (Cork Constitution) 1990 *E, S, F, W, Arg,* 1991 *F, W*(R), *S*(R), 1992 *S, F, NZ* 2(R)
Murphy, N A A (Cork Constitution) 1958 *A, E, S, W, F,* 1959 *E, S, W, F,* 1960 *E, S, W, F, SA,* 1961 *E, S, W,* 1962 *E,* 1963 *NZ,* 1964 *E, S, W, F,* 1965 *F, E, S, W, SA,* 1966 *F, E, S, W,* 1967 *A* 1, *E, S, W, F,* 1969 *F, E, S, W*
Murphy, N F (Cork Constitution) 1930 *E, W,* 1931 *F, E, S, W, SA,* 1932 *E, S, W,* 1933 *E*
Murphy-O'Connor, J (Bective Rangers) 1954 *E*
Murray, H W (Dublin) 1877 *S,* 1878 *E,* 1879 *E*
Murray, J B (UC Dublin) 1963 *F*
Murray, P F (Wanderers) 1927 *F,* 1929 *F, E, S,* 1930 *F, E, S, W,* 1931 *F, E, S, W, SA,* 1932 *E, S, W,* 1933 *E, W, S*
Murtagh, C W (Portadown) 1977 *S*
Myles, J (Dublin U) 1875 *E*

Nash, L C (Queen's Coll, Cork) 1889 *S,* 1890 *W, E,* 1891 *E, S, W*
Neely, M R (Collegians) 1947 *F, E, S, W*
Neill, H J (NIFC) 1885 *E, S* 1,2, 1886 *S,* 1887 *E, S, W,* 1888 *W, S*
Neill, J McF (Instonians) 1926 *F*
Nelson, J E (Malone) 1947 *A,* 1948 *E, S, W,* 1949 *F, E, S, W,* 1950 *F, E, S, W,* 1951 *F, E, W,* 1954 *F*
Nelson, R (Queen's Coll, Belfast) 1882 *E, S,* 1883 *S,* 1886 *S*
Nesdale, T J (Garryowen) 1961 *F*
Neville, W C (Dublin U) 1879 *S, E*
Nicholson, P C (Dublin U) 1900 *E, S, W*
Norton, G W (Bective Rangers) 1949 *F, E, S, W,* 1950 *F, E, S, W,* 1951 *F, E, S*
Notley, J R (Wanderers) 1952 *F, S*

O'Brien, B (Derry) 1893 *S, W*
O'Brien, B A P (Shannon) 1968 *F, E, S*
O'Brien, D J (London Irish, Cardiff, Old Belvedere) 1948 *E, S, W,* 1949 *F, E, S, W,* 1950 *F, E, S, W,* 1951 *F, E, S, W, SA,* 1952 *F, S, W, E*
O'Brien, K A (Broughton Park) 1980 *E,* 1981 *SA* 1 (R), 2
O'Brien-Butler, P E (Monkstown) 1897 *S,* 1898 *E, S,* 1899 *S, W,* 1900 *E*
O'Callaghan, C T (Carlow) 1910 *W, F,* 1911 *E, S, W, F,* 1912 *F*
O'Callaghan, M P (Sunday's Well) 1962 *W,* 1964 *E, F*
O'Callaghan, P (Dolphin) 1967 *A* 1, *E, A* 2, 1968 *F, E, S, W,* 1969 *F, E, S, W,* 1970 *SA, F, E, S, W,* 1976 *F, W, E, S, NZ*
O'Connell, K D (Sunday's Well) 1994 *F, E*(t)
O'Connell, P (Bective Rangers) 1913 *W, F,* 1914 *F, E, S, W*
O'Connell, W J (Lansdowne) 1955 *F*
O'Connor, H S (Dublin U) 1957 *F, E, S, W*
O'Connor, J (Garryowen) 1895 *S*
O'Connor, J H (Bective Rangers) 1888 *M,* 1890 *S, W, E,* 1891 *E, S,* 1892 *E, W,* 1893 *E, S,* 1894 *E, S, W,* 1895 *E,* 1896 *E, S, W*
O'Connor, J J (Garryowen) 1909 *F*
O'Connor, J J (UC Cork) 1933 *S,* 1934 *E, S, W,* 1935 *E, S, W, NZ,* 1936 *S, W,* 1938 *S*
O'Connor, P J (Lansdowne) 1887 *W*
Odbert, R V M (RAF) 1928 *F*
O'Donnell, R C (St Mary's Coll) 1979 *A* 1,2, 1980 *S, F, W*
O'Donoghue, P J (Bective Rangers) 1955 *F, E, S, W,* 1956 *W,* 1957 *F, E,* 1958 *A, E, S, W*
O'Driscoll, B J (Manchester) 1971 *F* (R), *E, S, W*
O'Driscoll, J B (London Irish, Manchester) 1978 *S,* 1979 *A* 1,2, 1980 *E, S, F, W,* 1981 *F, W, E, S, SA* 1,2, *A,* 1982 *W, E, S, F,* 1983 *S, F, W, E,* 1984 *F, W, E, S*
O'Flanagan, K P (London Irish) 1947 *A*
O'Flanagan, M (Lansdowne) 1948 *S*
O'Hanlon, B (Dolphin) 1947 *E, S, W,* 1948 *F, E, S, W,* 1949 *F, E, S, W,* 1950 *F*
O'Hara, P T J (Sunday's Well, Cork Const) 1988 *WS* (R), 1989 *F, W, E, NZ,* 1990 *E, S, F, W,* 1991 *Nm* 1, *[J],* 1993 *F, W, E*

O'Leary, A (Cork Constitution) 1952 *S, W, E*
O'Loughlin, D B (UC Cork) 1938 *E, S, W,* 1939 *E, S, W*
O'Meara, J A (UC Cork, Dolphin) 1951 *F, E, S, W, SA,* 1952 *F, S, W, E,* 1953 *F, E, S, W,* 1954 *NZ, F, E, S,* 1955 *F, E,* 1956 *S, W,* 1958 *W*
O'Neill, H O'H (Queen's U, Belfast, UC Cork) 1930 *E, S, W,* 1933 *E, S, W*
O'Neill, J B (Queen's U, Belfast) 1920 *S*
O'Neill, W A (UC Dublin, Wanderers) 1952 *E,* 1953 *F, E, S, W,* 1954 *NZ*
O'Reilly, A J F (Old Belvedere, Leicester) 1955 *F, E, S, W,* 1956 *F, E, S, W,* 1957 *F, E, S, W,* 1958 *A, E, S, W, F,* 1959 *E, S, W, F,* 1960 *E,* 1961 *E, F, SA,* 1963 *F, S, W,* 1970 *E*
Orr, P A (Old Wesley) 1976 *F, W, E, S, NZ,* 1977 *W, E, S, F,* 1978 *S, F, W, E, NZ,* 1979 *F, W, E, S, A* 1,2, 1980 *E, S, F, W,* 1981 *F, W, E, S, SA* 1,2, *A,* 1982 *W, E, S, F,* 1983 *S, F, W, E,* 1984 *F, W, E, S, A,* 1985 *S, F, W, E,* 1986 *F, S, R,* 1987 *E, S, F, W, [W, C, A]*
O'Shea, C M P (Lansdowne) 1993 *R,* 1994 *F, W, E, S*
O'Sullivan, A C (Dublin U) 1882 *S*
O'Sullivan, J M (Limerick) 1884 *S,* 1887 *S*
O'Sullivan, P J A (Galwegians) 1957 *F, E, S, W,* 1959 *E, S, W, F,* 1960 *SA,* 1961 *E, S,* 1962 *F, W,* 1963 *F, NZ*
O'Sullivan, W (Queen's Coll, Cork) 1895 *S*
Owens, R H (Dublin U) 1922 *E, S*

Parfrey, P (UC Cork) 1974 *NZ*
Parke, J C (Monkstown) 1903 *W,* 1904 *E, S, W,* 1905 *W, NZ,* 1906 *E, S, W, SA,* 1907 *E, S, W,* 1908 *E, S, W,* 1909 *E, S, W, F*
Parr, J S (Wanderers) 1914 *F, E, S, W*
Patterson, C S (Instonians) 1978 *NZ,* 1979 *F, W, E, S, A* 1,2, 1980 *E, S, F, W*
Patterson, R d'A (Wanderers) 1912 *F, S, W, SA,* 1913 *E, S, W, F*
Payne, C T (NIFC) 1926 *E,* 1927 *F, E, S, A,* 1928 *F, E, S, W,* 1929 *F, E, W,* 1930 *F, E, S, W*
Pedlow, A C (CIYMS) 1953 *W,* 1954 *NZ, F, E,* 1955 *F, E, S, W,* 1956 *F, E, S, W,* 1957 *F, E, S, W,* 1958 *A, E, S, W, F,* 1959 *E, S, W, F,* 1960 *E, S, W, F, SA,* 1961 *S,* 1962 *W,* 1963 *F*
Pedlow, J (Bessbrook) 1882 *S,* 1884 *W*
Pedlow, R (Bessbrook) 1891 *W*
Pedlow, T B (Queen's Coll, Belfast) 1889 *S, W*
Peel, T (Limerick) 1892 *E, S, W*
Peirce, W (Cork) 1881 *E*
Phipps, G C (Army) 1950 *E, W,* 1952 *F, W, E*
Pike, T O (Lansdowne) 1927 *E, S, W, A,* 1928 *F, E, S, W*
Pike, V J (Lansdowne) 1931 *E, S, W, SA,* 1932 *E, S, W,* 1933 *E, W, S,* 1934 *E, S, W*
Pike, W (Kingstown) 1879 *E,* 1881 *E, S,* 1882 *E,* 1883 *S*
Pinion, G (Belfast Collegians) 1909 *E, S, W, F*
Piper, O J S (Cork Constitution) 1909 *E, S, W, F,* 1910 *E, S, W, F*
Polden, S E (Clontarf) 1913 *W, F,* 1914 *F,* 1920 *F*
Popham, I (Cork Constitution) 1922 *S, W, F,* 1923 *F*
Popplewell, N J (Greystones) 1989 *NZ,* 1990 *Arg,* 1991 *Nm* 1,2, *[Z, S, A],* 1992 *W, E, S, F, NZ* 1,2, *A,* 1993 *S, F, W, E, R,* 1994 *F, W, E, S*
Potterton, H N (Wanderers) 1920 *W*
Pratt, R H (Dublin U) 1933 *E, W, S,* 1934 *E, S*
Price, A H (Dublin U) 1920 *S, F*
Pringle, J C (NIFC) 1902 *S, W*
Purcell, N M (Lansdowne) 1921 *E, S, W, F*
Purdon, H (NIFC) 1879 *S, E,* 1880 *E,* 1881 *E, S*
Purdon, W B (Queen's Coll, Belfast) 1906 *E, S, W*
Purser, F C (Dublin U) 1898 *E, S, W*

Quinlan, S V J (Blackrock Coll) 1956 *F, E, W,* 1958 *W*
Quinn, B T (Old Belvedere) 1947 *F*
Quinn, F P (Old Belvedere) 1981 *F, W, E*
Quinn, J P (Dublin U) 1910 *E, S,* 1911 *E, S, W, F,* 1912 *E, S, W,* 1913 *E, W, F,* 1914 *F, E, S*
Quinn, K (Old Belvedere) 1947 *F, A,* 1953 *F, E, S*
Quinn, M A M (Lansdowne) 1973 *F,* 1974 *F, W, E, S, P, NZ,* 1977 *S, F,* 1981 *SA* 2
Quirke, J M T (Blackrock Coll) 1962 *E, S,* 1968 *S*

Rainey, P I (Ballymena) 1989 *NZ*
Rambaut, D F (Dublin U) 1887 *E, S, W,* 1888 *W*

259

Rea, H H (Edinburgh U) 1967 *A* 1, 1969 *F*
Read, H M (Dublin U) 1910 *E, S,* 1911 *E, S, W, F,* 1912 *F, E, S, W, SA,* 1913 *E, S*
Rearden, J V (Cork Constitution) 1934 *E, S*
Reid, C (NIFC) 1899 *S, W,* 1900 *E,* 1903 *W*
Reid, J L (Richmond) 1934 *S, W*
Reid, P J (Garryowen) 1947 *A,* 1948 *F, E, W*
Reid, T E (Garryowen) 1953 *E, S, W,* 1954 *NZ, F,* 1955 *E, S,* 1956 *F, E,* 1957 *F, E, S, W*
Reidy, C J (London Irish) 1937 *W*
Reidy, G F (Dolphin, Lansdowne) 1953 *W,* 1954 *F, E, S, W*
Richey, H A (Dublin U) 1889 *W,* 1890 *S*
Ridgeway, E C (Wanderers) 1932 *S, W,* 1935 *E, S, W*
Rigney, B J (Greystones) 1991 *F, W, E, S, Nm* 1, 1992 *F, NZ* 1(R),2
Ringland, T M (Queen's U, Belfast, Ballymena) 1981 *A,* 1982 *W, E, F,* 1983 *S, F, W, E,* 1984 *F, W, E, S, A,* 1985 *S, F, W, E,* 1986 *F, W, E, S, R,* 1987 *E, S, F, W,* [*W, C, Tg, A*], 1988 *S, F, W, E* 1
Riordan, W F (Cork Constitution) 1910 *E*
Ritchie, J S (London Irish) 1956 *F, E*
Robb, C G (Queen's Coll, Belfast) 1904 *E, S, W,* 1905 *NZ,* 1906 *S*
Robbie, J C (Dublin U, Greystones) 1976 *A, F, NZ,* 1977 *S, F,* 1981 *F, W, E, S*
Robinson, B F (Ballymena, London Irish) 1991 *F, W, E, S, Nm* 1,2, [*Z, S, A*], 1992 *W, E, S, F, NZ* 1,2, *A,* 1993 *W, E, R,* 1994 *F, W, E, S*
Robinson, T T H (Wanderers) 1904 *E, S,* 1905 *E, S, W, NZ,* 1906 *SA,* 1907 *E, S, W*
Roche, J (Wanderers) 1890 *S, W, E,* 1891 *E, S, W,* 1892 *W*
Roche, R E (UC Galway) 1955 *E, S,* 1957 *S, W*
Roche, W J (UC Cork) 1920 *E, S, F*
Roddy, P J (Bective Rangers) 1920 *S, F*
Roe, R (Lansdowne) 1952 *E,* 1953 *F, E, S, W,* 1954 *F, E, S, W,* 1955 *F, E, S, W,* 1956 *F, E, S, W,* 1957 *F, E, S, W*
Rolland, A C (Blackrock Coll) 1990 *Arg*
Rooke, C V (Dublin U) 1891 *E, W,* 1892 *F, E, S,* 1893 *E, S, W,* 1894 *E, S, W,* 1895 *E, S, W,* 1896 *E, S, W,* 1897 *E, S*
Ross, D J (Belfast Academy) 1884 *E,* 1885 *S* 1,2, 1886 *E, S*
Ross, G R P (CIYMS) 1955 *W*
Ross, J F (NIFC) 1886 *S*
Ross, J P (Lansdowne) 1885 *E, S* 1,2, 1886 *E, S*
Ross, N G (Malone) 1927 *F, E*
Ross, W McC (Queen's U, Belfast) 1932 *E, S, W,* 1933 *E, W, S,* 1934 *E, S,* 1935 *NZ*
Russell, J (UC Cork) 1931 *F, E, S, W, SA,* 1933 *E, W, S,* 1934 *E, S, W,* 1935 *E, S, W,* 1936 *E, S, W,* 1937 *E, S*
Russell, P (Instonians) 1990 *E,* 1992 *NZ* 1,2, *A*
Rutherford, W G (Tipperary) 1884 *E, S,* 1885 *E, S* 1, 1886 *E,* 1888 *W*
Ryan, E (Dolphin) 1937 *W,* 1938 *E, S*
Ryan, J (Rockwell Coll) 1897 *E,* 1898 *E, S, W,* 1899 *E, S, W,* 1900 *S, W,* 1901 *E, S, W,* 1902 *E,* 1904 *E*
Ryan, J G (UC Dublin) 1939 *E, S, W*
Ryan, M (Rockwell Coll) 1897 *E, S,* 1898 *E, S, W,* 1899 *E, S, W,* 1900 *E, S, W,* 1901 *E, S, W,* 1903 *E,* 1904 *E, S*

Saunders, R (London Irish) 1991 *F, W, E, S, Nm* 1,2, [*Z, J, S, A*], 1992 *W,* 1994 *F*(t)
Sayers, H J M (Lansdowne) 1935 *E, S, W,* 1936 *E, S, W,* 1938 *W,* 1939 *E, S, W*
Schute, F (Wanderers) 1878 *E,* 1879 *E*
Schute, F G (Dublin U) 1912 *SA,* 1913 *E, S*
Scott, D (Malone) 1961 *F, SA,* 1962 *S*
Scott, R D (Queen's U, Belfast) 1967 *E, F,* 1968 *F, E, S*
Scovell, R H (Kingstown) 1883 *E,* 1884 *E*
Scriven, G (Dublin U) 1879 *S, E,* 1880 *E, S,* 1881 *E,* 1882 *S,* 1883 *E, S*
Sealy, J (Dublin U) 1896 *E, S, W,* 1897 *S,* 1899 *E, S, W,* 1900 *E, S*
Sexton, J F (Dublin U, Lansdowne) 1988 *E* 2, *WS, It,* 1989 *F*
Sexton, W J (Garryowen) 1984 *A,* 1988 *S, E* 2
Shanahan, T (Lansdowne) 1885 *E, S* 1,2, 1886 *E,* 1888 *S, W*
Shaw, G M (Windsor) 1877 *S*
Sheehan, M D (London Irish) 1932 *E*

Sherry, B F (Terenure Coll) 1967 *A* 1, *E, S, A* 2, 1968 *F, E*
Sherry, M J A (Lansdowne) 1975 *F, W*
Siggins, J A E (Belfast Collegians) 1931 *F, E, S, W, SA,* 1932 *E, S, W,* 1933 *E, W, S,* 1934 *E, S, W,* 1935 *E, S, W, NZ,* 1936 *E, S, W,* 1937 *E, S, W*
Slattery, J F (UC Dublin, Blackrock Coll) 1970 *SA, F, E, S, W,* 1971 *F, E, S, W,* 1972 *F* 1, *E, F* 2, 1973 *NZ, E, S, W, F,* 1974 *F, W, E, S, P, NZ,* 1975 *E, S, F, W,* 1976 *A,* 1977 *S, F,* 1978 *S, F, W, E, NZ,* 1979 *F, W, E, S, A* 1,2, 1980 *E, S, F, W,* 1981 *F, W, E, S, SA* 1,2, *A,* 1982 *W, E, S, F,* 1983 *S, F, W, E,* 1984 *F*
Smartt, F N B (Dublin U) 1908 *E, S,* 1909 *E*
Smith, B A (Oxford U, Leicester) 1989 *NZ,* 1990 *S, F, W, Arg,* 1991 *F, W, E, S*
Smith, J H (London Irish) 1951 *F, E, S, W, SA,* 1952 *F, S, W, E,* 1954 *NZ, W, F*
Smith, R E (Lansdowne) 1892 *E*
Smith, S J (Ballymena) 1988 *E* 2, *WS, It,* 1989 *F, W, E, S, NZ,* 1990 *E,* 1991 *F, W, E, S, Nm* 1,2, [*Z, S, A*], 1992 *W, E, S, F, NZ* 1,2, 1993 *S*
Smithwick, F F S (Monkstown) 1898 *S, W*
Smyth, J T (Queen's U, Belfast) 1920 *F*
Smyth, P J (Belfast Collegians) 1911 *E, S, F*
Smyth, R S (Dublin U) 1903 *E, S,* 1904 *E*
Smyth, T (Malone, Newport) 1908 *E, S, W,* 1909 *E, S, W,* 1910 *E, S, W, F,* 1911 *E, S, W,* 1912 *E*
Smyth, W S (Belfast Collegians) 1910 *W, F,* 1920 *E*
Solomons, B A H (Dublin U) 1908 *E, S, W,* 1909 *E, S, W, F,* 1910 *E, S*
Spain, A W (UC Dublin) 1924 *NZ*
Sparrow, W (Dublin U) 1893 *W,* 1894 *E*
Spillane, B J (Bohemians) 1985 *S, F, W, E,* 1986 *F, W, E,* 1987 *F, W,* [*W, C, A*(R)], 1989 *E* (R)
Spring, D E (Dublin U) 1978 *S, NZ,* 1979 *S,* 1980 *S, F, W,* 1981 *W*
Spring, R M (Lansdowne) 1979 *F, W, E*
Spunner, H F (Wanderers) 1881 *E, S,* 1884 *W*
Stack, C R R (Dublin U) 1889 *S*
Stack, G H (Dublin U) 1875 *E*
Staples, J E (London Irish) 1991 *W, E, S, Nm* 1,2, [*Z, J, S, A*], 1992 *W, E, NZ* 1,2, *A*
Steele, H W (Ballymena) 1976 *E,* 1977 *F,* 1978 *F, W, E,* 1979 *F, W, E, A* 1,2
Stephenson, G V (Queen's U, Belfast, London Hosp) 1920 *F,* 1921 *E, S, W, F,* 1922 *E, S, W, F,* 1923 *E, S, W, F,* 1924 *F, E, S, W, NZ,* 1925 *F, E, S, W,* 1926 *F, E, S, W,* 1927 *F, E, S, W, A,* 1928 *F, E, S, W,* 1929 *F, E, W,* 1930 *F, E, S, W*
Stephenson, H W V (United Services) 1922 *S, W, F,* 1924 *F, E, S, W, NZ,* 1925 *F, E, S, W,* 1927 *A,* 1928 *E*
Stevenson, J (Dungannon) 1888 *M,* 1889 *S*
Stevenson, J B (Instonians) 1958 *A, E, S, W, F*
Stevenson, R (Dungannon) 1887 *E, S, W,* 1888 *M,* 1889 *S, W,* 1890 *S, W, E,* 1891 *W,* 1892 *W,* 1893 *E, S, W*
Stevenson, T H (Belfast Acad) 1895 *E, W,* 1896 *E, S, W,* 1897 *E, S*
Stewart, A L (NIFC) 1913 *W, F,* 1914 *F*
Stewart, W J (Queen's U, Belfast, NIFC) 1922 *F,* 1924 *S,* 1928 *F, E, S, W,* 1929 *F, E, S, W*
Stoker, E W (Wanderers) 1888 *W, S*
Stoker, F O (Wanderers) 1886 *S,* 1888 *W, M,* 1889 *S,* 1891 *W*
Stokes, O S (Cork Bankers) 1882 *E,* 1884 *E*
Stokes, P (Garryowen) 1913 *E, S,* 1914 *F,* 1920 *E, S, W, F,* 1921 *E, S, F,* 1922 *W, F*
Stokes, R D (Queen's Coll, Cork) 1891 *S, W*
Strathdee, E (Queen's U, Belfast) 1947 *E, S, W, A,* 1948 *W, F,* 1949 *E, S, W*
Stuart, C P (Clontarf) 1912 *SA*
Stuart, I M B (Dublin U) 1924 *E, S*
Sugars, H S (Dublin U) 1905 *NZ,* 1906 *SA,* 1907 *S*
Sugden, M (Wanderers) 1925 *F, E, S, W,* 1926 *F, E, S, W,* 1927 *E, S, W, A,* 1928 *F, E, S, W,* 1929 *F, E, S, W,* 1930 *F, E, S, W,* 1931 *F, E, S, W*
Sullivan, D B (UC Dublin) 1922 *E, S, W, F*
Sweeney, J A (Blackrock Coll) 1907 *E, S, W*
Symes, G R (Monkstown) 1895 *E*
Synge, J S (Lansdowne) 1929 *S*

Taggart, T (Dublin U) 1887 *W*
Taylor, A S (Queen's Coll, Belfast) 1910 *E, S, W,* 1912 *F*
Taylor, D R (Queen's Coll, Belfast) 1903 *E*

Taylor, J (Belfast Collegians) 1914 *E, S, W*
Taylor, J W (NIFC) 1879 *S*, 1880 *E, S*, 1881 *S*, 1882 *E, S*, 1883 *E, S*
Tector, W R (Wanderers) 1955 *F, E, S*
Tedford, A (Malone) 1902 *E, S, W*, 1903 *E, S, W*, 1904 *E, S, W*, 1905 *E, S, W, NZ*, 1906 *E, S, W, SA*, 1907 *E, S, W*, 1908 *E, S, W*
Teehan, C (UC Cork) 1939 *E, S, W*
Thompson, C (Belfast Collegians) 1907 *E, S*, 1908 *E, S, W*, 1909 *E, S, W, F*, 1910 *E, S, W, F*
Thompson, J A (Queen's Coll, Belfast) 1885 *S* 1,2
Thompson, J K S (Dublin U) 1921 *W*, 1922 *E, S, F*, 1923 *E, S, W, F*
Thompson, R G (Lansdowne) 1882 *W*
Thompson, R H (Instonians) 1951 *SA*, 1952 *F*, 1954 *NZ, F, E, S, W*, 1955 *F, S, W*, 1956 *W*
Thornhill, T (Wanderers) 1892 *E, S, W*, 1893 *E*
Thrift, T (Dublin U) 1904 *W*, 1905 *E, S, W, NZ*, 1906 *E, W, SA*, 1907 *E, S, W*, 1908 *E, S, W*, 1909 *E, S, W, F*
Tierney, D (UC Cork) 1938 *S, W*, 1939 *E*
Tillie, C R (Dublin U) 1887 *E, S*, 1888 *W, S*
Todd, A W P (Dublin U) 1913 *W, F*, 1914 *F*
Torrens, J D (Bohemians) 1938 *W*, 1939 *E, S, W*
Tucker, C C (Shannon) 1979 *F, W*, 1980 *F* (R)
Tuke, B B (Bective Rangers) 1890 *E*, 1891 *E, S*, 1892 *E*, 1894 *E, S, W*, 1895 *E, S*
Turley, N (Blackrock Coll) 1962 *E*
Tydings, J J (Young Munster) 1968 *A*
Tyrrell, W (Queen's U, Belfast) 1910 *F*, 1913 *E, S, W, F*, 1914 *F, E, S, W*

Uprichard, R J H (Harlequins, RAF) 1950 *S, W*

Waide, S L (Oxford U, NIFC) 1932 *E, S, W*, 1933 *E, W*
Waites, J (Bective Rangers) 1886 *S*, 1888 *M*, 1889 *W*, 1890 *S, W, E*, 1891 *E*
Waldron, O C (Oxford U, London Irish) 1966 *S, W*, 1968 *A*
Walker, S (Instonians) 1934 *E, S*, 1935 *E, S, W, NZ*, 1936 *E, S, W*, 1937 *E, S, W*, 1938 *E, S, W*
Walkington, D B (NIFC) 1887 *E, W*, 1888 *W*, 1890 *W, E*, 1891 *E, S, W*
Walkington, R B (NIFC) 1875 *E*, 1876 *E*, 1877 *E, S*, 1878 *E*, 1879 *S*, 1880 *E, S*, 1882 *E, S*
Wall, H (Dolphin) 1965 *S, W*
Wallace, Jas (Wanderers) 1904 *E, S*
Wallace, Jos (Wanderers) 1903 *S, W*, 1904 *E, S, W*, 1905 *E, S, W, NZ*, 1906 *W*
Wallace R M (Garryowen) 1991 *Nm* 1(R), 1992 *W, E, S, F, A*, 1993 *S, F, W, E, R*, 1994 *F, W, E, S*
Wallace, T H (Cardiff) 1920 *E, S, W*
Wallis, A K (Wanderers) 1892 *E, S, W*, 1893 *E, W*
Wallis, C O'N (Old Cranleighans, Wanderers) 1935 *NZ*
Wallis, T G (Wanderers) 1921 *F*, 1922 *E, S, W, F*

Wallis, W A (Wanderers) 1880 *S*, 1881 *E, S*, 1882 *W*, 1883 *S*
Walmsley, G (Bective Rangers) 1894 *E*
Walpole, A (Dublin U) 1888 *S, M*
Walsh, E J (Lansdowne) 1887 *E, S, W*, 1892 *E, S, W*, 1893 *E*
Walsh, H D (Dublin U) 1875 *E*, 1876 *E*
Walsh, J C (UC Cork, Sunday's Well) 1960 *S, SA*, 1961 *E, S, F, SA*, 1963 *E, S, W, NZ*, 1964 *E, S, W, F*, 1965 *F, S, W, SA*, 1966 *F, S, W*, 1967 *E, S, W, F, A 2*
Ward, A J P (Garryowen, St Mary's Coll, Greystones) 1978 *S, F, W, E, NZ*, 1979 *F, W, E, S*, 1981 *W, E, S, A*, 1983 *E* (R), 1984 *E, S*, 1986 *S*, 1987 [*C, Tg*]
Warren, J P (Kingstown) 1883 *E*
Warren, R G (Lansdowne) 1884 *W*, 1885 *E, S* 1,2, 1886 *E*, 1887 *E, S, W*, 1888 *W, S, M*, 1889 *S, W*, 1890 *S, W, E*
Watson, R (Wanderers) 1912 *SA*
Wells, H G (Bective Rangers) 1891 *S, W*, 1894 *E, S*
Westby, A J (Dublin U) 1876 *E*
Wheeler, G H (Queen's Coll, Belfast) 1884 *S*, 1885 *E*
Wheeler, J R (Queen's U, Belfast) 1922 *E, S, W, F*, 1924 *E*
Whelan, P C (Garryowen) 1975 *E, S*, 1976 *NZ*, 1977 *W, E, S, F*, 1978 *S, F, W, E, NZ*, 1979 *F, W, E, S*, 1981 *F, W, E*
White, M (Queen's Coll, Cork) 1906 *E, S, W, SA*, 1907 *E, W*
Whitestone, A M (Dublin U) 1877 *E*, 1879 *S, E*, 1880 *E*, 1883 *S*
Whittle, D (Bangor) 1988 *F*
Wilkinson, C R (Malone) 1993 *S*
Wilkinson, R W (Wanderers) 1947 *A*
Williamson, F W (Dolphin) 1930 *E, S, W*
Willis, W J (Lansdowne) 1879 *E*
Wilson, F (CIYMS) 1977 *W, E, S*
Wilson, H G (Glasgow U, Malone) 1905 *E, S, W, NZ*, 1906 *E, S, W, SA*, 1907 *E, S, W*, 1908 *E, S, W*, 1909 *E, S, W*, 1910 *W*
Wilson, W H (Bray) 1877 *E, S*
Withers, H H C (Army, Blackheath) 1931 *F, E, S, W, SA*
Wolfe, E J (Armagh) 1882 *E*
Wood, G H (Dublin U) 1913 *W*, 1914 *F*
Wood, B G M (Garryowen) 1954 *E, S*, 1956 *F, E, S, W*, 1957 *F, E, S, W*, 1958 *A, E, S, W, F*, 1959 *E, S, W, F*, 1960 *E, S, W, F, SA*, 1961 *E, S, W, F, SA*
Woods, D C (Bessbrook) 1888 *M*, 1889 *S*
Wright, R A (Monkstown) 1912 *S*

Yeates, R A (Dublin U) 1889 *S, W*
Young, G (UC Cork) 1913 *E*
Young, R M (Collegians) 1965 *F, E, S, W, SA*, 1966 *F, E, S, W*, 1967 *W, F*, 1968 *W, A*, 1969 *F, E, S, W*, 1970 *SA, F, E, S, W*, 1971 *F, E, S, W*

IRISH INTERNATIONAL RECORDS

Both team and individual records are for official Ireland international matches up to 31 March 1994.

TEAM RECORDS

Highest score
60 v Romania (60-0) 1986 Dublin
v individual countries
20 v Argentina (20-18) 1990 Dublin
27 v Australia (27-12) 1979 Brisbane
46 v Canada (46-19) 1987 Dunedin
26 v England (26-21) 1974 Twickenham
25 v France { (25-5) 1911 Cork
{ (25-6) 1975 Dublin

31 v Italy (31-15) 1988 Dublin
32 v Japan (32-16) 1991 Dublin
15 v Namibia (15-26) 1991 Windhoek
21 v N Zealand (21-24) 1992 Dunedin
60 v Romania (60-0) 1986 Dublin
15 v S Africa (15-23) 1981 Cape Town
26 v Scotland (26-8) 1953 Murrayfield
32 v Tonga (32-9) 1987 Brisbane

21 v Wales
- (21-24) 1979 Cardiff
- (21-7) 1980 Dublin
- (21-9) 1985 Cardiff
- (21-21) 1991 Cardiff

49 v W Samoa (49-22) 1988 Dublin
55 v Zimbabwe (55-11) 1991 Dublin

Biggest winning points margin
60 v Romania (60-0) 1986 Dublin
v individual countries
 2 v Argentina (20-18) 1990 Dublin
15 v Australia (27-12) 1979 Brisbane
27 v Canada (46-19) 1987 Dunedin
22 v England (22-0) 1947 Dublin
24 v France (24-0) 1913 Cork
16 v Italy (31-15) 1988 Dublin
16 v Japan (32-16) 1991 Dublin
No win v Namibia
No win v N Zealand
60 v Romania (60-0) 1986 Dublin
 3 v S Africa (9-6) 1965 Dublin
21 v Scotland (21-0) 1950 Dublin
23 v Tonga (32-9) 1987 Brisbane
16 v Wales (19-3) 1925 Belfast
27 v W Samoa (49-22) 1988 Dublin
44 v Zimbabwe (55-11) 1991 Dublin

Longest winning sequence
6 matches 1968-69

Highest score by opposing team
59 N Zealand (6-59) 1992 Wellington
by individual countries
18 Argentina (20-18) 1990 Dublin
42 Australia (17-42) 1992 Dublin
19 Canada (46-19) 1987 Dunedin
38 England (9-38) 1992 Twickenham
44 France (12-44) 1992 Paris
15 Italy (31-15) 1988 Dublin
16 Japan (32-16) 1991 Dublin
26 Namibia (15-26) 1991 Windhoek
59 N Zealand (6-59) 1992 Wellington
 3 Romania (25-3) 1993 Dublin
38 S Africa (0-38) 1912 Dublin
37 Scotland (21-37) 1989 Murrayfield
 9 Tonga (32-9) 1987 Brisbane
34 Wales (9-34) 1976 Dublin
22 W Samoa (49-22) 1988 Dublin
11 Zimbabwe (55-11) 1991 Dublin

Biggest losing points margin
53 v N Zealand (6-59) 1992 Wellington

v individual countries
25 v Australia (17-42) 1992 Dublin
32 v England (3-35) 1988 Twickenham
32 v France (12-44) 1992 Paris
11 v Namibia (15-26) 1991 Windhoek
53 v N Zealand (6-59) 1992 Wellington
38 v S Africa (0-38) 1912 Dublin
23 v Scotland (9-32) 1984 Dublin
29 v Wales (0-29) 1907 Cardiff
No defeats v Argentina, Canada, Italy, Japan, Romania, Tonga, W Samoa or Zimbabwe

Longest losing sequence
11 matches 1991-93

Most tries by Ireland in an international
10 v Romania (60-0) 1986 Dublin

Most tries against Ireland in an international
10 by S Africa (0-38) 1912 Dublin

Most points by Ireland in International Championship in a season – 71
in season 1982-83

Most tries by Ireland in International Championship in a season – 12
in seasons 1927-28 and 1952-53

INDIVIDUAL RECORDS

Most capped player
C M H Gibson   69   1964-79
in individual positions
Full-back
T J Kiernan   54   1960-73
Wing
K D Crossan   41   1982-92
Centre
B J Mullin   45[1]   1984-92
Fly-half
J W Kyle   46   1947-58
Scrum-half
M T Bradley   34   1984-94
Prop
P A Orr   58   1976-87
Hooker
K W Kennedy   45   1965-75

Lock
W J McBride   63   1962-75
Flanker
J F Slattery   61   1970-84
No 8
W P Duggan   39(41)[2]   1975-84
[1]*C M H Gibson won 40 caps as a centre, 25 at fly-half and 4 as a wing*
[2]*Duggan won 39 caps at No 8 and 2 as a flanker*

Longest international career
A J F O'Reilly 16 seasons 1955-70
C M H Gibson 16 seasons 1964-79
Gibson's career ended during a Southern Hemisphere season

Most consecutive Tests – 52
W J McBride 1964-75

Most internationals as captain – 24
T J Kiernan   1963-73

Most points in internationals – 308
M J Kiernan (43 matches) 1982-91

Most points in International Championship in a season – 52
S O Campbell (4 matches) 1982-83

Most points in an international – 23
R P Keyes v Zimbabwe 1991 Dublin

Most tries in internationals – 15
B J Mullin (45 matches) 1984-92

Most tries in International Championship in a season – 5
J E Arigho (3 matches) 1927-28

Most tries in an international – 4
B F Robinson v Zimbabwe 1991 Dublin

Most conversions in internationals – 40
M J Kiernan (43 matches) 1982-91

Most conversions in International Championship in a season – 7
R A Lloyd (4 matches) 1912-13

Most conversions in an international – 7
M J Kiernan v Romania 1986 Dublin

Most dropped goals in internationals – 7
R A Lloyd (19 matches) 1910-20
S O Campbell (22 matches) 1976-84

Most dropped goals in an international – 2
C M H Gibson v Australia 1967 Dublin
W M McCombe v France 1975 Dublin
S O Campbell v Australia 1979 Sydney
E P Elwood v England 1993 Dublin

Most penalty goals in internationals – 62
M J Kiernan (43 matches) 1982-91

Most penalty goals in International Championship in a season – 14
S O Campbell (4 matches) 1982-83
E P Elwood (4 matches) 1993-94

Most penalty goals in an international – 6
S O Campbell v Scotland 1982 Dublin
E P Elwood v Romania 1993 Dublin

Most points for Ireland on overseas tour – 60
S O Campbell (5 appearances) 1979 Australia
M J Kiernan scored 65 points in Japan 1985, but this was not on a major tour

Most points in any match on tour – 19
A J P Ward v Australian Capital Territory 1979 Canberra
S O Campbell v Australia 1979 Brisbane
M J Kiernan scored 25 points in the second match against Japan 1985, but this was not on a major tour

Most tries in any match on tour – 3
A T A Duggan v Victoria 1967 Melbourne
J F Slattery v SA President's XV 1981 East London
M J Kiernan v Gold Cup XV 1981 Oudtshoorn, SA
T M Ringland scored 3 tries v Japan at Osaka 1985, but this was not on a major tour

THE REVENGE OF THE 'FEATHER DUSTERS'

THE 1993-94 SEASON IN WALES
John Billot *Western Mail*

Ieuan Evans led a doomed command against Canada in November which plunged a nation into mourning. Yet the season ended in triumph with Wales as Five Nations champions. From the wooden spoon in 1993 to the top team in Europe (on scoring difference) was an impossible dream come true. It might be said to be the revenge of the 'feather dusters'.

Who imagined that Wales would be going for the Grand Slam at Twickenham after the humiliation of home defeat at the hands of Canada? Wales had opened the season with a record 55-5 victory over Japan at the Arms Park (though there had been an 82-6 success against Japan in Tokyo in 1975 in a non-cap match) and the Canadian disaster cast a deep gloom. Welsh attackers impaled themselves on tackles in a misconceived Geronimo plan. Rupert Moon, the scrum-half, repeatedly joined his back row on the charge and there was not even a try to show for it. Neil Jenkins put over a world record-equalling eight penalty goals in this 26-24 defeat, but Welsh rugby used to be all about tries. Shame is a word not expressed lightly: it was how a nation felt.

A multiplicity of problems had existed in Welsh teams for far too long, but it seemed that considerable progress had been made during the summer tour of Zimbabwe and Namibia. Now hope was replaced by old fears that the side would again prove irredeemably poor. Not even victory over a surprisingly supine Scotland, reeling from the ravages of the All Blacks, convinced the doubters that rescue was on its way. Scotland, it was considered, would be the easiest game: Ireland presented a vastly different prospect since the Green Gladiators would be met on their home ground.

So it proved, and had Eric Elwood's kick not hit the upright in the closing minutes, Ireland would have stolen the match with five penalty goals instead of losing 17-15. Some Irish supporters thought it the worst disaster since the Potato Famine. Still, fortune has been less than generous as far as the Welsh team are concerned and this little bit of Lansdowne Road luck was the turning-point.

At last the whole team appeared to be imbued with the vital spark of self-belief and this rediscovered confidence took France aback in Cardiff. Gareth Llewellyn, leading in the absence of the injured Ieuan Evans, fired his pack to a supreme effort in a significant renaissance. Of course, this is not the France of old: in the general dilution of quality throughout Northern Hemisphere rugby, they have suffered their share. Without a Jean-Pierre Rives, a Jacques Fouroux or a Daniel Dubroca to rally them, they lost to Wales for the first time in 12 years. The 24-15 victory

The Wales team which beat France at Cardiff. L-R, back row: I W Jones (replacement), H Williams-Jones (replacement), J D Davies, R L Evans, P T Davies, E W Lewis, L S Quinnell, M A Perego, R C McBryde (replacement), A H Copsey (replacement); front row: R N Jones (replacement), M A Rayer, N Walker, S D Hill, M R Hall, G O Llewellyn (capt), R H St J B Moon, A Clement, G R Jenkins, N R Jenkins, H T Taylor (replacement).

was notable for the invigorating performance of 21-year-old Scott Quinnell. His audacious try, which he modestly admitted was lucky as he slipped three tackles, set the game alight with a winning glitter for the home side.

There was a worrying French recovery and Llewellyn confessed: 'We were on the verge of cracking.' But there was a new steel about the Welsh forwards while yet again Neil Jenkins was on target to kick four penalty goals and a conversion from the touchline. Wales have been plagued with some penurious packs; barren of line-out substance in the post-Robert Norster era, and deficient in back-row speed over recent years. Only against equally deprived packs have they shown a measure of control, albeit mostly unsustainable. But with Phil Davies recalled to help stoke the fires of response, this was a team with a mission. The Grand Slam, alas, proved a match too far, and defeat at Twickenham was comprehensive. Nevertheless, the lessons of the tactical blunder against Canada had been absorbed and wherever possible Wales looked to run at space and work the ball wide: the old, winning Welsh way. Coach Alan Davies tempered his delight at the success of his 'feather dusters' with a sobering comment: 'We still have a long way to go.' To come back as cocks of the walk must be the aim.

Two leading players turned to Rugby League during the season. Richard Webster left for Salford in September, lured by a package deal worth around £150,000, the first Welsh international to defect for three years. Another Swansea star, Scott Gibbs, joined St Helens in April on a five-year contract, said to be irresistible at somewhere in the region of £300,000. Gibbs signed shortly after the announcement of plans for the WRU lottery. The start date was July 1994 and the expected revenue, £1.5 million annually, to be divided among participating clubs, prizes and a trust fund. This trust fund will receive £300,000 each year for distribution to players when they retire from the game. Obviously, Scott Gibbs was not impressed!

Denis Evans was dismissed as WRU secretary in October 1993 for 'grave misconduct', and his assistant, Edwards Jones, was appointed in his place, the fourth man to hold the office in the last five years.

THE STALKING HORSE STRIKES

SWALEC CUP 1993-94
John Billot   *Western Mail*

7 May, Cardiff Arms Park
Cardiff 15 (1G 1PG 1T)   **Llanelli 8** (1PG 1T)

Most critics considered Llanelli, winners for the previous three years, favourites for this 23rd Cup final, but the Stradey team had reservations: they saw in Cardiff the stalking horse of the competition. To the horror of Llanelli supporters this proved an accurate assessment. Llanelli made a brave contribution to a thrill-packed event, though without the conviction that had brought them nine Cups and 11 previous appearances in finals. This time, the team with a reputation for peaking on the big occasion looked distinctly peaky. They were locked for long periods in a grim grip of doom.

Llanelli's hopes of a fourth triumph to equal the four in a row they achieved back in 1973-76 declined abruptly with Mike Hall's smart try for Cardiff after just three minutes, when Neil Boobyer missed a high kick. It was inevitable that he would be tested with a sky-screamer as a centre having to deputise at full-back. Adrian Davies converted, but then a Colin Stephens penalty shot and a try by Ieuan Evans – virtually a ritual event for the wing who has scored a record 45 tries in 36 ties (seven in finals) – put the Scarlets in front 8-7 after 15 minutes.

Alas, their scoring burst was over. Instead Davies fired in a penalty goal and Mike Rayer dived in for one of his big-match special tries for Cardiff. There was no scoring in the second half, in which Derwyn Jones, the 6 foot 10 Cardiff lock, dominated the line-out and the Llanelli pack were shorn of momentum.

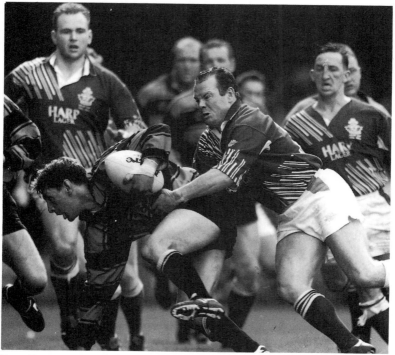

Ieuan Evans of Llanelli tackles Andy Moore, the Cardiff scrum-half, in the 1994 SWALEC Cup final.

Andy Moore, the Cardiff scrum-half, won the Lloyd Lewis Memorial Award as the outstanding performer, though Rayer's efforts were equally influential as a much-criticised Cardiff came good to regain the Cup after seven unsuccessful years.

With some justification, Llanelli can claim they paid a high price for providing the bulk of the national team, sacrificing their own squad training. Hands on hearts, there are few who would exchange the Cup or League title for Wales winning the Grand Slam. Club rugby is the lifeblood of the Welsh game and they don't mind sparing a few pints for the national side, but with the game's fast-changing pattern, a large transfusion is likely to be a worrying factor in future. League prize-money and relegation can be more significant than international success and there is support for the idea of delaying the Five Nations Championship to the end of the season.

Cardiff: M A Rayer; S Ford, M R Hall (*capt*), C Laity, N Walker; A Davies, A Moore; M Griffiths, J Humphreys, L Mustoe, A P Rees, D Jones, M Bennett, O Williams, M Budd *Replacement* V Davies for Budd (temp)
Scorers *Tries:* Hall, Rayer   *Conversion:* Davies   *Penalty Goal:* Davies
Llanelli: N Boobyer; I C Evans, S Davies, N G Davies, W T Proctor; C J Stephens, R H StJ B Moon (*capt*); R L Evans, A E Lamerton, H Williams-Jones, P T Davies, A H Copsey, E W Lewis, L S Quinnell, M A Perego *Replacements* I W Jones for S Davies (53 mins); P M Jones for P T Davies (58 mins)
Scorers *Try:* I C Evans   *Penalty Goal:* Stephens
Referee R Yeman (Taibach)

Two semi-final tries in the space of two minutes right at the end saw Llanelli finally subdue gallant Maesteg at the Gnoll 23-7 after the Old Parish had led for most of the game. It was 7-5 to the underdogs, who had been given no chance until, after 26 minutes of the second half, Stephens put the Scarlets in front 8-7 with a penalty shot. Such a cruel blow was undeserved by the team who had produced all the adventure and scored the best try. Mark Watts, a perceptive fly-half, was the scorer from a midfield burst by Roddy Boobyer, sweeping past his twin, Neil, in the Llanelli centre. Watts converted, but Llanelli's Ieuan Evans crossed wide out on a quick spread from a scrum five and from then on the Scarlets were the only scorers. After Stephens' penalty goal, Scott Quinnell's long stride pattern carried him out of a tackle and over for Stephens to convert. Two minutes later, Moon's searing break launched a try for Ricky Evans. Jason Strange completed matters with a dropped goal.

In the other semi-final, at Rodney Parade, Crispin Cormack, as stand-in for the record-breaking goal-kicker Neil Jenkins, injured the previous week against Swansea, fired over two penalty goals to give Pontypridd a 6-0 lead by half-time. But he missed a number of attempts in the tricky wind, one hitting a post, and Cardiff stole the match 8-6. Victory came with a try by Colin Laity midway through the second half after Adrian Davies had closed the gap with a penalty shot. Davies set up the try with a hanging punt that arrived in the drop zone at the same time as Laity. Pontypridd's rolling maul was superbly executed, but the absence of Jenkins really reduced their chances.

The quarter-finals brought a capacity April crowd of 10,000 to Neath to witness a repeat of the previous year's final, in which Llanelli were again successful. This time it was 7-3 to the Scarlets as the Fortress Gnoll ground record fell to a Moon try, converted by Stephens. Paul Thorburn kicked a home penalty goal. Cardiff lacked cohesion and assertiveness in disposing of a stubborn South Wales Police side by 20-13. Pontypridd's 32-10 defeat of Newbridge was virtually a solo performance by Neil Jenkins, who scored two tries in a.tally of 27 points. Maesteg's physical superiority enabled them to recover from 9-10 during the second half and defeat Tenby United 35-17.

Bridgend failed to reach the quarter-finals for the first time in ten years as they slipped to a 15-6 defeat against Cardiff in the Arms Park mud in the sixth round. Swansea went out at this stage, beaten 13-3 at Pontypridd, where Jenkins kicked two penalty goals and converted the try by Mark Rowley, who ploughed across on Swansea's throw-in at a close-up line-out.

The fifth round produced grief once more for Newport as they suffered defeat for a second time against a village team. It had been 4-0 at Penclawdd in 1980 and now it was 10-9 at Ystradgynlais. Mike Lewis, a former Newport fly-half, kicked a penalty goal and added the points to a try by wing Ian Michael. A sad day, indeed, for the big boys.

The fourth round, played in quagmire conditions, produced keen disappointment for Treorchy, who went on to win the Division 2 title. They failed 28-6 at Pontypridd. Equally disappointed were Fleur-de-Lys, who had been responsible for Aberavon's shock exit the previous season. Fleur went out in the first round 17-11 against Felinfoel and had four players sent off. It was not really the stuff of a giant-killing story!

RESULTS

Third Round

Abercarn 6, Gwernyfed 3; Amman Utd 0, Nantymoel 3; Blackwood 30, Old Illtydians 7; Blaina 10, Abercrave 33; Briton Ferry 3, Pyle 35; Brynamman 6, Tonyrefail 25; Bryncoch 3, Hendy 9; Caerphilly 30, Aberavon Quins 8; Chepstow 15, Pwllheli 3; Croesyceiliog 11, Ystradgynlais 12; Garndiffaith 23, Beddau 25; Glynneath 39, Bridgend Sports Club 5; Hollybush 3, Felinfoel 7; Kidwelly 22, Pontypool Utd 15; Llantrisant 30, Kenfig Hill 3; Loughor 5, New Dock Stars 19; Machen 17, Gowerton 16; Mold 24, Llandybie 16; Newport Saracens 11, Abergavenny 0; Neyland 8, Seven Sisters 30; Oakdale 18, Carmarthen 8; Old Penarthians 21, Morriston 8; Pencoed 12, Cardigan 8; Penygraig 8, Fairwater 11; Pontycymmer 3, Maesteg Celtic 12; Porthcawl 6, Crumlin 17; Resolven 0, Builth Wells 33; Rhymney 25, Waunarlwydd 8; Risca 11, Rhiwbina 18; Rumney 23, Tredegar 6; Taff's Well 7, Wrexham 26; Tondu 32, UC Cardiff 14; Tumble 13, Cardiff Institute of Education 32; Vardre 3, Abercynon 16; Wattstown 26, Pontyberem 6; Whitland 7, Ynysybwl 18

Fourth Round

Abercarn 6, Pyle 26; Abercynon 56, Pencoed 5; Abertillery 3, Neath 13; Bonymaen 13, Tonyrefail 8; Bridgend 21,

Penarth 8; Caerphilly 17, Hendy 13; Cardiff 16, Pontypool 6; Cardiff Quins 20, Nantymoel 21; Cross Keys 5, Glamorgan Wanderers 9; Crumlin 6, Maesteg 17; Dunvant 18, Mountain Ash 0; Fairwater 14, Newport 23; Kidwelly 28, Machen 9; Llanharan 22, Chepstow 0; Llantrisant 5, Llanelli 40; Maesteg Celtic 19, Rhymney 18; Mold 21, Beddau 10; New Dock Stars 16, Llandovery 25; Oakdale 25, Builth Wells 8; Old Penarthians 9, Seven Sisters 20; Pontypridd 28, Treorchy 6; Rhiwbina 3, Aberavon 37; Rumney 8, Felinfoel 9; St Peter's 10, Abercrave 14; Swansea 21, Ebbw Vale 13; Talywain 15, Cardiff Institute of Education 11; Tenby Utd 43, Blackwood 5; Tondu 13, Newport Saracens 0; Wattstown 11, Narberth 13; Wrexham 10, Newbridge 48; Ynysybwl 5, SW Police 18; Ystradgynlais 21, Glynneath 15

Fifth Round

Abercynon 12, Neath 19; Bonymaen 6, Tondu 0; Bridgend 29, Felinfoel 6; Cardiff 27, Oakdale 3; Dunvant 39, Pyle 10; Kidwelly 6, Llanelli 49; Llandovery 13, Mold 3; Maesteg 9, Glamorgan Wanderers 5; Maesteg Celtic 8, Talywain 3; Narberth 16, Nantymoel 6; Newbridge 32, Llanharan 3; Pontypridd 29, Aberavon 0; SW Police 10, Caerphilly 3; Swansea 70, Seven Sisters 6; Tenby Utd 18, Abercrave 13; Ystradgynlais 10, Newport 9

Sixth Round

Cardiff 15, Bridgend 6; Dunvant 8, Newbridge 16; Llanelli 57, Llandovery 5; Maesteg 11, Bonymaen 9; Maesteg Celtic

14, SW Police 37; Pontypridd 13, Swansea 3; Tenby Utd 25, Narberth 14; Ystradgynlais 3, Neath 26

Seventh Round

Cardiff 20, SW Police 13; Maesteg 35, Tenby Utd 17; Neath 3, Llanelli 7; Pontypridd 32, Newbridge 10

Semi-finals

Llanelli 23, Maesteg 7
(at Neath); Cardiff 9, Pontypridd 6
(at Newport)

FINAL *(at Cardiff Arms Park)*
Cardiff 15 Llanelli 8

Previous finals
(all at Cardiff Arms Park)

1972	Neath 15 Llanelli 9
1973	Llanelli 30 Cardiff 7
1974	Llanelli 12 Aberavon 10
1975	Llanelli 15 Aberavon 6
1976	Llanelli 15 Swansea 4
1977	Newport 16 Cardiff 15
1978	Swansea 13 Newport 9
1979	Bridgend 18 Pontypridd 12
1980	Bridgend 15 Swansea 9
1981	Cardiff 14 Bridgend 6
1982*	Cardiff 12 Bridgend 12
1983	Pontypool 18 Swansea 6
1984	Cardiff 24 Neath 19
1985	Llanelli 15 Cardiff 14
1986	Cardiff 28 Newport 21
1987	Cardiff 16 Swansea 15
1988	Llanelli 28 Neath 13
1989	Neath 14 Llanelli 13
1990	Neath 16 Bridgend 10
1991	Llanelli 24 Pontypool 9
1992	Llanelli 16 Swansea 7
1993	Llanelli 21 Neath 18

* *Winners on 'most tries' rule*

SWANSEA FIRST TO REGAIN TITLE
THE HEINEKEN LEAGUES 1993-94

Swansea became the first team to regain the Championship title despite innumerable frustrations that might well have daunted many sides. In September, Richard Webster took the northern shilling and then injuries to key players proved a handicap. Scott Gibbs played only ten League games before a serious knee injury put him out and probably nudged him towards an April decision to follow Webster into the Rugby League ranks. Skipper Stuart Davies missed much of the season and Aled Williams, the leading goal-scorer and fly-half, was out for two months. Despite all this, Swansea triumphed, fulfilling the confidence of coaching supremo Mike Ruddock. The Whites were unbeaten at home in all matches and lost only two League games, at Neath (40-18) and Llanelli (20-13). Success brought the top prize of £14,000.

For a long time, Neath were considered favourites. They were unbeaten in their first ten games after opening with a 22-22 draw against Pontypridd at the Gnoll, where no League sides were to succeed. But Gareth Llewellyn's team had to settle for second place, a whisker ahead of Pontypridd, who enjoyed the distinction of having Neil Jenkins chosen as Welsh Player of the Year and his scrum-half partner, Paul John, as Most Promising Player.

Cardiff, in fourth place, scored most tries with 87, but after an encouraging start seldom did themselves justice against the stronger sides. Llanelli, with a record for the Stradey club of nine players capped against Ireland, and ten in the season, found that the sacrifice of national squad training destroyed their League aspirations. Pontypool escaped relegation by winning their last two games, but there was no reprieve for Cross Keys, doomed without a win. Dunvant thoroughly deserved to stay up after holding Neath to 10-10 at Broadacre. Their success in their last match, against Bridgend, meant relegation for Aberavon. The Wizards lost their last game 7-5 to Pontypridd and returned to Division 2 after two seasons at the top level.

Treorchy became the second club outside the recognised major teams to win promotion and joined Dunvant after taking the Division 2 title with just one defeat (34-18 by South Wales Police). The Zebras recruited eagerly, signing former Wales internationals Paul Knight (Pontypridd), Luc Evans (Bridgend) and David Evans (Cardiff), supplemented by Keith Orrell (Newport), Justin Burnell (Newbridge) and Darryl Hughes (Pontypridd). Abertillery, despite having their captain, Mark Rossiter, a busy scrum-half, sent off in their final match, returned to the First Division. They lost their first three games before finding pattern and confidence.

Abercynon were defeated in their second game, 15-8 by visitors Tredegar, but that was their only reverse as they hastened towards the Division 3 Championship to replace Glamorgan Wanderers, who plunged from Division 2, sadly in their centenary season. The Wanderers lost their first 11 games and there was no way back, though they finished with a flourish with three victories, including a 23-13 success over third-placed Maesteg. Abercynon, incidentally, set a League record of 20 consecutive wins. Bonymaen required three tries as well as victory for promotion in their final game, and managed to score four in their 32-10 win at Tredegar.

Builth Wells, inspired by former Wales and Neath prop Jeremy Pugh, won the Division 4 title ahead of Caerphilly, who gained promotion in their first season in the Heineken League. A fifth division is added for the 1994-95 season and comprises Abercarn, Cardiff Quins, Cardigan, Felinfoel, Garndiffaith, Hendy, Merthyr, Pwellheli, Rumney, Seven Sisters, Tonmawr and Wrexham.

HEINEKEN LEAGUES
Division 1

	P	W	D	L	F	A	Pts
Swansea	22	20	0	2	549	264	40
Neath	22	17	2	3	581	286	36
Pontypridd	22	17	1	4	571	299	35
Cardiff	22	15	2	5	668	240	32
Llanelli	22	13	1	8	461	366	27
Bridgend	22	10	1	11	466	434	21
Newport	22	8	2	12	362	472	18
Newbridge	22	7	1	14	367	440	15
Pontypool	22	7	0	15	312	626	14
Dunvant	22	6	1	15	288	464	13
Aberavon	22	6	1	15	242	464	13
Cross Keys	22	0	0	22	239	751	0

Division 2

	P	W	D	L	F	A	Pts
Treorchy	22	20	1	1	425	200	41
Abertillery	22	15	1	6	473	242	31
Maesteg	22	13	1	8	376	259	27
SW Police	22	12	0	10	367	333	24
Tenby Utd	22	10	0	12	308	366	20
Llanharan	22	9	2	11	259	349	20
Narberth	22	10	0	12	273	294	20
Penarth	22	9	0	13	291	372	18
Ebbw Vale	22	8	2	12	279	321	18
Llandovery	22	8	1	13	269	370	17
Mountain Ash	22	8	0	14	275	333	16
Glam Wands	22	6	0	16	262	418	12

Division 3

	P	W	D	L	F	A	Pts
Abercynon	22	21	0	1	563	242	42
Bonymaen	22	17	0	5	369	244	34
Ystradgynlais	22	17	0	5	429	226	34
Kenfig Hill	22	13	1	8	407	339	27
Blackwood	22	10	1	11	413	450	21
Tredegar	22	10	0	12	341	333	20
Pontypool U	22	10	0	12	354	375	20
Aberavon Qs	22	9	0	13	285	367	18
Tondu	22	7	1	14	251	311	15
Blaina	22	5	2	15	283	465	12
St Peter's	22	5	1	16	338	482	11
Tumble	22	5	0	17	241	439	10

Division 4

	P	W	D	L	F	A	Pts
Builth Wells	22	19	0	3	370	169	38
Caerphilly	22	17	1	4	446	201	35
Pyle	22	15	0	7	396	265	30
Vardre	22	12	0	10	333	315	24
Whitland	22	11	1	10	263	282	23
Carmarthen	22	10	1	11	310	293	21
Oakdale	22	10	1	11	314	265	21
Kidwelly	22	9	3	10	288	218	21
Rumney	22	10	1	11	257	267	21
Cardiff Qs	22	9	0	13	331	442	18
Wrexham	22	4	0	18	171	382	8
Garndiffaith	22	2	0	20	184	564	4

Promoted to Division 4 for 1994-95: Llantrisant, Glynneath, Rhymney, Cardiff Institute.
New Division 5 for 1994-95: Abercarn, Cardiff Quins, Cardigan, Felinfoel, Garndiffaith, Hendy, Merthyr, Pwllheli, Rumney, Seven Sisters, Tonmawr, Wrexham.

FEEDER LEAGUES
EAST DISTRICT CHAMPIONSHIP

Division 1	P	W	D	L	Pts
Cardiff Inst	16	13	3	0	29
Pencoed	16	13	1	2	27
O Penarthians	16	12	0	4	24
O Illtydians	16	9	1	6	19
Rhiwbina	16	8	1	7	17
Llandaff	16	4	0	12	8
Llandaff North	16	3	1	12	7
Pentyrch	16	3	1	12	7
Pontyclun	16	3	0	13	6

Division 2 finishing order: Dinas Powys, St Joseph's, Barry, Heol-y-Cyw, Cowbridge, Taffs Well, Llantwit Major, Llanishen, Cardiff University

CENTRAL DISTRICT CHAMPIONSHIP

Division 1	P	W	D	L	Pts
Tonmawr	18	15	1	2	31
Maesteg Celtic	18	14	0	4	28
Bridgend Ath	18	12	0	6	24
Bridgend SC	18	10	2	6	22
Nantymoel	18	11	0	7	22
Neath Athletic	18	7	1	10	15
Nantyffyllon	18	7	1	10	15
Porthcawl	18	5	3	10	13
British Steel	18	4	0	14	8
Cefn Cribbwr	18	1	0	17	2

Division 2 finishing order: Aberavon Green Stars, Blaengarw, Taibach, Maesteg Quins, Pontycymmer, Cwmavon, Briton Ferry, Ogmore Vale

MID-DISTRICT CHAMPIONSHIP

Division 1	P	W	D	L	Pts
Llantrisant	18	17	0	1	34
Merthyr	18	15	1	2	25
Tonyrefail	18	11	0	7	22
Ystrad Rhondda	17	9	0	8	17
Hirwaun	18	7	1	10	15
Ynysybwl	18	7	1	10	15
Beddau	17	7	0	10	14
Nelson	18	6	1	11	13
Senghenydd	18	5	2	11	12
Cilfyndd	18	2	2	14	6

Division 2 finishing order: Rhydyfelin, Gilfach Goch, Penygraig, Treherbert, Bargoed, Llantwit Fardre, Cefn Coed, Brecon, Aberaman, Tylorstown

PEMBROKESHIRE CHAMPIONSHIP

	P	W	D	L	Pts
Cardigan	18	15	2	2	32
Pembroke	18	14	2	2	30
Pembroke DQ	18	14	1	3	29
Milford Haven	18	7	4	7	18
Haverfordwest	18	7	4	7	18
Neyland	18	8	1	9	17
Aberystwyth	18	7	0	11	14
F'guard & G'wick	18	3	2	13	8
St David's	18	4	0	14	8
Llangwm	18	3	0	15	6

NORTH WALES LEAGUE

Group A	P	W	D	L	Pts
Mold	12	12	0	0	24
Rhyl	12	10	0	2	20
Dolgellau	12	6	0	6	12
Ruthin	12	5	1	6	11
Welshpool	12	5	1	6	11
Caernarfon	12	2	0	10	4
UCNW	12	1	0	11	2

Group B					
Pwllheli	10	10	0	0	20
Newtown	10	7	0	3	14
Colwyn Bay	10	5	1	4	11
Llandudno	10	5	1	4	11
Denbigh	10	2	0	8	4
Bangor	10	0	0	10	0

Semi-finals: Mole 30, Newtown 10; Pwllheli 17, Rhyl 7
Final: Mold 9, Pwllheli 9 (*aet at Mold: Pwllheli won on away rule*)

MONMOUTHSHIRE CHAMPIONSHIP

Division 1	P	W	D	L	Pts
Rhymney	18	14	2	2	30
Abercarn	18	14	0	4	28
Talywain	18	11	1	6	23
Bedwas	18	11	0	7	22
Abergavenny	18	9	1	8	19
Tredegar Irons	18	8	1	9	17
Blaenau Gwent	18	6	1	11	13
Pill Harriers	18	5	1	12	11
Newport Saras	18	4	2	12	10
Newport HSOB	18	3	1	14	7

Division 2 finishing order: Croesyceiliog, Fleur de Lys, Cwmbran, Brynmawr, Monmouth, Chepstow, Llanhilleth, RTB (Ebbw Vale), Risca, Machen
Division 3 finishing order: Crumlin, Blaenavon, Usk, Caldicot, Trinant, Nantyglo, Ynysddu

WEST WALES CHAMPIONSHIP

Section A	P	W	D	L	Pts
Glynneath	18	15	1	2	31
Seven Sisters	18	13	0	5	26
Hendy	18	12	0	6	24
Felinfoel	18	11	1	6	23
Morriston	18	10	0	8	20
Llandeilo	18	9	0	9	18
Cwmgwrach	18	8	0	10	16
Pontarddulais	18	6	0	12	12
Trimsaran	18	5	0	13	10
Carmarthen Ath	18	0	0	18	0

Section B finishing order: Llandybie, New Dock Stars, Waunarlwydd, Amman Utd, Loughor, Resolven, Ystalyfera, Glais, Alltwen, Furnace Utd
Division B finishing order: Abercrave, Pontyberem, Brynamman, Penygroes, Skewen, Ammanford, Gowerton, Bryncoch, Cryant, Llangennech
Section C finishing order: Laugharne, Trebanos, Gorseinon, Mumbles, Lampeter Town, Bynea, Cefneithin, Pontardawe, Pontyates, Llanybydder
Division C finishing order: Cwmgors, Penclewdd, Newcastle Emlyn, Tonna, Tycroes, Cwmllynfell, Llanelli Wanderers, Byrry Port, Swansea Uplands, BP Llandarcy

273

WELSH INTERNATIONAL PLAYERS
(up to 31 March 1994)

ABBREVIATIONS

A – Australia; *Arg* – Argentina; *Bb* – Barbarians; *C* – Canada; *E* – England; *F* – France; *Fj* – Fiji; *I* – Ireland; *J* – Japan; *M* – Maoris; *Nm* – Namibia; *NZ* – New Zealand; *NZA* – New Zealand Army; *R* – Romania; *S* – Scotland; *SA* – South Africa; *Tg* – Tonga; *US* – United States; *WS* – Western Samoa; *Z* – Zimbabwe; (R) – Replacement; (t) – temporary replacement. Entries in square brackets [ ] indicate appearances in the World Cup.

Note: Years given for Five Nations' matches are for second half of season; eg 1972 means season 1971-72. Years for all other matches refer to the actual year of the match. When a series has taken place, figures have been used to denote the particular matches in which players have featured. Thus 1969 *NZ* 2 indicates that a player appeared in the second Test of the series.

Ackerman, R A (Newport, London Welsh) 1980 *NZ*, 1981 *E, S, A*, 1982 *I, F, E, S*, 1983 *S, I, F, R*, 1984 *S, I, F, E, A*, 1985 *S, I, F, E, Fj*
Alexander, E P (Llandovery Coll, Cambridge U) 1885 *S*, 1886 *E, S*, 1887 *E, I*
Alexander, W H (Llwynypia) 1898 *I, E*, 1899 *E, S, I*, 1901 *S, I*
Allen, A G (Newbridge) 1990 *F, E, I*
Allen, C P (Oxford U, Beaumaris) 1884 *E, S*
Andrews, F (Pontypool) 1912 *SA*, 1913 *E, S, I*
Andrews, F G (Swansea) 1884 *E, S*
Andrews, G E (Newport) 1926 *E, S*, 1927 *E, F, I*
Anthony, L (Neath) 1948 *E, S, F*
Arnold, P (Swansea) 1990 *Nm* 1,2, *Bb*, 1991 *E, S, I, F1, A*, [*Arg; A*], 1993 *F*(R),*Z2*
Arnold, W R (Swansea) 1903 *S*
Arthur, C S (Cardiff) 1888 *I, M*, 1891 *E*
Arthur, T (Neath) 1927 *S, F, I*, 1929 *E, S, F, I*, 1930 *E, S, I, F*, 1931 *E, S, F, I, SA*, 1933 *E, S*
Ashton, C (Aberavon) 1959 *E, S, I*, 1960 *E, S, I*, 1962 *I*
Attewell, S L (Newport) 1921 *E, S, F*

Badger, O (Llanelli) 1895 *E, S, I*, 1896 *E*
Baker, A (Neath) 1921 *I*, 1923 *E, S, F, I*
Baker, A M (Newport) 1909 *S, F*, 1910 *S*
Bancroft, J (Swansea) 1909 *E, S, F, I*, 1910 *F, E, S, I*, 1911 *E, F, I*, 1912 *E, S, I*, 1913 *I*, 1914 *E, S, F*
Bancroft, W J (Swansea) 1890 *S, E, I*, 1891 *E, S, I*, 1892 *E, S, I*, 1893 *E, S, I*, 1894 *E, S, I*, 1895 *E, S, I*, 1896 *E, S, I*, 1897 *E*, 1898 *I, E*, 1899 *E, S, I*, 1900 *E, S, I*, 1901 *E, S, I*
Barlow, T M (Cardiff) 1884 *I*
Barrell, R J (Cardiff) 1929 *S, F, I*, 1933 *I*
Bartlett, J D (Llanelli) 1927 *S*, 1928 *E, S*
Bassett, A (Cardiff) 1934 *I*, 1935 *E, S, I*, 1938 *E, S*
Bassett, J A (Penarth) 1929 *E, S, F, I*, 1930 *E, S, I*, 1931 *E, S, F, I, SA*, 1932 *E, S, I*
Bateman, A G (Neath) 1990 *S, I, Nm* 1,2
Bayliss, G (Pontypool) 1933 *S*
Bebb, D I E (Carmarthen TC, Swansea) 1959 *E, S, I, F*, 1960 *E, S, I, F, SA*, 1961 *E, S, I, F*, 1962 *E, S, F, I*, 1963 *E, F, NZ*, 1964 *E, S, F, SA*, 1965 *E, S, I, F*, 1966 *F, A*, 1967 *S, I, F, E*
Beckingham, G (Cardiff) 1953 *E, S*, 1958 *F*
Bennett, I (Aberavon) 1937 *I*
Bennett, P (Cardiff Harlequins) 1891 *E, S*, 1892 *S, I*
Bennett, P (Llanelli) 1969 *F* (R), 1970 *SA, S, F*, 1972 *S* (R), *NZ*, 1973 *E, S, I, F, A*, 1974 *S, I, F, E*, 1975 *S* (R), *I*, 1976 *E, S, I, F*, 1977 *I, F, E, S*, 1978 *E, S, I, F*
Bergiers, R T E (Cardiff Coll of Ed, Llanelli) 1972 *E, S, F, NZ*, 1973 *E, S, I, F, A*, 1974 *S*, 1975 *I*
Bevan, G W (Llanelli) 1947 *E*
Bevan, J A (Cambridge U) 1881 *E*
Bevan, J C (Cardiff, Cardiff Coll of Ed) 1971 *E, S, I, F*, 1972 *S, F, NZ*, 1973 *E, S*
Bevan, J D (Aberavon) 1975 *F, E, S, A*
Bevan, S (Swansea) 1904 *I*
Beynon, B (Swansea) 1920 *E, S*
Beynon, G E (Swansea) 1925 *F, I*
Bidgood, R A (Newport) 1992 *S*, 1993 *Z1,2, Nm, J*(R)
Biggs, N W (Cardiff) 1888 *M*, 1889 *I*, 1892 *I*, 1893 *E, S, I*, 1894 *E, S*
Biggs, S H (Cardiff) 1895 *E, S*, 1896 *S*, 1897 *E*, 1898 *I, E*, 1899 *S, I*, 1900 *I*

Birch, J (Neath) 1911 *S, F*
Birt, F W (Newport) 1911 *E, S*, 1912 *E, S, I, SA*, 1913 *E*
Bishop, D J (Pontypool) 1984 *A*
Bishop, E H (Swansea) 1889 *S*
Blackmore, J H (Abertillery) 1909 *E*
Blackmore, S W (Cardiff) 1987 *I*, [*Tg* (R), *C, A*]
Blake, J (Cardiff) 1899 *E, S, I*, 1900 *E, S, I*, 1901 *E, S, I*
Blakemore, R E (Newport) 1947 *E*
Bland, A F (Cardiff) 1887 *E, S, I*, 1888 *S, I, M*, 1890 *S, E, I*
Blyth, L (Swansea) 1951 *SA*, 1952 *E, S*
Blyth, W R (Swansea) 1974 *E*, 1975 *S* (R), 1980 *F, E, S, I*
Boobyer, N (Llanelli) 1993 *Z1*(R), 2, *Nm*
Boon, R W (Cardiff) 1930 *S, F*, 1931 *E, S, F, I, SA*, 1932 *E, S, I*, 1933 *E, I*
Booth, J (Pontymister) 1898 *I*
Boots, J G (Newport) 1898 *I, E*, 1899 *I*, 1900 *E, S, I*, 1901 *E, S, I*, 1902 *E, S, I*, 1903 *E, S, I*, 1904 *E*
Boucher, A W (Newport) 1892 *E, S, I*, 1893 *E, S, I*, 1894 *E*, 1895 *E, S, I*, 1896 *E, I*, 1897 *E*
Bowcott, H M (Cardiff, Cambridge U) 1929 *S, F, I*, 1930 *E, I*, 1931 *E, S*, 1933 *E, I*
Bowdler, F A (Cross Keys) 1927 *A*, 1928 *E, S, I, F*, 1929 *E, S, F, I*, 1930 *E, I*, 1931 *SA*, 1932 *E, S, I*, 1933 *I*
Bowen, B (S Wales Police, Swansea) 1983 *R*, 1984 *S, I, F, E*, 1985 *Fj*, 1986 *E, S, I, F, Fj, Tg, WS*, 1987 [*C, E, NZ*], *US*, 1988 *E, S, I, F, WS*, 1989 *S, I*
Bowen, C A (Llanelli) 1896 *E, S, I*, 1897 *E*
Bowen, D H (Llanelli) 1883 *E*, 1886 *E, S*, 1887 *E*
Bowen, G E (Swansea) 1887 *S, I*, 1888 *S, I*
Bowen, W (Swansea) 1921 *S, F*, 1922 *E, S, I, F*
Bowen, Wm A (Swansea) 1886 *E, S*, 1887 *E, S, I*, 1888 *M*, 1889 *S, I*, 1890 *E, S, I*, 1891 *E, S*
Brace, D O (Llanelli, Oxford U) 1956 *E, S, I, F*, 1957 *E*, 1960 *S, I, F*, 1961 *I*
Braddock, K J (Newbridge) 1966 *A*, 1967 *S, I*
Bradshaw, K (Bridgend) 1964 *E, S, I, F, SA*, 1966 *E, S, I, F*
Brewer, T J (Newport) 1950 *E*, 1955 *E, S*
Brice, A B (Aberavon) 1899 *E, S, I*, 1900 *E, S, I*, 1901 *E, S, I*, 1902 *E, S, I*, 1903 *E, S, I*, 1904 *E, S, I*
Bridges, C J (Neath) 1990 *Nm* 1,2, *Bb*, 1991 *E*(R), *I, F1, A*
Bridie, R H (Newport) 1882 *I*
Britton, G R (Newport) 1961 *S*
Broughton, A S (Treorchy) 1927 *A*, 1929 *S*
Brown, A (Newport) 1921 *I*
Brown, J (Cardiff) 1925 *I*
Brown, J A (Cardiff) 1907 *E, S, I*, 1908 *E, S, F*, 1909 *E*
Brown, M (Pontypool) 1983 *R*, 1986 *E, S,Fj* (R), *Tg, WS*
Bryant, D J (Bridgend) 1988 *NZ* 1,2, *WS, R*, 1989 *S, I, F, E*
Buchanan, A (Llanelli) 1987 [*Tg, E, NZ, A*], 1988 *I*
Burcher, D H (Newport) 1977 *I, F, E, S*
Burgess, R C (Ebbw Vale) 1977 *I, F, E, S*, 1981 *I, F*, 1982 *F, E, S*
Burnett, R (Newport) 1953 *E*
Burns, J (Cardiff) 1927 *F, I*
Bush, P F (Cardiff) 1905 *NZ*, 1906 *E, SA*, 1907 *I*, 1908 *E, S*, 1910 *S, I*
Butler, E T (Pontypool) 1980 *F, E, S, I, NZ* (R), 1982 *S*, 1983 *E, S, I, F, R*, 1984 *S, I, F, E, A*

Dowell, W H (Newport) 1907 *E, S, I*, 1908 *E, S, F, I*
Dyke, J C M (Penarth) 1906 *SA*
Dyke, L M (Penarth, Cardiff) 1910 *I*, 1911 *S, F, I*

Edmunds, D A (Neath) 1990 *I* (R), *Bb*
Edwards, A B (London Welsh, Army) 1955 *E, S*
Edwards, B O (Newport) 1951 *I*
Edwards, D (Glynneath) 1921 *E*
Edwards, G O (Cardiff, Cardiff Coll of Ed) 1967 *F, E, NZ, 1968 E, S, I, F, 1969 S, I, F, E, NZ 1,2, A, 1970 SA, S, E, I, F, 1971 E, S, I, F, 1972 E, S, F, NZ, 1973 E, S, I, F, A, 1974 S, I, F, E, 1975 F, E, S, I, A, 1976 E, S, I, F, 1977 I, F, E, S, 1978 E, S, I, F*
Eidman, I H (Cardiff) 1983 *S, R*, 1984 *I, F, E, A*, 1985 *S, I, Fj*, 1986 *E, S, I, F*
Elliott, J E (Cardiff) 1894 *I*, 1898 *I, E*
Elsey, W J (Cardiff) 1895 *E*
Emyr, Arthur (Swansea) 1989 *E, NZ*, 1990 *F, E, S, I, Nm* 1,2, 1991 *F* 1,2, [*WS, Arg, A*]
Evans, A C (Pontypool) 1924 *E, I, F*
Evans, B (Swansea) 1933 *S*
Evans, B (Llanelli) 1933 *E, S*, 1936 *E, S, I*, 1937 *E*
Evans, B S (Llanelli) 1920 *E*, 1922 *E, S, I, F*
Evans, C (Pontypool) 1960 *E*
Evans, D (Penygraig) 1896 *S, I*, 1897 *E*, 1898 *E*
Evans, D B (Swansea) 1926 *E*
Evans, D D (Cheshire, Cardiff U) 1934 *E*
Evans, D P (Llanelli) 1960 *SA*
Evans, D W (Cardiff) 1889 *S, I*, 1890 *E, I*, 1891 *E*
Evans, D W (Oxford U, Cardiff) 1989 *F, E, NZ*, 1990 *F, E, S, I, Bb*, 1991 *A*(R), *F2*(R), [*A*(R)]
Evans, E (Llanelli) 1937 *E*, 1939 *S, I*
Evans, F (Llanelli) 1921 *S*
Evans, G (Cardiff) 1947 *E, S, F, I, A*, 1948 *E, S, F, I*, 1949 *E, S, I*
Evans, G (Maesteg) 1981 *S* (R), *I, F, A*, 1982 *I, F, E, S*, 1983 *F, R*
Evans, G L (Newport) 1977 *F* (R), 1978 *F, A* 2 (R)
Evans, I (London Welsh) 1934 *S, I*
Evans, I (Swansea) 1922 *E, S, I, F*
Evans, I C (Llanelli) 1987 *F, E, S, I*, [*I, C, E, NZ, A*], 1988 *E, S, I, F, NZ* 1,2, 1989 *I, F, E*, 1991 *E, S, I, F1, A, F2*, [*WS, Arg, A*], 1992 *I, F, E, S, A*, 1993 *E, S, I, F, J, C*, 1994 *S, I, E*
Evans, I L (Llanelli) 1991 *F2*(R)
Evans, J (Llanelli) 1896 *S, I*, 1897 *E*
Evans, J (Blaina) 1904 *E*
Evans, J (Pontypool) 1907 *E, S, I*
Evans, J D (Cardiff) 1958 *I, F*
Evans, J E (Llanelli) 1924 *S*
Evans, J R (Newport) 1934 *E*
Evans, O J (Cardiff) 1887 *E, S*, 1888 *S, I*
Evans, P D (Llanelli) 1951 *E, F*
Evans, R (Cardiff) 1889 *S*
Evans, R (Bridgend) 1963 *S, I, F*
Evans, R L (Llanelli) 1993 *E, S, I, F*, 1994 *S, I, F, E*
Evans, R T (Newport) 1947 *F, I*, 1950 *E, S, I, F*, 1951 *E, S, I, F*
Evans, S (Swansea, Neath) 1985 *F, E*, 1986 *Fj, Tg, WS*, 1987 *F, E*, [*I, Tg*]
Evans, T (Swansea) 1924 *I*
Evans, T G (London Welsh) 1970 *SA, S, E, I*, 1972 *E, S, F*
Evans, T H (Llanelli) 1906 *I*, 1907 *E, S, I*, 1908 *I, A*, 1909 *E, S, F, I*, 1910 *F, E, S, I*, 1911 *E, S, F, I*
Evans, T P (Swansea) 1975 *F, E, S, I, A*, 1976 *E, S, I, F*, 1977 *I*
Evans, V (Neath) 1954 *I, F, S*
Evans, W (Llanelli) 1958 *A*
Evans, W F (Rhymney) 1882 *I*, 1883 *S*
Evans, W G (Brynmawr) 1911 *I*
Evans, W H (Llwynypia) 1914 *E, S, F, I*
Evans, W J (Pontypool) 1947 *S*
Evans, W R (Bridgend) 1958 *A, E, S, I, F*, 1960 *SA*, 1961 *E, S, I, F*, 1962 *E, S, I*
Everson, W A (Newport) 1926 *S*

Faulkner, A G (Pontypool) 1975 *F, E, S, I, A*, 1976 *E, S, I, F*, 1978 *E, S, I, F, A* 1,2, *NZ*, 1979 *S, I, F*
Faull, J (Swansea) 1957 *I, F*, 1958 *A, E, S, I, F*, 1959 *E, S, I*, 1960 *E, F*
Fauvel, T J (Aberavon) 1988 *NZ* 1 (R)
Fear, A G (Newport) 1934 *S, I*, 1935 *S, I*
Fender, N H (Cardiff) 1930 *I, F*, 1931 *E, S, F, I*

Fenwick, S P (Bridgend) 1975 *F, E, S, A*, 1976 *E, S, I, F*, 1977 *I, F, E, S*, 1978 *E, S, I, F, A* 1,2, *NZ*, 1979 *S, I, F, E*, 1980 *F, E, S, I, NZ*, 1981 *E, S*
Finch, E (Llanelli) 1924 *F, NZ*, 1925 *F, I*, 1926 *F*, 1927 *A*, 1928 *I*
Finlayson, A A J (Cardiff) 1974 *I, F, E*
Fitzgerald, D (Cardiff) 1894 *S, I*
Ford, F J V (Welch Regt, Newport) 1939 *E*
Ford, I (Newport) 1959 *E, S*
Ford, S P (Cardiff) 1990 *I, Nm* 1,2, *Bb*, 1991 *E, S, I, A*
Forward, A (Pontypool, Mon Police) 1951 *S, SA*, 1952 *E, S, I, F*
Fowler, I J (Llanelli) 1919 *NZA*
Francis, D G (Llanelli) 1919 *NZA*, 1924 *S*
Francis, P (Maesteg) 1987 *S*

Gabe, R T (Cardiff, Llanelli) 1901 *I*, 1902 *E, S, I*, 1903 *E, S, I*, 1904 *E, S, I*, 1905 *E, S, I, NZ*, 1906 *E, I, SA*, 1907 *E, S, I*, 1908 *E, S, F, I*
Gale, N R (Swansea, Llanelli) 1960 *I*, 1963 *E, S, I, NZ*, 1964 *E, S, I, F, SA*, 1965 *E, S, I, F*, 1966 *E, S, I, F, A*, 1967 *E, NZ*, 1968 *E*, 1969 *NZ* 1 (R), 2, *A*
Gallacher, I S (Llanelli) 1970 *F*
Garrett, R M (Penarth) 1888 *M*, 1889 *S*, 1890 *S, E, I*, 1891 *S, I*, 1892 *E*
Geen, W P (Oxford U, Newport) 1912 *SA*, 1913 *E, I*
George, E E (Pontypridd, Cardiff) 1895 *S, I*, 1896 *E*
George, G M (Newport) 1991 *E, S*
Gething, G I (Neath) 1913 *F*
Gibbs, I S (Neath, Swansea) 1991 *E, S, I, F1, A, F2*, [*WS, Arg, A*], 1992 *I, F, E, S, A*, 1993 *E, S, I, F, J, C*
Gibbs, R A (Cardiff) 1906 *S, I*, 1907 *E, S*, 1908 *E, S, F, I*, 1910 *F, E, S, I*, 1911 *E, S, F, I*
Giles, R (Aberavon) 1983 *R*, 1985 *Fj* (R), 1987 [*C*]
Girling, B E (Cardiff) 1881 *E*
Goldsworthy, S J (Swansea) 1884 *I*, 1885 *E, S*
Gore, J H (Blaina) 1924 *I, F, NZ*, 1925 *E*
Gore, W (Newbridge) 1947 *S, F, I*
Gould, A J (Newport) 1885 *E, S*, 1886 *E, S*, 1887 *E, S, I*, 1888 *S*, 1889 *I*, 1890 *S, E, I*, 1892 *E, S, I*, 1893 *E, S, I*, 1894 *E, S*, 1895 *E, S, I*, 1896 *E, S, I*, 1897 *E*
Gould, G H (Newport) 1892 *I*, 1893 *S, I*
Gould, R (Newport) 1882 *I*, 1883 *E, S*, 1884 *E, S, I*, 1885 *E, S*, 1886 *E*, 1887 *E, S*
Graham, T C (Newport) 1890 *I*, 1891 *S, I*, 1892 *E, S*, 1893 *E, S, I*, 1894 *E, S*, 1895 *E, S*
Gravell, R W R (Llanelli) 1975 *F, E, S, I, A*, 1976 *E, S, I, F*, 1978 *E, S, I, F, A* 1,2, *NZ*, 1979 *S, I*, 1981 *I, F*, 1982 *F, E, S*
Gray, A J (London Welsh) 1968 *E, S*
Greenslade, D (Newport) 1962 *S*
Greville, H G (Llanelli) 1947 *A*
Griffin, Dr J (Edinburgh U) 1883 *S*
Griffiths, C (Llanelli) 1979 *E* (R)
Griffiths, D (Llanelli) 1888 *M*, 1889 *I*
Griffiths, G (Llanelli) 1889 *I*
Griffiths, G M (Cardiff) 1953 *E, S, I, F, NZ*, 1954 *I, F, S*, 1955 *I, F*, 1957 *E, S*
Griffiths, J L (Llanelli) 1988 *NZ* 2, 1989 *S*
Griffiths, M (Bridgend, Cardiff) 1988 *WS, R*, 1989 *S, I, F, E, NZ*, 1990 *F, E, Nm* 1,2, *Bb*, 1991 *I, F1,2*, [*WS, Arg, A*], 1992 *I, F, E, S, A*, 1993 *Z1,2, Nm, J, C*
Griffiths, V M (Newport) 1924 *S, I, F*
Gronow, B (Bridgend) 1910 *F, E, S, I*
Gwilliam, J A (Cambridge U, Newport) 1947 *A*, 1948 *I*, 1949 *E, S, I, F*, 1950 *E, S, I, F*, 1951 *E, S, I, SA*, 1952 *E, S, I, F*, 1953 *E, I, F, NZ*, 1954 *E*
Gwynn, D (Swansea) 1883 *E*, 1887 *S*, 1890 *E, I*, 1891 *E, S*
Gwynn, W H (Swansea) 1884 *E, S, I*, 1885 *E, S*

Hadley, A M (Cardiff) 1983 *R*, 1984 *S, I, F, E*, 1985 *F, E, Fj*, 1986 *E, S, I, F, Fj, Tg*, 1987 *S* (R), *I*, [*I, Tg, C, E, NZ, A*], *US*, 1988 *E, S, I, F*
Hall, I (Aberavon) 1967 *NZ*, 1970 *SA, S, E*, 1971 *S*, 1974 *S, I, F*
Hall, M R (Cambridge U, Bridgend, Cardiff) 1988 *NZ* 1 (R) 2, *WS, R*, 1989 *S, I, F, E, NZ*, 1990 *F, E, S*, 1991 *A, F2*, [*WS, Arg, A*], 1992 *I, F, E, S, A*, 1993 *E, S, I*, 1994 *S, I, F, E*
Hall, W H (Bridgend) 1988 *WS*
Hancock, F E (Cardiff) 1884 *I*, 1885 *E, S*, 1886 *S*
Hannan, J (Newport) 1888 *M*, 1889 *S, I*, 1890 *S, E, I*,

1891 E, **1892** E, S, I, **1893** E, S, I, **1894** E, S, I, **1895** E, S, I

Harding, A F (London Welsh) 1902 E, S, I, 1903 E, S, I, 1904 E, S, I, 1905 E, S, I, NZ, 1906 E, S, I, SA, 1907 I, 1908 E, S

Harding, G F (Newport) 1881 E, 1882 I, 1883 E, S

Harding, R (Swansea, Cambridge U) 1923 E, S, F, I, 1924 I, F, NZ, 1925 F, I, 1926 E, I, F, 1927 E, S, F, I, 1928 E

Harding, T (Newport) 1888 M, 1889 S, I

Harris, D J E (Pontypridd, Cardiff) 1959 I, F, 1960 S, I, F, SA, 1961 E, S

Harris, T (Aberavon) 1927 A

Hathway, G F (Newport) 1924 I, F

Havard, Rev W T (Llanelli) 1919 NZA

Hawkins, F (Pontypridd) 1912 I, F

Hayward, D (Newbridge) 1949 E, F, 1950 E, S, I, F, 1951 E, S, I, F, SA, 1952 E, S, I, F

Hayward, D J (Cardiff) 1963 E, NZ, 1964 S, I, F, SA

Hayward, G (Swansea) 1908 S, F, I, A, 1909 E

Hellings, R (Llwynypia) 1897 E, 1898 I, E, 1899 S, I, 1900 E, I, 1901 E, S

Herrerá, R C (Cross Keys) 1925 S, F, I, 1926 E, S, I, F, 1927 E

Hiams, H (Swansea) 1912 I, F

Hickman, A (Neath) 1930 E, 1933 S

Hiddlestone, D D (Neath) 1922 E, S, I, F, 1924 NZ

Hill, A F (Cardiff) 1885 S, 1886 E, S, 1888 S, I, M, 1889 S, 1890 S, I, 1893 E, S, I, 1894 E, S, I

Hill, S D (Cardiff) 1993 Z1,2, Nm, 1994 I(R), F

Hinam, S (Cardiff) 1925 I, 1926 E, S, I, F

Hinton, J T (Cardiff) 1884 I

Hirst, G L (Newport) 1912 S, 1913 S, 1914 E, S, F, I

Hodder, W (Pontypool) 1921 E, S, F

Hodges, J J (Newport) 1899 E, S, I, 1900 E, S, I, 1901 E, S, 1902 E, S, I, 1903 E, S, I, 1904 E, S, 1905 E, S, I, NZ, 1906 E, S, I

Hodgson, G T R (Neath) 1962 I, 1963 E, S, I, F, NZ, 1964 E, S, I, F, SA, 1966 S, I, F, 1967 I

Hollingdale, H (Swansea) 1912 SA, 1913 E

Hollingdale, T H (Neath) 1927 A, 1928 E, S, I, F, 1930 E

Holmes, T D (Cardiff) 1978 A 2, NZ, 1979 S, I, F, E, 1980 F, E, S, I, NZ, 1981 A, 1982 I, F, E, 1983 E, S, I, F, 1984 E, 1985 S, I, F, E, Fj

Hopkin, W H (Newport) 1937 S

Hopkins, K (Cardiff, Swansea) 1985 E, 1987 F, E, S, [Tg, C(R)], US

Hopkins, P L (Swansea) 1908 A, 1909 E, I, 1910 E

Hopkins, R (Maesteg) 1970 E (R)

Hopkins, T (Swansea) 1926 E, S, I, F

Hopkins, W J (Aberavon) 1925 E, S

Howells, B (Llanelli) 1934 E

Howells, W G (Llanelli) 1957 E, S, I, F

Howells, W H (Swansea) 1888 S, I

Hughes, D (Newbridge) 1967 NZ, 1969 NZ 2, 1970 SA, S, E, I

Hughes, G (Penarth) 1934 E, S, I

Hughes, H (Cardiff) 1887 S, 1889 S

Hughes, K (Cambridge U, London Welsh) 1970 I, 1973 A, 1974 S

Hullin, W (Cardiff) 1967 S

Hurrell, J (Newport) 1959 F

Hutchinson, F (Neath) 1894 I, 1896 S, I

Huxtable, R (Swansea) 1920 F, I

Huzzey, H V P (Cardiff) 1898 I, E, 1899 E, S, I

Hybart, A J (Cardiff) 1887 E

Ingledew, H M (Cardiff) 1890 I, 1891 E, S

Isaacs, I (Cardiff) 1933 E, S

Jackson, T H (Swansea) 1895 E

James, B (Bridgend) 1968 E

James, C R (Llanelli) 1958 A, F

James, D (Swansea) 1891 I, 1892 S, I, 1899 E

James, D R (Treorchy) 1931 F, I

James, E (Swansea) 1890 S, 1891 I, 1892 S, I, 1899 E

James, M (Cardiff) 1947 A, 1948 E, S, F, I

James, T O (Aberavon) 1935 I, 1937 S

James, W J (Aberavon) 1983 E, S, I, F, R, 1984 S, 1985 S, I, F, E, Fj, 1986 E, S, I, F, Fj, Tg, WS, 1987 E, S, I

James, W P (Aberavon) 1925 E, S

Jarman, H (Newport) 1910 E, S, I, 1911 E

Jarrett, K S (Newport) 1967 E, 1968 E, S, 1969 S, I, F, E, NZ 1,2, A

Jeffery, J J (Cardiff Coll of Ed, Newport) 1967 NZ

Jenkin, A M (Swansea) 1895 I, 1896 E

Jenkins, A (Llanelli) 1920 E, S, F, I, 1921 S, F, 1922 F, 1923 E, S, F, I, 1924 NZ, 1928 S, I

Jenkins, D M (Treorchy) 1926 E, S, I, F

Jenkins, D R (Swansea) 1927 A, 1929 E

Jenkins, E (Newport) 1910 S, I

Jenkins, E M (Aberavon) 1927 S, F, I, A, 1928 E, S, I, F, 1929 F, 1930 E, S, I, F, 1931 E, S, F, I, SA, 1932 E, S, I

Jenkins, G R (Pontypool, Swansea) 1991 F2, [WS(R), Arg, A], 1992 I, F, E, S, A, 1993 C, 1994 S, I, F, E

Jenkins, J C (London Welsh) 1906 SA

Jenkins, J L (Aberavon) 1923 S, F

Jenkins, L H (Mon TC, Newport) 1954 I, 1956 E, S, I, F

Jenkins, N R (Pontypridd) 1991 E, S, I, F1, 1992 I, F, E, S, 1993 E, S, I, F, Z1,2, Nm, J, C, 1994 S, I, F, E

Jenkins, V G J (Oxford U, Bridgend, London Welsh) 1933 E, I, 1934 S, I, 1935 E, S, NZ, 1936 E, S, I, 1937 E, 1938 E, S, 1939 E

Jenkins, W (Cardiff) 1912 I, F, 1913 S, I

John, B (Llanelli, Cardiff) 1966 A, 1967 S, NZ, 1968 E, S, I, F, 1969 S, I, F, E, NZ 1,2, A, 1970 SA, S, E, I, 1971 E, S, I, F, 1972 E, S, F

John, D A (Llanelli) 1925 I, 1928 E, S, I

John, D E (Llanelli) 1923 F, I, 1928 E, S, I

John, E R (Neath) 1950 E, S, I, F, 1951 E, S, I, F, SA, 1952 E, S, I, F, 1953 E, S, I, F, NZ, 1954 E

John, G (St Luke's Coll, Exeter) 1954 E, F

John, J H (Swansea) 1926 E, S, I, F, 1927 E, S, F, I

Johnson, T A (Cardiff) 1921 E, F, I, 1923 E, S, F, 1924 E, S, NZ, 1925 E, S, F

Johnson, W D (Swansea) 1953 E

Jones, A H (Cardiff) 1933 E, S

Jones, B (Abertillery) 1914 E, S, F, I

Jones, Bert (Llanelli) 1934 S, I

Jones, Bob (Llwynypia) 1901 I

Jones, B J (Newport) 1960 I, F

Jones, B Lewis (Devonport Services, Llanelli) 1950 E, S, I, F, 1951 E, S, SA, 1952 E, I, F

Jones, C W (Cambridge U, Cardiff) 1934 E, S, I, 1935 E, S, I, NZ, 1936 E, S, I, 1938 E, S, I

Jones, C W (Bridgend) 1920 E, S, F

Jones, D (Neath) 1927 A

Jones, D (Aberavon) 1897 E

Jones, D (Swansea) 1947 E, F, I, 1949 E, S, I, F

Jones, D (Treherbert) 1902 S, I, 1903 E, S, I, 1905 E, S, I, NZ, 1906 E, S, SA

Jones, D (Newport) 1926 E, S, I, F, 1927 E

Jones, D (Llanelli) 1948 E

Jones, D K (Llanelli, Cardiff) 1962 E, S, F, I, 1963 E, F, NZ, 1964 E, S, SA, 1966 E, S, I, F

Jones, D P (Pontypool) 1907 I

Jones, E H (Neath) 1929 E, S

Jones, E L (Llanelli) 1930 F, 1933 E, S, I, 1935 E

Jones, Elvet L (Llanelli) 1939 S

Jones, G (Ebbw Vale) 1963 S, I, F

Jones, G (Llanelli) 1988 NZ 2, 1989 F, E, NZ, 1990 F

Jones, G G (Cardiff) 1930 S, 1933 I

Jones, H (Penygraig) 1902 S, I

Jones, H (Neath) 1904 I

Jones, H (Swansea) 1930 I, F

Jones, Iorwerth (Llanelli) 1927 A, 1928 E, S, I, F

Jones, I C (London Welsh) 1968 I

Jones, Ivor E (Llanelli) 1924 E, S, 1927 S, F, I, A, 1928 E, S, I, F, 1929 E, S, F, I, 1930 E, S

Jones, J (Aberavon) 1901 E

Jones, J (Swansea) 1924 F

Jones, Jim (Aberavon) 1919 NZA, 1920 E, S, 1921 S, F, I

Jones, J A (Cardiff) 1883 S

Jones, J P (Tuan) (Pontypool) 1913 S

Jones, J P (Pontypool) 1908 A, 1909 E, S, F, I, 1910 F, E, 1912 E, F, 1913 F, I, 1920 F, I, 1921 E

Jones, K D (Cardiff) 1960 SA, 1961 E, S, I, 1962 E, F, 1963 E, S, I, NZ

Jones, K J (Newport) 1947 E, S, F, I, A, 1948 E, S, F, I, 1949 E, S, I, F, 1950 E, S, I, F, 1951 E, S, I, F, SA, 1952 E, S, I, F, 1953 E, S, I, F, NZ, 1954 E, I, F, S, 1955 E, S, I, F, 1956 E, S, I, F, 1957 S

Jones, K W J (Oxford U, London Welsh) 1934 E

Morgan, E T (London Welsh) 1902 *E, S, I,* 1903 *I,* 1904 *E, S, I,* 1905 *E, S, I, NZ,* 1906 *E, S, I, SA,* 1908 *F*
Morgan, F L (Llanelli) 1938 *E, S, I,* 1939 *E*
Morgan, H J (Abertillery) 1958 *E, S, I, F,* 1959 *I, F,* 1960 *E,* 1961 *E, S, I, F,* 1962 *E, S, F, I,* 1963 *S, I, F,* 1965 *E, S, I, F,* 1966 *E, S, I, F, A*
Morgan, H P (Newport) 1956 *E, S, I, F*
Morgan, I (Swansea) 1908 *A,* 1909 *E, S, F, I,* 1910 *F, E, S, I,* 1911 *E, F, I,* 1912 *S*
Morgan, J L (Llanelli) 1912 *SA,* 1913 *E*
Morgan, M E (Swansea) 1938 *E, S, I,* 1939 *E*
Morgan, N (Newport) 1960 *S, I, F*
Morgan, P E J (Aberavon) 1961 *E, S, F*
Morgan, P J (Llanelli) 1980 *S* (R), *I, NZ* (R), 1981 *I*
Morgan, R (Newport) 1984 *S*
Morgan, T (Llanelli) 1889 *I*
Morgan, W G (Cambridge U) 1927 *F, I,* 1929 *E, S, F, I,* 1930 *I, F*
Morgan, W L (Cardiff) 1910 *S*
Moriarty, R D (Swansea) 1981 *A,* 1982 *I, F, E, S,* 1983 *E,* 1984 *S, I, F, E,* 1985 *S, I, F,* 1986 *Fj, Tg, WS,* 1987 *[I, Tg, C(R), E, NZ, A]*
Moriarty, W P (Swansea) 1986 *I, F, Fj, Tg, WS,* 1987 *F, E, S, I, [I, Tg, C, E, NZ, A], US,* 1988 *E, S, I, F, NZ* 1
Morley, J C (Newport) 1929 *E, S, F, I,* 1930 *E, I,* 1931 *E, S, F, I, SA,* 1932 *E, S, I*
Morris, G L (Swansea) 1882 *I,* 1883 *E, S,* 1884 *E, S*
Morris, H T (Cardiff) 1951 *F,* 1955 *I, F*
Morris, J I T (Swansea) 1924 *E, S*
Morris, M S (S Wales Police, Neath) 1985 *S, I, F,* 1990 *I, Nm* 1,2, *Bb,* 1991 *I, F1, [WS(R)],* 1992 *E*
Morris, R R (Swansea, Bristol) 1933 *S,* 1937 *S*
Morris, S (Cross Keys) 1920 *E, S, F, I,* 1922 *E, S, I, F,* 1923 *E, S, F, I,* 1924 *E, S, F, NZ,* 1925 *E, S, F*
Morris, W (Abertillery) 1919 *NZA,* 1920 *F,* 1921 *I*
Morris, W (Llanelli) 1896 *S, I,* 1897 *E*
Morris, W D (Neath) 1967 *F, E,* 1968 *E, S, I, F,* 1969 *S, I, F, E, NZ* 1,2, *A,* 1970 *SA, S, E, I, F,* 1971 *E, S, I, F,* 1972 *E, S, F, NZ,* 1973 *E, S, I, A,* 1974 *S, I, F, E*
Morris, W (Newport) 1965 *S,* 1966 *F*
Morris, W J (Pontypool) 1963 *S, I*
Moseley, K (Pontypool, Newport) 1988 *NZ* 2, *R,* 1989 *S, I,* 1990 *F,* 1991 *F2, [WS, Arg, A]*
Murphy, C D (Cross Keys) 1935 *E, S, I*

Nash, D (Ebbw Vale) 1960 *SA,* 1961 *E, S, I, F,* 1962 *F*
Newman, C H (Newport) 1881 *E,* 1882 *I,* 1883 *E, S,* 1884 *E, S,* 1885 *E, S,* 1886 *E,* 1887 *E*
Nicholas, D L (Llanelli) 1981 *E, S, I, F*
Nicholas, T J (Cardiff) 1919 *NZA*
Nicholl, C B (Cambridge U, Llanelli) 1891 *I,* 1892 *E, S, I,* 1893 *E, S, I,* 1894 *E, S,* 1895 *E, S, I,* 1896 *E, S, I*
Nicholl, D W (Llanelli) 1894 *I*
Nicholls, E G (Cardiff) 1896 *S, I,* 1897 *E,* 1898 *I, E,* 1899 *E, S, I,* 1900 *S, I,* 1901 *E, S, I,* 1902 *E, S, I,* 1903 *I,* 1904 *E,* 1905 *I, NZ,* 1906 *E, S, I, SA*
Nicholls, F E (Cardiff Harlequins) 1892 *I*
Nicholls, H (Cardiff) 1958 *I*
Nicholls, S H (Cardiff) 1888 *M,* 1889 *S, I,* 1891 *S*
Norris, C H (Cardiff) 1963 *F,* 1966 *F*
Norster, R L (Cardiff) 1982 *S,* 1983 *E, S, I, F,* 1984 *S, I, F, E, A,* 1985 *S, I, F, E, Fj,* 1986 *I, Tg, WS,* 1987 *F, E, S, I, [I, C, E], US,* 1988 *E, S, I, F, NZ* 1, *WS,* 1989 *F, E*
Norton, W B (Cardiff) 1882 *I,* 1883 *E, S,* 1884 *E, S, I*

O'Connor, A (Aberavon) 1960 *SA,* 1961 *E, S,* 1962 *F, I*
O'Connor, R (Aberavon) 1957 *E*
O'Neill, W (Cardiff) 1904 *S, I,* 1905 *E, S, I,* 1907 *E, I,* 1908 *E, S, F, I*
O'Shea, J P (Cardiff) 1967 *S, I,* 1968 *S, I, F*
Oliver, G (Pontypool) 1920 *E, S, F, I*
Osborne, W T (Mountain Ash) 1902 *E, S, I,* 1903 *E, S, I*
Ould, W J (Cardiff) 1924 *E, S*
Owen, A (Swansea) 1924 *E*
Owen, G D (Newport) 1955 *I, F,* 1956 *E, S, I, F*
Owen, R M (Swansea) 1901 *I,* 1902 *E, S, I,* 1903 *E, S, I,* 1904 *E, S, I,* 1905 *E, S, I, NZ,* 1906 *E, S, I, SA,* 1907 *E, S,* 1908 *F, I, A,* 1909 *E, S, F, I,* 1910 *F, E,* 1911 *E, S, F, I,* 1912 *E, S*

Packer, H (Newport) 1891 *E,* 1895 *S, I,* 1896 *E, S, I,* 1897 *E*

Palmer, F (Swansea) 1922 *E, S, I*
Parfitt, F C (Newport) 1893 *E, S, I,* 1894 *E, S, I,* 1895 *S,* 1896 *S, I*
Parfitt, S A (Swansea) 1990 *Nm* 1(R), *Bb*
Parker, D S (Swansea) 1924 *I, F, NZ,* 1925 *E, S, F, I,* 1929 *F, I,* 1930 *E*
Parker, T (Swansea) 1919 *NZA,* 1920 *E, S, I,* 1921 *E, S, F, I,* 1922 *E, S, I, F,* 1923 *E, S, F*
Parker, W (Swansea) 1899 *E, S*
Parsons, G W (Newport) 1947 *E*
Pascoe, D (Bridgend) 1923 *F, I*
Pask, A E J (Abertillery) 1961 *F,* 1962 *E, S, F, I,* 1963 *E, S, I, F, NZ,* 1964 *E, S, I, F, SA,* 1965 *E, S, I, F,* 1966 *E, S, L, F, A,* 1967 *S, I*
Payne, G W (Army, Pontypridd) 1960 *E, S, I*
Payne, H (Swansea) 1935 *NZ*
Peacock, H (Newport) 1929 *S, F, I,* 1930 *S, I, F*
Peake, E (Chepstow) 1881 *E*
Pearce, G P (Bridgend) 1981 *I, F,* 1982 *I* (R)
Pearson, T W (Cardiff, Newport) 1891 *E, I,* 1892 *E, S,* 1894 *S, I,* 1895 *E, S, I,* 1897 *E,* 1898 *I, E,* 1903 *E*
Pegge, E V (Neath) 1891 *E*
Perego, M A (Llanelli) 1990 *S,* 1993 *F, Z1, Nm*(R), 1994 *S, I, F, E*
Perkins, S J (Pontypool) 1983 *S, I, F, R,* 1984 *S, I, F, E, A,* 1985 *S, I, F, E, Fj,* 1986 *E, S, I, F*
Perrett, F L (Neath) 1912 *SA,* 1913 *E, S, F, I*
Perrins, V C (Newport) 1970 *SA, S*
Perry, W (Neath) 1911 *E*
Phillips, A J (Cardiff) 1979 *E,* 1980 *F, E, S, I, NZ,* 1981 *E, S, I, F, A,* 1982 *I, F, E, S,* 1987 *[C, E, A]*
Phillips, B (Aberavon) 1925 *E, S, F, I,* 1926 *E*
Phillips, D H (Swansea) 1952 *F*
Phillips, H P (Newport) 1892 *E,* 1893 *E, S, I,* 1894 *E, S*
Phillips, H T (Newport) 1927 *E, S, F, I, A,* 1928 *E, S, I, F*
Phillips, K H (Neath) 1987 *F, [I, Tg, NZ], US,* 1988 *E, NZ* 1, 1989 *NZ,* 1990 *F, E, S, I, Nm* 1,2, *Bb,* 1991 *E, S, I, F1, A*
Phillips, L A (Newport) 1900 *E, S, I,* 1901 *S*
Phillips, R (Neath) 1987 *US,* 1988 *E, S, I, F, NZ* 1,2, *WS,* 1989 *S, I*
Phillips, W D (Cardiff) 1881 *E,* 1882 *I,* 1884 *E, S, I*
Pickering, D F (Llanelli) 1983 *E, S, I, F, R,* 1984 *S, I, F, E, A,* 1985 *S, I, F, E, Fj,* 1986 *E, S, I, F, Fj,* 1987 *F, E, S*
Plummer, R C S (Newport) 1912 *S, I, F, SA,* 1913 *E*
Pook, T (Newport) 1895 *S*
Powell, G (Ebbw Vale) 1957 *I, F*
Powell, J (Cardiff) 1906 *I*
Powell, J (Cardiff) 1923 *I*
Powell, R W (Newport) 1888 *S, I*
Powell, W C (London Welsh) 1926 *S, I, F,* 1927 *E, F, I,* 1928 *S, I, F,* 1929 *E, S, F, I,* 1930 *S, I, F,* 1931 *E, S, F, I, SA,* 1932 *E, S, I,* 1935 *E, S, I*
Powell, W J (Cardiff) 1920 *E, S, F, I*
Price, B (Newport) 1961 *I, F,* 1962 *E, S,* 1963 *E, S, F, NZ,* 1964 *E, S, I, F, SA,* 1965 *E, S, I, F,* 1966 *E, S, I, F, A,* 1967 *S, I, F, E,* 1969 *S, I, F, NZ* 1,2, *A*
Price, G (Pontypool) 1975 *F, E, S, I, A,* 1976 *E, S, I, F,* 1977 *I, F, E, S,* 1978 *E, S, I, F, A* 1,2, *NZ,* 1979 *S, I, F, E,* 1980 *F, E, S, I, NZ,* 1981 *E, S, I, F, A,* 1982 *I, F, E, S,* 1983 *E, I, F*
Price, M J (Pontypool, RAF) 1959 *E, S, I, F,* 1960 *E, S, I, F,* 1962 *E*
Price, R E (Weston) 1939 *S, I*
Price, T G (Llanelli) 1965 *E, S, I, F,* 1966 *E, A,* 1967 *S, F*
Priday, A J (Cardiff) 1958 *I,* 1961 *I*
Pritchard, C (Pontypool) 1928 *E, S, I, F,* 1929 *E, S, F, I*
Pritchard, C C (Newport, Pontypool) 1904 *S, I,* 1905 *NZ,* 1906 *E, S*
Pritchard, C M (Newport) 1904 *I,* 1905 *E, S, NZ,* 1906 *E, S, I, SA,* 1907 *E, S, I,* 1908 *E,* 1910 *F, E*
Proctor, W T (Llanelli) 1992 *A,* 1993 *E, S, Z1,2, Nm, C,* 1994 *I*
Prosser, D R (Neath) 1934 *S, I*
Prosser, G (Neath) 1934 *E, S, I,* 1935 *NZ*
Prosser, J (Cardiff) 1921 *I*
Prosser, T R (Pontypool) 1956 *S, F,* 1957 *E, S, I, F,* 1958 *A, E, S, I, F,* 1959 *E, S, I, F,* 1960 *S, I, F, SA,* 1961 *I, F*
Prothero, G J (Bridgend) 1964 *S, I, F,* 1965 *E, S, I, F,*

Thomas, Bob (Swansea) 1900 *E, S, I*, 1901 *E*
Thomas, Brian (Neath, Cambridge U) 1963 *E, S, I, F, NZ*, 1964 *E, S, I, F, SA*, 1965 *E, S, I*, 1966 *E, S, I*, 1967 *NZ*, 1969 *S, I, F, E, NZ* 1,2
Thomas, C (Bridgend) 1925 *E, S*
Thomas, C J (Newport) 1888 *I, M*, 1889 *S, I*, 1890 *S, E, I*, 1891 *E, I*
Thomas, D (Aberavon) 1961 *I*
Thomas, D (Llanelli) 1954 *I*
Thomas, Dick (Mountain Ash) 1906 *SA*, 1908 *F, I*, 1909 *S*
Thomas, D J (Swansea) 1904 *E*, 1908 *A*, 1910 *E, S, I*, 1911 *E, S, F, I*, 1912 *E*
Thomas, D J (Swansea) 1930 *S, I*, 1932 *E, S, I*, 1933 *E, S*, 1934 *E*, 1935 *E, S, I*
Thomas, D L (Neath) 1937 *E*
Thomas, E (Newport) 1904 *S, I*, 1909 *S, F, I*, 1910 *F*
Thomas, G (Llanelli) 1923 *E, S, F, I*
Thomas, G (Newport) 1888 *M*, 1890 *I*, 1891 *S*
Thomas, H (Llanelli) 1912 *F*
Thomas, H (Neath) 1936 *E, S, I*, 1937 *E, S, I*
Thomas, H W (Swansea) 1912 *SA*, 1913 *E*
Thomas, I (Bryncethin) 1924 *E*
Thomas, L C (Cardiff) 1885 *E, S*
Thomas, M C (Newport, Devonport Services) 1949 *F*, 1950 *E, S, I, F*, 1951 *E, S, I, F, SA*, 1952 *E, S, I, F*, 1953 *E*, 1956 *E, S, I, F*, 1957 *E, S*, 1958 *E, S, I, F*, 1959 *I, F*
Thomas, M G (St Bart's Hospital) 1919 *NZA*, 1921 *S, F, I*, 1923 *F*, 1924 *E*
Thomas, R (Pontypool) 1909 *F, I*, 1911 *S, F*, 1912 *E, S, SA*, 1913 *E*
Thomas, R C C (Swansea) 1949 *F*, 1952 *I, F*, 1953 *S, I, F, NZ*, 1954 *I, F, S*, 1955 *S, I*, 1956 *E, S, I*, 1957 *E*, 1958 *A, E, S, I, F*, 1959 *E, S, I, F*
Thomas, R L (London Welsh) 1889 *S, I*, 1890 *I*, 1891 *E, S, I*, 1892 *E*
Thomas, S (Llanelli) 1890 *S, E*, 1891 *I*
Thomas, W D (Llanelli) 1966 *A*, 1968 *S, I, F*, 1969 *E, NZ* 2, *A*, 1970 *SA, S, E, I, F*, 1971 *E, S, I, F*, 1972 *E, S, F, NZ*, 1973 *E, S, I, F*, 1974 *E*
Thomas, W G (Llanelli, Waterloo, Swansea) 1927 *E, S, F, I*, 1929 *E, S, I*, 1931 *E, S, SA*, 1932 *E, S, I*, 1933 *E, S, I*
Thomas, W H (Llandovery Coll, Cambridge U) 1885 *S*, 1886 *E, S*, 1887 *E, S*, 1888 *S, I*, 1890 *E, I*, 1891 *S, I*
Thomas, W J (Cardiff) 1961 *F*, 1963 *F*
Thomas, W L (Newport) 1894 *E, S*, 1895 *E, I*
Thomas, W T (Abertillery) 1930 *E*
Thompson, J F (Cross Keys) 1923 *E*
Thorburn, P H (Neath) 1985 *F, E, Fj*, 1986 *E, S, I, F*, 1987 *F, [I, Tg, C, E, NZ, A], US*, 1988 *S, I, F, WS, R* (R), 1989 *S, I, F, E, NZ*, 1990 *F, E, S, I, Nm* 1,2, *Bb*, 1991 *E, S, I, F1, A*
Titley, M H (Bridgend, Swansea) 1983 *R*, 1984 *S, I, F, E, A*, 1985 *S, I, Fj*, 1986 *F, Fj, Tg, WS*, 1990 *F, E*
Towers, W H (Swansea) 1887 *I*, 1888 *M*
Travers, G (Pill Harriers) 1903 *E, S, I*, 1905 *E, S, I, NZ*, 1906 *E, S, I, SA*, 1907 *E, S, I*, 1908 *E, S, F, I, A*, 1909 *E, S, I*, 1911 *S, F, I*
Travers, W H (Newport) 1937 *S, I*, 1938 *E, S, I*, 1939 *E, S, I*, 1949 *E, S, I, F*
Treharne, E (Pontypridd) 1881 *E*, 1883 *E*
Trew, W J (Swansea) 1900 *S, E, I*, 1901 *E, S*, 1903 *S*, 1905 *S*, 1906 *S*, 1907 *E, S*, 1908 *E, S, F, I, A*, 1909 *E, S, F, I*, 1910 *F, E, S*, 1911 *E, S, I*, 1912 *S*, 1913 *S, F*
Trott, R F (Cardiff) 1948 *E, S, F, I*, 1949 *E, S, I, F*
Truman, W H (Llanelli) 1934 *E*, 1935 *E*
Trump, L C (Newport) 1912 *E, S, I, F*
Turnbull, B R (Cardiff) 1925 *I*, 1927 *E, S*, 1928 *E, F*, 1930 *S*
Turnbull, M J L (Cardiff) 1933 *E, I*
Turner, P (Newbridge) 1989 *I* (R), *F, E*

Uzzell, H (Newport) 1912 *E, S, I, F*, 1913 *S, F, I*, 1914 *E, S, F, I*, 1920 *E, S, F, I*
Uzzell, J R (Newport) 1963 *NZ*, 1965 *E, S, I, F*

Vickery, W E (Aberavon) 1938 *E, S, I*, 1939 *E*
Vile, T H (Newport) 1908 *E, S*, 1910 *I*, 1912 *I, F, SA*, 1913 *E, I*, 1921 *S*
Vincent, H C (Bangor) 1882 *I*

Wakeford, J D M (S Wales Police) 1988 *WS, R*

Waldron, R (Neath) 1965 *E, S, I, F*
Walker, N (Cardiff) 1993 *I, F, J*, 1994 *S, F, E*
Waller, P D (Newport) 1908 *A*, 1909 *E, S, F, I*, 1910 *F*
Walters, N (Llanelli) 1902 *E*
Wanbon, R (Aberavon) 1968 *E*
Ward, W S (Cross Keys) 1934 *S, I*
Warlow, J (Llanelli) 1962 *I*
Waters, D R (Newport) 1986 *E, S, I, F*
Waters, K (Newbridge) 1991 [WS]
Watkins, D (Newport) 1963 *E, S, I, F, NZ*, 1964 *E, S, I, F, SA*, 1965 *E, S, I, F*, 1966 *E, S, I, F*, 1967 *I, F, E*
Watkins, E (Neath) 1924 *E, S, I, F*
Watkins, E (Blaina) 1926 *S, I, F*
Watkins, E (Cardiff) 1935 *NZ*, 1937 *S, I*, 1938 *E, S, I*, 1939 *E, S*
Watkins, H (Llanelli) 1904 *S, I*, 1905 *E, S, I*, 1906 *E*
Watkins, I J (Ebbw Vale) 1988 *E* (R), *S, I, F, NZ* 2, *R*, 1989 *S, I, F, E*
Watkins, L (Oxford U, Llandaff) 1881 *E*
Watkins, M J (Newport) 1984 *I, F, E, A*
Watkins, S J (Newport, Cardiff) 1964 *S, I, F*, 1965 *E, S, I, F*, 1966 *E, S, I, F, A*, 1967 *S, I, F, E, NZ*, 1968 *E, S*, 1969 *S, I, F, E, NZ* 1, 1970 *E, I*
Watkins, W R (Newport) 1959 *F*
Watts, D (Maesteg) 1914 *E, S, F, I*
Watts, J (Llanelli) 1907 *E, S, I*, 1908 *E, S, F, I, A*, 1909 *S, F, I*
Watts, W (Llanelli) 1914 *E*
Watts, W H (Newport) 1892 *E, S, I*, 1893 *E, S, I*, 1894 *E, S, I*, 1895 *E, I*, 1896 *E*
Weaver, D (Swansea) 1964 *E*
Webb, J (Abertillery) 1907 *S*, 1908 *E, S, F, I, A*, 1909 *E, S, F, I*, 1910 *F, E, S, I*, 1911 *E, S, F, I*, 1912 *E, S*
Webb, J E (Newport) 1888 *M*, 1889 *S*
Webbe, G M C (Bridgend) 1986 *Tg* (R), *WS*, 1987 *F, E, S*, [*Tg*], *US*, 1988 *F* (R), *NZ* 1, *R*
Webster, R E (Swansea) 1987 [A], 1990 *Bb*, 1991 [*Arg, A*], 1992 *I, F, E, S, A*, 1993 *E, S, I, F*
Wells, G T (Cardiff) 1955 *E, S*, 1957 *I, F*, 1958 *A, E, S*
Westacott, D (Cardiff) 1906 *I*
Wetter, H (Newport) 1912 *SA*, 1913 *E*
Wetter, J J (Newport) 1914 *S, F, I*, 1920 *E, S, F, I*, 1921 *E*, 1924 *I, NZ*
Wheel, G A D (Swansea) 1974 *I, E* (R), 1975 *F, E, I, A*, 1976 *E, S, I, F*, 1977 *I, E, S*, 1978 *E, S, I, F, A* 1,2, *NZ*, 1979 *S, I*, 1980 *F, E, S, I*, 1981 *E, S, I, F, A*, 1982 *I*
Wheeler, P J (Aberavon) 1967 *NZ*, 1968 *E*
Whitefoot, J (Cardiff) 1984 *A* (R), 1985 *S, I, F, E, Fj*, 1986 *E, S, I, F, Fj, Tg, WS*, 1987 *F, E, S, I*, [*I, C*]
Whitfield, J (Newport) 1919 *NZA*, 1920 *E, S, F, I*, 1921 *E*, 1922 *E, S, I, F*, 1924 *S, I*
Whitson, G K (Newport) 1956 *F*, 1960 *S, I*
Williams, A (Bridgend) 1990 *Nm* 2(R)
Williams, B (Llanelli) 1920 *S, F, I*
Williams, B L (Cardiff) 1947 *E, S, F, I, A*, 1948 *E, S, F, I*, 1949 *E, S, I*, 1951 *I, SA*, 1952 *S, I*, 1953 *E, S, I, F, NZ*, 1954 *S*, 1955 *E*
Williams, B R (Neath) 1990 *S, I, Bb*, 1991 *E, S*
Williams, C (Llanelli) 1924 *NZ*, 1925 *E*
Williams, C (Aberavon, Swansea) 1977 *E, S*, 1980 *F, E, S, I, NZ*, 1983 *E*
Williams, C D (Cardiff, Neath) 1955 *F*, 1956 *F*
Williams, D (Ebbw Vale) 1963 *E, S, I, F*, 1964 *E, S, I, F, SA*, 1965 *E, S, I, F*, 1966 *E, S, I, A*, 1967 *F, E, NZ*, 1968 *E*, 1969 *S, I, F, E, NZ* 1,2, *A*, 1970 *SA, S, E, I*, 1971 *E, S, I, F*
Williams, D B (Newport, Swansea) 1978 *A* 1, 1981 *E, S*
Williams, E (Neath) 1924 *NZ*, 1925 *F*
Williams, E (Aberavon) 1925 *E, S*
Williams, F L (Cardiff) 1929 *S, F, I*, 1930 *E, S, I, F*, 1931 *F, I, SA*, 1932 *E, S, I*, 1933 *I*
Williams, G (Aberavon) 1936 *E, S, I*
Williams, G (London Welsh) 1950 *I, F*, 1951 *E, S, I, F, SA*, 1952 *E, S, I, F*, 1953 *NZ*, 1954 *E*
Williams, G (Bridgend) 1981 *I, F*, 1982 *E* (R), *S*
Williams, G P (Bridgend) 1980 *NZ*, 1981 *E, S, A*, 1982 *I*
Williams, J (Blaina) 1920 *E, S, F, I*, 1921 *S, F, I*
Williams, J F (London Welsh) 1905 *I, NZ*, 1906 *S, SA*
Williams, J J (Llanelli) 1973 *F* (R), *A*, 1974 *S, I, F, E*, 1975 *F, E, S, I, A*, 1976 *E, S, I, F*, 1977 *I, F, E, S*, 1978 *E, S, I, F, A* 1,2, *NZ*, 1979 *S, I, F, E*
Williams, J L (Cardiff) 1906 *SA*, 1907 *E, S, I*, 1908

E, S, I, A, 1909 E, S, F, I, 1910 I, 1911 E, S, F, I
Williams, J P R (London Welsh, Bridgend) 1969 S, I,
F, E, NZ 1,2, A, 1970 SA, S, E, I, F, 1971 E, S, I, F,
1972 E, S, F, NZ, 1973 E, S, I, F, A, 1974 S, I, F, 1975
F, E, S, I, A, 1976 E, S, I, F, 1977 I, F, E, S, 1978 E,
S, I, F, A 1,2, NZ, 1979 S, I, F, E, 1980 NZ, 1981 E, S
Williams, L (Llanelli, Cardiff) 1947 E, S, F, I, A, 1948
I, 1949 E
Williams, L H (Cardiff) 1957 S, I, F, 1958 E, S, I, F,
1959 E, S, I, 1961 F, 1962 E, S
Williams, M (Newport) 1923 F
Williams, O (Bridgend) 1990 Nm 2
Williams, O (Llanelli) 1947 E, S, A, 1948 E, S, F, I
Williams, R (Llanelli) 1954 S, 1957 F, 1958 A
Williams, R D G (Newport) 1881 E
Williams, R F (Cardiff) 1912 SA, 1913 E, S, 1914 I
Williams, R H (Llanelli) 1954 I, F, S, 1955 S, I, F,
1956 E, S, I, 1957 E, S, I, F, 1958 A, E, S, I, F, 1959
E, S, I, F, 1960 E
Williams, S (Llanelli) 1947 E, S, F, I, 1948 S, F
Williams, S A (Aberavon) 1939 E, S, I
Williams, T (Pontypridd) 1882 I
Williams, T (Swansea) 1888 S, I
Williams, T (Swansea) 1912 I, 1913 F, 1914 E, S, F, I
Williams, Tudor (Swansea) 1921 F
Williams, T G (Cross Keys) 1935 S, I, NZ, 1936 E, S,
I, 1937 S, I
Williams, W A (Crumlin) 1927 E, S, F, I
Williams, W A (Newport) 1952 I, F, 1953 E
Williams, W E O (Cardiff) 1887 S, I, 1889 S, 1890 S, E

Williams, W H (Pontymister) 1900 E, S, I, 1901 E
Williams, W O G (Swansea, Devonport Services) 1951
F, SA, 1952 E, S, I, F, 1953 E, S, I, F, NZ, 1954 E, I,
F, S, 1955 E, S, I, F, 1956 E, S, I
Williams, W P J (Neath) 1974 I, F
Williams-Jones, H (S Wales Police) 1989 S(R), 1990
F(R), I, 1991 A, 1992 S, A, 1993 E, S, I, F, Z1, Nm
Willis, W R (Cardiff) 1950 E, S, I, F, 1951 E, S, I, F,
SA, 1952 E, S, 1953 S, NZ, 1954 E, I, F, S, 1955 E, S,
I, F
Wiltshire, M L (Aberavon) 1967 NZ, 1968 E, S, F
Windsor, R W (Pontypool) 1973 A, 1974 S, I, F, E,
1975 F, E, S, I, A, 1976 E, S, I, F, 1977 I, F, E, S,
1978 E, S, I, F, A 1,2, NZ, 1979 S, I, F
Winfield, H B (Cardiff) 1903 I, 1904 E, S, I, 1905 NZ,
1906 E, S, I, 1907 S, I, 1908 E, S, F, I, A
Winmill, S (Cross Keys) 1921 E, S, F, I
Wintle, R V (London Welsh) 1988 WS(R)
Wooller, W (Sale, Cambridge U, Cardiff) 1933 E, S, I,
1935 E, S, I, NZ, 1936 E, S, I, 1937 E, S, I, 1938 S, I,
1939 E, S, I
Wyatt, M A (Swansea) 1983 E, S, I, F, 1984 A, 1985 S,
I, 1987 E, S, I

Young, D (Swansea, Cardiff) 1987 [E, NZ], US, 1988
E, S, I, F, NZ 1,2, WS, R, 1989 S, NZ, 1990 F
Young, G A (Cardiff) 1886 E, S
Young, J (Harrogate, RAF, London Welsh) 1968 S, I,
F, 1969 S, I, F, E, NZ 1, 1970 E, I, F, 1971 E, S, I, F,
1972 E, S, F, NZ, 1973 E, S, I, F

WELSH INTERNATIONAL RECORDS

Both team and individual records are for official Welsh international matches up to 31 March 1994.

TEAM RECORDS

Highest score
55 v Japan (55-5) 1993 Cardiff
v individual countries
16 v Argentina (16-7) 1991 Cardiff
28 v Australia (28-3) 1975 Cardiff
40 v Canada (40-9) 1987 Invercargill
34 v England (34-21) 1967 Cardiff
49 v France (49-14) 1910 Swansea
40 v Fiji (40-3) 1985 Cardiff
34 v Ireland (34-9) 1976 Dublin
55 v Japan (55-5) 1993 Cardiff
38 v Namibia (38-23) 1993 Windhoek
16 v N Zealand (16-19) 1972 Cardiff
 9 v Romania (9-15) 1988 Cardiff
35 v Scotland (35-12) 1972 Cardiff
 6 v S Africa (6-6) 1970 Cardiff
29 v Tonga (29-16) 1987 Palmerston North
46 v United States (46-0) 1987 Cardiff
32 v W Samoa (32-14) 1986 Apia
42 v Zimbabwe (42-13) 1993 Harare

25 v Australia (28-3) 1975 Cardiff
31 v Canada (40-9) 1987 Invercargill
25 v England (25-0) 1905 Cardiff
42 v France (47-5) 1909 Colombes
37 v Fiji (40-3) 1985 Cardiff
29 v Ireland (29-0) 1907 Cardiff
50 v Japan (55-5) 1993 Cardiff
15 v Namibia (38-23) 1993 Windhoek
 5 v N Zealand (13-8) 1953 Cardiff
23 v Scotland $\begin{cases} (35\text{-}12) \ 1972 \text{ Cardiff} \\ (29\text{-}6) \ 1994 \text{ Cardiff} \end{cases}$
13 v Tonga (29-16) 1987 Palmerston North
46 v United States (46-0) 1987 Cardiff
22 v W Samoa (28-6) 1988 Cardiff
29 v Zimbabwe (42-13) 1993 Harare
No wins v Romania or South Africa

Longest winning sequence
11 matches – 1907-10

Biggest winning points margin
50 v Japan (55-5) 1993 Cardiff
v individual countries
 9 v Argentina (16-7) 1991 Cardiff

Highest score by opposing team
63 Australia (6-63) 1991 Brisbane

v individual countries
7 Argentina (16-7) 1991 Cardiff
63 Australia (6-63) 1991 Brisbane
26 Canada (24-26) 1993 Cardiff
34 England (6-34) 1990 Twickenham
36 France (3-36) 1991 Paris
15 Fiji (22-15) 1986 Suva
21 Ireland { (24-21) 1979 Cardiff
(7-21) 1980 Dublin
(9-21) 1985 Cardiff
(21-21) 1991 Cardiff
5 Japan (55-5) 1993 Cardiff
30 Namibia (34-30) 1990 Windhoek
54 N Zealand (9-54) 1988 Auckland
24 Romania (6-24) 1983 Bucharest
35 Scotland (10-35) 1924 Inverleith
24 S Africa (3-24) 1964 Durban
16 Tonga (29-16) 1987 Palmerston North
0 United States (46-0) 1987 Cardiff
16 W Samoa (13-16) 1991 Cardiff
13 Zimbabwe (42-13) 1993 Harare

Biggest losing points margin
57 v Australia (6-63) 1991 Brisbane
v individual countries
57 v Australia (6-63) 1991 Brisbane
2 v Canada (24-26) 1993 Cardiff
28 v England (6-34) 1990 Twickenham
33 v France (3-36) 1991 Paris
16 v Ireland (3-19) 1925 Belfast
49 v N Zealand (3-52) 1988 Christchurch
18 v Romania (6-24) 1983 Bucharest
25 v Scotland (10-35) 1924 Inverleith
21 v S Africa (3-24) 1964 Durban
3 v W Samoa (13-16) 1991 Cardiff
No defeats v Argentina, Fiji, Japan, Namibia, Tonga, United States or Zimbabwe

Longest losing sequence
5 matches – 1989-90

Most tries by Wales in an international
11 v France (47-5) 1909 Colombes

Most tries against Wales in an international
13 by England 1881 Blackheath

Most points by Wales in International Championship in a season – 102
in season 1975-76

Most tries by Wales in International Championship in a season – 21
in season 1909-10

INDIVIDUAL RECORDS

Most capped player
J P R Williams 55 1969-81
in individual positions
Full-back
J P R Williams 54(55)[1] 1969-81
Wing
K J Jones 44[2] 1947-57
Centre
S P Fenwick 30[3] 1975-81
Fly-half
C I Morgan 29[3] 1951-58
Scrum-half
G O Edwards 53 1967-78
Prop
G Price 41 1975-83
Hooker
B V Meredith 34 1954-62
Lock
A J Martin 34 1973-81
R L Norster 34 1982-89
Flanker
W D Morris 32(34)[4] 1967-74
No 8
T M Davies 38[5] 1969-76
[1]Williams won one cap as a flanker
[2]T G R Davies, 46 caps, won 35 as a wing, 11 as a centre
[3]M G Ring, 32 caps, won 27 at centre, 4 at fly-half and 1 as a full-back. P Bennett, 29 caps, played 25 times as a fly-half
[4]Morris won his first two caps as a No 8
[5]P T Davies, 39 caps, has won 24 as a No 8, 2 as a flanker and 13 as a lock

Longest international career
W J Trew
14 seasons 1899-1900 to 1912-13
T H Vile
14 seasons 1907-08 to 1920-21
H Tanner
14 seasons 1935-36 to 1948-49

Most consecutive internationals – 53★
G O Edwards 1967-78
★entire career

Most internationals as captain – 18
A J Gould 1889-97
I C Evans 1991-94

Most points in internationals – 304
P H Thorburn (37 matches) 1985-91

**Most points in International
Championship in a season – 52**
P H Thorburn (4 matches) 1985-86

Most points in an international – 24
N R Jenkins v Canada 1993 Cardiff

Most tries in internationals – 20
G O Edwards (53 matches) 1967-78
T G R Davies (46 matches) 1966-78

**Most tries in International
Championship in a season – 6**
R A Gibbs (4 matches) 1907-08
M C R Richards (4 matches) 1968-69

Most tries in an international – 4
W M Llewellyn* v England 1899 Swansea
R A Gibbs v France 1908 Cardiff
M C R Richards v England 1969 Cardiff
I C Evans v Canada 1987 Invercargill
on first appearance

Most conversions in internationals – 43
P H Thorburn (37 matches) 1985-91

**Most conversions in International
Championship in a season – 11**
J Bancroft (4 matches) 1908-09

Most conversions in an international – 8
J Bancroft v France 1910 Swansea

Most dropped goals in internationals – 13
J Davies (27 matches) 1985-88

Most dropped goals in an international – 2
J Shea v England 1920 Swansea
A Jenkins v Scotland 1921 Swansea
B John v England 1971 Cardiff
M Dacey v England 1984 Twickenham
J Davies v Ireland 1987 Wellington
J Davies v Scotland 1988 Cardiff

Most penalty goals in internationals – 70
P H Thorburn (37 matches) 1985-91

**Most penalty goals in International
Championship in a season – 16**
P H Thorburn (4 matches) 1985-86

Most penalty goals in an international – 8
N R Jenkins v Canada 1993 Cardiff

Most points on major overseas tour – 89
N R Jenkins (6 matches) Africa 1993

Most points in a tour match – 28
M Rayer v N Region 1990 Namibia
*P Bennett scored 34 points v Japan in Tokyo in 1975, but
this was not on a major tour*

Most tries in a tour match – 3
M C R Richards v Otago 1969 Dunedin,
NZ
S Fealey v Welwitschia 1990 Swakop-
mund, Namibia
Several others have scored 3 in matches on non-major tours

FROM GLORY TO DOUBT, AND AGAIN FRANCE HAVE A TEAM TO BUILD

THE 1993-94 SEASON IN FRANCE
Bob Donahue *International Herald Tribune*

The season began in hope after French success on tour in South Africa in June and July. It had been expected that this tour might resemble that of 1975, when a modest side lost both Tests but emerged rebuilt as the powerful team of 1976 and 1977. Instead the tour echoed 1958, France drawing the First Test and winning the Second. The future looked rosy.

Jean-François (Jeff) Tordo, who had succeeded Marc Cecillon as captain early in the 1992-93 season, was raked out of contention in the second tour match, against Western Province, and needed 50 stitches in his right cheek. Olivier Roumat took over – just as Lucien Mias had taken over from Michel Celaya 35 years before. When the Durban Test was drawn 20-20, *Midi Olympique* used letters two and a half inches high to ask, 'LIKE IN 1958?' One of some 600 faxes from France was a message of encouragement from Dr Mias. After victory in Johannesburg by 18-17, another giant headline exulted, 'THEY DID IT!'

Defence, ball-winning and composure were strengths in Johannesburg as the French fell behind 8-0 but fought back to win. Said Roumat: 'We may not be a great team but we're good. The confidence that we're starting to show makes me think a great adventure is beginning.' The tour launched the international career of Olivier Merle, a 20-stone lock from Grenoble.

The road ahead to the 1995 World Cup suddenly looked promising. Coach Pierre Berbizier stressed that much methodical work remained to be done, yet he, too, gave way to optimism. Since the basics seemed to be in place, he declared: 'Our mission from now on is to play rugby that people can dream about.' It was a dangerous promise to many critics of his team's dogged style, and he would come to regret it.

A 51-0 trouncing of Romania in October kept spirits up. Leon Loppy, of Toulon, stood in for the injured Laurent Cabannes. Loppy was the first of seven new caps during the season but the only one who had been on the South Africa tour. In other words, as a team-building venture, the tour was a disappointment. The season's other newcomers would be Emile N'tamack (Toulouse) against Wales, William Téchoueyres (Bordeaux) and Laurent Benezech (Racing Club) against England, and Yann Delaigue (Toulon), Alain Macabiau (Perpignan) and Olivier Brouzet (Grenoble) against Scotland.

Since Australia were holders of the 1991 World Cup and France were the 1993 Five Nations champions, their two-Test series was billed as an unofficial world championship. This was nonsense, of course, as everyone knew. Still, French victory in Bordeaux by 16-13 was yet

The France team which lost to England at Parc des Princes. L-R, back row: J-M Gonzalez, L Benezech, P Gallart, L Cabannes, P Benetton, O Merle, A Benazzi; front row: P Saint-André, P Sella, T Lacroix, F Galthié, O Roumat (capt), J-L Sadourny, A Penaud, W Téchoueyres.

another piece of good news. Emphatic defeat in Paris, by 24-3 and a 2-0 try-count, brought French supporters back down to earth. Even without Nick Farr-Jones (who played with the French Barbarians against his countrymen), Australia were patently superior. The challenge for Berbizier and Roumat was to build an attacking game on strong defence. As lacklustre match succeeded lacklustre match, pressure mounted to change the half-backs, Aubin Hueber and Alain Penaud. The glory from South Africa was by now much dimmed.

The Five Nations campaign would extinguish the glow altogether. Two late tries against Ireland in Paris made for a flattering final score, 35-15. Fabien Galthié was back at scrum-half, and Thierry Lacroix amassed 20 points. But an ambush awaited France a month later in Cardiff, where Scott Quinnell and company richly deserved their 24-15 victory. Well, hadn't the mighty English fallen at home to Ireland? Over-confident France and England had been looking ahead at each other instead of at the current opposition, and both had tripped over it. But there was still time to beat England in Paris and save the season.

Instead, Rob Andrew and the rest of Will Carling's winning machine made Roumat's team look ordinary. Berbizier's head was on the block. Roumat, Penaud and Galthié were dropped, the captaincy passing to Philippe Saint-André. Modest victory in Edinburgh (France's first there since 1978) saved the coach. Supporters were left with a fleeting vision, a fragment of a dream: young Delaigue accelerating head-high into a decisive gap. Scarcely noticed was the extraordinary figure of 18 penalty goals conceded by France in four matches, an all-time Championship record. (The previous worst was 17, also conceded by France, in 1982.)

In the final phase of club play, Christophe Deylaud, the 29-year-old Toulouse fly-half, looked to some a potential saviour for the coming tour to Canada and New Zealand. In any case, it was clear that France's major problem in 1993-94 had been behind the scrum. Of the 14 backs selected for this tour, only four (Saint-André, Lacroix, Jean-Luc Sadourny and Philippe Sella) had been in South Africa a year earlier.

Sella by now totalled 98 caps, having equalled Serge Blanco's world record of 93 in the First Test against Australia. He had played for France under 11 captains since his debut against Romania in 1982, in addition to leading France himself in the 1992 Championship. His 29th international try came against Wales in 1994. His 98 appearances were in 61 victories, five draws and 32 defeats. Sella of Agen, like Blanco of Biarritz, is a man of just one club.

FRENCH INTERNATIONAL PLAYERS
(up to 31 March 1994)

ABBREVIATIONS

A – Australia; *Arg* – Argentina; *B* – British Forces and Home Union Teams; *C* – Canada; *Cz* – Czechoslovakia; *E* – England; *Fj* – Fiji; *G* – Germany; *I* – Ireland; *It* – Italy; *J* – Japan; *K* – New Zealand Services; *M* – Maoris; *NZ* – New Zealand; *R* – Romania; *S* – Scotland; *SA* – South Africa; *US* – United States of America; *W* – Wales; *Z* – Zimbabwe; (R) – Replacement; (t) – temporary replacement. Entries in square brackets [ ] indicate appearances in the World Cup.

Club Abbreviations: ASF – Association Sportive Française; BEC – Bordeaux Etudiants Club; CASG – Club Athlétique des Sports Généraux; PUC – Paris Université Club; RCF – Racing Club de France; SB – Stade Bordelais; SBUC – Stade Bordelais Université Club; SCUF – Sporting Club Universitaire de France; SF – Stade Français; SOE – Stade Olympien des Etudiants; TOEC – Toulouse Olympique Employés Club.

Note: Years given for Five Nations' matches are for second half of season, eg 1972 refers to season 1971-72. Years for all other matches refer to the actual year of the match. When a series has taken place, or more than one match has been played against a country in the same year, figures have been used to denote the particular matches in which players have featured. Thus 1967 *SA* 2,4 indicates that a player appeared in the second and fourth Tests of the 1967 series against South Africa. This list includes only those players who have appeared in FFR International Matches '*donnant droit au titre d'international*'.

Abadie, A (Pau) 1964 *I*
Abadie, A (Graulhet) 1965 *R*, 1967 *SA* 1,3,4, *NZ*, 1968 *S, I*
Abadie, L (Tarbes) 1963 *R*
Aguerre, R (Biarritz O) 1979 *S*
Aguilar, D (Pau) 1937 *G*
Aguirre, J-M (Bagnères) 1971 *A* 2, 1972 *S*, 1973 *W, I, J, R*, 1974 *I, W, Arg* 2, *R, SA* 1, 1976 *W*(R), *E, US, A* 2, *R*, 1977 *W, E, S, I, Arg* 1,2, *NZ* 1,2, 1978 *E, S, I, W, R*, 1979 *I, W, E, S, NZ* 1,2, *R*, 1980 *W, I*
Ainciart, E (Bayonne) 1933 *G*, 1934 *G*, 1935 *G*, 1937 *G, It*, 1938 *G* 1
Albaladejo, P (Dax) 1954 *E, It*, 1960 *W, I, It, R*, 1961 *S, SA, E, W, I, NZ* 1,2, *A*, 1962 *S, E, W, I*, 1963 *S, I, E, W, It*, 1964 *S, NZ, W, It, I, SA, Fj*
Alvarez, A-J (Tyrosse) 1945 *B* 2, 1946 *B, I, K, W*, 1947 *S, I, W, E*, 1948 *I, A, S, W, E*, 1949 *I, E, W*, 1951 *S, E, W*
Amand, H (SF) 1906 *NZ*
Ambert, A (Toulouse) 1930 *S, I, E, G, W*
Amestoy, J-B (Mont-de-Marsan) 1964 *NZ, E*
André, G (RCF) 1913 *SA, E, W, I*, 1914 *I, W, E*
Andrieu, M (Nîmes) 1986 *Arg* 2, *NZ* 1, *R* 2, *NZ* 2, 1987 [*R, Z*], *R*, 1988 *E, S, I, W, Arg* 1,2,3,4, *R*, 1989 *I, W, E, S, NZ* 2, *B, A* 2, 1990 *W, E, I*(R)
Anduran, J (SCUF) 1910 *W*
Araou, R (Narbonne) 1924 *R*
Arcalis, R (Brive) 1950 *S, I*, 1951 *I, E, W*
Arino, M (Agen) 1962 *R*
Aristouy, P (Pau) 1948 *S*, 1949 *Arg* 2, 1950 *S, I, E, W*
Armary, L (Lourdes) 1987 [*R*], *R*, 1988 *S, I, W, Arg* 3,4, *R*, 1989 *W, S, A* 1,2, 1990 *W, E, S, I, A* 1,2,3, *NZ* 1, 1991 *W2*, 1992 *S, I, R, Arg* 1,2, *SA* 1,2, *Arg*, 1993 *E, S, I, W, SA1,2, R2, A1,2*, 1994 *I, W*
Arnal, J-M (RCF) 1914 *I, W*
Arnaudet, M (Lourdes) 1964 *I*, 1967 *It, W*
Arotca, R (Bayonne) 1938 *R*
Arrieta, J (SF) 1953 *E, W*
Arthapignet, P (see Harislur-Arthapignet)
Astre, R (Béziers) 1971 *R*, 1972 *I* 1, 1973 *E* (R), 1975 *E, S, I, SA* 1,2, *Arg* 2, 1976 *A* 2, *R*
Augé, J (Dax) 1929 *S, W*
Augras-Fabre, L (Agen) 1931 *I, S, W*
Averous, J-L (La Voulte) 1975 *S, I, SA* 1,2, 1976 *I, W, E, US, A* 1,2, *R*, 1977 *W, E, S, I, Arg* 1, *R*, 1978 *E, S, I*, 1979 *NZ* 1,2, 1980 *E, S*, 1981 *A* 2
Azarete, J-L (Dax, St Jean-de-Luz) 1969 *W, R*, 1970 *S, I, W, R*, 1971 *S, I, E, SA* 1,2, *A* 1, 1972 *E, W, I* 2, *A* 1, *R*, 1973 *NZ, W, I, R*, 1974 *I, R, SA* 1,2, 1975 *W*

Bader, E (Primevères) 1926 *M*, 1927 *I, S*
Badin, C (Chalon) 1973 *W, I*, 1975 *Arg* 1
Baillette, M (Perpignan) 1925 *I, NZ, S*, 1926 *W, M*, 1927 *I, W, G* 2, 1929 *G*, 1930 *S, I, E, G*, 1931 *I, S, E*, 1932 *G*
Baladie, G (Agen) 1945 *B* 1,2, *W*, 1946 *B, I, K*
Ballarin, J (Tarbes) 1924 *E*, 1925 *NZ, S*

Baquey, J (Toulouse) 1921 *I*
Barbazanges, A (Roanne) 1932 *G*, 1933 *G*
Barrau, M (Beaumont, Toulouse) 1971 *S, E, W*, 1972 *E, W, A* 1,2, 1973 *S, NZ, E, I, J, R*, 1974 *I, S*
Barrère, P (Toulon) 1929 *G*, 1931 *W*
Barrière, R (Béziers) 1960 *R*
Barthe, E (SBUC) 1925 *W, E*
Barthe, J (Lourdes) 1954 *Arg* 1,2, 1955 *S*, 1956 *I, W, It, E, Cz*, 1957 *S, I, E, W, R* 1,2, 1958 *S, E, A, W, It, I, SA* 1,2, 1959 *S, E, It, W*
Basauri, R (Albi) 1954 *Arg* 1
Bascou, P (Bayonne) 1914 *E*
Basquet, G (Agen) 1945 *W*, 1946 *B, I, K, W*, 1947 *S, I, W, E*, 1948 *I, A, S, W, E*, 1949 *I, E, W, Arg* 1, 1950 *S, I, E, W*, 1951 *S, I, E, W*, 1952 *S, I, SA, W, E, It*
Bastiat, J-P (Dax) 1969 *R*, 1970 *S, I, W*, 1971 *S, A* 2, 1972 *S, A* 1, 1973 *E, I*, 1974 *Arg* 1,2, *SA* 2, 1975 *W, Arg* 1,2, *R*, 1976 *S, I, W, E, A* 1,2, *R*, 1977 *W, E, S, I*, 1978 *E, S, I, W*
Baudry, N (Montferrand) 1949 *S, I, W, Arg* 1,2
Baulon, R (Vienne, Bayonne) 1954 *S, NZ, W, E, It*, 1955 *I, E, W, It*, 1956 *S, I, W, It, E, Cz*, 1957 *S, I, It*
Baux, J-P (Lannemezan) 1968 *NZ* 1,2, *SA* 1,2
Bavozet, J (Lyon) 1911 *S, E, W*
Bayard, J (Toulouse) 1923 *S, W, E*, 1924 *W, R, US*
Bayardon, J (Chalon) 1964 *S, NZ, E*
Beaurin-Gressier, C (SF) 1907 *E*, 1908 *E*
Bégu, J (Dax) 1982 *Arg* 2 (R), 1984 *E, S*
Béguerie, C (Agen) 1979 *NZ* 1
Beguet, L (RCF) 1922 *I*, 1923 *S, W, E, I*, 1924 *S, I, E, R, US*
Behoteguy, A (Bayonne, Cognac) 1923 *E*, 1924 *S, I, E, W, R, US*, 1926 *E*, 1927 *E, G* 1,2, 1928 *A, I, E, G, W*, 1929 *S, W, E*
Behoteguy, H (RCF, Cognac) 1923 *W*, 1928 *A, I, E, G, W*
Belascain, C (Bayonne) 1977 *R*, 1978 *E, S, I, W, R*, 1979 *I, W, E, S, I, A* 2, *R*, 1983 *E, S, I, W*
Belletante, G (Nantes) 1951 *I, E, W*
Benazzi, A (Agen) 1990 *A* 1,2, *NZ* 1,2, 1991 *E, US*1(R),2, [*R, Fj, C*], 1992 *SA* 1(R),2, *Arg*, 1993 *E, S, I, W, A*1,2, 1994 *I, W, E, S*
Bénésis, R (Narbonne) 1969 *W, R*, 1970 *S, I, W, E, R*, 1971 *S, I, E, W, A* 2, *R*, 1972 *S, I* 1, *E, W, I* 2, *A* 1, *R*, 1973 *NZ, E, W, I, R*, 1974 *I, W, E, S*
Benetière, J (Roanne) 1954 *It, Arg* 1
Benetton, P (Agen) 1989 *B*, 1990 *NZ* 2, 1991 *US2*, 1992 *Arg* 1,2(R), *SA* 1(R),2, *Arg*, 1993 *E, S, I, W, SA*1,2, *R2, A*1,2, 1994 *I, W, E, S*
Benezech, L (RCF) 1994 *E, S*
Berbizier, P (Lourdes, Agen) 1981 *S, I, W, E, NZ* 1,3, 1982 *I, R*, 1983 *S, I*, 1984 *S* (R), *NZ* 1,2, 1985 *Arg* 1,2, 1986 *S, I, W, E, R* 1, *Arg* 1, *A, NZ* 1, *R* 2, *NZ* 2,3, 1987 *W, E, S, I, [S, R, Fj, A, NZ], R*, 1988 *E, S, I, W, Arg* 1,2, 1989 *I, W, E, S, NZ* 1,2, *B, A* 1, 1990 *W, E*, 1991 *S, I, W1, E*
Berejnoi, J-C (Tulle) 1963 *R*, 1964 *S, W, It, I, SA, Fj*,

R, 1965 S, I, E, W, It, R, 1966 S, I, E, W, It, R, 1967 S, A, E, It, W, I, R
Berges, B (Toulouse) 1926 I
Berges-Cau, R (Lourdes) 1976 E (R)
Bergese, F (Bayonne) 1936 G 2, 1937 G, It, 1938 G 1, R, G 2
Bergougnan, Y (Toulouse) 1945 B 1, W, 1946 B, I, K, W, 1947 S, I, W, E, 1948 S, W, E, 1949 S, E, Arg 1,2
Bernard, R (Bergerac) 1951 S, I, E, W
Bernat-Salles, P (Pau) 1992 Arg, 1993 R1, SA1,2, R2, A1,2, 1994 I
Bernon, J (Lourdes) 1922 I, 1923 S
Bérot, J-L (Toulouse) 1968 NZ 3, A, 1969 S, I, 1970 E, R, 1971 S, I, E, W, SA 1,2, A 1,2, R, 1972 S, I 1, E, W, A 1, 1974 I
Bérot, P (Agen) 1986 R 2, NZ 2,3, 1987 W, E, S, I, R, 1988 E, S, I, Arg 1,2,3,4, R, 1989 S, NZ 1,2
Bertrand, P (Bourg) 1951 I, E, W, 1953 S, I, E, W, It
Bertranne, R (Bagnères) 1971 E, W, SA 2, A 1,2, 1972 S, I 1, 1973 NZ, E, J, R, 1974 I, W, E, S, Arg 1,2, R, SA 1,2, 1975 W, E, S, I, SA 1,2, Arg 1,2, R, 1976 S, I, W, E, US, A 1,2, R, 1977 W, E, S, I, Arg 1,2, NZ 1,2, R, 1978 E, S, I, W, R, 1979 I, W, E, S, R, 1980 W, E, S, I, SA, R, 1981 S, I, W, E, R, NZ 1,2
Berty, D (Toulouse) 1990 NZ 2, 1992 R(R), 1993 R2
Besset, E (Grenoble) 1924 S
Besset, L (SCUF) 1914 W, E
Besson, M (CASG) 1924 I, 1925 I, E, 1926 S, W, 1927 I
Besson, P (Brive) 1963 S, I, E, 1965 R, 1968 SA 1
Bianchi, J (Toulon) 1986 Arg 1
Bichindaritz, J (Biarritz O) 1954 It, Arg 1,2
Bidart, L (La Rochelle) 1953 W
Biemouret, P (Agen) 1969 E, W, 1970 I, W, E, 1971 W, SA 1,2, A 1, 1972 E, W, I 2, A 2, 1973 S, NZ, E, W, I
Biénès, R (Cognac) 1950 S, I, E, W, 1951 S, I, E, W, 1952 S, I, SA, W, E, It, 1953 S, I, E, 1954 S, I, NZ, W, E, Arg 1,2, 1956 S, I, W, It, E
Bigot, C (Quillan) 1930 S, E, 1931 I, S
Bilbao, L (St Jean de Luz) 1978 I, 1979 I
Billac, E (Bayonne) 1920 S, E, W, I, US, 1921 S, W, 1922 W, 1923 E
Billière, M (Toulouse) 1968 NZ 3
Bioussa, A (Toulouse) 1924 W, US, 1925 I, NZ, S, E, 1926 S, I, E, 1928 E, G, W, 1929 I, S, W, E, 1930 S, I, E, G, W
Bioussa, C (Toulouse) 1913 W, I, 1914 I
Biraben, M (Dax) 1920 W, I, US, 1921 S, W, E, I, 1922 S, E, I
Blain, A (Carcassonne) 1934 G
Blanco, S (Biarritz O) 1980 SA, R, 1981 S, W, E, A 1, 2, R, NZ 1,2, 1982 W, E, S, I, R, Arg 1,2, 1983 E, S, I, W, 1984 I, W, E, S, NZ 1,2, R, 1985 E, S, I, W, Arg 1,2, 1986 S, I, W, E, R 1, Arg 2, A, NZ 1, R 2, NZ 2,3, 1987 W, E, S, I, [S, R, Fj, A, NZ], R, 1988 E, S, I, W, Arg 1,2,3,4, R, 1989 I, W, E, S, NZ 1,2, B, A 1, 1990 E, S, I, R, A 1,2,3, NZ 1,2, 1991 S, I, W1, E, R, US1,2, W2, [R, Fj, C, E]
Blond, J (SF) 1935 G, 1936 G 2, 1937 G, 1938 G 1, R, G 2
Blond, X (RCF) 1990 A 3, 1991 S, I, W1, E
Boffelli, V (Aurillac) 1971 A 2, R, 1972 S, I 1, 1973 J, R, 1974 I, W, E, S, Arg 1,2, R, SA 1,2, 1975 W, S, I
Bonal, J-M (Toulouse) 1968 E, W, Cz, NZ 2,3, SA 1, 2, R, 1969 S, I, E, R, 1970 W, E
Bonamy, R (SB) 1928 A, I
Boniface, A (Mont-de-Marsan) 1954 I, NZ, W, E, It, Arg 1,2, 1955 S, I, 1956 S, I, W, It, Cz, 1957 S, I, W, R 2, 1958 S, E, 1959 E, 1961 NZ 1,3, A, R, 1962 E, W, I, It, R, 1963 S, I, E, W, It, R, 1964 S, NZ, E, W, It, 1965 W, It, R, 1966 S, I, E, W
Boniface, G (Mont-de-Marsan) 1960 W, I, It, R, Arg 1, 2,3, 1961 S, SA, E, W, It, I, NZ 1,2,3, R, 1962 R, 1963 S, I, E, W, It, R, 1964 S, I, E, W, It, R, 1966 S, I, E, W
Bonnes, E (Narbonne) 1924 W, R, US
Bonneval, E (Toulouse) 1984 NZ 2 (R), 1985 W, Arg 1, 1986 W, E, R 1, Arg 1,2, A, R 2, NZ 2,3, 1987 W, E, S, I, [Z], 1988 E
Bonnus, F (Toulon) 1950 S, I, E, W
Bonnus, M (Toulon) 1937 It, 1938 G 1, R, G 2, 1940 B
Bontemps, D (La Rochelle) 1968 SA 2
Borchard, G (RCF) 1908 E, 1909 E, W, I, 1911 I
Borde, F (RCF) 1920 I, US, 1921 S, W, E, 1922 S, W,

1923 S, I, 1924 E, 1925 I, 1926 E
Bordenave, L (Toulon) 1948 A, S, W, E, 1949 S
Boubée, J (Tarbes) 1921 S, E, I, 1922 E, W, 1923 E, I, 1925 NZ, S
Boudreaux, R (SCUF) 1910 W, S
Bouet, D (Dax) 1989 NZ 1,2, B, A 2, 1990 A 3
Bouguyon, G (Grenoble) 1961 SA, E, W, It, I, NZ 1,2, 3, A
Boujet, C (Grenoble) 1968 NZ 2, A (R), SA 1
Bouquet, J (Bourgoin, Vienne) 1954 S, 1955 E, 1956 S, I, W, It, E, Cz, 1957 S, E, W, R 2, 1958 S, E, 1959 S, It, W, I, 1960 S, E, W, I, R, 1961 S, SA, E, W, It, I, R, 1962 S, E, W, I
Bourdeu, J R (Lourdes) 1952 S, I, SA, W, E, It, 1953 S, I, E
Bourgarel, R (Toulouse) 1969 R, 1970 S, I, E, R, 1971 W, SA 1,2, 1973 S
Bourguignon, G (Narbonne) 1988 Arg 3, 1989 I, E, B, A 1, 1990 R
Bousquet, A (Béziers) 1921 E, I, 1924 R
Bousquet, R (Albi) 1926 M, 1927 I, S, W, E, G 1, 1929 W, E, 1930 W
Boyau, M (SBUC) 1912 I, S, W, E, 1913 W, I
Boyer, P (Toulon) 1935 G
Branca, G (SF) 1928 S, 1929 I, S
Branlat, A (RCF) 1906 NZ, E, 1908 W
Brejassou, R (Tarbes) 1952 S, I, SA, W, E, 1953 W, E, 1954 S, I, NZ, 1955 S, I, E, W, It
Brethes, R (St Sever) 1960 Arg 2
Bringeon, A (Biarritz O) 1925 W
Brouzet, O (Grenoble) 1994 S
Brun, G (Vienne) 1950 E, W, 1951 S, E, W, 1952 S, I, SA, W, E, It, 1953 E, W, It
Bruneau, M (SBUC) 1910 W, E, 1913 SA, E
Brunet, Y (Perpignan) 1975 SA 1, 1977 Arg 1
Buchet, E (Nice) 1980 R, 1982 E, R (R), Arg 1,2
Buisson, H (see Empereur-Buisson)
Buonomo, Y (Béziers) 1971 A 2, R, 1972 I 1
Burgun, M (RCF) 1909 I, 1910 W, S, I, 1911 S, E, 1912 I, S, 1913 S, E, 1914 E
Bustaffa, D (Carcassonne) 1977 Arg 1,2, NZ 1,2, 1978 W, R, 1980 W, E, S, SA, R
Buzy, C-E (Lourdes) 1946 K, W, 1947 S, I, W, E, 1948 I, A, S, W, E, 1949 S, I, E, W, Arg 1,2

Cabanier, J-M (Montauban) 1963 R, 1964 S, Fj, 1965 S, I, W, It, R, 1966 S, I, E, W, It, R, 1967 S, A, E, It, W, I, SA 1,3, NZ, R, 1968 S, I
Cabannes, L (RCF) 1990 NZ 2(R), 1991 S, I, W1, E, US2, W2, [R, Fj, C, E], 1992 W, I, R, Arg 2, SA 1,2, 1993 E, S, I, W, R1, SA1,2, 1994 E, S
Cabrol, H (Béziers) 1972 A 1 (R), A 2, 1973 J, 1974 SA 2
Cadenat, J (SCUF) 1910 S, E, 1911 W, I, 1912 W, E, 1913 I
Cadieu, J-M (Toulouse) 1991 R, US1, [R, Fj, C, E], 1992 W, I, R, Arg 1,2, SA 1
Cahuc, F (St Girons) 1922 S
Cals, R (RCF) 1938 G 1
Calvo, G (Lourdes) 1961 NZ 1,3
Camberabero, D (La Voulte, Béziers) 1982 R, Arg 1,2, 1983 E, W, 1987 [R(R), Z, Fj(R), A, NZ], 1988 I, 1989 B, A 1, 1990 W, S, I, R, A 1,2,3, NZ 1,2, 1991 S, I, W1, E, R, US1,2, W2, [R, Fj, C], 1993 E, S, I
Camberabero, G (La Voulte) 1961 NZ 3, 1962 R, 1964 R, 1967 A, E, It, W, I, SA 1,3,4, 1968 S, E, W
Camberabero, L (La Voulte) 1964 R, 1965 S, I, 1966 E, W, 1967 A, E, It, W, I, 1968 S, E, W
Cambré, T (Oloron) 1920 E, W, I, US
Camel, A (Toulouse) 1928 S, A, I, E, G, W, 1929 W, E, G, 1930 S, I, E, G, W, 1935 G
Camel, M (Toulouse) 1929 S, W, E
Camicas, F (Tarbes) 1927 G 2, 1928 S, I, E, G, W, 1929 I, S, W, E
Camo, E (Villeneuve) 1931 I, S, W, E, G, 1932 G
Campaes, A (Lourdes) 1965 W, 1967 NZ, 1968 S, I, E, W, Cz, NZ 1,2, A, 1969 S, W, 1972 R, 1973 NZ
Campan, O (Agen) 1993 SA1(R), 2(R), R2(R)
Cantoni, J (Béziers) 1970 W, R, 1971 S, I, E, W, SA 1, 2, A 1, R, 1972 S, I 1, 1973 S, NZ, W, I, 1975 W (R)
Capdouze, J (Pau) 1964 SA, Fj, R, 1965 S, I, E
Capendeguy, J-M (Begles) 1967 NZ, R
Capitani, P (Toulon) 1954 Arg 1,2
Capmau, J-L (Toulouse) 1914 E

289

Carabignac, G (Agen) 1951 *S, I*, 1952 *SA, W, E*, 1953 *S, I*
Carbonne, J (Perpignan) 1927 *W*
Carminati, A (Béziers) 1986 *R* 2, *NZ* 2, 1987 [*R, Z*], 1988 *I, W, Arg* 1,2, 1989 *I, W, S, NZ* 1(R),2, *A* 2, 1990 *S*
Caron, L (Lyon O, Castres) 1947 *E*, 1948 *I, A, W, E*, 1949 *S, I, E, W, Arg* 1
Carpentier, M (Lourdes) 1980 *E, SA, R*, 1981 *S, I, A* 1, 1982 *E, S*
Carrère, C (Toulon) 1966 *R*, 1967 *S, A, E, W, I, SA* 1, 3,4, *NZ, R*, 1968 *S, I, E, W, Cz, NZ* 3, *A, R*, 1969 *S, I*, 1970 *S, I, W, E*, 1971 *E, W*
Carrère, J (Vichy, Toulon) 1956 *S*, 1957 *E, W, R* 2, 1958 *S, SA* 1,2, 1959 *I*
Carrère, R (Mont-de-Marsan) 1953 *E, It*
Casaux, L (Tarbes) 1959 *I, It*, 1962 *S*
Cassagne, P (Pau) 1957 *It*
Cassayet-Armagnac, A (Tarbes, Narbonne) 1920 *S, E, W, US*, 1921 *W, E, I*, 1922 *S, E, W*, 1923 *S, W, E, I*, 1924 *S, E, W, R, US*, 1925 *I, NZ, S, W*, 1926 *S, I, E, W, M*, 1927 *I, S, W*
Cassiède, M (Dax) 1961 *NZ* 3, *A, R*
Castets, J (Toulon) 1923 *W, E, I*
Caujolle, J (Tarbes) 1909 *E*, 1913 *SA, E*, 1914 *W, E*
Caunègre, R (SB) 1938 *R, G* 2
Caussade, A (Lourdes) 1978 *R*, 1979 *I, W, E, NZ* 1,2, *R*, 1980 *W, E, S*, 1981 *S* (R), *I*
Caussarieu, G (Pau) 1929 *I*
Cayrefourcq, E (Tarbes) 1921 *E*
Cazals, P (Mont-de-Marsan) 1961 *NZ* 1, *A, R*
Cazenave, A (Pau) 1927 *E, G* 1, 1928 *S, A, G*
Cazenave, F (RCF) 1950 *E*, 1952 *S*, 1954 *I, NZ, W, E*
Cecillon, M (Bourgoin) 1988 *I, W, Arg* 2,3,4, *R*, 1989 *I, E, NZ* 1,2, *A* 1, 1991 *S, I, E* (R), *R, US*1, *W*2, [*E*], 1992 *W, E, S, I, R, Arg* 1,2, *SA* 1,2, 1993 *E, S, I, W, R*1, *SA*1,2, *R*2, *A*1,2, 1994 *I, W*
Celaya, M (Biarritz O, SBUC) 1953 *E, W, It*, 1954 *I, E, It, Arg* 1,2, 1955 *S, I, E, W, It*, 1956 *S, I, W, It, E, Cz*, 1957 *S, I, E, W, R* 2, 1958 *S, E, A, W, It*, 1959 *S, E*, 1960 *S, E, W, I, R, Arg* 1,2,3, 1961 *S, SA, E, W, It, I, NZ* 1,2,3, *A, R*
Celhay, M (Bayonne) 1935 *G*, 1936 *G* 1, 1937 *G, It*, 1938 *G* 1, 1940 *B*
Cessieux, N (Lyon) 1906 *NZ*
Cester, E (TOEC, Valence) 1966 *S, I, E*, 1967 *W*, 1968 *S, I, E, W, Cz, NZ* 1,3, *A, SA* 1,2, *R*, 1969 *S, I, E, W*, 1970 *S, I, W, E*, 1971 *A* 1, 1972 *R*, 1973 *S, NZ, W, I, J, R*, 1974 *I, W, E, S*
Chaban-Delmas, J (CASG) 1945 *B* 2
Chabowski, H (Nice, Bourgoin) 1985 *Arg* 2, 1986 *R* 2, *NZ* 2, 1989 *B*(R)
Chadebech, P (Brive) 1982 *R, Arg* 1,2, 1986 *S, I*
Champ, E (Toulon) 1985 *Arg* 1,2, 1986 *I, W, E, R* 1, *Arg* 1,2, *A, NZ* 1, *R* 2, *NZ* 2,3, 1987 *W, E, S, I*, [*S, R, Fj, A, NZ*], *R*, 1988 *E, S, Arg* 1,3,4, *R*, 1989 *W, S, A* 1,2, 1990 *W, E, NZ* 1, 1991 *R, US*1, [*R, Fj, C, E*]
Chapuy, L (SF) 1926 *S*
Charpentier, G (SF) 1911 *E*, 1912 *W, E*
Charton, P (Montferrand) 1940 *B*
Charvet, D (Toulouse) 1986 *W, E, R* 1, *Arg* 1, *A, NZ* 1,3, 1987 *W, E, S, I*, [*S, R, Z, Fj, A, NZ*], *R*, 1989 *E*(R), 1990 *W, E*, 1991 *S, I*
Chassagne, J (Montferrand) 1938 *G* 1
Chatau, A (Bayonne) 1913 *SA*
Chaud, E (Toulon) 1932 *G*, 1934 *G*, 1935 *G*
Chenevay, C (Grenoble) 1968 *SA* 1
Chevallier, B (Montferrand) 1952 *S, I, SA, W, E, It*, 1953 *E, W, It*, 1954 *S, I, NZ, W, Arg* 1, 1955 *S, I, E, W, It*, 1956 *S, I, W, It, E, Cz*, 1957 *S*
Chiberry, J (Chambéry) 1955 *It*
Chilo, A (RCF) 1920 *S, W*, 1925 *I, NZ*
Cholley, G (Castres) 1975 *E, S, I, SA* 1,2, *Arg* 1,2, *R*, 1976 *S, I, W, E, A* 1,2, *R*, 1977 *W, E, S, I, Arg* 1,2, *NZ* 1,2, *R*, 1978 *E, S, I, W, R*, 1979 *I, S*
Choy, J (Narbonne) 1930 *S, I, E, G, W*, 1931 *I*, 1933 *G*, 1934 *G*, 1935 *G*, 1936 *G* 2
Cimarosti, J (Castres) 1976 *US* (R)
Clady, A (Lezignan) 1929 *G*, 1931 *I, S, E, G*
Clarac, H (St Girons) 1938 *G* 1
Claudel, R (Lyon) 1932 *G*, 1934 *G*
Clauzel, F (Béziers) 1924 *E, W*, 1925 *W*
Clavé, J (Agen) 1936 *G* 2, 1938 *R, G* 2
Claverie, H (Lourdes) 1954 *NZ, W*

Clément, G (RCF) 1931 *W*
Clément, J (RCF) 1921 *S, W, E*, 1922 *S, E, W, I*, 1923 *S, W, I*
Clemente, M (Oloron) 1978 *R*, 1980 *S, I*
Cluchague, L (Biarritz O) 1924 *S*, 1925 *E*
Coderc, J (Chalon) 1932 *G*, 1933 *G*, 1934 *G*, 1935 *G*, 1936 *G* 1
Codorniou, D (Narbonne) 1979 *NZ* 1,2, *R*, 1980 *W, E, S, I*, 1981 *S, W, E, A* 2, 1983 *E, S, I, W, A* 1,2, *R*, 1984 *I, W, E, S, NZ* 1,2, *R*, 1985 *E, S, I, W, Arg* 1,2
Coeurveille, C (Agen) 1992 *Arg* 1(R),2
Cognet, L (Montferrand) 1932 *G*, 1936 *G* 1,2, 1937 *G, It*
Colombier, J (St Junien) 1952 *SA, W, E*
Colomine, G (Narbonne) 1979 *NZ* 1
Combe, J (SF) 1910 *S, E, I*, 1911 *S*
Combes, G (Fumel) 1945 *B* 2
Communeau, M (SF) 1906 *NZ, E*, 1907 *E*, 1908 *E, W*, 1909 *E, W, I*, 1910 *S, E, I*, 1911 *S, E, I*, 1912 *I, S, W, E*, 1913 *SA, E, W*
Condom, J (Boucau, Biarritz O) 1982 *R*, 1983 *E, S, I, W, A* 1,2, *R*, 1984 *I, W, E, S, NZ* 1,2, *R*, 1985 *E, S, I, W, Arg* 1,2, 1986 *S, I, W, E, R* 1, *Arg* 1,2, *NZ* 1, *R* 2, *NZ* 2,3, 1987 *W, E, S, I*, [*S, R, Z, A, NZ*], *R*, 1988 *E, S, W, Arg* 1,2,3,4, *R*, 1989 *I, W, E, S, NZ* 1,2, *A* 1, 1990 *I, R, A* 2,3(R)
Conilh de Beyssac, J-J (SBUC) 1912 *I, S*, 1914 *I, W, E*
Constant, G (Perpignan) 1920 *W*
Coscolla, G (Béziers) 1921 *S, W*
Costantino, J (Montferrand) 1973 *R*
Costes, F (Montferrand) 1979 *E, S, NZ* 1,2, *R*, 1980 *W, I*
Couffignal, H (Colomiers) 1993 *R*1
Coulon, E (Grenoble) 1928 *S*
Courtiols, M (Bègles) 1991 *R, US*1, *W*2
Crabos, R (RCF) 1920 *S, E, W, I, US*, 1921 *S, W, E, I*, 1922 *S, E, W, I*, 1923 *S, I*, 1924 *S, I*
Crampagne, J (Begles) 1967 *SA* 4
Crancee, R (Lourdes) 1960 *Arg* 3, 1961 *S*
Crauste, M (RCF, Lourdes) 1957 *R* 1,2, 1958 *S, E, A, W, It, I*, 1959 *E, It, W, I*, 1960 *S, E, W, I, It, R, Arg* 1, 3, 1961 *S, SA, E, W, It, I, NZ* 1,2,3, *A, R*, 1962 *S, E, W, I, It, R*, 1963 *S, I, E, W, It, R*, 1964 *S, NZ, E, W, It, I, SA, Fj, R*, 1965 *S, I, E, W, It, R*, 1966 *S, I, E, W, It*
Cremaschi, M (Lourdes) 1980 *R*, 1981 *R, NZ* 1,2, 1982 *W, S*, 1983 *A* 1,2, *R*, 1984 *I, W*
Crichton, W H (Le Havre) 1906 *NZ, E*
Cristina, J (Montferrand) 1979 *R*
Cussac, P (Biarritz O) 1934 *G*
Cutzach, A (Quillan) 1929 *G*

Daguerre, F (Biarritz O) 1936 *G* 1
Daguerre, J (CASG) 1933 *G*
Dal Maso, M (Mont-de-Marsan) 1988 *R*(R), 1990 *NZ* 2
Danion, J (Toulon) 1924 *I*
Danos, P (Toulon, Béziers) 1954 *Arg* 1,2, 1957 *R* 2, 1958 *S, E, W, It, I, SA* 1,2, 1959 *S, E, It, W, I*, 1960 *S, E*
Darbos, P (Dax) 1969 *R*
Darracq, R (Dax) 1957 *It*
Darrieussecq, A (Biarritz O) 1973 *E*
Darrieussecq, J (Mont-de-Marsan) 1953 *It*
Darrouy, C (Mont-de-Marsan) 1957 *I, E, W, It, R* 1, 1959 *E*, 1961 *R*, 1963 *S, I, E, W, It*, 1964 *NZ, E, W, It, I, SA, Fj, R*, 1965 *S, I, E, It, R*, 1966 *S, I, E, W, It, R*, 1967 *S, A, E, It, W, I, SA* 1,2,4
Daudignon, G (SF) 1928 *S*
Dauga, B (Mont-de-Marsan) 1964 *S, NZ, E, W, It, I, SA, Fj, R*, 1965 *S, I, E, W, It, R*, 1966 *S, I, E, W, It, R*, 1967 *S, A, E, It, W, I, SA* 1,2,3,4, *NZ, R*, 1968 *S, I, NZ* 1,2,3, *A, SA* 1,2, *R*, 1969 *S, I, E, W, R*, 1970 *S, I, W, E, R*, 1971 *S, I, E, W, SA* 1,2, *A* 1,2, 1972 *S, I* 1, *W*
Dauger, J (Bayonne) 1945 *B* 1,2, 1953 *S*
Daulouede, P (Tyrosse) 1937 *G, It*, 1938 *G* 1, 1940 *B*
Decamps, R (RCF) 1911 *S*
Dedet, J (SF) 1910 *S, E, I*, 1911 *W, I*, 1912 *S*, 1913 *E, I*
Dedeyn, P (RCF) 1906 *NZ*
Dedieu, P (Béziers) 1963 *E, It*, 1964 *W, It, I, SA, Fj, R*, 1965 *S, I, E, W*
De Gregorio, J (Grenoble) 1960 *S, E, W, I, It, R, Arg* 1,2, 1961 *S, SA, E, W, I, It*, 1962 *S, E, W*, 1963 *S, W, It*, 1964 *NZ, E*

290

Dehez, J-L (Agen) 1967 *SA* 2, 1969 *R*
de Jouvencel, E (SF) 1909 *W, I*
de Laborderie, M (RCF) 1921 *I*, 1922 *I*, 1925 *W, E*
Delage, C (Agen) 1983 *S, I*
de Malherbe, H (CASG) 1932 *G*, 1933 *G*
de Malmann, R (RCF) 1908 *E, W*, 1909 *E, W, I*, 1910 *E, I*
de Muizon, J J (SF) 1910 *I*
Delaigue, G (Toulon) 1973 *J, R*
Delaigue, Y (Toulon) 1994 *S*
Delque, A (Toulouse) 1937 *It*, 1938 *G* 1, *R, G* 2
Descamps, P (SB) 1927 *G* 2
Desclaux, F (RCF) 1949 *Arg* 1,2, 1953 *It*
Desclaux, J (Perpignan) 1934 *G*, 1935 *G*, 1936 *G* 1,2, 1937 *G, It*, 1938 *G* 1, *R, G* 2, 1945 *B* 1
Deslandes, C (RCF) 1990 *A* 1, *NZ* 2, 1991 *W*1, 1992 *R, Arg* 1,2
Desnoyer, L (Brive) 1974 *R*
Destarac, L (Tarbes) 1926 *S, I, E, W, M*, 1927 *W, E, G* 1,2
Desvouges, R (SF) 1914 *W*
Detrez, P-E (Nîmes) 1983 *A* 2 (R), 1986 *Arg* 1(R),2, *A* (R), *NZ* 1
Devergie, T (Nîmes) 1988 *R*, 1989 *NZ* 1,2, *B, A* 2, 1990 *W, E, S, I, R, A* 1,2,3, 1991 *US*2, *W*2, 1992 *R* (R), *Arg* 2(R)
Deygas, M (Vienne) 1937 *It*
Deylaud, C (Toulouse) 1992 *R, Arg* 1,2, *SA* 1
Dintrans, P (Tarbes) 1979 *NZ* 1,2, *R*, 1980 *E, S, I, SA, R*, 1981 *S, I, W, E, A* 1,2, *R, NZ* 1,2, 1982 *W, E, S, I, R, Arg* 1,2, 1983 *E, W, A* 1,2, *R*, 1984 *I, W, E, S, NZ* 1,2, *R*, 1985 *E, S, I, W, Arg* 1,2, 1987 [*R*], 1988 *Arg* 1,2,3, 1989 *W, E, S*, 1990 *R*
Dizabo, P (Tyrosse) 1948 *A, S, E*, 1949 *S, I, E, W, Arg* 2, 1950 *S, I*, 1960 *Arg* 1,2,3
Domec, A (Carcassonne) 1929 *W*
Domec, H (Lourdes) 1953 *W, It*, 1954 *S, I, NZ, W, E, It*, 1955 *S, I, E, W*, 1956 *I, W, It*, 1958 *E, A, W, It, I* 1,2, 1958 *S, E, It*, 1959 *It*, 1960 *S, E, W, I, It, R, Arg* 1,2,3, 1961 *S, SA, E, W, It, I, NZ* 1,2,3, *A, R*, 1962 *S, E, W, I, It, R*, 1963 *W, It*
Domercq, J (Bayonne) 1912 *I, S*
Dorot, J (RCF) 1935 *E*
Dospital, P (Bayonne) 1977 *R*, 1980 *I*, 1981 *S, I, W, E*, 1982 *I, R, Arg* 1,2, 1983 *E, S, I, W*, 1984 *E, S, NZ* 1,2, *R*, 1985 *E, S, I, W, Arg* 1
Dourthe, C (Dax) 1966 *R*, 1967 *S, A, E, W, I, SA* 1,2, 3, *NZ*, 1968 *W, NZ* 3, *SA* 1,2, 1969 *W*, 1971 *SA* 2 (R), *R*, 1972 *I* 1,2, *A* 1,2, *R*, 1973 *S, NZ, E*, 1974 *I, Arg* 1,2, *SA* 1,2, 1975 *W, E, S*
Doussau, E (Angoulême) 1938 *R*
Droitecourt, M (Montferrand) 1972 *R*, 1973 *NZ* (R), *E*, 1974 *E, S, Arg* 1, *SA* 2, 1975 *SA* 1,2, *Arg* 1,2, *R*, 1976 *S, I, W, A* 1, 1977 *Arg* 2
Dubertrand, A (Montferrand) 1971 *A* 2, *R*, 1972 *I* 2, 1974 *I, W, E, SA* 2, 1975 *Arg* 1,2, *R*, 1976 *S, US*
Dubois, D (Bègles) 1971 *S*
Dubroca, D (Agen) 1979 *NZ* 2, 1981 *NZ* 2 (R), 1982 *E, S*, 1984 *W, E, S*, 1985 *Arg* 2, 1986 *S, I, W, E, R* 1, *Arg* 2, *A, NZ* 1, *R* 2, *NZ* 2,3, 1987 *W, E, S, I*, [*S, Z, Fj, A, NZ*], *R*, 1988 *E, S, I, W*
Duché, A (Limoges) 1929 *G*
Duclos, A (Lourdes) 1931 *S*
Ducousso, J (Tarbes) 1925 *S, W, E*
Dufau, G (RCF) 1948 *I, A*, 1949 *I, W*, 1950 *S, E, W*, 1951 *S, I, E, W*, 1952 *SA, W*, 1953 *S, I, E, W*, 1954 *S, I, NZ, W, E, It*, 1955 *S, I, E, W, It*, 1956 *S, I, W, It*, 1957 *S, I, E, W, It, R* 1
Dufau, J (Biarritz) 1912 *I, S, W, E*
Duffaut, Y (Agen) 1954 *Arg* 1,2
Duffour, R (Tarbes) 1911 *W*
Dufourcq, J (SBUC) 1906 *NZ, E*, 1907 *E*, 1908 *W*
Duhard, Y (Bagnères) 1980 *E*
Duhau, J (SF) 1928 *I*, 1930 *I, G*, 1931 *I, S, W*, 1933 *G*
Dulaurens, C (Toulouse) 1926 *I*, 1928 *S*, 1929 *W*
Duluc, A (Béziers) 1934 *G*
Du Manoir, Y LeP (RCF) 1925 *I, NZ, S, W, E*, 1926 *S*, 1927 *I, S*
Dupont, C (Lourdes) 1923 *S, W, I*, 1924 *S, I, W, R*, *US*, 1925 *S*, 1927 *E, G* 1,2, 1928 *A, G, W*, 1929 *I*
Dupont, J-L (Agen) 1983 *S*
Dupont, L (RCF) 1934 *G*, 1935 *G*, 1936 *G* 1,2, 1938 *R*,

G 2
Dupouy, A (SB) 1924 *W, R*
Duprat, B (Bayonne) 1966 *E, W, It, R*, 1967 *S, A, E, SA* 2,3, 1968 *S, I*, 1972 *E, W, I* 2, *A* 1
Dupré, P (RCF) 1909 *W*
Dupuy, J (Tarbes) 1956 *S, I, W, It, E, Cz*, 1957 *S, I, E, W, It, R* 2, 1958 *S, E, SA* 1,2, 1959 *S, E, It, W, I*, 1960 *W, I, It, Arg* 1,3, 1961 *S, SA, E, NZ* 2, *R*, 1962 *S, E, W, I, It*, 1963 *W, It, R*, 1964 *S*
Du Souich, C J (see Judas du Souich)
Dutin, B (Mont-de-Marsan) 1968 *NZ* 2, *A, SA* 2, *R*
Dutour, F X (Toulouse) 1911 *E, I*, 1912 *S, W, E*, 1913 *S*
Dutrain, H (Toulouse) 1945 *W*, 1946 *B, I*, 1947 *E*, 1949 *I, E, W, Arg* 1
Dutrey, J (Lourdes) 1940 *B*
Duval, R (SF) 1908 *E, W*, 1909 *E*, 1911 *E, W, I*

Echavé, L (Agen) 1961 *S*
Elissalde, E (Bayonne) 1936 *G* 2, 1940 *B*
Elissalde, J-P (La Rochelle) 1980 *SA, R*, 1981 *A* 1,2, *R*
Empereur-Buisson, H (Béziers) 1931 *E, G*
Erbani, D (Agen) 1981 *A* 1,2, *NZ* 1,2, 1982 *Arg* 1,2, 1983 *S* (R), *I, W, A* 1,2, *R*, 1984 *W, E, R*, 1985 *E, W*(R), *Arg* 2, 1986 *S, I, W, E, R* 1, *Arg* 2, *NZ* 1,2(R), 3, 1987 *W, E, S, I*, [*S, R, Fj, A, NZ*], 1988 *E, S*, 1989 *I*(R), *W, E, S, NZ* 1, *A* 2, 1990 *W, E*
Escaffre, P (Narbonne) 1933 *G*, 1934 *G*
Escommier, M (Montelimar) 1955 *It*
Esponda, J-M (RCF) 1967 *SA* 1,2, *R*, 1968 *NZ* 1,2, *SA* 2, *R*, 1969 *S, I, E*
Estève, A (Béziers) 1971 *SA* 1, 1972 *I* 1, *E, W, I* 2, *A* 2, *R*, 1973 *S, NZ, E, I*, 1974 *I, W, E, S, R, SA* 1,2, 1975 *W, E*
Estève, P (Narbonne, Lavelanet) 1982 *R, Arg* 1,2, 1983 *E, S, I, W, A* 1,2, *R*, 1984 *I, W, E, S, NZ* 1,2, *R*, 1985 *E, S, I, W*, 1986 *S, I*, 1987 [*S, Z*]
Etcheberry, J (Rochefort, Cognac) 1923 *W, I*, 1924 *S, I, E, W, R, US*, 1926 *S, I, E, M*, 1927 *I, S, W, G* 2
Etchenique, J-M (Biarritz O) 1974 *R, SA* 1, 1975 *E, Arg* 2
Etchepare, A (Bayonne) 1922 *I*
Etcheverry, M (Pau) 1971 *S, I*
Eutrope, A (SCUF) 1913 *I*

Fabre, E (Toulouse) 1937 *It*, 1938 *G* 1,2
Fabre, J (Toulouse) 1963 *S, I, E, W, It*, 1964 *S, NZ, E*
Fabre, L (Lezignan) 1930 *G*
Fabre, M (Béziers) 1981 *A* 1, *R, NZ* 1,2, 1982 *I, R*
Failliot, P (RCF) 1911 *S, W, I*, 1912 *I, S, E*, 1913 *E, W*
Fargues, G (Dax) 1923 *I*
Fauré, F (Tarbes) 1914 *I, W, E*
Fauvel, J-P (Tulle) 1980 *R*
Favre, M (Lyon) 1913 *E, W*
Ferrand, L (Chalon) 1940 *B*
Ferrien, R (Tarbes) 1950 *S, I, E, W*
Finat, R (CASG) 1932 *G*, 1933 *G*
Fite, R (Brive) 1963 *W, It*
Forestier, J (SCUF) 1912 *W*
Forgues, F (Bayonne) 1911 *S, E, W*, 1912 *I, W, E*, 1913 *S, SA, W*, 1914 *I, E*
Fort, J (Agen) 1967 *It, W, I, SA* 1,2,3,4
Fourcade, G (BEC) 1909 *E, W*
Foures, H (Toulouse) 1951 *S, I, E, W*
Fournet, F (Montferrand) 1950 *W*
Fouroux, J (La Voulte) 1972 *I* 2, *R*, 1974 *W, E, Arg* 1,2, *R, SA* 1,2, 1975 *W, Arg* 1, *R*, 1976 *S, I, W, E, US, A* 1, 1977 *W, E, S, I, Arg* 1,2, *NZ* 1,2, *R*
Francquenelle, A (Vaugirard) 1911 *S*, 1913 *W, I*
Furcade, R (Perpignan) 1952 *S*

Gabernet, S (Toulouse) 1980 *E, S*, 1981 *S, I, W, E, A* 1,2, *R, NZ* 1,2, 1982 *I*, 1983 *A* 2, *R*
Gachassin, J (Lourdes) 1961 *S, I*, 1963 *R*, 1964 *S, NZ, E, W, It, I, SA, Fj, R*, 1965 *S, I, E, W, It, R*, 1966 *S, I, E, W*, 1967 *S, A, It, W, I, NZ*, 1968 *I, E*, 1969 *S, I*
Galau, H (Toulouse) 1924 *S, I, E, W, US*
Galia, J (Quillan) 1927 *E, G* 1,2, 1928 *S, A, I, E, W*, 1929 *I, E, G*, 1930 *S, I, E, G, W*, 1931 *S, W, E, G*
Gallart, P (Béziers) 1990 *R, A* 1,2(R),3, 1992 *S, I, R, Arg* 1,2, *SA* 1,2, *Arg*, 1994 *I, S, R*
Gallion, J (Toulon) 1978 *E, S, I, W*, 1979 *I, W, E, S, NZ* 2, *R*, 1980 *W, E, S, I*, 1983 *A* 1,2, *R*, 1984 *I, W, E, S, R*, 1985 *E, S, I, W*, 1986 *Arg* 2

A 3(R), *NZ* 2, 1991 *S, I, W*1, *E, R, US*1, *W*2, [*R*(R), *Fj, C, E*], 1992 *W, E, S, I*(R), *SA* 2, 1993 *E, S, I, W*
Lagisquet, P (Bayonne) 1983 *A* 1,2, *R*, 1984 *I, W, NZ* 1,2, 1986 *R* 1 (R), *Arg* 1,2, *A*, *NZ* 1, 1987 [*S, R, Fj, A, NZ]*, *R*, 1988 *S, I, W, Arg* 1,2,3,4, *R*, 1989 *I, W, E, S, NZ* 1,2, *B, A* 1,2, 1990 *W, E, S, I, A* 1,2,3, 1991 *S, I, US*2, [*R*]
Lagrange, J-C (RCF) 1966 *It*
Lalande, M (RCF) 1923 *S, W, I*
Lane, G (RCF) 1906 *NZ, E*, 1907 *E*, 1908 *E, W*, 1909 *E, W, I*, 1910 *W, E*, 1911 *S, W*, 1912 *I, W, E*, 1913 *S*
Langlade, J-C (Hyères) 1990 *R, A* 1, *NZ* 1
Laporte, G (Graulhet) 1981 *I, W, E, R, NZ* 1,2, 1986 *S, I, W, E, R* 1, *Arg* 1, *A* (R), 1987 [*R, Z*(R), *Fj*]
Larreguy, P (Bayonne) 1954 *It*
Larribau, J (Périgueux) 1912 *I, S, W, E*, 1913 *S*, 1914 *I, E*
Larrieu, J (Tarbes) 1920 *I, US*, 1921 *W*, *1923 S, W, E, I*
Larrieux, M (SBUC) 1927 *G* 2
Larrue, H (Carmaux) 1960 *W, I, It, R, Arg* 1,2,3
Lasaosa, P (Dax) 1950 *I*, 1952 *S, I, E, It*, 1955 *It*
Lascubé, G (Agen) 1991 *S, I, W*1, *E, US*2, *W*2, [*R, Fj, C, E*], 1992 *W, E*
Lassegue, J-B (Toulouse) 1946 *W*, 1947 *S, I, W*, 1948 *W*, 1949 *I, E, W, Arg* 1
Lasserre, F (René) (Bayonne, Cognac, Grenoble) 1914 *I*, 1920 *S*, 1921 *S, W, I*, 1922 *S, E, W, I*, 1923 *W, E*, 1924 *S, I, R, US*
Lasserre, J-C (Dax) 1963 *It*, 1964 *S, NZ, E, W, It, I, Fj*, 1965 *W, It, R*, 1966 *R*, 1967 *S*
Lasserre, M (Agen) 1967 *SA* 2,3, 1968 *E, W, Cz, NZ* 3, *A, SA* 1,2, 1969 *S, I, E*, 1970 *E*, 1971 *E, W*
Laterrade, G (Tarbes) 1910 *E, I*, 1911 *S, E, I*
Laudouar, J (Soustons, SBUC) 1961 *NZ* 1,2, *R*, 1962 *I, R*
Lauga, P (Vichy) 1950 *S, I, E, W*
Laurent, A (Biarritz O) 1925 *NZ, S, W, E*, 1926 *W*
Laurent, J (Bayonne) 1920 *S, E, W*
Laurent, M (Auch) 1932 *G*, 1933 *G*, 1934 *G*, 1935 *G*, 1936 *G* 1
Lavail, G (Perpignan) 1937 *G*, 1940 *B*
Lavaud, R (Carcassonne) 1914 *I, W*
Lavergne, P (Limoges) 1950 *S*
Lavigne, B (Agen) 1984 *R*, 1985 *E*
Lavigne, J (Dax) 1920 *E, W*
Lazies, H (Auch) 1954 *Arg* 2, 1955 *It*, 1956 *E*, 1957 *S*
Le Bourhis, R (La Rochelle) 1961 *R*
Lecointre, M (Nantes) 1952 *It*
Le Droff, J (Auch) 1963 *It, R*, 1964 *S, NZ, E*, 1970 *E, R*, 1971 *S, I*
Lefevre, R (Brive) 1961 *NZ* 2
Lefort, J-B (Biarritz O) 1938 *G* 1
Le Goff, R (Métro) 1938 *R, G* 2
Legrain, M (SF) 1909 *I*, 1910 *I*, 1911 *S, E, W, I*, 1913 *S, SA, E, I*, 1914 *I, W*
Lemeur, Y (RCF) 1993 *R*1
Lenient, J-J (Vichy) 1967 *R*
Lepatey, J (Mazamet) 1954 *It*, 1955 *S, I, E, W*
Lepatey, L (Mazamet) 1924 *S, I, E*
Lescarboura, J-P (Dax) 1982 *W, E, S, I*, 1983 *A* 1,2, *R*, 1984 *I, W, E, S, NZ* 1,2, *R*, 1985 *E, S, I, W, Arg* 1, 2, 1986 *Arg* 2, *A*, *NZ* 1, *R* 2, *NZ* 2, 1988 *S, W*, 1990 *R*
Lesieur, E (SF) 1906 *E*, 1908 *E, W*, 1909 *E, W, I*, 1910 *S, E, I*, 1911 *E, I*, 1912 *W*
Leuvielle, M (SBUC) 1908 *W*, 1913 *S, SA, E, W*, 1914 *W, E*
Levasseur, R (SF) 1925 *W, E*
Levée, H (RCF) 1906 *NZ*
Lewis, E W (Le Havre) 1906 *E*
Lhermet, J-M (Montferrand) 1990 *S, I*, 1993 *R*1
Libaros, G (Tarbes) 1936 *G* 1, 1940 *B*
Lira, M (La Voulte) 1962 *R*, 1963 *I, E, W, It, R*, 1964 *W, It, I, SA*, 1965 *S, I, R*
Llari, J (Carcassonne) 1926 *S*
Lobies, J (RCF) 1921 *S, W, E*
Lombard, F (Narbonne) 1934 *G*, 1937 *It*
Lombarteix, R (Montferrand) 1938 *R, G* 2
Londios, J (Montauban) 1967 *SA* 3
Loppy, L (Toulon) 1993 *R*2
Lorieux, A (Grenoble, Aix) 1981 *A* 1, *R, NZ* 1,2, 1982 *W*, 1983 *A* 2, *R*, 1984 *I, W, E*, 1985 *Arg* 1,2(R), 1986 *R* 2, *NZ* 2,3, 1987 *W, E*, [*S, Z, Fj, A, NZ*], 1988 *S, I, W*, *Arg* 1,2,4, 1989 *W, A* 2
Loury, A (RCF) 1927 *E, G* 1,2, 1928 *S, A, I*

Loustau, M (Dax) 1923 *E*
Lubin-Lebrère, M-F (Toulouse) 1914 *I, W, E*, 1920 *S, E, W, I, US*, 1921 *S*, 1922 *S, E, W*, 1924 *W, US*, 1925 *I*
Lubrano, A (Béziers) 1972 *A* 2, 1973 *S*
Lux, J-P (Tyrosse, Dax) 1967 *E, It, W, I, SA* 1,2,4, *R*, 1968 *I, E, Cz, NZ* 3, *A, SA* 1,2, 1969 *S, I, E*, 1970 *S, I, W, E, R*, 1971 *S, I, E, W, A* 1,2, 1972 *S, I* 1, *E, W, I* 2, *A* 1,2, *R*, 1973 *S, NZ, E*, 1974 *I, W, E, S, Arg* 1,2, 1975 *W*

Macabiau, A (Perpignan) 1994 *S*
Maclos, P (SF) 1906 *E*, 1907 *E*
Magnanou, C (RCF) 1923 *E*, 1925 *W, E*, 1926 *S*, 1929 *S, W*, 1930 *S, I, E, W*
Magnol, L (Toulouse) 1928 *S*, 1929 *S, W, E*
Magois, H (La Rochelle) 1968 *SA* 1,2, *R*
Majerus, R (SF) 1928 *W*, 1929 *I, S*, 1930 *S, I, E, G, W*
Malbet, J-C (Agen) 1967 *SA* 2,4
Maleig, A (Oloron) 1979 *W, E, NZ* 2, 1980 *W, E, SA, R*
Malquier, Y (Narbonne) 1979 *S*
Manterola, T (Lourdes) 1955 *It*, 1957 *R* 1
Mantoulan, C (Pau) 1959 *I*
Marcet, J (Albi) 1925 *I, NZ, S, W, E*, 1926 *I, E*
Marchal, J-F (Lourdes) 1979 *S, R*, 1980 *W, S, I*
Marchand, R (Poitiers) 1920 *S, W*
Marfaing, M (Toulouse) 1992 *R, Arg* 1
Marocco, P (Montferrand) 1986 *S, I, W, E, R* 1, *Arg* 1,2, *A*, 1988 *Arg* 4, 1989 *I*, 1990 *E*(R), *NZ* 1(R), 1991 *S, W*1, *E, US*2, [*R, Fj, C, E*]
Marot, A (Brive) 1969 *R*, 1970 *S, I, W*, 1971 *SA* 1, 1972 *I* 2, 1976 *A* 1
Marquesuzaa, A (RCF) 1958 *It, SA* 1,2, 1959 *S, E, It, W*, 1960 *S, E, Arg* 1
Marracq, H (Pau) 1961 *R*
Martin, C (Lyon) 1909 *I*, 1910 *W, S*
Martin, H (SBUC) 1907 *E*, 1908 *W*
Martin, J-L (Béziers) 1971 *A* 2, *R*, 1972 *S, I* 1
Martin, R (Pau) 1948 *I, A, S, W, E*, 1950 *S*
Martine, R (Lourdes) 1952 *S, I, It*, 1953 *It*, 1954 *S, I, NZ, W, E, It, Arg* 2, 1955 *S, I, W*, 1958 *A, W, It, I, SA* 1,2, 1960 *S, E, Arg* 3, 1961 *S, It*
Martinez, G (Toulouse) 1982 *W, E, S, Arg* 1,2, 1983 *E, W*
Mas, F (Béziers) 1962 *R*, 1963 *S, I, E, W*
Maso, J (Perpignan, Narbonne) 1966 *It, R*, 1967 *S, R*, 1968 *S, W, Cz, NZ* 1,2,3, *A, R*, 1969 *S, I, W*, 1971 *SA* 1,2, *R*, 1972 *E, W, A* 2, 1973 *W, I, J, R*
Massare, J (PUC) 1945 *B* 1,2, *W*, 1946 *B, I, W*
Massé, A (SBUC) 1908 *W*, 1909 *E, W*, 1910 *W, S, E, I*
Masse, H (Grenoble) 1937 *G*
Matheu-Cambas, J (Agen) 1945 *W*, 1946 *B, I, K, W*, 1947 *S, I, W, E*, 1948 *I, A, S, W, E*, 1949 *S, I, E, W, Arg* 1,2, 1950 *E, W*, 1951 *S, I*
Mauduy, G (Périgueux) 1957 *It, R* 1,2, 1958 *S, E*, 1961 *W, It*
Mauran, J (Castres) 1952 *SA, W, E, It*, 1953 *I, E*
Mauriat, P (Lyon) 1907 *E*, 1908 *E, W*, 1909 *W, I*, 1910 *W, S, E, I*, 1911 *S, E, W, I*, 1912 *I, S, W*, 1913 *S, SA, W, I*
Maurin, G (ASF) 1906 *E*
Maury, A (Toulouse) 1925 *I, NZ, S, W, E*, 1926 *S, I, E*
Mayssonnié, A (Toulouse) 1908 *E, W*, 1910 *W*
Mazas, L (Colomiers) 1992 *Arg*
Melville, E (Toulon) 1990 *I*(R), *A* 1,2,3, *NZ* 1, 1991 *US*2
Menrath, R (SCUF) 1910 *W*
Menthiller, Y (Romans) 1964 *W, It, SA, R*, 1965 *E*
Meret, F (Tarbes) 1940 *B*
Mericq, S (Agen) 1959 *I*, 1960 *S, E, W*, 1961 *I*
Merle, O (Grenoble) 1993 *SA*1,2, *R*2, *A* 1,2, 1994 *I, W, E, S*
Merquey, J (Toulon) 1950 *S, I, E, W*
Mesnel, F (RCF) 1986 *NZ* 2(R),3, 1987 *W, E, S, I*, [*S, Z, Fj, A, NZ*], *R*, 1988 *E, Arg* 1,2,3,4, 1989 *I, W, E, S, NZ* 1, *A* 1,2, 1990 *E, S, I, A* 2,3, *NZ* 1,2, 1991 *S, I, W*1, *E, R, US*2, *W*2, [*R, Fj, C, E*], 1992 *W, E, S, I, SA* 1,2, 1993 *E*(R), *S, I, W*
Mesny, P (RCF, Grenoble) 1979 *NZ* 1,2, 1980 *SA, R*, 1981 *I, W*(R), *A* 1,2, *R, NZ* 1,2, 1982 *I, Arg* 1,2
Meyer, G-S (Périgueux) 1960 *S, E, It, R, Arg* 2
Meynard, J (Cognac) 1954 *Arg* 1, 1956 *Cz*
Mias, L (Mazamet) 1951 *S, I, E, W*, 1952 *I, SA, W, E, It*, 1953 *S, I, W, It*, 1954 *S, I, NZ, W*, 1957 *R* 2, 1958 *S, E, A, W, I, SA* 1,2, 1959 *S, It, W, I*

Milliand, P (Grenoble) 1936 *G* 2, 1937 *G, It*
Minjat, R (Lyon) 1945 *B* 1
Mir, J-H (Lourdes) 1967 *R*, 1968 *I*
Mir, J-P (Lourdes) 1967 *A*
Modin, R (Brive) 1987 [*Z*]
Moga, A-M-A (Bègles) 1945 *B* 1,2, *W*, 1946 *B, I, K, W*, 1947 *S, I, W, E*, 1948 *I, A, S, W, E*, 1949 *S, I, E, W, Arg* 1,2
Mommejat, B (Cahors, Albi) 1958 *It, I, SA* 1,2, 1959 *S, E, It, W, I*, 1960 *S, E, I, R*, 1962 *S, E, W, I, It, R*, 1963 *S, I, W*
Moncla, F (RCF, Pau) 1956 *Cz*, 1957 *I, E, W, It, R* 1, 1958 *SA* 1,2, 1959 *S, E, It, W, I*, 1960 *S, E, W, I, It, R, Arg* 1,2,3, 1961 *S, SA, E, W, It, I, NZ* 1,2,3
Monié, R (Perpignan) 1956 *Cz*, 1957 *E*
Monier, R (SBUC) 1911 *I*, 1912 *S*
Monniot, M (RCF) 1912 *W, E*
Montade, A (Perpignan) 1925 *I, NZ, S, W*, 1926 *W*
Montlaur, P (Agen) 1992 *E*(R), 1994 *S*(R)
Moraitis, B (Toulon) 1969 *E, W*
Morel, A (Grenoble) 1954 *Arg* 2
Morere, J (Toulouse) 1927 *E, G* 1, 1928 *S, A*
Moscato, V (Bègles) 1991 *R, US*1, 1992 *W, E*
Mougeot, C (Bègles) 1992 *W, E, Arg*
Mouniq, P (Toulouse) 1911 *S, E, W, I*, 1912 *I, E*, 1913 *S, SA, E*
Moure, H (SCUF) 1908 *E*
Moureu, P (Béziers) 1920 *I, US*, 1921 *W, E, I*, 1922 *S, W, I*, 1923 *S, W, E, I*, 1924 *S, I, E, W*, 1925 *E*
Mournet, A (Bagnères) 1981 *A* 1 (R)
Mouronval, F (SF) 1909 *I*
Muhr, A H (RCF) 1906 *NZ, E*, 1907 *E*
Murillo, G (Dijon) 1954 *It, Arg* 1

Namur, R (Toulon) 1931 *E, G*
Noble, J-C (La Voulte) 1968 *E, W, Cz, NZ* 3, *A, R*
Normand, A (Toulouse) 1957 *R* 1
Novès, G (Toulouse) 1977 *NZ* 1,2, *R*, 1978 *W, R*, 1979 *I, W*
N'Tamack, E (Toulouse) 1994 *W*

Olive, D (Montferrand) 1951 *I*, 1952 *I*
Ondarts, P (Biarritz O) 1986 *NZ* 3, 1987 *W, E, S, I*, [*S, Z, Fj, A, NZ*], *R*, 1988 *E, I, W, Arg* 1,2,3,4, *R*, 1989 *I, W, E, NZ* 1,2, *A* 2, 1990 *W, E, S, I, R*(R), *NZ* 1,2, 1991 *S, I, W*1, *E, US*2, *W*2, [*R, Fj, C, E*]
Orso, J-C (Nice, Toulon) 1982 *Arg* 1,2, 1983 *E, S, A* 1, 1984 *E* (R), *S, NZ* 1, 1985 *I* (R), *W*, 1988 *I*
Othats, J (Dax) 1960 *Arg* 2,3
Ougier, S (Toulouse) 1992 *R, Arg* 1, 1993 *E*(R)

Paco, A (Béziers) 1974 *Arg* 1,2, *R, SA* 1,2, 1975 *W, E, Arg* 1,2, 1976 *S, I, W, E, US, A* 1,2, *R*, 1977 *W, E, S, I, NZ* 1,2, *R*, 1978 *E, S, I, W, R*, 1979 *I, W, E, S*, 1980 *W*
Palat, J (Perpignan) 1938 *G* 2
Palmié, M (Béziers) 1975 *SA* 1,2, *Arg* 1,2, *R*, 1976 *S, I, W, E, US*, 1977 *W, E, S, I, Arg* 1,2, *NZ* 1,2, *R*, 1978 *E, S, I, W*
Paoli, R (see Simonpaoli)
Paparemborde, R (Pau) 1975 *SA* 1,2, *Arg* 1,2, *R*, 1976 *S, I, W, E, US, A* 1,2, *R*, 1977 *W, E, S, I, Arg* 1, *NZ* 1,2, 1978 *E, S, I, W, R*, 1979 *I, W, E, S, NZ* 1,2, *R*, 1980 *W, E, S, SA, R*, 1981 *S, I, W, E, A* 1,2, *R, NZ* 1,2, 1982 *W, I, R, Arg* 1,2, 1983 *E, S, I, W*
Pardo, L (Hendaye) 1924 *I, E*
Pardo, L (Bayonne) 1980 *SA, R*, 1981 *S, I, W, E, A* 1, 1982 *W, E, S*, 1983 *A* 1 (R), 1985 *S, I, Arg* 2
Pargade, J-H (Lyon U) 1953 *It*
Paries, L (Biarritz O) 1968 *SA* 2, *R*, 1970 *S, I, W*, 1975 *E, S, I*
Pascalin, P (Mont-de-Marsan) 1950 *I, E, W*, 1951 *S, I, E, W*
Pascarel, J-R (TOEC) 1912 *W, E*, 1913 *S, SA, E, I*
Pascot, J (Perpignan) 1922 *S, E, I*, 1923 *S*, 1926 *I*, 1927 *G* 2
Paul, R (Montferrand) 1940 *B*
Pauthe, G (Graulhet) 1956 *E*
Pebeyre, E-J (Fumel, Brive) 1945 *W*, 1946 *I, K, W*, 1947 *S, I, W, E*
Pebeyre, M (Vichy, Montferrand) 1970 *E, R*, 1971 *I, SA* 1,2, *A*, 1973 *W*
Pecune, J (Tarbes) 1974 *W, E, S*, 1975 *Arg* 1,2, *R*, 1976 *I, W, E, US*

Pedeutour, P (Begles) 1980 *I*
Pellissier, L (RCF) 1928 *A, I, E, G, W*
Penaud, A (Brive) 1992 *W, E, S, I, R, Arg* 1,2, *SA* 1,2, *Arg*, 1993 *R*1, *SA*1,2, *R*2, *A*1,2, 1994 *I, W, E*
Peron, P (RCF) 1975 *SA* 1,2
Perrier, P (Bayonne) 1982 *W, E, S, I* (R)
Pesteil, J-P (Béziers) 1975 *SA* 1, 1976 *A* 2, *R*
Petit, C (Lorrain) 1931 *W*
Peyrelade, H (Tarbes) 1940 *B*
Peyroutou, G (Périgueux) 1911 *S, E*
Phliponeau, J-F (Montferrand) 1973 *W, I*
Piazza, A (Montauban) 1968 *NZ* 1, *A*
Picard, T (Montferrand) 1985 *Arg* 2, 1986 *R* 1 (R), *Arg* 2
Pierrot, G (Pau) 1914 *I, W, E*
Pilon, J (Périgueux) 1949 *E*, 1950 *E*
Piqué, J (Pau) 1961 *NZ* 2,3, *A*, 1962 *S, It*, 1964 *NZ, E, W, It, I, SA, Fj, R*, 1965 *S, I, E, W, It*
Piquemal, M (Tarbes) 1927 *I, S*, 1929 *I, G*, 1930 *S, I, E, G, W*
Piquiral, E (RCF) 1924 *S, I, E, W, R, US*, 1925 *E*, 1926 *S, I, E, W, M*, 1927 *I, S, W, E, G* 1,2, 1928 *E*
Piteu, R (Pau) 1921 *S, W, E, I*, 1922 *S, E, W, I*, 1923 *E*, 1924 *E*, 1925 *I, NZ, W, E*, 1926 *E*
Plantefol, A (RCF) 1967 *SA* 2,3,4, *NZ, R*, 1968 *E, W, Cz, NZ* 2, 1969 *E, W*
Plantey, S (RCF) 1961 *A*, 1962 *It*
Podevin, G (SF) 1913 *W, I*
Poeydebasque, F (Bayonne) 1914 *I, W*
Poirier, A (SCUF) 1907 *E*
Pomathios, M (Agen, Lyon U, Bourg) 1948 *I, A, S, W, E*, 1949 *S, I, E, W, Arg* 1,2, 1950 *S, I, W*, 1951 *S, I, E, W*, 1952 *W, E*, 1953 *S, I, W*, 1954 *S*
Pons, P (Toulouse) 1920 *S, E, W*, 1921 *S, W*, 1922 *S*
Porra, M (Lyon) 1931 *I*
Porthault, A (RCF) 1951 *S, E, W*, 1952 *I*, 1953 *S, I, It*
Portolan, C (Toulouse) 1986 *A*, 1989 *I, E*
Potel, A (Begles) 1932 *G*
Prat, J (Lourdes) 1945 *B* 1,2, *W*, 1946 *B, I, K, W*, 1947 *S, I, W, E*, 1948 *I, A, S, W, E*, 1949 *S, I, E, W, Arg* 1, 2, 1950 *S, I, E, W*, 1951 *S, E, W*, 1952 *S, I, SA, W, E, It*, 1953 *S, I, E, W, It*, 1954 *S, I, NZ, W, E, It*, 1955 *S, I, E, W, It*
Prat, M (Lourdes) 1951 *I*, 1952 *S, I, SA, W, E*, 1953 *S, I, E*, 1954 *I, NZ, W, E, It*, 1955 *S, I, E, W, It*, 1956 *I, W, It, Cz*, 1957 *S, I, W, It, R* 1, 1958 *A, W, I*
Prevost, A (Albi) 1926 *M*, 1927 *I, S, W*
Prin-Clary, J (Cavaillon, Brive) 1945 *B* 1,2, *W*, 1946 *B, I, K, W*, 1947 *S, I, W*
Puech, L (Toulouse) 1920 *S, E, I*, 1921 *E, I*
Puget, M (Toulouse) 1961 *It*, 1966 *S, I, It*, 1967 *SA* 1,3,4, *NZ*, 1968 *Cz, NZ* 1,2, *SA* 1,2, *R*, 1969 *E, R*, 1970 *W*
Puig, A (Perpignan) 1926 *S, E*
Pujol, A (SOE Toulouse) 1906 *NZ*
Pujolle, M (Nice) 1989 *B, A* 1, 1990 *S, I, R, A* 1,2, *NZ* 2

Quaglio, A (Mazamet) 1957 *R* 2, 1958 *S, E, A, W, I, SA* 1,2, 1959 *S, E, It, W, I*
Quilis, A (Narbonne) 1967 *SA* 1,4, *NZ*, 1970 *R*, 1971 *I*

Ramis, R (Perpignan) 1922 *E, I*, 1923 *W*
Rancoule, H (Lourdes, Toulon, Tarbes) 1955 *E, W, It*, 1958 *A, W, It, I, SA* 1, 1959 *S, It, W*, 1960 *I, It, R, Arg* 1,2, 1961 *SA, E, W, It, NZ* 1,2, 1962 *S, E, W, I, It*
Rapin, A (SBUC) 1938 *R*
Raymond, F (Toulouse) 1925 *S*, 1927 *W*, 1928 *I*
Raynal, F (Perpignan) 1935 *G*, 1936 *G* 1,2, 1937 *G, It*
Raynaud, F (Carcassonne) 1933 *G*
Razat, J-P (Agen) 1962 *R*, 1963 *S, I, R*
Rebujent, R (RCF) 1963 *E*
Revailler, D (Graulhet) 1981 *S, I, W, E, A* 1,2, *R, NZ* 1,2, 1982 *W, S, I, R, Arg* 1
Revillon, J (RCF) 1926 *I, E*, 1927 *S*
Ribère, E (Perpignan, Quillan) 1924 *I*, 1925 *I, NZ, S*, 1926 *S, I, W, M*, 1927 *I, S, W, E, G* 1,2, 1928 *S, A, I, E, G, W*, 1929 *I, E, G*, 1930 *S, I, E, W*, 1931 *I, S, W, E, G*, 1932 *G*, 1933 *G*
Rives, J-P (Toulouse, RCF) 1975 *E, S, I, Arg* 1,2, *R*, 1976 *S, I, W, E, US, A* 1,2, *R*, 1977 *W, E, S, I, Arg* 1,2, *R*, 1978 *E, S, I, W, R*, 1979 *I, W, E, S, NZ* 1,2, *R*, 1980 *W, E, S, I, SA*, 1981 *S, I, W, E, A* 2, 1982 *W, E, S, I, R*, 1983 *E, S, I, W, A* 1,2, *R*, 1984 *I, W, E, S*

Rochon, A (Montferrand) 1936 *G* 1
Rodrigo, M (Mauléon) 1931 *I*, *W*
Rodriguez, L (Mont-de-Marsan, Montferrand, Dax) 1981 *A* 1,2, *R*, *NZ* 1,2, 1982 *W*, *E*, *S*, *I*, *R*, 1983 *E*, *S*, 1984 *I*, *NZ* 1,2, *R*, 1985 *E*, *S*, *I*, *W*, 1986 *Arg* 1, *A*, *R* 2, *NZ* 2,3 1987 *W*, *E*, *S*, *I*, [*S*, *Z*, *Fj*, *A*, *NZ*], *R*, 1988 *E*, *S*, *I*, *W*, *Arg* 1,2,3,4, *R*, 1989 *I*, *E*, *S*, *NZ* 1,2, *B*, *A* 1, 1990 *W*, *E*, *S*, *I*, *NZ* 1
Rogé, L (Béziers) 1952 *It*, 1953 *E*, *W*, *It*, 1954 *S*, *Arg* 1,2, 1955 *S*, *I*, 1956 *W*, *It*, *E*, 1957 *S*, 1960 *S*, *E*
Rollet, J (Bayonne) 1960 *Arg* 3, 1961 *NZ* 3, *A*, 1962 *It*, 1963 *I*
Romero, H (Montauban) 1962 *S*, *E*, *W*, *I*, *It*, *R*, 1963 *E*
Romeu, J-P (Montferrand) 1972 *R*, 1973 *S*, *NZ*, *E*, *W*, *I*, *R*, 1974 *W*, *E*, *S*, *Arg* 1,2, *R*, *SA* 1,2 (*R*), 1975 *W*, *SA* 2, *Arg* 1,2, *R*, 1976 *S*, *I*, *W*, *E*, *US*, 1977 *W*, *E*, *S*, *I*, *Arg* 1,2, *NZ* 1,2, *R*
Roques, A (Cahors) 1958 *A*, *W*, *It*, *I*, *SA* 1,2, 1959 *S*, *E*, *W*, *I*, 1960 *S*, *E*, *W*, *I*, *It*, *Arg* 1,2,3, 1961 *S*, *SA*, *E*, *W*, *It*, *I*, 1962 *S*, *E*, *W*, *I*, *It*, 1963 *S*
Roques, J-C (Brive) 1966 *S*, *I*, *It*, *R*
Rossignol, J-C (Brive) 1972 *A* 2
Rouan, J (Narbonne) 1953 *S*, *I*
Roucaries, G (Perpignan) 1956 *S*
Rouffia, L (Narbonne) 1945 *B* 2, *W*, 1946 *W*, 1948 *I*
Rougerie, J (Montferrand) 1973 *J*
Rougé-Thomas, P (Toulouse) 1989 *NZ* 1,2
Roujas, F (Tarbes) 1910 *I*
Roumat, O (Dax) 1989 *NZ* 2(R), *B*, 1990 *W*, *E*, *S*, *I*, *R*, *A* 1,2,3, *NZ* 1,2, 1991 *S*, *I*, *W*1, *E*, *R*, *US*1, *W*2, [*R*, *Fj*, *C*, *E*], 1992 *W*(R), *E*(R), *S*, *I*, *SA* 1,2, *Arg*, 1993 *E*, *S*, *I*, *W*, *R*1, *SA*1,2, *R*2, *A*1,2, 1994 *I*, *W*, *E*
Rousie, M (Villeneuve) 1931 *S*, *G*, 1932 *G*, 1933 *G*
Rousset, G (Béziers) 1975 *SA* 1, 1976 *US*
Ruiz, A (Tarbes) 1968 *SA* 2, *R*
Rupert, J-J (Tyrosse) 1963 *R*, 1964 *S*, *Fj*, 1965 *E*, *W*, *It*, 1966 *S*, *I*, *E*, *W*, *It*, 1967 *It*, *R*, 1968 *S*

Sadourny, J-L (Colomiers) 1991 *W*2(R), [*C*(R)], 1992 *E*(R), *S*, *I*, *Arg* 1(R),2, *SA* 1,2, 1993 *R*1, *SA*1,2, *R*2, *A*1,2, 1994 *I*, *W*, *E*, *S*
Sagot, P (SF) 1906 *NZ*, 1908 *E*, 1909 *W*
Sahuc, A (Métro) 1945 *B* 1,2
Sahuc, F (Toulouse) 1936 *G* 2
Saint-André, P (Montferrand) 1990 *R*, *A* 3, *NZ* 1,2, 1991 *I*(R), *W*1, *E*, *US*1,2, *W*2, [*R*, *Fj*, *C*, *E*], 1992 *W*, *E*, *S*, *I*, *R*, *Arg* 1,2, *SA* 1,2, 1993 *E*, *S*, *I*, *W*, *SA*1,2, *A*1,2, 1994 *I*, *W*, *E*, *S*
Saisset, O (Béziers) 1971 *R*, 1972 *S*, *I*, *A* 1,2, 1973 *S*, *NZ*, *E*, *W*, *I*, *J*, *R*, 1974 *I*, *Arg* 2, *SA* 1,2, 1975 *W*
Salas, P (Narbonne) 1979 *NZ* 1,2, *R*, 1980 *W*, *E*, 1981 *A* 1, 1982 *Arg* 2
Salinié, R (Perpignan) 1923 *E*
Sallefranque, M (Dax) 1981 *A* 2, 1982 *W*, *E*, *S*
Salut, J (TOEC) 1966 *R*, 1967 *S*, 1968 *I*, *E*, *Cz*, *NZ* 1, 1969 *I*
Samatan, R (Agen) 1930 *S*, *I*, *E*, *G*, *W*, 1931 *I*, *S*, *W*, *E*, *G*
Sanac, A (Perpignan) 1952 *It*, 1953 *S*, *I*, 1954 *E*, 1956 *Cz*, 1957 *S*, *I*, *E*, *W*, *It*
Sangalli, F (Narbonne) 1975 *I*, *SA* 1,2, 1976 *S*, *A* 1,2, *R*, 1977 *W*, *E*, *S*, *I*, *Arg* 1,2, *NZ* 1,2
Sanz, H (Narbonne) 1988 *Arg* 3,4, *R*, 1989 *A* 2, 1990 *S*, *I*, *R*, *A* 1,2, *NZ* 2, 1991 *W*2
Sappa, M (Nice) 1973 *J*, *R*, 1977 *R*
Sarrade, R (Pau) 1929 *I*
Saux, J-P (Pau) 1960 *W*, *It*, *Arg* 1,2, 1961 *SA*, *E*, *W*, *It*, *I*, *NZ* 1,2,3, *A*, 1962 *S*, *E*, *W*, *I*, *It*, 1963 *S*, *I*, *E*, *It*
Savitsky, M (La Voulte) 1969 *R*
Savy, M (Montferrand) 1931 *I*, *S*, *W*, *E*, 1936 *G* 1
Sayrou, J (Perpignan) 1926 *W*, *M*, 1928 *E*, *G*, *W*, 1929 *S*, *W*, *E*, *G*
Scohy, R (BEC) 1931 *S*, *W*, *E*, *G*
Sébedio, J (Tarbes) 1913 *S*, *E*, 1914 *I*, 1920 *S*, *I*, *US*, 1922 *S*, *E*, 1923 *S*
Seguier, N (Béziers) 1973 *J*, *R*
Seigne, L (Agen, Merignac) 1989 *B*, *A* 1, 1990 *NZ* 1, 1993 *E*, *S*, *I*, *W*, *R*1, *A*1,2 1994 *S*
Sella, P (Agen) 1982 *R*, *Arg* 1,2, 1983 *E*, *S*, *I*, *W*, *A* 1,2, *R*, 1984 *I*, *W*, *E*, *S*, *NZ* 1,2, *R*, 1985 *E*, *S*, *I*, *W*, *Arg* 1,2, 1986 *S*, *I*, *W*, *E*, *R* 1, *Arg* 1,2, *A*, *NZ* 1, *R* 2, *NZ* 2,3, 1987 *W*, *E*, *S*, *I*, [*S*, *R*, *Z*(R), *Fj*, *A*, *NZ*], 1988 *E*, *S*, *I*, *W*, *Arg* 1,2,3,4, *R*, 1989 *I*, *W*, *E*, *S*, *NZ* 1,2, *B*, *A* 1,2, 1990 *W*, *E*, *S*, *I*, *A* 1,2,3, 1991 *W*1, *E*, *R*, *US*1,2,

*W*2, [*Fj*, *C*, *E*], 1992 *W*, *E*, *S*, *I*, *Arg*, 1993 *E*, *S*, *I*, *W*, *R*1, *SA*1,2, *R*2, *A*1,2, 1994 *I*, *W*, *E*, *S*
Semmartin, J (SCUF) 1913 *W*, *I*
Senal, G (Béziers) 1974 *Arg* 1,2, *R*, *SA* 1,2, 1975 *W*
Sentilles, J (Tarbes) 1912 *W*, *E*, 1913 *S*, *SA*
Serin, L (Béziers) 1928 *E*, 1929 *W*, *E*, *G*, 1930 *S*, *I*, *E*, *G*, *W*, 1931 *I*, *W*, *E*
Serre, P (Perpignan) 1920 *S*, *E*
Serrière, P (RCF) 1986 *A*, 1987 *R*, 1988 *E*
Servole, L (Toulon) 1931 *I*, *S*, *W*, *E*, *G*, 1934 *G*, 1935 *G*
Sicart, N (Perpignan) 1922 *I*
Sillières, J (Tarbes) 1968 *R*, 1970 *S*, *I*, 1971 *S*, *I*, *E*, 1972 *E*, *W*
Siman, M (Montferrand) 1948 *E*, 1949 *S*, 1950 *S*, *I*, *E*, *W*
Simon, S (Bègles) 1991 *R*, *US*1
Simonpaoli, R (SF) 1911 *I*, 1912 *I*, *S*
Sitjar, M (Agen) 1964 *W*, *It*, *I*, *R*, 1965 *It*, *R*, 1967 *A*, *E*, *It*, *W*, *I*, *SA* 1,2
Skrela, J-C (Toulouse) 1971 *SA* 2, *A* 1,2, 1972 *I* 1 (R), *E*, *W*, *I* 2, *A* 1, 1973 *W*, *J*, *R*, 1974 *W*, *E*, *S*, *Arg* 1, *R*, 1975 *W* (R), *E*, *S*, *I*, *SA* 1,2, *Arg* 1,2, *R*, 1976 *S*, *I*, *W*, *E*, *US*, *A* 1,2, *R*, 1977 *W*, *E*, *S*, *I*, *Arg* 1,2, *NZ* 1,2, *R*, 1978 *E*, *S*, *I*, *W*
Soler, M (Quillan) 1929 *G*
Soro, R (Lourdes, Romans) 1945 *B* 1,2, *W*, 1946 *B*, *I*, *K*, 1947 *S*, *I*, *W*, *E*, 1948 *I*, *A*, *S*, *W*, *E*, 1949 *S*, *I*, *E*, *W*, *Arg* 1,2
Sorondo, L-M (Montauban) 1946 *K*, 1947 *S*, *I*, *W*, *E*, 1948 *I*
Soulié, E (CASG) 1920 *E*, *I*, *US*, 1921 *S*, *E*, *I*, 1922 *E*, *W*, *I*
Sourgens, J (Begles) 1926 *M*
Spanghero, C (Narbonne) 1971 *E*, *W*, *SA* 1,2, *A* 1,2, *R*, 1972 *S*, *E*, *W*, *I* 2, *A* 1,2, 1974 *I*, *W*, *E*, *S*, *R*, *SA* 1, 1975 *E*, *S*, *I*
Spanghero, W (Narbonne) 1964 *SA*, *Fj*, *R*, 1965 *S*, *I*, *E*, *W*, *It*, *R*, 1966 *S*, *I*, *E*, *W*, *It*, *R*, 1967 *S*, *A*, *E*, *SA* 1,2,3,4, *NZ*, 1968 *S*, *I*, *E*, *W*, *NZ* 1,2,3, *A*, *SA* 1,2, *R*, 1969 *S*, *I*, *W*, 1970 *R*, 1971 *E*, *W*, *SA* 1, 1972 *E*, *I* 2, *A* 1,2, *R*, 1973 *S*, *NZ*, *E*, *W*, *I*
Stener, G (PUC) 1956 *S*, *I*, *E*, 1958 *SA* 1,2
Struxiano, P (Toulouse) 1913 *W*, *I*, 1920 *S*, *E*, *W*, *I*, *US*
Sutra, G (Narbonne) 1967 *SA* 2, 1969 *W*, 1970 *S*, *I*
Swierczinski, C (Begles) 1969 *E*, 1977 *Arg* 2

Tachdjian, M (RCF) 1991 *S*, *I*, *E*
Taffary, M (RCF) 1975 *W*, *E*, *S*, *I*
Taillantou, J (Pau) 1930 *I*, *G*, *W*
Tarricq, P (Lourdes) 1958 *A*, *W*, *It*, *I*
Tavernier, H (Toulouse) 1913 *I*
Techoueyres, W (SBUC) 1994 *E*, *S*
Terreau, M-M (Bourg) 1945 *W*, 1946 *B*, *I*, *K*, *W*, 1947 *S*, *I*, *W*, *E*, 1948 *I*, *A*, *W*, *E*, 1949 *W*, *Arg* 1,2, 1951 *S*
Theuriet, A (SCUF) 1909 *E*, *W*, 1910 *S*, 1911 *W*, 1913 *E*
Thevenot, M (SCUF) 1910 *W*, *E*, *I*
Thierry, R (RCF) 1920 *S*, *E*, *W*, *US*
Thiers, P (Montferrand) 1936 *G* 1,2, 1937 *G*, *It*, 1938 *G* 1,2, 1940 *B*, 1945 *B*, 1,2
Tignol, P (Toulouse) 1953 *S*, *I*
Tilh, H (Nantes) 1912 *W*, *E*, 1913 *S*, *SA*, *E*, *W*
Tolot, J-L (Agen) 1987 [*Z*]
Tordo, J-F (Nice) *US*1(R), 1992 *W*, *E*, *S*, *I*, *R*, *Arg* 1,2, *SA* 1, *Arg*, 1993 *E*, *S*, *I*, *W*, *R*1
Torreilles, S (Perpignan) 1956 *S*
Tourte, R (St Girons) 1940 *B*
Trillo, J (Begles) 1967 *SA* 3,4, *NZ*, *R*, 1968 *S*, *I*, *NZ* 1,2,3, *A*, 1969 *I*, *E*, *W*, 1970 *E*, *R*, 1971 *S*, *I*, *SA* 1,2, *A* 1,2, 1972 *S*, *A* 1,2, *R*, 1973 *S*, *E*
Triviaux, R (Cognac) 1931 *E*, *G*
Tucoo-Chala, M (PUC) 1940 *B*

Ugartemendia, J-L (St Jean-de-Luz) 1975 *S*, *I*

Vaills, G (Perpignan) 1928 *A*, 1929 *G*
Vallot, C (SCUF) 1912 *S*, *I*
van Heerden, A (Tarbes) 1992 *E*, *S*
Vannier, M (RCF, Chalon) 1953 *W*, 1954 *S*, *I*, *Arg* 1,2, 1955 *S*, *I*, *E*, *W*, *It*, 1956 *S*, *I*, *W*, *E*, 1957 *S*, *I*, *E*, *W*, *It*, *R* 1,2, 1958 *E*, *A*, *W*, *It*, *I*, 1960 *S*, *E*, *W*, *I*, *It*, *R*, *Arg* 1,3, 1961 *SA*, *E*, *W*, *It*, *I*, *NZ* 1, *A*
Vaquer, F (Perpignan) 1921 *S*, *W*, 1922 *W*

295

Vaquerin, A (Béziers) 1971 *R*, 1972 *S*, *I* 1, *A* 1, 1973 *S*, 1974 *W*, *E*, *S*, *Arg* 1,2, *R*, *SA* 1,2, 1975 *W*, *E*, *S*, *I*, 1976 *US*, *A* 1(R), 2, *R*, 1977 *Arg* 2, 1979 *W*, *E*, 1980 *S*, *I*
Vareilles, C (SF) 1907 *E*, 1908 *E*, *W*, 1910 *S*, *E*
Varenne, F (RCF) 1952 *S*
Varvier, T (RCF) 1906 *E*, 1909 *E*, *W*, 1911 *E*, *W*, 1912 *I*
Vassal, G (Carcassonne) 1938 *R*, *G* 2
Vaysse, J (Albi) 1924 *US*, 1926 *M*
Vellat, E (Grenoble) 1927 *I*, *E*, *G* 1,2, 1928 *A*
Verger, A (SF) 1927 *W*, *E*, *G* 1, 1928 *I*, *E*, *G*, *W*
Verges, L (Bègles) 1993 *R*1(R)
Verges, S-A (SF) 1906 *NZ*, *E*, 1907 *E*
Viard, G (Narbonne) 1969 *W*, 1970 *S*, *R*, 1971 *S*, *I*
Viars, S (Brive) 1992 *W*, *E*, *I*, *R*, *Arg* 1,2, *SA* 1,2(R), *Arg*, 1993 *R*1
Vigerie, M (Agen) 1931 *W*
Vigier, R (Montferrand) 1956 *S*, *W*, *It*, *E*, *Cz*, 1957 *S*, *E*, *W*, *It*, *R* 1,2, 1958 *S*, *E*, *A*, *W*, *It*, *I*, *SA* 1,2, 1959 *S*, *E*, *It*, *W*, *I*

Vigneau, A (Bayonne) 1935 *G*
Vignes, C (RCF) 1957 *R* 1,2, 1958 *S*, *E*
Vila, E (Tarbes) 1926 *M*
Vilagra, J (Vienne) 1945 *B* 2
Villepreux, P (Toulouse) 1967 *It*, *I*, *SA* 2, *NZ*, 1968 *I*, *Cz*, *NZ* 1,2,3, *A*, 1969 *S*, *I*, *E*, *W*, *R*, 1970 *S*, *I*, *W*, *E*, *R*, 1971 *S*, *I*, *E*, *W*, *A* 1,2, *R*, 1972 *S*, *I* 1, *E*, *W*, *I* 2, *A* 1,2
Viviès, B (Agen) 1978 *E*, *S*, *I*, *W*, 1980 *SA*, *R*, 1981 *S*, *A* 1, 1983 *A* 1 (R)
Volot, M (SF) 1945 *W*, 1946 *B*, *I*, *K*, *W*

Weller, S (Grenoble) 1989 *A* 1,2, 1990 *A* 1, *NZ* 1
Wolf, J-P (Béziers) 1980 *SA*, *R*, 1981 *A* 2, 1982 *E*

Yachvili, M (Tulle, Brive) 1968 *E*, *W*, *Cz*, *NZ* 3, *A*, *R*, 1969 *S*, *I*, *R*, 1971 *E*, *SA* 1,2, *A* 1, 1972 *R*, 1975 *SA* 2

Zago, F (Montauban) 1963 *I*, *E*

FRENCH INTERNATIONAL RECORDS

Both team and individual records are for official French international matches, up to 31 March 1994.

TEAM RECORDS

Highest score
70 v Zimbabwe (70-12) 1987 Auckland
v individual countries
37 v Argentina (37-3) 1960 Buenos Aires
34 v Australia (34-6) 1976 Parc des Princes
19 v Canada (19-13) 1991 Agen
28 v Czechoslovakia (28-3) 1956 Toulouse
37 v England (37-12) 1972 Colombes
33 v Fiji (33-9) 1991 Grenoble
38 v Germany (38-17) 1933 Parc des Princes
44 v Ireland (44-12) 1992 Parc des Princes
60 v Italy (60-13) 1967 Toulon
30 v Japan (30-18) 1973 Bordeaux
24 v N Zealand (24-19) 1979 Auckland
59 v Romania (59-3) 1924 Colombes
28 v Scotland (28-22) 1987 Parc des Princes
29 v S Africa (29-16) 1992 Parc des Princes
41 v United States (41-9) 1991 Denver
36 v Wales (36-3) 1991 Parc des Princes
70 v Zimbabwe (70-12) 1987 Auckland

Biggest winning points margin
58 v Zimbabwe (70-12) 1987 Auckland
v individual countries
34 v Argentina (37-3) 1960 Buenos Aires
28 v Australia (34-6) 1976 Parc des Princes
6 v Canada (19-13) 1991 Agen
25 v Czechoslovakia (28-3) 1956 Toulouse
25 v England (37-12) 1972 Colombes
24 v Fiji (33-9) 1991 Grenoble

34 v Germany (34-0) 1931 Colombes
32 v Ireland (44-12) 1992 Parc des Princes
47 v Italy (60-13) 1967 Toulon
12 v Japan (30-18) 1973 Bordeaux
13 v N Zealand (16-3) 1986 Nantes
56 v Romania (59-3) 1924 Colombes
20 v Scotland (23-3) 1977 Parc des Princes
13 v S Africa (29-16) 1992
  Parc des Princes
32 v United States (41-9) 1991 Denver
33 v Wales (36-3) 1991 Parc des Princes
58 v Zimbabwe (70-12) 1987 Auckland

Longest winning sequence
10 matches – 1931-37

Highest score by opposing team
49 Wales (14-49) 1910 Swansea
S Africa beat 'France' 55-6 at Parc des Princes on 3 January 1907, but it is not regarded as an official international match
by individual countries
27 Argentina (31-27) 1974 Buenos Aires
48 Australia (31-48) 1990 Brisbane
13 Canada (19-13) 1991 Agen
6 Czechoslovakia (19-6) 1968 Prague
41 England (13-41) 1907 Richmond
16 Fiji (31-16) 1987 Auckland
17 Germany { (16-17) 1927 Frankfurt
          { (38-17) 1933 Parc des
          { Princes

25 Ireland { (5-25) 1911 Cork
{ (6-25) 1975 Dublin
13 Italy (60-13) 1967 Toulon
18 Japan (30-18) 1973 Bordeaux
38 N Zealand (8-38) 1906 Parc des
   Princes
21 Romania (33-21) 1991 Bucharest
31 Scotland (3-31) 1912 Inverleith
         { (5-38) 1913 Bordeaux
38 S Africa { (25-38) 1975
         { Bloemfontein
17 United States (3-17) 1924 Colombes
49 Wales (14-49) 1910 Swansea
12 Zimbabwe (70-12) 1987 Auckland

Biggest losing points margin
42 v Wales (5-47) 1909 Colombes
The 6-55 defeat by S Africa in Paris in 1907 is regarded as unofficial

v individual countries
12 v Argentina (6-18) 1988 Buenos Aires
21 v Australia (3-24) 1993 Parc des Princes
37 v England (0-37) 1911 Twickenham
 3 v Germany (0-3) 1938 Frankfurt
24 v Ireland (0-24) 1913 Cork
30 v N Zealand (8-38) 1906 Parc des
   Princes
15 v Romania (0-15) 1980 Bucharest
28 v Scotland (3-31) 1912 Inverleith
33 v S Africa (5-38) 1913 Bordeaux
14 v United States (3-17) 1924 Colombes
42 v Wales (5-47) 1909 Colombes
No defeats v Canada, Czechoslovakia, Fiji, Italy, Japan or Zimbabwe

Longest losing sequence
18 matches – 1911-20

Most tries by France in an international
13 v Romania (59-3) 1924 Paris

Most tries against France in an international
11 by Wales (5-47) 1909 Colombes

Most points by France in International Championship in a season – 98
in season 1985-86

Most tries by France in International Championship in a season – 13
in seasons 1975-76 and 1985-86

INDIVIDUAL RECORDS

Most capped player
P Sella 98 1982-94
in individual positions
Full-back
S Blanco 81(93)[1] 1980-91
Wing
P Lagisquet 46 1983-91
Centre
P Sella 91(98)[2] 1982-94
Fly-half
J-P Romeu 33(34)[3] 1972-77
Scrum-half
P Berbizier 56 1981-91
Prop
R Paparemborde 55 1975-83
Hooker
P Dintrans 50 1979-90
Lock
J Condom 61[4] 1982-90
Flanker
J-P Rives 59[4] 1975-84
No 8
G Basquet 33[4] 1945-52
[1] *S Blanco won 12 caps as a wing*
[2] *Sella has won 6 caps as a wing and one as a full-back*
[3] *Romeu was capped once as a replacement full-back. F Mesnel, 52 caps, won 29 as a centre and 23 at fly-half. D Camberabero, 36 caps, has won 30 at fly-half, 3 on the wing and 3 at full-back*
[4] *B Dauga and M Crauste, 63 caps each, are France's most-capped forwards. Dauga was capped as a lock and No 8; Crauste as a flanker and No 8*

Longest international career
F Haget 14 seasons 1974-87

Most consecutive Tests – 46
R Bertranne 1973-79

Most internationals as captain – 34
J-P Rives 1978-84

Most points in internationals – 354
D Camberabero (36 matches) 1982-93

Most points in International Championship in a season – 54
J-P Lescarboura (4 matches) 1983-84

Most points in an international – 30
D Camberabero v Zimbabwe 1987 Auckland

Most tries in internationals – 38
S Blanco (93 matches) 1980-91

Most tries in International Championship in a season – 5
P Estève (4 matches) 1982-83
E Bonneval (4 matches) 1986-87

Most tries in an international – 4
A Jauréguy v Romania 1924 Colombes
M Celhay v Italy 1937 Parc des Princes

Most conversions in internationals – 48
D Camberabero (36 matches) 1982-93

Most conversions in International Championship in a season – 7
P Villepreux (4 matches) 1971-72

Most conversions in an international – 9
G Camberabero v Italy 1967 Toulon
D Camberabero v Zimbabwe 1987 Auckland
Father and son

Most dropped goals in internationals – 15
J-P Lescarboura (28 matches) 1982-90

Most dropped goals in an international – 3
P Albaladejo v Ireland 1960 Paris
J-P Lescarboura v England 1985 Twickenham
J-P Lescarboura v New Zealand 1986 Christchurch
D Camberabero v Australia 1990 Sydney

Most penalty goals in internationals – 59
D Camberabero (36 matches) 1982-93

Most penalty goals in International Championship in a season – 10
J-P Lescarboura (4 matches) 1983-84

Most penalty goals in an international – 6
J M Aguirre v Argentina 1977 Buenos Aires

Most points on major tour – 112
S Viars (7 matches) 1992 Argentina

Most points in any match on tour – 28
P Lagisquet v Paraguayan XV 1988 Ascunción
P Estève scored 32 points against East Japan in 1984, but this was not on a major tour

Most tries in a tour match – 7
P Lagisquet v Paraguayan XV 1988 Ascunción
P Estève scored 8 tries v East Japan in 1984, but this was not on a major tour

THE IMPOSING SHADOW OF LUYT

THE 1993 SEASON IN SOUTH AFRICA
Deon Viljoen

South Africa's first full season back in international competition will be remembered not so much for the exploits of the national side, at best indifferent, as for the remorseless rise of the house of Luyt. Yes, Louis Luyt – loathed by some, admired by others and discounted as a formidable presence in the South African rugby firmament only by the foolhardy – cast an imposing shadow over the domestic season through Transvaal, the union he had painstakingly rebuilt from scratch into a near-professional, highly gifted outfit in the space of a decade.

Not only did Luyt achieve his long-cherished dream of placing the golden Currie Cup trophy in the Ellis Park boardroom for the first time in 21 years, but Transvaal's unprecedented four title wins stood as a monument to his administrative and commercial acumen. At the beginning of the term, the erstwhile fertiliser mogul showed profound promotional and marketing insight by changing Transvaal's dour turn-of-the-century emblem to a more saleable golden lion rampant. The golden lion crest would be established with a great deal of panache as the team fulfilled its predatory mission in the M-Net Night Series, the inaugural Southern Hemisphere Super-10 tournament, the Lion Cup knock-out competition and, of course, the Currie Cup.

Transvaal had been on the losing side in four Currie Cup finals since 1986, and their successful thrust for the premier prize took place primarily at the expense of neighbours Northern Transvaal. In a hard-to-fathom blunder, the Blue Bulls hierarchy declined to counter a cash carrot offered to their most valued asset, hooker Uli Schmidt, and a number of other durable performers. Even Gavin Johnson, admittedly a relatively obscure player, was allowed to bound free of the Loftus Versfeld corral. On reflection, it was no coincidence that both Schmidt and Johnson had close ties with Pretoria Harlequins, a club which spawned Transvaal's tactical masterminds in coach Kitch Christie and his assistant, Ray Mordt. Nor was it entirely unexpected when Schmidt and Johnson exerted a decisive influence on the Currie Cup final, in which Transvaal wrested the pennant from Natal in front of its Durban faithful. Schmidt, playing in what appeared to be the last representative match of an extraordinary career, fittingly scored a last-gasp try which sealed a 21-15 victory (see page 129). Johnson contributed 16 points to emerge as the find of the season, an accolade that would later be amplified when, summoned as a late replacement during the South Africa's tour of Argentina, he celebrated his international debut with a record 22-point haul in the 52-23 Second Test eclipse of the Pumas.

That Johnson was thought to be fit only as a substitute for the Argentinian adventure reflected the insecure state of the national side in

1993. For all Transvaal's dominance at provincial level, the South African selectors and coach Ian McIntosh largely failed to recreate the recipe on the world stage. This anomaly was mainly attributable to three factors: international inexperience, poor domestic refereeing standards and the general indiscipline of the South African players. The last two aspects in particular would dog the Springboks throughout their home contest with France and the subsequent trip to Australia.

Against the Tricolours, South Africa salvaged a 20-20 draw in the First Test in Durban, only to lose the series by the odd point in 75 through a heartbreaking 18-17 Second Test defeat under floodlights at Ellis Park. France, it must be said, deserved the honours but a measure of their good fortune was that centre Thierry Lacroix's match-winning penalty kick hit the inside of the post, then bounced over.

If the gods seemed to smile on France rather than South Africa, there was no such excuse in Australia. Heady heights were achieved through a fine 19-12 victory (three tries to nil) in the floodlit First Test in Sydney – South Africa's best result since the end of isolation in 1992 – and there was promise of more to come when Queensland were snuffed out 17-3 before the Second Test. But that, as they say, was that. South Africa had reached the summit of their capability and the fall was thankfully limited to only seven days. The Wallabies, superior in every facet of play, bounced back 28-20 to square the series in Brisbane. James Small was the first Springbok to be sent off in an international, and for the seemingly innocuous misdemeanour of back-chatting the referee. This controversial incident alone took a great deal of wind out of South Africa's sails, though without obscuring the fact that in both the Second and decisive Tests (the latter was won 19-12 by Australia in Sydney a week later) the Springbok forwards were thoroughly outplayed. Moreover, McIntosh's 'direct rugby' philosophy was shown to be too inflexible by a side infinitely more blessed with ideas.

With the trip to Argentina in early summer, McIntosh had an opportunity to atone for earlier setbacks, and to some extent he did manage to cement his authority, though the process was not without its anxious moments. A shameful bout of fisticuffs in a midweek game against Tucumán was a preamble to a not-so-convincing 29-26 First Test win, insufficient to quell restless public opinion back home.

Happily for McIntosh, a rapidly overhauled side made amends through a forceful 52-23 Second Test victory – South Africa's highest total in an international since the 44-0 annihilation of Scotland at Murrayfield in 1951, though in those days, of course, a try counted for only three points. A promising feature was South Africa's refreshing willingness to carry the ball wide. It suggested that McIntosh had finally seen the sense of playing to the team's strengths.

LION CUP FINAL: Transvaal 20, Natal 11
M-NET NIGHT SERIES FINAL: Transvaal 12, Northern Transvaal 12

SOUTH AFRICAN INTERNATIONAL PLAYERS *(up to 31 March 1994)*

ABBREVIATIONS

A – Australia; *Arg* – Argentina; *BI* – British Isles teams; *Cv* – New Zealand Cavaliers; *E* – England; *F* – France; *I* – Ireland; *NZ* – New Zealand; *S* – Scotland; *S Am* – South America; *US* – United States of America; *W* – Wales; *Wld* – World Invitation XV; (R) – Replacement; (t) – temporary replacement.

PROVINCIAL ABBREVIATIONS

Bor – Border; Bol – Boland; EP – Eastern Province; GW – Griqualand West; N – Natal; NT – Northern Transvaal; OFS – Orange Free State; R – Rhodesia; SET – South East Transvaal; SWA – South West Africa; SWD – South West Districts; Tvl – Transvaal; WP – Western Province; WT – Western Transvaal; Z-R – Zimbabwe-Rhodesia.

Note: When a series has taken place, figures denote the particular matches in which players featured. Thus 1968 *BI* 1,2,4 indicates that a player appeared in the first, second and fourth Tests of the 1968 series against the British Isles.

Ackermann, D S P (WP) 1955 *BI* 2,3,4, 1956 *A* 1,2, *NZ* 1,3, 1958 *F* 2
Albertyn, P K (SWD) 1924 *BI* 1,2,3,4
Alexander, E (GW) 1891 *BI* 1,2
Allan, J (N) 1993 *A* 1(R), *Arg* 1,2(R)
Allen, P B (EP) 1960 *S*
Allport, P (WP) 1910 *BI* 2,3
Anderson, J A (WP) 1903 *BI* 3
Anderson, J H (WP) 1896 *BI* 1,3,4
Andrew, J B (Tvl) 1896 *BI* 2
Andrews, K S (WP) 1992 *E*, 1993 *F* 1,2, *A* 1(R),2,3, *Arg* 1(R),2
Antelme, M J G (Tvl) 1960 *NZ* 1,2,3,4, 1960-61 *F*
Apsey, J T (WP) 1933 *A* 4,5, 1938 *BI* 2
Ashley, S (WP) 1903 *BI* 2
Aston, F T D (Tvl) 1896 *BI* 1,2,3,4
Atherton, S (N) 1993 *Arg* 1,2
Aucamp, J (WT) 1924 *BI* 1,2

Baard, A P (WP) 1960-61 *I*
Babrow, L (WP) 1937 *A* 1,2, *NZ* 1,2,3
Barnard, A S (EP) 1984 *S Am* 1,2, 1986 *Cv* 1,2
Barnard, J H (Tvl) 1965 *S*, *A* 1,2, *NZ* 3,4
Barnard, R W (Tvl) 1970 *NZ* 2(R)
Barnard, W H M (NT) 1949 *NZ* 4, 1951-52 *W*
Barry, J (WP) 1903 *BI* 1,2,3
Bartmann, W J (Tvl, N) 1986 *Cv* 1,2,3,4, 1992 *NZ*, *A*, *F* 1,2
Bastard, W E (N) 1937 *A* 1, *NZ* 1,2,3, 1938 *BI* 1,3
Bates, A J (WT) 1969-70 *E*, 1970 *NZ* 1,2, 1972 *E*
Bayvel, P C R (Tvl) 1974 *BI* 2,4, *F* 1,2, 1975 *F* 1,2, 1976 *NZ* 1,2,3,4
Beck, J J (WP) 1981 *NZ* 2(R), 3 (R), *US*
Bedford, T P (N) 1963 *A* 1,2,3,4, 1964 *W*, *F*, 1965 *I*, *A* 1,2, 1968 *BI* 1,2,3,4, *F* 1,2, 1969 *A* 1,2,3,4, 1969-70 *S*, *E*, *I*, *W*, 1971 *F* 1,2
Bekker, H J (WP) 1981 *NZ* 1,3
Bekker, H P J (NT) 1951-52 *E*, *F*, 1953 *A* 1,2,3,4, 1955 *BI* 2,3,4, 1956 *A* 1,2, *NZ* 1,2,3,4
Bekker, M J (NT) 1960 *S*
Bekker, R P (NT) 1953 *A* 3,4
Bergh, W F (SWD) 1931-32 *W*, *I*, *E*, *S*, 1933 *A* 1,2,3,4,5, 1937 *A* 1,2, *NZ* 1,2,3, 1938 *BI* 1,2,3
Bestbier, A (OFS) 1974 *F* 2(R)
Bester, J J N (WP) 1924 *BI* 2,4
Bester, J L A (WP) 1938 *BI* 2,3
Beswick, A M (Bor) 1896 *BI* 2,3,4
Bezuidenhoudt, C E (NT) 1962 *BI* 2,3,4
Bezuidenhoudt, N S E (NT) 1972 *E*, 1974 *BI* 2,3,4, *F* 1,2, 1975 *F* 1,2, 1977 *Wld*
Bierman, J N (Tvl) 1931-32 *I*
Bisset, W M (WP) 1891 *BI* 1,3
Blair, R (WP) 1977 *Wld*
Bosch, G R (Tvl) 1974 *BI* 2, *F* 1,2, 1975 *F* 1,2, 1976 *NZ* 1,2,3,4
Bosman, N J S (Tvl) 1924 *BI* 2,3,4
Botha, D S (NT) 1981 *NZ* 1
Botha, H E (NT) 1980 *S Am* 1,2, *BI* 1,2,3,4, *S Am* 3,4, *F*, 1981 *I* 1,2, *NZ* 1,2,3, *US*, 1982 *S Am* 1,2, 1986 *Cv* 1,2,3,4, 1989 *Wld* 1,2, 1992 *NZ*, *A*, *F* 1,2, *E*
Botha, J (Tvl) 1903 *BI* 3
Botha, J P F (NT) 1962 *BI* 2,3,4

Botha, P H (Tvl) 1965 *A* 1,2
Boyes, H C (GW) 1891 *BI* 1,2
Brand, G H (WP) 1928 *NZ* 2,3, 1931-32 *W,I, E, S*, 1933 *A* 1,2,3,4,5, 1937 *A* 1,2, *NZ* 2,3, 1938 *BI* 1
Bredenkamp, M (GW) 1896 *BI* 1,3
Breedt, J C (Tvl) 1986 *Cv* 1,2,3,4, 1989 *Wld* 1,2, 1992 *NZ*, *A*
Brewis, J D (NT) 1949 *NZ* 1,2,3,4, 1951-52 *S*, *I*, *W*, *E*, *F*, 1953 *A* 1
Briers, T P D (WP) 1955 *BI* 1,2,3,4, 1956 *NZ* 2,3,4
Brink, D J (WP) 1906 *S*, *W*, *E*
Brooks, D (Bor) 1906 *S*
Brown, C (WP) 1903 *BI* 1,2,3
Brynard, G S (WP) 1965 *A* 1, *NZ* 1,2,3,4, 1968 *BI* 3,4
Buchler, J U (Tvl) 1951-52 *S*, *I*, *W*, *E*, *F*, 1953 *A* 1,2,3,4, 1956 *A* 2
Burdett, A F (WP) 1906 *S*, *I*
Burger, J M (WP) 1989 *Wld* 1,2
Burger, M B (NT) 1980 *BI* 2(R), *S Am* 3, 1981 *US* (R)
Burger, S W P (WP) 1984 *E* 1,2, 1986 *Cv* 1,2,3,4
Burger, W A G (Bor) 1906 *S*, *I*, *W*, 1910 *BI* 2

Carelse, G (EP) 1964 *W*, *F*, 1965 *I*, *S*, 1967 *F* 1,2,3, 1968 *F* 1,2, 1969 *A* 1,2,3,4, 1969-70 *S*
Carlson, R A (WP) 1972 *E*
Carolin, H W (WP) 1903 *BI* 3, 1906 *S*, *I*
Castens, H H (WP) 1891 *BI* 1
Chignell, T W (WP) 1891 *BI* 3
Cilliers, G D (OFS) 1963 *A* 1,3,4
Claassen, J T (WT) 1955 *BI* 1,2,3,4, 1956 *A* 1,2, *NZ* 1,2,3,4, 1958 *F* 1,2, 1960 *S*, *NZ* 1,2,3, 1960-61 *W*, *I*, *E*, *S*, *F*, 1961 *I*, *A* 1,2, 1962 *BI* 1,2,3,4
Claassen, W (N) 1981 *I* 1,2, *NZ* 2,3, *US*, 1982 *S Am* 1,2
Clarke, W H (Tvl) 1933 *A* 3
Clarkson, W A (N) 1921 *NZ* 1,2, 1924 *BI* 1
Cloete, H A (WP) 1896 *BI* 4
Cockrell, C H (WP) 1969-70 *S*, *I*, *W*
Cockrell, R J (WP) 1974 *F* 1,2, 1975 *F* 1,2, 1976 *NZ* 1,2, 1977 *Wld*, 1981 *NZ* 1,2(R),3, *US*
Coetzee, J H H (WP) 1974 *BI* 1, 1975 *F* 2(R), 1976 *NZ* 1,2,3,4
Cope, D (Tvl) 1896 *BI* 2
Cotty, W (GW) 1896 *BI* 3
Crampton, G (GW) 1903 *BI* 2
Craven, D H (WP) 1931-32 *W*, *I*, *S*, 1933 *A* 1,2,3,4,5, 1937 *A* 1,2, *NZ* 1,2,3, 1938 *BI* 1,2,3
Cronje, P A (Tvl) 1971 *F* 1,2, *A* 1,2,3, 1974 *BI* 3,4
Crosby, J H (Tvl) 1896 *BI* 2
Crosby, N J (Tvl) 1910 *BI* 1,3
Currie, C (GW) 1903 *BI* 2

D'Alton, G (WP) 1933 *A* 1
Daneel, G M (WP) 1928 *NZ* 1,2,3,4, 1931-32 *W*, *I*, *E*, *S*
Daneel, H J (WP) 1906 *S*, *I*, *W*, *E*
Davidson, M (EP) 1910 *BI* 1
De Bruyn, J (OFS) 1974 *BI* 3
De Jongh, H P K (WP) 1928 *NZ* 3
De Klerk, I J (Tvl) 1969-70 *E*, *I*, *W*
De Klerk, K B H (Tvl) 1974 *BI* 1,2,3(R), 1975 *F* 1,2, 1976 *NZ* 2(R),3,4, 1980 *S Am* 1,2, *BI* 2, 1981 *I* 1,2

301

Jennings, C B (Bor) 1937 *NZ* 1
Johnson, G (Tvl) 1993 *Arg* 2
Johnstone, P G A (WP) 1951-52 *S, I, W, E, F,* 1956 *A*
1, *NZ* 1,2,4
Jones, C H (Tvl) 1903 *BI* 1,2
Jones, P S T (WP) 1896 *BI* 1,3,4
Jordaan, R P (NT) 1949 *NZ* 1,2,3,4
Joubert, A J (OFS,N) 1989 *Wld* 1 (R), 1993 *A* 3, *Arg* 1
Joubert, S J (WP) 1906 *I, W, E*

Kahts, W J H (NT) 1980 *BI* 1,2,3, *S Am* 3,4, *F,* 1981
I 1,2, *NZ* 2, 1982 *S Am* 1,2
Kaminer, J (Tvl) 1958 *F* 2
Kebble, G R (N) 1993 *Arg* 1,2
Kelly, E W (GW) 1896 *BI* 3
Kenyon, B J (Bor) 1949 *NZ* 4
Kipling, H G (GW) 1931-32 *W, I, E, S,* 1933 *A* 1,2,3,4,5
Kirkpatrick, A I (GW) 1953 *A* 2, 1956 *NZ* 2, 1958 *F* 1,
1960 *S, NZ* 1,2,3,4, 1960-61 *W, I, E, S, F*
Knight, A S (Tvl) 1912-13 *S, I, W, E, F*
Knoetze, F (WP) 1989 *Wld* 1,2
Koch, A C (Bol) 1949 *NZ* 2,3,4, 1951-52 *S, I, W, E, F,*
1953 *A* 1,2,4, 1955 *BI* 1,2,3,4, 1956 *A* 1, *NZ* 2,3, 1958
F 1,2, 1960 *NZ* 1,2
Koch, H V (WP) 1949 *NZ* 1,2,3,4
Kotze, G J M (WP) 1967 *F* 1,2,3,4
Krantz, E F W (OFS) 1976 *NZ* 1, 1981 *I* 1
Krige, J D (WP) 1903 *BI* 1,3, 1906 *S, I, W*
Kritzinger, J L (Tvl) 1974 *BI* 3,4, *F* 1,2, 1975 *F* 1,2,
1976 *NZ* 4
Kroon, C M (EP) 1955 *BI* 1
Kruger, P E (Tvl) 1986 *Cv* 3,4
Kruger, R J (NT) 1993 *Arg* 1,2
Kruger, T L (Tvl) 1921 *NZ* 1,2, 1924 *BI* 1,2,3,4, 1928
NZ 1,2
Kuhn, S P (Tvl) 1960 *NZ* 3,4 1960-61 *W, I, E, S, F,*
1961 *I, A* 1,2, 1962 *BI* 1,2,3,4, 1963 *A* 1,2,3, 1965 *I, S*

La Grange, J B (WP) 1924 *BI* 3,4
Larard, A (Tvl) 1896 *BI* 2,4
Lategan, M T (WP) 1949 *NZ* 1,2,3,4, 1951-52 *S, I, W,*
E, F, 1953 *A* 1,2
Lawless, M J (WP) 1964 *F,* 1969-70 *E* (R), *I, W*
Ledger, S H (GW) 1912-13 *S, I, E, F*
Le Roux, H P (Tvl) 1993 *F* 1,2
Le Roux, M (OFS) 1980 *BI* 1,2,3,4, *S Am* 3,4, *F,* 1981
I 1
Le Roux, P A (WP) 1906 *I, W, E*
Little, E M M (GW) 1891 *BI* 1,3
Lochner, G P (WP) 1955 *BI* 3, 1956 *A* 1,2, *NZ* 1,2,3,4,
1958 *F* 1,2
Lochner, G P (EP) 1937 *NZ* 3, 1938 *BI* 1,2
Lockyear, R J (GW) 1960 *NZ* 1,2,3,4, 1960-61 *I, F*
Lombard, A C (EP) 1910 *BI* 2
Lötter, D (Tvl) 1993 *F* 2, *A* 1,2
Lotz, J W (Tvl) 1937 *A* 1,2, *NZ* 1,2,3, 1938 *BI* 1,2,3
Loubser, J A (WP) 1903 *BI* 3, 1906 *S, I, W, E,* 1910 *BI*
1,3
Lourens, M J (NT) 1968 *BI* 2,3,4
Louw, J S (Tvl) 1891 *BI* 1,2,3
Louw, M J (Tvl) 1971 *A* 2,3
Louw, M M (WP) 1928 *NZ* 3,4, 1931-32 *W, I, E, S,*
1933 *A* 1,2,3,4,5, 1937 *A* 1,2, *NZ* 2,3, 1938 *BI* 1,2,3
Louw, R J (WP) 1980 *S Am* 1,2, *BI* 1,2,3,4, *S Am* 3,4,
F, 1981 *I* 1,2, *NZ* 1,3, 1982 *S Am* 1,2, 1984 *E* 1,2, *S Am*
1,2
Louw, S C (WP) 1933 *A* 1,2,3,4,5, 1937 *A* 1, *NZ* 1,2,3,
1938 *BI* 1,2,3
Luyt, F P (WP) 1910 *BI* 1,2,3, 1912-13 *S, I, W, E*
Luyt, J D (EP) 1912-13 *S, W, E, F*
Luyt, R R (WP) 1910 *BI* 2,3, 1912-13 *S, I, W, E, F*
Lyons, D (EP) 1896 *BI* 1
Lyster, P J (N) 1933 *A* 2,5, 1937 *NZ* 1

McCallum, I D (WP) 1970 *NZ* 1,2,3,4, 1971 *F* 1,2, *A*
1,2,3, 1974 *BI* 1,2
McCallum, R J (WP) 1974 *BI* 1
McCulloch, J D (GW) 1912-13 *E, F*
MacDonald, A W (R) 1965 *A* 1, *NZ* 1,2,3,4
Macdonald, D A (WP) 1974 *BI* 2
Macdonald, I (Tvl) 1992 *NZ, A,* 1993 *F* 1, *A* 3
McDonald, J A J (WP) 1931-32 *W, I, E, S*
McEwan, W M C (Tvl) 1903 *BI* 1,3
McHardy, E E (OFS) 1912-13 *S, I, W, E, F*

McKendrick, J A (WP) 1891 *BI* 3
Malan, A S (Tvl) 1960 *NZ* 1,2,3,4, 1960-61 *W, I, E, S,*
F, 1962 *BI* 1, 1963 *A* 1,2,3, 1964 *W,* 1965 *I, S*
Malan, A W (NT) 1989 *Wld* 1,2, 1992 *NZ, A, F* 1,2, *E*
Malan, E (NT) 1980 *BI* 3(R),4
Malan, G F (WP) 1958 *F* 2, 1960 *NZ* 1,3,4, 1960-61 *E,*
S, F, 1962 *BI* 1,2,3, 1963 *A* 1,2,4, 1964 *W,* 1965 *A* 1,2,
NZ 1,2
Malan, P (Tvl) 1949 *NZ* 4
Mallett, N V H (WP) 1984 *S Am* 1,2
Mans, W J (WP) 1965 *I, S*
Marais, F P (Bol) 1949 *NZ* 1,2, 1951-52 *S,* 1953 *A* 1,2
Marais, J F K (WP) 1963 *A* 3, 1964 *W, F,* 1965 *I, S, A*
2, 1968 *BI* 1,2,3,4, *F* 1,2, 1969 *A* 1,2,3,4, 1969-70 *S, E,*
I, W, 1970 *NZ* 1,2,3,4, 1971 *F* 1,2, *A* 1,2,3, 1974 *BI*
1,2,3,4, *F* 1,2
Maré, D S (Tvl) 1906 *S*
Marsberg, A F W (GW) 1906 *S, W, E*
Marsberg, P A (GW) 1910 *BI* 1
Martheze, W C (GW) 1903 *BI* 2, 1906 *I, W*
Martin, H J (Tvl) 1937 *A* 2
Mellett, T (GW) 1896 *BI* 2
Mellish, F W (WP) 1921 *NZ* 1,3, 1924 *BI* 1,2,3,4
Merry, J (EP) 1891 *BI* 1
Metcalf, H D (Bor) 1903 *BI* 2
Meyer, C du P (WP) 1921 *NZ* 1,2,3
Meyer, P J (GW) 1896 *BI* 1
Michau, J M (Tvl) 1921 *NZ* 1
Michau, J P (WP) 1921 *NZ* 1,2,3
Millar, W A (WP) 1906 *E,* 1910 *BI* 2,3, 1912-13 *I, W, F*
Mills, W J (WP) 1910 *BI* 2
Moll, T (Tvl) 1910 *BI* 2
Montini, P E (WP) 1956 *A* 1,2
Moolman, L C (NT) 1977 *Wld,* 1980 *S Am* 1,2, *BI*
1,2,3,4, *S Am* 3,4, *F,* 1981 *I* 1,2, *NZ* 1,2,3, *US,* 1982 *S*
Am 1,2, 1984 *S Am* 1,2, 1986 *Cv* 1,2,3,4
Mordt, R H (Z-R, NT) 1980 *S Am* 1,2, *BI* 1,2,3,4, *S*
Am 3,4, *F,* 1981 *I* 2, *NZ* 1,2,3, *US,* 1982 *S Am* 1,2, 1984
S Am 1,2
Morkel, A O (Tvl) 1903 *BI* 1
Morkel, D F T (Tvl) 1906 *I, E,* 1910 *BI* 1,3, 1912-13 *S,*
I, W, E, F
Morkel, H J (WP) 1921 *NZ* 1
Morkel, H W (WP) 1921 *NZ* 1,2
Morkel, J A (WP) 1921 *NZ* 2,3
Morkel, J W H (WP) 1912-13 *S, I, W, E, F*
Morkel, P G (WP) 1912-13 *S, I, W, E, F,* 1921 *NZ*
1,2,3
Morkel, P K (WP) 1928 *NZ* 4
Morkel, W H (WP) 1910 *BI* 3, 1912-13 *S, I, W, E, F,*
1921 *NZ* 1,2,3
Morkel, W S (Tvl) 1906 *S, I, W, E*
Moss, C (N) 1949 *NZ* 1,2,3,4
Mostert, P J (WP) 1921 *NZ* 1,2,3, 1924 *BI* 1,2,4, 1928
NZ 1,2,3,4, 1931-32 *W, I, E, S*
Muller, G H (WP) 1969 *A* 3,4, 1969-70 *S, W,* 1970 *NZ*
1,2,3,4, 1971 *F* 1,2, 1972 *E,* 1974 *BI* 1,3,4
Muller, H L (OFS) 1986 *Cv* 4 (R), 1989 *Wld* 1(R)
Muller, H S V (Tvl) 1949 *NZ* 1,2,3,4, 1951-52 *S, I, W,*
E, F, 1953 *A* 1,2,3,4
Muller, L J J (N) 1992 *NZ, A*
Muller, P G (N) 1992 *NZ, A, F* 1,2, *E,* 1993 *F* 1,2, *A*
1,2,3, *Arg* 1,2
Myburgh, F R (EP) 1896 *BI* 1
Myburgh, J L (NT) 1962 *BI* 1, 1963 *A* 4, 1964 *W, F,*
1968 *BI* 1,2,3, *F* 1,2, 1969 *A* 1,2,3,4, 1969-70 *E, I, W,*
1970 *NZ* 3,4
Myburgh, W H (WT) 1924 *BI* 1

Naude, J P (WP) 1963 *A* 4, 1965 *A* 1,2, *NZ* 1,3,4, 1967
F 1,2,3,4, 1968 *BI* 1,2,3,4
Neethling, J B (WP) 1967 *F* 1,2,3,4, 1968 *BI* 4, 1969-70
S, 1970 *NZ* 1,2
Nel, J A (Tvl) 1960 *NZ* 1,2, 1963 *A* 1,2, 1965 *A* 2, *NZ*
1,2,3,4, 1970 *NZ* 3,4
Nel, J J (WP) 1956 *A* 1,2, *NZ* 1,2,3,4, 1958 *F* 1,2
Nel, P A R O (Tvl) 1903 *BI* 1,2,3
Nel, P J (N) 1928 *NZ* 1,2,3,4, 1931-32 *W, I, E, S,* 1933
A 1,3,4,5, 1937 *A* 1,2, *NZ* 2,3
Nimb, C F (WP) 1961 *I*
Nomis, S H (Tvl) 1967 *F* 4, 1968 *BI* 1,2,3,4, *F* 1,2,
1969 *A* 1,2,3,4, 1969-70 *S, E, I, W,* 1970 *NZ* 1,2,3,4,
1971 *F* 1,2, *A* 1,2,3, 1972 *E*
Nykamp, J L (Tvl) 1933 *A* 2

Van Der Merwe, A J (Bol) 1955 *BI* 2,3,4, 1956 *A* 1,2, *NZ* 1,2,3,4, 1958 *F* 1, 1960 *S*, *NZ* 2
Van Der Merwe, A V (WP) 1931-32 *W*
Van Der Merwe, B S (NT) 1949 *NZ* 1
Van Der Merwe, H S (NT) 1960 *NZ* 4, 1963 *A* 2,3,4, 1964 *F*
Van Der Merwe, J P (WP) 1969-70 *W*
Van Der Merwe, P R (SWD, WT, GW) 1981 *NZ* 2,3, *US*, 1986 *Cv* 1,2, 1989 *Wld* 1
Vanderplank, B E (N) 1924 *BI* 3,4
Van Der Schyff, J H (GW) 1949 *NZ* 1,2,3,4, 1955 *BI* 1
Van Der Watt, A E (WP) 1969-70 *S* (R), *E*, *I*
Van Der Westhuizen, J C (WP) 1928 *NZ* 2,3,4, 1931-32 *I*
Van Der Westhuizen, J H (WP) 1931-32 *I*, *E*, *S*
Van Der Westhuizen, J H (NT) 1993 *Arg* 1,2
Van Druten, N J V (Tvl) 1924 *BI* 1,2,3,4, 1928 *NZ* 1,2,3,4
Van Heerden, A J (Tvl) 1921 *NZ* 1,3
Van Heerden, J L (NT, Tvl) 1974 *BI* 3,4, *F* 1,2, 1975 *F* 1,2, 1976 *NZ* 1,2,3,4, 1977 *Wld*, 1980 *BI* 1,3,4, *S Am* 3,4, *F*
Van Jaarsveld, C J (Tvl) 1949 *NZ* 1
Van Jaarsveldt, D C (R) 1960 *S*
Van Niekerk, J A (WP) 1928 *NZ* 4
Van Reenen, G L (WP) 1937 *A* 2, *NZ* 1
Van Renen, C G (WP) 1891 *BI* 3, 1896 *BI* 1,4
Van Renen, W (WP) 1903 *BI* 1,3
Van Rensburg, J T J (Tvl) 1992 *NZ*, *A*, *E*, 1993 *F* 1,2, *A* 1
Van Rooyen, G W (Tvl) 1921 *NZ* 2,3
Van Ryneveld, R C B (WP) 1910 *BI* 2,3
Van Schoor, R A M (R) 1949 *NZ* 2,3,4, 1951-52 *S*, *I*, *W*, *E*, *F*, 1953 *A* 1,2,3,4
Van Vollenhoven, K T (NT) 1955 *BI* 1,2,3,4, 1956 *A* 1,2, *NZ* 3
Van Vuuren, T F (EP) 1912-13 *S*, *I*, *W*, *E*, *F*
Van Wyk, C J (Tvl) 1951-52 *S*, *I*, *W*, *E*, *F*, 1953 *A* 1,2,3,4, 1955 *BI* 1
Van Wyk, J F B (NT) 1970 *NZ* 1,2,3,4, 1971 *F* 1,2, *A* 1,2,3, 1972 *E*, 1974 *BI* 1,3,4, 1976 *NZ* 3,4
Van Wyk, S P (WP) 1928 *NZ* 1,2
Van Zyl, B P (WP) 1961 *I*
Van Zyl, C G P (OFS) 1965 *NZ* 1,2,3,4
Van Zyl, G H (WP) 1958 *F* 1, 1960 *S*, *NZ* 1,2,3,4, 1960-61 *W*, *I*, *E*, *S*, *F*, 1961 *I*, *A* 1,2, 1962 *BI* 1,3,4
Van Zyl, H J (Tvl) 1960 *NZ* 1,2,3,4, 1960-61 *I*, *E*, *S*, 1961 *I*, *A* 1,2
Van Zyl, P J (Bol) 1961 *I*

Veldsman, P E (WP) 1977 *Wld*
Venter, F D (Tvl) 1931-32 *W*, *S*, 1933 *A* 3
Versfeld, C (WP) 1891 *BI* 3
Versfeld, M (WP) 1891 *BI* 1,2,3
Vigne, J T (Tvl) 1891 *BI* 1,2,3
Viljoen, J F (GW) 1971 *F* 1,2, *A* 1,2,3, 1972 *E*
Viljoen, J T (N) 1971 *A* 1,2,3
Villet, J V (WP) 1984 *E* 1,2
Visagie, P J (GW) 1967 *F* 1,2,3,4, 1968 *BI* 1,2,3,4, *F* 1,2, 1969 *A* 1,2,3,4, 1969-70 *S*, *E*, 1970 *NZ* 1,2,3,4, 1971 *F* 1,2, *A* 1,2,3
Visagie, R G (OFS, N) 1984 *E* 1,2, *S Am* 1,2, 1993 *F* 1
Visser, J de V (WP) 1981 *NZ* 2, *US*
Visser, P J (Tvl) 1933 *A* 2
Viviers, S S (OFS) 1956 *A* 1,2, *NZ* 2,3,4
Vogel, M L (OFS) 1974 *BI* 2(R)

Wagenaar, C (NT) 1977 *Wld*
Wahl, J J (WP) 1949 *NZ* 1
Walker, A P (N) 1921 *NZ* 1,3, 1924 *BI* 1,2,3,4
Walker, H N (OFS) 1953 *A* 3, 1956 *A* 2, *NZ* 1,4
Walker, H W (Tvl) 1910 *BI* 1,2,3
Walton, D C (N) 1964 *F*, 1965 *I*, *S*, *NZ* 3,4, 1969 *A* 1,2, 1969-70 *E*
Waring, F W (WP) 1931-32 *I*, *E*, 1933 *A* 1,2,3,4,5
Wegner, N (WP) 1993 *F* 2, *A* 1,2,3
Wessels, J J (WP) 1896 *BI* 1,2,3
Whipp, P J M (WP) 1974 *BI* 1,2, 1975 *F* 1, 1976 *NZ* 1,3,4, 1980 *S Am* 1,2
White, J (Bor) 1931-32 *W*, 1933 *A* 1,2,3,4,5, 1937 *A* 1,2, *NZ* 1,2
Wiese, J J (Tvl) 1993 *F* 1
Williams, A E (GW) 1910 *BI* 1
Williams, A P (WP) 1984 *E* 1,2
Williams, C M (WP) 1993 *Arg* 2
Williams, D O (WP) 1937 *A* 1,2 *NZ* 1,2,3, 1938 *BI* 1,2,3
Williams, J G (NT) 1971 *F* 1,2, *A* 1,2,3, 1972 *E*, 1974 *BI* 1,2,4, *F* 1,2, 1976 *NZ* 1,2
Wilson, L G (WP) 1960 *NZ* 3,4, 1960-61 *W*, *I*, *E*, *F*, 1961 *I*, *A* 1,2, 1962 *BI* 1,2,3,4, 1963 *A* 1,2,3,4, 1964 *W*, *F*, 1965 *I*, *S*, *A* 1,2, *NZ* 1,2,3,4
Wolmarans, B J (OFS) 1977 *Wld*
Wright, G D (EP, Tvl) 1986 *Cv* 3,4, 1989 *Wld* 1,2, 1992 *F* 1,2, *E*
Wyness, M R K (WP) 1962 *BI* 1,2,3,4, 1963 *A* 2

Zeller, W C (N) 1921 *NZ* 2,3
Zimerman, M (WP) 1931-32 *W*, *I*, *E*, *S*

SOUTH AFRICAN INTERNATIONAL RECORDS

Both team and individual records are for official South African international matches, up to 31 March 1994.

TEAM RECORDS

Highest score

52 v Argentina (52-23) 1993 Buenos Aires
v individual countries
52 v Argentina (52-23) 1993 Buenos Aires
30 v Australia (30-11) 1969 Johannesburg
34 v B Isles (34-14) 1962 Bloemfontein
35 v England (35-9) 1984 Johannesburg
38 v France { (38-5) 1913 Bordeaux
{ (38-25) 1975 Bloemfontein
38 v Ireland (38-0) 1912 Dublin

24 v N Zealand { (24-12) 1981 Wellington
{ (24-27) 1992 Johannesburg
33 v NZ Cavaliers (33-18) 1986 Pretoria
50 v S America (50-18) 1982 Pretoria
44 v Scotland (44-0) 1951 Murrayfield
38 v United States (38-7) 1981 New York
24 v Wales (24-3) 1964 Durban

Biggest winning points margin
44 v Scotland (44-0) 1951 Murrayfield
v individual countries
29 v Argentina (52-23) 1993 Buenos Aires
25 v Australia (28-3) 1961 Johannesburg
20 v B Isles (34-14) 1962 Bloemfontein
26 v England (35-9) 1984 Johannesburg
33 v France (38-5) 1913 Bordeaux
38 v Ireland (38-0) 1912 Dublin
17 v N Zealand (17-0) 1928 Durban
15 v NZ Cavaliers (33-18) 1986 Pretoria
32 v S America (50-18) 1982 Pretoria
44 v Scotland (44-0) 1951 Murrayfield
31 v United States (38-7) 1981 New York
21 v Wales (24-3) 1964 Durban

Longest winning sequence
10 matches – 1949-53

Highest score by opposing team
33 England (16-33) 1992 Twickenham
by individual countries
26 Argentina (29-26) 1993 Buenos Aires
28 Australia (20-28) 1993 Brisbane
28 B Isles (9-28) 1974 Pretoria
33 England (16-33) 1992 Twickenham
29 France (16-29) 1992 Parc des Princes
15 Ireland (23-15) 1981 Cape Town
25 N Zealand (22-25) 1981 Auckland
19 NZ Cavaliers (18-19) 1986 Durban
21 S America (12-21) 1982 Bloemfontein
10 Scotland (18–10) 1960 Port Elizabeth
 7 United States (38-7) 1981 New York
 6 Wales (6-6) 1970 Cardiff

Biggest losing points margin
23 v Australia (3-26) 1992 Cape Town
v individual countries
23 v Australia (3-26) 1992 Cape Town
19 v B Isles (9-28) 1974 Pretoria
17 v England (16-33) 1992 Twickenham
13 v France (16-29) 1992 Parc des Princes
 3 v Ireland (6-9) 1965 Dublin
17 v N Zealand (3-20) 1965 Auckland
 1 v NZ Cavaliers (18-19) 1986 Durban
 9 v S America (12-21) 1982 Bloemfontein
 6 v Scotland (0-6) 1906 Glasgow
No defeats v Argentina, United States or Wales

Longest losing sequence
7 matches – 1964-65

Most tries by South Africa in an international
10 v Ireland (38-0) 1912 Dublin

Most tries against South Africa in an international
5 $\begin{cases} \text{by B Isles (22-23) 1955 Johannesburg} \\ \text{by N Zealand (3-20) 1965 Auckland} \\ \text{by B Isles (9-28) 1974 Pretoria} \end{cases}$

Most points on overseas tour (all matches)
753 in Australia/N Zealand (26 matches) 1937

Most tries on overseas tour (all matches)
161 in Australia/N Zealand (26 matches) 1937

INDIVIDUAL RECORDS

Most capped player
F C H du Preez $\big\}$ 38 $\big\{$ 1960-71
J H Ellis $\qquad\qquad$ 1965-76
in individual positions
Full-back
L G Wilson $\quad$ 27 $\quad$ 1960-65
Wing
J P Engelbrecht $\quad$ 33 $\quad$ 1960-69
Centre
J L Gainsford $\quad$ 33 $\quad$ 1960-67
Fly-half
H E Botha $\quad$ 28 $\quad$ 1980-92
Scrum-half
D J de Villiers $\quad$ 25 $\quad$ 1962-70
Prop
J F K Marais $\quad$ 35 $\quad$ 1963-74
Hooker
G F Malan $\quad$ 18 $\quad$ 1958-65
Lock
F C H du Preez $\quad$ 31(38)[1] $\quad$ 1960-71
Flanker
J H Ellis $\quad$ 38 $\quad$ 1965-76
No 8
D J Hopwood $\quad$ 22[2] $\quad$ 1960-65
[1]*du Preez won 7 caps as a flanker*
[2]*T P Bedford, 25 caps, won 19 at No 8 and 6 as a flanker*

Longest international career
J M Powell 13 seasons 1891-1903
B H Heatlie 13 seasons 1891-1903

D M Gerber 13 seasons 1980-1992/3
H E Botha 13 seasons 1980-1992/3
Gerber's and Botha's careers ended during a Northern
Hemisphere season

Most consecutive internationals 25
S H Nomis 1967-72

Most internationals as captain
D J de Villiers 22 1965-70

Most points in internationals – 312
H E Botha (28 matches) 1980-92

Most points in an international – 22
G R Bosch v France 1975 Pretoria
G Johnson v Argentina 1993
    Buenos Aires

Most tries in internationals – 19
D M Gerber (24 matches) 1980-92

Most tries in an international – 3
E E McHardy v Ireland 1912 Dublin
J A Stegmann v Ireland 1912 Dublin
K T van Vollenhoven v B Isles
    1955 Cape Town
H J van Zyl v Australia 1961 Johannesburg
R H Mordt v New Zealand 1981 Auckland
R H Mordt v United States
    1981 New York
D M Gerber v S America 1982 Pretoria
D M Gerber v England 1984 Johannesburg

Most conversions in internationals – 50
H E Botha (28 matches) 1980-92

Most conversions in an international – 7
A Geffin v Scotland 1951 Murrayfield

Most dropped goals in internationals – 18
H E Botha (28 matches) 1980-92

Most dropped goals in an international – 3
H E Botha { v S America 1980 Durban
           { v Ireland 1981 Durban

Most penalty goals in internationals – 50
H E Botha (28 matches) 1980-92

Most penalty goals in an international – 6
G R Bosch v France 1975 Pretoria

Most points in international series – 69
H E Botha (4 appearances) v
    NZ Cavaliers 1986

**Most points in international series
on tour – 35**
H E Botha (3 appearances)
    1981 N Zealand

**Most tries in international series
on tour – 6**
E E McHardy (5 appearances) 1912-13
    B Isles/France

Most points on overseas tour – 190
G H Brand (20 appearances) 1937
    Australia/N Zealand

Most tries on overseas tour – 22
J A Loubser (20 appearances) 1906-07
    B Isles/France

Most points in a tour match – 35
W J de Wet Ras v British Schools OB
    1980 Montevideo

Most tries in a tour match – 6
R G Dryburgh v Queensland 1956
    Brisbane

FINAL DESTINATIONS UNKNOWN

THE 1993 SEASON IN NEW ZEALAND
Donald Cameron *New Zealand Herald*

New Zealand rugby in 1993 was no place for the traditionalist. At the year's end, New Zealand were contemplating an All Black side which had been outplayed and outpointed by England at Twickenham – the start of one of the saddest and sorriest weeks of New Zealand rugby.

The close season brought the findings of a Melbourne-based firm of consultants which had been engaged by the New Zealand Rugby Football Union to suggest the future path of the game going into the 21st century. And at a time when the top brass of New Zealand rugby were looking eagerly into a domestic crystal ball, the view of more and more provincial unions was being tempted by overseas and/or international competition, further weakening the basic club structure of the game.

If all the above suggests that New Zealand rugby is on some higgledy-piggledy course and unsure of its final destination then that uncertain finding is probably very accurate. There are so many parts of the New Zealand rugby mainstream branching off in different directions that one hesitates to suggest where it will all end.

On the playing side, the All Blacks, under Laurie Mains' increasingly dominant leadership, defeated the British Lions 2-1 without convincing anyone that the result could not have been turned the other way. An under-prepared Wallaby side yielded up the Bledisloe Cup at Carisbrook, and the All Blacks settled into a more effective rhythm in turning back the first Test challenge offered by Western Samoa, the personality side of the home season during a brief but spectacular tour.

Then came the tour to Britain, the amazingly big win over Scotland and then the loss to England at Twickenham. Just as a sorrowing country was trying to accept that England was the better team the incredible news came that Mike Brewer, in Britain on business, had been drafted into the Twickenham Test reserves ahead of players selected for the tour, and in fact he made a brief appearance as a replacement against the Barbarians at Cardiff a week later.

Mains coldly rebuffed home criticism of his action by saying it did not affect him. He received a mild slap on the wrist from NZRFU when he returned. Months later, Brewer's few minutes on the field at Cardiff allowed him to claim the same share as everyone else from the All Blacks' payment pool. Mains was heavily involved in this direction, too, being one of the mainsprings behind the setting up of the All Blacks Club, which was designed to attract corporate and public financial support to be allocated to needy All Blacks.

A further curiosity occurred when Mains, who had supported the new ruck-maul-pile-up legislation, did an about-turn in the off season and said he no longer thought the new regulations were a good idea.

Just as the arguments surrounding the All Black tour were dying down the wide-ranging survey on New Zealand rugby was drip-fed to the public and the domestic unions. Not everyone liked some parts of the report. At a time when the Super-10 was promising to fly higher than in its first year the report suggested more second-level international competition, including the hoary old chestnut of New South Wales and Queensland playing in the New Zealand National Championship.

Two salient points emerged. The survey suggested that an élite group of perhaps ten unions should play at the major grounds for maximum financial return, leaving the other unions to act as feeder grounds for the élite group while going about their second-and third-division activities away from metropolitan eyes. And we have yet to find out how the 19-man NZRFU council will react to the survey's recommendation that administration control should be handled by about half the council's present number.

No one is quite sure whether the survey suggestions will be used, or put out of sight in a convenient pigeon-hole – the fate of a previous wide-ranging survey a few years ago. And the survey might disregard the fact that at representative level the game in New Zealand is throbbing with life and special accomplishment.

Waikato achieved instant fame by taking the Ranfurly Shield from Auckland, ending Auckland's run of 61 defences since 1985, and then overcame a challenge from Otago.

NATIONAL CHAMPIONSHIP

Division 1	P	W	D	L	F	A	Pts
Waikato	8	6	0	2	219	106	26
Auckland	8	6	0	2	356	131	25
North Harbour	8	6	0	2	257	161	24
Otago	8	5	1	2	221	141	23
Wellington	8	4	1	3	174	166	20
Canterbury	8	4	0	4	188	235	16
King Country	8	2	0	6	90	317	9
Taranaki	8	2	0	6	175	338	8
Hawke's Bay	8	0	0	8	157	242	3

Semi-finals: Auckland 43, North Harbour 20; Otago 36, Waikato 22 **Final:** Auckland 27, Otago 18 **Relegated:** Hawke's Bay

Division 2	P	W	D	L	F	A	Pts
N Auckland	8	7	0	1	322	162	29
S Canterbury	8	6	0	2	238	138	25
Counties	8	6	0	2	401	135	24
Bay of Plenty	8	6	0	2	318	189	24
Manawatu	8	4	1	3	224	242	18
Southland	8	3	0	5	199	230	14
Nelson Bays	8	2	0	6	182	275	9
Wairarapa-Bush	8	0	2	6	105	300	4
Poverty Bay	8	0	1	7	80	393	3

Semi-finals: Bay of Plenty 41, North Auckland 26; Counties 33, South Canterbury 18
Final: Counties 38, Bay of Plenty 10
Promoted: Counties **Relegated:** Poverty Bay

Division 3	P	W	D	L	F	A	Pts
Wanganui	8	7	0	1	317	114	28
Mid-Canterbury	8	6	0	2	223	138	25
Horowhenua	8	5	0	3	262	118	22
Thames Valley	8	5	0	3	211	141	21
Marlborough	8	5	0	3	186	202	21
Buller	8	4	0	4	160	149	17
North Otago	8	2	0	6	139	275	9
East Coast	8	2	0	6	113	272	9
West Coast	8	0	0	8	102	304	2

Semi-finals: Wanganui 30, Thames Valley 14; Horowhenua 30, Mid-Canterbury 22
Final: Horowhenua 15, Wanganui 9
Promoted: Horowhenua

RANFURLY SHIELD

Auckland 80, Horowhenua 17;
Auckland 48, Buller 3; Auckland 69,
Hawke's Bay 31; Auckland 139, North
Otago 5; Auckland 51, Wellington 14;
Waikato 17, Auckland 6; Waikato 28,
Otago 11

NEW ZEALAND INTERNATIONAL PLAYERS (*up to 31 March 1994*)

ABBREVIATIONS

A – Australia; *Arg* – Argentina; *AW* – Anglo-Welsh; *BI* – British Isles teams; *C* – Canada; *E* – England; *F* – France; *Fj* – Fiji; *I* – Ireland; *It* – Italy; *R* – Romania; *S* – Scotland; *SA* – South Africa; *US* – United States; *W* – Wales; *Wld* – World Invitation XV; *WS* – Western Samoa; (R) – Replacement; (t) – temporary replacement. Entries in square brackets [ ] indicate appearances in the Rugby World Cup.

Note: When a series has taken place, figures denote the particular matches in which players featured. Thus 1959 *BI* 2,4 indicates that a player appeared in the second and fourth Tests of the 1959 series against the British Isles.

Abbott, H L (Taranaki) 1906 *F*
Aitken, G G (Wellington) 1921 *SA* 1,2
Allen, F R (Auckland) 1946 *A* 1,2 1947 *A* 1,2, 1949 *SA* 1,2
Allen, M R (Taranaki) 1993 *WS* (t)
Allen, N H (Counties) 1980 *A* 3, *W*
Alley, G T (Canterbury) 1928 *SA* 1,2,3
Anderson, A (Canterbury) 1983 *S, E,* 1984 *A* 1,2,3, 1987 [*Fj*]
Anderson, B L (Wairarapa-Bush) 1986 *A* 1
Archer, W R (Otago, Southland) 1955 *A* 1,2, 1956 *SA* 1,3
Argus, W G (Canterbury) 1946 *A* 1,2, 1947 *A* 1,2
Arnold, D A (Canterbury) 1963 *I, W,* 1964 *E, F*
Arnold, K D (Waikato) 1947 *A* 1,2
Ashby, D L (Southland) 1958 *A* 2
Asher, A A (Auckland) 1903 *A*
Ashworth, B G (Auckland) 1978 *A* 1,2
Ashworth, J C (Canterbury, Hawke's Bay) 1978 *A* 1,2,3, 1980 *A* 1,2,3, 1981 *SA* 1,2,3, 1982 *A* 1,2, 1983 *BI* 1,2,3,4, 1984 *F* 1,2 *A* 1,2,3, 1985 *E* 1,2, *A*
Atkinson, H (West Coast) 1913 *A* 1
Avery, H E (Wellington) 1910 *A* 1,2,3

Bachop, G T M (Canterbury) 1989 *W, I,* 1990 *S* 1,2, *A* 1,2,3, *F* 1,2, 1991 *Arg* 1,2, *A* 1,2, [*E, US, C, A, S*], 1992 *Wld* 1
Badeley, C E O (Auckland) 1921 *SA* 1,2
Baird, J A S (Otago) 1913 *A* 2
Ball, N (Wellington) 1931 *A,* 1932 *A* 2,3, 1935 *W,* 1936 *E*
Barrett, J (Auckland) 1913 *A* 2,3
Barry, E F (Wellington) 1934 *A* 2
Batty, G B (Wellington, Bay of Plenty) 1972 *W, S,* 1973 *E* 1, *I, F, E* 2, 1974 *A* 1,3, *I,* 1975 *S,* 1976 *SA* 1,2,3,4, 1977 *BI* 1
Batty, W (Auckland) 1930 *BI* 1,3,4, 1931 *A*
Beatty, G E (Taranaki) 1950 *BI* 1
Bell, R H (Otago) 1951 *A* 3, 1952 *A* 1,2
Bellis, E A (Wanganui) 1921 *SA* 1,2,3
Bennet, R (Otago) 1905 *A*
Berghan, T (Otago) 1938 *A* 1,2,3
Berry, M J (Wairarapa-Bush) 1986 *A* 3 (R)
Bevan, V D (Wellington) 1949 *A* 1,2, 1950 *BI* 1,2,3,4
Birtwistle, W M (Canterbury) 1965 *SA* 1,2,3,4, 1967 *E, W, S*
Black, J E (Canterbury) 1977 *F* 1, 1979 *A,* 1980 *A* 3
Black, N W (Auckland) 1949 *SA* 3
Black, R S (Otago) 1914 *A* 1
Blake, A W (Wairarapa) 1949 *A* 1
Boggs, E G (Auckland) 1946 *A* 2, 1949 *SA* 1
Bond, J G (Canterbury) 1949 *A* 2
Booth, E E (Otago) 1906 *F,* 1907 *A* 1,3
Boroevich, K G (Wellington) 1986 *F* 1, *A* 1, *F* 3 (R)
Botica, F M (North Harbour) 1986 *F* 1, *A* 1,2,3, *F* 2,3, 1989 *Arg* 1 (R)
Bowden, N J G (Taranaki) 1952 *A* 2
Bowers, R G (Wellington) 1954 *I, F*
Bowman, A W (Hawke's Bay) 1938 *A* 1,2,3
Braid, G J (Bay of Plenty) 1983 *S, E*
Bremner, S G (Auckland, Canterbury) 1952 *A* 2, 1956 *SA* 2
Brewer, M R (Otago) 1986 *F* 1, *A* 1,2,3, *F* 2,3, 1988 *A* 1, 1989 *A, W, I,* 1990 *S* 1,2, *A* 1,2,3, *F* 1,2, 1992 *I* 2, *A* 1
Briscoe, K C (Taranaki) 1959 *BI* 2, 1960 *SA* 1,2,3,4, 1963 *I, W,* 1964 *E, S*
Brooke, R M (Auckland) 1992 *I* 2, *A* 1,2,3, *SA,* 1993 *BI* 1,2,3, *A, WS*

Brooke, Z V (Auckland) 1987 [*Arg*], 1989 *Arg* 2 (R), 1990 *A* 1,2,3, *F* 1 (R), 1991 *Arg* 2, *A* 1,2, [*E, It, C, A, S*], 1992 *A* 2,3, *SA,* 1993 *BI* 1,2,3(R), *WS*(R), *S, E*
Brooke-Cowden, M (Auckland) 1986 *F* 1, *A* 1, 1987 [*W*]
Brown, C (Taranaki) 1913 *A* 2,3
Brown, O M (Auckland) 1992 *I* 2, *A* 1,2,3, *SA,* 1993 *BI* 1,2,3, *A, S, E*
Brown, R H (Taranaki) 1955 *A* 3, 1956 *SA* 1,2,3,4, 1957 *A* 1,2 1958 *A* 1,2,3, 1959 *BI* 1,3, 1961 *F* 1,2,3, 1962 *A* 1
Brownlie, C J (Hawke's Bay) 1924 *W,* 1925 *E, F*
Brownlie, M J (Hawke's Bay) 1924 *I, W,* 1925 *E, F,* 1928 *SA* 1,2,3,4
Bruce, J A (Auckland) 1914 *A* 1,2
Bruce, O D (Canterbury) 1976 *SA* 1,2,4, 1977 *BI* 2,3,4, *F* 1,2, 1978 *A* 1,2, *I, W, E, S*
Bryers, R F (King Country) 1949 *A* 1
Budd, T A (Southland) 1946 *A* 2, 1949 *A* 2
Bullock-Douglas, G A H (Wanganui) 1932 *A* 1,2,3, 1934 *A* 1,2
Bunce, F E (North Harbour) 1992 *Wld* 1,2,3, *I* 1,2, *A* 1,2,3, *SA,* 1993 *BI* 1,2,3, *A, WS, S, E*
Burgess, G A J (Auckland) 1981 *SA* 2
Burgess, G F (Southland) 1905 *A*
Burgess, R E (Manawatu) 1971 *BI* 1,2,3, 1972 *A* 3, *W,* 1973 *I, F*
Burke, P S (Taranaki) 1955 *A* 1, 1957 *A* 1,2
Burns, P J (Canterbury) 1908 *AW* 2, 1910 *A* 1,2,3, 1913 *A* 3
Bush, R G (Otago) 1931 *A*
Bush, W K (Canterbury) 1974 *A* 1,2, 1975 *S,* 1976 *I, SA* 2,4, 1977 *BI* 2,3,4(R), 1978 *I, W,* 1979 *A*
Buxton, J B (Canterbury) 1955 *A* 3, 1956 *SA* 1

Cain, M J (Taranaki) 1913 *US,* 1914 *A* 1,2,3
Callesen, J A (Manawatu) 1974 *A* 1,2,3, 1975 *S*
Cameron, D (Taranaki) 1908 *AW* 1,2,3
Cameron, L M (Manawatu) 1980 *A* 3, 1981 *SA* 1(R),2,3, *R*
Carleton, S R (Canterbury) 1928 *SA* 1,2,3, 1929 *A* 1,2,3
Carrington, K R (Auckland) 1971 *BI* 1,3,4
Carter, M P (Auckland) 1991 *A* 2, [*It, A*]
Casey, S T (Otago) 1905 *S, I, E, W,* 1907 *A* 1,2,3, 1908 *AW* 1
Catley, E H (Waikato) 1946 *A* 1, 1947 *A* 1,2, 1949 *SA* 1,2,3,4
Caughey, T H C (Auckland) 1932 *A* 1,3, 1934 *A* 1,2, 1935 *S, I,* 1936 *E, A* 1, 1937 *SA* 3
Caulton, R W (Wellington) 1959 *BI* 2,3,4, 1960 *SA* 1,4 1961 *F* 2, 1963 *E* 1,2, *I, W,* 1964 *E, S, F, A* 1,2,3
Cherrington, N P (North Auckland) 1950 *BI* 1
Christian, D L (Auckland) 1949 *SA* 4
Clamp, M (Wellington) 1984 *A* 2,3
Clark, D W (Otago) 1964 *A* 1,2
Clark, W H (Wellington) 1953 *W,* 1954 *I, E, S,* 1955 *A* 1,2, 1956 *SA* 2,3,4
Clarke, A H (Auckland) 1958 *A* 3, 1959 *BI* 4, 1960 *SA* 1
Clarke, D B (Waikato) 1956 *SA* 3,4, 1957 *A* 1,2, 1958 *A* 1,3, 1959 *BI* 1,2,3,4, 1960 *SA* 1,2,3,4, 1961 *F* 1,2,3, 1962 *A* 1,3,4,5, 1963 *E* 1,2, *I, W,* 1964 *E, S, F, A* 2,3
Clarke, E (Auckland) 1992 *Wld* 2,3, *I* 1,2, 1993 *BI* 1,2, *S*(R), *E*
Clarke, I J (Waikato) 1953 *W,* 1955 *A* 1,2,3, 1956 *SA* 1,2,3,4, 1957 *A* 1,2 1958 *A* 1,3, 1959 *BI* 1,2, 1960 *SA* 2,4, 1961 *F* 1,2,3, 1962 *A* 1,2,3, 1963 *E* 1,2

Clarke, R L (Taranaki) 1932 *A* 2,3
Cobden, D G (Canterbury) 1937 *SA* 1
Cockerill, M S (Taranaki) 1951 *A* 1,2,3
Cockroft, E A P (South Canterbury) 1913 *A* 3, 1914 *A* 2,3
Codlin, B W (Counties) 1980 *A* 1,2,3
Collins, A H (Taranaki) 1932 *A* 2,3, 1934 *A* 1
Collins, J L (Poverty Bay) 1964 *A* 1, 1965 *SA* 1,4
Colman, J T H (Taranaki) 1907 *A* 1,2, 1908 *AW* 1,3
Connor, D M (Auckland) 1961 *F* 1,2,3, 1962 *A* 1,2,3, 4,5, 1963 *E* 1,2, 1964 *A* 2,3
Conway, R J (Otago, Bay of Plenty) 1959 *BI* 2,3,4, 1960 *SA* 1,3,4, 1965 *SA* 1,2,3,4
Cooke, A E (Auckland, Wellington) 1924 *I*, *W*, 1925 *E*, *F*, 1930 *BI* 1,2,3,4
Cooke, R J (Canterbury) 1903 *A*
Cooksley, M S B (Counties) 1992 *Wld* 1, 1993 *BI* 2,3(R), *A*
Cooper, G J L (Auckland, Otago) 1986 *F* 1, *A* 1,2, 1992 *Wld* 1,2,3, *I* 1
Cooper, M J A (Waikato) 1992 *I* 2, *SA*(R), 1993 *BI* 1(R), 3(t), *WS*(t), *S*
Corner, M M N (Auckland) 1930 *BI* 2,3,4, 1931 *A*, 1934 *A* 1, 1936 *E*
Cossey, R R (Counties) 1958 *A* 1
Cottrell, A I (Canterbury) 1929 *A* 1,2,3, 1930 *BI* 1,2, 3,4 1931 *A*, 1932 *A* 1,2,3
Cottrell, W D (Canterbury) 1968 *A* 1,2, *F* 2,3, 1970 *SA* 1, 1971 *BI* 1,2,3,4
Couch, M B R (Wairarapa) 1947 *A* 1, 1949 *A* 1,2
Coughlan, T D (South Canterbury) 1958 *A* 1
Creighton, J N (Canterbury) 1962 *A* 4
Crichton, S (Wellington) 1983 *S*, *E*
Cross, T (Canterbury) 1904 *BI*, 1905 *A*
Crowley, K J (Taranaki) 1985 *E* 1,2, *A*, *Arg* 1,2, 1986 *A* 3, *F* 2,3, 1987 [*Arg*], 1990 *S* 1,2, *A* 1,2,3, *F* 1,2, 1991 *Arg* 1,2, [*A*]
Crowley, P J B (Auckland) 1949 *SA* 3,4, 1950 *BI* 1,2,3,4
Cummings, W (Canterbury) 1913 *A* 2,3
Cundy, R T (Wairarapa) 1929 *A* 2(R)
Cunningham, G R (Auckland) 1979 *A*, *S*, *E*, 1980 *A* 1,2
Cunningham, W (Auckland) 1905 *S*, *I*, 1906 *F*, 1907 *A* 1,2,3, 1908 *AW* 1,2,3
Cupples, L F (Bay of Plenty) 1924 *I*, *W*
Currie, C J (Canterbury) 1978 *I*, *W*
Cuthill, J E (Otago) 1913 *A* 1, *US*

Dalley, W C (Canterbury) 1924 *I*, 1928 *SA* 1,2,3,4
Dalton, A G (Counties) 1977 *F* 2, 1978 *A* 1,2,3, *I*, *W*, *E*, *S*, 1979 *F* 1,2, *S*, 1981 *S* 1,2, *SA* 1,2,3, *R*, *F* 1,2, 1982 *A* 1,2,3, 1983 *BI* 1,2,3,4, *A*, 1984 *F* 1,2, *A* 1,2,3, 1985 *E* 1,2, *A*
Dalton, D (Hawke's Bay) 1935 *I*, *W*, 1936 *A* 1,2, 1937 *SA* 1,2,3, 1938 *A* 1,2
Dalton, R A (Wellington) 1947 *A* 1,2
Dalzell, G N (Canterbury) 1953 *W*, 1954 *I*, *E*, *S*, *F*
Davie, M G (Canterbury) 1983 *E*(R)
Davies, W A (Auckland, Otago) 1960 *SA* 4, 1962 *A* 4,5
Davis, K (Auckland) 1952 *A* 2, 1953 *W*, 1954 *I*, *E*, *S*, *F*, 1955 *A* 2, 1958 *A* 1,2,3
Davis, L J (Canterbury) 1976 *I*, 1977 *BI* 3,4
Davis, W L (Hawke's Bay) 1967 *A*, *E*, *W*, *F*, *S*, 1968 *A* 1,2, *F* 1, 1969 *W* 1,2, 1970 *SA* 2
Deans, I B (Canterbury) 1988 *W* 1,2, *A* 1,2,3, 1989 *F* 1,2, *Arg* 1,2, *A*
Deans, R G (Canterbury) 1905 *S*, *I*, *E*, *W*, 1908 *AW* 3
Deans, R M (Canterbury) 1983 *S*, *E*, 1984 *A* 1(R),2,3
Delamore, G W (Wellington) 1949 *SA* 4
Dewar, H (Taranaki) 1913 *A* 1, *US*
Diack, E S (Otago) 1959 *BI* 2
Dick, J (Auckland) 1937 *SA* 1,2, 1938 *A* 3
Dick, M J (Auckland) 1963 *I*, *W*, 1964 *E*, *S*, *F*, 1965 *SA* 3, 1966 *BI* 4, 1967 *A*, *E*, *W*, *F*, 1969 *W* 1,2, 1970 *SA* 1,4
Dixon, M J (Canterbury) 1954 *I*, *E*, *S*, *F*, 1956 *SA* 1,2,3,4, 1957 *A* 1,2
Dobson, R L (Auckland) 1949 *A* 1
Dodd, E H (Wellington) 1905 *A*
Donald, A J (Wanganui) 1983 *S*, *E*, 1984 *F* 1,2, *A* 1,2,3
Donald, J G (Wairarapa) 1921 *SA* 1,2
Donald, Q (Wairarapa) 1924 *I*, *W*, 1925 *E*, *F*
Donaldson, M W (Manawatu) 1977 *F* 1,2, 1978 *A* 1, 2,3, *I*, *E*, *S*, 1979 *F* 1,2, *A*, *S* (R), 1981 *SA* 3(R)
Dougan, J P (Wellington) 1972 *A* 1, 1973 *E* 2

Dowd, C W (Auckland) 1993 *BI* 1,2,3, *A*, *WS*, *S*, *E*
Dowd, G W (North Harbour) 1992 *I* 1(R)
Downing, A J (Auckland) 1913 *A* 1, *US*, 1914 *A* 1,2,3
Drake, J A (Auckland) 1986 *F* 2,3, 1987 [*Fj*, *Arg*, *S*, *W*, *F*], *A*
Duff, R H (Canterbury) 1951 *A* 1,2,3, 1952 *A* 1,2, 1955 *A* 2,3, 1956 *SA* 1,2,3,4
Duncan, J (Otago) 1903 *A*
Duncan, M G (Hawke's Bay) 1971 *BI* 3(R), 4
Duncan, W D (Otago) 1921 *SA* 1,2,3
Dunn, E J (North Auckland) 1979 *S*, 1981 *S* 1
Dunn, I T W (North Auckland) 1983 *BI* 1,4, *A*
Dunn, J M (Auckland) 1946 *A* 1

Earl, A T (Canterbury) 1986 *F* 1, *A* 1, *F* 3(R), 1987 [*Arg*], 1989 *W*, *I*, 1991 *Arg* 1(R), 2, *A* 1, [*E*(R), *US*, *S*], 1992 *A* 2,3(R)
Eastgate, B P (Canterbury) 1952 *A* 1,2, 1954 *S*
Elliott, K G (Wellington) 1946 *A* 1,2
Ellis, M C G (Otago) 1993 *S*, *E*
Elsom, A E G (Canterbury) 1952 *A* 1,2, 1953 *W*, 1955 *A* 1,2,3
Elvidge, R R (Otago) 1946 *A* 1,2, 1949 *SA* 1,2,3,4, 1950 *BI* 1,2,3
Erceg, C P (Auckland) 1951 *A* 1,2,3, 1952 *A* 1
Evans, D A (Hawke's Bay) 1910 *A* 2
Eveleigh, K A (Manawatu) 1976 *SA* 2,4, 1977 *BI* 1,2

Fanning, A H N (Canterbury) 1913 *A* 3
Fanning, B J (Canterbury) 1903 *A*, 1904 *BI*
Farrell, C P (Auckland) 1977 *BI* 1,2
Fawcett, C L (Auckland) 1976 *SA* 2,3
Fea, W R (Otago) 1921 *SA* 3
Finlay, B E L (Manawatu) 1959 *BI* 1
Finlay, J (Manawatu) 1946 *A* 1
Finlayson, I (North Auckland) 1928 *SA* 1,2,3,4, 1930 *BI* 1,2
Fitzgerald, J T (Wellington) 1952 *A* 1
Fitzpatrick, B B J (Wellington) 1953 *W*, 1954 *I*, *F*
Fitzpatrick, S B T (Auckland) 1986 *F* 1, *A* 1, *F* 2,3, 1987 [*It*, *Fj*, *Arg*, *S*, *W*, *F*], *A*, 1988 *W* 1,2, *A* 1,2,3, 1989 *F* 1,2, *Arg* 1,2, *A*, *W*, *I*, 1990 *S* 1,2, *A* 1,2,3, *F* 1,2, 1991 *Arg* 1,2, *A* 1,2, [*E*, *US*, *It*, *C*, *A*, *S*], 1992 *Wld* 1,2,3, *I* 1,2, *A* 1,2,3, *SA*, 1993 *BI* 1,2,3, *A*, *WS*, *S*, *E*
Fleming, J K (Wellington) 1979 *S*, *E*, 1980 *A* 1,2,3
Fletcher, C J C (North Auckland) 1921 *SA* 3
Fogarty, R (Taranaki) 1921 *SA* 1,3
Ford, B R (Marlborough) 1977 *BI* 3,4, 1978 *I*, 1979 *E*
Forster, S T (Otago) 1993 *S*, *E*
Fox, G J (Auckland) 1985 *Arg* 1, 1987 [*It*, *Fj*, *Arg*, *S*, *W*, *F*], *A*, 1988 *W* 1,2, *A* 1,2,3, 1989 *F* 1,2, *Arg* 1,2, *A*, *W*, *I*, 1990 *S* 1,2, *A* 1,2,3, *F* 1,2, 1991 *Arg* 1,2, *A* 1,2, [*E*, *It*, *C*, *A*], 1992 *Wld* 1,2(R), *A* 1,2,3, *SA*, 1993 *BI* 1,2,3, *A*, *WS*
Francis, A R H (Auckland) 1905 *A*, 1907 *A* 1,2,3, 1908 *AW* 1,2,3, 1910 *A* 1,2,3
Francis, W C (Wellington) 1913 *A* 2,3, 1914 *A* 1,2,3
Fraser, B G (Wellington) 1979 *S*, *E*, 1980 *A* 3, *W*, 1981 *S* 1,2, *SA* 1,2,3, *R*, *F* 1,2, 1982 *A* 1,2,3, 1983 *BI* 1,2,3,4, *A*, *S*, *E*, 1984 *A* 1
Frazer, H F (Hawke's Bay) 1946 *A* 1,2, 1947 *A* 1,2, 1949 *SA* 2
Fryer, F C (Canterbury) 1907 *A* 1,2,3, 1908 *AW* 2
Fuller, W B (Canterbury) 1910 *A* 1,2
Furlong, B D M (Hawke's Bay) 1970 *SA* 4

Gallagher, J A (Wellington) 1987 [*It*, *Fj*, *S*, *W*, *F*], *A*, 1988 *W* 1,2, *A* 1,2,3, 1989 *F* 1,2, *Arg* 1,2, *A*, *W*, *I*
Gallaher, D (Auckland) 1903 *A*, 1904 *BI*, 1905 *S*, *E*, *W*, 1906 *F*
Gard, P C (North Otago) 1971 *BI* 4
Gardiner, A J (Taranaki) 1974 *A* 3
Geddes, J H (Southland) 1929 *A* 1
Geddes, W McK (Auckland) 1913 *A* 2
Gemmell, B McL (Auckland) 1974 *A* 1,2
George, V L (Southland) 1938 *A* 1,2,3
Gilbert, G D M (West Coast) 1935 *S*, *I*, *W*, 1936 *E*
Gillespie, C T (Wellington) 1913 *A* 2
Gillespie, W D (Otago) 1958 *A* 3
Gillett, G A (Canterbury, Auckland) 1905 *S*, *I*, *E*, *W*, 1907 *A* 2,3, 1908 *AW* 1,3
Gillies, C C (Otago) 1936 *A* 2
Gilray, C M (Otago) 1905 *A*

1982 *A* 1,2,3, 1983 *BI* 1,2,3,4, *A*, 1984 *F* 1,2, *A* 1,2,3, 1985 *E* 1,2, *A*, 1986 *A* 2,3
Knight, L G (Poverty Bay) 1977 *BI* 1,2,3,4, *F* 1,2
Koteka, T T (Waikato) 1981 *F* 2, 1982 *A* 3
Kreft, A J (Otago) 1968 *A* 2

Laidlaw, C R (Otago, Canterbury) 1964 *F*, *A* 1, 1965 *SA* 1,2,3,4, 1966 *BI* 1,2,3,4, 1967 *E*, *W*, *S*, 1968 *A* 1,2, *F* 1,2, 1970 *SA* 1,2,3
Laidlaw, K F (Southland) 1960 *SA* 2,3,4
Lambert, K K (Manawatu) 1972 *S*(R), 1973 *E* 1, *I*, *F*, *E* 2, 1974 *I*, 1976 *SA* 1,3,4, 1977 *BI* 1,4
Lambourn, A (Wellington) 1934 *A* 1,2, 1935 *S*, *I*, *W*, 1936 *E*, 1937 *SA* 1,2,3, 1938 *A* 3
Larsen, B P (North Harbour) 1992 *Wld* 2,3, *I* 1
Le Lievre, J M (Canterbury) 1962 *A* 4
Lendrum, R N (Counties) 1973 *E* 2
Leslie, A R (Wellington) 1974 *A* 1,2,3, *I*, 1975 *S*, 1976 *I*, *SA* 1,2,3,4
Leys, E T (Wellington) 1929 *A* 3
Lilburne, H T (Canterbury, Wellington) 1928 *SA* 3,4, 1929 *A* 1,2,3, 1930 *BI* 1,4, 1931 *A*, 1932 *A* 1, 1934 *A* 2
Lindsay, D F (Otago) 1928 *SA* 1,2,3
Lineen, T R (Auckland) 1957 *A* 1,2, 1958 *A* 1,2,3, 1959 *BI* 1,2,3,4, 1960 *SA* 1,2,3
Lister, T N (South Canterbury) 1968 *A* 1,2, *F* 1, 1969 *W* 1,2, 1970 *SA* 1,4, 1971 *BI* 4
Little, P F (Auckland) 1961 *F* 2,3, 1962 *A* 2,3,5, 1963 *I*, *W*, 1964 *E*, *S*, *F*
Little, W K (North Harbour) 1990 *S* 1,2, *A* 1,2,3, *F* 1,2, 1991 *Arg* 1,2, *A* 1, [*It*, *S*], 1992 *Wld* 1,2,3, *I* 1,2, *A* 1,2,3, *SA*, 1993 *BI* 1, *WS*(R)
Loader, C J (Wellington) 1954 *I*, *E*, *S*, *F*
Lochore, B J (Wairarapa) 1964 *E*, *S*, 1965 *SA* 1,2,3,4, 1966 *BI* 1,2,3,4, 1967 *A*, *E*, *W*, *F*, *S*, 1968 *A* 1, *F* 2,3, 1969 *W* 1,2, 1970 *SA* 1,2,3,4, 1971 *BI* 3
Loe, R W (Waikato) 1987 [*It*, *Arg*], 1988 *W* 1,2, *A* 1,2,3, 1989 *F* 2, *Arg* 1,2, *A*, *W*, *I*, 1990 *S* 1,2, *A* 1,2,3, *F* 1,2, 1991 *Arg* 1,2, *A* 1,2, [*E*, *It*, *C*, *A*, *S*], 1992 *Wld* 1,2,3, *I* 1, *A* 1,2,3, *SA*
Long, A J (Auckland) 1903 *A*
Loveridge, D S (Taranaki) 1978 *W*, 1979 *S*, *E*, 1980 *A* 1,2,3, 1981 *S* 1,2, *SA* 1,2,3, *R*, *F* 1,2, 1982 *A* 1,2,3, 1983 *BI* 1,2,3,4, *A*, 1985 *Arg* 2
Lucas, F W (Auckland) 1924 *I*, 1925 *F*, 1928 *SA* 4, 1930 *BI* 1,2,3,4
Lunn, W A (Otago) 1949 *A* 1,2
Lynch, T W (South Canterbury) 1913 *A* 1, 1914 *A* 1,2,3
Lynch, T W (Canterbury) 1951 *A* 1,2,3

McAtamney, F S (Otago) 1956 *SA* 2
McCahill, B J (Auckland) 1987 [*Arg*, *S*(R), *W*(R)], 1989 *Arg* 1(R), 2(R), 1991 *A* 2, [*E*, *US*, *C*, *A*]
McCaw, W A (Southland) 1951 *A* 1,2,3, 1953 *W*, 1954 *F*
McCool, M J (Wairarapa-Bush) 1979 *A*
McCormick, W F (Canterbury) 1965 *SA* 4, 1967 *E*, *W*, *F*, *S*, 1968 *A* 1,2, *F* 1,2,3, 1969 *W* 1,2, 1970 *SA* 1,2,3, 1971 *BI* 1
McCullough, J F (Taranaki) 1959 *BI* 2,3,4
McDonald, A (Otago) 1905 *S*, *I*, *E*, *W*, 1907 *A* 1, 1908 *AW* 1, 1913 *A* 1, *US*
Macdonald, H H (Canterbury, North Auckland) 1972 *W*, *S*, 1973 *E* 1, *I*, *F*, *E* 2, 1974 *I*, 1975 *S*, 1976 *I*, *SA* 1,2,3
McDowell, S C (Auckland, Bay of Plenty) 1985 *Arg* 1,2, 1986 *A* 2,3, *F* 2,3, 1987 [*It*, *Fj*, *S*, *W*, *F*], *A*, 1988 *W* 1,2, *A* 1,2,3, 1989 *F* 1,2, *Arg* 1,2, *A*, *W*, *I*, 1990 *S* 1,2, *A* 1,2,3, *F* 1,2, 1991 *Arg* 1,2, *A* 1,2, [*E*, *US*, *It*, *C*, *A*, *S*], 1992 *Wld* 1,2,3, *I* 1,2
McEldowney, J T (Taranaki) 1977 *BI* 3,4
MacEwan, I N (Wellington) 1956 *SA* 2, 1957 *A* 1,2, 1958 *A* 1,2,3, 1959 *BI* 1,2,3, 1960 *SA* 1,2,3,4, 1961 *F* 1,2,3, 1962 *A* 1,2,3,4
McGrattan, B (Wellington) 1983 *S*, *E*, 1985 *Arg* 1,2, 1986 *F* 1, *A* 1
McGregor, A J (Auckland) 1913 *A* 1, *US*
McGregor, D (Canterbury, Southland) 1903 *A*, 1904 *BI*, 1905 *E*, *W*
McGregor, N P (Canterbury) 1924 *W*, 1925 *E*
McGregor, R W (Auckland) 1903 *A*, 1904 *BI*
McHugh, M J (Auckland) 1946 *A* 1,2, 1949 *SA* 3
McIntosh, D N (Wellington) 1956 *SA* 1,2, 1957 *A* 1,2
McKay, D W (Auckland) 1961 *F* 1,2,3, 1963 *E* 1,2

McKechnie, B J (Southland) 1977 *F* 1,2, 1978 *A* 2(R),3, *W*(R), *E*, *S*, 1979 *A*, 1981 *SA* 1(R), *F* 1
McKellar, G F (Wellington) 1910 *A* 1,2,3
McKenzie, R J (Wellington) 1913 *A* 1, *US*, 1914 *A* 2,3
McKenzie, R McC (Manawatu) 1934 *A* 1, 1935 *S*, 1936 *A* 1, 1937 *SA* 1,2,3, 1938 *A* 1,2,3
McLachlan, J S (Auckland) 1974 *A* 2
McLaren, H C (Waikato) 1952 *A* 1
McLean, A L (Bay of Plenty) 1921 *SA* 2,3
McLean, H F (Wellington, Auckland) 1930 *BI* 3,4, 1932 *A* 1,2,3, 1934 *A* 1, 1935 *I*, *W*, 1936 *E*
McLean, J K (King Country, Auckland) 1947 *A* 1, 1949 *A* 2
McLeod, B E (Counties) 1964 *A* 1,2,3, 1965 *SA* 1,2,3,4, 1966 *BI* 1,2,3,4, 1967 *E*, *W*, *F*, *S*, 1968 *A* 1,2, *F* 1,2,3, 1969 *W* 1,2, 1970 *SA* 1,2
McMinn, A F (Wairarapa, Manawatu) 1903 *A*, 1905 *A*
McMinn, F A (Manawatu) 1904 *BI*
McMullen, R F (Auckland) 1957 *A* 1,2, 1958 *A* 1,2,3, 1959 *BI* 1,2,3, 1960 *SA* 2,3,4
McNab, J R (Otago) 1949 *SA* 1,2,3, 1950 *BI* 1,2,3
McNaughton, A M (Bay of Plenty) 1971 *BI* 1,2,3
McNeece, J (Southland) 1913 *A* 2,3, 1914 *A* 1,2,3
McPhail, B E (Canterbury) 1959 *BI* 1,4
Macpherson, D G (Otago) 1905 *A*
MacPherson, G L (Otago) 1986 *F* 1
MacRae, I R (Hawke's Bay) 1966 *BI* 1,2,3,4, 1967 *A*, *E*, *W*, *F*, *S*, 1968 *F* 1,2, 1969 *W* 1,2, 1970 *SA* 1,2,3,4
McRae, J A (Southland) 1946 *A* 1(R),2
McWilliams, R G (Auckland) 1928 *SA* 2,3,4, 1929 *A* 1,2,3, 1930 *BI* 1,2,3,4
Mackrell, W H C (Auckland) 1906 *F*
Macky, J V (Auckland) 1913 *A* 2
Maguire, J R (Auckland) 1910 *A* 1,2,3
Mahoney, A (Bush) 1935 *S*, *I*, *W*, 1936 *E*
Mains, L W (Otago) 1971 *BI* 2,3,4, 1976 *I*
Major, J (Taranaki) 1967 *A*
Manchester, J E (Canterbury) 1932 *A* 1,2,3, 1934 *A* 1,2, 1935 *S*, *I*, *W*, 1936 *E*
Mason, D F (Wellington) 1947 *A* 2(R)
Masters, R R (Canterbury) 1924 *I*, *W*, 1925 *E*, *F*
Mataira, H K (Hawke's Bay) 1934 *A* 2
Matheson, J D (Otago) 1972 *A* 1,2,3, *W*, *S*
Max, D S (Nelson) 1931 *A*, 1934 *A* 1,2
Meads, C E (King Country) 1957 *A* 1,2, 1958 *A* 1,2,3, 1959 *BI* 2,3,4, 1960 *SA* 1,2,3,4, 1961 *F* 1,2,3, 1962 *A* 1,2,3,5, 1963 *E* 1,2, *I*, *W*, 1964 *E*, *S*, *F*, *A* 1,2,3, 1965 *SA* 1,2,3,4 1966 *BI* 1,2,3,4, 1967 *A*, *E*, *W*, *F*, *S*, 1968 *A* 1,2, *F* 1,2,3, 1969 *W* 1,2, 1970 *SA* 3,4, 1971 *BI* 1,2,3,4
Meads, S T (King Country) 1961 *F* 1, 1962 *A* 4,5, 1963 *I*, 1964 *A* 1,2,3, 1965 *SA* 1,2,3,4, 1966 *BI* 1,2,3,4
Meates, K F (Canterbury) 1952 *A* 1,2
Meates, W A (Otago) 1949 *SA* 2,3,4, 1950 *BI* 1,2,3,4
Metcalfe, T C (Southland) 1931 *A*, 1932 *A* 1
Mexted, G G (Wellington) 1950 *BI* 4
Mexted, M G (Wellington) 1979 *S*, *E*, 1980 *A* 1,2,3, *W*, 1981 *S* 1,2, *SA* 1,2,3, *R*, *F* 1,2, 1982 *A* 1,2,3, 1983 *BI* 1,2,3,4, *A*, *S*, *E*, 1984 *F* 1,2, *A* 1,2,3, 1985 *E* 1,2, *A*, *Arg* 1,2
Mill, J J (Hawke's Bay, Wairarapa) 1924 *W*, 1925 *E*, *F*, 1930 *BI* 1
Milliken, H M (Canterbury) 1938 *A* 1,2,3
Milner, H P (Wanganui) 1970 *SA* 3
Mitchell, N A (Southland, Otago) 1935 *S*, *I*, *W*, 1936 *E*, *A* 2, 1937 *SA* 3, 1938 *A* 1,2
Mitchell, T W (Canterbury) 1976 *SA* 4(R)
Mitchell, W J (Canterbury) 1910 *A* 2,3
Mitchinson, F E (Wellington) 1907 *A* 1,2,3, 1908 *AW* 1,2,3, 1910 *A* 1,2,3, 1913 *A* 1(R), *US*
Moffitt, J E (Wellington) 1921 *SA* 1,2,3
Moore, G J T (Otago) 1949 *A* 1
Moreton, R C (Canterbury) 1962 *A* 3,4, 1964 *A* 1,2,3, 1965 *SA* 2,3
Morgan, J E (North Auckland) 1974 *A* 3, *I*, 1976 *SA* 2,3,4
Morris, T J (Nelson Bays) 1972 *A* 1,2,3
Morrison, T C (South Canterbury) 1938 *A* 1,2,3
Morrison, T G (Otago) 1973 *E* 2(R)
Morrissey, P J (Canterbury) 1962 *A* 3,4,5
Mourie, G N K (Taranaki) 1977 *BI* 3,4, *F* 1,2, 1978 *I*, *W*, *E*, *S*, 1979 *F* 1,2, *A*, *S*, *E*, 1980 *W*, 1981 *S* 1,2, *F* 1,2, 1982 *A* 1,2,3
Muller, B L (Taranaki) 1967 *A*, *E*, *W*, *F*, 1968 *A* 1,

F 1, 1969 *W* 1, 1970 *SA* 1,2,4, 1971 *BI* 1,2,3,4
Mumm, W J (Buller) 1949 *A* 1
Murdoch, K (Otago) 1970 *SA* 4, 1972 *A* 3, *W*
Murdoch, P H (Auckland) 1964 *A* 2,3, 1965 *SA* 1,2,3
Murray, H V (Canterbury) 1913 *A* 1, *US*, 1914 *A* 2,3
Murray, P C (Wanganui) 1908 *AW* 2
Myers, R G (Waikato) 1978 *A* 3
Mynott, H J (Taranaki) 1905 *I*, *W*, 1906 *F*, 1907 *A* 1,2,3, 1910 *A* 1,3

Nathan, W J (Auckland) 1962 *A* 1,2,3,4,5, 1963 *E* 1,2, *W*, 1964 *F*, 1966 *BI* 1,2,3,4, 1967 *A*
Nelson, K A (Otago) 1962 *A* 4,5
Nepia, G (Hawke's Bay, East Coast) 1924 *I*, *W*, 1925 *E*, *F*, 1929 *A* 1, 1930 *BI* 1,2,3,4
Nesbit, S R (Auckland) 1960 *SA* 2,3
Newton, F (Canterbury) 1905 *E*, *W*, 1906 *F*
Nicholls, H E (Wellington) 1921 *SA* 1
Nicholls, M F (Wellington) 1921 *SA* 1,2,3, 1924 *I*, *W*, 1925 *E*, *F*, 1928 *SA* 4, 1930 *BI* 2,3
Nicholson, G W (Auckland) 1903 *A*, 1904 *BI*, 1907 *A* 2,3

Norton, R W (Canterbury) 1971 *BI* 1,2,3,4, 1972 *A* 1,2,3, *W*, *S*, 1973 *E* 1, *I*, *F*, *E* 2, 1974 *A* 1,2,3, *I*, 1975 *S*, 1976 *I*, *SA* 1,2,3,4, 1977 *BI* 1,2,3,4

O'Brien, J G (Auckland) 1914 *A* 1
O'Callaghan, M W (Manawatu) 1968 *F* 1,2,3
O'Callaghan, T R (Wellington) 1949 *A* 2
O'Donnell, D H (Wellington) 1949 *A* 2
Old, G H (Manawatu) 1981 *SA* 3, *R*(R), 1982 *A* 1(R)
O'Leary, M J (Auckland) 1910 *A* 1,3, 1913 *A* 2,3
Oliver, C J (Canterbury) 1929 *A* 1,2, 1934 *A* 1, 1935 *S*, *I*, *W*, 1936 *E*
Oliver, D J (Wellington) 1930 *BI* 1,2
Oliver, D O (Otago) 1954 *I*, *F*
Oliver, F J (Southland, Otago, Manawatu) 1976 *SA* 4, 1977 *BI* 1,2,3,4, *F* 1,2, 1978 *A* 1,2,3, *I*, *W*, *E*, *S*, 1979 *F* 1,2, 1981 *SA* 2
Orr, R W (Otago) 1949 *A* 1
Osborne, W M (Wanganui) 1975 *S*, 1976 *SA* 2(R), 4(R), 1977 *BI* 1,2,3,4, *F* 1(R),2, 1978 *I*, *W*, *E*, *S*, 1980 *W*, 1982 *A* 1,3
O'Sullivan, J M (Taranaki) 1905 *S*, *I*, *E*, *W*, 1907 *A* 3
O'Sullivan, T P A (Taranaki) 1960 *SA* 1, 1961 *F* 1, 1962 *A* 1,2

Page, J R (Wellington) 1931 *A*, 1932 *A* 1,2,3, 1934 *A* 1,2
Palmer, B P (Auckland) 1929 *A* 2, 1932 *A* 2,3
Parker, J H (Canterbury) 1924 *I*, *W*, 1925 *E*
Parkhill, A A (Otago) 1937 *SA* 1,2,3, 1938 *A* 1,2,3
Parkinson, R M (Poverty Bay) 1972 *A* 1,2,3, *W*, *S*, 1973 *E* 1,2
Paterson, A M (Otago) 1908 *AW* 2,3, 1910 *A* 1,2,3
Paton, H (Otago) 1910 *A* 1,3
Pene, A R B (Otago) 1992 *Wld* 1(R),2,3, *I* 1,2, *A* 1,2(R), 1993 *BI* 3, *A*, *WS*, *S*, *E*
Phillips, W J (King Country) 1937 *SA* 2, 1938 *A* 1,2
Philpott, S (Canterbury) 1991 [*It*(R), *S*(R)]
Pickering, E A R (Waikato) 1958 *A* 2, 1959 *BI* 1,4
Pierce, M J (Wellington) 1985 *E* 1,2, *A*, *Arg* 1, 1986 *A* 2,3, *F* 2,3, 1987 [*It*, *Arg*, *S*, *W*, *F*], *A*, 1988 *W* 1,2, *A* 1,2,3, 1989 *F* 1,2, *Arg* 1,2, *A*, *W*, *I*
Pokere, S T (Southland, Auckland) 1981 *SA* 3, 1982 *A* 1,2,3, 1983 *BI* 1,2,3,4, *A*, *S*, *E*, 1984 *F* 1,2, *A* 2,3, 1985 *E* 1,2, *A*
Pollock, H R (Wellington) 1932 *A* 1,2,3, 1936 *A* 1,2
Porter, C G (Wellington) 1925 *F*, 1929 *A* 2,3, 1930 *BI* 1,2,3,4
Preston, J P (Canterbury, Wellington) 1991 [*US*, *S*], 1992 *SA*(R), 1993 *BI* 2,3, *A*, *WS*
Procter, A C (Otago) 1932 *A* 1
Purdue, C A (Southland) 1905 *A*
Purdue, E (Southland) 1905 *A*
Purdue, G B (Southland) 1931 *A*, 1932 *A* 1,2,3
Purvis, G H (Waikato) 1991 [*US*], 1993 *WS*
Purvis, N A (Otago) 1976 *I*

Quaid, C E (Otago) 1938 *A* 1,2

Rangi, R E (Auckland) 1964 *A* 2,3, 1965 *SA* 1,2,3,4, 1966 *BI* 1,2,3,4
Rankin, J G (Canterbury) 1936 *A* 1,2, 1937 *SA* 2
Reedy, W J (Wellington) 1908 *AW* 2,3

Reid, A R (Waikato) 1952 *A* 1, 1956 *SA* 3,4, 1957 *A* 1,2
Reid, H R (Bay of Plenty) 1980 *A* 1,2, *W*, 1983 *S*, *E*, 1985 *Arg* 1,2, 1986 *A* 2,3
Reid, K H (Wairarapa) 1929 *A* 1,3
Reid, S T (Hawke's Bay) 1935 *S*, *I*, *W*, 1936 *E*, *A* 1,2, 1937 *SA* 1,2,3
Reside, W B (Wairarapa) 1929 *A* 1
Rhind, P K (Canterbury) 1946 *A* 1,2
Richardson, J (Otago, Southland) 1921 *SA* 1,2,3, 1924 *I*, *W*, 1925 *E*, *F*
Rickit, H (Waikato) 1981 *S* 1,2
Ridland, A J (Southland) 1910 *A* 1,2,3
Roberts, E J (Wellington) 1914 *A* 1,2,3, 1921 *SA* 2,3
Roberts, F (Wellington) 1905 *S*, *I*, *E*, *W*, 1907 *A* 1,2,3, 1908 *AW* 1,3, 1910 *A* 1,2,3
Roberts, R W (Taranaki) 1913 *A* 1, *US*, 1914 *A* 1,2,3
Robertson, B J (Counties) 1972 *A* 1,3, *S*, 1973 *E* 1, *I*, *F*, 1974 *A* 1,2,3, *I*, 1976 *I*, *SA* 1,2,3,4, 1977 *BI* 1,3,4, *F* 1,2, 1978 *A* 1,2,3, *W*, *E*, *S*, 1979 *F* 1,2, *A*, 1980 *A* 2,3, *W*, 1981 *S* 1,2
Robertson, D J (Otago) 1974 *A* 1,2,3, *I*, 1975 *S*, 1976 *I*, *SA* 1,3,4, 1977 *BI* 1
Robilliard, A C C (Canterbury) 1928 *SA* 1,2,3,4
Robinson, C E (Southland) 1951 *A* 1,2,3, 1952 *A* 1,2
Rollerson, D L (Manawatu) 1980 *W*, 1981 *S* 2, *SA* 1,2,3, *R*, *F* 1(R), 2
Roper, R A (Taranaki) 1949 *A* 2, 1950 *BI* 1,2,3,4
Rowley, H C B (Wanganui) 1949 *A* 2
Rutledge, L M (Southland) 1978 *A* 1,2,3, *I*, *W*, *E*, *S*, 1979 *F* 1,2, *A*, 1980 *A* 1,2,3
Ryan, J (Wellington) 1910 *A* 2, 1914 *A* 1,2,3

Sadler, B S (Wellington) 1935 *S*, *I*, *W*, 1936 *A* 1,2
Salmon, J L B (Wellington) 1981 *R*, *F* 1,2(R)
Savage, L T (Canterbury) 1949 *SA* 1,2,4
Saxton, C K (South Canterbury) 1938 *A* 1,2,3
Schuler, K J (Manawatu, North Harbour) 1990 *A* 2(R), 1992 *A* 2
Schuster, N J (Wellington) 1988 *A* 1,2,3, 1989 *F* 1,2, *Arg* 1,2, *A*, *W*, *I*
Scott, R W H (Auckland) 1946 *A* 1,2, 1947 *A* 1,2, 1949 *SA* 1,2,3,4, 1950 *BI* 1,2,3,4, 1953 *W*, 1954 *I*, *E*, *S*, *F*
Scown, A I (Taranaki) 1972 *A* 1,2,3, *W*(R), *S*
Scrimshaw, G (Canterbury) 1928 *SA* 1
Seear, G A (Otago) 1977 *F* 1,2, 1978 *A* 1,2,3, *I*, *W*, *E*, *S*, 1979 *F* 1,2, *A*
Seeling, C E (Auckland) 1904 *BI*, 1905 *S*, *I*, *E*, *W*, 1906 *F*, 1907 *A* 1,2, 1908 *AW* 1,2,3
Sellars, G M V (Auckland) 1913 *A* 1, *US*
Shaw, M W (Manawatu, Hawke's Bay) 1980 *A* 1,2,3(R), *W*, 1981 *S* 1,2, *SA* 1,2, *R*, *F* 1,2, 1982 *A* 1,2,3, 1983 *BI* 1,2,3,4, *A*, *S*, *E*, 1984 *F* 1,2, *A* 1, 1985 *E* 1,2, *A*, *Arg* 1,2, 1986 *A* 3
Shelford, F N K (Bay of Plenty) 1981 *SA* 3, *R*, 1984 *A* 2,3
Shelford, W T (North Harbour) 1986 *F* 2,3, 1987 [*It*, *Fj*, *S*, *W*, *F*], *A*, 1988 *W* 1,2, *A* 1,2,3, 1989 *F* 1,2, *Arg* 1,2, *A*, *W*, *I*, 1990 *S* 1,2,
Siddells, S K (Wellington) 1921 *SA* 3
Simon, H J (Otago) 1937 *SA* 1,2,3
Simpson, J G (Auckland) 1947 *A* 1,2, 1949 *SA* 1,2,3,4, 1950 *BI* 1,2,3
Simpson, V L J (Canterbury) 1985 *Arg* 1,2
Sims, G S (Otago) 1972 *A* 2
Skeen, J R (Auckland) 1952 *A* 2
Skinner, K L (Otago, Counties) 1949 *SA* 1,2,3,4, 1950 *BI* 1,2,3,4, 1951 *A* 1,2,3, 1952 *A* 1,2, 1953 *W*, 1954 *I*, *E*, *S*, *F*, 1956 *SA* 3,4
Skudder, G R (Waikato) 1969 *W* 2
Sloane, P H (North Auckland) 1979 *E*
Smith, A E (Taranaki) 1969 *W* 1,2, 1970 *SA* 1
Smith, B W (Waikato) 1984 *F* 1,2, *A* 1
Smith, G W (Auckland) 1905 *S*, *I*
Smith, I S T (Otago, North Otago) 1964 *A* 1,2,3, 1965 *SA* 1,2,4, 1966 *BI* 1,2,3
Smith, J B (North Auckland) 1946 *A* 1, 1947 *A* 2, 1949 *A* 1,2
Smith, R M (Canterbury) 1955 *A* 1
Smith, W E (Nelson) 1905 *A*
Smith, W R (Canterbury) 1980 *A* 1, 1982 *A* 1,2,3, 1983 *BI* 2,3, *S*, *E*, 1984 *F* 1,2, *A* 1,2,3, 1985 *E* 1,2, *A*, *Arg* 2
Snow, E M (Nelson) 1929 *A* 1,2,3
Solomon, F (Auckland) 1931 *A*, 1932 *A* 2,3
Sonntag, W T C (Otago) 1929 *A* 1,2,3

Speight, M W (Waikato) 1986 *A* 1
Spencer, J C (Wellington) 1905 *A*, 1907 *A* 1(R)
Spiers, J E (Counties) 1979 *S, E,* 1981 *R, F* 1,2
Spillane, A P (South Canterbury) 1913 *A* 2,3,
Stanley, J T (Auckland) 1986 *F* 1, *A* 1,2,3, *F* 2,3, 1987
[*It, Fj, Arg, S, W, F*], *A*, 1988 *W* 1,2, *A* 1,2,3, 1989 *F*
1,2, *Arg* 1,2, *A, W, I,* 1990 *S* 1,2
Stead, J W (Southland) 1904 *BI*, 1905 *S, I, E,* 1906 *F,*
1908 *AW* 1,3
Steel, A G (Canterbury) 1966 *BI* 1,2,3,4, 1967 *A, F, S,*
1968 *A* 1,2
Steel, J (West Coast) 1921 *SA* 1,2,3, 1924 *W,* 1925 *E, F*
Steele, L B (Wellington) 1951 *A* 1,2,3
Steere, E R G (Hawke's Bay) 1930 *BI* 1,2,3,4, 1931 *A,*
1932 *A* 1
Stensness, L (Auckland) 1993 *BI* 3, *A, WS*

Stephens, O G (Wellington) 1968 *F* 3
Stevens, I N (Wellington) 1972 *S,* 1973 *E* 1, 1974 *A* 3
Stewart, A J (Canterbury, South Canterbury) 1963 *E*
1,2, *I, W,* 1964 *E, S, F, A* 3
Stewart, J D (Auckland) 1913 *A* 2,3
Stewart, K W (Southland) 1973 *E* 2, 1974 *A* 1,2,3, *I,*
1975 *S,* 1976 *I, SA* 1,3, 1979 *S, E,* 1981 *SA* 1,2
Stewart, R T (South Canterbury, Canterbury) 1928 *SA*
1,2,3,4, 1930 *BI* 2
Stohr, L B (Taranaki) 1910 *A* 1,2,3
Stone, A M (Waikato, Bay of Plenty) 1981 *F* 1,2, 1983
BI 3(R), 1984 *A* 3, 1986 *F* 1, *A* 1,3, *F* 2,3
Storey, P W (South Canterbury) 1921 *SA* 1,2
Strachan, A D (Auckland, North Harbour) 1992 *Wld*
2,3, *I* 1,2, *A* 1,2,3, *SA,* 1993 *BI* 1
Strahan, S C (Manawatu) 1967 *A, E, W, F, S,* 1968 *A*

All Black John Timu (20 caps), with team-mate Frank Bunce (16 caps) in support.

315

NEW ZEALAND INTERNATIONAL RECORDS

Both team and individual records are for official New Zealand international matches, up to 31 March 1994.

TEAM RECORDS

Highest score
74 v Fiji (74-13) 1987 Christchurch

v individual countries
60 v Argentina (60-9) 1989 Dunedin
38 v Australia $\begin{cases} (38\text{-}13) \ 1936 \ \text{Dunedin} \\ (38\text{-}3) \ 1972 \ \text{Auckland} \end{cases}$
38 v B Isles (38-6) 1983 Auckland
29 v Canada (29-13) 1991 Lille
42 v England (42-15) 1985 Wellington
74 v Fiji (74-13) 1987 Christchurch
38 v France (38-8) 1906 Paris
59 v Ireland (59-6) 1992 Wellington
70 v Italy (70-6) 1987 Auckland
14 v Romania (14-6) 1981 Bucharest
27 v S Africa (27-24) 1992 Johannesburg
51 v Scotland (51-15) 1993 Murrayfield
51 v United States (51-3) 1913 Berkeley
54 v Wales (54-9) 1988 Auckland
35 v W Samoa (35-13) 1993 Auckland

Biggest winning points margin
64 v Italy (70-6) 1987 Auckland

v individual countries
51 v Argentina (60-9) 1989 Dublin
35 v Australia (38-3) 1972 Auckland
32 v B Isles (38-6) 1983 Auckland
16 v Canada (29-13) 1991 Lille
27 v England (42-15) 1985 Wellington
61 v Fiji (74-13) 1987 Christchurch
30 v France (38-8) 1906 Paris
53 v Ireland (59-6) 1992 Wellington
64 v Italy (70-6) 1987 Auckland
8 v Romania (14-6) 1981 Bucharest
17 v S Africa (20-3) 1965 Auckland
36 v Scotland (51-15) 1993 Murrayfield
48 v United States (51-3) 1913 Berkeley
49 v Wales (52-3) 1988 Christchurch
22 v W Samoa (35-13) 1993 Auckland

Longest winning sequence
17 matches – 1965-69

Highest score by opposing team
30 Australia (16-30) 1978 Auckland

by individual countries
21 Argentina (21-21) 1985 Buenos Aires
30 Australia (16-30) 1978 Auckland
20 B Isles (7-20) 1993 Wellington
13 Canada (29-13) 1991 Lille
16 England (10-16) 1973 Auckland
13 Fiji (74-13) 1987 Christchurch
24 France (19-24) 1979 Auckland
21 Ireland (24-21) 1992 Dunedin
21 Italy (31-21) 1991 Leicester
6 Romania (14-6) 1981 Bucharest
24 S Africa $\begin{cases} (12\text{-}24) \ 1981 \ \text{Wellington} \\ (27\text{-}24) \ 1992 \ \text{Johannesburg} \end{cases}$
25 Scotland (25-25) 1983 Edinburgh
6 United States (46-6) 1991 Gloucester
16 Wales (19-16) 1972 Cardiff
13 W Samoa (35-13) 1993 Auckland

Biggest losing points margin
17 v S Africa (0-17) 1928 Durban

v individual countries
16 v Australia (10-26) 1980 Sydney
13 v B Isles (7-20) 1993 Wellington
13 v England (0-13) 1936 Twickenham
13 v France (3-16) 1986 Nantes
17 v S Africa (0-17) 1928 Durban
5 v Wales (8-13) 1953 Cardiff
No defeats v Argentina, Canada, Fiji, Ireland, Italy, Romania, Scotland, United States or Western Samoa

---

Longest losing sequence
6 matches – 1949

Most tries by New Zealand in an international
13 v United States (51-3) Berkeley

Most tries against New Zealand in an international
5 by $\begin{cases} \text{S Africa (6-17) 1937 Auckland} \\ \text{Australia (16-30) 1978 Auckland} \\ \text{World XV (54-26) 1992 Wellington} \end{cases}$

Most points on overseas tour (all matches)
868 in B Isles/France (33 matches) 1905-06

Most tries on overseas tour
215 in B Isles/France (33 matches) 1905-06

INDIVIDUAL RECORDS

Most capped player
G W Whetton   58   1981-91
J J Kirwan   58   1984-93
in individual positions
Full-back
D B Clarke   31   1956-64
Wing
J J Kirwan   58   1984-93
Centre (includes 2nd five-eighth)
B J Robertson   34   1972-81
1st five-eighth
G J Fox   46   1985-93
Scrum-half
S M Going   29   1967-77
Prop
S C McDowell   46   1985-92
Hooker
S B T Fitzpatrick   56   1986-93
Lock
G W Whetton   58   1981-91
Flanker
K R Tremain   36(38)[1]   1959-68
I A Kirkpatrick   36(39)[2]   1967-77
No 8
M G Mexted   34   1979-85
[1]*Tremain won 2 caps as a No 8*
[2]*Kirkpatrick won 3 caps as a No 8*

Longest international career
E Hughes   15 seasons   1907-21
C E Meads   15 seasons   1957-71

Most consecutive internationals – 54
S B T Fitzpatrick 1986-93

Most internationals as captain – 30
W J Whineray 1958-65

Most points in internationals – 645
G J Fox (46 matches) 1985-93

Most points in an international – 26
A R Hewson v Australia 1982 Auckland
G J Fox v Fiji 1987 Christchurch

Most tries in internationals – 34
J J Kirwan (58 matches) 1984-93

Most tries in an international – 4
D McGregor v England 1905 Crystal Palace
C I Green v Fiji 1987 Christchurch

J A Gallagher v Fiji 1987 Christchurch
J J Kirwan v Wales 1988 Christchurch

Most conversions in internationals – 118
G J Fox (46 matches) 1985-93

Most conversions in an international – 10
G J Fox v Fiji 1987 Christchurch

Most dropped goals in internationals – 7
G J Fox (46 matches) 1985-93

Most dropped goals in an international – 2
O D Bruce v Ireland 1978 Dublin
F M Botica v France 1986 Christchurch

Most penalty goals in internationals – 128
G J Fox (46 matches) 1985-93

Most penalty goals in an international – 7
G J Fox v W Samoa 1993 Auckland

Most points in international series – 46
A R Hewson (4 appearances) v B Isles 1983

Most points in international series on tour – 38
G J Fox (2 appearances) 1990 France

Most tries in international series on tour – 5
K Svenson (4 appearances) 1924-25
   B Isles/France
Svenson scored in each match of the international series

Most points on tour – 230
W J Wallace (25 appearances) 1905-06
   B Isles/France

Most tries on tour – 42
J Hunter (23 appearances) 1905-06
   B Isles/France

Most points in a tour match – 43
R M Deans v South Australia 1984
   Adelaide

Most tries in a tour match – 8
T R Heeps v Northern NSW 1962
   Quirindi

CHAMPION QUALITY TO THE FORE

THE 1993 SEASON IN AUSTRALIA
Greg Campbell

This was a season in which the Wallabies faced wide and varied challenges, mounting pressure and abnormal adversity through injury and illness. Although they lost three Tests, one more than in the two previous seasons combined, they continued to rewrite the record books and, in the eyes of most judges, maintained their status as the number one team in the world. It was a season in which Australia were forced to rely on their true grit and character rather than the skill and flair which had been their signature in previous years. It was also a year which brought sadness with the passing of Australian Rugby Football Union president and chairman Mr Joe French, a much-loved and admired man who led the game in this country away from the trapdoor of failure and into the penthouse of success.

During the year, the Wallabies toured three different countries, were led by two different Test captains and capped nine new internationals, taking the tally to an amazing 15 Test debutants in two years. The Bledisloe Cup was lost to New Zealand but the Ford Australia Cup was secured with a 2-1 series win over South Africa at home, while the Bicentenary Trophy was retained against France, thanks to a record winning margin in Paris. New Zealand, South Africa and France were among the five nations the Wallabies tackled with the remaining opponents being the physical Tongans and the vastly improving Canadians.

The highlight of the domestic season was the tour to Australia by South Africa. It was their first visit since the demonstration-marred 1971 tour and they attracted record crowds, including ground records at the Sydney Football Stadium and at Ballymore. The Australians prepared for the South Africans with a Test against Tonga, which saw the Wallabies manage a record 52-14 victory before the one-off Bledisloe Cup encounter against the All Blacks in Dunedin, the timing which was far from ideal for the Wallabies.

The All Blacks were well prepared to take on the Wallabies after the Test series against the British Lions and the Wallabies' winning plans were further dented by the injury to scrum-half Peter Slattery and the severe stomach illness to captain Michael Lynagh, which forced him to have emergency surgery and, as a result, sidelined him for the remainder of the domestic season. Added to these fracturing blows were the loss of world-class lock John Eales and powerhouse flanker Willie Ofahengaue for the entire year because of injury.

The Test series with South Africa also saw the ARFU break new ground by playing a Test under lights. This First Test proved to be a marvellous spectacle with a record crowd, soaring television ratings and widespread interest across the country. But unfortunately the script did not go according to plan for the Wallabies as the South Africans recorded a deserved 19-12 win, scoring three tries to nil in the process. The Wallabies were now facing a series defeat and had registered successive losses. Public criticism and media inquests followed, and the national team had their backs to the wall. But the Wallabies' champion qualities surfaced in the do-or-die Second Test in Brisbane and, despite an early intercept try by South Africa, they responded magnificently to win 28-20 with new cap Ilie Tabua leading the charge. The series decider in Sydney was clinched 19-12 through a controlled performance and the dash of the mercurial David Campese.

At the end of the year, the Wallabies headed off to North America and France. The North American leg saw the Australians play a non-Test match against the American Eagles in heatwave temperatures before encountering freezing, snow-driven conditions in their next match, against Canada B in Calgary. It was hardly the ideal build-up to the Test against Canada days later, but the Wallabies had enough class to run away 43-16, Campese adding three touchdowns and extending his world record to 57 tries.

In France, never a happy hunting-ground for past touring teams, the Wallabies enjoyed unprecedented success, losing only the First Test (16-13) and one tour match. The First Test loss in Bordeaux once again raised doubts over the team and pressure was building, particularly on coach Bob Dwyer, who was seeking reappointment until after the 1995 World Cup. The Wallabies' 24-3 Second Test win in Paris was their first ever in this city and furthermore the 21-point winning margin was a record. On his return, Dwyer was re-elected until after the World Cup and Peter Falk was named manager ahead of John Breen.

The year saw Marty Roebuck announce his retirement while Nick Farr-Jones once again closed his representative career after responding to an SOS call from the selectors after Slattery was injured against Tonga. Also announcing his retirement was experienced Test referee Sandy MacNeill. On the administration side, long-serving treasurer John Howard stepped down after 17 distinguished years in office.

In sevens rugby, the Wallabies reached the semi-final of the Hong Kong Sevens, where they were beaten by runners-up Fiji, and lost to England in the final of the inaugural Rugby World Cup Sevens in Scotland.

The game in Australia continued to grow at grass-roots level and statistics revealed that the number of rugby players under 19 years of age had soared by 54.7 per cent since 1990. Queensland were the dominant state side, winning the Digital State of the Union series 2-0 over New South Wales, while both state teams failed to reach the final of the Super-10 championship. At club level, Gordon won their first Sydney premiership since 1976, beating Warringah in the grand final, while Southern Districts successfully defended their Brisbane title with victory over one of Brisbane's emerging clubs, Sunnybank.

AUSTRALIAN INTERNATIONAL PLAYERS *(up to 31 March 1994)*

ABBREVIATIONS

Arg – Argentina; *BI* – British Isles teams; *C* – Canada; *E* – England; *F* – France; *Fj* – Fiji; *I* – Ireland; *It* – Italy; *J* – Japan; *M* – Maoris; *NZ* – New Zealand; *S* – Scotland; *SA* – South Africa; *SK* – South Korea; *Tg* – Tonga; *US* – United States of America; *W* – Wales; *WS* – Western Samoa; (R) – Replacement; (t) – temporary replacement. Entries in square brackets [ ] indicate appearances in the Rugby World Cup.

STATE ABBREVIATIONS

ACT – Australian Capital Territory; NSW – New South Wales; Q – Queensland; V – Victoria; WA – Western Australia.

N.B. In the summer of 1986, the ARU retrospectively granted full Australian Test status to the five international matches played by the 1927-28 touring team to Europe. In 1988 Test status was extended to all those who played overseas in the 1920s.

Note: When a series has taken place, figures denote the particular matches in which players featured. Thus 1963 *SA* 2,4 indicates that a player appeared in the second and fourth Tests of the 1963 series against South Africa.

Abrahams, A M F (NSW) 1967 *NZ*, 1968 *NZ* 1, 1969 *W*
Adams, N J (NSW) 1955 *NZ* 1
Adamson, R W (NSW) 1912 *US*
Allan, T (NSW) 1946 *NZ* 1, *M*, *NZ* 2, 1947 *NZ* 2, *S*, *I*, *W*, 1948 *E*, *F*, 1949 *M* 1,2,3, *NZ* 1,2
Anlezark, E A (NSW) 1905 *NZ*
Armstrong, A R (NSW) 1923 *NZ* 1,2
Austin, L R (NSW) 1963 *E*

Baker, R L (NSW) 1904 *BI* 1,2
Baker, W H (NSW) 1914 *NZ* 1,2,3
Ballesty, J P (NSW) 1968 *NZ* 1,2, *F*, *I*, *S*, 1969 *W*, *SA* 2,3,4
Bannon, D P (NSW) 1946 *M*
Bardsley, E J (NSW) 1928 *NZ* 1,3, *M* (R)
Barker, H S (NSW) 1952 *Fj* 1,2, *NZ* 1,2, 1953 *SA* 4, 1954 *Fj* 1,2
Barnett, J T (NSW) 1907 *NZ* 1,2,3, 1908 *W*, 1909 *E*
Barry, M J (Q) 1971 *SA* 3
Barton, R F D (NSW) 1899 *BI* 3
Batch, P G (Q) 1975 *S*, *W*, 1976 *E*, *Fj* 1,2,3, *F* 1,2, 1978 *W* 1,2, *NZ* 1,2,3, 1979 *Arg* 2
Batterham, R P (NSW) 1967 *NZ*, 1970 *S*
Battishall, B R (NSW) 1973 *E*
Baxter, A J (NSW) 1949 *M* 1,2,3, *NZ* 1,2, 1951 *NZ* 1,2, 1952 *NZ* 1,2
Baxter, T J (Q) 1958 *NZ* 3
Beith, B McN (NSW) 1914 *NZ* 3
Bell, K R (Q) 1968 *S*
Bennett, W G (Q) 1931 *M*, 1933 *SA* 1,2,3
Bermingham, J V (Q) 1934 *NZ* 1,2, 1937 *SA* 1
Berne, J E (NSW) 1975 *S*
Besomo, K S (NSW) 1979 *I* 2
Betts, T N (Q) 1951 *NZ* 2,3, 1954 *Fj* 2
Biilmann, R R (NSW) 1933 *SA* 1,2,3,4
Birt, R (Q) 1914 *NZ* 2
Black, J (NSW) 1985 *C* 1,2, *NZ*, *Fj* 1
Blackwood, J G (NSW) 1923 *NZ* 1,2,3, 1925 *NZ*, 1927 *I*, *W*, *S*, 1928 *E*, *F*
Blair, M R (NSW) 1928 *F*, 1931 *M*, *NZ*
Bland, G V (NSW) 1928 *NZ* 3, *M*, 1932 *NZ* 1,2,3, 1933 *SA* 1,2,4,5
Blomley, J (NSW) 1949 *M* 1,2,3, *NZ* 1,2, 1950 *BI* 1,2
Boland, S B (Q) 1899 *BI* 3,4, 1903 *NZ*
Bond, J H (NSW) 1921 *NZ*
Bonis, E T (Q) 1929 *NZ* 1,2,3, 1930 *BI*, 1931 *M*, *NZ*, 1932 *NZ* 1,2,3, 1933 *SA* 1,2,3,4,5, 1934 *NZ* 1,2, 1936 *NZ* 1,2, *M*, 1937 *SA* 1, *NZ* 1
Bosler, J M (NSW) 1953 *SA* 1
Bouffler, R G (NSW) 1899 *BI* 3
Bourke, T K (Q) 1947 *NZ* 2
Bowen, S (NSW) 1993 *SA* 1,2,3
Bowers, A J A (NSW) 1923 *NZ* 3, 1925 *NZ*, 1927 *I*
Boyce, E S (NSW) 1962 *NZ* 1,2, 1964 *NZ* 1,2,3, 1965 *SA* 1,2, 1966 *W*, *S*, 1967 *E*, *I* 1, *F*, *I* 2
Boyce, J S (NSW) 1962 *NZ* 3,4,5, 1963 *E*, *SA* 1,2,3,4, 1964 *NZ* 1,3, 1965 *SA* 1,2

Boyd, A (NSW) 1899 *BI* 3
Boyd, A F McC (Q) 1958 *M* 1
Brass, J E (NSW) 1966 *BI* 2, *W*, *S*, 1967 *E*, *I* 1, *F*, *I* 2, *NZ*, 1968 *NZ* 1, *F*, *I*, *S*
Breckenridge, J W (NSW) 1927 *I*, *W*, *S*, 1928 *E*, *F*, 1929 *NZ* 1,2,3, 1930 *BI*
Brial, M C (NSW) 1993 *F* 1(R), 2
Bridle, O L (V) 1931 *M*, 1932 *NZ* 1,2,3, 1933 *SA* 3,4,5, 1934 *NZ* 1,2, 1936 *NZ* 1,2, *M*
Broad, E G (Q) 1949 *M* 1
Brockhoff, J D (NSW) 1949 *M* 2,3, *NZ* 1,2, 1950 *BI* 1,2, 1951 *NZ* 2,3
Brown, B R (Q) 1972 *NZ* 1,3
Brown, J V (NSW) 1956 *SA* 1,2, 1957 *NZ* 1,2, 1958 *W*, *I*, *E*, *S*, *F*
Brown, R C (NSW) 1975 *E* 1,2
Brown, S W (NSW) 1953 *SA* 2,3,4
Bryant, H (NSW) 1925 *NZ*
Buchan, A J (NSW) 1946 *NZ* 1,2, 1947 *NZ* 1,2, *S*, *I*, *W*, 1948 *E*, *F*, 1949 *M* 3
Bull, D (NSW) 1928 *M*
Buntine, H (NSW) 1923 *NZ* 1(R)
Burdon, A (NSW) 1903 *NZ*, 1904 *BI* 1,2, 1905 *NZ*
Burge, A B (NSW) 1907 *NZ* 3, 1908 *W*
Burge, P H (NSW) 1907 *NZ* 1,2,3
Burge, R (NSW) 1928 *NZ* 1,2,3(R), *M* (R)
Burke, B T (NSW) 1988 *S* (R)
Burke, C T (NSW) 1946 *NZ* 2, 1947 *NZ* 1,2, *S*, *I*, *W*, 1948 *E*, *F*, 1949 *M* 2,3, *NZ* 1,2, 1950 *BI* 1,2, 1951 *NZ* 1,2,3, 1953 *SA* 2,3,4, 1954 *Fj* 1, 1955 *NZ* 1,2,3, 1956 *SA* 1,2
Burke, M (NSW) 1993 *SA* 3(R), *F* 1
Burke, M P (NSW) 1984 *E* (R), *I*, 1985 *C* 1,2, *NZ*, *Fj* 1,2, 1986 *It*(R), *F*, *Arg* 1,2, *NZ* 1,2,3, 1987 *SK*, [*US*, *J*, *I*, *F*, *W*], *NZ*, *Arg* 1,2
Burnet, D R (NSW) 1972 *F* 1,2, *NZ* 1,2,3, *Fj*
Butler, O F (NSW) 1969 *SA* 1,2, 1970 *S*, 1971 *SA* 2,3, *F* 1,2

Calcraft, W J (NSW) 1985 *C* 1, 1986 *It*, *Arg* 2
Caldwell, B C (NSW) 1928 *NZ* 3
Cameron, A S (NSW) 1951 *NZ* 1,2,3, 1952 *Fj* 1,2, *NZ* 1,2, 1953 *SA* 1,2,3,4, 1954 *Fj* 1,2, 1955 *NZ* 1,2,3, 1956 *SA* 1,2, 1957 *NZ* 1, 1958 *I*
Campbell, J D (NSW) 1910 *NZ* 1,2,3
Campbell, W A (Q) 1984 *Fj*, 1986 *It*, *F*, *Arg* 1,2, *NZ* 1,2,3, 1987 *SK*, [*E*, *US*, *J*(R), *I*, *F*], *NZ*, 1988 *E*, 1989 *BI* 1,2,3, *NZ*, 1990 *NZ* 2,3
Campese, D I (ACT, NSW) 1982 *NZ* 1,2,3, 1983 *US*, *Arg* 1,2, *NZ*, *It*, *F* 1,2, 1984 *Fj*, *NZ* 1,2,3, *E*, *I*, *W*, *S*, 1985 *Fj* 1,2, 1986 *It*, *F*, *Arg* 1,2, *NZ* 1,2,3, 1987 [*E*, *US*, *J*, *I*, *F*, *W*], *NZ*, 1988 *E* 1,2, *NZ* 1,2,3, *E*, *S*, *It*, 1989 *BI* 1,2,3, *NZ*, *F* 1,2, 1990 *F* 2,3, *US*, *NZ* 1,2,3, 1991 *W*, *E*, *NZ* 1,2, [*Arg*, *WS*, *W*, *I*, *NZ*, *E*], 1992 *S* 1,2, *NZ* 1,2,3, *SA*, *I*, *W*, 1993 *Tg*, *NZ*, *SA* 1,2,3, *C*, *F* 1,2
Canniffe, W D (Q) 1907 *NZ* 2
Carberry, C M (NSW, Q) 1973 *Tg* 2, *E*, 1976 *I*, *US*, *Fj* 1,2,3, 1981 *F* 1,2, *I*, *W*, *S*, 1982 *E*

321

Manning, R C S (Q) 1967 *NZ*
Mansfield, B W (NSW) 1975 *J* 2
Marks, H (NSW) 1899 *BI* 1,2
Marks, R J P (Q) 1962 *NZ* 4,5, 1963 *E, SA* 2,3,4, 1964 *NZ* 1,2,3, 1965 *SA* 1,2, 1966 *W, S,* 1967 *E, I* 1, *F, I* 2
Marrott, W J (NSW) 1923 *NZ* 1,2
Marshall, J S (NSW) 1949 *M* 1
Martin, G J (Q) 1989 *BI* 1,2,3, *NZ, F* 1,2, 1990 *F* 1,3 (R), *NZ* 1
Martin, M C (NSW) 1980 *Fj, NZ* 1,2, 1981 *F* 1,2, *W* (R)
Massey-Westropp, M (NSW) 1914 *NZ* 3
Mathers, M J (NSW) 1980 *Fj, NZ* 2 (R)
Maund, J W (NSW) 1903 *NZ*
Meadows, J E C (V, Q) 1974 *NZ* 1, 1975 *S, W,* 1976 *I, US, Fj* 1,3, *F* 1,2, 1978 *NZ* 1,2,3, 1956 *SA* 1,2, 1957 1982 *E, NZ* 2,3, 1983 *US, Arg* 2, *NZ*
Meadows, R W (NSW) 1958 *M* 1,2,3, *NZ* 1,2,3
Meagher, F W (NSW) 1923 *NZ* 3, 1925 *NZ,* 1927 *I, W*
Meibusch, J H (Q) 1904 *BI* 3
Meibusch, L S (Q) 1912 *US*
Melrose, T C (NSW) 1978 *NZ* 3, 1979 *I* 1,2, *NZ, Arg* 1,2
Messenger, H H (NSW) 1907 *NZ* 2,3
Middleton, S A (NSW) 1909 *E,* 1910 *NZ* 1,2,3
Miller, A R (NSW) 1952 *Fj* 1,2, *NZ* 1,2, 1953 *SA* 1,2,3,4, 1954 *Fj* 1,2, 1955 *NZ* 1,2,3, 1956 *SA* 1,2, 1957 *NZ* 1,2, 1958 *W, E, S, F, M* 1,2,3, 1959 *BI* 1,2, 1961 *Fj* 1,2,3, *SA* 2, *F,* 1962 *NZ* 1,2, 1966 *BI* 1,2, *W, S,* 1967 *I* 1, *F, I* 2, *NZ*
Miller, J M (NSW) 1962 *NZ* 1, 1963 *E, SA* 1, 1966 *W, S,* 1967 *E*
Miller, J S (Q) 1986 *NZ* 2,3, 1987 *SK, [US, I, F], NZ, Arg* 1,2, 1988 *E* 1,2, *NZ* 2,3,4, *E, S, It,* 1989 *BI* 1,2,3, *NZ,* 1990 *F* 1,3, 1991 *W, [WS, W, I]*
Miller, S W J (NSW) 1899 *BI* 3
Mingey, N (NSW) 1923 *NZ* 1,2
Monaghan, L E (NSW) 1973 *E,* 1974 *NZ* 1,2,3, 1975 *E* 1,2, *S, W,* 1976 *E, I, US, F* 1, 1978 *W* 1,2, *NZ* 1, 1979 *I* 1,2
Monti, C I A (Q) 1938 *NZ* 2
Moon, B J (Q) 1978 *NZ* 2,3, 1979 *I* 1,2, *NZ, Arg* 1,2, 1980 *Fj, NZ* 1,2,3, 1981 *F* 1,2, *I, W, S,* 1982 *E, S* 1,2, 1983 *US, Arg* 1,2, *NZ, It, F* 1,2, 1984 *Fj, NZ* 1,2,3, *E,* 1986 *It, F, Arg* 1,2
Mooney, T P (Q) 1954 *Fj* 1,2
Moran, H M (NSW) 1908 *W*
Morgan, G (Q) 1992 *NZ* 1(R), 3(R), *W,* 1993 *Tg, NZ, SA* 1,2,3, *C, F* 1,2
Morrissey, C V (NSW) 1925 *NZ*
Morrissey, W (Q) 1914 *NZ* 2
Morton, A R (NSW) 1957 *NZ* 1,2, 1958 *F, M* 1,2,3, 1959 *BI* 1,2
Mossop, R P (NSW) 1949 *NZ* 1,2, 1950 *BI* 1,2, 1951 *NZ* 1
Moutray, I E (NSW) 1963 *SA* 2
Munsie, A (NSW) 1928 *NZ* 2
Murdoch, A (NSW) 1993 *F* 1
Murphy, P J (Q) 1910 *NZ* 1,2,3, 1913 *NZ* 1,2,3, 1914 *NZ* 1,2,3
Murphy, W (Q) 1912 *US*

Nasser, B P (Q) 1989 *F* 1,2, 1990 *F* 1,2,3, *US, NZ* 2, 1991 *[WS]*
Nicholson, F C (Q) 1904 *BI* 3
Nicholson, F V (Q) 1903 *NZ,* 1904 *BI* 1
Niuqila, A S (NSW) 1988 *S, It,* 1989 *BI* 1
Nothling, O E (NSW) 1921 *NZ,* 1923 *NZ* 1,2,3
Nucifora, D V (Queensland) 1991 *[Arg*(R)], 1993 *C*(R)

O'Brien, F W H (NSW) 1937 *SA* 2, 1938 *NZ* 3
O'Connor, J A (NSW) 1928 *NZ* 1,2,3, *M*
O'Connor, M D (ACT, Q) 1979 *Arg* 1,2, 1980 *Fj, NZ* 1,2,3, 1981 *F* 1,2, *I,* 1982 *E, S* 1,2
O'Donnell, C (NSW) 1913 *NZ* 1,2
O'Donnell, I C (NSW) 1899 *BI* 1,2
O'Donnell, J B (NSW) 1928 *NZ* 1,3, *M*
O'Donnell, J M (NSW) 1899 *BI* 4
O'Gorman, J F (NSW) 1961 *Fj* 1, *SA* 1,2, *F,* 1962 *NZ* 2, 1963 *E, SA* 1,2,3,4, 1965 *SA* 1,2, 1966 *W, S,* 1967 *E, I* 1, *F, I* 2
O'Neill, D J (Q) 1964 *NZ* 1,2
O'Neill, J M (Q) 1952 *NZ* 1,2, 1956 *SA* 1,2
Ofahengaue, V (NSW) 1990 *NZ* 1,2,3, 1991 *W, E, NZ*

1,2, *[Arg, W, I, NZ, E],* 1992 *S* 1,2, *SA, I, W*
Osborne, D H (V) 1975 *E* 1,2, *J* 1
Outterside, R (NSW) 1959 *BI* 1,2
Oxenham, A McE (Q) 1904 *BI* 2, 1907 *NZ* 2
Oxlade, A M (Q) 1904 *BI* 2,3, 1905 *NZ,* 1907 *NZ* 2
Oxlade, B D (Q) 1938 *NZ* 1,2,3

Palfreyman, J R L (NSW) 1929 *NZ* 1, 1930 *BI,* 1931 *NZ,* 1932 *NZ* 3
Papworth, B (NSW) 1985 *Fj* 1,2, 1986 *It, Arg* 1,2, *NZ* 1,2,3, 1987 *[E, US, J* (R), *I, F], NZ, Arg* 1,2
Parker, A J (Q) 1983 *Arg* 1 (R), 2, *NZ*
Parkinson, C E (Q) 1907 *NZ* 2
Pashley, J J (NSW) 1954 *Fj* 1,2, 1958 *M* 1,2,3
Pauling, T P (NSW) 1936 *NZ* 1, 1937 *SA* 1
Pearse, G K (NSW) 1975 *W* (R), 1976 *I, US, Fj* 1,2,3, 1978 *NZ* 1,2,3
Penman, A P (NSW) 1905 *NZ*
Perrin, P D (Q) 1962 *NZ* 1
Perrin, T D (NSW) 1931 *M, NZ*
Phelps, R (NSW) 1955 *NZ* 2,3, 1956 *SA* 1,2, 1957 *NZ* 1,2, 1958 *W, I, E, S, F, M* 1, *NZ* 1,2,3, 1961 *Fj* 1,2,3, *SA* 1,2, *F,* 1962 *NZ* 1,2
Phipps, J A (NSW) 1953 *SA* 1,2,3,4, 1954 *Fj* 1,2, 1955 *NZ* 1,2,3, 1956 *SA* 1,2
Phipps, W J (NSW) 1928 *NZ* 2
Pilecki, S J (Q) 1978 *W* 1,2, *NZ* 1,2, 1979 *I* 1,2, *NZ, Arg* 1,2, 1980 *Fj, NZ* 1,2, 1982 *S* 1,2, 1983 *US, Arg* 1,2, *NZ*
Piper, B J C (NSW) 1946 *NZ* 1, *M, NZ* 2, 1947 *NZ* 1, *S, I, W,* 1948 *E, F,* 1949 *M* 1,2,3
Poidevin, S P (NSW) 1980 *Fj, NZ* 1,2,3, 1981 *F* 1,2, *I, W, S,* 1982 *E, NZ* 1,2,3, 1983 *US, Arg* 1,2, *NZ, It, F* 1,2, 1984 *Fj, NZ* 1,2,3, *E, I, W, S,* 1985 *C* 1,2, *NZ, Fj* 1,2, 1986 *It, F, Arg* 1,2, *NZ* 1,2,3, 1987 *SK, [E, J, I, F, W], Arg* 1, 1988 *NZ* 1,2,3, 1989 *NZ,* 1991 *E, NZ* 1,2, *[Arg, W, I, NZ, E]*
Pope, A M (Q) 1968 *NZ* 2 (R)
Potter, R T (Q) 1961 *Fj* 2
Potts, J M (NSW) 1957 *NZ* 1,2, 1958 *W, I,* 1959 *BI* 1
Prentice, C W (NSW) 1914 *NZ* 3
Prentice, W S (NSW) 1908 *W,* 1909 *E,* 1910 *NZ* 1,2,3, 1912 *US*
Price, R A (NSW) 1974 *NZ* 1,2,3, 1975 *E* 1,2, *J* 1,2, 1976 *US*
Primmer, C J (Q) 1951 *NZ* 1,3
Proctor, I J (NSW) 1967 *NZ* 1
Prosser, R B (NSW) 1967 *E, I* 1,2, *NZ,* 1968 *NZ* 1,2, *F, I, S,* 1969 *W, SA* 1,2,3,4, 1971 *SA* 1,2,3, *F* 1,2, 1972 *F* 1,2, *NZ* 1,2,3, *Fj*
Pugh, G H (NSW) 1912 *US*
Purcell, M P (Q) 1966 *W, S,* 1967 *I* 2
Purkis, E M (NSW) 1958 *S, M* 1

Ramalli, C (NSW) 1938 *NZ* 2,3
Ramsay, K M (NSW) 1936 *M,* 1937 *SA* 1, 1938 *NZ* 1,3
Rankin, R (NSW) 1936 *NZ* 1,2, *M,* 1937 *SA* 1,2, 1938 *NZ* 1,2
Rathie, D S (Q) 1972 *F* 1,2
Raymond, R L (NSW) 1921 *NZ*
Redwood, C (Q) 1903 *NZ,* 1904 *BI* 1,2,3
Reid, E J (NSW) 1925 *NZ*
Reid, T W (NSW) 1961 *Fj* 1,2,3, *SA* 1, 1962 *NZ* 1
Reilly, N P (Q) 1968 *NZ* 1,2, *F, I, S,* 1969 *W, SA* 1,2,3,4
Reynolds, L J (NSW) 1910 *NZ* 2 (R), 3
Reynolds, R J (NSW) 1984 *Fj, NZ* 1,2,3, 1985 *Fj* 1,2, 1986 *Arg* 1,2, *NZ* 1, 1987 *[J]*
Richards, E W (Q) 1904 *BI* 1,3, 1905 *NZ,* 1907 *NZ* 1 (R), 2
Richards, G (NSW) 1978 *NZ* 2 (R), 3, 1981 *F* 1
Richards, T J (Q) 1908 *W,* 1909 *E,* 1912 *US*
Richards, V S (NSW) 1936 *NZ* 1,2 (R), *M,* 1937 *SA* 1, 1938 *NZ* 1
Richardson, G C (Q) 1971 *SA* 1,2,3, 1972 *NZ* 2,3, *Fj,* 1973 *Tg* 1,2, *W*
Rigney, W A (NSW) 1925 *NZ*
Riley, S A (NSW) 1903 *NZ*
Roberts, B T (NSW) 1956 *SA* 2
Roberts, H F (Q) 1961 *Fj* 1,3, *SA* 2, *F*
Robertson, I J (NSW) 1975 *J* 1,2
Roche, C (Q) 1982 *S* 1,2, *NZ* 1,2,3, 1983 *US, Arg* 1,2, *NZ, It, F* 1,2, 1984 *Fj, NZ* 1,2,3, *I*
Rodriguez, E E (NSW) 1984 *Fj, NZ* 1,2,3, *E, I, W, S,*

1985 *C* 1,2, *NZ*, *Fj* 1, 1986 *It*, *F*, *Arg* 1,2, *NZ* 1,2,3, 1987 *SK*, [*E*, *J*, *W* (R)], *NZ*, *Arg* 1,2
Roebuck, M C (NSW) 1991 *W*, *E*, *NZ* 1,2, [*Arg*, *WS*, *W*, *I*, *NZ*, *E*], 1992 *S* 1,2, *NZ* 2,3, *SA*, *I*, *W*, 1993 *Tg*, *SA* 1,2,3, *C*, *F* 2
Rose, H A (NSW) 1967 *I* 2, *NZ*, 1968 *NZ* 1,2, *F*, *I*, *S*, 1969 *W*, *SA* 1,2,3,4, 1970 *S*
Rosenblum, M E (NSW) 1928 *NZ* 1,2,3, *M*
Rosenblum, R G (NSW) 1969 *SA* 1,3, 1970 *S*
Rosewell, J S H (NSW) 1907 *NZ* 1,3
Ross, A W (NSW) 1927 *I*, *W*, *S*, 1928 *E*, *F*, 1929 *NZ* 1, 1930 *BI*, 1931 *M*, *NZ*, 1932 *NZ* 2,3, 1933 *SA* 5, 1934 *NZ* 1,2
Ross, W S (Q) 1979 *I* 1,2, *Arg* 2, 1980 *Fj*, *NZ* 1,2,3, 1982 *S* 1,2, 1983 *US*, *Arg* 1,2, *NZ*
Rothwell, P R (NSW) 1951 *NZ* 1,2,3, 1952 *Fj* 1
Row, F L (NSW) 1899 *BI* 1,3,4
Row, N E (NSW) 1907 *NZ* 1,3, 1909 *E*, 1910 *NZ* 1,2,3
Rowles, P G (NSW) 1972 *Fj*, 1973 *E*
Roxburgh, J R (NSW) 1968 *NZ* 1,2, *F*, 1969 *W*, *SA* 1,2,3,4, 1970 *S*
Ruebner, G (NSW) 1966 *BI* 1,2
Russell, C J (NSW) 1907 *NZ* 1,2,3, 1908 *W*, 1909 *E*
Ryan, J R (NSW) 1975 *J* 2, 1976 *I*, *US*, *Fj* 1,2,3
Ryan, K J (Q) 1958 *E*, *M* 1, *NZ* 1,2,3
Ryan, P F (NSW) 1963 *E*, *SA* 1, 1966 *BI* 1,2

Sampson, J H (NSW) 1899 *BI* 4
Sayle, J L (NSW) 1967 *NZ*
Schulte, B G (Q) 1946 *NZ* 1, *M*
Scott, P R I (NSW) 1962 *NZ* 1,2
Scott-Young, S J (Q) 1990 *F* 2,3 (R), *US*, *NZ* 3, 1992 *NZ* 1,2,3
Shambrook, G G (Q) 1976 *Fj* 2,3
Shaw, A A (Q) 1973 *W*, *E*, 1975 *E* 1,2, *J* 2, *S*, *W*, 1976 *E*, *I*, *US*, *Fj* 1,2,3, *F* 1,2, 1978 *W* 1,2, *NZ* 1,2,3, 1979 *I* 1,2, *NZ*, *Arg* 1,2, 1980 *Fj*, *NZ* 1,2,3, 1981 *F* 1,2, *I*, *W*, *S*, 1982 *S* 1,2
Shaw, C (NSW) 1925 *NZ* (R)
Shaw, G A (NSW) 1969 *W*, *SA* 1 (R), 1970 *S*, 1971 *SA* 1,2,3, *F* 1,2, 1973 *W*, *E*, 1974 *NZ* 1,2,3, 1975 *E* 1,2, *J* 1,2, *W*, 1976 *E*, *I*, *US*, *Fj* 1,2,3, *F* 1,2, 1979 *NZ*
Sheehan, W B J (NSW) 1923 *NZ* 1,2,3, 1927 *W*, *S*
Shehadie, N M (NSW) 1947 *NZ* 2, 1948 *E*, *F*, 1949 *M* 1,2,3, *NZ* 1,2, 1950 *BI* 1,2, 1951 *NZ* 1,2,3, 1952 *Fj* 1,2, *NZ* 2, 1953 *SA* 1,2,3,4, 1954 *Fj* 1,2, 1955 *NZ* 1,2,3, 1956 *SA* 1, 1957 *NZ* 2, 1958 *W*, *I*
Sheil, A G R (Q) 1956 *SA* 1
Shepherd, D J (V) 1964 *NZ* 3, 1965 *SA* 1,2, 1966 *BI* 1,2
Simpson, R J (NSW) 1913 *NZ* 2
Skinner, A J (NSW) 1969 *W*, *SA* 4, 1970 *S*
Slack, A G (Q) 1978 *W* 1,2, *NZ* 1,2, 1979 *NZ*, *Arg* 1,2, 1980 *Fj*, 1981 *I*, *W*, *S*, 1982 *E*, *S* 1, *NZ* 3, 1983 *US*, *Arg* 1,2, *NZ*, *It*, 1984 *Fj*, *NZ* 1,2,3, *E*, *I*, *W*, *S*, 1986 *It*, *F*, *NZ* 1,2,3, 1987 *SK*, [*E*, *US*, *J*, *I*, *F*, *W*]
Slater, S H (NSW) 1910 *NZ* 3
Slattery, P J (Q) 1990 *US* (R), 1991 *W*(R), *E*(R), [*WS*(R), *W*, *I*(R)], 1992 *I*, *W*, 1993 *Tg*, *C*, *F* 1,2
Smairl, A M (NSW) 1928 *NZ* 1,2,3
Smith, B A (Q) 1987 *SK*, [*US*, *J*, *I* (R), *W*], *Arg* 1
Smith, D (Q) 1993 *SA* 1,2,3, *C*, *F* 2
Smith, F B (NSW) 1905 *NZ*, 1907 *NZ* 1,2,3
Smith, L M (NSW) 1905 *NZ*
Smith, N C (NSW) 1923 *NZ* 1
Smith, P V (NSW) 1967 *NZ*, 1968 *NZ* 1,2, *F*, *I*, *S*, 1969 *W*, *SA* 1
Smith, R A (NSW) 1971 *SA* 1,2, 1972 *F* 1,2, *NZ* 1,2 (R), 3, *Fj*, 1975 *E* 1,2, *J* 1,2, *S*, *W*, 1976 *E*, *I*, *US*, *Fj* 1,2,3, *F* 1,2
Smith, T S (NSW) 1921 *NZ*, 1925 *NZ*
Snell, H W (NSW) 1928 *NZ* 3
Solomon, H J (NSW) 1949 *M* 3, *NZ* 2, 1950 *BI* 1,2, 1951 *NZ* 1,2, 1952 *Fj* 1,2, *NZ* 1,2, 1953 *SA* 1,2,3, 1955 *NZ* 1
Spragg, S A (NSW) 1899 *BI* 1,2,3,4,
Stanley, R G (NSW) 1921 *NZ*, 1923 *NZ* 1,2,3
Stapleton, E T (NSW) 1951 *NZ* 1,2,3, 1952 *Fj* 1,2, *NZ* 1,2, 1953 *SA* 1,2,3,4, 1954 *Fj* 1, 1955 *NZ* 1,2,3, 1958 *NZ* 1
Steggall, J C (Q) 1931 *M*, *NZ*, 1932 *NZ* 1,2,3, 1933 *SA* 1,2,3,4,5
Stegman, T R (NSW) 1973 *Tg* 1,2
Stephens, O G (NSW) 1973 *Tg* 1,2, *W*, 1974 *NZ* 2,3
Stewart, A A (NSW) 1979 *NZ*, *Arg* 1,2

Stone, A H (NSW) 1937 *SA* 2, 1938 *NZ* 2,3
Stone, C G (NSW) 1938 *NZ* 1
Stone, J M (NSW) 1946 *M*, *NZ* 2
Storey, G P (NSW) 1927 *I*, *W*, *S*, 1928 *E*, *F*, 1929 *NZ* 3 (R), 1930 *BI*
Storey, K P (NSW) 1936 *NZ* 2
Storey, N J D (NSW) 1962 *NZ* 1
Strachan, D J (NSW) 1955 *NZ* 2,3
Street, N O (NSW) 1899 *BI* 2
Streeter, S F (NSW) 1978 *NZ* 1
Stuart, R (NSW) 1910 *NZ* 2,3
Stumbles, B D (NSW) 1972 *NZ* 1 (R), 2,3, *Fj*
Sturtridge, G S (V) 1929 *NZ* 2, 1932 *NZ* 1,2,3, 1933 *SA* 1,2,3,4,5
Sullivan, P D (NSW) 1971 *SA* 1,2,3, *F* 1,2, 1972 *F* 1,2, *NZ* 1,2, *Fj*, 1973 *Tg* 1,2, *W*
Summons, A J (NSW) 1958 *W*, *I*, *E*, *S*, *M* 2, *NZ* 1,2,3, 1959 *BI* 1,2
Suttor, D C (NSW) 1913 *NZ* 1,2,3
Swannell, B I (NSW) 1905 *NZ*
Sweeney, T L (Q) 1953 *SA* 1

Taafe, B S (NSW) 1969 *SA* 1, 1972 *F* 1,2
Tabua, I (Q) 1993 *SA* 2,3, *C*, *F* 1
Tancred, A J (NSW) 1927 *I*, *W*, *S*
Tancred, J L (NSW) 1928 *F*
Tanner, W H (Q) 1899 *BI* 1,2
Tasker, W G (NSW) 1913 *NZ* 1,2,3, 1914 *NZ* 1,2,3
Tate, M J (NSW) 1951 *NZ* 3, 1952 *Fj* 1,2, *NZ* 1,2, 1953 *SA* 1, 1954 *Fj* 1,2
Taylor, D A (Q) 1968 *NZ* 1,2, *F*, *I*, *S*
Taylor, H C (NSW) 1923 *NZ* 1,2,3
Taylor, J I (NSW) 1971 *SA* 1, 1972 *F* 1,2, *Fj*
Teitzel, R G (Q) 1966 *W*, *S*, 1967 *E* 1 1, *F*, *I* 2, *NZ*
Thompson, C E (NSW) 1923 *NZ* 1
Thompson, E G (Q) 1929 *NZ* 1,2,3, 1930 *BI*
Thompson, F (NSW) 1913 *NZ* 1,2,3, 1914 *NZ* 1,2,3
Thompson, J (Q) 1914 *NZ* 1
Thompson, P D (Q) 1950 *BI* 1
Thompson, R J (WA) 1971 *SA* 3, *F* 2 (R), 1972 *Fj*
Thorn, A M (NSW) 1921 *NZ*
Thorn, E J (NSW) 1923 *NZ* 1,2,3
Thornett, J E (NSW) 1955 *NZ* 1,2,3, 1956 *SA* 1,2, 1958 *W*, *I*, *S*, *F*, *M* 2,3, *NZ* 2,3, 1959 *BI* 1,2, 1961 *Fj* 2,3, *SA* 1,2, *F*, 1962 *NZ* 2,3,4,5, 1963 *E*, *SA* 1,2,3,4, 1964 *NZ* 1,2,3, 1965 *SA* 1,2, 1966 *BI* 1,2, 1967 *F*
Thornett, R N (NSW) 1961 *Fj* 1,2,3, *SA* 1,2, *F*, 1962 *NZ* 1,2,3,4,5
Thorpe, A C (NSW) 1929 *NZ* 1 (R)
Timbury, F R V (Q) 1910 *NZ* 1,2
Tindall, E N (NSW) 1973 *Tg* 2
Toby, A E (NSW) 1925 *NZ*
Tolhurst, H A (NSW) 1931 *M*, *NZ*
Tombs, R C (NSW) 1992 *S* 1,2
Tonkin, A E J (NSW) 1947 *S*, *I*, *W*, 1948 *E*, *F*, 1950 *BI* 2
Tooth, R M (NSW) 1951 *NZ* 1,2,3, 1954 *Fj* 1,2, 1955 *NZ* 1,2,3, 1957 *NZ* 1,2
Towers, C H T (NSW) 1927 *I*, 1928 *E*, *F*, *NZ* 1,2,3, *M*, 1929 *NZ* 1,3, 1930 *BI*, 1931 *M*, *NZ*, 1934 *NZ* 1,2, 1937 *SA* 1,2
Trivett, R K (Q) 1966 *BI* 1,2
Turnbull, A (V) 1961 *Fj* 3
Turnbull, R V (NSW) 1968 *I*
Tuynman, S N (NSW) 1983 *F* 1,2, 1984 *E*, *I*, *W*, *S*, 1985 *C* 1,2, *NZ*, *Fj* 1,2, 1986 *It*, *F*, *Arg* 1,2, *NZ* 1,2,3, 1987 *SK*, [*E*, *US*, *J*, *I*, *W*], *NZ*, *Arg* 1 (R), 2, 1988 *E*, *It*, 1989 *BI* 1,2,3, *NZ*, 1990 *NZ* 1
Tweedale, E (NSW) 1946 *NZ* 1,2, 1947 *NZ* 2, *S*, *I*, 1948 *E*, *F*, 1949 *M* 1,2,3

Vaughan, D (NSW) 1983 *US*, *Arg* 1, *It*, *F* 1,2
Vaughan, G N (V) 1958 *E*, *S*, *F*, *M* 1,2,3
Verge, A (NSW) 1904 *BI* 1,2

Walden, R J (NSW) 1934 *NZ* 2, 1936 *NZ* 1,2, *M*
Walker, A K (NSW) 1947 *NZ* 1, 1948 *E*, *F*, 1950 *BI* 1,2
Walker, A S B (NSW) 1912 *US*, 1921 *NZ*
Walker, L F (NSW) 1988 *NZ* 2,3, *S*, *It*, 1989 *BI* 1,2,3, *NZ*
Walker, L R (NSW) 1982 *NZ* 2,3
Wallace, A C (NSW) 1921 *NZ*, 1927 *I*, *W*, *S*, 1928 *E*, *F*
Wallach, C (NSW) 1913 *NZ* 1,3, 1914 *NZ* 1,2,3
Walsh, J J (NSW) 1953 *SA* 1,2,3,4

Walsh, P B (NSW) 1904 *BI* 1,2,3
Walsham, K P (NSW) 1962 *NZ* 3, 1963 *E*
Ward, P G (NSW) 1899 *BI* 1,2,3,4
Ward, T (Q) 1899 *BI* 2
Watson, G W (Q) 1907 *NZ* 1
Watson, W T (NSW) 1912 *US*, 1913 *NZ* 1,2,3, 1914 *NZ* 1
Waugh, W W (NSW) 1993 *SA* 1
Weatherstone, L J (ACT) 1975 *E* 1,2, *J* 1,2, *S* (R), 1976 *E*, *I*
Webb, W (NSW) 1899 *BI* 3,4
Wells, B G (NSW) 1958 *M* 1
Westfield, R E (NSW) 1928 *NZ* 1,2,3, *M*, 1929 *NZ* 2,3
White, C J B (NSW) 1899 *BI* 1, 1903 *NZ*, 1904 *BI* 1
White, J M (NSW) 1904 *BI* 3
White, J P L (NSW) 1958 *NZ* 1,2,3, 1961 *Fj* 1,2,3, *SA* 1,2, *F*, 1962 *NZ* 1,2,3,4,5, 1963 *E*, *SA* 1,2,3,4, 1964 *NZ* 1,2,3, 1965 *SA* 1,2
White, M C (Q) 1931 *M*, *NZ*, 1932 *NZ* 1,2, 1933 *SA* 1,2,3,4,5
White, S W (NSW) 1956 *SA* 1,2, 1958 *I*, *E*, *S*, *M* 2,3
White, W G S (Q) 1933 *SA* 1,2,3,4,5, 1934 *NZ* 1,2, 1936 *NZ* 1,2, *M*
White, W J (NSW) 1928 *NZ* 1, *M*, 1932 *NZ* 1
Wickham, S M (NSW) 1903 *NZ*, 1904 *BI* 1,2,3, 1905 *NZ*
Williams, D (Q) 1913 *NZ* 3, 1914 *NZ* 1,2,3

Williams, I M (NSW) 1987 *Arg* 1,2, 1988 *E* 1,2, *NZ* 1,2,3, 1989 *BI* 2,3, *NZ*, *F* 1,2, 1990 *F* 1,2,3, *US*, *NZ* 1
Williams, J L (NSW) 1963 *SA* 1,3,4
Williams, S A (NSW) 1980 *Fj*, *NZ* 1,2, 1981 *F* 1,2, 1982 *E*, *NZ* 1,2,3, 1983 *US*, *Arg* 1 (R), 2, *NZ*, *It*, *F* 1,2, 1984 *NZ* 1,2,3, *E*, *I*, *W*, *S*, 1985 *C* 1,2, *NZ*, *Fj* 1,2
Wilson, B J (NSW) 1949 *NZ* 1,2
Wilson, C R (Q) 1957 *NZ* 1, 1958 *NZ* 1,2,3
Wilson, D J (Q) 1992 *S* 1,2, *NZ* 1,2,3, *SA*, *I*, *W*, 1993 *Tg*, *NZ*, *SA* 1,2,3, *C*, *F* 1,2
Wilson, V W (Q) 1937 *SA* 1,2, 1938 *NZ* 1,2,3
Windon, C J (NSW) 1946 *NZ* 1,2, 1947 *NZ* 1, *S*, *I*, *W*, 1948 *E*, *F*, 1949 *M* 1,2,3, *NZ* 1,2, 1951 *NZ* 1,2,3, 1952 *Fj* 1,2, *NZ* 1,2
Windon, K S (NSW) 1937 *SA* 1,2, 1946 *M*
Windsor, J C (Q) 1947 *NZ* 2
Winning, K C (Q) 1951 *NZ* 1
Wogan, L W (NSW) 1913 *NZ* 1,2,3, 1914 *NZ* 1,2,3, 1921 *NZ*
Wood, F (NSW) 1907 *NZ* 1,2,3, 1910 *NZ* 1,2,3, 1913 *NZ* 1,2,3, 1914 *NZ* 1,2,3
Wood, R N (Q) 1972 *Fj*
Woods, H F (NSW) 1925 *NZ*, 1927 *I*, *W*, *S*, 1928 *E*
Wright, K J (NSW) 1975 *E* 1,2, *J* 1, 1976 *US*, *F* 1,2, 1978 *NZ* 1,2,3

Yanz, K (NSW) 1958 *F*

AUSTRALIAN INTERNATIONAL RECORDS

Both team and individual records are for official Australian international matches, up to 31 March 1994.

TEAM RECORDS

Highest score
67 v United States (67-9) 1990 Brisbane
v individual countries
39 v Argentina (39-19) 1986 Brisbane
30 v British Isles (30-12) 1989 Sydney
59 v Canada (59-3) 1985 Sydney
40 v England (40-15) 1991 Sydney
52 v Fiji (52-28) 1985 Brisbane
48 v France (48-31) 1990 Brisbane
42 v Ireland (42-17) 1992 Dublin
55 v Italy (55-6) 1988 Rome
50 v Japan (50-25) 1975 Brisbane
30 v N Zealand (30-16) 1978 Auckland
37 v Scotland { (37-12) 1984 Murrayfield
              { (37-13) 1992 Brisbane
28 v South Africa (28-20) 1993 Brisbane
65 v South Korea (65-18) 1987 Brisbane
52 v Tonga (52-14) 1993 Brisbane
67 v United States (67-9) 1990 Brisbane
63 v Wales (63-6) 1991 Brisbane
 9 v Western Samoa (9-3) 1991 Pontypool

v individual countries
26 v Argentina (26-0) 1986 Sydney
18 v British Isles (30-12) 1989 Sydney
56 v Canada (59-3) 1985 Sydney
25 v England (40-15) 1991 Sydney
24 v Fiji (52-28) 1985 Brisbane
21 v France (24-3) 1993 Parc des Princes
25 v Ireland (42-17) 1992 Dublin
49 v Italy (55-6) 1988 Rome
30 v Japan (37-7) 1975 Sydney
16 v N Zealand (26-10) 1980 Sydney
25 v Scotland (37-12) 1984 Murrayfield
23 v South Africa (26-3) 1992 Cape Town
47 v South Korea (65-18) 1987 Brisbane
38 v Tonga (52-14) 1993 Brisbane
58 v United States (67-9) 1990 Brisbane
57 v Wales (63-6) 1991 Brisbane
 6 v Western Samoa (9-3) 1991 Pontypool

Biggest winning points margin
58 v United States (67-9) 1990 Brisbane

Longest winning sequence
10 matches 1991-92

Highest score by opposing team

38 { N Zealand (13-38) 1936 Dunedin
     { N Zealand (3-38) 1972 Auckland

by individual countries

27 Argentina (19-27) 1987 Buenos Aires
31 British Isles (0-31) 1966 Brisbane
16 Canada (43-16) 1993 Calgary
28 England (19-28) 1988 Twickenham
28 Fiji (52-28) 1985 Brisbane
34 France (6-34) 1976 Paris
27 Ireland (12-27) 1979 Brisbane
18 Italy (39-18) 1986 Brisbane
25 Japan (50-25) 1975 Brisbane

38 { N Zealand (13-38) 1936 Dunedin
     { N Zealand (3-38) 1972 Auckland

24 Scotland (15-24) 1981 Murrayfield
30 South Africa (11-30) 1969 Johannesburg
18 South Korea (65-18) 1987 Brisbane
16 Tonga (11-16) 1973 Brisbane
12 United States (47-12) 1987 Brisbane
28 Wales (3-28) 1975 Cardiff
 3 Western Samoa (9-3) 1991 Pontypool

Biggest losing points margin

35 v N Zealand (3-38) 1972 Auckland

v individual countries

15 v Argentina (3-18) 1983 Brisbane
31 v British Isles (0-31) 1966 Brisbane
17 v England { (3-20) 1973 Twickenham
              { (6-23) 1976 Twickenham
 2 v Fiji { (15-17) 1952 Sydney
          { (16-18) 1954 Sydney
28 v France (6-34) 1976 Paris
15 v Ireland (12-27) 1979 Brisbane
35 v New Zealand (3-38) 1972 Auckland
 9 v Scotland (15-24) 1981 Murrayfield
25 v South Africa (3-28) 1961 Johannesburg
 5 v Tonga (11-16) 1973 Brisbane
25 v Wales (3-28) 1975 Cardiff
No defeats v Canada, Italy, Japan, South Korea, United States or Western Samoa.

Longest losing sequence

10 matches { 1899-1907
           { 1937-47

Most tries by Australia in an international

13 v South Korea (65-18) 1987 Brisbane

Most tries against Australia in an international

9 by N Zealand (13-38) 1936 Dunedin

Most points on overseas tour (all matches)

500 in B Isles/France (35 matches)
    1947-48

Most tries on overseas tour (all matches)

115 in B Isles/France (35 matches)
    1947-48

INDIVIDUAL RECORDS

Most capped player

D I Campese   80   1982-93

in individual positions

Full-back

R G Gould   25   1980-87

Wing

D I Campese   64(80)[1]   1982-93

Centre

A G Slack   39   1978-87

Fly-half

M P Lynagh   56(64)[2]   1984-93

Scrum-half

N C Farr-Jones   62(63)[3]   1984-93

Prop

A J McIntyre   38   1982-89

Hooker

P G Johnson   42   1959-71

Lock

S A G Cutler   40   1982-91

Flanker

S P Poidevin   59   1980-91

No 8

S N Tuynman   28(34)[4]   1983-90
B T Gavin   28(30)[4]   1988-93

[1]*Campese has played 16 times as a full-back*
[2]*Lynagh has played 7 times as a centre and once as a replacement full-back*
[3]*Farr-Jones was capped once as a replacement wing*
[4]*Tuynman played 6 times as a flanker and Gavin twice as a replacement lock*

Longest international career

G M Cooke 16 seasons 1932-1947/8
A R Miller 16 seasons 1952-1967
Cooke's career ended during a Northern hemisphere season

Most consecutive internationals – 37

P G Johnson 1959-68

Most internationals as captain – 36
N C Farr-Jones   1988-92
Includes wins against the British Isles and all senior IB nations

Most points in internationals – 783
M P Lynagh (64 matches) 1984-93

Most points in an international – 24
M P Lynagh v France 1990 Brisbane
M P Lynagh v United States 1990 Brisbane

Most tries in internationals – 57
D I Campese (80 matches) 1982-93

Most tries in an international – 4
G Cornelsen v N Zealand 1978 Auckland
D I Campese v United States 1983 Sydney

Most conversions in internationals – 129
M P Lynagh (64 matches) 1984-93

Most conversions in an international – 8
M P Lynagh v Italy 1988 Rome
M P Lynagh v United States 1990 Brisbane

Most dropped goals in internationals – 9
P F Hawthorne (21 matches) 1962-67
M P Lynagh (64 matches) 1984-93

Most dropped goals in an international – 3
P F Hawthorne v England 1967
  Twickenham

Most penalty goals in internationals – 150
M P Lynagh (64 matches) 1984-93

Most penalty goals in an international – 6
M P Lynagh v France 1986 Sydney
M P Lynagh v England 1988 Brisbane

Most points in international series on tour – 42
M P Lynagh (4 appearances) 1984
  B Isles

Most tries in international series on tour – 4
G Cornelsen (3 appearances) 1978
  N Zealand
M G Ella (4 appearances) 1984
  B Isles
Ella scored in each match of the international series

Most points on overseas tour – 154
P E McLean (18 appearances) B Isles
  1975-76

Most tries on overseas tour – 23
C J Russell B Isles 1908-09

Most points in a tour match – 26
A J Leeds v Buller (NZ) 1986 Westport

Most tries in a tour match – 6
J S Boyce v Wairarapa (NZ) 1962
  Masterton

INTERNATIONAL MATCH APPEARANCES FOR BRITISH ISLES TEAMS (*up to 31 March 1994*)

From 1910 onwards, when British Isles teams first became officially representative of the four Home Unions. (*Uncapped when first selected to play in a Test match for the British Isles.*)

ABBREVIATIONS

A – Australia; *NZ* – New Zealand; *SA* –South Africa; (R) – Replacement; (t) – temporary replacement.

CLUB ABBREVIATIONS

NIFC – North of Ireland Football Club; CIYMS – Church of Ireland Young Men's Society

Note: When a series has taken place, figures have been used to denote the particular matches in which players have featured. Thus 1962 *SA* 1,4 indicates that a player appeared in the first and fourth Tests of a series.

Aarvold, C D (Cambridge U, Blackheath and England) 1930 *NZ* 1,2,3,4, *A*
Ackerman, R A (London Welsh and Wales) 1983 *NZ* 1,4(R)
Ackford, P J (Harlequins and England) 1989 *A* 1,2,3
Alexander, R (NIFC and Ireland) 1938 *SA* 1,2,3
Andrew, C R (Wasps and England) 1989 *A* 2,3, 1993 *NZ* 1,2,3
Arneil, R J (Edinburgh Acads and Scotland) 1968 *SA* 1,2,3,4
Ashcroft, A (Waterloo and England) 1959 *A* 1, *NZ* 2

Bainbridge, S J (Gosforth and England) 1983 *NZ* 3,4
Baird, G R T (Kelso and Scotland) 1983 *NZ* 1,2,3,4
Baker, A M (Newport and Wales) 1910 *SA* 3
Baker, D G S (Old Merchant Taylors' and England) 1955 *SA* 3,4
Bassett, J (Penarth and Wales) 1930 *NZ* 1,2,3,4, *A*
Bayfield, M C (Northampton and England) 1993 *NZ* 1,2,3
Beamish, G R (Leicester, RAF and Ireland) 1930 *NZ* 1,2,3,4, *A*
Beattie, J R (Glasgow Acads and Scotland) 1983 *NZ* 2(R)
Beaumont, W B (Fylde and England) 1977 *NZ* 2,3,4, 1980 *SA* 1,2,3,4
Bebb, D I E (Swansea and Wales) 1962 *SA* 2,3, 1966 *A* 1,2, *NZ* 1,2,3,4
Bennett, P (Llanelli and Wales) 1974 *SA* 1,2,3,4, 1977 *NZ* 1,2,3,4
Bevan, J C (Cardiff Coll of Ed, Cardiff and Wales) 1971 *NZ* 1
Black, A W (Edinburgh U and Scotland) 1950 *NZ* 1,2
Black, B H (Oxford U, Blackheath and England) 1930 *NZ* 1,2,3,4, *A*
Blakiston, A F (Northampton and England) 1924 *SA* 1,2,3,4
Bowcott, H M (Cambridge U, Cardiff and Wales) 1930 *NZ* 1,2,3,4, *A*
Boyle, C V (Dublin U and Ireland) 1938 *SA* 2,3
Brand, T N (NIFC and *Ireland) 1924 *SA* 1,2
Bresnihan, F P K (UC Dublin and Ireland) 1968 *SA* 1,2,4
Brophy, N H (UC Dublin and Ireland) 1962 *SA* 1,4
Brown, G L (W of Scotland and Scotland) 1971 *NZ* 3,4, 1974 *SA* 1,2,3, 1977 *NZ* 2,3,4
Budge, G M (Edinburgh Wands and Scotland) 1950 *NZ* 4
Burcher, D H (Newport and Wales) 1977 *NZ* 3
Burnell, A P (London Scottish and Scotland) 1993 *NZ* 1
Butterfield, J (Northampton and England) 1955 *SA* 1,2,3,4

Calder, F (Stewart's-Melville FP and Scotland) 1989 *A* 1,2,3
Calder, J H (Stewart's-Melville FP and Scotland) 1983 *NZ* 3
Cameron, A (Glasgow HSFP and Scotland) 1955 *SA* 1,2
Campbell, S O (Old Belvedere and Ireland) 1980 *SA* 2(R), 3,4, 1983 *NZ* 1,2,3,4

Campbell-Lamerton, M J (Halifax, Army and Scotland) 1962 *SA* 1,2,3,4, 1966 *A* 1,2, *NZ* 1,3
Carleton, J (Orrell and England) 1980 *SA* 1,2,4, 1983 *NZ* 2,3,4
Carling, W D C (Harlequins and England) 1993 *NZ* 1
Chalmers, C M (Melrose and Scotland) 1989 *A* 1
Clarke, B B (Bath and England) 1993 *NZ* 1,2,3
Cleaver, W B (Cardiff and Wales) 1950 *NZ* 1,2,3
Clifford, T (Young Munster and Ireland) 1950 *NZ* 1,2,3, *A* 1,2
Cobner, T J (Pontypool and Wales) 1977 *NZ* 1,2,3
Colclough, M J (Angoulême and England) 1980 *SA* 1,2,3,4, 1983 *NZ* 1,2,3,4
Connell, G C (Trinity Acads and Scotland) 1968 *SA* 4
Cotton, F E (Loughborough Colls, Coventry and England) 1974 *SA* 1,2,3,4, 1977 *NZ* 2,3,4
Coulman, M J (Moseley and England) 1968 *SA* 3
Cove-Smith, R (Old Merchant Taylors' and England) 1924 *SA* 1,2,3,4
Cowan, R C (Selkirk and Scotland) 1962 *SA* 4
Cromey, G E (Queen's U, Belfast and Ireland) 1938 *SA* 3
Cunningham, W A (Lansdowne and Ireland) 1924 *SA* 3

Dancer, G T (Bedford) 1938 *SA* 1,2,3
Davies, C (Cardiff and Wales) 1950 *NZ* 4
Davies, D M (Somerset Police and Wales) 1950 *NZ* 3,4, *A* 1
Davies, D S (Hawick and Scotland) 1924 *SA* 1,2,3,4
Davies, H J (Newport and Wales) 1924 *SA* 2
Davies, T G R (Cardiff, London Welsh and Wales) 1968 *SA* 3, 1971 *NZ* 1,2,3,4
Davies, T J (Llanelli and Wales) 1959 *NZ* 2,4
Davies, T M (London Welsh, Swansea and Wales) 1971 *NZ* 1,2,3,4, 1974 *SA* 1,2,3,4
Davies, W G (Cardiff and Wales) 1980 *SA* 2
Davies, W P C (Harlequins and England) 1955 *SA* 1,2,3
Dawes, S J (London Welsh and Wales) 1971 *NZ* 1,2,3,4
Dawson, A R (Wanderers and Ireland) 1959 *A* 1,2, *NZ* 1,2,3,4
Dixon, P J (Harlequins and England) 1971 *NZ* 1,2,4
Dodge, P W (Leicester and England) 1980 *SA* 3,4
Dooley, W A (Preston Grasshoppers and England) 1989 *A* 2,3
Doyle, M G (Blackrock Coll and Ireland) 1968 *SA* 1
Drysdale, D (Heriot's FP and Scotland) 1924 *SA* 1,2,3,4
Duckham, D J (Coventry and England) 1971 *NZ* 2,3,4
Duggan, W P (Blackrock Coll and Ireland) 1977 *NZ* 1,2,3,4
Duff, P L (Glasgow Acads and Scotland) 1938 *SA* 2,3

Edwards, G O (Cardiff and Wales) 1968 *SA* 1,2, 1971 *NZ* 1,2,3,4, 1974 *SA* 1,2,3
Evans, G (Maesteg and Wales) 1983 *NZ* 3,4
Evans, G L (Newport and Wales) 1977 *NZ* 2,3,4
Evans, I C (Llanelli and Wales) 1989 *A* 1,2,3, 1993 *NZ* 1,2,3
Evans, R T (Newport and Wales) 1950 *NZ* 1,2,3,4, *A* 1,2
Evans, T P (Swansea and Wales) 1977 *NZ* 1

Evans, W R (Cardiff and Wales) 1959 *A* 2, *NZ* 1,2,3

Farrell, J L (Bective Rangers and Ireland) 1930 *NZ* 1,2,3,4, *A*
Faull, J (Swansea and Wales) 1959 *A* 1, *NZ* 1,3,4
Fenwick, S P (Bridgend and Wales) 1977 *NZ* 1,2,3,4
Fitzgerald, C F (St Mary's Coll and Ireland) 1983 *NZ* 1,2,3,4
Foster, A R (Queen's U, Belfast and Ireland) 1910 *SA* 1,2

Gibbs, I S (Swansea and Wales) 1993 *NZ* 2,3
Gibson, C M H (Cambridge U, NIFC and Ireland) 1966 *NZ* 1,2,3,4, 1968 *SA* 1(R),2,3,4, 1971 *NZ* 1,2,3,4
Giles, J L (Coventry and England) 1938 *SA* 1,3
Gravell, R W R (Llanelli and Wales) 1980 *SA* 1 (R),2,3,4
Graves, C R A (Wanderers and Ireland) 1938 *SA* 1,3
Greenwood, J T (Dunfermline and Scotland) 1955 *SA* 1,2,3,4
Grieve, C F (Oxford U and Scotland) 1938 *SA* 2,3
Griffiths, G M (Cardiff and Wales) 1955 *SA* 2,3,4
Griffiths, V M (Newport and Wales) 1924 *SA* 3,4
Guscott, J C (Bath and England) 1989 *A* 2,3, 1993 *NZ* 1,2,3

Hall, M R (Bridgend and Wales) 1989 *A* 1
Handford, F G (Manchester and England) 1910 *SA* 1,2,3
Harding, W R (Cambridge U, Swansea and Wales) 1924 *SA* 2,3,4
Harris, S W (Blackheath and England) 1924 *SA* 3,4
Hastings, A G (London Scottish, Watsonians and Scotland) 1989 *A* 1,2,3, 1993 *NZ* 1,2,3
Hastings, S (Watsonians and Scotland) 1989 *A* 2,3
Hay, B H (Boroughmuir and Scotland) 1980 *SA* 2,3,4
Hayward, D J (Newbridge and Wales) 1950 *NZ* 1,2,3
Henderson, N J (Queen's U, Belfast, NIFC and Ireland) 1950 *NZ* 3
Henderson, R G (Northern and Scotland) 1924 *SA* 3,4
Hendrie, K G P (Heriot's FP and Scotland) 1924 *SA* 2
Hewitt, D (Queen's U, Belfast, Instonians and Ireland) 1959 *A* 1,2, *NZ* 1,3,4, 1962 *SA* 4
Higgins, R (Liverpool and England) 1955 *SA* 1
Hinshelwood, A J W (London Scottish and Scotland) 1966 *NZ* 2,4, 1968 *SA* 2
Hodgson, J McD (Northern and *England) 1930 *NZ* 1,3
Holmes, T D (Cardiff and Wales) 1983 *NZ* 1
Hopkins, R (Maesteg and Wales) 1971 *NZ* 1(R)
Horrocks-Taylor, J P (Leicester and England) 1959 *NZ* 3
Horton, A L (Blackheath and England) 1968 *SA* 2,3,4
Howard, W G (Old Birkonians) 1938 *SA* 1
Howie, R A (Kirkcaldy and Scotland) 1924 *SA* 1,2,3,4

Irvine, A R (Heriot's FP and Scotland) 1974 *SA* 3,4, 1977 *NZ* 1,2,3,4, 1980 *SA* 2,3,4
Irwin, D G (Instonians and Ireland) 1983 *NZ* 1,2,4
Isherwood, G A M (Old Alleynians, Sale) 1910 *SA* 1,2,3

Jackson, P B (Coventry and England) 1959 *A* 1,2, *NZ* 1,3,4
Jarman, H (Newport and Wales) 1910 *SA* 1,2,3
Jeeps, R E G (Northampton and *England) 1955 *SA* 1,2,3,4, 1959 *A* 1,2, *NZ* 1,2,3, 1962 *SA* 1,2,3,4
Jenkins, V G J (Oxford U, London Welsh and Wales) 1938 *SA* 1
John, B (Cardiff and Wales) 1968 *SA* 1, 1971 *NZ* 1,2,3,4
John, E R (Neath and Wales) 1950 *NZ* 1,2,3,4, *A* 1,2
Johnson, M O (Leicester and England) 1993 *NZ* 2,3
Jones, B L (Devonport Services, Llanelli and Wales) 1950 *NZ* 4, *A* 1,2
Jones, D K (Llanelli, Cardiff and Wales) 1962 *SA* 1,2,3, 1966 *A* 1,2, *NZ* 1
Jones, E L (Llanelli and *Wales) 1938 *SA* 1,3
Jones, Ivor (Llanelli and Wales) 1930 *NZ* 1,2,3,4, *A*
Jones, J P (Newport and Wales) 1910 *SA* 1,2,3
Jones, K D (Cardiff and Wales) 1962 *SA* 1,2,3,4
Jones, K J (Newport and Wales) 1950 *NZ* 1,2,4
Jones, R N (Swansea and Wales) 1989 *A* 1,2,3
Jones, S T (Pontypool and Wales) 1983 *NZ* 2,3,4

Keane, M I (Lansdowne and Ireland) 1977 *NZ* 1
Kennedy, K W (CIYMS, London Irish and Ireland) 1966 *A* 1,2, *NZ* 1,4
Kiernan, M J (Dolphin and Ireland) 1983 *NZ* 2,3,4
Kiernan, T J (Cork Const and Ireland) 1962 *SA* 3, 1968 *SA* 1,2,3,4
Kininmonth, P W (Oxford U, Richmond and Scotland) 1950 *NZ* 1,2,4
Kinnear, R M (Heriot's FP and *Scotland) 1924 *SA* 1,2,3,4
Kyle, J W (Queen's U, Belfast, NIFC and Ireland) 1950 *NZ* 1,2,3,4, *A* 1,2

Laidlaw, F A L (Melrose and Scotland) 1966 *NZ* 2,3
Laidlaw, R J (Jedforest and Scotland) 1983 *NZ* 1(R), 2,3,4
Lamont, R A (Instonians and Ireland) 1966 *NZ* 1,2,3,4
Lane, M F (UC Cork and Ireland) 1950 *NZ* 4, *A* 2
Larter, P J (Northampton, RAF and England) 1968 *SA* 2
Leonard, J (Harlequins and England) 1993 *NZ* 2,3
Lewis, A R (Abertillery and Wales) 1966 *NZ* 2,3,4
Lynch, J F (St Mary's Coll and Ireland) 1971 *NZ* 1,2,3,4

McBride, W J (Ballymena and Ireland) 1962 *SA* 3,4, 1966 *NZ* 2,3,4, 1968 *SA* 1,2,3,4, 1971 *NZ* 1,2,3,4, 1974 *SA* 1,2,3,4
Macdonald, R (Edinburgh U and Scotland) 1950 *NZ* 1, *A* 2
McFadyean, C W (Moseley and England) 1966 *NZ* 1,2,3,4
McGeechan, I R (Headingley and Scotland) 1974 *SA* 1,2,3,4, 1977 *NZ* 1,2,3(R),4
McKay, J W (Queen's U, Belfast and Ireland) 1950 *NZ* 1,2,3,4, *A* 1,2
McKibbin, H R (Queen's U, Belfast and Ireland) 1938 *SA* 1,2,3
McLauchlan, J (Jordanhill and Scotland) 1971 *NZ* 1,2,3,4, 1974 *SA* 1,2,3,4
McLeod, H F (Hawick and Scotland) 1959 *A* 1,2, *NZ* 1,2,3,4
McLoughlin, R J (Gosforth, Blackrock Coll and Ireland) 1966 *A* 1,2, *NZ* 4
MacNeill, H P (Oxford U and Ireland) 1983 *NZ* 1,2, 4(R)
Macpherson, N C (Newport and Scotland) 1924 *SA* 1,2,3,4
Macrae, D J (St Andrew's U and Scotland) 1938 *SA* 1
McVicker, J (Collegians and Ireland) 1924 *SA* 1,3,4
Marques, R W D (Harlequins and England) 1959 *A* 2, *NZ* 2
Marsden-Jones, D (London Welsh and Wales) 1924 *SA* 1,2
Martin, A J (Aberavon and Wales) 1977 *NZ* 1
Martindale, S A (Kendal and England) 1930 *A*
Matthews, J (Cardiff and Wales) 1950 *NZ* 1,2,3,4, *A* 1,2
Maxwell, R B (Birkenhead Park) 1924 *SA* 1
Mayne, R B (Queen's U, Belfast and Ireland) 1938 *SA* 1,2,3
Meredith, B V (Newport and Wales) 1955 *SA* 1,2,3,4, 1962 *SA* 1,2,3,4
Meredith, C C (Neath and Wales) 1955 *SA* 1,2,3,4
Millar, S (Ballymena and Ireland) 1959 *A* 1,2, *NZ* 2, 1962 *SA* 1,2,3,4, 1968 *SA* 1,2
Milliken, R A (Bangor and Ireland) 1974 *SA* 1,2,3,4
Milne, K S (Heriot's FP and Scotland) 1993 *NZ* 1
Moore, B C (Nottingham, Harlequins and England) 1989 *A* 1,2,3, 1993 *NZ* 2,3
Morgan, C I (Cardiff and Wales) 1955 *SA* 1,2,3,4
Morgan, D W (Stewart's-Melville FP and Scotland) 1977 *NZ* 3(R),4
Morgan, G J (Clontarf and Ireland) 1938 *SA* 3
Morgan, H J (Abertillery and Wales) 1959 *NZ* 3,4, 1962 *SA* 2,3
Morgan, M E (Swansea and Wales) 1938 *SA* 1,2
Morley, J C (Newport and Wales) 1930 *NZ* 1,2,3
Morris, C D (Orrell and England) 1993 *NZ* 1,2,3
Mulcahy, W A (UC Dublin and Ireland) 1959 *A* 1, *NZ* 4, 1962 *SA* 1,2,3,4
Mullen, K D (Old Belvedere and Ireland) 1950 *NZ* 1,2, *A* 2

Mulligan, A A (Wanderers, London Irish and Ireland) 1959 *NZ* 4
Mullin, B J (London Irish and Ireland) 1989 *A* 1
Murphy, N A A (Cork Const and Ireland) 1959 *A* 2, *NZ* 1,2,4, 1966 *A* 1,2, *NZ* 2,3
Murray, P F (Wanderers and Ireland) 1930 *NZ* 1,2,4, *A*

Neale, M E (Bristol, Blackheath and *England) 1910 *SA* 1,2,3
Neary, A (Broughton Park and England) 1977 *NZ* 4
Nelson, J E (Malone and Ireland) 1950 *NZ* 3,4, *A* 1,2
Nicholson, B E (Harlequins and England) 1938 *SA* 2
Norris, C H (Cardiff and Wales) 1966 *NZ* 1,2,3
Norster, R L (Cardiff and Wales) 1983 *NZ* 1,2, 1989 *A* 1
Novis, A L (Blackheath and England) 1930 *NZ* 2,4, *A*

O'Donnell, R C (St Mary's Coll and Ireland) 1980 *SA* 1
O'Driscoll, J B (London Irish and Ireland) 1980 *SA* 1,2,3,4, 1983 *NZ* 2,4
O'Neill, H O'H (Queen's U, Belfast and Ireland) 1930 *NZ* 1,2,3,4, *A*
O'Reilly, A J F (Old Belvedere and Ireland) 1955 *SA* 1,2,3,4, 1959 *A* 1,2, *NZ* 1,2,3,4
Orr, P A (Old Wesley and Ireland) 1977 *NZ* 1
O'Shea, J P (Cardiff and Wales) 1968 *SA* 1

Parker, D (Swansea and Wales) 1930 *NZ* 1,2,3,4, *A*
Pask, A E I (Abertillery and Wales) 1962 *SA* 1,2,3, 1966 *A* 1,2, *NZ* 1,3,4
Patterson, C S (Instonians and Ireland) 1980 *SA* 1,2,3
Patterson, W M (Sale and *England) 1959 *NZ* 2
Paxton, I A M (Selkirk and Scotland) 1983 *NZ* 1,2,3,4
Pedlow, A C (CIYMS and Ireland) 1955 *SA* 1,4
Pillman, C H (Blackheath and England) 1910 *SA* 2,3
Piper, O J S (Cork Const and Ireland) 1910 *SA* 1
Poole, H (Cardiff) 1930 *NZ* 3
Popplewell, N J (Greystones and Ireland) 1993 *NZ* 1,2,3
Preece, I (Coventry and England) 1950 *NZ* 1
Prentice, F D (Leicester and England) 1930 *NZ* 2, *A*
Price, B (Newport and Wales) 1966 *A* 1,2, *NZ* 1,4
Price, G (Pontypool and Wales) 1977 *NZ* 1,2,3,4, 1980 *SA* 1,2,3,4, 1983 *NZ* 1,2,3,4
Price, M J (Pontypool and Wales) 1959 *A* 1,2, *NZ* 1,2,3
Prosser, T R (Pontypool and Wales) 1959 *NZ* 4
Pullin, J V (Bristol and England) 1968 *SA* 2,3,4, 1971 *NZ* 1,2,3,4

Quinnell, D L (Llanelli and *Wales) 1971 *NZ* 3, 1977 *NZ* 2,3, 1980 *SA* 1,2

Ralston, C W (Richmond and England) 1974 *SA* 4
Reed, A I (Bath and Scotland) 1993 *NZ* 1
Rees, H E (Neath and *Wales) 1977 *NZ* 4
Reeve, J S R (Harlequins and England) 1930 *NZ* 1,3,4, *A*
Reid, T E (Garryowen and Ireland) 1955 *SA* 2,3
Renwick, J M (Hawick and Scotland) 1980 *SA* 1
Rew, H (Blackheath, Army and England) 1930 *NZ* 1,2,3,4
Reynolds, F J (Old Cranleighans and England) 1938 *SA* 1,2
Richards, D (Leicester and England) 1989 *A* 1,2,3, 1993 *NZ* 1,2,3
Richards, D S (Swansea and Wales) 1980 *SA* 1
Richards, M C R (Cardiff and Wales) 1968 *SA* 1,3,4
Richards, T J (Bristol and Australia) 1910 *SA* 1,2
Rimmer, G (Waterloo and England) 1950 *NZ* 3
Ringland, T M (Ballymena and Ireland) 1983 *NZ* 1
Risman, A B W (Loughborough Colls and England) 1959 *A* 1,2, *NZ* 1,4
Robbie, J C (Greystones and Ireland) 1980 *SA* 4
Robins, J D (Birkenhead Park and Wales) 1950 *NZ* 1,2,3, *A* 1,2
Robins, R J (Pontypridd and Wales) 1955 *SA* 1,2,3,4
Rogers, D P (Bedford and England) 1962 *SA* 1,4
Rowlands, K A (Cardiff and Wales) 1962 *SA* 1,2,4
Rutherford, D (Gloucester and England) 1966 *A* 1
Rutherford, J Y (Selkirk and Scotland) 1983 *NZ* 3

Savage, K F (Northampton and England) 1968 *SA* 1,2,3,4

Scotland, K J F (Cambridge U, Heriot's FP and Scotland) 1959 *A* 1,2, *NZ* 1,3,4
Sharp, R A W (Oxford U, Redruth and England) 1962 *SA* 3,4
Slattery, J F (Blackrock Coll and Ireland) 1974 *SA* 1,2,3,4
Slemen, M A C (Liverpool and England) 1980 *SA* 1
Smith, A R (Edinburgh Wands, London Scottish and Scotland) 1962 *SA* 1,2,3
Smith, D F (Richmond and England) 1910 *SA* 1,2,3
Smith, D W C (London Scottish and Scotland) 1950 *A* 1
Smith, G K (Kelso and Scotland) 1959 *A* 1,2, *NZ* 1,3
Smith, I S (Oxford U, London Scottish and Scotland) 1924 *SA* 1,2
Smyth, T (Malone, Newport and Ireland) 1910 *SA* 2,3
Sole, D M B (Edinburgh Acads and Scotland) 1989 *A* 1,2,3
Spong, R S (Old Millhillians and England) 1930 *NZ* 1,2,3,4, *A*
Spoors, J A (Bristol) 1910 *SA* 1,2,3
Squire, J (Newport, Pontypool and Wales) 1977 *NZ* 4, 1980 *SA* 1,2,3,4, 1983 *NZ* 1
Squires, P J (Harrogate and England) 1977 *NZ* 1
Stagg, P K (Oxford U, Sale and Scotland) 1968 *SA* 1,3,4
Steele, W C C (Bedford, RAF and Scotland) 1974 *SA* 1,2
Stephens, I (Bridgend and Wales) 1983 *NZ* 1
Stephens, J R G (Neath and Wales) 1950 *A* 1,2
Stevenson, R C (St Andrew's U and Scotland) 1910 *SA* 1,2,3

Tanner, H (Swansea and Wales) 1938 *SA* 2
Taylor, A R (Cross Keys and Wales) 1938 *SA* 1,2
Taylor, J (London Welsh and Wales) 1971 *NZ* 1,2,3,4
Taylor, R B (Northampton and England) 1968 *SA* 1,2,3,4
Teague, M C (Gloucester, Moseley and England) 1989 *A* 2,3, 1993 *NZ* 2(t)
Telfer, J W (Melrose and Scotland) 1966 *A* 1,2, *NZ* 1,2,4, 1968 *SA* 2,3,4
Thomas, M C (Devonport Services, Newport and Wales) 1950 *NZ* 2,3, *A* 1, 1959 *NZ* 2
Thomas, R C C (Swansea and Wales) 1955 *SA* 3,4
Thomas, W D (Llanelli and *Wales) 1966 *NZ* 2,3, 1968 *SA* 3(R),4, 1971 *NZ* 1,2,4(R)
Thompson, R H (Instonians, London Irish and Ireland) 1955 *SA* 1,2,4
Travers, W H (Newport and Wales) 1938 *SA* 2,3
Tucker, C C (Shannon and Ireland) 1980 *SA* 3,4
Turner, J W C (Gala and Scotland) 1968 *SA* 1,2,3,4

Underwood, R (RAF, Leicester and England) 1989 *A* 1,2,3, 1993 *NZ* 1,2,3
Unwin, E J (Rosslyn Park, Army and England) 1938 *SA* 1,2
Uttley, R M (Gosforth and England) 1974 *SA* 1,2,3,4

Voyce, A T (Gloucester and England) 1924 *SA* 3,4

Waddell, G H (Cambridge U, London Scottish and Scotland) 1962 *SA* 1,2
Waddell, H (Glasgow Acads and Scotland) 1924 *SA* 1,2,4
Walker, S (Instonians and Ireland) 1938 *SA* 1,2,3
Wallace, W (Percy Park) 1924 *SA* 1
Waller, P D (Newport and Wales) 1910 *SA* 1,2,3
Ward, A J P (Garryowen and Ireland) 1980 *SA* 1
Waters, J A (Selkirk and Scotland) 1938 *SA* 3
Watkins, D (Newport and Wales) 1966 *A* 1,2, *NZ* 1,2,3,4
Watkins, S J (Newport and Wales) 1966 *A* 1,2,*NZ* 3
Webb, J (Abertillery and Wales) 1910 *SA* 1,2,3
Welsh, W B (Hawick and Scotland) 1930 *NZ* 4
Weston, M P (Richmond, Durham City and England) 1962 *SA* 1,2,3,4, 1966 *A* 1,2
Wheeler, P J (Leicester and England) 1977 *NZ* 2,3,4, 1980 *SA* 1,2,3,4
White, D B (London Scottish and Scotland) 1989 *A* 1
Whitley, H (Northern and *England) 1924 *SA* 1,3,4
Willcox, J G (Oxford U, Harlequins and England) 1962 *SA* 1,2,4
Williams, B L (Cardiff and Wales) 1950 *NZ* 2,3,4, *A* 1,2

Williams, C (Swansea and Wales) 1980 *SA* 1,2,3,4
Williams, D (Ebbw Vale and Wales) 1966 *A* 1,2, *NZ* 1,2,4
Williams, D B (Cardiff and *Wales) 1977 *NZ* 1,2,3
Williams, J J (Llanelli and Wales) 1974 *SA* 1,2,3,4, 1977 *NZ* 1,2,3
Williams, J P R (London Welsh and Wales) 1971 *NZ* 1,2,3,4, 1974 *SA* 1,2,3,4
Williams, R H (Llanelli and Wales) 1955 *SA* 1,2,3,4, 1959 *A* 1,2, *NZ* 1,2,3,4
Williams, S H (Newport and *England) 1910 *SA* 1,2,3
Williams, W O G (Swansea and Wales) 1955 *SA* 1,2,3,4
Willis, W R (Cardiff and Wales) 1950 *NZ* 4, *A* 1,2
Wilson, S (London Scottish and Scotland) 1966 *A* 2, *NZ* 1,2,3,4
Windsor, R W (Pontypool and Wales) 1974 *SA* 1,2,3,4, 1977 *NZ* 1

Winterbottom, P J (Headingley, Harlequins and England) 1983 *NZ* 1,2,3,4, 1993 *NZ* 1,2,3
Wood, B G M (Garryowen and Ireland) 1959 *NZ* 1,3
Wood, K B (Leicester) 1910 *SA* 1,3
Woodward, C R (Leicester and England) 1980 *SA* 2,3

Young, A T (Cambridge U, Blackheath and England) 1924 *SA* 2
Young, D (Cardiff and Wales) 1989 *A* 1,2,3
Young, J (Harrogate, RAF and Wales) 1968 *SA* 1
Young, J R C (Oxford U, Harlequins and England) 1959 *NZ* 2
Young, R M (Queen's U, Belfast, Collegians and Ireland) 1966 *A* 1,2, *NZ* 1, 1968 *SA* 3

The fleet-footed Lion Rory Underwood, who scored three tries on the British Isles 1993 tour of New Zealand.

RESULTS OF BRITISH ISLES MATCHES
(*up to 31 March 1994*)

From 1910 onwards – the tour to South Africa in that year was the first fully representative one in which the four Home Unions co-operated.

v SOUTH AFRICA

Played 30   British Isles won 8, South Africa won 18, Drawn 4

1910 *1* Johannesburg
South Africa 1G 3T (14) to 1DG 2T (10)

2 Port Elizabeth
British Isles 1G 1T (8) to 1T (3)

3 Cape Town
South Africa 3G 1PG 1T (21) to 1G (5)
South Africa won series 2-1

1924 *1* Durban
South Africa 1DG 1T (7) to 1T(3)

2 Johannesburg
South Africa 1G 1PG 3T (17) to 0

3 Port Elizabeth
Drawn 1T (3) each

4 Cape Town
South Africa 1DG 4T (16) to 1PG 2T (9)
South Africa won series 3-0, with 1 draw

1938 *1* Johannesburg
South Africa 4G 2PG (26) to 4PG (12)

2 Port Elizabeth
South Africa 2G 2PG 1T (19) to 1T (3)

3 Cape Town
British Isles 1G 1PG 1DG 3T (21) to 2G 1PG 1T (16)
South Africa won series 2-1

1955 *1* Johannesburg
British Isles 4G 1T (23) to 2G 2PG 2T (22)

2 Cape Town
South Africa 2G 5T (25) to 1PG 2T (9)

3 Pretoria
British Isles 1PG 1DG 1T (9) to 2PG (6)

4 Port Elizabeth
South Africa 2G 1DG 3T (22) to 1G 1T (8)
Series drawn 2-2

1962 *1* Johannesburg
Drawn 1T (3) each

2 Durban
South Africa 1PG (3) to 0

3 Cape Town
South Africa 1G 1PG (8) to 1DG (3)

4 Bloemfontein
South Africa 5G 2PG 1T (34) to 1G 1PG 2T (14)
South Africa won series 3-0, with 1 draw

1968 *1* Pretoria
South Africa 2G 4PG 1T (25) to 1G 5PG (20)

2 Port Elizabeth
Drawn 2PG (6) each

3 Cape Town
South Africa 1G 2PG (11) to 2PG (6)

4 Johannesburg
South Africa 2G 1DG 2T (19) to 2PG (6)
South Africa won series 3-0, with 1 draw

1974 *1* Cape Town
British Isles 3PG 1DG (12) to 1DG (3)

2 Pretoria
British Isles 1G 1PG 1DG 4T (28) to 2PG 1DG (9)

3 Port Elizabeth
British Isles 1G 2PG 2DG 2T (26) to 3PG (9)

4 Johannesburg
Drawn British Isles 1G 1PG 1T (13) South Africa 3PG 1T (13)
British Isles won series 3-0, with 1 draw

1980 *1* Cape Town
South Africa 3G 2T (26) to 5PG 1DG 1T (22)

2 Bloemfontein
South Africa 2G 2PG 2T (26) to 1G 3PG 1T (19)

3 Port Elizabeth
South Africa 1G 1PG 1DG (12) to 2PG 1T (10)

4 Pretoria
British Isles 1G 1PG 2T (17) to 3PG 1T (13)
South Africa won series 3-1

v NEW ZEALAND

Played 31   British Isles won 6, New Zealand won 23, Drawn 2

1930 *1* Dunedin
British Isles 2T (6) to 1T (3)

2 Christchurch
New Zealand 2G 1GM (13) to 2G (10)

3 Auckland
New Zealand 1G 1DG 2T (15)
to 2G (10)

4 Wellington
New Zealand 2G 4T (22) to 1G 1PG (8)
New Zealand won series 3-1

1950 *1* Dunedin
Drawn 1PG 2T (9) each

2 Christchurch
New Zealand 1G 1T (8) to 0

3 Wellington
New Zealand 1PG 1T (6) to 1PG (3)

4 Auckland
New Zealand 1G 1DG 1T (11)
to 1G 1PG (8)
New Zealand won series 3-0, with 1 draw

1959 *1* Dunedin
New Zealand 6PG (18)
to 1G 1PG 3T (17)

2 Wellington
New Zealand 1G 2T (11) to 1G 1PG (8)

3 Christchurch
New Zealand 2G 1PG 1DG 2T (22)
to 1G 1PG (8)

4 Auckland
British Isles 3T (9) to 2PG (6)
New Zealand won series 3-1

1966 *1* Dunedin
New Zealand 1G 2PG 1DG 2T (20)
to 1PG (3)

2 Wellington
New Zealand 2G 1PG 1T (16)
to 3PG 1DG (12)

3 Christchurch
New Zealand 2G 2PG 1T (19) to 2T (6)

4 Auckland
New Zealand 3G 1PG 1DG 1T (24)
to 1G 1PG 1T (11)
New Zealand won series 4-0

1971 *1* Dunedin
British Isles 2PG 1T (9) to 1PG (3)

2 Christchurch
New Zealand 2G 1PG 3T (22)
to 1PG 1DG 2T (12)

3 Wellington
British Isles 2G 1DG (13) to 1T (3)

4 Auckland
Drawn British Isles 1G 2PG 1DG (14)
New Zealand 1G 2PG 1T (14)
British Isles won series 2-1, with 1 draw

1977 *1* Wellington
New Zealand 2G 1T (16) to 4PG (12)

2 Christchurch
British Isles 3PG 1T (13) to 3PG (9)

3 Dunedin
New Zealand 1G 2PG 1DG 1T (19)
to 1PG 1T (7)

4 Auckland
New Zealand 2PG 1T (10) to 1G 1PG (9)
New Zealand won series 3-1

1983 *1* Christchurch
New Zealand 3PG 1DG 1T (16)
to 3PG 1DG (12)

2 Wellington
New Zealand 1G 1PG (9) to 0

3 Dunedin
New Zealand 1G 3PG (15) to 2T (8)

4 Auckland
New Zealand 4G 2PG 2T (38) to 2PG (6)
New Zealand won series 4-0

1993 *1* Christchurch
New Zealand 5PG 1T (20) to 6PG (18)

2 Wellington
British Isles 4PG 1DG 1T (20) to 1G (7)

3 Auckland
New Zealand 3G 3PG (30) to 1G 2PG (13)
New Zealand won series 2-1

v AUSTRALIA

Played 10   British Isles won 8, Australia won 2, Drawn 0

1930 *1* Sydney
Australia 2T (6) to 1G (5)

1950 *1* Brisbane
British Isles 2G 2PG 1DG (19)
to 2PG (6)

2 Sydney
British Isles 3G 1PG 2T (24) to 1T (3)
British Isles won series 2-0

1959 *1* Brisbane
British Isles 1G 2PG 1DG 1T (17)
to 2PG (6)

2 Sydney
British Isles 3G 1PG 2T (24) to 1PG (3)
British Isles won series 2-0

1966 *1* Sydney
British Isles 1G 1PG 1T (11)
to 1G 1PG (8)

2 Brisbane
British Isles 5G 1PG 1DG (31) to 0
British Isles won series 2-0

1989 *1* Sydney
Australia 4G 1PG 1DG (30)
to 3PG 1DG (12)

2 Brisbane
British Isles 1G 2PG 1DG 1T (19)
to 1G 2PG (12)

3 Sydney
British Isles 5PG 1T (19) to 1G 4PG (18)
British Isles won series 2-1

BRITISH ISLES RECORDS
(*up to 31 March 1994*)

From 1910 onwards – the tour to South Africa in that year was the first fully representative one in which the four Home Unions co-operated.

TEAM RECORDS

Highest score
31 v Australia (31-0) 1966 Brisbane
v individual countries
28 v S Africa (28-9) 1974 Pretoria
20 v New Zealand (20-7) 1993 Wellington
31 v Australia (31-0) 1966 Brisbane

Biggest winning points margin
31 v Australia (31-0) 1966 Brisbane
v individual countries
19 v S Africa (28-9) 1974 Pretoria
13 v New Zealand (20-7) 1993 Wellington
31 v Australia (31-0) 1966 Brisbane

Highest score by opposing team
38 New Zealand (6-38) 1983 Auckland
by individual countries
34 S Africa (14-34) 1962 Bloemfontein
38 New Zealand (6-38) 1983 Auckland
30 Australia (12-30) 1989 Sydney

Biggest losing points margin
32 v New Zealand (6-38) 1983 Auckland
v individual countries
20 v S Africa (14-34) 1962 Bloemfontein
32 v New Zealand (6-38) 1983 Auckland
18 v Australia (12-30) 1989 Sydney

Most tries by B Isles in an international
5 {
v Australia (24-3) 1950 Sydney
v S Africa (23-22) 1955 Johannesburg
v Australia (24-3) 1959 Sydney
v Australia (31-0) 1966 Brisbane
v S Africa (28-9) 1974 Pretoria
}

Most tries against B Isles in an international
7 by South Africa (9-25) 1955 Cape Town

Most points on overseas tour (all matches)
842 in Australia, New Zealand and Canada (33 matches) 1959
(includes 582 points in 25 matches in New Zealand)

Most tries on overseas tour (all matches)
165 in Australia, New Zealand and Canada (33 matches) 1959
(includes 113 tries in 25 matches in New Zealand)

INDIVIDUAL RECORDS

Most capped player
W J McBride 17 1962-74
in individual positions
Full-back
J P R Williams 8[1] 1971-74
Wing
A J F O'Reilly 9(10)[2] 1955-59
Centre
C M H Gibson 8(12)[3] 1966-71
Fly-half
P Bennett 8 1974-77
Scrum-half
R E G Jeeps 13 1955-62
Prop
G Price 12 1977-83
Hooker
B V Meredith 8 1955-62
Lock
W J McBride 17 1962-74
Flanker
N A A Murphy 8 1959-66
No 8
T M Davies 8[4] 1971-74

[1] *A R Irvine, 9 Tests, played 7 times at full-back and twice as a wing*
[2] *O'Reilly played once as a centre*
[3] *Gibson played 4 times as a fly-half. I R McGeechan, 8 Tests, played 7 times as a centre and once, as a replacement, on the wing*
[4] *Both A E I Pask and J W Telfer (8 Tests each), played 4 Tests at No 8 and 4 Tests at flanker*

Longest international career
W J McBride   13 seasons   1962-74

Most consecutive Tests – 15
W J McBride 1966-74

Most internationals as captain – 6
A R Dawson 1959

Most points in internationals – 66
A G Hastings (6 appearances) 1989-93

Most points in an international – 18
A J P Ward v S Africa 1980 Cape Town
A G Hastings v New Zealand 1993
   Christchurch

Most tries in internationals – 6
A J F O'Reilly (10 appearances) 1955-59

Most tries in an international – 2
C D Aarvold v New Zealand 1930
   Christchurch
J E Nelson v Australia 1950 Sydney
M J Price v Australia 1959 Sydney
M J Price v New Zealand 1959 Dunedin
D K Jones v Australia 1966 Brisbane
T G R Davies v New Zealand 1971
   Christchurch
J J Williams v S Africa 1974 Pretoria
J J Williams v S Africa 1974 Port Elizabeth

Most conversions in internationals – 6
S Wilson (5 matches) 1966

Most conversions in an international – 5
S Wilson v Australia 1966 Brisbane

Most dropped goals in internationals – 2
D Watkins (6 matches) 1966
B John (5 matches) 1968-71
P Bennett (8 matches) 1974-77
C R Andrew (5 matches) 1989-93
(P F Bush also dropped 2 goals in Tests played by British teams prior to 1910)

Most dropped goals in an international – 2
P Bennett v S Africa 1974 Port Elizabeth

Most penalty goals in internationals – 20
A G Hastings (6 matches) 1989-93

Most penalty goals in an international – 6
A G Hastings v New Zealand 1993
   Christchurch

Most points for B Isles on overseas tour – 188
B John (17 appearances) 1971 Australia/
   N Zealand
(including 180 points in 16 appearances in
   N Zealand)

Most tries for B Isles on overseas tour – 22★
A J F O'Reilly (23 appearances) 1959
   Australia/N Zealand/Canada
(includes 17★ tries in 17 appearances in
   N Zealand)
★Includes one penalty try

Most points for B Isles in international series – 38
A G Hastings (3 appearances) 1993
   New Zealand

Most tries for B Isles in international series – 4
J J Williams (4 appearances) 1974 S Africa

Most points for B Isles in any match on tour – 37
A G B Old v South Western Districts
   1974 Mossel Bay, S Africa

Most tries for B Isles in any match on tour – 6
D J Duckham v West Coast-Buller 1971
   Greymouth, N Zealand
J J Williams v South Western Districts
   1974 Mossel Bay, S Africa
(A R Irvine scored 5 tries from full-back
   v King Country-Wanganui 1977
   Taumarunui, N Zealand)

LEADING CAP-WINNERS
(up to 31 March 1994)

ENGLAND

R Underwood	65
P J Winterbottom	58
C R Andrew	57
W A Dooley	55
B C Moore	50
W D C Carling	47
A Neary	43
J V Pullin	42
P J Wheeler	41
J A Probyn	37
D J Duckham	36
G S Pearce	36
D Richards	36
D P Rogers	34
W B Beaumont	34
J P Scott	34
J M Webb	33
P W Dodge	32
W W Wakefield	31
F E Cotton	31
M A C Slemen	31
E Evans	30
J Leonard	30
R Cove-Smith	29
C R Jacobs	29
M P Weston	29
P J Squires	29
R J Hill	29
J Butterfield	28
S J Smith	28
P A G Rendall	28
J C Guscott	28
A T Voyce	27
J S Tucker	27
M C Teague	27
J Carleton	26
C N Lowe	25
J D Currie	25
M S Phillips	25
C B Stevens	25
W H Hare	25
M J Colclough	25

SCOTLAND

J M Renwick	52
C T Deans	52
A R Irvine	51
A B Carmichael	50
A G Hastings	50
S Hastings	50
A J Tomes	48
R J Laidlaw	47
A F McHarg	44
K W Robertson	44
I G Milne	44
D M B Sole	44
J McLauchlan	43
J Y Rutherford	42
D B White	41
J Jeffrey	40
H F McLeod	40
D M D Rollo	40
J MacD Bannerman	37
I Tukalo	37
I A M Paxton	36
C M Chalmers	35
A G Stanger	35
A P Burnell	34
F Calder	34
A R Smith	33
I S Smith	32
F A L Laidlaw	32
I R McGeechan	32
D G Leslie	32
N S Bruce	31
I H P Laughland	31
G L Brown	30
G Armstrong	30
K S Milne	30
W I D Elliot	29
S R P Lineen	29
D F Cronin	29
W M Simmers	28
P K Stagg	28
J W Y Kemp	27
K J F Scotland	27
P C Brown	27
J H Calder	27
D I Johnston	27
G R T Baird	27
W E Maclagan	26
D Drysdale	26
J C McCallum	26
G P S Macpherson	26
J B Nelson	25
J P Fisher	25
J R Beattie	25
J W Telfer	25

IRELAND

C M H Gibson	69
W J McBride	63
J F Slattery	61
P A Orr	58
T J Kiernan	54
D G Lenihan	52
M I Keane	51
J W Kyle	46
K W Kennedy	45
B J Mullin	45
M J Kiernan	43
G V Stephenson	42
N A A Murphy	41
W P Duggan	41
K D Crossan	41
N J Henderson	40
R J McLoughlin	40
P M Matthews	38
S Millar	37
H P MacNeill	37
J R Kavanagh	35
W A Mulcahy	35
E O'D Davy	34
T M Ringland	34
D C Fitzgerald	34
M T Bradley	34
P M Dean	32
A C Pedlow	30
G T Hamlet	30
W E Crawford	30
J D Clinch	30
J L Farrell	29
B G M Wood	29
A J F O'Reilly	29
M Sugden	28
J S McCarthy	28
A M Magee	27
A R Dawson	27
M G Molloy	27
J J Moloney	27
W A Anderson	27
J C Walsh	26
R M Young	26
J B O'Driscoll	26
G R Beamish	25
K D Mullen	25
F P K Bresnihan	25
A T A Duggan	25
B J McGann	25
T O Grace	25
S A McKinney	25
C F Fitzgerald	25
D G Irwin	25
S J Smith	25
N P J Francis	25

WALES

J P R Williams	55
G O Edwards	53
R N Jones	47
T G R Davies	46
K J Jones	44
G Price	41
I C Evans	41
P T Davies	39
T M Davies	38
P H Thorburn	37
D Williams	36
R M Owen	35
B V Meredith	34
D I E Bebb	34
W D Morris	34
A J Martin	34
R L Norster	34
W J Bancroft	33

B Price	32
J R G Stephens	32
G A D Wheel	32
M G Ring	32
J J Williams	30
S P Fenwick	30
W J Trew	29
C I Morgan	29
P Bennett	29
J Squire	29
M R Hall	29
R W Windsor	28
M Griffiths	28
A J Gould	27
W C Powell	27
M C Thomas	27
H J Morgan	27
A M Hadley	27
J Davies	27
R C C Thomas	26
A E I Pask	26
S J Watkins	26
J Taylor	26
A Clement	26
G Travers	25
H Tanner	25
B John	25
N R Gale	25
W D Thomas	25
T D Holmes	25
G O Llewellyn	25

FRANCE

P Sella	98
S Blanco	93
R Bertranne	69
M Crauste	63
B Dauga	63
J Condom	61
J-P Rives	59
P Berbizier	56
L Rodriguez	56
R Paparemborde	55
A Domenech	52
F Mesnel	52
J Prat	51
W Spanghero	51
J-L Joinel	51
M Celaya	50
P Dintrans	50
A Boniface	48
J-P Lux	47
J-C Skréla	46
D Erbani	46
P Lagisquet	46
M Vannier	43
O Roumat	43
J-P Garuet	42
E Champ	42
P Ondarts	42
J Dupuy	40
C Darrouy	40
F Haget	40
L Armary	40

J-M Aguirre	39
M Cecillon	39
G Dufau	38
D Camberabero	36
J-B Lafond	36
G Boniface	35
E Cester	35
A Paco	35
P Saint-André	35
E Ribère	34
J Bouquet	34
P Villepreux	34
J Iraçabal	34
J-P Romeu	34
G Basquet	33
C Lacaze	33
C Dourthe	33
D Dubroca	33
J Gachassin	32
J-P Bastiat	32
A Cassayet	31
A Jauréguy	31
M Prat	31
F Moncla	31
G Cholley	31
D Codorniou	31
P Albaladéjo	30
A Roques	30
R Bénésis	30
A Lorieux	30
R Biénès	29
L Mias	29
J Trillo	28
J-P Lescarboura	28
L Cabannes	28
H Rancoule	27
P Lacroix	27
J-C Berejnoi	27
C Carrère	27
J Fouroux	27
J Gallion	27
B Chevallier	26
J Barthe	26
J-M Cabanier	26
A Gruarin	26
J-L Azarète	26
A Vaquerin	26
M Andrieu	26
R Martine	25
J Maso	25
J-L Averous	25
P Estève	25

SOUTH AFRICA

F C H Du Preez	38
J H Ellis	38
J F K Marais	35
J P Engelbrecht	33
J L Gainsford	33
J T Claassen	28
H E Botha	28
F du T Roux	27
L G Wilson	27

T P Bedford	25
D J de Villiers	25
P J F Greyling	25
S H Nomis	25
P J Visagie	25
L C Moolman	24
D M Gerber	24
D J Hopwood	22
A C Koch	22
M Du Plessis	22
J A du Rand	21
M T S Stofberg	21
J S Germishuys	20

NEW ZEALAND

G W Whetton	58
J J Kirwan	58
S B T Fitzpatrick	56
C E Meads	55
S C McDowell	46
G J Fox	46
A M Haden	41
I A Kirkpatrick	39
K R Tremain	38
B G Williams	38
R W Loe	38
G A Knight	36
A G Dalton	35
A J Whetton	35
B J Robertson	34
S S Wilson	34
M G Mexted	34
M N Jones	33
W J Whineray	32
I D Jones	32
D B Clarke	31
M W Shaw	30
T J Wright	30
S M Going	29
R W Norton	27
J T Stanley	27
M J Pierce	26
B J Lochore	25
B E McLeod	24
K F Gray	24
I J Clarke	24
J C Ashworth	24
D S Loveridge	24
W T Taylor	24
R A White	23
B G Fraser	23
Z V Brooke	23
W K Little	23
D J Graham	22
D Young	22
W T Shelford	22
G N K Mourie	21
M J B Hobbs	21
K L Skinner	20
C R Laidlaw	20
I N MacEwan	20
P J Whiting	20
C I Green	20
J K R Timu	20

AUSTRALIA

		A J Daly	33	J K Lenehan	24
		T J Horan	33	J P L White	24
D I Campese	80	E J A McKenzie	32	J W Cole	24
M P Lynagh	64	N M Shehadie	30	G Fay	24
N C Farr-Jones	63	P E McLean	30	R Phelps	23
S P Poidevin	59	B T Gavin	30	M P Burke	23
P G Johnson	42	J S Little	29	M C Roebuck	23
A R Miller	41	M E Loane	28	R A Smith	22
T A Lawton	41	S A Williams	28	J E C Meadows	22
S A G Cutler	40	K W Catchpole	27	W A Campbell	22
G V Davis	39	G A Shaw	27	E T Bonis	21
A G Slack	39	C T Burke	26	P F Hawthorne	21
A J McIntyre	38	E E Rodriguez	26	R J Heming	21
J E Thornett	37	J S Miller	26	A N McGill	21
J N B Hipwell	36	R B Prosser	25	W H Cerutti	21
A A Shaw	36	G Cornelsen	25	A S Cameron	20
P N Kearns	36	M G Ella	25	B J Ellwood	20
B J Moon	35	R G Gould	25	C J Windon	20
S N Tuynman	34	P C Grigg	25		
R J McCall	34	M J Hawker	25		

WORLD'S LEADING CAP-WINNERS
(up to 31 March 1994)

For purposes of comparison, the following list includes appearances for individual countries in major international matches.

P Sella	France	98	S B T Fitzpatrick	New Zealand	56
S Blanco	France	93	C E Meads	New Zealand	55
D I Campese	Australia	80	J P R Williams	Wales	55
C M H Gibson	Ireland	69	R Paparemborde	France	55
R Bertranne	France	69	W A Dooley	England	55
R Underwood	England	65	T J Kiernan	Ireland	54
M P Lynagh	Australia	64	G O Edwards	Wales	53
M Crauste	France	63	A Domenech	France	52
W J McBride	Ireland	63	J M Renwick	Scotland	52
B Dauga	France	63	C T Deans	Scotland	52
N C Farr-Jones	Australia	63	F Mesnel	France	52
J Condom	France	61	J Prat	France	51
J F Slattery	Ireland	61	W Spanghero	France	51
J-P Rives	France	59	A R Irvine	Scotland	51
S P Poidevin	Australia	59	M I Keane	Ireland	51
P A Orr	Ireland	58	J-L Joinel	France	51
G W Whetton	New Zealand	58	M Celaya	France	50
P J Winterbottom	England	58	A B Carmichael	Scotland	50
J J Kirwan	New Zealand	58	P Dintrans	France	50
C R Andrew	England	57	A G Hastings	Scotland	50
L Rodriguez	France	56	B C Moore	England	50
P Berbizier	France	56	S Hastings	Scotland	50

The following list incorporates appearances by home countries' players for British Isles teams (the Lions) in international matches against New Zealand, Australia and South Africa (up to 31 March 1994). The number of Lions appearances is shown in brackets.

P Sella	France	98		J P R Williams	Wales	63	(8)
S Blanco	France	93		M Crauste	France	63	
C M H Gibson	Ireland	81	(12)	B Dauga	France	63	
W H McBride	Ireland	80	(17)	N C Farr-Jones	Australia	63	
D I Campese	Australia	80		C R Andrew	England	62	(5)
R Underwood	England	71	(6)	J Condom	France	61	
R Bertranne	France	69		A R Irvine	Scotland	60	(9)
J F Slattery	Ireland	65	(4)	T J Kiernan	Ireland	59	(5)
P J Winterbottom	England	65	(7)	J-P Rives	France	59	
M P Lynagh	Australia	64		P A Orr	Ireland	59	(1)
G O Edwards	Wales	63	(10)	S P Poidevin	Australia	59	

G W Whetton	New Zealand	58	
J J Kirwan	New Zealand	58	
W A Dooley	England	57	(2)
L Rodriguez	France	56	
P Berbizier	France	56	
S B T Fitzpatrick	New Zealand	56	
A G Hastings	Scotland	56	(6)
C E Meads	New Zealand	55	
R Paparemborde	France	55	
B C Moore	England	55	(5)
J M Renwick	Scotland	53	(1)
G Price	Wales	53	(12)
A Domenech	France	52	
C T Deans	Scotland	52	
J W Kyle	Ireland	52	(6)
M I Keane	Ireland	52	(1)
F Mesnel	France	52	
S Hastings	Scotland	52	(2)
J Prat	France	51	
W Spanghero	France	51	
T G R Davies	Wales	51	(5)
J McLauchlan	Scotland	51	(8)
J-L Joinel	France	51	
R J Laidlaw	Scotland	51	(4)
M Celaya	France	50	
A B Carmichael	Scotland	50	
P Dintrans	France	50	
R N Jones	Wales	50	(3)

Most appearances for the Lions are by W J McBride (Ireland) 17, R E G Jeeps (England) 13, C M H Gibson (Ireland) 12, G Price (Wales) 12, and A J F O'Reilly (Ireland), R H Williams (Wales), and G O Edwards (Wales) 10 each, up to 31 March 1994.

Hooker Brian Moore joins the world's leading cap-winners list with 50 for England and 5 for the Lions.

INTERNATIONAL REFEREES 1993-94

Leading Referees

Up to 31 March 1994, in major international matches. These include all matches for which senior members of the International Board have awarded caps, and also all matches played in the World Cup final stages.

12 or more internationals

C Norling	Wales	25	F Palmade	France	17
K D Kelleher	Ireland	23	B S Cumberlege	England	16
D G Walters	Wales	23	D I H Burnett	Ireland	15
W D Bevan	Wales	23	C H Gadney	England	15
M Joseph	Wales	22	O E Doyle	Ireland	15
R C Williams	Ireland	21	S R Hilditch	Ireland	15
K V J Fitzgerald	Australia	21	I David	Wales	14
F A Howard	England	20	Dr I R Vanderfield	Australia	14
J M Fleming	Scotland	20	R G Byres	Australia	13
A M Hosie	Scotland	19	J P Murphy	New Zealand	13
D J Bishop	New Zealand	19	N R Sanson	Scotland	13
Capt M J Dowling	Ireland	18	K H Lawrence	New Zealand	13
A E Freethy	Wales	18	R F Johnson	England	12
R C Quittenton	England	18	T D Schofield	Wales	12
J R West	Ireland	18	T H Vile	Wales	12
J B Anderson	Scotland	18	W Williams	England	12
R Hourquet	France	18	A R MacNeill	Australia	12
D P D'Arcy	Ireland	17			

Major international match appearances 1993-94

Matches controlled between 1 April 1993 and 31 March 1994.

1993

R v F	B W Stirling (Ireland)	Arg v SA(2)	W D Bevan (Wales)
Z v W	*I Rogers (South Africa)	W v C	O E Doyle (Ireland)
Z v W	*I Anderson (South Africa)	I v R	*R Yeman (Wales)
Nm v W	K W McCartney (Scotland)	S v NZ	F Burger (South Africa)
NZ v BI	B Kinsey (Australia)	E v NZ	F Burger (South Africa)
NZ v BI(2)	P Robin (France)		
SA v F	S R Hilditch (Ireland)	**1994**	
SA v F	E F Morrison (England)	F v I	J M Fleming (Scotland)
A v Tg	*B Leask (Australia)	W v S	P Robin (France)
NZ v A	W D Bevan (Wales)	S v E	L L McLachlan (New Zealand)
NZ v WS	J M Fleming (Scotland)	I v W	A J Spreadbury (England)
A v SA	L L McLachlan (New Zealand)	E v I	*P Thomas (France)
A v SA(2)	E F Morrison (England)	W v F	L L McLachlan (New Zealand)
C v A	W D Bevan (Wales)	F v E	S R Hilditch (Ireland)
W v J	E F Morrison (England)	I v S	E F Morrison (England)
F v R	J M Fleming (Scotland)	S v F	W D Bevan (Wales)
F v A(2)	D J Bishop (New Zealand)	E v W	J M Fleming (Scotland)

*Denotes debut in a major international

Referees dismissing players in a major international

A E Freethy	E v NZ	1925	N R Sanson (two)	W v I	1977
K D Kelleher	S v NZ	1967	D I H Burnett	E v W	1980
R T Burnett	A v E	1975	C Norling	F v I	1984
W M Cooney	A v Fj	1976	K V J Fitzgerald	NZ v W	1987*

F A Howard	A v W	1987*	C Norling	A v F	1990
K V J Fitzgerald	Fj v E	1988	C J Hawke	E v Arg	1990
O E Doyle	Arg v F	1988	E F Morrison	R v F	1991
B W Stirling (two)	E v Fj	1989	J M Fleming (two)	Arg v WS	1991*
F A Howard	W v F	1990	S R Hilditch (two)	F v E	1992
F A Howard	S v F	1990	D J Bishop	NZ v Wld	1992
F A Howard	Nm v W	1990	E F Morrison	A v SA	1993
A J Spreadbury	A v F	1990			

World Cup matches

INTERNATIONAL REFEREES

The list which follows shows referees who have controlled major internationals (i.e. games for which a senior member country of the IB has awarded caps, or the final stages of the official World Cup) since 1876, when referees were first appointed, up to 31 March 1994.

ABBREVIATIONS

A – Australia; Arg – Argentina; AW – Anglo-Welsh; B – British Forces' and Home Union Teams; Bb – Barbarians; BI – British Isles; C – Canada; Cv – New Zealand Cavaliers; Cz – Czechoslovakia; E – England; F – France; Fj – Fiji; GB – Great Britain; G – Germany; I – Ireland; It – Italy; J – Japan; K – New Zealand Kiwis; M – New Zealand Maoris; Nm – Namibia; NZ – New Zealand; NZA – New Zealand Army; P – President's XV; R – Romania; S – Scotland; SA – South Africa; SAm – South America; SK – South Korea; Tg – Tonga; US – United States of America; W – Wales; Wld– World XV; WS – Western Samoa; Z – Zimbabwe; (C) – Special Centenary Match; (R) – Replacement. Entries in square brackets [ ] indicate matches in the World Cup final stages.

N.B. The Australian Rugby Union now recognises the internationals played by the New South Wales touring teams of the 1920s as cap matches.

Ackermann, C J (South Africa) 1953 *SA v A* (2), 1955 *SA v BI*, 1958 *SA v F*
Acton, W H (Ireland) 1926 *W v E, E v S*
Adams, A (South Africa) 1991 *US v F* (2)
Alderson, F H R (England) 1903 *S v I*
Allan, M A (Scotland) 1931 *I v W, I v SA,* 1933 *E v I, I v W,* 1934 *I v E,* 1935 *E v I, I v W,* 1936 *I v E,* 1937 *I v W,* 1947 *I v E,* 1948 *I v W*
Allen, J W (Ireland) 1906 *W v S, S v E*
Anderson, C (Scotland) 1928 *I v F*
Anderson, I (South Africa) 1993 *Z v W*
Anderson, J B (Scotland) 1981 *W v E, I v A,* 1982 *R v F,* 1983 *I v E, A v NZ,* 1984 *E v W,* 1986 *W v F, NZ v A,* 1987 [*A v US, A v I, F v A*], 1988 *A v NZ*(2), 1989 *I v F, R v E, F v B,* 1991 [*E v It, Arg v WS*]
Anderson, J H (South Africa) 1903 *SA v GB*
Angus, A W (Scotland) 1924 *W v E,* 1927 *I v A*
Ashmore, H L (England) 1890 *S v I,* 1891 *S v W,* 1892 *S v I,* 1894 *I v S,* 1895 *S v I*
Austin, A W C (Scotland) 1952 *W v F,* 1953 *I v E,* 1954 *I v W*
Austry, R (France) 1972 *E v I*

Badger, Dr (England) 1900 *I v S*
Baise, M (South Africa) 1967 *SA v F* (2), 1968 *SA v BI* (2), 1969 *SA v A,* 1974 *SA v BI* (2)
Baise, S (South Africa) 1969 *SA v A*
Barnes, P (Australia) 1938 *A v NZ*
Baxter, J (England) 1913 *F v S, S v I,* 1914 *I v S,* 1920 *S v I,* 1921 *W v S, I v S,* 1923 *W v S,* 1925 *W v S, I v W*
Bean, A S (England) 1939 *W v S,* 1945 *W v F,* 1946 *F v W,* 1947 *F v W, W v A,* 1948 *S v F, W v F,* 1949 *S v I*
Beattie, R A (Scotland) 1937 *E v W,* 1938 *W v E,* 1945 *B v F,* 1947 *W v E, I v A,* 1948 *E v W,* 1949 *I v E,* 1950 *E v I, I v W*
Beattie, W H (Australia) 1899 *A v GB,* 1904 *A v GB*
Bell, T (Ireland) 1932 *S v W,* 1933 *E v W*
Bevan, W D (Wales) 1985 *E v R,* 1986 *F v E, NZ v A* (2), 1987 [*NZ v Fj, F v Z*], 1989 *I v W,* 1990 *NZ v S,* 1991 *I v F,* [*F v Fj, S v WS, E v A*], 1992 *S v E, E v I, NZ v Wld* (2), 1993 *F v S, NZ v A, C v A, Arg v SA* (2), 1994 *S v F*

Beves, G (South Africa) 1896 *SA v GB*
Bezuidenhout, G P (South Africa) 1976 *SA v NZ* (3)
Bishop, D J (New Zealand) 1986 *Fj v W, R v F, I v R,* 1987 [*W v Tg, W v C*], 1988 *A v E* (2), *E v A, S v A,* 1990 *S v E, I v W,* 1991 *S v W, W v I,* [*A v Arg, F v E*], 1992 *NZ v Wld, SA v A,* 1993 *F v A* (2)
Bisset, W M (South Africa) 1896 *SA v GB*
Bonnet, J-P (France) 1979 *W v E,* 1980 *S v E, SA v BI* (2), 1981 *I v E, Arg v E* (2), 1982 *W v S*
Bott, J G (Scotland) 1931 *W v S,* 1933 *W v S*
Boundy, L M (England) 1955 *S v I,* 1956 *W v S,* 1957 *F v S, I v F, S v I, R v F,* 1958 *S v F,* 1959 *S v I,* 1961 *S v SA*
Bowden, G (Scotland) 1910 *F v E*
Bowen, D H (Wales) 1905 *E v S*
Bradburn, T J (England) 1928 *F v A,* 1929 *F v G*
Bressy, Y (France) 1988 *W v S*
Brook, P G (England) 1963 *F v W,* 1964 *W v S,* 1965 *W v I, I v SA,* 1966 *F v I, It v F, R v F*
Brown, A (Australia) 1907 *A v NZ*
Brown, D A (England) 1960 *I v W, It v F*
Brunton, J (England) 1924 *W v NZ*
Buchanan, A (Scotland) 1877 *I v S,* 1880 *S v I*
Bullerwell, I M (England) 1988 *W v R,* 1990 *F v R*
Burger, F (South Africa) 1989 *F v A* (2), 1990 *S v Arg,* 1992 *S v F, F v I, Arg v F* (2), 1993 *S v NZ, E v NZ*
Burmeister, R D (South Africa) 1949 *SA v NZ* (2), 1953 *SA v A,* 1955 *SA v BI* (2), 1960 *SA v NZ* (2), 1961 *SA v A*
Burnand, F W (England) 1890 *I v W*
Burnet, W (Scotland) 1932 *I v E,* 1934 *W v I*
Burnett, D I H (Ireland) 1977 *W v E,* 1979 *F v W,* 1980 *E v W,* 1981 *S v W, E v S,* 1982 *W v F, F v Arg,* 1983 *E v F,* 1984 *S v E, A v NZ,* 1985 *E v F, NZ v A,* 1986 *S v F,* 1987 [*S v Z, NZ v S*]
Burnett, R T (Australia) 1973 *A v Tg,* 1974 *A v NZ,* 1975 *A v E, A v J,* 1978 *A v W*
Burrell, G (Scotland) 1958 *E v I,* 1959 *W v I*
Burrell, R P (Scotland) 1966 *I v W,* 1967 *I v F, F v NZ,* 1969 *I v E, F v W*
Butt, C C (Australia) 1914 *A v NZ*
Byres, R G (Australia) 1976 *A v Fj,* 1978 *A v W,* 1979

343

A v I (2), *A v NZ*, 1980 *A v NZ*, 1981 *NZ v S*, 1982 *A v S* (2), 1983 *NZ v BI* (2), 1984 *I v W, W v F*

Calitz, M (South Africa) 1961 *SA v I*
Calmet, R (France) 1970 *E v W*
Calver, E W (England) 1914 *F v I*
Camardon, A (Argentina) 1960 *Arg v F*
Campbell, A (New Zealand) 1908 *NZ v AW* (2)
Carlson, K R V (South Africa) 1962 *SA v BI*
Cartwright, V H (England) 1906 *I v S*, 1909 *S v I*, 1910 *I v S, F v I*, 1911 *S v I*
Castens, H H (South Africa) 1891 *SA v GB*
Ceccon, A (France) 1991 *I v E, R v S*
Chambers, J (Ireland) 1888 *W v S, I v M*, 1890 *S v E*, 1891 *E v S*
Chapman, W S (Australia) 1938 *A v NZ* (2)
Charman, R (England) 1919 *W v NZA*
Chevrier, G (France) 1980 *I v S*
Chiene, Dr J (Scotland) 1879 *I v S*
Clark, K H (Ireland) 1973 *E v F*, 1974 *S v F*, 1976 *F v E*
Cochrane, C B (Australia) 1907 *A v NZ*
Coffey, J J (Ireland) 1912 *S v F*
Colati, L (Fiji) 1991 [*I v J*]
Coles, P (England) 1903 *W v I*, 1905 *S v I*
Collett C K (Australia) 1981 *NZ v S*
Combe, A (Ireland) 1876 *I v E*
Cook, H G (Ireland) 1886 *S v E*
Cooney, R C (Australia) 1929 *A v NZ*, 1930 *A v BI*, 1932 *A v NZ*, 1934 *A v NZ*
Cooney, W M (Australia) 1972 *A v F*, 1975 *A v E, A v J*, 1976 *A v Fj*
Cooper, Dr P F (England) 1952 *I v W*, 1953 *S v W, W v I, F v It, W v NZ*, 1954 *I v NZ, W v S, It v F*, 1956 *F v I, W v F, It v F*, 1957 *F v W*
Corley, H H (Ireland) 1906 *S v SA*, 1908 *S v E*
Corr, W S (Australia) 1899 *A v GB* (2)
Costello, J (Fiji) 1972 *Fj v A*
Craven, W S D (England) 1920 *F v W*
Crawford, S H (Ireland) 1913 *W v E, S v W*, 1920 *S v W*, 1921 *S v E*
Cross, W (Scotland) 1877 *S v E*
Crowe, K J (Australia) 1965 *A v SA*, 1966 *A v BI*, 1968 *A v NZ*, 1976 *A v Fj*
Cumberlege, B S (England) 1926 *S v I, W v I*, 1927 *S v F, I v S, I v W*, 1928 *S v I*, 1929 *F v I, S v F, I v S*, 1930 *I v F, S v I*, 1931 *I v S*, 1932 *S v SA, S v I*, 1933 *I v S*, 1934 *S v I*
Cunningham, J G (Scotland) 1913 *W v I*, 1921 *F v I*
Cuny, Dr A (France) 1976 *W v S*
Curnow, P (Canada) 1976 *US v F*
Currey, F I (England) 1887 *S v W*

Dallas, J D (Scotland) 1905 *W v NZ*, 1908 *I v W*, 1909 *W v E, I v E*, 1910 *E v W, I v W*, 1911 *I v E*, 1912 *I v W*
D'Arcy, D P (Ireland) 1967 *E v F, E v S, F v W, F v R*, 1968 *E v W, S v E, F v SA*, 1969 *E v F, W v E*, 1970 *W v S*, 1971 *W v E*, 1973 *F v NZ, F v W, F v R*, 1975 *E v S, F v Arg, W v A*
David, I (Wales) 1938 *E v S*, 1939 *S v E*, 1947 *E v S*, 1952 *F v I, I v S, E v I*, 1953 *S v I*, 1954 *S v F, E v NZ, S v NZ, F v NZ, F v E*, 1955 *I v F*, 1956 *F v E*
Davidson, I G (Ireland) 1911 *S v W*
Day, H L V (England) 1934 *S v W*
Day, P W (South Africa) 1903 *SA v GB*
Dedet, L (France) 1906 *F v NZ, F v E*
De Bruyn, C J (South Africa) 1969 *SA v A*, 1974 *SA v BI* (2)
Delany, M G (Ireland) 1899 *S v W*, 1900 *S v E*
Desclaux, M (France) 1992 *W v S*
Dickie, A I (Scotland) 1954 *F v I, E v I, W v F*, 1955 *I v E, W v I*, 1956 *E v I, I v W*, 1957 *W v E, I v E*, 1958 *W v A, W v F*
Dodds, J (Ireland) 1898 *S v E*
Domercq, G (France) 1972 *S v NZ*, 1973 *W v E, E v W*, 1977 *S v W*, 1978 *I v W*
Donaldson, S (Ireland) 1937 *S v E*
Donaldson, W P (South Africa) 1903 *SA v GB*
Don Wauchope, A R (Scotland) 1889 *W v I*, 1890 *E v I*, 1893 *I v E*
Doocey, T F (New Zealand) 1976 *NZ v I*, 1983 *E v S, F v W*
Douglas, W M (Wales) 1891 *I v E*, 1894 *E v I*, 1896 *S v E*, 1903 *E v S*
Doulcet, J-C (France) 1989 *S v W*

Dowling, M J (Ireland) 1947 *S v W*, 1950 *W v S, S v E, W v F*, 1951 *W v E, S v W, F v W, E v S, S v SA*, 1952 *W v S, F v SA, S v E*, 1953 *W v E, E v S*, 1954 *E v W*, 1955 *S v W*, 1956 *S v F, S v E*
Downes, A D (New Zealand) 1913 *NZ v A*
Doyle, O E (Ireland) 1984 *W v S, R v S, W v A*, 1987 *E v S*, 1988 *F v E, Arg v F* (2), *W v WS*, 1989 *F v S*, 1990 *F v E*, 1991 [*It v US, Fj v R*], 1992 *W v F*, 1993 *F v W, W v C*
Drennan, V (Ireland) 1914 *W v S*
Duffy, B (New Zealand) 1977 *NZ v BI*
Dumé, J (France) 1993 *W v E, S v W*
Duncan, J (New Zealand) 1908 *NZ v AW*
Durand, C (France) 1969 *E v S*, 1970 *I v S*, 1971 *E v S*

Eckhold, A E (New Zealand) 1923 *NZ v A*
Elliott, H B (England) 1955 *F v S, F v It*, 1956 *I v S*
Engelbrecht, Dr G K (South Africa) 1964 *SA v W*
Evans, F T (New Zealand) 1904 *NZ v GB*
Evans, G (England) 1905 *E v NZ*, 1908 *W v A*
Evans, W J (Wales) 1958 *I v A, F v E*

Farquhar, A B (New Zealand) 1961 *NZ v F* (3), 1962 *NZ v A* (2), 1964 *NZ v A*
Faull, J W (Wales) 1936 *E v NZ, S v I*, 1937 *E v I*
Ferguson, C F (Australia) 1963 *A v E*, 1965 *A v SA*, 1968 *A v F*, 1969 *A v W*, 1971 *A v SA* (2)
Ferguson, P (Australia) 1914 *A v NZ*
Findlay, D G (Scotland) 1895 *I v E*, 1896 *E v W, E v I*, 1897 *I v E*, 1898 *E v I*, 1899 *I v E*, 1900 *E v I*
Findlay, J C (Scotland) 1902 *I v W*, 1903 *I v E*, 1904 *E v W, I v W*, 1905 *I v NZ*, 1911 *I v F*
Finlay, A K (Australia) 1961 *A v Fj*, 1962 *A v NZ*
Fitzgerald, K V J (Australia) 1985 *I v F, W v I, NZ v E* (2), *Arg v NZ* (2), 1987 [*I v W, E v US, NZ v W, NZ v F*], 1988 *Fj v E*, 1989 *S v I, W v S, A v Wld* (2), 1990 *A v US*, 1991 *F v W, S v I*, [*Fj v C, NZ v It, S v E*]
Fleming, G R (Scotland) 1879 *S v E*
Fleming, J M (Scotland) 1985 *I v E*, 1986 *A v Arg* (2), 1987 *E v F*, [*A v F, Fj v Arg*], *F v R*, 1989 *F v W*, 1990 *NZ v A*, 1991 *W v F*, [*E v NZ, Arg v WS* (R), *I v A, NZ v A*], 1992 *A v NZ*, 1993 *S v F, NZ v WS, F v R*, 1994 *F v I, E v W*
Fleury, A L (New Zealand) 1959 *NZ v BI*
Fong, A S (New Zealand) 1946 *NZ v A*, 1950 *NZ v BI*
Fordham, R J (Australia) 1986 *E v W, F v I, Arg v F* (2), 1987 [*NZ v It, F v R*]
Fornès, E (Argentina) 1954 *Arg v F* (2)
Forsyth, R A (New Zealand) 1958 *NZ v A*
Frames, P R (South Africa) 1891 *SA v GB*
Francis, R C (New Zealand) 1984 *E v A, I v A*, 1985 *Arg v F* (2), 1986 *W v S, S v E, WS v W*
Freeman, W L (Ireland) 1932 *E v SA*
Freethy, A E (Wales) 1923 *F v E*, 1924 *E v F, I v NZ, F v US*, 1925 *E v NZ, I v S, S v E, F v E*, 1926 *E v F*, 1927 *F v E*, 1928 *I v E, E v F*, 1929 *E v I, F v E*, 1930 *I v E, E v F*, 1931 *E v I, F v E*
Fright, W H (New Zealand) 1956 *NZ v SA* (2)
Frood, J (New Zealand) 1952 *NZ v A*
Fry, H A (England) 1945 *F v B*
Furness, D C (Australia) 1952 *A v Fj* (2), 1954 *A v Fj*

Gadney, C H (England) 1935 *S v NZ, W v NZ*, 1936 *S v W, W v I*, 1937 *W v S, I v S*, 1938 *S v W, S v I*, 1939 *I v S*, 1940 *F v B*, 1946 *F v B*, 1947 *F v S, S v I*, 1948 *F v A, I v S*
Games, J (Wales) 1909 *A v A*, 1913 *E v F*, 1914 *F v E*
Gardiner, F (Ireland) 1912 *S v E*
Gardner, J A (Scotland) 1884 *E v W*, 1887 *W v I*
Garling, A F (Australia) 1981 *A v NZ* (2)
Garrard, W G (New Zealand) 1899 *A v GB*
Gilchrist, N R (New Zealand) 1936 *M v A*
Gillespie, J I (Scotland) 1907 *W v E*, 1911 *W v E*
Gilliard, P (England) 1902 *W v S*
Gillies, C R (New Zealand) 1958 *NZ v A* (2), 1959 *NZ v BI* (2)
Gilliland, R W (Ireland) 1964 *It v F*, 1965 *S v W, E v F, F v W, F v R*, 1966 *E v W*, 1967 *F v A*
Gillmore, W N (Ireland) 1956 *F v Cz*, 1958 *I v S, It v F*
Glasgow, O B (Ireland) 1953 *F v S, F v W*, 1954 *S v E*, 1955 *W v E, F v W*
Goulding, W J (Ireland) 1882 *I v W*
Gourlay, I W (South Africa) 1976 *SA v NZ*

Gouws, Dr J (South Africa) 1977 *SA v Wld*
Greenlees, Dr J R C (Scotland) 1913 *I v E*, 1914 *E v W*
Grierson, T F E (Scotland) 1970 *I v SA*, 1971 *F v R*, 1972 *F v E* , 1973 *W v I*, 1975 *E v F*
Griffin, Dr J (South Africa) 1891 *SA v GB*
Griffiths, A A (New Zealand) 1946 *M v A*, 1952 *NZ v A*
Guillemard, A G (England) 1877 *E v I*, 1878 *E v S*, 1879 *E v I*, 1880 *E v S*, 1881 *E v I*, *E v W*
Gurdon, E T (England) 1898 *I v S*, 1899 *S v I*

Hamilton, F M (Ireland) 1902 *S v E*
Harland, R W (Ireland) 1922 *F v W*, 1925 *W v F*, 1926 *F v W*, 1928 *W v E*, *S v W*, *F v W*, 1929 *E v W*, 1931 *W v F*
Harnett, G H (England) 1896 *W v S*, 1901 *S v I*, *W v I*
Harris, G A (Ireland) 1910 *S v F*
Harrison, G L (New Zealand) 1980 *Fj v A*, 1981 *A v F*, 1983 *A v US*, *F v A* (2), 1984 *Fj v A*
Harrison, H C (England) 1922 *F v S*
Hartley, A (England) 1900 *W v S*
Haslett, F W (Ireland) 1934 *W v E*, *E v S*, 1935 *E v W*, *W v S*, 1936 *W v E*
Hawke, C J (New Zealand) 1990 *I v Arg*, *E v Arg*, 1992 *A v S*
Haydon, N V (Australia) 1957 *A v NZ*
Helliwell, D (England) 1926 *S v W*, 1927 *W v A*, 1929 *W v S*, 1930 *F v S*, *W v I*, *G v F*, *F v W*
Herbert, D (Wales) 1883 *W v E*
Herck, M (Romania) 1938 *F v G*
High, C J (England) 1987 *F v W*, *W v US*, 1990 *NZ v S*
Hilditch, S R (Ireland) 1984 *S v A*, 1985 *W v Fj*, 1987 [*R v Z*, *S v R*], 1988 *E v W*, 1989 *E v F*, *NZ v A*, *S v R*, 1991 *E v S*, [*F v C*, *S v NZ*], 1992 *F v E*, *E v SA*, 1993 *SA v F*, 1994 *F v E*
Hill, A (England) 1902 *I v S*
Hill, E D (New Zealand) 1949 *NZ v A*
Hill, G R (England) 1883 *S v W*, 1884 *S v I*, *W v I*, 1885 *S v W*, 1886 *S v I*, 1887 *W v E*, *I v S*, 1888 *I v W*, 1889 *E v M*, 1891 *I v S*, 1893 *I v S*
Hill, W W (Australia) 1913 *US v NZ*
Hinton, W P (Ireland) 1921 *S v F*
Hodgson, J (England) 1892 *W v S*
Hofmeyr, E W (South Africa) 1949 *SA v NZ* (2), 1961 *SA v A*, 1963 *SA v A*
Hollander, S (New Zealand) 1930 *NZ v BI* (3), 1931 *NZ v A*
Hollis, M (England) 1931 *F v G*
Holmes, E (England) 1931 *W v SA*, 1932 *W v I*
Holmes, E B (England) 1892 *I v W*, 1894 *W v S*, 1895 *S v W*, *W v I*, 1896 *I v S*, *I v W*, 1897 *S v I*
Horak, A T (South Africa) 1938 *SA v BI*
Hosie, A M (Scotland) 1973 *I v E*, 1974 *F v I*, 1975 *W v E*, 1976 *E v I*, *F v A*, 1977 *F v W*, *I v F*, , 1979 *W v I*, *I v E*, 1980 *W v F*, *F v I*, 1981 *E v F*, *R v NZ*, 1982 *E v I*, *NZ v A* (2), 1983 *I v F*, *E v NZ*, 1984 *F v E*
Hourquet, R (France) 1983 *S v NZ*, 1984 *E v I*, *SA v E* (2), *SA v SAm* (2), 1985 *S v W*, 1987 *I v E*, [*E v J*, *W v E*], 1988 *I v E*, 1989 *A v BI* (2), 1990 *W v S*, *NZ v A* (2), 1991 [*W v Arg*, *Z v J*]
Howard, F A (England) 1984 *I v S*, 1986 *I v W*, *A v F*, *NZ v F*, 1987 [*F v S*, *I v C*, *A v W*], 1988 *W v F*, *A v NZ*, 1989 *NZ v F*(2), 1990 *W v F*, *S v F*, *Nm v W*(2), *W v Bb*, 1991 *A v W*, [*S v I*, *NZ v C*], 1992 *I v W*
Hughes, D M (Wales) 1965 *F v It*, 1966 *S v F*, *I v S*, 1967 *I v E*, *S v I*
Hughes, J (England) 1935 *I v S*
Hughes, P E (England) 1977 *F v R*, 1978 *I v S*
Humphreys, W H (England) 1893 *S v W*, *W v I*

Ireland, J C H (Scotland) 1938 *I v E*, *W v I*, 1939 *E v W*, *E v I*, *I v W*
Irving, A L C (Australia) 1934 *A v NZ*, 1937 *A v SA*

Jackson, W H (England) 1926 *F v M*, 1927 *W v S*, *W v F*, *F v G*, *G v F*
Jamison, G A (Ireland) 1972 *W v S*
Jardine, A (Scotland) 1906 *E v W*
Jeffares, R W (Ireland) 1930 *W v E*, *E v S*, 1931 *S v F*, 1935 *S v E*, *I v NZ*
Jeffares, R W (Sen) (Ireland) 1901 *S v W*, *E v S*, 1902 *E v W*, 1909 *S v W*
Jeffreys, M (England) 1920 *F v US*
Johns, E A (Wales) 1911 *E v F*
Johnson, R F (England) 1969 *F v R*, 1970 *F v I*, *E v W*

(R), 1971 *W v I*, 1972 *I v F*, *W v NZ*, 1973 *I v F*, 1974 *W v S*, *I v NZ*, *F v SA*, 1975 *S v I*, *S v A*
Jones, A O (England) 1906 *W v SA*, 1907 *S v I*, 1911 *F v S*, 1912 *F v I*, *W v F*
Jones, T (Wales) 1947 *E v F*, 1948 *E v I*, *F v E*, 1949 *E v F*, 1950 *S v F*, 1951 *I v E*
Jones, W (Wales) 1984 *S v F*, *NZ v F* (2), 1988 *S v E*
Jones, W K M (Wales) 1968 *I v A*, 1970 *F v E*, 1971 *S v I*
Joseph, M (Wales) 1966 *S v A*, 1967 *I v A*, 1968 *I v S*, *E v I*, *R v F*, 1969 *S v I*, *S v SA*, 1970 *S v E*, 1971 *I v E*, *S v E*(C), 1972 *S v F*, *S v A*, 1973 *I v NZ*, *S v P*(C), *F v J*, 1974 *E v I*, 1975 *F v Arg*, 1976 *E v A*, *F v A*, 1977 *E v S*, *S v I*, *F v S*
Joynson, D C (Wales) 1955 *E v S*

Keenan, H (England) 1962 *It v F*, 1963 *I v NZ*
Kelleher, J C (Wales) 1973 *E v S*, 1974 *F v E*, 1976 *R v F*, 1977 *E v F*
Kelleher, K D (Ireland) 1960 *W v S*, 1961 *W v E*, *E v S*, 1962 *S v E*, *W v F*, 1963 *W v E*, *F v It*, 1964 *E v W*, *R v F*, 1965 *F v S*, *W v E*, 1966 *S v E*, *W v F*, *W v A*, 1967 *E v A*, *F v S*, *S v W*, *S v NZ*, 1968 *S v F*, 1969 *S v W*, *E v SA*, 1970 *W v F*, 1971 *F v S*
Kelly, H C (Ireland) 1881 *I v S*, 1883 *I v S*, *S v E*, 1885 *S v I*
Kemsley, H B (South Africa) 1896 *SA v GB*
Kennedy, G H B (Ireland) 1905 *S v W*, 1910 *W v S*, *S v E*
Kennedy, W (Ireland) 1905 *S v NZ*
Kilner, W F B (Australia) 1937 *A v SA*
King, J S (New Zealand) 1937 *NZ v SA* (2)
King, M H R (England) 1961 *S v I*
Kinsey, B (Australia) 1986 *Tg v W*, 1990 *Arg v E* (2), 1991 *Fj v E*, 1992 *F v SA* (2), 1993 *NZ v BI*
Knox, J (Argentina) 1949 *Arg v F*
Krembs, M (Germany) 1938 *G v F*

Lacroix, M (Belgium) 1962 *R v F*
Laidlaw, H B (Scotland) 1963 *I v E*, 1964 *W v F*, 1965 *I v E*, 1968 *F v E*, *W v F*
Lamb, G C (England) 1968 *F v I*, *W v S*, *F v SA*, 1969 *F v S*, *I v F*, 1970 *S v F*, *W v SA*, *I v W*, *R v F*, 1971 *I v F*, *F v A*
Lambert, N H (Ireland) 1947 *S v A*, 1948 *E v A*, *S v E*, 1949 *W v E*, *S v W*, *E v S*, *F v W*, 1950 *E v W*, *F v E*, 1951 *W v SA*, 1952 *E v W*
Lang, J S (Scotland) 1884 *I v E*
Larkin, F A (Australia) 1932 *A v NZ*
Lathwell, H G (England) 1946 *I v F*
Lawrence, K H (New Zealand) 1985 *A v C* (2), 1986 *A v It*, 1987 *F v S*, *S v W*, [*Fj v It*, *A v E*], *Arg v A* (2), 1989 *A v BI*, 1991 *E v F*, [*I v Z*, *W v A*]
Lawrie, A A (Scotland) 1924 *I v F*, 1925 *E v W*, 1926 *I v F*
Leask, B (Australia) 1993 *A v Tg*
Lee, S (England) 1904 *S v E*
Lefevre, C (Ireland) 1905 *W v E*, 1907 *S v W*
Leith, H S (New Zealand) 1928 *M v A*
Leslie, D (Scotland) 1990 *E v W*, 1993 *I v F*
Lewis, C P (Wales) 1885 *W v E*
Lewis, E M (Wales) 1971 *F v A*
Lewis, M S (Wales) 1975 *F v S*, 1976 *I v S*
Lewis, R (Wales) 1970 *E v I*, 1971 *E v F*, 1972 *F v I*, 1973 *S v I*, *E v A*, 1974 *Arg v F* (2)
Lieprand, M (Germany) 1934 *G v F*
Llewellyn, A (Wales) 1906 *E v I*
Llewellyn, V S (Wales) 1951 *E v F*
Llewellyn, W J (Wales) 1926 *F v S*, *I v E*, 1927 *S v A*
Lloyd, D M (Wales) 1975 *I v F*, 1976 *S v E*
Lloyd, R A (Ireland) 1922 *S v W*, *E v S*
Louw, L L (South Africa) 1953 *SA v A*
Luff, A C (England) 1963 *W v I*, 1964 *I v S*, *I v W*
Lyle, T R (Ireland) 1887 *E v S*
Lyne, H S (Wales) 1885 *E v I*

McAllister, E (Ireland) 1889 *S v W*, 1890 *W v S*
Macassey, L E (New Zealand) 1937 *NZ v SA*
McAuley, C J (New Zealand) 1937 *NZ v SA*
McCartney, K W (Scotland) 1990 *F v I*, 1991 *NZ v A*, 1992 *F v R*, 1993 *Nm v W*
McDavitt, P A (New Zealand) 1972 *NZ v A*, 1975 *NZ v S*, 1977 *NZ v BI*
McEwan, M C (Scotland) 1892 *E v W*

Simmonds, G (Wales) 1992 *E v C*
Simpson, J W (Scotland) 1906 *I v W*
Simpson, R L (New Zealand) 1913 *NZ v A*, 1921 *NZ v A*, 1923 *NZ v A*
Sklar, E (Argentina) 1991 [*NZ v US*]
Slabber, M J (South Africa) 1955 *SA v BI*, 1960 *SA v NZ*
Smith, J A (Scotland) 1892 *E v I*, 1894 *E v W*, 1895 *W v E*
Spreadbury, A J (England) 1990 *A v F*, 1992 *I v S*, *W v A*, 1994 *I v W*
Stanton, R W (South Africa) 1910 *SA v GB* (3)
Steyn, M (Germany) 1932 *G v F*
Stirling, B W (Ireland) 1989 *E v Fj*, 1991 *Arg v NZ* (2), 1993 *E v S*, *R v F*
Strasheim, Dr E A (South Africa) 1958 *SA v F*, 1960 *SA v S*, *SA v NZ*, 1962 *SA v BI* (2), 1964 *SA v F*, 1967 *SA v F*, 1968 *SA v BI*
Strasheim, Dr J J (South Africa) 1938 *SA v BI*
Strydom, S (South Africa) 1979 *Arg v A* (2), 1982 *SA v SAm*, 1985 *S v I*, *F v W*, 1986 *F v NZ* (2)
Sturrock, J C (Scotland) 1921 *E v W*, *F v E*, 1922 *W v I*
Sullivan, G (New Zealand) 1950 *NZ v BI*
Sutherland, F E (New Zealand) 1925 *NZ v A*, 1928 *NZ v A* (2), 1930 *NZ v BI*
Swainston, E (England) 1878 *I v E*

Tagnini, S (Italy) 1968 *Cz v F*
Taylor, A R (New Zealand) 1965 *NZ v SA* (R), 1972 *NZ v A*
Taylor, J A S (Scotland) 1957 *W v I*, 1960 *E v W*, *F v E*, *W v SA*, 1961 *F v It*, 1962 *E v W*, *F v I*, *I v W*
Tennent, J M (Scotland) 1920 *I v F*, 1921 *I v W*, 1922 *W v E*, *E v F*, *I v F*, *I v E*, 1923 *I v W*
Thomas, C (Wales) 1979 *S v I*, 1980 *E v I*
Thomas, C G P (Wales) 1977 *F v NZ*, 1978 *S v F*, *F v I*
Thomas, P (France) 1994 *E v I*
Tierney, A T (Australia) 1957 *A v NZ*, 1958 *A v M*, 1959 *A v BI*
Tindill, E W T (New Zealand) 1950 *NZ v BI* (2), 1955 *NZ v A*
Titcomb, M H (England) 1966 *W v S*, 1967 *W v I*, *W v NZ*, 1968 *I v W*, *S v A*, 1971 *S v W*, *E v P* (C), 1972 *W v F*
Tolhurst, H A (Australia) 1951 *A v NZ* (2)
Tomalin, L C (Australia) 1947 *A v NZ*, 1949 *A v M* (2) 1950 *A v BI*
Treharne, G J (Wales) 1960 *I v SA*, 1961 *E v SA*, *I v E*, *I v F*, 1963 *S v I*
Trigg, J A F (England) 1981 *F v R*, 1982 *S v F*, 1983 *W v I*
Tulloch, J T (Scotland) 1906 *I v SA*, *E v SA*, 1907 *I v E*, 1908 *E v W*, 1912 *E v W*, 1913 *E v SA*, 1914 *I v W*, 1920 *W v E*, 1924 *W v I*
Turnbull, A (Scotland) 1898 *I v W*, 1899 *W v E*, *W v I*, 1900 *E v W*, *I v W*, 1901 *W v E*, *I v E*

Vanderfield, Dr I R (Australia) 1956 *A v SA*, 1958 *A v M*, 1961 *A v Fj* (2), *A v F*, 1962 *A v NZ*, 1966 *A v BI*, 1967 *A v I*, 1968 *A v NZ*, 1970 *A v S*, 1971 *A v SA*, 1973 *A v Tg*, 1974 *A v NZ* (2)
Van der Horst, A W (South Africa) 1933 *SA v A*
Van der Merwe, A (Germany) 1936 *G v F*
Vile, T H (Wales) 1923 *S v F*, *E v I*, *I v S*, *S v E*, 1924 *I v E*, *S v I*, *E v S*, 1925 *E v I*, 1927 *E v I*, 1928 *E v A*, *E v S*, 1931 *F v I*

Waldron, C A (Australia) 1986 *F v R*, 1987 *A v SK*
Waldron, H (England) 1957 *F v It*
Walsh, L (New Zealand) 1949 *NZ v A*
Walters, D G (Wales) 1959 *F v S*, *I v E*, *E v S*, *I v F*, 1960 *S v F*, *E v I*, *I v S*, *F v I*, 1961 *F v SA*, *E v F*, 1962 *E v I*, *F v E*, 1963 *E v S*, *F v R*, 1964 *E v I*, *F v E*, *F v I*, *F v Fj*, 1965 *I v F*, *S v I*, *E v S*, *S v SA*, 1966 *F v E*
Warden, G (England) 1946 *F v K*
Warren, R G (Ireland) 1892 *S v E*
Warren, T H H (Scotland) 1928 *W v I*
Watson, D H (Scotland) 1881 *S v E*
Waugh, Dr R (Australia) 1903 *A v NZ*
Welsby, A (England) 1976 *F v I*, 1978 *W v F*, 1981 *F v W*, 1982 *F v I*
Welsh, R (Scotland) 1902 *E v I*, 1903 *W v E*, 1905 *I v E*
West, J R (Ireland) 1974 *E v W*, 1975 *S v W*, 1976 *W v F*, 1977 *F v NZ*, 1978 *W v S*, *S v E*, *S v NZ*, 1979 *E v F*, *NZ v F* (2), 1980 *S v F*, *SA v F*, *W v NZ*, 1981 *F v NZ*, *W v A*, 1982 *F v Arg*, 1983 *W v E*, 1984 *R v F*
Wheeler, Dr E de C (Ireland) 1925 *S v F*
Wheeler, Dr J R (Ireland) 1929 *S v E*, 1930 *S v W*, 1931 *E v W*, *S v E*, 1932 *E v S*, 1933 *S v E*
Whittaker, J B G (England) 1947 *I v F*, *W v I*
Wiesse, M (Germany) 1936 *G v F*
Wilkins, H E B (England) 1925 *F v NZ*, 1928 *G v F*, 1929 *W v F*
Wilkins, W H (Wales) 1893 *E v S*, 1894 *S v E*, 1895 *E v S*
Williams, J (New Zealand) 1905 *NZ v A*
Williams, R C (Ireland) 1957 *S v W*, *E v F*, 1958 *E v W*, *E v A*, *S v A*, *S v E*, 1959 *W v E*, *S v W*, *E v F*, 1960 *S v E*, 1961 *F v S*, *S v W*, *F v R*, 1962 *S v F*, 1963 *F v S*, *S v W*, *W v NZ*, 1964 *S v F*, *S v NZ*, *F v NZ*, *S v E*
Williams, T (Wales) 1904 *E v I*
Williams, W (England) 1904 *I v S*, 1905 *W v I*, 1907 *E v F*, 1908 *W v S*, *I v S*, *W v F*, 1909 *E v F*, *F v W*, *I v F*, 1910 *W v F*, 1911 *F v W*, 1913 *F v SA*
Wolstenholme, B H (New Zealand) 1955 *NZ v A*
Woolley, A (South Africa) 1970 *SA v NZ*
Wyllie, W D (Australia) 1949 *A v M*

Yché, J-C (France) 1983 *S v I*, *R v W*, *It v A*, 1985 *A v Fj* (2)
Yeman, R (Wales) 1993 *I v R*
Young, J (Scotland) 1971 *F v W*, 1972 *E v W*, *R v F*, 1973 *E v NZ*

WORLD INTERNATIONAL RECORDS

Both team and individual records are for official cap matches played by senior members of the International Board, up to 31 March 1994.

TEAM RECORDS

Highest score – 74
New Zealand (74-13) v Fiji 1987
  Christchurch

Biggest winning margin – 64
New Zealand (70-6) v Italy 1987 Auckland

Most tries in an international – 13
England v Wales 1881 Blackheath
New Zealand v United States 1913 Berkeley
France v Romania 1924 Paris
France v Zimbabwe 1987 Auckland

Most conversions in an international – 10
New Zealand v Fiji 1987 Christchurch

Most penalty goals in an international – 8
Wales v Canada 1993 Cardiff

**Most consecutive international
  victories – 17**
New Zealand between 1965 and 1969

**Most consecutive internationals
  undefeated – 23**
New Zealand between 1987 and 1990

**Most points in an international
  series – 109**
New Zealand v Argentina (2 matches)
  1989 in New Zealand

Most tries in an international series – 18
New Zealand v Wales (2 matches) 1988
  in New Zealand

**Most points in Five Nations
Championship in a season – 118**
England 1991-92

**Most tries in Five Nations
Championship in a season – 21**
Wales 1909-10

**Most points on an overseas tour
(all matches) – 868**
New Zealand to B Isles/France
  (33 matches) 1905-06

**Most tries on an overseas tour
(all matches) – 215**
New Zealand to B Isles/France
  (33 matches) 1905-06

**Biggest win on a major tour
(all matches)**
117-6 New Zealand v S Australia 1974
  Adelaide

INDIVIDUAL RECORDS

*including appearances for British Isles,
shown in brackets*

Most capped player
P Sella (France) 98 1982-94
in individual positions
Full-back
S Blanco (France) 81[1] 1980-91
Wing
R Underwood (England) 71(6)[2] 1984-94
Centre (includes 2nd five-eighth)
P Sella (France) 91[3] 1982-94
Fly-half (includes 1st five-eighth)
C R Andrew (England) 61(5)[4] 1985-94

Scrum-half
G O Edwards (Wales) 63(10)[5] 1967-78
Prop
P A Orr (Ireland) 59(1) 1976-87
Hooker
S B T Fitzpatrick (N Zealand) 56 1986-93
Lock
W J McBride (Ireland) 80(17) 1962-75
Flanker
J F Slattery (Ireland) 65(4) 1970-84
P J Winterbottom (England) 65(7) 1982-93
No 8
T M Davies (Wales) 46(8)[6] 1969-76

[1] *Blanco also played 12 times as a wing*
[2] *D I Campese (Australia), 80 caps, has won 64 as a wing*
[3] *Sella has also played 6 times on the wing and once at full-back*
[4] *Andrew has also played once for England as a full-back. M P Lynagh (Australia), 64 caps in all, has played 56 times at fly-half, and 8 times in the centre*
[5] *N C Farr-Jones, 63 caps for Australia, won 62 as a scrum-half and one as a replacement wing*
[6] *Several French utility forwards won more caps than Davies, but none has played as frequently at No 8*

Most consecutive internationals for a country – 54
S B T Fitzpatrick (N Zealand) 1986-93

Most internationals as captain – 40
W D C Carling (England) 1988-94

Most points in internationals – 783
M P Lynagh (Australia) (64 matches) 1984-93

Most points in an international – 30
D Camberabero (France) v Zimbabwe 1987 Auckland

Most tries in internationals – 57
D I Campese (Australia) (80 matches) 1982-93

Most tries in an international – 5
G C Lindsay (Scotland) v Wales 1887 Edinburgh
D Lambert (England) v France 1907 Richmond
R Underwood (England) v Fiji 1989 Twickenham

Most conversions in internationals – 129
M P Lynagh (Australia) (64 matches) 1984-93

Most conversions in an international – 10
G J Fox (New Zealand) v Fiji 1987 Christchurch

Most dropped goals in internationals – 18
H E Botha (South Africa) (28 matches) 1980-92
C R Andrew (England) (57 matches) and (B Lions) (5 matches) 1985-94

Most dropped goals in an international – 3
P Albaladejo (France) v Ireland 1960 Paris
P F Hawthorne (Australia) v England 1967 Twickenham
H E Botha (South Africa) v S America 1980 Durban
H E Botha (South Africa) v Ireland 1981 Durban
J-P Lescarboura (France) v England 1985 Twickenham
J-P Lescarboura (France) v New Zealand 1986 Christchurch
D Camberabero (France) v Australia 1990 Sydney

Most penalty goals in internationals – 150
M P Lynagh (Australia) (64 matches) 1984-93

Most penalty goals in an international – 8
N R Jenkins (Wales) v Canada 1993 Cardiff

Fastest player to 100 points in internationals
G J Fox (New Zealand) in his 6th match

Fastest player to 200 points in internationals
G J Fox (New Zealand) in his 13th match

**Fastest player to 300 points in
internationals**
G J Fox (New Zealand) in his 18th match

**Fastest player to 400 points in
internationals**
G J Fox (New Zealand) in his 26th match

**Most points in a Five Nations
match – 24**
S Viars (France) v Ireland 1992

**Most points in Five Nations
Championship in a season – 67**
J M Webb (England) (4 matches)
1991-92

**Most tries in Five Nations
Championship in a season – 8**
C N Lowe (England) (4 appearances)
1913-14
I S Smith (Scotland) (4 appearances)
1924-25

**Tries in each match of a Five Nations
Championship**
H C Catcheside (England) 1923-24
A C Wallace (Scotland) 1924-25
P Estève (France) 1982-83
P Sella (France) 1985-86

**Most penalty goals in Five Nations
Championship in a season – 18**
S D Hodgkinson (England) (4 matches)
1990-91

**Most conversions in Five Nations
Championship in a season – 11**
J Bancroft (Wales) (4 appearances)
1908-09
J M Webb (England) (4 matches)
1991-92

**Most dropped goals in Five Nations
Championship in a season – 5**
G Camberabero (France) (3 appearances)
1966-67
J-P Lescarboura (France) dropped a goal in each Championship match 1983-84, a unique feat

Most points on an overseas tour – 230
W J Wallace (NZ) (25 appearances) in
B Isles/France 1905-06

Most tries on an overseas tour – 42
J Hunter (NZ) (23 appearances) in
B Isles/France 1905-06

Most points in any match on tour – 43
R M Deans (NZ) v South Australia 1984
Adelaide

Most tries in any match on tour – 8
T R Heeps (NZ) v Northern NSW 1962
P Estève scored 8 for France v East Japan in 1984, but this was not on a major tour

PARTNERSHIP RECORDS
Centre threequarters
S Hastings and S R P Lineen
(Scotland) 28
Half-backs
M P Lynagh and N C Farr-Jones
(Australia) 47
Front row
S C McDowell, S B T Fitzpatrick and
R W Loe (New Zealand) 33
Second row
A J Martin and G A D Wheel (Wales) 27
Back row
J Matheu, G Basquet and J Prat (France) 22

OTHER INTERNATIONAL MATCH RECORDS

Up to 31 March 1994. These are included for comparison and cover performances since 1971 by teams and players in Test matches for nations which are not senior members of the International Board.

Most points in a match
By a team
111 Zimbabwe v Nigeria 1987 Nairobi
By a player
31 M Grobler Zimbabwe v Nigeria 1987
29 S Bettarello Italy v Canada 1983

Most tries in a match
By a team
20 Zimbabwe v Nigeria 1987 Nairobi
By a player
5 R Tsimba Zimbabwe v Nigeria 1987
5 M Neill Zimbabwe v Nigeria 1987

Most conversions in a match
By a team
14 Zimbabwe v Nigeria Nairobi 1987
By a player
14 M Grobler Zimbabwe v Nigeria 1987

Most penalty goals in a match
By a team
8 Canada v Scotland 1991 St John
By a player
8 M A Wyatt Canada v Scotland 1991
  St John

Most dropped goals in a match
By a team
3 Argentina v SA Gazelles 1971 Pretoria
3 Argentina v Australia 1979
  Buenos Aires
3 Argentina v New Zealand 1985
  Buenos Aires

By a player
3 T A Harris-Smith
  Argentina v SA Gazelles 1971
3 H Porta Argentina v Australia 1979
3 H Porta Argentina v New Zealand 1985

Most points in matches
530 H Porta Argentina/South America
483 S Bettarello Italy

Most tries in matches
21 M Marchetto Italy

Most conversions in matches
54 H Porta Argentina/South America
46 S Bettarello Italy

Most penalty goals in matches
109 H Porta Argentina/South America
104 S Bettarello Italy

Most dropped goals in matches
25 H Porta Argentina/South America
17 S Bettarello Italy

Most matches as captain
43 H Porta Argentina/South America

Biggest win on a major tour
128-0 W Samoa v Marlborough
  (N Zealand) 1993 Blenheim

WORLD CUP RECORDS

(final stages only)

LEADING SCORERS

Most points in the competition

126	G J Fox	New Zealand	1987
82	M P Lynagh	Australia	1987
68	R P Keyes	Ireland	1991
66	M P Lynagh	Australia	1991
62	A G Hastings	Scotland	1987

Most tries in the competition

6	C I Green	New Zealand	1987
6	J J Kirwan	New Zealand	1987
6	D I Campese	Australia	1991
6	J-B Lafond	France	1991

Most conversions in the competition

30	G J Fox	New Zealand	1987
20	M P Lynagh	Australia	1987
16	A G Hastings	Scotland	1987

Most penalty goals in the competition

21	G J Fox	New Zealand	1987
16	R P Keyes	Ireland	1991
14	J M Webb	England	1991
13	A G Hastings	Scotland	1991

Most dropped goals in the competition

3	J Davies	Wales	1987
2	by several players		

MOST POINTS IN A MATCH

By a team

74	New Zealand v Fiji	1987
70	New Zealand v Italy	1987
70	France v Zimbabwe	1987
60	England v Japan	1987
60	Scotland v Zimbabwe	1987

By a player

30	D Camberabero	France v Zimbabwe	1987
27	A G Hastings	Scotland v Romania	1987
26	G J Fox	New Zealand v Fiji	1987
24	J M Webb	England v Italy	1991
23	G Laporte	France v Romania	1987
23	R P Keyes	Ireland v Zimbabwe	1991
22	G J Fox	New Zealand v Italy	1987
22	G J Fox	New Zealand v Argentina	1987
22	G J Fox	New Zealand v Scotland	1987

MOST TRIES IN A MATCH

By a team

13	France v Zimbabwe	1987
12	New Zealand v Italy	1987
12	New Zealand v Fiji	1987
11	Scotland v Zimbabwe	1987

By a player

4	I C Evans	Wales v Canada	1987
4	C I Green	New Zealand v Fiji	1987
4	J A Gallagher	New Zealand v Fiji	1987

MOST CONVERSIONS IN A MATCH

By a team

10	New Zealand v Fiji	1987
9	France v Zimbabwe	1987
8	New Zealand v Italy	1987
8	France v Romania	1987
8	Scotland v Zimbabwe	1987
8	Scotland v Romania	1987

By a player

10	G J Fox	New Zealand v Fiji	1987
9	D Camberabero	France v Zimbabwe	1987
8	G J Fox	New Zealand v Italy	1987
8	G Laporte	France v Romania	1987
8	A G Hastings	Scotland v Zimbabwe	1987
8	A G Hastings	Scotland v Romania	1987

MOST PENALTY GOALS IN A MATCH

By a team

6	New Zealand v Scotland	1987
6	New Zealand v Argentina	1987
5	Argentina v Italy	1987
5	Zimbabwe v Scotland	1987
5	Ireland v Zimbabwe	1991

By a player

6	G J Fox	New Zealand v Scotland	1987
6	G J Fox	New Zealand v Argentina	1987
5	H Porta	Argentina v Italy	1987
5	M Grobler	Zimbabwe v Scotland	1987
5	R P Keyes	Ireland v Zimbabwe	1991

MOST DROPPED GOALS IN A MATCH

By a team

3	Fiji v Romania	1991
2	Wales v Ireland	1987
2	Ireland v Canada	1987
2	Argentina v Australia	1991

By a player

2	J Davies	Wales v Ireland	1987
2	L Arbizu	Argentina v Australia	1991
2	T Rabaka	Fiji v Romania	1991

OBITUARY 1993-94 (*up to 1 May 1994*)

Ian ANDERSON, the South African referee who controlled Wales' Second Test against Zimbabwe in 1993, died in a road accident in January 1994, aged 30.

Edward Fitzgerald BARRY (Wellington, Wanganui, New Zealand), a policeman who died on 12 December 1993, aged 88, toured Australia with the 1932 and 1934 All Blacks, making two Test appearances on the latter tour. His son Kevin was an All Black in the 1960s and his grandson Liam toured Britain with last autumn's New Zealand team. The Barrys, all of whom were back-row forwards, are the only family to date which has produced three generations of All Blacks.

Surg Capt Edward BINGHAM CBE (Dublin U), the distinguished polar explorer who died on 1 September 1993, aged 92, was a regular member of the Trinity College, Dublin XVs in the 1920s.

Charles BRAY, the freelance writer who covered the Normandy landings and regularly reported cricket and rugby after the war, died in September 1993, aged 95.

Sir Thomas Harcourt Clarke CAUGHEY (Auckland, New Zealand) was one of New Zealand's most exciting midfield attacking players of the 1930s. His three tours with the All Blacks included the 1935-36 visit to Britain and Ireland, where he was the party's leading try-scorer. Although his Test career was spread over five years, his three international tries were all scored in one match: against Scotland at Murrayfield in 1935. Knighted for his services to the Auckland Hospital Board, he died in Auckland on 4 August 1993, aged 81.

William Ruben COLLINS (Poverty Bay, East Coast, Hawke's Bay, New Zealand) was the giant lock of the Hawke's Bay team which won the Ranfurly Shield in 1934. Strong performances in provincial games the following year helped book his passage to Britain with the Third All Blacks, for whom he played only seven times on tour. Injury precipitated his premature retirement from serious rugby. He died in Auckland on 9 September 1993, aged 82.

Lt Cmdr Wilfrid Hornby CRAWFORD (United Services, Scotland), who died on 6 June 1993, aged 77, was a robust forward who doubled as first-choice place-kicker for Scotland. His last-minute penalty against Wales on his debut in 1938 was the match-winning kick which set Scotland on course for the Triple Crown. He went on to score 21 points in five internationals before war cut short his rugby career.

Bill DICKINSON (Jordanhill College) was the first coach appointed to advise the Scotland international team. He took up the appointment in 1971 after guiding his club to the unofficial Scottish club championship title. During his six-year stewardship, Scotland won half of their matches, Mr Dickinson restoring pride to a nation which had endured more than its fair share of rugby misery in the 1950s and 1960s. He died in Irvine on 7 April 1994, aged 77.

Sir Ernest Edward DUNLOP AC, CMG, OBE, the Australian surgeon whose heroism was an inspiration to countless captives of the Japanese during the war, died in Melbourne on 2 July 1993, aged 85. As a medical student at Melbourne University in the 1930s, he was twice capped by Australia against New Zealand. Just before the war, he studied at St Mary's Hospital, turning out regularly for their strong rugby XV.

Clement DUPONT (Lourdes, Rouen, SBUC France), the grand old gentleman of French rugby, died in Bordeaux on 1 November 1993, aged 95. He won 16 caps between 1923 and 1929 and was the scrum-half in France's first wins against England (3-0 in 1927) and Wales (8-3 in 1928).

Kevin Columba FITZGERALD (London Irish), the well-known broadcaster and thriller writer who died in November 1993, aged 91, was an energetic playing member of London Irish and a regular county player with Staffordshire in the 1920s.

James Train FITZGERALD (Otago, Wellington, New Zealand) died in Christchurch on 13 May 1993, aged 64. Best remembered in Britain as an enterprising centre with Bob Stuart's 1953-54 All Blacks, Jim Fitzgerald's only Test was at Christchurch against the 1952 Wallabies. He scored an early try in that match but was one of several All Blacks axed after a 14-9 defeat. On tour in Britain he faced stiff competition from Brian Fitzpatrick, Colin Loader and Doug Wilson for a Test place.

Allen FORWARD (Pontypool, Wales), the loose forward who won six Welsh caps, died in January 1994, aged 72. When he was first listed in the Welsh team, in 1951, uninformed critics believed the Welsh selectors had named a ringer for A N Other. But he made his presence felt in the loose and became an invaluable member of Wales' 1952 Grand Slam team. A retired police sergeant, he was a life member of Pontypool RFC.

Robert FRAME (Coventry, Bristol), one of the finest post-war centres never capped by England, died in January 1994, aged 52. In the early 1960s, Bob Frame was an indispensable member of the famous Warwickshire side which won the County Championship four seasons running – the last county to do so.

Joseph Phillip FRENCH (Queensland), the respected Australian coach and administrator, died in Brisbane on 30 December 1993, aged 78. In his youth he was a dashing full-back whose passion for flowing rugby earned him state recognition in 1935 and 1936. He went on to coach first his club, Brothers, then Queensland, and between 1961 and 1970 he was in demand as a national selector. Never a tub-thumper, he later turned his analytical mind to administration and during his five-year stint as president and chairman of the Australian Rugby Union, the state of Rugby Union in a country dominated by League and Aussie Rules rapidly improved.

Col Evan Michael Pearce HARDY OBE (Blackheath, Headingley, Army, England) formed with Denis Shuttleworth one of the most effective half-back pairings in English rugby in the early 1950s. They were twinned for Headingley, the Army and Combined Services, and played together once for England, in the Calcutta Cup win of 1951. Mike Hardy, who won three caps altogether, died on 13 January 1994, aged 66.

Lester Robert HARVEY (Otago, New Zealand), the All Black who died on 3 June 1993, aged 74, was first-choice lock for his country during two hard-fought series – against South Africa in 1949 and at home to the Lions of 1950. A late developer, he did not make his Test debut until he was 30, but he adapted rapidly to the fray of international rugby and was named the outstanding forward of the 1950 rubber.

Reginald James HAYTER, the proprietor of Britain's foremost sporting news agency, died in Northwood on 13 March 1994, aged 80. His services to rugby included contributions to earlier editions of this Yearbook.

Hugh Francis Winnington HOLMES (Cambridge U), the retired Sherborne schoolmaster who died there on 18 September 1993, aged 83, was a robust forward who regularly appeared for Eastern Counties between the wars. As a schoolboy at Haileybury, he led the English Public Schools XV, and later, at Cambridge, narrowly missed a Blue.

Gordon HUDSON (Gloucester), who died in December 1993, aged 78, was a popular flanker whose 300-plus appearances for Gloucester spanned 18 seasons, 1935 to 1954. His father, Arthur, played for England in the early 1900s.

Marcos IACHETTI (Hindu, Argentina), scaling two metres, was the tallest forward capped by Argentina in the late 1970s. He made his Test debut alongside his brother, Alejandro, against New Zealand at Dunedin in 1979 and his handful of international caps included appearances against Australia and South Africa. He died on 10 July 1993, aged 38, from injuries sustained in a car accident.

William Roy JONES (Swansea, Wales), a loyal servant of Swansea RFC, died in July 1993, aged 90. He won two caps for Wales as a centre in 1927-28, finishing on the losing side both times. Later he was elected president of his club.

James Maurice KILBURN, the cricket and rugby football correspondent of the *Yorkshire Post* from 1934 to 1975, died at Harrogate on 28 August 1993, aged 84.

Paul Francis LITTLE (Auckland, New Zealand), the inventive centre who was never on the losing side in his ten Tests for the All Blacks between 1961 and 1964, died of cancer in Auckland on 7 August 1993, aged 58. With the Fifth All Blacks in Europe in 1963-64 he mastered a variety of conditions and excelled at creating scoring chances for his wings.

William Ross LOGAN (Edinburgh U, Edinburgh Wands, Scotland), who died in Edinburgh on 26 November 1993, aged 84, was the outstanding Scottish scrum-half of the 1930s. Altogether he won 20 caps between 1931 and 1937, when he captained his country, and formed an effective pairing with 'Kilty' Jackson in Scotland's Triple Crown season of 1933. He also represented Scotland at cricket and was the president of the SRU in 1964-65.

Sir Richard Edmonds LUYT, GCMG, KCVO, DCM (Oxford U), former vice-chancellor of the University of Cape Town and, from 1968 to 1980, the governor of British Guyana, died in Cape Town on 12 February 1994, aged 78. A keen sportsman, he played rugby and cricket for Oxford and appeared in the 1938 Varsity Match, which his team narrowly lost.

Robert Henry Craig MacKENZIE (Wellington, New Zealand) was an All Black five-eighth who represented his country twice in 1928 but never played in a Test. In 1929 he captained the New Zealand Universities but an ankle injury two years later ended a promising career. 'Crow' MacKenzie died in Wellington on 19 July 1993, aged 89.

William John MUMM (Buller, New Zealand), one of the small band of All Blacks capped out of Buller province, died in Westport on 11 December 1993, aged 70. On the light side for a prop, he won his sole cap against Australia at Wellington in 1949.

Harry PATEMAN (Coventry, Nuneaton), a steady full-back who was deprived of full England honours by the war, died in April 1994, aged 79. He was no stranger, however, to representative rugby. He made his first England trial appearance in 1938, was in the Warwickshire side which won the County Championship in 1939, played for England XVs in three of the Victory internationals in 1945-46, and was still giving polished performances for his county in the 1952 County Championship semi-finals.

Thomas Neill PEARCE OBE, TD (Old Blues), the popular all-round sportsman and administrator known as 'Burly T' on cricket and rugby grounds across Britain, died in Worthing on 10 April 1994, aged 88. In rugby he was a front-row forward who regularly played for Middlesex, though it was as an international referee that he distinguished himself. Between 1948 and 1952, he took control of 11 Five Nations matches, five of them in Paris.

Ernest Frederick ROBINSON (Coventry, England), a no-nonsense Midlands hooker who died in Coventry on 2 July 1993, aged 67, spent most of his career in the international shadow of Eric Evans. Ernie played more than 300 times for Coventry, the club he captained in 1956-57, but won only four caps for England. He deputised for Evans at Murrayfield in 1954 when England won the Triple Crown, and was recalled to play three matches seven years later.

Jack TAYLOR (Cambridge U, Leicester, Musselburgh), Scotland's international referee who controlled eight matches between 1957 and 1962, died on 16 May 1993. As a youth he was a gifted games-player. He represented Scotland at cricket and came close to winning a rugby Blue at Cambridge as an outside-half. He taught Classics at Loretto School and was for many years the honorary secretary of the Scottish Schools Rugby Union.

Armand VAQUERIN (Béziers, France) was the larger-than-life figure who anchored the Béziers pack that won ten French Club Championship titles in the 1970s. An extremely mobile loose head with safe hands, he was first capped for France as a 20-year-old in 1971. But difficulties meeting international training demands put his Test place in jeopardy and although he won 26 caps in nine years, for most of his career he had to play second fiddle to Gerard Cholley. He died in Béziers on 10 July 1993 from gunshot wounds sustained in a game of Russian roulette. He was 42.

Kenneth James WILSON (Gloucester, England), who won his only cap as a prop against France at Twickenham in 1963, died in Oldham on 1 December 1993, aged 55. 'Tug' Wilson, who was also an RAF heavyweight boxing champion, went north after winning his England cap and represented Oldham with distinction for ten years.

Birnie WOLSTENHOLME (Hawke's Bay), the New Zealand referee who controlled the final Test of the 1955 Bledisloe Cup series, died in Gisborne on 9 July 1993, aged 77.

CLUBS SECTION

Records of most-capped players are complete up to 30 April 1994

ENGLAND
Bath

Year of formation 1865
Ground Recreation Ground, London Road, Bath   Tel: Bath (0225) 425192
Colours Blue, white and black
Most capped player D M B Sole (Scotland) 44 caps
Captain 1993-94 J P Hall
Courage League Div 1 *Winners* **Pilkington Cup** *Winners* Beat Leicester 21-9 (final)

League Record 1993-94

Date	Venue	Opponents	Result	Scorers
11 Sept	A	Bristol	18-10	*T:* Catt (2) *C:* Callard *PG:* Callard, Barnes
18 Sept	H	Northampton	37-9	*T:* Lumsden (2), Clarke, Callard *C:* Callard (4) *PG:* Callard (3)
25 Sept	A	Orrell	18-15	*T:* Guscott, Callard *C:* Callard *PG:* Callard, Barnes
2 Oct	H	Gloucester	46-17	*T:* Ubogu (2), Clarke, Guscott, Hill, Adebayo *C:* Callard (5) *PG:* Callard (2)
9 Oct	A	Wasps	19-13	*T:* Catt, Clarke *PG:* Callard (3)
13 Nov	H	Newcastle Gosforth	46-3	*T:* Clarke, Hill, Bamsey, Dawe, Lumsden *C:* Callard (2), Chilcott *PG:* Callard (5)
20 Nov	A	Leicester	6-9	*PG:* Barnes (2)

Bath's Victor Ubogu on the break in the Pilkington Cup final, in which Bath beat Leicester 21-9 to record their third League and Cup double.

4 Dec	A	Harlequins	14-12	*T:* Robinson *PG:* Barnes (2), Catt
11 Dec	H	London Irish	28-8	*T:* Catt, Lloyd, de Glanville, Hill *C:* Callard *PG:* Callard (2)
8 Jan	H	Bristol	9-0	*PG:* Callard (3)
15 Jan	A	Northampton	30-9	*T:* Swift (2), de Glanville, pen try *C:* Callard (2) *PG:* Callard (2)
29 Jan	H	Orrell	13-7	*T:* Swift *C:* Callard *PG:* Callard (2)
12 Feb	A	Gloucester	16-6	*T:* Ojomoh *C:* Callard *PG:* Callard (3)
12 Mar	H	Wasps	24-8	*T:* Callard (2) *C:* Callard *PG:* Callard (3) *DG:* Barnes
26 Mar	A	Newcastle Gosforth	29-5	*T:* Haag (2), Catt, Sanders *C:* Callard (3) *PG:* Callard
9 Apr	H	Leicester	14-6	*T:* Swift *PG:* Callard (3)
23 Apr	H	Harlequins	32-13	*T:* Clarke, de Glanville, Hilton, Hall *C:* Callard (3) *PG:* Callard (2)
30 Apr	A	London Irish	32-31	*T:* Egerton (2), Woodman *C:* Rayner *PG:* Rayner (4) *DG:* Rayner

Bristol

Year of formation 1888
Ground Memorial Ground, Filton Avenue, Horfield, Bristol   Tel: Bristol (0272) 514448
Colours Navy blue and white
Most capped player J V Pullin (England) 42 caps
Captain 1993-94 D J Eves
Courage League Div 1 4th **Pilkington Cup** Lost 9-14 to Bath (5th round)

League Record 1993-94

Date	Venue	Opponents	Result	Scorers
11 Sept	H	Bath	10-18	*T:* Saverimutto *C:* Tainton *PG:* Tainton
18 Sept	A	London Irish	16-0	*T:* Wring *C:* Tainton *PG:* Tainton (3)
25 Sept	A	Harlequins	20-15	*T:* Eves, Saverimutto *C:* Tainton (2) *PG:* Tainton (2)
2 Oct	H	Northampton	22-31	*T:* Hull (2), Saverimutto, Eves *C:* Hull
9 Oct	A	Orrell	13-16	*T:* Saverimutto *C:* Tainton *PG:* Tainton (2)
13 Nov	H	Gloucester	16-12	*T:* Knibbs *C:* Tainton *PG:* Tainton (3)
20 Nov	A	Wasps	8-34	*T:* Bracken *PG:* Tainton
4 Dec	H	Newcastle Gosforth	26-0	*T:* Hull, Saverimutto, John *C:* Tainton *PG:* Tainton (3)
11 Dec	A	Leicester	9-21	*PG:* Tainton (3)
8 Jan	A	Bath	0-9	
29 Jan	H	Harlequins	20-16	*T:* Blackmore, John, Knibbs *C:* Tainton *PG:* Tainton
12 Feb	A	Northampton	19-22	*T:* Barrow, Eves *PG:* Tainton (3)
12 Mar	H	Orrell	30-17	*T:* Hull (2), Bracken *C:* Tainton (3) *PG:* Tainton (3)
26 Mar	A	Gloucester	24-6	*T:* Kitchin (2), Saverimutto *C:* Tainton (3) *DG:* Tainton
2 Apr	H	London Irish	21-8	*T:* Saverimutto, Kitchin *C:* Tainton *PG:* Tainton (3)
19 Apr	H	Wasps	15-16	*PG:* Tainton (5)
23 Apr	A	Newcastle Gosforth	22-13	*T:* Saverimutto *C:* Tainton *PG:* Tainton (4) *DG:* Knibbs
30 Apr	H	Leicester	40-22	*T:* Hull (2), Patten (2), Denney *C:* Tainton (3) *PG:* Tainton (3)

Gloucester

Year of formation 1873
Ground Kingsholm, Kingsholm Road, Gloucester   Tel: Gloucester (0452) 520901
Colours Cherry and white

Most capped player A T Voyce (England)/M C Teague (England) 27 caps
Captain 1993-94 I R Smith
Courage League Div 1 8th **Pilkington Cup** Lost 3-10 to Orrell (quarter-final)

League Record 1993-94

Date	Venue	Opponents	Result	Scorers
11 Sept	H	Wasps	9-9	*PG:* T Smith (2) *DG:* Cummins
18 Sept	A	Newcastle Gosforth	12-12	*PG:* T Smith (2), Beech (2)
25 Sept	H	Leicester	14-23	*T:* Holford *PG:* T Smith (2), Beech
2 Oct	A	Bath	17-46	*T:* Cummins, Holford *C:* T. Smith, Beech *PG:* Beech
9 Oct	H	London Irish	9-10	*PG:* Roberts (3)
13 Nov	A	Bristol	12-16	*PG:* Johnson (4)
20 Nov	H	Northampton	19-14	*T:* Deacon *C:* Johnson *PG:* Johnson (2), T Smith (2)
4 Dec	A	Orrell	10-6	*T:* Johnson *C:* T Smith *PG:* T Smith
11 Dec	H	Harlequins	24-20	*T:* Nicholson, Fenley, Windo, Deacon *C:* T Smith (2)
8 Jan	A	Wasps	18-29	*T:* Fenley, pen try *C:* T Smith *PG:* T Smith (2)
15 Jan	H	Newcastle Gosforth	15-9	*T:* Holford, pen try *C:* T Smith *PG:* T Smith
29 Jan	A	Leicester	8-28	*T:* Sims *PG:* T Smith
12 Feb	H	Bath	6-16	*PG:* T Smith *DG:* Cummins
12 Mar	A	London Irish	15-12	*PG:* T Smith (4) *DG:* T Smith
26 Mar	H	Bristol	6-24	*PG:* Fenwick (2)
9 Apr	A	Northampton	3-19	*DG:* Cummins
23 Apr	H	Orrell	30-25	*T:* Sharp (2), Morris, Fenley *C:* T Smith (2) *PG:* T Smith (2)
30 Apr	A	Harlequins	20-38	*T:* Windo, Kearsey, T Smith *C:* Beech *PG:* T Smith

Andy Deacon of Gloucester celebrates the try by fellow prop Tony Windo in the home League game against Harlequins.

Harlequins

Year of formation 1866
Ground Stoop Memorial Ground, Craneford Way, Twickenham, Middlesex
Tel: 081-892 0822
Colours Light blue, magenta, chocolate, French grey, black and light green
Most capped player P J Winterbottom (England) 58 caps
Captain 1993-94 A R Mullins
Courage League Div 1 6th **Pilkington Cup** Lost 25-26 to Bath (semi-final)

League Record 1993-94

Date	Venue	Opponents	Result	Scorers
11 Sept	H	London Irish	30-15	*T:* O'Leary (2), Challinor, Glenister
				C: Challinor (2) *PG:* Challinor (2)
18 Sept	A	Wasps	15-18	*T:* Leonard, Glenister *C:* Bray *PG:* Bray
25 Sept	H	Bristol	15-20	*PG:* Bray (5)
2 Oct	A	Newcastle Gosforth	22-3	*T:* O'Leary, Snow *PG:* Bray (3), Challinor
9 Oct	H	Northampton	15-7	*PG:* Bray (5)
13 Nov	A	Leicester	10-3	*T:* O'Leary, Carling
20 Nov	A	Orrell	20-21	*T:* O'Leary, Challinor *C:* Bray (2) *PG:* Bray (2)
4 Dec	H	Bath	12-14	*PG:* Bray (4)
11 Dec	A	Gloucester	20-24	*T:* Bray, Keyter, Jardine-Brown *C:* Bray
				PG: Bray
8 Jan	A	London Irish	33-7	*T:* Russell, Glenister, O'Leary, Thompson
				C: Bray (2) *PG:* Bray (3)
15 Jan	H	Wasps	22-17	*T:* O'Leary *C:* Bray *PG:* Bray (4)
				DG: Challinor
29 Jan	A	Bristol	16-20	*T:* Glenister, Snow *PG:* Bray (2)
12 Feb	H	Newcastle Gosforth	12-6	*PG:* Challinor (4)
12 Mar	A	Northampton	14-15	*T:* O'Leary *PG:* Challinor (3)
26 Mar	H	Leicester	13-25	*T:* Keyter *C:* Challinor *PG:* Challinor (2)
9 Apr	H	Orrell	13-20	*T:* Keyter *C:* Bray *PG:* Bray (2)
23 Apr	A	Bath	13-32	*T:* Thompson *C:* Bray *PG:* Bray (2)
30 Apr	H	Gloucester	38-20	*T:* O'Leary (2), Carling, Keyter *C:* Bray (3)
				PG: Bray (4)

Leicester

Year of formation 1880
Ground Welford Road, Leicester Tel: Leicester (0533) 540276 or 541607
Colours Scarlet, green and white
Most capped player R Underwood (England) 65 caps
Captain 1993-94 D Richards
Courage League Div 1 2nd **Pilkington Cup** Lost 9-21 to Bath (final)

League Record 1993-94

Date	Venue	Opponents	Result	Scorers
11 Sept	A	Northampton	10-19	*T:* T Underwood *C:* Harris *PG:* Harris
18 Sept	H	Orrell	23-18	*T:* Cockerill, Potter *C:* Liley (2) *PG:* Liley
				DG: Harris (2)
25 Sept	A	Gloucester	23-14	*T:* Hackney (2), Back *C:* Liley *PG:* Liley
				DG: Harris
2 Oct	H	Wasps	38-6	*T:* Back, Wells, Poole, Richards *C:* Harris (3)
				PG: Harris (3) *DG:* Harris
9 Oct	A	Newcastle Gosforth	22-13	*T:* Back *C:* Harris *PG:* Harris (4)
				DG: Harris
13 Nov	H	Harlequins	3-10	*PG:* Liley
20 Nov	H	Bath	9-6	*PG:* Liley (2) *DG:* Harris
4 Dec	A	London Irish	22-10	*T:* Kardooni, Harris *PG:* Harris (2)
				DG: Harris (2)

11 Dec	H	Bristol	21-9	*PG:* Harris (7)
8 Jan	H	Northampton	36-9	*T:* Kilford, T Underwood, Poole *C:* Harris (3)
				PG: Harris (3) *DG:* Harris (2)
15 Jan	A	Orrell	18-0	*T:* Boyle, Harris, Kilford *PG:* Harris
29 Jan	H	Gloucester	28-8	*T:* T Underwood *C:* Harris *PG:* Harris (7)
12 Feb	A	Wasps	15-13	*PG:* Harris (4) *DG:* Harris
12 Mar	H	Newcastle Gosforth	66-5	*T:* T Underwood (4), Hackney (2), Back (2),
				Robinson, Rowntree *C:* Harris (5)
				PG: Harris (2)
26 Mar	A	Harlequins	25-13	*T:* Back, Potter, Richards *C:* Harris (2)
				PG: Harris (2)
9 Apr	A	Bath	6-14	*PG:* Harris (2)
23 Apr	H	London Irish	38-3	*T:* Hackney, Potter, Boyle, T Underwood, Smith
				C: Harris (2) *PG:* Harris (3)
30 Apr	A	Bristol	22-40	*T:* Tarbuck, Johnson, Reynolds *C:* Liley (2)
				PG: Liley

London Irish

Year of formation 1898
Ground The Avenue, Sunbury-on-Thames, Middlesex   Tel: Sunbury (0932) 783034
Colours Emerald green
Most capped player K W Kennedy (Ireland) 45 caps
Captain 1993-94 P C Collins
Courage League Div 1 9th *relegated* **Pilkington Cup** Lost 10-43 to Leicester (5th round)

League Record 1993-94

Date	*Venue*	*Opponents*	*Result*	*Scorers*
11 Sept	A	Harlequins	15-30	*T:* Geoghegan, Halpin, Corcoran
18 Sept	H	Bristol	0-16	
25 Sept	A	Northampton	12-23	*PG:* Burke (3) *DG:* Burke
2 Oct	H	Orrell	19-6	*T:* Geoghegan *C:* Burke *PG:* Burke (4)
9 Oct	A	Gloucester	10-9	*T:* Dooley *C:* Burke *PG:* Burke
20 Nov	A	Newcastle Gosforth	13-9	*T:* Hennessy *C:* Corcoran *PG:* Burke (2)
4 Dec	H	Leicester	10-22	*T:* Geoghegan *C:* Corcoran *DG:* Cobbe
11 Dec	A	Bath	8-28	*T:* Collins *PG:* Corcoran
8 Jan	H	Harlequins	7-33	*T:* Domoni *C:* Cobbe
29 Jan	H	Northampton	13-16	*T:* Henderson, Jenkins *PG:* Corcoran
12 Feb	A	Orrell	3-24	*PG:* Corcoran
26 Feb	H	Wasps	14-29	*T:* Geoghegan *PG:* Corcoran (3)
12 Mar	H	Gloucester	12-15	*PG:* Corcoran (4)
26 Mar	A	Wasps	22-21	*T:* Corcoran *C:* Corcoran *PG:* Corcoran (5)
2 Apr	A	Bristol	8-21	*T:* Corcoran *PG:* Corcoran
9 Apr	H	Newcastle Gosforth	17-19	*T:* Hennessy *PG:* Cathcart (2), Corcoran (2)
23 Apr	A	Leicester	3-38	*PG:* Cathcart
30 Apr	H	Bath	31-32	*T:* Cathcart, Henderson, Higgins, Donovan
				C: Cathcart *PG:* Cathcart (3)

London Scottish

Year of formation 1878
Ground Richmond Athletic Ground, Richmond, Surrey   Tel: 081-332 2473
Colours Blue jersey with red lion crest
Most capped player A G Hastings (Scotland) 50 caps
Captain 1993-94 D Millard
Courage League Div 2 8th **Pilkington Cup** Lost 6-8 to Fylde (4th round)

League Record 1993-94

Date	*Venue*	*Opponents*	*Result*	*Scorers*
11 Sept	H	Sale	3-12	*PG:* Grecian

18 Sept	A	Waterloo	17-13	*T:* Leckie, Millard *C:* Grecian (2) *PG:* Walker
25 Sept	H	Otley	3-11	*PG:* Walker
2 Oct	A	Rugby	5-7	*T:* Grecian
9 Oct	H	Moseley	16-8	*T:* Eriksson *C:* Russell *PG:* Russell (3)
13 Nov	A	Wakefield	11-17	*T:* Walker *PG:* Wichary (2)
20 Nov	H	Nottingham	21-14	*T:* Eriksson, Walker *C:* Wichary *PG:* Wichary (3)
4 Dec	A	West Hartlepool	19-21	*T:* Wichary *C:* Wichary *PG:* Wichary (2) *DG:* Millard, Troup
11 Dec	H	Saracens	12-37	*PG:* Russell (4)
15 Jan	H	Waterloo	9-18	*PG:* Wichary (3)
29 Jan	A	Otley	6-13	*PG:* Wichary (2)
12 Feb	H	Rugby	22-11	*T:* Appleson, McLellan, Sly *C:* Walker (2) *PG:* Walker
19 Feb	A	Sale	12-28	*T:* Eriksson, Cronin *C:* Walker
12 Mar	A	Moseley	12-27	*PG:* Walker (4)
26 Mar	H	Wakefield	11-37	*T:* Cronin *PG:* Walker (2)
9 Apr	A	Nottingham	18-23	*PG:* Walker (4) *DG:* Walker (2)
23 Apr	H	West Hartlepool	24-22	*T:* Appleson, Eriksson *C:* Walker *PG:* Walker *DG:* Walker (3)
30 Apr	A	Saracens	11-6	*T:* Grecian *PG:* Walker (2)

Moseley

Year of formation 1873
Ground The Reddings, Reddings Road, Moseley, Birmingham   Tel: 021-499 2149
Colours Red and black
Most capped player M C Teague (England) 27 caps
Captain 1993-94 P Shillingford
Courage League Div 2 5th **Pilkington Cup** Lost 6-12 to Leicester (quarter-final)

League Record 1993-94

Date	Venue	Opponents	Result	Scorers
11 Sept	A	Saracens	10-14	*T:* Teague *C:* Hamlin *PG:* Hamlin
18 Sept	H	Wakefield	20-11	*T:* Linnett (2) *C:* Kerr (2) *PG:* Kerr (2)
25 Sept	A	Nottingham	25-6	*T:* Anderson (2), Lloyd *C:* Kerr (2) *PG:* Kerr (2)
2 Oct	H	West Hartlepool	9-31	*PG:* Kerr (3)
9 Oct	A	London Scottish	8-16	*T:* Dossett *PG:* Hodgkinson
13 Nov	H	Sale	9-3	*PG:* Kerr (3)
20 Nov	A	Waterloo	5-12	*T:* Morris
4 Dec	H	Otley	30-22	*T:* Teague, Linnett, Raymond, Moon *C:* Hodgkinson (2) *PG:* Hodgkinson (2)
11 Dec	A	Rugby	3-6	*PG:* Hodgkinson
8 Jan	H	Saracens	15-16	*PG:* Hodgkinson (5)
15 Jan	A	Wakefield	12-13	*PG:* Kerr (4)
29 Jan	H	Nottingham	17-0	*T:* Poll *PG:* Hodgkinson (4)
12 Feb	A	West Hartlepool	15-16	*PG:* Hodgkinson (4) *DG:* Kerr
12 Mar	H	London Scottish	27-12	*T:* Smith, Watson, Shillingford, Linnett *C:* Hodgkinson (2) *PG:* Hodgkinson
26 Mar	A	Sale	16-13	*T:* Becconsall *C:* Hodgkinson *PG:* Hodgkinson (3)
9 Apr	H	Waterloo	6-6	*PG:* Hodgkinson (2)
23 Apr	A	Otley	26-12	*T:* Watson, Bonney, Corbett, Ball *C:* Hodgkinson (2), Kerr
30 Apr	H	Rugby	13-11	*T:* Linnett *C:* Kerr *PG:* Kerr (2)

Newcastle Gosforth

Year of formation 1877
Ground Kingston Park, Brunton Road, Kenton Bank Foot, Newcastle-upon-Tyne
Tel: Tyneside (091) 214 0422

Colours Green and white
Most capped player R J McLoughlin (Ireland) 40 caps
Captain 1993-94 N Frankland
Courage League Div 1 10th *relegated* **Pilkington Cup** Lost 7-12 to Orrell (5th round)

League Record 1993-94

Date	Venue	Opponents	Result	Scorers
11 Sept	A	Orrell	12-42	*PG:* Johnson (3) *DG:* Willcox
18 Sept	H	Gloucester	12-12	*PG:* Johnson (4)
25 Sept	A	Wasps	21-38	*T:* Vanzandvliet, Wilkinson *C:* Johnson *PG:* Johnson (3)
2 Oct	H	Harlequins	3-22	*PG:* Johnson
9 Oct	H	Leicester	13-22	*T:* Arnold *C:* Willcox *PG:* Willcox (2)
13 Nov	A	Bath	3-46	*PG:* Willcox
20 Nov	H	London Irish	9-13	*PG:* Willcox (2) *DG:* Willcox
4 Dec	A	Bristol	0-26	
11 Dec	H	Northampton	8-28	*T:* Douglas *DG:* Willcox
15 Jan	A	Gloucester	9-15	*PG:* Johnson (3)
29 Jan	H	Wasps	16-18	*T:* Corry, Douglas *PG:* Johnson *DG:* Johnson
12 Feb	A	Harlequins	6-12	*PG:* Johnson (2)
12 Mar	A	Leicester	5-66	*T:* Wilkinson
26 Mar	H	Bath	5-29	*T:* Corry
9 Apr	A	London Irish	19-17	*T:* Douglas, Vanzandvliet, Wilkinson *C:* Johnson (2)
16 Apr	H	Orrell	13-12	*T:* Frankland *C:* Johnson *PG:* Johnson (2)
23 Apr	H	Bristol	13-22	*T:* Wilkinson, Penn *PG:* Johnson
30 Apr	A	Northampton	23-43	*T:* Corry, Casado, Penn *C:* Johnson *PG:* Johnson (2)

Northampton

Year of formation 1888
Ground Franklins Gardens, Weedon Road, Northampton
Tel: Northampton (0604) 751543
Colours Black, green and gold
Most capped player G S Pearce (England) 36 caps
Captain 1993-94 C J Olver
Courage League Div 1 5th **Pilkington Cup** Lost 6-11 to Gloucester (5th round)

League Record 1993-94

Date	Venue	Opponents	Result	Scorers
11 Sept	H	Leicester	19-10	*T:* Packman *C:* Grayson *PG:* Grayson (3) *DG:* Steele
18 Sept	A	Bath	9-37	*PG:* Grayson (3)
25 Sept	H	London Irish	23-12	*T:* Fielden (2) *C:* Grayson (2) *PG:* Grayson (3)
2 Oct	A	Bristol	31-22	*T:* Grayson (2), Walton *C:* Grayson (2) *PG:* Grayson (3) *DG:* Grayson
9 Oct	A	Harlequins	7-15	*T:* Dawson *C:* Grayson
13 Nov	H	Orrell	9-13	*PG:* Grayson (2), Hunter
20 Nov	A	Gloucester	14-19	*T:* Beal *PG:* Grayson (3)
4 Dec	H	Wasps	15-17	*PG:* Steele (4) *DG:* Steele
11 Dec	A	Newcastle Gosforth	28-8	*T:* Hunter, Beal, Dawson, Merlin *C:* Grayson *PG:* Grayson (2)
8 Jan	A	Leicester	9-36	*PG:* Grayson (3)
15 Jan	H	Bath	9-30	*PG:* Steele (3)
29 Jan	A	London Irish	16-13	*T:* Thorneycroft *C:* Grayson *PG:* Grayson (3)
12 Feb	H	Bristol	22-19	*T:* Fletcher *C:* Grayson *PG:* Grayson (5)
12 Mar	H	Harlequins	15-14	*T:* Morgan (2) *C:* Grayson *PG:* Grayson

26 Mar	A	Orrell	6-27	*PG:* Grayson (2)
9 Apr	H	Gloucester	19-3	*T:* Rodber *C:* Beal *PG:* Beal (4)
23 Apr	A	Wasps	11-24	*T:* Moir *PG:* Beal *DG:* Beal
30 Apr	H	Newcastle Gosforth	43-23	*T:* Thorneycroft, Steele, Walton, Bayfield, Morgan *C:* Beal (3) *PG:* Beal (4)

Nottingham

Year of formation 1877
Ground Ireland Avenue, Beeston, Nottingham   Tel: Nottingham (0602) 254238
Colours White and green
Most capped player C R Andrew (England) 57 caps
Captain 1993-94 C A Gray
Courage League Div 2 6th **Pilkington Cup** Lost 9-29 to Gloucester (4th round)

League Record 1993-94

Date	Venue	Opponents	Result	Scorers
11 Sept	H	Otley	25-30	*T:* Gregory *C:* Gregory *PG:* Gregory (5) *DG:* Gregory
18 Sept	A	Rugby	14-16	*T:* Brackenbury *PG:* Gregory (3)
25 Sept	H	Moseley	6-25	*PG:* Gregory (2)
2 Oct	A	Wakefield	6-6	*PG:* Gregory (2)
9 Oct	A	Saracens	3-13	*PG:* Gallagher
13 Nov	H	West Hartlepool	9-17	*PG:* Gregory (2) *DG:* Gregory
20 Nov	A	London Scottish	14-21	*T:* Smallwood *PG:* Gregory (3)
4 Dec	H	Sale	9-30	*PG:* Gregory (3)
11 Dec	A	Waterloo	19-8	*T:* Bradley *C:* Gregory *PG:* Gregory (3) *DG:* Gregory
8 Jan	A	Otley	18-12	*T:* Bradley, Furley *C:* Gregory *PG:* Gregory *DG:* Gregory
15 Jan	H	Rugby	17-16	*T:* Jackson, West *C:* Gregory (2) *PG:* Gregory
29 Jan	A	Moseley	0-17	
12 Feb	H	Wakefield	16-13	*T:* Bradley, West *PG:* Gregory (2)
12 Mar	H	Saracens	18-9	*PG:* Gregory (6)
26 Mar	A	West Hartlepool	23-13	*T:* Bradley, Smallwood *C:* Gregory (2) *PG:* Gregory (2) *DG:* Gregory
9 Apr	H	London Scottish	23-18	*T:* Smallwood, West *C:* Gregory (2) *PG:* Gregory (3)
23 Apr	A	Sale	7-41	*T:* Smallwood *C:* Gregory
30 Apr	H	Waterloo	27-21	*T:* Smallwood, Royer *C:* Gregory *PG:* Gregory (5)

Orrell

Year of formation 1927
Ground Edge Hall Road, Orrell, Lancashire   Tel: Upholland (0695) 623193
Colours Black and amber
Most capped player J Carleton (England) 26 caps
Captain 1993-94 S Taberner
Courage League Div 1 7th **Pilkington Cup** Lost 18-31 to Leicester (semi-final)

League Record 1993-94

Date	Venue	Opponents	Result	Scorers
11 Sept	H	Newcastle Gosforth	42-12	*T:* Naylor (2), Morris (2), Taberner, Hamer *C:* Langford (2), Peacock *PG:* Langford (2)
18 Sept	A	Leicester	18-23	*T:* Ashurst, Cleary *C:* Langford *PG:* Langford (2)

25 Sept	H	Bath	15-18	*PG:* Langford (5)
2 Oct	A	London Irish	6-19	*PG:* Langford (2)
9 Oct	H	Bristol	16-13	*T:* Naylor *C:* Ainscough *PG:* Ainscough (2), Langford
13 Nov	A	Northampton	13-9	*T:* Cleary *C:* Ainscough *PG:* Ainscough (2)
20 Nov	H	Harlequins	21-20	*T:* Morris, Cleary *C:* Ainscough *PG:* Ainscough (3)
4 Dec	H	Gloucester	6-10	*PG:* Ainscough, Peacock
11 Dec	A	Wasps	16-28	*T:* Hamer *C:* Langford *PG:* Langford (2), Peacock
15 Jan	H	Leicester	0-18	
29 Jan	A	Bath	7-13	*T:* Morris *C:* Langford
12 Feb	H	London Irish	24-3	*T:* Bibby, Taberner, Wynn *C:* Langford (2), Ainscough *PG:* Ainscough
12 Mar	A	Bristol	17-30	*T:* Hayter, Hamer *C:* Ainscough (2) *PG:* Langford
26 Mar	H	Northampton	27-6	*T:* Naylor (2), Johnson, Langford *C:* Ainscough, Langford *PG:* Ainscough
9 Apr	A	Harlequins	20-13	*T:* French, Johnson *C:* Ainscough, Langford *PG:* Langford (2)
16 Apr	A	Newcastle Gosforth	12-13	*T:* Hamer, Bibby *C:* Ainscough
23 Apr	A	Gloucester	25-30	*T:* Winstanley, Langford, Johnson *C:* Ainscough, Langford *PG:* Ainscough, Langford
30 Apr	H	Wasps	42-24	*T:* Naylor (2), Wynn (2), Johnson, French *C:* Ainscough (3) *PG:* Ainscough (2)

Otley

Year of formation 1865 (reformed 1907)
Ground Cross Green, Otley, West Yorkshire   Tel: Otley (0943) 461180
Colours Black and white hoops
Most capped player A H Bateson (England) 4 caps
Captain 1993-94 M Winterbottom
Courage League Div 2 10th *relegated* **Pilkington Cup** Lost 7-58 to Sale (5th round)

League Record 1993-94

Date	*Venue*	*Opponents*	*Result*	*Scorers*
11 Sept	A	Nottingham	30-25	*T:* Rutledge, Melville, Atkinson *PG:* Rutledge (3) *DG:* Petyt (2)
18 Sept	H	West Hartlepool	11-28	*T:* Atkinson *PG:* Rutledge (2)
25 Sept	A	London Scottish	11-3	*T:* Atkinson *PG:* Rutledge (2)
2 Oct	H	Sale	9-5	*PG:* Rutledge (3)
9 Oct	A	Waterloo	16-39	*T:* Rutledge *C:* Rutledge *PG:* Rutledge (3)
13 Nov	H	Saracens	9-11	*PG:* Rutledge (3)
20 Nov	H	Rugby	3-3	*PG:* Petyt
4 Dec	A	Moseley	22-30	*T:* Scott, Atkinson, pen try *C:* Rutledge (2) *PG:* Rutledge
11 Dec	H	Wakefield	0-22	
8 Jan	H	Nottingham	12-18	*T:* Flint, Carroll *C:* Rutledge
15 Jan	A	West Hartlepool	20-48	*T:* Atkinson, Farrar, A Scott *C:* Rutledge *PG:* Rutledge
29 Jan	H	London Scottish	13-6	*T:* Atkinson *C:* Rutledge *PG:* Rutledge *DG:* Petyt
12 Feb	A	Sale	9-88	*PG:* Rutledge (2) *DG:* Petyt
12 Mar	H	Waterloo	15-21	*T:* Scott, Wilson *C:* Rutledge *PG:* Rutledge
26 Mar	A	Saracens	19-31	*T:* Rutledge *C:* Rutledge *PG:* Rutledge (3) *DG:* Petyt
9 Apr	A	Rugby	10-19	*T:* Tipping *C:* Rutledge *DG:* Petyt
23 Apr	H	Moseley	12-26	*T:* Atkinson, Flint *C:* Rutledge
30 Apr	A	Wakefield	14-26	*T:* Balmer *PG:* Rutledge (3)

Rugby

Year of formation 1873
Ground Webb Ellis Road (off Bilton Road), Rugby   Tel: Rugby (0788) 542252
Colours Orange, black and white
Most capped player G S Conway (England) 18 caps
Captain 1993-94 D Bishop
Courage League Div 2 9th *relegated* **Pilkington Cup** Lost 13-17 to Sale (4th round)

League Record 1993-94

Date	Venue	Opponents	Result	Scorers
11 Sept	A	Wakefield	16-48	*T:* Mapletoft *C:* Mapletoft *PG:* Mapletoft (3)
18 Sept	H	Nottingham	16-14	*T:* Saunders *C:* Mapletoft *PG:* Mapletoft (3)
25 Sept	A	West Hartlepool	19-28	*T:* Mapletoft (2), Saunders *C:* Mapletoft (2)
2 Oct	H	London Scottish	7-5	*T:* Mapletoft *C:* Mapletoft
9 Oct	A	Sale	3-16	*PG:* Mapletoft
13 Nov	H	Waterloo	3-8	*PG:* Mapletoft
20 Nov	A	Otley	3-3	*PG:* Mapletoft
4 Dec	A	Saracens	3-6	*DG:* Mapletoft
11 Dec	H	Moseley	6-3	*PG:* Mapletoft (2)
8 Jan	H	Wakefield	16-12	*T:* Watson, Rennell *PG:* Mapletoft *DG:* Pell
15 Jan	A	Nottingham	16-17	*T:* Pell *C:* Mapletoft *PG:* Mapletoft (2) *DG:* Pell
29 Jan	H	West Hartlepool	6-27	*PG:* Mapletoft (2)
12 Feb	A	London Scottish	11-22	*T:* Mapletoft *PG:* Macleod *DG:* Macleod
12 Mar	H	Sale	8-21	*T:* Bishop *PG:* Mapletoft
26 Mar	A	Waterloo	17-19	*T:* Riley, Watson *C:* Mapletoft (2) *PG:* Mapletoft
9 Apr	H	Otley	19-10	*T:* Mills *C:* Mapletoft *PG:* Mapletoft (3) *DG:* Mapletoft
23 Apr	H	Saracens	6-30	*PG:* Mapletoft *DG:* Pell
30 Apr	A	Moseley	11-13	*T:* Revan *PG:* Mason (2)

Sale

Year of formation 1861
Ground Heywood Road, Brooklands, Sale, Cheshire   Tel: Manchester (061) 973 6348
Colours Blue and white
Most capped player F E Cotton (England) 31 caps
Captain 1993-94 M Kenrick
Courage League Div 2 *Winners – promoted* **Pilkington Cup** Lost 13-26 to Harlequins (quarter-final)

League Record 1993-94

Date	Venue	Opponents	Result	Scorers
11 Sept	A	London Scottish	12-3	*PG:* Turner (4)
18 Sept	H	Saracens	52-3	*T:* Erskine (2), Young (2), Kenrick, Stocks, Mallinder, Baldwin *C:* Turner (6)
25 Sept	H	Waterloo	15-6	*T:* Birt (2) *C:* Turner *PG:* Turner
2 Oct	A	Otley	5-9	*T:* Baldwin
9 Oct	H	Rugby	16-3	*T:* Warr *C:* Turner *PG:* Turner (3)
13 Nov	A	Moseley	3-9	*PG:* Turner
20 Nov	H	Wakefield	11-11	*T:* Kenrick *PG:* Jee *DG:* Turner
4 Dec	A	Nottingham	30-9	*T:* Duthie, Kenrick, Diamond, Verbickas *C:* Turner (2) *PG:* Turner (2)
11 Dec	H	West Hartlepool	28-12	*T:* McCartney, Verbickas, Warr *C:* Turner (2) *PG:* Turner (3)
15 Jan	A	Saracens	8-3	*T:* Verbickas *PG:* Turner
29 Jan	A	Waterloo	28-10	*T:* Verbickas (2), Diamond *C:* Turner (2) *PG:* Turner (3)

12 Feb	H	Otley	88-9	*T:* Verbickas (5), Warr (3), Erskine, Mallinder, Turner, Whitcombe, Young, pen try *C:* Turner (9)
19 Feb	H	London Scottish	28-12	*T:* Young, Verbickas, Whitcombe, Erskine *C:* Jee *PG:* Turner, Jee
12 Mar	A	Rugby	21-8	*T:* Verbickas (2), Mallinder *PG:* Jee (2)
26 Mar	H	Moseley	13-16	*T:* Mallinder, Verbickas *PG:* Turner
9 Apr	A	Wakefield	28-19	*T:* Erskine, Mallinder, Whitcombe *C:* Turner (2) *PG:* Turner (2) *DG:* Turner
23 Apr	H	Nottingham	41-7	*T:* Baldwin, O'Grady, Young, Birt, Verbickas, Mallinder *C:* Turner (4) *PG:* Turner
30 Apr	A	West Hartlepool	11-11	*T:* Verbickas *PG:* Turner (2)

Saracens

Year of formation 1876
Ground Bramley Sports Ground, Green Road, Southgate, London N14
Tel: 081-449 3770
Colours Black with red star and crescent
Most capped player J Leonard (England) 30 caps
Captain 1993-94 B Davies
Courage League Div 2 3rd **Pilkington Cup** Lost 6-23 to Bath (quarter-final)

League Record 1993-94

Date	*Venue*	*Opponents*	*Result*	*Scorers*
11 Sept	H	Moseley	14-10	*T:* Van Poortvliet *PG:* Tunningley (2) *DG:* Tunningley
18 Sept	A	Sale	3-52	*PG:* Tunningley
25 Sept	H	Wakefield	20-10	*T:* Tunningley, Kemp, Green *C:* Tunningley *PG:* Tunningley
2 Oct	A	Waterloo	12-12	*PG:* Tunningley (3), G Hughes
9 Oct	H	Nottingham	13-3	*T:* Ravenscroft *C:* Tunningley *PG:* Tunningley *DG:* G Hughes
13 Nov	A	Otley	11-9	*T:* Davies *PG:* Tunningley (2)
20 Nov	H	West Hartlepool	8-14	*T:* Crawley *PG:* Tunningley
4 Dec	H	Rugby	6-3	*PG:* Tunningley (2)
11 Dec	A	London Scottish	37-12	*T:* Lee (2), Tunningley, Hill *C:* Tunningley (4) *PG:* Tunningley (3)
8 Jan	A	Moseley	16-15	*T:* Tunningley (2) *PG:* Tunningley (2)
15 Jan	H	Sale	3-8	*PG:* Tunningley
29 Jan	A	Wakefield	23-14	*T:* Buckton, Green *C:* Tunningley (2) *PG:* Tunningley (3)
12 Feb	H	Waterloo	37-0	*T:* Hill (2), Hughes (2), Ravenscroft *C:* Tunningley (3) *PG:* Tunningley (2)
12 Mar	A	Nottingham	9-18	*PG:* Tunningley (3)
26 Mar	H	Otley	31-19	*T:* Harries (2), Davies, Langley *C:* Tunningley *PG:* Tunningley (3)
9 Apr	A	West Hartlepool	20-22	*T:* Harries, Tunningley *C:* Tunningley (2) *PG:* Tunningley *DG:* Lee
23 Apr	A	Rugby	30-6	*T:* Hill (2), Andrews, Butler *C:* Lee (2) *PG:* Lee (2)
30 Apr	H	London Scottish	6-11	*DG:* G Hughes (2)

Wakefield

Year of formation 1901
Ground Pinderfields Road, College Grove, Wakefield   Tel: Wakefield (0924) 372038
Colours Black and gold hoops
Most capped player M E Harrison (England) 15 caps
Captain 1993-94 D Scully
Courage League Div 2 4th **Pilkington Cup** Lost 17-18 to West Hartlepool (4th round)

League Record 1993-94

Date	Venue	Opponents	Result	Scorers
11 Sept	H	Rugby	48-16	T: Sleightholme (2), Edwards, Scully, Maynard C: Liley (4) PG: Liley (5)
18 Sept	A	Moseley	11-20	T: Sleightholme PG: Liley (2)
25 Sept	A	Saracens	10-20	T: pen try C: Liley PG: Liley
2 Oct	H	Nottingham	6-6	PG: Liley (2)
9 Oct	A	West Hartlepool	13-13	T: Sleightholme C: Liley PG: Liley (2)
13 Nov	H	London Scottish	17-11	T: Thompson PG: Liley (4)
20 Nov	A	Sale	11-11	T: Green PG: Liley (2)
4 Dec	H	Waterloo	47-6	T: Sleightholme (2), Green, Croft, Stewart, Scully C: Liley (3), Jackson PG: Liley (3)
11 Dec	A	Otley	22-0	T: Garnett, Sleightholme PG: Jackson (4)
8 Jan	A	Rugby	12-16	PG: Jackson (4)
15 Jan	H	Moseley	13-12	T: Scully, Thompson PG: Jackson
29 Jan	H	Saracens	14-23	T: Sleightholme PG: Jackson (3)
12 Feb	A	Nottingham	13-16	T: Thompson C: Jackson PG: Jackson (2)
12 Mar	H	West Hartlepool	10-11	T: Edwards C: Jackson PG: Jackson
26 Mar	A	London Scottish	37-11	T: Thompson (2), Cowling, Stewart C: Jackson (4) PG: Jackson (3)
9 Apr	H	Sale	19-28	T: Sleightholme C: Jackson PG: Jackson (4)
23 Apr	A	Waterloo	18-6	T: Sleightholme (2) C: Jackson PG: Jackson (2)
30 Apr	H	Otley	26-14	T: Thompson (2), Day, Sleightholme PG: Cowling, Scully

Wasps

Year of formation 1867
Ground Repton Avenue (off Rugby Road), Sudbury, Middlesex   Tel: 081-902 4220
Colours Black with gold wasp on left breast
Most capped player C R Andrew (England) 57 caps
Captain 1993-94 D Ryan
Courage League Div 1 3rd **Pilkington Cup** Lost 11-24 to Bath (4th round)

League Record 1993-94

Date	Venue	Opponents	Result	Scorers
11 Sept	A	Gloucester	9-9	PG: Andrew (3)
18 Sept	H	Harlequins	18-15	T: Holmes, D Hopley C: Andrew PG: Andrew (2)
25 Sept	H	Newcastle Gosforth	38-21	T: D Hopley (2), Oti (2), Andrew C: Andrew (2) PG: Andrew (3)
2 Oct	A	Leicester	6-38	PG: Andrew (2)
9 Oct	H	Bath	13-19	T: Childs C: Andrew PG: Andrew (2)
20 Nov	H	Bristol	34-8	T: D Hopley (2), Buzza, Andrew C: Andrew (4) PG: Andrew (2)
4 Dec	A	Northampton	17-15	T: Shortland PG: Andrew (3) DG: Andrew
11 Dec	H	Orrell	28-16	T: Bates C: Andrew PG: Andrew (7)
8 Jan	H	Gloucester	29-18	T: Ryan, Shortland C: Andrew (2) PG: Andrew (5)
15 Jan	A	Harlequins	17-22	T: Oti PG: Andrew (4)
29 Jan	A	Newcastle Gosforth	18-16	T: Dallaglio, White C: Andrew PG: Andrew (2)
12 Feb	H	Leicester	13-13	T: P Hopley C: Andrew PG: Andrew (2)
26 Feb	A	London Irish	29-14	T: P Hopley, Dallaglio, Ryan, Bates C: Andrew (3) PG: Andrew
12 Mar	A	Bath	8-24	T: Hunter PG: P Hopley
26 Mar	H	London Irish	21-22	T: Greenstock, Maddock C: Maddock PG: Maddock (2) DG: Davies
19 Apr	A	Bristol	16-15	T: Ryan, P Hopley PG: Braithwaite (2)
23 Apr	H	Northampton	24-11	T: Braithwaite, P Hopley C: Braithwaite PG: Braithwaite (3), Maddock

| 30 Apr | A | Orrell | 24-42 | T: Probyn, Shortland   C: Braithwaite |
| | | | | PG: Braithwaite (3)   DG: Braithwaite |

Waterloo

Year of formation 1882
Ground St Anthony's Road, Blundellsands, Liverpool   Tel: Liverpool (051) 924 4552
Colours Green, red and white
Most capped player H G Periton (England) 21 caps
Captain 1993-94 P Hackett
Courage League Div 2 7th **Pilkington Cup** Lost 3-22 to Northampton (4th round)

League Record 1993-94

Date	Venue	Opponents	Result	Scorers
11 Sept	A	West Hartlepool	11-30	T: Greenwood PG: Swindells (2)
18 Sept	H	London Scottish	13-17	T: Meredith C: Handley PG: Handley (2)
25 Sept	A	Sale	6-15	PG: Handley (2)
2 Oct	H	Saracens	12-12	PG: Swindells (4)
9 Oct	H	Otley	39-16	T: J Ashcroft (2), Saverimutto, Aitchison, Meredith C: Emmett (2), Swindells (2) PG: Emmett, Swindells
13 Nov	A	Rugby	8-3	T: Fletcher PG: Swindells
20 Nov	H	Moseley	12-5	PG: Swindells (4)
4 Dec	A	Wakefield	6-47	PG: Swindells, Emmett
11 Dec	H	Nottingham	8-19	T: Craig PG: Swindells
8 Jan	H	West Hartlepool	15-25	PG: Swindells (5)
15 Jan	A	London Scottish	18-9	PG: Swindells (5) DG: Craig
29 Jan	H	Sale	10-28	T: Hill C: Swindells DG: Ryan
12 Feb	A	Saracens	0-37	
12 Mar	A	Otley	21-15	PG: Swindells (6) DG: Aitchison
26 Mar	H	Rugby	19-17	T: Greenhalgh C: Swindells PG: Swindells (4)
9 Apr	A	Moseley	6-6	PG: Swindells (2)
23 Apr	H	Wakefield	6-18	PG: Handley (2)
30 Apr	A	Nottingham	21-27	T: Swindells (2) C: Swindells PG: Swindells (3)

West Hartlepool

Year of formation 1881
Ground Brierton Lane, Hartlepool   Tel: Hartlepool (0429) 272640
Colours Red, green and white hoops
Most capped player C D Aarvold (England) 16 caps
Captain 1993-94 J Stabler
Courage League Div 2 2nd *promoted* **Pilkington Cup** Lost 15-23 to Harlequins (5th round)

League Record 1993-94

Date	Venue	Opponents	Result	Scorers
11 Sept	H	Waterloo	30-11	T: Hodder, Wrigley, Cooke C: Stabler (3) PG: Stabler (3)
18 Sept	A	Otley	28-11	T: Cooke (2), Wrigley C: Stabler (2) PG: Stabler (3)
25 Sept	H	Rugby	28-19	T: Watson, Dixon, Stabler C: Stabler (2) PG: Stabler (3)
2 Oct	A	Moseley	31-9	T: Cooke, Mitchell, Wrigley, Oliphant C: Stabler (4) PG: Stabler
9 Oct	H	Wakefield	13-13	T: Dixon C: Stabler PG: Stabler (2)
13 Nov	A	Nottingham	17-9	T: Lancaster, Mitchell C: Stabler (2) PG: Stabler
20 Nov	A	Saracens	14-8	T: Hodder PG: Stabler (2) DG: Hodder
4 Dec	H	London Scottish	21-19	T: P Evans, O Evans C: Stabler PG: Stabler (2) DG: Stabler

11 Dec	A	Sale	12-28	*PG:* Stabler (2), Oliphant *DG:* Stabler
8 Jan	A	Waterloo	25-15	*T:* Watson, Wrigley, Evans *C:* Oliphant (2) *PG:* Oliphant (2)
15 Jan	H	Otley	48-20	*T:* O Evans (2), Brown, Cooke, Hodder, Wrigley, pen try *C:* Oliphant (5) *PG:* Oliphant
29 Jan	A	Rugby	27-6	*T:* P Evans, Lee *C:* Oliphant *PG:* Oliphant (5)
12 Feb	H	Moseley	16-15	*T:* Brown, Wrigley *PG:* Oliphant (2)
12 Mar	A	Wakefield	11-10	*T:* P Evans *PG:* Parker (2)
26 Mar	H	Nottingham	13-23	*T:* Wrigley *C:* Stabler *PG:* Oliphant, Stabler
9 Apr	H	Saracens	22-20	*T:* Watson *C:* Oliphant *PG:* Oliphant (4) *DG:* Parker
23 Apr	A	London Scottish	22-24	*T:* S Mitchell, Watson *PG:* Oliphant (3) *DG:* Parker
30 Apr	H	Sale	11-11	*T:* Watson *PG:* Oliphant (2)

SCOTLAND
Ayr

Year of formation 1897
Ground Millbrae, Alloway, Ayr KA7 4PJ   Tel: Alloway (0292) 441944
Colours Pink and black
Most capped player S Munro (Scotland) 10 caps
Captain 1993-94 George McMillan
1st XV 1993-94 P30 W8 D0 L21 Ab1 F414 A703
McEwan's/SRU Div 2 14th *relegated*

League Record 1993-94

Date	Venue	Opponents	Result	Scorers
11 Sept	A	Clarkston	27-9	*T:* George McMillan, Magorian (2), Moore *C:* Hay (2) *PG:* Hay
18 Sept	H	Musselburgh	6-13	*PG:* Hay (2)
25 Sept	A	Haddington	11-18	*T:* Buchanan *PG:* Hay (2)
2 Oct	H	Kirkcaldy	3-13	*PG:* Menzies
9 Oct	H	Peebles	15-17	*T:* George McMillan, Magorian *C:* George McMillan *PG:* George McMillan
16 Oct	A	Glasgow High/K'side	16-76	*T:* Magorian, K Nicol *PG:* George McMillan (2)
6 Nov	H	Wigtownshire	8-25	*T:* Gilmour *PG:* Courtney
27 Nov	A	Preston Lodge FP	12-24	*PG:* Kemp (4)
22 Jan	A	Edinburgh Wands	17-18	*T:* Stewart Kerr, A Nicol *C:* Kemp (2) *PG:* Kemp
12 Feb	H	Biggar	18-7	*T:* Fairgrieve, Logan *C:* Kemp *PG:* Kemp (2)
26 Feb	A	Grangemouth	6-14	*PG:* Kemp (2)
12 Mar	H	Glasgow Acads	19-0	*T:* Robertson *C:* Kemp *PG:* Kemp (4)
26 Mar	H	Dundee HSFP	10-27	*T:* Horne *C:* Kemp *PG:* Kemp

Biggar

Year of formation 1975
Ground Hartree Mill, Biggar   Tel: Biggar (0899) 21219
Colours Black jersey with red collar and cuffs
Captain 1993-94 Alan Harvey
1st XV 1993-94 P24 W10 D2 L12 F519 A429
McEwan's/SRU: Div 2 joint 11th

League Record 1993-94

Date	Venue	Opponents	Result	Scorers
11 Sept	H	Wigtownshire	38-6	*T:* Brown, F A W Jack, McAlpine (2), A Stewart *C:* Lavery (5) *PG:* Lavery

18 Sept	A	Preston Lodge	14-17	*T:* Aspinall *PG:* Lavery (3)
25 Sept	H	Dundee HSFP	3-17	*PG:* Lavery
2 Oct	A	Edinburgh Wands	10-34	*T:* S Jack *C:* Bruce *PG:* Lavery
9 Oct	A	Kirkcaldy	13-22	*T:* pen try *C:* Bruce *PG:* Bruce (2)
16 Oct	H	Grangemouth	8-8	*T:* Steel *PG:* Graham
6 Nov	A	Glasgow Acads	31-31	*T:* Graham, A McAlpine, Young (2) *C:* Lavery (4) *PG:* Bruce
4 Dec	H	Clarkston	24-13	*T:* E McAlpine, Steele (2) *PG:* Lavery (3)
22 Jan	H	Haddington	11-14	*T:* Graham *PG:* Lavery (2)
29 Jan	A	Musselburgh	26-11	*T:* Graham (2), S Jack *C:* Lavery *PG:* Lavery (3)
12 Feb	A	Ayr	7-18	*T:* Graham *C:* Lavery
26 Feb	H	Peebles	14-26	*T:* Graham *PG:* Lavery (3)
12 Mar	A	Glasgow High/K'side	3-23	*DG:* Graham

Boroughmuir

Year of formation 1919 (Boroughmuir FP until 1974)
Ground Meggetland, Colinton Road, Edinburgh EH14 1AS   Tel: 031-443 7571
Colours Blue and green quarters
Most capped player S R P Lineen (Scotland) 29 caps
Captain 1993-94 S J Reid
1st XV 1993-94 P33 W20 D2 L11 F797 A521
McEwan's/SRU Div 1 11th

League Record 1993-94

Date	*Venue*	*Opponents*	*Result*	*Scorers*
11 Sept	A	Stewart's-Melville FP	15-20	*T:* Smith, Stark *C:* Easson *PG:* Easson
18 Sept	H	Gala	23-28	*T:* Wilson *PG:* Easson (6)
25 Sept	H	Heriot's FP	6-21	*PG:* Easson (2)
2 Oct	A	West of Scotland	32-14	*T:* Reid, Stark (3) *C:* Easson (3) *PG:* Easson *DG:* Easson
9 Oct	H	Selkirk	18-16	*T:* Hall, Stark *C:* Easson *PG:* Easson (2)
16 Oct	A	Jedforest	21-15	*T:* Jennings, Reid, Wright *PG:* Easson (2)
6 Nov	H	Currie	11-23	*T:* McCallum *PG:* Easson (2)
18 Dec	A	Melrose	3-14	*PG:* Easson
8 Jan	H	Watsonians	23-30	*T:* Laird, Reid, Stark *C:* Easson *PG:* Easson (2)
22 Jan	A	Edinburgh Acads	15-24	*T:* Macrae, Wilson *C:* Easson *PG:* Easson
12 Feb	H	Stirling County	25-20	*T:* Knight, Stark *PG:* Easson (5)
12 Mar	H	Kelso	22-3	*T:* Jennings, Mardon, Stark *C:* Easson (2) *PG:* Easson

Clarkston

Year of formation 1937
Ground Braidholm, Braidholm Road, Giffnock, Glasgow G46 6EB Tel: 041-637 5850
Colours Red, white and green hoops
Captain 1993-94 K Fairbairn
1st XV 1993-94 P28 W10 D0 L18 F473 A679
McEwan's/SRU Div 2 joint 11th *relegated*

League Record 1993-94

Date	*Venue*	*Opponents*	*Result*	*Scorers*
11 Sept	H	Ayr	9-27	*PG:* Langley (3)
18 Sept	A	Peebles	13-24	*T:* Price *C:* Langley *PG:* Langley (2)
25 Sept	H	Glasgow High/K'side	10-41	*T:* Aitken *C:* Langley *PG:* Langley
2 Oct	A	Wigtownshire	3-35	*PG:* Langley
9 Oct	H	Preston Lodge FP	25-12	*T:* T Greenshields, Manson, Menzies, Orsi *C:* Menzies *PG:* Menzies

16 Oct	A	Dundee HSFP	0-95	
6 Nov	H	Edinburgh Wands	8-24	*T:* Price *PG:* Langley
4 Dec	A	Biggar	13-24	*T:* Price (2) *PG:* A C B Greenshields
8 Jan	H	Grangemouth	5-22	*T:* Keith
22 Jan	A	Glasgow Acads	19-16	*T:* Aitken, Price *PG:* A C B Greenshields (3)
12 Feb	A	Kirkcaldy	6-14	*PG:* A C B Greenshields (2)
12 Mar	A	Haddington	20-15	*T:* Dawes (2), Robertson
				C: A C B Greenshields *PG:* A C B Greenshields
26 Mar	H	Musselburgh	27-8	*T:* Gerry, Goldie, Price, Robertson
				C: A C B Greenshields (2)
				PG: A C B Greenshields

Currie

Year of formation 1970
Ground Malleny Park, Balerno, Edinburgh EH14 5HA   Tel: 031-449 2432
Colours Amber and black
Captain 1993-94 A Donaldson
1st XV 1993-94 P25   W15   D0   L10   F538   A433
McEwan's/SRU Div 1 joint 8th

League Record 1993-94

Date	Venue	Opponents	Result	Scorers
11 Sept	A	Watsonians	53-10	*T:* Carson, Laugerson, McIntyre, Rayasi, Te Whaiti (2), Wilson *C:* Donaldson (6) *DG:* Donaldson (2)
18 Sept	H	Edinburgh Acads	13-33	*T:* Tonkin *C:* Donaldson *PG:* Donaldson (2)
25 Sept	A	Stirling County	18-22	*T:* Dickson (2) *C:* Donaldson *PG:* Donaldson (2)
2 Oct	H	Hawick	12-6	*PG:* Donaldson (4)
9 Oct	A	Kelso	24-11	*T:* Scott, Te Whaiti *C:* Donaldson *PG:* Donaldson (3) *DG:* Donaldson
16 Oct	H	Stewart's-Melville FP	15-6	*PG:* Donaldson (5)
6 Nov	A	Boroughmuir	23-11	*T:* Hamilton, Rayasi *C:* Donaldson (2) *PG:* Donaldson (2) *DG:* Donaldson
18 Dec	H	Heriot's FP	9-21	*PG:* Donaldson (3)
22 Jan	H	Selkirk	18-10	*T:* Donaldson, Forrester *C:* Donaldson *PG:* Donaldson (2)
29 Jan	A	West of Scotland	16-38	*T:* Laugerson, Wilson *PG:* Donaldson (2)
12 Feb	A	Jedforest	19-43	*T:* Forrester, McIntyre, Morrison *C:* Morrison (2)
12 Mar	H	Melrose	10-74	*T:* Plumb *C:* Morrison *PG:* Morrison

Dundee High School FP

Year of formation 1880
Ground Mayfield, Arbroath Road, Dundee   Tel: Dundee (0382) 453517 (ground) and 451045 (clubhouse)
Colours Blue and red
Most capped player D G Leslie (Scotland) 32 caps
Captain 1993-94 A D Nicol
1st XV 1993-94 P30   W23   D0   L6   Ab1   F860   A345
McEwan's/SRU Div 2 2nd *promoted*

League Record 1993-94

Date	Venue	Opponents	Result	Scorers
11 Sept	H	Kirkcaldy	20-14	*T:* Jardine *PG:* J R Newton (5)
18 Sept	H	Edinburgh Wands	54-0	*T:* Cairney, Keyes, Lamont, J R Newton (2), Nicol, Waite, pen try *C:* J R Newton (7)
25 Sept	A	Biggar	17-3	*T:* Cousin *PG:* J R Newton (2) *DG:* J R Newton (2)

9 Oct	A	Glasgow Acads	17-3	*T:* Herrington *PG:* J R Newton (3) *DG:* Rouse
16 Oct	H	Clarkston	95-0	*T:* Batchelor, Cairney, Campbell, Cousin (2), Lamont, C R H Newton (4), J R Newton (2), Nicol (2) *C:* J R Newton (11) *PG:* J R Newton
6 Nov	A	Musselburgh	17-10	*T:* Cairney *PG:* Jon Newton (4)
18 Dec	H	Grangemouth	43-13	*T:* Allan, Cousin, Manson, S Newton, Ritchie *C:* C R H Newton (3) *PG:* C R H Newton (3), S Newton
22 Jan	H	Peebles	26-0	*T:* Allan, Cairney, Cousin *C:* J R Newton *PG:* J R Newton (3)
12 Feb	A	Glasgow High/K'side	10-17	*T:* Nicol *C:* J R Newton *PG:* J R Newton
26 Feb	H	Wigtownshire	22-7	*T:* Cousin (2), Nicol *C:* J R Newton (2) *PG:* J R Newton
12 Mar	A	Preston Lodge FP	42-3	*T:* Allan, Cousin (2), J R Newton, Nicol (2) *C:* J R Newton (3) *PG:* J R Newton (2)
26 Mar	A	Ayr	27-10	*T:* Batchelor, Cousin *C:* J R Newton *PG:* J R Newton (5)

Edinburgh Academicals

Year of formation 1857
Ground Raeburn Place, Stockbridge, Edinburgh EH4 1HQ   Tel: 031-332 1070
Colours Blue and white hoops
Most capped player D M B Sole (Scotland) 44 caps
Captain 1993-94 D J McIvor
1st XV 1993-94   P27   W14   D1   L11   Ab1   F620   A489
McEwan's/SRU Div 1 3rd

League Record 1993-94

Date	Venue	Opponents	Result	Scorers
11 Sept	H	Jedforest	17-3	*T:* Patterson, Scott, Wilson *C:* Shepherd
18 Sept	A	Currie	33-13	*T:* Changleng, McIvor (2), Patterson (2) *C:* Shepherd *PG:* Shepherd *DG:* Hay-Smith
25 Sept	H	Melrose	16-17	*T:* Burns, Simmers *PG:* Hay-Smith (2)
2 Oct	A	Watsonians	31-21	*T:* Changleng (2), Shepherd *C:* Hay-Smith (2) *PG:* Hay-Smith (4)
9 Oct	A	Gala	3-30	*PG:* Hay-Smith
16 Oct	H	Stirling County	13-13	*T:* Mitchell *C:* Hay-Smith *PG:* Hay-Smith (2)
6 Nov	A	Hawick	22-3	*T:* Hay-Smith, Shepherd, Wainwright *C:* Hay-Smith (2) *PG:* Hay-Smith
27 Nov	H	Kelso	23-14	*T:* Adamson, Changleng, Jackson *C:* Hay-Smith *PG:* Hay-Smith (2)
8 Jan	A	Stewart's-Melville FP	11-13	*T:* Porter *PG:* Hay-Smith (2)
22 Jan	H	Boroughmuir	24-15	*T:* Griffiths, Hay-Smith *C:* Hay-Smith *PG:* Hay-Smith (4)
12 Feb	A	Heriot's FP	25-17	*T:* Patterson, Shepherd, Wilson *C:* Hay-Smith (2) *PG:* Hay-Smith (2)
26 Feb	H	West of Scotland	11-21	*T:* Swanson *PG:* Hay-Smith (2)
12 Mar	A	Selkirk	36-3	*T:* McWhannall (2), Shepherd, Simmers, Wilson *C:* Shepherd (4) *DG:* Shepherd

Edinburgh Wanderers

Year of formation 1868
Ground Murrayfield, Edinburgh EH12 5QG   Tel: 031-337 2196
Colours Red and black
Most capped player A R Smith (Scotland) 33 caps
Captain 1993-94 S Dennis
1st XV 1993-94   P31   W16   D0   L15   F593   A675
McEwan's/SRU Div 2 4th

League Record 1993-94

Date	Venue	Opponents	Result	Scorers
11 Sept	H	Preston Lodge FP	14-6	*T:* Boswell *PG:* Bremner (3)
18 Sept	A	Dundee HSFP	0-54	
25 Sept	A	Kirkcaldy	15-36	*T:* Boswell, Brown *C:* Cropper *PG:* Cropper
2 Oct	H	Biggar	34-10	*T:* Dennis, Graham, L A B Hamilton, Hastie *C:* Bremner (4) *PG:* Bremner (2)
9 Oct	A	Grangemouth	13-7	*T:* L A B Hamilton *C:* Bremner *PG:* Bremner (2)
16 Oct	H	Glasgow Acads	26-11	*T:* S Dennis, Gillan, Hepburn *C:* Bremner *PG:* Bremner (3)
6 Nov	A	Clarkston	24-8	*T:* Hepburn, Lorrain-Smith, Wands *C:* Bremner (3) *PG:* Bremner
4 Dec	H	Musselburgh	13-18	*T:* Lorrain-Smith *C:* Bremner *PG:* Bremner (2)
22 Jan	H	Ayr	18-17	*T:* G W M Hamilton, Kava *C:* Bremner *PG:* Bremner (2)
12 Feb	A	Peebles	18-13	*T:* Dennis, Kava *C:* Bremner *PG:* Bremner *DG:* Bremner
19 Feb	A	Haddington	7-5	*T:* Godfrey *C:* Bremner
26 Feb	H	Glasgow High/K'side	15-45	*T:* Gillan, Lorrain-Smith *C:* Bremner *PG:* Bremner
12 Mar	A	Wigtownshire	17-21	*T:* Cropper, Gillan, pen try *C:* Cropper

Gala

Year of formation 1875
Ground Netherdale, Nether Road, Galashiels TD1 3HE   Tel: Galashiels (0896) 55145
Colours Maroon
Most capped player P C Brown (Scotland) 27 caps
Captain 1993-94 H A Hunter
1st XV 1993-94   P26   W19   D1   L6   F673   A477
McEwan's/SRU Div 1 2nd

League Record 1993-94

Date	Venue	Opponents	Result	Scorers
11 Sept	A	Melrose	14-13	*T:* Dalgleish *PG:* Dods (2) *DG:* G P J Townsend
18 Sept	A	Boroughmuir	28-23	*T:* Dalgleish, Swan, G P J Townsend *C:* Dods (2) *PG:* Dods (2) *DG:* G P J Townsend
25 Sept	H	Watsonians	39-6	*T:* Dalgleish (2), Paterson, Waddell *C:* Dods (2) *PG:* Dods (5)
2 Oct	A	Heriot's FP	20-35	*T:* Dods, Waddell (2) *C:* Dods *PG:* Dods
9 Oct	H	Edinburgh Acads	30-3	*T:* Dalgleish, Swan Weir (2) *C:* Dods (2) *PG:* Dods (2)
16 Oct	A	West of Scotland	33-10	*T:* Crooks, Dalgleish, Dods, Waddell (2) *C:* Dods *PG:* Dods *DG:* Changleng
6 Nov	H	Stirling County	9-20	*PG:* Dods (3)
18 Dec	A	Selkirk	20-13	*T:* Paterson, Swan, Waddell (2)
22 Jan	A	Jedforest	10-33	*T:* Amos *C:* Dods *PG:* Dods
12 Feb	H	Kelso	23-20	*T:* Corcoran, Paterson *C:* Dods (2) *PG:* Dods (3)
12 Mar	H	Stewart's-Melville FP	26-17	*T:* Amos, G P J Townsend, Waddell *C:* Dods *PG:* Dods (3)
26 Mar	H	Hawick	22-21	*T:* Corcoran, Waddell *PG:* Maitland (3) *DG:* Maitland

Glasgow Academicals

Year of formation 1867

Ground New Anniesland, Helensburgh Drive, Glasgow   Tel: 041-959 1101
Colours Navy blue and white hoops
Most capped player W M Simmers (Scotland) 28 caps
Captain 1993-94 J F Mason
1st XV 1993-94 P24 W7 D1 L16 F366 A713
McEwan's/SRU Div 2 7th

League Record 1993-94

Date	Venue	Opponents	Result	Scorers
11 Sept	H	Peebles	23-14	T: McAslan, J F Mason C: C G MacGregor (2) PG: C G MacGregor (2) DG: C G MacGregor
18 Sept	A	Glasgow High/K'side	9-31	PG: C G MacGregor (3)
25 Sept	H	Wigtownshire	16-8	T: C G MacGregor, Mitchell PG: C G MacGregor (2)
2 Oct	A	Preston Lodge FP	19-13	T: Fletcher C: C G MacGregor PG: C G MacGregor (4)
9 Oct	H	Dundee HSFP	3-17	PG: C G MacGregor
16 Oct	A	Edinburgh Wands	11-26	T: Jarvie PG: C G MacGregor (2)
6 Nov	H	Biggar	31-31	T: Christini, McAslan, Mortimer, Semple C: C G MacGregor PG: C G MacGregor (3)
27 Nov	A	Grangemouth	39-15	T: C G MacGregor, Mason (3), Richmond, Turner C: C G MacGregor (3) PG: C G MacGregor
22 Jan	H	Clarkston	16-19	T: Fletcher C: Simmers PG: Simmers (3)
29 Jan	A	Kirkcaldy	3-43	PG: Simmers
12 Feb	A	Musselburgh	11-24	T: Fletcher PG: Simmers (2)
12 Mar	A	Ayr	0-19	
26 Mar	H	Haddington	62-16	T: Eccles, McAslan (3), J F Mason, Mitchell, Pirrie, Simmers (2), Spence C: Simmers (6)

Glasgow High/Kelvinside

Year of formation 1982 (on amalgamation of Glasgow High RFC and Kelvinside Academicals)
Ground Old Anniesland, 637 Crow Road, Glasgow   Tel: 041-959 1154
Colours Navy blue, green and white
Most capped player A G J Watt (Scotland) 2 caps (before amalgamation J M Bannerman (Glasgow HSFP) was capped 37 times and D M White (Kelvinside Academicals) 4 times, both for Scotland)
Captain 1993-94 M I Wallace
1st XV 1993-94 P30 W28 D1 L1 F936 A321
McEwan's/SRU Div 2 *Winners – promoted*

League Record 1993-94

Date	Venue	Opponents	Result	Scorers
11 Sept	A	Grangemouth	54-12	T: Bassi, Busby, Dow, C E Little, Manning, Sanderson, Wilson C: Bassi (5) PG: Bassi (3)
18 Sept	H	Glasgow Acads	31-9	T: Busby (2), C E Little, S Little C: Bassi PG: Bassi (3)
25 Sept	A	Clarkston	41-10	T: Breckenridge, Busby, Hawkes (2), Manning, Watt C: Bassi (4) PG: Bassi
2 Oct	H	Musselburgh	23-6	T: Hawkes, McDiarmid C: Bassi (2) PG: Bassi (3)
9 Oct	A	Haddington	13-0	T: Busby, Sanderson PG: Bassi
16 Oct	H	Ayr	76-16	T: Hawkes (2), C E Little (4), McKee, Malcolm, Manning, M I Wallace, Watt C: Bassi (6) PG: Bassi (3)
6 Nov	A	Peebles	30-7	T: Breckenridge, Hawkes, Sanderson, F D Wallace C: Bassi (2) PG: Bassi DG: Breckenridge

18 Dec	H	Kirkcaldy	26-9	*T:* C E Little *PG:* Breckenridge (6), MacDonald
8 Jan	H	Wigtownshire	42-13	*T:* Breckenridge (2), Eason, Glasgow (2), Manning *C:* Bassi (3) *PG:* Bassi (2)
22 Jan	A	Preston Lodge FP	19-6	*T:* Breckenridge *C:* Breckenridge *PG:* Bassi (2), Breckenridge (2)
12 Feb	H	Dundee HSFP	17-10	*T:* Watt *PG:* Bassi (2) *DG:* Breckenridge (2)
26 Feb	A	Edinburgh Wands	45-15	*T:* Bassi, C E Little (2), Malcolm, Waddell *C:* Bassi (4) *PG:* Bassi (4)
12 Mar	H	Biggar	23-3	*T:* Eason, Manning *C:* Bassi (2) *PG:* Bassi (3)

Grangemouth

Year of formation 1929
Ground Glensburgh, Glensburgh Road, Grangemouth
Tel: Grangemouth (0324) 486142
Colours Red and black hoops
Captain 1993-94 G Jesty
1st XV 1993-94 P28 W9 D2 L16 Ab1 F420 A666
McEwan's/SRU Div 2 10th

League Record 1993-94

Date	Venue	Opponents	Result	Scorers
11 Sept	H	Glasgow High/K'side	12-54	*PG:* Rennie (4)
18 Sept	A	Wigtownshire	30-5	*T:* Crossan, Holmes, Penman *C:* Rennie (3) *PG:* Rennie (3)
25 Sept	H	Preston Lodge FP	33-34	*T:* Campbell, Laurentson, Lyon, Penman, Rutherford *C:* Rennie (4)
9 Oct	H	Edinburgh Wands	7-13	*T:* Rutherford *C:* Rennie
16 Oct	A	Biggar	8-8	*T:* Mackenzie *DG:* Mackenzie
6 Nov	A	Kirkcaldy	6-38	*PG:* Rennie (2)
27 Nov	H	Glasgow Acads	15-39	*T:* Crossan, Smith *C:* Jesty *PG:* Rennie
18 Dec	A	Dundee HSFP	13-43	*T:* Mackenzie *C:* Rennie *PG:* Rennie (2)
8 Jan	A	Clarkston	22-5	*T:* Holmes, Innes *PG:* Rennie (4)
22 Jan	H	Musselburgh	18-10	*T:* Holmes, McGregor *C:* Halliday *PG:* Halliday (2)
12 Feb	A	Haddington	11-13	*T:* Campbell *PG:* Halliday (2)
26 Feb	H	Ayr	14-6	*T:* Rennie *PG:* Halliday (3)
12 Mar	A	Peebles	12-25	*PG:* Halliday (4)

Haddington

Year of formation 1911
Ground Neilson Park, Haddington EH41 4DB   Tel: Haddington (062082) 3702
Colours Scarlet
Captain 1993-94 B A Craig
1st XV 1993-94 P24 W11 D0 L13 F354 A425
McEwan's/SRU Div 2 joint 8th

League Record 1993-94

Date	Venue	Opponents	Result	Scorers
11 Sept	A	Musselburgh	6-19	*PG:* Craig (2)
18 Sept	H	Kirkcaldy	16-27	*T:* McGeary *C:* Brownlee *PG:* Brownlee (2) *DG:* Craig
25 Sept	H	Ayr	18-11	*T:* Craig, McGeary *C:* Brownlee *PG:* Craig, Brownlee
2 Oct	A	Peebles	13-30	*T:* Brownlee *C:* Brownlee *PG:* Craig (2)
9 Oct	H	Glasgow High/K'side	0-13	
16 Oct	A	Wigtownshire	13-6	*T:* McKenzie *C:* Brownlee *PG:* Brownlee *DG:* Craig

6 Nov	H	Preston Lodge FP	16-3	*T:* Kenny *C:* Brownlee *PG:* Brownlee (2) *DG:* Craig
22 Jan	A	Biggar	14-11	*T:* Craig *PG:* Craig (3)
12 Feb	H	Grangemouth	13-11	*T:* McGeary *C:* Craig *PG:* Brownlee, Craig
19 Feb	H	Edinburgh Wands	5-7	*T:* McGeary
12 Mar	H	Clarkston	15-20	*PG:* Brownlee (5)
26 Mar	A	Glasgow Acads	16-62	*T:* Brownlee *C:* Brownlee *PG:* Brownlee (3)

Hawick

Year of formation 1873
Ground Mansfield Park, Mansfield Road, Hawick, Roxburghshire
Tel: Hawick (0450) 74291
Colours Dark green
Most capped player J M Renwick (Scotland)/C T Deans (Scotland) 52 caps
Captain 1993-94 J A Hay
1st XV 1993-94 P27 W15 D3 L9 F510 A416
McEwan's/SRU Div 1 joint 6th

League Record 1993-94

Date	Venue	Opponents	Result	Scorers
11 Sept	H	West of Scotland	17-17	*T:* Stanger *PG:* Welsh (4)
18 Sept	A	Selkirk	19-10	*T:* Scott *C:* Welsh *PG:* Sharp (2), Welsh *DG:* Welsh
25 Sept	H	Jedforest	18-14	*T:* Crowford, Stanger *C:* Welsh *PG:* Welsh *DG:* Welsh
2 Oct	A	Currie	6-12	*PG:* Murdie (2)
9 Oct	H	Melrose	10-12	*T:* Renwick, Suddon
16 Oct	A	Watsonians	13-34	*T:* Sharp, Suddon *PG:* Sharp
6 Nov	H	Edinburgh Acads	3-22	*PG:* Sharp
22 Jan	H	Kelso	28-19	*T:* Stanger, Suddon (2) *C:* Welsh (2) *PG:* Welsh (3)
29 Jan	A	Stirling County	12-8	*PG:* Welsh (2) *DG:* Welsh (2)
12 Feb	A	Stewart's-Melville FP	22-5	*T:* Stanger *C:* Welsh *PG:* Welsh (2) *DG:* Welsh (3)
12 Mar	A	Heriot's FP	49-3	*T:* Graham, Murray, Oliver, Sharp (2), Stanger, Willison (2) *C:* Oliver (3) *PG:* Oliver
26 Mar	A	Gala	21-22	*T:* Stanger, Suddon, Willison *PG:* Oliver (2)

Heriot's FP

Year of formation 1890
Ground Goldenacre, Bangholm Terrace, Edinburgh EH3 5QN
Tel: 031-552 5925 (ground staff) and 031-552 5925 (clubhouse)
Colours Blue and white horizontal stripes
Most capped player A R Irvine (Scotland) 51 caps
Captain 1993-94 M J de G Allingham
1st XV 1993-94 P24 W16 D0 L8 F574 A431
McEwan's/SRU Div 1 joint 4th

League Record 1993-94

Date	Venue	Opponents	Result	Scorers
11 Sept	A	Kelso	12-18	*T:* Adam, Robertson *C:* Whitaker
18 Sept	H	Stewart's-Melville FP	24-13	*T:* Buchanan-Smith, Murray *C:* Glasgow *PG:* Glasgow (4)
25 Sept	A	Boroughmuir	21-6	*T:* H R Gilmour, Whitaker *C:* Glasgow *PG:* Glasgow (3)
2 Oct	H	Gala	35-20	*T:* Adam, Allingham, Glasgow, K S Milne (2) *C:* Glasgow (2) *PG:* Glasgow (2)

9 Oct	H	West of Scotland	24-14	*T:* Allingham, H R Gilmour, M W Livingstone
				C: Glasgow (3) *PG:* Glasgow
16 Oct	A	Selkirk	32-10	*T:* Dall, K S Milne (2), Whitaker
				C: Glasgow (3) *PG:* Glasgow *DG:* Whitaker
6 Nov	H	Jedforest	15-3	*T:* K S Milne, Whitaker *C:* Glasgow
				PG: Glasgow
18 Dec	A	Currie	21-9	*T:* Hewitt, Simpson *C:* Hewitt
				PG: Hewitt (3)
8 Jan	H	Melrose	19-37	*T:* H R Gilmour *C:* Hewitt *PG:* Hewitt (4)
22 Jan	A	Watsonians	7-20	*T:* H R Gilmour *C:* Hewitt
12 Feb	H	Edinburgh Acads	17-25	*T:* H R Gilmour, Robertson, Stoddart
				C: Murray
12 Mar	H	Hawick	3-49	*PG:* Glasgow

Jedforest

Year of formation 1885
Ground Riverside Park, Jedburgh   Tel: Jedburgh (0835) 62855
Colours Royal blue
Most capped player R J Laidlaw (Scotland) 47 caps
Captain 1993-94 N A McIlroy
1st XV 1993-94   P28   W16   D1   L11   F609   A416
McEwan's/SRU Div 1 joint 8th

League Record 1993-94

Date	Venue	Opponents	Result	Scorers
11 Sept	A	Edinburgh Acads	3-17	*PG:* McKechnie
18 Sept	H	Stirling County	12-25	*PG:* McKechnie (4)
25 Sept	A	Hawick	14-18	*T:* C J Brown *PG:* G Armstrong (3)
2 Oct	H	Kelso	28-3	*T:* C J Brown (2), Kirkpatrick, Pringle *C:* Amos
				PG: Amos (2)
9 Oct	A	Stewart's-Melville FP	17-7	*T:* C J Brown, A J Douglas, Hogg *C:* Hogg
16 Oct	H	Boroughmuir	15-21	*T:* G Armstrong, C J Brown *C:* Hogg
				PG: Hogg
6 Nov	A	Heriot's FP	3-15	*PG:* Amos
18 Dec	H	West of Scotland	17-6	*T:* Liddle *PG:* Richards (4)
22 Jan	H	Gala	33-10	*T:* G Armstrong, A J Douglas, Hogg,
				Kirkpatrick (2) *C:* Richards *PG:* Richards (2)
29 Jan	A	Selkirk	11-5	*T:* Liddle *PG:* Richards (2)
12 Feb	H	Currie	43-19	*T:* Amos, C J Brown, Hynd, G G Scott (2), Yule
				C: McKechnie (5) *PG:* McKechnie
12 Mar	H	Watsonians	13-24	*T:* Amos, Hynd *PG:* McKechnie
26 Mar	A	Melrose	22-29	*T:* Yule *C:* Richards *PG:* Richards (5)

Kelso

Year of formation 1876
Ground Poynder Park, Bowmont Street, Kelso, Roxburghshire
Tel: Kelso (0573) 224300 or 223773
Colours Black and white
Most capped player J Jeffrey (Scotland) 40 caps
Captain 1993-94 G J Aitchison
1st XV 1993-94   P28   W13   D0   L15   F575   A507
McEwan's/SRU Div 1 13th *relegated*

League Record 1993-94

Date	Venue	Opponents	Result	Scorers
11 Sept	H	Heriot's FP	18-12	*PG:* Aitchison (6)
18 Sept	A	West of Scotland	6-34	*PG:* Aitchison *DG:* Barton
25 Sept	H	Selkirk	17-11	*T:* J Jeffrey *PG:* Aitchison (4)

2 Oct	A	Jedforest	3-28	*PG:* Aitchison
9 Oct	H	Currie	11-24	*T:* Bennett *PG:* Aitchison (2)
16 Oct	A	Melrose	17-46	*T:* Aitchison, Barton, Roxburgh *C:* Aitchison
6 Nov	H	Watsonians	12-17	*PG:* Lang (4)
27 Nov	A	Edinburgh Acads	14-23	*T:* Aitchison, R Laing *C:* Aitchison (2)
22 Jan	A	Hawick	19-28	*T:* Baird *C:* Aitchison *PG:* Aitchison (4)
12 Feb	A	Gala	20-23	*T:* Roxburgh, pen try *C:* Aitchison (2) *PG:* Aitchison (2)
26 Feb	H	Stewart's-Melville FP	15-10	*T:* Howlett, Lang *C:* Aitchison *PG:* Aitchison
12 Mar	A	Boroughmuir	3-22	*PG:* Aitchison
26 Mar	H	Stirling County	20-18	*T:* Aitchison *PG:* Aitchison (5)

Kirkcaldy

Year of formation 1873
Ground Beveridge Park, Balwearie Road, Kirkcaldy   Tel: Kirkcaldy (0592) 263470
Colours Royal blue
Most capped player D D Howie (Scotland)/R Howie (Scotland) 9 caps
Captain 1993-94 A D Henderson
1st XV 1993-94   P29   W22   D0   L7   F742   A390
McEwan's/SRU Div 2 3rd

League Record 1993-94

Date	Venue	Opponents	Result	Scorers
11 Sept	A	Dundee HSFP	14-20	*T:* Ferguson, Reddick *C:* Ferguson (2)
18 Sept	A	Haddington	27-16	*T:* R R Dewar, Hannah, J R Mitchell *PG:* J R Mitchell (3) *DG:* J R Mitchell
25 Sept	H	Edinburgh Wands	36-15	*T:* Carruthers, Hannah (2), Stewart (2), J W Thomson *C:* J R Mitchell (3)
2 Oct	A	Ayr	13-3	*T:* J R Mitchell *C:* J R Mitchell *PG:* J R Mitchell *DG:* Ferguson
9 Oct	H	Biggar	22-13	*T:* Bonner, R R Dewar, Hannah *C:* J R Mitchell (2) *PG:* J R Mitchell
16 Oct	A	Peebles	12-10	*T:* Hannah, J R Mitchell *C:* Carruthers
6 Nov	H	Grangemouth	38-6	*T:* Black, Hannah (2), Macdonald *C:* J R Mitchell (3) *PG:* J R Mitchell (4)
18 Dec	A	Glasgow High/K'side	9-26	*PG:* J R Mitchell (3)
22 Jan	A	Wigtownshire	21-22	*PG:* J R Mitchell (7)
29 Jan	H	Glasgow Acads	43-3	*T:* Bonner, Ferguson, J R Mitchell (2), Reddick (2) *C:* J R Mitchell (2) *PG:* J R Mitchell (3)
12 Feb	H	Clarkston	14-6	*T:* Wyllie *PG:* J R Mitchell (3)
26 Feb	A	Preston Lodge FP	12-3	*PG:* J R Mitchell (4)
12 Mar	H	Musselburgh	16-6	*T:* R R Dewar, Ferguson *PG:* J R Mitchell (2)

Melrose

Year of formation 1877
Ground The Greenyards, Melrose, Roxburghshire TD6 9SA
Tel: Melrose (089682) 2993 (office) and 2559 (clubrooms)
Colours Yellow and black hoops
Most capped player K W Robertson (Scotland) 44 caps
Captain 1993-94 C M Chalmers
1st XV 1993-94   P25   W24   D0   L1   F842   A274
McEwan's/SRU Div 1 *Winners*

League Record 1993-94

Date	Venue	Opponents	Result	Scorers
11 Sept	H	Gala	13-14	*T:* Ross Brown *C:* Parker *PG:* Parker (2)

18 Sept	H	Watsonians	65-23	*T:* Robbie Brown, Ross Brown (2), M G Browne, McLeish, Parker, A C Redpath, Shiel, Weir, pen try *C:* Parker (6) *PG:* Parker
25 Sept	A	Edinburgh Acads	17-16	*T:* Parker *PG:* Parker (4)
2 Oct	H	Stirling County	17-9	*T:* M G Browne *PG:* Parker (4)
9 Oct	A	Hawick	12-10	*PG:* Parker (4)
16 Oct	H	Kelso	46-17	*T:* M G Browne, Chalmers, Hogg, Parker, A C Redpath, B W Redpath, pen try *C:* Parker (4) *PG:* Parker
6 Nov	A	Stewart's-Melville FP	18-10	*T:* Parker, Simpson, Weir *PG:* Parker
18 Dec	H	Boroughmuir	14-3	*T:* Joiner *PG:* Parker (3)
8 Jan	A	Heriot's FP	37-19	*T:* Brotherstone, Chalmers, Hogg, Joiner, Parker *C:* Parker (3) *PG:* Parker (2)
22 Jan	H	West of Scotland	30-21	*T:* Chalmers, Kerr, A C Redpath, B W Redpath *C:* Parker (2) *PG:* Parker *DG:* Parker
12 Feb	A	Selkirk	38-18	*T:* Joiner (2), Parker (2), B W Redpath *C:* Parker (2) *PG:* Parker (3)
12 Mar	A	Currie	74-10	*T:* Brotherstone (2), Robbie Brown, Ross Brown (2), Chalmers, Hogg, Parker, Shiel, Weir, pen try *C:* Parker (8) *PG:* Parker
26 Mar	H	Jedforest	29-22	*T:* Ross Brown, Parker, A C Redpath, White *C:* Parker (3) *PG:* Parker

Musselburgh

Year of formation 1921
Ground Stoneyhill, Stoneyhill Farm Road, Musselburgh   Tel: 031-665 3435
Colours Navy blue with narrow white hoops
Captain 1993-94 A McLeod
1st XV 1993-94   P26   W14   D1   L11   F530   A492
McEwan's/SRU Div 2 5th

League Record 1993-94

Date	Venue	Opponents	Result	Scorers
11 Sept	H	Haddington	19-6	*T:* McLeod, McMillan, pen try *C:* C Livingstone (2)
18 Sept	A	Ayr	13-6	*T:* Stewart *C:* C Livingstone *PG:* C Livingstone (2)
25 Sept	H	Peebles	21-5	*T:* C Livingstone, Lockhart *C:* C Livingstone *PG:* Livingstone (3)
2 Oct	A	Glasgow High/K'side	6-23	*PG:* C Livingstone (2)
9 Oct	H	Wigtownshire	14-6	*T:* Hawkins *PG:* C Livingstone (3)
16 Oct	A	Preston Lodge FP	44-16	*T:* Horsburgh (2), Lockhart, McLeod (4), pen try *C:* C Livingstone, Lockhart
6 Nov	H	Dundee HSFP	10-17	*T:* Ramsay *C:* C Livingstone *PG:* Livingstone
4 Dec	A	Edinburgh Wands	18-13	*T:* McLeod, McMillan *C:* C Livingstone *PG:* C Livingstone *DG:* C Livingstone
22 Jan	A	Grangemouth	10-18	*T:* Scott *C:* C Livingstone *PG:* C Livingstone
29 Jan	H	Biggar	11-26	*T:* MacColl *PG:* C Livingstone (2)
12 Feb	H	Glasgow Acads	24-11	*T:* Dickson, MacColl, Ramsay *PG:* C Livingstone (3)
12 Mar	A	Kirkcaldy	6-16	*PG:* C Livingstone (2)
26 Mar	A	Clarkston	8-27	*T:* Weatherhead *PG:* Weatherhead

Peebles

Year of formation 1923
Ground Hay Lodge Park, Neidpath Road, Peebles EH45 8NN
Tel: Peebles (0721) 21600
Colours Red and white hoops
Captain 1993-94 J Currie

1st XV 1993-94   P24   W8   D0   L16   F348   A437
McEwan's/SRU Div 2 6th

League Record 1993-94

Date	Venue	Opponents	Result	Scorers
11 Sept	A	Glasgow Acads	14-23	*T:* Murray, Nisbet *C:* Mutch (2)
18 Sept	H	Clarkston	24-13	*T:* Gray (2), Mutch, Wilson *C:* McBride, Mutch
25 Sept	A	Musselburgh	5-21	*T:* N Raeburn
2 Oct	H	Haddington	30-13	*T:* Knox, Nisbet (2), Renwick *C:* McBride (2) *PG:* Renwick (2)
9 Oct	A	Ayr	17-15	*T:* Gray, Nisbet *C:* McBride (2) *PG:* McBride
16 Oct	H	Kirkcaldy	10-12	*T:* Knox *C:* McBride *PG:* McBride
6 Nov	H	Glasgow High/K'side	7-30	*T:* G Wilson *C:* Nisbet
27 Nov	A	Wigtownshire	5-12	*T:* Nisbet
22 Jan	A	Dundee HSFP	0-26	
29 Jan	H	Preston Lodge FP	30-10	*T:* Gray, Kilner (2), Nisbet, Gordon Wilson *C:* Renwick *PG:* Renwick
12 Feb	H	Edinburgh Wands	13-18	*T:* G Wilson *C:* Nisbet *PG:* Nisbet (2)
26 Feb	A	Biggar	26-14	*T:* Gray, Nisbet, pen try *C:* Mullen *PG:* Mullen, Nisbet (2)
12 Mar	H	Grangemouth	25-12	*T:* Gray, Kilner, Nisbet *C:* Mullen, Nisbet *PG:* Kilner, Nisbet

Preston Lodge FP

Year of formation 1929
Ground Pennypit Park, Rope Walk, Prestonpans, East Lothian EH32 9BN
Tel: 0875 810309
Colours Black with maroon band edged in white
Most capped player R F Cunningham (Scotland) 3 caps
Captain 1993-94 G McSorley
1st XV 1993-94 P27   W9   D0   L18   F508   A654
McEwan's/SRU Div 2 joint 11th

League Record 1993-94

Date	Venue	Opponents	Result	Scorers
11 Sept	A	Edinburgh Wands	6-14	*PG:* M Allan (2)
18 Sept	H	Biggar	17-14	*T:* Smith *PG:* M Allan (4)
25 Sept	A	Grangemouth	34-33	*T:* Gordon, Smith (2) *C:* M Allan (2) *PG:* M Allan (5)
2 Oct	H	Glasgow Acads	13-19	*T:* M Allan *C:* M Allan *PG:* M Allan (2)
9 Oct	A	Clarkston	12-25	*PG:* McPhee (4)
16 Oct	H	Musselburgh	16-44	*T:* Payne *C:* McPhee *PG:* McPhee (3)
6 Nov	A	Haddington	3-16	*PG:* McPhee
27 Nov	H	Ayr	24-12	*PG:* McPhee (8)
22 Jan	H	Glasgow High/K'side	6-19	*PG:* McPhee *DG:* Haig
29 Jan	A	Peebles	10-30	*T:* Haig *C:* Sandilands *PG:* Sandilands
12 Feb	A	Wigtownshire	11-6	*T:* Gordon *PG:* Sandilands (2)
26 Feb	H	Kirkcaldy	3-12	*PG:* M Allan
12 Mar	H	Dundee HSFP	3-42	*PG:* D Allan

Selkirk

Year of formation 1907
Ground Philiphaugh, Selkirk   Tel: Selkirk (0750) 20403
Colours Navy blue

Most capped player J Y Rutherford (Scotland) 42 caps
Captain 1993-94 R L Pow
1st XV 1993-94　P25　W7　D2　L16　F326　A507
McEwan's/SRU Div 1 14th *relegated*

League Record 1993-94

Date	Venue	Opponents	Result	Scorers
11 Sept	A	Stirling County	16-44	*T:* Jaffray, Pow　*PG:* Pow (2)
18 Sept	H	Hawick	10-19	*T:* Gentleman　*C:* Pow　*PG:* Pow
25 Sept	A	Kelso	11-17	*T:* Johnston　*PG:* Pow (2)
2 Oct	H	Stewart's-Melville FP	3-3	*PG:* Pow
9 Oct	A	Boroughmuir	16-18	*T:* S A Nichol　*C:* Brett　*PG:* Brett (3)
16 Oct	H	Heriot's FP	10-32	*T:* Minto　*C:* Pow　*PG:* Pow
6 Nov	A	West of Scotland	13-16	*T:* McConnell, Tukalo　*PG:* Lindores
18 Dec	H	Gala	13-20	*T:* Tukalo　*C:* Brett　*PG:* Brett (2)
22 Jan	A	Currie	10-18	*T:* Tukalo　*C:* Pow　*PG:* Pow
29 Jan	H	Jedforest	5-11	*T:* McConnell
12 Feb	H	Melrose	18-38	*T:* Johnston, S A Nichol　*C:* Pow　*PG:* Pow (2)
26 Feb	A	Watsonians	10-40	*T:* S A Nichol　*C:* Lindores　*PG:* S A Nichol
12 Mar	H	Edinburgh Acads	3-36	*PG:* S A Nichol

Stewart's-Melville FP

Year of formation 1973 (on amalgamation of Daniel Stewart's College FP and Melville College FP)
Ground Inverleith, Ferry Road, Edinburgh EH5 2DW　Tel: 031-552 1515
Colours Scarlet with broad black and narrow gold bands
Most capped player F Calder (Scotland) 38 caps
Captain 1993-94 D S Wyllie
1st XV 1993-94　P29　W14　D2　L13　F583　A490
McEwan's/SRU Div 1 10th

League Record 1993-94

Date	Venue	Opponents	Result	Scorers
11 Sept	H	Boroughmuir	20-15	*T:* Kittle, Thomson, pen try　*C:* Wyllie *PG:* Thomson
18 Sept	A	Heriot's FP	13-24	*T:* Flockhart, Penny　*PG:* Thomson
25 Sept	H	West of Scotland	23-18	*T:* MacKenzie (2), Milligan　*C:* Stirling *PG:* Stirling *DG:* Wyllie
2 Oct	A	Selkirk	3-3	*PG:* Stirling
9 Oct	H	Jedforest	7-17	*T:* MacKenzie　*C:* Wyllie
16 Oct	A	Currie	6-15	*PG:* Flockhart (2)
6 Nov	H	Melrose	10-18	*T:* Milligan　*C:* Thomson　*PG:* Thomson
27 Nov	A	Watsonians	24-3	*T:* Burns, Milligan, MacKenzie *C:* Thomson (3)　*PG:* Thomson
8 Jan	H	Edinburgh Acads	13-11	*T:* MacKenzie　*C:* Thomson *PG:* Thomson (2)
22 Jan	A	Stirling County	6-3	*PG:* Thomson (2)
12 Feb	H	Hawick	5-22	*T:* Burns
26 Feb	A	Kelso	10-15	*T:* Milligan　*C:* Thomson　*PG:* Thomson
12 Mar	A	Gala	17-26	*T:* Burns, Kittle, Lockie　*C:* Flockhart

Stirling County

Year of formation 1904
Ground Bridgehaugh Park, Causewayhead Road, Stirling　Tel: Stirling (0786) 74827
Colours Red, white and black
Most capped player K M Logan (Scotland) 2 caps

Captain 1993-94 J S Hamilton
1st XV 1993-94 P26 W14 D1 L11 F674 A472
McEwan's/SRU Div 1 joint 6th

League Record 1993-94

Date	Venue	Opponents	Result	Scorers
11 Sept	H	Selkirk	44-16	*T:* Brough, Imrie, Ireland, Logan, Turner
				C: M McKenzie (2) *PG:* M McKenzie (5)
18 Sept	A	Jedforest	25-12	*T:* Jardine, Mackay, Robertson
				C: M McKenzie (2) *PG:* M McKenzie (2)
25 Sept	H	Currie	22-18	*T:* Jardine *C:* M McKenzie *PG:* Logan,
				M McKenzie (4)
2 Oct	A	Melrose	9-17	*PG:* M McKenzie (3)
9 Oct	H	Watsonians	30-6	*T:* Brough, Harper, Logan *C:* M McKenzie (3)
				PG: M McKenzie (3)
16 Oct	A	Edinburgh Acads	13-13	*T:* Mackay *C:* M McKenzie
				PG: M McKenzie (2)
6 Nov	A	Gala	20-9	*T:* M McKenzie, Wright *C:* M McKenzie (2)
				PG: M McKenzie (2)
22 Jan	H	Stewart's-Melville FP	3-6	*PG:* M McKenzie
29 Jan	H	Hawick	8-12	*T:* Mackay *PG:* M McKenzie
12 Feb	A	Boroughmuir	20-25	*T:* Parsons *PG:* Williamson (5)
12 Mar	A	West of Scotland	15-9	*T:* Hamilton, Williamson *C:* Williamson
				PG: Williamson
26 Mar	A	Kelso	18-20	*T:* Brough, Logan *C:* Logan *PG:* Logan (2)

Watsonians

Year of formation 1875
Ground Myreside, Myreside Road, Edinburgh EH10 5DB   Tel: 031-447 5200
Colours Maroon and white hoops
Most capped player A G Hastings (Scotland)/S Hastings (Scotland) 50 caps
Captain 1993-94 J D MacDonald
1st XV 1993-94 P27 W15 D0 L12 F645 A663
McEwan's/SRU Div 1 joint 4th

League Record 1992-93

Date	Venue	Opponents	Result	Scorers
11 Sept	H	Currie	10-53	*T:* S A Aitken *C:* Hodge *PG:* Hodge
18 Sept	A	Melrose	23-65	*T:* Kerr, Maxwell *C:* Hodge, Thomson
				PG: Thomson *DG:* Hodge (2)
25 Sept	A	Gala	6-39	*PG:* Hodge (2)
2 Oct	H	Edinburgh Acads	21-31	*T:* Kerr (2) *C:* Hodge *PG:* Hodge (3)
9 Oct	A	Stirling County	6-30	*PG:* Hodge (2)
16 Oct	H	Hawick	34-13	*T:* A G Hastings, F M Henderson, Kerr
				C: Hodge (2) *PG:* Hodge (4) *DG:* Hodge
6 Nov	A	Kelso	17-12	*T:* S Hastings (2) *C:* Hodge (2) *PG:* Hodge
27 Nov	H	Stewart's-Melville FP	3-24	*PG:* Hodge
8 Jan	A	Boroughmuir	30-23	*T:* F M Henderson, Mathieson *C:* Hodge
				PG: A G Hastings (2), Hodge (3) *DG:* Hodge
22 Jan	H	Heriot's FP	20-7	*T:* A G Hastings *PG:* A G Hastings (3),
				Hodge *DG:* Hodge
12 Feb	A	West of Scotland	42-17	*T:* A D Aitken, A G Hastings,
				F M Henderson (2), Kerr *C:* Hodge (4)
				PG: Hodge (3)
26 Feb	H	Selkirk	40-10	*T:* A G Hastings, S Hastings, D S Henderson,
				MacDonald (2) *C:* A G Hastings (3)
				PG: A G Hastings (2) *DG:* Hodge
12 Mar	H	Jedforest	24-13	*T:* Garry, S Hastings (2) *C:* A G Hastings (3)
				PG: A G Hastings

West of Scotland

Year of formation 1865
Ground Burnbrae, Glasgow Road, Milngavie, Glasgow G62 6HX
Tel: 041-956 3116 or 041-956 1960
Colours Red and yellow hoops
Most capped player A B Carmichael (Scotland) 50 caps
Captain 1993-94 J Lonergan
1st XV 1993-94   P26   W12   D1   L13   F577   A429
McEwan's/SRU Div 1 12th

League Record 1993-94

Date	Venue	Opponents	Result	Scorers
11 Sept	A	Hawick	17-17	*T:* Fleming, Lonergan, Munro *C:* Barrett
18 Sept	H	Kelso	34-6	*T:* Barrett, Lonergan, McIntosh, Macpherson, Munro *C:* Barrett (3) *PG:* Barrett
25 Sept	A	Stewart's-Melville FP	18-23	*T:* Hastie, Stott *C:* Barrett *PG:* Barrett (2)
2 Oct	H	Boroughmuir	14-32	*T:* Fletcher, McIntosh *C:* Barrett, Williamson
9 Oct	A	Heriot's FP	14-24	*T:* Carmichael *PG:* Barrett, Williamson (2)
16 Oct	H	Gala	10-33	*T:* McIntosh *C:* Williamson *PG:* Williamson
6 Nov	H	Selkirk	16-13	*T:* Williamson *C:* Barrett *PG:* Barrett (3)
18 Dec	A	Jedforest	6-17	*PG:* Barrett *DG:* Barrett
22 Jan	A	Melrose	21-30	*PG:* Barrett (6) *DG:* Barrett
29 Jan	H	Currie	38-16	*T:* Barrett, Lonergan, Munro, Newell, Stott *C:* Barrett (2) *PG:* Barrett (2) *DG:* Lonergan
12 Feb	H	Watsonians	17-42	*T:* Munro, Newell, Shaw *C:* Barrett
26 Feb	A	Edinburgh Acads	21-11	*T:* Stott (2) *C:* Barrett *PG:* Barrett (2) *DG:* Barrett
12 Mar	H	Stirling County	9-15	*PG:* Barrett (2), Williamson

Wigtownshire

Year of formation 1922
Ground London Road Playing Fields, Ladies Walk, Stranraer   Tel: Stranraer (0776) 4133
Colours Royal blue
Captain 1993-94 R Stevenson
1st XV 1993-94   P27   W15   D0   L12   F417   A513
McEwan's/SRU Div 2 joint 8th

League Record 1993-94

Date	Venue	Opponents	Result	Scorers
11 Sept	A	Biggar	6-38	*PG:* David Drysdale (2)
18 Sept	H	Grangemouth	5-30	*T:* Scott Kerr
25 Sept	A	Glasgow Acads	8-16	*T:* David Drysdale *PG:* David Drysdale
2 Oct	H	Clarkston	35-3	*T:* Alan Drysdale (3), McTurk *C:* Gibson (3) *PG:* Gibson (3)
9 Oct	A	Musselburgh	6-14	*PG:* Gibson (2)
16 Oct	H	Haddington	6-13	*PG:* Gibson, H Hannah
6 Nov	A	Ayr	25-8	*T:* Dougie Drysdale, Paxton *PG:* I Hannah, M I Hose (4)
27 Nov	H	Peebles	12-5	*T:* I Hannah, M I Hose *C:* M I Hose
8 Jan	A	Glasgow High/K'side	13-42	*T:* Dougie Drysdale *C:* M I Hose *PG:* M I Hose (2)
22 Jan	H	Kirkcaldy	22-21	*T:* Andrew Hose *C:* M I Hose *PG:* M I Hose (5)
12 Feb	H	Preston Lodge FP	6-11	*PG:* M I Hose (2)
26 Feb	A	Dundee HSFP	7-22	*T:* David Drysdale *C:* M I Hose
12 Mar	H	Edinburgh Wands	21-17	*T:* A Drysdale, David Drysdale, Andrew Hose *C:* M I Hose (3)

IRELAND
Ballina

Year of formation 1914
Ground Creggs Road, Ballina   Tel: Ballina 21562
Colours Green
Captain 1993-94 M Byrne
1st XV 1993-94 P31   W9   D2   L20   F278   A428
Insurance Corporation League Div 2 11th *relegated* **Smithwick's Connacht Senior Cup** Lost 9-13 to Galway Corinthians (semi-final)

League Record 1993-94

Date	Venue	Opponents	Result	Scorers
19 Sept	A	Old Crescent	9-31	*PG:* Carey (3)
25 Sept	H	Malone	6-17	*PG:* Carey (2)
2 Oct	A	Ballymena	16-48	*T:* Roe *C:* Ruane *PG:* Ruane (2), Carey
20 Nov	H	Old Belvedere	6-19	*PG:* Carey (2)
9 Jan	A	Sunday's Well	3-32	*PG:* Carey
22 Jan	H	Instonians	10-52	*T:* pen try *C:* Carey *PG:* Carey
26 Feb	A	Bangor	8-14	*T:* Gorham *PG:* Carey
12 Mar	H	Galwegians	5-22	*T:* Meech
19 Mar	A	Terenure Coll	3-51	*DG:* Carey
16 Apr	H	Dolphin	6-23	*PG:* Carey (2)

Ballymena

Year of formation 1922
Ground Eaton Park, Raceview Road, Ballymena   Tel: Ballymena 656746
Colours Black
Most capped player W J McBride (Ireland) 63 caps
Captain 1993-94 D McAleese
1st XV 1993-94   P28   W23   D0   L5   F730   A381
Insurance Corporation League Div 2 3rd **First Trust Bank Ulster Senior Cup** Lost 13-16 to Instonians (semi-final)

League Record 1993-94

Date	Venue	Opponents	Result	Scorers
18 Sept	A	Malone	9-6	*PG:* McAleese (2) *DG:* McAleese
2 Oct	H	Ballina	48-16	*T:* Smyth (2), Pollock (2), Matchett *C:* McAleese (4) *PG:* McAleese (5)
9 Oct	A	Old Belvedere	23-8	*T:* Rainey, Smyth *C:* McAleese (2) *PG:* McAleese (3)
20 Nov	H	Sunday's Well	19-22	*T:* Smith *C:* McAleese *PG:* McAleese (4)
8 Jan	A	Instonians	16-23	*T:* McMaster *C:* McAleese *PG:* McAleese (3)
22 Jan	H	Bangor	32-3	*T:* Caskey, Tweed, Pollock, Robinson *C:* McAleese (3) *PG:* McAleese *DG:* McAleese
26 Feb	A	Galwegians	13-3	*T:* Smyth *C:* McMaster *PG:* McAleese (2)
12 Mar	H	Terenure Coll	12-22	*PG:* McAleese (4)
19 Mar	A	Dolphin	29-16	*T:* Matchett, Rainey, Smyth, Logan *C:* McMaster (3) *DG:* McAleese
9 Apr	H	Old Crescent	13-6	*T:* Matchett *C:* McAleese *PG:* McAleese (2)

Bangor

Year of formation 1885
Ground Uprichard Park, Bloomfield Road South, Bangor   Tel: Bangor 462670
Colours Old gold, royal blue and black

Most capped player J J McCoy (Ireland) 16 caps
Captain 1993-94 M McCall
1st XV 1993-94 P25 W15 D0 L9 F461 A408
Insurance Corporation League Div 2 5th **First Trust Bank Ulster Senior Cup**
Lost 13-33 to Ballymena (2nd round)

League Record 1993-94

Date	Venue	Opponents	Result	Scorers
25 Sept	H	Galwegians	14-6	*T:* Tinman *PG:* Strutt (2) *DG:* Strutt
2 Oct	A	Terenure Coll	8-5	*T:* Jackson *PG:* Strutt
9 Oct	H	Dolphin	20-15	*T:* Maxwell *PG:* Strutt (5)
20 Nov	A	Old Crescent	20-32	*T:* Strutt, Maxwell *C:* Strutt (2) *PG:* Strutt (2)
8 Jan	H	Malone	19-11	*T:* Dawson *C:* Strutt *PG:* Strutt (4)
22 Jan	A	Ballymena	3-32	*PG:* Strutt
26 Feb	H	Ballina	14-8	*T:* McKinty, Whittle *C:* Strutt (2)
12 Mar	A	Old Belvedere	7-22	*T:* Long *C:* Strutt
19 Mar	H	Sunday's Well	12-20	*T:* Whittle, Long *C:* Strutt
9 Apr	A	Instonians	5-38	*T:* Maxwell

Blackrock College

Year of formation 1882
Ground Stradbrook Road, Blackrock, Dublin   Tel: Dublin 2805967
Colours Royal blue and white hoops
Most capped player J F Slattery (Ireland) 61 caps
Captain 1993-94 J McGovern
1st XV 1993-94 P29 W18 D2 L9 F528 A400
Insurance Corporation League Div 1 3rd **Aluset Leinster Senior Cup** Lost 26-31 to
Greystones (semi-final)

League Record 1993-94

Date	Venue	Opponents	Result	Scorers
18 Sept	H	St Mary's Coll	21-18	*T:* Byrne, Mullin, Woods *C:* McGowan (3)
25 Sept	A	Dungannon	11-6	*T:* McDermott *PG:* McGowan (2)
2 Oct	H	Old Wesley	20-6	*T:* Woods *PG:* McGowan (5)
1 Dec	A	Wanderers	25-9	*T:* Kavanagh *C:* McGowan *PG:* McGowan (6)
8 Jan	H	Greystones	12-8	*PG:* McGowan (4)
12 Feb	A	Shannon	18-6	*T:* Woods, Assaf *C:* McGowan *PG:* McGowan (2)
12 Mar	A	Young Munster	3-10	*PG:* McGowan
19 Mar	H	Lansdowne	10-16	*T:* pen try *C:* McGowan *PG:* McGowan
2 Apr	H	Cork Const	14-11	*T:* Wallace *PG:* McGowan (3)
9 Apr	A	Garryowen	3-9	*PG:* McGowan

Cork Constitution

Year of formation 1892
Ground Temple Hill, Ballintemple, Cork   Tel: Cork 292563
Colours White
Most capped player T J Kiernan (Ireland) 54 caps
Captain 1993-94 C Murphy
1st XV 1993-94 P31 W25 D0 L6 F902 A376
Insurance Corporation League Div 1 2nd **Carling Munster Senior Cup** Lost 8-12 to
Young Munster (semi-final)

League Record 1993-94

Date	Venue	Opponents	Result	Scorers
18 Sept	H	Garryowen	8-0	*T:* Smith *PG:* Hennebry
25 Sept	A	St Mary's Coll	10-12	*T:* Hennebry *C:* K Murphy *PG:* Hennebry
2 Oct	H	Dungannon	12-17	*PG:* O'Sullivan (4)
9 Oct	A	Old Wesley	28-22	*T:* O'Dowd (2), Murray *C:* O'Sullivan (2)
				PG: O'Sullivan (2) *DG:* O'Sullivan
20 Nov	H	Greystones	23-6	*T:* O'Sullivan, Corkery *C:* O'Sullivan (2)
				PG: O'Sullivan (3)
8 Jan	H	Wanderers	35-12	*T:* K Murphy, Corkery, Walsh *C:* O'Sullivan
				PG: O'Sullivan (5) *DG:* O'Sullivan
12 Mar	A	Shannon	18-6	*T:* Bradley (2) *C:* O'Sullivan
				PG: O'Sullivan (2)
19 Mar	H	Young Munster	27-11	*T:* O'Dowd (2) *C:* O'Sullivan
				PG: O'Sullivan (4) *DG:* O'Sullivan
2 Apr	A	Blackrock Coll	11-14	*T:* Dinneen *PG:* O'Sullivan (2)
9 Apr	A	Lansdowne	29-23	*T:* Murray (3), O'Dowd *PG:* O'Sullivan (3)

Dolphin

Year of formation 1902
Ground Musgrave Park, Cork   Tel: Cork 962435
Colours Navy blue, yellow and white
Most capped player M J Kiernan (Ireland) 43 caps
Captain 1993-94 S Holden
1st XV 1993-94   P28   W9   D0   L19   F425   A591
Insurance Corporation League Div 2 9th **Carling Munster Senior Cup** Lost 3-16 to Sunday's Well (1st round)

League Record 1993-94

Date	Venue	Opponents	Result	Scorers
18 Sept	H	Old Belvedere	14-15	*T:* O'Shea *PG:* Byrne (2) *DG:* Byrne
25 Sept	A	Sunday's Well	11-16	*T:* Clarke *PG:* Byrne (2)
2 Oct	H	Instonians	11-17	*T:* Clarke *PG:* Byrne *DG:* Byrne
9 Oct	A	Bangor	15-20	*T:* Byrne, O'Neill *C:* O'Shea *PG:* O'Shea
20 Nov	H	Galwegians	13-9	*T:* Quaid *C:* Keary *PG:* Keary (2)
8 Jan	A	Terenure Coll	9-14	*PG:* Keary (3)
26 Feb	H	Old Crescent	15-12	*T:* Clarke, Abbott *C:* Kiernan *PG:* Cotir
12 Mar	A	Malone	12-6	*PG:* Kiernan (4)
19 Mar	H	Ballymena	16-29	*T:* Keogh, Abbott *PG:* Kiernan (2)
16 Apr	A	Ballina	23-6	*T:* Kiernan, Quaid, Kelleher *C:* Kiernan
				PG: Kiernan (2)

Dungannon

Year of formation 1873
Ground Stevenson Park, Dungannon   Tel: Dungannon 22387
Colours Blue and white hoops
Most capped player W A Anderson (Ireland) 27 caps
Captain 1993-94 H McCaughey
1st XV 1993-94   P30   W18   D1   L11   F741   A457
Insurance Corporation League Div 1 4th **First Trust Bank Ulster Senior Cup** *Winners* Beat Instonians 14-10 (final)

League Record 1993-94

Date	Venue	Opponents	Result	Scorers
18 Sept	A	Shannon	9-15	*PG:* McGarry (2) *DG:* McGarry

25 Sept	H	Blackrock Coll	6-11	*PG:* McGarry (2)
2 Oct	A	Cork Const	17-12	*T:* Patterson *PG:* McGarry (2)
				DG: McGarry, Blair
9 Oct	H	Young Munster	43-16	*T:* Davidson, McDowell, Howe, John Hastings
				C: McGarry (4) *PG:* McGarry (3)
				DG: McGarry, Blair
20 Nov	A	Garryowen	16-19	*T:* Davidson *C:* McGarry *PG:* McGarry (3)
8 Jan	A	Lansdowne	27-9	*T:* Carey, Burns *C:* McGarry
				PG: McGarry (3) *DG:* Blair (2)
22 Jan	H	St Mary's Coll	17-19	*T:* Carey *PG:* McGarry (4)
12 Mar	H	Old Wesley	14-16	*T:* Archer *PG:* McGarry (2) *DG:* McGarry
19 Mar	A	Wanderers	19-10	*T:* Carey, Archer *PG:* McGarry (3)
9 Apr	H	Greystones	13-3	*T:* Weir *C:* McGarry *PG:* McGarry (2)

Galwegians

Year of formation 1922
Ground Crowley Park, Glenina, Galway   Tel: Galway 53435
Colours Sky blue
Most capped player P J A O'Sullivan (Ireland) 15 caps
Captain 1993-94 S Carty
1st XV 1993-94   P27   W9   D0   L18   F327   A434
Insurance Corporation League Div 2 10th *relegated* **Smithwick's Connacht Senior Cup** Lost 9-12 to Galway Corinthians (1st round)

League Record 1993-94

Date	Venue	Opponents	Result	Scorers
18 Sept	H	Instonians	14-18	*T:* Gavin *PG:* McGowan (3)
25 Sept	A	Bangor	6-14	*PG:* McGowan (2)
9 Oct	H	Terenure Coll	18-9	*T:* Murphy, Taylor *C:* McGowan
				PG: McGowan (2)
20 Nov	A	Dolphin	9-13	*PG:* McGowan (3)
8 Jan	H	Old Crescent	6-12	*PG:* McGowan (2)
22 Jan	A	Malone	12-13	*T:* Murphy, Guerin *C:* Murphy
26 Feb	H	Ballymena	3-13	*PG:* Mitchell
12 Mar	A	Ballina	22-5	*T:* pen try *C:* Mitchell *PG:* Mitchell (5)
19 Mar	H	Old Belvedere	23-13	*T:* Gavin, Guerin *C:* Mitchell (2)
				PG: Mitchell (3)
9 Apr	A	Sunday's Well	0-14	

Garryowen

Year of formation 1884
Ground Dooradoyle, Limerick   Tel: Limerick 227672
Colours Light blue with white five-pointed star
Most capped player B G M Wood (Ireland) 29 caps
Captain 1993-94 P Hogan
1st XV 1993-94   P27   W16   D0   L11   F525   A410
Insurance Corporation League Div 1 *Winners* **Carling Munster Senior Cup** Lost 3-18 to Young Munster (1st round)

League Record 1993-94

Date	Venue	Opponents	Result	Scorers
18 Sept	A	Cork Const	0-8	
25 Sept	H	Young Munster	23-9	*T:* Smith, Sheenhan, Wallace *C:* Smith
				PG: Smith (2)
2 Oct	A	Lansdowne	26-19	*T:* Sheenhan, Wallace *C:* Smith (2)
				PG: Smith (3) *DG:* P Murphy

20 Nov	H	Dungannon	19-16	T: Costello C: Smith PG: Smith (4)
8 Jan	H	St Mary's Coll	13-12	T: Wallace C: Smith PG: Smith
				DG: P Murphy
22 Jan	A	Old Wesley	16-6	T: Ronan, Wood PG: Smith (2)
12 Feb	A	Wanderers	39-23	T: Smith, Larkin, Wood, Cronin C: Smith (2)
				PG: Smith (5)
12 Mar	H	Greystones	27-6	T: Wallace, Coughlan, Danaher C: Smith (3)
				PG: Smith (2)
19 Mar	A	Shannon	0-6	
9 Apr	H	Blackrock Coll	9-3	PG: Smith (2) DG: P Murphy

Greystones

Year of formation 1937
Ground Dr J J Hickey Park, Delgany Road, Greystones, Co Wicklow
Tel: Dublin 2874640
Colours Green and white narrow hoops
Most capped player N J Popplewell (Ireland) 16 caps
Captain 1993-94 M Carney
1st XV 1993-94   P36   W20   D1   L15   F661   A577
Insurance Corporation League Div 1 10th *relegated* **Aluset Leinster Senior Cup**
Lost 8-12 to Terenure College (final)

League Record 1993-94

Date	Venue	Opponents	Result	Scorers
18 Sept	H	Old Wesley	12-6	PG: Harvey (3), Keyes
25 Sept	A	Wanderers	24-13	T: Harvey, Barrett C: Harvey
				PG: Harvey (3), Keyes
9 Oct	H	Shannon	9-6	PG: Keyes (2) DG: Harvey
20 Nov	A	Cork Const	6-23	PG: Harvey (2)
8 Jan	A	Blackrock Coll	8-12	T: Murphy PG: Dunne
22 Jan	H	Young Munster	11-14	T: Power PG: Keyes, Evans
26 Feb	H	Lansdowne	0-30	
12 Mar	A	Garryowen	6-27	PG: Harvey (2)
19 Mar	H	St Mary's Coll	18-12	PG: Harvey (5) DG: Harvey
9 Apr	A	Dungannon	3-13	PG: Harvey

Instonians

Year of formation 1919
Ground Shane Park, Stockmans Lane, Belfast   Tel: Belfast 660629
Colours Purple, yellow and black
Most capped player K D Crossan (Ireland) 41 caps
Captain 1993-94 G Bell
1st XV 1993-94   P32   W26   D0   L6   F870   A335
Insurance Corporation League Div 2 *Winners – promoted* **First Trust Bank Ulster Senior Cup** Lost 10-14 to Dungannon (final)

League Record 1993-94

Date	Venue	Opponents	Result	Scorers
18 Sept	A	Galwegians	18-14	PG: Laing (4) DG: Laing, Russell
25 Sept	H	Terenure Coll	9-3	PG: Laing (3)
2 Oct	A	Dolphin	17-11	T: Russell PG: Laing (4)
9 Oct	H	Old Crescent	21-9	T: Croft, Crossan, Russell PG: Laing
				DG: Russell
20 Nov	A	Malone	6-8	PG: Laing (2)
8 Jan	H	Ballymena	23-16	T: Bell PG: Laing (5) DG: Wyllie

22 Jan	A	Ballina	52-10	*T:* Bell, McCluskey, O'Donnell, McKibben, Crossan, Boyd, Russell *C:* Laing (4) *PG:* Laing (3)
26 Feb	H	Old Belvedere	12-9	*PG:* Laing (4)
12 Mar	A	Sunday's Well	9-15	*PG:* Russell (3)
9 Apr	H	Bangor	38-5	*T:* McCausland, McCluskey, Russell, Cornelius, Wyllie *C:* Russell (2) *PG:* Russell (3)

Lansdowne

Year of formation 1872
Ground Lansdowne Road, Dublin   Tel: Dublin 6689300
Colours Red, yellow and black
Most capped player M I Keane (Ireland) 51 caps
Captain 1993-94 J Sexton
1st XV 1993-94   P33   W17   D1   L15   F626   A545
Insurance Corporation League Div 1 5th **Aluset Leinster Senior Cup** Lost 13-26 to Greystones (2nd round replay)

League Record 1993-94

Date	Venue	Opponents	Result	Scorers
18 Sept	A	Young Munster	10-6	*T:* O'Shea *C:* Elwood *PG:* O'Shea
2 Oct	H	Garryowen	19-26	*T:* O'Shea *C:* O'Shea *PG:* O'Shea (4)
9 Oct	A	St Mary's Coll	24-19	*T:* Woods, Dillon *C:* O'Shea *PG:* O'Shea (4)
20 Nov	A	Old Wesley	9-16	*PG:* O'Shea (2), Elwood
8 Jan	H	Dungannon	9-27	*PG:* Elwood (2), O'Shea
22 Jan	H	Shannon	6-23	*PG:* O'Shea (2)
22 Feb	H	Wanderers	16-11	*T:* O'Shea *C:* Elwood *PG:* Elwood (2), O'Shea
26 Feb	A	Greystones	30-0	*T:* Glennon (2), Kearin (2) *C:* O'Shea (2) *PG:* O'Shea (2)
19 Mar	A	Blackrock Coll	16-10	*T:* Sexton (2) *PG:* Elwood *DG:* Elwood
9 Apr	H	Cork Const	23-29	*T:* Glennon (2) *C:* O'Shea (2) *PG:* O'Shea (3)

Malone

Year of formation 1892
Ground Gibson Park, Gibson Park Avenue, Belfast   Tel: Belfast 451312
Colours White
Most capped player A Tedford (Ireland) 23 caps
Captain 1993-94 D McBride
1st XV 1993-94   P25   W13   D1   L11   F446   A322
Insurance Corporation League Div 2 7th **First Trust Bank Ulster Senior Cup**
Lost 6-11 to Instonians (2nd round)

League Record 1993-94

Date	Venue	Opponents	Result	Scorers
18 Sept	H	Ballymena	6-9	*PG:* Bush (2)
25 Sept	A	Ballina	17-6	*T:* Field (2), McBride *C:* Bush
2 Oct	H	Old Belvedere	16-19	*T:* Smith *C:* Bush *PG:* Bush (2) *DG:* Bush
9 Oct	A	Sunday's Well	17-13	*T:* Hooks *PG:* Bush (4)
20 Nov	H	Instonians	8-6	*T:* McAllister *PG:* Wilkinson
8 Jan	A	Bangor	11-19	*T:* Duncan *PG:* Wilkinson, Cullen
22 Jan	H	Galwegians	13-12	*T:* Harbinson *C:* Wilkinson *PG:* Wilkinson, Cullen
26 Feb	A	Terenure Coll	14-14	*T:* Porter *PG:* Brown, Wilkinson *DG:* Brown
12 Mar	H	Dolphin	6-12	*PG:* Brown *DG:* Brown
19 Mar	A	Old Crescent	17-31	*T:* Harbinson, Potter *C:* Brown (2) *PG:* Brown

Old Belvedere

Year of formation 1930
Ground Angelsea Road, Ballsbridge, Dublin   Tel: Dublin 6689748
Colours Black and white hoops
Most capped player A J F O'Reilly (Ireland) 29 caps
Captain 1993-94 D Rock
1st XV 1993-94   P33   W19   D0   L14   F651   A482
Insurance Corporation League Div 2 4th **Aluset Leinster Senior Cup** Lost 6-9 to
Terenure College (2nd round)

League Record 1993-94

Date	Venue	Opponents	Result	Scorers
18 Sept	A	Dolphin	15-14	*PG:* Murphy (5)
25 Sept	H	Old Crescent	9-6	*PG:* Murphy (3)
2 Oct	A	Malone	19-16	*T:* Gavin *C:* Murphy *PG:* Murphy (3) *DG:* Murphy
9 Oct	H	Ballymena	8-23	*T:* Norse *PG:* Murphy
20 Nov	A	Ballina	19-6	*T:* McDowell *C:* Murphy *PG:* Murphy (4)
22 Jan	H	Sunday's Well	15-12	*T:* Gavin, Norse *C:* Murphy *PG:* Murphy
26 Feb	A	Instonians	9-12	*PG:* Murphy (3)
12 Mar	H	Bangor	22-7	*T:* Murphy, McDonnell, Malone *C:* Murphy, Philpott *PG:* Philpott
19 Mar	A	Galwegians	13-23	*T:* Norse *C:* Philpott *PG:* Philpott (2)
9 Apr	H	Terenure Coll	12-6	*PG:* Philpott (4)

Old Crescent

Year of formation 1947
Ground Rosbrien, Limerick   Tel: Limerick 228083
Colours Navy blue and white hoops
Most capped player P Lane (Ireland) 1 cap
Captain 1993-94 P Boland
1st XV 1993-94   P25   W12   D0   L13   F393   A423
Insurance Corporation League Div 2 8th **Carling Munster Senior Cup** Lost 15-18 to
Sunday's Well (2nd round)

League Record 1993-94

Date	Venue	Opponents	Result	Scorers
19 Sept	H	Ballina	31-9	*T:* O'Sullivan, Reddan (2), Begley *C:* Begley *PG:* Begley (3)
25 Sept	A	Old Belvedere	6-9	*PG:* Begley (2)
3 Oct	H	Sunday's Well	22-25	*T:* Reddan, Begley *PG:* Begley (4)
9 Oct	A	Instonians	9-21	*PG:* Begley (2), Barrett
20 Nov	H	Bangor	32-20	*T:* Browne, Toland, Forde *C:* Begley *PG:* Begley (5)
8 Jan	A	Galwegians	12-6	*PG:* Begley (3) *DG:* Tuohy
22 Jan	H	Terenure Coll	12-15	*PG:* Begley (4)
26 Feb	A	Dolphin	12-15	*T:* O'Sullivan, Dwyer *C:* Barrett
19 Mar	H	Malone	31-17	*T:* O'Sullivan, Clohessy, Boland, Begley *C:* Barrett *PG:* Barrett (3)
9 Apr	A	Ballymena	6-13	*PG:* Barrett (2)

Old Wesley

Year of formation 1891
Ground Donnybrook, Dublin   Tel: Dublin 6609893
Colours White with blue and red band

Most capped player P A Orr (Ireland) 58 caps
Captain 1993-94 R Love
1st XV 1993-94   P33   W20   D2   L11   F705   A516
Insurance Corporation League Div 1 9th **Aluset Leinster Senior Cup** Lost 3-22 to Blackrock College (2nd round)

League Record 1993-94

Date	Venue	Opponents	Result	Scorers
18 Sept	A	Greystones	6-12	*PG:* Farren (2)
25 Sept	H	Shannon	6-3	*PG:* Farren (2)
2 Oct	A	Blackrock Coll	6-20	*PG:* Farren (2)
9 Oct	H	Cork Const	22-28	*T:* Younger, Pim *PG:* Farren, Hawe
				DG: Farren, Hawe
20 Nov	H	Lansdowne	16-9	*T:* Pim *C:* Farren *PG:* Farren
				DG: Moloney (2)
8 Jan	A	Young Munster	3-6	*PG:* Farren
22 Jan	H	Garryowen	6-16	*PG:* Hawe (2)
26 Feb	A	St Mary's Coll	9-13	*PG:* Farren (2) *DG:* Hawe
12 Mar	A	Dungannon	16-14	*T:* Moloney *C:* Farren *PG:* Farren (3)
16 Apr	H	Wanderers	24-17	*T:* Hurley, Moloney *C:* Farren
				PG: Farren (3) *DG:* Farren

Shannon

Year of formation 1884
Ground Thomond Park, Limerick   Tel: Limerick 452350
Colours Black and blue hoops
Most capped player G A J McLoughlin (Ireland) 18 caps
Captain 1993-94 N O'Shea
1st XV 1993-94   P31   W17   D1   L13   F545   A369
Insurance Corporation League Div 1 8th **Carling Munster Senior Cup** Lost 10-13 to Sunday's Well (semi-final)

League Record 1993-94

Date	Venue	Opponents	Result	Scorers
18 Sept	H	Dungannon	15-9	*T:* Galvin, Foley *C:* W O'Shea *PG:* W O'Shea
25 Sept	A	Old Wesley	3-6	*PG:* Galvin
2 Oct	H	Wanderers	19-10	*T:* McDermott, N O'Shea *PG:* W O'Shea (2)
				DG: Galvin
9 Oct	A	Greystones	6-9	*PG:* W O'Shea *DG:* Galvin
22 Jan	A	Lansdowne	23-6	*T:* Foley, McCormack *C:* W O'Shea (2)
				PG: W O'Shea (3)
14 Feb	H	Blackrock Coll	6-18	*PG:* W O'Shea (2)
26 Feb	A	Young Munster	5-6	*T:* Foley
12 Mar	H	Cork Const	6-18	*PG:* Thompson (2)
19 Mar	H	Garryowen	6-0	*PG:* Thompson, Galvin
30 Apr	A	St Mary's Coll	18-22	*T:* W O'Shea, Murray *C:* W O'Shea
				PG: Galvin *DG:* Galvin

St Mary's College

Year of formation 1900
Ground Templeville Road, Templeogue, Dublin   Tel: Dublin 900440
Colours Royal blue with white five-pointed star
Most capped player P M Dean (Ireland) 32 caps
Captain 1993-94 S Jameson
1st XV 1993-94   P26   W13   D0   L13   F551   A453
Insurance Corporation League Div 1 6th **Aluset Leinster Senior Cup** Lost 16-24 to University College, Dublin (2nd round)

League Record 1993-94

Date	Venue	Opponents	Result	Scorers
18 Sept	A	Blackrock Coll	18-21	*T:* White, Gillen, Dowling *PG:* White
25 Sept	H	Cork Const	12-10	*PG:* White (4)
2 Oct	A	Young Munster	3-18	*PG:* White
9 Oct	H	Lansdowne	19-24	*T:* White *C:* White *PG:* White (4)
8 Jan	A	Garryowen	12-13	*PG:* Barry (4)
22 Jan	A	Dungannon	19-17	*T:* Potts *C:* Barry *PG:* Barry (4)
26 Feb	H	Old Wesley	13-9	*T:* Lavin *C:* Barry *PG:* Barry (2)
12 Mar	H	Wanderers	27-15	*T:* Gillen, Keane, Devlin *C:* Barry (3) *PG:* Barry (2)
19 Mar	A	Greystones	12-18	*PG:* Barry (3) *DG:* Barry
30 Apr	H	Shannon	22-18	*T:* Halpin, Gillen, Burke *C:* Barry (2) *PG:* Barry

Sunday's Well

Year of formation 1923
Ground Musgrave Park, Tramore Road, Cork   Tel: Cork 965735
Colours Red, green and white hoops
Most capped player J C Walsh (Ireland) 26 caps
Captain 1993-94 K O'Connell
1st XV 1993-94 P36 W29 D0 L7 F784 A482
Insurance Corporation League Div 2 2nd *promoted* **Carling Munster**
Senior Cup *Winners* Beat Young Munster 20-9 (final)

League Record 1992-93

Date	Venue	Opponents	Result	Scorers
18 Sept	A	Terenure Coll	15-10	*T:* O'Riordan (2) *C:* Daly *PG:* Daly
25 Sept	H	Dolphin	16-11	*T:* Horgan *C:* Haly *PG:* Haly (3)
3 Oct	A	Old Crescent	25-22	*T:* Murphy *C:* Haly *PG:* Haly (6)
9 Oct	H	Malone	13-17	*T:* Hayes *C:* Haly *PG:* Haly (2)
20 Nov	A	Ballymena	22-19	*T:* Daly *C:* Daly *PG:* Daly (4) *DG:* Daly
9 Jan	H	Ballina	32-3	*T:* McCahill, Daly, Roche, Cummins *C:* Daly (3) *PG:* Daly (2)
22 Jan	A	Old Belvedere	12-15	*PG:* Daly (2) *DG:* Crotty (2)
12 Mar	H	Instonians	15-9	*T:* Haly, Daly *C:* Daly *PG:* Haly
19 Mar	A	Bangor	20-12	*T:* Murphy, O'Connell *C:* Daly (2) *PG:* Daly (2)
9 Apr	H	Galwegians	14-0	*T:* O'Connell *PG:* Daly (3)

Terenure College

Year of formation 1941
Ground Lakelands Park, Greenlea, Terenure, Dublin   Tel: Dublin 907572
Colours Purple, black and white hoops
Most capped player M L Hipwell (Ireland) 12 caps
Captain 1993-94 N Hogan
1st XV 1993-94 P34 W20 D3 L11 F663 A505
Insurance Corporation League Div 2 6th **Aluset Leinster Senior Cup** *Winners* Beat Greystones 12-8 (final)

League Record 1993-94

Date	Venue	Opponents	Result	Scorers
18 Sept	H	Sunday's Well	10-15	*T:* Clarke *C:* Walsh *PG:* Walsh
25 Sept	A	Instonians	3-9	*PG:* Lynagh
2 Oct	H	Bangor	5-8	*T:* Walsh
9 Oct	A	Galwegians	9-18	*PG:* Cullen, Walsh *DG:* Cullen

8 Jan	H	Dolphin	14-9	*T:* Coleman *PG:* Lynagh (2) *DG:* Walsh
22 Jan	A	Old Crescent	15-12	*PG:* Lynagh (3), O'Farrell *DG:* O'Farrell
26 Feb	H	Malone	14-14	*T:* Walsh *PG:* Lynagh (3)
12 Mar	A	Ballymena	22-12	*T:* Hogan *C:* Lynagh *PG:* Lynagh (5)
19 Mar	H	Ballina	51-3	*T:* Lynagh (2), Bruce, Hogan, Kavanagh, Kelly, Quinn, Walsh *C:* Lynagh (4) *PG:* Lynagh
9 Apr	A	Old Belvedere	6-12	*PG:* Lynagh (2)

Wanderers

Year of formation 1870
Ground Lansdowne Road, Dublin   Tel: Dublin 689277
Colours Blue, black and white
Most capped player J R Kavanagh (Ireland) 35 caps
Captain 1993-94 J O'Riordan
1st XV 1993-94 P28 W7 D1 L20 F404 A592
Insurance Corporation League Div 1 11th *relegated* **Aluset Leinster Senior Cup**
Lost 5-39 to St Mary's College (1st round)

League Record 1993-94

Date	Venue	Opponents	Result	Scorers
25 Sept	H	Greystones	13-24	*T:* McGoey *C:* Daly *PG:* Daly *DG:* Barlow
2 Oct	A	Shannon	10-19	*T:* Daly *C:* Daly *PG:* Daly
20 Nov	H	Young Munster	21-6	*PG:* Daly (7)
1 Dec	H	Blackrock Coll	9-25	*PG:* Daly (2) *DG:* Wyse
8 Jan	A	Cork Const	12-35	*PG:* Daly (4)
12 Feb	H	Garryowen	23-39	*T:* Lesur, Finnegan, Garth *C:* Daly *PG:* Daly (2)
22 Feb	A	Lansdowne	11-16	*T:* Leahy *PG:* Garth (2)
12 Mar	A	St Mary's Coll	15-27	*T:* McGoey, Cosgrave *C:* Wyse *PG:* Wyse
19 Mar	H	Dungannon	10-19	*T:* Byrne *C:* Mahon *PG:* Mahon
16 Apr	A	Old Wesley	17-24	*T:* Finnegan *PG:* Mahon (3) *DG:* Mahon

Young Munster

Year of formation 1895
Ground Tom Clifford Park, Greenfields, Limerick   Tel: Limerick 228433
Colours Black and amber hoops
Most capped player T Clifford (Ireland) 14 caps
Captain 1993-94 R Ryan
1st XV 1993-94 P27 W17 D2 L8 F451 A320
Insurance Corporation League Div 1 7th **Carling Munster Senior Cup** Lost 9-20 to
Sunday's Well (final)

League Record 1993-94

Date	Venue	Opponents	Result	Scorers
18 Sept	H	Lansdowne	6-10	*PG:* A O'Halloran (2)
25 Sept	A	Garryowen	9-23	*PG:* A O'Halloran (3)
2 Oct	H	St Mary's Coll	18-3	*T:* P Clohessy, M O'Halloran *C:* A O'Halloran *PG:* A O'Halloran *DG:* A O'Halloran
9 Oct	A	Dungannon	16-43	*T:* McNamara *C:* A O'Halloran *PG:* A O'Halloran (3)
20 Nov	A	Wanderers	6-21	*PG:* A O'Halloran (2)
8 Jan	H	Old Wesley	6-3	*PG:* A O'Halloran (2)
22 Jan	A	Greystones	14-11	*T:* McMahon *PG:* A O'Halloran (2) *DG:* A O'Halloran
26 Feb	H	Shannon	6-5	*PG:* A O'Halloran (2)
12 Mar	H	Blackrock Coll	10-3	*T:* Coventry *C:* A O'Halloran *PG:* A O'Halloran
19 Mar	A	Cork Const	11-27	*T:* Earls *PG:* A O'Halloran (2)

WALES
Aberavon

Year of formation 1876
Ground Talbot Athletic Ground, Manor Street, Port Talbot, West Glamorgan
Tel: Port Talbot (0639) 882427
Colours Red and black hoops
Most capped player A J Martin (Wales) 34 caps
Captain 1993-94 J Jardine
1st XV 1993-94   P44   W21   D1   L22   F732   A762
Heineken League Div 1 11th *relegated* **SWALEC Cup** Lost 0-29 to Pontypridd
(5th round)

League Record 1993-94

Date	Venue	Opponents	Result	Scorers
4 Sept	A	Cardiff	3-59	*PG:* D Love
11 Sept	A	Dunvant	18-12	*T:* B Shenton, J Williams *C:* L Lewis *PG:* L Lewis, G Thomas
18 Sept	H	Cross Keys	42-15	*T:* J Jardine (2), W Morris, K Allen, J Williams, B Roach *C:* N Forrester (3) *PG:* L Lewis, N Forrester
25 Sept	A	Llanelli	21-24	*T:* I Spender, M Evans *C:* L Lewis *PG:* N Forrester (2), G Thomas
2 Oct	H	Neath	0-10	
9 Oct	H	Newbridge	8-28	*T:* M Evans *PG:* L Lewis
23 Oct	A	Pontypool	11-16	*T:* S Hutchinson *PG:* N Forrester (2)
30 Oct	H	Bridgend	12-12	*PG:* N Griffiths (2), G Thomas *DG:* N Griffiths
6 Nov	A	Newport	6-30	*PG:* J Davies (2)
13 Nov	H	Swansea	3-10	*PG:* I Bebb
20 Nov	A	Pontypridd	7-28	*T:* S Hutchinson *C:* I Bebb
27 Nov	H	Cardiff	3-17	*PG:* N Griffiths
4 Dec	H	Dunvant	23-12	*T:* D Griffiths, I Bebb, P Middleton *C:* I Bebb *PG:* I Bebb (2)
11 Dec	A	Cross Keys	15-12	*T:* P Middleton, J Jardine *C:* I Bebb *PG:* I Bebb
8 Jan	A	Newbridge	6-19	*PG:* I Bebb (2)
29 Jan	A	Neath	3-27	*PG:* J Morgan
5 Mar	H	Pontypool	11-9	*T:* L Lewis *PG:* I Bebb (2)
26 Mar	A	Bridgend	20-59	*T:* A Bucknall, G Thomas *C:* I Bebb (2) *PG:* I Bebb (2)
5 Apr	H	Llanelli	9-5	*PG:* J Morgan (2), G Thomas
9 Apr	H	Newport	13-21	*T:* D Griffiths, K Allen *PG:* J Morgan
23 Apr	A	Swansea	3-32	*PG:* J Morgan
30 Apr	H	Pontypridd	5-7	*T:* S Hutchinson

Abertillery

Year of formation 1884
Ground The Park, Abertillery, Gwent   Tel: Abertillery (0495) 212555
Colours Green and white quarters
Most capped player H J Morgan (Wales) 27 caps
Captain 1993-94 M Rossiter
1st XV 1993-94   P39   W25   D1   L13   F765   A528
Heineken League Div 2 2nd *promoted* **SWALEC Cup** Lost 3-13 to Neath (4th round)

League Record 1993-94

Date	Venue	Opponents	Result	Scorers
4 Sept	A	S Wales Police	7-15	*T:* G Gladwyn *C:* B Hayward

11 Sept	H	Treorchy	16-21	T: G Gladwyn C: B Hayward
				PG: B Hayward (2) DG: B Hayward
18 Sept	A	Maesteg	11-21	T: G Gladwyn PG: B Hayward (2)
25 Sept	H	Tenby Utd	44-13	T: D Jones, J Williams, M McCluney, B Corlett,
				M Rossiter C: B Hayward (5)
				PG: B Hayward (2) DG: M Williams
2 Oct	A	Mountain Ash	15-10	T: D John, A Hillman C: B Hayward
				PG: B Hayward
9 Oct	H	Ebbw Vale	28-3	T: B Corlett, M Rossiter, R Roberts
				C: B Hayward (2) PG: B Hayward (3)
23 Oct	A	Glamorgan Wands	41-21	T: G Gladwyn, E Glastonbury, D John, B Collett,
				B Hayward, M Williams C: B Hayward (4)
				PG: B Hayward
30 Oct	A	Llandovery	29-9	T: R McCorduck, A Richards C: B Hayward (2)
				PG: B Hayward (4) DG: B Hayward
6 Nov	H	Narberth	20-9	T: B Hayward PG: B Hayward (5)
13 Nov	A	Llanharan	6-6	PG: B Hayward (2)
20 Nov	H	Penarth	47-3	T: M Williams (2), E Glastonbury, D John,
				M Rossiter, A Richards, B Hayward
				C: B Hayward (3) PG: B Hayward
				DG: B Hayward
27 Nov	H	S Wales Police	36-10	T: A Dobbs, M Williams, B Hayward
				C: B Hayward (3) PG: B Hayward (5)
3 Dec	A	Treorchy	10-26	T: A Richards C: B Hayward PG: B Hayward
11 Dec	H	Maesteg	22-13	T: J Williams, M Williams PG: B Hayward (4)
3 Jan	A	Tenby Utd	12-15	T: D John, J Williams C: B Hayward
29 Jan	H	Mountain Ash	8-6	T: D John PG: B Hayward
5 Mar	A	Ebbw Vale	24-3	T: D John, B Corlett C: B Hayward
				PG: B Hayward (4)
26 Mar	H	Glamorgan Wands	19-6	T: M Williams C: M Williams
				PG: M Williams (4)
9 Apr	H	Llandovery	13-6	T: pen try C: B Hayward PG: B Hayward (2)
16 Apr	A	Narberth	21-0	T: J Williams, M Picton C: B Hayward
				PG: B Hayward (3)
23 Apr	H	Llanharan	38-8	T: M Picton, M McCluney, W Ford, M Griffiths
				C: B Hayward (3) PG: B Hayward (4)
30 Apr	A	Penarth	6-18	PG: B Hayward (2)

Bridgend

Year of formation 1878
Ground Brewery Field, Tondu Road, Bridgend, Mid-Glamorgan
Tel: Bridgend (0656) 659032
Colours Blue and white hoops
Most capped player J P R Williams (Wales) 55 caps
Captain 1993-94 D J Bryant
1st XV 1993-94 P38   W21   D1   L16   F926   A696
Heineken League Div 1 6th **SWALEC Cup** Lost 6-15 to Cardiff (6th round)

League Record 1993-94

Date	Venue	Opponents	Result	Scorers
4 Sept	A	Cross Keys	17-16	T: J Derrick, D Davies, R Howley C: G Wilkins
7 Sept	H	Llanelli	11-18	T: G Wilkins PG: G Wilkins DG: M Lewis
11 Sept	A	Neath	11-33	T: G Davies PG: G Wilkins (2)
18 Sept	H	Pontypool	74-20	T: G Evans (2), N Spender (2), R Howley (2),
				G Webbe, G Wilkins, M Lewis, P Wintle
				C: G Wilkins (9) PG: G Wilkins
				DG: M Lewis
25 Sept	A	Pontypridd	14-26	T: S Gale PG: G Wilkins (3)
2 Oct	A	Newport	24-11	T: I Greenslade, P Wintle, G Webbe
				C: G Wilkins (3) PG: G Wilkins
23 Oct	H	Swansea	16-20	T: G Webbe C: D Davies PG: D Davies (3)
30 Oct	A	Aberavon	12-12	PG: D Davies (4)

6 Nov	H	Cardiff	3-29	*PG:* D Davies
20 Nov	H	Dunvant	15-6	*T:* G Webbe, P Wintle *C:* M Lewis
				PG: M Lewis
27 Nov	H	Cross Keys	30-0	*T:* B Grabham, K Mably, P Wintle, D Davies,
				S Jenkins *C:* D Davies *PG:* M Lewis
1 Dec	A	Llanelli	20-19	*T:* S Gale, G Evans, K Mably *C:* M Lewis
				PG: M Lewis
6 Dec	H	Neath	15-37	*T:* G Webbe, K Mably, G Wilkins
11 Dec	A	Pontypool	23-29	*T:* G Webbe (2), M Lewis *C:* M Lewis
				PG: M Lewis (2)
3 Jan	H	Pontypridd	5-27	*T:* S Gale
29 Jan	H	Newport	17-14	*T:* K Mably, C Bradshaw *C:* M Lewis (2)
				PG: M Lewis
5 Mar	A	Swansea	14-23	*T:* P Jones, G Jones *C:* M Lewis (2)
26 Mar	H	Aberavon	59-20	*T:* G Webbe (2), C Bradshaw (2), N Spender,
				M Lewis, J Daley, S Gale, P Jones, D Bryant
				C: M Lewis, G Wilkins, R Howley *PG:* M Lewis
9 Apr	A	Cardiff	13-22	*T:* G Jones *C:* M Lewis *PG:* M Lewis (2)
16 Apr	A	Newbridge	38-11	*T:* G Wilkins (2), P Jones, N Jones, R Howley
				C: M Lewis (5) *PG:* M Lewis
23 Apr	H	Newbridge	22-18	*T:* M Lewis, G Jones, pen try *C:* M Lewis (2)
				PG: M Lewis
30 Apr	A	Dunvant	13-23	*T:* pen try *C:* M Lewis *PG:* M Lewis (2)

Cardiff

Year of formation 1876
Ground Cardiff Arms Park, Westgate Street, Cardiff   Tel: Cardiff (0222) 383546
Colours Cambridge blue and black
Most capped player G O Edwards (Wales) 53 caps
Captain 1993-94 M R Hall
1st XV 1993-94   P46   W32   D2   L12   F1288   A621
Heineken League Div 1 4th **SWALEC Cup** *Winners* Beat Llanelli 15-8 (final)

League Record 1993-94

Date	Venue	Opponents	Result	Scorers
4 Sept	H	Aberavon	59-3	*T:* A Booth (2), A Davies, N Walker, M Hall,
				H Stone, M Rayer, S Hill *C:* A Davies (5)
				PG: A Davies (3)
7 Sept	A	Pontypridd	24-17	*T:* O Thomas, N Walker *C:* A Davies
				PG: A Davies (3) *DG:* A Davies
11 Sept	A	Newbridge	36-0	*T:* A Booth, M Rayer, S Hill, N Walker, M Budd
				C: M Rayer *PG:* A Davies (3)
18 Sept	H	Dunvant	55-3	*T:* M Hall (2), S Hill (2), A Moore (2),
				J Humphreys, C Laity *C:* M Rayer (6)
				PG: M Rayer
25 Sept	A	Cross Keys	61-21	*T:* O Thomas (2), C John, M Budd, M Rayer,
				C Laity, A Booth, P Sedgemore, H Stone
				C: M Rayer (3), C John (2) *PG:* M Rayer (2)
2 Oct	H	Llanelli	9-15	*PG:* A Davies (3)
23 Oct	A	Neath	6-11	*PG:* A Davies *DG:* A Davies
30 Oct	H	Pontypool	78-0	*T:* A Moore (2), C John (2), S Ford, S Hill,
				M Rayer (2), A Davies, H Taylor, C Mills
				C: A Davies (10) *DG:* A Davies
6 Nov	A	Bridgend	29-3	*T:* O Williams, S Ford, C John, A Davies
				C: A Davies (3) *PG:* A Davies
13 Nov	H	Newport	52-3	*T:* N Walker (2), S Ford (2), H Bevan (2),
				H Taylor *C:* A Davies (4) *PG:* A Davies (3)
20 Nov	A	Swansea	6-22	*PG:* A Davies (2)
27 Nov	A	Aberavon	17-3	*T:* A Davies, S Hill *C:* A Davies (2)
				PG: M Rayer
1 Dec	H	Pontypridd	10-15	*T:* H Stone *C:* A Davies *PG:* A Davies

5 Dec	H	Newbridge	33-3	*T:* S Ford (2), A Davies, M Hall *C:* A Davies (2) *PG:* A Davies (3)
11 Dec	A	Dunvant	8-6	*T:* M Hall *PG:* A Davies
29 Jan	A	Llanelli	19-19	*T:* H Taylor *C:* A Davies *PG:* A Davies (4)
16 Feb	H	Cross Keys	72-14	*T:* A Moore (3), O Thomas (2), S Ford, C Laity, C John, M Bennett, O Williams, M Griffiths, pen try *C:* A Davies (6)
5 Mar	H	Neath	14-8	*T:* A Davies *PG:* A Davies (3)
26 Mar	A	Pontypool	17-16	*T:* N Walker, S Hill *C:* M Rayer (2) *PG:* M Rayer
9 Apr	H	Bridgend	22-13	*T:* V Davies, H Stone, O Thomas *C:* M Rayer, C John *PG:* C John
23 Apr	A	Newport	22-22	*T:* N Walker, A Moore, S Hill *C:* A Davies (2) *PG:* A Davies
30 Apr	H	Swansea	19-23	*T:* O Thomas, A Palfrey, pen try *C:* C John (2)

Cross Keys

Year of formation 1885
Ground Pandy Park, Cross Keys, Gwent   Tel: Cross Keys (0495) 270289
Colours Black and white hoops
Most capped player S Morris (Wales) 19 caps
Captain 1993-94 P Withers
1st XV 1993-94   P36   W10   D0   L26   F668   A939
Heineken League Div 1 12th *relegated*   **SWALEC Cup** Lost 5-9 to Glamorgan Wands (4th round)

League Record 1993-94

Date	Venue	Opponents	Result	Scorers
4 Sept	H	Bridgend	16-17	*T:* J Powell *C:* M Fleet *PG:* M Fleet (3)
8 Sept	A	Newport	20-23	*T:* P Withers, M Fleet, S Marshall *C:* M Fleet *PG:* M Fleet
11 Sept	H	Swansea	3-19	*PG:* P Withers
18 Sept	A	Aberavon	15-42	*T:* P Withers, R Nicholls *C:* M Fleet *PG:* M Fleet
25 Sept	H	Cardiff	21-61	*T:* pen try, C Weed *C:* M Fleet *PG:* M Fleet (3)
2 Oct	A	Newbridge	6-25	*PG:* J Parfitt, M Fleet
23 Oct	H	Dunvant	15-24	*PG:* M Fleet (5)
30 Oct	H	Pontypridd	10-20	*T:* G Gittings, R Nicholls
6 Nov	A	Llanelli	10-43	*T:* R Nicholls *C:* M Fleet PG: N Davies
20 Nov	A	Pontypool	3-17	*PG:* M Fleet
27 Nov	A	Bridgend	0-30	
1 Dec	H	Newport	7-13	*T:* R Nicholls *C:* M Fleet
4 Dec	A	Swansea	22-95	*T:* J Parfitt (2), R Nicholls *C:* J Parfitt (2) *PG:* J Parfitt
11 Dec	H	Aberavon	12-15	*PG:* P Withers (3) *DG:* P Withers
29 Jan	H	Newbridge	3-42	*PG:* S Smith
16 Feb	A	Cardiff	14-72	*T:* K Gregory, M Price *C:* J Parfitt (2)
5 Mar	A	Dunvant	8-50	*T:* R Nicholls *PG:* I Gladwyn
8 Mar	H	Neath	11-17	*T:* D Rees *PG:* D Rees (2)
26 Mar	A	Pontypridd	5-25	*T:* J Powell
9 Apr	H	Llanelli	11-21	*T:* M Price *PG:* I Gladwyn, S Smith
23 Apr	A	Neath	10-56	*T:* M Price *C:* D Rees *PG:* D Rees
30 Apr	H	Pontypool	17-24	*T:* R Gladwyn, R Nicholls *C:* D Rees (2) *PG:* D Rees

Dunvant

Year of formation 1888
Ground Broadacre, Killay, Swansea   Tel: Swansea (0792) 207291
Colours Red and green hoops

Captain 1993-94 D Crane
Heineken League Div 1 10th **SWALEC Cup** Lost 8-18 to Newbridge (6th round)

League Record 1993-94

Date	Venue	Opponents	Result	Scorers
4 Sept	H	Newport	12-7	*PG:* M Thomas (3) *DG:* M Thomas
8 Sept	A	Swansea	11-37	*T:* M Jones *PG:* M Thomas (2)
11 Sept	H	Aberavon	12-18	*PG:* M Thomas (4)
18 Sept	A	Cardiff	3-55	*PG:* M Thomas
25 Sept	H	Newbridge	20-6	*T:* N Bolton, M Thomas *C:* M Thomas (2) *PG:* M Thomas (2)
23 Oct	A	Cross Keys	24-15	*T:* N Lloyd, D Evans *C:* M Thomas *PG:* M Thomas (4)
30 Oct	H	Llanelli	10-43	*T:* P Morris *C:* M Thomas *PG:* M Thomas
6 Nov	A	Neath	14-26	*T:* W Lloyd, P Roberts *C:* M Thomas (2)
13 Nov	H	Pontypool	13-10	*T:* pen try *C:* M Thomas *PG:* M Thomas (2)
20 Nov	A	Bridgend	6-15	*PG:* M Thomas (2)
27 Nov	A	Newport	9-13	*PG:* M Thomas (3)
1 Dec	H	Swansea	13-14	*T:* R Llewellyn *C:* M Thomas *PG:* M Thomas (2)
4 Dec	A	Aberavon	12-23	*T:* D Niblo, P Farnworth *C:* M Thomas
11 Dec	H	Cardiff	6-8	*PG:* M Thomas (2)
29 Jan	A	Pontypridd	8-53	*T:* P Farnworth *PG:* M Thomas
12 Feb	A	Newbridge	0-16	
5 Mar	H	Cross Keys	50-8	*T:* C Hutchings (2), C Davies (2), D Niblo, R Greenwood, P Hopkins, C Young *C:* M Thomas (5)
22 Mar	H	Pontypridd	9-29	*PG:* M Thomas (3)
26 Mar	A	Llanelli	20-27	*T:* P Hopkins, R Williams *C:* M Thomas (2) *PG:* M Thomas (2)
9 Apr	H	Neath	10-10	*T:* R Williams, P Hopkins
23 Apr	A	Pontypool	3-18	*PG:* M Thomas
30 Apr	H	Bridgend	23-13	*T:* R Greenwood, W Lloyd *C:* M Thomas (2) *PG:* M Thomas (3)

Ebbw Vale

Year of formation 1880
Ground Eugene Cross Park, Ebbw Vale, Gwent   Tel: Ebbw Vale (0495) 302995
Colours Red, white and green
Most capped player D Williams (Wales) 36 caps
Captain 1993-94 P Booth
1st XV 1993-94 P34 W10 D3 L21 F423 A680
Heineken League Div 2 9th **SWALEC Cup** Lost 13-21 to Swansea (4th round)

League Record 1993-94

Date	Venue	Opponents	Result	Scorers
4 Sept	A	Treorchy	5-6	*T:* R Dixon
11 Sept	H	Maesteg	20-32	*T:* S Fealey, R Dixon, C Price *C:* J Strange *PG:* J Strange
18 Sept	A	Tenby Utd	13-24	*T:* D Morris *C:* J Strange *PG:* J Strange (2)
25 Sept	H	Mountain Ash	27-0	*T:* M Davies (2), C Scully, J Strange *C:* J Strange (2) *PG:* J Strange
2 Oct	A	Glamorgan Wands	32-5	*T:* A Allen (2), S Jones, C Grant, J Strange *C:* J Strange (2) *PG:* J Strange
9 Oct	A	Abertillery	3-28	*PG:* J Strange
23 Oct	H	Llandovery	29-0	*T:* C Butler (3), M Davies *C:* J Strange (3) *PG:* J Strange
30 Oct	A	Narberth	15-13	*T:* J Strange, S Fealey *C:* J Strange *PG:* J Strange

6 Nov	H	Llanharan	3-3	*PG:* J Strange
13 Nov	A	Penarth	15-11	*T:* G Jones, D Harris *C:* J Strange
				PG: J Strange
20 Nov	H	S Wales Police	8-20	*T:* J Lapham *PG:* J Strange
27 Nov	H	Treorchy	10-15	*T:* D Harris *C:* M Jones *PG:* M Jones
3 Dec	A	Maesteg	6-6	*PG:* M Jones (2)
11 Dec	H	Tenby Utd	13-9	*T:* A Thomas *C:* M Jones *PG:* M Jones
				DG: M Davies
22 Jan	A	Mountain Ash	3-28	*PG:* M Jones
29 Jan	H	Glamorgan Wands	12-10	*PG:* M Jones (4)
5 Mar	H	Abertillery	3-24	*PG:* M Jones
26 Mar	A	Llandovery	0-25	
16 Apr	A	Llanharan	6-9	*PG:* M Jones (2)
19 Apr	H	Narberth	23-10	*T:* C Lake *PG:* M Jones (6)
23 Apr	H	Penarth	17-20	*T:* N Edwards, D Morris *C:* M Jones (2)
				PG: M Jones
30 Apr	A	S Wales Police	16-23	*T:* G Lawrence *C:* M Jones *PG:* M Jones (3)

Glamorgan Wanderers

Year of formation 1893
Ground The Memorial Ground, Stirling Road, Ely, Cardiff   Tel: Cardiff (0222) 591039
Colours Cambridge blue, black and white
Captain 1993-94 D St John
1st XV 1993-94   P36   W10   D0   L26   F463   A773
Heineken League Div 2 12th *relegated* **SWALEC Cup** Lost 5-9 to Maesteg (5th round)

League Record 1993-94

Date	*Venue*	*Opponents*	*Result*	*Scorers*
4 Sept	A	Tenby Utd	6-22	*PG:* M Jones (2)
11 Sept	H	Llanharan	20-22	*T:* D Paris, D St John *C:* M Jones (2)
				PG: M Jones (2)
18 Sept	H	Mountain Ash	13-17	*T:* M Burley, D Smith *PG:* N Richards
25 Sept	A	Penarth	13-17	*T:* S Collins *C:* N Richards *PG:* N Richards (2)
2 Oct	H	Ebbw Vale	5-32	*T:* R Calcaterra
9 Oct	A	S Wales Police	12-28	*T:* D Flint, D Gibbon *C:* D Smith
23 Oct	H	Abertillery	21-41	*T:* D Flint, B Patterson, D Smith *PG:* M Jones (2)
30 Oct	A	Treorchy	0-24	
6 Nov	H	Llandovery	14-34	*T:* B Patterson, S Collins *C:* M Burley (2)
13 Nov	A	Maesteg	5-24	*T:* M Thomas
20 Nov	H	Narberth	0-23	
27 Nov	H	Tenby Utd	21-9	*T:* D St John (2) *C:* R Marshall
				PG: R Marshall (3)
3 Dec	A	Llanharan	3-11	*PG:* R Marshall
11 Dec	A	Mountain Ash	30-7	*T:* B Patterson, D St John, R Calcaterra, D Smith
				C: R Marshall (2) *PG:* R Marshall (2)
29 Jan	A	Ebbw Vale	10-12	*T:* D Gibbon *C:* R Marshall *PG:* R Marshall
26 Feb	H	Penarth	6-3	*PG:* R Marshall (2)
5 Mar	H	S Wales Police	0-20	
26 Mar	A	Abertillery	6-19	*PG:* R Marshall (2)
9 Apr	H	Treorchy	0-13	
16 Apr	A	Llandovery	17-10	*T:* D Gibbon, T Henson, M Burley *C:* R Marshall
23 Apr	H	Maesteg	23-13	*T:* D Flint, B Patterson, D Paris *C:* D Smith
				PG: D Smith (2)
30 Apr	A	Narberth	37-17	*T:* M Thomas (2), D Flint (2), D Gibbon, D Smith,
				T Henson *C:* D Smith

Llandovery

Year of formation 1878
Ground Church Bank, Llandovery, Dyfed   Tel: Llandovery (0550) 21389
Colours Red and white hoops

Most capped player C P Lewis (Wales) 5 caps
Captain 1993-94 H Thomas
1st XV 1993-94   P29   W12   D1   L16   F418   A528
Heineken League Div 2 10th   **SWALEC Cup** Lost 5-57 to Llanelli (6th round)

League Record 1993-94

Date	Venue	Opponents	Result	Scorers
4 Sept	A	Penarth	16-9	*T:* N Clarke *C:* D Lloyd-Jones *PG:* D Lloyd-Jones (3)
11 Sept	H	S Wales Police	3-10	*DG:* D Lloyd-Jones
18 Sept	A	Treorchy	6-25	*PG:* D Lloyd-Jones (2)
25 Sept	H	Maesteg	20-10	*T:* A Hodgkinson, A Jones *C:* D Lloyd-Jones (2) *PG:* D Lloyd-Jones *DG:* D Lloyd-Jones
2 Oct	A	Tenby Utd	13-22	*T:* D Lloyd-Jones *C:* D Lloyd-Jones *PG:* D Lloyd-Jones (2)
9 Oct	H	Mountain Ash	9-8	*PG:* D Lloyd-Jones (3)
23 Oct	A	Ebbw Vale	0-29	
30 Oct	H	Abertillery	9-29	*PG:* D Lloyd-Jones (3)
6 Nov	A	Glamorgan Wands	34-14	*T:* A Hodgkinson, H Thomas, M Rees, A Evans *C:* D Lloyd-Jones (4) *PG:* D Lloyd-Jones (2)
13 Nov	A	Narberth	0-6	
20 Nov	H	Llanharan	22-15	*T:* A Hodgkinson (2), H Jones *C:* H Jones, R Dix *PG:* R Dix
27 Nov	H	Penarth	11-21	*T:* D Giles *PG:* H Jones, A Williams
4 Dec	A	S Wales Police	19-37	*T:* A Hodgkinson (2), A Davies *C:* R Dix (2)
11 Dec	H	Treorchy	11-11	*T:* A Williams *PG:* R Dix (2)
29 Jan	H	Tenby Utd	9-24	*PG:* R Dix (3)
22 Mar	A	Maesteg	10-26	*T:* D Lloyd-Jones *C:* D Lloyd-Jones *PG:* D Lloyd-Jones
26 Mar	H	Ebbw Vale	25-0	*T:* R Dix *C:* R Dix *PG:* R Dix (6)
2 Apr	A	Mountain Ash	22-12	*T:* A Williams, A Thomas, A Hodgkinson *C:* D Lloyd-Jones (2) *PG:* D Lloyd-Jones
9 Apr	A	Abertillery	6-13	*PG:* R Dix (2)
16 Apr	H	Glamorgan Wands	10-17	*T:* H Thomas *C:* D Lloyd-Jones *PG:* D Lloyd-Jones
23 Apr	H	Narberth	14-3	*T:* J Hughes *PG:* R Dix (3)
30 Apr	A	Llanharan	0-19	

Llanelli

Year of formation 1872
Ground Stradey Park, Llanelli, Dyfed   Tel: Llanelli (0554) 774060
Colours Scarlet
Most capped player I C Evans (Wales) 41 caps
Captain 1993-94 R H St J B Moon
1st XV 1993-94   P38   W27   D1   L10   F979   A553
Heineken League Div 1 5th   **SWALEC Cup** Lost 8-15 to Cardiff (final)

League Record 1993-94

Date	Venue	Opponents	Result	Scorers
4 Sept	H	Pontypool	31-17	*T:* R Moon, W Proctor, L Jones, E Lewis *C:* C Stephens *PG:* C Stephens (3)
7 Sept	A	Bridgend	18-11	*T:* A Richards, R Moon *C:* C Stephens *PG:* C Stephens (2)
11 Sept	H	Newport	44-8	*T:* I Jones (3), A Richards, E Lewis, N Davies *C:* H Williams (4) *PG:* H Williams (2)
18 Sept	A	Swansea	12-22	*PG:* C Stephens (4)
25 Sept	H	Aberavon	24-21	*T:* M Wintle, A Lamerton, S Quinnell, H Williams *C:* H Williams (2)
2 Oct	A	Cardiff	15-9	*T:* P Young, P Jones *C:* H Williams *PG:* H Williams

Ian Jones of Llanelli gets the ball away before being tackled by Cardiff's Mike Hall in the Scarlets' 15-9 League win at Cardiff in October.

23 Oct	H	Newbridge	35-14	*T:* I Evans (2), G Jones, S Quinnell (2)
				C: H Williams (2) *PG:* H Williams (2)
30 Oct	A	Dunvant	43-10	*T:* R Moon (3), S Quinnell (2), N Davies,
				W Proctor *C:* H Williams (4)
6 Nov	H	Cross Keys	43-10	*T:* H Harries (2), S Davies, N Davies, A Richards,
				M Wintle *C:* I Jones (5) *PG:* I Jones
13 Nov	H	Pontypridd	8-6	*T:* A Lamerton *PG:* C Stephens
20 Nov	A	Neath	5-27	*T:* R Moon
27 Nov	A	Pontypool	20-9	*T:* W Proctor, A Richards, A Copsey
				C: A Richards *PG:* H Williams
1 Dec	H	Bridgend	19-20	*T:* H Harries (2), A Richards *C:* A Richards (2)
4 Dec	A	Newport	14-22	*T:* P Davies *PG:* A Richards (3)
11 Dec	H	Swansea	20-13	*T:* I Jones, A Richards, J Strange *C:* J Strange
				PG: J Strange
29 Jan	H	Cardiff	19-19	*T:* S Davies *C:* C Stephens *PG:* C Stephens (4)
5 Mar	A	Newbridge	20-37	*T:* I Jones, P Young, G Jones *C:* C Stephens
				PG: C Stephens
26 Mar	H	Dunvant	27-20	*T:* L Davies, N Boobyer, P Jones, J Strange,
				I Evans *C:* J Strange
5 Apr	A	Aberavon	5-9	*T:* M Wintle
9 Apr	A	Cross Keys	21-11	*T:* I Evans, L Davies, G Jones *PG:* J Strange (2)
23 Apr	A	Pontypridd	7-31	*T:* W Proctor *C:* J Strange
30 Apr	H	Neath	11-20	*T:* S Davies *PG:* J Strange (2)

Llanharan

Year of formation 1891
Ground Dairy Field, Bridgend Road, Llanharan, Mid-Glamorgan
Tel: Llanharan (0443) 222209
Colours Black and sky blue hoops
Captain 1993-94 J Pick
1st XV 1993-94 P35   W13   D3   L19   F269   A191
Heineken League Div 2 6th **SWALEC Cup** Lost 3-32 to Newbridge (5th round)

League Record 1993-94

Date	Venue	Opponents	Result	Scorers
4 Sept	H	Narberth	8-20	*T:* A Price *PG:* J Morris
11 Sept	A	Glamorgan Wands	22-20	*T:* G Hiscock *C:* J Morris *PG:* J Morris (5)
18 Sept	A	Penarth	17-6	*T:* M Reynolds, pen try *C:* J Morris (2) *PG:* J Morris
25 Sept	H	S Wales Police	16-12	*T:* G Pritchard *C:* J Morris *PG:* J Morris (2) *DG:* J Morris
2 Oct	A	Treorchy	11-31	*T:* N Berbillion *PG:* J Morris (2)
9 Oct	H	Maesteg	5-24	*T:* M Taylor
23 Oct	A	Tenby Utd	6-19	*PG:* R Langmead (2)
30 Oct	H	Mountain Ash	5-13	*T:* B Lewis
6 Nov	A	Ebbw Vale	3-3	*PG:* R Cogbill
13 Nov	H	Abertillery	6-6	*PG:* R Cogbill (2)
20 Nov	A	Llandovery	15-22	*T:* W Merry, S Price *C:* S Hughes *PG:* S Hughes
27 Nov	A	Narberth	3-14	*PG:* S Hughes
3 Dec	H	Glamorgan Wands	11-3	*T:* M Reynolds *PG:* R Langmead (2)
11 Dec	H	Penarth	18-15	*T:* C Langdon, M Reynolds *C:* J Morris *PG:* R Langmead (2)
5 Mar	A	Maesteg	17-23	*T:* D Collins, W Merry *C:* R Langmead, J Morris *PG:* J Morris
16 Mar	A	S Wales Police	14-11	*T:* D Emyr *PG:* J Morris (3)
26 Mar	H	Tenby Utd	21-13	*T:* J Morris (2) *C:* J Morris *PG:* J Morris (3)
9 Apr	A	Mountain Ash	11-30	*T:* P Hughes *PG:* W Jervis *DG:* W Jervis
13 Apr	H	Treorchy	14-20	*T:* W Merry *PG:* W Jervis (3)
16 Apr	H	Ebbw Vale	9-6	*PG:* J Morris *DG:* J Morris (2)
23 Apr	A	Abertillery	8-38	*T:* G Davies *PG:* J Morris
30 Apr	H	Llandovery	19-0	*T:* P Hughes, K Jones, K Cornelius *C:* J Morris (2)

Maesteg

Year of formation 1882
Ground Old Parish Ground, Llynfi Road, Maesteg, Mid-Glamorgan
Tel: Maesteg (0656) 732283
Colours Black and amber hoops
Most capped player G Evans (Wales) 10 caps
Captain 1993-94 L Harvey
1st XV 1993-94 P47 W24 D3 L20 F865 A781
Heineken League Div 2 3rd **SWALEC Cup** Lost 7-23 to Llanelli (semi-final)

League Record 1993-94

Date	Venue	Opponents	Result	Scorers
4 Sept	H	Mountain Ash	9-5	*PG:* M Watts (2) *DG:* D Williams
11 Sept	A	Ebbw Vale	32-20	*T:* P Riley, V Price, N Stent, A Williams *C:* M Watts (3) *PG:* M Watts (2)
18 Sept	H	Abertillery	21-11	*T:* D Neill, L Gilbey *C:* M Watts *PG:* M Watts (3)
25 Sept	A	Llandovery	10-20	*T:* A Williams *C:* M Watts *PG:* M Watts
2 Oct	H	Narberth	17-10	*T:* J Hopkins *PG:* M Watts (4)
9 Oct	A	Llanharan	24-5	*T:* H Lewis, B Davey, P Thomas *C:* M Watts (3) *PG:* M Watts
23 Oct	H	Penarth	36-0	*T:* G Harry, G Wilcox, H Lewis, L Morgan, B Davey *C:* M Watts (4) *DG:* M Watts
30 Oct	A	S Wales Police	10-15	*T:* G Wilcox *C:* M Watts *PG:* M Watts
6 Nov	H	Treorchy	9-19	*PG:* M Watts (3)
13 Nov	H	Glamorgan Wands	24-5	*T:* H Lewis, B Davey, S Thomas *C:* M Watts (3) *PG:* M Watts
20 Nov	A	Tenby Utd	5-3	*T:* H Lewis
27 Nov	A	Mountain Ash	6-12	*PG:* M Watts (2)
3 Dec	H	Ebbw Vale	6-6	*PG:* M Watts (2)

11 Dec	A	Abertillery	13-22	T: H Lewis C: M Watts PG: M Watts (2)
29 Jan	A	Narberth	23-12	T: P Riley, pen try C: M Watts (2) PG: M Watts (3)
5 Mar	H	Llanharan	23-17	T: R Jarvis, J Hopkins C: M Watts (2) PG: M Watts (2) DG: M Watts
22 Mar	H	Llandovery	26-10	T: R Boobyer, M Watts, H Lewis C: M Watts PG: M Watts (2) DG: M Watts
26 Mar	A	Penarth	6-10	PG: M Watts (2)
19 Apr	A	Treorchy	12-20	PG: M Watts (3) DG: M Watts
23 Apr	A	Glamorgan Wands	13-23	T: D Neil C: M Watts PG: M Watts (2)
26 Apr	H	S Wales Police	22-6	T: R Boobyer C: M Watts PG: M Watts (4) DG: M Watts
30 Apr	H	Tenby Utd	29-8	T: L Gilbey, M Wareham, P Buckle, N Walsh C: M Watts (3) PG: M Watts

Mountain Ash

Year of formation 1875
Ground Recreation Ground, Woodland Street, Mountain Ash
Tel: Mountain Ash (0443) 472918
Colours Black and amber
Most capped player L J Manfield (Wales) 7 caps
Captain 1993-94 N Eynon
1st XV 1993-94   P40   W21   D1   L18   F746   A541
Heineken League Div 2 11th *relegated* **SWALEC Cup** Lost 0-18 to Dunvant
(4th round)

League Record 1993-94

Date	Venue	Opponents	Result	Scorers
4 Sept	A	Maesteg	5-9	T: R Johnson
11 Sept	H	Tenby Utd	21-9	T: R Johnson, J Gibbon C: C Conway PG: C Conway (3)
18 Sept	A	Glamorgan Wands	17-13	T: S Pascoe PG: C Conway (4)
25 Sept	A	Ebbw Vale	0-27	
2 Oct	H	Abertillery	10-15	T: S Pascoe C: C Conway PG: C Conway
9 Oct	A	Llandovery	8-9	T: D Moseley PG: C Conway
23 Oct	H	Narberth	11-21	T: R Johnson PG: J Mason (2)
30 Oct	A	Llanharan	13-5	T: D Moseley C: K Price PG: K Price, J Mason
6 Nov	H	Penarth	19-29	T: J Mason, N Williams, J Downes C: J Mason (2)
20 Nov	H	Treorchy	9-18	PG: J Mason (3)
27 Nov	H	Maesteg	12-6	PG: K Price (3) DG: K Price
4 Dec	A	Tenby Utd	14-22	T: N Williams PG: K Price (3)
11 Dec	H	Glamorgan Wands	7-30	T: K Price C: J Mason
22 Jan	H	Ebbw Vale	28-3	T: K Price, M Bennett, N Williams C: J Mason (2) PG: J Mason (3)
29 Jan	A	Abertillery	6-8	PG: J Mason (2)
12 Mar	A	S Wales Police	3-15	PG: K Price
26 Mar	A	Narberth	8-12	T: M Cushion PG: N Price
2 Apr	H	Llandovery	12-22	PG: J Mason (4)
9 Apr	H	Llanharan	30-11	T: N Eynon, pen try C: J Mason PG: J Mason (4) DG: C Conway, M Bennett
16 Apr	A	Penarth	11-6	T: M Butts PG: J Mason (2)
23 Apr	H	S Wales Police	20-6	T: N Williams PG: J Mason (5)
30 Apr	A	Treorchy	11-37	T: M Cushion PG: J Mason (2)

Narberth

Year of formation 1882
Ground Lewis Lloyd Ground, Spring Gardens, Narberth, Dyfed
Tel: Narberth (0834) 860462
Colours Sky blue and navy hoops

Captain 1993-94 D Setaro
1st XV 1993-94   P42   W22   D1   L19   F677   A582
Heineken League Div 2 7th   **SWALEC Cup** Lost 14-25 to Tenby Utd (6th round)

League Record 1993-94

Date	Venue	Opponents	Result	Scorers
4 Sept	A	Llanharan	20-8	*T:* C Phillips, B Evans, M Roderick *C:* S Pearce *DG:* S Pearce
11 Sept	H	Penarth	21-13	*T:* M Roderick, C Phillips *C:* S Pearce *PG:* S Pearce (2) *DG:* B Evans
18 Sept	A	S Wales Police	15-21	*T:* M Roderick, S Pearce *C:* S Pearce *DG:* S Pearce
25 Sept	H	Treorchy	8-20	*T:* S Gerrard *PG:* S Pearce
2 Oct	A	Maesteg	10-17	*T:* G Jones *C:* S Pearce *PG:* S Pearce
17 Oct	H	Tenby Utd	3-6	*PG:* S Pearce
23 Oct	A	Mountain Ash	21-11	*T:* I Matthews, C Phillips *C:* S Pearce *PG:* S Pearce (2) *DG:* S Pearce
30 Oct	H	Ebbw Vale	13-15	*T:* I Jones *C:* S Pearce *PG:* S Pearce (2)
6 Nov	A	Abertillery	9-20	*PG:* S Pearce (2) *DG:* S Pearce
13 Nov	H	Llandovery	6-0	*PG:* S Pearce (2)
20 Nov	A	Glamorgan Wands	23-0	*T:* C Phillips (2), R Jones *C:* S Pearce *PG:* S Pearce (2)
27 Nov	H	Llanharan	14-3	*T:* R Jones *PG:* S Pearce (3)
4 Dec	A	Penarth	14-10	*T:* A Young *PG:* S Pearce (3)
11 Dec	H	S Wales Police	14-3	*T:* C Phillips *PG:* S Pearce (2) *DG:* S Pearce
8 Jan	A	Treorchy	10-14	*T:* D Setaro *C:* S Pearce *PG:* S Pearce
29 Jan	H	Maesteg	12-23	*PG:* S Pearce (4)
5 Mar	A	Tenby Utd	18-7	*T:* I Jones (2) *C:* S Pearce *PG:* S Pearce (2)
26 Mar	H	Mountain Ash	12-8	*PG:* S Pearce (3) *DG:* S Pearce
16 Apr	H	Abertillery	0-21	
19 Apr	A	Ebbw Vale	10-23	*T:* R Evans *C:* S Pearce *PG:* S Pearce
23 Apr	A	Llandovery	3-14	*PG:* S Pearce
30 Apr	H	Glamorgan Wands	17-37	*T:* C Phillips *PG:* L Rogers (4)

Neath

Year of formation 1871
Ground The Gnoll, Gnoll Park Road, Neath, West Glamorgan   Tel: Neath (0639) 636547
Colours Black with white Maltese cross
Most capped player P H Thorburn (Wales) 37 caps
Captain 1993-94 G O Llewellyn
1st XV 1993-94   P40   W33   D2   L5   F1131   A404
Heineken League Div 1 2nd   **SWALEC Cup** Lost 3-7 to Llanelli (semi-final)

League Record 1993-94

Date	Venue	Opponents	Result	Scorers
4 Sept	H	Pontypridd	22-22	*T:* M Singer *C:* P Thorburn *PG:* P Thorburn (5)
8 Sept	A	Pontypool	43-20	*T:* A Varney (2), J Reynolds (2), R Jones, pen try *C:* P Thorburn (2) *PG:* P Thorburn (3)
11 Sept	H	Bridgend	33-11	*T:* M Singer (2), B Williams *C:* P Thorburn (3) *PG:* P Thorburn (4)
18 Sept	A	Newport	19-16	*T:* Barrie Williams, M McCarthy *PG:* P Thorburn (3)
25 Sept	H	Swansea	40-18	*T:* J Davies, A Varney, Brian Williams, N Lewis, pen try *C:* P Thorburn (3) *PG:* P Thorburn (3)
2 Oct	A	Aberavon	10-0	*T:* A Shaw *C:* P Thorburn *PG:* P Thorburn
23 Oct	H	Cardiff	11-6	*T:* M McCarthy *PG:* P Thorburn, M McCarthy
30 Oct	A	Newbridge	17-11	*T:* R Jones, S Williams (2) *C:* M McCarthy
6 Nov	H	Dunvant	26-14	*T:* A Harries (2), S Crandon, A Shaw *C:* P Thorburn (3)

20 Nov	H	Llanelli	27-5	*T:* A Shaw, M McCarthy, C Bridges
				C: P Thorburn (3) *PG:* P Thorburn (2)
27 Nov	A	Pontypridd	12-27	*PG:* P Thorburn (4)
30 Nov	H	Pontypool	71-10	*T:* I Boobyer (3), N Lewis (2), A Shaw (2), R Rees,
				P Thorburn, J Davies, H Woodland
				C: P Thorburn (8)
6 Dec	A	Bridgend	37-15	*T:* S Williams (4), H Woodland
				C: P Thorburn (3) *PG:* P Thorburn (2)
11 Dec	H	Newport	28-17	*T:* R Rees (2), pen try *C:* P Thorburn (2)
				PG: P Thorburn (3)
29 Jan	H	Aberavon	27-3	*T:* Glyn Llewellyn, P Thorburn, A Harries, pen try
				C: P Thorburn (2) *PG:* P Thorburn
5 Mar	A	Cardiff	8-14	*T:* H Woodland *PG:* P Thorburn
8 Mar	A	Cross Keys	17-11	*T:* M Morris *PG:* P Thorburn (4)
23 Mar	A	Swansea	0-15	
26 Mar	H	Newbridge	47-20	*T:* R Jones (2), J Reynolds (2), H Woodland (2),
				P Thorburn *C:* P Thorburn (2), J Bird
				PG: P Thorburn (2)
9 Apr	A	Dunvant	10-10	*T:* H Woodland, J Davies
23 Apr	H	Cross Keys	56-10	*T:* J Reynolds (2), P Thorburn, A Harries,
				H Woodland, M McCarthy, C Bridges, B Williams,
				I Boobyer, R Jones *C:* J Bird (2), P Thorburn
30 Apr	A	Llanelli	20-11	*T:* Glyn Llewellyn, S Crandon, R Jones
				C: P Thorburn *PG:* P Thorburn

Newbridge

Year of formation 1888
Ground The Welfare Ground, Bridge Street, Newbridge, Gwent
Tel: Newbridge (0495) 243247
Colours Blue and black hoops
Most capped player D Hayward (Wales) 15 caps
Captain 1993-94 A Collins
1st XV 1993-94 P40 W21 D1 L18 F937 A605
Heineken League Div 1 8th **SWALEC Cup** Lost 10-32 to Pontypridd (quarter-final)

League Record 1993-94

Date	Venue	Opponents	Result	Scorers
4 Sept	H	Swansea	11-15	*T:* A Glasson *PG:* A Green (2)
11 Sept	H	Cardiff	0-36	
18 Sept	H	Pontypridd	17-21	*T:* A Harries *PG:* A Green (4)
25 Sept	A	Dunvant	6-20	*PG:* W Taylor (2)
2 Oct	H	Cross Keys	25-6	*T:* J Hawker, W Taylor, P Crane *C:* A Green (2)
				PG: A Green (2)
9 Oct	A	Aberavon	28-8	*T:* J Churcher, A Griffiths, A Green, S Reed
				C: A Green *PG:* W Taylor, A Green
23 Oct	A	Llanelli	14-35	*T:* W Taylor, J Churcher *C:* A Green, W Taylor
30 Oct	H	Neath	11-17	*T:* G Harding *PG:* A Green (2)
6 Nov	A	Pontypool	25-0	*T:* J Churcher, W Grimstead *PG:* A Green (2),
				J Churcher (2), W Taylor
20 Nov	A	Newport	17-17	*T:* A Lucas, J Hawker *C:* A Green (2)
				PG: A Green
27 Nov	A	Swansea	6-26	*PG:* A Green *DG:* J Churcher
5 Dec	A	Cardiff	3-33	*PG:* A Green
11 Dec	A	Pontypridd	18-43	*T:* D Roberts, S Fealey *C:* A Green
				PG: A Green (2)
8 Jan	H	Aberavon	19-6	*T:* P Crane (2) *PG:* A Green (3)
29 Jan	A	Cross Keys	42-3	*T:* S Fealey (2), P Edwards, J Hawker, D Hooper,
				A Green, P Kawulok, K Waters *C:* A Green
12 Feb	H	Dunvant	16-0	*T:* D Hooper, A Lucas *PG:* W Taylor, A Green
5 Mar	H	Llanelli	37-20	*T:* G Harding (2), K Waters, A Gibbs, P Edwards,
				W Taylor *C:* A Green (2) *PG:* A Green

26 Mar	A	Neath	20-47	*T:* D Roberts, S Reed *C:* A Green (2) *PG:* A Green *DG:* A Green
9 Apr	H	Pontypool	10-11	*T:* A Sutton *C:* W Taylor *PG:* A Green
16 Apr	H	Bridgend	11-38	*T:* K Waters *PG:* A Green (2)
23 Apr	A	Bridgend	18-22	*T:* A Gibbs, S Fealey *C:* A Green *PG:* A Green, W Taylor
30 Apr	H	Newport	13-16	*T:* D Churchill *C:* A Green *PG:* A Green (2)

Newport

Year of formation 1874
Ground Rodney Parade, Rodney Road, Newport, Gwent
Tel: Newport (0633) 258193 or 267410
Colours Black and amber hoops
Most capped player K J Jones (Wales) 44 caps
Captain 1993-94 R A Bidgood
1st XV 1993-94 P39 W20 D2 L17 F891 A735
Heineken League Div 1 7th **SWALEC Cup** Lost 9-10 to Ystradgynlais (5th round)

League Record 1993-94

Date	*Venue*	*Opponents*	*Result*	*Scorers*
4 Sept	A	Dunvant	7-12	*T:* M Yendle *C:* D Rees
8 Sept	H	Cross Keys	23-20	*T:* D Rees, D Hughes *C:* D Rees (2) *PG:* D Rees (2), J Williams
11 Sept	A	Llanelli	8-44	*T:* S McCracken *PG:* D Rees
18 Sept	H	Neath	16-19	*T:* R Bidgood *C:* D Rees *PG:* D Rees (3)
25 Sept	A	Pontypool	35-21	*T:* J Goodchild (2), J Alvis, D Hughes, S McCracken *C:* D Rees (2) *PG:* D Rees (2)
2 Oct	H	Bridgend	11-24	*T:* D Llewellyn *PG:* D Rees (2)
23 Oct	A	Pontypridd	14-31	*T:* A Carter *PG:* D Rees (2) *DG:* J Williams
30 Oct	A	Swansea	3-30	*PG:* D Rees
6 Nov	H	Aberavon	30-6	*T:* D Llewellyn (2), J Alvis, D Rees *C:* D Rees (2) *PG:* D Rees (2)
13 Nov	A	Cardiff	3-52	*PG:* D Rees
20 Nov	H	Newbridge	17-17	*T:* R Bidgood *PG:* D Rees (4)
27 Nov	H	Dunvant	13-9	*T:* D Gray *C:* D Rees *PG:* D Rees (2)
1 Dec	A	Cross Keys	13-7	*T:* A Lewis *C:* J Williams *PG:* J Williams, D Rees
4 Dec	H	Llanelli	22-14	*T:* C Wyatt (2), A Lewis *C:* D Rees (2) *DG:* D Rees
11 Dec	A	Neath	17-28	*T:* D Rees, D Llewellyn *C:* D Rees (2) *PG:* D Rees
8 Jan	H	Pontypool	5-14	*T:* J Williams
29 Jan	A	Bridgend	14-17	*T:* J Goodchild, R Goodey *C:* D Hughes (2)
5 Mar	H	Pontypridd	30-32	*T:* M Yendle (2), I Jeffreys *C:* D Hughes (3) *PG:* D Hughes (3)
26 Mar	H	Swansea	22-27	*T:* R Goodey, A Lewis *PG:* G Rees (4)
9 Apr	A	Aberavon	21-13	*T:* G Rees, B Atkins *C:* G Rees *PG:* G Rees (3)
23 Apr	H	Cardiff	22-22	*T:* A Dibble, D Llewellyn *PG:* G Rees (4)
30 Apr	A	Newbridge	16-13	*T:* B Atkins, M Evans *PG:* D Hughes (2)

Penarth

Year of formation 1880
Ground Athletic Field, Lavernock Road, Penarth, South Glamorgan
Tel: Penarth (0222) 708402
Colours Royal blue with white chevron
Most capped player J A Bassett (Wales) 15 caps
Captain 1993-94 T Crothers
1st XV 1993-94 P36 W15 D0 L21 F599 A589
Heineken League Div 2 8th **SWALEC Cup** Lost 8-21 to Bridgend (4th round)

League Record 1993-94

Date	Venue	Opponents	Result	Scorers
4 Sept	H	Llandovery	9-16	*PG:* C Miller (3)
11 Sept	A	Narberth	13-21	*T:* T Crothers *C:* M Thomas *PG:* M Thomas (2)
18 Sept	H	Llanharan	6-17	*PG:* A Rosser (2)
25 Sept	H	Glamorgan Wands	17-13	*T:* I Fifield, C Miller *C:* C Miller (2) *PG:* C Miller
2 Oct	A	S Wales Police	22-8	*T:* S Crothers, A Rosser, I Fifield *C:* C Miller (2) *PG:* C Miller
9 Oct	H	Treorchy	8-20	*T:* M Parry *PG:* C Miller
23 Oct	A	Maesteg	0-36	
30 Oct	H	Tenby Utd	25-33	*T:* C Miller (2), R Phillips *C:* A Rosser (2) *PG:* A Rosser *DG:* A Rosser
6 Nov	A	Mountain Ash	29-19	*T:* I Fifield, M Parry, R Phillips, M Edwards *C:* A Rosser (3) *PG:* A Rosser
13 Nov	H	Ebbw Vale	11-15	*T:* S Crothers *PG:* A Rosser (2)
20 Nov	A	Abertillery	3-47	*PG:* A Rosser
27 Nov	A	Llandovery	21-11	*T:* M Liddiat, R Phillips, S Thomas *PG:* A Rosser (2)
4 Dec	H	Narberth	10-14	*T:* I Fifield *C:* C Miller *PG:* C Miller
11 Dec	A	Llanharan	15-18	*T:* P Cousins, D Williams *C:* C Miller *PG:* C Miller
26 Feb	A	Glamorgan Wands	3-6	*PG:* A Rosser
26 Mar	H	Maesteg	10-6	*T:* T Crothers *C:* C Miller *PG:* C Miller
2 Apr	A	Treorchy	14-18	*T:* C Miller *PG:* C Miller (3)
9 Apr	A	Tenby Utd	11-3	*T:* T Crothers *PG:* C Miller (2)
13 Apr	H	S Wales Police	20-17	*T:* C Howells, M Edwards, J Allen *C:* C Miller *PG:* C Miller
16 Apr	H	Mountain Ash	6-11	*PG:* C Miller (2)
23 Apr	A	Ebbw Vale	20-17	*T:* S Crothers, J Allen *C:* C Miller (2) *PG:* C Miller *DG:* C Miller
30 Apr	H	Abertillery	18-6	*T:* M Thomas, A Rosser *C:* C Miller *PG:* C Miller (2)

Pontypool

Year of formation 1868 (reconstituted 1901)
Ground The Park, Pontypool, Gwent   Tel: Pontypool (0495) 763492 or 762524
Colours Red, white and black hoops
Most capped player G Price (Wales) 41 caps
Captain 1993-94 M G Ring
1st XV 1993-94   P38   W17   D1   L20   F721   A867
Heineken League Div 1 9th **SWALEC Cup** Lost 6-16 to Cardiff (4th round)

League Record 1993-94

Date	Venue	Opponents	Result	Scorers
4 Sept	A	Llanelli	17-31	*T:* N Hope, S White *C:* I Bebb (2) *PG:* I Bebb
8 Sept	H	Neath	20-43	*T:* G Taylor (2) *C:* I Bebb (2) *PG:* I Bebb (2)
11 Sept	A	Pontypridd	18-51	*T:* B Taylor, M Taylor *C:* I Bebb *PG:* I Bebb (2)
18 Sept	A	Bridgend	20-74	*T:* I Bebb, M Bernard *C:* M Ring (2) *PG:* M Ring (2)
25 Sept	H	Newport	21-35	*T:* A Newbury, B Taylor *C:* M Ring *PG:* M Ring (3)
2 Oct	A	Swansea	10-30	*T:* L Jones *C:* M Ring *PG:* M Ring
23 Oct	H	Aberavon	16-11	*T:* pen try *C:* M Ring *PG:* M Ring (3)
30 Oct	A	Cardiff	0-78	
6 Nov	H	Newbridge	0-25	
13 Nov	A	Dunvant	10-13	*T:* J McCarthy *C:* M Ring *PG:* M Ring
20 Nov	H	Cross Keys	17-3	*T:* M Ring *PG:* M Ring (2) *DG:* M Taylor, L Jones
27 Nov	H	Llanelli	9-20	*PG:* M Ring (2) *DG:* M Ring

30 Nov	A	Neath	10-71	*T:* L Jones *C:* M Ring *PG:* M Ring
5 Dec	H	Pontypridd	14-39	*T:* pen try *PG:* M Ring (3)
11 Dec	H	Bridgend	29-23	*T:* G Taylor, H Jones *C:* M Ring (2)
				PG: M Ring (3), I Reynolds *DG:* M Ring
· 8 Jan	A	Newport	14-5	*T:* H Jones *PG:* M Ring (3)
29 Jan	H	Swansea	9-16	*PG:* M Ring (3)
5 Mar	A	Aberavon	9-11	*PG:* M Ring (3)
26 Mar	H	Cardiff	16-17	*T:* M Ring *C:* M Ring *PG:* M Ring (2)
				DG: M Ring
9 Apr	A	Newbridge	11-10	*T:* Mark Taylor *PG:* J Williams (2)
23 Apr	H	Dunvant	18-3	*T:* Mark Taylor, P Hewitt *C:* J Williams
				PG: J Williams, M Ring
30 Apr	A	Cross Keys	24-17	*PG:* J Williams (8)

Pontypridd

Year of formation 1876
Ground Sardis Road Ground, Pwllgwaun, Pontypridd   Tel: Pontypridd (0433) 405006
Colours Black and white hoops
Most capped player N R Jenkins (Wales) 21 caps
Captain 1993-94 N Bezani
1st XV 1993-94 P43 W34 D1 L8 F1210 A512
Heineken League Div 1 3rd **SWALEC Cup** Lost 6-8 to Cardiff (semi-final)

League Record 1993-94

Date	*Venue*	*Opponents*	*Result*	*Scorers*
4 Sept	A	Neath	22-22	*T:* D Manley (3) *C:* N Jenkins (2)
				PG: N Jenkins
7 Sept	H	Cardiff	17-24	*T:* P Thomas *PG:* N Jenkins (4)
11 Sept	H	Pontypool	51-18	*T:* G Prosser (2), M Lloyd (2), P John, D Manley
				C: N Jenkins (3) *PG:* N Jenkins (5)
18 Sept	A	Newbridge	21-17	*T:* D Manley (2) *C:* N Jenkins
				PG: N Jenkins (3)
25 Sept	H	Bridgend	26-14	*T:* O Robbins, D Manley *C:* N Jenkins (2)
				PG: N Jenkins (3) *DG:* N Jenkins
23 Oct	H	Newport	31-14	*T:* N Jenkins, C Cormack, R Davies
				C: N Jenkins (2) *PG:* N Jenkins (4)
30 Oct	A	Cross Keys	20-10	*T:* D Manley (2), O Robbins, N Jenkins
6 Nov	H	Swansea	15-25	*PG:* N Jenkins (5)
13 Nov	A	Llanelli	6-8	*PG:* N Jenkins (2)
20 Nov	H	Aberavon	28-7	*T:* R Collins (2), N Jenkins *C:* N Jenkins (2)
				PG: N Jenkins (3)
27 Nov	H	Neath	27-12	*T:* D Manley (2) *C:* N Jenkins
				PG: N Jenkins (5)
1 Dec	A	Cardiff	15-10	*PG:* N Jenkins (5)
5 Dec	A	Pontypool	39-14	*T:* D Manley (2) *C:* C Cormack
				PG: N Jenkins (9)
11 Dec	H	Newbridge	43-18	*T:* P John, O Robbins, M Back, N Jenkins
				C: N Jenkins (4) *PG:* N Jenkins (5)
3 Jan	A	Bridgend	27-5	*T:* D Manley, O Robbins, D McIntosh, pen try
				C: N Jenkins (2) *PG:* N Jenkins
29 Jan	H	Dunvant	53-8	*T:* C Cormack (2), J Lewis, D Manley, G Prosser,
				M Lloyd, R Collins, N Jenkins *C:* N Jenkins (5)
				PG: N Jenkins
5 Mar	A	Newport	32-30	*T:* D McIntosh, O Robbins, G Jones, S Lewis,
				J Lewis *C:* C Cormack (2) *PG:* C Cormack
22 Mar	A	Dunvant	29-9	*T:* C Cormack, S Lewis *C:* N Jenkins (2)
				PG: N Jenkins (4) *DG:* N Jenkins
26 Mar	H	Cross Keys	25-5	*T:* M Back, pen try, P John *C:* C Cormack (2)
				PG: C Cormack (2)
9 Apr	A	Swansea	6-17	*PG:* N Jenkins (2)
23 Apr	H	Llanelli	31-7	*T:* N Jenkins (2), G Jones, N Bezani, P John
				C: N Jenkins (3)
30 Apr	A	Aberavon	7-5	*T:* D Manley *C:* C Cormack

South Wales Police

Year of formation 1969
Ground Waterton Cross, Bridgend, Mid-Glamorgan   Tel: Bridgend (0656) 655555 ext 218
Colours Red shirts with white shorts and blue stockings
Most capped player B Bowen (Wales) 22 caps
Captain 1993-94 R Williams
1st XV 1993-94 P40   W25   D1   L14   F801   A616
Heineken League Div 2 4th **SWALEC Cup** Lost 13-20 to Cardiff (quarter-final)

League Record 1993-94

Date	Venue	Opponents	Result	Scorers
4 Sept	H	Abertillery	15-7	T: J Griffiths, J Price C: J Price PG: J Price
11 Sept	A	Llandovery	10-3	T: C Higgs, J Payne
18 Sept	H	Narberth	21-15	T: S Parfitt, A Davies C: A Hughes PG: A Hughes (2), J Price
25 Sept	A	Llanharan	12-16	T: S Parfitt, pen try C: J Price
2 Oct	H	Penarth	8-22	T: C Higgs DG: J Price
9 Oct	H	Glamorgan Wands	28-12	T: J Payne, D Thomas, J Price C: J Price (2) PG: J Price (3)
23 Oct	A	Treorchy	18-34	PG: G Jones (5) DG: G Jones
30 Oct	H	Maesteg	15-10	PG: J Price (4) DG: J Price
6 Nov	A	Tenby Utd	12-14	T: M Cox, C Higgs C: J Price
20 Nov	A	Ebbw Vale	20-8	T: J Williams (2), R Erskine, S Legge
27 Nov	A	Abertillery	10-36	T: C Higgs C: J Price PG: J Price
4 Dec	H	Llandovery	37-19	T: I Hemburrow (2), M Cox (2), J Price C: J Price (3) PG: J Price (2)
11 Dec	A	Narberth	3-14	PG: J Price
5 Mar	A	Glamorgan Wands	20-0	T: I Hemburrow (2) C: J Price (2) PG: J Price (2)
12 Mar	H	Mountain Ash	15-3	T: J Apsee, A Phillips C: J Price PG: J Price
16 Mar	H	Llanharan	11-14	T: R Williams PG: J Price (2)
26 Mar	H	Treorchy	13-10	T: I Hemburrow, J Apsee PG: J Price
13 Apr	A	Penarth	17-20	T: I Hemburrow, J Williams C: J Price (2) PG: J Price
16 Apr	H	Tenby Utd	47-18	T: D Thomas, I Hemburrow, A Hughes, J Price, M Cox, G Bundock C: J Price (4) PG: J Price (3)
23 Apr	A	Mountain Ash	6-20	PG: J Price (2)
26 Apr	A	Maesteg	6-22	PG: J Price (2)
30 Apr	H	Ebbw Vale	23-16	T: C Hillman, S Legge C: J Price (2) PG: J Price (3)

Swansea

Year of formation 1873
Ground St Helen's, Bryn Road, Swansea, West Glamorgan   Tel: Swansea (0792) 466593
Colours All white
Most capped player R N Jones (Wales) 47 caps
Captain 1993-94 Stuart Davies
1st XV 1993-94 P40   W36   D1   L3   F1185   A552
Heineken League Div 1 *Winners* **SWALEC Cup** Lost 3-13 to Pontypridd (6th round)

League Record 1993-94

Date	Venue	Opponents	Result	Scorers
4 Sept	A	Newbridge	15-11	T: R Webster (2), Simon Davies
8 Sept	H	Dunvant	37-11	T: S Barclay (2), Stuart Davies, J Ball, G Jenkins, R Webster C: B Childs (2) PG: B Childs
11 Sept	A	Cross Keys	19-3	T: M Titley, I Davies, Simon Davies C: A Williams (2)

18 Sept	H	Llanelli	22-12	*T:* R Webster *C:* A Williams
				PG: A Williams (5)
25 Sept	A	Neath	18-40	*T:* M Titley, Stuart Davies *C:* B Childs
				PG: B Childs (2)
2 Oct	H	Pontypool	30-10	*T:* A Clement, A Williams *C:* A Williams
				PG: A Williams (5) *DG:* A Williams
23 Oct	A	Bridgend	20-16	*T:* A Williams (2) *C:* A Williams (2)
				PG: A Williams (2)
30 Oct	H	Newport	30-3	*T:* D Weatherley, S Barclay, S Gibbs, A Williams
				C: A Williams (2) *PG:* A Williams (2)
6 Nov	A	Pontypridd	25-15	*T:* P Arnold *C:* A Williams *PG:* A Williams (5)
				DG: A Williams
13 Nov	A	Aberavon	10-3	*T:* S Gibbs, I Davies
20 Nov	H	Cardiff	22-6	*T:* Simon Davies, S Gibbs, I Davies
				C: A Williams (2) *PG:* A Williams
27 Nov	H	Newbridge	26-6	*T:* R Jones, I Davies *C:* A Williams (2)
				PG: A Williams (3) *DG:* A Williams
1 Dec	A	Dunvant	14-13	*T:* Simon Davies *PG:* A Williams (3)
4 Dec	H	Cross Keys	95-22	*T:* I Jones (3), D Weatherley (2), S Barclay (2),
				M Titley (2), I Davies (2), I Lewis, A Williams,
				M Evans, R Jones *C:* M Titley (2), A Williams (7)
11 Dec	A	Llanelli	13-20	*T:* R Appleyard *C:* A Williams
				PG: A Williams (2)
29 Jan	A	Pontypool	16-9	*T:* I Davies, Simon Davies *PG:* A Williams (2)
5 Mar	H	Bridgend	23-14	*T:* Simon Davies (2), I Jones *C:* J Ball
				PG: J Ball (2)
23 Mar	H	Neath	15-0	*T:* R Jones, A Reynolds *C:* P Withers
				PG: P Withers
26 Mar	A	Newport	27-22	*T:* P Withers, A Reynolds, A Clement, P Arnold,
				Simon Davies *C:* P Withers
9 Apr	H	Pontypridd	17-6	*T:* P Withers, Stuart Davies, R Jones
				C: P Withers
23 Apr	H	Aberavon	32-3	*T:* Simon Davies, P Arnold, G Jenkins, pen try
				C: A Williams (3) *PG:* A Williams (2)
30 Apr	A	Cardiff	23-19	*T:* J Forster, J Ball *C:* P Withers (2)
				PG: P Withers *DG:* A Booth, D Weatherley

Tenby United

Year of formation 1901
Ground Heywood Lane, Tenby, Dyfed   Tel: Tenby (0834) 842909 and 843501
Colours Black and scarlet hoops
Captain 1993-94 M Evans
1st XV 1993-94 P36 W21 D1 L14 F691 A548
Heineken League Div 2 5th **SWALEC Cup** Lost 17-35 to Maesteg (quarter-final)

League Record 1993-94

Date	*Venue*	*Opponents*	*Result*	*Scorers*
4 Sept	H	Glamorgan Wands	22-6	*T:* J Bainbridge *C:* P Sutton *PG:* P Sutton (3),
				G Thomas (2)
11 Sept	A	Mountain Ash	9-21	*PG:* P Sutton (3)
18 Sept	H	Ebbw Vale	24-13	*T:* M Evans, P Sutton, D Balkwill
				PG: P Sutton (3)
25 Sept	A	Abertillery	13-44	*T:* D Hadley *C:* P Sutton *PG:* P Sutton (2)
2 Oct	H	Llandovery	32-13	*T:* J Bainbridge, C Goodwin, R Evans, S Hartland,
				P Sutton *C:* P Sutton (2) *DG:* P Sutton
17 Oct	A	Narberth	6-3	*PG:* P Sutton (2)
23 Oct	H	Llanharan	19-6	*T:* P Morris, M Griffiths *PG:* J Richards (2)
				DG: J Richards
30 Oct	A	Penarth	33-25	*T:* S Hartland, M Griffiths, C Goodwin
				C: P Sutton (3) *PG:* P Sutton (4)
6 Nov	H	S Wales Police	14-12	*T:* R Evans (2) *C:* P Sutton, G Thomas
13 Nov	A	Treorchy	5-12	*T:* R Evans

20 Nov	H	Maesteg	3-5	*PG:* G Scotcher
27 Nov	A	Glamorgan Wands	9-21	*PG:* P Sutton (3)
4 Dec	H	Mountain Ash	22-14	*T:* M Griffiths, C Goodwin *PG:* P Sutton (4)
11 Dec	A	Ebbw Vale	9-13	*PG:* P Sutton (3)
3 Jan	H	Abertillery	15-12	*T:* S Hartland, G Thomas *C:* P Sutton *PG:* P Sutton
29 Jan	A	Llandovery	24-9	*T:* M Evans, R Evans, D Balkwill *C:* G Scotcher (3) *PG:* G Scotcher
5 Mar	H	Narberth	7-18	*T:* C Goodwin *C:* P Sutton
26 Mar	A	Llanharan	13-21	*T:* N Truman *C:* G Scotcher *PG:* G Scotcher *DG:* G Scotcher
9 Apr	H	Penarth	3-11	*PG:* D Bowen
16 Apr	A	S Wales Police	18-47	*T:* J Bainbridge (2) *C:* D Bowen *PG:* D Bowen (2)
23 Apr	H	Treorchy	0-11	
30 Apr	A	Maesteg	8-29	*T:* C Goodwin *PG:* D Bowen

Treorchy

Year of formation 1886
Ground The Zebras, The Oval, Treorchy, Rhondda Tel: Treorchy (0443) 434671
Colours Black and white hoops
Most capped player W Cummins (Wales)/D Jenkins (Wales) 4 caps
Captain 1993-94 P Knight
1st XV 1993-94 P36 W29 D1 L6 F777 A444
Heineken League Div 2 *Winners – promoted* **SWALEC Cup** Lost 6-28 to Pontypridd
(4th round)

League Record 1993-94

Date	*Venue*	*Opponents*	*Result*	*Scorers*
4 Sept	H	Ebbw Vale	6-5	*PG:* L Evans *DG:* L Evans
11 Sept	A	Abertillery	21-16	*PG:* L Evans (6) *DG:* A Dunn
18 Sept	H	Llandovery	25-6	*T:* K Orrell, S Evans, D Hughes, R Davies *C:* L Evans *PG:* L Evans
25 Sept	A	Narberth	20-8	*T:* A Jones (2) *C:* A Dunn, D Lloyd *PG:* A Dunn (2)
2 Oct	H	Llanharan	31-11	*T:* P Thomas, A Jones, L Evans *C:* L Evans (2) *PG:* L Evans (4)
9 Oct	A	Penarth	20-8	*T:* D Evans *PG:* L Evans (4), D Evans
23 Oct	H	S Wales Police	34-18	*T:* C Hammans (2), L Evans (2), D Hughes *C:* L Evans (3) *PG:* L Evans
30 Oct	H	Glamorgan Wands	24-0	*T:* K Jones, D Jones, K Orrell, D Hughes *C:* D Lloyd (2)
6 Nov	A	Maesteg	19-9	*T:* K Orrell, C Greedy *PG:* L Evans (3)
13 Nov	H	Tenby Utd	12-5	*PG:* L Evans (4)
20 Nov	A	Mountain Ash	18-9	*T:* K Orrell, C Greedy *C:* L Evans *PG:* L Evans (2)
27 Nov	A	Ebbw Vale	15-10	*T:* D Lloyd, D Hughes *C:* D Evans *PG:* D Evans
3 Dec	H	Abertillery	26-10	*T:* D Hughes, D Evans *C:* L Evans (2) *PG:* L Evans (4)
11 Dec	A	Llandovery	11-11	*T:* L Evans *PG:* L Evans (2)
8 Jan	H	Narberth	14-10	*T:* D Evans *PG:* L Evans (2) *DG:* L Evans
26 Mar	A	S Wales Police	10-13	*T:* L Evans *C:* L Evans *PG:* L Evans
2 Apr	H	Penarth	18-14	*T:* S Williams, J Burnell *C:* D Evans *PG:* D Evans *DG:* L Evans
9 Apr	A	Glamorgan Wands	13-0	*T:* M Rowe *C:* L Evans *PG:* L Evans (2)
13 Apr	A	Llanharan	20-14	*T:* K Orrell, C Hammans, M Jones *C:* D Evans *PG:* D Evans
19 Apr	H	Maesteg	20-12	*T:* M Rowe *PG:* D Evans (4) *DG:* D Evans
23 Apr	A	Tenby Utd	11-0	*T:* L Evans *PG:* D Evans (2)
30 Apr	H	Mountain Ash	37-11	*T:* P Thomas, K Orrell, A Jones, S Williams, G Owen, D Lloyd *C:* D Evans (2) *PG:* D Evans

THE GAME GROWS EVER LARGER IN ENGLAND'S CHAMPIONSHIP YEAR

WOMEN'S RUGBY 1993-94
Alice Cooper

WORLD CHAMPIONSHIPS
11-24 April 1994, Edinburgh

The second World Cup was renamed the World Championships to avoid confusion with the men's game but it had more than enough confusion of its own. For reasons that remain both curious and clouded, the Dutch organisers pulled out of the tournament on 1 January, news which was greeted with universal dismay. The ensuing gloom soon lifted, however, when the Scots picked up the tournament and got it back on its feet and running smoothly. In just 90 days, they organised an outstanding event in which the host team came fifth – an extraordinary achievement considering they did not play their first full international until February 1993.

However, of the original 16 entries, only 12 registered for the new event – New Zealand were banned by the NZRFU and the Dutch, Italian and Arabian Gulf teams withdrew. To add to the organisational nightmares, Spain pulled out due to financial problems just two weeks before the tournament. The Scottish Students stepped in to take their place but with the middle tier of ability missing, the pool rounds were tediously one-sided affairs. Only Pool D – from which Kazakhstan emerged as the new rugby nation to watch – had a competitive edge to it.

In the semi-finals, Wales met America and, despite losing 15-56, fully exposed the weakness of the American forwards. At the end of the game, the Welsh captain declined an invitation to teach the Americans how to do a rolling maul. In the other semi, a lacklustre performance by England produced an unconvincing win over France by 18-6. By the final, the Americans looked unbeatable with an astonishing average of 91 points. Their opponents, England, had used their full squad during the other matches and, unlike in the 1991 final, when the first XV had been exhausted, the first-choice English players were fit and ready.

The final was an outstanding demonstration of women's rugby at its best. The Americans were totally dominated in the forwards and gave away two penalty tries by collapsing five-metre scrums. But once their backs got the ball, their speed and handling was a delight. England, however, played to their strengths, taking several penalties as scrums. Captain Karen Almond provided consistently precise kicking from fly-half, and, despite their excellent backs, the Americans never looked like winning.

During the World Cup, 11 countries attended a conference held to form an international organisation for controlling and co-ordinating

England's Gill Burns wins a line-out in the 1994 Women's World Championship final, in which the English overcame the USA by 38-23.

the women's game prior to full IRFB integration. The Women's International Advisory Committee for Rugby was established and the following executive was elected: chair: Canada (Jill Zonneveld), secretary: England (Rosie Golby), treasurer: Wales (Frances Marguerison), PR and marketing: USA (Ellen Cunningham).

WORLD CHAMPIONSHIP FINAL: ENGLAND 38 (5G 1PG)   USA 23 (1PG 4T)

England: J Mitchell (Berkeley); V Blackett (Clifton), J Edwards (Blackheath), G Prangnell (Wasps), A Cole (Saracens); K Almond (Saracens) *(capt)*, E Mitchell (Saracens); J Mangham (Waterloo), N Ponsford (Clifton), S Ewing (Wasps), S Wenn (Clifton), H Stirrup (Wasps), J Ross (Saracens), G Burns (Waterloo), G Shaw (Wasps) *Replacements* P George (Wasps) for Edwards; J Chambers (Richmond) for Wenn **Scorers** *Tries:* pen tries (2), Mitchell, Edwards, Burns   *Conversions:* Almond (5) *Penalty Goal:* Almond

USA: J Crawford (Berkeley); K McFarren (New Orleans), C Orsini (Florida), E Huffer (Peninsula Chaos), P Jervey (Florida); J Bergman (BASH), P Connell (Beantown); A Flavin (Beantown), J Gray (Twin City Amazons), M Sorrenson (Philadelphia), J Rutkowski (Beantown), T Flanagan (UCLA), S Hunt (San Diego Surfers), B Bond (BASH) *(capt)*, L Spicer-Bourdon (Beantown) **Scorers** *Tries:* Crawford (2), Jervey, Connell   *Penalty Goal:* Bergman

RESULTS

Pool A *(Melrose):* 11 Apr: USA 111, Sweden 0; 13 Apr: Sweden 5, Japan 10; 15 Apr: USA 121, Japan 0
Pool B *(Boroughmuir):* 11 Apr: England 66, Russia 0; 13 Apr: Scotland 51, Russia 0; 15 Apr: Scotland 0, England 26
Pool C *(West of Scotland):* 11 Apr: France 77, Scottish Students 0; 13 Apr: Scottish Students 5, Ireland 18; 15 Apr: France 31, Ireland 0
Pool D *(Gala):* 11 Apr: Canada 5, Wales 11; 13 Apr: Wales 29, Kazakhstan 8; 15 Apr: Canada 28, Kazakhstan 0
Quarter-finals 17 Apr: USA 76, Ireland 0 *(Boroughmuir);* England 24, Canada 10 *(Gala);* France 99, Japan 0 *(Edinburgh Acads);* Wales 8, Scotland 0 *(Melrose)*

Semi-finals: *20 April, Gala:* USA 56, Wales 15; England 18, France 6,
23 April, Boroughmuir
Shield 3rd-4th Play-off: Japan 3, Ireland 11
Shield Final: Scotland 11, Canada 5
24 April, Edinburgh Acads
3rd-4th Play-off: France 27, Wales 0
FINAL: England 38, USA 23
Plate Final: Kazakhstan 29, Sweden 12

Other International Results
19 Dec: Scotland 0, Wales 23 *(Burnbrae);* 13 *Feb:* Wales 10, England 11 *(Bridgend);* 13 Feb: Ireland 0, Scotland 5 *(Ravenhill, Belfast);* 19 *Feb:* England A 15, Wales A 13 *(Wolverhampton);* England 36, France 8 *(Castlecroft)*

WRFU 1993-94

This season saw the expansion continue, still without sponsorship, in the women's game. Clubs now total over 200, and sincere worries about the size and unwieldy nature of the union were expressed repeatedly. As a result, at the AGM in May 1994, the WRFU was finally dissolved and the Ireland WRFU, the Welsh WRFU and England's RFUW emerged from the old organisation. This is a sound evolution following the successful departure of Scotland, who affiliated with the SRU at the end of the 1992-93 season.

In the last full season under the WRFU system, the First Division saw the same three clubs battling it out for the titles – Saracens, Wasps and Richmond. After Saracens' clean sweep last year, Richmond were the first team to beat the title-holders for 18 months – something they achieved twice in ten days, in a League fixture and in the National Cup final.

In Division 2, Waterloo took the title to return to their rightful place in Division 1 following a curious decision over Lampeter's repeated defaulting in the 1992-93 season. Lampeter had stayed up, pushed Waterloo down and then promptly folded during the first weeks of 1993-94 season.

National Cup: Richmond 18, Saracens 10 (*Blackheath*) **National Sevens:** Saracens (*Clifton*) **Divisionals:** London 22, South 8; North 55, Midlands 0; North 5, London 25; London 5, Midlands 0; South 48, Midlands 0

Division 1

	P	W	D	L	F	A	Pts
Saracens	12	10	1	1	371	66	31
Richmond*	11	8	0	2	263	79	27
Wasps*	11	7	1	3	193	117	25
Blackheath	12	6	0	6	142	202	15
Clifton*	10	4	2	4	169	121	14
Cardiff	11	2	1	8	101	265	6
Eton Manor*	10	0	0	10	35	401	0

* 1 game defaulted

Division 2

	P	W	D	L	F	A	Pts
Waterloo	12	12	0	0	333	66	33
Leeds*	11	9	0	2	188	38	27
Richmond	12	9	0	3	213	146	21
Wasps II	12	7	0	5	215	144	21
N'ton OS**	11	3	0	1	52	219	10
Sale	12	2	0	10	90	247	6
Medway*	11	0	1	9	48	196	1

* 1 game defaulted ** 7 games defaulted

Division 3 Midlands

	P	W	D	L	F	A	Pts
Old Leams	10	9	1	0	288	15	29
Selly Oak	10	6	2	2	82	49	24
Northampton	10	6	1	3	228	116	23
Sudbury*	10	4	1	3	155	183	17
Norwich	10	2	1	7	66	263	15
Witham**	10	0	0	5	22	165	5

* 2 games defaulted ** 5 games defaulted

Division 3 London

	P	W	D	L	F	A	Pts
St Albans	10	9	0	1	284	19	28
Teddington	10	9	0	1	204	45	28
Southend	10	4	1	5	162	169	19
Saracens II	10	4	1	5	128	173	19
Wimbledon	10	3	0	7	141	127	16
London Wesh*	10	0	0	7	5	391	7

* 3 games defaulted

Division 3 South

	P	W	D	L	F	A	Pts
Staines	10	7	3	0	79	39	24
Alton	10	6	2	2	93	64	24
Cheltenham	10	6	1	3	164	39	23
Richmond III*	10	4	1	4	93	117	18
Exeter*	10	3	0	6	51	106	15
Crawley*	10	2	0	7	13	127	13

* 1 game defaulted

Division 3 North

	P	W	D	L	F	A	Pts
Novos**	7	7	0	0	340	0	21
Manchester	9	6	0	3	115	145	21
York**	7	6	0	1	260	13	19
Wharfedale*	8	5	0	3	207	96	18
Northern	9	4	0	5	62	247	17
Whitchurch**	7	4	0	3	191	99	15
Waterloo*	8	3	0	5	100	174	14
Vale of Lune**	7	1	5	1	57	171	10
N Ribb*	7	0	1	6	25	337	8
Congleton†	6	1	0	5	52	127	8

* 1 game defaulted ** 2 games defaulted
† 3 games defaulted

Division 3 Wales

	P	W	D	L	F	A	Pts
Swansea Uplds	8	8	0	0	280	5	24
Blaenau Gwent	8	6	0	2	186	76	20
Aberystwyth*	8	4	0	3	45	168	15
Neath	7	1	0	6	36	144	7
Brecon**	7	0	0	4	10	164	4

* 1 game defaulted ** 3 games defaulted

Division 4 Midlands West

	P	W	D	L	F	A	Pts
Sutton Cldfld	10	9	1	0	229	10	29
Notts Casuals	10	8	0	2	166	35	26
Hereford	10	5	1	3	53	64	20
Newbold-on-A	10	6	0	3	32	103	15
Shipston-on-St	10	3	0	6	20	144	15
King's Norton	10	1	0	5	22	166	8

Division 4 South-West

	P	W	D	L	F	A	Pts
Supermarine	6	6	0	0	244	12	18
Clifton II	6	5	0	1	157	32	16
Hornets	6	4	0	2	180	38	14
Valley Cats	6	3	0	3	81	58	12
Lychett Minster	6	2	0	4	58	105	10
Tor	6	1	0	5	51	238	8
Kingswood	6	0	0	6	0	288	6

Division 5 South-West

	P	W	D	L	F	A	Pts
Brixham	6	5	1	0	268	22	17
Tavistock	6	5	0	1	126	52	16
Penpyn	6	4	1	1	157	36	15
Bodmin*	6	3	0	2	168	59	11
Bude	6	2	0	4	41	226	10
Truro	6	1	0	5	45	196	8
Liskeard*	6	0	0	5	22	236	5

* 1 game defaulted

Division Merit League West Midlands

	P	W	D	L	F	A	Pts
Pershore	8	7	1	0	198	45	23
O Halesonians	8	5	0	3	98	101	18
Atherstone	8	3	2	3	67	76	16
Lichfield*	8	0	1	5	44	152	14
Chipping N*	8	0	1	5	44	91	7

* 2 games defaulted

SCOTTISH RESULTS

Scottish Cup: Edinburgh Academicals **SWRU National Sevens:** Heriot Watt University

Division 1

	P	W	D	L	F	A	Pts
Edin Acads	10	8	1	1	370	30	27
W of Scotland	10	6	2	2	167	89	24
Aberdeen U*	9	4	2	3	32	80	19
Heriot Watt U*	9	4	2	3	82	189	19
Edinburgh U	10	2	1	7	33	255	15
Biggar*	9	1	2	6	60	101	13

* 1 game defaulted

Division 2

	P	W	D	L	F	A	Pts
Glasgow U	6	5	1	0	157	7	17
Perthshire	6	5	0	1	226	44	16
St Andrews U*	7	3	1	3	71	161	14
Stirling U	8	1	3	4	44	204	13
Dundee U*	5	0	1	4	30	112	6

* 1 game defaulted

Division 3

	P	W	D	L	F	A	Pts
Edin Acads II	7	7	0	0	178	15	21
West II	7	6	0	1	125	47	19
Mull	7	5	0	2	34	73	17
Dundee HSFP*	6	4	0	2	45	49	14
RDVC*	6	3	0	3	51	37	12
Kirkcaldy	7	2	0	5	40	57	11
Edin U II**	4	1	0	3	0	170	6
Musselburgh†	1	0	0	1	0	25	1

* 1 game defaulted   ** 3 games defaulted
† 6 games defaulted

FIXTURES 1994-95

Venues and fixtures are understood to be correct at the time of going to press, but are subject to alteration. We should like to thank all those who have assisted in the compilation of this list, especially those at the various headquarters of the Home Unions.

Friday, 26 August

Cheltenham v Rosslyn Park

Saturday, 27 August

WRU Heineken Leagues
Division 1
Cardiff v Bridgend
Dunvant v Newport
Llanelli v Swansea
Neath v Treorchy
Newbridge v Abertillery
Pontypool v Pontypridd
Division 2
Abercynon v Cross Keys
Llanharan v Ebbw Vale
Maesteg v Aberavon
Narberth v Bonymaen
Penarth v Llandovery
S Wales Police v Tenby Utd

Sale v Lansdowne
Stroud v Rosslyn Park

Thursday, 1 September

Newbold-on-Avon v Coventry
Northampton v Met Police
Preston Lodge v Ross High
Tynedale v Watsonians
Wakefield v Morley
West of Scotland v Ayr

Saturday, 3 September

Bath v Barbarians

WRU Heineken Leagues
Division 1
Abertillery v Llanelli
Bridgend v Dunvant
Neath v Pontypool
Newport v Newbridge
Pontypridd v Cardiff
Swansea v Treorchy
Division 2
Aberavon v Penarth
Bonymaen v Llanharan
Cross Keys v Narberth

Ebbw Vale v Maesteg
Llandovery v S Wales Police
Tenby Utd v Abercynon

Ballymena v Hawick
Bristol v Blackheath
Gala v West Hartlepool
Glasgow Acads v Stewart's-Melville FP
Harrogate v Wakefield
Highfield v Dungannon
Kendal v Fylde
Lansdowne v Heriot's FP
Leeds v Morley
Leicester v Saracens
Melrose v Kelso
Moseley v Bedford
Newcastle Gosforth v Boroughmuir
Northampton v Coventry
Preston Grasshoppers v Preston Lodge
Rosslyn Park v Havant
Rugby v London Scottish
Selkirk v Jedforest
Stirling County v Sale
Tynedale v Dundee HSFP
Vale of Lune v West of Scotland
Wasps v Instonians

Sunday, 4 September

Kelso Sevens

Tuesday, 6 September

Collegians v Instonians
Richmond v Wasps

Wednesday, 7 September

WRU Heineken Leagues
Division 1
Abertillery v Newport
Cardiff v Neath
Dunvant v Pontypridd
Newbridge v Bridgend
Pontypool v Swansea
Treorchy v Llanelli

Division 2
Llanharan v Cross Keys
Maesteg v Bonymaen
Narberth v Abercynon
Penarth v Ebbw Vale
S Wales Police v Aberavon
Tenby Utd v Llandovery

Moseley v Cheltenham
West Hartlepool v Middlesbrough

Saturday, 10 September

RFU Courage Leagues
Division 1
Bath v Bristol
Leicester v Northampton
Sale v Harlequins
Wasps v Gloucester
West Hartlepool v Orrell
Division 2
Coventry v Wakefield
Fylde v Nottingham
London Irish v London Scottish
Moseley v Saracens
Waterloo v Newcastle Gosforth
Division 3
Clifton v Otley
Morley v Exeter
Richmond v Harrogate
Rosslyn Park v Blackheath
Rugby v Bedford
Division 4
Aspatria v Leeds
Havant v Redruth
Liverpool St Helens v Broughton Park
Reading v Plymouth
Rotherham v Askeans

SRU McEwan's Leagues

Division 1
Edinburgh Acads v Dundee HSFP
Glasgow High/Kelvinside v Boroughmuir
Hawick v Heriot's FP
Melrose v Currie
Stewart's-Melville FP v Gala
Stirling County v West of Scotland
Watsonians v Jedforest
Division 2
Biggar v Kelso
Edinburgh Wands v Wigtownshire
Glasgow Acads v Corstorphine
Gordonians v Haddington
Grangemouth v Peebles
Musselburgh v Kirkcaldy
Selkirk v Preston Lodge

RFU Pilkington Cup: *1st round*
RFU Pilkington Junior Clubs Cup:
1st round

Bridgend v S Wales Police
Cardiff v Pontypool
Dungannon v Old Crescent
Neath v Narberth
Penarth v Newbridge
Swansea v Aberavon
Terenure Coll v Instonians
Torquay Ath v Newport

Tuesday, 13 September

Aberavon v Glam Wands
Llanhilleth v Newbridge
Mountain Ash v S Wales Police

Friday, 16 September

Newport v Cardiff

Saturday, 17 September

ROMANIA v WALES (Bucharest)

RFU Courage Leagues
Division 1
Bristol v Sale
Gloucester v West Hartlepool
Harlequins v Wasps
Northampton v Bath
Orrell v Leicester
Division 2
London Scottish v Waterloo
Newcastle Gosforth v Fylde
Nottingham v Coventry
Saracens v London Irish
Wakefield v Moseley
Division 3
Bedford v Clifton
Blackheath v Rugby
Exeter v Rosslyn Park
Harrogate v Morley
Otley v Richmond
Division 4
Askeans v Liverpool St Helens
Broughton Park v Aspatria
Leeds v Havant
Plymouth v Rotherham
Redruth v Reading
Division 5 North
Birmingham Solihull v Stoke-on-Trent
Lichfield v Stourbridge

Nuneaton v Kendal
Preston Grasshoppers v Barkers Butts
Sheffield v Hereford
Wharfedale v Winnington Park
Division 5 South
Barking v Met Police
Berry Hill v Henley
Camborne v Basingstoke
High Wycombe v Weston-super-Mare
London Welsh v Tabard
Lydney v North Walsham

SRU McEwan's Leagues
Division 1
Boroughmuir v Stewart's-Melville FP
Currie v Watsonians
Dundee HSFP v Stirling County
Gala v Melrose
Heriot's FP v Glasgow High/Kelvinside
Jedforest v Edinburgh Acads
West of Scotland v Hawick
Division 2
Corstorphine v Gordonians
Haddington v Musselburgh
Kelso v Grangemouth
Kirkcaldy v Selkirk
Peebles v Glasgow Acads
Preston Lodge v Edinburgh Wands
Wigtownshire v Biggar

IRFU Insurance Corporation Leagues
Division 1
Blackrock Coll v Garryowen
Cork Const v Lansdowne
Instonians v Dungannon
Shannon v St Mary's Coll
Sunday's Well v Old Wesley
Division 2
Bangor v Terenure Coll
Bective Rangers v Ballymena
Greystones v Dolphin
Old Belvedere v Malone
Wanderers v Old Crescent
Division 3
City of Derry v Galway Corinthians
De La Salle Palmerston v Clontarf
Galwegians v Athlone
NIFC v Monkstown
Waterpark v Ballina
Division 4
Ards v City of Armagh
CIYMS v Bohemians
Collegians v Skerries

WRU SWALEC Cup: *1st round*

Newbridge v Cross Keys
Pontypool v Aberavon
Pontypridd v S Wales Police
Tenby Utd v Treorchy

Monday, 19 September

Caerleon v Newport

Saturday, 24 September
RFU Courage Leagues
Division 1
Bath v Orrell
Bristol v Harlequins
Leicester v Gloucester
Sale v Northampton
West Hartlepool v Wasps
Division 2
Coventry v Newcastle Gosforth
Fylde v London Scottish
Moseley v Nottingham
Wakefield v Saracens
Waterloo v London Irish
Division 3
Blackheath v Exeter
Morley v Otley
Richmond v Bedford
Rosslyn Park v Harrogate
Rugby v Clifton
Division 4
Askeans v Broughton Park
Havant v Aspatria
Liverpool St Helens v Plymouth
Reading v Leeds
Rotherham v Redruth
Division 5 North
Barkers Butts v Walsall
Hereford v Lichfield
Kendal v Birmingham Solihull
Stoke-on-Trent v Sheffield
Stourbridge v Wharfedale
Winnington Park v Preston Grasshoppers
Division 5 South
Basingstoke v High Wycombe
Henley v London Welsh
Met Police v Sudbury
North Walsham v Berry Hill
Tabard v Barking
Weston-super-Mare v Lydney

SRU McEwan's Leagues
Division 1
Edinburgh Acads v Currie

Gala v Boroughmuir
Glasgow High/Kelvinside v
    West of Scotland
Hawick v Dundee HSFP
Stewart's-Melville FP v Heriot's FP
Stirling County v Jedforest
Watsonians v Melrose
Division 2
Biggar v Preston Lodge
Edinburgh Wands v Selkirk
Glasgow Acads v Kelso
Gordonians v Peebles
Grangemouth v Wigtownshire
Kirkcaldy v Haddington
Musselburgh v Corstorphine

IRFU Insurance Corporation Leagues
Division 1
Dungannon v Sunday's Well
Lansdowne v Blackrock Coll
St Mary's Coll v Instonians
Young Munster v Cork Const
Division 2
Ballymena v Greystones
Bective Rangers v Wanderers
Dolphin v Terenure Coll
Malone v Bangor
Old Crescent v UC Dublin
Division 3
Athlone v De La Salle Palmerston
Ballina v NIFC
Clontarf v Galwegians
Galway Corinthians v Waterpark
Monkstown v Highfield
UC Cork v City of Derry
Division 4
Bohemians v Sligo
City of Armagh v Queen's U, Belfast
Dublin U v CIYMS
Skerries v Ards
UC Galway v Portadown

WRU Heineken Leagues
Division 1
Bridgend v Newport
Llanelli v Pontypool
Neath v Dunvant
Pontypridd v Newbridge
Swansea v Cardiff
Treorchy v Abertillery
Division 2
Aberavon v Llandovery
Abercynon v Llanharan
Bonymaen v Penarth

Cross Keys v Maesteg
Ebbw Vale v S Wales Police
Narberth v Tenby Utd

Manchester v Vale of Lune

Sunday, 25 September

IRFU Insurance Corporation Leagues
Division 1
Garryowen v Shannon

Wednesday, 28 September

Cambridge U v Cambridge City

Saturday, 1 October

ITALY v ROMANIA

RFU Courage Leagues
Division 1
Gloucester v Bath
Harlequins v West Hartlepool
Northampton v Bristol
Orrell v Sale
Wasps v Leicester
Division 2
London Irish v Fylde
London Scottish v Coventry
Newcastle Gosforth v Moseley
Nottingham v Wakefield
Saracens v Waterloo
Division 3
Bedford v Morley
Clifton v Richmond
Exeter v Rugby
Harrogate v Blackheath
Otley v Rosslyn Park
Division 4
Aspatria v Reading
Broughton Park v Havant
Leeds v Rotherham
Redruth v Liverpool St Helens
Plymouth v Askeans
Division 5 North
Birmingham Solihull v Nuneaton
Lichfield v Stoke-on-Trent
Preston Grasshoppers v Stourbridge
Sheffield v Kendal
Walsall v Winnington Park
Wharfedale v Hereford
Division 5 South
Barking v Henley
Berry Hill v Weston-super-Mare

High Wycombe v Camborne
London Welsh v North Walsham
Lydney v Basingstoke
Sudbury v Tabard

SRU McEwan's Leagues
Division 1
Currie v Stirling County
Dundee HSFP v Glasgow High/Kelvinside
Heriot's FP v Boroughmuir
Jedforest v Hawick
Melrose v Edinburgh Acads
Watsonians v Gala
West of Scotland v Stewart's-Melville FP
Division 2
Corstorphine v Haddington
Edinburgh Wands v Kirkcaldy
Kelso v Gordonians
Peebles v Musselburgh
Preston Lodge v Grangemouth
Selkirk v Biggar
Wigtownshire v Glasgow Acads

IRFU Insurance Corporation Leagues
Division 1
Blackrock Coll v Young Munster
Instonians v Garryowen
Old Wesley v Dungannon
Shannon v Lansdowne
Sunday's Well v St Mary's Coll
Division 2
Bangor v Ballymena
Greystones v Bective Rangers
Terenure Coll v Old Crescent
UC Dublin v Malone
Wanderers v Old Belvedere
Division 3
City of Derry v Monkstown
Clontarf v Ballina
Galwegians v De La Salle Palmerston
Highfield v Athlone
NIFC v Galway Corinthians
Waterpark v UC Cork
Division 4
Ards v Dublin U
CIYMS v City of Armagh
Portadown v Collegians
Queen's U, Belfast v UC Galway
Sligo v Skerries

WRU Heineken Leagues
Division 1
Abertillery v Bridgend
Cardiff v Llanelli

Dunvant v Swansea
Newbridge v Neath
Newport v Pontypridd
Pontypool v Treorchy
Division 2
Llandovery v Ebbw Vale
Llanharan v Narberth
Maesteg v Abercynon
Penarth v Cross Keys
S Wales Police v Bonymaen
Tenby Utd v Aberavon

Tuesday, 4 October
Newport v Barbarians
Cambridge U v Crawshay's Welsh

Bedford v Oxford U
Rosslyn Park v Wasps
S Wales Police v Newbridge

Wednesday, 5 October
Abertillery v Aberavon

Saturday, 8 October
RFU Courage Leagues
Division 1
Bath v Wasps
Bristol v Orrell
Leicester v West Hartlepool
Northampton v Harlequins
Sale v Gloucester
Division 2
Coventry v London Irish
Fylde v Waterloo
Moseley v London Scottish
Nottingham v Saracens
Wakefield v Newcastle Gosforth

SRU McEwan's Leagues
Division 1
Boroughmuir v West of Scotland
Edinburgh Acads v Watsonians
Gala v Heriot's FP
Glasgow High/Kelvinside v Jedforest
Hawick v Currie
Stewart's-Melville FP v Dundee HSFP
Stirling County v Melrose
Division 2
Biggar v Edinburgh Wands
Glasgow Acads v Preston Lodge
Gordonians v Wigtownshire
Grangemouth v Selkirk

Haddington v Peebles
Kirkcaldy v Corstorphine
Musselburgh v Kelso

IRFU Insurance Corporation Leagues
Division 1
Blackrock Coll v Dungannon
Cork Const v St Mary's Coll
Instonians v Sunday's Well
Shannon v Old Wesley
Division 2
Ballymena v UC Dublin
Bective Rangers v Bangor
Malone v Terenure Coll
Old Belvedere v Greystones
Old Crescent v Dolphin
Division 3
Athlone v NIFC
Clontarf v Waterpark
De La Salle Palmerston v City of Derry
Galwegians v Highfield
Monkstown v Ballina
UC Cork v Galway Corinthians
Division 4
Ards v CIYMS
Collegians v Queen's U, Belfast
Dublin U v Sligo
Portadown v Bohemians
UC Galway v City of Armagh

RFU Pilkington Cup: *2nd round*
RFU Pilkington Junior Clubs Cup:
 2nd round

Aberavon v Llanelli
Cambridge U v Cardiff
Ebbw Vale v Newbridge
Newport v Loughborough U
Pontypool v S Wales Police
Treorchy v Narberth

Sunday, 9 October

IRFU Insurance Corporation Leagues
Division 1
Young Munster v Garryowen

Wednesday, 12 October

WALES v ITALY (Cardiff)

Blackheath v Aspen, Colorado
Cambridge U v St Mary's Hosp

Saturday, 15 October

RFU Courage Leagues
Division 1
Gloucester v Bristol
Harlequins v Leicester
Orrell v Northampton
Wasps v Sale
West Hartlepool v Bath
Division 2
London Irish v Moseley
London Scottish v Wakefield
Newcastle Gosforth v Nottingham
Saracens v Fylde
Waterloo v Coventry
Division 3
Blackheath v Otley
Exeter v Harrogate
Morley v Clifton
Rosslyn Park v Bedford
Rugby v Richmond
Division 4
Askeans v Redruth
Liverpool St Helens v Leeds
Plymouth v Broughton Park
Reading v Havant
Rotherham v Aspatria
Division 5 North
Hereford v Preston Grasshoppers
Kendal v Lichfield
Nuneaton v Sheffield
Stoke-on-Trent v Wharfedale
Stourbridge v Walsall
Winnington Park v Barkers Butts
Division 5 South
Basingstoke v Berry Hill
Cambridge v Lydney
Henley v Sudbury
North Walsham v Barking
Tabard v Met Police
Weston-super-Mare v London Welsh

SRU McEwan's Leagues
Division 1
Currie v Glasgow High/Kelvinside
Dundee HSFP v Boroughmuir
Edinburgh Acads v Gala
Jedforest v Stewart's-Melville FP
Melrose v Hawick
Watsonians v Stirling County
West of Scotland v Heriot's FP
Division 2
Biggar v Kirkcaldy
Edinburgh Wands v Grangemouth
Kelso v Haddington

423

Peebles v Corstorphine
Preston Lodge v Gordonians
Selkirk v Glasgow Acads
Wigtownshire v Musselburgh

IRFU Insurance Corporation Leagues
Division 1
Dungannon v Cork Const
Garryowen v Lansdowne
Old Wesley v Blackrock Coll
St Mary's Coll v Young Munster
Division 2
Bangor v Old Belvedere
Dolphin v Malone
Greystones v Wanderers
Terenure Coll v Ballymena
UC Dublin v Bective Rangers
Division 3
Ballina v UC Cork
City of Derry v Galwegians
Highfield v De La Salle Palmerston
Galway Corinthians v Monkstown
NIFC v Clontarf
Waterpark v Athlone
Division 4
Bohemians v Queen's U, Belfast
City of Armagh v Collegians
CIYMS v UC Galway
Skerries v Portadown
Sligo v Ards

WRU Heineken Leagues
Division 1
Llanelli v Dunvant
Neath v Newport
Pontypool v Abertillery
Pontypridd v Bridgend
Swansea v Newbridge
Treorchy v Cardiff
Division 2
Abercynon v Penarth
Bonymaen v Llandovery
Cross Keys v S Wales Police
Ebbw Vale v Aberavon
Llanharan v Tenby Utd
Narberth v Maesteg

Sunday, 16 October

IRFU Insurance Corporation Leagues
Division 1
Sunday's Well v Shannon

Tuesday, 18 October

Rosslyn Park v Cambridge U

S Wales Police v Swansea
Wasps v Oxford U

Wednesday, 19 October

Aberavon v Treorchy
Mountain Ash v Llanharan
Newport v Maesteg

Friday, 21 October

Hawick v Langholm
Jedforest v Kelso

Saturday, 22 October

Cardiff v South Africans
Connacht v Scottish North & Midlands
Glasgow Dist v Leinster
Munster v Edinburgh Dist
South of Scotland v Ulster

RFU Courage Leagues
Division 1
Bath v Leicester
Bristol v Wasps
Harlequins v Orrell
Northampton v Gloucester
Sale v West Hartlepool
Division 2
Coventry v Fylde
Moseley v Waterloo
Newcastle Gosforth v Saracens
Nottingham v London Scottish
Wakefield v London Irish
Division 3
Bedford v Blackheath
Clifton v Rosslyn Park
Otley v Exeter
Richmond v Morley
Rugby v Harrogate
Division 4
Aspatria v Liverpool St Helens
Broughton Park v Reading
Havant v Rotherham
Leeds v Askeans
Redruth v Plymouth
Division 5 North
Barkers Butts v Stourbridge
Lichfield v Nuneaton
Preston Grasshoppers v Stoke-on-Trent
Sheffield v Birmingham Solihull
Walsall v Hereford
Wharfedale v Kendal

Division 5 South
Barking v Weston-super-Mare
Berry Hill v Camborne
London Welsh v Basingstoke
Lydney v High Wycombe
Met Police v Henley
Sudbury v North Walsham

WRU Heineken Leagues
Division 1
Newbridge v Llanelli

WRU SWALEC Cup: *2nd round*

Abertillery v S Wales Police
Ayr v Boroughmuir
Cambridge U v Dublin U
Cross Keys v Newport
Dungannon v UC Dublin
Dunvant v Tenby Utd
Edinburgh Wands v Currie
Gala v Selkirk
Glasgow Acads v Kilmarnock
Glasgow High/Kelvinside v Instonians
Grangemouth v West of Scotland
Heriot's FP v Kirkcaldy
Melrose v Ballymena
Pontypridd v Aberavon
Preston Lodge v Hillhead Jordanhill
Stirling County v Dundee HSFP

Tuesday, 25 October

Cambridge U v Bedford
Mountain Ash v Cardiff
Oxford U v Northampton

Wednesday, 26 October

Wales A v South Africans (Newport)

Friday, 28 October

Kelso v Gala

Saturday, 29 October

Llanelli v South Africans
Edinburgh Dist v Connacht
Leinster v South of Scotland
Scottish North & Midlands v Munster
Ulster v Glasgow Dist

RFU Courage Leagues
Division 1
Bath v Harlequins

Gloucester v Orrell
Leicester v Sale
Wasps v Northampton
West Hartlepool v Bristol
Division 2
Coventry v Saracens
Fylde v Moseley
London Irish v Nottingham
London Scottish v Newcastle Gosforth
Waterloo v Wakefield
Division 3
Blackheath v Clifton
Exeter v Bedford
Harrogate v Otley
Morley v Rugby
Rosslyn Park v Richmond
Division 4
Askeans v Aspatria
Broughton Park v Redruth
Liverpool St Helens v Havant
Plymouth v Leeds
Rotherham v Reading
Division 5 North
Birmingham Solihull v Lichfield
Hereford v Barkers Butts
Kendal v Preston Grasshoppers
Nuneaton v Wharfedale
Stoke-on-Trent v Walsall
Stourbridge v Winnington Park
Division 5 South
Basingstoke v Barking
Camborne v London Welsh
Henley v Tabard
High Wycombe v Berry Hill
North Walsham v Met Police
Weston-super-Mare v Sudbury

WRU Heineken Leagues
Division 1
Abertillery v Pontypridd
Bridgend v Neath
Cardiff v Pontypool
Dunvant v Treorchy
Newport v Swansea
Division 2
Aberavon v Bonymaen
Llandovery v Cross Keys
Maesteg v Llanharan
Penarth v Narberth
S Wales Police v Abercynon
Tenby Utd v Ebbw Vale

Ayr v Jedforest
Cambridge U v Loughborough U
Collegians v Dungannon

Corstorphine v Preston Lodge
Edinburgh Wands v Glasgow High/
  Kelvinside
Glasgow Acads v Watsonians
Grangemouth v Dundee HSFP
Langholm v Melrose
Royal High v Heriot's FP
Selkirk v Hawick
West of Scotland v Gordonians

Tuesday, 1 November

Ireland Development XV v Namibians
  (Galway)

Northampton v Cambridge U

Wednesday, 2 November

Neath v South Africans
Bangor v Instonians
Durham City v West Hartlepool
Penarth v Cardiff

Friday, 4 November

Bridgend v Canterbury

Saturday, 5 November

IRELAND v NAMIBIA (Dublin)
Swansea v South Africans

RFU Courage Leagues
Division 1
Bristol v Leicester
Harlequins v Gloucester
Northampton v West Hartlepool
Orrell v Wasps
Sale v Bath
Division 2
Moseley v Coventry
Newcastle Gosforth v London Irish
Nottingham v Waterloo
Saracens v London Scottish
Wakefield v Fylde

SRU McEwan's Leagues
Division 1
Boroughmuir v Jedforest
Gala v West of Scotland
Glasgow High/Kelvinside v Melrose
Hawick v Watsonians
Heriot's FP v Dundee HSFP
Stewart's-Melville FP v Currie
Stirling County v Edinburgh Acads

Division 2
Corstorphine v Kelso
Glasgow Acads v Edinburgh Wands
Gordonians v Selkirk
Grangemouth v Biggar
Haddington v Wigtownshire
Kirkcaldy v Peebles
Musselburgh v Preston Lodge

WRU Heineken Leagues
Division 1
Cardiff v Abertillery
Llanelli v Newport
Neath v Pontypridd
Pontypool v Dunvant
Treorchy v Newbridge
Division 2
Abercynon v Llandovery
Bonymaen v Ebbw Vale
Cross Keys v Aberavon
Llanharan v Penarth
Maesteg v Tenby Utd
Narberth v S Wales Police

RFU Pilkington Cup: *3rd round*
RFU Pilkington Junior Clubs Cup:
  3rd round

Bective Rangers v Instonians
Dungannon v City of Derry
Kelso v Melrose
Vale of Lune v Liverpool St Helens

Monday, 7 November

Leinster v Canterbury (Dublin)

Tuesday, 8 November

Cambridge U v Romanians
Ireland U-21 v England U-21 (Belfast)

Blackheath v Maidstone
Cardiff v Gloucester

Wednesday, 9 November

Scotland A v South Africans (Melrose)
Irish Us v Namibians
Cornwall v Canterbury

Friday, 11 November

Bristol v Coventry
Kelso v Currie
Stirling County v Glasgow High/
  Kelvinside

Saturday, 12 November

ENGLAND v ROMANIA (Twickenham)
Scottish Districts v South Africans
  (Glasgow)
Leinster v Namibians (Dublin)
Connacht v Irish Exiles
Munster v Ulster

RFU CIS County Championship
Midlands Group A
Staffordshire v Leicestershire
Midlands Group B
East Midlands v Notts, Lincs & Derbys

West Hartlepool v Canterbury

RFU Courage Leagues
Division 3
Bedford v Harrogate
Clifton v Exeter
Otley v Rugby
Richmond v Blackheath
Rosslyn Park v Morley
Division 4
Aspatria v Plymouth
Havant v Askeans
Leeds v Redruth
Reading v Liverpool St Helens
Rotherham v Broughton Park

WRU Heineken Leagues
Division 1
Abertillery v Neath
Bridgend v Llanelli
Dunvant v Cardiff
Newbridge v Pontypool
Newport v Treorchy
Pontypridd v Swansea
Division 2
Aberavon v Abercynon
Ebbw Vale v Cross Keys
Llandovery v Narberth
Penarth v Maesteg
S Wales Police v Llanharan
Tenby Utd v Bonymaen

Bath v Loughborough U
City of Armagh v Instonians
Dundee HSFP v Musselburgh
Edinburgh Acads v Ayr
Edinburgh Wands v Kilmarnock
Fylde v Walsall
Gala v Hawick
Grangemouth v Clarkston

Harlequins v Cambridge U
Heriot's FP v Preston Lodge
Kirkcaldy v Stewart's-Melville FP
Melrose v Jedforest
Moseley v Wasps
Northampton v Newcastle Gosforth
Saracens v Sale
Vale of Lune v Sandal
Wakefield v Orrell
Watsonians v Haddington

Tuesday, 15 November

Scottish Selection v South Africans
  (Aberdeen)

RFU CIS County Championship
Northern Group
Durham v Yorkshire
Cheshire v Lancashire
Cumbria v Northumberland

Moseley v Canterbury

Exeter v Bristol
Northampton v London Welsh

Thursday, 17 November

Coventry v Canterbury

Rugby v East Ontario

Friday, 18 November

Boroughmuir v Heriot's FP
Clarkston v Dundee HSFP
Hawick v Melrose
Hillhead Jordanhill v Glasgow
  High/Kelvinside
Jedforest v Gala
Kelso v Langholm
Musselburgh v Watsonians
Portadown v Dungannon
Stirling County v Kilmarnock
West of Scotland v Peebles

Saturday, 19 November

SCOTLAND v SOUTH AFRICA
  (Murrayfield)

RFU CIS Divisional Championship
North v Midlands
South-West v London

Leinster v Irish Exiles
Ulster v Connacht

RFU CIS County Championship
Northern Group
Cheshire v Cumbria
Lancashire v Durham
Northumberland v Yorkshire
Midland Group A
Leicestershire v North Midlands
Midland Group B
Notts, Lincs & Derbys v Warwickshire
Southern Group Pool 1
Surrey v Hertfordshire
Southern Group 2
Buckinghamshire v Sussex
Gloucestershire v Devon
Southern Group 3
Hampshire v Oxfordshire
Kent v Eastern Counties
Southern Group 4
Cornwall v Middlesex
Dorset & Wilts v Berkshire

Gloucester v Canterbury

WRU Heineken Leagues
Division 1
Cardiff v Newbridge
Dunvant v Abertillery
Llanelli v Pontypridd
Pontypool v Newport
Swansea v Neath
Treorchy v Bridgend
Division 2
Abercynon v Ebbw Vale
Cross Keys v Bonymaen
Llanharan v Llandovery
Maesteg v S Wales Police
Narberth v Aberavon
Penarth v Tenby Utd

WRU SWALEC Cup: *3rd round*

Broughton Park v Fylde
Coventry v Bath
Morley v Saracens
Newcastle Gosforth v West Hartlepool
Oxford U v Leicester
Rosslyn Park v Moseley
Vale of Lune v Durham U
Wakefield v Northampton
Wasps v Cambridge U

Tuesday, 22 November

Pontypridd v South Africans
Bristol v Canterbury
428

Berry Hill v Newbridge
Mountain Ash v Penarth

Wednesday, 23 November

Cambridge U v M R Steele-Bodger's XV
Pontypool v Bath

Friday, 25 November

Ulster v Canterbury (Belfast)
Wales U-21 v Romania U-21

Cardiff v Aberavon
Instonians v Collegians
Treorchy v Mountain Ash

Saturday, 26 November

WALES v SOUTH AFRICA (Cardiff)
RFU CIS Divisional Championship
London v North
Midlands v South-West

Connacht v Leinster
Irish Exiles v Munster

RFU CIS County Championship
Northern Group
Cheshire v Northumberland
Cumbria v Durham
Yorkshire v Lancashire
Midland Group A
North Midlands v Staffordshire
Midland Group B
Warwickshire v East Midlands
Southern Group 1
Hertfordshire v Somerset
Southern Group 2
Devon v Sussex
Gloucestershire v Buckinghamshire
Southern Group 3
Hampshire v Kent
Oxfordshire v Eastern Counties
Southern Group 4
Cornwall v Dorset & Wilts
Middlesex v Berkshire

SRU McEwan's Leagues
Division 1
Currie v Boroughmuir
Dundee HSFP v West of Scotland
Edinburgh Acads v Hawick
Jedforest v Heriot's FP
Melrose v Stewart's-Melville FP
Stirling County v Gala
Watsonians v Glasgow High/Kelvinside

Division 2
Biggar v Glasgow Acads
Edinburgh Wands v Gordonians
Grangemouth v Kirkcaldy
Kelso v Peebles
Preston Lodge v Haddington
Selkirk v Musselburgh
Wigtownshire v Corstorphine

RFU Pilkington Junior Clubs Cup:
4th round

Bath v Oxford U
Cambridge U v Leicester
Dungannon v CIYMS
Fylde v Blackheath
Harrogate v Newcastle Gosforth
Morley v Liverpool St Helens
Moseley v Sale
Northampton v Bedford
Nottingham v West Hartlepool
Nuneaton v Rugby
Rosslyn Park v London Scottish
Saracens v Bristol
Wakefield v Otley

Sunday, 27 November

Coventry v Newport
Wasps v London Irish

Tuesday, 29 November

Combined Provinces v South Africans
(Belfast)

Edinburgh Wands v Boroughmuir
Northampton v Crusaders

Wednesday, 30 November

Bedford v RAF
Rugby v Met Police

Thursday, 1 December

Cambridge LX Club v Oxford Greyhounds

Moseley v Combined Services

Saturday, 3 December

Barbarians v South Africans (Dublin)
RFU CIS Divisional Championship
London v Midlands
North v South-West (Sale)

Glasgow Dist v Scottish North & Midlands
South of Scotland v Scottish Exiles

RFU CIS County Championship
Northern Group
Cumbria v Lancashire
Northumberland v Durham
Yorkshire v Cheshire
Midland Group: Semi-finals
Southern Group 1
Somerset v Surrey
Southern Group 2
Buckinghamshire v Devon
Sussex v Gloucestershire
Southern Group 3
Eastern Counties v Hampshire
Kent v Oxfordshire
Southern Group 4
Berkshire v Cornwall
Dorset & Wilts v Middlesex

WRU Heineken Leagues
Division 1
Abertillery v Swansea
Bridgend v Pontypool
Neath v Llanelli
Newbridge v Dunvant
Newport v Cardiff
Pontypridd v Treorchy
Division 2
Aberavon v Llanharan
Bonymaen v Abercynon
Ebbw Vale v Narberth
Llandovery v Maesteg
S Wales Police v Penarth
Tenby Utd v Cross Keys

Aberdeen GSFP v Preston Lodge
Aspatria v Kelso
Ballymena v Instonians
Bedford v Gloucester
Blackheath v Lydney
Boroughmuir v Glasgow High/Kelvinside
Bristol v Moseley
Coventry v Wanderers
Dundee HSFP v Gordonians
Edinburgh Wands v Hutchesons'
Fylde v Sheffield
Gala v Hartlepool Rovers
Glasgow Acads v Melrose
Heriot's FP v Ayr
Kilmarnock v Perthshire
Leicester v Loughborough U

London Scottish v Wasps
Morley v Wakefield
Newcastle Gosforth v Sale
Northampton v Harrogate
Nottingham v Bath
Orrell v Rugby
Saracens v Rosslyn Park
Stewart's-Melville FP v Jedforest
Terenure Coll v Dungannon
Tynedale v Hawick
Watsonians v Edinburgh Acads
Wigtownshire v West of Scotland

Sunday, 4 December

France A v Italy

Tuesday, 6 December

Oxford U v Cambridge U (Twickenham)

Wednesday, 7 December

Cardiff v Penarth

Friday, 9 December

Leicester v Otley
Rugby v Bristol

Saturday, 10 December

ENGLAND v CANADA (Twickenham)
Scottish Exiles v Glasgow Dist
**Scottish North & Midlands v
    Edinburgh Dist**
Irish Exiles v Ulster (Sale)
Leinster v Munster

RFU CIS County Championship
Northern Group
Durham v Cheshire
Lancashire v Northumberland
Yorkshire v Cumbria

WRU Heineken Leagues
Division 1
Abertillery v Newbridge
Bridgend v Cardiff
Newport v Dunvant
Pontypridd v Pontypool
Swansea v Llanelli
Treorchy v Neath
Division 2
Aberavon v Maesteg
Bonymaen v Narberth
Cross Keys v Abercynon

Ebbw Vale v Llanharan
Llandovery v Penarth
Tenby Utd v S Wales Police

Bedford v Sale
Blackheath v Saracens
Boroughmuir v Kelso
City of Derry v Instonians
Dundee HSFP v Jedforest
Dunfermline v Edinburgh Wands
Dungannon v Clontarf
Fylde v Aspatria
Gala v Ayr
Gloucester v Coventry
Grangemouth v Edinburgh Acads
Haddington v West of Scotland
Harlequins v West London Inst
Hawick v Selkirk
Heriot's FP v Kilmarnock
Kirkcaldy v Watsonians
Melrose v Wakefield
Moseley v Northampton
Preston Lodge v Trinity Acads
Rosslyn Park v Basingstoke
Rotherham v Morley
Wasps v Newcastle Gosforth
West Hartlepool v Waterloo
Wharfedale v Vale of Lune

Wednesday, 14 December

South of Scotland v Edinburgh Dist

Friday, 16 December

Dungannon v NIFC
Instonians v CIYMS

Saturday, 17 December

Edinburgh Dist v Glasgow Dist
**Scottish North & Midlands v South of
    Scotland**
Munster v Connacht
Ulster v Leinster
RFU Pilkington Cup: *4th round*
RFU Pilkington Junior Clubs Cup:
    5th round
WRU SWALEC Cup: *4th round*

Ayr v Hillhead Jordanhill
Boroughmuir v Dundee HSFP
Broughton Park v Rugby
Edinburgh Acads v Edinburgh Wands
Grangemouth v Royal High
Hartlepool Rovers v Hawick

Jedforest v Langholm
Kelso v Heriot's FP
Kendal v Vale of Lune
Kilmarnock v Gala
Selkirk v Melrose
Sheffield v Morley
Stewart's-Melville FP v Preston Lodge
West of Scotland v Stirling County

Wednesday, 21 December

**Scottish Exiles v Scottish North &
  Midlands**

Saturday, 24 December

Edinburgh Dist v Scottish Exiles
Glasgow Dist v South of Scotland

WRU Heineken Leagues
Division 1
Cardiff v Pontypridd
Dunvant v Bridgend
Llanelli v Abertillery
Newbridge v Newport
Pontypool v Neath
Treorchy v Swansea
Division 2
Abercynon v Tenby Utd
Llanharan v Bonymaen
Maesteg v Ebbw Vale
Narberth v Cross Keys
Penarth v Aberavon
S Wales Police v Llandovery

Bedford v Coventry
Bradford & Bingley v Morley
Edinburgh Wands v Trinity Acads
Gala v Stewart's-Melville FP
Grangemouth v Corstorphine
Instonians v Malone
Jedforest v Kirkcaldy
Langholm v Hawick
Leeds v Wakefield
Melrose v Ayr
Middlesbrough v Newcastle Gosforth
Sale v Kendal
Vale of Lune v Fylde
Watsonians v Heriot's FP
West of Scotland v Glasgow High/
  Kelvinside

Monday, 26 December

Aberavon v Neath
Ballymena v Dungannon

Bedford v Old Paulines
Bristol v Newport
Broughton Park v Sale
Coventry v Warwickshire XV
Fylde v Preston Grasshoppers
Glasgow High/Kelvinside v Glasgow Acads
Hartlepool Rovers v West Hartlepool
Hawick v Jedforest
Kelso v Selkirk
Llanelli v London Welsh
Melrose v Gala
Moseley v Rugby
Newbridge v Glam Wands
Newcastle Gosforth v Northern
Northampton v Stirling County
Whitland v Narberth

Tuesday, 27 December

Leicester v Barbarians
Harlequins v Richmond
Preston Lodge v Musselburgh

Saturday, 31 December

Scotland Trial (Murrayfield)

WRU Heineken Leagues
Division 1
Bridgend v Newbridge
Llanelli v Treorchy
Neath v Cardiff
Newport v Abertillery
Pontypridd v Dunvant
Swansea v Pontypool
Division 2
Abercynon v Narberth
Aberavon v S Wales Police
Bonymaen v Maesteg
Cross Keys v Llanharan
Ebbw Vale v Penarth

Ayr v Howe of Fife
Bedford v London Welsh
Clifton v Bristol
Coventry v Orrell
Dungannon v Malone
Edinburgh Wands v Watsonians
Gala v Kelso
Glasgow High/Kelvinside v Stewart's-
  Melville FP
Gloucester v Moseley
Grangemouth v Stirling County
Jedforest v Tynedale
London Irish v Blackheath

Melrose v Langholm
Morley v Waterloo
Newcastle Gosforth v Alnwick
NIFC v Instonians
Nottingham v Northampton
Preston Grasshoppers v Vale of Lune
Sale v Winnington Park
Tenby Utd v Pembroke Dock Quins
Wakefield v Liverpool St Helens
West Hartlepool v Stockton
West of Scotland v Ardrossan Acads

Monday, 2 January 1995

Heriot's FP v Hawick
Kelso v Jedforest
Melrose v Glasgow High/Kelvinside
Novocastrians v Newcastle Gosforth
Rosslyn Park v Harlequins
Saracens v Wasps
Selkirk v Gala

Tuesday, 3 January

Haddington v Preston Lodge

Saturday, 7 January

Scotland A v Italy

RFU Courage Leagues
Division 1
Bristol v Bath
Gloucester v Wasps
Harlequins v Sale
Northampton v Leicester
Orrell v West Hartlepool
Division 2
London Scottish v London Irish
Newcastle Gosforth v Waterloo
Nottingham v Fylde
Saracens v Moseley
Wakefield v Coventry
Division 3
Blackheath v Morley
Exeter v Richmond
Harrogate v Clifton
Otley v Bedford
Rugby v Rosslyn Park
Division 4
Askeans v Reading
Broughton Park v Leeds
Liverpool St Helens v Rotherham
Plymouth v Havant
Redruth v Aspatria

Division 5 North
Barkers Butts v Stoke-on-Trent
Lichfield v Sheffield
Preston Grasshoppers v Nuneaton
Walsall v Kendal
Wharfedale v Birmingham Solihull
Winnington Park v Hereford
Division 5 South
Barking v Camborne
Berry Hill v Lydney
London Welsh v High Wycombe
Met Police v Weston-super-Mare
Sudbury v Basingstoke
Tabard v North Walsham

IRFU Insurance Corporation Leagues
Division 1
Cork Const v Blackrock Coll
Lansdowne v Instonians
Old Wesley v St Mary's Coll
Shannon v Young Munster
Division 2
Ballymena v Old Belvedere
Dolphin v Bangor
Malone v Wanderers
Old Crescent v Greystones
Terenure Coll v UC Dublin
Division 3
Athlone v Galway Corinthians
City of Derry v Clontarf
De La Salle Palmerston v NIFC
Galwegians v Waterpark
Highfield v Ballina
Monkstown v UC Cork
Division 4
Ards v Bohemians
City of Armagh v Portadown
CIYMS v Queen's U, Belfast
Collegians v Sligo
Dublin U v Skerries

WRU Heineken Leagues
Division 1
Abertillery v Treorchy
Cardiff v Swansea
Dunvant v Neath
Newbridge v Pontypridd
Newport v Bridgend
Pontypool v Llanelli
Division 2
Llandovery v Aberavon
Llanharan v Abercynon
Maesteg v Cross Keys
Penarth v Bonymaen
S Wales Police v Ebbw Vale
Tenby Utd v Narberth

Ayr v Kilmarnock
Currie v Grangemouth
Dundee HSFP v Stewart's-Melville FP
Dungannon v Bective Rangers
Glasgow High/Kelvinside v Heriot's FP
Hawick v Kelso
Jedforest v Glasgow Acads
Langholm v Gala
Melrose v Selkirk
Stirling County v Watsonians
West of Scotland v Edinburgh Wands

Sunday, 8 January

IRFU Insurance Corporation Leagues
Division 1
Garryowen v Sunday's Well

Tuesday, 10 January

Newbridge v Aberavon
S Wales Police v Mountain Ash

Wednesday, 11 January

Moseley v Loughborough U

Saturday, 14 January

RFU Courage Leagues
Division 1
Bath v Northampton
Leicester v Orrell
Sale v Bristol
Wasps v Harlequins
West Hartlepool v Gloucester
Division 2
Coventry v Nottingham
Fylde v Newcastle Gosforth
London Irish v Saracens
Moseley v Wakefield
Waterloo v London Scottish
Division 3
Clifton v Bedford
Morley v Harrogate
Richmond v Otley
Rosslyn Park v Exeter
Rugby v Blackheath
Division 4
Askeans v Rotherham
Broughton Park v Liverpool St Helens
Leeds v Aspatria
Plymouth v Reading
Redruth v Havant
Division 5 North
Birmingham Solihull v Preston
 Grasshoppers

Hereford v Stourbridge
Kendal v Barkers Butts
Nuneaton v Walsall
Sheffield v Wharfedale
Stoke-on-Trent v Winnington Park
Division 5 South
Basingstoke v Met Police
Camborne v Sudbury
High Wycombe v Barking
Lydney v London Welsh
North Walsham v Henley
Weston-super-Mare v Tabard

SRU McEwan's Leagues
Division 1
Boroughmuir v Melrose
Gala v Dundee HSFP
Glasgow High/Kelvinside v Edinburgh
 Acads
Hawick v Stirling County
Heriot's FP v Currie
Stewart's-Melville FP v Watsonians
West of Scotland v Jedforest
Division 2
Corstorphine v Preston Lodge
Glasgow Acads v Grangemouth
Gordonians v Biggar
Haddington v Selkirk
Kirkcaldy v Kelso
Musselburgh v Edinburgh Wands
Peebles v Wigtownshire

IRFU Insurance Corporation Leagues
Division 1
Blackrock Coll v Shannon
Dungannon v Garryowen
Instonians v Cork Const
Lansdowne v Old Wesley
Young Munster v Sunday's Well
Division 2
Bangor v Old Crescent
Greystones v Malone
Old Belvedere v Bective Rangers
UC Dublin v Dolphin
Wanderers v Ballymena
Division 3
Ballina v De La Salle Palmerston
City of Derry v Highfield
Galway Corinthians v Clontarf
Monkstown v Waterpark
NIFC v Galwegians
UC Cork v Athlone
Division 4
Ards v Collegians

433

Bohemians v Dublin U
CIYMS v Skerries
Queen's U, Belfast v Portadown
Sligo v UC Galway

WRU Heineken Leagues
Division 2
Llandovery v Tenby Utd

Aberavon v Pontypridd
Cambridge U v Durham U
Cardiff v Maesteg
Cross Keys v Newbridge
Narberth v Treorchy

Tuesday, 17 January

Aberavon v Swansea
Mountain Ash v Pontypridd

Wednesday, 18 January

Cambridge U v RAF

Friday, 20 January

Ireland A v England A (Dublin)
Ireland Students v England Students

Bective Rangers v Northampton
Cardiff v Bristol
Mountain Ash v Oakdale
Newport v Gloucester
Old Belvedere v Leicester
St Mary's Coll v Fylde
Tenby Utd v Kidwelly

Saturday, 21 January

IRELAND v ENGLAND (Dublin)
FRANCE v WALES (Paris)
SCOTLAND v CANADA
  (Murrayfield)
Scotland A v France A

Edinburgh Wands v Hawick
Glasgow Acads v West of Scotland
Glasgow High/Kelvinside v Peebles
Harlequins v Blackheath
Heriot's FP v Stewart's-Melville FP
Jedforest v Hartlepool Rovers
Kilmarnock v Dalziel HSFP
Langholm v Kelso
London Irish v Bath
London Scottish v Bedford
Morley v Broughton Park
Newbridge v Coventry
Newcastle Gosforth v Leeds

Nuneaton v Moseley
Preston Lodge v Dunfermline
Rosslyn Park v London Welsh
Sale v Waterloo
Saracens v Richmond
Sheffield v Cambridge U
Wakefield v Gala
Wanderers v Wasps
Watsonians v Dundee HSFP
Winnington Park v Vale of Lune

Wednesday, 25 January

Penarth v Mountain Ash
Sale v Loughborough U

Saturday, 28 January

RFU Pilkington Cup: *5th round*
RFU Pikington Junior Clubs Cup:
  6th round

SRU McEwan's Leagues
Division 1
Currie v West of Scotland
Edinburgh Acads v Stewart's-Melville FP
Hawick v Gala
Jedforest v Dundee HSFP
Melrose v Heriot's FP
Stirling County v Glasgow High/
  Kelvinside
Watsonians v Boroughmuir
Division 2
Biggar v Musselburgh
Edinburgh Wands v Haddington
Glasgow Acads v Kirkcaldy
Grangemouth v Gordonians
Preston Lodge v Peebles
Selkirk v Corstorphine
Wigtownshire v Kelso

WRU SWALEC Cup: *5th round*

Bedford v Nottingham
Blackheath v Cambridge U
Cardiff v Moseley
Coventry v Harrogate
Ebbw Vale v Mountain Ash
Instonians v Greystones
Leeds v West Hartlepool
Liverpool St Helens v Fylde
London Scottish v Bath
Newport v Harlequins
Northampton v London Irish
Otley v Newcastle Gosforth
Richmond v Bristol
Rosslyn Park v Walsall

Rugby v Sale
Wakefield v Bradford & Bingley
Wasps v Swansea

Tuesday, 31 January

Northampton v Loughborough U

Wednesday, 1 February

Edinburgh Wands v Heriot's FP

Thursday, 2 February

Ayr v Glasgow High/Kelvinside
Instonians v City of Armagh
Kelso v Old Wesley

Friday, 3 February

Scotland A v Ireland A
Scotland U-21 v Ireland U-21

Cambridge U v Askeans
Clarkston v Kilmarnock
Coventry v Leicester
Dunfermline v Stewart's-Melville FP
Gala v Bective Rangers
Hawick v Dungannon
Jedforest v Selkirk
Newbridge v Bath
Northampton v Moseley
Sale v Broughton Park
West of Scotland v Hillhead Jordanhill

Saturday, 4 February

SCOTLAND v IRELAND (Murrayfield)
ENGLAND v FRANCE (Twickenham)

WRU Heineken Leagues
Division 1
Bridgend v Abertillery
Llanelli v Cardiff
Neath v Newbridge
Pontypridd v Newport
Swansea v Dunvant
Treorchy v Pontypool
Division 2
Aberavon v Tenby Utd
Abercynon v Maesteg
Bonymaen v S Wales Police
Cross Keys v Penarth
Ebbw Vale v Llandovery
Narberth v Llanharan

Fylde v Morley
Harlequins v Nottingham
London Irish v Bristol

London Welsh v Blackheath
Newcastle Gosforth v Durham City
Orrell v Wakefield
Saracens v Bedford
Vale of Lune v Wigton
Wasps v Racing Club de France

Tuesday, 7 February

WRU Heineken Leagues
Division 1
Abertillery v Pontypool
Bridgend v Pontypridd
Cardiff v Treorchy
Dunvant v Llanelli
Newbridge v Swansea
Newport v Neath
Division 2
Aberavon v Ebbw Vale
Llandovery v Bonymaen
Maesteg v Narberth
Penarth v Abercynon
S Wales Police v Cross Keys

Wednesday, 8 February

Royal Navy v Cambridge U

Saturday, 11 February

RFU Courage Leagues
Division 1
Gloucester v Leicester
Harlequins v Bristol
Northampton v Sale
Orrell v Bath
Wasps v West Hartlepool
Division 2
London Irish v Waterloo
London Scottish v Fylde
Newcastle Gosforth v Coventry
Nottingham v Moseley
Saracens v Wakefield
Division 3
Bedford v Rugby
Blackheath v Rosslyn Park
Exeter v Morley
Harrogate v Richmond
Otley v Clifton
Division 4
Aspatria v Broughton Park
Havant v Leeds
Liverpool St Helens v Askeans
Reading v Redruth
Rotherham v Plymouth

Division 5 North
Barkers Butts v Nuneaton
Preston Grasshoppers v Sheffield
Stourbridge v Stoke-on-Trent
Walsall v Birmingham Solihull
Wharfedale v Lichfield
Winnington Park v Kendal
Division 5 South
Barking v Lydney
Henley v Weston-super-Mare
London Welsh v Berry Hill
Met Police v Camborne
Sudbury v High Wycombe
Tabard v Basingstoke

SRU McEwan's Leagues
Division 1
Boroughmuir v Edinburgh Acads
Dundee HSFP v Currie
Gala v Jedforest
Glasgow High/Kelvinside v Hawick
Heriot's FP v Watsonians
Stewart's-Melville FP v Stirling County
West of Scotland v Melrose
Division 2
Corstorphine v Edinburgh Wands
Gordonians v Glasgow Acads
Haddington v Biggar
Kelso v Preston Lodge
Kirkcaldy v Wigtownshire
Musselburgh v Grangemouth
Peebles v Selkirk

IRFU Insurance Corporation Leagues
Division 1
Garryowen v Old Wesley
St Mary's Coll v Dungannon
Sunday's Well v Lansdowne
Young Munster v Instonians
Division 2
Ballymena v Dolphin
Bective Rangers v Terenure Coll
Malone v Old Crescent
Old Belvedere v UC Dublin
Wanderers v Bangor
Division 3
Athlone v Monkstown
City of Derry v NIFC
Clontarf v UC Cork
De La Salle Palmerston v Galway
    Corinthians
Galwegians v Ballina
Highfield v Waterpark
Division 4
City of Armagh v Sligo

Dublin U v Collegians
Portadown v CIYMS
Skerries v Bohemians
UC Galway v Ards

WRU Heineken Leagues
Division 2
Tenby Utd v Llanharan

Aberavon v Bridgend
Cambridge U v West London Inst
Newbridge v Ebbw Vale
Penarth v Newport
S Wales Police v Pontypool
Swansea v Cardiff

Sunday, 12 February

IRFU Insurance Corporation Leagues
Division 1
Cork Const v Shannon

Tuesday, 14 February

Aberavon v Newbridge
Abercarn v Newport
Pontypool v Mountain Ash
Rugby v Coventry
Treorchy v S Wales Police

Thursday, 16 February

Kilmarnock v Glasgow High/Kelvinside

Friday, 17 February

France A v Wales A

Aberavon v Blackheath
Bath v Swansea
Bedford v Leicester
Boroughmuir v Stewart's-Melville FP
Bridgend v Moseley
Bristol v Pontypridd
Cardiff v London Welsh
Clarkston v West of Scotland
Coventry v Northampton
Hendy v Tenby Utd
Hillhead Jordanhill v Grangemouth
Jedforest v Boroughmuir
Kelso v Hawick
Llanelli v Wasps
Mountain Ash v Nottingham
Newbridge v Penarth
Preston Lodge v Gala
S Wales Police v Abertillery

Saturday, 18 February

WALES v ENGLAND (Cardiff)
FRANCE v SCOTLAND (Paris)

IRFU Insurance Corporation Leagues
Division 1
Dungannon v Shannon
Garryowen v Cork Const
Lansdowne v Young Munster
Old Wesley v Instonians
St Mary's Coll v Blackrock Coll
Division 2
Bangor v Greystones
Dolphin v Bective Rangers
Old Crescent v Ballymena
Terenure Coll v Old Belvedere
UC Dublin v Wanderers
Division 3
Ballina v Athlone
Galway Corinthians v Galwegians
Monkstown v Clontarf
NIFC v Highfield
UC Cork v De La Salle Palmerston
Waterpark v City of Derry
Division 4
Bohemians v City of Armagh
Collegians v UC Galway
Portadown v Dublin U
Queen's U, Belfast v Skerries
Sligo v CIYMS

Edinburgh Wands v Portobello
Exeter v Saracens
Glasgow Acads v Ayr
Harlequins v Rugby
Harrogate v Melrose
Morley v Newcastle Gosforth
Orrell v Fylde
Otley v West Hartlepool
Richmond v Cambridge U
Rosslyn Park v Sudbury
Sale v Liverpool St Helens
Vale of Lune v Durham City
Wakefield v Broughton Park

Wednesday, 22 February

Cambridge U v Army

Saturday, 25 February

RFU Pilkington Cup: *quarter-finals*
RFU Junior Clubs Cup: *quarter-finals*

RFU Courage Leagues
Division 3
Blackheath v Harrogate
Morley v Bedford
Richmond v Clifton
Rosslyn Park v Otley
Rugby v Exeter
Division 4
Aspatria v Havant
Broughton Park v Askeans
Leeds v Reading
Plymouth v Liverpool St Helens
Redruth v Rotherham
Division 5 North
Birmingham Solihull v Barkers Butts
Kendal v Stourbridge
Lichfield v Preston Grasshoppers
Nuneaton v Winnington Park
Sheffield v Walsall
Stoke-on-Trent v Hereford
Division 5 South
Basingstoke v Henley
Berry Hill v Barking
Camborne v Tabard
High Wycombe v Met Police
Lydney v Sudbury
Weston-super-Mare v North Walsham

SRU McEwan's Leagues
Division 1
Currie v Jedforest
Edinburgh Acads v Heriot's FP
Glasgow High/Kelvinside v Gala
Hawick v Stewart's-Melville FP
Melrose v Dundee HSFP
Stirling County v Boroughmuir
Watsonians v West of Scotland
Division 2
Biggar v Corstorphine
Edinburgh Wands v Peebles
Glasgow Acads v Musselburgh
Gordonians v Kirkcaldy
Grangemouth v Haddington
Preston Lodge v Wigtownshire
Selkirk v Kelso

IRFU Insurance Corporation Leagues
Division 3
Highfield v UC Cork
Division 4
Queen's U, Belfast v Sligo
UC Galway v Dublin U

WRU Heineken Leagues
Division 1
Llanelli v Newbridge

Neath v Bridgend
Pontypool v Cardiff
Pontypridd v Abertillery
Swansea v Newport
Treorchy v Dunvant
Division 2
Abercynon v S Wales Police
Bonymaen v Aberavon
Cross Keys v Llandovery
Ebbw Vale v Tenby Utd
Llanharan v Maesteg
Narberth v Penarth

Cambridge U v London Welsh
Fylde v Middlesbrough
Instonians v Ballina
London Irish v Harlequins
Moseley v Bath
Northampton v Saracens
Sale v Nottingham
Wasps v Coventry
West Hartlepool v Wakefield

Tuesday, 28 February

S Wales Police v Glam Wands
Treorchy v Aberavon

Wednesday, 1 March

Cambridge U v Luddites
Mountain Ash v Ebbw Vale

Thursday, 2 March

Dungannon v Bangor
Portadown v Instonians

Friday, 3 March

Scotland U-21 v Wales U-21
Ireland Students v France Students

Clarkston v Glasgow High/Kelvinside
Edinburgh Acads v S Wales Police
Hawick v Aberavon
Heriot's FP v Selkirk
Jedforest v Peebles
Kelso v Melrose
Kirkcaldy v Gala
Newbridge v Bath
Newport v Cross Keys
Watsonians v Cardiff
West of Scotland v Currie

Saturday, 4 March

SCOTLAND v WALES (Murrayfield)
IRELAND v FRANCE (Dublin)
Royal Navy v Army (Twickenham)

RFU Courage Leagues
Division 1
Bath v Gloucester
Bristol v Northampton
Leicester v Wasps
Sale v Orrell
West Hartlepool v Harlequins
Division 2
Coventry v London Scottish
Fylde v London Irish
Moseley v Newcastle Gosforth
Wakefield v Nottingham
Waterloo v Saracens
Division 3
Bedford v Rosslyn Park
Clifton v Morley
Harrogate v Exeter
Otley v Blackheath
Richmond v Rugby
Division 4
Askeans v Plymouth
Havant v Broughton Park
Liverpool St Helens v Redruth
Reading v Aspatria
Rotherham v Leeds
Division 5 North
Barkers Butts v Sheffield
Hereford v Kendal
Preston Grasshoppers v Wharfedale
Stourbridge v Nuneaton
Walsall v Lichfield
Winnington Park v Birmingham Solihull
Division 5 South
Barking v London Welsh
Henley v Camborne
Met Police v Lydney
North Walsham v Basingstoke
Sudbury v Berry Hill
Tabard v High Wycombe

Ardrossan Acads v Kilmarnock
Royal High v Preston Lodge

Wednesday, 8 March

Llanharan v Mountain Ash
Rugby v Royal Navy

Saturday, 11 March

RFU CIS County Championship:
Semi-finals

SRU McEwan's Leagues
Division 1
Boroughmuir v Hawick
Dundee HSFP v Watsonians
Gala v Currie
Heriot's FP v Stirling County
Jedforest v Melrose
Stewart's-Melville FP v Glasgow High/
 Kelvinside
West of Scotland v Edinburgh Acads
Division 2
Corstorphine v Grangemouth
Haddington v Glasgow Acads
Kelso v Edinburgh Wands
Kirkcaldy v Preston Lodge
Musselburgh v Gordonians
Peebles v Biggar
Wigtownshire v Selkirk

IRFU Insurance Corporation Leagues
Division 1
Dungannon v Lansdowne
Instonians v Blackrock Coll
Old Wesley v Young Munster
St Mary's Coll v Garryowen
Division 2
Dolphin v Wanderers
Malone v Bective Rangers
Old Crescent v Old Belvedere
Terenure Coll v Greystones
UC Dublin v Bangor
Division 3
Ballina v City of Derry
Clontarf v Athlone
De La Salle Palmerston v Monkstown
Galway Corinthians v Highfield
Galwegians v UC Cork
NIFC v Waterpark
Division 4
Bohemians v Collegians
City of Armagh v Dublin U
Queen's U, Belfast v Ards
Skerries v UC Galway
Sligo v Portadown

WRU Heineken Leagues
Division 1
Abertillery v Cardiff
Bridgend v Swansea
Dunvant v Pontypool
Newbridge v Treorchy
Newport v Llanelli
Pontypridd v Neath
Division 2
Aberavon v Cross Keys
Ebbw Vale v Bonymaen

Llandovery v Abercynon
Penarth v Llanharan
S Wales Police v Narberth
Tenby Utd v Maesteg

Bristol v Bedford
Coventry v Sale
Fylde v Rugby
Harlequins v Wakefield
Leicester v Moseley
London Irish v Rosslyn Park
Nottingham v Wasps
Orrell v Morley
Richmond v Northampton
Saracens v London Welsh
West Hartlepool v Newcastle Gosforth

Sunday, 12 March

IRFU Insurance Corporation Leagues
Division 1
Sunday's Well v Cork Const

Tuesday, 14 March

Blackheath v Askeans
Mountain Ash v Treorchy
Northampton v RAF
S Wales Police v Pontypridd

Wednesday, 15 March

Coventry v Nuneaton

Thursday, 16 March

Instonians v Queen's U, Belfast

Friday, 17 March

Wales A v Ireland A
Wales U-21 v Ireland U-21

Aberavon v Bristol
Ayr v Stirling County
Bedford v Kelso
Cardiff v Bath
Howe of Fife v Edinburgh Wands
Gloucester v Newport
Kirkcaldy v Dundee HSFP
Mountain Ash v Terenure Coll
Musselburgh v Stewart's-Melville FP
Northampton v Gala
Nottingham v Leicester
Preston Lodge v West of Scotland
Rugby v Jedforest
Saracens v Harrogate
Wasps v Melrose

Saturday, 18 March

ENGLAND v SCOTLAND
  (Twickenham)
WALES v IRELAND (Cardiff)

Aspatria v Vale of Lune
Harlequins v Coventry
London Welsh v Hawick
Moseley v Richmond
Sale v Fylde
Wakefield v Sheffield
West Hartlepool v Morley

Sunday, 19 March

Rosslyn Park v Bridgend

Wednesday, 22 March

UAU: *Final* (Twickenham)

Newport v Newport & Dist RU

Saturday, 25 March

RFU Courage Leagues
Division 1
Gloucester v Sale
Harlequins v Northampton
Orrell v Bristol
Wasps v Bath
West Hartlepool v Leicester
Division 2
London Irish v Coventry
London Scottish v Moseley
Newcastle Gosforth v Wakefield
Saracens v Nottingham
Waterloo v Fylde
Division 3
Blackheath v Bedford
Exeter v Otley
Harrogate v Rugby
Morley v Richmond
Rosslyn Park v Clifton
Division 4
Aspatria v Rotherham
Broughton Park v Plymouth
Havant v Reading
Leeds v Liverpool St Helens
Redruth v Askeans
Division 5 North
Birmingham Solihull v Stourbridge
Kendal v Stoke-on-Trent
Lichfield v Barkers Butts
Nuneaton v Hereford

Sheffield v Winnington Park
Wharfedale v Walsall
Division 5 South
Basingstoke v Weston-super-Mare
Berry Hill v Met Police
Camborne v North Walsham
High Wycombe v Henley
London Welsh v Sudbury
Lydney v Tabard

WRU SWALEC Cup: *6th round*
RFU Schools' Day (Twickenham)

Boroughmuir v Watsonians
Bridgend v Aberavon
Dundee HSFP v Ayr
Dunvant v Tenby Utd
Edinburgh Wands v Royal High
Glasgow Acads v Gala
Greystones v Dungannon
Kelso v Stewart's-Melville FP
Kirkcaldy v Hawick
Langholm v Jedforest
Maesteg v Newport
Malone v Instonians
Melrose v Kilmarnock
Mountain Ash v Pontypool
Musselburgh v Heriot's FP
Trinity Acads v Grangemouth
West of Scotland v Dunfermline

Wednesday, 29 March

Army v RAF (Twickenham)

Saturday, 1 April

RFU Pilkington Cup: *Semi-finals*
RFU Pilkington Junior Clubs Cup:
  Semi-finals

RFU Courage Leagues
Division 3
Bedford v Exeter
Clifton v Blackheath
Otley v Harrogate
Richmond v Rosslyn Park
Rugby v Morley
Division 4
Askeans v Leeds
Liverpool St Helens v Aspatria
Plymouth v Redruth
Reading v Broughton Park
Rotherham v Havant

IRFU Insurance Corporation Leagues
Division 1
Blackrock Coll v Sunday's Well
Cork Const v Old Wesley
Lansdowne v St Mary's Coll
Shannon v Instonians
Young Munster v Dungannon
Division 2
Ballymena v Malone
Bective Rangers v Old Crescent
Greystones v UC Dublin
Old Belvedere v Dolphin
Wanderers v Terenure Coll
Division 3
Athlone v City of Derry
Clontarf v Highfield
Galway Corinthians v Ballina
Monkstown v Galwegians
UC Cork v NIFC
Waterpark v De La Salle Palmerston
Division 4
Collegians v CIYMS
Dublin U v Queen's U, Belfast
Portadown v Ards
Skerries v City of Armagh
UC Galway v Bohemians

WRU Heineken Leagues
Division 1
Cardiff v Dunvant
Llanelli v Bridgend
Neath v Abertillery
Pontypool v Newbridge
Swansea v Pontypridd
Treorchy v Newport
Division 2
Abercynon v Aberavon
Bonymaen v Tenby Utd
Cross Keys v Ebbw Vale
Llanharan v S Wales Police
Maesteg v Penarth
Narberth v Llandovery

Scotland U-21 v Italy U-21
Spain U-18 v Scotland U-18

Ayr v Clarkston
Coventry v Bristol
Fylde v West Hartlepool
Harlequins v Saracens
Newcastle Gosforth v Northampton
Orrell v Moseley
Sale v Wakefield
Waterloo v Wasps

Tuesday, 4 April

Glam Wands v Aberavon

Wednesday, 5 April

Royal Navy v RAF (Twickenham)

Saturday, 8 April

RFU Courage Leagues
Division 1
Bath v West Hartlepool
Bristol v Gloucester
Leicester v Harlequins
Northampton v Orrell
Sale v Wasps
Division 2
Coventry v Waterloo
Fylde v Saracens
Moseley v London Irish
Nottingham v Newcastle Gosforth
Wakefield v London Scottish
Division 3
Bedford v Otley
Clifton v Harrogate
Morley v Blackheath
Richmond v Exeter
Rosslyn Park v Rugby
Division 4
Aspatria v Askeans
Havant v Liverpool St Helens
Leeds v Plymouth
Reading v Rotherham
Redruth v Broughton Park
Division 5 North
Barkers Butts v Wharfedale
Hereford v Birmingham Solihull
Stoke-on-Trent v Nuneaton
Stourbridge v Sheffield
Walsall v Preston Grasshoppers
Winnington Park v Lichfield
Division 5 South
Henley v Lydney
Met Police v London Welsh
North Walsham v High Wycombe
Sudbury v Barking
Tabard v Berry Hill
Weston-super-Mare v Camborne

WRU SWALEC Cup: *Quarter-finals*
Melrose Sevens
Scotland U-19 v England U-19
Scotland U-18 v Ireland U-18

Aberavon v Pontypool
Bridgend v Mountain Ash

Narberth v Whitland
Old Wesley v Ayr
Treorchy v Tenby Utd

Thursday, 13 April

WRU Heineken Leagues
Division 1
Newbridge v Cardiff

Saturday, 15 April

Cardiff v Barbarians

RFU Courage Leagues
Division 1
Gloucester v Northampton
Leicester v Bath
Orrell v Harlequins
Wasps v Bristol
West Hartlepool v Sale
Division 2
Fylde v Coventry
London Irish v Wakefield
London Scottish v Nottingham
Saracens v Newcastle Gosforth
Waterloo v Moseley
Division 3
Blackheath v Richmond
Exeter v Clifton
Harrogate v Bedford
Morley v Rosslyn Park
Rugby v Otley
Division 4
Askeans v Havant
Broughton Park v Rotherham
Liverpool St Helens v Reading
Plymouth v Aspatria
Redruth v Leeds

WRU Heineken Leagues
Division 1
Abertillery v Dunvant
Bridgend v Treorchy
Neath v Swansea
Newport v Pontypool
Pontypridd v Llanelli
Division 2
Aberavon v Narberth
Bonymaen v Cross Keys
Ebbw Vale v Abercynon
Llandovery v Llanharan
S Wales Police v Maesteg
Tenby Utd v Penarth

442

Wales U-19 v Scotland U-19
Vale of Lune v Preston Grasshoppers

Monday, 17 April

Swansea v Barbarians

Aberavon v Abertillery
Newport v London Welsh
Preston Grasshoppers v Fylde

Saturday, 22 April

SCOTLAND v ROMANIA
   (Murrayfield)
RFU CIS County Championship: *Final*
   (Twickenham)

RFU Courage Leagues
Division 1
Bristol v West Hartlepool
Harlequins v Bath
Northampton v Wasps
Orrell v Gloucester
Sale v Leicester
Division 2
Moseley v Fylde
Newcastle Gosforth v London Scottish
Nottingham v London Irish
Saracens v Coventry
Wakefield v Waterloo

WRU SWALEC Cup: *Semi-finals*
Jedforest Sevens

Bedford v Cardiff
Mountain Ash v Aberavon
Pontypool v Rugby
Richmond v Newport
S Wales Police v Newbridge
Tynedale v Vale of Lune

Wednesday, 26 April

Cheltenham v Moseley

Saturday, 29 April

RFU Courage Leagues
Division 1
Bath v Sale
Gloucester v Harlequins
Leicester v Bristol
Wasps v Orrell
West Hartlepool v Northampton

Division 2
Coventry v Moseley
Fylde v Wakefield
London Irish v Newcastle Gosforth
London Scottish v Saracens
Waterloo v Nottingham
Division 3
Bedford v Richmond
Clifton v Rugby
Exeter v Blackheath
Harrogate v Rosslyn Park
Otley v Morley
Division 4
Aspatria v Redruth
Havant v Plymouth
Leeds v Broughton Park
Reading v Askeans
Rotherham v Liverpool St Helens

WRU Heineken Leagues
Division 1
Cardiff v Newport
Dunvant v Newbridge
Llanelli v Neath
Pontypool v Bridgend
Swansea v Abertillery

Treorchy v Pontypridd
Division 2
Abercynon v Bonymaen
Cross Keys v Tenby Utd
Llanharan v Aberavon
Maesteg v Llandovery
Narberth v Ebbw Vale
Penarth v S Wales Police

Ulster Senior Cup: *Final*

Monday, 1 May

National Tens (Gloucester)

Saturday, 6 May

ITALY v IRELAND (provisional)
RFU Pilkington Cup: *Final*
(Twickenham)
WRU SWALEC Cup: *Final* (Cardiff)
RFU Pilkington Junior Clubs Cup: *Final*
(Twickenham)
France U-21 v Wales U-21

Saturday, 13 May

Middlesex Sevens (Twickenham)

RFU CIS INSURANCE COUNTY CHAMPIONSHIP 1994-95

November

12	*Midlands*	
	Group A:	Staffordshire v Leicestershire
	Group B:	East Midlands v Notts, Lincs and Derbys
15	*North*	Durham v Yorkshire
		Cheshire v Lancashire
		Cumbria v Northumberland

These fixtures may be played on Sunday or other midweek date if mutually agreed

19	*South*	
	Pool 1:	Surrey v Hertfordshire
	Pool 2:	Gloucestershire v Devon
		Buckinghamshire v Sussex
	Pool 3:	Hampshire v Oxfordshire
		Kent v Eastern Counties
	Pool 4:	Cornwall v Middlesex
		Dorset/Wilts v Berkshire

	Midlands	
	Group A:	Leicestershire v North Midlands
	Group B:	Notts, Lincs and Derbys v Warwickshire
	North	Cheshire v Cumbria
		Lancashire v Durham
		Northumberland v Yorkshire

26	*South*	
	Pool 1:	Hertfordshire v Somerset
	Pool 2:	Devon v Sussex
		Gloucestershire v Buckinghamshire
	Pool 3:	Oxfordshire v Eastern Counties
		Hampshire v Kent
	Pool 4:	Middlesex v Berkshire
		Cornwall v Dorset/Wilts
	Midlands	
	Group A:	North Midlands v Staffordshire
	Group B:	Warwickshire v East Midlands
	North	Yorkshire v Lancashire
		Cheshire v Northumberland
		Cumbria v Durham

December

3	*South*	
	Pool 1:	Somerset v Surrey
	Pool 2:	Buckinghamshire v Devon
		Sussex v Gloucestershire
	Pool 3:	Kent v Oxfordshire
		Eastern Counties v Hampshire
	Pool 4:	Dorset/Wilts v Middlesex
		Berkshire v Cornwall
	Midlands	Semi-finals
	North	Yorkshire v Cheshire
		Northumberland v Durham
		Cumbria v Lancashire
10	*Midlands*	Finals
	North	Durham v Cheshire
		Lancashire v Northumberland
		Yorkshire v Cumbria

The South will have their quarter-final play-off on or before 28 January 1995. By mutual arrangement, games in the southern sector may be played on the Sunday of the weekend indicated

March

11	Semi-finals

April

22	FINAL	(Twickenham)

MAJOR TOURS 1994-95

South Africans to Scotland, Wales and Ireland

October

22 **Cardiff**
26 **Wales A** (Newport)
29 **Llanelli**

November

2 **Neath**
5 **Swansea**
9 **Scotland A** (Melrose)
12 **Scottish Districts** (Glasgow)
15 **Scottish Selection** (Aberdeen)
19 **SCOTLAND** (Murrayfield)
22 **Pontypridd**
26 **WALES** (Cardiff)
29 **Combined Irish Provinces** (Belfast)

December

3 **Barbarians** (Dublin)

Namibians to Ireland

November

1 **Irish Development XV** (Galway)
5 **IRELAND** (Dublin)
9 **Irish Universities**
12 **Leinster** (Dublin)

MAJOR FIXTURES IN EUROPE 1994-95

September

17 **ROMANIA v WALES** (Bucharest)

October

12 **WALES v ITALY** (Cardiff)

November

5   **IRELAND v NAMIBIA** (Dublin)
12 **ENGLAND v ROMANIA**
    (Twickenham)
19 **SCOTLAND v SOUTH AFRICA**
    (Murrayfield)
26 **WALES v SOUTH AFRICA**
    (Cardiff)

December

3   **Barbarians v South Africans**
    (Dublin)
6   **Oxford U v Cambridge U**
    (Twickenham)
10 **ENGLAND v CANADA**
    (Twickenham)
31 **Scotland Trial** (Murrayfield)

January

7   **Scotland A v Italy**
20 **Ireland A v England A**
21 **IRELAND v ENGLAND**
    (Dublin)
    FRANCE v WALES (Paris)
    SCOTLAND v CANADA
    (Murrayfield)
    Scotland A v France A

February

3   **Scotland A v Ireland A**
4   **ENGLAND v FRANCE**
    (Twickenham)
    SCOTLAND v IRELAND
    (Murrayfield)
17 **France A v Wales A**
18 **WALES v ENGLAND**
    (Cardiff)
    FRANCE v SCOTLAND (Paris)

March

4   **SCOTLAND v WALES**
    (Murrayfield)
    IRELAND v FRANCE (Dublin)
    Royal Navy v Army (Twickenham)
17 **Wales A v Ireland A**
18 **ENGLAND v SCOTLAND**
    (Twickenham)
    WALES v IRELAND (Cardiff)
22 **UAU Final** (Twickenham)
29 **Army v RAF** (Twickenham)

April

5   **Royal Navy v RAF** (Twickenham)
22 **SCOTLAND v ROMANIA**
    (Murrayfield)
    County Championship Final
    (Twickenham)

May

6   **ITALY v IRELAND** (provisional)
    RFU Cup Final (Twickenham)
    WRU Cup Final (Cardiff)

RUGBY WORLD CUP

European Zone Play-off

September

17 **ROMANIA v WALES** (Bucharest)

October

1 **ITALY v ROMANIA**
12 **WALES v ITALY** (Cardiff)
All three qualify: winners go to finals as Europe 1, runners-up as Europe 2 and third-placed nation as Europe 3)

Asian Zone Play-off

October

21-29 (in Malaysia)

RUGBY WORLD CUP FINALS 1995

May
25 **South Africa v Australia**
(Cape Town) (A)
26 **Scotland v Ivory Coast**
(Rustenburg) (D)
France v Tonga (Pretoria) (D)
Canada v Europe 3
(Port Elizabeth) (A)
27 **Western Samoa v Europe 2**
(East London) (B)
Europe 1 v Asian Qualifier
(Bloemfontein) (C)
England v Argentina (Durban) (B)
New Zealand v Ireland
(Johannesburg) (C)
30 **Western Samoa v Argentina**
(East London) (B)
South Africa v Europe 3
(Cape Town) (A)
France v Ivory Coast
(Rustenburg) (D)
Scotland v Tonga (Pretoria) (D)
31 **Australia v Canada**
(Port Elizabeth) (A)
Ireland v Asian Qualifier
(Bloemfontein) (C)
England v Europe 2 (Durban) (B)
New Zealand v Europe 1
(Johannesburg) (C)

June
3 **Tonga v Ivory Coast**
(Rustenburg) (D)
Australia v Europe 3
(Stellenbosch) (A)
Scotland v France (Pretoria) (D)
South Africa v Canada
(Port Elizabeth) (A)
4 **Argentina v Europe 2**
(East London) (B)
New Zealand v Asian Qualifier
(Bloemfontein) (C)
Ireland v Europe 1
(Johannesburg) (C)
England v Western Samoa
(Durban) (B)
10 **Quarter-final:** Winner (D) v
Runner-up (C) (Durban)
Quarter-final: Winner (A) v
Runner-up (B) (Johannesburg)
11 **Quarter-final:** Winner (B) v
Runner-up (A) (Cape Town)
Quarter-final: Winner (C) v
Runner-up (D) (Pretoria)
17 **Semi-final:** Winner 1st quarter-
final v Winner 2nd quarter-final
(Durban)
18 **Semi-final:** Winner 3rd quarter-
final v Winner 4th quarter-final
(Cape Town)
22 **Third/fourth-place play-off**
(Pretoria)
24 **FINAL** (Johannesburg)

A selection of non-fiction from Headline

ROTHMANS FOOTBALL YEARBOOK 1994-95	Jack Rollin	£16.99 ☐
ROTHMANS RUGBY LEAGUE YEARBOOK 1994-95	Fletcher/Howes	£15.99 ☐
PLAYFAIR FOOTBALL ANNUAL 1994-95	Jack Rollin	£4.50 ☐
EUROPEAN FOOTBALL ANNUAL 1994-95:		
ROTHMANS PUBLICATIONS	Bruce Smith	£17.99 ☐
CANTONA: MY STORY	Eric Cantona	£15.99 ☐
GRAEME SOUNESS: A SOCCER REVOLUTIONARY	Stephen Kelly	£16.99 ☐
MATCH OF MY LIFE	Ray French	£16.99 ☐
VENABLES: THE INSIDE STORY	Harris/Curry	£16.99 ☐

All Headline books are available at your local bookshop or newsagent, or can be ordered direct from the publisher. Just tick the titles you want and fill in the form below. Prices and availability subject to change without notice.

Headline Book Publishing Ltd, Cash Sales Department, Bookpoint, 39 Milton Park, Abingdon, OXON OX14 4TD, UK. If you have a credit card you may order by telephone – 0235 400400.

Please enclose a cheque or postal order made payable to Bookpoint Ltd to the value of the cover price and allow the following for postage and packing:
UK & BFPO: £1.00 for the first book, 50p for the second book and 30p for each additional book ordered up to a maximum charge of £3.00.
OVERSEAS & EIRE: £2.00 for for the first book, £1.00 for the second book, and 50p for each additional book.

Name ....

Address ....

....

....

If you would prefer to pay by credit card, please complete:
Please debit my Visa/Access/Diner's Card/American Express (delete as applicable) card no:

Signature..Expiry Date........................